American
Higher
Education
Transformed,
1940–2005

American Higher Education Transformed, 1940–2005

Documenting the National Discourse

Edited by
Wilson Smith and
Thomas Bender

The Johns Hopkins
University Press

BALTIMORE

The Johns Hopkins University Press
2715 North Charles Street
Baltimore, Maryland 21218-4363
www.press.jhu.edu

Library of Congress Cataloging-in-Publication Data
American higher education transformed, 1940–2005 :
documenting the national discourse /
edited by Wilson Smith and Thomas Bender.
p. cm.
Includes bibliographical references and index.
ISBN-13: 978-0-8018-8671-3 (hardcover : alk. paper)
ISBN-10: 0-8018-8671-6 (hardcover : alk. paper)
1. Education, Higher—United States—History—
20th century.
I. Smith, Wilson (Francis Wilson), 1922–
II. Bender, Thomas.
LA226.A64 2007
378.73'09044—dc22   2007006284

A catalog record for this book is available
from the British Library.

*Special discounts are available for
bulk purchases of this book.
For more information,
please contact Special Sales at
410-516-6936
or specialsales@press.jhu.edu.*

Contents

Part IV. Graduate Studies

Part V. Disciplines and Interdisciplinarity

Part VI. Academic Profession

Preface

The people who transformed American colleges and universities in the half-century after World War II pursued a variety of purposes. Their efforts, documented here, continue a story that, as late as the 1940s, was told in *American Higher Education, A Documentary History,* edited in 1961 by Richard Hofstadter and Wilson Smith. The scope and magnitude of the changes over the past half-century could easily fill several volumes. What we record in this collection is necessarily and happily selective. We emphasize a discourse that speaks to the national ways, means, and aims of higher learning. We exclude the social life of students, the business of intercollegiate athletics, and institutional budgets in favor of questions of access, the diversity of students, their studies, and their place in educational change. We stress the curriculum and the ideal of liberal learning in an age of mass education, the position and leadership of universities in society, the role of the federal government, including its courts, and academic life as a profession.

Not only did the numbers of students and faculty expand at an unprecedented rate during this half-century, so also did the fields of inquiry and teaching with their challenges of disciplinary development. Coming to the fore was an unprecedented shift toward new studies of nature in the modern sciences underwritten by generous financing that overshadowed inquiries into the human condition historically central to the humanities disciplines.

With it all, more than three thousand institutions of higher education in the United States themselves came to be marked by astonishing degrees of differentiation.

The changes we document and the reflexive statements we reprint are part of a persistent national discourse that continues to ask: What is the role of higher learning in a democratic-industrial-technological society? Where can the inevitable tensions between equality and excellence be softened? How can universities meet their responsibility to lead the way toward both equality and excellence? The voices in the pages that follow do not shrink from these difficult issues in a society that aspires to equality in educational opportunities and a common enticement to learning without expecting uniform achievements.

We hope the reader will bear in mind the theme for these endeavors that long ago was put simply by the father of American public higher education. Thomas Jefferson in 1807 wrote: "The field of knolege is the common property of all mankind." This documentary account of transformation carries that belief.

Note: Footnotes are omitted from most of the documents. When faced with many possible references, the bibliography in each headnote is meant to cite the most informative and relevant supplementary readings.

Acknowledgments

We are grateful to all who helped put together this large volume of documents. In its early stage, three graduate students in the History Department at the University of California, Davis, who later received their doctorates, tracked down sources and, in that age of technological antiquity, used typewriters. The three were Mary Agnes Dougherty, Anita Gentry, and Carolyn Lawes. Later on, Kelly Hopkins, Dr. David Barber, Lia Schraeder, Dan Constable, and Andreas Agocs introduced the documents to the age of scanners and computers. In the final computer preparations for the press, Chris Doyle, Beth Slutsky, and Marie Basile put in long hours as excellent keyboarders and discerning guides to the marvels of electronic communication. Kevin Bryant, technological wizard for the department, helped too at crucial times.

At New York University, we are indebted to the International Center for Advanced Study and its administrator, Jeryl Martin-Hannibal, as well as to Calvin Nguyen, who helped with permissions. Felice Batlin, at that time a doctoral student and now a professor of law at Chicago-Kent School of Law, contributed both creative document research and valuable substantive suggestions. David Gibney and Paula Segal, then undergraduates at NYU, helped to "clean up" and verify the text of scanned documents.

We thank all at the Johns Hopkins University Press who contributed their skills to this endeavor. We particularly appreciate the cordial guidance of Henry Tom, our executive editor, and our happy working relationship with his assistant editor, Claire McCabe Tamberino.

We both are grateful to Kathryn Reed Smith for her constant encouragement of this long project, her stylistic preferences, and her generous financial support.

American
Higher
Education
Transformed,
1940–2005

Introduction

The transformation of the postwar American university was so extensive that it resulted in a wholly new institution, qualitatively different from that of the first half of the century. The expansion of higher education after 1945 was transformative, both at the level of individual institutions and the national system as a whole. While research had been a core component of the American university since the closing decades of the nineteenth century, before 1945 it had been more of a teaching institution than it would be afterward. Colleges and universities had an important place in American society before 1945, but their constituency had been limited and quite homogeneous. Even the most distinguished institutions were regional rather than national; only after the war did the top-tier research universities and liberal arts colleges develop national constituencies. Government policy—especially research funding, policies on race and gender equity, and student financial aid—along with the influence of national professional organizations affecting university personnel from admissions officers to professors had the effect of nationalizing a wide range of institutional practices.

At the same time, the leading postwar universities became the premier sites of knowledge production. They, along with a clutch of liberal arts colleges, became open to wider and more diverse constituencies, becoming in this sense more democratic. Meritocratic values became more influential in admissions as higher education became more important for the society and for individuals. By 1960, institutions of higher learning were incorporated into the center of American society.[1] With the emergence of a postindustrial economy, a term that entered popular discourse with the publication of *The Coming of Postindustrial Society* (1973) by Daniel Bell, knowledge became the engine of economic development, and in that process universities, with what Clark Kerr called their "invisible product," assumed an unprecedented role.[2] By the last quarter of the century, America's research universities were recognized as being the world's leaders, and the national system the most democratic, at least by way of making higher education accessible to a vast and very diverse population (I, 16–17).[3]

At the same time, university administrators and civic leaders dreamed of new domains of activity and resources. They hoped to replicate the symbiotic relations between universities and business enterprises that had developed in California's Silicon Valley and Route 128 in Massachusetts, where in each case a pair of distinguished universities anchored a regional culture of technological and corporate innovation.[4] Universities began actively to commercialize their research capacity with private sector partners and many, even some of the most

prestigious, extended their "classrooms" through new technologies that were managed on a for-profit business model. Indeed, Harvard University was advised by a marketing consultant that they had "a global brand without a global distribution."[5]

The social character of higher education was also transformed. Though not exclusively or uniformly so, prewar American colleges served mostly a white male constituency drawn from roughly the upper quartile of American families measured by wealth and income. The President's Commission on Higher Education convened by Harry Truman strongly urged a vast expansion of higher education to serve a much larger and more diverse segment of the American population. Its ambitious report, the first presidential-level engagement with a national higher education policy, included a passage that criticized existing economic and racial barriers to equal education; indeed, the commitment to racial equality that it voiced was strong enough to prompt several commissioners, including scientist Arthur H. Compton and historian Douglas S. Freeman, to register their dissent to that part of the report. The report also recommended a system of higher education that would better suit the various needs of different students, even as it insisted on a curriculum that would promote a sense of common culture and citizenship (II, 1).

These hopes for higher education were largely realized over the next half-century: women, people of color, and students from families of modest incomes (initially with the support of the G.I. Bill of Rights and later with other federally sponsored financial aid) all entered the halls of American colleges and universities in increasing numbers. Student bodies became more representative, and the trend continued into the twenty-first century: the proportion of African Americans rose from 10 percent in 1993 to 13 percent in 2003, with gains also by Latino (4% to 10%) and Asian (4% to 7%) students. Community colleges provided the most generous access for these underrepresented students, who totaled 36 percent of their enrollment in 2002.[6] Focusing on enrollment rates can be misleading, however; the more important measure is graduation, particularly at the undergraduate level, and these rates are less representative of the general population, reflecting race- and class-based inequalities in the quality of prior preparation and the limited financial resources available to many students.[7] The number and variety of postsecondary institutions swelled in the same span, revealing a pattern of growth that responded to the highly differentiated capacities and aspirations of the growing numbers of students, who often seek vocational rather than liberal educations (VI, 18).

The G.I. Bill is regularly mentioned in discussions of the expansion of educational opportunity—and rightly so (VIII, 1). Between 1938 and 1948, the number of college students doubled, mostly as a result of the G.I. Bill. That it "masculinized" campus life and aided whites far more than African Americans is not regularly mentioned, but it should be.[8] As should the spike in tuition income produced by this infusion of federal money. Public colleges and universities especially benefited, since the program paid out-of-state tuition rates for all students. Given the numbers involved, the impact was significant. In 1947–48, the Veterans Administration paid for almost half of the male college students in the United States, and by 1962 higher education had received $5.5 billion from that source on behalf of veterans of World War II and the Korean War. This produced windfalls for many universities; the University of California used these funds particularly creatively and effectively. In 1947–48, these fees brought the university $12 million, a sum roughly equal to the total budget of Columbia University at the time.[9] This unrestricted revenue—which continued to flow into the coffers in the years to follow—enabled Robert Sproul and Clark Kerr to leverage Berkeley to the premier position it achieved a decade later.[10]

Faculties were expanded. The National Defense Education Act, a response to Sputnik, increased the number and quality of doctoral fellowships, thereby contributing to the diversification in the social background of graduate students and thus college and university teachers (VIII, 4). (The Vietnam War and the domestic turmoil surrounding it also drew growing numbers of students from more diverse backgrounds into graduate work, especially in the humanities and social sciences.) As one might expect, the more nearly that faculty and students approached the range of socioeconomic and cultural diversity of the nation at large, the more that the tensions and conflicts of the larger culture began to play themselves out in institutions of higher learning. Certain conventions, from teas for faculty wives hosted by the president's wife to the dynamics of interaction in the classroom, had to be rethought, and the notion of a common curriculum, not problematic when academic culture was homogeneous, became a difficult challenge, producing debate and conflict on campus and even in the wider public (III, 8–13).

Accommodating such difference was only part of the challenge, however. The sharp increase in the number of faculty and students raised new challenges for university leaders, ranging from governance, advisement, student services, and, most obviously, adequate space for classrooms, laboratories, offices, dormitories, recreational facilities, and parking. Building on the previous enlargement of college students produced by the G.I. Bill, enrollments tripled between 1960 and 1980. This was the largest percentage increase since the 1875–95 period, when the American research university was invented and the curriculum modernized. In both eras, strains proved to be inevitable.[11] In the 1960s, however, students challenged what they saw as an alienating education machine complicit in increasingly disturbing social issues at home—poverty, race, and injustice—and war abroad. Military research was often a focal point, and ROTC was a local symbol of militarism that mobilized protest on many campuses (VII, 7–10).

Before World War I, many of the most ambitious and talented American scientists and scholars had sought advanced training abroad. During the interwar years, however, the American university became self-sufficient, and the academic leaders of the postwar era were mostly American-trained, though in some fields they were significantly influenced by the émigré scientists and scholars who had fled European fascism (VI, 1). Indeed, the Nazi regime and the Holocaust not only sent extraordinary academic talent to the United States (with positive help from the Rockefeller Foundation), the German horrors also delivered a message that prompted Americans to end discriminatory practices in higher education, particularly those limiting Jews and segregating African Americans who sought admission or faculty appointments.[12]

The quarter-century following the war has been characterized as a "golden age" for higher education, and with good reason. But we must not forget that academe suffered under the dark cloud of McCarthyism; its destructive challenges to academic freedom ruined lives and distorted scholarship (X, 1–4).[13] Higher education was also marked by the color line during those years, with formal segregation in the southern states and considerable discouragement to African-American students in many northern institutions. Women were increasing their numbers as students, but for those with academic inclinations it was more difficult for women to obtain faculty positions than it had been thirty or forty years earlier (II, 10–15). Still, the postwar decades were remarkable for higher education in the United States. The problem that these years and the "golden age" label caused later in the century was its transformation into a presumed norm to be recovered rather than a unique conjuncture of international challenges and a domestic political commitment to social investment.

Higher education experienced not only expansion but also a leveling up. The movement was vertical, enabling institutions to climb up the ladder of quality, but it was also lateral and geographical. Regional inequalities were narrowed. Research and training was no longer dominated by a few select institutions like Chicago and the Ivies. Distinction was as likely to be found in major public institutions (Berkeley, Ann Arbor, Madison) as in private ones, in the South (North Carolina and Texas) as in the Northeast, the Great Lakes region, or the West (IV, 1–3).[14]

Racial change was contested and slow. Officially,

public institutions were desegregated in the South, but integration required courage and fortitude from African-American student pioneers; prior to the late 1960s they too frequently "endured isolation, shunning, and sabotage." Elite private institutions—Tulane, Emory, Vanderbilt—lagged well behind the slow-moving public ones. Historically black institutions retained a regional role and, in fact, became an important staging ground for civil rights protest in the South.[15] After a considerable struggle, southern colleges became generally accessible to African Americans who had heretofore been restricted to historically black colleges (II, 16–20).

A postwar European visitor with continental research institutions as a point of reference would have been struck by the organization (not to say system, which the visitor would have thought to be missing) and funding of higher education in the United States. The American practice of combining advanced research and undergraduate education in the same institution, the product of a decision educators made at the beginning of the century, would have seemed novel.[16] When massive amounts of new funding flowed into research, it went to colleges and universities; very few independent or government research institutes were established, and those that were created typically had ties to a university or consortium of universities. Second, such a visitor would be surprised not only by the vast number and diversity of the institutions of higher education but also by the knowledge that most were organized by local initiative rather than by national policy. If relatively few gained resources from the expanded federal investment in research, over the course of the half-century all of them benefited from federally funded student aid, a form of aid massive in its aggregate impact yet compatible with institutional autonomy and individual choice by students. By 1997–98, the largest federal program, Pell Grants, begun in 1972, was spending nearly $4 billion on 3.8 million students.[17]

The quantity and quality of American science after the war cannot be measured with any precision, but even crude measures impress. For example, 80 percent of all citations in electronic retrieval systems are in English, and 44 percent of the most frequently cited articles in science and engineering are the products of U.S. universities.[18] The postwar history of the Nobel Prizes is another mark of American scientific leadership. Before 1946, one in seven Nobel Prizes went to Americans; between 1946 and 1975, Americans received one in two.[19] And in 2005 American universities employed 70 percent of living Nobel Laureates.[20] There is much talk from time to time about the influence of foreign scholars and scholarship—French theory in the 1980s, for example. But in fact Americans borrow little from abroad. Although scientists and scholars are more cosmopolitan than the general population of the United States, the professoriate, particularly in the humanities and social sciences, are monolingual

and rather insular in their intellectual tastes, while the publishing industry of the United States translates very few books—no other advanced industrial country translates fewer. On the other hand, foreign scholars and scientists study in the United States and follow research done by Americans, and American scholarship and science circulates everywhere without translation, much like American music, software, movies, and style.

It was not always so. When Abraham Flexner reported on the quality of universities in the United States, Great Britain, and Germany in 1930, he found American institutions falling short. Twenty years later, a major appraisal of prewar social science and humanities research recorded recent improvement but argued that the larger pattern was nonetheless marked and marred by "fact finding," "over-specialization," and "trivial investigations."[21] Yet the same report presciently noted that the genteel professoriate of the interwar years was changing, becoming more worldly, more professionally ambitious, and, given the more diverse social origins of the postwar cohort, more aggressive, fueled by aspirations to upward mobility.

After the war, there was a strong sense that more would be expected of higher education, hence the substantial investment in university science (I, 1–2). But the humanities were also to be mobilized. It was widely believed that science and technology had advanced faster than the understanding of the social and moral challenges posed, with nuclear annihilation only the most obvious. The humanities were charged with remedying the situation. To devise an education to address the disjuncture, Harvard President James B. Conant turned to his faculty, who took his request with a seriousness appropriate to the times. In 1945 they delivered their curriculum report, *General Education in a Free Society* (1945), which became known as the "Red Book" (I, 1). This enormously influential document made a case for studying both science and the texts of the European humanist tradition, which were understood to sustain the American values of freedom and democracy in the emerging Cold War contest with the Soviet Union. The historical disciplines, it was argued, were essential to develop in citizens the capacity to understand and manage the social and ethical issues they would have to confront—first and foremost, rapid social, scientific, and technological change. The past was thus placed in the service of the future, and this provided a rationale for the broad liberal arts emphasis characteristic of the postwar American college experience.

Over the course of the half-century, however, the faculty became less and less committed to the program of general education. Disciplinary agendas trumped local, institutional ones, and research, not teaching, became the measure of academic distinction (VI, 17). Moreover, an ever-tighter disciplinary specialization and engagement with the cutting edge of disciplinary development, rather than worrisome issues of civic education, shaped the faculty and the curriculum (V, 3). By the end of the century, it was common for critics to insist that what the faculty wanted to teach was not what the students needed to learn and that what the students needed to learn, the faculty could not or would not teach. The prescriptions of curricular reformers and faculty committees devoted to general education were politely received but were difficult to implement.

The Red Book itself provides a premonitory example. Whereas it had asked philosophers to investigate and teach "the place of human aspirations and ideals in the total scheme of things," the postwar discipline, embracing logical positivism and the inward-looking and donnish analytical movement, eschewed such a civic role. Even among humanists, whose disciplines were increasingly professionalized and self-consciously scientific, such a civic role was embarrassing for its moralism and sentiment. The authors of the Red Book knew their colleagues and sensed these trends, pointing out that "one of the subtlest and most prevalent effects of specialism has been that . . . subjects have tended to be conceived and taught with an eye . . . to their own internal logic rather than their larger usefulness to students."[22]

There was a much better fit between the faculty agenda and graduate education, which was expanding as funding grew and graduate schools sought to meet the demand for qualified faculty to staff the ever-increasing classrooms (IV, 1–3). Enrollment in Ph.D. programs doubled between 1940 and 1950 and then increased by a factor of four between 1950 and 1970.[23] To manage this challenge, the various disciplines, with support from the Carnegie Corporation of New York, responded with self studies to guide their efforts to expand and upgrade training for the next generation of teachers and researchers.[24]

Foundations had entered the world of higher education and advanced research early in the twentieth century (VIII, 11). The Rockefeller Foundation, the earliest, played a particularly prominent role in the development of university medical education, the natural sciences, and the social sciences early in the twentieth century, creating the Rockefeller Institute (today's Rockefeller University) and strongly supporting the development of the social sciences at the University of Chicago and through the vehicle of the Social Science Research Council. Later, it could also claim credit for the creation of the discipline of biochemistry.[25] After the war, however, the Ford Foundation brought new ideas, energy, resources, and its own agenda to higher education philanthropy. The settlement of the estates of Henry Ford and his son Edsel brought a massive increase in the endowment of the foundation the family had established in 1936, making it the world's richest philanthropic foundation. In 1949, a study group headed by H. Rowan Gaither established five areas of human welfare to define the program of the Ford Foundation—peace, democracy, economics, education in its broadest

definition, and the study of individual behavior and human relations (VIII, 12). All of them, one can say, were a direct response to the first half of the twentieth century, which had been brutal: two world wars, a devastating depression, totalitarian governments of the right and the left, and the specter of nuclear annihilation.

It was widely hoped—and believed—that just as the technology of the bomb had brought the war to an end, an increase in social knowledge might make the second half of the century more peaceful and humane than the first. The Ford Foundation took particular leadership in two areas of study that had a direct and substantial impact on higher education—understanding human behavior and increasing knowledge of the different societies of the world. Their investments in these fields transformed the social sciences and created international and area studies. Like Vannevar Bush's report to the president in 1945, *Science, The Endless Frontier* (I, 2), the authors of the Ford report—along with much of the educated public—had a neo-Enlightenment faith that reason, science, and the rigor of scientific methods could solve social problems after the fashion of the Manhattan Project, which had produced what they considered to be the decisive weapon in the war, or of DDT, with its promise to wipe out malaria. Understanding human behavior, they were sure, would point to ways of ensuring a rational politics, social instability, and peace.[26]

If Henry Ford was something of a xenophobic isolationist, the foundation his wealth created played a decisive role in bringing international studies and area studies, which had heretofore been the province of missionaries, business leaders, diplomats, and journalists, into the curriculum and research agendas of American higher education.[27] Carnegie had been first into the field with the Foreign Studies and Research Fellowship Program, which was administered by the Social Science Research Council. Ford took over that activity in 1952 and began a systematic program of support for foreign area studies, first with fellowships and then with institutional grants to develop area studies programs. This required courage, for Ford's support of international studies and the behavioral sciences was subject to criticism in the McCarthy era, and in 1953 a congressional committee investigating foundations was particularly critical of Ford's support for the "inherently collectivist" social sciences and for their "internationalist view point."[28] Political attacks notwithstanding, between 1952 and 1966 Ford invested $270 million in foreign area studies, making area studies a "core component" of U.S. higher education. Before 1940, the total production of dissertations completed in American universities on nonwestern parts of the world was about sixty, including those dealing with antiquity.[29] It is important to note here the distinctive midcentury American pattern in which both the government and foundations turned to universities, not to independent research institutes, to provide research in the national interest.

The Ford Foundation also invested heavily in academic social science. However, the rubric that gave a name to their interest was a novel one: "behavioral sciences," distinctly in the plural to suggest interdisciplinary collaboration among disciplines rather than a grand theory of behavior. The naming had other reasons, one political and the other intellectual with political implications. The Ford Foundation feared that Americans were prone to confuse social science with socialism and socialism with communism and the Cold War enemy, the Soviet Union. The other reason was to emphasize the importance of the individual.[30] In contrast to the classic social sciences, which took society as their focus, the behavioral sciences focused on the individual actor, how individuals behaved in various social circumstances. This framing implied particular research strategies (survey research, for example) and associated the work with the American tradition of individualism, a theme prominent in American Cold War rhetoric.

To prime research on "individual behavior and human relations," the Ford Foundation established the Center for Advanced Study in the Behavioral Sciences at Palo Alto, California, in 1952. There, it was hoped, current leaders of the relevant fields would form the leaders of the next generation of academic social scientists.[31] More funds went directly to universities. Over the course of the twelve years from 1946 to 1958, support by foundations for academic social science amounted to $85 million, of which 48 percent went to three institutions (Harvard, Columbia, and Berkeley).[32] Over the following five years, the big three foundations (Ford, Rockefeller, and Carnegie) bestowed nearly $100 million on political science departments to develop behavioral approaches for the discipline, half of which went to the same three institutions.[33] These investments in the behavioral sciences emphasized scientific rigor, especially the use of quantitative evidence, partly for its own value but also to distinguish it from the subjective and ideological scholarship thought to have characterized the social sciences in the 1930s.

The advent of the behavioral sciences was part of a larger shift in American academic life and intellectual life generally toward the center, toward theories of social consensus, with reference to both the past and present. Marxism disappeared from the discourse of intellectuals, as did other grand theories. Historians described a nation of limited social division, emphasizing consensus on core values.[34] Middle range and equilibrium theories prevailed in the social sciences, identified respectively with the era's two most influential social theorists, Robert Merton and Talcott Parsons.[35] The method of science was widely embraced. One finds the rhetoric of science across the humanities and social sciences, ranging from literary criticism (the New Criticism) to

philosophy (analytic philosophy, positivism) to economics (mathematical modeling). All of this amounted to what Carl Schorske has denoted "the new rigorism" (V, 3).[36] Such approaches produced certainty and were supposedly free of ideology. With both grand theory and ideology dismissed, it was possible for Daniel Bell, a sociologist and leading American intellectual, to announce the end of the ideologies that had plagued the twentieth century.[37] This spirit of scientism was the context for the publication of *The Structure of Scientific Revolutions* by Thomas S. Kuhn in 1962, and it explains the extraordinary response to and controversy around its revitalization of historicism (V, 1).

In the postwar decades, the financial foundations of higher education were not only expanded but also reconfigured. Between 1945 and 1995, the budget of Columbia University, for example, increased on average 10 percent annually, leaping by a multiple of 100, from $11 million to approximately $1.1 billion, and it has doubled in the decade since.[38] Over the same period, the role of federal funding for higher education moved from nearly nothing to indispensable, particularly in two areas—research and student aid. Between 1950 and 1970, the federal government's expenditures for student aid and the research activities of higher education rose from $2.2 billion to $23.4 billion and from there to $31 billion in 1991, and with some shifts in emphasis this pattern of growth continued into the new century.[39]

A considerable portion of research, including basic research, was funded by the Department of Defense. Dwight Eisenhower's worry about the military-industrial complex is well remembered. Less so is his warning in the same speech that government support of university research might overwhelm the "free university, historically the fountainhead of free ideas and scientific discoveries." Might the "government contract" become a "substitute for intellectual curiosity"?[40] When Frederick Terman, Stanford's provost, urged the chair of the economics department to support its graduate students with federal funds, Kenneth Arrow replied that the Office of Naval Research, the principal source of relevant funds, supported mathematical approaches. While that was the area of his own work, for which he had funding from ONR, there were other important areas of economics that the department considered important and worth pursuing that would be pushed aside by too great a focus on externally funded research: resource allocation, social security, and comparative economics systems.[41] As it turned out, Arrow went on to win the Nobel Prize for his mathematical work in economic theory, and the discipline as a whole followed the funds provided by the National Science Foundation and a variety of private foundations, leaving the research areas noted by Arrow on the margins of the discipline at Stanford and elsewhere.

Before the war, private foundations were the

principal source of research funds, but after the war the federal government led the way. World War I had involved individual scientists but not universities, except for some programs for training officers.[42] During World War II, individual scholars were drawn from universities to work for the Office of Strategic Services (historians, political scientists, and anthropologists) or the Manhattan Project (physicists) or the Office of Operations Research (economists), yet, again, excepting the short-lived Army Special Training Program in 1943 (V, 5), there was no structural integration or fusion of the university and the state. After the war, however, a broad recognition of the importance of knowledge for national security and the high costs of the relevant research brought the government and universities into a tight partnership, indispensable to each— both in respect to funding research and the support of students. At the leading science and engineering institutions, military research had what one historian, referring to MIT, characterized as a "predominant influence." The military agenda gave direction to the development of "Big Science" at MIT to such a degree that physicists there were not even consulted about plans for a radiation laboratory on the campus.[43] The new relation between the universities and the federal government raised a variety of issues, ranging from autonomy and academic balance to management, and it was periodically examined by the government and universities (V, 5; VIII, 5, 6, 8).

The costs of ordinary laboratory science, to say nothing of "Big Science," quickly rose beyond the capacity of philanthropy (VIII, 9). Already in 1954 the federal government was providing 69 percent of the funding for university research, with the foundations' portion dropping to 11 percent. The universities' absorptive capacity was still increasing every year; by 1961, 85 percent of the $100 million dispersed by the National Science Foundation went to universities. After Sputnik, the cost of big science and the federal government's escalating commitment to research translated into to an even greater expansion of the federal role. In 1958, federal funds allocated to "basic university research" totaled $178 million; in 1968, only ten years later, support had risen to almost $1.3 billion, and the figure continued to grow through the end of the century.[44] In the 1990s, reflecting current public policy ideas that particularly valued public-private partnerships, joint private and public funding for science became increasingly common, with one party seeking leverage from the other. At the University of Illinois, the W. M. Keck Foundation offered to build a state-of-the-art center for genomics research—on the condition that the university match their contribution, resulting in the W. M. Keck Center for Comparative and Functional Genomics. In 2000, the University of California system leveraged $100 million of state money for each of three "Institutes for Science and Innovation," producing a total of $900 million that produced an increase in research

capacity that was measurable even in the gigantic U.C. system.[45]

The infusion of funds from various sources expanded the research capacity of the whole complex of American research universities. Between 1960 and 1990, the exclusive club of research-intensive universities tripled in size, and research capacity was distributed more evenly. In 1963, 80 percent of university-based R&D expenditures were made at 20 percent of the institutions. By 1990, there had been a significant shift; that percentage of the total was now distributed among 45 percent of the universities.[46] Access to such funds from outside the university—especially in the sciences but also in some of the social sciences—gave the faculty members who pulled in this money leverage against the university, which made them freer to follow their personal course or that of their funders rather than any path laid out by the institutional mission, whether in research or teaching.[47]

The humanities, by contrast, have been more dependent on the university's internal resources; there is evidence that in the 1980s and 1990s university administrators moved discretionary funds, partly in a compensatory way, toward the humanities, something most visibly evident in the proliferation of humanities institutes, many of which offered residential research fellowships.[48] Such administrative protection for the humanities faculty recognized their larger role in carrying on the teaching burden, particularly by assuming heavy responsibility for the general education portion of the curriculum and thus protecting the tuition income of the institution.

Between 1940 and 1990, federal funds for higher education increased by a factor of twenty-five, enrollment by ten, and the average teaching load was cut in half.[49] So as resources increased, the conditions of work for faculty improved. It was systemic, but, of course, the enhancement of professional careers at the richest and most elite institutions was well above average. Though it may seem a reduction of the work load at these universities, it was more precisely a shift, whether or not appropriate or properly balanced, toward more research and more supervision of doctoral students. At Harvard, to give the most notable example, the arts and science faculty increased seven times faster than the number of students, yet the proportion of undergraduate courses in the college decreased by 28 percent.[50]

For four decades following the war, faculty values —merit, research opportunities, greater autonomy, and better students—increasingly shaped the culture of colleges and universities (VI, 2–7, 14–17). This incorporation of faculty values was characterized at the time by Christopher Jencks and David Riesman as an "academic revolution."[51] As a consequence of these developments, faculty participation and influence in university governance increased. That moved the university in a democratic direction. Yet these values had a different relationship to the larger pattern of democratization of higher education.

The implications for the students were more complex. Did more emphasis on research and more faculty autonomy respond to student educational aspirations? Increased emphasis on merit, an idea vigorously promoted by the faculty, weakened the institutional and local commitments of professors. And by vastly increasing the geography of the institution's potential student constituency, this standard undercut an older tie between the college and its students from the local community. Faculty, students, and administrators surely agreed on the importance of moving admissions in the direction of merit rather than class and family, which had been so important before the war. But the meaning of merit was not transparent. It could be and sometimes was interpreted as undermining democratic access, if democracy is taken to mean equality of access for all.[52] Such was the concern of those who demanded greater local access, most notably in the movement for "open admissions" at New York's City College (II, 5, 24–26).

The administrations of John F. Kennedy and Lyndon B. Johnson broadened federal science policy into a higher education policy and ultimately, with student aid and affirmative action, into a social policy. While reaffirming the peer review process for research grants, a policy that had been established with the founding of the National Science Foundation, both administrations urged government funding agencies to expand the regional diversity and the types of institutions (including community colleges) eligible for funding, mostly by providing resources to develop adequate physical facilities. These New Frontier and Great Society policies also extended research support to include the social sciences, the humanities, and even the visual and performing arts.[53] As this flow of federal funds leveled off and even declined, tuition became an increasingly important source of income for colleges and universities, especially after about 1980. In 1945, tuition charges were quite modest. Tuition was free or close to it at public colleges and universities, but even in private institutions the cost was calculated in hundreds of dollars, not the tens of thousands common by the end of the century.

When Harvard's Henry Rosovsky claimed in 1987 that American research universities were the best in the world, he was not challenged (I, 16). Yet even as American educational leaders and the public recognized this standing, many commentators on higher education began to sense an emerging crisis in the American system. A number of books extremely critical of higher education and of the professoriate in particular were widely discussed in the 1990s (III, 8–10).[54] *The University in Ruins,* a book by a literary scholar arguing that the university's historical meaning and legitimacy had largely been lost, won wide readership among education leaders and university faculty (I, 19). And the new century exposed another weakness: the dependence on foreign students in science and engineering graduate programs and laboratories. In the years following the destruction of the World Trade Center in New York City in 2001, the national security policies of the United States discouraged applications from international students. Inequalities in institutional resources were prompting worries too. The richest academic institutions were getting richer, with the poor falling farther behind. In a competitive market environment, the wealthiest institutions accumulated ever larger resources—and the talented faculties and students that that money would buy. Many feared that the pervasiveness of market competition for faculty and students threatened to undermine the remnants of commitment to the community of scholars.

Higher education did not move in this direction entirely out of choice. The withdrawal of public support in higher education as in other areas of common benefit forced a move toward what is called "privatization" of various public goods. Following the emergence of the anti-tax movement that began in California in 1978 with Proposition 13, which limited local taxes, resources were withdrawn from public colleges and universities as well as from other domains of public provision. This shift accelerated in the 1990s, becoming increasingly problematic in the new century. State support for colleges and universities accounted for 74 percent of their budgets in 1991; in 2004, that figure dropped to 64 percent. This decline particularly affected the teaching-oriented colleges, rather than the research-intensive flagship campuses that had more access to federal, foundation, and corporate resources. In fact, by 2005 many of these flagship campuses were operating virtually as private institutions. At Michigan's Ann Arbor campus, only 18 percent of the budget came from state funds; the University of Virginia received only 8 percent.[55] This shift in funding inevitably produced distortions, weakening the institution's commitment to serving the state's research needs (agriculture in farm states, for example) and the education of state residents. John D. Wiley, the chancellor at the University of Wisconsin, Madison, a major research institution much less vulnerable than UW-Oshkosh or UW-River Falls, worried that the United States was "dismantling" the public system of higher education built up after the war, a system that had midwifed the dramatic expansion of the American middle class in the postwar decades.[56]

While public institutions were operating under ever more severe fiscal constraints, private institutions—at least the strongest of them—were accumulating greater and greater resources, launching billion-dollar (and up) development campaigns, finding parents able to pay tuitions in excess of thirty thousand dollars per year and recruiting faculty at salaries that public institutions generally could not match. Clearly these private institutions benefited from the growing accumulation of wealth in private hands, thus recreating and greatly widening a divide between public and private institutions, something that had been narrowed to the vanishing point in the first two decades of the postwar era.[57]

By the end of the century there were worrisome signs that the post–World War II vision of expansion and diversification was at risk. The social movements and public policies committed to widening educational opportunity and pluralizing the system had lost public support. Affirmative action, which sought to increase the opportunity of African Americans and other underrepresented groups to gain access to top-tier or "selective" institutions, was excoriated by conservatives and eviscerated by the courts and state legislatures, even though the number of institutions applying sufficient selectivity in admissions to be affected was quite limited. These one hundred institutions represented a small part of higher education; together in the late 1990s they enrolled fewer than 150,000 of the 1.2 million students going from high school to four-year colleges (IX, 4–6).[58] Oddly, there is no similar objection expressed toward preferences given to athletes, a much larger affirmative action project that has no civic purpose and is at odds with the fundamental values of academe.[59]

In conservative times, university faculties tend to be more progressive than the general society on issues of racial and gender equality, personal lifestyles and speech rights, multicultural diversity and cosmopolitan internationalism, among other issues, and this tends to weaken their public standing and, consequently, their support. Quite unlike the situation in 1945, there was at the end of the twentieth century substantial distrust of universities, prompting unprecedented levels of regulation with talk of more to come. A half-century earlier, the federal government regulated business but not universities, while the new century marked the age of deregulation for business and a vast body of rules and regulations for universities and proposals for "assessments."[60]

Colleges and universities have always been at once a part of society and a sanctuary outside of it; perhaps they can be described as semi-cloistered institutions. The line of distinction, never absolute, had gotten more difficult to specify at the beginning of the twenty-first century. Perhaps the most worrisome index of the change was the increased acceptance of market values—something accelerated by both public policy and market innovations, including the growing number of privately conducted rankings of colleges and universities. The race for high ratings in these publications—which translate into tuition-paying students—began to transform academic culture. This competition for "preferred students" produced an inevitable result: more stratification among colleges and their students.[61]

If in the years after the war the university was incorporated into society, the closing decade or so of the century witnessed significant incorporation into the market.[62] Of course, the university has never been outside of either society or the market. It has been and remains always a question of balance or articulation. In 2003 David Kirp worried about what he saw as a severe imbalance: "the university at its truest and best" cherishes values "that the market does not honor." The professor is a "pursuer of truth," not an "entrepreneur," and the student is not a "consumer whose preferences are to be satisfied" but rather a neophyte whose preferences will be formed as part of his or her educational experience.[63]

Tight budgets, competition, and scale encouraged more hierarchical management of universities. Faculty governance weakened toward the end of the century, and universities as institutions began to resemble more closely public bureaucracies and private corporations. At the same time, wholly new for-profit companies were entering the higher education business. The Apollo Group, whose University of Phoenix had 150,000 students in 2002 and has absolutely no faculty governance, saw its stock rise on Wall Street by 368 percent between 2000 and 2003 (I, 20). The faculty and administrators of mainstream colleges and universities were instantly contemptuous of these for-profit institutions, but the for-profit education industry indirectly raised questions quite beyond the scope of its business plans that warranted serious consideration (I, 21). They effectively provided education for an underserved population, at least in the career-oriented fields they emphasized. Less affluent students, many of them immigrants or children of immigrants, decided that the struggle to pay the tuition at these institutions is worth it: they found the teaching efficient and effective, the schedule accommodating, and future white collar employment a reasonable expectation. DeVry University, with twenty-five campuses, placed 95 percent of its graduates within six months. The student body at its Fremont, California, campus represents sixty-four language groups, and the institution graduated more black and Latino engineers than any other college in the country.[64]

Technology transfer, another focus of university administrators, raised similar issues of commercialization. Earning income from patents was not a novelty, but the Bayh-Dole Act of 1980 vastly increased the practice. Passed at a time when American technological innovation seemed to be lagging behind that of other nations, particularly Japan, this legislation sought to accelerate technology transfers or, put differently, to get patented discoveries that relied upon government funding more quickly into the economy. The legislation authorized universities to make commercial agreements with corporations to do just that. In addition, novel forms of corporate finance for university research were sought, bringing academic values and practices into contact (conflict, in the minds of some) with those of major corporations (VIII, 13–14).[65] The move into the patent market was, however, a financial windfall for leading universities. In 1995, for example, Columbia University earned $24 million from patent and licensing fees, a figure equal to the annual drawdown on an endowment of $480 million.[66] In 2002, Stanford pushed its technology transfer income up to $50 million, in part by offering faculty a "cut" of the income—fair enough, perhaps, but certainly evidence of the deepening penetration of market values.[67]

In 1945 education was understood as a public good, and research was a national resource; the government invested heavily to enhance the cultural stature of the United States and its national security, both commitments admittedly driven by the Cold War. Beginning in the 1980s, education, like research, lost much of its intrinsic value; it was discussed more and more in terms of the market, as an individual investment in human capital. Increasingly higher education was treated as a private good, a product to be purchased for personal benefit, hence the notion of student loan programs, which amounts to a capital investment in oneself, in contrast to a scholarship signifying a collective investment in a public good. This change produced the student as consumer, too often more interested in certification than in inquiry. The tuition-paying student became a customer to be satisfied, creating a relationship that corrupts pedagogy by discouraging the use of "negative sanctions."[68] Clark Kerr identified this trend as early as 1980, when he declared that student consumerism is "one of the greatest reversals of direction in the history of American higher education."[69]

The era of higher education that began with World War II came to an end as the century closed. If the decades immediately after the war witnessed the self-conscious development of a higher education *system* as a public good—best represented by the California Master Plan (II, 6)—that vision is today clouded. Such policy ideas were replaced by market principles, shaped by a commercial ranking system begun in 1983 by a popular magazine using a questionable methodology and imitated by various other ranking services. In 1945 universities did not "compete" for students; most were local. By 2000 all of them did. The most selective institutions were competing on a national basis for quality, while lesser institutions were competing, still locally, for numbers to fill the classrooms and to bring in tuition and per capita state funding. An obsession with ranking focused attention on hierarchy, but the undercurrent in American education since 1945 has been lateral: diffusion, expansion, and differentiation, in which 3,600 institutions employing a half million faculty found their niches (VI, 18).

The present volume appears at a moment for reflection—by the higher education establishment, by government officials, and by all of us as citizens. There are large issues of autonomy and accountability, of purpose and means; there are choices to be made. Who should make these choices within the university and for the public? How should they be made? Is university governance capable of ensuring wide participation and decisiveness? Has federal government shown itself sufficiently capable of grasping the complexity, subtlety, and magnitude of the moral and intellectual stakes involved in higher education to make the big decisions facing it?[70] Or should we expect the states to take charge?[71] And are they any more capable of doing so than the federal government?

If reflection about the fundamental issues before higher education is to be productive, then those who engage in that necessary work must engage the public discussions of their predecessors who had earlier explored and debated the aims and the issues of American higher education. The documents in this volume are a contribution to the history of American higher education since 1945. But along with two volumes of documents that preceded it,[72] this volume is designed for a larger and more public role. It is intended to provide a foundation for continuing the national discourse on higher education that will shape the next half century.

NOTES

1. Edward Shils, *The Constitution of Society* (Chicago, 1982), ch. 10, esp. 259.

2. Clark Kerr, *The Uses of the University*, 4th ed. (Cambridge, MA, 1995), xiv (quotation).

3. See the "Higher Education" special survey in *The Economist*, September 10, 2005.

4. Walter E. Massey, "Can the Research University Adapt to a Changing Future?" in *The Research University in a Time of Discontent*, ed. Jonathan R. Cole, Elinor G. Barber, and Stephen Graubard (Baltimore, 1994), 193.

5. Morton Keller and Phyllis Keller, *Making Harvard Modern: The Rise of America's University* (New York, 2001), 491.

6. Jamilah Evelyn, "College Enrollments Grow More Diverse, More Numerous, and More Female, 2 Government Reports Say," *Chronicle Daily News*, June 2, 2005. Available at chronicle.com/daily/2005/06/2005060203n.htm.

7. There is a huge gap in B.A. attainment rates that separates students from high- and low-income families. The top quartile has a completion rate of 78.2 percent, while the bottom quartile is 42.2 percent. See William Bowen, Martin Kurzweil, and Eugene Tobin, *Equity and Excellence in American Higher Education* (Charlottesville, VA, 2005), 91–92.

8. John R. Thelin points out these issues in his *History of American Higher Education* (Baltimore, 2004), 267 (quotation). See also Micaela di Leonardo, "White Lies, Black Myths," in *The Gender/Sexuality Reader*, ed. Roger Lancaster and Micaela di Leonardo (New York, 1997), 57–58.

9. Jonathan Cole, "Balancing Acts: Dilemmas of Choice Facing Research Universities," in *The Research University in a Time of Discontent*, ed. Cole, Barber, and Graubard, 3.

10. Roger Geiger, *Research and Relevant Knowledge: American Research Universities since World War II* (New York, 1993), 41.

11. Richard Freeland, *Academia's Golden Age: Universities in Massachusetts, 1945–1970* (New York, 1992), 88; David Damrosch, *We Academics: Changing the Culture of the University* (Cambridge, MA, 1995), 24.

12. For an exceptionally illuminating first-person account of the color line in respect to faculty appointments by the first black scholar to chair a department in other than at a historically black university, see John Hope Franklin, *Mirror to America: The Autobiography of John Hope Franklin* (New York, 2005).

13. Ellen Schrecker, *No Ivory Tower: McCarthyism and the Universities* (New York, 1986).

14. For the discipline of history as an example of this naturalization, see Thomas Bender, Philip M. Katz, Colin Palmer, and the Committee on Graduate Education of the American Historical Association, *The Education of Historians for the Twenty-First Century* (Urbana, IL, 2004), 7–9.

15. Thelin, *A History of American Higher Education,* 304–6.

16. Nathan Reingold, *Science, American Style* (New Brunswick, NJ, 1991), chs. 9–10.

17. Thelin, *A History of American Higher Education,* 325.

18. David L. Featherman, "What Does Society Need from Higher Education," *Items* 47 (1993), 41. Of course, Great Britain, a considerable center for scholarship and science, and the substantial English-speaking research establishments in the countries that were once part of the British empire and are still part of the Commonwealth contribute to this figure. On the most cited articles, see *The Economist,* September 10, 2005, 14.

19. Data from Robert Wuthnow, *The Restructuring of American Religion: Society and Faith since World War II* (Princeton, NJ, 1988), 155.

20. *The Economist,* September 10, 2005, 14.

21. Abraham Flexner, *Universities: American, English, German* (New York, 1930); Merle Curti, "The Setting and the Problem," in *American Scholarship in the Twentieth Century,* ed. Merle Curti (Cambridge, MA, 1953), 15.

22. Harvard University Committee on the Objectives of a General Education in a Free Society, *General Education in a Free Society* (Cambridge, MA, 1946), 71, 74. Precisely this mismatch of interests emerged in a faculty conference on general education organized by a Harvard faculty committee with a mandate from the dean of the college to rethink the undergraduate curriculum (2003).

23. Thelin, *A History of American Higher Education,* 281–82.

24. See, for example, Dexter Perkins and John L. Snell, *The Education of Historians in the United States* (New York, 1962), which was one of the best of several sponsored by the Carnegie Corporation in New York and published by McGraw-Hill.

25. On the foundation's role in biochemistry, see Robert Kohler, *Partners in Science: Foundations and Natural Scientists, 1900–1945* (Chicago, 1991).

26. The report remains an impressive document, one that was in important respects courageous, making unambiguous reference to the dangers to thought and policy posed by references to "un-American activities" and other aspects of the era of McCarthyism. Ford Foundation, *Report of the Study for the Ford Foundation on Policy and Program* (Detroit, 1949).

27. Robert A. McCaughey, *International Studies and Academic Enterprise: A Chapter in the Enclosure of American Learning* (New York, 1984).

28. Quoted in ibid., 160–61.

29. David Szanton, "Introduction: The Origin, Nature, and Challenge of Area Studies in the United States," in *The Politics of Knowledge: Area Studies and the Disciplines,* ed. David Szanton (Berkeley, 2004), 11, 6.

30. See Bernard Berelson, "Behavioral Sciences," in *International Encyclopedia of the Social Sciences,* ed. David Sills (17 vols., New York, 1968), 41–45; and Ford Foundation, *Report of the Study for the Ford Foundation,* 43–48. See also Ron Robin, *The Making of the Cold War Enemy: Culture and Politics in the Military-Intellectual Complex* (Princeton, NJ, 2001).

31. Ford Foundation, *Report of the Study for the Ford Foundation,* 43–48, 90–99; and Ralph Tyler, "Report of the Planning Group," Center for Advanced Study in the Behavioral Sciences, June 1952. Files, Center for Advanced Study in the Behavioral Sciences, Palo Alto, California.

32. Geiger, *Research and Relevant Knowledge,* 105–6.

33. Albert Somit and Joseph Tanenhaus, *The Development of American Political Science: From Burgess to Behavioralism* (Boston, 1967), 168–69.

34. The most explicit example of this historiography was Louis Hartz, *The Liberal Tradition in America* (New York, 1955). This interpretive frame was named by John Higham, "Cult of 'American Consensus': Homogenizing Our History," *Commentary* (1959), 93–100.

35. Robert K. Merton, *Social Theory and Social Structure* (Glencoe, IL, 1949; enlarged ed. 1957); Talcott Parsons, *The Structure of Social Action,* 2nd ed. (Glencoe, IL, 1949).

36. See Thomas Bender and Carl E. Schorske, eds., *American Academic Culture in Transformation* (Princeton, NJ, 1998).

37. Daniel Bell, *The End of Ideology: On the Exhaustion of Political Ideas in the Fifties* (New York, 1962).

38. Cole, "Balancing Acts," 3; Jonathan R. Cole, "Academic Freedom Under Fire," *Daedalus* 134 (2005): 5.

39. David Damrosch, *We Academics.*

40. Quoted in Rebecca Lowen, *Creating the Cold War University: The Transformation of Stanford* (Berkeley, 1997), 147 (first quotation); Stuart W. Leslie, *The Cold War and American Science: The Military-Industrial-Academic Complex at MIT and Stanford* (New York, 1993), 2 (second quotation).

41. Lowen, *Creating the Cold War University,* 161.

42. Carol Gruber, *Mars and Minerva: World War I and the Uses of Higher Learning in America* (Baton Rouge, LA, 1975).

43. Leslie, *The Cold War and American Science,* 14 (quotation), 22.

44. Hugh Davis Graham and Nancy Diamond, *The Rise of American Research Universities: Elites and Challengers in the Postwar Era* (Baltimore, 1997), 32, 34; R. C. Lewontin, "The Cold War and the Transformation of the Academy," in *The Cold War and the University,* ed. [André Schiffrin] (New York, 1997), 16.

45. Roger L. Geiger, *Knowledge and Money: Research Universities and the Paradox of the Marketplace* (Stanford, CA, 2004), 72–73.

46. Massey, "Can the Research University Adapt to a Changing Future?" 195–96.

47. This point is made in Lewontin, "The Cold War and the Transformation of the Academy," 2.

48. See John D'Arms, "Funding Trends in the Academic Humanities, 1970–1995," in *What's Happened to the Humanities?* ed. Alvin Kernan (Princeton, NJ, 1997), 44–45.

49. Kerr, *The Uses of the University,* 142.

50. Phyllis Keller, *Getting at the Core: Curricular Reform at Harvard* (Cambridge, MA, 1982), 39.

51. Christopher Jencks and David Riesman, *The Academic Revolution* (Garden City, NY, 1968). See also Freeland, *Academia's Golden Age.*

52. Morton Keller and Phyllis Keller, *Making Harvard Modern,* 29–30.

53. Graham and Diamond, *The Rise of American Research Universities,* 27.

54. For a sample, see William J. Bennett, *To Reclaim a Legacy: A Report on the Humanities in Higher Education* (Washington, D.C., 1984); Charles T. Sykes, *ProfScam: Professors and the Demise of Higher Education* (New York, 1990); Dinesh D'Souza, *Illiberal Education: The Politics of Race and Sex on Campus* (New York, 1991); and Roger Kimball, *Tenured Radicals* (New York, 1990). Complaints about the quality of teaching continued beyond the 1990s into the new century. See Andrew Hacker, "The Truth About the Colleges," *The New York Review of Books,* November 3, 2005, 51–54.

55. Sam Dillon, "At Public Universities, Warnings of Privatization," *The New York Times,* October 16, 2005, 12.

56. Ibid. The rate of tuition increase at public institutions has run at approximately three times the rate of inflation since 1980. Jennifer Washburn, *University, Inc.: The Corporate Corruption of Higher Education* (New York, 2005), xiii.

57. Clark Kerr, *The Great Transformation in Higher Education, 1960–1980* (Albany, NY, 1991), 35–37.

58. See William G. Bowen and Derek Bok, *The Shape of the River: Long-Term Consequences of Considering Race in College and University Admissions* (Princeton, NJ, 1998).

59. Bowen, Kurzweil, and Tobin, *Equity and Excellence in American Higher Education,* 166. See also James L. Shulman and William G. Bowen, *The Game of Life: College Sports and Educational Values* (Princeton, NJ, 2001); and John R. Thelin, *Scandal and Reform in Intercollegiate Athletics* (Baltimore, 1994).

60. Thelin, *A History of the American University,* 342.

61. Geiger, *Knowledge and Money,* 264–65.

62. See Sheila Slaughter and Larry L. Leslie, *Academic Capitalism: Politics, Policies, and the Entrepreneurial University* (Baltimore, 1997).

63. David L. Kirp, *Shakespeare, Einstein, and the Bottom Line: The Marketing of Higher Education* (Cambridge, MA, 2003), 7.

64. Ibid., 243, 250.

65. See Derek Bok, *Universities in the Marketplace: The Commercialization of Higher Education* (Princeton, NJ, 2003), 2–3; Geiger, *Knowledge and Money*; Kirp, *Shakespeare, Einstein, and the Bottom Line*; and Washburn, *University, Inc.*

66. Cole, "Balancing Acts," 31.

67. Washburn, *University, Inc.,* 138.

68. Geiger, *Knowledge and Money,* 247.

69. Quoted in ibid., 99.

70. See Cole, "Balancing Acts," 6; and Kenneth Prewitt, "America's Research Universities under Public Scrutiny," in *The Research University in a Time of Discontent,* ed. Cole, Barber, and Graubard, 204–5.

71. Patrick M. Callan, "Government and Higher Education," in *Higher Learning in America, 1980–2000,* ed. Arthur Levine (Baltimore, 1993), 5.

72. We refer to Richard Hofstadter and Wilson Smith, eds., *American Higher Education, A Documentary History,* vols. 1–2 (Chicago, 1961).

Part I   The Terrain

How far did the terrain of higher learning extend in the United States during the second half of the twentieth century? Educational leaders and policy-makers asked themselves the harder question of what it ought to encompass. What array of institutions and institutional forms would provide higher learning for a society professedly egalitarian but deeply divided by region, class, race, religion, and gender? They were motivated to understand this issue in a new way for the challenging era of global responsibility. What is the relation of higher learning to public purpose, to the making of informed citizens, to personal enrichment of American lives, and to the economic well-being of individuals and the society as a whole?

The Harvard University Report, *Education for a Free Society* (1) and the Truman Commission's Report on Higher Education (II, 1) both addressed these large issues and outlined the initial response of American higher education to the challenge of extending the ideal of liberal education into a greatly enlarged academic establishment. As late as 1940, the scholarly world had a strongly Christian aura; thereafter, one of the great transformations was the secularization of American intellectual life (6). Secular and ever more democratic definitions of the humanities and liberal learning were proposed (9, 10). The successful mobilization of science in World War II encouraged an ambitious investment in academic science and international studies during the Cold War (2–4; VIII, 2, 12). It also seemed to be important to increase the numbers and diversity of the college-educated. The President's Commission insisted that neither race nor class (nor, eventually, gender) should limit access to higher learning (II, 1, 10–22). While accommodating these larger social and democratic agendas, academe was looking to maintain its historic liberal arts tradition (9–11, 14, 15). What, leaders asked, is the role and proper con-

tent of higher education in a democracy in a dangerous world—more dangerous than ever before, at least from an American perspective?

The decades immediately after World War II brought the United States to unprecedented economic growth and public sector investments, including higher education. Public institutions especially experienced giddy growth. Clark Kerr of the University of California embraced the transformative impact of this growth and the new institutional scale it implied (I, 12). Others, however, feared that such a "multiversity," as he called it, undermined the core values of the university (13). For many of those devoted to liberal learning, a sense of community—or connection—absent in the multiversity was fundamental (14, 15). Kerr himself, who had had such an experience as an undergraduate, came to recognize this, supporting the creation of cluster colleges at the new Santa Cruz campus in the 1960s. But in the end it found few imitators.

By the final decade of the century, the designs of the 1940s and 1950s had been largely swept aside. Developments within academic culture and beyond academe undercut what had momentarily been a national consensus on the meaning of American academic life. At century's end, different voices (18–23) alternately described and prescribed various presents and futures for American higher education. These visions ranged from postmodern critique (19) to civic hopefulness (22).

If at the beginning of the half-century there was confidence that the American economy could support substantial public investments in higher education, such was not the case at the end of the twentieth century. Nor were either national leaders or the general public so convinced that higher education was the important public good it had seemed to them after the war.

The Harvard Report on General Education

1. Harvard Committee, *General Education in a Free Society,* 1945

The dominant curricular statement of James Bryant Conant's presidency of Harvard University (1933–53) was widely known, after the color of its cover, as the "Red Book." Written at the request of their president by eleven eminent faculty members, the report was aimed at the nation and addressed the educational challenges of the postwar world. Conant (1893–1978) had been disturbed and by 1939 alarmed at the threat of totalitarian governments to liberal learning and liberal societies. Foreseeing a postwar surge in enrollments, he advised the committee in 1943 to point the undergraduate curriculum toward "the continuance of a liberal and humane tradition." The committee's chair was Paul H. Buck (History); its vice chair John H. Finley (Classics), joined by professors of biology, education, English, government, history, and philosophy.

Although the intellectual aims of the Red Book had been introduced at Columbia and Chicago in the 1920s, the Harvard program went beyond Great Ideas and Great Books to stress preparation for intelligent democratic citizenship at the college level. It was in keeping with Conant's description of himself as a "tough-minded" Jeffersonian idealist promoting national opportunities for education, with advancement going to individuals who merit it. "Endow the talented" with scholarships was one of his watchwords. The Red Book served as a model for curricular debate at many liberal arts colleges, secondary schools, and state boards of education. It stressed the importance of the humanities to undergird a liberal arts bachelor's degree in an increasingly technological and scientific age. By 1950, its sales had exceeded forty thousand copies. But at Harvard, ironically, General Education gradually lost faculty support due to professorial specialism with its proliferation of courses.

Besides his Harvard presidency, Conant, earlier an award-winning professor of chemistry (1919–33), pursued a public life in the militarization and administration of national applied science. During World War I in the Army Chemical Warfare Service he oversaw the manufacture of poison gas. In the 1940s he succeeded Vannevar Bush as chair of the National Defense Research Committee, where he recruited the nation's scientists for the secret wartime Manhattan Project to plan, develop, and finally use the atomic bomb. President Eisenhower appointed him High Commissioner of the postwar German Federal Republic (1953–55) and ambassador to West Germany (1955–57). Retaining his distrust of Soviet communism during these years, he saw himself as "a cold-war warrior." When he came home, he turned to reform of public high schools, charging them with insufficient rigor and urging them to emphasize basic liberal subjects that would nourish responsible citizenship. One of his several books, *The American High School Today* (1959), sold a half million copies.

Reprinted by permission of the publisher from General Education in a Free Society: Report of the Harvard Committee, pp. 43–58, Cambridge, Mass.: Harvard University Press, Copyright © 1945. Further reading: Conant, *My Several Lives: Memoirs of a Social Inventor* (New York, 1970); James G. Hershberg, *James B. Conant: Harvard to Hiroshima and the Making of the Nuclear Age* (New York, 1993); Phyllis Keller, *Getting at the Core* (Cambridge, MA, 1982); Morton Keller and Phyllis Keller, *Making Harvard Modern: The Rise of America's University* (New York, 2001); Ernest L. Boyer and Arthur Levine, *A Quest for Common Learning: The Aims of General Education* (Princeton, NJ, 1981); and Russell Thomas, *The Search for a Common Learning: General Education, 1800–1960* (New York, 1962). For Conant and admission tests, see II, 5; on academic freedom, see X, 2.

[A] supreme need of American education is for a unifying purpose and idea. As recently as a century ago, no doubt existed about such a purpose; it was to train the Christian citizen. Nor was there doubt how this training was to be accomplished. The student's logical powers were to be formed by mathematics, his taste by the Greek and Latin classics, his speech by rhetoric, and his ideals by Christian ethics. College catalogues commonly began with a specific statement about the influence of such a training on the mind and character. The reasons why this enviable certainty both of goal and of means has largely disappeared have already been set forth. For some decades the mere excitement of enlarging the curriculum and making place for new subjects, new methods, and masses of new students seems quite pardonably to have absorbed the energies of schools and colleges. It is fashionable now to criticize the leading figures of that expansive time for failing to replace, or even to see the need of replacing, the unity which they destroyed. But such criticisms, if just in themselves, are hardly just historically. A great and necessary task of modernizing and broadening education waited to be done, and there is credit enough in its accomplishment. In recent times, however, the question of unity has become insistent. We are faced with a diversity of education which, if it has many virtues, nevertheless works against the good of society by helping to destroy the common ground of training and outlook on which any society depends.

It seems that a common ground between some, though not all, of the ideas underlying our educational practice is the sense of heritage. The word heritage is not here taken to mean mere retrospection. The purpose of all education is to help students live their own lives. The appeal to heritage is partly to the authority, partly to the clarification of the past about what is important in the present. All Catholic and many Protestant institutions thus appeal to the Christian view of man and history as providing both final meaning and immediate standards for life. As observed at the outset, it is less than a century since such was the common practice of American education generally, and certainly this impulse to mold students to a pattern sanctioned by the past can, in one form or another, never be absent from education. If it were, society would become discontinuous.

In this concern for heritage lies a close similarity

between religious education and education in the great classic books. Exponents of the latter have, to be sure, described it as primarily a process of intellectual discipline in the joint arts of word and number, the so-called *trivium* (grammar, logic, rhetoric) and *quadrivium* (arithmetic, geometry, astronomy, music). But, since the very idea of this discipline goes back to antiquity and since the actual books by which it is carried out are in fact the great books of the Western tradition, it seems fairer, without denying the disciplinary value of such a curriculum, to think of it as primarily a process of opening before students the intellectual forces that have shaped the Western mind. There is a sense in which education in the great books can be looked at as a secular continuation of the spirit of Protestantism. As early Protestantism, rejecting the authority and philosophy of the medieval church, placed reliance on each man's personal reading of the Scriptures, so this present movement, rejecting the unique authority of the Scriptures, places reliance on the reading of those books which are taken to represent the fullest revelation of the Western mind. But be this as it may, it is certain that, like religious education, education in the great books is essentially an introduction of students to their heritage.

Nor is the sense of heritage less important, though it may be less obvious, a part of education for modern democratic life. To the degree that the implications of democracy are drawn forth and expounded, to that degree the long-standing impulse of education toward shaping students to a received ideal is still pursued. Consider the teaching of American history and of modern democratic life. However ostensibly factual such teaching may be, it commonly carries with it a presupposition which is not subject to scientific proof: namely, the presupposition that democracy is meaningful and right. Moreover, since contemporary life is itself a product of history, to study it is to tread unconsciously, in the words of the hymn, where the saints have trod. To know modern democracy is to know something at least of Jefferson, though you have not read him; to learn to respect freedom of speech or the rights of the private conscience is not to be wholly ignorant of the *Areopagitica* or the *Antigone*, though you know nothing about them. Whether, as philosophers of history argue, being conditioned by the present we inevitably judge the past by what we know in the present (since otherwise the past would be unintelligible) or whether human motives and choices do not in reality greatly change with time, the fact remains that the past and the present are parts of the same unrolling scene and, whether you enter early or late, you see for the most part the still-unfinished progress of the same issues.

Here, then, in so far as our culture is adequately reflected in current ideas on education, one point about it is clear: it depends in part on an inherited view of man and society which it is the function, though not the only function, of education to pass on. It is not and cannot be true that all possible choices are open to us individually or collectively. We are part of an organic process, which is the American, and, more broadly, the Western evolution. Our standards of judgment, ways of life, and form of government all bear the marks of this evolution, which would accordingly influence us, though confusedly, even if it were not understood. Ideally it should be understood at several degrees of depth which complement rather than exclude each other. To study the American present is to discern at best the aims and purposes of a free society animating its imperfections. To study the past is immensely to enrich the meaning of the present and at the same time to clarify it by the simplification of the writings and the issues which have been winnowed from history. To study either past or present is to confront, in some form or another, the philosophic and religious fact of man in history and to recognize the huge continuing influence alike on past and present of the stream of Jewish and Greek thought in Christianity. There is doubtless a sense in which religious education, education in the great books, and education in modern democracy may be mutually exclusive. But there is a far more important sense in which they work together to the same end, which is belief in the idea of man and society that we inherit, adapt, and pass on.

This idea is described in many ways, perhaps most commonly in recent times, as that of the dignity of man. To the belief in man's dignity must be added the recognition of his duty to his fellow men. Dignity does not rest on any man as a being separate from all other beings, which he in any case cannot be, but springs from his common humanity and exists positively as he makes the common good his own. This concept is essentially that of the Western tradition: the view of man as free and not as slave, an end in himself and not a means. It may have what many believe to be the limitations of humanism, which are those of pride and arise from making man the measure of all things. But it need not have these limitations, since it is equally compatible with a religious view of life. Thus it is similar to the position described at the end of the last chapter as cooperation without uniformity, agreement on the good of man at the level of performance without the necessity of agreement on ultimates. But two points have now been added. First, thus stated, the goal of education is not in conflict with but largely includes the goals of religious education, education in the Western tradition, and education in modern democracy. For these in turn have been seen to involve necessary elements in our common tradition, each to a great extent implied in the others as levels at which it can be understood. Certainly no fruitful way of stating the belief in the dignity and mutual obligation of man can present it as other than, at one and the same time, effective in the present, emerging from the past, and partaking of the nature not of fact but of faith. Second, it has become clear that the common ground between these various views—namely, the impulse to rear students to a received idea of the good—is in fact necessary to education. It is impossible to escape the realization that our society, like any society, rests on common beliefs and that a major task of education is to perpetuate them.

This conclusion raises one of the most fundamental problems of education, indeed of society itself: how to reconcile this necessity for common belief with the equally obvious necessity for new and independent insights leading to change. We approach here the one previously mentioned concept of education which was not included under the idea of heritage: namely, the views associated with the names of James and Dewey and having to do with science, the scientific attitude, and pragmatism. This is hardly the place to try to summarize this body of thought or even to set forth in detail its application by Mr. Dewey to education. To do so would be virtually to retrace the educational controversies of the last forty years. But, at the risk of some injustice to Mr. Dewey's thought as a whole, a few points can be made about it. It puts trust in the scientific method of thought, the method which demands that you reach conclusions from tested data only, but that, since the data may be enlarged or the conclusions themselves combined with still other conclusions, you must hold them only tentatively. It emphasizes that full truth is not known and that we must be forever led by facts to revise our approximations of it. As a feeling of commitment and of allegiance marks the sense of heritage, so a tone of tough-mindedness and curiosity and a readiness for change mark this pragmatic attitude.

Here, then, is a concept of education, founded on obedience to fact and well disposed, even hospitable, to change, which appears at first sight the antithesis of any view based on the importance of heritage. Such hostility to tradition well reflects one side of the modern mind. It is impossible to contemplate the changes even of the last decades, much less the major groundswell of change since the Renaissance, without feeling that we face largely new conditions which call for new qualities of mind and outlook. Moreover, it is obviously no accident that this pragmatic philosophy has been worked out most fully in the United States. Yet, in spite of its seeming conflict with views of education based on heritage, strong doubt exists whether the questioning, innovating, experimental attitude of pragmatism is in fact something alien to the Western heritage, or whether it is not, in the broadest sense of the word, a part of it.

The rest of the present volume would hardly suffice for this sweeping subject. But it can be observed even here that we look back on antiquity not simply out of curiosity but because ancient thought is sympathetic to us. The Greek idea of an orderly universe, of political freedom under rationally constructed laws, and of the inner life itself as subject to the sway of reason, was certainly not achieved without skepticism, observation, or the test of experience. The ancient atomists and medical writers and, to a large extent, Socrates himself relied precisely on induction from observed facts. Socrates, the teacher and the gadfly of the Athenian city, impressed on his pupils and the public at large the duty of man to reflect on his beliefs and to criticize his presuppositions. Socrates was an individualist proclaiming that man should form his opinions by his own reasoning and not receive them by social indoctrination. And yet, it was this same Socrates who died in obedience to the judgment of the state, even though he believed this judgment to be wrong. Again, historical Christianity has been expressly and consistently concerned with the importance of this life on earth. The doctrine of the Incarnation, that God took the form of man and inhabited the earth, declares this concern. While perhaps for Greek thought, only the timeless realm had importance, in Christian thought the process of history is vested with absolute significance. If the ideal of democracy was rightly described above in the interwoven ideas of the dignity of man (that is, his existence as an independent moral agent) and his duty to his fellow men (that is, his testing by outward performance), the debt of these two ideas to the similarly interwoven commandments of the love of God and the love of neighbor is obvious.

These evidences of a consistent and characteristic appeal through Western history to the test of reason and experience are not adduced for the purpose of minimizing the huge creativeness of the modern scientific age or of glossing over its actual break from the past. In the well-known opening chapters of his *Science and the Modern World* in which he inquires into the origin of modern science, Mr. Whitehead pictures it as inspired by a revolt against abstract reasoning and a respect for unique fact. So considered, the first impulse of modern science was antirational or, better, antitheoretical, in the sense that it was a reaction against the most towering intellectual system which the West has known, namely, scholasticism. But be this question of origin as it may, there is no doubt that the modern mind received one of its characteristic bents in the empiricism, the passion for observation, and the distrust of abstract reasoning which have attended the origin and growth of science.

But there also seems no doubt that what happened was a shift, perhaps to some degree a restoration, of emphasis within the Western tradition itself rather than a complete change in its nature. It is a mistake to identify the older Western culture with traditionalism. Classical antiquity handed on a working system of truth which relied on both reason and experience and was designed to provide a norm for civilized life. Its import was heightened and vastly intensified by its confluence with Christianity. But when, in its rigid systematization in the late Middle Ages, it lost touch with experience and individual inquiry, it violated its own nature and provoked the modernist revolt. The seeming opposition that resulted between traditionalism and modernism has been a tragedy for Western thought. Modernism rightly affirms the importance of inquiry and of relevance to experience. But as scholasticism ran the danger of becoming a system without vitality, so modernism runs the danger of achieving vitality without pattern.

While, then, there are discontinuities between the classical and the modern components of our Western culture, there are also continuities. For instance, it would be wrong to construe the scientific outlook as inimical to human values. Even if it were true that science is concerned with means only, it would not follow that science ignores the intrinsic worth of man. For the values of human life cannot be achieved within a physical vacuum; they require for their fulfillment the existence of material conditions. To the extent that classical civilization failed to mitigate the evils of poverty, disease, squalor, and a generally low level of living among the masses, to that extent it failed to liberate man. Conversely, to the extent that science, especially in its medical and technological applications, has succeeded in dealing with these evils, it has contributed to the realization of human values. Thus science has implemented the humanism which classicism and Christianity have proclaimed.

Science has done more than provide the material basis of the good life; it has directly fostered the spiritual values of humanism. To explain, science is both the outcome and the source of the habit of forming objective, disinterested judgments based upon exact evidence. Such a habit is of particular value in the formation of citizens for a free society. It opposes to the arbitrariness of authority and "first principles" the direct and continuing appeal to things as they are. Thus it develops the qualities of the free man. It is no accident that John Locke, who set forth the political doctrine of the natural rights of man against established authority, should have been also the man who rejected the authority of innate ideas.

Students of antiquity and of the Middle Ages can therefore rightly affirm that decisive truths about the human mind and its relation to the world were laid hold of then, and yet agree that, when new application of these truths was made through a more scrupulous attention to fact, their whole implication and meaning were immensely enlarged. Modern civilization has seen this enlargement of meaning and possibility; yet it is not a new civilization but the organic development of an earlier civilization. The true task of education is therefore so to reconcile the sense of pattern and direction deriving from heritage with the sense of experiment and innovation deriving from science that they may exist fruitfully together, as in varying degrees they have never ceased to do throughout Western history.

Belief in the dignity and mutual obligation of man is the common ground between these contrasting but mutually necessary forces in our culture. As was pointed out earlier, this belief is the fruit at once of religion, of the Western tradition, and of the American tradition. It equally inspires the faith in human reason which is the basis for trust in the future of the democracy. And if it is not, strictly speaking, implied in all statements of the scientific method, there is no doubt that science has become its powerful instrument. In this tension between the opposite forces of heritage and change poised only in the faith in man, lies something like the old philosophic problem of the knowledge of the good. If you know the good, why do you seek it? If you are ignorant of the good, how do you recognize it when you find it? You must evidently at one and the same time both know it and be ignorant of it. Just so, the tradition which has come down to us regarding the nature of man and the good society must inevitably provide our standard of good. Yet an axiom of that tradition itself is the belief that no current form of the received ideal is final but that every generation, indeed every individual, must discover it in a fresh form. Education can therefore be wholly devoted neither to tradition nor to experiment, neither to the belief that the ideal in itself is enough nor to the view that means are valuable apart from the ideal. It must uphold at the same time tradition and experiment, the ideal and the means, subserving, like our culture itself, change within commitment.

GENERAL AND SPECIAL EDUCATION

In the previous section we have attempted to outline the unifying elements of our culture and therefore of American education as well. In the present section we shall take the next step of indicating in what ways these cultural strands may be woven into the fabric of education. Education is broadly divided into general and special education; our topic now is the difference and the relationship between the two. The term, general education, is somewhat vague and colorless; it does not mean some airy education in knowledge in general (if there be such knowledge), nor does it mean education for all in the sense of universal education. It is used to indicate that part of a student's whole education which looks first of all to his life as a responsible human being and citizen; while the term, special education, indicates that part which looks to the student's competence in some occupation. These two sides of life are not entirely separable, and it would be false to imagine education for the one as quite distinct from education for the other—more will be said on this point presently. Clearly, general education has somewhat the meaning of liberal education, except that, by applying to high school as well as to college, it envisages immensely greater numbers of students and thus escapes the invidium which, rightly or wrongly, attaches to liberal education in the minds of some people. But if one clings to the root meaning of liberal as that which befits or helps to make free men, then general and liberal education have identical goals. The one may be thought of as an earlier stage of the other, similar in nature but less advanced in degree.

The opposition to liberal education—both to the phrase and to the fact—stems largely from historical causes. The concept of liberal education first appeared in a slave-owning society, like that of Athens, in which the community was divided into free men and slaves, rulers and subjects. While the slaves carried on the specialized occupations of menial work, the freemen were primarily concerned with the rights and duties of citizenship. The training of the former was purely vocational; but as the freemen were not only a ruling class but also a leisure class, their education was exclusively in the liberal arts, without any utilitarian tinge. The freemen were trained in the reflective pursuit of the good life; their education was unspecialized as well as unvocational; its aim was to produce a rounded person with a full understanding of himself and of his place in society and in the cosmos.

Modern democratic society clearly does not regard labor as odious or disgraceful; on the contrary, in this country at least, it regards leisure with suspicion and expects its "gentlemen" to engage in work. Thus we attach no odium to vocational instruction. Moreover, in so far as we surely reject the idea of freemen who are free in so far as they have slaves or subjects, we are apt strongly to deprecate the liberal education which went with the structure of the aristocratic ideal. Herein our society runs the risk of committing a serious fallacy. Democracy is the view that not only the few but that all are free, in that everyone governs his own life and shares in the responsibility for the management of the community. This being the case, it follows that all human beings stand in need of an ampler and rounded education. The task of modern democracy is to preserve the ancient ideal of liberal education and to extend it as far as possible to all the members of the community. In short, we have been apt to confuse accidental with fundamental factors, in our suspicion of the classical ideal. To believe in the equality of human beings is to believe that the good life, and the education which trains the citizen for the good life, are equally the privilege of all. And these are the touchstones of the liberated man; first, is he free; that is to say, is he able to judge and plan for himself, so that he can truly govern himself? In order to do this, his must be a mind capable of self-criticism; he must lead that self-examined life which according to Socrates is alone worthy of a freeman. Thus he will possess inner freedom, as well as social freedom. Second, is he universal in his motives and sympathies? For the civilized man is a citizen of the entire universe; he has overcome provincialism, he is objective, and is a "spectator of all time and all existence." Surely these two are the very aims of democracy itself.

But the opposition to general education does not stem from causes located in the past alone. We are living in an age of specialism, in which the avenue to success for the student often lies in his choice of a specialized career, whether as a chemist, or an engineer, or a doctor, or a specialist in some form of business or of manual or technical work. Each of these specialties makes an increasing demand on the time and on the interest of the student. Specialism is the means for advancement in our mobile social structure; yet we must envisage the fact that a society controlled wholly by specialists is not a wisely ordered society. We cannot, however, turn away from specialism. The problem is how to save general education and its values within a system where specialism is necessary.

The very prevalence and power of the demand for special training makes doubly clear the need for a concurrent, balancing force in general education. Specialism enhances the centrifugal forces in society. The business of providing for the needs of society breeds a great diversity of special occupations; and a given specialist does not speak the language of the other specialists. In order to discharge his duties as a citizen adequately, a person must somehow be able to grasp the complexities of life as a whole. Even from the point of view of economic success, specialism has its peculiar limitations. Specializing in a vocation makes for inflexibility in a world of fluid possibilities. Business demands minds capable of adjusting themselves to varying situations and of managing complex human institutions. Given the pace of economic progress, techniques alter speedily; and even the work in which the student has been trained may no longer be useful when he is ready to earn a living, or soon after. Our conclusion, then, is that the aim of education should be to prepare an individual to become an expert both in some particular vocation or art and in the general art of the freeman and the citizen. Thus the two kinds of education once given separately to different social classes must be given together to all alike.

In this epoch in which almost all of us must be experts in some field in order to make a living, general education therefore assumes a peculiar importance. Since no one can become an expert in all fields, everyone is compelled to trust the judgment of other people pretty thoroughly in most areas of activity. I must trust the advice of my doctor, my plumber, my lawyer, my radio repairman, and so on. Therefore I am in peculiar need of a kind of sagacity by which to distinguish the expert from the quack, and the better from the worse expert. From this point of view, the aim of general education may be defined as that of providing the broad critical sense by which to recognize competence in any field. William James said that an educated person knows a good man when he sees one. There are standards and a style for every type of activity—manual, athletic, intellectual, or artistic; and the educated man should be one who can tell sound from shoddy work in a field outside his own. General education is especially required in a democracy where the public elects its leaders and officials; the ordinary citizen must be discerning enough so that he will not be deceived by appearances and will elect the candidate who is wise in his field.

Both kinds of education—special as well as general—contribute to the task of implementing the pervasive forces of our culture. Here we revert to what was said at the start of this chapter on the aims of education in our society. It was argued there that two complementary forces are at the root of our culture: on the one hand, an ideal of man and society distilled from the past but at the same time transcending the past as a standard of judgment valid in itself, and, on the other hand, the belief that no existent expressions of this ideal are final but that all alike call for perpetual scrutiny and change in the light of new knowledge. Specialism is usually the vehicle of this second force. It fosters the open-mindedness and love of investigation which are the wellspring of change, and it devotes itself to the means by which change is brought about. The fact may not always be obvious. There is a sterile specialism which hugs accepted knowledge and ends in the bleakest conservatism. Modern life also calls for many skills which, though specialized, are repetitive and certainly do not conduce to inquiry. These minister to change but unconsciously. Nevertheless, the previous statement is true in the sense that specialism is concerned primarily with knowledge in action, as it advances into new fields and into further applications.

Special education comprises a wider field than vocationalism; and correspondingly, general education extends beyond the limits of merely literary preoccupation. An example will make our point clearer. A scholar—let us say a scientist (whether student or teacher)—will, in the laudable aim of saving himself from narrowness, take a course in English literature, or perhaps read poetry and novels, or perhaps listen to good music and generally occupy himself with the fine arts. All this, while eminently fine and good, reveals a misapprehension. In his altogether unjustified humility, the scientist wrongly interprets the distinction between liberal and illiberal in terms of the distinction between the humanities and the sciences. Plato and Cicero would have been very much surprised to hear that geometry, astronomy, and the sciences of nature in general, are excluded from the humanities. There is also implied a more serious contempt for the liberal arts, harking back to the fallacy which identifies liberal education with the aristocratic ideal. The implication is that liberal education is something only genteel. A similar error is evident in the student's attitude towards his required courses outside his major field as something to "get over with," so that he may engage in the business of serious education, identified in his mind with the field of concentration.

Now, a general education is distinguished from special education, not by subject matter, but in terms of method and outlook, no matter what the field. Literature, when studied in a technical fashion, gives rise to the special science of philology; there is also the highly specialized historical approach to painting. Specialism is interchangeable, not with natural science, but with the method of science, the method which abstracts material from its context and handles it in complete isolation. The reward of scientific method is the utmost degree of precision and exactness. But, as we have seen, specialism as an educational force has its own limitations; it does not usually provide an insight into general relationships.

A further point is worth noting. The impact of specialism has been felt not only in those phases of education which are necessarily and rightly specialistic; it has affected also the whole structure of higher and even of secondary education. Teachers, themselves products of highly technical disciplines, tend to reproduce their knowledge in class. The result is that each subject, being taught by an expert, tends to be so presented as to attract potential experts. This complaint is perhaps more keenly felt in colleges and universities, which naturally look to scholarship. The undergraduate in a college receives his teaching from professors who, in their turn, have been trained in graduate schools. And the latter are dominated by the ideal of specialization. Learning now is diversified and parceled into a myriad of specialties. Correspondingly, colleges and universities are divided into large numbers of departments, with further specialization within the departments. As a result, a student in search of a general course is commonly frustrated. Even an elementary course is devised as an introduction to a specialism within a department; it is significant only as the beginning of a series of courses of advancing complexity. In short, such introductory courses are planned for the specialist, not for the student seeking a general education. The young chemist in the course in literature and the young writer in the course in chemistry find themselves in thoroughly uncomfortable positions so long as the purpose of these courses is primarily to train experts who will go on to higher courses rather than to give some basic understanding of science as it is revealed in chemistry or of the arts as they are revealed in literature.

It is most unfortunate if we envisage general education as something formless—that is to say, the taking of one course after another; and as something negative, namely, the study of what is not in a field of concentration. Just as we regard the courses in concentration as having definite relations to one another, so should we envisage general education as an organic whole whose parts join in expounding a ruling idea and in serving a common aim. And to do so means to abandon the view that all fields and all departments are equally valuable vehicles of general education. It also implies some prescription. At the least it means abandoning the usual attitude of regarding "distribution" as a sphere in which the student exercises a virtually untrammeled freedom of choice. It may be objected that we are proposing to limit the liberty of the student in the very name of liberal education. Such an objection would only indicate an ambiguity in the conception of liberal education. We must distinguish between liberalism in education and education in liberalism. The former, based as it is on the doctrine of individualism, expresses the view that the student should be free in his choice of courses. But education in liberalism is an altogether different matter; it is education which has a pattern of its own, namely, the pattern associated with the liberal outlook. In this view, there are truths which none can be free to ignore, if one is to have that wisdom through which life can become useful. These are the truths concerning the structure of the good life and concerning the factual conditions by which it may be achieved, truths comprising the goals of the free society.

Finally, the problem of general education is one of combining fixity of aim with diversity in application. It is not a question of providing a general education which will be uniform through the same classes of all schools and colleges all over the country, even were such a thing possible in our decentralized system. It is rather to adapt general education to the needs and intentions of different groups and, so far as possible, to carry its spirit into special education. The effectiveness of teaching has always largely depended on this willingness to adapt a central unvarying purpose to varying outlooks. Such adaptation is as much in the interest of the quick as of the slow, of the bookish as of the unbookish, and is the necessary protection of each. What is wanted, then, is a general education capable at once of taking on many different forms and yet of representing in all its forms the common knowledge and the common values on which a free society depends.

Science

2. Vannevar Bush,
Science, the Endless Frontier, 1945

This design for the organization and federal support of postwar basic research in the physical sciences was a pathmarking and welcomed document among the nation's scientists. Vannevar Bush (1890–1974) forwarded the report in 1945 to Franklin D. Roosevelt at the president's request. Not until 1950 did the National Research Foundation, which Bush foresaw, finally receive congressional approval. It was delayed because it separated biological from medical research (the two were soon merged), did not consider economic and social issues, stepped on the toes of existing civilian and military agencies, and was belatedly modified to make the director of the new foundation responsible to a new president, Harry S. Truman. The renamed National Science Foundation had a limited budget until the launch of the Soviet Russian satellite *Sputnik* in 1957, when nationwide alarm

at the American lag in this field and the resultant urgency to create a pool of young physicists brought ever-increasing funding.

A gifted scientist and administrator, Bush was well prepared to produce this report, supported by several appended committee recommendations. After a professorship in electrical engineering at the Massachusetts Institute of Technology (1919–38), where he invented an early analog computer (differential analyzer) and code-breaking machines used by the Navy, he moved to the presidency of the Carnegie Institution of Washington to oversee a collection of research institutes. There he became increasingly involved with people who were considering the probable mobilization of science for war. Introduced to President Roosevelt in 1940, his ideas were well received, and he thereafter had the ear of the president. Roosevelt appointed him to chair the National Defense Research Committee and, in 1941, to direct the new umbrella Office of Scientific Research and Development. In his work he was abetted by two colleagues from his Cambridge days: James B. Conant of Harvard and Karl T. Compton of MIT. Their theme in the early war years was the urgent need for team efforts in wartime weapons research under efficient federal coordination, a theme partly transformed to peacetime purposes in this famous schematic report.

Vannevar Bush, *Science, the Endless Frontier: A Report to the President on a Program for Postwar Scientific Research* (1945; repr. Washington, D.C., 1960), 5–12, 31–34, 40. Further reading: Bush's autobiographical *Pieces of Action* (New York, 1970) and his widely read *Modern Arms and Free Men: A Discussion of the Role of Science in Preserving Democracy* (New York, 1949); Nathan Reingold, "Vannevar Bush," in *American National Biography,* ed. John M. Garraty and Mark C. Carnes, vol. 4 (New York, 2000), 77–81; Patrick J. McGrath, *Science, Business, and the State, 1890–1960* (Chapel Hill, NC, 2002); Daniel J. Kevles, *The Physicists: The History of a Scientific Community in Modern America* (New York, 1977, revised with new preface 1995); and Sally Gregory Kohlstedt, Michael M. Sokal, and Bruce V. Lewenstein, *The Establishment of Science in America: 150 Years of the American Association for the Advancement of Science* (New Brunswick, NJ, 1999). Jeffrey J. Williams, "The Post–Welfare State University," *American Literary History* 18 (Spring 2006): 190–216, valuably summarizes a growing critical literature on institutional control and support and the situation of academic workers within "academic capitalism" entering the twenty-first century.

SUMMARY OF THE REPORT

Progress in the war against disease depends upon a flow of new scientific knowledge. New products, new industries, and more jobs require continuous additions to knowledge of the laws of nature, and the application of that knowledge to practical purposes. Similarly, our defense against aggression demands new knowledge so that we can develop new and improved weapons. This essential, new knowledge can be obtained only through basic scientific research.

Science can be effective in the national welfare only as a member of a team, whether the conditions be peace or war. But without scientific progress no amount of achievement in other directions can insure our health, prosperity, and security as a nation in the modern world. . . .

The responsibility for basic research in medicine and the underlying sciences, so essential to progress in the war against disease, falls primarily upon the medical schools and universities. Yet we find that the traditional sources of support for medical research in the medical schools and universities, largely endowment income, foundation grants, and private donations, are diminishing and there is no immediate prospect of a change in this trend. Meanwhile, the cost of medical research has been rising. If we are to maintain the progress in medicine which has marked the last 25 years, the Government should extend financial support to basic medical research in the medical schools and in universities. . . .

One of our hopes is that after the war there will be full employment. To reach that goal the full creative and productive energies of the American people must be released. To create more jobs we must make new and better and cheaper products. We want plenty of new, vigorous enterprises. But new products and processes are not born full-grown. They are founded on new principles and new conceptions which in turn result from basic scientific research. Basic scientific research is scientific capital. Moreover, we cannot any longer depend upon Europe as a major source of this scientific capital. Clearly, more and better scientific research is one essential to the achievement of our goal of full employment.

How do we increase this scientific capital? First, we must have plenty of men and women trained in science, for upon them depends both the creation of new knowledge and its application to practical purposes. Second, we must strengthen the centers of basic research which are principally the colleges, universities, and research institutes. These institutions provide the environment which is most conducive to the creation of new scientific knowledge and least under pressure for immediate, tangible results. With some notable exceptions, most research in industry and in Government involves application of existing scientific knowledge to practical problems. It is only the colleges, universities, and a few research institutes that devote most of their research efforts to expanding the frontiers of knowledge.

Expenditures for scientific research by industry and Government increased from $140,000,000 in 1930 to $309,000,000 in 1940. Those for the colleges and universities increased from $20,000,000 to $31,000,000, while those for research institutes declined from $5,200,000 to $4,500,000 during the same period. If the colleges, universities, and research institutes are to meet the rapidly increasing demands of industry and Government for new scientific knowledge, their basic research should be strengthened by use of public funds. . . .

The responsibility for the creation of new scientific knowledge—and for most of its application— rests on that small body of men and women who understand the fundamental laws of nature and are skilled in the techniques of scientific research. We shall have rapid or slow advance on any scientific frontier depending on the number of highly qualified and trained scientists exploring it.

The deficit of science and technology students who, but for the war, would have received bachelor's degrees is about 150,000. It is estimated that the deficit of those obtaining advanced degrees in these fields will amount in 1955 to about 17,000—for it takes at least 6 years from college entry to achieve a doctor's degree or its equivalent in science or engineering. The real ceiling on our productivity of new scientific knowledge and its application in the war against disease, and the development of new products and new industries, is the number of trained scientists available.

The training of a scientist is a long and expensive process. Studies clearly show that there are talented individuals in every part of the population, but with few exceptions, those without the means of buying higher education go without it. If ability, and not the circumstance of family fortune, determines who shall receive higher education in science, then we shall be assured of constantly improving quality at every level of scientific activity. The Government should provide a reasonable number of undergraduate scholarships and graduate fellowships in order to develop scientific talent in American youth. The plans should be designed to attract into science only that proportion of youthful talent appropriate to the needs of science in relation to the other needs of the Nation for high abilities. . . .

The Government should accept new responsibilities for promoting the flow of new scientific knowledge and the development of scientific talent in our youth. These responsibilities are the proper concern of the Government, for they vitally affect our health, our jobs, and our national security. It is in keeping also with basic United States policy that the Government should foster the opening of new frontiers and this is the modern way to do it. For many years the Government has wisely supported research in the agricultural colleges and the benefits have been great. The time has come when such support should be extended to other fields.

The effective discharge of these new responsibilities will require the full attention of some over-all agency devoted to that purpose. There is not now in the permanent governmental structure receiving its funds from Congress an agency adapted to supplementing the support of basic research in the colleges, universities, and research institutes, both in medicine and the natural sciences, adapted to supporting research on new weapons for both Services, or adapted to administering a program of science scholarships and fellowships.

Therefore I recommend that a new agency for these purposes be established. Such an agency should be composed of persons of broad interest and experience, having an understanding of the peculiarities of scientific research and scientific education. It should have stability of funds so that long-range programs may be undertaken. It should recognize that freedom of inquiry must be preserved and should leave internal control of policy, personnel, and the method and scope of research to the institutions in which it is carried on. It should be fully responsible to the President and through him to the Congress for its program.

Early action on these recommendations is imperative if this Nation is to meet the challenge of science in the crucial years ahead. On the wisdom with which we bring science to bear in the war against disease, in the creation of new industries, and in the strengthening of our Armed Forces depends in large measure our future as a nation.

INTRODUCTION

In 1939 millions of people were employed in industries which did not even exist at the close of the last war—radio, air conditioning, rayon and other synthetic fibers, and plastics are examples of the products of these industries. But these things do not mark the end of progress—they are but the beginning if we make full use of our scientific resources. New manufacturing industries can be started and many older industries greatly strengthened and expanded if we continue to study nature's laws and apply new knowledge to practical purposes.

Great advances in agriculture are also based upon scientific research. Plants which are more resistant to disease and are adapted to short growing seasons, the prevention and cure of livestock diseases, the control of our insect enemies, better fertilizers, and improved agricultural practices, all stem from painstaking scientific research.

Advances in science when put to practical use mean more jobs, higher wages, shorter hours, more abundant crops, more leisure for recreation, for study, for learning how to live without the deadening drudgery which has been the burden of the common man for ages past. Advances in science will also bring higher standards of living, will lead to the prevention or cure of diseases, will promote conservation of our limited national resources, and will assure means of defense against aggression. But to achieve these objectives—to secure a high level of employment, to maintain a position of world leadership—the flow of new scientific knowledge must be both continuous and substantial.

Our population increased from 75 million to 130 million between 1900 and 1940. In some countries comparable increases have been accompanied by famine. In this country the increase has been accompanied by more abundant food supply, better living, more leisure, longer life, and better health. This is, largely, the product of three factors—the free play of initiative of a vigorous people under democracy, the heritage of great natural wealth, and the advance of science and its application.

Science, by itself, provides no panacea for individual, social, and economic ills. It can be effective in the national welfare only as a member of a team, whether the conditions are peace or war. But without scientific progress no amount of achievement in other directions can insure our health, prosperity, and security as a nation in the modern world.

It has been basic United States policy that Government should foster the opening of new frontiers. It opened the seas to clipper ships and furnished land for pioneers. Although these frontiers have more or less disappeared, the frontier of science remains. It is in keeping with the American tradition—one which has made the United States great—that new frontiers shall be made accessible for development by all American citizens.

Moreover, since health, well-being, and security are proper concerns of Government, scientific progress is, and must be, of vital interest to Government. Without scientific progress the national health would deteriorate; without scientific progress we could not hope for improvement in our standard of living or for an increased number of jobs for our citizens; and without scientific progress we could not have maintained our liberties against tyranny. . . .

We have no national policy for science. The Government has only begun to utilize science in the Nation's welfare. There is no body within the Government charged with formulating or executing a national science policy. There are no standing committees of the Congress devoted to this important subject. Science has been in the wings. It should be brought to the center of the stage—for in it lies much of our hope for the future.

There are areas of science in which the public interest is acute but which are likely to be cultivated inadequately if left without more support than will come from private sources. These areas—such as research on military problems, agriculture, housing, public health, certain medical research, and research involving expensive capital facilities beyond the capacity of private institutions—should be advanced by active Government support. To date, with the exception of the intensive war research conducted by the Office of Scientific Research and Development, such support has been meager and intermittent.

For reasons presented in this report we are entering a period when science needs and deserves increased support from public funds.

The publicly and privately supported colleges, universities, and research institutes are the centers of basic research. They are the wellsprings of knowledge and understanding. As long as they are vigorous and healthy and their scientists are free to pursue the truth wherever it may lead, there will be a flow of new scientific knowledge to those who can apply it to practical problems in Government, in industry, or elsewhere.

Many of the lessons learned in the war-time application of science under Government can be profitably applied in peace. The Government is peculiarly fitted to perform certain functions, such as the coordination and support of broad programs on problems of great national importance. But we must proceed with caution in carrying over the methods which work in wartime to the very different conditions of peace. We must remove the rigid controls which we have had to impose, and recover freedom of inquiry and that healthy competitive scientific spirit so necessary for expansion of the frontiers of scientific knowledge.

Scientific progress on a broad front results from the free play of free intellects, working on subjects of their own choice, in the manner dictated by their curiosity for exploration of the unknown. Freedom of inquiry must be preserved under any plan for Government support of science in accordance with the Five Fundamentals listed [below].

The study of the momentous questions presented in President Roosevelt's letter has been made by able committees working diligently. This report presents conclusions and recommendations based upon the studies of these committees which appear in full as the appendices. Only in the creation of one overall mechanism rather than several does this report depart from the specific recommendations of the committees. The members of the committees have reviewed the recommendations in regard to the single mechanism and have found this plan thoroughly acceptable.

THE MEANS TO THE END

One lesson is clear from the reports of the several committees attached as appendices. The Federal Government should accept new responsibilities for promoting the creation of new scientific knowledge and the development of scientific talent in our youth.

The extent and nature of these new responsibilities are set forth in detail in the reports of the committees whose recommendations in this regard are fully endorsed.

In discharging these responsibilities Federal funds should be made available. We have given much thought to the question of how plans for the use of Federal funds may be arranged so that such funds will not drive out of the picture funds from local governments, foundations, and private donors. We believe that our proposals will minimize that effect, but we do not think that it can be completely avoided. We submit, however, that the Nation's need for more and better scientific research is such that the risk must be accepted.

It is also clear that the effective discharge of these responsibilities will require the full attention of some over-all agency devoted to that purpose. There

should be a focal point within the Government for a concerted program of assisting scientific research conducted outside of Government. Such an agency should furnish the funds needed to support basic research in the colleges and universities, should coordinate where possible research programs on matters of utmost importance to the national welfare, should formulate a national policy for the Government toward science, should sponsor the interchange of scientific information among scientists and laboratories both in this country and abroad, and should ensure that the incentives to research in industry and the universities are maintained. . . .

Nowhere in the governmental structure receiving its funds from Congress is there an agency adapted to supplementing the support of basic research in the universities, both in medicine and the natural sciences; adapted to supporting research on new weapons for both Services; or adapted to administering a program of science scholarships and fellowships.

A new agency should be established, therefore, by the Congress for the purpose. Such an agency, moreover, should be an independent agency devoted to the support of scientific research and advanced scientific education alone. Industry learned many years ago that basic research cannot often be fruitfully conducted as an adjunct to or a subdivision of an operating agency or department. Operating agencies have immediate operating goals and are under constant pressure to produce in a tangible way, for that is the test of their value. None of these conditions is favorable to basic research. Research is the exploration of the unknown and is necessarily speculative. It is inhibited by conventional approaches, traditions, and standards. It cannot be satisfactorily conducted in an atmosphere where it is gauged and tested by operating or production standards. Basic scientific research should not, therefore, be placed under an operating agency whose paramount concern is anything other than research. Research will always suffer when put in competition with operations. The decision that there should be a new and independent agency was reached by each of the committees advising in these matters.

I am convinced that these new functions should be centered in one agency. Science is fundamentally a unitary thing. The number of independent agencies should be kept to a minimum. Much medical progress, for example, will come from fundamental advances in chemistry. Separation of the sciences in tight compartments, as would occur if more than one agency were involved, would retard and not advance scientific knowledge as a whole.

There are certain basic principles which must underlie the program of Government support for scientific research and education if such support is to be effective and if it is to avoid impairing the very things we seek to foster. These principles are as follows:

(1) Whatever the extent of support may be, there must be stability of funds over a period of years so that long-range programs may be undertaken.

(2) The agency to administer such funds should be composed of citizens selected only on the basis of their interest in and capacity to promote the work of the agency. They should be persons of broad interest in and understanding of the peculiarities of scientific research and education.

(3) The agency should promote research through contracts or grants to organizations outside the Federal Government. It should not operate any laboratories of its own.

(4) Support of basic research in the public and private colleges, universities, and research institutes must leave the internal control of policy, personnel, and the method and scope of the research to the institutions themselves. This is of the utmost importance.

(5) While assuring complete independence and freedom for the nature, scope, and methodology of research carried on in the institutions receiving public funds, and while retaining discretion in the allocation of funds among such institutions, the Foundation proposed herein must be responsible to the President and the Congress. Only through such responsibility can we maintain the proper relationship between science and other aspects of a democratic system. The usual controls of audits, reports, budgeting, and the like, should, of course, apply to the administrative and fiscal operations of the Foundation, subject, however, to such adjustments in procedure as are necessary to meet the special requirements of research.

Basic research is a long-term process—it ceases to be basic if immediate results are expected on short-term support. Methods should therefore be found which will permit the agency to make commitments of funds from current appropriations for programs of five years duration or longer. Continuity and stability of the program and its support may be expected (a) from the growing realization by the Congress of the benefits to the public from scientific research, and (b) from the conviction which will grow among those who conduct research under the auspices of the agency that good quality work will be followed by continuing support....

The job of long range research involving application of the newest scientific discoveries to military needs should be the responsibility of those civilian scientists in the universities and in industry who are best trained to discharge it thoroughly and successfully. It is essential that both kinds of research go forward and that there be the closest liaison between the two groups.

Placing the civilian military research function in the proposed agency would bring it into close relationship with a broad program of basic research in both the natural sciences and medicine. A balance between military and other research could thus readily be maintained....

It is my judgment that the national interest in scientific research and scientific education can best be promoted by the creation of a National Research Foundation.

The National Research Foundation should develop and promote a national policy for scientific research and scientific education, should support basic research in nonprofit organizations, should develop scientific talent in American youth by means of scholarships and fellowships, and should by contract and otherwise support long-range research on military matters....

The National Research Foundation herein proposed meets the urgent need of the days ahead. The form of the organization suggested is the result of considerable deliberation. The form is important. The very successful pattern of organization of the National Advisory Committee for Aeronautics, which has promoted basic research on problems of flight during the past thirty years, has been carefully considered in proposing the method of appointment of Members of the Foundation and in defining their responsibilities. Moreover, whatever program is established it is vitally important that it satisfy the Five Fundamentals.

The Foundation here proposed has been described only in outline. The excellent reports of the committees which studied these matters are attached as appendices. They will be of aid in furnishing detailed suggestions.

Legislation is necessary. It should be drafted with great care. Early action is imperative, however, if this Nation is to meet the challenge of science and fully utilize the potentialities of science. On the wisdom with which we bring science to bear against the problems of the coming years depends in large measure our future as a Nation.

3. Alan T. Waterman, "Introduction," *Science, the Endless Frontier*, 1960

Introducing the reprinting of Vannevar Bush's *Science, the Endless Frontier* (1945), Alan Waterman (1892–1967) in 1960 emphasized the accomplishments of the National Science Foundation during its first decade. His comments were an admirer's testimonial to Bush's shrewd insights, stressing how the foundation had followed Bush's guidelines by initiating programs on basic scientific research. As a young agency in postwar Washington funded by a low (though increasing) budget and overshadowed by competing atomic, defense, and health agencies, the NSF struggled to survive. It was at times a political football, tossed by officials from Congress, the budget bureau, or the White House. That it funded projects only in the basic sciences and data collection kept it generally pointed toward Bush's premise. Waterman, first director of the NSF (1950–63), remained adept at protecting the foundation. He was a prudent and cautious administrator, loath to lead his people into uncertain terrain yet able to keep the respect of physical scientists. His father was a professor of physics at Smith College; he took all his degrees at Princeton and filled a distinguished professorship in physics at Yale (1919–42). During the Second

World War he came under Karl Compton's wing, serving first in radar work, next as deputy to Compton in the Office of Scientific Research and Development, and finally chairing the Field Service of the OSRD (1945–46).

Alan T. Waterman, "Introduction," in Vannevar Bush, *Science, the Endless Frontier,* repr. ed. (Washington, D.C., 1960), xv–xvii, xxv. Further reading: Nathan Reingold, "Alan Tower Waterman," in *American National Biography,* ed. John A. Garraty and Mark C. Carnes, vol. 22 (New York, 2000), 777–79; Milton Lomask, *A Minor Miracle: An Informal History of the National Science Foundation* (Washington, D.C., 1976); J. Merton England, *A Patron for Pure Science* (Washington, D.C., 1983); and I, 2.

Dr. Bush and his advisory committee on education were concerned (1) with broadening the base from which students with scientific aptitude and talents could be drawn, and (2) with filling the wartime deficit in young scientists and engineers. They were concerned with quality and with the full operation of the democratic process. They felt that all boys and girls should be able to feel that, if they have what it takes, there is no limit to the opportunity. A ceiling should not be imposed on a young person's educational opportunities either by limited family means or negative family attitudes.

Science, the Endless Frontier also emphasized the importance of teaching in these words: "Improvement in the teaching of science is imperative; for students of latent scientific ability are particularly vulnerable to high school teaching which fails to awaken interest or to provide adequate instruction."

The specific recommendations of the Bush Report in the area of science education were for the establishment of a national program of science scholarships and science fellowships and for the subsequent enrollment of the recipients of these awards in a National Science Reserve upon which the Government could draw in times of emergency.

In the establishment and operation of the Foundation's program of education in the sciences, there has been fundamental and perhaps unanimous agreement with the Bush thesis. The methods and techniques by which these objectives are to be accomplished do not coincide at every point with the rather general proposals set forth in the Bush Report; nevertheless, I think it can be said that all the programs that the Foundation has initiated and supported have contributed in significant measure to the principal recommendation of Dr. Bush, namely, that the Nation's pool of scientific talent should be strengthened and improved.

In the very first year of operation with its total budget only $3.5 million, the Foundation awarded 575 predoctoral and postdoctoral fellowships. Over the ten-year period the fellowship program has been gradually expanded to include fellowships in other categories, and more than 12,000 fellowships in all categories have been awarded.

The Foundation has not embarked upon a program of scholarship support for a number of reasons, the principal one being the conviction of the National Science Board that an undergraduate program of scholarship support should not be limited to a particular field of science or even to science and engineering generally. The Foundation does, however, support several programs of a different type which provide to gifted students, at both the undergraduate and secondary-school levels, research experience and educational opportunities far beyond those afforded by the normal curriculum.

Financial assistance for undergraduate students was anticipated by Dr. Bush and his Committee. Although Public Law 346 (G.I. Bill of Rights) had been passed in 1944 and is mentioned at some length in *Science, the Endless Frontier,* its ultimate impact was not apparent at that time. The final summing up is impressive. Of the more than 7.5 million veterans who took advantage of this training, more than two million pursued courses in schools of higher learning. Almost 10 per cent of the total (744,000) pursued courses in scientific fields. The engineering profession attracted 45,000 and medicine and related courses more than 180,000. The remaining 113,000 who elected to study in the natural sciences were variously distributed among geology, chemistry, geography, metallurgy, physics, medicine, dentistry, and others.

About two million veterans of the Korean conflict received similar educational opportunities under the Veterans Readjustment Assistance Act of 1952. Engineering, medical, dental, and scientific fields attracted about a quarter million of these.

Other sources of financial aid for undergraduate students include the National Merit Scholarship Corporation, a nonprofit institution established and supported by philanthropic foundations and business organizations, and the National Defense Education Act of 1958, which provides for loans to students in institutions of higher education.

Dr. Bush's urgent plea that the generation in uniform should not be lost seems to have been abundantly answered. The evidence suggests also that the military services are making constructive efforts to utilize both draftees and officers in positions in which they can make use of specialized skills and training. The services also have interesting programs for continuing the advanced education of highly qualified men through such mediums as the Navy Postgraduate School and through direct subsidy of advanced education for military men in colleges and universities.

A comparison of the support levels for scientific personnel and education recommended in *Science, the Endless Frontier* and those that actually obtain is difficult. The Bush recommendation of $7 million for the first year, rising to $29 million by the fifth year, was based on an annual program of 6,000 undergraduate scholarships and 300 graduate fellowships. The National Science Foundation's obligations for scientific personnel, education and manpower, which in the early years were devoted largely to graduate fellowship support, totaled approximately $1.5 million the first year and $4 million about the fifth year. During this period, of course, Federal funds for education were also available through the G.I. Bill, through the fellowships of the National Institutes of Health, and the Atomic Energy Commission, as well as from other sources.

By 1960 the Foundation's obligations for scientific personnel and education totaled more than $65 million, of which more than half went for institutes to improve the teaching of mathematics and science principally in—but not limited to—the high school. The institutes program initiated by the Foundation on an experimental basis in 1953 appealed particularly to Congress and for several succeeding years funds have been specifically appropriated by Congress for this purpose.

A significant assessment of the impact and value of these programs is difficult at close range. A number of years, possibly a generation, will be required before we may be able to judge fairly the extent to which Federal-support programs have met their objectives.

In the National Science Foundation, quality rather than numbers has been stressed. We have felt that it was important for the whole broad rank and file of students to be made aware of the opportunities and intellectual satisfactions of science as well as other fields; it has seemed to us especially important that those with special aptitudes and ability from whatever walk of life should have the fullest opportunity for the realization of their talents.

The Foundation is trying to the extent possible to meet the problem at its source. It agrees fully with the Bush stress upon the importance of the teaching of science at the high school level. It has been apparent that in order to teach modern science effectively, teachers must not only be adequately trained themselves but must have the opportunity to work with up-to-date curriculums and course content and with proper laboratories and equipment.

Beginning with the work of the Physical Sciences Study Group at M.I.T., the Foundation is supporting studies looking toward the complete revision and up-dating of course content in physics, mathematics, chemistry, and biology. This work has included the preparation of new textbooks and teaching aids and the introduction of imaginative and stimulating new equipment.

It seems reasonable to assume that these constructive efforts must by their very nature influence for the better the teaching of science. Nevertheless, nothing that has been accomplished thus far provides reason for complacency. As a nation we still seem a long way from a universal understanding and appreciation for intellectual activity generally and probably will remain so until we attach roughly the same importance to academic achievement as we do, for example, to prowess in sports.

In order to understand the whole support situation it is necessary to look beyond a bare statistical comparison of Dr. Bush's recommendations and the Foundation's financial resources. As previously mentioned, Dr. Bush had visualized the Foundation as the sole support of basic research in the Government. This has been far from the fact. As already noted, a number of agencies began actively to support basic research during the five years of legislative debate of the National Science Foundation bills. It is estimated that in 1956 the Federal Government obligated about $200 million for basic research. Of this amount somewhat less than $120 million went for basic research related to "national defense" (Department of Defense $72 million, and Atomic Energy Commission $45 million). Twenty-six million dollars represents the total basic research reported by the National Institutes of Health for the year. The remainder of the $200 million is variously distributed among the Departments of Agriculture, Commerce, Interior, National Advisory Committee for Aeronautics, National Science Foundation, and the Smithsonian Institution.

Rough estimates indicate that about $115 million of the $200 million total 1956 obligation for basic research went to nonprofit institutions, including colleges and universities, research centers, research institutions, hospitals, and so on. Thus it would appear from these estimates that although the Foundation itself had not reached the projected level of basic research support proposed for its fifth year the Federal Government as a whole was providing the kind of basic research support visualized by Dr. Bush at a level somewhat higher than he projected.

4. Bentley Glass, "The Academic Scientist, 1940–1960," 1960

The geneticist Bentley Glass (1906–2005) emerged in the postwar era as a standard-bearer for the work of academic scientists. His presidential address to the Association of American University Professors briefly traced rapid changes in the national importance of science over two decades and then went on to underscore five challenges confronting the college and university science teacher or researcher. These were: to maintain the quality and future integrity of scientific inquiry and its practitioners, to establish wage equity among professors; to preserve academic freedom unthreatened by secrecy in scientific research; to improve science teaching in the nation's public schools; and to place science at the center of the college liberal arts curriculum.

Born in China to American missionary parents, Glass earned his doctorate in genetics at the University of Texas (1932). Most of his academic career was spent in Baltimore, first at Goucher College (1938–47) and next in a distinguished tenure at Johns Hopkins (1947–65). He moved to the State University of New York at Stony Brook as academic vice president (1965–71) and Distinguished Professor of Biology (1965–76). Along the way he was elected president of the American Association for the Advancement of Science (1960) as well as several other scientific organizations and was also elected president of the American Civil Liberties Union.

Bentley Glass, "The Academic Scientist, 1940–1960," *AAUP Bulletin* 46 (June 1960): 149–55. Copyright © by the American Association of University Professors. All rights reserved. Abridged with the kind permission of the author and the AAUP. Further reading: Glass, *Science and Liberal Education* (Baton Rouge, LA, 1959); Garland E. Allen, *Life Science in the Twentieth Century* (New York, 1975); L. C. Dunn, *A Short History of Genetics* (New York, 1965); Philip J. Pauly, *Biologists and the Promise of American Life: From Meriwether Lewis to Alfred Kinsey* (Princeton, NJ, 2000); Toby A. Appel, *Shaping Biology: The National Science Foundation and American Biological Research, 1945–1975* (Baltimore, 2000); and William Bechtel, *Discovering Cell Mechanisms: The Creation of Modern Cell Biology* (Cambridge, MA, 2006). For the continuing problems of recruitment, teacher training, and the science curriculum, see the *Journal of Science Teaching* and the *Journal of Research in Science Teaching*.

Among academic subjects, the natural sciences and mathematics have come, since World War II, to occupy a favored position in the United States, in respect to the support received from the federal government and from industry. The trend began long before the sputnik era and was an outgrowth of the part played by scientific developments in winning the war. It gained added strength from the rivalry of the chief powers in the Cold War. This was the period that saw the establishment of the National Science Foundation in 1950, and growing attention to the utilization and training of American scientists. The past two years have seen a flurry of added excitement and anxiety as the American public came to perceive that in at least some scientific and technological respects the Russians have exceeded us, and that in advanced education they are far outstripping us in quantity of trained personnel if not in the quality. General concern has led to another unprecedented increase in the effort to hold our own by subsidizing. scientific research and development and by improving the educative process that permits further growth. The National Defense Education Act, vast increases in appropriations to existing agencies for science education and scientific research, and new roles of science in the political sphere alike show what enormous concern about these problems now prevails in the executive and legislative branches of our government and in the political life of our people. . . .

It is surely time to take stock of the altering status in education of the academic scientist (that is, the scientist holding an academic post)—time to appraise the influence upon university and college education, as a whole, of the new emphasis on science and technology. What reorientation of existing relations is required? What developing imbalances necessitate compensatory emphasis elsewhere? Is there truly a danger that other, essential aspects of education will be so neglected that our social structure will resemble a giant on puny legs?

Census figures for the decade from 1941 to 1950 show that workers in science and technology were rapidly overhauling teachers as the largest of professional groups. In that decade the scientists and engineers almost doubled in numbers, while the teachers increased by only 10 percent. (It is worth noting that the census put persons who were both scientists and teachers into the category of teachers.) If there has been anywhere near a proportionate increase in the decade 1951–60, professional workers in science and technology now greatly outnumber both teachers and professional workers in health and constitute about 30 percent of the entire professional element of our population (6 to 7 million persons). The task of the academic scientists is to continue to train this rapidly growing body of professional people, even though their own numbers are increasing much more slowly.

Full-time teachers in universities, colleges, and junior colleges are estimated (by the National Education Association) to number at present about 250,000 persons, of whom 78,000 are teachers of science and mathematics (31.2 percent). To these should be added some 3000 teachers of dentistry and 10,350 full-time teachers in medical schools, to make a total of approximately 91,000. The annual output of persons with doctor's degrees in the sciences and mathematics (exclusive of dentistry and medicine) was 4,611 in 1956–57 and amounted to 52.6 percent of doctor's degrees in all academic subjects (exclusive of law, dentistry, and medicine). These figures seem to indicate that there is an especially critical shortage of college and university teachers in the sciences and mathematics, since less than one-third of the teachers are producing half of the output of college graduates and Ph.D.'s. This is as would be expected in a rapidly expanding professional field.

In economic status the academic scientist is faring considerably better than his colleague in the humanities or social studies. There are three principal reasons for this. First, the demand on the part of industry, and to a smaller extent of government, for trained personnel in the sciences, engineering, and mathematics has made it not uncommon for a young man just receiving his Ph.D. degree to step into a position carrying a considerably higher income than that of the associate professor, or even the full professor, who has trained him. . . . Administrators have long since recognized that in order to have any engineers, geologists, mathematicians, physicists, or chemists of standing on their faculties whatsoever, they must remunerate them on a different scale from that applicable to teachers of history, languages, or literature. Psychologists have recently come to profit more and more from the same pressures. Only biologists, among the scientific groups, seem less favored, because industry has had less demand for them (except in the pharmaceutical industry), and because the applied branches of biology—medicine and agriculture—are recognized as distinct professions or occupations.

The second economic factor that enhances the

status of the academic scientist is the availability to him of outside work as a consultant. Individuals who are in considerable demand can more than double their university salaries in this way, although they pay the price for it by overworking on weekends and at night until health and sanity may suffer.

The third and final factor is one that has developed since World War II, in connection with federal research grants or contracts. This is the factor of the "research salary," originally allowed to academic scientists on 9 or 10 months' university duty, who were free to spend 1 or 2 months of their summer time uninterruptedly upon their government-supported research program. Research salary was therefore figured at the equivalent of the monthly college or university salary. Later, because this obviously worked to the disadvantage of scientists on 12-month annual appointments, who might actually be devoting just as much time to the research program as those nominally on 9-month appointments, the system of payment was made more flexible by considering it as compensation for a definite fraction of the scientist's total 12-months' working time. Thus, an academic scientist may now receive, as additional salary connected with a government grant or contract, as much as one-third of his academic salary. . . .

For all of these reasons, members of the science faculties possess a considerable economic advantage over their colleagues, except for the occasional writer of a book that becomes a bestseller or is widely adopted for use as a textbook, or the economist, for example, who obtains numerous fees as a consultant. The resulting situation is one that has long had a parallel in our medical schools, where very often the professors of clinical subjects have outside practices and may enjoy large incomes while the professors of the preclinical subjects are forced to the level of an ordinary professor's income. . . . The general principle which might well serve is that, regardless of supply and demand, equal service should be rewarded with equal compensation throughout the several professorial ranks.

The picture of the academic scientist of 1960 is not complete without some further description of the modest empires over which many of them now preside. Let us consider an example. In 1940, an assistant professor of biology, a fairly typical scientist, had no special funds for his research. An amount not exceeding $100 annually came from the departmental budget and was used for consumable supplies. He had for his use one moderately good compound microscope and one good binocular dissecting microscope. He made all his own media, did his own sterilizing in a Sears Roebuck pressure cooker, kept his own stocks without assistance, and was grateful for some help in washing up the glassware. Without even a chest to run at a controlled temperature, he worked during the hot summer weeks in a dusty, normally unused, but cool basement room. Still the research went on, in spite of the fact that perhaps 80 percent of the scientist's time

was spent in routine chores. In 1960 the professor has charge of two research laboratories, both supported by funds from the federal government. A senior research associate operates one of these laboratories semi-independently, with a research assistant to aid him. Two research assistants work in the other laboratory. In addition, there are two part-time laboratory assistants to wash bottles, keep animals, and prepare media. The annual research budget of the group is close to $50,000, not including the scientist's university salary, and none of this sum comes from the regular department budget. There is no lack of equipment. There are compound microscopes of the best quality; binocular dissecting microscopes for each worker; phase microscopes; photomicrographic equipment; an x-ray machine; a cold room; constant-temperature incubators, refrigerators, and deep-freeze; air-conditioning for the laboratories; special supplies of chemicals; special rooms and equipment for preparing and sterilizing media and washing glassware; animal quarters—in short, everything that is really needed for an experimental program of some size.

One might be moved to say, "But this is exceptional. It reflects seniority as well as the change of the times." On the contrary, junior members in the same department are about equally well established. The changed situation is perhaps best reflected in the departmental budget, which at the end of World War II was about $70,000 per annum and today is close to $1 million, while the size of the staff has perhaps doubled. This is not atypical of science departments in our larger universities, although colleges where research is quite secondary to teaching have not altered greatly. True, government grants or contracts for research are open to every applicant on the basis of merit, but heavy teaching loads often prevent faculty scientists from capitalizing on the opportunity. The cleavage is thus deepening between colleges which are primarily teaching institutions and universities where teaching is secondary to research, whether the criterion is expenditure or staff time. . . .

According to statements of the National Science Foundation, last year over 10 billions of dollars were spent in the United States for research and development. Of that vast amount, less than 8 percent was for basic scientific research, most of which is done in the universities and colleges. Yet even 8 percent means an annual sum that is over $800 million, and in addition there are large sums for science education in the form of fellowship programs, summer and academic-year institutes, and the like. The President's Committee on Education beyond the High School estimated that as a nation we are currently spending $3 billion annually for higher education. It seems reasonable to suppose, therefore, that approximately one-fourth of the entire budget for higher education is now coming from the federal government in the form of funds for scientific research and science education. Since many institutions are still but little involved in these programs, others must be so largely supported by them that *in fact*, public or private, they would collapse if federal aid were to be withdrawn.

In return for the abundant financial aid now available from governmental agencies and private foundations, the scientist must give ever more freely of his time to serve on innumerable advisory committees and panels for judging the relative merits of applications for research grants and for fellowships —undergraduate, graduate, postdoctoral, and even more senior. There is today a sort of scientific Washington Merry-Go-Round where the scientists who form these boards, committees, and panels meet their friends and, from time to time, exchange places. To be sure, it is gratifying that the government agencies consult the scientists themselves in making awards. No scientist would choose to be judged other than by his own peers. The very multiplicity of the granting agencies and their panels, moreover, provides a guarantee that everyone will have a good opportunity to win a prize, since if one agency fails to award the guerdon, another is very likely to be more generous. . . .

Another development growing out of the current recognition by government of the importance of science is the budding and burgeoning of programs for the improvement of science education. . . .

The day of the college or university scientist who held himself professionally aloof from the problems of elementary and secondary school teaching has ended. The realization has been sharply forced upon us that the foundation of good college and graduate training in the sciences, as well as our supply of scientific manpower, depends on the excellence of science education throughout the elementary and secondary school systems. The outcry against the practice of training teachers how to teach but giving little attention to teaching them what to teach has roused the conscience of many a college or university science teacher who has until now been satisfied to teach his classes with only future physicists, mathematicians, or biologists in mind. This is demonstrated by the willingness and enthusiasm with which the college scientists have responded to the opportunity to participate in these curriculum studies. . . .

All of these developments in science education are obviously of great benefit, on the one hand to the nation, on the other to the participating scientists themselves. They do, nevertheless, require time, time, and more time. They take the scientist out of his own classroom and out of his laboratory. The very function to be served demands the academic scientist and no substitute; yet the increasing number of calls made on him make it less and less possible for him to remain an academic scientist.

In the past two decades the academic scientist has become increasingly involved in politics. That was inevitable, from the day the Manhattan Project was initiated. It became quite apparent with the exploding of atomic bombs over Hiroshima and Nagasaki. The atomic scientists were for the most part academic people on leave from their posts, from Robert Oppenheimer down to the youngest Ph.D.'s. The formation of the Federation of American Scientists and the foundation of the *Bulletin of the Atomic Scientists* were symptoms of the awakened political conscience of men appalled at what they had let loose in the world. The secret preparations for chemical and biological warfare embroiled chemists and biologists in the same schizophrenia that the conscience-stricken physicists were in. The era of nuclear testing brought more and more scientists into the prolonged argument over the relative weight to be given the need for military security and the harm done by radioactive fallout. Linus Pauling and Edward Teller became familiar figures to Americans. Meanwhile the disloyalty and defection of a few scientists engaged in secret work made it all the easier for the late Senator McCarthy to hale academic scientists before his committee and to pry into their political opinions. A rash of "loyalty oaths" and disclaimer affidavits spread round the land, unfortunately to remain with us long after the hysteria of the McCarthy era had died down.

Scientists have become increasingly concerned about the effect of security regulations on the rate of scientific advance. In 1958 the house Special Subcommittee on Government Information concluded that "the Federal Government has mired the American scientist in a swamp of secrecy" and that classification of scientific information played a real part in "the nation's loss of the first lap in the race into space." A year later the Constitutional Rights Subcommittee of the Senate Judiciary Committee made public letters from 17 American Nobel prizewinning scientists, who agreed almost unanimously that undue secrecy is gravely impeding scientific progress and development in the United States. It is obviously much easier to classify a paper as top-secret than it is to declassify even the most innocuous or ancient document. I have myself had the experience of preparing for the State Department, after a tour of scientific visits in West Germany in 1950–51, a report which was so rigorously classified that after it was once handed in I was never able to see it again, since I was not sufficiently cleared to be allowed to examine such top-secret information. Although that report is antiquated beyond any conceivable remaining value after the passage of 10 years, no efforts to get it and similar reports declassified for general scientific reference have ever succeeded.

The disease of secrecy is probably even more serious in other agencies, such as the Atomic Energy Commission and the Department of Defense, and many similar anecdotes could be told. Orders to declassify and refrain from classifying have made only a little dent in the monolithic system of secrecy. Last summer, when an international scientific conference was held at Pugwash in Nova Scotia on the dangers of chemical and biological warfare, no chemists or biologists who had been at all recently associated with such activities could be found to participate. The most personally informed scientist in attendance had been dissociated from such work for no less than 12 years. It is no wonder that, as a consequence, the academic scientists discussing such a problem are very academic and theoretical indeed. The experts who are really informed about actual developments are unable to speak. The consequence, as in the nuclear area, is that representatives of the military services can make almost any claims they wish without fear of contradiction. Let us honor, therefore, such scientists as Linus Pauling, Ralph Lapp, Eugene Rabinowitch, and others who have run the risk of being sometimes egregiously in error in order to dispel the miasma of secrecy that is choking scientific advance.

Let me say, parenthetically, that I do not at all wish to imply that I advocate any weakening, during these critical times, of the free world's strength. Obviously, one can negotiate only from a position of strength. But it may be stoutly argued that scientific advance will be far greater and more rapid when there is maximum access to new discoveries than when each scientist and engineer is restricted in the information he may obtain.

Nature discovered this truth long ago. Evolutionary progress depends upon the occurrence of rare, fortuitous, advantageous mutations, and even more upon the lucky combinations of these that happen to work best in a particular environment . . . even so with the transmission of ideas and the generation of new discoveries. As every scientist knows, the free interplay of thoughts between minds far outstrips in productivity the isolated, clonal generation of ideas, even by a genius.

Science is truly in politics to stay, and the academic scientist is rapidly becoming highly political in outlook. This is evident, on the one hand, in the government itself, evident from the growing significance of the President's Science Advisory Committee. . . . On the international scene, the open letter which Bertrand Russell and Albert Einstein addressed to all scientists, urging them to bestir themselves before it was too late to arouse the world to a realization of the overwhelming disaster implicit in any nuclear war, and to talk candidly with one another, as scientists should, about the relationship of science to world peace, has resulted in the formation of the Pugwash movement. The five conferences of this group during the past three years have done much to lay a foundation for a real solution of some critical world problems.

CONCLUSION

In recent months there has been considerable discussion of C. P. Snow's thought-provoking Rede lecture entitled "The Two Cultures and the Scientific Revolution." Is it in fact true that scientists and "literary intellectuals" now represent two poles of culture so remote that they have lost all real communication with one another, and live in different worlds? Are the misunderstandings that separate us irreconcilable?

To this extent I must agree: that the major problem of higher education today is the need to cure this growing schizophrenia. The sciences must become the core of a liberal education, as I have argued elsewhere, although "in teaching science we must not forget . . . that it is simultaneously social study and creative art, a history of ideas, a philosophy, and a supreme product of esthetic ingenuity." The humanities and social sciences, on their part, must do more than merely recognize that the natural sciences exist. They must become permeated with the knowledge and spirit of science if they are to be more than relics of a departed age.

The academic scientist represents more than a growing proportion of the teaching profession. He will be, whether we like it or not, the dominant figure in higher education in a very few decades. He is a strange, harsh figure to many of us, a figure tormented by a growing world-conscience, aware of dawning power but blind to his own limitations. The scientist passionately defends the freedom of science and fails to perceive that it and academic freedom are one. Academic scientists have been rather ordinary participants in the defense of academic freedom and the elevation of the standards of their profession. They are underrepresented in general organizations with these aims, and they do not support their own special organizations and societies with either the vigor or the funds that physicians, lawyers, and members of labor unions expend in support of theirs. This growing and awakening giant, the academic scientist, has indeed much to learn as he moves toward leadership. As Bertrand Russell has so well said, science can enhance among men two great evils, tyranny and war. And which, I wonder, is preferable, to perish in a nuclear holocaust or to live under a scientific tyranny?

5. David Baltimore, "Limiting Science," 1978

Midcentury applied science, especially in the fields of atomic weaponry, biology, and health, continued to trouble many people in science, just as it did the atomic physicists at Alamogordo, New Mexico, in 1945. More and more, two questions were being raised: Is basic science overreaching? Should limits be placed upon some areas of scientific inquiry? These questions lurked both in government-supported laboratories and in private research centers. Here David Baltimore (1938–) examines these concerns, declaring that in his view they have chiefly to do with basic science and not, generally, with its technological applications.

Baltimore is president of the California Institute of Technology (1997–). He was born in New York City, took up microbiology on his own as an undergraduate at Swarthmore College (B.A. 1960), and received his doctorate at Rockefeller University (1964), where he later served as its president (1990–91). He long held a distinguished tenure at the Massachusetts Institute of Technology studying nucleic acids, cancer, and viruses as the American Cancer Professor of Microbiology (1973–84) and, jointly, director of the Whitehead Institute for Biomedical Research (1982–90, 1991–97). In the 1970s he received honors from several scientific organizations, capped in 1975 by the Nobel Prize for Physiology and Medicine.

David Baltimore, "Limiting Science: A Biologist's Perspective," in *Daedalus* 107 (Spring 1978): 37–45. © 1978 by the American Academy of Arts and Sciences, abridged with permission. Further reading: In the same issue of *Daedalus,* Baltimore's confident tone was muted or challenged, notably by Sissela Bok, Robert S. Morison, and Robert L. Sinsheimer. A biography is Shane Crotty, *Ahead of the Curve: David Baltimore's Life in Science* (Berkeley, 2001); Daniel J. Kevles, *The Baltimore Case: A Trial of Politics, Science, and Character* (New York, 1998) reveals the complex politics of modern science by studying a case in which Baltimore was exonerated.

Contemporary research in molecular biology has grown up in an era of almost complete permissiveness. Its practitioners have been allowed to decide their own priorities and have met with virtually no restraints on the types of work they can do. Viewed as a whole, the field has not even met with fiscal restraints because, relative to "big science," molecular biology has been a relatively cheap enterprise.

Some of the funds that fueled the initial, seminal investigations in molecular biology were granted because of the medical implications of work in basic biology. Most continue to come from agencies concerned with health. Although basic research in biology has yet to have a major impact on the prevention and treatment of human disease, a backlash already seems to be developing in which various groups in our society question whether the freedom that has characteristically been granted to research biologists by a permissive public requires modification. Among the numerous elements prompting this questioning are impatience with the lack of practical results, and fears that direct hazards might result from the experimentation, that basic research may not be an appropriate investment of significant funds, and that dangerous new technologies may flow from discoveries in basic biology. Lay critics as well as a few members of the profession have argued that molecular biologists should concentrate their efforts in certain areas of research, like fertility mechanisms, while other areas, like genetics or aging, are possibly dangerous and certainly not worthy of financial support from the public. These critics believe that they can channel contemporary biology to fit their own conception of appropriate research.

I wish to argue that the traditional pact between society and its scientists in which the scientist is given the responsibility for determining the direction of his work is a necessary relationship if basic science is to be an effective endeavor. This does not mean that society is at the mercy of science, but rather that society, while it must determine the pace of basic scientific innovation, should not attempt to prescribe its directions.

What we call molecular biology today had its origins in individual decisions of a small number of scientists during the period from the late 1930s through the early 1950s. These people were trained in diverse fields, among them physics, medicine, microbiology, and crystallography. They created molecular biology out of the realization that the problems posed by genetics were central to understanding the structures of living systems. No one channeled them towards this line of thinking, no one cajoled them to tackle these problems; rather, their own curiosity and sense of timing led them to try to elucidate these mysteries. This history provides a model of how the most effective science is done.

It is partly the successes of molecular biology that have brought on the questioning of whether scientists should be allowed their freedom of decision. It is therefore worthwhile tracing the development of concerns about whether certain areas of science should be closed to investigation. Molecular biology is the science that has revealed to us the nature of one of the most fundamental of all substances of life, the gene. There is a very simple underlying reality to the transmission of characteristics from parents to children: a code based on four different chemicals, denoted by the letters A, T, G, and C, is used to store the information of heredity. The order in which these four chemicals appear in a virtually endless polymer, called DNA, is the language of life.

Knowing that DNA was the physical storehouse of the genes, Watson and Crick in 1953 first solved the problem of how the DNA is organized to assure that information is transferred with almost perfect reliability from parent cells to progeny cells. . . .

Following the monumental discovery of the structure of DNA, many scientists have contributed to learning how to make DNA, how to read DNA, how to cut DNA, how to rejoin DNA, and in general, how to manipulate at will the genes of very simple organisms.

What good has all of this new knowledge brought to the average person? First, and of great importance, is the contribution that scientific advances make to human culture. The continued accumulation of knowledge about ourselves and our environment is a crucial cultural aspect of contemporary life. Science as well as art illuminates man's view of himself and his relation to others. Our knowledge of how we work, how one person differs from and is similar to another, what is health and what disease, what we need to support health, etc., helps to set the ground rules for the debates of politics and the productions of art.

The more practical benefits of biology can be expected to come in the future in the form of medical advances, or increases in food production, or in other manipulations of life processes that will be able to provide positive contributions to civilization. But molecular biology, for all of its power as a basic science, has not been easily translated into tangible benefits. This is a situation that could change very soon. New discoveries are rapidly bringing molecular biology closer to an ability to affect the lives of the general public.

RECOMBINANT DNA

Of the advances that have occurred, a critical one has been the development of a process called recombinant DNA research. This is a technique whereby different pieces of DNA are sewn together using enzymes; the chimeric DNA is then inserted into a bacterium where it can be multiplied indefinitely. Because the method allows genes from any species in the world to be put into a common type of bacterium, there is a theoretical possibility of hazard in this research. The potential for unforeseen occurrences led a number of scientists, including me, to issue in 1974 a call for restraint in the application of these new methods. We were addressing a limited problem, whether there could be a recognizable hazard in the performance of certain experiments. That limited question opened a floodgate; other questions came pouring out and are still coming. They have led to front cover stories in weekly magazines, to serious attempts at federal legislation, to a demoralization of some of the community of basic research biologists, and, most significantly, to a deep questioning of whether further advances in biology are likely to be beneficial or harmful to our society.

Much of the discussion about recombinant DNA research has centered on whether the work is likely to create hazardous organisms. The mayor of Cambridge, Massachusetts, raised the specter of Frankenstein monsters emerging from MIT and Harvard laboratories, and speculations about the possibility of inadvertent development of a destructive organism like the fictitious Andromeda Strain have been much in the news. I am personally satisfied that most of such talk is simply science fiction and that the research can be made as safe as any other research. The people who understand infectious diseases best make the arguments most strongly that recombinant DNA research is not going to create monsters. But rather than defend my judgment that the safety issue has been blown out of proportion, I want to consider some of the more general issues that have been raised by the controversy.

GENETIC ENGINEERING

If safety were the most important consideration behind the debate about recombinant DNA then we might expect the debate to focus on the hazards of doing recombinant DNA experiments. Instead, many of the discussions that start considering such questions, soon turn to a consideration of genetic engineering. . . .

Genetic engineering of human beings is not the same as recombinant DNA research. Genetic engineering is a process carried out on human beings; recombinant DNA methods are ways to purify genes. Such genes might be used in genetic engineering procedures but are much more likely to be used as tools in studies of biological organization or as elements in a biological manufacturing process. Although genetic engineering is not the same as recombinant DNA research, the two are rightly linked, because recombinant DNA work is hastening the day when genetic engineering will be a feasible process for use on certain human diseases. Since recombinant DNA work is also bringing closer the discovery of many other possible new medical treatments, and is likely to bring other new capabilities, why is there so much focus on genetic engineering? I believe that genetic engineering, because of its tabloid appeal, has become a symbol to many people of the frightening potential of modern-day technology. Rather than seeing in molecular biology the same complex mixtures of appropriate and inappropriate applications that characterize all powerful sciences, many people have allowed the single negative catch phrase, genetic engineering, to dominate discussions. People worry that if the possibility of curing a genetic defect by gene therapy should ever become a reality, the inevitable result would be "people made to order." It is argued that unless we block recombinant DNA research now we will never have another chance to control our fate.

LIMITS TO BASIC BIOLOGY

To see the form of the argument against recombinant DNA research most clearly and to highlight its danger to intellectual freedom and creativity, we should realize that similar arguments have been put forward relative to other areas of basic biology. . . .

Certain people believe that there are areas of research that should be taboo because their outcome might be, or in some scenarios will be, detrimental to the stable relationships that characterize contemporary society. I have heard the argument in a different and more pernicious form from members of a Boston area group called Science for the People. They argue that some research in genetics should not go on because its findings might be detrimental to the relationships they believe should characterize a just society. Such arguments are reminiscent of those surrounding the eugenics movements that developed in Germany and Russia in the 1920s. After a period of intense debate, these countries with opposing ideologies settled on opposing analyses of the role of genetics in determining human diversity. German scientists and politicians espoused a theory of racial purification by selective breeding, while Russia accepted the Lamarckian principle of transmission of acquired characteristics. In both cases, science was forced into a mold created by political and social ideology, and in both cases the results were disastrous.

NECESSITY OF FREEDOM

As I see it, we are being faced today with the following question: should limits be placed on biological research because of the danger that new knowledge can present to the established or desired order of our society? Having thus posed the question, I believe that there are two simple, and almost universally applicable, answers. First, the criteria determining what areas to restrain inevitably express certain sociopolitical attitudes that reflect a dominant ideology. Such criteria cannot be allowed to guide scientific choices. Second, attempts to restrain directions of scientific inquiry are more likely to be generally disruptive of science than to provide the desired specific restraints. These answers to the question of whether limits should be imposed can be stated in two arguments. One is that science should not be the servant of ideology, because ideology assumes answers, but science asks questions. The other is that attempts to make science serve ideology will merely make science impotent without assuring that only desired questions are investigated. I am stating simply that we should not control the direction of science and, moreover, that we cannot do so with any precision.

Before trying to substantiate these arguments I must make a crucial distinction. The arguments pertain to basic scientific research, not to the technological applications of science. As we go from the fundamental to the applied, my arguments fall away. There is every reason why technology should and must serve specific needs. Conversely, there are many technological possibilities that ought to be restrained.

To return to basic research, let me first consider the danger of restricting types of investigation because their outcome could be disruptive to society. There are three aspects of danger. One is the fallacy that you can predict what society will be like even in the near future. To say, for instance, that it would be bad for Americans to live longer assumes that the birth rate will stay near where it is. But what happens if the birth rate falls even lower than it is now in the United States and also stabilizes elsewhere in the world? We might welcome a readjustment of the life span. In any case, we have built a world around a given human life span; we could certainly adjust to a longer span and it would be hard to predict whether in the long run the results would be better or worse.

In a general form, I would call this argument for restricting research the Error of Futurism. The Futurist believes that the present holds enough readable clues about the future to provide a good basis for prediction. I doubt this assumption; to think that the data of today can be analyzed well enough to predict the future with any accuracy seems nonsensical to me.

The second danger in restricting areas of scientific investigation is more crucial: although we often worry most about keeping society stable, in fact societies need certain kinds of upheaval and renewal to stay vital. The new ideas and insights of science, much as we may fight against them, provide an important part of the renewal process that maintains the fascination of life. Freedom is the range of opportunities available to an individual—the more he has to choose from, the freer his choice. Science creates freedom by widening our range of understanding and therefore the possibilities from which we can choose.

Finally, attempts to dictate scientific limits on political or social considerations have another disastrous implication. Scientific orthodoxy is usually dictated by the state when its leaders fear that truths could undermine their power. Their repressive dicta are interpreted by the citizens as an admission of the leaders' insecurity, and may thus lead to unrest requiring further repression. A social system that leaves science free to explore, and encourages scientific discoveries rather than trying to make science serve it by producing the truths necessary for its stability, transmits to the members of that society strength, not fear, and can endure. . . .

Although they would fail to produce their desired result, attempts explicitly to control the directions of basic research would hardly be benign. Instead disruption and demoralization would follow from attempts to determine when a scientist was doing work in approved directions and when he was not. Creative people would shun whole areas of science if they knew that in those areas their creativity would be channeled, judged, and limited. The net effect of constraining biologists to approved lines of investigation would be to degrade the effectiveness of the whole science of biology.

Put this way, the penalty for trying to control lines of investigation seems to me greater than any conceivable benefit. I conclude that society can choose to have either more science or less science, but choosing *which* science to have is not a feasible alternative.

Faith and Modernity

6. William F. Buckley Jr., *God and Man at Yale*, 1951

Fresh from an undergraduate degree and controversial chair of the *Yale Daily News*, William F. Buckley Jr. (1925–) published his first book, excerpted here, which sold widely and established him in the front rank of American conservatives. Overnight he became the *enfant terrible* of liberal academic people. This report on Yale judged each prominent lecturing professor in the humanities and social sciences. He found that few gave room, let alone credence, to religious faith in their lectures. He dismissed professorial neutrality, countering that Yale's ancient chartered commitment to a religious context for learning was being ignored in favor of secularized and collectivist teachings. In passing, he scoffed at two contemporary assessments of higher education—the Red Book and the *Report of the President's Commission on*

Higher Education (see I, 1; II, 1)—and finally presented his own meaning of academic freedom.

Buckley went on to become a dominant voice for his credo of Christian faith, individualism, and limited government. Founder and editor-in-chief of the *National Review* (1955–90), he aired his beliefs in many books, wrote adventure novels, and was a syndicated columnist, a keen debater, host of his own television program (1966–99), and Conservative Party candidate for mayor of New York City in 1965. He received thirty honorary degrees as well as the Presidential Medal of Freedom in 1991. Along the way he was also a skilled ocean sailor and passionate devotee of Bach's music.

William F. Buckley Jr., *God and Man at Yale: The Superstitions of "Academic Freedom"* (Chicago, 1951), 3–5, 38–42, 114–15, 174–77, 180–84. Reprinted with the permission of Henry Regnery. Further reading: Buckley, *Miles Gone By, A Literary Autobiography* (Chicago, 2004); *Rumbles Left and Right, A Book about Troublesome People and Ideas* (New York, 1963); as editor, *Did You Ever See a Dream Walking?: American Conservative Thought in the Twentieth Century* (Indianapolis, 1970). John B. Judis, *William F. Buckley, Jr., Patron Saint of the Conservatives* (New York, 1988), a biography; William C. Ringenberg, *The Christian College: A History of Protestant Higher Education in America*, 2nd ed. (Grand Rapids, MI, 2006). Critical judgments can be found in Allen Gutman, *The Conservative Tradition in America* (New York, 1967); J. David Hoeveler Jr., *Watch on the Right: Conservative Intellectuals in the Reagan Era* (Madison, WI, 1991), ch. 2; and Charles W. Dunn and J. David Woodard, *American Conservatism from Burke to Bush, An Introduction* (Lanham, MD, 1991), ch. 2.

I call on all members of the faculty, as members of a thinking body, freely to recognize the tremendous validity and power of the teachings of Christ in our life-and-death struggle against the forces of selfish materialism. If we lose that struggle, judging from present events abroad, scholarship as well as religion will disappear.

PRESIDENT CHARLES SEYMOUR
Inaugural Address, October 16, 1937

In evaluating the role of Christianity and religion at Yale, I have not in mind the ideal that the University should be composed of a company of scholars exclusively or even primarily concerned with spreading the Word of the Lord. I do not feel that Yale should treat her students as potential candidates for divinity school. It has been said that there are those who "want to make a damned seminary" out of Yale. There may be some who do, but I do not count myself among these.

But we can, without going that far, raise the question whether Yale fortifies or shatters the average student's respect for Christianity. There are, of course, some students who will emerge stronger Christians from any institution, and others who will reject religion wherever they are sent. But if the atmosphere of a college is overwhelmingly secular, if the influential members of the faculty tend to discourage religious inclinations, or to persuade

the student that Christianity is nothing more than "ghost-fear," or "twentieth-century witchcraft," university policy quite properly becomes a matter of concern to those parents and alumni who deem active Christian faith a powerful force for good and for personal happiness.

I think of Yale, then, as a nondenominational educational institution not exclusively interested in the propagation of Christianity. The question must then arise whether or not the weight of academic activity at Yale tends to reinforce or to subvert Christianity, or to do neither the one nor the other. It is clear that insight into this problem cannot be had from counting the number of faculty members who believe as opposed to those that do not believe. Some instructors deal with subject matter that has little, if any, academic bearing upon religion. Some have more influence than others. Some teach classes that as a matter of course attract a large number of students, while others seldom address more than a half dozen or so.

The handiest arguments of those who vaunt the pro-religious atmosphere at Yale is that the University has a large religion department, a great number of strong and influential men whose beliefs are strongly pro-Christian on its faculty, and a powerful and pervasive "religious tradition."

To a greater or lesser extent, these statements are true. And yet, it remains that Yale, corporately speaking, is neither pro-Christian, nor even, I believe, neutral toward religion.

To begin with, it is impossible to gauge the Christian purpose of a college by counting the number of courses offered in religion. It is, of course, of interest that such courses are offered, because this serves as an official indication, at least, that the University recognizes religion as an important field of learning, worthy of the student's academic endeavor. But it is important to remember that a student may major in Christianity and not be pro-Christian, just as he can major in Far Eastern Studies and be anti-oriental.

If we are, indeed, witnessing a religious revival, it would seem to be only against the rigid resistance of probably the most influential, and certainly the best publicized, policy-makers in education. The two most widely circularized attempts to analyze the plight of education at the half-century point are revealing. The first of these was sponsored by Harvard; after exhaustive consultations, an expenditure of $60,000, and three years' work, the project appeared in 1945 and under the title *General Education in a Free Society*.

In this exhaustive work, religion is mentioned only a few times, and then merely to note the historic association of Christianity with democracy and humanism. The importance which the educators who drafted this document attached to religion is symbolized by their acknowledgement of the educational value of Harvard's glee club and orchestra, while saying "nothing of the chapel or of Brooks House, long a center of religious and social service." The Report is explicit when it states:

We are not at all unmindful of the importance of religious belief in the completely good life. But, given the American scene with its varieties of faith and even of unfaith, we did not feel justified in proposing religious instruction as a part of the curriculum.

The report emphatically discards religion as a potential source of the desired "unifying purpose and idea" of education: "Whatever one's views, religion is not now for most colleges a practicable [or desirable, the report urges throughout] source of intellectual unity."

Some comfort is yet to be derived from the report's stipulation of goals: The student should learn *"to think effectively, to communicate thought, to make relevant judgments, to discriminate among values"* (italics in the original).

The second influential document to which I refer is the Report of the [U.S.] President's Commission on Higher Education, *Higher Education for American Democracy*. While this report is primarily a highly controversial package of political and economic ideas looking to increasing educational benefits, more student subsidies, and tripled college enrolments in the next ten years, the document, by indirection, deals a body blow to religion, whose relevance it does not so much as acknowledge. Pages are spent in a discussion of democratic ideals, and much is made of our cultural heritage. The report, where education is concerned, is one more victory for the secularists. . . .

On the sixth of October 1950, A. Whitney Griswold was confirmed as sixteenth president of Yale University in the simple and impressive ritual that has marked presidential inaugurations for 250 years. According to custom, the new president delivers an inaugural address, an oration of some interest since it is customarily interpreted as a fundamental pronouncement of his educational policy.

The incessantly cited Christian "symbols" of Yale were forthright and unambiguous; all was in keeping with the Connecticut Charter of 1701 which conferred upon the president and the Fellows of Yale "liberty to erect a collegiate school wherein youth may be instructed in the arts and sciences and who through the blessings of almighty God may be fitted for public employment both for church and civil state." Indeed, of the four men who raised their voices on that afternoon, three were clergymen, one of them the presiding bishop of the Episcopal Church of America. Hymns were sung, and a footnote on the program extended an invitation to tea to the members of the "congregation."

The traditions and the atmosphere had no apparent effect on President Griswold's thinking as revealed in his address. He did not cite or pay tribute to the contribution to the good life which for so many generations was regarded as the distinctive attribute of Christian education. He did not mention religion. . . .

Too much significance can, of course, be attributed to an inaugural address. President Sey-

mour had made a clarion call for a return to Christian values in 1937, but that did not exorcise the extreme secularism that characterized Yale at least during the last four years of his administration:

Yale was dedicated to the upraising of spiritual leaders [President Seymour had said]. We betray our trust if we fail to explore the various ways in which the youth who come to, us may learn to appreciate spiritual values, whether by the example of our own lives or through the cogency of our philosophical arguments. The simple and direct way is through the maintenance and upbuilding of the Christian religion as a vital part of university life.

For, after all, it is the policies of the university president that count: "No observer of the college scene can take undiluted delight in the mere fact that lots of colleges go through the motions. The motions must be meaningful or they are worse than meaningless."

President Seymour's devotion to Christianity and his scholarly appreciation of religious values are on the record for all to see. What I call a failure to Christianize Yale was not due to any lack of sympathy or understanding of religion on his part. It was due, rather, to the shibboleths of "academic freedom" that have so decisively hamstrung so many educators in the past fifty years. . . .

President Griswold, as an alumnus himself, is known to feel strongly that alumni interest in Yale is dependent upon full understanding of the university as a great educational center; that the alumni are adults and should be treated as such.

Yale Alumni Magazine, March 1950

If the alumni wish secular and collectivist influences to prevail at Yale, that is their privilege. What is more, if that is what they want, they need bestir themselves very little. The task has been done for them. There remains only a mopping-up operation to eliminate the few outspoken and influential figures who stand in the way of real unity in Yale's intellectual drive toward agnosticism and collectivism.

Let me add something else: if the present generation of Yale graduates does not check the University's ideological drive, the next generation most probably will not *want* to. I should be disrespectful of Yale if I did not credit her with molding the values and thinking processes of the majority of her students. Many of these, of course, withstand Yale's influence even while living in her cloistered halls for four years; and many more, in the course of future experience, learn to be first skeptical and then antagonistic to the teachings of some of the college professors they once revered.

But my contention that the values and biases of the University linger with the majority of graduates is surely not controversial. It is basic to education and to human experience that this be so, and I have no reason to doubt that it is so. If Yale Alumni come to be dissatisfied with the international, national, and community influence of the forthcoming generation of Yale graduates, they can only do so with the irrationality of the Scotsman who complained that his new dictaphone had the worst Aberdeen accent he had ever heard.

And so I repeat: unless something is done now, or soon, by collective or individual alumni action, nothing in all probability will be done in the future about Yale's predominant biases, because these will be in full accord with the wishes of the next generation of alumni.

The question arises, of course, whether or not the alumni have the power or the right to interfere if they are in disagreement with Yale's educational policy. My contention on both points is yes, they have the power and they have the right to "interfere." But I go one step farther than some people; for I maintain they also have the *duty* to "interfere." . . .

The presumption, of course, is that the values behind individualism and Christianity will not endure, and that therefore, Yale, stubbornly clinging to an outworn creed, would one day find itself a desert inhabited by deadened and spiritless intellectual prostitutes.

This is the crucial point. It is, moreover, the most frequently cited defense of *laissez-faire* education. If we adhere to a formula of education such as yours, the argument runs, wouldn't progress halt? Wouldn't we still be teaching Copernicus, fundamentalism, and divine right of kings, instead of Galileo, evolution, and republicanism?

To explore the charge calls for a preliminary distinction between *refining* a given set of values, and *displacing* them altogether in favor of others. It is true that a college must, ultimately, be flexible enough to do both.

Now, I see no problem as regards *refining* our values, modifying them, and reinterpreting them, under the educational philosophy I envision. There is great and decisive freedom to be found within the sense-making limits of orthodoxy. Free enterprise can and should be examined, criticized, and fashioned from the heart of an institution nevertheless dedicated, until something better comes along, to reserving its general outline. Similarly, no one can criticize a Christian whose allegiance and devotion to his faith lead him to criticize and to seek to reform the temporal, ritualistic, or even organic inadequacies of his religion.

The critics of any orthodoxy, of value inculcation, are quick to presuppose a rigid, insensitive administration as a necessary feature of such an institution. I fail to see why this assumption should be valid, just as I fail to see why there is reason to believe that the wide powers conferred by the Constitution on the Congress of the United States will inevitably be misused. Ultimately we are all at the mercy of the collective action of men. There is no alternative to faith that men will act reasonably. If pessimism about this prevailed, societal life would be impossible.

It is to be borne constantly in mind that the alumni of a private educational institution are the ultimate overseers of university policy. They can be presumed sufficiently human, sufficiently sensitive to new experience and changing situations, to move along, if circumstance warrants, to "new ideas," even if this means the complete displacement of previously cherished values. In fact, to intimate otherwise, to predict a rigidity of ideas in face of overwhelming contradictory evidence, is to gainsay in the most dramatic sense the validity of democracy. For if we cannot rely on the elite among our citizenry—the beneficiaries of higher education—to accommodate newly perceived truth and to adjust their thinking and acts correspondingly, there is little to be said for conferring on the people at large the reins of our destiny.

But who will advance these new ideas if the faculty is constrained to teach existing ones? Who will unearth them? This raises the question of *who will do research,* while our concern here is with the question of *who will do the teaching.* The tradition that the same men do both bears re-examination. . . . But we can rest confident that the governing body of an educational institution composed, we presume, of sensitive men of good faith, will honestly confront new experience as it is unearthed, wherever it is unearthed, and will be always prepared to jettison traditional ideas if the situation warrants.

President Seymour's most frequently quoted statement is "We shall seek the truth and endure the consequences." Unimaginable though the advent of such a truth is, I too should be willing to face the consequences of new experience that, for example, rendered individualism infeasible. But *this hasn't yet happened.*

In the meanwhile, at any given time, society is confronted with value alternatives, as with atheism versus faith, collectivism versus individualism. One value or the other, after thoughtful examination, ought to be embraced. . . .

I cannot sufficiently stress the responsibility of the faculty to insist upon student examination of other and even unfriendly creeds; but notwithstanding, again I find myself in accord with Mr. Seymour when he says: "In the intellectual and in the moral, our teachers cannot be either subservient or neutral." I hasten to dissociate myself from the school of thought, largely staffed by conservatives, that believes teachers ought to be "at all times neutral." Where values are concerned, effective teaching is difficult and stilted, if not impossible, in the context of neutrality; and further, I believe such a policy to be a lazy denial of educational responsibility.

I believe, therefore, that the attitude of the teacher ought to reveal itself, and that, assuming the overseers of the university in question to have embraced democracy, individualism, and religion, the attitudes of the faculty ought to conform to the university's. Consequently, while reading and studying Marx or Hitler, Laski or the Webbs, Huxley or Dewey, I should expect the teacher, whose competence, intelligence, and profundity I take for granted, to "deflate" the arguments advanced; similarly, I should expect an institution whose alumni sought to promulgate different values, to seek out a competent faculty whose concern would be to deflate Locke and Jefferson, Smith and Ricardo, Jesus and Paul.

Ultimately, of course, the student must decide for himself. If he chooses to repudiate the values of his instructor, he is free—and ought to be free—to do so. No coercion of any sort, whether through low examination grades, ridicule, or academic bullying, would be tolerable. The teacher must rest his case after he has done his best to show why one value is better than another. He can do no more. The institution can do no more. Neither should try to do more. Both have discharged their responsibilities to steer the student toward the truth as they see it. But can they do less than that?

THE HOAX OF ACADEMIC FREEDOM

I have left for the last a direct examination of the term "academic freedom," that handy slogan that is constantly wielded to bludgeon into impotence numberless citizens who waste away with frustration as they view in their children and in their children's children the results of *laissez-faire* education. We must determine whether freedom is violated by the administration of a private educational institution which insists upon a value orthodoxy.

The hoax to which so many of us have succumbed can only be understood after a fastidious analysis of the functions of the scholar. *We must bear in mind that the scholar has had not one but two functions, and that, further, they are not inherently related.* These pursuits are (1) scholarship, and (2) teaching. They are related solely by convenience, by tradition, and by economic exigency. This would seem clear: a man gifted in research in genetics is not thereby gifted in the art of *transmitting* to the pupil his knowledge of biology. In fact, this is periodically brought to mind in widespread student resentment at the retention by many universities of scholars who, while often distinguished in research, are miserably inept in teaching.

However, since the scholar, like his fellow-man, must earn his keep, tradition has it that in the afternoon he will utilize the university's libraries and laboratories, generally to satisfy his own desires, while in the morning he will use the classrooms to satisfy other people's desires. In short, the student pays not only for the scholar's morning work, of which the student is properly the direct beneficiary, but also, in effect, for his afternoon work, which may concern or interest the student not at all.

Now, the implications of this double role are manifold. We have in focus the methodological confusion that impedes purposive discussion of "academic freedom"; for in today's controversy, the critic is taking exception to *unlicensed teaching*, while the professors are actually basing their case on the rights of *unlicensed personal scholarship*. And

while the two sides are constantly at loggerheads, they should not be at all, for both are right.

Let us remember that it is *the scholars* who have systematized the modern conception of academic freedom. They have constructed an appealing and compact philosophical package, labeled it "truth," and tossed it for enshrinement to that undiscriminating fellow, the liberal. It is understandable that the modern rationale of "academic freedom" originated with and is a product of the scholar. To the pure scholar, the bread of life is research, theory, creation. It is horrifying to him—as it ought to be to anyone who respects the individual—that anyone other than himself should seek to prescribe the method or the orientation or the findings of his research—except, of course, in those cases where he is hired to perform a specific service.

His position here is certainly unassailable. A researcher ought to be free to seek out his own conclusions, to make his own generalizations on the basis of his discoveries. To think otherwise is, at best, to think awkwardly. It is a self-contained paradox to endow a researcher or a research organization with funds and to assert simultaneously what shall come out of the investigations for which the funds are to be used. For obviously, under such a formula, there is no reason for the investigation to be undertaken at all.

But, legend notwithstanding, the proverbial long-haired professor can, at the margin, take stock of the facts of life, and these are that *research* is in large part subsidized by the consumers of *teaching*. Therefore, cannily, he distends the protective cloak of research to include his activities as a *teacher*, thereby insuring to himself license in the laboratory, which is right and proper, and license in the classroom, which is wrong and improper.

The educational overseer—the father who sends his son to school, or the trustee who directs the policy of the school—is violating no freedom I know of if he insists, let us say, that individualism instead of collectivism be inculcated in the school. Rather, he is asserting his own freedom. For if the educational overseer, in the exercise of his freedom, espouses a set of values, his is the inescapable duty and privilege to give impetus to these values in the classroom just as he does, from time to time, in the polling booth.

7. John Tracy Ellis,
American Catholics and the Intellectual Life, 1956

Historian and documentarian of American Catholicism John Tracy Ellis (1905–92) in 1955 delivered this indictment of American Catholic intellectual life. Catholics were significantly underrepresented in the faculties of leading institutions except within the Catholic education system, where the university was separate and self-enclosed. It was this circumstance that Ellis exposed. Though disputed by a few indignant voices within his faith, his paper would become a classic for Catholic educators. Monsignor Ellis, a midwesterner, taught from 1938 to 1964 at the Catholic University of America (Ph.D. 1928) and chaired the history department at the University of San Francisco (1964–76). Through his histories, biographies, and documentaries of American Catholicism, Ellis was widely viewed and honored as the leading American Catholic scholar.

John Tracy Ellis, *American Catholics and the Intellectual Life* (Chicago, 1956), 15–17, 42–50, 54–57, first published in *Thought* 30 (Autumn 1955): 351–88. Footnotes here omitted. Reprinted with the permission of Fordham University Press © 1956. Further reading: self-identity and the ensuing "crisis of confidence" among Catholic thinkers, largely initiated by Monsignor Ellis's paper, are discussed by Philip Gleason in "What Made Catholic Identity a Problem?" in *The Challenge and Promise of a Catholic University*, ed. Theodore M. Hesburgh, C.S.C. (Notre Dame, IN, and London, 1994), 91–102. See also Gleason's *Contending with Modernity: Catholic Higher Education in the Twentieth Century* (New York, 1995); and John T. McGreevy, "Thinking on One's Own: Catholics in the American Intellectual Imagination," in *Journal of American History* 84 (1997): 97–131, and "Catholics, Catholicism, and the Humanities since World War II," in *The Humanities and the Dynamics of Inclusion since World War II*, ed. David A. Hollinger (Baltimore, 2006), ch. 7, a brief but comprehensive survey of this subject.

Fourteen years ago one of the most perceptive of living foreign observers of American life and institutions, Denis W. Brogan, professor of political science in the University of Cambridge, stated in a book on the United States: ". . . in no Western society is the intellectual prestige of Catholicism lower than in the country where, in such respects as wealth, numbers, and strength of organization, it is so powerful." No well-informed American Catholic will attempt to challenge that statement. Admittedly, the weakest aspect of the Church in this country lies in its failure to produce national leaders and to exercise commanding influence in intellectual circles, and this at a time when the number of Catholics in the United States is exceeded only by those of Brazil and Italy, and their material resources are incomparably superior to those of any other branch of the universal Church. What, one may ask, is the explanation of this striking discrepancy? . . .

The first point is, namely, that the implanting in this soil of a deep anti-Catholic prejudice by the original English settlers in the early seventeenth century, requires no elaborate proof for any educated American. . . . In the spring of 1942 I had the fact brought home to me in a forceful way when Professor Arthur M. Schlesinger, Sr., of Harvard University, one of the outstanding authorities in American social history, remarked to me during a friendly chat in Cambridge, "I regard the bias against your Church as the most persistent prejudice in the history of the American people." . . .

The American intellectual climate has been aloof and unfriendly to Catholic thought and ideas, when it has not been openly hostile, and it places no burden upon the imagination to appreciate how this factor has militated against a strong and vibrant intellectual life among the Catholics of this country. . . .

Part of the reason why American Catholics have not made a notable impression on the intellectual life of their country is due, I am convinced, to what might be called a betrayal of that which is peculiarly their own. The nature of that betrayal has been highlighted during the last quarter of a century by such movements as the scholastic revival in philosophy. . . . Meanwhile the Catholic universities were engrossed in their mad pursuit of every passing fancy that crossed the American educational scene, and found relatively little time for distinguished contributions to scholastic philosophy. Woefully lacking in the endowment, training, and equipment to make them successful competitors of the secular universities in fields like engineering, business administration, nursing education, and the like, the Catholic universities, nonetheless, went on multiplying these units and spreading their budgets so thin—in an attempt to include everything—that the subjects in which they could, and should, make a unique contribution were sorely neglected.

That American educators expect Catholic institutions to be strong in the humanities and the liberal arts—to say nothing of theology and philosophy—is not surprising. Eighteen years ago Robert M. Hutchins . . . criticized the Catholic institutions for failing to emphasize that tradition in a way that would make it come alive in American intellectual circles. He thought the ideals of Catholic educators were satisfactory, but as far as actual practice was concerned, he said, "I find it necessary to level against you a scandalous accusation." He then went on:

> In my opinion . . . you have imitated the worst features of secular education and ignored most of the good ones. There are some good ones, relatively speaking—high academic standards, development of habits of work, and research. . . .

Hutchins listed the bad features he had in mind as athleticism, collegiatism, vocationalism, and anti-intellectualism. In regard to the first two we can claim, I think, that in recent years Catholic institutions have shown improvement, just as all other educational groups have done. As for the second two, vocationalism and anti-intellectualism, I find no striking evidence of reform in the Church's colleges and universities since 1937. Regarding the three good features of secular institutions which Hutchins named, high academic standards, development of habits of work, and the ideal of research, I would say that a better showing has been made here and there on the first, but in the development of habits of work and a cherished ideal of research, I cannot personally see much by way of a fundamental change.

A second major defect in Catholic higher education that helps to account for its paucity of scholars of distinction, is what I would call our betrayal of one another. By that I mean the development within the last two decades of numerous and competing graduate schools, none of which is adequately endowed, and few of which have the trained personnel, the equipment in libraries and laboratories, and the professional wage scales to warrant their ambitious undertakings. The result is a perpetuation of mediocrity and the draining away from each other of the strength that is necessary if really superior achievements are to be attained. I am speaking here; incidentally, only of the graduate schools, and not, of the competition—amounting in certain places to internecine warfare—among the more than 200 Catholic colleges of the land. . . . The Catholic institutions of higher learning in this country may soon face the peril of financial bankruptcy. I realize that this may sound extreme, but in my judgment the danger of insolvency, and that alone, will put an end to the senseless duplication of effort and the wasteful proliferation that have robbed Catholic graduate schools of the hope of superior achievement in the restricted area of those academic disciplines where their true strength and mission lie. Hutchins had that in mind when he closed his address to the Catholic educators at Chicago in 1937 by saying, "The best service Catholic education can perform for the nation and all education is to show that the intellectual tradition can again be made the heart of higher education."

An additional point which should find a place in an investigation of this kind is the absence of a love of scholarship for its own sake among American Catholics, and that even among too large a number of Catholics who are engaged in higher education. It might be described as the absence of a sense of dedication to an intellectual apostolate. This defect, in turn, tends to deprive many of those who spend their lives in the universities of the American Church of the admirable industry and unremitting labor in research and publication which characterize a far greater proportion of their colleagues on the faculties of the secular universities. I do not pretend to know precisely what the cause of this may be, but I wonder if it is not in part due to the too literal interpretation which many churchmen and superiors of seminaries and religious houses have given to St. Paul's oft-quoted statement that "Here we have no permanent city, but we seek for the city that is to come. . . ."

Closely connected with the question of the prevailing Catholic attitudes in education is the overemphasis which some authorities of the Church's educational system in the United States have given to the school as an agency for moral development, with an insufficient stress on the role of the school as an instrument for fostering intellectual excellence. That fact has at times led to a confusion of aims and to a neglect of the school as a training ground for the intellectual virtues. No sensible person will for a moment question that the inculcation of moral virtue is one of the principal reasons for having Catholic schools in any circumstances. But that goal should never be permitted to overshadow the fact that the school, at whatever level one may consider it, must maintain a strong emphasis on the cultivation of intellectual excellence. Given superior minds, out of the striving for the intellectual virtues there will flow, with its attendant religious instruction, the formation of a type of student who will not only be able to withstand the strains which life will inevitably force upon his religious faith, but one who will have been so intellectually fortified that he will reflect distinction upon the system of which he is a product. . . .

A volume published three years ago by R. H. Knapp and H. B. Goodrich . . . sifted 18,000 names from among the 43,500 scientists listed in two editions of *American Men of Science*. From these selected names they then drew up a list of the fifty institutions which had led in the production of scientists, but no Catholic college or university received a place among the fifty leaders. . . .

If the Catholic scientists should have begun to think that an undue amount of stress has been placed on the dearth of distinguished names among their kind, they can be quickly reassured. The picture in the sacred sciences, the liberal arts, and the humanities is no brighter on that score, for the studies which I have examined reveal no higher proportion of distinction in these fields than they do in science. . . .

While it is gratifying to learn that so many of the graduates of Catholic institutions pursue their studies beyond college by fitting themselves for the legal and medical professions, it is to be regretted that a proportionately high number do not manifest a like desire, or find a similarly strong stimulation, to become trained scholars in the fields where the Catholic tradition of learning is the strongest. In that connection the work of Robert H. Knapp and Joseph J. Greenbaum published two years ago is enlightening. The principal objective of these authors was to determine, from the undergraduate backgrounds of the younger generation of Americans who had won distinction in graduate schools during the years 1946–1952, which colleges had produced the largest number of promising scholars. . . .

The roster assembled by Knapp and Greenbaum contained in all the names of 562 institutions, but among the fifty top-ranking colleges for men in the production of scholars in science, social science, and the humanities, no Catholic school found a place. . . .

The one bright spot of the Knapp-Greenbaum study, insofar as Catholics are concerned, relates to the women's colleges. . . . These facts would tend to bear out a fairly common opinion that in a number of ways the Catholic women's colleges are in advance of the institutions for men. The over-all impression left by the Knapp-Greenbaum work is, therefore, anything but flattering to the Catholic institutions of this country, especially in fields like the humanities and the social sciences.

In conclusion, then, one may say that it has been a combination of all the major points made in this paper, along with others which I may have failed to consider, that has produced in American Catholics generally, as well as in the intellectuals, a pervading spirit of separatism from their fellow citizens of other religious faiths. They have suffered from the timidity that characterizes minority groups, from the effects of a ghetto they have themselves fostered, and, too, from a sense of inferiority induced by their consciousness of the inadequacy of Catholic scholarship. But who, one may rightly ask, has been responsible in the main for its inadequacy? Certainly not the Church's enemies, for if one were to reason on that basis St. Augustine would never have written the *City of God,* St. Robert Bellarmine the *Tractatus de potestate summi pontificis,* nor would Cardinal Baronius have produced the *Annales ecclesiastici.* In fact, it has been enmity and opposition that have called forth some of the greatest monuments to Catholic scholarship. The major defect, therefore, lies elsewhere than with the unfriendly attitude of some of those outside the Church. The chief blame, I firmly believe, lies with Catholics themselves. It lies in their frequently self-imposed ghetto mentality which prevents them from mingling as they should with their non-Catholic colleagues, and in their lack of industry and the habits of work, to which Hutchins alluded in 1937. It lies in their failure to have measured up to their responsibilities to the incomparable tradition of Catholic learning of which they are the direct heirs.

The Newman Report

8. Frank Newman et al., *Report on Higher Education,* 1971

Among widely publicized assessments of higher education during the Vietnam War years, the Newman Report was exceptional. Like the others, it did address some of the internal institutional sources of contemporary student unrest. But its major theme was ways in which higher education could better serve the needs of all Americans beyond "the exclusionary" college-age population. Its prose was blunt and brief. It asked whether higher education need be academic education. It asserted that the academic enterprise is indeed a national enterprise, one that requires accountability from all who are engaged with it or who profit from it. One of its insights, reprinted here, describes the price paid nationally for the professionalization of learning.

Frank Newman (1927–2004) chaired the task force that wrote this report, which had first been requested by Robert Fitch, secretary of health, education, and welfare. His successor, Elliot Richardson, was its recipient. Newman was joined by seven others on the task force who were chosen for their ability "to think about conventional problems in unconventional ways." Five were from uni-

versity faculties and two were from HEW. The task force published two more studies over the next five years calling for easier access, wiser financing, and accreditation for American colleges. Frank Newman was educated at Bucknell, Brown, Oxford University, Columbia (M.S. 1955), and Stanford (Ph.D. 1981). Before serving as president of the University of Rhode Island (1974–83), he had worked in administration and public relations at Stanford (1967–74) and had run unsuccessfully for Congress. From 1983–97 he presided over the Education Commission of the States, an advisory group on education policy. His last appointments were the directorship of the Futures Project at Brown University and as a visiting professor at Teachers College.

Frank Newman et al., *Report on Higher Education, March 1971* (Washington, D.C., 1971), v–vii, x, 17–19. Further reading: On the history and critical reception of this report, see *Change* 3 (Summer 1971): 11–13, and 4 (May 1972): 28–37; and Arthur Levine, "For Frank Newman, Anything was Possible," *Chronicle of Higher Education,* June 18, 2004, B16. Echoing in some respects his 1971 report was *The Future of Higher Education: Rhetoric Reality and the Risks of the Market,* edited with Laura Couturier and Jamie Scurry (San Francisco, 2004), to which Newman contributed before he died.

THE PROFESSIONALIZATION OF LEARNING

The faculties educated and then hired by our colleges and universities in the past 30 years have brought extraordinary benefits to the Nation. They have produced research of enormous importance to our national growth and international position; they have made our graduate schools the envy of the world; they have educated more knowledgeable and sophisticated undergraduates than ever before. Yet these triumphs of academic professionalism have come at the expense of millions of individuals seeking an education. While the population seeking higher education is becoming ever more diverse—in class and social background, age, academic experience, and ability—our colleges and universities have come to assume that there is only one mode of teaching and learning—the academic mode. . . .

The professionalization of academic faculties has shaped the character of higher education in many ways. Increasingly, being a teacher has become part of a broader role centering around one's professional colleagues—attending professional conferences, writing and reviewing articles, sponsoring and recruiting apprentices into the discipline. Faculties at universities and the more prestigious colleges have come to view themselves as independent professionals responsible to their guilds rather than to the institutions which pay their salaries. They have established at their institutions a system of tenure and promotion designed to preserve their professional objectives. Those who slight the academic obligations of specialization, research, and publication are themselves slighted in promotion, esteem, and influence.

Professional faculties have, with few exceptions,

organized their institutions in ways that reflect their training and are congenial to their interests. Almost all of the 2,500 institutions of higher education are organized in terms of departments based on academic disciplines. Collectively, the faculty interest has asserted itself in favor of rounding out the campus to become similar to a broad-gauged university. Each faculty member tends to see himself as a member of a particular discipline which requires a department on campus. Status accrues to those campuses noted for research activity. Hence, normal schools and agricultural colleges have changed their names to "State College"; and, a decade later, to "State University at . . ." Institutions with specialized programs—even prestigious institutions such as the Massachusetts Institute of Technology and the California Institute of Technology—have decided to round out their offerings.

This organization of college curriculums into the mold of the academic specialties has been accompanied by a strong faculty bias toward the acquisition of theoretical knowledge. In the graduate schools, the social science and even the humanities faculties have strained to build disciplines modeled after the pure sciences. In the undergraduate schools, courses tend to be taught as if the development of theoretical knowledge were the only proper business of liberal education. Those individuals who cannot see themselves as recruits to an academic discipline are slighted in favor of the few (out of the total student population) who display an interest and talent for theoretical training.

The professionalization of faculties has influenced not only the content but the methods of undergraduate education. These faculties assume that their students will learn best the way they themselves learned best—by sitting in class, listening to professors, and reading books. All too infrequently is an undergraduate course organized or taught on the assumption that students might learn best through subjective or practical experiences. Sometimes faculty members will try to bring practitioners into the classroom to supplement their lectures, but rarely are courses organized around such individuals, and almost never are they brought into the academic inner sanctum. Rarely are there politicians or lawyers in political science departments, novelists, clergymen, or practicing psychiatrists in psychology departments, or engineers asked to help teach courses in the department of physics.

Moreover, seldom do the majority of faculty members spend any time in jobs outside the university. The drive to obtain tenure plays a crucial role in the faculty lockstep. The young faculty members with an interest in spending a few years in government or industry find that such broadening experiences count for little. More important, only the most courageous dare lose their place in line or their chance at one more publication. By the time the safety of tenure is reached, most have been socialized to the prevailing faculty role.

The Humanities

9. Lionel Trilling, *The Last Decade,* 1974

On various occasions Lionel Trilling (1905–75) assessed the condition of the humanities. His writings were generally "literary-historical" inquiries. As social criticism they arose from a singular engagement with the cultivated mind and the moral experience of the examined self facing the contingencies of the modern world. Drawing on the classics of western literature and the modern social sciences—attending to Freud, though no Freudian, and to Marx, though no Marxist—he sought to deepen and enlarge the "liberal imagination."

Still, Trilling was a career-long classroom teacher and an institutional man, in contrast to other eminent literary critics in mid–twentieth century America like Edmund Wilson and Alfred Kazin. He belonged to Columbia University, where he took his degrees (Ph.D. 1938), reversed an English Department decision to let him go as a young assistant professor, went on to become the first Jewish tenured professor of English, and was awarded the University Professorship in 1970.

This essay, first presented at the Aspen Institute the year before he died, was his response to the question "What were the factors in contemporary society which worked for or against the likelihood that, in the late twentieth century, there would emerge an effectual ideal of education which would be integrally related to the humanistic educational traditions of the past?"

Lionel Trilling, "The Uncertain Future of the Humanistic Educational Ideal," in *The Last Decade: Essays and Reviews, 1965–75,* ed. Diana Trilling (New York, 1979): 160–61, 163–76. Copyright © 1974 by Lionel Trilling Estate. Reprinted with the permission of The Wylie Agency, Inc. Further reading: of Lionel Trilling's several works, those that are relevant here include *The Liberal Imagination: Essays on Literature and Society* (New York, 1950); *Sincerity and Authenticity* (Cambridge, MA, 1972); *Mind in the Modern World* (New York, 1972). Biographies include Edward Joseph Shoben, *Lionel Trilling* (New York, 1981); Stephen Tanner, *Lionel Trilling* (New York, 1988); William M. Chace, *Lionel Trilling, Criticism and Politics* (New York, 1980); and VII, 11.

Partly for Socratic reasons, but chiefly because it is my actual belief, I shall take the view that at the present time in American society, there are few factors to be perceived, if any at all, which make it likely that within the next quarter-century there will be articulated in a convincing and effectual way an educational ideal that has a positive and significant connection with the humanistic educational traditions of the past. At the moment, it seems to me that the indications point the opposite way and urge upon us the conclusion that our society will tend increasingly to alienate itself from the humanistic educational ideal.

Yet, although I would argue the necessity of this conclusion from the evidence before us, I think it necessary to stipulate, as I have done, that the state of affairs to which I refer is one that exists "at the moment." I wish, that is, to express my sense of how readily the winds of American educational doctrine shift, and that they do so at the behest of all manner of circumstances which are hard to discern, let alone predict.

A Columbia man is perhaps in a particularly good position to comment on the impermanence of educational theory, especially of such theory as takes account of the traditional humanistic conceptions of what education properly is. The history of my university over most of the last hundred years might be told in terms of its alternations of attitude toward these conceptions. . . .

After the First World War, for a variety of reasons, . . . "professional option" became much less popular than it had formerly been, and the "generous and reflective use of leisure" established itself as a proper mode of life for the young men of Columbia College. It was John Erskine, a scholar of Renaissance English literature, who gave it its most effectual form by initiating what elsewhere came to be known as the Great Books Program; at Columbia, the Great Books were read in a rather exigent two-year course for juniors and seniors which was called General Honors and remembered with gratitude and pride by everyone who was permitted to take it. . . .

Erskine put his mark on Columbia, and, indeed, on educational theory throughout the country. Mortimer Adler as a very young graduate student was one of the first teachers in that enchanting General Honors course that Erskine had devised, and the mention of his name will suggest the response to the Great Books idea at the University of Chicago and at St. John's College and at the innumerable other schools that were led to believe, though of course with varying degrees of intensity, that the study of the preeminent works of the past, chiefly those in the humanities, with what this study implied of the development of the "whole man"—no one then thought of the necessity of saying the "whole person"—was the best possible direction that undergraduate education could take.

The purpose of my historical reference has been only to put us in mind of how recently it could be conceived that a traditionally humanistic education had a bearing upon contemporary American life and deserved to be given an honored place in it. I recall my experience as a college teacher through the thirties, forties, and fifties as having been a peculiarly fortunate one: I inhabited an academic community which was informed by a sense not merely of scholarly, but of educational purpose, and which was devoted to making ever more cogent its conception of what a liberal and humane education consists in. . . .

I speak of the thirties, the forties, and the fifties. But by the sixties, something had happened to reduce the zeal for such education as set store by its being general, and defined its purpose as being the cultivation of general intelligence in the young. For reasons which, to my knowledge, have not yet been formulated, but which I cannot doubt to have been of great cultural moment, this concern lost its characteristic urgency. At Columbia College, the consciousness of this change in our educational ethos was made explicit when, in 1964, the dean of the College, David Truman, asked Daniel Bell to look into the state of general education in the College and report on it to the faculty. I shall not touch upon the substance of Bell's brilliant report, which was later published under the title of *The Reforming of General Education*. I wish only to commemorate as a sad and significant event in the culture of our time the response of the Columbia College faculty to the questions the report raised and sought to answer. From my long experience of the College, I can recall no meetings on an educational topic that were so poorly attended and so lacking in vivacity as those in which the report was considered. If I remember correctly, these meetings led to no action whatever, not even to the resolve to look further into the matter. Through some persuasion of the *Zeitgeist*, the majority of the faculty were no longer concerned with general education in the large and honorific meaning of the phrase.

Nothing could be further from my intention than to say that they had become cynical about their function as teachers. Actually, indeed, it was in some part the seriousness with which they took their teacherly function that led them to withdraw their interest from the large questions of educational theory; periodically the answers to these questions become platitudinous and boring, mere pious protestations, and at such times a teacher might naturally and rightly feel that he does most for his students not by speculating about what shape and disposition their minds ought eventually to have, but by simply pressing upon them the solid substance and the multitudinous precisions of his own particular intellectual discipline. I think there can be no doubt, too, that the growing indifference to the ideals of general education was in some considerable part an aspect of the new mode of political anxiety that was manifesting itself at the time. The urgency of the problems, the sordidness of the problems, which pressed in upon us from the surrounding world made speculation on educational theory seem almost frivolous.

But no sooner have we taken note of how things stood in 1964 and in the years of violent disruption of university life that followed . . . than we have to observe that the doctrinal winds are shifting once more, that the feeling about general education is changing yet again: we perceive that in certain circles, the circumferences of which tend to enlarge themselves, general education is being represented as a subject of ultimate and urgent importance.

Among those who have a professional concern with education, there is now a strong inclination to make the humanities salient in the ideal curriculums they project. . . . Of the three categories of learning, this is the one that lays least claim to immediate practicality, to being effectual in what we call problem-solving, yet among those who are prophetically concerned with education the feeling seems to grow, and to be affirmed in conference after conference, in seminar after seminar, that in the humanities is to be found the principle that must inform our educational enterprise, the principle that directs us to see to the development of the critical intelligence, of the critical moral intelligence, without which—so it is increasingly said—we shall perish, or at least painfully deteriorate.

I speak of our society as being at the present time animated by a renewed interest in the kind of higher education whose moral content will help us in the right ordering of social and political existence. This is the interest in and the conception of higher education that is entertained by the educated middle classes and made articulate by those among them—among *us*—who have a professional concern with the process and goals of education and who are habituated to connect them with the welfare of society at large. But we can scarcely fail to be aware that this large, ultimate, and ideal concern is concomitant with, and possibly a remonstrative response to, an interest in higher education that has both a different source and a different purpose. What I refer to is the interest in higher education of people for whom its salient characteristic is that they have not had any of it. . . .

But the grievance of those who have been debarred from higher education is not wholly understood if it is thought of as having reference to economic deprivation alone. Those who feel the grievance—or at least many of those who feel it—are not merely saying that because they have not had college educations they cannot make as much money as those who have. Nor are they quite talking about their unsatisfactory social status only in the simple way that associates it immediately and directly with income. Their grievance is social in a more complex sense, in the sense that it is cultural. Its nature is vividly described in a book called *The Hidden Injuries of Class,* by Richard Sennett and Jonathan Cobb. . . .

These urban workers want to become educated persons; they believe that being educated is to their advantage. They do not exactly know why this is so, and Sennett, the professional observer and recorder of such desires and beliefs as they entertain, cannot say with any definiteness what the advantage might be. As I say, he rules out crass economic advantage and such social gains as follow directly from it. He seems to suggest that the desire to be educated is associated with the diminished force of the ethos of class, that the people who think it would be good for them and their children to be "cultured" feel that they have lost a class idiom and a class bond—they want to be "cultured" because they have been deprived of the community once provided by class. They think of themselves, that is, as postulants for membership in a new, larger, and more complex community to which they are as yet extraneous. They conceive education, higher education, as the process of initiation into membership in that community. . . .

But if, following Sennett's lead, I suggest that there is an affinity between the way in which higher education is conceived by traditional humanism and the way in which it is conceived, instinctually as it were, by a significant group of uneducated people who want to be educated, have I not in effect said that the educational ideal of traditional humanism can count upon being ceaselessly sustained and renewed? And if I have done that, then how can I maintain the opinion expressed at the beginning of this paper, that there is but little likelihood that in our time there will be articulated in a convincing and effectual way an educational ideal that has a positive connection with the humanistic educational traditions of the past?

I have used the word *initiation* to suggest the ritually prescribed stages by which a person is brought into a community whose members are presumed to have attained to a state of being superior to his own. Such ritual procedures typically involve a test, which, by reason of its difficulty or danger or pain or hardship, is commonly called an ordeal. It is from this exigent experience that the process of initiation is thought to derive its validity. The ordeal is presumed to bring about a change in the postulant, a state of illumination and power. . . .

If I am right in saying that humanistic educational traditions of the past were grounded in strenuous effort and that the idea of ordeal was essential to them, it will be obvious, I think, that our American culture will not find these educational traditions congenial. . . .

Very likely this feeling on the part of many Americans that being taught or required to learn is an arbitrary denial of autonomy goes far toward explaining the state of primary and secondary education in our country. Everyone seems to act as if that cause is wholly and irretrievably lost and to conclude that the best way of dealing with this significant defeat of the democratic-ideal is to put it behind us, to say nothing more about it, and to place our hope for education wholly in its higher branches. At the several conferences and seminars that I have attended through the past year . . . any attempt to suggest that the quality of higher education might have some relation to the quality of primary and secondary education was unfailingly met with irritated resistance as being an obstructive irrelevance. This would have greatly surprised—would have appalled—John Milton or any theorist of humanistic education of the past.

Yet will we be fair to our society if we let those old theorists of humanistic education have the last word? Will we be doing justice to our system of education in its totality if we take the view that we fail in our duty to our young people because we do not see to it that they are really taught, that they are really required to learn traditional substantive subjects, that they are early and compulsorily subjected to such fashioning, forming, shaping as will prepare them for further *Bildung* at the university? As I have said, there is pretty wide agreement that this is not how our primary and secondary schools understand their function. But might it not be a question whether, in the light of precisely our most conscientiously forward-looking and hopeful cultural sentiment, there is any real need for them to regard their function in this way? Consider the following estimate of young people who have entered the universities after having had the presumably inadequate training our schools give: "The present generation of young people in our universities are the best informed, the most intelligent, and the most idealistic this country has ever known. This is the experience of teachers everywhere." I am citing the opening paragraph of the *Report of the Fact-Finding Commission Appointed to Investigate the Disturbances at Columbia University in April and May 1968*. It was written by the chairman of the commission, Professor Archibald Cox of the Harvard Law School. The statement, we may presume, was not carelessly made.

Although when I first read Professor Cox's statement my response was one of natural bewilderment, upon further consideration perhaps I have come to see how Professor Cox arrived at this remarkable judgment. Ours is a culture of which a chief characteristic is its self-awareness. Not only that aspect of our culture which we refer to as "high" is largely given over to enhancing this alertness to our condition—no less intense and overt in this effort is what we might call the institutional-popular section of our culture, which includes advertising, television in its various genres, journalism in its various modes. Through the agency of one segment of the culture or another, there is unceasingly being borne in upon us the consciousness that we live in circumstances of an unprecedented sort. And through these agencies we are provided with the information and the attitudes that enable us to believe not only that we can properly identify the difficulties presented by the society but also that we can cope with them, at least in spirit, and that in itself our consciousness of difficulties to be coped with gives us moral distinction. The young share with their elders this alertness to our condition; and the consciousness, together with the moral validation it confers, appears in the young at an increasingly early age, the rate of social and cultural maturation having radically accelerated in recent years, doubtless as a consequence of extreme alterations in the mores of the family and in the mores of sexuality. The excitement about the problems of our world (perhaps not the less heady for being touched by apprehensiveness) and the emotions of mastery (perhaps not the less cherished for showing some color of factiousness) that are so abundantly generated in our culture make a convincing simulacrum of a serious address to, and comprehension of, the society.

In his high estimate of the young, Professor Cox accepted the simulacrum for the real thing: he celebrated as knowledge and intelligence what in actuality is merely a congeries of "advanced" public attitudes. When he made his affirmation of the enlightenment of the young, he affirmed his own enlightenment and that of others who would agree with his judgment—for it is from the young and not from his own experience that he was deriving his values, and for values to have this source is, in the view of a large part of our forward-looking culture, all the certification that is required to prove that the values are sound ones. But surely more important than the deference to youth that was implicit in Professor Cox's high estimate of the attainment of this generation of students was his readiness to accept another of the master traits of our contemporary culture: its willingness—its eagerness—to forgo the particularization of conduct. Recognizing the great store now placed on selfhood and the energies of the self, Professor Cox met and matched the culture in its principled indifference to the intellectual and moral forms in which the self chooses to be presented.

If we consider the roadblocks in the path of a reestablishment of traditional humanistic education, surely none is so effectually obstructing as the tendency of our culture to regard the mere energy of impulse as being in every mental and moral way equivalent and even superior to defined intention. We may remark, as exemplary of this tendency, the fate of an idea that once was salient in Western culture: the idea of "making a life," by which was meant conceiving human existence, one's own or another's, as if it were a work of art upon which one might pass judgment, assessing it by established criteria. This idea of a conceived and executed life is a very old one and was in force until relatively recently; we regard it as characteristic of the Victorian age, but it of course lasted even longer than that. It was what virtually all novels used to be about: how you were born, reared, and shaped, and then how you took over and managed for yourself as best you could. And cognate with the idea of making a life, a nicely proportioned one, with a beginning, a middle, and an end, was the idea of making a self, a good self. Yeats speaks of women dealing with their outward selves as works of art, laboring to be beautiful; just so does Castiglione in *The Book of the Courtier* represent men laboring to come up to standard, to be all that men might reasonably hope to be, partly for the satisfaction of being so, partly for the discharge of rather primitive political functions.

This desire to fashion, to shape, a self and a life has all but gone from a contemporary culture whose emphasis, paradoxically enough, is so much on self. If we ask why this has come about, the answer of course involves us in a giant labor of social history. But there is one reason which can be readily isolated and which, I think, explains much. It is this: if you set yourself to shaping a self, a life, you limit yourself to that self and that life. You preclude any other kind of selfhood remaining available to you. You close out other options, other possibilities which might have been yours. Such limitation, once acceptable, now goes against the cultural grain—it is almost as if the fluidity of the contemporary world demands an analogous limitlessness in our personal perspective. Any doctrine, that of the family, religion, the school, that does not sustain this increasingly felt need for a multiplicity of options and instead offers an ideal of a shaped self, a formed life, has the sign on it of a retrograde and depriving authority, which, it is felt, must be resisted.

For anyone concerned with contemporary education at whatever level, the assimilation that contemporary culture has made between social idealism, even political liberalism, and personal fluidity —a self without the old confinements—is as momentous as it is recalcitrant to correction. Among the factors in the contemporary world which militate against the formulation of an educational ideal related to the humanistic traditions of the past, this seems to me to be the most decisive.

10. Joseph Duffey, "The Social Meaning of the Humanities," 1980

Joseph Duffey (1932–), equipped with divinity degrees from Andover Newton (1957), Yale (1964), and Hartford (Ph.D. 1969), became a Congregationalist minister (1957–60). He entered public and academic life as chairman of Americans for Democratic Action (1969–70), ran unsuccessfully for the U.S. Senate from Connecticut in 1970, was general secretary of the American Association of University Professors (1974–76), chaired the National Endowment for the Humanities (1978–81), and later became director of the United States Information Agency (1993–98). He also served as chancellor of the University of Massachusetts at Amherst (1982–91) and president of American University (1991–93). From these manifold experiences, he discussed the humanities in an exceptionally open-minded and generous way.

Joseph Duffey, "The Social Meaning of the Humanities," *Change* 12 (February–March 1980), 40–42. Reprinted with permission of the Helen Dwight Reid Educational Foundation. Published by Heldref Publications, 1319 Eighteenth St. NW, Washington, D.C. 20036-1802. Copyright © 1980. Further reading: Thomas Bender, "Locality and Worldliness," in *The Transformation of Humanistic Studies in the Twenty-first Century: Opportunities and Perils*, ACLS Occasional Papers Series, 40 (New York, 1997); Jill M. Bystydzienski, Sharon R. Bird, eds., *Removing Barriers: Women in Academic Science, Technology, Engineering, and Mathematics* (Bloomington, IN, 2006); and I, 1, 9, 11; III, 2–7.

All too often those of us who cherish the work of the humanities are called upon to defend such endeavors on utilitarian grounds—to say what problems such studies solve, what needs they fulfill. Even in the eloquent report of the Commission on the Human-

ities which led to the founding of the NEH-15 years ago, a key section was called, "America's Need of the Humanities." The language of that report seems in part to argue that the solution of major problems of American life—the need for national vision, the relationship of democracy and wisdom, the position of the United States in world public opinion, and the expansion of leisure time—required the contributions of the "resources" of the humanities.

Fifteen years have passed. Hundreds of projects have been funded by NEH and it is difficult to argue that the humanities have helped in a major way to "solve" these problems. But of course the business of the humanities is not to solve such problems; it is to explore them, to clarify them, redefine their terms, connect them to older questions, perhaps to rephrase them and ask them anew. This is difficult work and it is immensely frustrating to those seeking clear, crisp, action-oriented answers.

Thus although I would like to think of myself as a humanitarian as well as one concerned with the humanities, I would agree with [Irving] Babbitt that the humanities are less than efficient agents for social good. The United States has many pressing social problems. We have some effective programs for ameliorating them. But the major rationale for public assistance to research and teaching in the humanities cannot be based upon the contribution of these disciplines to problem solving. . . .

I am more than a little uncomfortable with vaulting assertions about the contributions of the humanities to society that describe those contributions in terms of social purpose. But I believe that learning in these fields not only contributes to individual enrichment and insight but may contribute as well to the enrichment and strength of society. It might be helpful then, in clarifying this larger role of humanistic learning, to assert here the difference between social *purpose* and social *meaning*.

The social purposes of the humanities are problematic. They don't solve practical problems. For example, studies of the history of religious thought or of philosophical ethics are forms of humanistic inquiry. But learning in these disciplines is not an effective substitute for religion and morality in making people more decent, even more "humane." The mastery of learning in some fields of the humanities may in fact be trivialized into a haughty badge of assumed social superiority or an ornament of one's background or formal education, but such self-display has little to do with the essentially critical and humble spirit of learning in the humanities.

In the academic world today the most common use of the term humanities is to designate a number of disciplines. As a result of either a fateful loss of innocence or increasing sophistication—take your choice—we no longer maintain, as Babbitt did, that what these areas of learning share is their relation to a unitary philosophy or sense of a transcendent cultural heritage. But the complexity of humanistic inquiry would be lost by simply defining these disciplines as plots of intellectual no-man's-land be-tween the sciences and the social sciences. . . . For my own part I believe that at a minimum, humanistic studies can be described as nonquantitative inquiry into the continuities and discontinuities of human history; critical inquiry that aspires to the interpretation and understanding of human experience.

It is in relation to these concerns for interpretation and understanding that the social *meaning* of the humanities is inescapable. In the 70 years since Babbitt wrote, we have come to view culture more as a continuing human construction than as an inheritance passed intact from one generation to another. The meaning of ordinary realities and works of art alike is conceived and developed in the convergence of minds, in the agreement that this should be so and that not. . . .

We have become aware that the study of the humanities is shaped in part by changing social circumstances, by history. In our generation we have often seen scholars in these disciplines turn to subjects of contemporary significance—examining the histories of women and ethnic groups, studying the cultural complexities of Southeast Asia, or, more recently, of the Islamic Near East. But more subtly, scholars have also altered the sorts of conceptions and assumptions with which they frame their studies even of conventional subjects—regarding religious orthodoxy and ritualism more seriously and more critically than they did a generation ago; emphasizing the local aspects of historical events; seeing fictional characters and social activity as forms of quasi-theatrical "roles"; stressing the developmental perspective in life histories.

These conceptual shifts are the ways in which cultural meanings change. They are not the product of individual minds, nor do they occur suddenly. They are the work of many thoughtful men and women, developed slowly and cooperatively. The notion, for example, that Americans still cherish their ethnic group loyalties despite decades of assimilation cannot be traced to the "discovery" of any particular scholar or scholarly discipline. Indeed, our common understanding of ethnic diversity has been the product of as many outside the academic profession—social workers, clergy, politicians, journalists—as of sociologists and historians.

What role, then, do humanists in particular play in the development of social meaning for the whole culture? By virtue of their training and skills scholars in the humanities can help to unmask the apparent "givenness" of the cultural world around us. They can show us that our thoughts and acts have historical precedents, philosophical implications, imaginative possibilities. By becoming conscious of these humanistic contexts for contemporary life, we can recognize that our world is not a given, a natural prison from which we can never escape, but a continuing process in which each generation affirms, rejects, and transforms various aspects of the cultural heritage it receives from its past. . . .

In taking our ideas seriously, in reflecting upon them against the backdrop of various historical, philosophical, and imaginative contexts, the humanist performs his most significant task. He helps all of us shape our changing visions of the human condition: How free do we think man is, and how determined? How individualistic should we be, and how much a part of a community? How much change do we want, and how much stability and order?

Even the most esoteric research in the humanities may thus contribute to shaping our sense of social meaning. In the greatest of scholars this vision is clear in every part of their work. . . .

At particular moments in the history of academic life, perhaps most in times of economic woes, some scholars succumb to excessive boasting about the obscurity of the work they perform. So where campus paths were decked in the 1960s with banners of "relevance," now the call in many quarters is for the "self-referentiality" of scholarship. The adoption of structuralist jargon by students of religion and literature, or of behaviorist "methodological paradigms" by students of society and history, has sapped some of the pleasure (and the elegance) of the humanities, just as a decade or so ago too much straining after relevance unsinewed some of their intellectual coherence and discipline.

In the end the cause of social meaning will win out. For the humanities differ from other kinds of specialized knowledge in one key respect: They can transact their business in the language of ordinary discourse. Not in simple language, mind you, but . . . language at once clear and fertile. Clear enough to state accurately the scholar's perception of historical fact. Fertile enough to teach us about ourselves as well as about Machiavelli. . . .

Public debate today is rarely conducted with reference to the traditions of political and moral philosophy. Even the conduct of private life is seldom appraised any longer in such humanistic language; it has been swamped by behaviorist psychologies and the mass-market fantasies of popular culture. Small wonder, then, that the humanities, once the privileged center of the college curriculum, now occupy only a small fraction of the enterprise of higher education in the U.S.

How should the humanities respond to this situation? Surely the worst answer would be to draw ourselves into a tight circle, crouch into a timid or defensive stance toward the world, and devote ourselves only to endless pedantic commentaries on scholarly work. The growth of a technical civilization is a challenge, not an insult, to the intelligence of those who study the humanities. Humanistic inquiry can reveal the historical patterns that have led to our current images of "Psychological Man" and "Man as Part of System." Humanistic inquiry can expose the social and logical clarities and confusions of the present time. Through inquiry into the perspectives of other societies and historical cultures, humanistic learning can create representations of life that are alternatives to the present. . . .

11. Alvin Kernan,
"Change in the Humanities," 1997

Introducing a collection of essays on the declining institutional condition of the humanities, Alvin Kernan (1923–) here briefly noted the radically changing fortunes of higher education in the late twentieth century. His word for what in his opinion had supplanted Clark Kerr's "multiversity" is *demoversity*. The neologism describes a grasp of events that Kernan recorded in his witty and engaging autobiography, *In Plato's Cave* (1999). His entry into academic life was common to many young veterans of World War II who chose this career path. Yet his was an exceptional examination of life in two Ivy League institutions. He recounted the struggles for tenure and its meaning, the ways of departmental and university-wide politics, effective teaching, and the varying and unsettling episodes in the office of a professor turned administrator during the 1960s and 1970s.

Kernan took bachelors degrees at Williams College (1949) and Oxford University (1952) after naval service in World War II in the Pacific for which he was decorated with the Navy Cross and the Distinguished Flying Cross. His doctorate came at Yale (1954), where he rose through the professorial ranks in English (1959–73) and served as provost (1965–68, 1970). He moved to Princeton in 1973 as professor of English and dean of the graduate school (1973–77), then retired in 1988 after eleven years as Andrew Mellon and Avalon Professor of the Humanities.

Alvin Kernan, "Change in the Humanities and Higher Education," in *What's Happened to the Humanities?* ed. Kernan, vii–viii. Reprinted by permission of Princeton University Press © 1997. Statistical figures deleted. Further reading: Francis Oakley, "Data Deprivation and Humanities Indicators," in Robert M. Solow et al., *Making the Humanities Count: The Importance of Data* (Cambridge, MA, 2002), ch. 2, tempers the tone of Kernan and Hunt (IV, 7) five years later by urging more quantitative work on humanities enrollments, which may put into question the discouraging comments of the 1970s and 1980s; David A. Hollinger, ed., *The Humanities and the Dynamics of Inclusion since World War II* (Baltimore, 2006).

Institutionally, in the standard academic table of organization, the university catalogue—the knowledge tree of contemporary western culture—the humanities are the subjects regularly listed under that heading: literature, philosophy, art history, music, religion, languages, and sometimes history. This branch of knowledge is separated from the branch of the social sciences and from the branch of the biological and physical sciences. These three branches together form the arts and sciences, or the liberal arts, as they are sometimes known, which are as a group separated in turn from the professional disciplines—such as medicine, education, business, and law—which, at least at one time, concentrated on practice rather than theory.

Historically, the humanities are the old subjects, which in many forms and under a variety of names —the nine muses; the liberal arts; quadrivium and trivium; rhetoric, dialectic, and logic; humane letters—were the major part of Western education for over two millennia. In the modern college and university they have mutated into a number of specialized subjects, such as art history, religious studies, classics, national literatures, and musicology. Perhaps because they are the old subjects, they are also the least abstract, the most immediate—not the most prestigious, but the most intimate—to humanity's sense of itself in the world. They shape the stories we tell, our ways of thinking, what our collective past has been, how we communicate and persuade with language, and, perhaps most powerfully of all, the music that stirs our depths: these are, *inutatis mutandis*, the basic humanistic ways of knowing, the most instrumental to life as it is ordinarily lived.

Socially, in the latter twentieth century, the humanities, along with some of the "softer" social sciences like anthropology and sociology, have been the battlefields of an extended *Kulturkampf*. These subjects have proven extremely sensitive to pressures for social change in the society at large, to the wave of populist democracy, to technological changes in communication, to relativistic epistemologies, to demands for increased tolerance, and to various social causes, such as black studies, feminism, and gay rights. Every liberal cause—from freedom of speech and the Vietnam War to anticolonialism and the nonreferentiality of language—has fought bitter and clamorous battles in these subjects. The revolutionary spirit extended into the intellectual realm, and truth itself as well as fact, the foundations of Western rational inquiry, were confronted by deconstructive philosophies that replaced knowledge with interpretation and dethroned objectivity in the name of subjectivity. Where the old humanities were once ethnocentric in their concentration on western Europe, they have become increasingly multicultural, pluralistic, and politicized.

This turmoil in the humanities has been part of, and offers an insight into, a much larger change in American higher education as a whole that has been taking place since World War II. "A substantial change of scale is a change of enterprise," remarks Christopher Ricks, and a few numbers establish the nature and direction of the change of "enterprise" in higher education. In the years between 1960 and 1990, according to figures from the National Center for Educational Statistics, the number of institutions of higher education increased from 2,000 to 3,595. The greatest increase was in the publics, which grew from 700 to 1,576, while the privates, which had earlier dominated higher education went from 1,300 to 2,019. Full-time enrollments increased from 3.5 to 15.3 million, with the share accounted for by the public institutions increasing from 60 to 80 percent of the total. The area of the greatest growth was in the new community colleges, which enrolled only

400,000 students in 1960 but had 6.5 million by 1990. The proportion of women increased from 37 to 51 percent of the total of undergraduate enrollments in this time period, and that of minorities from 12 to 28 percent. To support this growth, federal aid to students went from $5.1 to $11.2 billion. To provide teachers for the increased number of students, the number of doctoral degrees granted grew from about 10,000 to over 38,000 a year, and overall faculty numbers increased from approximately 281,000 to over 987,000. Research payments were increased accordingly by the federal government, which between 1960 and 1990 increased R&D funds from $2 billion constant 1960 dollars to $12 billion.

These numerical changes are of course the substructure of much more visible surface disturbances. Socrates said that "the modes of music are never disturbed without unsettling of the most fundamental political and social conditions," but who would have thought that the sounds of Elvis and the Beatles, electrically amplified until they drowned out every other sound, would announce new political and social conditions on campus? The sweet smell of marijuana floated through the dormitories, and the sound of gunfire crackled in the groves of academe. *Et in Arcadia ego!* Free-speech movements coarsened the vocabulary of higher education, and student protests, strikes, and sit-ins were only the most visible of many continuing challenges to *in loco parentis* authority. Democratic egalitarianism found its intellectual counterparts in pluralism, a multi-cultural curriculum, and the relativistic concept of truth—one person's ideas are as good as another's—which has been the intellectual "loss leader" on campus for many years now. In time, new manners and new epistemologies were followed by new politics. Affirmative action brought increasing numbers of minorities into the classrooms, a feminist movement established itself at the center of academic concerns, and all intellectual activities were declared to be means of seeking power. Margery Sabin sums up the pattern of change in the following way: "radical social protest in the late 1960s; deconstruction in the 1970s; ethnic, feminist, and Marxist cultural studies in the 1980s; postmodern sexuality in the 1990s; and rampant careerism from beginning to end."

Educational institutions, like all other social institutions—the family, the state, the church—obviously do change radically from time to time. In *The Uses of the University* (1967), Clark Kerr noted the appearance as early as the 1950s and 1960s of a new kind of institution of higher education, which he called the "multiversity, a city of infinite variety," a term he coined to call attention to a progressive weakening of any unifying force at the educational center—either geographical, curricular, or philosophical—of the old research universities, which he defined as a "unified community of masters and students with a single 'soul' or purpose." In the

thirty years since Kerr told us that a "multiversity" was replacing the old research universities, the democratic social revolution in education has continued to the point that by now it might be better to call the new institution a "demoversity," if you will allow the word, tending toward the empowerment of the many rather than the unified one, questioning traditional centralized authority and all forms of elitism.

These tectonic shifts in higher education have not, I think it is fair to say, been kind to the liberal arts in general, and to the humanities in particular. . . . While the absolute numbers of bachelor's and doctoral degrees in the humanities have increased slightly in the last thirty years, the humanities have lost ground at both levels as a percentage of the total number of degrees conferred in a time of maximum growth. Where bachelor's degrees in the humanities were 20.7 percent of the total awarded in 1966, in 1993 they were only 12.7 percent; and where doctoral degrees in the humanities were 13.8 percent of the total awarded in 1966, in 1993 they made up only 9.1 percent. It is true that both bachelor's and doctoral degrees have recovered somewhat from a deeper slump in the 1980s, and it has been argued that the numbers for the mid-1960s—the point at which reliable figures are first available—are perhaps historically high. Furthermore, the liberal arts in general, not just the humanities, have lost ground during this period. But the inescapable point would still seem to be that as the demoversity has taken shape, the humanities, in plain words, have become a less and less significant part of higher education. This is not . . . so much the case in the elite institutions as in the community colleges and more service-oriented educational institutions, where vocationalism has swept the board. Yet this does not change the fact that the humanities are playing a less important part within the totality of higher education in America. During the same period the social sciences little more than held their own in percentages of bachelor's and doctoral degrees, but the natural sciences were hit as hard as the humanities. . . .

The Multiversity

12. Clark Kerr, *The Uses of the University*, 1964

Clark Kerr (1911–2003) painted this portrait of the modern American research university in the Godkin Lectures at Harvard. It became the most enduring and concise description of the "multiversity," Kerr's neologism, to come out of the 1960s. For thousands of readers, his book defined mass higher education and its problems in an industrial and technocratic democratic culture. By 2001 it had gone into four revisions and had been translated into six languages. While preparing these lectures, Kerr was in the midst of his presidency (1958–67) of the University of California system, having earlier been chancellor of the Berkeley campus (1952–58), professor of industrial relations (1945–52), and recipient of a Ph.D. in economics (1939). He was well equipped for administrative posts by virtue of his experiences in industrial and governmental labor arbitrations throughout the 1940s and 1950s. These honed his skill, essential to university leaders, for eliciting or fashioning consensus among many expert, inner-directed, and often competing academic groups. His background, moreover, as a "convinced" (not born) member of the Society of Friends and honors graduate (later a lifetime manager) of the related Swarthmore College (1932) disposed him toward a principled but practical and mediating, even conciliatory outlook. Notwithstanding his politically maneuvered dismissal from the university presidency in 1967, his record was one of remarkable accomplishments: three campuses expanded, three new ones created, the excellence of Berkeley among all public campuses in the nation certified, and a rapid attainment of academic prestige at UCLA. Thereafter Kerr increased his stature as a national guide for higher education by chairing the Carnegie Commission of Higher Education (1967–73) and its Council on Policy Studies in Higher Education (1974–79). Out of this connection he oversaw some 137 publications on academic affairs.

Reprinted by permission of the publisher, the author, and abridged from *The Uses of the University* by Clark Kerr, pp. 1–2, 6, 8–9, 17–20, 28–31, 33, 36–38, 114, 116–18, 121, Cambridge, Mass.: Harvard University Press. Copyright © 1964. Further reading: Kerr, *The Gold and the Blue: A Personal Memoir of the University of California, 1949–1967,* vol. 1, *Academic Triumphs* (Berkeley, 2001), vol. 2, *Political Turmoil* (Berkeley, 2003); and *The Great Transformation in Higher Education, 1960–1980* (Albany, NY, 1991). See also Jeff Lustig, "The Mixed Legacy of Clark Kerr, A Personal View," *Academe* 90 (July–August 2004): 51–53; John Douglass, *The California Idea and American Higher Education, 1850 to the 1960 Master Plan* (Stanford, CA, 2000), chs. 9–10; Roger L. Geiger, "Research Universities in a New Era: From the 1980s to the 1990s," in *Higher Learning in America, 1980–2000,* ed. Arthur Levine (Baltimore, 1983), ch. 4; and I, 13; II, 2–4.

The university started as a single community—a community of masters and students. It may even be said to have had a soul in the sense of a central animating principle. Today the large American university is, rather, a whole series of communities and activities held together by a common name, a common governing board, and related purposes. This great transformation is regretted by some, accepted by many, gloried in, as yet, by few. But it should be understood by all.

The university of today can perhaps be understood, in part, by comparing it with what it once was—with the academic cloister of Cardinal Newman, with the research organism of Abraham Flexner. Those are the ideal types from which it has derived, ideal types which still constitute the illusions of some of its inhabitants. The modern American university, however, is not Oxford nor is it Berlin; it is a new type of institution in the world. As a new type of institution, it is not really private and it is not really public; it is neither entirely of the world nor entirely apart from it. It is unique. . . .

By 1930, American universities had moved a long way from Flexner's "Modern University" where "The heart of a university is a graduate school of arts and sciences, the solidly professional schools (mainly, in America, medicine and law) and certain research institutes." They were becoming less and less like a "genuine university," by which Flexner meant "an organism, characterized by highness and definiteness of aim, unity of spirit and purpose." The "Modern University" was as nearly dead in 1930 when Flexner wrote about it, as the old Oxford was in 1852 when Newman idealized it. History moves faster than the observer's pen. Neither the ancient classics and theology nor the German philosophers and scientists could set the tone for the really modern university—the multiversity.

"The Idea of a Multiversity" has no bard to sing its praises; no prophet to proclaim its vision; no guardian to protect its sanctity. It has its critics, its detractors, its transgressors. It also has its barkers selling its wares to all who will listen—and many do. But it also has its reality rooted in the logic of history. It is an imperative rather than a reasoned choice among elegant alternatives. . . .

Newman's "Idea of a University" still has its devotees—chiefly the humanists and the generalists and the undergraduates. Flexner's "Idea of a Modern University" still has its supporters—chiefly the scientists and the specialists and the graduate students. "The Idea of a Multiversity" has its practitioners—chiefly the administrators, who now number many of the faculty among them, and the leadership groups in society at large. The controversies are still around in the faculty clubs and the student coffee houses; and the models of Oxford and Berlin and modern Harvard all animate segments of what was once a "community of masters and students" with a single vision of its nature and purpose. These several competing visions of true purpose, each relating to a different layer of history, a different web of forces, cause much of the malaise in the university communities of today. The university is so many things to so many different people that it must, of necessity, be partially at war with itself. . . .

Out of all these fragments, experiments, and conflicts a kind of unlikely consensus has been reached. Undergraduate life seeks to follow the British, who have done the best with it, and an historical line that goes back to Plato; the humanists often find their sympathies here. Graduate life and research follow the Germans, who once did best with them, and an historical line that goes back to Pythagoras; the scientists lend their support to all this. The "lesser" professions (lesser than law and medicine) and the service activities follow the American pattern, since the Americans have been best at them, and an historical line that goes back to the Sophists; the social scientists are most likely to be sympathetic. Lowell found his greatest interest in the first, Eliot in the second, and James Bryant Conant (1934 to 1954) in the third line of development and in the synthesis. The resulting combination does not seem plausible but it has given America a remarkably effective educational institution. A university anywhere can aim no higher than to be as British as possible for the sake of the undergraduates, as German as possible for the sake of the graduates and the research personnel, as American as possible for the sake of the public at large—and as confused as possible for the sake of the preservation of the whole uneasy balance.

The multiversity is an inconsistent institution. It is not one community but several—the community of the undergraduate and the community of the graduate; the community of the humanist, the community of the social scientist, and the community of the scientist; the communities of the professional schools; the community of all the nonacademic personnel; the community of the administrators. Its edges are fuzzy—it reaches out to alumni, legislators, farmers, businessmen, who are all related to one or more of these internal communities. As an institution, it looks far into the past and far into the future, and is often at odds with the present. It serves society almost slavishly—a society it also criticizes, sometimes unmercifully. Devoted to equality of opportunity, it is itself a class society. A community, like the medieval communities of masters and students, should have common interests; in the multiversity, they are quite varied, even conflicting. A community should have a soul, a single animating principle; the multiversity has several—some of them quite good, although there is much debate on which souls really deserve salvation. . . .

Flexner thought of a university as an "organism." In an organism, the parts and the whole are inextricably bound together. Not so the multiversity—many parts can be added and subtracted with little effect on the whole or even little notice taken or any blood spilled. It is more a mechanism—a series of processes producing a series of results—a mechanism held together by administrative rules and powered by money.

Hutchins once described the modern university as a series of separate schools and departments held together by a central heating system. In an area where heating is less important and the automobile more, I have sometimes thought of it as a series of individual faculty entrepreneurs held together by a common grievance over parking.

It is, also, a system of government like a city, or a city state: the city state of the multiversity. It may be inconsistent but it must be governed—not as the guild it once was, but as a complex entity with greatly fractionalized power. . . .

The general rule is that the administration everywhere becomes, by force of circumstances if not by choice, a more prominent feature of the university. As the institution becomes larger, administration becomes more formalized and separated as a distinct function; as the institution becomes more complex, the role of administration becomes more central in integrating it; as it becomes more related to the once external world, the administration assumes the burdens of these relationships. The managerial revolution has been going on also in the university.

It is sometimes said that the American multiversity president is a two-faced character. This is not so. If he were, he could not survive. He is a many-faced character, in the sense that he must face in many directions at once while contriving to turn his back on no important group. In this he is different in degree from his counterparts of rectors and vice chancellors, since they face in fewer directions because their institutions have fewer doors and windows to the outside world. The difference, however, is not one of kind. And intensities of relationships vary greatly; the rector of a Latin American university, from this point of view, may well have the most trying task of all, though he is less intertwined in a range of relationships than the North American university president.

The university president in the United States is expected to be a friend of the students, a colleague of the faculty, a good fellow with the alumni, a sound administrator with the trustees, a good speaker with the public, an astute bargainer with the foundations and the federal agencies, a politician with the state legislature, a friend of industry, labor, and agriculture, a persuasive diplomat with donors, a champion of education generally, a supporter of the professions (particularly law and medicine), a spokesman to the press, a scholar in his own right, a public servant at the state and national levels, a devotee of opera and football equally, a decent human being, a good husband and father, an active member of a church. Above all he must enjoy traveling in airplanes, eating his meals in public, and attending public ceremonies. No one can be all of these things. Some succeed at being none.

He should be firm, yet gentle; sensitive to others, insensitive to himself; look to the past and the future, yet be firmly planted in the present; both visionary and sound; affable, yet reflective; know the value of a dollar and realize that ideas cannot be bought; inspiring in his visions yet cautious in what he does; a man of principle yet able to make a deal; a man with broad perspective who will follow the details conscientiously; a good American but ready to criticize the status quo fearlessly; a seeker of truth where the truth may not hurt too much; a source of public policy pronouncements when they do not reflect on his own institution. He should sound like a mouse at home and look like a lion abroad. He is one of the marginal men in a democratic society—of whom there are many others—on the margin of many groups, many ideas, many endeavors, many characteristics. He is a marginal man but at the very center of the total process. . . .

To the faculty, he is usually not a hero-figure. Hutchins observed that the faculty really "prefer anarchy to any form of government"—particularly the presidential form.

The issue is whether the president should be "leader" or "officeholder," as Hutchins phrased it;

"educator" or "caretaker," as Harold W. Dodds stated it; "creator" or "inheritor," as Frederick Rudolph saw it; "initiator" as viewed by James L. Morrill or consensus-seeker as viewed by John D. Millett; the wielder of power or the persuader, as visualized by Henry M. Wriston; "pump" or "bottleneck" as categorized by Eric Ashby. . . .

Hutchins was the last of the giants in the sense that he was the last of the university presidents who really tried to change his institution and higher education in any fundamental way. Instead of the not always so agreeable autocracy, there is now the usually benevolent bureaucracy, as in so much of the rest of the world. Instead of the Captain of Erudition or even David Riesman's "staff sergeant," there is the Captain of the Bureaucracy who is sometimes a galley slave on his own ship; and "no great revolutionary figure is likely to appear." . . .

The president in the multiversity is leader, educator, creator, initiator, wielder of power, pump; he is *also* officeholder, caretaker, inheritor, consensus-seeker, persuader, bottleneck. But he is mostly a mediator. . . .

The president becomes the central mediator among the values of the past, the prospects for the future, and the realities of the present. He is the mediator among groups and institutions moving at different rates of speed and sometimes in different directions; a carrier of change—as infectious and sometimes as feared as a "Typhoid Mary." He is not an innovator for the sake of innovation, but he must be sensitive to the fruitful innovation. He has no new and bold "vision of the end." He is driven more by necessity than by voices in the air. . . .

The ends are already given—the preservation of the eternal truths, the creation of new knowledge, the improvement of service wherever truth and knowledge of high order may serve the needs of man. The ends are there; the means must be ever improved in a competitive dynamic environment. There is no single "end" to be discovered; there are several ends and many groups to be served. . . .

Knowledge is now central to society. It is wanted, even demanded, by more people and more institutions than ever before. The university as producer, wholesaler and retailer of knowledge cannot escape service. Knowledge, today, is for everybody's sake. . . .

The university must range itself on the side of intelligent solutions to sometimes unintelligent questions. These questions more and more arise from abroad as well as at home; and the quality of the answers has been made all the more crucial in a world swept by Communist and nationalist revolutions.

There are those who fear the further involvement of the university in the life of society. They fear that the university will lose its objectivity and its freedom. But society is more desirous of objectivity and more tolerant of freedom than it used to be. The university can be further ahead of the times and further behind the times, further to the left of the public and further to the right of the public—and

still keep its equilibrium—than was ever the case before, although problems in this regard are not yet entirely unknown. There are those who fear that the university will be drawn too far from basic to applied research and from applied research to application itself. But the lines dividing these never have been entirely clear and much new knowledge has been generated at the borders of basic and applied research, and even of applied knowledge and its application.

Growth and shifting emphases and involvement in society all take money; and which universities get it in the largest quantities will help determine which of them excel a decade or two hence. Will federal support be spent according to merit or according to political power? Will private donors continue to do as well as they recently have for those universities that have done well already? Will the states find new sources of revenue or will their expenditures be held under a lid of no new taxes? The answers to these questions will help predict the standings on the next rating scale of universities.

However this turns out, the scene of American higher education will continue to be marked by great variety, and this is one of its great strengths. The large and the small, the private and the public, the general and the specialized all add their share to over-all excellence. The total system is extraordinarily flexible, decentralized, competitive—and productive. The new can be tried, the old tested with considerable skill and alacrity. Pluralism in higher education matches the pluralistic American society. The multiversity, in particular, is the child of middle-class pluralism; it relates to so much of the variety of the surrounding society and is thus so varied internally.

The general test of higher education is not how much is done poorly, and some is; rather it is how much is done superbly, and a great deal is, to the nation's great benefit. Although it has been said that the best universities in America have been caught in a "stalemate of success," there is no stalemate; there is some success. . . .

The great university is of necessity elitist—the elite of merit—but it operates in an environment dedicated to an egalitarian philosophy. How may the contribution of the elite be made clear to the egalitarians, and how may an aristocracy of intellect justify itself to a democracy of all men? It was equality of opportunity, not equality *per se*, that animated the founding fathers and the progress of the American system; but the forces of populist equality have never been silent, the battle between Jeffersonianism and Jacksonianism never finally settled.

13. Robert Paul Wolff, *The Ideal of the University*, 1969

A radical critic of American educational and political ways, Robert Paul Wolff (1933–) watched the student uprising at Columbia University in 1968 with "an irritated uneasiness" while teaching in the philosophy department. The book he issued the next year offered not only an indictment of Clark Kerr's modern university but also his own proposals for ideal and fundamental changes in the undergraduate curriculum. A New Yorker, Wolff earned his B.A. (1953) and his Ph.D. (1957) at Harvard, then taught at Harvard (1958–61) and Chicago (1961–64) before going to Columbia (1964–71). Thereafter he became a professor of philosophy and next of Afro-American studies at the University of Massachusetts (1971–   ).

The Ideal of the University by Robert Paul Wolff, Copyright © 1969 by Robert Paul Wolff. Reprinted by permission of Beacon Press, Boston. pp. 36–42. Abridged with the permission of the author. Further reading: Wolff, *A Critique of Pure Tolerance* [*Beyond Tolerance*] (Boston, 1965) and *In Defense of Anarchism* (New York, 1970).

Throughout his essay, Kerr speaks of the multiversity as responding to social needs or as satisfying demands made upon it by society. . . .

The difficulty with these and countless other assertions in Kerr's book is their complete failure to draw a sharp distinction between the concepts of *effective or market demand* and *human or social need*. Dr. Kerr's discussion commits exactly the same error which lies at the heart of classical laissez-faire economic theory. In this way, his book serves as a perfect expression of liberal ideology.

The point is a simple one and many critics since Marx have elaborated it: A *human or social need* is a want, a lack, the absence of something material or social, whose presence would contribute to physical and emotional health, to the full and unalienated development of human power—in a word, to true happiness. . . .

Effective or market demand, on the other hand, is simply the existence in a market economy of buyers who are in the market place, have money in hand, and are prepared to spend it for a particular commodity. Hence the familiar expression, "He is in the market for" this or that. Demand is said to be *effective* when it is capable of eliciting a response in the form of a supply. . . .

The rationale of the classical free market rests on two assumptions, both of which have for quite a long time now been known to be wrong. The first assumption is that all human and social needs are *felt needs*. The second assumption is that felt needs in a free market society are always expressible as *effective demand*. Thus, if men *need* food, they *feel* hungry. If they *feel* hungry, then they go into the market to *buy* food. The demand for food drives up the price, which drives up the profit, which attracts investors, who increase the supply, which drives down the price again *and satisfies the need.* A continuing rolling adjustment of resources to needs takes place, in a way which guarantees the fullest satisfaction possible with the resources and technology available.

In the classical theory, no moral judgments are permitted concerning "true" versus "false" needs, or "higher" versus "lower" pleasures. Happiness is assumed to be the only thing intrinsically good; and happiness, it is supposed, consists in the satisfaction of whatever desires one actually has. So when men want poetry, their expressed demand will elicit poetry from some source or other in society; when they want pornography, pornography will appear.

There is a case to be made for this pristine doctrine, although I confess that it has always seemed to me more aesthetically pleasing by virtue of its simplicity, than persuasive or plausible. But quite frequently, an author will appear who systematically identifies *effective market demand* with *true human need,* while not subscribing at all to the postulates and presuppositions which . . . underlie such an identification. That is, he will talk as though a demand in the market automatically expressed a human or social need, while at the same time talking as though he made moral judgments about true versus false needs. The result is not an argument, nor is it exactly just a confusion. The result is a covert ideological rationalization for whatever human or social desires happen to be backed by enough money or power to translate them into effective demands. I shall try briefly to show that Clark Kerr is guilty of exactly just such ideological rhetoric. . . .

When Kerr speaks repeatedly of the multiversity's responsiveness to national *needs,* he is describing nothing more than its tendency to adjust itself to effective *demand* in the form of government grants, scholarship programs, corporate or alumni underwriting, and so forth. But his language encourages the reader to suppose that the demands to which the multiversity responds are expressions of genuine human and social needs, needs which make a moral claim upon the effort and attention of the academy. It takes very little thought to see the weakness of this implicit claim.

The nation *needs* more engineers and scientists, Kerr says. Only three fourths of the *demand* will be met at current rates of enrollment. But the shortage of engineers in America is due entirely to the enormous space program, which absorbs tens of thousands of highly trained personnel in an enterprise of very dubious social priority. When Kerr speaks of the "demand" for engineers as one to which the multiversity ought to respond, he is covertly (and probably unwittingly) endorsing the space program. He would hardly view the matter that way, I should imagine. But the alternative is to assume without question that the multiversity should accept the goals and values of whoever in America has the money to pay for them. Instead of calling his essay *The Uses of the University,* he could more appropriately have titled it *University for Hire!* . . .

Surely it should be obvious that the academy must make its own judgment about the social value of the tasks it is called upon to perform. Even if the federal government wants war research or political stability studies or officer training, the professors and students of the university may decide that the government is *wrong* and that its desires should be resisted. If someone asks what right the professors and students have to question the will of the federal government, we can only reply, what right has the federal government to impose its will upon free men and women?

But there are material conditions of freedom, as a Marxist might say, and a university too heavily dependent upon federal grants will find itself unable to take a stand against programs and directions of development which it believes to be wrong. It is honorable for the workers in a government agency to accept the policy direction of Congress and the President. They exist to effect the will of the people, which expresses itself through its elected representatives. But it is *dishonorable* for a university to become a government agency by forfeiting the active exercise of its power of independent evaluation. . . . Kerr's voice is the voice of praise, but his words are an unwitting indictment of the modern university.

So we come to our last criticism of the multiversity. If it is an *instrument* of national purpose, then it cannot be a *critic* of national purpose, for an instrument is a means, not an evaluator of ends. In America today the power of the federal government has grown so great that there is almost no independent center of activity with the authority to challenge its policies. Within the broad consensus of practical politics there are countless disagreements and conflicts of belief or interest, but when the very premises of that consensus are wrong, who is to combat them? The great universities stand alone as institutions rich enough, powerful enough, possessed of sufficient moral and intellectual authority to cry Nay, Nay, when every other voice says Yea, Yea. There is no better example of this "power of negation," as the Hegelians might say, than the case of the Vietnam Teach-ins. Without overestimating their role in the great shift of opinion which eventually brought Johnson down and drove the government to the peace table, I think it is fair to say that the public debates staged by dissenting professors and students were the turning point in the history of America's involvement in Vietnam.

Clark Kerr's vision of the university of social service poses a great choice to those of us who care about the future of the academy. Shall the university accept the symbiotic interactions with government which are now offered? Shall it devote its resources to the satisfaction of those social desires which make themselves felt as effective demands? Or shall it remain institutionally aloof and counterpose itself to the momentum of government, foundation, and industry? It won't do to strike for a middle course, thinking that we can accept the government's money and be admitted to the council chambers while yet remaining free to dissent. Perhaps we might persuade ourselves that such a course was honorable, but I fear we would soon find it in practice impossible.

Connecting
14. John William Ward, "Convocation Address," 1976

Liberal arts college presidents often speak to the advantages of their college community in a secular context. Their remarks, except in faith-based colleges, are distant from the religious premises of the old-time moral-philosopher presidents, yet they are often equally distant from the addresses of modern university presidents. In a convocation talk John William Ward (1922–85), president of Amherst College (1971–79), spoke to the meaning of the academic community, especially in its tension with the individual finding a place within it. This tension, in larger historical ways, had been long studied by the historian Ward. A Harvard graduate (1947), he earned his doctorate (1953) in American Studies at the University of Minnesota, then occupied two teaching posts, at Princeton (1952–64) and at Amherst (1964–79). Before his untimely death, he was president of the American Council of Learned Societies (1982–85).

John William Ward, "Convocation Address" *Amherst* (Fall 1976): 7–8. Copyright © 1976 by *Amherst Alumni Magazine*. Reprinted with the kind permission of Amherst College. Further reading: Ward, *Red, White, and Blue: Men, Books, and Ideas in American Culture* (New York, 1969), and Wilson Smith, "John William Ward," in *American National Biography*, ed. John M. Garraty and Mark C. Carnes, vol. 22 (New York, 1999), 639–40.

If we inquire closely into this moment, and the unease I suspect attends any attempt to insist upon its collective aspect, we come upon a major question in American values, the relation of the individual to the community. But rather than turn to history and the society at large, let us turn to this place, this community.

Words are important. They make a claim on us if we choose to understand our lives by the sense of the words we use. To refer to the "community" makes a moral claim on us, and unless we are clear what we mean by the word it may well be an illegitimate claim. . . .

What does it mean to speak of this place as a community? The question derives from the essential nature of modern society as well as from the particular nature of an educational institution. More than one hundred years ago, in 1861 to be precise, the English scholar, Sir Henry Maine, explored the same question when he defined modern society as the movement from status to contract; that is, the movement from who one is to what one can do. The classic text, of course, is the German sociologist, Ferdinand Tönnies, in his book *Gemeinschaft und Gesellschaft*, in 1887.

By *Gemeinschaft*, Tönnies meant associations among people which are built upon intimate relations and emotional feeling, most especially, of course, within the family. Such associations, which may include the neighborhood, ethnic comradeship, friendship, are—more importantly—noncalculating relationships. They are their own justification; their worth is measured by what they are in themselves, not by some end beyond them. They define a shared sense of community.

Gesellschaft, on the other hand, describes an association which is contractual, in which people come together or associate together to pursue or to further some end in common, irrespective of their kinship or personal affection; an association organized on the basis of rationally determined and relatively impersonal goals. They define a functional society.

As we consider Amherst College, clearly we are an instance of *Gesellschaft*, a contractual association. We come together from fifty states and foreign countries by virtue of what we can do, not by reason of who we are. We are not kin, we did not grow together in the same neighborhood. We are not bound by a common faith or an ethnic identity. We come together for a season to pursue a particular end in common, namely, learning. Our end determines who we are in relation to one another as we pursue our transient lives together. We are part of a corporate body defined by a particular interest which draws us together to pursue together, students for four years, faculty for varying lengths of time, a rationally determined end, namely education.

We come together not out of love and friendship but for learning and the fellowship of the mind. To say so, I have discovered from students I have taught now these many years, sounds cold, impersonal, affectless, distant. I would argue not so, but one should, I think, give the complaint full weight. One should, because not to recognize the nature of the institution, the kind of contractual association it is, one may be too easily seduced into a false sentimentality, or suffer the unearned guilt of not satisfying the false expectations of others because one happens to be together with them at this time in this place. To evade reality has its own and special corruptions.

Education is the process by which an individual ceaselessly strives to arrive at as intense a self-consciousness as possible about the grounds of one's beliefs and actions. The purpose of the College, the purpose of our association together, should be to give institutional form and support to that essential process.

Note that I say "should." I believe that education is a deeply moral enterprise. It has built into it a host of moral imperatives. Not "moral" in the debased sense of whether one sleeps around or gets slovenly drunk, as irritating as that may be to others, or troublesome to the poor deans in the case of students when it becomes public. But moral in the sense that education presumes the equal worth of all in the dialogue which is its substance; I do not mean a condescending tolerance for the opinions of others, but a lively interest in what one may learn from the other, from different experience and perspective. Moral in the sense that, out of mutual respect, force or coercion or unquestioned authority, ide-

ally, have no place in it. Moral, not in the sense of particular views to be arrived at, but moral in the sense of the integrity of the very process by which one arrives at tentative judgments and considered positions of value, with the will to act upon them, but open always to the possibility that new experience and new evidence may test and change them.

When I say that education is about the achievement of as intense a self-consciousness as possible, I ask for much and leave out much. Self-consciousness will drive the mind inward, toward one's single self, to understand one's emotions and instinctual urges; self-consciousness will drive the mind outward, to society and to history, to understand the effect of one's place in the structure of society and in historical time. Such self-consciousness may not make you happy; it may not make you rich. I rather doubt it will do either. But for education, it is an imperative, a necessary given, a good in and of itself.

But how does this view of education get us in from out of the cold? I would suggest two ways, although I admit the first is an evasion of the question. The first would be to say that, although an insistence on the achievement of a heightened awareness of self asks for much, it leaves out much. It may be the essence of learning, but there are other and more important things by far: the embrace of love which is its own justification; the clasp of friendship which sets no standard of achievement or merit to justify it. There is much else to life than education's imperative demands for a heightened self-consciousness. That answer has its indubitable appeal. It says this is what we do: do not look for too much, surely not for everything, in what we do.

But there is a second answer which is better, I think. We may discover in our commitment to the primary and essential purpose of education that each of us is involved in the endless quest which defines our common humanity.

Education, if we mean by it the process of as intense a self-consciousness as one may achieve, education never ends. It is not defined by four years of college, nor is it defined by an advanced degree and the publication of books. It is an endless process because the self is not something achieved, not a hard and massy particle which moves unchanged through space and time. We are caught in history. We are involved with each other. Our awareness of who we are. our respect for our individual self and achievement depends—if we are truly self-aware—on our awareness of all the others with whom we live our lives and a sacred respect for them. The tension between the self and others will be with us all our lives, because the process of self-discovery goes on all our lives to the end.

As some start out and some return, perhaps in the busyness of other business, some of you may pause to think about what it means that you happen to be in this place. Perhaps we might turn a contractual society of teachers and students into a community of learners together.

15. Francis Oakley, *Community of Learning*, 1992

Francis Oakley (1931–), president of Williams College (1985–94), took leave from his duties to survey the condition of higher learning and to publish his findings. His book was meant "to make some sense of the current discontent" with the American undergraduate experience. There Oakley displayed the historical meaning of the liberal arts and recorded much of the polemical literature and statistical findings on academic life from the 1960s to the 1980s. Oakley's long footnote is included here to guide the reader who wishes to pursue these matters. An Oxonian and medievalist, Oakley was born in Liverpool and came to Williams College after serving in the British army and earning his doctorate at Yale. He arrived at Williams and 1961 and has been affiliated with Williams even into retirement. He chaired the board of directors of the American Council of Learned Societies (1993–97) and presided over the Medieval Academy of America (1999–2002).

From *Community of Learning: The American College and the Liberal Arts Tradition* by Francis Oakley, copyright © 1992 by Francis Oakley. Used by permission of Francis Oakley and Oxford University Press, Inc. pp. 3–8, 62–66, 93–103, 175–76. Footnotes omitted except 1–3. Further reading: Frederick Rudolph, *Curriculum, A History of the American Undergraduate Course of Study since 1636* (San Francisco, 1977) offers a larger historical perspective. See also Bruce A. Kimball, *Orators and Philosophers: A History of the Idea of Liberal Education* (New York, 1995); William J. Bennett, *To Reclaim a Legacy: A Report on the Humanities in Higher Education* (Washington, 1984); Ernest L. Boyer and Arthur Levine, *A Quest for Common Learning: The Aims of General Education* (Princeton, NJ, 1981); Derek Bok, *Our Underachieving Colleges* (Princeton, NJ, 2006); and I, 1; pt. III; IV, 7.

The important thing is to realize that the American college is deficient, and unnecessarily deficient, alike in earnestness and in pedagogical intelligence; that in consequence our college students are, and for the most part emerge, flighty, superficial and immature, lacking, as a class, concentration, seriousness and thoroughness.

ABRAHAM FLEXNER (1908)

[B]eyond cavil is the fact that, as in Aristotle's time, there is little agreement about what liberal education should be. Both theory and practice are confused and contradictory.

THOMAS WOODY (1951)

What we have on many of our campuses is an unclaimed legacy, a course of studies in which the humanities have been siphoned off, diluted, or so adulterated that the students graduate knowing little of their heritage.

WILLIAM J. BENNETT (1984)

The genre is quasi-apocalyptic; the mood, in best American fashion, resolutely masochistic; the cumulative message, in disappointing degree, quite myopic. About the recent collective jeremiad of reports, articles and books focused on American higher education in general and the state of the liberal arts and the undergraduate course of study in particular, there is little enough to rejoice; in their contents still less to encourage.[1] The line of march generally pursued is drearily familiar; in its overall direction and the staging points that punctuate it, by now almost canonical. A golden age of educational coherence and curricular integrity is evoked or implied. If its precise location is no more than foggily determined, that it has been succeeded by a more or less catastrophic fall from grace is not left in doubt. The recent history of undergraduate education in the United States emerges as a deplorable descent from the realms of gold to our current age

---

1. I would divide these publications into two groups. The first, a series of reports and analyses, all of them somewhat discouraging in tone but lacking the harder edge that characterizes the second group, which includes some works of markedly punitive and vituperative bent. The first group includes such works as William J. Bennett, *To Reclaim a Legacy: A Report on the Humanities in Higher Education* (Washington, D.C.: The National Endowment for the Humanities, 1984); Ernest L. Boyer, *College: The Undergraduate Experience in America* (New York, 1987); Lynne V. Cheney, *Humanities in America: A Report to the President, the Congress, and the American People* (Washington, D.C.: The National Endowment for the Humanities, 1988); idem, *Tyrannical Machines: A Report on Educational Practices Gone Wrong and Our Best Hopes for Setting Them Right* (Washington, D.C.: The National Endowment for the Humanities, 1990); Mark H. Curtis et al., *Integrity in the College Curriculum: A Report to the Academic Community* (Association of American Colleges; Washington, D.C., 1985). In the second group I would place such works as Allan Bloom, *The Closing of the American Mind: How Higher Education Has Failed Democracy and Impoverished the Souls of Today's Students* (New York, 1987); Dinesh D'Souza, *Illiberal Education: The Politics o f Race and Sex on Campus* (New York, 1991); Roger Kimball, *Tenured Radicals: How Politics Has Corrupted Our Higher Education* (New York, 1990); Chester E. Finn, Jr., "Higher Education on Trial: An Indictment," *Current* (Oct. 1984), 14–24; idem, "The Campus: 'An Island of Repression in a Sea of Freedom' " *Commentary*, 86 (Sept. 1989), 17–23; Page Smith, *Killing the Spirit: Higher Education in America* (New York, 1990); Charles T. Sykes, *ProfScam: Professors and the Demise of Higher Education* (New York, 1990).

The gloomy phrases quoted below are drawn from works in both groups. With the possible exception of the last four authors listed above, none, I should concede, is more negative about the state of American undergraduate education than was Abraham Flexner *Universities: American, English, German* (New York, 1930), pp. 46–72. None, certainly, can match the vituperative exuberance Flexner brought to the subject some sixty years ago. It should be noted, however, that having belabored Columbia College, Chicago and Wisconsin mightily for their sins, he excluded from his strictures such institutions as Harvard College, Yale, Princeton, Swarthmore, Vanderbilt, Amherst, Williams, Bryn Mawr, Smith, and Wellesley. These, he conceded (p. 64), offered in his day "a varied and solid curriculum to undergraduate students who may care to be educated." Few of our latter-day critics would be so generous in their exclusion.

of iron—an age distinguished by declining academic standards, curricular incoherence, creeping consumerism, rampant vocationalism and wavering sense of mission.

"The undergraduate college," we are told, "is a troubled institution," often "more successful in credentialing than in providing a quality education" for its students. As for the undergraduate degree, "evidence of decline and devaluation is everywhere." In our day "a profound crisis" has overtaken undergraduate education. We are beset, in effect, by nothing less than a "crisis of liberal education" itself—a crisis reflecting (variously) the distortion of our universities and colleges by the research ethos and a concomitant neglect of teaching, the fragmentation of knowledge and the growth of hyperspecialization in the academic disciplines, the corrosive inroads of cultural relativism, the intrusion of a marketplace philosophy into the curriculum, its politicization and the subordination of "our studies [accordingly] to contemporary prejudices." Coupled with a "collective loss of nerve and faith on the part of both faculty and administrators during the late 1960s and early 1970s," as well as an abandonment of the old commitment to mediate to successive generations of students the richnesses of the Western cultural tradition, these developments have eventuated, alas, in "the decay of the humanities" and the dissolution of the curriculum. In sum, our "educational failures" as a nation are lovingly caressed, a sense of time running out is evoked in the manner formerly made fashionable by the denizens of the Club of Rome, and the compelling need to respond to the challenge thus posed is urged with a vigor redolent of other, less cerebral, realms of discourse.

In all of this, despite the pervasive sense that somewhere and at some time things used surely to be better, the golden age evoked remains, historically speaking, remarkably elusive. Few of the recent critics of the American undergraduate experience seem disposed to seek the interpretative leverage afforded by a comparative perspective, either by looking back in time beyond the provincial simplicities of the curriculum dominant in the American colonial colleges or by examining the texture of higher education in other regions of our own contemporary world. Little is made, accordingly, of the central role played by professional needs in the origin and development of the university itself. And, in our own era, little attention is drawn to the comparatively greater commitment of some of the European systems of higher education (those, for example, of Sweden, the German Federal Republic and the Soviet Union) to specialized and vocational studies. Eyes are discreetly averted, moreover, from the truly enormous gap (evident from the ancient world down to our own day) between ringing theoretical affirmations of commitment to the plentitude of liberal arts instruction and the more humdrum realities of what has actually been going on amid the day-to-day confusions and disruptions of educational life as it has usually been lived in the pedagogic trenches. Still less does one detect the presence of any historically informed sense of the range, looseness, variability and flexibility of the liberal arts tradition itself across the course of its longer history, or of the tensions which have wracked it for centuries and may well account for much of its enduring vitality and strength. That tradition, after all, still bears the mark left by the fateful decision of the early Christian communities in the Graeco-Roman world not to establish their own schools but rather to adapt to their purposes a pagan educational tradition of essentially Hellenistic provenance. As the history of Plato scholarship well exemplifies, this helped set up a tension that was still making its presence felt in Europe as recently as the late nineteenth and early twentieth century. Similarly, historians have detected the continued presence in the tradition of an even more enduring tension, that between the rhetorical vision of liberal education as pivoting on the cultivation of the ancient classics or their derivatives and the philosophical-scientific model driven by the urge for critical originality and advancing via the overthrow of received assumptions. The former has traditionally been directed to the development of the skills pertinent to public expression and legal and political persuasion, as well as to the inculcation in those destined for lives of public service of the hallowed values and traditions inherited from the past. The latter, instead, has persistently been targeted on the advancement of knowledge and understanding and on the development of critical rationality. Between the hammer and the anvil of these competing approaches little peace over the centuries has been able to grow.

About such things our critics say next to nothing. Nor, perhaps more surprisingly, do they allude at any great length to the impact on our colleges and universities of the cultural and demographic factors that loomed so large in the world of higher education in the 1960s and 1970s. And three of these loomed very large indeed. First, the growing and wholly unprecedented diversity (in terms of gender, race, age, ethnicity and social class) of our undergraduate population during the years since the Second World War. Second, the understandable push given to a cautious vocationalism among college students by uncertain job prospects amid the turbulent economic conditions of the 1970s. Third, and above all, the truly enormous pressures brought to bear on the whole apparatus of higher education by the G.I. bill, the baby-boom of the postwar years and the entry into college of a higher percentage of the young adult cohort, and then, in the 1980s and 1990s, by the progressive dwindling of that cohort—leading, among the less secure institutions, to a competitive scramble for students, a reduction in the number of liberal arts courses required, and the addition of a growing array of purely vocational majors.

The willingness to slight the impact of such demographic factors on the academic vitality of our colleges and universities is the more surprising at a time when historians of higher education in Europe have been quick to emphasize "the importance of the rise and fall of student numbers in affecting the quality of life at the universities," insisting (in relation to the early-modern period) that "so widespread were these movements and so dramatic in their impact on the universities, that in the future much of the history of higher education is going to have to be articulated around them."[2] Certainly, the comparative success of the much-maligned American system of higher education in adjusting to the enormous growth in undergraduate population since the Second World War (and without the swamping of existing institutions by students of differing expectations and capacities so evident in parts of Europe) might be taken to suggest that, despite the unevenness in academic quality that is their inevitable concomitant, there is something healthy and praiseworthy about the characteristics of independence, autonomy and sheer institutional variety which distinguish that system from systems of higher education abroad.

Of such thoughts, however, we find little trace in the recent spate of gloomy commentary on the college experience in America. . . . About this and other related disagreements in the current debate there is, nothing particularly surprising. The issues involved are complex and intricate. It would be too much to expect them to yield readily to resolution. Nor is there anything particularly novel about the shape of such disagreements. During the course of the present century, the writing of national reports on the status of liberal education in America has been endemic. So, too, has been the criticism of such reports, as well as the emasculation or rejection of their findings. . . .

The outcome, as a result, has been a sort of educational war of attrition. It is a war in which the contending sides surge back and forth across a desolate Great War-style battleground, terrain dominated by the same enduring set of issues, punctuated by the rubble of earlier high-minded experiments, and strewn with the remnants of discarded curricular equipment. It is also a war whose monotony is relieved by the introduction of few strategies not already tried, and whose long-established course, marked by an almost liturgical predictability, suggests the unwisdom of expecting, however intense the fighting, that any permanent victories are likely in the future to be won. Even if one were to be tempted accordingly to seek refuge in a stance of war-weary detachment, one would confront the chastening fact that such a temptation has itself, over the years, become an integral part of the script. Some thirty years ago, in the wake of another era of intense debate about higher education and the undergraduate course of study, President Conant of Harvard described the "sense of distasteful weariness" aroused in him by debates about the meaning of the word "education." "I feel," he said, "as though I were starting to see a badly scratched film of a poor movie for the second or third time."

But as one of Conant's distinguished successors has done well to remind us, "the fact that curricular debates are inconclusive does not mean that they are unimportant."[3] And detachment is hardly an option

---

2. Thus Lawrence Stone in Lawrence Stone, ed., *The University Society, I. Oxford and Cambridge from the 14th to the Early 19th Century* (Princeton, 1976), p. vii, where he continues: "We can now dimly see the shape of a vast seismic shift in west European cultural arrangements over the last four centuries. First came a period of astonishing growth after the middle of the 16th century, so that by 1640 in England, Germany, and Spain (and also, as Professor Kagan is discovering, in France and Italy) a staggering number of students were pouring into the universities. This boom was followed everywhere by a long period of decline and low enrollment which lasted from the middle of the 17th century until the first decade of the 19th. Then came another period of huge expansion, first immediately after the Napoleonic Wars and then again after 1860."

3. Derek Bok, *Higher Learning*, p. 44. He makes that observation having just set forth (pp. 40–44) as clear and succinct a statement of the points at issue as any I have seen. "There are," he says, "three perennial issues in discussion about the liberal arts curriculum. The first of these is how much to prescribe and how much to leave to the freedom of students. Those who argue for detailed requirements claim that college students are too young to know what subjects are truly important and too disposed toward courses of immediate or practical relevance. Those who favor more electives believe that students are much too varied in their interests to be forced into a single curricular mold. . . . The second curricular issue is how to achieve breadth in each student's education. Through decades of discussion three major camps have pressed their rival claims. One group emphasizes the transmission of a defined body of learning, often captured in a list of the great works of human thought. . . . Another school of thought stresses an acquaintance with the principal ways by which the human mind apprehends the world—methods of understanding and inquiring about literature, art, moral philosophy, history, economy, and society, as well as physical and biological phenomena. . . . The third camp advocates achieving breadth by simply requiring students to take a certain number of courses in each of several diverse categories, such as social science, natural sciences, and humanities. . . . The last of the curricular questions is how to achieve integration—how to teach students to synthesize what they have learned, to connect different modes of analysis and bodies of thought to illumine issues of human importance. . . . In fairness, however, we need to recognize that no one has yet progressed very far in creating a body of insights, generalizations, and concepts that will help students understand how to integrate the learning from different disciplines and modes of inquiry."

Preparing themselves in 1943 for the ending of the Second World War and the entry of the veterans into

today for those charged with the stewardship of the nation's institutions of higher education. Those debates hold, I believe, a particular importance for those of us who pursue our calling at one or other of the nation's free-standing liberal arts colleges, by their very nature committed to vindicating the importance of undergraduate education. Especially so, I would argue, for those fortunate enough to be affiliated with the small sub-group of those colleges usually designated as "highly selective." If the colleges of that sub-group constitute no more than a tiny fraction of the nation's institutions of higher education, nonetheless they are a group exceptionally favored by the quality of their students and faculty, the clarity of their mission, and the strength of their financial resources.

Such advantages impose, I believe, certain obligations. And, not least among them, a cheerful willingness to enter the curricular arena, or to do so at least to the extent necessary to reflect on the educational mission appropriate to the free-standing liberal arts college if it is to discharge its responsibilities at this particular juncture in our educational history and in the intellectual and institutional climate now prevailing. . . .

It is hardly surprising that the understanding in twentieth-century America of what constitutes a liberal education has been one of formidable complexity. It has been characterized by considerable (though not necessarily mounting) confusion, and punctuated accordingly by periodic bursts of self-criticism and reforming zealotry—of which the current one, especially if compared with the great wave of self-examination stimulated by the Second World War, is not necessarily the most prominent instance.

The German university ideal, with its stress on the primacy of research had meshed uneasily with the whole Anglo-American approach to undergraduate education. Nonetheless, at the liberal arts colleges and the undergraduate colleges of the large universities alike, far-reaching attempts were made to accommodate that ideal. The multiplication of discrete academic departments, the proliferation of courses available for undergraduates to elect, and, during the long and influential presidency of

Charles William Eliot at Harvard; (1869–1909), the widespread adoption of the free-elective system, all represented such an attempt. So, too, did the creation of undergraduate majors permitting a high degree of concentration or specialization in a single discipline—a concept first mentioned, it seems, in the Johns Hopkins catalogue of 1877–78. And so, again, the later adoption of honors programs designed for the more intellectually gifted undergraduates and pioneered most notably in the 1920s by Frank Aydelotte, then president of Swarthmore College. So far as the conception of a liberal arts education is concerned, a version of Bruce A. Kimball's liberal-free ideal has clearly been in the ascendant. So much so, indeed, that in 1960 a nationwide study of the attitude of liberal arts faculty members found that they "equated liberal arts education to a major in the liberal arts" and viewed "as liberal any discipline which offers a student an opportunity to prove his intellectual ability by becoming competent in a narrow discipline."

But that is only part of the story. Earlier in the century, the widespread adoption by colleges and universities either of distribution requirements (classically in the humanities, social sciences and natural sciences) or of some sort of core curriculum comprised of courses required of all students had reflected a concern to ensure that an undergraduate education would involve an appropriate measure of breadth as well as depth. It had reflected also the reaction of faculties to the excesses of the free elective system and their unwillingness wholly to abandon the notion that a liberal education should be one broadly based in the liberal arts. Given the fact that the major had clearly come to stay, much of the attention of those concerned about the possibility that undergraduates were no longer being given a truly liberal education came to focus on the non-major part of the curriculum. And, since the Second World War, at least, it is largely over the fate of that particular piece of curricular territory that the defenders of liberal or general education (the terms are now sometimes used synonymously) have raised their defiant banners.

The general education movement is often taken to be much older than it is. That that should be so is readily understandable. With its overall preoccupation with the mediation of the cultural heritage, and its reverential canonization of a selection of Greek and Roman classics (or, at least, of such classics in translation along with other "great books of the Western tradition"), it has represented among other things an attempt to recapture for the benefit of a broader, democratized clientele some of the values traditionally embedded in the rhetorical version of the old liberal arts ideal. Redolent though it is of a more distant and aristocratic past, and despite the recent rallying of some of the more conservative of educational critics to its standard, the movement is, in effect, a twentieth-century novelty. Though its deepest roots reach back beyond 1914, its growth

institutions of higher education, the members of the American Association of Colleges' Committee on the Re-Statement of the Nature and Aims of Liberal Education expressed similar sentiments. "Liberal education," they wrote, "as a creative enterprise of free men, is in perennial need of re-examination and reform. The tendency of all institutions, including educational institutions, is to lose sight of their ultimate objective, to adopt mechanical procedures, and to succumb to the inertia of static rigidity. This tendency can be combated only by periodic reappraisal."—see James P. Baxter, 3rd., "Commission on Liberal Education Report," *Association of American Colleges Bulletin*, 29 (1943), 269–99 at 295–6 (the report itself 275–79). It should be noted that, at the time, the debate about undergraduate education in America was even more intense than it has been in the past few years.

really got under way only in the wake of the First World War. The important benchmarks were the launching in 1919 of the "Contemporary Civilization" course at Columbia College, the creation in 1927 of Alexander Meiklejohn's Experimental College within the University of Wisconsin, and the general education core curriculum developed at the University of Chicago during the 1930s and 1940s under the presidency of Robert Maynard Hutchins. And it was only during and after the Second World War that the movement came finally of age. Things could scarcely have been otherwise. Only in the context of a deepening global engagement on the part of the United States, and of the recovery of independence and vitality by ancient "non-Western" societies and cultures once deemed moribund, could the highly self-conscious preoccupation with the mediation of "the Western tradition" and the "revelation of the Western mind," which one finds, for example, in the influential Harvard Redbook of 1945, have become so salient a feature of the American educational consciousness. That preoccupation, indeed, may properly be taken to reflect the first uneasy stirrings of widespread cultural self-doubt.

It is worthy of note, however, that while the Redbook speaks the language of heritage and affirms the abiding importance of the great classic books, it inclines more to the philosophical approach to liberal education than to the rhetorical. Nowhere do the names of Isocrates or Quintilian appear, and Cicero is mentioned but once. The canonical names, instead, are Socrates, Plato and Aristotle. . . . In this it may be said to share something of a common spirit with such earlier proponents of the general education movement as Hutchins and Meiklejohn, perhaps also with such recent contributors to discussion of the undergraduate course of studies as William J. Bennett and Lynne V. Cheney. And much of the daunting complexity of twentieth-century debate about liberal education springs from the extraordinarily intricate and constantly shifting accommodations being made between the old rhetorical version of the liberal arts ideal and the more modern scientifico-philosophical liberal-free ideal.

In those accommodations, it seems clear, the bulk of the ground has been conceded to the liberal-free ideal, with its stress on the centrality of the individual critical intellect in its free, skeptical, and unending pursuit of the truth. But unfashionable though it has come to be over the course of the past century, the old, rhetorical vision of liberal arts education in its purer form has not been lost sight of entirely. And, as recently as 1976, some of its classic virtues were evoked, appropriately enough, and with characteristic clarity and firmness, by the scholar to whom we owe so much for our understanding of its history: Paul Oskar Kristeller.

He did so in a paper "Liberal Education and Western Humanism" delivered at the Columbia University seminar "Liberalism and Liberal Education." Resisting the linkage suggested by the title of the series, he insisted that political liberalism and liberal education were not "related or interdependent," that liberal education neither produced nor was itself produced by political liberalism, and that "in a broad sense [it had] existed for many centuries before political liberalism was even heard of." It is to be identified, instead, with that humanistic education in the classics which had its roots in antiquity, had risen and fallen across the centuries, but in one form or another had flourished especially between the fifteenth and the early twentieth century. In its Renaissance form it had focused exclusively upon the humanities defined as grammar, rhetoric, poetry, history and moral philosophy, and it was predicated on the assumption that the best way "to teach and study them is to read and interpret the Greek and Latin classics in their original text." Advocating "the ideal of a general culture and of a continuing education in the service of this culture" and expressing sympathy with "the programs in the humanities and western civilization at Columbia College and elsewhere" which at least seek to teach the ancient classics (even if "in a hurry" and, regrettably, in English translation), he confessed that he himself remained "convinced of the intrinsic value of classical studies" pursued via study of the texts in Greek and Latin. They serve to foster precision and coherence in both thought and expression, and they convey a body of knowledge that in no way stifles "originality or creativity." "Ancient literature, historiography, and philosophy still provide us with valid standards of excellence," and "the student who develops critical judgment does not lose his freedom when he submits to what is true and valid." Indeed, without such ties "with our past and tradition" the present would be "thrown back on its own resources," and these Kristeller frankly judged to be "intellectually, culturally, and morally inadequate."

In sharp contrast, Charles Frankel, in a paper presented earlier in the same series, clearly aligned himself, not with the rhetorical understanding of the liberal arts tradition but with something close to the liberal-free ideal. Arguing that "at least seven [different] important meanings" could be distinguished for the term "liberalism," he saw a certain affinity between liberal education and some of the features characteristic especially of what he called "philosophic liberalism" and "the liberal style and temperament." Among those characteristics, it would seem, are the "affirmative interest in the promotion of diversity and of the qualities of mind which encourage empathetic understanding and critical appreciation of the many-sided possibilities of human life," and "the belief in the supremacy of rational methods of inquiry" in which are the very presupposition of such a commitment to pluralism. In order to be open to diversity, the new, the different and the idiosyncratic, "without destroying itself, . . . [liberalism] must also generate a capacity to judge, to sift and weigh evidence and, in the end, to resist the meretricious." While a university cannot be political "in the sense that it cannot be bound to the uncriticized and unchallenged defense of a given economic system or of a given political system or social structure," it must be committed to certain "long-term aspirations" to which liberalism, in its broader meaning, is itself committed. And thus it is the purpose of a liberal education "to protect the liberal emphasis on critical method and a pluralistic, competitive society." To that end, a primary objective at a university cannot be "anything but the criticism of inherited ideas, institutions and cultures—and the pursuit of truth in this broad sense." To that end, also, we must exemplify "certain attitudes, certain principles. One of these principles is tolerance. Another is free speech. Another is the sovereignty of rational methods." And if, in education, "a principle is adopted as a basic guiding principle, it . . . becomes a goal in itself. Thus [he concluded] I view toleration as an end-value and not simply a means.

It is not surprising, then, that twentieth-century discourse about liberal education should be widely viewed as being in something of a muddle. But despite the intricate accommodations and confusions by which it is characterized, it has clearly not lost sight of the ancient tension between the competing rhetorical and philosophical ideals. . . . It is a tension which Kristeller views as being at the very heart of the frequently misunderstood clash between scholastics and humanists during the Renaissance era. It is a tension the presence of which Sheldon Rothblatt has detected in the debates about education at Oxford in the nineteenth century, and the longer history of which Bruce A. Kimball has mapped out in considerable detail, with great clarity and much persuasive force, arguing for its continuation right down to the present. In its absence, it would indeed be hard to make adequate sense of the point-counterpoint of the recurrent rounds of debate about liberal education in our own century. And failure to recognize its presence almost certainly dooms us to misinterpreting the current round which may be said to have begun with the publication in 1977 of the Carnegie Council's report *Missions of the College Curriculum,* which moved to the forefront of the public consciousness with the publication in 1984 of William J. Bennett's characteristically forceful statement, *To Reclaim a Legacy,* and which now seems destined to continue on into the 1990s.

Given the crucial importance of the role that faculty members play in the educative process, it is much to be regretted that so few attempts have been made to collect at the national level a full array of pertinent quantitative data concerning them. For full-time faculty, overall counts and figures on average salaries have been available, along with data generated by periodic surveys of faculty opinion, but not a great deal more. As a result, much of the pertinent terrain has been left available very much as unfenced grazing land for peripatetic commenta-tors prone to rampant anecdotalism. And, of late, the more apoplectically critical among them have made effective use of the license accorded to them thereby.

In 1987, happily, the National Center for Education Statistics of the U.S. Department of Education initiated for the first time since 1963 a National Survey of Postsecondary Faculty designed to collect data on faculty and faculty issues. Its stated plan was to collect such data at regular intervals, and to do so from three sources: faculty members themselves, department chairs, and institutional academic officers. The first cycle of the study was completed in 1988 and an overview of the data was published in 1990. It was based on an institutional sampling selected from an overall "universe" of some 3,159 nonprofit accredited institutions offering a two-year associate's or higher degree. The data presented from the survey are broken down on many issues by age, gender, race, part-time or full-time status, tenure status or academic rank. They are also broken down by institutional control (public or private), and institutional sector—with nine categories employed: public research, private research, public doctoral, private doctoral, public comprehensive, private comprehensive, liberal arts, public two-year, and other. While these categories lack the precision of the full range of Carnegie Classifications and are not fully aligned with them, they are close enough to permit useful comparison.

Of the plethora of data garnered by this survey only a handful need be highlighted here. First, the basics: even if one excludes from the count the 100,000 and more temporary, adjunct, or visiting faculty, there were in 1987 around 670,000 faculty members at the more than 3,000 institutions covered by the survey. Of these, approximately 494,000 were full-time, 176,000 part-time. Of the full-time faculty approximately 28 percent taught at research universities, 26 percent at comprehensive institutions, 19 percent at public two-year colleges, and 8 percent at liberal arts colleges of one sort or another. The distribution of part-time faculty was sharply different. No less than 46 percent of them were concentrated in the two-year colleges, with the next largest group (approximately 18%) at the comprehensive institutions, and only 11 and 8 percent, respectively, at the research universities and liberal arts colleges. A similar contrast is evident in the percentages (35 versus 19%) of full-time and part-time faculty teaching in the arts and sciences.

Of the full-time faculty at both four-year and two-year institutions, some 60 percent were tenured, ranging from a high of 69 percent at the public research universities to a low of 48 percent at the private doctoral institutions, with the liberal arts colleges coming in towards the low end at 51 percent, and with above-average tenured cohorts in the arts and sciences. The mean age of the full-time group was forty-seven; at forty-four their part-time colleagues were slightly younger. Of the full-time faculty, only 2 percent were under thirty, 40 percent were between thirty and forty-four, and 55 percent between forty-five and sixty-four. On this dimension, no statistically significant differences were evident across either subject area or institutional sector. The same is almost as true among both part-time and full-time faculty for representation of the several racial or ethnic groupings across the several institutional sectors. Eighty-nine percent of the full-time and 90 percent of the part-time faculty were white. Asians constituted some 4 percent of the total; blacks, Hispanics and Native Americans 3, 2 and 1 percent respectively. So far as gender is concerned, however, there is a fairly marked difference between full-time and part-time faculty. Whereas men constituted 73 percent of the full-time contingent, they totaled no more than 56 percent of the part-timers. Not surprisingly, then, in terms at least of their overall average of 27 percent, women were comparatively overrepresented at the public two-year institutions (38%), and underrepresented at the research universities (approximately 20%). At 29 percent, they possessed a comparatively strong presence in the liberal arts colleges.

From the responses of faculty members to the 1988 survey, we learn that in the fall semester 1987 they reported themselves as working, on average, some 53 hours per week at all their professional activities, whether paid or unpaid. Eighty-seven percent of that average workload involved work at their academic institutions, while mean hours of unremunerated professional service constituted 6 percent, and mean hours of such remunerated outside work as consulting, 7 percent of the total. Faculty at the public and private research and at the public doctoral universities put in the longest hours (at 57, 56 and 54 hours per week); those at the two-year colleges (at 47 hours) the shortest. The amount of time devoted to outside professional work, whether paid or unpaid, differed little across the several institutional sectors, but mean hours of work at the institution itself did. Faculty teaching at the two-year colleges averaged, at 40 hours per week, less than those at any of the four-year institutions; those at the private and public research and at the public doctoral universities exceeded, at 52, 50 and 49 hours per week, the overall average of 46.

Academic rank seemed to make no appreciable difference in the number of working hours devoted either to the institution itself or to outside professional activities, whether remunerated or not. Field of study or program area, however, did make such a difference. Faculty in the fine arts, for example, while putting in the same number of hours as the overall mean and as the mean for unpaid professional services "outside," committed less time to the institution (44 hours) and more to paid outside activities (6 hours). In contrast, faculty in the humanities, who also aligned with the mean in relation both to overall workload and to amount of time devoted to outside unpaid professional services, devoted more time to the institution (48 hours) and less to outside remunerated activities (2 hours).

Differences in the way in which faculty members allocated their working hours show up also by institutional sector. At all types of institution teaching activities naturally accounted for the bulk of that time, with the overall mean being 56 percent for teaching, student advising, grading, course preparation and so on, 16 percent for scholarly research (and, presumably, writing), 13 percent for administrative and governance activities of one sort or another, and 15 percent for such other activities as working with student organizations, community or public service, and outside counseling or free-lance work. But so far as the balance between teaching and research is concerned, whereas faculty at the two-year colleges devoted 71 percent of their time to teaching and only 3 percent to research, those at the private research universities (not surprisingly) devoted an average of only 40 percent to teaching but 30 percent to research. The comparable distribution of time for faculty members at the liberal arts colleges was 65 percent to teaching, 8 percent to research. At all types of institutions, moreover, academic rank made a difference in the differential amounts of time allocated to teaching, research, and administrative activities. Full professors devoted 51 percent of their time to teaching, 20 percent to research and 16 percent to administrative duties; assistant professors, on the other hand, spent 56 percent of their time teaching, 18 percent pursuing research and, understandably, only 10 percent on administrative matters. Similarly, differences show up when one controls for academic field or program area, with the extremes being set by faculty in agriculture and home economics (46% teaching; 28% research), and in the humanities (61% teaching; 17% research).

For their efforts, full-time faculty respondents to the 1987 survey reported themselves to be receiving on average a total annual income from all sources in the neighborhood of $49,000. Apart from an obvious differentiation in earnings by academic rank, institutional sector and program area or field also accounted for substantial differences in mean annual incomes. The highest average income (about $75,000) was reported by faculty members teaching at private research universities; the lowest (about $33,000) by faculty at liberal arts colleges. Interestingly enough, faculty teaching at the public two-year colleges earned somewhat more than that (approximately $39,000). When broken down by academic field or program area—and whatever the institutional sector involved—those in the health sciences emerge as the best remunerated ($75,000); those in the humanities the worst ($39,000). And that discrepancy reflects not only the differential in the income they received from their institutions but also a very marked differential in the income they received from outside consulting work ($9,431 per annum as opposed to $663). For full-time faculty, overall average income from such outside consulting work was $8,000. That average, however, conceals marked differences both in the amounts received in general and in the amounts received by faculty in different academic fields and at different types of institutions. In general, only 42 percent earned any income from consulting work and over half of that group earned less than $2,500. Nine percent earned $10,000 or more. Faculty members teaching in the health sciences were most likely to be in receipt of outside consulting income, and they earned most from that source; in contrast, faculty teaching in the humanities were least likely to make any money from consulting, and those who did so earned less on average than faculty in any other academic field. Similarly, if one breaks the data down by institutional sector faculty teaching at private research universities were most likely to be engaged in outside consulting work (61%) and to earn most from that source. In contrast, faculty teaching at two-year institutions were least likely (24%) to engage in such outside consulting work, though they earned somewhat more on average for their efforts than the 32 percent of faculty at liberal arts colleges who took on such assignments.

In the case of faculty, it is harder to make reliable comparisons with the past or to chart the process of change across the past three decades than it was either with the institutions themselves or with the bodies of students who enrolled in them. . . . What we do have . . . are surveys and studies by scholars like Lipset, Ladd, Howard R. Bowen, Schuster, Fulton, Trow and Boyer, drawing in part on the faculty surveys conducted at intervals since 1969 (and most recently in 1989) by the Carnegie Commission on Higher Education and the American Council on Education. And these surveys and studies do help fill the gap. The Carnegie surveys have all included questions pertaining to the topic. And the appropriately weighted data generated thereby (and we are assured that they "may be taken as reasonably representative of the entire population of teaching faculty at colleges and universities in the United States") are extremely interesting. In common with the 1988 data they strongly suggest that the typical faculty member in the United States places a much higher priority on teaching and a lower priority on research and publication than is often alleged to be the case. Thus the data from the 1989 survey reveal that 70 percent of the professoriate reported their interests as lying primarily with teaching rather than research, that 56 percent had never published or edited a book, whether alone or in collaboration (although 6%, presumably composed of compulsive recidivists, had published six or more), that 59 percent had published *in toto* no more than five articles in an academic or professional journal, 26 percent none at all, and that 62 percent believed that teaching effectiveness should be the primary criteria for promotion of faculty.

The data generated by that Carnegie survey in 1989 did attest to some movement in a research-oriented direction across the two decades since 1969, when 76 percent of the professoriate had considered themselves as primarily committed to teaching (as opposed to the 70% of 1979 and 1989) and 69 percent (as opposed to 56) had never published or edited a book. Such changes, however, are dwarfed by other developments which, despite the incommensurability of some of the data, are easy enough to identify. The most obvious is the sheer growth in the overall size of the professoriate. In 1900 there were only 24,000 faculty members at American colleges and universities. By 1920 that number had risen to 45,000, by 1940 to 147,000, by 1972 to 603,000. As Ladd and Lipset point out, the biggest jump (of about 150,000) came between 1965 and 1970, "with the number of *new* positions created and filled exceeding the *entire number* of faculty slots that [had] existed in 1940."After the early 1970s, however, as student enrollment levels stabilized, the demand for new faculty dried up and the growth rate accordingly slowed down.

With the dramatic process of expansion had come, however, an equally dramatic shift in the institutional location of the bulk of faculty members. In 1963, for example, one faculty member in six taught at a liberal arts college; by 1980, only one in twelve did so, and by 1988 the number had dropped to something closer to one in thirteen. On the other hand, whereas in 1963 only one faculty member in ten taught at a two-year college, by 1988 the figure was one in five, and their numbers, since then have grown still further.

Although for the earlier years information about the age distribution of the faculty is not readily available, the enormous influx of new people clearly led to a significant drop in the average age of the professoriate, with the steady-state conditions of the 1970s and 1980s leading to a subsequent reversal of that change. . . .

The roller-coaster conditions prevailing in the academic employment market across the years between 1960 and the present also had a marked impact on the economic status of the profession. Embedded in the figures reported in the 1988 survey for annual income is the effect of some demoralizing swings, as the excess demand for faculty generated by the surging enrollments of the 1960s (and prevailing until 1969) was replaced in subsequent years by a surplus in the number of candidates available for the rapidly dwindling number of openings. As a result, while "the rapid expansion of higher education in the 1960s was accompanied by the only significant, sustained improvement in the real income of faculty members since World War II," the subsequent slowdown led between 1970–71 and 1983–84 to a 19 percent decline in faculty salaries (in terms of real, non-inflated dollars), while, in contrast, "compensation in most other occupational categories more or less kept up with inflation." Over the period 1960–61 to 1983–84, most occupational groups "experienced increases in real [non-inflated] earnings of at least 20 per cent." In contrast, "average real faculty salaries in 1983–84 were no higher than they had been in 1960–61."

Linked with these ups and downs in the economic well-being of the profession was the shifting relationship across these years of the number of enrollments in our colleges and universities and the size of the pool of Ph.D.s being generated by our graduate schools. During the 1960s the size of that pool grew dramatically as the graduate schools scrambled to keep up with the demand for new faculty. Between 1958 and 1972, indeed, there was a fourfold increase (8,800 to 33,000) in the overall number of Ph.D.s awarded by American universities. The rate of production then stabilized and has since fluctuated within the 30,000 to 33,000 range. . . .

By now, even the most patient and long-suffering of readers will have been tempted to conclude that they have been told altogether more than they want to know about the numbers, types, characteristic commitments, concerns and challenges confronting the institutions, students and faculty that together make up the world of American higher education. About that barrage of numbers, proportions and percentages I have, however, no apologies to make. We have well been reminded of the fact that "in thinking about education, many of us are autobiographical." That is to say, "we tend to make judgments about the future on the basis of our own experiences and the experiences of friends." Not only does that make it difficult for us "to anticipate changes in circumstances" and to plan properly for them, it also dims our awareness of the sheer scope and variety of the whole enterprise of higher education in America and the changes that have overtaken it even in our own lifetime.

That these changes have been massive, almost overwhelming, the array of data . . . leaves no room for doubt. The rapid increase over the past thirty years in the number of institutions of higher education and the sectors in which it has largely been concentrated have conspired to nudge the center of institutional gravity away, somewhat, from the leading research universities and liberal arts colleges and more in the direction of the comprehensive institutions and two-year colleges. The characteristic concerns of those leading institutions and the academic standards they set are now much less likely than they once were to set the tone for the whole enterprise. Similarly, the dramatic increase in the size of the student body, the opening up of access and the presence in far greater numbers on our campuses of women, members of racial minority groups, older students, part-time students, students who commute to their classes—all of these developments, which are destined to continue on into the future, have helped turn many of our colleges and universities in new directions and have left none of them totally unaffected. As we peer anxiously into the future, we simply cannot afford to forget for a moment that "roughly one-half of the students in the classroom of 2000 would not have been there if the composition of [the American student body as it was in] 1960 had been continued. And there have been parallel, if less dramatic, changes in the overall numbers, age, gender, race and typical institutional context of the faculty members charged with the teaching of those students. Such transformations, crammed into the narrow compass of no more than three decades, must necessarily inform the perspective from which we make our judgments about the current undergraduate experience in America—its overall quality, the changes it reflects, the threat or promise it holds for the future.

Primacy of American Higher Education

16. Henry Rosovsky, "Our Universities Are the World's Best," 1987

In the line of widely respected faculty managers at Harvard, Henry Rosovsky (1927–) served as dean of the Faculty of Arts and Sciences (1973–84). He was an academic wunderkind. Polish-born, he came with no command of English to the United States in 1940, served as a first lieutenant in the Army (1946–47, 1950–52), earned an A.B. from the College of William and Mary (1949) and his Ph.D. from Harvard (1959). As an economist specializing in Japan, he rose to full professor at Berkeley (1958–65) and then in 1965 went to the Harvard economics department, where he occupied a chair (1975–84), finally becoming Geyser University Professor in 1984 (Emeritus 1996). He was one of the few professors in modern Harvard history to be appointed to the Harvard University Corporation (1985–97).

Henry Rosovsky, "Highest Education," *The New Republic,* July 13, 1987, 13–14. Reprinted by permission of *The New Republic,* © 1987, *The New Republic,* LLC. Further reading: Rosovsky, *The University: An Owner's Manual* (Cambridge, MA, 1990); Morton Keller and Phyllis Keller, *Making Harvard Modern* (New York, 2001); and I, 17.

In these days when foreign economic rivals seem to be surpassing us in one field after another, it may be reassuring to know that there is one vital industry where America unquestionably dominates the world: higher education. Between two-thirds and three-quarters of the world's best universities are located in the United States. This fact has been ignored by the many recent critics of higher education in America. (We also are home to a large share of the world's worst colleges and universities, but that is beside the point.)

What other sector of our economy can make a similar statement? There are baseball, football, and basketball teams—but that pretty much exhausts the list. No one has suggested that today America is home to two-thirds of the best steel mills, automobile factories, chip manufacturers, banks, or government agencies. . . .

A recent exercise by Asian scholars, published in the *Asian Wall Street Journal,* produced the following rankings: 1. Harvard; 2. Cambridge/Oxford; 3. Stanford; 4. Berkeley; 5. MIT; 6. Yale; 7. Tokyo; 8. Paris-Sorbonne; 9. Cornell; 10. Michigan, Princeton. I attach no real importance to individual rank order. What does have validity . . . is the group as a whole. . . . I believe that if this list were expanded to 20 or 30 institutions, the U.S. proportion would not decline. Columbia, Chicago, UCLA, Cal Tech, Wisconsin, and many others would find little competition abroad. . . .

Some may argue that the very notion of rankings or "the best" is invidious, crude, and meaningless. I do not share that view if we adopt a sufficiently broad interpretation of these terms. The universities we are considering lead the world in basic science research. They provide a significant share of the most competitive graduate programs. They are generally at the cutting edge—rather blunt these days— of the social sciences. Students from all over the world . . . seek entry in large numbers.

Why this happy result? Our national wealth, large population, government support especially of science have to be significant explanatory factors. The constructive influence of Hitler refugees undoubtedly was important in setting new standards of quality beginning in the 1930s. The American habit of private philanthropy remains crucial. These are influential factors, but in my opinion there are less obvious and perhaps more important considerations.

An unusual characteristic of American university life is its competitiveness. Institutions of the same class compete for faculty, research funds, students, public attention—and much else. That Harvard and Stanford, for example, actively recruit and compete for students—undergraduate, graduate, and professional—is quite incomprehensible to establishments such as Tokyo or Kyoto universities, where an entrance examination determines all. It is almost equally unusual in most parts of the world for one institution to hire professors away from another by offering a higher salary and/or better working conditions. In Japan, and to a lesser extent elsewhere, universities hire almost exclusively their own graduates. Inbreeding is rampant—a sharp contrast with most departments in top American universities.

Institutional competitiveness has some negative consequences—particularly if your university loses too many encounters with the market. The dark side includes too much movement by professorial stars from one university to another in relentless pursuit of personal gain, and a consequently lower level of institutional loyalty. Competition also leads to invidious comparisons among fields of study, with excessive advantages within the university going to those subjects where "market power" is strong (computer sciences, yes; English, no). Not least, competition can lead to a Wall Street–like mentality that focuses too much on short-term highly visible achievements at the expense of the long run and the unfashionable.

However, the benefits of American-style competi-

tition among universities outweigh the costs. It has prevented complacency and spurred the drive for excellence and change. . . .

American practices also differ in the selection of faculty for "permanent employment," or tenure. Despite the ubiquity of security of employment in our society, faculty tenure at universities seems to be an inordinately vexing subject. Critics complain that teaching ability is ignored and that deadwood is encouraged to remain in place for many years. Without discussing these criticisms—and I do not agree with them—this much is clear: in our leading universities, the granting of tenure is taken with utmost seriousness. It is not merely a question of time. Tenure is awarded only after a long period of probationary service (usually eight years), and extensive inside and outside peer review; it is a highly competitive selection process. . . . All of these schools correctly assume that the quality of the faculty is the most important factor in maintaining their reputation and position. The best faculty attracts the finest students, produces the highest quality research, gains the most outside support. . . .

Governance is another area in which American universities are unusual. . . . The American system is unitary. Ultimately one person—a president—is in charge. Typically, educational policy—curriculum, nature of degrees, selection of faculty, admissions, etc.—is initiated by or delegated to academics. But budgets, management of endowment, decisions on new programs, long-range plans, and similar matters are in the hands of a hierarchy headed by a president who is responsible to a board of trustees. . . . Chairmen, deans, provosts, and similar levels of senior and middle management are appointed, not elected, and they can be dismissed. This is crucial because academic elections tend to result in weak leadership. What professors in their right minds would vote for a dean who advocated cuts in their departments? . . . Relatively independent trustees serve both public and private schools, giving considerable protection from political interference even to state universities. We have a system of governance that permits nonconsensual and unpopular decisions to be made when necessary. We have learned that not everything is improved by making it more democratic. We also have learned that university governance functions best when conflict of interest is minimized. . . .

In the rest of the world . . . more often than not universities are state-run, under the direction of a ministry of education or some form of national grants committee disbursing government funds. Professors tend to be civil servants subject to many bureaucratic regulations; logrolling all too easily replaces competition. An election administration— another common feature—ensures that leadership is weak: those who are strong and espouse change are unlikely to be popular favorites. . . .

I suspect another factor: . . . regional pride. It may exist elsewhere in the world, but not nearly to the same degree. Many of our best institutions—public and private—are clear expressions of local patriotism.... In our large and decentralized country, each region wants its share of the best, and sometimes these ambitions are fulfilled. In less than a hundred years, with the help of a growing population and tax base, great local ambition, new wealth, and a wonderful climate, the state of California has created an astonishing number of universities with international reputations. And all are far removed from the traditional cultural centers of the Northeast. In America the pre-emptive power of Paris, Tokyo, or pre-war Berlin simply does not exist—thank goodness.

In higher education, "made in America" still is the finest label. My only advice is to add "handle with care," lest we too descend to the level of most other American industrial performance.

17. Charles M. Vest,
Pursuing the Endless Frontier, 2005

Seventeen years after Harvard's Henry Rosovsky voiced his pride in the primacy of American universities (I, 16), the president of a neighboring university published a book that briefly itemized his own explanation of academic excellence in the United States: Charles M. Vest (1941–) at the time had been president of the Massachusetts Institute of Technology (1990–99). After a bachelor's degree in mechanical engineering from West Virginia University and his higher degrees from the University of Michigan (1964, 1967), he became full professor in the mechanical engineering faculty at Michigan (1968–77) and then dean of engineering and provost. His research interests concerned the thermal sciences and the engineering applications of lasers and coherent optics. During and after his presidency of MIT, Vest served in public advisory capacities, including membership in the President's Council of Advisors on Science and Technology (1994–). Significantly, he oversaw an increase in the number of female faculty members in science and engineering and was succeeded in the presidency by a female scientist.

Charles M. Vest, *Pursuing the Endless Frontier: Essays on MIT and the Role of Research Universities* (Cambridge, MA, 2005): 259–61. Reprinted with kind permission of the MIT Press, © 2004. Further reading: Roger L. Geiger, "Research Universities in a New Era: From the 1980s to the 1990s," in *Higher Learning in America, 1980–2000*, ed. Arthur Levine (Baltimore, 1983), ch. 4; and I, 16.

A basic question I have been asked innumerable times, especially when traveling abroad, is, Why is America's system of higher education so good? It is, as has been said all too often, the envy of the world.

I think that there are seven primary reasons for the excellence of U.S. higher education relative to that in other countries:

- We have a broad diversity of institutions ranging from small liberal arts colleges to Ivy League schools, to the great land grant universities, and to somewhat more focused institutions like MIT or Caltech. This diversity provides a wealth of environments and opportunities, from which individual students can select a school that best matches their needs and capabilities.

- We offer new assistant professors a wide-open field of freedom to choose what they teach and the topics of research and scholarship they engage. We reject the hierarchical systems of many other nations in which junior faculty are subservient to, and indeed apprenticed to, senior professors. We therefore enjoy a constant flow of new ideas, passions, and approaches that keep us fresh and robust.

- In our research universities we meaningfully weave together teaching and research. This too brings a freshness, intensity, and constant renewal that is a critical component of institutional excellence.

- We welcome to our nation and our institutions students, scholars, and faculty from other countries. It is not possible to overstate the intellectual and cultural richness that immigrants have brought to U.S. campuses. They have joined us to create what we are. Even the constant flow of international visitors to our campuses, and our faculty to theirs, is critically important.

- We have an implicit national science and technology policy that recognizes the support of frontier research in our universities as an important responsibility of the federal government. This policy is intended to provide financial support to researchers, in whatever institution they are located, based on their merit in a competitive marketplace of ideas. It has the additional feature, elegant in its simplicity, that funding for infrastructure is attached to grants and contracts, and therefore flows to the researchers with the most meritorious ideas and track records.

- We have a tradition of individual philanthropy through which our alumni and others who believe in excellent education support our colleges and universities. They enable talented students from families of modest means to attend even the most costly schools. We have tax laws that encourage and enable such support, to an extent that is unique in the world.

- We have a system of free competition for faculty and students. Such inter-institutional competition, though it may be the bane of academic administrators' daily lives, drives excellence.

As has been explained in my reports during the last thirteen years, most of these seven factors are constantly in danger. The political winds shift and change—raising barriers to international flow of students and scholars, corrupting the merit-based, peer-reviewed award of federal research funds through rampant "pork barrel" congressional earmarking of projects and facilities, and raising the specter of price controls on higher education rather than emphasizing financial aid for needy students. Some private foundations and philanthropists blow hot and cold on supporting the academic enterprise, and often suppress creative forces by being overly prescriptive. Governing boards, especially in public institutions, occasionally attempt to interfere inappropriately with the freedom of faculty to choose the subjects of their research and teaching.

All those who believe that it is important for the United States to have the best system of higher education in the world must therefore be constantly vigilant and advocate effectively for sustaining these elements of success. . . .

Horizons

18. Michael Gibbons et al., *The New Production of Knowledge*, 1994

A team of international social scientists in the early 1990s examined the shifting collaborative formations and inventive connections among the sciences and, to a limited and problematic degree, within the humanities that are producing "new knowledge." The turn toward changeable methods, dimensions, and perspectives of inquiry (called here Mode 2) is a departure from, if not a full replacement of, the older, widely diffused, complex but controlling model of Newtonian scientific inquiry (called here Mode 1). The newer mode is at work in the academic sciences and among people asking questions about general public policy. The thrust of this piece is largely directed at the sciences, but the theme of integrating scholarship is one of long standing. In the 1960s Mark Van Doren asserted that "the connectedness of things is what the educator contemplates to the limit of his capacity." In 1967 Michael Polanyi spoke of "overlapping [academic] neighborhoods." Clifford Geertz wrote about "blurred genres as the refiguration of social thought" in 1980. And Ernest Boyer emphasized the "scholarship of integration" in 1990.

Michael Gibbons (1939–), secretary general of the Association of Commonwealth Universities (1996–), was the academic coordinator of five people who joined him in these studies. The distinguished group included Camille Limoges (1942–) of the Université du Quebec à Montreal, Helga Nowotny (1937–) from the University of Vienna, Simon Schwartzman (1939–) of the Universidade de São Paulo, Peter Scott (1946–) of Kingston University, and Martin Trow (1926–) of the University of California at Berkeley.

Reprinted by permission of Sage Publications Ltd. from Michael Gibbons et al., *The New Production of Knowledge: The Dynamics of Science and Research in Contemporary Societies* (London and Thousand Oaks, CA, 1994) Copyright © 1994: vii, 32–38. Further reading: Eric Von Hippel, *The Sources of Innovation* (New York, 1989); David Harvey, *The Condition of Postmodernity: An Enquiry into the Origins of Cultural Change* (London, 1989); Vannevar Bush, *Endless Horizons* (Washington, D.C., 1946); Paul S. Adler, ed., *Technology and the Future of Work* (Oxford, 1992); Gary W. Matkin, *Technology Transfer and the University* (New York, 1990); Cristina Gonzalez, Debbie A. Niemeier, and Alexandra Navrotsky, "The New Generation of American Scholars," *Academe* (July–August 2003): 56–60; and I, 16; IV, 8–11; V, 12; VI, 18; XII, 5.

To help in the description of the changes observed, we have distinguished the new mode—Mode 2—from the more familiar mode—Mode 1. Our view is that while Mode 2 may not be replacing Mode 1, Mode 2 is different from Mode 1—in nearly every respect. The new mode operates within a context of application in that problems are not set within a disciplinary framework. It is transdisciplinary rather than mono- or multidisciplinary. It is carried out in non-hierarchical, heterogeneously organised forms which are essentially transient. It is not being institutionalised primarily within university structures. Mode 2 involves the close interaction of many actors throughout the process of knowledge production and this means that knowledge production is becoming more socially accountable. One consequence of these changes is that Mode 2 makes use of a wider range of criteria in judging quality control. Overall, the process of knowledge production is becoming more reflexive and affects at the deepest levels what shall count as 'good science.' . . .

In discussing knowledge production in terms of the emergence of Mode 1 alongside Mode 2, we have to clarify where the differences lie. Of these, an essential one concerns changes in the mechanisms which assess the quality of knowledge produced. In Mode 1 for both scientific and technological knowledge this is a matter of establishing a provisional consensus among a community of practitioners. The judgements of this community form a powerful selection mechanism of problems, methods, people and results. It is a crucial social process to maintain standards and its prerogatives are protected because rigorous control of quality is seen to be the principal way to maintain autonomy over the internal affairs of the community. Quality control has two main components; one is institutional and concerns the spatial position of a particular research activity in the cognitive landscape; the other is cognitive and pertains to the social organisation in which such research is performed.

The dependence of quality control on institutional space. In Mode 1, control is exercised by different types of knowledge producing institutions each of which has its own boundaries, structures of apprenticeship and rules of behaviour. Such institutions include, for example, universities, national academies and the professional societies. Each has different ways of controlling membership, some provide training, establishing procedures whereby knowledge is produced and validated. Because knowledge production in Mode 2 occurs within transient contexts of application it is unlikely that the communities of practitioners who exercise quality control will be backed up by relatively stable institutions such as one finds in Mode 1. Looked at from the point of view of Mode 1 such a process of quality control necessarily appears as dislocated. It takes on transient and temporary forms, exhibits fluid contours and provisional norms, and occupies temporary institutional spaces which can accommodate knowledge producers with many different institutional affiliations, either simultaneously or sequentially.

The dependence of quality control on the social organisation of research. The second component of quality control relates to mechanisms that define what problems are to be pursued, how they are to be tackled and which results shall count as valid. This involves a shift from control located within disciplines to more diffuse kinds of control that reflect the transdisciplinary nature of the problems being addressed. In Mode 2, success is defined differently from that in Mode 1. Success in Mode 1 might perhaps be summarily described as excellence defined by disciplinary peers. In Mode 2 success would have to include the additional criteria such as efficiency or usefulness, defined in terms of the contribution the work has made to the overall solution of transdisciplinary problems. In both cases success reflects a perception of quality as judged by a particular community of practitioners. But, all quality control is linked, legitimated and, ultimately, receives its credibility and scientific authority from an idea, image, or concept of what constitutes good science including best practice. For example, at different times in history what constitutes good science has been guided by the ideal of truth and the search for unitary principles. In Mode 2, the issue of assessing the quality of good research is twofold. One has to do with the fact that the community of practitioners is transient and transdisciplinary, as we have already shown, the other arising out of the fact that the criteria of quality are not solely those that obtain in Mode 1 but include the additional criteria that arise out of context of application.

Currently conventional wisdom is that discovery must precede application. Although this has not always been the case it has provided a powerful image of how things ought to be. By contrast, Mode 2 quality control is additionally guided by a good deal of practical, societal, policy-related concerns, so that whatever knowledge is actually produced, the environment already structured by application or use will have to be taken into account. When knowledge is actually produced in the context of application, it is not applied science, because discovery and applications cannot be separated, the relevant science being produced in the very course of providing solutions to problems defined in the context of application. Those who exert quality control in Mode 2 have learned to use multiple criteria not only in general, but in relation to the specific results produced by the particular configuration of researchers involved.

THE DYNAMICS OF MODE 2 KNOWLEDGE PRODUCTION

In order to understand better the growth and diffusion of Mode 2 a distinction will be drawn between homogeneous and heterogeneous growth. Within the scientific enterprise an example of homogeneous growth would be the expansion of a given entity, say papers in nuclear physics, where the rate of growth often follows a logarithmic curve. In this case, growth essentially consists of the production of more of the same, whether these are numbers of papers produced or numbers of scientists working in a given field. The result is exponential growth which would continue indefinitely were it not for the fact that resources are finite (De Solla Price, 1963). Heterogeneous growth, by contrast, refers to a process of differentiation through which rearrangements of component elements take place within a given process or set of activities. In these cases it is the number of rearrangements that grow rather than solely the number of outputs, that is, a shift in the pace of internal differentiation occurs. Considering only national research and development (R&D) statistics in the aggregate, or listening exclusively to the rhetoric of the institutional leaders of the scientific community, may mask the phenomenon, but it is evident that deep-seated structural changes are taking place in the relationships both within and between the scientific communities and society at large, with knowledge becoming socially distributed to ever wider segments of society. The globalisation of science and R&D sourcing and the role that specialised knowledge has come to play in technological innovation result in a highly differentiated, heterogeneous form of growth of knowledge. This is expressed tellingly in authorship patterns of scientific papers, the traditional vehicle of scientific communications. Not only is the average number of authors per paper increasing, but much more significantly, so are the diversity of specialisms and disciplines involved in the writing of a single paper and the range of institutions and organisations from which the authors originate. In addition, the geographical distribution of these institutions continues to broaden. In Mode 2, not only are more actors involved in the genesis of knowledge but they remain socially distributed.

What kind of model, or analytical framework, might best describe this process of heterogeneous growth, a process of diffusion in which the numbers of linkages between entities increases and new configurations are set up, which dissolve and re-emerge in different combinations? Communication plays a central role in this process and the density of communication appears to be the key variable. . . .

During the past decades most industrial countries have been putting in place the basic infrastructure for a dynamic knowledge production system based upon specialisation and disciplinary structures. . . . In an unplanned and unforeseen way these past investments have established the essential preconditions for the numbers of communication linkages to become large enough to change existing patterns of knowledge production in a fundamental way. The density of communication between the elements of the global research system has reached the criticality which makes a significant expansion of communication linkages a certain, though unintended outcome. The expansion of the number, nature and range of communicative interactions between the different sites of knowledge production leads not only to more knowledge being produced but also to more knowledge of different kinds; not only to sharing of resources, but to their continuous configuration. Each new configuration becomes itself a potential source of new knowledge production which in turn is transformed into the site of further possible configurations. The multiplication of the numbers and kinds of configurations are at the core of the diffusion process resulting from increasing density of communication. Its precondition is the vast increase in the numbers of communicative interactions of many kinds, because only a fraction of these will result in new configurations, which are sufficiently stable to become sites for further knowledge production. This process has been greatly aided by information technologies which not only speed up the rate of communication, but also create more new linkages. . . .

Communication between science and society. This is the widest, and by the very nature of the communication link, the most loosely linked web of communication. Traditionally, communication between science and society was essentially one-way: scientists were the holders of privileged expert knowledge, while the lay public was to be enlightened and educated. In the past various forms of popularisation of scientific knowledge have shaped this relationship, without altering the basic underlying conception. The pressure for increased accountability arises in two distinct but related ways. First, in all countries there is now much greater pressure to justify public expenditures on science. Financial accountability is essentially about justifying expenditure, about ensuring that financial resources have been spent in the manner stipulated in the allocation process. But, second, this is only one aspect of a much broader social concern with the conduct and goals of scientific research. There has been an increased demand for social as well as financial accountability.

Enhanced social accountability, particularly evident in the last few decades, arose as a better educated citizenry placed new demands on science. These demands were nurtured against the background of a number of techno-political controversies. In the public debates around these controversies it became obvious that a strong requirement for social assessment of science and technology had taken root in society. The previous one-way communication process from scientific experts to the lay public perceived to be scientifically illiterate and in need of education by experts has been supplanted by politically backed demands for accountability of science and technology and new public discussions in which experts have to communicate a more 'vernacular' science than ever before. The most sensitive domains so far have centred upon technological risks, notably those connected with nuclear power

and other hazardous large technical facilities, environmental concerns covering a wide range of topics from the ozone layer to biodiversity, and potential dangers or ethical issues associated with biotechnology and genetic engineering. In all these cases, technology has perhaps been more implicated than science per se, while in the mind of the public the two are seen as closely intertwined. What is at issue very often is the claim that research knows no limits—with the counterargument asserting that not everything research can learn or do, should actually be learned or done, nor is it always beneficial to society. A related argument is that it is no longer possible to contain scientific and technical experiments in the laboratories properly speaking and that society itself has become a laboratory for experiments that ought to be controlled in a more societal and tighter way.

The new demands for accountability and for more communication between the community of scientific and technical experts and the 'attentive' public are interconnected and emanate from the spread of higher education through society. The increased level of education of the population in highly industrialised societies, and the widespread use of technological applications in households, workplaces and in other public (for example, transport) and private (for example, health) places all accelerated the wide diffusion of scientific and technological knowledge into society. As many detailed studies of market-oriented technological innovation have shown, the presence of potential buyers and users directly in the contexts of development influence the direction that innovative lines of research will take (Von Hippel, 1976, 1988).

New forms of knowledge production can, as they diffuse, make for ambiguous situations as older demarcation lines and boundaries become more porous or break down altogether. For example, universities can adopt 'values' from the corporate culture of industry, bringing forth an entirely new type of academic entrepreneur. Conversely, big firms adopt some of the norms of academic culture, for example when they give employees sabbaticals or provide other forms of training possibilities. On a broader level, intellectual 'property rights' have become a major issue on the campus, thereby giving new roles to the lawyers rather than committees in resolving conflicts and in regulating the conditions under which research is performed. The list of examples can be extended almost indefinitely. Through what mechanisms do such 'borrowing' or transfers of norms and practices occur, and how does each sub-system maintain its distinct identity and founding values according to which it resolves other conflicts?

The mixing of norms and values in different segments of society is part of a diffusion process which at the same time fosters further communication among them by creating a common culture and language. In addition, a variety of inter-systemic agencies or intermediary bodies establish themselves in the interstices between established institutions or their components; examples from the United States might be the Occupational and Safety and Health Administration, or the Friends of the Earth, a governmental agency and a private organisation respectively, both concerned with environmental quality, both crossing disciplinary lines and both involving public, private and scientific interests, people, resources and powers. Thus while different kinds of institutions are able to maintain their own distinctive character and functions, they continually generate new forms of communication to link them together. This partially explains the emergence of new hybrid communities, consisting of people who have been socialised in different subsystems, disciplines or working environments, but who subsequently learn different styles of thought, modes of behaviour, knowledge and social competence that originally they did not possess. Hybridisation reflects the need of different communities to speak in more than one language in order to communicate at the boundaries and in the spaces between systems and subsystems. The availability and willingness of large numbers of people to become members of such hybrid communities, however, is also due to the spilling over of scientific attitudes, (which we have loosely defined as a greater readiness to ask questions, and to seek answers through reason, and evidence and the acceptance of change in general), from universities and laboratories to society at large.

Thus, communication between research and society increasingly takes the form of diffusion processes that carry scientific and technological knowledge into society while social norms and expectations held by different institutions and communities are brought home more forcefully to the research communities. At the same time, the sites in which knowledge is created proliferate, increasing both the possibilities and the need for such diffusion. Communication becomes more dense in line with the evolution of overall societal complexity.

19. Bill Readings, *The University in Ruins*, 1996

The work of Bill Readings stands in contrast to the preceding source (I, 18), which stresses the role of science in the "new production of knowledge." Generally bypassing science, Readings argues that the very idea of knowledge "production" must be questioned. Under our domineering monitor of "Culture," vapid in its endless repetitions and now without specific content, no new knowledge, he contends, is being produced. Radical intellectual change may revive a university in its ruins. Unshackled thinkers without academic identity may engage one another in conceiving the university as only a necessary place, distinguished from "a capitalist bureaucratic-apparatus for the production, distribution, and consumption of knowledge." This locus of thinkers becomes a "dissensual community" that is not affirmed as an ideal but as a question of what being-together means.

Readings (1960–94), born in Cornwall and recipient of degrees from Balliol College, Oxford (B.A. 1981; Ph.D. 1985), taught at the University of Geneva (1984–87) and Syracuse University (1987–91) before settling in at the Université de Montreal as a professor of comparative literature. After a study of postmodernism (1993), he turned his thinking to the condition of the modern university. The resulting book was published after his death in an airplane crash. Considered by many to be a penetrating and brilliant, though often repetitious and unconventional—not to say eccentric—projection of an ideal university future drawn by a candid man of letters, the book has acquired a steadily increasing readership in academic circles.

Reprinted by permission of the publisher from *The University in Ruins* by Bill Readings, pp. 14, 15, 16–18, 19–20, 124–126, 127, 128–129, 163–165, 168, 176, 177, 178–179, 191, 192, 193, Cambridge, Mass.: Harvard University Press, Copyright © 1996 by the Estate of Bill Readings. Further reading: Stanley N. Katz, "Choosing Justice Over Excellence," *Chronicle of Higher Education,* May 17, 2002, B7–9; Michael A. Olivas, "Race, Raza, and Ruins," *Journal of College and University Law* 24 (Summer 1997): 127–29 is a law professor's retort. Jeffrey J. Williams, "The Post–Welfare State University," *American Literary History* 18 (Spring 2006): 190–216, valuably summarizes a growing critical literature on institutional control, support, and the situation of academic workers within "academic capitalism" entering the twenty-first century. See also III, 3, 8, 11.

[W]hen I speak of the "modern" University I am referring to the German model, widely copied, that Humboldt instituted at the University of Berlin and that still served for the postwar expansion of tertiary education in the West. I would argue that we are now in the twilight of this model, as the University becomes posthistorical. In this context, Allan Bloom's *The Closing of the American Mind* seems to me to be more in touch with reality than the liberal nostrums of Jaroslav Pelikan in his *The Idea of the University,* which recalls us to a lost mission of liberal education. Bloom's conservative jeremiad at least recognizes that the autonomy of knowledge as an end in itself is threatened, because there is no longer a *subject* that might incarnate this principle, hence Bloom's repeated ridiculing of much of what goes on in the University as unintelligible and irrelevant to any student (read young-white-male-American student). . . . I am inclined to agree with Bloom's conclusion that the story of what he calls "the adventure of a liberal education" no longer has a hero. Neither a student hero to embark upon it, nor a professor hero as its end. . . .

I argue that the discourse of excellence gains purchase precisely from the fact that the link between the University and the nation-state no longer holds in an era of globalization. The University thus shifts from being an ideological apparatus of the nation-state to being a relatively independent bureaucratic system. The economics of globalization mean that the University is no longer called upon to train citizen subjects, while the politics of the end of the Cold War mean that the University is no longer called upon to uphold national prestige by producing and legitimating national culture. The University is thus analogous to a number of other institutions—such as national airline carriers—that face massive reductions in foreseeable funding from increasingly weakened states, which are no longer the privileged sites of investment of popular will. . . .

The history of previous ways of understanding the function of the University can be roughly summarized by saying that the modern University has had three ideas: the Kantian concept of reason, the Humboldtian idea of culture, and now the techno-bureaucratic notion of excellence. The historical narrative that I propose (reason—culture—excellence) is not simply a sequential one, however. . . . What I want to emphasize throughout this book is that the debate on the University is made up of divergent and non-contemporaneous discourses, even if one discourse dominates over the others at certain moments. . . .

The German Idealists, from Schiller to Humboldt . . . assign a more explicitly political role to the structure determined by Kant, and they do this by replacing the notion of reason with that of culture. Like reason, culture serves a particularly *unifying* function for the University. . . . Under the rubric of culture, the University is assigned the dual task of research and teaching, respectively the production and inculcation of national self-knowledge. As such, it becomes the institution charged with watching over the spiritual life of the people of the rational state, reconciling ethnic tradition and statist rationality. The University, in other words, is identified as the institution that will give reason to the common life of the people, while preserving their traditions and avoiding the bloody, destructive example of the French Revolution. This, I argue, is the decisive role accorded to the modern University until the present. . . .

The British and Americans give a particularly *literary* turn to the German Idealists' notion of culture. In the late nineteenth and early twentieth centuries, the English, notably Newman and Arnold, carried forward the work of Humboldt and Schlegel by placing literature instead of philosophy as the central discipline of the University and hence also of national culture. . . . The study of a tradition of national literature comes to be the primary mode of teaching students what it is to be French, or English, or German. In the case of the United States, this process is regulated in terms of the study of a *canon* rather than a tradition, in exemplary republican fashion. The canon matters in the United States because the determination of the canon is taken to be the result of an exercise of republican will. The autonomous *choice* of a canon, rather than submission to the blind weight of tradition, parallels the choice of a government rather than submission to hereditary monarchy. The role of literary study in the formation of national subjects is consequently what explains the massive institutional weight accumulated by literature departments, especially through their traditional control of the University-wide "composition course" requirement in many American universities. . . .

We are now seeing a decline in national literary studies and the increasing emergence of "Cultural Studies" as the strongest disciplinary model in the humanities in the Anglo-American University. In this context, the radical claims of Cultural Studies display rather more continuity than might be expected with the redemptive claim that underpinned the literary model of culture, however much they oppose its institutional forms. I argue that the institutional success of Cultural Studies in the 1990s is owing to the fact that it preserves the structure of the literary argument, while recognizing that literature can no longer work—throwing out the baby and keeping the bathwater, as it were. Cultural Studies does not propose culture as a regulatory ideal for research and teaching, so much as seek to preserve the structure of an argument for redemption through culture, while recognizing the inability of culture to function any longer as such an idea. To put it in the cruelest terms—terms that apply only to the attempt to make Cultural Studies into a hegemonic institutional project and not to any specific work calling itself "Cultural Studies"—Cultural Studies presents a vision of culture that is appropriate for the age of excellence.

And even like "excellence" itself, "culture" no longer has a specific content. Everything, given a chance, can be or become culture. Cultural Studies thus arrives on the scene along with a certain exhaustion. The very fecundity and multiplicity of work in Cultural Studies is enabled by the fact that culture no longer functions as a specific referent to any one thing or set of things—which is why Cultural Studies can be so popular while refusing general theoretical definition. Cultural Studies, in its current incarnation as an institutional project for the 1990s, proceeds from a certain sense that no more *knowledge* can be produced, since there is nothing to be said about culture that is not itself cultural, and vice versa. Everything is culturally determined, as it were, and culture ceases to mean anything *as such*.

I will also refer to this process as "dereferentialization." By this I mean to suggest that what is crucial about terms like "culture" and "excellence" (and even "University" at times) is that they no longer have specific referents; they no longer refer to a specific set of things or ideas. In using the term "dereferentialization," however, I do not want simply to introduce another bulky piece of jargon into our vocabulary; rather my design is to give a name to what I will argue is a crucial shift in thinking that has dramatic consequences for the University. In these terms, we can say that the rise of Cultural Studies becomes possible only when culture is dereferentialized and ceases to be the principle of study in the University. In the age of Cultural Studies, culture becomes merely one object among others for the system to deal with. This polemical argument does not denounce the history of work in Cultural Studies so much as criticize attempts—however well-meaning—to make Cultural Studies into the discipline that will save the University by giving it back its lost truth. . . .

The institutional pragmatism that I call for in place of either Enlightenment faith or Romantic nostalgia leads to an investigation . . . of the way in which we can rethink the modernist claim that the University provides a model of the rational community, a microcosm of the pure form of the public sphere. This claim for an ideal community in the University still exerts its power, despite its glaring inaccuracy—evident to anyone who has ever sat on a faculty committee. I argue that we should recognize that the loss of the University's cultural function opens up a space in which it is possible to think the notion of community otherwise, without recourse to notions of unity, consensus, and communication. At this point, the University becomes no longer a model of the ideal society but rather a place where the impossibility of such models can be thought—practically thought, rather than thought under ideal conditions. Here the University loses its privileged status as the model of society and does not regain it by becoming the model of the absence of models. Rather, the University becomes one site among others where *the question of being-together is raised*, raised with an urgency that proceeds from the absence of the institutional forms (such as the nation-state), which have historically served to mask that question for the past three centuries or so.

So what is the point of the University, if we realize that we are no longer to strive to realize a national identity, be it an ethnic essence or a republican will? In asking such a question I am not suggesting that I want to blow up the University, or even to resign from my job. I am neither pessimistic nor optimistic, since I do not think that the temporality implied by such terms is appropriate. . . . We need no new identity for the University, not even the supplement will save us. Rather we need to recognize that the dereferentialization of the University's function opens a space in which we can think the notions of community and communication differently.

A resistance to the technocratic University that does not ground itself in a pious claim to know the true referent of the University, the one that will redeem it, is difficult to characterize. The vast majority of those who speak about the University adopt one of two positions: either nostalgic calls for a return to the Humboldtian ideals of modular community and social functioning, or technocratic demands that the University embrace its corporate identity and become more productive, more efficient. Merely disdaining appeals to "excellence" will not do. The contemporary geopolitical situation

seems to me to disbar any thought of return to the levels of state funding that characterized the Western University during the Cold War, when culture (in both the human and the natural sciences) was a field of superpower competition. The ensuing economic pressures mean that we cannot hope to expand toward a fuller realization of the Humboldtian ideal, even if the narrative of national culture still had a subject that could act as its referent.

The challenge of the present conjuncture is a difficult one, but I do not think that what is required of us is the building of a better institution, the production of another model of efficiency, another unified and unifying project. Being smart in the present situation requires another kind of thinking altogether, one that does not seek to lend work in the University a unified ideological function. . . . The University has to find a new language in which to make a claim for its role as a locus of higher education—a role which nothing in history says is an inevitably necessary one.

The three functions that are still invoked in the contemporary University are *research, teaching,* and *administration*. The last of these is, of course, the most rapidly expanding field in terms of the allocation of resources, and, as I have argued, its expansion is symptomatic of the breakdown of the German Idealist contract between research and teaching. Indeed, I would be inclined to argue that the University of Excellence is one in which a general principle of administration replaces the dialectic of teaching and research, so that teaching and research, as aspects of professional life, are subsumed under administration.

A great deal of the current attack on the University claims that a too-exclusive focus on research is harming teaching. For the humanities this complaint is as old as the modern University. However, the terms of its contemporary resurgence are, I have suggested, different in that the complaint is symptomatic of a more fundamental breakdown: the breakdown of the metanarrative that centers the University around the production of a national subject. The University no longer has a hero for its grand narrative, and a retreat into "professionalization" has been the consequence. Professionalization deals with the loss of the subject-referent of the educational experience by integrating teaching and research as aspects of the general administration of a closed system: teaching is the administration of students by professors; research is the administration of professors by their peers; administration is the name given to the stratum of bureaucrats who administer the whole. In each case, administration involves the processing and evaluation of information according to criteria of excellence that are internal to the system: the value of research depends on what colleagues think of it; the value of teaching depends upon the grades professors give and the evaluations the students make; the value of administration depends upon the ranking of a University among its peers. Significantly, the synthesizing evaluation takes place at the level of administration. . . .

Now that we can no longer make a redemptive claim for research, can no longer believe that the imagined community of scholars mirrors in microcosm the potential community of the nation-state, we have to think how to reimagine the notion of community itself. Hence I shall argue that, far from community being the locus of unity and identity, the question of the proximity of thinkers in the University should be understood in terms of a *dissensual community* that has relinquished the regulatory ideal of communicational transparency, which has abandoned the notion of identity or unity. I shall attempt to sketch an account of the production and circulation of knowledges that imagines *thinking without identity,* that refigures the University as a locus of dissensus. In these terms, the University becomes one place among others where the question of being-together is posed, rather than an ideal community. My call is for a more radical and uncomfortable dissensus even than that proposed by Gerald Graff's call to "teach the conflicts." For behind Graff's laudable desire to displace the monologic authority of disciplinary discourse lies a desire for final consensus, the consensus that would permit the determination and transmission of "the conflict" as a unified object of professorial discourse. . . .

It is with regard to the *institution* that I think we need most urgently to rethink the terms within which we address the function of the University. In particular, the recognition that the University as we know it is a historically specific institution, is one with which academics have a hard time coming to terms. History grants no essential or eternal role to the modern research University, and it is necessary to contemplate the horizon of the disappearance of that University. Not to embrace the prospect of its vanishing, but to take seriously the possibility that the University, as presently constituted, holds no lien on the future. . . . Rather than offering new pious dreams of salvation, a new unifying idea, or a new meaning for the University, I will call for an institutional pragmatism. This pragmatism recognizes that thought begins where we are and does away with alibis. By thinking without alibis, I mean ceasing to justify our practices in the name of an idea from "elsewhere," an idea that would release us from responsibility for our immediate actions. Neither reason, nor culture. Neither excellence, nor an appeal to a transcendence that our actions struggle to realize, trying as we may to justify our deeds and absolve ourselves.

Such a pragmatism, I shall argue, requires that we accept that the modern University is a *ruined* institution. Those ruins must not be the object of a romantic nostalgia for a lost wholeness but the site of an attempt to transvalue the fact that the University no longer inhabits a continuous history of progress, of the progressive revelation of a unifying idea. Dwelling in the ruins of the University thus means giving a serious attention to the present complexity of its space, undertaking an endless work of *détournement* of the spaces willed to us by a history whose temporality we no longer inhabit. Like the inhabitants of some Italian city, we can seek neither to rebuild the Renaissance city-state nor to destroy its remnants and install rationally planned tower-blocks; we can seek only to put its angularities and winding passages to new uses, learning from and enjoying the cognitive dissonances that enclosed piazzas and non-signifying *campanile* induce. . . .

The question of the University cannot be answered by a program of reform that either produces knowledge more efficiently or produces more efficient knowledge. Rather, the analogy of production itself must be brought into question: the analogy that makes the University into a bureaucratic apparatus for the production, distribution, and consumption of knowledge. For what is at stake here is the extent to which the University *as an institution* participates in the capitalist-bureaucratic system. It seems to me dishonest to pretend that it does not. The University as an institution can deal with all kinds of knowledges, even oppositional ones, so as to make them circulate to the benefit of the system as a whole. This is something we know very well: radicalism sells well in the University marketplace. Hence the futility of the radicalism that calls for a University that will produce more radical kinds of knowledge, more radical students, more of anything. Such appeals, because they do not take into account the institutional status of the University as a capitalist bureaucracy, are doomed to confirm the very system they oppose. The ideological content of the knowledges produced in the University is increasingly indifferent to its functioning as a bureaucratic enterprise; the only proviso is that such radical knowledges fit into the cycle of production, exchange, and consumption. Produce what knowledge you like, only produce more of it, so that the system can speculate on knowledge differentials, can profit from the accumulation of intellectual capital. . . .

My argument is that the University is developing toward the status of a transnational corporation. To recognize the transnational framework within which the question of the University is posed is to have to acknowledge that teaching cannot be understood either as structurally independent of a generalized system of exchange or as exhaustively contained within any one closed system of exchange. This, it seems to me, is the situation in which we find ourselves now, one of both limitation and openness. We are more free than we used to be in our teaching, but we can no longer see what it is that our freedom is freedom from. How can we raise the question of accountability without always already giving in to the logic of accounting? In some sense, we cannot. People have to be paid, get scholarships, etc. The question, then, is how we can raise the question of accountability as something that *exceeds* the logic of accounting. The exponential growth in the commodification of information itself, thanks to new technologies, renders the current situation even more acute.

If pedagogy is to pose a challenge to the ever-increasing bureaucratization of the University as a whole, it will need to decenter our vision of the educational process, not merely adopt an oppositional stance in teaching. Only in this way can we hope to open up pedagogy, to lend it a temporality that resists commodification, by arguing that *listening to Thought* is not the spending of time in the production of an autonomous subject (even an oppositional one) or of an autonomous body of knowledge. Rather, to listen to Thought, to think beside each other and beside ourselves, is to explore an open network of obligations that keeps the question of meaning open as a locus of debate. Doing justice to Thought, listening to our interlocutors, means trying to hear that which cannot be said but that which tries to make itself heard. And this is a process incompatible with the production of (even relatively) stable and exchangeable knowledge. Exploring the question of value means recognizing that there exists no homogeneous standard of value that might unite all poles of the pedagogical scene so as to produce a single scale of evaluation. . . .

Institutional pragmatism . . . means, for me, recognizing the University today for what it is: an institution that is losing its need to make transcendental claims for its function. The University is no longer simply modern, insofar as it no longer needs a grand narrative of culture in order to work. As a bureaucratic institution of excellence, it can incorporate a very high degree of internal variety without requiring its multiplicity of diverse idioms to be unified into an ideological whole. Their unification is no longer a matter of ideology but of their exchange-value within an expanded market. Administering conflict thus does not mean resolving it, as one might take the example of the Cold War to have demonstrated. The non-ideological role of the University deprives disruption of any claim to automatic radicalism, just as it renders radical claims for a new unity susceptible to being swallowed up by the empty unity of excellence. . . .

What I am calling for . . . is not a generalized interdisciplinary space but a certain rhythm of disciplinary attachment and detachment, which is designed so as not to let the question of disciplinarity disappear, sink into routine. Rather, disciplinary structures would be forced to answer to the name of Thought, to imagine what kinds of thinking they make possible, and what kinds of thinking they exclude. It is perhaps a lesson of structuralism that, when faced with a disciplinary project, a crucial way of situating that project is by considering what it is *not*, what it excludes. Thus a concentration in European philosophy, for example, would be obliged—by the nature of the interruptive pattern that I

propose—to address both non-European philosophy and European non-philosophy. . . .

I propose an abandonment of disciplinary grounding but an abandonment that retains as structurally essential the *question of the disciplinary form that can be given to knowledges.* This is why the University should not exchange the rigid and outmoded disciplines for a simply amorphous interdisciplinary space in the humanities (as if we could still organize knowledge around the figure of "Man"). Rather, the loosening of disciplinary structures has to be made the opportunity for the installation of disciplinarity as a *permanent question.* The short-term projects I suggest are designed to keep open the question of what it means to group knowledges in certain ways, and what it has meant that they have been so grouped in the past. This keeps open the question of disciplinarity at the heart of any proposal for the grouping of knowledges in a constellation such as "Modern Art History" or "African-American Literature." Only by being constrained periodically to reinvent themselves can such groupings remain attentive to the terms of their production and reproduction. . . .

Given the prospect of such a generalized disciplinary regroupment, it seems to me necessary that we engage in a consideration of how the University might function as a place where a community of thinkers dwell, with the proviso that we rethink critically the notion of community, so as to detach it from both the organicist tradition and the feudal corporation. On this basis, it may become possible to provide some hints as to the kinds of institutional politics that might be pursued in order to transvalue the process of dereferentialization, to make the destruction of existing cultural forms by the encroachment of the open market into an opportunity for Thought rather than an occasion for denunciation or mourning. . . .

In a global economy, the University can no longer be called upon to provide a model of community, an intellectual Levittown. And the appeal to the University as a model of community no longer serves as the *answer* to the question of the social function of the University. Rather, the University will have to become one place, among others, where the attempt is made to think the social bond without recourse to a unifying idea, whether of culture or of the state. In the University, thought goes on alongside other thoughts. But do we think together? Is our thinking integrated into a unity? There is no property in thought, no proper identity, no subjective ownership. Neither Kant's *concordia discors,* nor Humboldt's organic idea, nor Habermas's consensual community can integrate or unify thinking. Working out the question of how thoughts stand beside other thoughts is, I believe, an act which can push the impulse of Cultural Studies beyond the work of mourning for a lost idea of culture that needs political renewal.

Such is the force of my suggestions concerning

disciplinarity. Instead of a new interdisciplinary space that will once and for all reunify the University, I have attempted to propose a shifting disciplinary structure that holds open the question of whether and how thoughts fit together. This question is not merely worthy of study; it is the massive challenge that faces us. An order of knowledge and an institutional structure are now breaking down, and in their place comes the discourse of excellence that tells teachers and students simply not to worry about how things fit together, since that is not their problem. All they have to do is get on with doing what they always have done, and the general question of integration will be resolved by the administration with the help of grids that chart the achievement of goals and tabulate efficiency. . . .

The problem that students and teachers face is thus not so much the problem of what to believe as the problem of what kind of analysis of institutions will allow any belief to count for anything at all. What kind of belief will not simply become fodder for evaluation in terms of excellence? At the same time, the very openness to activity that the process of dereferentialization fosters in the University of Excellence allows considerable room for maneuver, provided that students and teachers are ready to abandon nostalgia and try to move in ways that keep questions open.

The thought of community that abandons either expressive identity or transactional consensus as means to unity seems to me to refer to what the posthistorical University may be. . . .

Such a thought as I am proposing . . . does not mean the abandonment of social responsibility. Real responsibility, ethical probity, is simply not commensurate with the grand narrative of nationalism that has up to now underpinned accounts of the social action of University research and teaching. The abandonment of that legitimating metanarrative is a frightening prospect, but it seems to me that it is inevitable. Such an abandonment will occur gradually without us, if we ignore it. Hence I suggest we pay attention to the prospect of this dereferentialization that will make the preservation of the activity of thinking considerably more difficult. That a major shift in the role and function of the intellectual is occurring is clear. What it will come to have meant is an issue upon which those in the University should attempt to have an impact. An attention to this problematic is necessary. How we pay attention to it is not determined. Therein lies both the freedom and the enormous responsibility of Thought at the end of the twentieth century, which is also the end of what has been the epoch of the nation-state.

20. The University of Phoenix, Inc., 1999

The University of Phoenix is a leading example of the rapid expansion of for-profit institutions of higher education. Relying upon part-time faculties and new digital technologies in teaching, sometimes online, sometimes in classrooms, they have attracted students with vocational ambitions in new fields related to these new technologies, but established fields, like accounting, and new quasi-professional lifestyle oriented careers as well. Some even train in technical fields, including engineering. Reprinted here is an announcement from the University of Phoenix, a part of the Apollo Group.

The documents reproduced here were found at the Apollo Group website, www.apollogrp.edu, and later subjected to revisions. This copyrighted material used by permission of Apollo Group, Inc. 2005. All rights reserved. Further reading: Ted Marchese, "Not-So-Distant Competitors: How New Providers Are Remaking the Postsecondary Marketplace," AAHE *Bulletin* 50 (May 1998): 3–7; James Traub, "Drive-Thru U: Higher Education for People Who Mean Business," *New Yorker*, October 20, 1997; and I, 21.

MISSION

The University of Phoenix is a private, for-profit higher education institution whose mission is to provide high quality education to working adult students. The University identifies educational needs and provides, through innovative methods, including distance education technologies, educational access to working adults regardless of their geographical location. The University provides general education and professional programs that prepare students to articulate and advance their personal and professional goals. The University's educational philosophy and operational structure embody participative, collaborative, and applied problem-solving strategies that are facilitated by a faculty whose advanced academic preparation and professional experience help integrate academic theory with current practical application. The University assesses both the effectiveness of its academic offerings and the academic achievement of its students, and utilizes the results of these assessments to improve academic and institutional quality.

PURPOSES

To facilitate cognitive and affective student learning—knowledge, skills, and values—and to promote use of that knowledge in the student's work place.

To develop competence in communication, critical thinking, collaboration, and information utilization, together with a commitment to lifelong learning for enhancement of students' opportunities for career success.

To provide instruction that bridges the gap between theory and practice through faculty members who bring to their classrooms not only advanced academic preparation, but also the skills that come from the current practice of their professions.

To use technology to create effective modes and means of instruction that expand access to learning resources and that enhance collaboration and communication for improved student learning.

To assess student learning and use assessment data to improve the teaching/learning system, curriculum, instruction, learning resources, counseling and student services.

To be organized as a for-profit institution in order to foster a spirit of innovation that focuses on providing academic quality, service excellence, and convenience to the working adult.

To generate the financial resources necessary to support the University's mission.

Apollo Group, Inc., through its subsidiaries, the University of Phoenix, Inc., the Institute for Professional Development, the College for Financial Planning Institutes Corporation and Western International University, Inc., is a leading provider of higher education programs for working adults.

UNIVERSITY OF PHOENIX, INC.

The University of Phoenix became the first accredited for-profit university in the United States with the sole mission of identifying and meeting the educational needs of working adult students. The University has been accredited by the North Central Association of Colleges and Schools (NCA) since 1978.

Beginning with a class of 8 working adults in 1976, University of Phoenix currently enrolls over 61,500 degree seeking adult students at its 81 campuses and learning centers. The University of Phoenix is one of the four largest regionally accredited private university [sic] in the United States—with locations in Arizona, California, Colorado, Florida, Hawaii, Louisiana, Michigan, Maryland, Nevada, New Mexico, Oklahoma, Oregon, Utah, Washington, Puerto Rico and Vancouver, Canada. The University of Phoenix also offers its degree programs through its online services.

For a listing of the degree programs offered at the University of Phoenix, please check out their catalog online.

THE INSTITUTE FOR PROFESSIONAL DEVELOPMENT, INC.

The Institute for Professional Development, established in 1973, assists private small to medium-sized accredited colleges and universities in providing specially designed programs for working adults. IPD's higher education management consulting services enable traditional colleges to establish viable and profitable programs serving working adults.

IPD currently provides these services to 20 regionally accredited private colleges and universities at 47 campuses and learning centers in 22 states including Connecticut, Delaware, Georgia, Illinois, Indiana, Iowa, Kansas, Kentucky, Massachusetts, Michigan, Minnesota, Mississippi, Missouri, New Jersey, New York, North Carolina, Ohio, South Carolina, Tennessee, Texas, Virginia, and Wisconsin.

IPD-affiliated institutions offer associates, bachelors and masters degree programs as well as a limited number of general education courses, certificate programs and areas of specialization.

COLLEGE FOR FINANCIAL PLANNING INSTITUTES CORPORATION

The College for Financial Planning® Institutes Corporation is the largest U.S. provider of financial planning education, including the Certified Financial Planner Professional Education Program. For more than 26 years, the College for Financial Planning has been a leader in educating financial service professionals. Today, its over 75,000 graduates continue to excel in their profession and are consistently cited as some of the best advisors in the country.

The College's course work is primarily offered as independent self-study, through both paper-based coursework and interactive, Internet-based courses. Many courses are also offered in a classroom setting through affiliate institutions, including the University of Phoenix. The College utilizes an Internet-based testing process (Exam on Demand) which provides students with immediate feedback on their final exams and access to testing in more than 900 locations around the United States.

The College for Financial Planning offerings encompass individual courses and programs in insurance, investments, tax, retirement and estate planning including the following degree and non-degree programs:

- Certified Financial Planner® Professional Education Program
- Master of Science Degree Program with emphasis in Financial Planning
- Accredited Tax Advisor® Program
- Accredited Asset Management Specialist® Program
- Chartered Mutual Fund Counselor® Program
- Financial Paraplanner Program®
- Chartered Retirement Plans Specialists℠ Program
- Chartered Retirement Planning Counselors℠ Program
- Chartered Financial Analyst Study/Review Program

Additional educational offerings include:

- 160 continuing education courses in numerous disciplines
- Chartered Financial Analyst® Level I and Level II Study Materials
- Internet Review for the Chartered Financial Analyst® Level I Examination
- Internet Review for the Certified Financial Planner® Certification Examination

Consistent with its goal of providing quality, innovative, and accessible educational opportunities to financial services professionals, the College offers web-based Continuing Professional Education through CPEInternet℠. In addition to the College's paper-based and audiocassette courses, CPEInternet offers more than 90 interactive courses, including courses on current topics in taxation, accounting, investments, retirement planning, and computer applications.

WESTERN INTERNATIONAL UNIVERSITY, INC.

Western International University was founded in 1978 and was recently acquired by Apollo Group, Inc. on September 1, 1995. While the majority of WIU's students are working adults, they also have a large portion of students who come from more than 40 different countries to learn English as a Second Language and continue on to pursue a degree in higher education. WIU's mission is to provide the educational foundation needed to prepare their students to achieve their full potential in a dynamic and complex global marketplace. WIU is accredited by the NCA.

ABOUT THE ONLINE PROGRAM

Online computer-mediated education was an outgrowth of the technological transformation of the work place and a response to the increasing use of computers and modems for communication. The University of Phoenix Online was formed in 1989 and currently enrolls degree-seeking adult students from all over the U.S. and the world. It is a group-based learning environment offering the kind of interaction and support which take place in a traditional face-to-face seminar-style classroom.

The University of Phoenix Online offers you the unparalleled convenience and flexibility of attending classes from your personal computer. In small groups of eight to thirteen, or working one-on-one with an instructor, students are discussing issues, sharing ideas, testing theories—essentially enjoying all of the advantages of an on-campus degree program, with one important exception. No commute!

21. Richard S. Ruch, *Higher Ed, Inc.*, 2001

College and university people who clung to the ideal of the liberal arts as an exposure to creative idea and critical thinking were challenged by the sudden appearance of for-profit schools. Sometimes overlooked by established academics, however, was the tradition of technical and applied schooling in the American past. Technical vocation skills were widely taught in the small American colonial seaboard cities; their memorable advocate was Benjamin Franklin. In the nineteenth century, mechanics' institutes, evening trade schools, workingmen's library associations, and college parallel or "scientific" curricula rose to meet the economic needs and hopes of working people. In the first half of the twentieth century, business, secretarial, proprietary commercial schools, and correspondence schools came to be familiar in the educational landscape. The birth and proliferation of education for and from the electronic computer age in the 1970s was a continuing part of this story.

The first author of a book that weighed the advantages of for-profit and nonprofit institutions was Richard S. Ruch (1949–). He had served in high administrative capacities in both kinds of institutions.

Ruch, Richard S. *Higher Ed. Inc., The Rise of the For-Profit University*, pp. 28, 46–49, 111–12, 115, 118, 138–39, 147–48. © 2001. Reprinted with the kind permission of The Johns Hopkins University Press. Further reading: a chronicle of independent or proprietary technical schooling is woven throughout Lawrence A. Cremin's monumental *American Education: The Colonial Experience, 1607–1783* (New York, 1970) and *American Education: The National Experience, 1783–1876* (New York, 1980). The fluctuating securities values of the for-profit institutions are regularly printed in the *Chronicle of Higher Education*. See also I, 20.

The phenomenal growth of the largest of the nation's private universities (whether non-profit or for-profit) is almost impossible to ignore. Attempts to dismiss the University of Phoenix as a kind of error, perhaps the academic equivalent of a stock-market correction (as the provost of a large state university recently suggested to me), are too often based on a combination of misinformation and wishful thinking.

The sheer size of the enterprise alone is intimidating, with an enrollment of more than 100,000 students whose average age is 35 and whose average annual income is $56,000. Nearly two-thirds of its students are women. The Apollo Group, the publicly traded holding company that owns the University of Phoenix, has grown so vigorously that even the Internet investment sites have not kept up with the business expansion. One hundred thousand students is nothing to sniff at and cannot be written off as simply a large case of misinformed student consumers. Clearly, the University of Phoenix appeals to adult working professionals who have reached a certain level of success in their careers and are probably fairly savvy educational consumers. Referring to the notion held by some accreditors and state licensing agencies that adult student consumers actually need several layers of regulatory protection against unscrupulous colleges and universities, John G. Sperling, the founder and CEO of Apollo, says, "They also believe that consumers of educational services—even intelligent, well-educated adults—cannot adequately judge the value of the services they receive."

It is difficult not to interpret Phoenix's aggressive growth and continued expansion as a threat to traditional higher education, and yet it is too easy to dismiss the Phoenix phenomenon as "Drive-Thru U" and "McEducation." The essential threat is not so much that Phoenix is taking away market share, for when a Phoenix campus enters a local market, it tends to generate additional enrollment gains in neighboring community colleges and general education programs. What is threatening about the University of Phoenix is that it represents radical change in higher education.

"Phoenix heralds a potential revolution in higher education," says Arthur Levine, president of Teachers College at Columbia University. Sperling, Phoenix's irascible founder and CEO, is often portrayed as the Clint Eastwood of higher education (armed with a Ph.D. from Cambridge University), arriving in town during the night, daring you to meet

Profiles of Five For-Profit Players

Name	Founded, IPO	Core Institutions	Campuses	Enrollment	Programs	Accreditation
Apollo Group, Inc. Phoenix, Ariz. (NASDAQ: APOL)	1976, 1994	University of Phoenix Institute for Professional Development Western International University College for Financial Planning	137 in United States and Puerto Rico	100,000	Diploma through master's	North Central plus other professional
Argosy Education Group Chicago, Ill. (NASDAQ: AEGY)	1975, 1999	American Schools of Professional Psychology University of Sarasota John Marshall Law School Prime-Tech Institute Ventura Group	17 in 7 states	5,000	Mainly doctorate and master's, also others	North Central, American Psychological Association
DeVry, Inc. Chicago, Ill. (NYSE: DV)	1931, 1991	DeVry Institutes of Technology Keller Graduate Schools of Management Denver Technical College Becker Conviser CPA Review	19 campuses in 10 states and Canada; 30 Keller sites	50,000	Certificate through master's	North Central, Accreditation Board for Engineering Technology
Education Management Corporation Pittsburgh, Pa. (NASDAQ: EDMC)	1962, 1996	Art Institutes International New York Restaurant School National Center for Paralegal Training	20 in 17 cities	20,000	Certificate through bachelor's	North Central, New England, Southern Association
Strayer Education, Inc. Washington, D.C. (NASDAQ: STRA)	1982, 1996	Strayer University	12 in 3 states	12,500	Associate through master's	Middle States

him in the street at noon to make his day. Indeed, unlike DeVry, Strayer, Argosy, and Education Management, which are quite content to inquire of accrediting bodies and state licensing agencies, "Tell us what the rules are and we will play by them," the Phoenix approach has been more like, "The rules have changed and you need to wake up." By sheer force of will, business acumen, and a ready multitude of students, the University of Phoenix has apparently ushered in a new era in American higher education.

The Phoenix story is essentially one of aggressive growth brought about by giving the education marketplace what it wants and then continuing to push the edges of that growth by harnessing the resources of a well-capitalized corporation. There are any number of ways to measure Phoenix's growth—enrollments, campus locations, revenue, assessment of outcomes, return to stockholders—and all of them show impressive results. . . .

The public academic voice of the University of Phoenix is Jorge de Alva, the university's president. De Alva is an erudite scholar and consummate debater who, after achieving the rank of full processor in anthropology at Princeton, followed by an en-

dowed chair at Berkeley, has now made the University of Phoenix the focus of his intellectual passion. De Alva was successful in terms of all of the standard measures academic success—NEH and NSF grants, a Guggenheim Fellowship, a Getty Scholarship, a Fulbright Scholarship, and 24 scholarly books—and it is difficult to dismiss him as a businessman who does not understand academia.

"If you look at the history of higher education in the West," he says, "it began pretty much as a for-profit affair. In fact, the University of Phoenix's roots are not outside of the academy, any more than Protestantism is outside of traditional Christianity." To the question whether the University of Phoenix is serving society or merely generating profits, De Alva replies, "We are educating tens of thousands of students at no taxpayer's expense and returning a significant portion of our revenues back into the economy for other uses." By "returning a significant portion of revenues" he is referring to the for-profit providers' payment of income taxes at the rate of approximately 40 percent earnings before taxes, through which they return more to the public treasury than they receive in the form of federally insured loan subsidies for their students.

The Phoenix phenomenon follows a simple and powerful logic, aligned with ideals less familiar to non-profit higher education than to the world of commerce and the market economy. Jorge de Alva explains it this way: "We seek to increase the productivity of individual students, who in turn increase the productivity of companies, which in turn increase the productivity of regions, which ultimately generates no small part of the tax base that helps people give to the endowments of non-profit universities." . . .

At the level of the classroom, however, for-profit universities have the ethos of typical academic institutions. If you woke up and found yourself in a classroom at a for-profit university, you would probably not be able to tell the difference between it and a typical college classroom. There would be nothing particularly unusual about the setting, the physical space, or the behavior of students and faculty. Many of the for-profits, especially those with degree programs that focus on high-technology fields such as telecommunications, information systems, electronics, and health care, annually invest significant resources in instructional technology, so you might notice more and newer computer equipment in the classrooms and laboratories. Nevertheless, even this would not be very different from the situation at a well-funded public university or private college. If the class you woke up in was a general education course, say, introduction to psychology, you would not be able to tell any difference between it and a similar course taught at other colleges.

If anything else struck you about the classroom, it might be that the room itself is tidier than many typical college classrooms. The chairs and tables would be in neat rows, with little or no trash lying around. If you looked out the window of your classroom, you would see that the grounds, though small, and the parking areas, though large, are clean and well maintained. At for-profit colleges the lawns will always be mowed, the snow always plowed (or the palm fronds trimmed), and the restrooms always cleaned, for it is part of corporate culture to do so. Because they are businesses in a service industry, most of the for-profits pay great attention to facilities maintenance, grounds, and housekeeping. Even if faced with revenue losses, most of the for-profit companies would probably not compromise facilities and maintenance.

If you woke up and found yourself in a for-profit faculty meeting, you might notice some differences. Nearly all the faculty would be in attendance, and they would arrive on time. They would probably know one another because they probably work in the same building, and while there would be a few new faces in the crowd, there would be many familiar faces. Typically, more than half of the faculty would have been employed there full time for five years or more, and half of them for ten or more years.

Faculty colleagues at the for-profit campus might appear to be somewhat more polite and reserved in their interactions with one another and with administrators than those at traditional universities. Without a system of tenure, and teaching in a work environment in which annual reviews are performance-based, faculty in the for-profits are at-will employees like everyone else. Faculty have no special job protection beyond that of other nonexempt employees, and they serve "at the will" of their employer. While there is a system of faculty rank from instructor to full professor (some for-profits add the fifth rank of senior professor), senior faculty generally do not evaluate the work of junior faculty for purposes of promotion. Faculty rank, therefore, tends to have less influence on relationships between colleagues in the for-profit environment.

The curriculum is managed centrally by professional curriculum specialists, so the faculty here engage in fewer ideological debates about the curriculum, the number of credit hours required in their fields as opposed to others, and the direction of the college's curriculum development. Still, you would witness lively conversation about subject matter and students and hear passionately held opinions about teaching methods. Conversation about teaching would probably reflect a fairly sophisticated level of thought about what it means to be a teacher, how to manage a classroom, and how to reach today's students. Most of the for-profit faculty would be teaching three or four courses a term, and some would be teaching one or two lab sections in addition. The standard teaching load for full-time faculty at most for-profits is equivalent to 12 hours at a traditional university, with some faculty teaching up to 15 hours a semester and some as few as six. Some faculty are given reductions in teaching load for performing administrative work, curriculum development projects, and completion of Ph.D. dissertations. Most faculty teach four days a week. The pace is typically rather incessant, however, with classes running year round . . .

In general, . . . the non-profit dean is an advocate, a strategist, and a politician, while the for-profit dean is an academic manager who is caught in the middle of the dynamic tension between the business and academic sides of the enterprise.

As a chief academic officer at a for-profit college, I often feel caught in this tension—some would call it conflict—myself. Like all academic leaders, I am expected to articulate and defend the values of teaching, learning, and, to a lesser extent, scholarly inquiry. I am the head cheerleader for high academic standards and excellence in teaching. I am expected to notice and encourage creativity and innovation in the classroom. In addition, I am the business manager who is held accountable for results, including making the numbers on such things as continuous improvement in student retention and completion rates, along with meeting targets for average class sizes and even ensuring reasonably consistent grade distributions among faculty members teaching the same courses. I am expected to develop accurate forecasts for several key performance indicators and report regularly on performance against goals. When push comes to shove, I need to deliver results like any manager in a business organization. If I do not, it will be reflected as poor performance in my annual performance review.

One of the peculiar challenges of working in this kind of for-profit environment, especially for those who, like me, come from traditional academic cultures, is that the senior managers, notably the institution presidents and those to whom they report, are basically operational managers and not academic leaders, This is especially the case in publicly traded companies that own and operate multiple campuses. Their first accountability is managing the bottom line, the primary number being the gross profit margin. At the corporate level, the regional vice presidents and other senior executives are business people, not academic types.

As a result, the academic voice at the top of these companies is silent, or at best a whisper. This is not unlike the relationship between many traditional colleges and universities and their boards of trustees, which are, for the most part, made up of business people who themselves lack a context for appreciating cumbersome academic decision-making processes and what they sometimes perceive as academic whining. The difference, I think, is that trustees can be managed, or at least to some extent intimidated, controlled, or otherwise humored. However, when the bosses are business people who do not have a Ph.D. and who bring a pragmatic and straightforward approach to supervising the work of professional teachers and scholars, it changes the nature of academic conversation within the institution. . . .

A discussion about effective teaching, for example, is basically reduced to a conversation about grade distributions, failure rates, withdrawal rates, and student progression to the next-level course, rather than, say, a conversation about teaching people to think critically. . . .

Both non-profits and for-profits care about both academic quality and a healthy bottom line. The difference is that the for-profits change the center of gravity by radically shifting the balance between academics and business in favor of sound business practices. The for-profit president is first and foremost a business executive, expected to exercise managerial control over all operations and make day-to-day decisions.

The faculty in the for-profits are the center of the academic life of the organization, but they do not run the institution or even hold most of the power. They are the skilled workhorses in the for-profit system. They teach the curriculum assigned to them. They participate in curriculum development, but they do not make the final decisions regarding the curriculum. Nor are they directly involved in the recruitment and admission of students, as these functions are handled entirely by professionals trained in marketing and sales.

In a real sense, faculty in the for-profits are viewed by the business side as being delivery people, as in delivery of the curriculum. The delivery mode in almost all the for-profit universities is classroom-based, with distance learning being a small part of the operation. At the University of Phoenix, which many people mistakenly think is an online institution, fewer than 7 percent of the 100,000 students are pursuing their degrees via distance learning. Similarly, at DeVry, Education Management, Strayer, and most others, distance learning is used only to supplement instruction in the accelerated and weekend programs, in which the bulk of instruction still occurs in the classroom. The perception within the for-profits of faculty as delivery people is built primarily upon the traditional model of classroom-based instruction. . . .

Higher education in America, from the classical colleges to the mechanical arts schools, and from the land-grant universities to the correspondence schools, is the product of both tradition and the imperative of contemporary market demands. Many traditional colleges have continued to emphasize the protection of tradition over the response to market demands. The for-profit providers pay homage to academic tradition, and indeed they must do so to gain regional association accreditation, but they place a higher value on meeting market demands. There is room for both of these purveyors of higher education, and although the distinction between them is blurring, both approaches can be carried out with integrity. . . .

But what about the intellectual center of an institution like the University of Phoenix, which employs part-time faculty almost exclusively? Can there be an intellectual center at an institution where nearly all the faculty are "adjuncts"? Jorge de Alva, Phoenix's president, recently addressed this question at a meeting of the Council for Higher Education Accreditation. He drew an interesting distinction: "To me," he said, "the fundamental difference is not between full-time and part-time faculty, but rather between practitioner faculty and self-employed faculty." Phoenix does not refer to its faculty as "adjuncts" because they are not "adjunctive" but are rather the instructional centerpiece of the institution. A condition of employment as a faculty member at Phoenix is full-time engagement as a practitioner in the field being taught. Phoenix's founder and CEO, John Sperling, puts it this way: "If you don't do it by day, you can't teach it at night."

De Alva, reflecting on his years as a tenured professor at Princeton and as the holder of an endowed chair at Berkeley, says: "The full-time faculty of many traditional institutions are essentially self-employed, independent agents, who are expected to advance their careers and bring acclaim to their institutions through scholarly publications, grants, fellowships, and prizes." Operating under such expectations, argues De Alva, these faculty are often absent from their campuses, absent from the classroom, and absent from direct involvement in governance, and they are therefore contributing not so much to the institution's intellectual center as to their own careers and to the advancement of knowledge in the disciplines. He suggests that Phoenix's faculty are actually more present and engaged than the full-time faculty at many traditional universities and therefore more able to contribute to the institution's intellectual center.

Whatever our conclusions about the intellectual center of the University of Phoenix (and the other for-profit providers), we must ask whether it matters at all to most undergraduate students. One suspects that it does not.

22. William Durden, "Liberal Arts for All," 2001

William Durden (1949–) was well positioned to compare the educational advantages of the growing distance-learning and for-profit companies with residential liberal arts colleges. He was president of Sylvan Academy and Sylvan Learning Systems, Inc., before assuming the presidency of Dickinson College, where he had graduated in 1971 as the first in his family to attend college. His doctorate was earned at Johns Hopkins in German language and literature.

William G. Durden, "Liberal Arts for All, Not Just the Rich," *Chronicle of Higher Education*, October 19, 2001, B20. Reprinted with the kind permission of William Durden, president of Dickinson College. Further reading: I, 21.

For years, many of our country's most wealthy and privileged families have ignored shifting educational fashions and continued to send their children to high-quality residential colleges and universities for a liberal-arts education. They are well aware of the many lifelong benefits of such an education. For example, an estimated 40 percent of the Fortune 500 chief executive officers in 2000 graduated from a liberal-arts college or received a degree with a liberal-arts major.

Yet every time poor, minority, immigrant, first-generation, or otherwise disadvantaged college students in the United States stand to benefit from a liberal-arts education, the rules of the game change. Education is suddenly redefined. The liberal arts are devalued, and "modern" educational theories—usually anti-intellectual, practical, student-centered, and vocational—are trumpeted.

The outcome has been clear. The rich have remained rich and powerful. And the poor have remained poor and disenfranchised because they have been diverted, yet again, from obtaining the type of education that has served as one of the primary avenues to leadership and power for generations.

The latest educational fad is distance learning, arriving just as the proportion of black and Hispanic college-aged youths in the general population

is predicted to rise substantially, yet their share of the college population will be much less. If we are not careful, many disadvantaged students will, once more, lose access to substantive leadership opportunities.

Why does a traditional liberal education foster leadership? People are "affinity beings" who possess an innate desire to learn among other people in the most comprehensive sense: to see them, hear them, exchange ideas, share food and drink, even to have sufficient stimuli to fantasize about them. The "24/7" nature of a residential liberal-arts institution forces the inevitability of learning through social interaction. Students are addressed by their names and recognized and differentiated by their appearance, distinctive pattern of speech, gestures, or written words. They see their thoughts and ideas received and discussed by others, providing external recognition that those thoughts and ideas have value.

At the same time, one can't just strike the "Delete" key or turn off the machine in a residential environment when confronted with a difficult human interaction or an intellectual disagreement. Affinity with others is a "built-in" program, not an option. Through a liberal education, students engage in the study of a wide range of subjects in the arts, humanities, sciences, and social sciences, directed by an instructor in ways that ensure that students move beyond what they already know. Such an education aims to free students from preconceptions and encourages them to consider many different, often conflicting, opinions. In an environment that encourages experimentation, students can reconcile their perspectives with the prevailing values of current authorities—represented by instructors and the individuals whom instructors recommend—as well as other students.

Having worked both in a distance-learning company and a residential liberal-arts college, I know firsthand that no existing form of distance learning can similarly affirm students as individuals and also force them to acknowledge the ideas of others. Liberal education is not defined by practicality or the immediacy of occupational goals—which would do little to challenge prejudice, bias, or authority. But a liberal education is ultimately useful; it give students the strong sense of self and habits of mind and action to become leaders. And, unfortunately, it is precisely the poor, minority, first-generation, immigrant, or otherwise disenfranchised students who most desperately need an educational environment that builds identity and gives them the confidence even to attempt leadership. . . .

Today, to encourage disadvantaged students to choose distance-learning offerings over a liberal-arts education, people use arguments strikingly similar to those used decades ago to embrace populist reforms. For example, in testimony before Congress's Web-Based Education Commission, Andrew M. Rosenfield, the head of UNext.com, which sells online courses, enthusiastically predicted, "Internet learning has the power fundamentally to transform educational opportunity and democratize access to education"—especially, Rosenfield noted, for "those who because of the happenstance of financial and geographical circumstance never could hope to attend a physical college or university."

Yet, of course, the only area of distance instruction that appears pedagogically effective for great numbers of learners—and adult learners specifically—is vocational knowledge, where a body of technical information is transferred in specific fields like business and information technology. Therefore, the only education that can effectively be delivered en masse to young people is, by necessity, vocational and practical—precisely the type of education advanced in the early 20th century by progressive educators for immigrants, minority groups, and the poor. . . .

Few observers doubt that distance learning will be an important platform for the delivery and sharing of information and practical knowledge in the coming decades. It is already effective at delivering workplace training and adult continuing education. Growing evidence also suggests that it may be a useful supplement to liberal education—providing discrete knowledge or even coursework not readily available in a particular residential setting.

But to predict the death of liberal education and to offer distance education as a viable alternative for college-aged youth is irresponsible. Where's the research that proves the effectiveness of virtual learning for that purpose? The claim is also unfortunate because it comes precisely when more and more disadvantaged youth are ready for college, and when liberal-arts colleges are poised to make it possible for them to attend in unprecedented numbers through financial aid and heightened recruitment efforts.

Disenfranchised students, as much as their affluent and advantaged peers, deserve a chance at a residential, liberal education—not an unproven alternative. Those students deserve the opportunity to break the destructive cycle, finally, and receive, not just placebos, but the education that they need. They deserve a chance to obtain the type of education that will substantially increase their access to power and success.

It is time to let the secret out beyond the privileged: A liberal-arts education equals leadership.

23. Sander L. Gilman, *Medicine and Education . . . Can We Live Forever?* 2000

Whatever its forms and facilities, ideal teaching has spoken to the future, to the continuity of generations. Adding his confident voice to "the long tradition of immortality" that reaches back to the Athenian age, Sander L. Gilman (1944–) concluded his small book of essays on the humanities with this profession of faith. As a humanist whose teachings and writings integrate a keen interest in the sciences, Gilman has served on the faculties of Cornell (1978–94), where he became Goldwyn Smith Professor (1987–94) teaching German history, Near Eastern studies, and the history of psychiatry; at the University of Chicago as the Henry R. Luce Professor of Liberal Arts in Human Biology (1995–2000); and then at the University of Illinois, Chicago as Distinguished Professor of Liberal Arts and Sciences and Medicine (2000–2004); he recently moved to Emory University to head a new Humanities Laboratory (2005–). Gilman's notably broad scholarship was recognized by his being named president of the Modern Language Association. His brief autobiographical comments are found in the preface to this collection of essays.

Sander L. Gilman, *The Fortunes of the Humanities, Thoughts for after the Year 2000* (Stanford, CA, 2000): 121–22. Copyright © 2000 by the Board of Trustees of the Leland Stanford Jr. University.

Can we live forever? And, if not, how will we die? At the end of the millennium, with its symbolic evocation of ends and beginnings, these two questions haunt us. Assuredly we can live forever, but not through medicine. I, as a teacher, stand in a long tradition of immortality. In 1997 archeologists uncovered the ruins of Aristotle's Lyceum, the school where he taught philosophy to the elite of Athens. Education too is a form of cloning, but one that permits radical change over time. Individual immortality is neither possible nor desirable, but the need to function as educated men and women in a world such as that of higher education makes us part of an immortal undertaking, part of a long chain not of genes but of knowledge. Not merely copies of the past, but new and exciting participants in the present, and shapers and molders of the future. Possessors of the past, creators of a brave new future-students stand both as our products and as the revolutionaries who overturn our past. Can we live forever? I certainly shall-through the students who will carry on my mission, that of educating a new world, either in my own ideals or in theirs.

CONTEXT

The President's Commission on Higher Education of 1947 not only anticipated a dramatic increase in the number of Americans seeking higher education after the war, it also recognized that that expansion would mean a growing "diversity of needs and interests" among college students. The more compelling parts of the report concerned equal opportunity for higher education: excluding students for reasons of economic means or racial difference represented the "gravest" failure of American education. Some of the commissioners strongly resisted mention of racial discrimination in southern segregated and unequal institutions. The report also outlined issues that remained for decades: it suggested "intercultural cooperation," which a half-century later was often called "multicultural understandings," and it spoke for internationalized programs, pointing to the present concern for an education for global citizenship (1).

Despite the specific references in the report to women, its readers doubtless understood the expansion of higher education to be driven by an increase in male students, many on the G.I. Bill. On leading university faculties, the first quarter-century after the war actually saw a diminution of the status and numbers of female faculty, especially in the sciences (10). Before the social movements of the 1960s and 1970s, there was little expectation that women (and other underrepresented groups) would fill a significant number of places in doctoral programs and ultimately faculties, but by the end of the century women outnumbered men in several humanities disciplines. Underrepresented minorities remained underrepresented; yet at the end of the century they had become an effective presence in the composition of faculties (10–23). Even those who supported a more diversified student body and faculty seem not to have grasped that such a change would dramatically alter academic culture, ranging from curricula to social relations, dress, and personal styles within departments. Many of those who anticipated such changes under the pressure of mass higher education mostly worried about the dissolution of what they saw as an intellectual elite (3). Few academic leaders committed to merit or certain notions of merit (exemplified in James B. Conant's

role in founding the Educational Testing Service) considered how that might complicate a parallel commitment to equality of access (5). Community colleges tended toward "open admissions," and pressure for such a policy was applied to some public four-year institutions as well (24–26). Even in community colleges, there were questions of whether there were fiscal—or other—limits to a public commitment to educate all those who sought a degree (9).

The great expansion was mostly accommodated by three-tier statewide public systems of higher education (flagship research universities, state colleges, and community colleges), and the worries of Clark Kerr were widely shared by leaders of state institutions: could they accommodate the continual growth in numbers (2, 6–9)? Most top-tier private institutions identified their particular character and value with limited size, leaving the challenge of expansion to the public sector. For three decades after the war, the necessary resources for expansion from the federal and most of the state governments were forthcoming. Higher education was understood as a public good, an investment in both citizens and the workforce (2, 4). By the end of the century, however, higher education was treated more as a private good—indeed, by some as an entitlement—than as a matter of public interest, and public funding leveled off and even declined. The ebullience that marked the decades of growth was gone. Public faith in what had become a "mature industry" had waned. At a time when a compelling new vision was required, university leaders were unable to project one; both the federal government and state governments demanded efficiencies and accountability. The closing decades of the century were marked by a pervasive sense of fundamental change—economic, technological, and cultural. Did higher education, which had transformed itself after World War II, have the energy and insight to meet the challenge of change again? Would higher education sink into stasis? Or were leaders beginning to grasp new understandings of higher education for the new century, perhaps pointing to a transformation enabled by new technologies (28)?

Truman Commission Report

1. *Higher Education for American Democracy,* 1947

An invasion of American colleges by thousands of World War II veterans in 1946 was met by overcrowded and inadequate facilities. This event introduced a new era of higher education. President Harry Truman wisely appointed a Presidential Commission on Higher Education in the summer of 1946. "We should now re-examine our system of higher education," he stated, "in terms of its objectives, methods, and facilities; and in the light of the social role it has to play." A commission of twenty-eight educators and laymen headed by George F. Zook, president of the American Council on Education, worked to produce by the end of 1947 a report consisting of six volumes. The first volume, *Establishing the Goals,* excerpted here, set the pattern for the others and summarized the Commission's conclusions.

Higher Education for Democracy: A Report of the President's Commission on Higher Education, Vol. I, *Establishing the Goals* (New York, 1947), pp. 1–3, 5–8, 25–29, 32–39, 47–49. Reprinted with the permission of Harper Collins, copyright © 1947. Further reading: Gail Kennedy, ed., *Education for Democracy: The Debate over the Report of the President's Commission on Higher Education* (Boston, 1952); Edward A. Tenney, "Thinking—by Commission," *Journal of General Education* 4 (January 1950): 136–40; Charles A. Quattlebaum, *Federal Aid to Students for Higher Education* (Washington, 1956); and I, 8, 11; VIII, 1, 4, 6.

The President's Commission on Higher Education has been charged with the task of defining the responsibilities of colleges and universities in American democracy and in international affairs—and, more specifically, with reexamining the objectives, methods, and facilities of higher education in the United States in the light of the social role it has to play.

The colleges and universities themselves had begun this process of reexamination and reappraisal before the outbreak of World War II. For many years they had been healthily dissatisfied with their own accomplishments, significant though these have been. Educational leaders . . . felt that somehow the colleges had not kept pace with changing social conditions, that the programs of higher education would have to be repatterned if they were to prepare youth to live satisfyingly and effectively in contemporary society.

One factor contributing to this sense of inadequacy has been the steadily increasing number of young people who seek a college education. As the national economy became industrialized and more complex, as production increased and national resources multiplied, the American people came in ever greater numbers to feel the need of higher education for their children. More and more American youth attended colleges and universities, but resources and equipment and curriculum did not keep pace with the growing enrollment or with the increasing diversity of needs and interests among the students.

World War II brought a temporary falling off in enrollment, but with the war's end and the enactment of Public Laws 16 and 346, the "Veterans' Rehabilitation Act," and "The G.I. Bill of Rights," the acceleration has resumed. The increase in numbers is far beyond the capacity of higher education in teachers, in buildings, and in equipment. Moreover, the number of veterans availing themselves of veterans' educational benefits falls short of the numbers that records of military personnel show could benefit from higher education. Statistics reveal that a doubling of the 1947–48 enrollment in colleges and universities will be entirely possible within 10 to 15 years, if facilities and financial means are provided.

This tendency of the American people to seek higher education in ever greater numbers has grown concurrently with an increasingly critical need for such education. To this need several developments have contributed:

(a) Science and invention have diversified natural resources, have multiplied new devices and techniques of production. These have altered in radical ways the interpersonal and intergroup relations of and Americans in their work, in their play, and in their duties as citizens. As a consequence, new skills and greater maturity are required of youth as they enter upon their adult roles. And the increasing complexity that technological progress has brought to our society has made a broader understanding of social processes and problems essential for effective living.

(b) The people of America are drawn from the peoples of the entire world. They live in contrasting regions. They are of different occupations, diverse faiths, divergent cultural backgrounds, and varied interests. The American Nation is not only a union of 48 different states; it is also a union of an indefinite number of diverse groups of varying size. Of and among these diversities our free society seeks to create a dynamic unity. Where there is economic, cultural, or religious tension, we undertake to effect democratic reconciliation, so as to make of the national life one continuous process of interpersonal, intervocational, and intercultural cooperation.

(c) With World War II and its conclusion has come a fundamental shift in the orientation of American foreign policy. Owing to the inescapable pressure of events, the Nation's traditional isolationism has been displaced by a new sense of responsibility in world affairs. The need for maintaining our democracy at peace with the rest of the world has compelled our initiative in the formation of the United Nations, and America's role in this and other agencies of international cooperation requires of our citizens a knowledge of other peoples —of their political and economic systems, their social and cultural institutions—such as has not hitherto been so urgent.

(d) The coming of the atomic age, with its ambivalent promise of tremendous good or tremendous evil for mankind, has intensified the uncertainties of the future. It has deepened and broadened the responsibilities of higher education for anticipating and preparing for the social and economic changes that will come with the application of atomic energy to industrial uses. At the same time it has underscored the need for education and research for the self-protection of our democracy, for demonstrating the merits of our way of life to other peoples.

Thus American colleges and universities face the need both for improving the performance of their traditional tasks and for assuming the new tasks created for them by the new internal conditions and external relations under which the American people are striving to live and to grow as a free people. . . .

THE ROLE OF EDUCATION

It is a commonplace of the democratic faith that education is indispensable to the maintenance and growth of freedom of thought, faith, enterprise, and association. Thus the social role of education in a democratic society is at once to insure equal liberty and equal opportunity to differing individuals and groups, and to enable the citizens to understand, appraise, and redirect forces, men, and events as these tend to strengthen or to weaken their liberties.

In performing this role, education will necessarily vary its means and methods to fit the diversity of its constituency, but it will achieve its ends more successfully if its programs and policies grow out of and are relevant to the characteristics and needs of contemporary society. Effective democratic education will deal directly with current problems.

This is not to say that education should neglect the past—only that it should not get lost in the past. No one would deny that a study of man's history can contribute immeasurably to understanding and managing the present. But to assume that all we need do is apply to present and future problems "eternal" truths revealed in earlier ages is likely to stifle creative imagination and intellectual daring. Such an assumption may blind us to new problems and the possible need for new solutions. It is wisdom in education to use the past selectively and critically, in order to illumine the pressing problems of the present.

At the same time education is the making of the future. Its role in a democratic society is that of critic and leader as well as servant; its task is not merely to meet the demands of the present but to alter those demands if necessary, so as to keep them always suited to democratic ideals. Perhaps its most important role is to serve as an instrument of social transition, and its responsibilities are defined in terms of the kind of civilization society hopes to build. If its adjustments to present needs are not to be mere fortuitous improvisations, those who formulate its policies and programs must have a vision of the

Nation and the world we want—to give a sense of direction to their choices among alternatives.

What America needs today, then, is "a schooling better aware of its aims." Our colleges need to see clearly what it is they are trying to accomplish. The efforts of individual institutions, local communities, the several States, the educational foundations and associations, and the Federal Government will all be more effective if they are directed toward the same general ends.

In the future as in the past, American higher education will embody the principle of diversity in unity: each institution, State, or other agency will continue to make its own contribution in its own way. But educational leaders should try to agree on certain common objectives that can serve as a stimulus and guide to individual decision and action.

A TIME OF CRISIS

It is essential today that education come decisively to grips with the world-wide crisis of mankind. This is no careless or uncritical use of words. No thinking person doubts that we are living in a decisive moment of human history.

Atomic scientists are doing their utmost to make us realize how easily and quickly a world catastrophe may come. They know the fearful power for destruction possessed by the weapons their knowledge and skill have fashioned. They know that the scientific principles on which these weapons are based are no secret to the scientists of other nations, and that America's monopoly of the engineering processes involved in the manufacture of atom bombs is not likely to last many years. And to the horror of atomic weapons, biological and chemical instruments of destruction are now being added.

But disaster is not inevitable. The release of atomic energy that has brought man within sight of world devastation has just as truly brought him the promise of a brighter future. The potentialities of atomic power are as great for human betterment as for human annihilation. Man can choose which he will have.

The possibility of this choice is the supreme fact of our day, and it will necessarily influence the ordering of educational priorities. We have a big job of reeducation to do. Nothing less than a complete reorientation of our thinking will suffice if mankind is to survive and move on to higher levels.

In a real sense the future of our civilization depends on the direction education takes, not just in the distant future, but in the days immediately ahead. . . .

The scientific knowledge and technical skills that have made atomic and bacteriological warfare possible are the products of education and research, and higher education must share proportionately in the task of forging social and political defenses against obliteration. The indirect way toward some longer view and superficial curricular tinkering can no longer serve. The measures higher education takes will have to match in boldness and vision the magnitude of the problem.

In the light of this situation, the President's Commission on Higher Education has attempted to select, from among the principal goals for higher education, those which should come first in our time. They are to bring to all the people of the Nation:

Education for a fuller realization of democracy in every phase of living.

Education directly and explicitly for international understanding and cooperation.

Education for the application of creative imagination and trained intelligence to the solution of social problems and to the administration of public affairs. . . .

RECORD OF GROWTH

The expansion of the American education enterprise since the turn of the century has been phenomenal. The 700,000 enrollment in high schools in the school year 1900 was equal to only 11 percent of the youth of usual high-school age, 14 through 17 years old. This increased in 1940 to over 7,000,000 students representing 73 percent of the youth.

Almost as spectacular has been the increase in college attendance. In 1900 fewer than 250,000 students, only 4 percent of the population 18 through 21 years of age, were enrolled in institutions of higher education. By 1940 the enrollment had risen to 1,500,000 students, equal to a little less than 16 percent of the 18–21-year-olds. In 1947, enrollments jumped to the theretofore unprecedented peak of 2,354,000 although approximately 1,000,000 of the students were veterans, older than the usual college age because World War II had deferred their education. The situation in the fall of 1947 gives every indication that the school year 1948 will witness even larger enrollments.

This record of growth is encouraging, but we are forced to admit nonetheless that the educational attainments of the American people are still substantially below what is necessary, either for effective individual living or for the welfare of our society.

According to the U. S. Bureau of the Census, almost 17,000,000 men and women over 19 years of age in 1947 had stopped their schooling at the sixth grade or less. Of these, 9,000,000 had never attended school or had stopped their schooling before completing the fifth grade. In 1947, about 1,600,000 or 19 percent of our high-school-age boys and girls were not attending any kind of school, and over two-thirds of the 18- and 19-year-old youths were not in school.

These are disturbing facts. They represent a sobering failure to reach the educational goals implicit in the democratic creed, and they are indefensible in a society so richly endowed with material resources as our own. We cannot allow so many of our people to remain so ill equipped either as human beings or as citizens of a democracy.

Great as the total American expenditure for education may seem, we have not been devoting any really appreciable part of our vast wealth to higher education.

BARRIERS TO EQUAL OPPORTUNITY

One of the gravest charges to which American society is subject is that of failing to provide a reasonable equality of educational opportunity for its youth. For the great majority of our boys and girls, the kind and amount of education they may hope to attain depends, not on their own abilities, but on the family or community into which they happened to be born or, worse still, on the color of their skin or the religion of their parents.

ECONOMIC BARRIERS

The old, comfortable idea that "any boy can get a college education who has it in him" simply is not true. Low family income, together with the rising costs of education, constitutes an almost impassable barrier to college education for many young people. For some, in fact, the barrier is raised so early in life that it prevents them from attending high school even when free public high schools exist near their homes.

Despite the upward trend in average per capita income for the past century and more, the earnings of a large part of our population are still too low to provide anything but the barest necessities of physical life. It is a distressing fact that in 1945, when the total national income was far greater than in any previous period in our history, half of the children under 18 were growing up in families which had a cash income of $2,530 or less. The educational significance of these facts is heightened by the relationship that exists between income and birth rate. Fertility is highest in the families with lowest incomes.

In the elementary and secondary schools the effects of these economic conditions are overcome to a considerable extent, though not entirely, by the fact that education is free and at certain ages is compulsory. But this does not hold true at the college level. . . .

Under the pressure of rising costs and of a relative lessening of public support, the colleges and universities are having to depend more and more on tuition fees to meet their budgets. As a result, on the average, tuition rates rose about 30 percent from 1939 to 1947.

Nor are tuition costs the whole of it. There are not enough colleges and universities in the country, and they are not distributed evenly enough to bring them within reach of all young people. Relatively few students can attend college in their home communities. So to the expense of a college education for most youth must be added transportation and living costs—by no means a small item.

This economic factor explains in large part why the father's occupation has been found in many studies to rank so high as a determining factor in a young person's college expectancy. A farm laborer earns less than a banker or a doctor, for instance, and so is less able to afford the costs of higher education for his children. The children, moreover, have less inducement to seek a college education because of their family background. In some social circles a college education is often considered a luxury which can be done without, something desirable perhaps, "but not for the likes of us."

The importance of economic barriers to post–high school education lies in the fact that there is little if any relationship between the ability to benefit from a college education and the ability to pay for it. . . .

By allowing the opportunity for higher education to depend so largely on the individual's economic status, we are not only denying to millions of young people the chance in life to which they are entitled; we are also depriving the Nation of a vast amount of potential leadership and potential social competence which it sorely needs. . . .

BARRIER OF A RESTRICTED CURRICULUM

We shall be denying educational opportunity to many young people as long as we maintain the present orientation of higher education toward verbal skills and intellectual interests. Many young people have abilities of a different kind, and they cannot receive "education commensurate with their native capacities" in colleges and universities that recognize only one kind of educable intelligence.

Traditionally the colleges have sifted out as their special clientele persons possessing verbal aptitudes and a capacity for grasping abstractions. But many other aptitudes—such as social sensitivity and versatility, artistic ability, motor skill and dexterity, and mechanical aptitude and ingenuity—also should be cultivated in a society depending, as ours does, on the minute division of labor and at the same time upon the orchestration of an enormous variety of talents.

If the colleges are to educate the great body of American youth, they must provide programs for the development of other abilities than those involved in academic aptitude, and they cannot continue to concentrate on students with one type of intelligence to the neglect of youth with other talents.

RACIAL AND RELIGIOUS BARRIERS

The outstanding example of these barriers to equal opportunity, of course, is the disadvantages suffered by our Negro citizens. The low educational attainments of Negro adults reflect the cumulative effects of a long period of unequal opportunity. In 1940 the schooling of the Negro was significantly below that of whites at every level from the first grade through college. At the college level, the difference is marked; 11 percent of the white population 20 years of age and over had completed at least 1 year of college and almost 5 percent had finished 4 years; whereas for the nonwhites (over 95 percent of whom are Negroes) only a little more than 3 percent had completed at least 1 year of college and less than 1.5 percent had completed a full course.

Gains Have Been Made. Noteworthy advances have been made toward eliminating the racial inequalities which in large measure are responsible for this low level of educational achievement by the Negroes. Between 1900 and 1940 the percentage of Negroes 5 to 20 years of age attending school rose from 31.0 percent to 64.4 percent. And the percentage of Negro youth 15 to 20 years old attending school increased from 17.5 in 1900 to 33.8 in 1940.

Institutions which accept both Negro and non-Negro students do not maintain separate record systems for Negroes, and so data on enrollment of Negroes are restricted to those institutions—usually located in the South—which accept only Negro students. In recent years, since 1932, these institutions have almost tripled their enrollments whereas the institutions for whites or which are unsegregated only about doubled theirs.

Inequalities Remain. But the numbers enrolled in school do not tell the whole story. Marked as has been the progress in Negro education in recent years, it cannot obscure the very great differences which still persist in educational opportunities afforded the Negro and the non-Negro.

In 17 states and the District of Columbia, segregation of the Negroes in education is established by law. In the *Gaines* decision, the U.S. Supreme Court ruled that "if a State furnishes higher education to white residents, it is bound to furnish [within the State] substantially equal advantages to Negro students." Although segregation may not legally mean discrimination as to the quality of the facilities it usually does so in fact. The schools maintained for the Negroes are commonly much inferior to those for the whites. The Negro schools are financed at a pitifully low level, they are often housed in buildings wholly inadequate for the purpose, and many of the teachers are sorely in need of more education themselves. Library facilities are generally poor or lacking altogether, and professional supervision is more a name than a reality. . . .

Segregation lessens the quality of education for the whites as well. To maintain two school systems side by side—duplicating even inadequately the buildings, equipment, and teaching personnel—means that neither can be of the quality that would be possible if all the available resources were devoted to one system, especially not when the States least able financially to support an adequate educational program for their youth are the very ones that are trying to carry a double load. . . .

Equality of education opportunity is not achieved by the mere physical existence of schools; it involves also the quality of teaching and learning that takes place in them.

The Quota System. At the college level a different form of discrimination is commonly practiced.

Many colleges and universities, especially in their professional schools, maintain a selective quota system for admission, under which the chance to learn, and thereby to become more useful citizens, is denied to certain minorities, particularly to Negroes and Jews.

This practice is a violation of a major American principle and is contributing to the growing tension in one of the crucial areas of our democracy.

The quota, or *numerus clausus,* is certainly un-American. It is European in origin and application, and we have lately witnessed on that continent the horrors to which, in its logical extension, it can lead. To insist that specialists in any field shall be limited by ethnic quotas is to assume that the Nation is composed of separate and self-sufficient ethnic groups and this assumption America has never made except in the case of its Negro population, where the result is one of the plainest inconsistencies with our national ideal.

The quota system denies the basic American belief that intelligence and ability are present in all ethnic groups, that men of all religious and racial origins should have equal opportunity to fit themselves for contributing to the common life.

Moreover, since the quota system is never applied to all groups in the Nation's population, but only to certain ones, we are forced to conclude that the arguments advanced to justify it are nothing more than rationalizations to cover either convenience or the disposition to discriminate. The quota system cannot be justified on any grounds compatible with democratic principles. . . .

It is obvious, then, that free and universal access to education, in terms of the interest, ability, and need of the student, must be a major goal in American education.

THE NEED FOR GENERAL EDUCATION

Present college programs are not contributing adequately to the quality of students' adult lives either as workers or citizens. This is true in large part because the unity of liberal education has been splintered by overspecialization.

For half a century and more the curriculum of the liberal arts college has been expanding and disintegrating to an astounding degree. The number of courses has so multiplied that no student could take all of them, or even a majority of them, in a lifetime . . .

This tendency to diversify the content of what was once an integrated liberal education is in part the consequence of the expansion of the boundaries of knowledge. New advances in every direction have added more and more subjects to the liberal arts curriculum and have at the same time limited the area of knowledge a single course could cover. This development is at once the parent and the child of specialization.

Specialization is a hallmark of our society, and its advantages to mankind have been remarkable. But in the educational program it has become a source

both of strength and of weakness. Filtering downward from the graduate and professional school levels, it has taken over the undergraduate years, too, and in the more extreme instances it has made of the liberal arts college little more than another vocational school, in which the aim of teaching is almost exclusively preparation for advanced study in one or another specialty.

This tendency has been fostered, if not produced, by the training of college teachers in the graduate school, where they are imbued with the single ideal of an ever-narrowing specialism.

The trend toward specialization has been reenforced by the movement toward democratization of higher education. The young people appearing in growing numbers on college campuses have brought with them widely diverse purposes, interests, capacities, and academic backgrounds. Some expect to enter one of the old-line professions; others want training in one of the numerous branches of agriculture, industry or commerce. Some consider college education a natural sequel to high school; others seek it as a road to higher social status.

The net result of the situation is that the college student is faced with a bewildering array of intensive courses from which to make up his individual program. . . . He, therefore, leaves college unacquainted with some of the fundamental areas of human knowledge and without the integrated view of human experience that is essential both for personal balance and for social wisdom.

Today's college graduate may have gained training in one field of work or another, but is only incidentally, if at all, made ready for performing his duties as citizen. Too often he is "educated" in that he has acquired competence in some particular occupation, yet falls short of that human wholeness and civic conscience which the cooperative activities of citizenship require. . . .

The crucial task of higher education today, therefore, is to prove a unified general education for American youth. Colleges must find the right relationship between specialized training on the one hand, aiming at a thousand different careers, and the transmission of a common cultural heritage toward a common citizenship on the other.

There have already been many efforts to define this relationship. Attempts to reach conclusions about the ends and means of general education have been a major part of debate and experimentation in higher education for at least two decades.

"General education" is the term that has come to be accepted for those phases of nonspecialized and nonvocational learning which should be the common experience of all educated men and women.

General education should give to the student the values, attitudes, knowledge, and skills that will equip him to live rightly and well in a free society. It should enable him to identify, interpret, select, and build into his own life those components of his cultural heritage that contribute richly to understanding and appreciation of the world in which he lives. It should therefore embrace ethical values, attitudes, scientific generalizations, and aesthetic conceptions, as well as an understanding of the purposes and character of the political, economic, and social institutions that men have devised.

But the knowledge and understanding which general education aims to secure, whether drawn from the past or from a living present, are not to be regarded as ends in themselves. They are means to a more abundant personal life and a stronger, freer social order.

Thus conceived, general education is not sharply distinguished from liberal education; the two differ mainly in degree, not in kind. General education undertakes to redefine liberal education in terms of life's problems as men face them, to give it human orientation and social direction, to invest it with content that is directly relevant to the demands of contemporary society. General education is liberal education with its matter and method shifted from its original aristocratic intent to the service of democracy. General education seeks to extend to all men the benefits of an education that liberates.

This purpose calls for a unity in the program of studies that a uniform system of courses cannot supply. The unity must come, instead, from a consistency of aim that will infuse and harmonize all teaching and all campus activities.

The Challenge of Expansion

2. Clark Kerr, "Just Ahead . . . Berkeley's Greatest Permanent Growth," 1955

In 1955 Clark Kerr (1911–2003) made the bold prediction that a flood of students equaling the tidal wave of postwar GIs of 1948 was about to hit Berkeley. Kerr then was chancellor at Berkeley (1952–58), where he earlier had been director of the Institute for Industrial Relations (1945–52).

Clark Kerr, "Just Ahead . . . Berkeley's Greatest Permanent Growth," *California Monthly* 66 (September 1955): 14–18. Copyright © 1955 by the California Alumni Association. Abridged with the permission of *California Monthly*. Further reading: Kerr, *The Gold and the Blue: A Personal Memoir of the University of California, 1949–1967*, vol. 1, *Academic Triumphs* (Berkeley, CA, 2001), pt. II; John Aubrey Douglass, *The California Idea and American Higher Education: 1850 to the 1960 Master Plan* (Stanford, CA, 2000), chs. 6–7; and II, 6.

Among the many concerns of the Berkeley administration these days, a major one is the flood of students now sweeping through the grades and high schools and soon to inundate the campus. The fact that we share this worry with administrations of colleges and universities across the country is comforting, but does not diminish our concern.

A tidal wave of students, some writers call it, but a tidal wave recedes, and this will stay, permanently. I prefer the flood metaphor, and am confident that the campus will ride it our successfully, adjusting to the changes that it brings.

Berkeley's enrollment has grown steadily from its early registration of 40 (1869) to 2,229 (1900), to 10,796 (1920), to 15,581 (1940), and, with the postwar GIs bringing what *was* a tidal wave, to 23,145 (1948). That tidal wave receded, and Berkeley's 1953 fall enrollment was 15,327. That, we suspect, may have been our last reasonably "normal" year.

This fall the number of students on the campus will continue rising, as it did last fall. By 1965 it is estimated that about 10,000 more students will be added to our annual rolls, an increase by about two-thirds in a single decade. We can only hope that we may never have to exceed the 25,000 students which will then populate our campus.

Of the many reasons for the flood of students soon due at Berkeley and elsewhere, let me cite four:

The rise in the birth rate. In 1935 the birth rate was 17 per thousand; in 1940 it was 18 per thousand; in 1945 it rose to 20, in 1950 to 24, in 1952 to 25. As research consultant Peter Drucker noted recently, the most important economic development of 1954 was that 4,060,000 babies were born in the United States, the largest baby crop ever. The war baby boom, so-called, is now on the doorstep of colleges and universities. It is easy to see why administrators, thinking of budgets, buildings and new faculty, often use figures of speech implying impending disaster.

The westward trek. California's population increase is due not only to the general increase in births, but to the great war and postwar migration that has placed it second in the nation. In part this represents a longtime national trend toward the west. The war helped it along by moving young men generously about the country. Many of them came, saw and settled in California.

Thus with more babies, and more people moving to California, there is a very predictable rise due in the number of college age youths. The State had 291,362 young people of college age in 1953. Estimates based on present figures indicate that it will have 962,063 in 1970, an increase of 230 per cent. (The national increase for the same period is figured at a mere 70 per cent.) Other western states have percentages nearly as high as California's.

The increasing demand for a college education. After World War I a high school education became for most young people a generally accepted thing. After World War II a college education has become a similarly generally accepted thing. This reflects our higher standard of living, and the continuing impact of our great American promise of equality of opportunity. Parents want greater advantages for their children than they had, in many cases, themselves. Employers more and more frequently ask for college trained employees. The colleges and universities must meet this demand if the nation is to furnish the leadership expected of it in the world today.

The private colleges and universities tend, facing the impending flood of students, *not* to plan to increase enrollment to any great extent. They feel that their special character and contribution may be lost if they expand extensively.

It is, therefore, chiefly up to State institutions like the University of California to grow to meet the challenge of tomorrow's youth. . . .

Enrollment figures for the years 1940–54 indicate the growing demand for graduate work at Berkeley. While total enrollment increased 1.8 per cent during those 14 years, graduate enrollment increased 37 per cent. Estimates are that total enrollment will have increased 15 per cent by 1959 and that graduate enrollment will have increased 45 per cent, or three times as fast.

However, Berkeley is very happy to retain the lower division because thereby it furnishes to some students the opportunity of taking a full four-year university course; because from the ranks of the four-year students are derived a high proportion of campus leaders; because having its own lower division courses Berkeley can set curricular standards helpful, as models by which to be guided and as yardsticks by which to be measured, for junior colleges and state colleges whose students transfer to Berkeley; and because with the lower division it can carry on the old time-hallowed customs and traditions that make up campus spirit. . . .

How can we retain the present level of distinction of our faculty while we add greatly (and also quickly) to its numbers, in order to carry the increased student load? And can we maintain at least our present student-faculty ratio, so that tomorrow's students will receive an education equal to that of today's? Our present ratio of 15.5 full-time students to full-time teaching staff (1954) compares none too favorably with ratios at some other outstanding universities.

Thus at Berkeley a faculty member teaches twice as many students as his colleague teaches at Harvard, Chicago, Princeton or Columbia. Despite this teaching load, the University at Berkeley has maintained high standards of scholarship, ranking in many fields with or above those institutions. This is a tribute to the excellence and vigor of the faculty members we have been able to attract. We want to continue to attract faculty of that calibre as we grow in the next decade.

Our present ratio of students to staff is related to today's student distribution: 36% lower division, 40% upper division, and 24% graduates. As we have noted, those percentages will shift, as we move into the next decade; furthermore, as the proportion of upper division and graduate students increases we shall need to lower our ratio, since graduate students, in particular, require much more individual attention.

Let us for the moment disregard what this changing distribution may be in the future, and suppose only that we move ahead holding to our present ratio. In 1960, with 19,000 students, at 15.5 to one, we should need 1226 faculty members, an increase

of 202 over today's staff of 1024. In 1956, with 25,000 students, we should need 1613 faculty members, an increase of 589.

Where, we wonder, shall we find them? For Harvard, Columbia, Chicago, Michigan, Iowa, Illinois, and all the other universities will be seeking new faculties, too. If one fact above all others shines clearly between the lines in the literature on the coming flood of students, it is that the market for trained teachers at the college level, especially for those of top quality, will be extremely competitive in the early 60s.

And how, we wonder further, thinking of the students themselves, can we make education more personal, with closer relations between teacher and student? For a significant trend in education today is on learning rather than teaching, on fewer large lecture halls, more small classes, more seminars where students can participate in discussion. This is a trend many of our faculty and students hope we can follow. We shall need also more reading rooms scattered about the campus, augmenting the great resources of the main library.

We hope, additionally, in the residence halls that are soon to rise, to have many small social units where students can learn from group living. In the new Student Union we hope to have lounges where faculty and students can meet informally and come to know each other better.

We want generally to have a campus atmosphere which will contribute in the fullest measure possible to the intellectual development and social maturity of the students. Such an atmosphere the alumni will remember from their own student days. We trust such an atmosphere may still be possible even with 25,000 students inside Sather Gate.

3. Douglas Bush, "Education for All Is Education for None," 1955

A champion of humane learning, Douglas Bush (1896–1983) in the mid-1950's saw higher education endangered by mass civilization and a "barbaric" invasion of thousands of new college students. Born in Canada, Bush earned his B.A. (1920) at the University of Toronto and his Ph.D. (1923) at Harvard University. With the exception of nine years (1927–36) at the University of Minnesota, he spent his academic career, distinguished by its studies of the classical tradition in English literature, at Harvard (1924–27, 1936–66), where he was appointed Gurney Professor of English in 1957.

Appended to Bush's text are two responses, from William G. Saltonstall (1905–89), then principal of Phillips Exeter Academy (1946–63), and George R. Geiger (1903–98), disciple of John Dewey and professor of philosophy at Antioch College (1937–68).

Douglas Bush, "Education for All is Education for None," abridged from New York Times, January 9, 1955, 13, 30–31, and January 23, 1955, 63. Copyright © 1955 by the New York Times Company. All rights reserved. Saltonstall and Geiger letters reprinted with the permission of the New York Times. Further reading: Roger Rosenblatt, "The Odd

Pursuit of Teaching Books," *Time*, March 28, 1983, 60–61; Jacques Barzun, *The House of Intellect* (New York, 1959), *The American University* (New York, 1968), and "The Wasteland of American Education," *New York Review of Books*, November 5, 1981, 34–36, in which Barzun advances Bush's general position, emphasizing that "Intellect" must stand aloof from the immediate demands of society, as contrasted to the role of "intelligence" in the modern university.

In schools, colleges and universities today, the results of the huge increase in the student body suggest a rather painful thought: the principle of education for all, however fine in theory, in practice ultimately leads to education for none. In other words, the ideal of education for all forces acceptance of the principle that the function of education is primarily social and political rather than purely intellectual; if school standards are geared to an almost invisibly low average there is not much real education available for anyone, even for the gifted.

To mention one of many examples, there has been an appalling growth of illiteracy at all levels, even in the graduate school. (Somehow stenographers are still literate, even if their college-bred employers are not.) At every commencement one wonders how many of the hordes of new bachelors of arts can speak and write their own language with elementary decency, or read it with understanding. After all, the polished mind is suspect, whether in a student, professor or Presidential candidate. And illiteracy, and contentment with illiteracy, are only symptoms of general shoddiness.

Obviously one main cause of this state of things has been the sheer pressure of numbers, along with a deplorable shrinkage in the number of qualified teachers. But the situation would not be so bad as it has been if the downward pressure of numbers had not been powerfully strengthened by misguided doctrine and practice. The training of teachers and the control of school curricula have been in the hands of colleges of education and their products, and these have operated on principles extracted from John Dewey's philosophy of barbarism.

(If that phrase seems unduly harsh, I may say that I have in mind Dewey's hostility to what he regarded as leisure-class studies; his anti-historical attitude, his desire—intensified in his followers—to immerse students in the contemporary and immediate; and his denial of a hierarchy of studies, his doctrine that all kinds of experience are equally or uniquely valuable; and it would not be irrelevant to add his notoriously inept writing.)

The lowest common denominator has been, not an evil, but an ideal. The substantial disciplines have been so denuded of content that multitudes of students, often taught by uneducated teachers, have been illiterate, uninformed, and thoroughly immature. There is no use in priding ourselves on the operation of the democratic principle if education loses much of its meaning in the process.

When we think, for instance, of education for citizenship, which has been the cry of modern pedagogy, we may think also of the volume and violence of popular support given to the anti-intellectual demagoguery of the last few years. Mass education tends to reflect mass civilization instead of opposing it. And even if education were everywhere working on the highest level, it would still face tremendous odds.

The great problem has been and will be, first, the preservation of minority culture against the many and insidious pressures of mass civilization and, secondly, the extension of that minority culture through wider and wider areas. The rising flood of students is very much like the barbarian invasions of the early Middle Ages, and then the process of education took a thousand years.

We hope for something less overwhelming and for a less protracted cure, but the principle is the same, and Graeco-Roman-Christian culture not only survived but triumphed, and with enrichment also. If we think of our problem in the light of that one, we shall not be disheartened, but recognize both as phases of man's perennial growing pains.

Throughout history it has been a more or less small minority that has created and preserved what culture and enlightenment we have and, if adverse forces are always growing, that minority is always growing, too. In spite of the low standards that have commonly prevailed in public education during the last fifty years, I think the top layer of college students now are proportionately more numerous than they were thirty years ago and are more generally serious and critical. . . .

Surely the state universities have the strength to set up bars and select their student body instead of admitting all who choose to walk in the front door and then, with much trouble and expense, trying to get rid of some through the back door. Doubtless such procedure would require a campaign of enlightenment and persuasion, but legislators always have an alert ear for the cry of economy, and the public must be convinced that higher education, or what passes for that, is neither a birthright nor a necessary badge of respectability and that useful and happy lives can be led without a college degree or even without membership in a fraternity or sorority.

As things are, we have an army of misfits, who lower educational standards and increase expense, and no branch of a university staff has grown more rapidly of late years than the psychiatric squad.

Secondly, many people have grounds for the belief that the multiplying junior colleges can and will drain off a large number of the young who, for various reasons, are unfitted for a really strenuous four-year course. Junior colleges, however, should not be recreational centers for the subnormal. . . .

We have grown so accustomed to a battalion of instructors teaching elementary composition to an army of freshmen that we take it as a normal part of college education, whereas, in fact, it is a monstrosity. Imagine a European university teaching the rudiments of expression! If high school graduates are illiterate, they have no business in college. For a long time and for a variety of reasons we have had slackness all along the line: somehow, some time, strictness and discipline have got to begin.

Increased enrollments have almost inevitably led to increased reliance upon large lecture courses. . . . I favor classes small enough to allow discussion, and that is expensive.

But there are possible economies that would be highly desirable in themselves. We do not need to maintain the naive doctrine that there has to be a course in anything in which anyone ever has been or might be interested. Further, a good many catalogues list courses that can only be called fantastic, and I don't think I am guilty of partisan prejudice if I say that these are rarely found among the humanities. At any rate, if we had fewer and less specialized courses, and if we did not have our armies of composition teachers, a considerable number of man-hours would be released for smaller classes. . . .

Finally, since I touched on the large number of young people who are in college and shouldn't be, I might mention those who are not in college and should be and who may be lost in the oncoming flood. Educators and others are more conscious than they once were of our failure to recognize and foster promising students who cannot afford college, and increasing efforts are being made in that direction, but we are still far behind England, for example, where bright students are picked out at the age of 10 or 11 and brought along on scholarships. If we spent on exceptional students a fraction of the time and money we have spent on nursing lame ducks, there would be a considerable change in the quality of education.

One last word on a different matter. Like everything else, the Ph.D. has been cheapened by quantitative pressure, and it might be earnestly wished that it were not a union card for the teaching profession. There are plenty of young men and women who would be good teachers without such a degree, and the degree itself ought to mean something more than it does. Along with that may go another earnest wish, that both administrators and members of departments would abandon the principle of "publish or perish." Socrates would never have had a chance at an assistant professorship.

To the editors:

Professor Bush has chosen to teach in order to preserve "minority culture against the many and insidious pressures of mass civilization." Most American school teachers are in the business because they believe that every human being has the right and responsibility, so far as possible, to develop his judgment and imagination, to become master of himself, and to increase his usefulness to others.

Education for all does not ultimately lead to education for none. It leads toward the realization of the American dream—equality of opportunity for every youngster to make the most of himself.

William G. Saltonstall,
Principal, Phillips Exeter Academy
Exeter, N.H.

To the editors:

Now, it is undignified for one professor to call another illiterate, but let's face it: Professor Bush has only heard about Dewey. (And I can even guess to whom he has been speaking.) He says that Dewey has an "anti-historical attitude": that, for Dewey, "all kinds of experience are equally valuable": and he seems to intimate that in Dewey's philosophy. "contemporary" and "immediate" are synonyms. Well, we simply have to be charitable and insist that Dewey has not been read—for the simple reason that Dewey's philosophy, celebrates the very *opposite* of all these.

George R. Geiger,
Professor of Philosophy, Antioch College
Yellow Springs, Ohio

4. John W. Gardner, *Excellence: Can We Be Equal and Excellent Too?* 1961

The major theme of educational excellence in the post-*Sputnik* years was increasingly posited in a sometimes tense relation to egalitarian social pressures of the 1960s. The little book from which this excerpt comes was at the time the most widely read delineation of this cultural problem in the American democracy.

A native of California, educated at Stanford (A.B. 1935) and the University of California (Ph.D. 1938), John William Gardner (1912–2002) had just served on President Kennedy's task force on education when he published this book. He then was president of the Carnegie Corporation of New York, with which he had been associated since 1946 after teaching psychology at Connecticut (1938–40) and Mount Holyoke (1940–42) colleges and serving with the Marines in World War II. Throughout the 1960s and the 1970s, Gardner was one of the nation's most respected and sought-after public servants. He served in President Johnson's cabinet as secretary of health, education, and welfare (1965–68), chaired the Urban Coalition (1968–70), and presided over Common Cause (1970–77). From 1989 to 1996 he was professor of public service at Stanford University. Among many honors, he was awarded the presidential Medal of Freedom in 1964.

John W. Gardner, *Excellence: Can We Be Equal and Excellent Too?* (New York, 1961), pp. 77–82, 84–86. Reprinted by permission of Sll/sterling Lord Literistic, Inc. Copyright by John W. Gardner.

The notion that so-called quality education and so-called mass education are mutually exclusive is woefully out of date. It would not have survived at all were there not a few remarkably archaic characters in our midst. We all know that some of the people calling most noisily for quality in education are those who were *never* reconciled to the widespread extension of educational opportunity. To such individuals there is something inherently vulgar about large numbers of people. At the other extreme are the fanatics who believe that the chief goal for higher education should be to get as many youngsters as possible—regardless of ability—into college classrooms. Such individuals regard quality as a concept smacking faintly of Louis XIV.

But neither extreme speaks for the American people, and neither expresses the true issues that pose themselves today. It would be fatal to allow ourselves to be tempted into an anachronistic debate. *We must seek excellence in a context of concern for all.* A democracy, no less than any other form of society, must foster excellence if it is to survive; and it should not allow the emotional scars of old battles to confuse it on this point.

Educating everyone up to the limit of his ability does not mean sending everyone to college. Part of any final answer to the college problem must be some revision of an altogether false emphasis which the American people are coming to place on college education. This false emphasis is the source of great difficulties for us. In Virginia they tell the story of the kindly Episcopal minister who was asked whether the Episcopal Church was the only path to salvation. The minister shook his head—a bit sadly, perhaps. "No, there are other paths," he said, and then added, "but no gentleman would choose them." Some of our attitudes toward college education verge dangerously on the same position.

There are some people who seem to favor almost limitless expansion of college attendance. One hears the phrase "everyone has a right to go to college." It is easy to dispose of this position in its extreme form. There are some youngsters whose mental deficiency is so severe that they cannot enter the first grade. There are a number of youngsters out of every hundred whose mental limitations make it impossible for them to get as far as junior high school. There are many more who can progress through high school only if they are placed in special programs which take into account their academic limitations. These "slow learners" could not complete high school if they were required to enroll in a college preparatory curriculum.

It is true that some who fall in this group would not be there if it were not for social and economic handicaps. But for most of them, there is no convincing evidence that social handicaps are a major factor in their academic limitations. Children with severe or moderate intellectual limitations appear not infrequently in families which are able to give them every advantage, and in which the possibilities of treatment have been exhaustively explored. Such children can be helped by intelligent attention, but the hope that any major change can be accomplished in their academic limitations is usually doomed to disappointment.

With each higher grade an increasing number of youngsters find it difficult or impossible to keep up with the work. Some drop out. Some transfer to vocational or industrial arts programs. A great many never complete high school.

Presumably, college students should only be drawn from the group which is able to get through high school. So the question becomes: "Should all high school graduates go to college?" The answer most frequently heard is that "all should go to college who are qualified for it"—but what do we mean by *qualified?* Probably less than 1 percent of the college-age population is qualified to attend the California Institute of Technology. There are other colleges where 10, 20, 40 or 60 per cent of the college-age population is qualified to attend.

It would be possible to create institutions with standards so low that 90 per cent of the college-age population could qualify. In order to do so it would be necessary only to water down the curriculum and provide simpler subjects. Pushed to its extreme, the logic of this position would lead us to the establishment of institutions at about the intellectual level of summer camps. We could then include almost all of the population in these make-believe colleges.

Let us pursue this depressing thought. If it were certain that almost all of the eighteen- to twenty-two-year-old population could benefit greatly by full-time attendance at "colleges" of this sort, no one could reasonably object. But one must look with extreme skepticism upon the notion that all high school graduates can profit by continued formal schooling. There is no question that they can profit by continued *education.* But the character of this education will vary from one youngster to the next. Some will profit by continued book learning; others by some kind of vocational training; still others by learning on the job. Others may require other kinds of growth experiences.

Because college has gained extraordinary prestige, we are. tempted to assume that the only useful learning and growth comes from attending such an institution; listening to professors talk from platforms, and reproducing required information on occasions called examinations. This is an extremely constricting notion. Even in the case of intellectually gifted individuals, it is a mistake to assume that the only kind of learning they can accomplish is in school. Many gifted individuals might be better off if they could be exposed to alternative growth experiences. . . .

Properly understood, the college or university is the instrument of *one kind of further education of those whose capacities fit them for that kind of education.* It should not be regarded as the sole means of establishing one's human worth. It should not be seen as the unique key to happiness, self respect and inner confidence.

We have all done our bit to foster these misconceptions. And the root of the difficulty is our bad habit of assuming that the only meaningful life is the "successful" life, defining success in terms of high personal attainment in the world's eyes. Today attendance at college has become virtually a prerequisite of high attainment in the world's eyes, so that it becomes, in the false value framework we have created, the only passport to a meaningful life. No wonder our colleges are crowded.

The crowding in our colleges is less regrettable than the confusion in our values. *Human dignity and worth should be assessed only in terms of those qualities of mind and spirit that are within the reach of every human being.*

This is not to say that we should not value achievement. We should value it exceedingly. It is simply to say that achievement should not be confused with human worth. Our recognition of the dignity and worth of the individual is based upon moral imperatives and should be of universal application. In other words, everyone has a "right" to that recognition. Being a college graduate involves qualities of mind which can never be universally possessed. Everyone does not have a right to be a college graduate, any more than everyone has a right to run a four-minute mile.

What we are really seeking is what James Conant had in mind when he said that the American people are concerned not only for equality of opportunity but for equality of respect. Every human being wishes to be respected regardless of his ability, and in moral terms we are bound to grant him that right. The more we allow the impression to get abroad that only the college man or woman is worthy of respect in our society, the more we contribute to a fatal confusion which works to the injury of all concerned. If we make the confusing assumption that college is the sole cradle of human dignity, need we be surprised that every citizen demands to be rocked in that cradle? . . .

In short, we reject the notion that excellence is something that can only be experienced in the most rarified strata of higher education. It may be experienced at every level and in every serious kind of higher education. . . .

We must make the same challenging demands of students. We must never make the insolent and degrading assumption that young people unfitted for the most demanding fields of intellectual endeavor are incapable of rigorous attention to *some sort of standards*. It is an appalling error to assume—as some of our institutions seem to have assumed—that young men and women incapable of the highest standards of intellectual excellence are incapable of any standards whatsoever, and can properly be subjected to shoddy, slovenly and trashy educational fare. College should be a demanding as well as an enriching experience—demanding for the brilliant youngster at a high level of expectation and for the less brilliant at a more modest level.

It is no sin to let average as well as brilliant youngsters into college. It *is* a sin to let any substantial portion of them—average or brilliant—drift through college without effort, without growth and without a goal. That is the real scandal in many of our institutions. . . .

The Origin of Admissions Testing

5. James B. Conant, *My Several Lives,* 1970

Before his wartime government service, James Bryant Conant (1893–1978) made an indelible mark on American education. As president of Harvard College (1933–53), he early sought to raise standards for admission to Harvard by admitting students from around the nation on the basis of academic merit proven by rigorous testing. His program endorsed a meritocratic style that spread throughout higher education and indeed throughout much of American corporate and governmental life. Conant admired Thomas Jefferson's educational proposals and Frederick Jackson Turner's frontier themes. By 1940 Conant was touting in *Atlantic Monthly* articles the Jeffersonian scheme of advancing gifted students at all school levels up an increasingly competitive and narrowing ladder to attain a leadership group of the best minds regardless of social or class background. This would result, he wrote, in true "social mobility"—a decidedly Turnerian phrase. Opening the doors to higher education to all who had qualified under the tests would be the educational device for a "classless" society resulting in an exceptional American "radicalism."

In his autobiography, excerpted here, Conant explains why he changed his emphasis from aptitude to achievement (multiple-choice) testing, the pattern of tests given to millions of young people in the last half of the twentieth century. Its designs and aims continue to be criticized and modified into this century. Its major vehicle, the SAT (first called the Scholastic Aptitude Test, then renamed the Scholastic Achievement Test, then the Scholastic Assessment Test, and now simply the SAT) was initially administered by the Educational Testing Service under the auspices of the College Entrance Examination Board where Conant, an influential director, steered his former Harvard assistant, Henry Chauncey, into the presidency of the ETS.

My Several Lives: Memoirs of a Social Inventor by James B. Conant, pp. 417–19, 423–24, 426, 428–32. Copyright © 1970 by James B. Conant, Reprinted by permission of Harper Collins Publishers. Further reading: see Conant's "Education for a Classless Society: The Jeffersonian Tradition," *The Atlantic Monthly,* May 1940, 593–602; "Wanted: American Radicals," *The Atlantic Monthly,* May 1943, 40–45; and *Thomas Jefferson and the Development of American Public Education* (Berkeley, CA, 1963). Among many books on testing, see especially Nicolas Lemann, *The Big Test: The Secret History of American Meritocracy* (New York, 1999); Jacques Steinberg, *The Gatekeepers: Inside the Admissions Process* (New York, 2002); Rebecca Zwick, *Fair Game? The Use of Standardized Admissions Tests in Higher Education* (New York, 2002); a survey of admissions testing and its problems, "College-Admissions Testing," *The Atlantic Monthly,* November 2003, 104–40; Michael C. Johanek, *A Faithful Mirror: Reflections on the College Board and Education in America* (New York, 2001); Jerome Karabel, *The Chosen: The Hidden History of Admission and Exclusion at Harvard, Yale, and Princeton* (Boston, 2005), rehearses the history of Ivy League admission policies, with comprehensive bibliography; and Malcolm Gladwell, "Getting In: The Social Logic of Ivy League Admissions," *New Yorker*, October 10, 2005, 80–86.

The Educational Testing Service is a nonprofit company located near Princeton, New Jersey. In 1966 it did nearly $25 million worth of business. Since one of its main activities is connected with the College Entrance Examination Board, the initials ETS are well known to school people all over the nation. Each year, not a few parents became aware of the Educational Testing Service through concern with the scores their offspring make on the Scholastic Aptitude Test (SAT) and the achievement tests prepared and graded by the organization.

Three separate testing enterprises were merged in 1947 in order to avoid overlapping and unproductive competition and in order to make available more resources for research and development; ETS was the result. An attempt in 1937–38 to bring about a similar consolidation had failed; the leaders in the testing movement were not then ready to join forces. After the war was over, it was suggested that another attempt be made. The successful merger was guided by the skillful hand of Devereux C. Josephs, at that time president of the Carnegie Corporation. Aware of my involvement in the prewar effort, he asked me to head a committee of educators to bring about what he had in mind. Because of my connection with two negotiations among testing experts, I became somewhat of a legend. Thus Henry Chauncey, the president of ETS, wrote me in 1961 when I retired from the Board of Trustees that the merger was my idea, "going back to 1937 or 1938. In 1946, it was put forward a second time. With the assistance of the Carnegie Corporation and after long negotiations in which you yourself took an active part, the merger was finally agreed upon."

President Chauncey was mistaken; a merger was not my idea in either 1937 or 1946. I was acting not as an inventor but as a promoter. If anyone is interested in naming the true inventors of ETS, he will have a hard time drawing up a list. Which illustrates an important point: if social inventions were covered by patents, the possibilities of litigation would be as endless as they are with the usual type of patent applying to new products, processes and procedures in the physical sciences.

I agreed in 1937 as a college president to lend a hand to the combining of several testing agencies because of my recently acquired enthusiasm for the Scholastic Aptitude Test. During the first year of my presidency, as I mentioned earlier, I turned to the Harvard Scholarship Committee to gain support for my idea of a new type of scholarship. Would it be possible to pick out from the applicants for admission to the college a few extremely able young men to whom we could award prize scholarships with reasonable certainty that the subsequent record of the recipients would be outstanding? To answer my question, a subcommittee was formed

consisting of Henry Chauncey, then an assistant dean of Harvard College, and Wilbur Bender. The report of this subcommittee recommended the use of the Scholastic Aptitude Test.

As far as I can remember, my conversations with Chauncey and other members of the Scholarship Committee were my first introduction to what psychologists had been doing in the field of examinations since World War I. I had heard of the psychological tests used by the Army during the war, but the opinion's about such tests were usually far from favorable. I was almost completely ignorant of what Professor Carl C. Brigham of Princeton had accomplished by developing a scholastic aptitude test which the College Entrance Examination Board started to give annually in 1926. It was hardly a new invention when we decided at Harvard to employ it as an instrument to differentiate among the incoming freshmen. Yet the more I learned about the use of the new objective tests and the more I became familiar with the concept of scholastic aptitude, the more I showed signs characteristic of a recent convert to a new religion. And it was a recognition of these signs that led half a dozen leaders in the testing movement to turn to me in 1937 when the question of a merger of testing agencies came up for discussion.

Like those of many converts, my beliefs included hopes that went too far. Looking back over the thirty-five years since my conversion, I recognize the almost naive faith with which I embraced the testers. It was easy to see the limitations of the college entrance examination system which then existed and had existed during the first decades of this century. In reacting against it, I was too ready to see in two new concepts—verbal aptitude and mathematical aptitude—the keys which would unlock all doors to a more promising future.

An historian of American higher education is apt to overlook the extent to which professors of Latin and Greek dominated the scene in the closing decades of the last century. They were fighting a rearguard action, to be sure, but as late as 1910 few of them realized that almost complete defeat was just a few years around the corner. . . .

The old-fashioned examinations were on the way out, not because some involved writing an essay, but because all were based on an old assumption in process of being discarded. I may call it the classical premise, which in the nineteenth century had been accepted as self-evident in Europe, England and the United States. In a word, it amounted to a definition of the knowledge that all educated men must have mastered before leaving school. Knowledge of ancient and modern languages and mathematics constituted much more than half the total content.

Once the classical premise was abandoned, the foundation of the college entrance examination system as it had existed rapidly disappeared. The schools would call the tune, each in its own right. Even within one school different pupils, could elect different programs, each according to the headmaster entirely suitable for a future college student. What a heresy! In place of the uniformity among pupils and schools which acceptance of the classical premise ensured, academic chaos was the order of the day. . . . My own orientation was determined by my ignorance of psychology on the one hand and by Harvard's success with the Scholastic Aptitude Test on the other. The word "aptitude" seemed to me to be the key to the new revelation. I proceeded to try to make it my own. . . .

I had become a firm believer in what I thought the proponents of the Scholastic Aptitude Test had postulated. I equated "aptitude" with "inherent ability"; I thought the psychologists had shown the constancy of inherent abilities from childhood on. I was later to see the error of my oversimplification, but for a number of years my thoughts about education reflected what might be called a Calvinistic view of intellectual ability. If better testing methods could be devised, I saw no reason why the inherent abilities of each child could not be determined as early as age twelve. How many separate abilities or aptitudes there might be, I could not say. But if aptitude for mathematics might be taken as an example, a proper measure of it would enable one to predict for a junior high school youngster the degree of success in mathematics courses in school and college, irrespective of the efforts of the teachers. Such were my assumptions.

The advantage of this point of view for a college admission officer was obvious. Measure the various aptitudes of a candidate for admission and choose only those with the highest scores. Since there were several aptitudes, those who guarded the college gates would have to decide as to what would be an acceptable balance of aptitudes in a youth who sought admission. Low aptitude for mathematics might be offset by high performance on a verbal aptitude test. The significant fact appeared to be that the school record was of little consequence. Subject-matter examinations were of slight value. The aptitude, not the schooling, was what counted. . . . As I was gradually to realize, the most perfect mathematical aptitude test yet devised could measure only a *developed* aptitude; exposure to good teaching in mathematics as contrasted with no exposure in grades 9, 10 and 11 did make a difference in development. . . .

If a definitive history of the testing movement or even of the Educational Testing Service is ever written, it will have to treat in detail the immediate postwar activities of W. S. Learned, Henry Chauncey (who became associate secretary of the College Entrance Examination Board in the summer of 1945), G. W. Mullins, the new officers of the Carnegie Corporation, Devereux Josephs (president), Charles Dollard (second-in-command), as well as O. C. Carmichael of Vanderbilt, who became president of the Carnegie Foundation for the Advancement of Teaching. I was in no way involved until late in March 1946, when Henry Chauncey came to

Cambridge to see me. He explained what had been going on since the end of the war. . . .

In the middle of May (1946) Carmichael appointed me chairman of the commission which Chauncey had foreseen. . . . The other members were: the presidents of Cornell, Brown, the University of Cincinnati, the University of California and the University of Minnesota; the dean of the Graduate School of the University of North Carolina; Alexander J. Stoddard, Superintendent of Schools at Philadelphia; and Francis Spaulding, only recently inaugurated as the Commissioner of Education for the State of New York. Mr. Stephen H. Stackpole, an officer of the Carnegie Foundation, served as secretary. Such a group of well-known educational administrators was regarded with considerable respect in those days. It was extremely likely that what we recommended would find acceptance in all the hostile camps.

The report was unanimous; we carried out the task which Josephs wished us to perform, recommending "that there be established the Cooperative Educational Testing Service," but we envisioned this new organization as "affiliated with the American Council on Education." Now it was the turn for the College Entrance Board to dissent. There were others also who questioned the report of our committee, among them Henry Dyer of Harvard and Paul Buck, the provost of Harvard University. . . .

On June 20, 1947, the secretary of the committee wrote to me as chairman that the representatives of the CEEB and ACE had come to an agreement. The Carnegie Corporation had already promised to contribute handsomely to the initial endowment. The Board of Trustees of the new Educational Testing Service met and elected Henry Chauncey as president. The new educational invention was ready to function, and function effectively it did, with a manifold expansion of its projects. On my return from Germany in 1957, I became a trustee and therefore can speak from personal knowledge when I testify to the importance of the research and development activities in support of which the merger had been originally conceived.

Since 1937 not only I but others have modified our views about tests and testing. The concept of aptitude as distinguished from achievement is no longer as clear-cut as it once was. What is assessed by aptitude tests is not an inborn set of dispositions but the resultant of the experiences of the youth in question. I long ago recognized the effect on the SAT results of differing school environments. And since I made a study of the schools in the big-city slums, I have begun to appreciate how much all test scores are influenced by the out-of-school environment—the home, the family and the neighborhood. Nevertheless the significance of the introduction by the College Board of multiple-choice achievement tests remains. These tests were so all-embracing that no syllabi for them could be written. This fact was of determining importance. (The *Definitions of Re-*

quirements, as I mentioned, were abolished in 1942.) Since the end of World War II it has been widely recognized that for the purpose of predicting subsequent success (or lack of it) in college, both achievement tests and aptitude tests, as well as the school record, should be carefully considered. The new type of this test of the knowledge acquired (the multiple-choice achievement test) is a far better test than the old College Board papers because, instead of five to ten questions, there are now many items; the element of luck as to what a candidate would find on the examination paper, so great in the old days, has been largely eliminated. Today we have much better methods of assessing what a boy or girl has mastered during the school years than before the new-type tests were introduced. Though there are still critics of the new procedures, few school or college people would wish to go back to the days of fifty years ago. The establishment of ETS was part of an educational revolution in which I am proud to have played a part.

California's Master Plan

6. *A Master Plan for Higher Education in California,* 1960

Assemblywoman Dorothy M. Donahoe (1911–60) was the spirited leader of the legislative movement to coordinate higher education in California. A constant worker for statewide educational improvements, she introduced Assembly Concurrent Resolution No. 88, adopted in the 1959 session, which provided for this master plan. Clark Kerr, president of the University of California (I, 11), and Roy E. Simpson, superintendent of public instruction, headed the liaison committee that in 1959 set up the master plan survey team that drew up this document. On that team, chaired by Arthur G. Coons of Occidental College, were representatives of the university, the state colleges, the junior colleges, and private institutions. With remarkable speed, the master plan was prepared and submitted to the legislature by February 1, 1960. At a special session of the legislature, called by Governor Edmund G. Brown, recommendations requiring legislative action were made into law.

A Master Plan for Higher Education in California, 1960–1975 (Sacramento, 1960), pp. 1–5, 8–9, 11–12, 14. Further reading: The master plan was anticipated by two earlier reports: M. E. Deutsch, A. A. Douglas, and G. D. Strayer, *A Report of a Survey of the Needs of California in Higher Education* (Berkeley, 1948) and T. C. Holy, T. R. McConnell, and H. H. Semans, *A Restudy of the Needs of California in Higher Education* (Sacramento, 1955). Neil J. Smelser, "California: A Multisegment System," in *Higher Learning in America, 1980–2000,* ed. Arthur Levine (Baltimore, 1983), ch. 7; John Aubrey Douglass, *The California Idea and American Higher Education: 1850 to the 1960 Master Plan* (Stanford, CA, 2000), a carefully detailed history of the University of California down through the master plan; Arthur G. Coons, *Crises in California Higher Education: Experience under the Master Plan and Problems of Coordination, 1959 to 1968* (Los Angeles, 1968) traces the history of the plan by a participant in its formation.

To the Regents of the University of California and the State Board of Education:

Your Liaison Committee reports that, pursuant to the provisions of Assembly Concurrent Resolution No. 88, adopted by the Legislature in 1959, and pursuant to action taken by the two Boards in joint session on April 15, 1959, it has directed a basic study and the preparation of a Master Plan for Higher Education in the State of California to meet the needs of the State during the next ten years and thereafter; and as a result of said Study recommends as follows:

It is recommended that:

1. An amendment be proposed to add a new section to Article IX of the California Constitution providing that: Public higher education shall consist of the junior colleges, the State College System, and the University of California. Each shall strive for excellence in its sphere, as assigned in this section.

2. The junior colleges shall be governed by local boards selected for the purpose from each district maintaining one or more junior colleges. The State Board of Education shall prescribe minimum standards for the formation and operation of junior colleges, and shall exercise general supervision over said junior colleges, as prescribed by law. Said public junior colleges shall offer instruction through but not beyond the fourteenth grade level including, but courses not for limited to, one or more of the following: (a) standard collegiate courses for transfer to higher institutions, (b) vocational-technical fields leading to employment, and (c) general, or liberal arts courses. Studies in these fields may lead to the Associate in Arts or Associate in Science degree. Nothing in this section shall be construed as altering the status of the junior college as part of the Public School System as defined elsewhere in the Constitution.

3. The State College System:

a. Shall constitute a public trust, to be administered by a body corporate known as "The Trustees of the State College System of California" with number, term of appointment, and powers closely paralleling those of the Regents.

b. The board shall consist of five ex-officio members: the Governor, the Lieutenant Governor, the Speaker of the Assembly, the Superintendent of Public Instruction, and the chief executive officer of the State College System; and 16 appointive members appointed by the Governor for terms of 16 years. The chief executive officer of the State College System shall also sit with The Regents in an advisory capacity, and the President of the University of California shall sit with the Trustees in an advisory capacity. The members of the State Board of Education shall serve ex officio as first Trustees, being replaced by regular appointees at the expiration of their respective terms.

c. The state colleges shall have as their primary function the provision of instruction in the liberal arts and sciences and in professions and applied fields which require more than two years of collegiate education and teacher education, both for undergraduate students and graduate students through the master's degree. The doctoral degree may be awarded jointly with the University of California, as hereinafter provided. Faculty research, using facilities provided for and consistent with the primary function of the state colleges, is authorized.

4. The University of California shall be governed by The Regents as provided in Section 9 of Article IX of the California Constitution. The University shall provide instruction in the liberal arts and sciences, and in the professions, including teacher education, and shall have exclusive jurisdiction over training for the professions (including but not by way of limitation), dentistry, law, medicine, veterinary medicine, and graduate architecture. The University shall have the sole authority in public higher education to award the doctor's degree in all fields of learning, *except that* it may agree with the state colleges to award joint doctor's degrees in selected fields. The University shall be the primary state-supported academic agency for research, and The Regents shall make reasonable provision for the use of its library and research facilities by qualified members of the faculties of other higher educational institutions, public and private.

5. An advisory body, the Co-ordinating Council for Higher Education:

a. Shall consist of 12 members, three representatives each from the University, the State College System, the junior colleges, and the independent colleges and universities. The University and the State College System each shall be represented by its chief executive officer and two board members appointed by the boards. The junior colleges shall be represented by (1) a member of the State Board of Education or its Chief Executive Officer; (2) a representative of the local governing boards; and (3) a representative of the local junior college administrators. The independent colleges and universities shall be represented as determined by agreement of the chief executive officers of the University and the State College System, in consultation with the association or associations of private higher educational institutions. All votes shall be recorded, but effective action shall require an affirmative vote of four of the six University and state college representatives; except that on junior college matters the junior college representatives shall have effective votes; and on the appointment and removal of a director of the Council all 12 shall be effective.

b. A director of the staff for the Co-ordinating Council shall be appointed by a vote of eight of the 12 Council members, and may be removed by a vote of eight members of the Council. He shall appoint such staff as the Council authorizes.

c. The Co-ordinating Council shall have the following functions, advisory to the governing boards and appropriate State officials:

(1) Review of the annual budget and capital outlay requests of the University and the State College System, and presentation to the Governor of comments on the general level of support sought.

(2) Interpretation of the functional differentiation among the publicly supported institutions provided in this section; and in accordance with the primary functions for each system as set forth above, advise The Regents and The Trustees on programs appropriate to each system.

(3) Development of plans for the orderly growth of higher education and making of recommendations to the governing boards on the need for and location of new facilities and programs.

d. The Council shall have power to require the public institutions of higher education to submit data on costs, selection and retention of students, enrollments, capacities, and other matters pertinent to effective planning and co-ordination.

ADMISSIONS POLICIES AND PROCEDURES

It is recommended that:

1. In order to raise materially standards for admission to the lower division, the state colleges select first-time freshmen from the top one-third (33⅓ per cent) and the University from the top one-eighth (12½ per cent) of all graduates of California public high schools with:

a. Continuation of existing special programs and curricula involving exceptions to this rule subject to approval by the respective boards, and these to be kept to a minimum, and those that are continued to be reported annually to the co-ordinating agency. Any new special programs and curricula involving such exceptions to be approved by the co-ordinating agency.

b. Graduates of private and out-of-state secondary schools to be held to equivalent levels.

2. Implementation of Recommendation Number 1 to be left of the two systems with the following provisions:

a. Each to have the new requirements in force for students admitted for Fall, 1962.

b. Inasmuch as the Survey Team favors acceptance in both systems of a requirement that all, or almost all, of the recommending units for admission shall be in college preparatory courses, that the application of such a requirement be carefully studied during 1960, and this principle be applied as fully as possible throughout both systems.

3. For both the state colleges and the University, freshman admissions through special procedures outside the basic requirements of recommending units of high school work and/or aptitude tests (such as specials and exceptions to the rules) be limited to 2 per cent of all freshman admissions in each system for a given year. Furthermore that all

"limited" students be required to meet regular admission standards.

4. Junior college functions now carried by state colleges and nondegree lower division programs at any state college or University campus (other than extension) be subject to the following rule:

The equivalent of junior college out-of-district tuition be charged beginning in Fall, 1960, against the counties of residence of all lower division students who are ineligible to admission by regular standards, and the funds collected paid to the General Fund of the State.

Furthermore, that such junior college functions now carried by state colleges at State expense be terminated not later than July 1, 1964, all admittees thereafter being required to meet standard entrance requirements.

5. The state colleges and the University require a minimum of at least 56 units of acceptable advanced standing credit before considering the admission of applicants ineligible to admission as freshmen because of inadequate grades in high school, except for curricula that require earlier transfer, and except also that each state college and campus of the University, through special procedures developed by each, be permitted to accept for earlier transfer not more than 2 per cent of all students who make application for advanced standing in any year.

6. Undergraduate applicants to the state colleges and the University who are legally resident in other states be required to meet higher entrance requirements than are required of residents of California, such out-of-state applicants to stand in the upper half of those ordinarily eligible. Furthermore, that there be developed and applied a common definition of legal residence for these public segments.

7. A study of the transfer procedures to both the University and the state colleges be undertaken through the co-ordinating agency during 1960 with the view of tightening them. Evidence available to the Master Plan Survey Team indicates the need for such action.

8. A continuing committee on selection, admission, and retention as a part of the co-ordinating agency be established....

9. Private institutions of higher education in California in the approaching period of heavy enrollments strive for increased excellence by adopting rigorous admission and retention standards....

ENROLLMENT LIMITATIONS AND PROJECTED PLANT NEEDS

It is recommended that:

1. With respect to the establishment of new state colleges and campuses of the University, the governing boards reaffirm their action taken in joint session on April 15, 1959, to the effect that "no new State Colleges or campuses of the University, other than those already approved, shall be established until adequate Junior College facilities have been provided, the determination of adequacy to be based on studies made under the direction of the Liaison Committee of the State Board of Education and The Regents of the University of California ... " with the further provision that the new state colleges and campuses of the University established by action of the Legislature in 1957, and by action of The Regents, also in 1957, be limited to upper division and graduate work until such time as adequate junior college opportunities are provided for the primary area served by these institutions.

2. The following full-time enrollment ranges be observed for existing institutions, for those authorized but not yet established, and for those later established:

Type of Institution	Minimum[1]	Optimum	Maximum
Junior Colleges	400	3,500	6,000*
State Colleges			
In densely populated areas in metropolitan centers	5,000	10,000	20,000
Outside metropolitan centers	3,000	8,000	12,000
University of California Campusees[2]	5,000	12,000	27,500

[1] These are to be attained within seven to ten years after students are first admitted.

[2] The minimum figure for the University assumes graduate work in basic disciplines and one or more professional schools.

*This maximum might be exceeded in densely populated areas in metropolitan centers.

FACULTY DEMAND AND SUPPLY

It is recommended that:

1. Much greater effort be made to divert a greater proportion of college graduates into graduate training preparatory to careers in college and university teaching. This diversion can best be accomplished by a concerted effort on the part of adequately staffed and supported counseling and guidance services at all levels of education, and with the full co-operation of all college and university faculty members.

2. More funds be secured to provide financial assistance to those in graduate training. The high attrition rate in graduate programs is, in large part, due to financial difficulty; and these withdrawals constitute not only a loss to the potential faculty supply but an economic waste to the state. Provision of fellowship and loan funds for graduate students is undoubtedly one of the best ways of reducing the attrition rate.

3. Greatly increased salaries and expanded fringe benefits, such as health and group life insurance, leaves, and travel funds to attend professional meetings, housing, parking and moving expenses, be provided for faculty members in order to make college and university teaching attractive as compared with business and industry.

4. Greater use be made of California-trained doctoral degree holders, especially in the shortage years immediately ahead. For the three-year period 1955–58 only 53 per cent of those so trained who entered teaching did so in California. Evidence indicates that those leaving California do not do so by choice.

5. Individual faculty members and their institutions jointly assume responsibility for both the initiative and opportunity for the faculty in-service preparation and self-improvement, so essential for the growth and development of the institutions.

6. Strengthening of the master's degree programs in all institutions offering such programs be undertaken by these institutions so that holders of this degree may be more effective additions to the faculties of colleges, universities, and junior colleges.

7. Reorientation of present doctoral programs offered by California institutions be undertaken to insure that those receiving the degree and planning to enter college and university teaching possess the qualities not only of scholars, but of scholar-teachers. Because the University of California awarded 54.6 per cent of the doctorates given by California institutions for the period 1952–53—1955–56, it has a particular responsibility for the implementing of this recommendation.

8. Because of the continual change in faculty demand and supply, the Co-ordinating agency annually collect pertinent data from all segments of higher education in the state and thereby make possible the testing of the assumptions underlying this report. . . .

STUDENT FEES

For the state colleges and the University of California it is recommended that:

1. The two governing boards reaffirm the long established principle that state colleges and the University of California shall be tuition free to all residents of the state.

2. Students who are residents of other states pay as follows:

a. All students except those exempt by law pay tuition sufficient to cover not less than the state's contribution to the average teaching expense per student. . . .

"Teaching expense is defined to include the cost of the salaries of the instructors involved in teaching for the proportion of their time which is concerned with instruction, plus the clerical salaries, supplies, equipment and organized activities related to teaching."

b. Other fees for services not directly related to instruction.

3. Each system devise a fee structure and collect sufficient revenues to cover such operating costs as those for laboratory fees, health, intercollegiate athletics, student activities, and other services incidental to, but not directly related to, instruction.

4. The operation of all such ancillary services for students as housing, feeding, and parking be self-supporting. Taxpayers' money should not be used to subsidize, openly or covertly, the operation of such services. . . .

Community Colleges

7. W. B. Devall, "Community Colleges," 1968

When he wrote this criticism of the American community college, W. B. Devall was an assistant professor in the department of sociology at the University of Alberta.

W. B. Devall, "Community Colleges: A Dissenting View," *Educational Record* 49, no. 2 (Spring 1968): 168–72. © 1968 by American Council on Education, Washington, D.C. Used by permission of *Educational Record*. Further reading: James J. Zigerell, "The Community College in Search of an Identity," *Journal of Higher Education* 41 (December 1970): 701–12; Arthur M. Cohen and Florence B. Brawer, *The American Community College* (San Francisco, 1982); and II, 8.

It is my belief that the community college movement, far from being a blessing, may indeed further distort and dilute post–high school education in America. I argue that the problems and needs for education that community colleges are attempting to fill, can be handled more rationally and effectively by other organizations in the society without resorting to the expansion of this bugaboo in American education.

Let me lay one argument to rest right now. I can hear my opponents shouting that the community college movement is already too far under way to turn back. With millions of dollars already invested, with faculties and physical plants created, we cannot waste these resources. We could have discouraged community colleges 30 years ago, but not now. We have too much invested. We must, instead, devise ways to improve the colleges internally.

To these persons, I say that it is true that Bigness and rapid growth are taken as measures of achievement and are held in high regard almost universally in America. But rapid growth may not be a virtue and Bigness may actually be a vice. We may be creating a two-headed monster in American higher education; and before it comes back to haunt our descendants, we should decide whether we should put more of our energy and money into this organization, or should direct them in other, more innovative channels. . . .

Given the social conditions—few jobs for the unskilled, desire to avoid the draft, social acceptance of continuing one's education—"staying in school" also has strong social and financial payoffs for the student. As a student, a youth has a legitimate social identity. . . .

Given this situation—the need for more technical training, the value we place on education *per se,* the demand for "continuing education"—what are the alternatives to community colleges? There are at least five: expansion of proprietary schools; on the job training; true universal military training; extension divisions of state universities; and universities in the fields. . . .

Proprietary schools have a long history of successful service in this country and, today, training in many vocations—barbers, hairdressers, masseurs, modeling, etc.—is found chiefly in these schools. In supporting such training, I follow the principle that those who receive benefit from a service should pay for it. . . . These proprietary schools have placement bureaus for their graduates, and indeed, in some cases, like the business colleges, graduates may be working part-time for an employer while finishing their course work. They are regulated by the state and must fulfill certain standards.

In other words, there is nothing inherently better or more efficient about technical-vocational training in community colleges than in proprietary schools. Furthermore, they would help to reduce the tax burden in the local community, and are flexible enough to handle student needs.

Another alternative, and one that has become increasingly important in recent years, is the employee training programs which corporations use to train their new employees and retrain old employees. Corporations like General Motors, Ford, Westinghouse, Bell Telephone, Bendix, General Dynamics, etc., have extensive and extremely efficient vocational and managerial training programs. . . .

It is one of the ironic facts of higher education in America, that educational institutions (whose motto is, "education is our business") when given contracts to set up new concepts in American education like the Job Corps training centers, have had to subcontract the real substance of these programs —the occupational training programs—to private corporations that know more about certain aspects of education than the professional educators.

If American high schools could be successful in graduating at least somewhat literate graduates, then the large corporations should be encouraged to take these graduates, and. with a combination of on-the-job training and formal instruction, make them productive, tax-paying, independent citizens faster than Community colleges can, and without the unpleasant side effects of community college education: continued dependency, unrealistic aspirations, and wasted "general education."

A third alternative for young people between 18 and 24 would be a true, unequivocal universal citizenship service. . . . The young people would receive occupational training for which they would be awarded credit when they return to civilian life, and the needs and requirements of the society would be served with greater social justice than the present system. The Armed Forces have the most extensive educational facilities in this society of any organization. A great appeal for recruitment during nonemergency times is the educational advantages available in the service. . . .

The last two alternatives to the community college are of a somewhat different nature than those discussed above. While I have been concerned, up to this point, mainly with vocational training, I shall now consider liberal education and adult education. Parenthetically, I might add, one of the greatest concerns of critics of the community colleges in this country is that they may become shallow imitations of the traditional, four-year colleges. Community colleges, in trying to legitimize their status in American education, are taking on the trappings—liberal arts courses, academic rank, faculty senates, etc.,— of traditional colleges without really understanding the meaning of "liberal education." In trying so hard to please so many people, the community colleges may fail to provide the needed impetus to higher education. . . .

With greater resources and more flexibility, with a strong administration, and the prestige of established colleges behind them, the university extension program could provide the type of liberal arts curriculum and instruction that students need much better than can the community colleges. Most public universities today have extension divisions that use physical facilities already existing in a community—high schools or college classrooms— thus eliminating costly capital investments made by junior colleges. They also use human resources in the community. There are always college faculty members who will repeat a course that they teach during the day for an evening credit class. There are also many people in large communities who can teach part-time. These include successful professionals who are capable of teaching a course in their specialty, or women who hold graduate degrees and are capable of teaching college courses, but who do not want a full-time job because they are raising a family, Some universities even fly faculty members to other cities one day a week to teach an extension class. In other words, a well administered extension division of a university may be more flexible in serving the educational demands for "liberal education" courses than a community college. . . .

I recommend expanding the divisions of continuing education of the universities to handle the needs for adult education and continuing education in our society. Let us send mobile school rooms into rural areas and small towns as we now send bookmobiles or traveling theatre groups. Let us vastly expand the use of television in teaching college courses. Let us give college credit for work-study programs in industry, hospitals, and service organizations. But most of all, let us not be tied to the idea that education can only take place on a campus. Or better still, let's conceive of the whole country as a campus. . . .

Community colleges are providing a great service to this society, but they are not the panacea for the problems that plague American education. Other more dramatic alternatives are available, and should be utilized.

8. Patrick M. Callan,
"Stewards of Opportunity," 1997

Active in western regional higher education coordinating and monitoring agencies, Patrick M. Callan (1942–) wrote this brief and pointed overview of community colleges in 1997. Two decades before this essay, community colleges had enrolled one third of the nation's college students. At that time less than one quarter of community college students went on to four-year schools.

Callan's received his bachelor's degree from the University of Santa Clara (1964), which he followed up with graduate work at UCLA and Stanford. He joined a higher educational committee of the California state legislature, became a director of the Montana State Commission for Postsecondary Education (1973–74), next led the Washington State Council for Postsecondary Education (1975–78), then returned to head the California Postsecondary Education System (1978–86). After spending three years with the Educational Commission of the States in Denver, he worked with the National Center for Public Policy and Higher Education, becoming its president in 1992.

Patrick M. Callan, "Stewards of Opportunity: America's Public Community Colleges," *Daedalus* (1997): 95–103, 105–6, 109–11. © 1997 by the American Academy of Arts and Sciences, abridged with permission. Further reading: Audrey Williams June, "Where Have All the Private 2-Year Colleges Gone?" *Chronicle of Higher Education,* September 12, 2003, A23–25; *Community and Junior College Journal* (1930–present) and *Community College Review* (1973–present); "Community Colleges," *Chronicle of Higher Education,* October 29, 2004, B16; and II, 7, 9.

America's public community colleges enroll almost half of all undergraduates in higher education's public sector. Universally perceived as the first way station on the road to social mobility, they are at the leading edge of educational opportunity. Millions of Americans and hundreds of communities benefit from their convenient locations, wide range of programs, and open admission policies. What are these community colleges? For many people, including more than a few in academe, they are terra incognita. The most impressive fact about them is their magnitude: some 1,036 publicly supported community colleges enroll over 5.3 million students. Equally impressive, although less obvious, is their diversity, a diversity so great that it defies almost any attempt at generalization. But typically—although there is no typical community college—the community colleges are two-year schools with three primary missions: 1) general education equivalent to the freshman and sophomore years at a four-year college or university; 2) vocational and occupational training; and 3) community service. Over time, and across and within states, these colleges vary widely in the emphasis given to each of these missions. Nevertheless, the faculty commitment to teaching is strong and pervasive, whether it be English 101, computer technology in vocational training, or conversational French for footloose suburbanites.

Although their origins are in the early years of the twentieth century, today's public community colleges are products of post–World War II America. Only after about 1960 did they become the primary instrument for the expansion of college opportunity. An analogy here is appropriate: After the Morrill Act in 1862, the land-grant colleges expanded the very definition of higher education, providing opportunities for a new population and extending the curriculum to the practical and applied. Likewise, a hundred years later, the community colleges have expanded prior conceptions of what constituted higher education and its students. And, like the land-grant colleges, the community colleges grew and flourished in an era of economic transition and were nurtured by democratic, egalitarian, and political impulses.

Generalizations about community colleges based on national—or even state—statistics have little applicability to individual institutions. These colleges remain true to their local origins. They are *community* colleges in reality as well as name, as diverse as the towns, cities, and neighborhoods that they serve. Governors and legislators, particularly those in our most populous states, sometimes inappropriately treat all community colleges in their states as if they were virtually identical. They find the task of tailoring laws to meet the needs of the many different members of so diverse a group to be beyond easy solution. Nor, I have found, is there an easy approach for those who write about community colleges; I can only promise to try to avoid too much oversimplification.

THE COLLEGES, THEIR FACULTY, AND THEIR STUDENTS

Of the country's 2,640 public higher education institutions, 604 are four-year colleges and universities and 1,036 are community colleges. Of the 11.1 million students, some 5.8 million, including those in graduate programs, are enrolled in four-year institutions and about 5.3 million are in the community colleges, some in academic programs, others in occupational training. The large number of community colleges is not surprising, for many states have had the goal of a community college within commuting distance of every citizen. In contrast, few states need—or can afford—more than one major research university.

After World War II higher education expanded in an almost phenomenal fashion, and the community colleges contributed a major share of this growth. As William Friday, longtime and distinguished president of the University of North Carolina, once commented, four-year colleges had previously been located "up isolated, little hollows" where the students would be sheltered from worldly temptations. In the last half of this century, however, the community colleges were brought to the people, the people responded, and the colleges grew in numbers and students. Financial considerations played a part in this growth: Local support in most states initially reduced the burden on state general funds, and low or no tuition attracted students who could not otherwise afford to leave their homes, families, or work.

The many patterns of funding and governing the community colleges—as many as there are states—are difficult to squeeze into useful categories. Two broad, relatively recent trends can be discerned. First, most colleges now rely much more heavily than in the past on state funds and student tuition. Originally, the community colleges were funded in the same manner as the public schools, with largely local support supplemented by state funds, and without tuition. State funds now provide the greatest share both nationally (39 percent) and in forty-two states. Nationally, revenue from tuition (20 percent) now slightly exceeds local funding (18 percent), and in four states the colleges receive the largest share of their support from it. The higher the tuition, of course, the greater the adverse impact on access for those who are most dependent on the colleges. Second, like the four-year colleges and universities, the community colleges are now much more likely than in the past to be part of a statewide or multicampus system. However, even though they are part of a system, most community colleges have some form of local board.

The apparent shift of both funding and governance from the local level to the state does not necessarily, I believe, justify sounding an alarm about creeping centralization. Nothing in my experience, having visited a variety of states, suggests that most community colleges are any more amenable now than they ever were to taking direction from outside their local community.

The Faculty

The number of faculty members in the public community colleges—now about 290,000—has roughly tripled over the past twenty years. Their average, nine-month salary of $41,000 in 1993–94 was some 25 percent less than the pay at public universities and 11 percent less than that at other public four-year institutions. Sixty percent of community-college faculty hold a master's degree, and, as might be expected in a teaching institution, fewer than 16 percent hold doctoral or professional degrees. At approximately 66 percent of the community colleges. the faculty are covered by a collective bargaining agreement, in contrast to 55 percent of the four-year institutions at which their counterparts teach. Ninety-two percent of community-college faculty believe that teaching effectiveness should be the primary criterion for the promotion of faculty, contrasted to 22 percent of their research university counterparts.

Although they have administrative responsibilities similar to those of their counterparts at four-year campuses, community-college faculty are highly unlikely to engage in research or other scholarly activity. Eighty-one percent consider teaching to be their principal activity, and they report spending far more time teaching than do four-year college faculty. Alexander Astin found that more than three-fourths of the community-college faculty teach more than twelve hours of classes per week, contrasted with only about one-third of four-year college faculty and about 10 percent of those at universities. A similar percentage believe that creating a positive undergraduate experience is a high or very high priority for the community colleges, compared to 55 percent at public universities.

Community-college faculty are more likely to be part-time instructors than are their counterparts in the public, four-year institutions. The part-time status of community-college faculty has increased steadily over the years. . . .

The Students

Community colleges draw their students from a much different population than do four-year institutions, and student characteristics strongly suggest the importance of these institutions for college opportunity:

1) With an average age of twenty-nine, community-college students are generally older than those in the four-year colleges and universities. Thirty-five percent are under twenty-one years of age, in contrast to 42 percent of four-year college students. And 36 percent are thirty years of age or older, in contrast to 23 percent of those at four-year campuses.

2) Some 47 percent of undergraduates at community colleges are employed for thirty-five or more hours per week, in contrast to 27 percent of those at four-year colleges. At the same time, about the same percentage of students at both types of institutions are not employed at all.

3) Community colleges enroll roughly half of the students in higher education who come from minority or ethnic backgrounds—for example, 45 percent of African-American students, 52 percent of Hispanic students, and 56 percent of Native Americans.

4) Of students at the community colleges, 40 percent are from families with incomes of less than $30,000 a year, in contrast to only 28 percent of first-year students at four-year colleges and universities.

A college's geographic location is usually a critical determinant of the characteristics of its students. A college in a major city much more likely than one "up a little hollow" to have a large and diverse student body, with a high proportion of older, part-time and minority students. Many of these urban colleges also face the same inner-city problems that trouble the public schools—problems that can range from youth gangs to students' lack of preparation or motivation. But whether large or small, urban or rural, community colleges share a common history. . . .

By 1970, the "junior colleges" had become "community colleges," in part because this was proposed in the 1948 "Truman Report." More substantively, I believe, that report authoritatively stated the case for broad and equal educational opportunity that has set the direction of American higher education —at least until now. The report urged an imperative, that "free and universal access to education, in terms of interest, ability, and need of the student, must be a major goal in American education." The community colleges were central to the report's plan for expanding opportunity, and their extensive development was recommended. Population growth, the baby boomers, and an expanding job market were influential. Equally important, a national consensus supported full development of human talent, and this consensus fueled both the expansion of American higher education generally and the explosive increase in both the number of and enrollment at community colleges. Between 1950 and 1970, the number of community colleges more than doubled, and enrollment increased from 217,000 to 1,630,000. As returning veterans and the subsequent baby-boom generation dramatically increased demand for college, the role of the community colleges as an "open door" for entry to the four-year institutions reemerged. In 1971, the Carnegie Commission on Higher Education reported that community colleges were being established at a rate of one a week. The colleges embraced the call for wider access. In this postwar period, a growing number of students were older and less affluent than those of the prewar years.

Enrollment has continued to grow; between 1969 and 1994 community-college enrollment increased by some 174 percent, contrasted with 47 percent for four-year institutions. Today, in 1997, "community colleges" retain their name but are increasingly characterized as "comprehensive community colleges." The major emphasis of the colleges has shifted from the transfer function to vocational training. Between 1970 and 1990, the number of associate degrees awarded in occupational fields increased from 43 percent of all degrees to 63 percent, and the number in academic fields decreased accordingly. Recent years have seen state governments, business, industry, and private foundations increase their financial support for vocational programs. At the same time, the two primary missions of academic and vocational education seem to have been eroded in what may be the colleges' excessive zeal to be all things to all people. In part, this zeal could be attributed to the desire to educate new or previously neglected populations, such as displaced housewives, ethnic minorities, immigrants, and older adults. Also, the colleges needed to maintain enrollments to obtain state financial support. . . .

As the end of the century approaches, the community colleges are undoubtedly a success. Collectively they are now clearly an integral part of American higher education, and most are, or aspire to be, "comprehensive" institutions. Individually, however, the colleges have not yet resolved questions about their particular institutional identity. Overly enthusiastic response to community needs has sometimes blurred the line between vocational training and avocational recreation. Resources are strained at many colleges by the needs of older students and, particularly, those of students from public schools of declining quality. Pressure from their local communities for them to be a social and cultural resource confuses and complicates full realization of primary educational missions. The community colleges have given America a new dimension of what constitutes higher education in this country. They have become a national presence and asset but remain a uniquely local phenomenon. A few, but not many, resemble traditional, four-year liberal-arts colleges. A few, but again not many, resemble specialized technical institutes. Most combine the functions of both, often with the added responsibilities of teaching, for example, English as a second language, citizenship, and—under contract with business or industry—highly specialized skills. The colleges, their faculty, and their students now face the uncertainties of demographic, economic, and technological change. . . .

The community colleges have relatively low costs. They are an efficient channel in targeting public financial resources for lower division and occupational instruction without increasing other expenditures such as those for residential facilities and research. Yet even with these cost advantages, the sheer volume of additional students, along with the financial constraints and competition, will, I believe, generate strong pressure for greater productivity and efficiency. . . .

The almost limitless reach of electronic communication and interaction can also make geographic and political boundaries obsolete. The fiefdoms contained by state lines and local community-college districts will be increasingly permeable by public and private competitors.

Technological advance carries the possibility— or threat—that states will bypass traditional institutions completely, including community colleges. John S. Daniel, vice chancellor of the Open University in the United Kingdom, has recently described eleven "mega-universities" throughout the world (none currently in the United States) that serve over 100,000 degree-seeking students through distance learning, doing so at costs far below even those of the community colleges. The nascent Western Governors University incorporates several characteristics of these institutions, including the separation of assessment and credentialing from instruction— an essential element of distance education, and one that is likely to increase the visibility of learning outcomes in our country. These alternatives and others that may emerge can become increasingly attractive investments to political leaders if the existing array of institutions—particularly community colleges, where most of the demand will initially come—are perceived as unable or unwilling to use the possibilities inherent in technologies to respond to emerging societal needs.

The colleges have been the nation's primary instrument for the expansion of educational opportunity, first to young high school graduates and then to adults of all ages, part-time students, and many others. They have often been on the cutting edge of innovation in American higher education—particularly with respect to the diversity of the students they have served, scheduling, instructional sites, and academic calendars. In these ways, the community colleges have shown great flexibility in organizing educational programs around the needs of their students; they have been less organized around the preferences of educational "providers" than most campuses in the four-year sector. In their methods of instruction, however, the community colleges have been less innovative, and, in common with the rest of higher education and the public schools, they rely heavily on the traditional, teacher-centered classroom and the lecture. This largely unexamined adherence to traditional teaching practice represents a major obstacle to significant improvement of teaching and learning. The reluctance to stray from well-traveled roads may be reinforced by faculty unionization to impede, for example, the adoption of electronic technology for both distance and campus instruction. And resistance to change is particularly in evidence when instructional change involves selective substitution of capital for labor. . . .

CONCLUSION

No sector of American higher education is better positioned than the community colleges for a world that will be characterized by relentless and simultaneous pressure for opportunity, educational quality, and cost effectiveness. The ability of community colleges to address these societal demands will depend on continued public commitment and on the adaptive capacity of the colleges. The fundamental challenge to the colleges will be developing and nurturing an intellectual culture undergirded by systematically rigorous attention to adult learning; to instructional contexts and methods that will best produce learning in a heterogeneous student population; and to the assessment of knowledge and skills derived from learning.

Almost by definition, community colleges challenge the conventional wisdom that correlates quality with *institutional* characteristics, not student *accomplishment*—that is, with "inputs" such as selective admissions, high levels of expenditure, and prestige derived from research reputation and institutional venerability. These measures are simply not applicable to the community colleges that, by design, were deliberately established as the primary institutions of mass higher education. The logic of mass education, and particularly of open admissions, leads inexorably to a concept of quality based on educational outcomes and assessment of added educational value. Absent such concept, accessibil-

ity often becomes a perceived substitute for quality, with a consequent erosion of public confidence and absence of essential information for educational improvement. Building, refining, and applying this concept of quality is the unfinished agenda of the community colleges in the twentieth century, and it is the indispensable condition for the radical transformation in teaching and learning that community colleges and their faculties must lead if they are to maintain and enhance their relevance and their capacity to serve society in the twenty-first century.

9. George B. Vaughan, "Redefining 'Open Access,'" (2003)

George B. Vaughan (1932–) has had long experience with American community colleges. He was successively president of Piedmont Virginia Community College and Mountain Empire Community College. Currently he is professor of higher education at North Carolina State University. His alternative view of community college programs in a time of fiscal limitations is reprinted here.

George B. Vaughan, "Redefining 'Open Access,'" *Chronicle of Higher Education,* December 5, 2003, B24. Copyright © 2003. Reprinted with the kind permission of George B. Vaughan.

REDEFINING "OPEN ACCESS"

Nothing is dearer to the heart and mind of a community-college leader than the belief that his or her institution can and should serve all eligible people who seek admittance. For decades, the "open-door" community college has been an often used and much revered metaphor for equal opportunity in higher education. Many community-college administrators, politicians, and members of the public have believed that community colleges can actually be all things to all people and serve all of the people all of the time.

In fact, one could view the history of community colleges in the United States as a three-act play in which open access is a key element of the plot. The curtain for Act 1 rose during the 1960s and early 1970s, when new community colleges opened at the rate of one a week. Act 2 occurred from the mid-1970s until the early 1990s, by which time community colleges were enrolling more than five million students. In that era, community colleges led the way in opening higher education to people who had previously been ignored, people often from low-income backgrounds or minority groups. As a result, about 60 percent of public-community-college students today are first generation, according to data from the National Center for Education Statistics.

Community colleges had apparently proved that open access worked. Throughout the 1990s, most of them continued to pack students in, although those students usually paid more tuition to attend than their predecessors. Today, however, one of the most important questions community-college leaders face is whether open access can continue or whether Act 3 will see the curtain fall on that noble undertaking.

Community colleges have indeed had an amazing run, receiving generous appropriations from state and local legislators for much of the past 40 years. And even when tax dollars have fallen short, presidents and governing boards have found ways to keep the door open: Adjuncts have replaced full-time faculty members, fewer and larger classes have been offered, and schedules have become less flexible. Defying common sense, community-college leaders have even enrolled thousands and thousands of students beyond the number for which their colleges have received tax revenues Last year, for example, community colleges in Washington State, which are heavily dependent on tax dollars, enrolled 9,000 students for whom they received no state money.

But now the difficult economy and continuing cuts in state appropriations are forcing more community-college leaders to face facts: As it has been practiced in the past, open access is a failure. Community colleges cannot serve all of the students who want to attend, nor can they continue to enroll large numbers of students for whom they receive no state financing—a practice that ultimately leads to fiscal irresponsibility. . . .

Such cutbacks often hurt the neediest students most. When classes are full, presidents usually cap enrollments as a first response, and the students who manage to gain admittance are often simply those best able to understand and negotiate the system. Such students are also, more often than not, affluent. Meanwhile, growing numbers of minority, lower-income, and immigrant students are finding themselves shut out. For example, this year California community colleges may turn away 20,000 black and Hispanic students.

Can open access be saved? The answer is yes—but only if community-college leaders abandon the idea that their mission is to serve practically everyone who shows up. Simply talking about limiting enrollments ignites the fires in the bellies of old-time community-college presidents who insist that the answer is to demand more money from local and state legislators. But still believing that the community college can be all things to all people simply makes no sense in today's economic environment—if, indeed, it ever did—and will ultimately lead to failure.

To be true to their mission, community colleges must serve all segments, but not all members, of society There is a big difference in the two commitments. For example, community colleges must provide access to minority students, poor white people, middle-class homemakers wanting to re-enter the work force, new immigrants who must take ESL courses to function in the United States, unemployed workers, transfer students, and many other constituencies. But community colleges cannot admit everyone from each of those groups who wants

to enroll and serve them all well. Paradoxically, to preserve open access, enrollments must be limited.

Presidents, as the most important interpreters of the community-college mission, must understand and communicate that open access can exist and thrive in today's environment—but not in the same way that it has in the past. Each president must work closely with his or her trustees, faculty and staff members, legislators, business leaders, and other community representatives to define the meaning of access as it relates to the institution's specific mission and service area. Priorities must be set: Maintaining open access requires that a college determine the programs and courses that the key constituencies it serves need most and then thoughtfully allocate available resources to meet those needs. At the same time, a comprehensive curriculum must remain intact, for a college that promises access with few or no choices in programs and courses is misleading students and the public.

The president must then take the lead in putting words into action—connecting the budget to the mission in ways that, in many cases, have not been done before. Whatever the institution's financial situation, it must spend limited resources so that it can best serve a wide variety of students. The budget should not be the sole determinant of what programs are offered, how many classes are provided, which students are admitted. That will require difficult decisions. . . .

Many community colleges have already established selective-admissions programs in high-demand fields such as nursing. It is now time to apply the same practice across the board. Community colleges should develop the courses and programs that contribute the most to their missions and constituencies, admit students up to the point that their resources support such efforts, then close the door—thereby ceasing the suicidal practice of enrolling students for whom the college receives no tax support. At the same time, they should preserve admission to the college for representatives from virtually all segments of society. Reserving slots, providing special counseling, and offering some financial aid will almost guarantee that some people who have lingered on the periphery of the admissions process will be enrolled, thus maintaining open access.

So, is open access worth preserving? Yes. Is it possible to do so in light of today's limited resources and demands? Again, the answer is yes. Will it happen? That answer depends on how community-college leaders interpret their institutions' commitment to open access and how they fulfill that commitment.

Diversification of Higher Education: Women

10. Margaret Rossiter,
Women Scientists, 1940–1972, 1995

Two of Margaret Rossiter's (1944–) early books are landmarks in the history of American professional women. The first recounted the "struggles and strategies" of women scientists up to 1940; the second, the introduction of which is partly reprinted here, took the story to its turning point toward affirmative action. These studies document the overlooked or marginalized status of women in science for over a century. With comprehensive, well-written, and penetrating scholarship, they set a tone of discovery and indignation by a historian whose preponderance of evidence durably carried her case and her conviction. Her books remain strong documentary support underlying the movement to expand the role of women in science and in academic institutions generally.

Included here are her brief comments on the now-forgotten rise of women scientists during World War II to make up (temporarily) around 12 percent of the national science faculty ranks, replacing men gone to wartime duties.

After her Radcliffe (A.B. 1966) and Yale (Ph.D. 1970) degrees, Rossiter held research associate posts at Berkeley (1976–82) and at the American Academy of Arts and Sciences (1977–86); visiting lectureships at Harvard (1983–86) and the National Science Foundation (1986–88); then a professorship at Cornell (1988–   ), where she became the Marie Underhill Noll Professor of History and Science in 1993.

Margaret W. Rossiter, *Women Scientists in America: Before Affirmative Action, 1940–1972* (Baltimore, 1995): xv–xviii, 24–26, 33–49, 66–67, 93–94. Reprinted with the kind permission of The Johns Hopkins University Press, Copyright © 1995. Further reading: Marilyn Bailey Ogilvie, *Women and Science, An Annotated Bibliography* (New York and London, 1996), esp. entries for Judy Green, Evelyn Fox Keller, Betty M. Vetter, and Mary Roth Walsh; William G. Bowen, Martin A. Kurzweil, and Eugene M. Tobin, in collaboration with Susanne C. Pichler, *Equity and Excellence in American Higher Education* (Charlottesville, VA, 2005), measures the underrepresentation of women educated for science and engineering; and II, 11–15; IV, 1, 6.

Although by all accounts the period 1940–72 was a golden age for science in America, it has generally been considered a very dark age for women in the professions. How could this have been? Were women not an integral part of American science by 1940? Why, then, in a period of record growth in almost every aspect of American science that one could count—money spent, persons trained, jobs created, articles published, even Nobel prizes won—were women so invisible? What had happened? Was this not at first the period of World War II, when women were told that they could do anything and were even recruited for certain scientific and technical projects? Was this not followed by the Cold War, when, because of the heightened manpower needs of a highly technological military-industrial complex, officials launched a campaign for "woman power," urging bright women to seek training in nontraditional areas such as science and engineering? Was this not a period when record numbers of women were earning doctorates in scientific and technical fields? What had happened to them? Were they congregated in areas or fields that did not grow as much as the men's? Did the scientific job market

work differently for them? Did marriage as then constituted (or, more broadly, marital status in general) have a differential impact on their scientific careers? Why were there these limits to the women's opportunities?

Unfortunately for the trained women of the 1940s through the 1960s, the evidence indicates that the growth and affluence of the period that could have made room for more and better-trained scientists of both sexes did not benefit the two equally; in fact, it generally unleashed certain forces that hastened the women's exit and subsequent marginalization and underutilization, which could then be cited to justify denying further training for their successors. Evidence presented here indicates that most of the women's traditional employers, such as women's colleges, teachers colleges, and colleges of home economics, were closing their doors to them, and they were not included on the faculties of the growing and new coeducational institutions. Much of this new exclusion was tied to marriage, as in the reinstatement of the antinepotism rules on most campuses after World War II. But even single women were ousted or just not hired in these pronatalist years, often for fear that they might later get married. Prestigious universities had never had many women in visible places, but in the affluent 1950s and 1960s less well regarded institutions began to aspire to become prestigious themselves. Thus the pattern was deliberate and grew widespread. Formerly ridiculed and poorly supported, these institutions began to seem ripe for upgrading and colonization; for the first time they could afford to pension off the older women and employ more men.

Large numbers of often older women also seemed to spur, though this was never stated publicly, a lot of ageism, sexism, and possibly homophobia. It was portrayed as a sign of progress to get rid of the old girls, raise salaries, reduce teaching loads, hire more Ph.D.'s, rename the school a state university, and urge the new faculty to get on with their research, all of which would forcibly upgrade the school's level of prestige. Indeed, much of the discussion in these decades of the need for higher salaries at the liberal arts colleges and elsewhere, usually by foundation officials and academic administrators, was a kind of code language for the masculinization of formerly female-dominated areas. After the mid-1950s this "chill" spread beyond employment to levels of recognition that earlier women scientists had achieved, such as election to certain professional offices and selection for coveted prizes. Thus, at a time when young male scientists faced enhanced opportunities at every turn, the young women were supposed to be home with the children, whether they had them or not or whether they wanted to be there or not.

For many years there was little consciousness that these attitudes and practices might constitute something as ugly as discrimination. It was just the way it was. Even respectable people behaved this way, and they were often proud of it. The prevailing assumption, considered so obvious that hardly any-one expressed it in the 1950s, was that though some women were present in science, they were at best invisible and at worst an embarrassment. They could be, and were, blithely omitted as either un-important or anomalous from accounts and think-ing about the profession. Thus, at the same time that some governmental officials were urging young women to greater efforts . . . previously trained women scientists were finding it hard to get hired or promoted or even to be taken seriously. Whether single or married, they had been defined as obsta-cles to overall progress, and their removal was a desired goal. There did not seem to be any way to stop the juggernaut. Any protests or complaints were unlikely to change anything, and they were likely to be dismissed as special pleading not worthy of consideration. . . .

A few women scientists noticed what was hap-pening. Some saw instances such as quotas but were reluctant to see a pattern. Most women and scien-tists of the time lacked the vocabulary (e.g., "sexist" or "male chauvinist") and the civil-rights concepts to recognize systematic patterns, identify the re-sponsible parties, and plan how to correct the situa-tion. A few individuals and even small groups did see a pattern and reported it, but because they were either grateful for their current status or desperate not to lose even that, they were reluctant to criticize the powerful and successful, especially when so little seemed likely to be gained from it. . . . Occasional individuals, such as Myra Sampson at Smith Col-lege, Frances Clayton at Brown University, and Jessie Bernard at Pennsylvania State University, col-lected data that showed that the women's colleges were no longer hiring many women but evidently preferred men. Yet for various reasons none was able to use this material effectively. In short, even those women who were most inclined to take an in-terest in the professional status of scientific and aca-demic women were themselves too much a product of the thinking and politics of the time to raise much "consciousness" or effect change.

Yet one suspects from the few actions that were taken that if the data had been interpreted other-wise, they would not have been published, or if they had been published, they would not have been taken seriously. It is more likely that they would have been ignored, as Sampson's data were, or dis-missed as the ideas of radical or crazy women. Cer-tainly federal legislation regarding employment or the internal workings of universities would have seemed intrusive and detrimental at a time of Mc-Carthyism. From this it took even the most po-litically astute women a minimum of about fifteen years to recover.

Although the prevailing mindset made it nearly impossible for the women of the time, including several social scientists, to glimpse the larger reality, suddenly in the early 1960s Betty Friedan and others began to put enough pieces together into a radically new but recognizable pattern. Alice Rossi, a well-trained sociologist of the 1950s, devoted several years in the early 1960s to rereading, rethinking, and reformulating the prevailing wisdom. Perhaps her new view was possible then because in the context of the civil-rights movement she could begin to see a pattern of oppressive attitudes and practices, that is, that the "victims" were a class that did not "de-serve" their fate and should not be blamed for it; that society could and should be changed; that laws would have to be passed by a reluctant Congress and then, what would be even harder, the executive branch would have to be pressured into enforcing them. As the women's numbers increased in the late 1960s (especially in the biological sciences) and their "consciousness" began to rise, the continuing discriminatory practices grew increasingly outrage-ous and intolerable. Hundreds of women and other feminists, becoming aware for the first time of the enormity of their marginalization and exploitation and the scale of the resources denied to them, were energized to seek change immediately. "Sisterhood" was exhilarating, and within a few months many of them began to fight back. Finally, about 1969 this anger coalesced into a movement, which called for the innumerable "status of women" reports of 1969–72. These in turn, as they documented and brought into full view the totality of the women's exclusion, angered even more persons. By 1970 these reports had become prime evidence in federal hear-ings on sex discrimination on campus and in the work force, which led to landmark legislation—equal pay and affirmative action in academia—by 1972.

Thus, women scientists were there in record numbers in the 1950s and 1960s, though one might have to look rather hard to find them. Trained to advanced levels, they were, to use some military terms of the period, "camouflaged" as housewives, mothers, and "other" and "stockpiled" in cities and college towns across America (where many still re-main), ready but uncalled for the big emergency that never came. . . .

Perhaps in wartime the citizens felt safer in men's hands. Certainly protest was more difficult then, since critics of governmental policy could all too easily be accused of unpatriotic behavior. In any case, even at the height of the war, when gender roles were being stretched and changed, traditional American antifeminism remained very strong and perhaps even intensified. Professional women were learning how few friends they had politically, de-spite their important contributions to the war effort. During the Depression it had seemed that the biggest obstacle to women's advancement was the economy, but now, when the economy was boom-ing, basic social attitudes remained quite conserva-tive, despite all the oft-proclaimed "shortages." The demand for qualified persons in high places could never have been stronger, and yet the antifeminism was so strong and so persistent at high levels that it held back women in good times as well as bad. A tremendous change in public opinion, as well as full employment, would be necessary to uproot this basic belief.

In assessing the war's overall impact on women's role in science, one is tempted to conclude that despite all the activity and publicity about their advances and wartime "firsts," the women came out of the war only slightly stronger than they had gone into it. Some women scientists, perhaps about 100, had held temporary jobs on governmental and industrial war projects. Many others, who had been unemployed in the 1930s, had apparently found temporary positions, especially in college teaching, during the war. Potentially more important, the numbers of women scientists had more than doubled in just four years, increasing by the hundreds if one counts only women with higher degrees, and by the thousands if one includes those with a bachelor's degree or less. But owing to the overall wartime recruitment of both sexes, as well as improved recordkeeping and a broadened definition of what constituted a scientist, the total number of scientists on the Roster also more than doubled in these years, from 131,440 in 1941 to 324,145 in 1945. The result was that, despite all the talk about women's advances in science during the war, their percentage of the total on the Roster rose almost imperceptibly from 4.0 percent in 1941 to just 4.1 percent in 1945. Even then most of the women were added mostly at the lower levels, and layers of bureaucracy were added above them.

Yet the main reason why the women scientists failed to capitalize on their wartime demand as effectively as they might have has to be the prevailing public opinion about women's role in American society. To a large extent, the women scientists shared this ambivalence themselves. Although some women's leaders were out front challenging industry spokesmen, testifying in front of governmental committees, and fighting those in power for larger opportunities for women, others, especially among scientists and academics, shrank from this role. They were not convinced that they were equal and deserved better jobs, and they were unsure whether, or how hard, to push for them. Their leaders, senior academic women chosen for the most part because of their success in a conservative profession, tended to be cautious and more inclined to dampen the fires of protest than to stoke them. They saw little value or possible gain in political activism and were more comfortable telling the other women to work harder to measure up to higher levels of discipline and achievement. Yet it is debatable what they could have accomplished if they had organized a unified onslaught against the pervasive discrimination; the barriers and villains were everywhere, while the allies were few and halfhearted. Nor did this very unwillingness of so many women to protest and push for advancement in wartime, when they were at least thought to be needed, bode well for their advancement in the postwar world.

By 1945, then, the women who had seemed in such demand and performed so well in wartime knew how weak and short-lived their welcome really was. Regardless of how well they performed, they were not promoted, and most expected to be ousted from their temporary positions. They were, as a whole, still the victims of social and economic forces they could not control, the reserve labor force that could be called up and channeled into certain levels of work as occasion required. They had no leverage or way of consolidating even these minimal wartime gains, and if all the expected layoffs took place, they might be as badly off in the late 1940s as they had been in the 1930s. Their only hope was that in science the highly publicized shortages would continue into the postwar world. Under such conditions of "full employment," the women might continue to be in as much demand as in wartime....

The quotas on women's enrollment at the graduate level in these years were even more restrictive than at the undergraduate level. In some cases the women's numbers, as well as their percentages, actually dropped, as departments and whole graduate schools reserved their places for male candidates. At Radcliffe Graduate School, the female part of the Harvard Graduate School of Arts and Sciences, the total enrollment was 400 in 1945–46, but a strict postwar quota pushed that back to fewer than 300 in 1946, while the male graduate enrollment at Harvard soared from 1,088 in 1946 to 1,960 in 1947. Moreover, Radcliffe's female enrollment level was not allowed to reach 400 again until 1957, despite a great increase in the number of applicants, especially married ones. Radcliffe authorities apparently did not protest this administrative policy publicly, though some students were upset by the continuing lack of fellowship support and rules discouraging married or part-time students. Similarly; at Johns Hopkins, where graduate admissions were controlled entirely by the departments, the total female enrollment fluctuated between 120 and 155 each year in 1946–51 (always 21–25 percent of the totals, as if a percentage quota were being applied).

Despite these caps on female admissions, the number of doctorates earned by women continued to rise. The number of science doctorates granted to women by American universities rose slowly but steadily from about 120 per year in 1940 to about 290 per year in 1954. Because the men's performance was far more volatile, however, reflecting the wartime plummet to about 700 in 1945 and its dramatic postwar resurgence to more than 4,500 per year by 1954 (with about 500 per year in engineering alone), the women were now earning only about 6 percent of the total. The remasculinization of science in the 1950s and 1960s was under way with a vengeance.

Not only women students were being pushed aside in the spring of 1946; pushed aside as well were many women faculty and deans of women, oftentimes the highest-ranking women administrators. . . .

Given the record student enrollments on most campuses in the late 1940s, the women faculty who had filled in during the war years might have expected to be kept on a while longer, but they too were pushed out in various ways. On some campuses the trustees reinstated the antinepotism rules that had been temporarily relaxed during the war. Thus, spouses (usually wives) who had been sought out in the emergency were now dismissed. At the University of Kansas, for example, the antinepotism rules were reinstated in 1949 for wives in the same department as their husbands and then a year later for all wives. Similarly, women faculty who married men who were also on the faculty immediately lost their jobs. . . . Other women faculty married graduate students—not all of the veterans were young—and then quit their tenure-track and even tenured positions to follow their husbands when training or a job took them (and so whole couples) elsewhere. . . .

In the postwar era any hint that American society might have flaws, that it might be functioning unfairly or hurting some groups within it unduly, was unacceptable not only in the political arena, where McCarthyism held sway, but even, as Ravenna Helson has shown, in psychological journals. The absence of complaints made it all the harder for the few remaining reformers to fight discrimination. . . . No one was willing to come forward, force the issue, or be a test case. Discrimination was just as severe as ever, perhaps worse, but everyone ignored the problem and tried to forget it. Although some later investigators would fallaciously interpret this lack of protest as evidence that the problem had evaporated or been "solved," it persisted and worsened until it was confronted by a revived civil-rights movement in the late 1950s and 1960s and the "women's liberation" movement after that. Postwar "adjustment" had smothered protest and postponed change, but it had not really solved anything. . . .

In 1960 Bernard Berelson, a former program director in the "behavioral sciences" (a term he popularized) at the powerful Ford Foundation, published *Graduate Education in the United States,* a major review of the nation's graduate schools and their needs. Three years in the making, supported by a grant of $100,000 from the Carnegie Corporation of New York, and based on consultations with forty-one male academics (listed in an appendix) and questionnaires completed by many of the deans of ninety-two graduate schools (omitting Radcliffe and Bryn Mawr), this presumably was an authoritative report. Although Berelson claimed not to speak for any foundation or to represent anyone other than himself, his background, source of sup-

port, and methods would lead one to expect him to reflect pretty accurately the prevailing views of the male graduate deans and the foundation world. Therefore it is important to note the brutally negative expectation that Berelson held out for women's future in academia. At a time when governmental committees were talking about "encouraging" women and Congress was appropriating millions of dollars to alleviate shortages of trained personnel, Berelson strongly asserted the graduate deans' contrary belief in a brief paragraph:

> So much is being said these days about the possibility of solving the "college teacher shortage" with women Ph.D. s. that it is perhaps worth noting that they constituted 10% of the doctorates in 1910 and not quite 11% last year. Except for the war years, they have never accounted for a much larger segment than that. Furthermore, as the National Opinion Research Center study shows, only about 15% of women graduate students prefer a full-time professional career for the first five years after completing their work. When these facts are combined with the reluctance of academic employers, not to mention the rules against joint husband-wife employment, they do not leave much room, in my judgment, for reliance on this "solution." It may be, as a foundation officer put it, that "we are losing half our brains" in this way, but it is hard to see much that can be done about it.

Thus, Berelson was not only using incorrect percentages about previous doctorates (and thus trivializing the important fact that women were earning record numbers of Ph.D.'s in the 1950s) but, even worse, twisting the intent of the women respondents to one of the very large (and also foundation supported) "opinion" or "survey research" projects of the time. Because those women graduate students polled "preferred" to be both married and pursuing a career, something that was only rarely feasible at the time, Berelson refused to believe that they or any women in graduate school would ever make any significant contribution to academia! It is hard to calculate the damage that such a devastating assessment by such an authoritative source must have done to the burgeoning interest in adding women to college faculties. . . .

When the Ford Foundation awarded a total of $41.5 million to ten prestigious graduate schools in 1967 to reduce attrition, it tied the money to the elusive goal of completing the Ph.D. within four years. In a later evaluation a former Ford Foundation employee admitted quite frankly that the money "had little effect on attrition" and "did not have a significant effect on the ways major universities conduct their Ph.D. training programs." For this he blamed such circumstances as the Vietnam War, the "PhD glut," and a certain subversion of the grant's purposes at the departmental level. Yet one suspects that the money might have been much better spent at those perhaps less prestigious graduate schools that were already showing signs of flexibility. What, after all, was wrong with eight years of part-time study if the point was, as the deans kept saying, to finish the degree?

Thus, despite all the governmental officials' talk about "womanpower" and all the deans' talk about the need to keep up the value of the doctorate by requiring full-time study; prestigious graduate programs, supported by the major philanthropies, especially the Ford Foundation, continued their traditionally inflexible and exclusionary ways. If the "womanpower" experts in and out of government had really thought that by simply increasing the fellowship funds available to women they would be meeting the faculty shortage or beating the Russians in research, they had grossly underestimated the resistance of graduate departments and academic traditions and prejudices. In fact graduate school officials at the most prestigious schools, which dominated this level of instruction, were proud of how well they had resisted any tampering or lowering of standards that might have made it easier for students to complete the Ph.D. degree. Even when the students were supported with thousands of fellowships, their attrition rate approached carnage proportions. Neither female philanthropy nor federal fellowships had been able to overcome the entrenched attitudes and practices of departments and professors. Officially "encouraged" to earn degrees in order to be ready to meet pressing national shortages, many bright women students were unable to fulfill their academic and scientific potential. Institutional attitudes and practices discouraged all but the most determined and persistent at even this lowest level of access to the academic world.

Nevertheless, record numbers of women were obtaining doctorates in the sciences in the 1950s and 1960s, with or without fellowships. They tended to be concentrated in some fields more than in others and to have completed degrees at a smaller range of institutions than had the men, partly because, except for those in biology and education, they tended to be in the fields where the money was not (e.g., psychology and home economics rather than physics or engineering). Yet even these highly trained women, in fact especially these women, would have a tough time in the job market. Although it was unlikely that they would fare very well in academia, where the very faculty who had expected so little of them as graduate students loomed even larger as employers, that was where the largest growth was expected to be. Just as during World War II, they would continue to be underemployed everywhere, all too often filling in around the men. And in a kind of fitting revenge, many of the "dropouts" would find that, contrary to most of the advice of the time, many of the jobs that were in practice open to women, such as those in laboratories, libraries, customer service, or governmental agencies, did not require doctorates after all.

11. Aurelia Henry Reinhardt, "Women in the American University," 1941

As one of the few women presidents of women's colleges between the two world wars, Aurelia Henry Reinhardt (1877–1948) imperiously presided over Mills College in Oakland, California, from 1916–43. She was a San Franciscan with a bachelor's degree in literature from Berkeley (1898) and a doctorate in English literature from Yale (1905). After teaching briefly in Idaho and then returning to teach at Berkeley with great success, she was appointed president of Mills. During her twenty-seven years there, the college added seventeen buildings and gained national, even worldwide favor. Much of this was due to Reinhardt's vigorous but personal—at times, dictatorial—leadership. She was national president of the American Association of University Women (1923–27), a Republican Elector for California in 1928, and first woman moderator of the American Unitarian Association (1940–42).

Aurelia Henry Reinhardt, "Women in the American University of the Future," in *The University and the Future of America* (Palo Alto, 1941), pp. 73, 77–78, 80–82, 87–88. Further reading: George Hedley, *Aurelia Henry Reinhardt: Portrait of a Whole Woman* (Oakland, 1961). Surveys of women's higher education include Mabel Newcomer, *A Century of Higher Education for American Women* (New York, 1959); and Barbara Miller Solomon, *In the Company of Educated Women: A History of Women and Higher Education in America* (New Haven, 1985). See also Rosalind Rosenberg, "Women in the Humanities, Taking Their Place," in *The Humanities and the Dynamics of Inclusion Since World War II*, ed. David A. Hollinger (Baltimore, 2006), ch. 9; and Marilyn J. Boxer, *When Women Ask the Questions: Creating Women's Studies in America* (Baltimore, 1998).

What does it matter when, why, what for, and how many women are now or may be associated with American universities when . . . century-old institutions in other lands are being reduced to heaps of rubble, when priceless libraries are consumed by flame, and women together with their brothers can enjoy no educational opportunity?

Many reasons might be quickly marshaled to testify that there *is* contemporary importance in the subject. The reply is as inclusive as the purpose of universities and the function of women in a democratic state. Because wars are spreading over the planet, destroying men and their achievements, increased effort must be made to assure the development of intelligence and strengthening of character and to utilize every influence making for stability, justice, creativity, and that kind of dwelling together and working together which is crammed into the dynamic monosyllable *peace*. Universities are such an influence. Women might be. When *peace* is brought to pass, reconciliation and reconstruction will be the result of intellectual effort, as well as of prayer and fasting.

With culture as with civilization, the uses of the *intellect* are concerned. With building as with destroying these group achievements, *women* are concerned, though it is astonishing low little until recently has been known of woman's part in human history. As archaeology, ethnology, anthropology have brought to light the distinctive contribution of primitive woman, research has turned its attention to women in classic times, in Reformation and Renaissance, in the settlement of the Americas. So, a literature begins to form—biologic, economic, educational. Still, almost everything remains to be done to establish the relationship of women, historically, either to the uses of the intellect or to the flowering of racial cultures and their stabilization into recognized civilizations. . . .

Women's story, as science and history begin to tell it, proves her creative intelligence and her capacity for loyalty. This era of world chaos finds her in every occupation, of national and international activity. . . .

It is approximately one hundred years ago since three synchronous opportunities came to American women. First, the founding of academies into which like that of Catherine Beecher, Emma Willard, and Mary Lyon, training was available for her in a curriculum much like the classic curriculum which had been enjoyed by men throughout the nation's history. These academies were later to become the women's colleges of today. A second opportunity was that in co-education. Oberlin College in 1833 made its courses of instruction available to women. This method of teaching was to be taken over eventually by practically all government high schools and universities. Her third opportunity was that of teaching and preparation for teaching. The normal schools taken from France and developed by Horace Mann became the avenue through which women were to enter in increasing numbers—the first profession outside the home into which they were widely welcomed.

This profession of teaching for women, concurrent with the development of the public school system of education and the demand for trained teachers, came to them with little opposition. The second profession which they made an effort to enter welcomed them not at all. Though women had been midwives and nurses since the dawn of history, they were not wanted as trained medical colleagues. . . .

As to graduate study, it became available to women shortly before the turn of the last century. In 1892 the Commissioner of Education said that only 189 doctorates had previously been granted to women in the country. His report listed 42 institutions conferring advanced degrees in that one year to 312 men and 31 women. Ten years later 362 men and 42 women received recognition in one commencement season. . . .

I learn from the materials in the files of the American Association of University Women at Washington, D.C., that the first fellowship was made available to women as early as 1884. This Association, for the six decades of its history, has done an excellent service for the higher education of women. Objectively, practically, without sentimentality, it has encouraged an inter-alumnae association, an inter-institutional organization for the support of educational opportunities for women, in the most enlightened meaning of that phrase. Its membership is lay and professional. Its interest in standards has encouraged all institutions offering post–high-school instruction to women to better their programs. . . . With admirable practicality it has endowed national and international fellowships for women, and has a lengthening role of distinguished scholars indebted to the American Association of University Women for their opportunities for research in a score of countries. . . .

Prejudice against women, not incompetence, stubbornly stood in the way of professional advancement. As tax-supported universities increased in number and in strength, and as economic need strengthened women's determination to profit by available avenues of training, women appeared in multiplying numbers. There is noticeable a disproportionate percentage of women accepted as students, and women accepted as colleagues. For example, in 1911, *The American Educational Review* noted that four universities—California, Maine, Cornell and the Massachusetts Institute of Technology—had an aggregate of 1,258 instructors, of whom 25 were women. Farther west, in the same year, Ohio University had 41 per cent women instructors—a high percentage explained partly by the large division devoted to the preparation of teachers of all grades.

In the profession of college teachers, the women's colleges have generally divided appointments between men and women. I quote an available reference made in 1931 by the Association of University Professors on its 176 institutional members. Twenty-nine universities and colleges with 2,000 professors had two women—one in Harvard Medical School, one in Yale School of Education.

Fourteen colleges for women with 989 instructors counted more than 25 per cent of them men—exactly 251.

During the last ten years women in larger numbers are being invited into university lecture rooms and laboratories. Influential in bringing this about is less the realization of the capacities of women than the pressure of larger and larger numbers of well-trained women, the increase in the political authority of women in educational boards since gaining the suffrage, the scarcity of men due to the keen competition and higher salaries of scientific and administrative work outside the university, and within recent months the opportunities which come to women in war emergency.

Despite a growing improvement in the recognition of professional competency, there remains a difference in salary scales based not on competency but on sex. . . .

The university of the future must be liberal, knowing the universe itself is not geocentric. It must resist the temptation to take over the cult of power because we live in a power civilization, or the cult of numbers because we admire size. The university must become and remain intellectual, because to human beings of intellect democracy looks to solve the infinitely complex problems of a technical and industrial civilization. The university must accept women objectively as it accepts men, testing them in their capacity as individual human beings and judging them finally as persons capable of achievement. . . .

The woman of tomorrow must cease to apologize for the possession of intellect or talent. It should be unrelated to her opportunities for marriage and her happiness in marriage. In other words, as the college for women and the university admitting women come of age, they will show their maturity in permitting women to come of age as unselfconsciously as their brothers, and enter into the inheritance of scholarship and intellectual achievement through the same means of application and experimentation as is permitted to the men of their country.

12. Alice Emerson, "Preface," *Toward a Balanced Curriculum,* 1984

President of Wheaton College (1975–91), Alice F. Emerson (1931–) was well prepared to write a preface to a book on the issues of gender on the college curriculum. After her bachelor's degree from Vassar (1953) she took her Ph.D. from Bryn Mawr (1964), then went to the University of Pennsylvania, where she served in the deanships for women and students (1966–75). In retirement she is a senior adviser at the Andrew W. Mellon Foundation.

Alice Emerson, Preface to *Toward a Balanced Curriculum: A Sourcebook for Initiating Gender Integration Projects,* ed. Bonnie Spanier et al. (Cambridge, MA, 1984). Reprinted with the permission of and copyright held by Schenkman Books, Inc., Rochester, VT. Further reading: Linda Eisemann, *Higher Education for Women in Postwar America, 1945–1965* (Baltimore, 2006) and II, 10–11, 13–16.

Educational institutions have a special social responsibility to be future-oriented and to take the largest possible view. The particular form and forces of an educational institution's efforts must and should depend in significant measure on the character, mission, opportunities, and values of that institution. Such efforts must be tailored to the particular institutional strengths and resources, and should reflect some combination of ideals and practicality.

This is a long way around to raising the specific issue that I want to speak to this morning, namely, why Wheaton made the integration of the study of women into our curriculum a high priority issue for us—in fact, our compelling endeavor for the last three years and the foreseeable future. There are three major elements that I think formed the backdrop of our coming to this effort. One was the general climate of education and of our society. A second had to do with the special climate of liberal arts colleges dedicated to the education of women; and the third related to specific factors at Wheaton.

First, the general climate. As everyone in this room is well aware, the decade of the seventies, especially the second half of that decade, reflected enormous change in the lives of women in our society. We all owe a debt to the women's movement for raising the consciousness of our entire society about what women could and ought to be able to do. So the consciousness of the importance of women's interests was heightened for all of us. At the same time, there was a great outpouring and a new awareness of the availability of new scholarship about women, a resource, which, while available in some measure historically, was much more present and known at this time.

The special climate of liberal arts colleges devoted to the education of women is something, I think, harder to describe in special terms in the late seventies; but, in combination with what was going on in the rest of the world, it becomes very important. I say this because I think that women's colleges were founded on the belief that what women do matters. This has never been something that has been an issue in women's colleges; it is our reason for being. In addition, women's colleges have historically had a much better gender balance in their faculties with much higher proportions of women faculty members relative to men than at other institutions. And faculty members at colleges for women teach there because they believe it is important for women to be educated to undertake significant work in the future. This combination of factors made women's colleges the logical institutions to pioneer on behalf of integrating the study of women into the curriculum.

I think also that we recognized, because we were a special species among colleges, that we had a responsibility to take up issues and take on projects which we were specially suited to do on behalf of others as well. We wanted to be able to say to ourselves that we were taking a share of the general social responsibility that educational institutions carry, that we were doing some piece of the important work of educational development which could be useful not only in the smaller setting of our own particular species of institution, but which would also have wider ramifications. All institutions have a social responsibility, and I think each institution tries to see how it can best fulfill its responsibility so as to contribute both to its particular mission and to the evolution of the educational endeavor generally.

Turning to Wheaton in particular, it seems to me that we were probably especially aware of the presence of these elements and the critical climate for undertaking this significant endeavor. We even appreciated this climate as a luxury, a luxury to be utilized, a luxury which was a responsibility. We were aware of the availability of new materials in increased measure in a whole range of fields. We had the presence of a critical mass of people who cared, a mix of committed faculty and administrators. . . .

Two other factors were important. First, I think that at Wheaton there was the conviction that incorporating the study of women as broadly as possible into the curriculum was a compelling obligation of an institution truly dedicated to the liberal arts and we were prepared to do everything we could to make that happen, to provide the support for people in terms of resources, in terms of time, and in terms of psychological support. Second, we considered this a significant intellectual challenge with potentially far-reaching effects. We could see that the fundamental canons on which thinking has historically rested would require re-examination and restatement in many instances, and we knew this would be very unsettling. In fact, in some ways the challenge is truly awesome because all of you who have thought through the implications of really bringing gender balance to all of our efforts to understand our past history and the basic tenets of contemporary knowledge recognize that the effects of such efforts are infinitely far-reaching. I don't think any of us can know what the end point will be.

In hindsight it is clear that what seemed at first overwhelming was in fact energizing; that as we began to explore the opportunities and to look at the issues, to examine old materials in new ways, we found that what seemed at the start like a lonely effort was in fact shared by many others in many guises. For us, and I'm sure for many of you, one of the wonderful parts of being engaged in this effort is the amazing expansion of the network of scholars and teachers who are committed to advancing the study of women and the integration of our rapidly expanding knowledge and insights about women into the curriculum.

13. Jill Ker Conway, "Women's Place," 1978

Jill Ker Conway (1935–) was an accomplished historian of family life and gender roles as well as a forthright advocate of women's higher education before she became president of Smith College (1975–85). Her writing about the needs and rewards of higher education for women was bolstered by her presidency of Smith, where she was the first woman to lead that institution (XII, 4). More impressive to the general public has been her warm and candid autobiography, which has appeared in three volumes. Her personal insights as well as extraordinary experiences from a girlhood on a sheep farm in Australia to eminence in higher education in the United States and Canada have made hers a remarkable voice from modern literature with much to say on educational matters as well.

Jill Conway, "Women's Place," *Change* 10 (March 1978): 8–9. Reprinted with permission of the Helen Dwight Reid Educational Foundation. Published by Heldref Publications, 1319 Eighteenth St. NW, Washington, D.C.

20036-1802. Copyright © 1980. Further reading: Conway, *The Road From Coorain* (New York, 1989), *True North: A Memoir* (New York, 1994), and *A Woman's Education* (New York, 2001). Studies and reports on the inequality of women in American higher education have appeared increasingly since the mid-1960s; they frequently can be read as a part of the even larger body of literature on the twentieth-century women's rights movement. Early bibliographies are Saul D. Feldman, *Escape from the Doll's House: Women in Graduate and Professional School Education* (New York, 1974), 141–49, and Jane Williamson, *New Feminist Scholarship: A Guide to Bibliographies* (Old Westbury, NY, 1979), 43–46. See also National Research Council, Committee on the Education and Employment of Women in Science and Engineering, *Climbing the Academic Ladder: Doctoral Women Scientists in Academe* (Washington, D.C., 1979); Linda Eisenmann, *Higher Education for Women in Postwar America, 1945–1965* (Baltimore, 2006); and XII, 4.

"In general, young men are best educated in the company of young women. Young women are best educated in the company of their own sex. These two principles are hard to reconcile." This remark, attributed to a New College don during the debate about admission of women to Oxford colleges in 1963, goes to the heart of the problem. As the don suggested, introducing women into an environment that concentrates on male talents only promotes that male-oriented goal. But creating a balanced educational community—with the signals, rewards, excitements, and emotional bonds that encourage the growth of both sexes at the same time—is a far more complex and a quite different order of problem.

"Educational equity" was never an aspiration of the American educational system until the decade of the 1970s. Now, with the passage of such federal legislation as Title IX of the Civil Rights Act and the Women's Educational Equity Act, it is a well-articulated goal. But how profound the commitment to achieve it, in society at large or in the educational community, is still to be determined.

To some, the higher education institutions that limit their student bodies to women may seem outside the new goal of educational equity, even old-fashioned. That is, I believe, a mistaken interpretation. The women's colleges are indeed "different." But that is because they function as utopias of a sort, showing the rest of society how institutions have to be run if they are to effectively educate women. . . .

Coeducation, when accepted in high schools and colleges in the 1830s and 1840s, was favored for complex reasons, but two major factors were operating. First, women were seen as a cheap source of teaching labor for publicly funded schools. Second, female students were considered by proponents of coeducation . . . as important resources for the educational environment of males. Once women were admitted, it was relatively easy to establish new streams in professional education that prepared female graduates for acceptable subordinate and non-intellectual roles. The University of California at Berkeley established home economics, social work, and public health nursing curricula for female students who might otherwise have fought to enter law and medicine.

By contrast, the late nineteenth-century founders of women's colleges meant what they said when they described their educational objectives. They sought to give women access to the same rigorous curriculum that was available in the best colleges for men. They believed that women's minds would benefit equally from intellectual stimulation, a truly revolutionary concept and one still articulated most unequivocally in women's institutions. Furthermore, many founders of women's colleges wanted to bring women's talents to bear on the world outside the college in professional, business, and artistic activities. M. Carey Thomas of Bryn Mawr was the most explicit in her hope that women would become creators of culture, and the Bryn Mawr Graduate School is still testimony to her vision and hope.

To return now to the contemporary problem: The educational environment that nurtures students comprises far more than the classroom, the library, and the mind of the scholar interacting with his (and occasionally her) students. Just as essential to learning are other significant components of the environment that affect motivation. The most critical of these might include:

- the status hierarchy, within and outside the university, and the kind of leadership figures it provides;
- the strength and importance of male and female sociability groups in work, leisure, politics, and business;
- resources for personal counseling and sponsorship;
- links with the experiences of earlier generations;
- links with the occupational structure of society.

Historically, the Oxford or Cambridge college and its dons exemplified, in very nearly perfect form, how such factors channeled the energies and talents of young men. The colleges' clear patterns of hierarchy provided students with unequivocal role models. The ties of the senior common room to the world of politics and economic power connected the young to worlds outside the university; it gave them a sure aim and a steady hand in the pursuit of similar eminence. By copying these models, the Ivy League and other colleges attempted to guarantee the self-realization of a male elite in America—albeit a democratically recruited male elite in the Harvards and Yales of the 1950s and 1960s.

A dichotomy arises, however, when one considers how these elements work within the coeducational universities and colleges of the 1970s. Although the same persons may be teaching the same male and female students, who have access to the same libraries and laboratories and meet in the same classrooms, these men and women are not necessarily having the same educational experience.

The dichotomy disappears in the single-sex colleges for women. These colleges traditionally have shown great sensitivity to the importance of significant female leadership figures. They have given the sociability groups of women—student governments, newspapers, self-governing student committees—both dignity and status. Historically, they have also invested more resources in personal and career counseling for their students than men's or coeducational institutions. It was very clear to those who led them (as it is to present leaders) that their aspirations for their students were at odds with the aims of society at large and that only energetic compensatory efforts could build links with women achievers and with an alien occupational structure. Because of the deep ties women's colleges have with their alumnae, they have enjoyed distinct advantages in placing their students in contact with women of earlier generations.

Women's colleges have not yet established strong ties to the elites of the professional and business world or to the world of politics that would pass for an informal recruiting system. (Nor, one might add, have any groups or institutions for women.) But they are beginning to promote the careers of their graduates with the same aggressive tactics long associated with the Ivy League. And to the extent that women are represented among corporate, professional, and political leaders, women's college graduates play a disproportionately large role.

Elizabeth Tidball has shown in her study reported in the Spring 1973 *Educational Record* that graduates of women's colleges were more than twice as likely to have been cited for career achievement than were women graduates of coeducational colleges. The Carnegie Commission on Higher Education, in its 1973 recommendation favoring the continuation of colleges for women, noted that "an unusual proportion of women leaders" are graduates of such institutions. Vera Kistaikowsky and Tidball found that women's colleges have produced many more women achievers in science and mathematics than have coeducational environments (*Science*, August 1976). Current figures from the Women's College Coalition suggest that participation in such career-critical areas of study as science, mathematics, and economics is far higher at women's colleges than for women undergraduates nationally.

The key question is whether this remarkable productivity of women's colleges, so evident in the past, will continue now that an equally talented group of female students is also being admitted to coeducational student bodies. In my view, the differential will continue to favor women's colleges.

Where else but in the women's colleges can we discover what a learning experience not shaped by male models might be like? It is hard to say where else. Yet we know that females are different from males—in rates of development, in the social messages they receive, in their access to career opportunities, and in the stages of their adult lives, particularly if they have children. We know female students have different learning experiences than males in an academic world where all the verbs for learning come from forms of combat historically assigned to males, e.g., "mastering" a field or "defending" a thesis. And we know that the environment that encourages intellectual mastery in females is usually not one of strong male/female relationships, but rather one in which women can engage in intellectual dispute free of sexual ambiguities.

From all of this, we know that no matter what social goals—or federal laws—may exist, it will be a long time before the informal social environment in America's male-dominated colleges and universities will serve women students as well as men. Until that time we need "for women only" educational institutions. In fact, in the unlikely event that the secure male network begins to crumble within the next generation because of effective affirmative action, society may even once again see a value in preserving educational institutions "for men only."

14. Jean W. Campbell, "Women Drop Back In," 1973

The women's movement of the 1960s and 1970s and affirmative action brought many women who had not had a college experience to higher education. Reentry into college ranks (known as "dropping back in") as well as new enrollment of women took place throughout all levels of American society. Here Jean Winter Campbell (1918–), who served for years at the Center for Continuing Education of Women at the University of Michigan (1964–), describes the important aspects of this social trend. Campbell received the Distinguished Service Award of the National University Continuing Education Association in 1981.

Jean W. Campbell, "Women Drop Back In: Educational Innovation in the Sixties," in *Academic Women on the Move*, ed. Alice S. Rossi and Ann Calderwood (New York, 1973), ch. 5. © 1979 Russell Sage Foundation, 112 East 64th Street, New York, NY 10021. Reprinted with permission.

Women are not yet assured equality of employment in higher education or equal access to achievement and leadership roles within the educational establishment. But there is progress—some of which was generated a decade and more ago in a creative period of feminist activity similar in many ways to the movement today. An examination of this earlier period may heighten our sense of continuity within the feminist movement and thus strengthen its base of support.

The present political, economic, and cultural conditions not only give rise to but make possible for the first time in history "the kind of change in role expectations and psychological orientation women's liberationists have been talking about. It does not mean only women's rights, it means the emancipation of both men and women from a sex-dominated archaic division of labor and from the values that sustain it" (Lerner 1971: 248). With this distinction in mind, we can trace the postwar changes in women's education as a response to the changing needs and demands of women, and examine the seeds of the present women's movement.

In the fifties, a growing belief in higher education for all, dramatized by the enthusiastic return of veterans to the campuses, gradually generated a renewed interest in women's education. . . . The much remarked-upon drop in recent years from prewar highs in the percentage of women earning higher degrees and participating in professional academic roles is related to the quotas set by institutions of higher learning in the mid-forties to absorb men on the GI bill. In our anxiety to dismantle the war machine and absorb veterans into the economy, we severely curtailed women's admission to higher education and sent them home from wartime jobs. Women did not protest their declining opportunities nor did they foresee that in a few years there would be fewer models of leadership and fewer women who felt justified in a commitment to achievement and equality. . . .

PROFILE OF RETURNING WOMEN STUDENTS

Who are the women returning to school? Why do they return? How do they fare? Characteristics of returning women vary somewhat with each program, but an examination of even one program in some detail is enlightening. The University of Michigan Center for Continuing Education of Women is a good example of programs that serve large university communities and are geared to the unique needs of their particular university—in this case a highly decentralized group of nineteen schools and colleges. The center is a service to the state and welcomes *all* women; at the same time it recognizes that there is a self-selection factor operating upon those who do come because of the unique nature of and the particular services offered by the center. Two out of three women return to school although one out of three postpones enrollment for a time. Not all of these women attend the University of Michigan when they do return.

As a part of the Office of Academic Affairs, the Michigan center reaches across the university and through all academic levels in seeking to lower the barriers or change university policies for qualified women with family or job commitments. The center provides information, counseling, referrals, a library, scholarships and grants-in-aid, an evening program of regular credit courses, conferences, and small discussion groups throughout the year, a series of publications, consultation with counselors and programs on other campuses, services to promote research on women's education and development and scholarship in women's studies. Those center participants attending the university are qualified mainstream students. Except for certain licensing programs, some professional schools and a few graduate departments, students may be on a part-time basis; they may transfer credits of any age; and they may establish their own residency apart from their husband's. Some have received credit by examination, and some have had residency requirements waived and credits transferred beyond the stated limit. Summer independent reading courses and other independent study programs are available as well as a degree program that entails no fixed course requirements.

In 1964–1965 approximately 500 women came to the Michigan center for individual consultation. The typical woman was 37 years old, married, living in the area, with a professional or student husband, two or three children, some college, or more likely than not a bachelor's degree. She wanted to prepare for employment (approximately 85 percent of the women gave this as a reason for attending the center); and she needed help in thinking through her job possibilities, in selecting an educational program appropriate to her goals, and in dealing with technical problems of admissions, registration, convenient class scheduling, and financial assistance. She was very likely to be interested in some phase of education, in the social sciences, humanities, or in social work or library science as a career. Surprisingly, as many women expressed an interest in business administration as in nursing and health (10 percent). Also 2 percent were interested in law, 4 percent in mathematics and engineering, 8 percent in the physical or natural sciences, and a negligible number in medicine.

To date, more than 4,000 women have talked with counselors at the center and the participant profile has changed. There is now a greater diversity of background among the women who come to the center. The average participant is remarkably younger (36 percent are under 25 in contrast to an earlier 7 percent); is more likely to be single, divorced, or widowed (30 percent compared to 14 percent); has fewer children (1.6) than the typical participant of even five years ago. She more often needs money to finance her education and she is somewhat more likely to be employed when she comes to the center. Her educational achievement, the kind of help she requests from the center (except for more financial assistance), and her interest in preparing for a good job have remained about the same. Very few women are interested in courses without credit, in volunteer work, or solely in self-improvement. There is a slight increase in interest in nontraditional fields for women and a slight shift away from public school teaching, but essentially the fields of interest remain those traditionally associated with women.

The center designs its programs with the changing needs of women in mind, and presumably this will determine to some extent who utilizes the center. Changing expectations among the under-thirty age group concerning education and life styles (for example, joint planning of student couples, willingness to postpone marriage and child bearing, a desire to reduce or eliminate periods of interruption in education) probably are reflected in these statistics. . . .

Today the returning woman may be one who dropped out to assess her goals and life style rather than one who dropped out to marry and bear children.

Whatever the reason for dropping out, when a woman returns to a degree program, she is serious and highly motivated. The investment of time, money, and energy required is not for the casual student. . . .

A reason very often given for returning to school is the need for a "feeling of achievement" or sense of competency. For some women this is a comment on the loss of self-esteem accompanying the traditional roles of housewife and mother. For others it is simply a recognition of the value of a fully certifiable training. . . .

Besides their strong motivation, seriousness of purpose, persistence, adaptability, and industry, the returning women were eager and enjoyed learning for its own sake: "And after just one course in art history, I was hooked. I knew that I had been a misplaced person all these years."

They expressed concern about the effect of their activities on their children, but their concern was essentially to provide good substitute care. The woman returnee recognized the inconclusive nature of the data on children and working mothers, and rationalized her activities: "I think this interest . . . in furthering . . . education is going to be the greatest thing in correcting the child-centered home." On the other hand, women ". . . *do* have guilt feelings. This is par for the course. You step out in fear and trembling and hope that what you are doing is not going to starve yourself or your husband or your children."

The attitudes of husbands were understood to be important. The supportive and interested husband or one who appreciated his wife's enhanced earning power was singled out:

I would just like to say that I just recently moved from a small town where *The Feminine Mystique* was known as a dirty book. They questioned me when I took it out of the library. . . . So, I just went back to school, and I find that as I grow interested in what I am learning and go home and talk to my husband about it. . . . He has developed pride in what I am doing. Frankly, I think he was a little tired of hearing me say, "What's new at work today?"

Returning women without husbands were particularly likely to elicit their children's cooperation and support in organizing their lives. To encourage other women, one center participant wrote a three-page "how to" statement in which she explained her family management techniques, and the convictions concerning human fulfillment on which they are based.

There is little doubt that returning adult women perform well in school. Fagerburg found that they perform better than other women students including very young returnees. In a University of Michigan report on grades over a three-year period, the grade-point averages of married women students were found to be higher than any other students. A recent survey of the center participants indicates that 91 percent earned grades as good as or better than their earlier records.

Women reported that family responsibilities and lack of money were the major barriers to returning to school. But some experienced discrimination as a barrier. An engineering student said,

One of the things that always comes up is the salary discrepancy. . . . We had a discussion of the number of companies that will not even interview women at all. . . . Their complaint . . . is that a woman . . . will not stay because she will get married. . . . I *am* married, I *have* three children . . . but the attitude is not too terribly different toward me. . . .

Information concerning the number of programs for returning women in the nation's colleges and universities and the number of women participating in them is limited. In 1962, a survey of 1,167 accredited colleges, junior colleges, and universities in the United Stares was made by the American Association of University Women's Educational Foundation. At that time, approximately 300 institutions indicated that they had programs designed especially for returning women or that they provided for the admission and special needs of these women in the regular academic program. Succeeding editions of a listing prepared by the Women's Bureau of the Department of Labor indicated that there were 375 such programs by 1968 and 436 by 1971. Of those, 212 programs existed on the college and university level by 1968 and 376 by 1971.

The American Association of University Women report, "Campus 1970—Where Do Women Stand", based on a survey of 454 institutions, indicated that less than 50 percent of these institutions made any institutional adjustments to fit the special needs and even fewer had special programs for returning women, but almost all indicate that they make it possible for women to return to a degree program. . . .

More interesting than size and growth are the common concerns and themes running through continuing education programs. Important among these are the need for flexibility in educational institutions, counseling, career development opportunities, and the availability of part-time jobs, daycare, and financial assistance, as well as for continuing research and evaluation of such programs.

15. Adele Simmons, "Princeton's Women," 1977

The turn to coeducation on the part of single-sex colleges took place increasingly in the 1960s and 1970s. This change at an Ivy League college was watched intently from many administrative quarters, not only by dubious Princeton alumni. After graduating from Radcliffe (1963)

and taking her Ph.D. at Oxford (1969), Adele Smith Simmons (1941–) went to the history faculty and served as dean of student affairs at Princeton (1972–77). She took over the presidency of Hampshire College from 1977 to 1989 and then went to the presidency of the John D. and Catherine T. MacArthur Foundation (1989–99). Thereafter she became associated with the Center for International Studies at the University of Chicago. Her memories of early coeducation at Princeton while she was dean are recorded here.

Adele Simmons, "Princeton's Women," *Change* (December 1977): 42–44. Reprinted with permission of the Helen Dwight Reid Educational Foundation. Published by Heldref Publications, 1319 Eighteenth St. NW, Washington, D.C. 20036-1802 Copyright © 1980. Further reading: Leslie Miller-Bernal and Susan L. Poulson, eds., *Going Coed: Women's Experiences in Formerly Men's Colleges and Universities, 1950–2000* (Nashville, 2004).

When the question of coeducation arose at Princeton, President Robert F. Goheen appointed a commission, chaired by Gardner Patterson, then professor of economics, to study the touchy issue. At the conclusion of a debate that generated anger and anxiety, the Patterson Commission produced an exhaustive study that recommended the admission of women. Nine years later the Patterson Report appears anachronistic and patronizing. Princeton, like many male colleges considering coeducation, had to make its strongest argument to doubting alumni. Hence, the report stressed the impact of coeducation on male undergraduates.

As its first argument the Commission listed the positive "effect of coeducation on the number and quality of male applicants." According to the report, Princeton was rounding out its class in 1967 with good but not truly outstanding applicants. Those who declined admission in 1966 and 1967 listed three reasons: the lack of women students, the general social atmosphere, and the club system.

The views of the students who turned down Princeton were echoed by Princeton's faculty. Seventy-five percent believed that admitting women would make Princeton more attractive to male students; 83 percent of the enrolled students—but only 47 percent of the alumni—agreed.

The Patterson Report next considered the impact of coeducation on the intellectual life of Princeton. This section dealt with the quaint question of whether a feminine presence on campus would distract men and wisely concluded, "We have found little to support the view that, in the highly selective colleges, women seriously distract men's attention in the classroom and the library."

Princeton faculty who had recently taught in coeducational institutions maintained that mixed classes were more satisfying. They believed that the presence of female undergraduates increased the variety of viewpoints and methods for approaching classroom material. Besides, the Commission argued, the addition of 1,200 female students would enable Princeton to add faculty in areas that needed strengthening, such as the arts, and would help Princeton to utilize more fully existing resources, classrooms, and facilities.

The 55-page report devoted only one page to the impact of coeducation on women themselves. This section was titled "Princeton's Opportunity for Service." One might have hoped for more thoughtful elaboration of the importance to women of gaining access to one of the country's great universities.

Princeton, of course, was not alone in its decision to admit both sexes. The rush to coeducation in the late 1960s is now history. Within a seven-year period both women's and men's colleges opened their campuses and classes to members of the opposite sex, some with greater enthusiasm than others: Of the men's colleges, Yale admitted women to its freshman class in 1969 while Wesleyan admitted transfer students that year and freshmen the next. In April 1969 the Princeton admissions office had two sets of letters addressed to its female applicants pending the outcome of the April trustees meeting. One explained that the trustees had decided not to admit women; a second said that Princeton would be admitting women and informed the applicant of her status. In part because funding was pledged during the meeting to build the required dormitory space, the trustees were able to tell anxious Admissions officers to mail the second set of letters. The following year Brown merged with Pembroke; Williams admitted women in 1971; Dartmouth followed in 1972; Amherst accepted transfer students in 1975 and freshmen in 1976; and Haverford now admits all but freshman women. Now that two student generations of women have attended these traditionally male colleges, it seems appropriate to reflect on the academic and social changes: The Princeton experience is illustrative.

In spite of the deficiencies in the Patterson Report, for the most part the first Princeton women have thrived, thanks to the strong commitment of faculty and senior officers. Unlike their confreres at institutions that have been coeducational for many years, Princeton faculty did not have a history of treating women as second-class citizens. Women arrived on campus after the feminist movement had begun and most faculty were willing to take them and their goals seriously. Those who opposed coeducation enjoyed little support.

Sometimes, of course, mistakes were made. In an effort to ensure safety, one dormitory and several units of another were identified as women's living areas. All entrances and exits were locked and only the women were given keys. But the administration quickly realized that assigning all women to one living area was a mistake: It only enhanced their conspicuousness. And the system of locks never worked. Within a year Princeton moved to coeducational living arrangements, with provisions for single-sex living areas for all who wished them. Deans listened patiently to the first women and in

response to their requests developed a program in sex education and a women's center. Even menus were adjusted to provide more yogurt and cottage cheese, a small gesture easy to implement but important to morale. It was this flexibility and concern that earned Princeton a reputation as a good place for female undergraduates.

Even so, the first years were difficult. The women knew that some students and many alumni did not want them. They realized that attitudes toward future women students would be shaped by their own successes and failures. Many Princeton men, in their efforts to acknowledge the presence of the women, only made things worse. The most consistent early complaint stemmed from encounters in the classroom. One woman, in a discussion about a Robert Frost poem, was asked to give the class "the romantic view." Another, in the process of switching majors, was asked by a faculty advisor whether she was following "some boy" into the new department. Yet another, who described herself as one of the "failures of coeducation," believed that being a girl at Princeton was "the same as being a freak." She went on to say, "I was always the center of attention, not as a date, but as the only girl. I was not able to handle that kind of attention. Faculty were always asking for the girls' opinion. . . . I felt like saying I'm dumb, but don't blame it on my being a girl." And as late as 1972 one faculty member refused to recommend a girl for a summer scholarship because he thought she should not travel independently in Latin America.

For the most part, however, the first women achieved in extraordinary ways. Princeton gives two major awards each year to students with outstanding academic records who have made unusual contributions to the community. In 1973 both these awards went to women. One of these women has since been elected to the board of trustees. Both the valedictorian and the salutatorian of the class of 1975 were women. Many earned places in prestigious graduate schools or found challenging jobs in banks, businesses, and government.

Moreover, as female undergraduates became part of the Princeton scene, the unusual pressures declined. One found that in her "junior and senior years it was a shock when people didn't stare and stand up when I walked into a room." The change was largely due to the dramatic increase in numbers. In 1969–70, 148 out of 3,400 students were women; by 1976–77, these numbers were 1,395 out of 4,360.

Interest in women's issues ran high at first, and the new women's center drew many active supporters. But as women gained confidence about themselves and their chosen careers, they turned less to consciousness-raising groups or women's center activities. Ironically, having brought about a measure of social change, the feminist movement per se came to occupy a less central position.

Then, too, traditional impulses were operating.

Many believed, rightly or wrongly, that they must choose between men and women, and that active involvement with women's issues would impede male-female relationships. At age 18, even for the so-called liberated, those relationships matter very much, yet they place many freshman women in traditional sex roles, usually with upperclass males. In a group of 16 unmarried senior women with whom I met last fall, one third had been engaged during their freshman year. By the time they were seniors, however, most had established far more independent social lives.

The social situation for women in former men's colleges is complicated. The ratios suggest that there should be no woman sitting alone at home on any night, ever. But many students are bewildered as traditional patterns of behavior disintegrate. It is no longer clear who should ask whom to do what—let alone pay for the activity. In addition some men find it easier to restrict their social life to weekends and their companions to imports who arrive on a Friday and leave on a Sunday. Princeton women still complain that "Princeton men don't like coeds." Students in the mid-1970s often have difficulty meeting each other in informal settings; there is no successor to the mixers of the 1950s or the peace marches of the 1960s. In a Princeton Triangle song, one group of women expressed a view that can be heard on most campuses today:

Moanin' alone in my room,
Sewn in a pocket of gloom,
Alumni write letters that sound pretty mad,
'Cause nowadays lads don't have the rules that they
    had.
At parties and orgies they think we abound,
They think undergrad life's gone clear
    underground.
Successful and rich, these alums might be right,
But there's nothing to do this Saturday night.
Alumni if you'd make your complaints more
    specific,
Maybe my love life would turn out terrific.
Until it comes true, I know where I'll be,
In bed with my arms around Chem 203.

The women at Princeton may be bright, articulate, and academically thriving, but they are singing a familiar refrain: They would like to have careers, they would like to marry, but they want partners who will support their careers and share in the responsibilities of home and family. Many wonder whether there are enough men with these qualities to go around. They say their male peers still choose the easy way out—the long-term relationship with a woman who has no particular ambition. They know they can survive independently, but most don't want to.

For many reasons, at predominantly male institutions, it is not always easy for women to talk intimately to each other. Every meal, every class (even physical education) is coeducational. Some are unhappy over this lack of community. Perhaps that is why last year over one third of the women at Princeton opted for single-sex living areas.

But the majority adapt to their setting, assuming the characteristics that are associated with highly competitive white men. The route is easy and the immediate rewards are often considerable. Successful women feel little need to challenge current expectations about professional school admissions or the organization of work. After all, most have not experienced overt sex discrimination; on the contrary, their admission to an elite male school was proof of their competence. Male faculty by and large take them seriously and may even buy more cups of coffee for them than for male students. The possibility that they, like other women, will one day experience sex discrimination seems improbable.

Women faculty could tell them otherwise. They could explain that being the colleague of a male professor poses far more problems than being his student, that one day they may be viewed as threatening competitors rather than as intellectual comrades. But because the number of women faculty has been small, these faculty-student discussions have not taken place often enough. In 1969–70 Princeton had two women assistant professors and one tenured professor out of a faculty of 709. By fall 1977 the faculty of 697 included 43 women assistant professors and 11 female tenured professors.

Each institution has its own peculiar pressures of course, but generally the more successful women in male institutions are those with a clear sense of themselves who are confident and comfortable about their own abilities. They speak out and are not intimidated by the male environment, either because they are the kind of people who are rarely intimidated or because they have consciously learned how to be effective in a male environment.

At the same time these women are providing a service to the University, though not the one intended by the Patterson Report. They have encouraged Princeton to make curricular changes, however modest, to reflect the new interest in women's studies. They have acted as catalysts for changes in hiring practices. Were there not female undergraduates at Princeton today, women would probably not hold two of the University's most senior academic deanships, dean of the graduate school and dean of the college. These women deans, in turn, will be sitting on the committee that makes promotion and tenure decisions. Undergraduate women are also educating their male peers to better understand the new generation. While undergraduate men can agree in principle with the ideals of the feminist movement, they still appear nervous about marrying a "liberated woman"; having women in the classroom may ease some of their fears.

How are Princeton's women doing? Quite well, it seems. But in one area, more needs to happen. At Princeton and on other campuses where most of the adult authority figures are still male, broad counseling efforts for women should be provided. In the

decade to come, these women and their male partners will be facing extremely complicated decisions
regarding careers and lifestyles. They need to learn
through discussions with faculty and advisors that
there are no easy, clean-cut solutions for dealing
with the same set of circumstances. One project
in this vein is Princeton's "Lifestyles Colloquium"
which offers opportunities for men and women undergraduates to talk with people who have organized their work and family lives in different ways—
dual career families, single parents, couples without
children. Universities have an obligation to push for
efforts of this kind, so long as the campus remains a
place where male values predominate.

Diversification of Higher Education: African Americans

16. James Meredith, *Three Years in Mississippi*, 1966

Born in Mississippi and a veteran of nine years in the Air
Force, James Howard Meredith (1933–   ) was enrolled at
Jackson State College when he applied for admission, at
first unsuccessfully, to complete his bachelor's degree in
political science at the University of Mississippi. When
Governor Ross Barnett personally refused to enroll Meredith in the fall of 1962, President John F. Kennedy proclaimed the supremacy of federal law and assumed
command of the Mississippi National Guard to insure
Meredith's entrance in the face of campus rioting. The
drama of his admission and first weeks as a student was
widely publicized, as was the admission of two African-
American students at the University of Alabama in 1963
over the protests of Governor George Wallace and other
state officials. Here is Meredith's account of his efforts
to matriculate and then to survive as the first African-
American student at "Ole Miss." Meredith went on to
get a law degree at Columbia University, to run unsuccessfully for Congress in Mississippi, and then to work as
a stockbroker, professor, and writer. In later years, defending his support of senator Jesse Helms of North Carolina and his endorsement of Ku Klux Klan leader David
Duke in Louisiana, Meredith claimed he was merely
"monitoring the enemy."

James Meredith, *Three Years in Mississippi* (Bloomington,
IN, 1966), pp. 59–61, 188–90, 207, 212–14, 226–28, 230,
274–77, 326. Copyright © 1966 by James Meredith. Re-
printed with the kind permission of the author. Fur-
ther reading: Meredith's case at law is *Meredith v. Fair*
(U.S.C.A.), 298 F. 2d (1962) and 305 F. 2d (1962); Rus-
sell H. Barrett, *Integration at Ole Miss* (Chicago, 1965);
Jack Bass, *Unlikely Heroes* (New York, 1981), ch. 9;
William Doyle, *An American Insurrection: The Battle of
Oxford, Mississippi, 1962* (New York, 2001); Paul Hen-
drickson, *Sons of Mississippi: A Study of Race and Its
Legacy* (New York, 2003); *Reporting Civil Rights: Part I,
American Journalism, 1941–1963* (New York, 2003); and
Charlayne Hunter-Gault, *In My Place* (New York, 1992).

February 7, 1961
To: The United States Justice Department . . .
My background: I was born on a small farm in
Attala County, Mississippi, the seventh of thirteen

children. I walked to school, over four miles each
way, every day for eleven years. Throughout these
years, the white school bus passed us each morning. There was no Negro school bus. I never had a
teacher during grade and high school with a college
degree. But I was fortunate, because I was able to
go to school. Each day I passed by one of the largest
farms in the county, and there I saw boys my own
age and younger working in the fields who to this
day cannot even read road signs. I have never
known how I could help solve this situation, but I
have always felt that I must do my best.

During my last year of high school, which was
spent in Florida, I entered an essay contest sponsored by the American Legion, and I was a winner
along with two white girls. The title of the essay was
"Why I Am Proud to Be an American." My theme
was that I was not proud because I was born with
as many or more of the desirable things of life as
the next man, but because in my country an individual has the opportunity to grow and develop according to his ability and ingenuity and because he
is not restricted from progress solely on the basis of
race. Basically, I still believe in this possibility.

I served nine years in the United States Air
Force. All of this time was spent in the so-called
"integrated" service; because of this experience I
feel that there is no logical reason to justify denying
a law-abiding citizen the rights of full citizenship
solely on the basis of race.

What do I want from you? I think that the power
and influence of the federal government should be
used where necessary to insure compliance with
the laws as interpreted by the proper authority. I
feel that the federal government can do more in
this area if it chooses and I feel that it should
choose to do so. In view of the above information I
simply ask that the federal agencies use the power
and prestige of their positions to insure the full
rights of citizenship for our people.

Sincerely,
JAMES H. MEREDITH

Then we settled down to the business of the day. . . .
At a long table were three chairs: one for [Governor
Ross] Barnett as Registrar, another for his assistant,
Ellis, and on the other side of the table, a chair for the
honored guest. I was surprised that they would let a
Negro sit with them. Ellis read a written statement
making Barnett the registrar, but he refused to give
the lawyer a copy, however. Then Barnett took out
his long proclamation, stamped with the seal of the
"Great and Sovereign State of Mississippi." I guess I
was supposed to say my lines at this point, but the
coordinators had failed to give me the script, so
Barnett finally wanted to know if there was any further business. I got the message and addressed myself to "Mr. Registrar," looking at Ellis, but the Governor informed me that he was the Registrar, so I had
to restate my intention to enroll to Registrar Barnett.
He then proceeded to read his proclamation.

MISSISSIPPI
EXECUTIVE DEPARTMENT
JACKSON
TO: JAMES H. MEREDITH, APPLICANT FOR
ADMISSION AS A STUDENT AT THE UNI-
VERSITY OF MISSISSIPPI:

Pursuant to the authority vested in me under the Constitution and the laws of the State of Mississippi, I, Ross R. Barnett, Governor of the State of Mississippi and for the protection of all citizens of the State of Mississippi, and all others who may be within the confines of the State of Mississippi.

Therefore, you, James H. Meredith, are hereby refused admission as a student to the University of Mississippi, and any other person or persons who, in my opinion, by such admission, would lead to a breach of the peace and be contrary to the administrative procedures and regulations of the University of Mississippi and the laws of the State of Mississippi.

Take due notice thereof and govern yourself accordingly.

IN WITNESS WHEREOF, I have hereunto set my hand and caused the Great Seal of the State of Mississippi to be affixed on this the 20th day of September, A.D., 1962.

GOVERNOR

ATTEST:
SECRETARY OF STATE

When he had finished reading it, he handed it to me. I was finally given a piece of the show, and at least I would have a souvenir to pass on to my children and their children and their children's children. The Justice Department spokesman, on stage now, attempted to protest and warned the Governor that action would be taken against him. However, he soon seemed to sense that the most logical thing to do was to get out of there. I thanked the Governor and we hastened out to our waiting car, which sped away with hordes of shouting, rock-throwing students hot on the chase. The state troopers led us on our way to the Tennessee line as fast as one could imagine. The first registration attempt was over.

THE CONTEMPT TRIALS

The United States government no longer faced a mere threat, but a direct and definite challenge. And now the only way for either side to escape a showdown was to remove me physically from the arena. The courts had rendered their decision. Every citizen of the United States, including me, a Negro in Mississippi, had the right to attend any publicly supported school anywhere in the several states, and especially in the state of his residence and birth. The state of Mississippi had elected to reject this decision and to resist with every available resource, including the use of organized violence. Mississippi had purposefully and forcefully rejected my right to attend the University of Mississippi. The federal government could either capitulate or retaliate.

There was no other way out as the events that were to follow proved.

The first contempt trial was held September 21, the day after Barnett's rejection. The Chancellor of the University of Mississippi, the Dean of the College of Liberal Arts, and the Registrar were charged with civil and criminal contempt, and the proceedings were heard in Mississippi before U.S. District Judge Mize. The Judge found all the officials "not guilty" and ordered their acquittal.

The case was moved to the Fifth Circuit Court of Appeals in New Orleans, where, in an unusual sitting of the court, all the justices except Ben F. Cameron of Mississippi sat to hear the case. . . . At this hearing on September 24 the university officials expressed willingness to comply with the court's order to register me. The court then ordered the board of trustees to rescind its action purporting to relieve the university officials of registration duties and to revoke the action naming the governor agent of the board in affairs pertaining to my enrollment.

But Mississippi with Barnett at the helm meant to stay a step or two in front. On that day, September 24, Governor Barnett issued a proclamation which declared that the federal government's action in the Meredith case was a "direct usurpation" of the reserved powers of the state "through the illegal use of judicial decree," and went on to assert:

> Now, therefore, I, Ross R. Barnett, Governor of the State of Mississippi, by the authority vested in me under the Constitution and laws of the State of Mississippi, do hereby proclaim and direct that the arrest or attempts to arrest, or the fining or the attempts to fine, of any state official in the performance of his official duties, by any representative of the Federal Government, is illegal and such representative or representatives of said Federal Government are to be summarily arrested and jailed by reason of any such illegal acts in violation of this executive order and in violation of the laws of the State of Mississippi.

The United States government could not tolerate this defiance and at 8:30 A.M. on September 25, 1962, the Court of Appeals for the Fifth Circuit entered a temporary restraining order. . . .

The two days—September 30 and October 1, 1962—may well go down in history as one of the supreme tests of the Union. The use of force to defy the legitimate mandates of the world's most powerful government is basically significant. Insurrection against the United States by the state of Mississippi became on these days a reality.

The state of Mississippi had clearly shown its intention not only to threaten to use violence, but to use it. In the face of this direct challenge the federal government had no choice but to act to enforce its authority. President John F. Kennedy acted at the crucial moment on September 30, 1962, by issuing a proclamation and executive order. . . .

Some newspapermen later asked me if I thought attending the university was worth all this death and destruction. The question really annoyed me. Of course, I was sorry! I hadn't wanted this to happen. I believe it could have been prevented by responsible political leadership in Mississippi. As for the federal government, the President and the Attorney General had all the intelligence facilities at their disposal, and I believe that they handled it to the best of their knowledge and ability. I think it would have been much worse if they had waited any longer. Social change is a painful thing, but the method by which it is achieved depends upon the people at the top. Here they were totally opposed—the state against the federal government. There was bound to be trouble, and there was.

There was no lingering or turning back now. At eight o'clock the three of us—McShane, Doar, and Meredith—with a retinue of marshals and soldiers left Baxter Hall for the Lyceum Building to get on with the long-delayed business of my registering as a student at the University of Mississippi. The signs of strife and warfare from the night before were everywhere. But at this moment the power of the United States was supreme. Even the Mississippi National Guard had proven without a doubt that its first loyalty was to the Commander-in-Chief of the Armed Forces of the United States—the President.

The border patrol car in which we rode to the administration building was a shattered example of the violence of social change. We had used this car to make our first attempt to enroll on September 20, 1962, and then it had been a spotless, unmarred specimen. Now it was battered and smashed: bullet holes had riddled the sides; the windows were all shot out. . . .

It was a dismal day. Even the newsmen were spiritless. Inside the room behind a desk sat Ellis, the Registrar. He was a lone stand-out, the only man on the scene with spirit—a spirit of defiance, even of contempt, if not hatred. Doar stated our purpose and the Registrar pointed to a group of forms to be filled out by me. I looked at them and filled out all but one—my class-schedule form. As I studied it, obviously Ellis knew what was on my mind. One course on my schedule not only was a duplicate of one with the same title which I had already completed with the grade of A, but when I got to the class, I found that the instructor was using the very same textbook. Ellis said to me, "Meredith (he is the only official at the university who did not address me with the usual title of courtesy), you may as well sign." I tried to discuss the matter with him, but it was no use. I signed and decided to take the matter up through other channels. The schedule was later changed to suit my needs.

We left the room. The press had been patient and I consented to stop and talk briefly with them. There was not too much to ask and less to say. The first question asked me was, "Now that you are finally registered, are you happy?" I could only express my true feeling that, "This is no happy occasion." Truly, this was no time for joy.

On my way out of the Lyceum Building, I encountered my first Negro. What would his reaction be? What would our relationship be? What would be our communication? He had his cleaning tools, as all Negroes on the campus must keep them visible, and under one arm was tucked a broom. As I walked past, he acted as if he had not even noticed anything unusual on the campus, but just as I passed he touched me with the handle of his broom and caught my eye. I got the message. Every Negro on the campus was on my team. Every black eye would be watching over me at the University of Mississippi. Later on, I got to know this fellow very well. He told me that he just had to let me know that they were with me all the way, and to bump me with the broom handle was the best way he could think of to communicate with me.

At nine I attended my first class; it was a course in Colonial American History. I was a few minutes late and was given a seat at the back of the room. The professor was lecturing on the English background, conditions in England at the time of the colonization of America, and he pretended to pay no special attention when I entered. When the U.S. marshals decided to come inside the room, however, he asked them to remain outside. This was a precedent that was followed during my entire stay at the university. I think there were about a dozen students in class. One said hello to me and the others were silent. I remember a girl—the only girl there, I think—and she was crying. But it might have been from the tear gas in the room. I was crying from it myself.

I had three classes scheduled that day. I went to two; the third did not meet because there was too much tear gas in the room.

RETURN TO BAXTER HALL

This day, October 1, 1962, was a turning point in my three years in Mississippi. The first phase—to breach the system of "White Supremacy"—had been accomplished; even if I only had a toehold in the door, the solid wall had been cracked. . . .

MY THOUGHTS DURING THE FIRST WEEKS

People seem always to want to know what I thought and how I felt during the first few weeks at the University of Mississippi, what was being said to me and how I reacted. I think a few excerpts from an article written at the end of the second week for the *Saturday Evening Post* can best depict my feelings and attitudes. . . .

As far as my relations with the students go, I make it a practice to be courteous. I do not force myself on them, but that is not my nature anyway. Many of them—most, I would say—have been courteous, and the faculty members certainly have been. When I hear the jeers and the catcalls—"We'll get you, nigger" and all that—I do not consider it personal. I get the idea people are just having a little fun. I think it's tragic that they have to have this kind of fun about me, but many of them are children of the men who lead Mississippi today, and I would not expect them to act any other way. They have to act the way they do. I think I understand human nature enough to understand that.

It has not been all bad. Many students have spoken to me very pleasantly. They have stopped banging doors and throwing bottles into my dormitory now.

One day a fellow from my home town sat down at my table in the cafeteria. "If you're here to get an education, I'm for you," he said. "If you're here to cause trouble, I'm against you." That seemed fair enough to me.

If the decision is made to keep the marshals and troops on the campus until I complete my course, it is all right with me, but I hope that will not be necessary. I think the marshals have been superb. They have had an image of America—that the law must be obeyed, no matter what they may think of it or what anybody else may think of it—but they are certainly a distraction on the campus. The thing that grieves me most about all this is that the students are not getting the best college results because they are spending too much time looking on at these various events involving me. I did not get much studying done that first week, and I don't think anybody else did. . . .

Later, in an article that was published in *Look,* I made the following comments:

> The job has just begun, and everywhere you look, you see things that reflect the inequalities still existing in our society. At the university, the saddest day of every week for me is Thursday—because that is ROTC day. When I go to class that morning, the Reserve Officer Candidates have on their uniforms. In the afternoon, I often go out to watch them drill up and down the streets near my dormitory. I know that not one Negro in Mississippi has the privilege of taking part in the ROTC program. Surely, there is one Negro in our state who would make officer material. The Regular Army units guarding the campus are fully integrated, including Negro officers, but the country does not get any Negro officers from Mississippi ROTC training. It's a loss for the country in general. For the Negro, it is more than a loss, individually or financially; it affects him even down to his soul.

I seldom paid any attention to the yells. The thing I did notice was the language the white students used, including the women students. I have always heard it said that Negroes use bad language, but the Negro cannot match the vileness of the words many white students yelled. And the part that was most difficult for me to understand was that they did not care who was listening; they did not show any respect for their women, or any instructor or parent. This to me indicated that our state had degenerated to an extremely low level. . . .

A TYPICAL CLASS DAY

I would usually awaken around five-thirty or a quarter to six to the click of the steel-plated heels of the soldier walking his post in the hallway from one end of my apartment to the other. I shaved and put on the sweet-smelling after-shave lotion that one of my many friends had given me for Christmas. At seven I would walk out the only way open, through the living room (the marshals' headquarters). All the other doors had been blocked. The team of marshals for the day would join me, and I would head down the long flight of steps outside the dorm toward the sidewalk. When I reached the second step one of my watchers would yell, "Hey, Nigger! There's that Nigger!" I had been at the university ten months before I ever descended the fifteen or twenty steps without someone calling me nigger. They must have kept their eyes on those steps twenty-four hours a day. As I walked the two blocks down the hill to the cafeteria, I could hear the routine window-to-window comments. I think I would have been very disturbed, if not thoroughly frightened, if I had walked the whole distance without anybody saying anything. I would have known that they were up to something very drastic. . . .

Since the class in History of the New South was at eight o'clock and I always liked to be the first one in the room, I usually went from the cafeteria by the back door to the Graduate Building where the class was held and read *The Mississippian* (university newspaper). The professor, an old-line Mississippi aristocrat, is the only instructor that I have ever had in any school with whom I have never had a conversation of any kind. Once, we met head on in a narrow corridor and he spoke. Also, he wrote a note on my midterm exam paper, saying that I could raise my B+ to an A on the final if I gave more substance to my answers. This was ironic because the moderates on campus felt that he just might fail me in his course, since he was a known conservative.

On my way to the course in the Legislative Process in the Political Science Building I would stop by the post office and pick up my mail. The post office was probably the only place where there was unsupervised contact with other students at the school. It was usually crowded. Every now and then one of the boys would stick his foot out in a gesture to trip me. Often I would kick back at a couple of them. Most of the students crowded in to their boxes, even if I were in the narrow corridor where the individual boxes were. A few, especially girls, would never come in while I was there; they just waited out in the hall and sneered.

This class was taught by my adviser and the head of the department. A fine man of high character and a native Mississippian, he went the full official and formal limit and no further. Personally, I would expect no more. He was the only professor on the first day that I attended classes to read to the students the letter from the university directing the school to comply with the court order. I vividly remember his shaken look on that day; he had been deeply grieved by the events that had taken place in his state.

After the political science class, I would stop by

the library to read for a little while in the reserved books reading room. There was less friction in the library. I cannot recall any rudeness or indifferent treatment from the library staff or from any of the students working there. Some students, of course, always left the room when I came in, but I am a firm believer in individual freedom of action. There were numerous occasions when the library had to be vacated because of "bomb scares." At one point, I stopped going to the library because I hated to see the other students suffering so much inconvenience.

The worst event of all, and the most dishonorable, was having my reading glasses stolen. I usually went upstairs to the commercial room to do my studying. On this day the room was full. I went to the washroom and left my books and reading glasses on the table. When I returned, the glasses were gone. The campus police were called and everyone was questioned, but naturally no one had seen a thing. A few days later, one of the witnesses couldn't live with his conscience any longer and came over to tell me who did it. He also confessed to the marshals on condition that it would go no further. He would not testify in public. I guess I could understand his predicament.

By noon I always liked to be in a good position in the "chow" line. This was the biggest meal. From habit, or principle, I always went to the right side of the dining hall. For some reason more students usually went through my line. Very often the other line would be much shorter, yet they would wait in the much longer line on the right. Of course, I don't know why this was so, but I used to tell the marshals it was because the best food was always on my side. The Negroes cooked the food and brought it to the line, but it was served by whites. The Negroes knew that if the white servers got a chance they would give me some bad pieces of food; therefore, the Negroes made certain that every bit of food that was put on my line was the best.

It was always a heartbreaking sight to see the young Negro boys and girls who should have been in junior high or high school wiping the tables and carrying the trays for white students.

In the afternoon I would go to the Peabody Building for a math class. It was made up primarily of freshmen students and had a personality of its own. The instructor of the algebra class was a retired Navy Captain and a native Mississippian, but I never had any reason to believe that he would not be perfectly fair to me as a student in his class.

At three o'clock I had a two-hour biology laboratory class. We spent two hours peeking through microscopes at green leaves and frog blood. I had less interest in this than I had in Barnett's genealogical history, but it was required because the general science course I took at Jackson State College did not have any equivalent at the University of Mississippi.

After biology lab, I stopped by the library to read for a while and wait until time to eat supper. Five minutes before the dining hall was due to open, I left the library in order to get an early place in the cafeteria line. When I got in the line on the right as usual, a bumpy-faced antagonist of mine got in the other line opposite me. He was absolutely the foulest-mouthed individual that I have ever met, and that is saying a lot, considering the run-of-the-mill student at the University of Mississippi. . . .

On our march to the Grove we passed through the Lyceum Building where the U.S. government had set up its headquarters on September 30, 1962, the day I came to the campus. As I passed, I took special notice of the bullet holes that were still there, a consequence of the fighting between the state of Mississippi and the federal government of the United States. I had looked at these bullet holes many times.

We marched on past the statue of the Confederate soldier, the symbol of the blood that had been shed one hundred years ago in defense of the system of "White Supremacy." It was at the foot of this statue that General Walker had spoken to the crowd on the night of the revolt of the state of Mississippi.

We ended our march in the Grove, where the graduation exercises were being held in the open air. This was near the Circle where most of the riot had taken place on September 30. To one who knows the realities of life in Mississippi, the most striking thing about the Grove was the Negroes scattered throughout the audience. They were there in large numbers. Frankly, I was very surprised to see so many Negroes, but very pleased indeed.

The Ceremony. After taking my place among the graduates, I looked out at the curious and staring audience. Cameras were clicking in every direction. There in the audience was my seventy-two-year-old father with my three-year-old son. Throughout his life he had given his all in an effort to make Mississippi and the world free for his children and his children's children. He had lived to see the day that he had always longed for but had never really expected to see. Sitting on his knee was my son, not yet aware of the existence of the system of "White Supremacy" that would seek in every possible way to render him less than human. He seemed quite amused by the events. My gratification came from the hope that my son might be a future Governor or President.

17. Patricia Roberts Harris, "The Negro College and Its Community," 1971

The social importance of a national network of black college alumnae was discussed by Patricia Roberts Harris (1924–85) in a notable issue of *Daedalus* devoted to the future of black colleges. An outstanding woman in American public life in the 1960s and 1970s, Harris graduated from Howard University in 1945 and received her J.D. from George Washington University Law Center in 1960, graduating first in her class of ninety-four students. She became a trial attorney for the Department of Justice (1960–61), and then dean and professor of law at Howard University School of Law (1961–65, 1967–69), interrupted by two years as ambassador to Luxembourg. A leader in Democratic Party affairs, she became secretary of health, education, and welfare in President Carter's cabinet (1977–80). Seen by some as a member of a new African-American middle class, Harris made her past clear when questioned by a senator at her confirmation hearing in 1977. She said "I'm a black woman, the daughter of a dining car waiter. I'm a black woman who even eight years ago could not buy a house in some parts of the District of Columbia. Senator, to say I'm not by and of and for the people is to show a lack of understanding of who I am and where I came from."

Patricia Roberts Harris, "The Negro College and Its Community," *Daedalus* 100, no. 3 (Summer 1971): 722–25. © 1971 by the American Academy of Arts and Sciences, abridged with permission. Quotation from Judith R. Johnson, "Patricia Roberts Harris" in *American National Biography*, ed. John A Garraty and Mark C. Carnes, vol. 10 (New York, 1999), 179–80. Further reading: Harris, "Problems and Solutions in Achieving Equality for Women," in *Women in Higher Education*, ed. W. Todd Furniss and Patricia Albjerg Graham (Washington, D.C., 1974); Charlayne Hunter-Gault, *In My Place* (New York, 1992); William G. Bowen and Derek Bok, *The Shape of the River: Long-Term Consequences of Considering Race in College and University Admissions* (Princeton, NJ, 1998): chs. 5–6; Linda M. Perkins, "The African American Female Elite: The Early History of African American Women in the Seven Sister Colleges, 1880–1960," *Harvard Educational Review* 67 (Winter 1977): 718–56.

The most significant role of the black college in serving the Negro community was that of providing a glimpse of life as it might be to a racial minority relegated to the lowest rung of the nation's economic and social larder. Although American life has never been conspicuously hospitable to the intellectual and the academician, the presence of some blacks in activities suggesting that brain as well as brawn resided inside black skins was an element that was useful in combatting the hopelessness now described as the absence of black pride. The characteristic American ambivalence toward intellectuality was also to be found, in abundance, among blacks. The low remuneration of college teachers, the disrespect shown by ignorant whites, and the high status accorded the businessman all contributed in some degree to the denigration of the black academician. The primacy of the black college president and his business manager in college policy-making and in community status was a reflection of the general American hostility to the intellectual. On the other hand, with notable exceptions in places such as Atlanta, Durham, and Birmingham, the black businessman never achieved in his community the reverence accorded to his white counterpart, probably because he was, whether undertaker or druggist, a small businessman whose influence in terms of service and employment of others was limited. The not so limited black college was, by contrast, usually a major black community employer,

and, through its graduates, consistently adding to its constituency.

Through the production of this constituency, the black college created a community, the middle-class black community. Whatever may have been the objective competence of the graduates of black colleges when tested against median performances of white college graduates, the alumni of black colleges became the new black bourgeoisie. The creation and replenishment of an entire community was the most significant role played by the Negro college.

Although E. Franklin Frazier, through his accurate but incomplete description, has given the black middle class a bad name, the existence of this group is largely due to the existence of the Negro college. Most of the members of the black bourgeoisie are the graduates of black colleges. As teachers in the elementary and secondary schools of the South and of northern segregated systems, these graduates provided not only literacy for their students, but also a vision of the possibility of life-styles other than those provided by contact with white employers. That this life-style was in fact the same life-style as that of their white counterparts (which is the element Frazier failed to make clear) was of little significance. What was significant was the creation of a black middle class which could make black aspiration to move into middle-class life-style patterns viable.

From this black middle class, created by the black college, came the core of the leadership that changed the status of blacks in the United States. Although W. E. B. Du Bois was the product of the best that white academies had to offer, Booker T. Washington was the product of a black college. Regardless of the merits of the Washington-Du Bois debate, most blacks would take Booker T. Washington's route to education even as they chose Du Bois' route to equality. From Martin Luther King to Stokely Carmichael, spokesmen for the black community have been recruited from among graduates of black colleges.

Thus, it is probable that the greatest community contribution of the Negro college has been the creation of a community. Although, it has been fashionable in the last quarter century to decry all bourgeois elements as decadent, the reality is that the changes wrought in the status of American blacks were due almost entirely to the efforts of the black middle class. The middle-class product of Negro colleges—physicians, dentists, lawyers, and ministers (admittedly not all college graduates)—supported and encouraged others to support civil rights activities. Largely independent of the white community, they could serve the cause of civil rights in relative safety.

Less independent were the elementary and secondary schoolteacher products of the black colleges, who were subject to the whims of white administrators and school boards well aware of the incongruity of their support of a growing black bourgeoisie, and, consequently, suspicious of their black teachers. The black public schoolteachers and administrators were, therefore, more cautious in assuming leadership roles than were the independent black professionals.

Nonetheless, the black professionals and teachers had found another community institution at the black college—the Negro fraternity and sorority. Some of these fraternities and sororities were founded on predominantly white campuses, but all achieved their psychological and philosophical comfort in chapters established during the twenties on Negro college campuses. Although the activities on the campus were disturbingly like those of the white fraternities during the Scott Fitzgerald era, there was a difference in the alumni activity. Activity in black college fraternities and sororities did not cease upon graduation, nor was it converted into mere symbolic identification at periodic smokers and rushing activities. The black college graduate (and many who were not graduated) maintained a relationship to the fraternal society, and these institutions became the major vehicle for black middle-class entertainment and community service activity. . . .

Greek letter fraternities and sororities based on black college campuses provided for the development of organizational techniques and leadership. Several successful contemporary black politicians learned their political skills in the black fraternities and sororities.

In addition, the tiny black middle-class community extended its influence by the use of the college based fraternity and sorority to establish communication among graduates of the several black institutions. The black college graduate was surprisingly mobile and there were frequently too few graduates of individual institutions in most cities to enable these graduates to establish alumni associations of any size or significance. The most active alumni association, bringing together graduates of several institutions, was the Greek letter fraternity.

Through the national meetings of these Greek letter societies, members living throughout the country met brothers and sorors from other institutions. One fraternity's national meeting was a regular gathering place for a large number of the presidents of Negro colleges, who were fraternity members. Another group seemed to have a monopoly on professional civil rights activists, and the regular national meetings of that group tended to have a subculture of concern for the life of the civil rights movement. Still another group provided the base for recruitment of volunteers and staff of major integrated social welfare agencies

In short, the college based fraternity and sorority provided a national community for the black middle class. This national community was fed by and could not have existed without the black college.

18. Hugh Gloster, "The Black College—Its Struggle for Survival and Success," 1978

This brief survey of the variety of black colleges in America and of their problems was written by a man devoted to the cause of black education throughout his lifetime. Hugh M. Gloster (1911–2002) came from Brownsville, Tennessee, and took his degrees at Morehouse College (1931) and Atlanta University (M.A. 1933) before receiving his Ph.D. in English from New York University (1943). After teaching at Morehouse (1941–43) and at Hampton Institute (1946–67), he presided over Morehouse for the rest of his career. A trustee of educational institutions, the College Entrance Examination Board, and the United Negro College Fund, he was recognized as a leading citizen representing African-American education. He was particularly known for founding and supporting the College Language Association.

Between 1977 and 1982 the National Advisory Committee on Black Higher Education and Black Colleges and Universities, which included fifteen black college presidents and other nongovernment people, made over one hundred recommendations in nine reports to the Department of Health, Education, and Welfare. By 1982 this committee charged that its reports had received only "perfunctory acknowledgment" from federal policymakers.

Hugh M. Gloster, "The Black College—Its Struggle for Survival and Success," *The Journal of Negro History* 63 (April 1978): 101–7; quotation from *Chronicle of Higher Education*, May 26, 1982, 19. Further reading: Gloster, *Negro Voices in American Fiction* (New York, 1976); Earl McGrath, *The Predominantly Negro Colleges and Universities in Transition* (New York, 1965); Christopher Jencks and David Riesman, *The Academic Revolution* (New York, 1968), ch. 10; "The Future of the Black Colleges," *Daedalus* 100 (Summer 1971), special issue; Henry N. Drewry and Humphrey Doermann, *Stand and Prosper: Private Black Colleges and Their Students* (Princeton, NJ, 2001); and II, 21.

Whenever I talk about black colleges I always emphasize at the outset that black colleges are not all alike. Some black colleges are rich, and others are poor. Hampton has an endowment in excess of $30 million one of the largest in the country for a school of its size and others are plagued with debts and deficits. Some are strong, and others are feeble. Fisk, Howard, and Morehouse have chapters of Phi Beta Kappa; and others are weak and unaccredited.

Some people say that all black colleges are inferior and should be closed. This statement is obviously untrue. According to any objective criteria, a number of black colleges are superior. For example, Morehouse leads most colleges her size in the percentage of Ph.D.'s on the faculty (63 percent); in faculty salaries (from $9,500 to $25,500 for nine months), in the percentage of seniors going on to graduate and professional schools (54 percent); in the percentage of Ph.D.'s, M.D.'s, D.D.S.'s, J.D.'s, and D.B.A.'s among alumni; in the number of new buildings constructed during the past seven years (nine); in the addition of new majors responsive to student and societal needs for example, Engineering, Accounting, Banking and Finance, Marketing, Urban Studies, Social Welfare, Community Psychology, African Studies, Afro-American Studies, Caribbean Studies, and International Studies; in the opening of a new medical school in the fall of 1978 to increase the number of black physicians so urgently needed to meet the health needs of our people; and in the amount of money raised so far in our national fundraising campaign (over $22 million, exceeding our goal of $20 million by more than $2 million). And we have done all of this in the 1970's without experiencing a deficit year. . . .

I also say to you that there are many more inferior and unaccredited white colleges than there are inferior and unaccredited black colleges. Nevertheless, educational experts who say that inferior and unaccredited black colleges should close rarely say that inferior and unaccredited white colleges should close.

Any discussion of black colleges in this country should give some consideration to the past from which these institutions have come; they still suffer from the handicaps of slavery and segregation. . . .

The initial purposes of most of these schools were to train illiterate ex-slaves and to prepare teachers and ministers; but from the beginning most called themselves institutes, normal schools, colleges, or universities, not because of what they were but because of what they hoped to be. Many of the black colleges became a fulfillment of this dream, and by 1895 they had produced over 1,100 graduates in contrast to the less than three dozen black graduates that white colleges had produced during the entire antebellum period.

As we all know, black colleges were started because Southern colleges generally barred blacks altogether and Northern colleges admitted them either in small numbers or not at all. With the doors of white colleges either closed entirely or only slightly ajar, private black colleges carried almost the full responsibility for the education of Afro-Americans until public black colleges began to bear a part of the load in the first quarter of this century. These schools trained most of the black leaders and professionals of the country during a period of disfranchisement and segregation, when the Ku Klux Klan intimidated blacks at the polls and terrorized them with marauding, mutilation, and murder. The most crushing legal blows of this period were the disfranchising clauses of the Southern states and the 14 separate-but-equal Supreme Court decision in the Plessy-versus-Ferguson case, which entrenched segregation in 1896.

Two and a half centuries of slavery and a century of segregation are the basic causes of the problems which plague black people today: the run-down farms and the blighted ghettos, the underfed and the underclothed, the undereducated and the underemployed, the thefts and the robberies, the looting and the vandalism, the rapes and the murders.

And in the weaker and unaccredited black colleges these problems are reflected in poorly prepared teachers and underachieving students, in inadequate libraries and poorly stocked laboratories, in shoestring budgets and limited endowments, in cultural isolation and intentional neglect. . . .

Prior to World War II black colleges employed most of the gifted black teachers, and there were strong concentrations of black scholars in some schools. For example, during my student days at Morehouse College the Atlanta University Center faculty included such names as W.E.B. DuBois, Ira DeA. Reid, Rayford Logan, Clarence Bacote, Mercer Cook, William Stanley Braithwaite, N. P. Tillman, G. Lewis Chandler, Saunders Redding, and many other distinguished professors who exerted tremendous influence upon black students with talent and potential. Since World War II, however, civil-rights pressures and legislation have forced white universities to recruit black administrators and teachers; and, as a result, black colleges have lost some personnel that they could have easily employed in earlier years.

Civil-rights pressures and legislation have also caused white colleges to seek superior black students and to offer them generous scholarships and other attractive inducements. This recruitment of outstanding black students by white colleges increased during the late 1960s but lessened during the 1970s. As a result, many black students, dissatisfied with minority status or social isolation at white colleges, are transferring to black colleges in increasing numbers.

It is my opinion that the stronger black colleges now forced to compete with all other American colleges for faculty, students, and support are now better centers of teaching and learning than ever. They have professors who are well-trained, students who are better prepared, and facilities which include good libraries and laboratories.

Despite the foregoing considerations, every black college is involved in a struggle for existence in which only the fittest will survive. This has been true in the past, this is true in the present, and this will be true in the future. Today not only our weakest, but some of our strongest colleges are trying to cope with huge deficits.

In this grim struggle for existence, in which their survival is at stake, black colleges have certain special disadvantages.

In the first place, their endowments are usually small and therefore generally yield limited returns. . . .

Secondly, black colleges get only 3 percent of the federal dollar and 1 percent of the foundation dollar although blacks constitute 11 percent of the population.

Although federal support is limited, Title III

funds are furnishing necessary program support for black colleges; and Work-Study, BEOG, SEOG, and loans are giving much-needed financial aid to black students. A strong move is now under way, however, to take Title III support away from schools in AIDP (the Advanced Institutional Development Program). If Title III support and federal financial aid are ever withdrawn, weaker black colleges will face bankruptcy or closing, and the rest will experience serious financial problems or crippling deficits.

As far as foundation support is concerned, major foundations are now contributing chiefly to a selected group of about fifteen to twenty black private colleges. This kind of selective giving means that the majority of the black private colleges are receiving little or no support from major foundations.

Thirdly, the sponsoring denominations of the church-related black colleges are giving insufficient support. The most liberal denominations in supporting black colleges are the United Methodists and the United Church of Christ, which have predominantly white congregations. A denomination that gives weak support because of its structure and subdivision is the Baptist Church. After the Civil War the Baptists opened at least one black college in every Southern state; but today the black Baptist colleges founded in Kentucky, Louisiana, Tennessee, and West Virginia are closed, and four are unaccredited.

Fourthly, most black colleges receive limited alumni support. Hampton, Morehouse, and several other colleges sometimes raise over $100,000 a year from alumni; but in most schools alumni giving is small in amount and far from 100 percent in participation. Many alumni feel that foundations, corporations, and government will take care of their schools; but this assumption is not correct.

Fifth and finally, black colleges receive limited and insufficient income from student fees.

Black colleges keep fees as low as possible and student aid as high as possible in order to stay within the reach of low-income black students. At the same time, however, they must compete for able teachers, talented students, and adequate financial support in order to survive; and they must pay the same prices as other schools for books, equipment, and facilities.

It is easy to understand the special financial problems of black colleges when one observes that there is not a single black private college that charges $2,000 a year for tuition but that there are many white private colleges that charge as much as $4,000 and several that charge as much as $5,000. This additional tuition income enables wealthier white schools to pay better salaries, to offer higher scholarships, and to have better facilities and programs.

The public black colleges have a special set of problems. In the first place, the Southern states are not letting any of the black state colleges develop into first-class universities with the full gamut of graduate and professional schools. Secondly, throughout the South some previously black state colleges are being integrated out of existence. This process started in the 1940's, when Louisville Municipal College was absorbed into the University of Louisville and only one member of its faculty was retained. Later, West Virginia State College, Bluefield State College, and Lincoln University of Missouri became predominantly white in enrollment.

Throughout the South, black public colleges are being brought under state control. For example, in Arkansas and Maryland, black public colleges have been made a part of the state university; and in Georgia, black public colleges have been made a part of the state university system administered by a Board of Regents.

Black public colleges in the same cities and sometimes only a few blocks away from white public universities have an especially uncertain future. For example, Florida A & M in Tallahassee with Florida State, Southern in the Baton Rouge area with Louisiana State, and Texas Southern in Houston with the University of Houston. Some pessimists predict that by the end of the century most black public colleges will be predominantly white in enrollment or will be absorbed into predominantly white universities.

We view these trends in the private and public sectors with apprehension and dismay. We freely admit that interested and qualified blacks should have the opportunity to attend white institutions and that interested and qualified whites should have the opportunity to attend black colleges, but we cannot trust other schools with the education of all black students. If black colleges fade away, we lose our main resources for the development of our youth and for the preservation of our culture. We cannot trust other colleges and universities to eliminate the academic deficiencies of disadvantaged black students, to make black students equal members of the college community, to inspire black students toward the highest achievement, to produce leaders and scholars who will solve the problems of black people, to sponsor the study and promotion of African and Afro-American culture, and to employ black teachers and administrators. We would like to be able to trust other colleges and universities with these important responsibilities, but we cannot do so after reviewing their performance records. If Jews need Brandeis and Yeshiva and if Catholics need Holy Cross and Notre Dame, then blacks need Morehouse and Spelman.

Our black colleges have come a long way since they were founded in plantation houses, church basements, Army barracks, box cars, and other humble places during the dark days after the Civil War. Though opposed by local whites and harassed by the Ku Klux Klan, many of them developed from elementary schools into first-class colleges and universities.

For almost a hundred years—from the Civil War

until the Supreme Court decision of 1954 banning public school segregation—black colleges carried the burden of the higher education of black youth and produced most of our black leaders, preachers, teachers, lawyers, physicians, dentists, librarians, journalists, social workers, businessmen, politicians, and military officers. Their alumni include W.E.B. DuBois, Booker T. Washington, James Weldon Johnson, Walter White, Martin Luther King Jr., and a host of other leaders who guided our people to responsible citizenship.

Along with black churches, black colleges fanned the fires of hope and pride and served as information and organization centers for the campaign against segregation. Their students played the major role in the sit-ins, stand-ins, wade-ins—anything as long as they got in—which broke the back of Jim Crow in the early 1960's.

From their earliest beginnings, black colleges cultivated an interest in African and Afro-American culture and developed pride in the racial past. When our detractors told us that our people were inferior and backward, black colleges taught us that we were important human beings who had made significant contributions to civilization in music, literature, art, science, and other areas of cultural achievement.

Today there is no question about the continuing need for black colleges. We need them to develop leaders who will protect our interests in a country where we are outnumbered ten to one. We need them to help solve the problems of health, housing, education, and employment that beset our people in rural areas and urban ghettos. We need them to promote and preserve African and Afro-American culture. We need them to provide a place where black students who are overwhelmed or isolated at white colleges and universities may feel comfortable, cared for, and at home.

19. Nathan Huggins, *Afro-American Studies: A Report to the Ford Foundation,* 1985

After teaching posts at Long Beach State, Lake Forest College, and at the University of Massachusetts at Boston, Nathan Huggins (1927–89) spent a decade each on the faculty at Columbia (1970–80) and Harvard (1980–90), at the latter as W. E. B. DuBois Professor of History and Director of the W. E. B. DuBois Center for Afro-American Studies. Author of *Harlem Renaissance* (1971) and *Black Odyssey* (1977) and biographer of Frederick Douglass, he also edited the *Journal of Ethnic Studies* (1979–89) and was a director of the American Council of Learned Societies and a trustee of Radcliffe College (1985–89). Reprinted here is an excerpt from his report to the Ford Foundation, an exemplary scholarly study, comprehensive yet clearly written from the author's point of view.

Nathan I. Huggins, *Afro-American Studies, A Report to the Ford Foundation* (New York, 1985): 5–15, 19–22, 46–51. Reprinted with kind permission from the Ford Foundation. Further reading: Jonathan Scott Holloway, "The Black Scholar, The Humanities, and the Politics of Racial Knowledge since 1945," in *The Humanities and the Dynamics of Inclusion Since World War II,* ed. David A. Hollinger (Baltimore, 2006): ch.8; Nowlie M. Rooks, "The Beginnings of Black Studies," *Chronicle of Higher Education,* February 10, 2006, B8–9; and II, 17–18, 20–21; V, 6–7; VII, 11–12.

In the quarter-century following World War II, the American university underwent enormous growth and a remarkable transformation. Both were unexpected. As late as 1941, Archibald MacLeish, referring to Harvard University, predicted "a period of organization within existing frontiers, rather than a period of extension of existing frontiers." In less than a decade, all discussion of higher education in America was attempting to comprehend unprecedented expansion and transformation. By 1963, Clark Kerr's Godkin Lectures were defining the American university in new terms: as the multiversity or the federal-grant university. Not only had it ballooned in size—numbers of students, faculty, and scale of physical plant—it had changed dramatically in character and purpose, departing both from Cardinal Newman's idealism and from the shaping influence of the German university.

Kerr merely articulated what had come to be commonly recognized: that the American university was no longer an academic cloister but was a major force in modern society—vital to industry, agriculture, medicine, government (in war and in peace), and social health and welfare. It was the major producer in what Kerr called the "knowledge industry," and crucial as such to economic and social progress and to national security. Perceiving itself (and generally being perceived) as essential to social and political change, the university naturally became an instrument for those demanding such change, blacks among them. . . .

By the sixties, Americans shared two very new assumptions: that nearly everyone could benefit from some postsecondary education and that everyone—without exception—was entitled to access to higher education. Chronic social inequities—in particular, the failure of one particular ethnic group, blacks, to move into the middle class—might, many thought, be explained by that group's systematic exclusion from most American colleges, universities, and professional schools.

While southern society in general, and southern, white universities and professional schools in particular, were early targets of the civil rights movement, northern institutions had been far from exemplary on racial matters. The liberal response to the demand of blacks for racial justice was, in part, to try to bring more black students into northern, white colleges and universities. The growth and democratization of the American university thus had racial consequences as well as those of class and scale.

Black migration northward and the G.I. Bill increased black enrollment in northern schools following World War II. From 1940 to 1950, the percentage of blacks residing outside the South increased from 23 to 32. C. H. Arce estimated that black enrollment in white colleges outside the South in 1947 was 61,000 (47 percent of all black enrollment but 3 percent of the total enrollment in those institutions). Black college enrollment was 6 percent of the total national enrollment that year, a rate not reached again until 1967.

Between 1967 and 1971 black college enrollment increased enormously, by the latter year reaching 8.4 percent of total college enrollment. The numbers leveled off for two years and then began, once again to grow, so that by October 1977 black enrollment accounted for 10.8 percent of total enrollment, a remarkable figure considering that in 1976 blacks made up 12.6 percent of the nation's 18-to-24-year-old, college-age population. These increases were the result of aggressive recruitment by northern institutions and vastly increased financial aid, mainly from the federal government.

In the fifties, modest support for black students was available through the National Scholarship Service and Fund for Negro Students. The funds of this group were later augmented by those of the National Defense Student Loan Program (1958) and the National Achievement Program (1964). The Higher Education Act of 1965 (Work Study, Educational Opportunity Grants, Guaranteed Student Loan Program) made additional funds available. These programs were followed in 1972 by the Basic Educational Opportunity Grant Program, which vested funds in individual students who could take them to the institutions of their choice. In 1976–77, $1.5 billion were awarded under this program, to nearly two million students. In addition to federal funds, state aid also became available. In 1977–78, for instance, there were $756 million in state aid programs.

These figures point to an important characteristic of the growth of black student enrollment in the sixties. Not only did many more black students attend predominantly white schools in the mid-sixties; those who did were a different social slice of the black population than those who had attended those schools in the fifties and before. Administrators deliberately set out to recruit poor youngsters from the inner city (so-called ghetto youth), imagining that the university might rectify failures in the secondary-school system and redeem these students so they might enter mainstream life. This policy implied a changing (or at least a rethinking) of standards for admission as they applied to these youngsters. It implied the establishment of remedial programs, a faculty and a student body genuinely sympathetic both to the means and the ends of this policy, and inner-city black students who would be grateful for the opportunity. These assumptions were only partly to be realized, contributing to the general malaise among black students in the mid-sixties and leading in turn to much of the black contribution to student unrest in those years.

Being a black student at a predominantly white institution had never been easy. Before the sixties, such students had always been few in number, hardly more than a dozen undergraduates at any time on any college campus. Sports and other extra-curricular activities were sometimes closed to them. Little deference was given them, and they were likely to feel themselves alternately exemplars of their race and altogether ignored. Unlike those who arrived in the mid-sixties, however, they had not been specially recruited. Those who went to these institutions had made conscious, deliberate choices to be there, and had undoubtedly made important personal sacrifices. There had been no special admissions considerations, and they probably assumed (following conventional black wisdom) that they had to be better than whites to do as well. They expected to overcome obstacles and discrimination based on race. There could be a source of pride in that. It was pride as well (and their limited numbers) that made them unwilling to call attention to themselves by complaining even about real grievances.

After 1965, black college students were less likely to share these assumptions. Proportionately fewer were motivated in quite the same way; proportionately fewer had the educational background or the study habits to do well in these colleges. In addition, events outside the colleges—the war in Vietnam and, particularly, the continuing struggle for racial justice—were distracting from conventional academic pursuits. To some students—black and white —it seemed that the goals and values of those outside occurrences were in conflict with the university as it defined itself. Ironically, the growing number of black students contributed to their own malaise. There came a point, as their numbers grew, when their isolation became conspicuous. In earlier years, the handful of black students managed to fit in, badly or well, nursing as private matters any hurts they felt. With larger numbers, it became possible (indeed, almost inevitable) to consider being black on a white campus a collective condition. Private hurts became public grievances.

The extraordinary mid-century growth of the American university only partly explains the demand for black studies programs. Equally important were the assumptions about the new role of the university—assumptions about the university as a force extending social justice and its benefits to disadvantaged groups by means of higher education. The university would find it difficult to serve both traditional values and its new role of social reformer.

The American university had changed not only in size and purpose but in substance. The explosion of information, of new knowledge, had prompted Clark Kerr's metaphor of scholarship as "the knowledge industry." The new university was, of course, producing much of that new information; it was also training the engineers, technicians, and scientists who would put that knowledge to practical use in industry and government. One aspect of the university—science and technology—was experiencing dramatic growth, while the rest was being carried in its wake. The university was becoming, more than ever, the port of entry into the professions. The social sciences could help train young people to serve the expanding bureaucracies of government and industry. A natural consequence of these developments was the growing preprofessionalism of the undergraduate curriculum. . . .

Public institutions, most having land-grant origins, from the beginning had appealed to their legislatures for funds by citing their immediate contribution to agriculture, mining, and business. They had always found it easy to design undergraduate curricula that allowed students to avoid "useless" courses in the humanities. In the postwar period, however, even the prestigious private universities tolerated an erosion of the liberal arts core.

"Relevance;" a word often used . . . to distinguish the modern university from the "ivory tower," became a student clarion call. Black students wanted courses and programs "relevant to our blackness," relevant to the lives of blacks in the ghettos and in the rural South. They wanted to make the university useful in ending racism in America (as others wanted to make it useful in ending poverty and the war in Vietnam). They would begin by confronting and excising the evil at the institution's heart. By the end of the hubristic sixties, university administrators and faculty were more than willing to recognize limits to their usefulness.

It is important to understand, however, that the emphasis on utility and relevance had already struck discordant notes among faculties, notes discordant with traditional views of the college and its curriculum. Utilitarianism seemed merely to emphasize the increasingly secondary place of the humanities in the university. . . .

One of the principal characteristics of the liberal arts lead always been *inutility*. The college graduate, according to the traditional conception, was not supposed to be able, on the basis of his education, to do anything; his education was, rather, supposed to do something to him. While faculty arguments over general education requirements often sounded suspiciously like squabbles over course enrollment (i.e., budget), matters of principle were at stake. Defenders of the liberal arts tradition found something superior in education for its own sake. John Henry Newman, in his *Idea of the University Defined* (1873), had characterized "useful knowledge" as a "deal of trash." The very process of distancing oneself from private concerns, of transcending mundane matters to glimpse the universal, was itself, he and many others felt, educational. Time enough later to train to make a living. . . .

Given the new democratic and utilitarian direction of the American university, a defense of the humanities in terms of their inutility seemed perverse. That the strongest proponents of the liberal arts were to be found in expensive private schools tended to confirm the elitism of the humanities. It was difficult, also, to shake the Veblenian assessment that the pursuit of the liberal arts was merely an example of the conspicuous display of wealth; who else but the rich could afford to spend four years in pursuit of an education having no practical end? Humanists also easily drew the charge of elitism because they tended to think of their work as having a *civilizing* influence, and because their work (particularly in literature, the fine arts, and music) called upon them to make judgments as to quality. Some works were better than others; some writers, artists, and musicians were better than others. Those artists and works of art not studied, discussed, and evaluated were, by implication, inferior.

In practice, the liberal arts curriculum reduced itself to courses concerned with not just civilization, but *Western* civilization. Sometimes emphasis was placed on the "disciplines," sometimes on interdisciplinary approaches to "great issues," sometimes on the "great books" approach. The object was always the same: Matthew Arnold's "acquainting ourselves with the best that has been known and said in the world." Though the "world" of Matthew Arnold was small, it probably did include "acquaintance" with Islamic and Asian Culture. Compared to Arnold's, the "world" of postwar American scholars in the humanities—products of university Ph.D. programs—was Lilliputian. It certainly did not encompass Asia, Africa, and Latin America. Most American teachers in the humanities assumed *our* heritage (their students' as well as their own) to be the history and culture of the West. They could hardly imagine an American youngster of whatever ethnic background challenging that assumption.

Most supporters of the liberal arts probably did not really believe that what they taught comprised the "world" or "civilization." Rather, they supposed certain concepts, ideals, principles, values, to be universal rather than particular to any people or culture. Those values were, nevertheless, accessible through certain texts and other cultural artifacts of a Western tradition, a tradition that could be studied as coherent and whole. *King Lear, Medea*, Machiavelli, Plato, Kant, Locke, Mill, Jefferson posed questions as relevant to a Chinese, a Malayan, a Ugandan, or a Nigerian as to an American of any ethnic background.

When, in the late sixties, black students challenged the curriculum, their main target was the parochial character of the humanities as taught. They saw the humanities as exclusive rather than universal. They saw humanists as arrogant white men in self-congratulatory identification with a grand European Culture. To those students, such arrogance justified the charge of "racism."

The woeful ignorance of most humanists about all cultures and traditions other than their own made it difficult for them to respond to the charge in a constructive way. Nothing in the training of

American scholars in the humanities—scholars who were becoming more and more specialized even within the tradition they knew and accepted—prepared them for the challenge. Not surprisingly, their response was dogmatic: what they taught was the best that could be taught; it was what truly educated men and women needed to know; it trained (that is, disciplined) the mind; it was our heritage.

The same defense had been raised against the utilitarians in the university. It is important to understand that black students were taking aim at the segment of the college that was already the most frequently attacked; theirs was merely the latest in a series of frontal assaults. To the embattled humanists, black students arguing for courses "relevant to our blackness" sounded much like engineering students demanding that they be exempted from courses not "relevant" to their professional training. Humanists thus saw themselves as holding the line against a new wave of Philistines. This time, however, the Philistines were poor and black, and, when not denouncing their courses as worthless, a deal of trash, they were demanding both remedial courses to help them read and write and the redesign of admission standards to make college more accessible to inner-city blacks with inadequate high school training.

The social science faculties were less central, but they, too, came under attack. Political scientists, sociologists, and economists had for some time been modeling themselves after the natural and physical scientists. Historical and "institutional" study had diminished in importance in these fields. Systems and model analysis had become dominant, and even theory had ceased to be broadly philosophical, becoming instead a matter of model definition and analysis. As positivists, social scientists tended to avoid a priori assumptions and value judgments; their mastery of sophisticated methodologies defined the objective condition of the subject under study, implying solutions.

Few social scientists took up questions having directly to do with Afro-American life and circumstances, and few courses offered could be said to have to do with blacks. Events outside the university nevertheless spoke loudly to the fact that questions regarding race were at the heart of American social, political, and economic problems. When social scientists discussed blacks at all, black students found, they often did so in pathological terms, asking why blacks had failed to move into the social mainstream more quickly. The most flagrant example was Daniel P Moynihan's *The Negro Family*—the so-called Moynihan Report—which seemed to place the blame for continued poverty among blacks on a dysfunctional black family.

Black students and scholars thus began to challenge the "objectivity" of mainstream social science. In most "scientific" discussions of "problems" a norm was assumed, that of the white middle class; the social scientist, himself, was at the center, defining all variation as deviation and "blaming the victim," as critics liked to say. The demand of black students was for a discussion of what they saw to be the inherent racism in these normative assumptions and for a shift in perspective that would destigmatize blacks and reexamine the "normalcy" of the white middle class.

Black students and their allies imagined that out of these demands—for the introduction of nonwhite subject matter into the curriculum and for the shift of normative perspective—would come a revolutionary transformation of the American university. . . .

Between 1966 and 1970, most American colleges and universities added to their curricula courses on Afro-American life and history, and most made efforts to include blacks on their faculties and administrative staffs. The fact that schools like Macalester, Bowdoin, Colby, Reed, Dartmouth, and Carleton (to pick just a few names), which were relatively free of pressure, joined the rush argues that there was something more to explain it than the threat of students disrupting academic life. Like all other aspects of the movements for peace and civil rights, the demand for university reform by black students was national in its impact as well as local in particular manifestations. In some sense, the urge for change was everywhere; whether or not a campus had militant black students making demands, the urge for reform was in the air.

I suggest three motives, independent of immediate student pressure, that compelled college administrators and faculty to join the march for change. First, there was, particularly among liberal-minded academics, a genuine sense of American higher education's complicity in the social inequities resulting from racism—indifference to black undergraduate enrollment, insensibility to nonwhite subject matter in the curriculum, and the discouragement of black scholars. Second, it had become fashionable to bring blacks onto staffs and faculties, just as it had earlier become fashionable to recruit "hardcore, inner-city kids" for admission. The sense of competition among institutions should not be discounted; the legitimate purpose of the act too often was joined by the wish to do at least as well as comparable institutions. Third, in their effort to attract the "best" applicants from a generation of teenagers noted for their social consciousness, college administrators felt it important to look reasonably open to change, to appear to be progressive without compromising integrity. A course or two on black history or culture could achieve that end.

The great majority of institutions added courses pertinent to Afro-Americans and, as a direct result or not, experienced little or no student disruption; most changes involved merely a course or two and could hardly be called a program in black studies. Yet, from 1966, student disorders were increasingly common, and no college or university could be indifferent to, or uninfluenced by, events at San Francisco State, Cornell, Harvard, Wesleyan, and so on. It was widely assumed that disruptions of the sort that had occurred at those institutions could be avoided, if at all, only by swift and significant reform.

With the spurt of black enrollment in 1966, students and administrators began a process of negotiation aimed at correcting the problems perceived by black students. One problem was that many black students felt themselves to be educationally disadvantaged compared to their white peers; they wanted remedial programs that would compensate for their poor high schools (poor because white society made them so) and poor study habits. Problems also arose because of a deep sense of alienation from the institutions and their goals. This alienation was often expressed by defining schools as "white," as a part of a "white, racist system." Blacks' success and achievement within these institutions could come only if they "whitewashed their minds" and alienated themselves from "their people" and "their community." In this view, while college may have been a necessary route to upward mobility, success within the college would be purchased through the denial of one's "blackness" and through co-optation by the system. This was the black version of the widespread (and, among many young Americans, the rampant) alienation from mainstream, conventional, middle-class America. For black undergraduates, the solution to this dilemma was an assertion of blackness: beauty, culture, community, etc. The newly developing black student associations, therefore, pressed to make the college environment congenial and hospitable to what they described as black values and culture. They wanted student activities for black students, black cultural centers. Sometimes they asked for separate dormitories (or black floors or sections of dormitories); they established black tables in dining halls and treated white students with the same hostility and contempt they assumed whites had for them. They almost always pressed for the appointment of black faculty and for the introduction of courses "relevant to us as black people."

Black student leaders found some sympathetic ears among faculty members, administrators, and white students, but their demands also created hostility among the same groups. To some, the demand for remediation only supported the belief that standards were being lowered to admit black students who were bound either to fail or to undermine the quality of education. The new black assertiveness could only antagonize those who held to the ideal of integration and of a color-blind system of merit. Black students were, in their view, racists who merely wanted to turn an evil on its head. Antagonism over these issues set the tone for the debate over black studies when it became a central issue, and it also affected the reception of these programs when they were established by the end of the decade.

For the most part, negotiations went quietly. Colleges like Bowdoin, Carleton, Macalester, and Dartmouth, removed from crosscurrents of student radicalism, were able to move at their own pace to increase black enrollment, appoint black faculty and staff, and introduce a few courses on topics of interest to Afro-Americans. In some conspicuous instances, however (Cornell, San Francisco State, Wesleyan), the students armed themselves, and the threat of riot and violence was quite real. At other institutions, calls for black studies courses and programs merely added to a general atmosphere of conflict and upheaval. To the most vociferous activists, Afro-American academic programs were likely to be of incidental or secondary importance; what they were really interested in was not an academic but a political revolution. . . .

The models on which Afro-American studies programs were built were influenced by ideology and conditions on individual campuses. Naturally, each particular form had intrinsic strengths and weaknesses.

THE PROGRAM

From an academic point of view, the "program" approach has been the most successful. It acknowledges the interdisciplinary character of Afro-American studies by using faculty from established departments. It relies on the president and the dean to guarantee the program through budget allocations to the departments involved. While a faculty member's appointment may be principally to offer courses and service to Afro-American studies, his or her membership remains within the department of discipline. By definition, all senior faculty in a program are jointly appointed to a department and to the program. Because of this structure, it is relatively easy for the program to exploit the curricula of other departments; it is not necessary for the program to provide all of the courses its students are expected to take.

Most Afro-American studies offerings in the country follow the program model. A good example is the Yale program. Its success had much to do with the willingness of student advocates to accept this plan rather than insist on "autonomy." It has been noted for the broad range of faculty involvement. Names like Sidney Mintz, Charles Davis, Robert Thompson, and John Blassingame have been associated with it. Davis, until his recent death, served as director; his place has been taken by Blassingame. Young scholars of remarkably high quality have been in the program—especially in literature. Names like Robert Stepto, Henry Gates, and Houston Baker come to mind. Apparently from the beginning, association with the program has been judged with approval in academic circles. The Yale program is one of the few in the country offering a graduate program leading to a master's degree.

The strengths of this model are obvious, but

principally they reside in its capacity to engage a wide range of departments and faculty in the service of Afro-American studies. This, of course, would not have been a strength to those of markedly separatist persuasion. Its major weakness, as those who argued for autonomy predicted, is its dependence for survival on the continued support and good will of others in the university: the president, dean, and the heads of cooperating departments, among others. Yale's program has not been troubled in this regard, but other programs have, especially when enrollments drop or when there is disagreement about standards or goals.

Programs like Yale's are designed to offer undergraduates a major (or field of concentration) for their degree. Not all programs do. Some merely offer a few courses with a focus on subject matter having to do with Afro-American life. Such courses may be accepted for credit by the student's major department (for example, economics) or may serve merely as an elective. Wesleyan, for instance, until recently had a complicated system in which an Afro-American studies major was possible but in which students found it difficult to put the necessary courses together; they thus majored elsewhere and took the one or two Afro-American studies courses as electives. (The Wesleyan program has undergone changes designed to strengthen and improve it.) The program at the University of Rhode Island is also of interest in this regard. It offers special courses: one, for example, on free-enterprise zones, and another on human resources. Such courses are designed to serve students interested in working in the community or in Third World countries. These courses do not lead to a degree in Afro-American studies, but they serve students in special programs such as a master's program in international development.

THE COLLEGE

The most radical kind of Afro-American studies program was that of the independent college—sometimes an all-black college—within the university. That was the demand at San Francisco State and at Cornell. The ethnic studies department at Berkeley, existing outside the College of Arts and Sciences, had for a while something of a de facto college status. Afro-American studies, however, defected and became a standing department in Arts and Sciences in 1974. No other major university came close to acceding to this extreme demand.

Local community colleges sometimes became de facto all-black colleges. That was surely the case with Malcolm X College in Chicago. It is a community college, supported by public funds, but located in an area almost wholly black. Formerly Crane Junior College, it became Malcolm X in 1968 when it moved to its present location. Its student population is about 80 percent black, 8 percent Hispanic, and 12 percent other. While it offers a range of black-oriented courses, it specializes in computer sciences and health services. Whether or not it was planned to be so, circumstance permits it to be the kind of college the separatists demanded. It is difficult to know how many other such community colleges there are.

THE DEPARTMENT

The more practical model for those who insisted on autonomy was the department. A department had its own budget, could appoint and dismiss its own faculty and staff, design its own curriculum, and service its student concentrators without any control or oversight by others. It was also assumed to be a more permanent structure than a program. Some institutions established Afro-American studies departments without much ado. In others, like Harvard, departmental status remained a bone of contention years after it was established. The more it was resisted, of course, the more it appeared to be worth fighting for and defending.

The argument against it was mainly that a department normally represented a discipline. Afro-American studies, being interdisciplinary in character, should, critics said, be organized into a program made up of faculty from the various departments serving it. Its defenders most often claimed it was a discipline defined by its particular perspective on a topic none of the other departments offered. In these terms the argument was tendentious. As defined by the nineteenth-century German university, departments were identical with academic disciplines. By 1969, however, that had ceased to be true of American university departments. Interdisciplinary departments had developed within the sciences, and occasionally area studies were departmentally organized. On the other hand, a perspective, which was what Afro-American studies offered, could hardly be thought of as a discipline. Whatever it once was, a department is now largely an administrative convenience. Afro-American studies departments have worked reasonably well in some institutions, Berkeley and the University of Indiana being examples. It did not work well at Harvard, and its problems illuminate some of the weaknesses of the model.

Departmental autonomy, it turns out, is not as absolute as some believed. Such autonomy as exists carries problems. Under a program, the president and dean can, in effect, direct departments to make searches and appoint competent faculty approved by the program's committee. The department has the power and budget to make recommendations for appointment, but, lacking other arrangements, it must find scholars willing to take positions in Afro-American studies alone. In practice, most senior scholars with major reputations insist on joint appointments with the departments of their discipline. So, most often, an Afro-American studies department's appointment is contingent on another department's approval of its candidate. Such arrangements presuppose good will and respect among the departments involved. In such ways, autonomy can work against the department's efforts. Furthermore, even when university budgets were more ample, it was impossible for an Afro-American studies department to provide faculty in all of the disciplines thought useful to it. As a result, they are forced to depend on a very limited program (history and literature) or rely on other departments' offerings.

Whatever the expectation of those who struggled to create departments rather than programs, joint appointments are the general rule throughout the country. Sometimes this resulted from administrative fiat, sometimes out of necessity. Ewart Guinier, the first chairman of Harvard's department, had no joint appointment himself and attempted to make the question of departmental autonomy and integrity rest on the power to promote a junior person to tenure from within. The president and the dean, responding to university-wide criticism of the department's program and standards, in 1974 made promotion from within the Afro-American studies department conditional upon joint appointment. Guinier failed in his effort to force this issue in his favor. This case illustrates another important limit to departmental autonomy. Appointment and tenure matters must be concurred in by university-wide and ad hoc committees (in Harvard's case these committees are made up of outside scholars appointed by the dean), and, finally, only the president makes appointments.

The practice of joint appointments is a good thing when it works well. It dispels suspicion about the quality of a department's faculty, especially necessary in a new field in which standards and reputation are in question. Furthermore, it gives Afro-American studies a voice and an advocate within the conventional departments, which is quite useful for communication and good will. In this regard, the practice achieves some of the good features of programs. Whether imposed by the administration or adopted as a matter of convenience, however, joint appointments may be the cause of problems and friction. A candidate may fail to win tenure in the second department, its faculty claiming a failure to meet their standards. Since questions of standards are seldom easy to resolve, these decisions are likely to cause antagonism and ill will. Joint appointments also raise questions of service, loyalty, and commitment of faculty to Afro-American studies. Once appointed, a faculty member may find it more congenial working in the field of his discipline; if he is tenured, little can be done. From the faculty member's point of view, moreover, joint appointments can pose problems. It is time-consuming to be a good citizen in two departments. Junior faculty, particularly, are likely to feel themselves to be serving two masters, each having its own expectations.

20. William G. Bowen and Derek Bok, *The Shape of the River,* 1998

Two former presidents of leading universities collaborated to publish an influential study of race as an aspect of college and university admissions. Each had earlier written on the vital role of higher education in American culture. This book was built upon extensive statistical inquiries made by the Mellon Foundation, called College and Beyond, in the mid-1990s and drawn from a group of "academically selective" institutions. They were:

Liberal Arts Colleges	Research Universities
Barnard College	Columbia University
Bryn Mawr College	Duke University
Denison University	Emory University
Hamilton University	Miami University (Ohio)
Kenyon College	Northwestern University
Oberlin College	Pennsylvania University
Smith College	Princeton University
Swarthmore College	Rice University
Wellesley College	Stanford University
Wesleyan College	Tufts University
Williams College	Tulane University
	University of Michigan at Ann Arbor
	University of North Carolina at Chapel Hill
	University of Pennsylvania
	Vanderbilt University
	Washington University
	Yale University

Part of their "summing up" is reprinted here. William G. Bowen (1933–) graduated from Denison (1955) took his doctorate at Princeton (1958), where he would become a professor of economics, provost (1967–72), and president (1972–88). He then went to head the Andrew W. Mellon Foundation (1988–2006). He is a regent emeritus of the Smithsonian Institution. Derek Bok (1930–) graduated from Stanford (1951), took his law degree at Harvard (1954) and was on the law school faculty and dean there (1958–71) before entering upon the Harvard presidency (1971–91). He was named the 300th Anniversary University Professorship in 1991.

William G. Bowen and Derek Bok in Collaboration with James Shulman, Thomas L. Nygren, Stacy Berg Dale, and Lauren A. Meserve, *The Shape Of The River: Long-Term Consequences of Considering Race in College and University Admissions.* © 1998 Princeton University Press. Reprinted by permission of Princeton University Press. Paperback with Foreword, 2000: 15, 276–87. Further reading: Douglas S. Massey, Camille Z. Charles, Garvey F. Lundy, and Mary J. Fischer, *The Source of the River: The Social Origins of Freshmen at America's Selective Colleges and Universities* (Princeton, NJ, 2003); Christopher Jencks and Meredith Phillips, eds., *The Black-White Test Score Gap* (Washington, D.C., 1998); Richard D. Kahlenberg, *The Remedy: Class, Race, and Affirmative Action* (New York, 1996); and Steven M. Cahn, ed., *The Affirmative Action Debate* (New York, 2002). For critical assessments, see Stephan and Abigail Thernstrom, *America in Black and White: One Nation Indivisible* (New York, 1997); Peter Sacks, *Standardized Minds: The High Price of*

America's Testing Culture and What We Can Do to Change It (New York, 1999) and "Class Rules: the Fiction of Egalitarian Higher Education," *Chronicle of Higher Education*, July 25, 2003, B7–10, wherein Sacks stresses the privileged class status of most college matriculants in 2003, in contrast to egalitarian voices and studies four decades earlier; and Ward Connerly, *Creating Equal: My Fight against Race Preferences* (San Francisco, 2000), 235–39, wherein Connerly explains his disagreement with Bowen and Bok.

We need to clear up two misconceptions that frequently creep into discussions about the role of race in the admissions process. One of the most common misunderstandings concerns the number of institutions that actually take account of race in making admissions decisions. Many people are unaware of how few colleges and universities have enough applicants to be able to pick and choose among them. There is no single, unambiguous way of identifying the number of such schools, but we estimate that only about 20 to 30 percent of all four-year colleges and universities are in this category. Nationally, the vast majority of undergraduate institutions accept all qualified candidates and thus do not award special status to any group of applicants, defined by race or on the basis of any other criterion.[1]

THE MEANING OF "MERIT"

One conclusion we have reached is that the meaning of "merit" in the admissions process must be articulated more clearly. "Merit," like "preference" and "discrimination," is a word that has taken on so much baggage we may have to re-invent it or find a substitute.

Still, it is an important and potentially valuable concept because it reminds us that we certainly do not want institutions to admit candidates who *lack* merit, however the term is defined. Most people

---

1. Both *Peterson's Guide* and *Barron's* classify colleges and universities by their degree of selectivity, using a combination of test scores, high school grades, and acceptance rates. The 1998 edition of *Peterson's Guide* placed only 212 four-year colleges and universities, or about 12 percent of all the U.S. institutions they classified, in one of their top two categories—the categories that include almost all of the undergraduate schools in the College and Beyond universe. The top two categories used by *Barron's* in 1982 include 90 institutions, and the top three include 229 schools.

Using regression analysis, Thomas J. Kane (forthcoming) has estimated that a marked degree of racial preference is given within only the top 20 percent of all four-year institutions; he found a very limited degree of preference in the next quintile and none in the remaining 60 percent of all four-year institutions. Michael T. Nettles and his collaborators have used a similar methodology and arrived at similar conclusions (Nettles, Perna, and Edelin [forthcoming], pp. 32ff).

would agree that rank favoritism (admitting a personal friend of the admissions officer, say) is inconsistent with admission "on the merits," that no one should be admitted who cannot take advantage of the educational opportunities being offered, and that using a lottery or some similar random numbers scheme to choose among applicants who are over the academic threshold is too crude an approach.

One reason why we care so much about who gets admitted "on the merits" is because, as this study confirms, admission to the kinds of selective schools included in the College and Beyond universe pays off handsomely for individuals of all races, from all backgrounds. But it is not individuals alone who gain. Substantial additional benefits accrue to society at large through the leadership and civic participation of the graduates and through the broad contributions that the schools themselves make to the goals of a democratic society. These societal benefits are a major justification for the favored tax treatment that colleges and universities enjoy and for the subsidies provided by public and private donors. The presence of these benefits also explains why these institutions do not allocate scarce places in their entering classes by the simple expedient of auctioning them off to the highest bidders. The limited number of places is an exceedingly valuable resource—valuable both to the students admitted and to the society at large—which is why admissions need to be based "on the merits."

Unfortunately, however, to say that considerations of merit should drive the admissions process is to pose questions, not answer them. There are no magical ways of automatically identifying those who merit admission on the basis of intrinsic qualities that distinguish them from all others. Test scores and grades are useful measures of the ability to do good work, but they are no more than that. They are far from infallible indicators of other qualities some might regard as intrinsic, such as a deep love of learning or a capacity for high academic achievement. Taken together, grades and scores predict only 15–20 percent of the variance among all students in academic performance and a smaller percentage among black students. . . . Moreover, such quantitative measures are even less useful in answering other questions relevant to the admissions process, such as predicting which applicants will contribute later in life to their professions and their communities.

Some critics believe, nevertheless, that applicants with higher grades and test scores are more deserving of admission because they presumably worked harder than those with less auspicious academic records. According to this argument, it is only "fair" to admit the students who have displayed the greatest effort. We disagree on several grounds.

To begin with, it is not clear that students who

receive higher grades and test scores have necessarily worked harder in school. Grades and test scores are a reflection not only of effort but of intelligence, which in turn derives from a number of factors, such as inherited ability, family circumstances, and early upbringing, that have nothing to do with how many hours students have labored over their homework. Test scores may also be affected by the quality of teaching that applicants have received or even by knowing the best strategies for taking standardized tests, as coaching schools regularly remind students and their parents. For these reasons, it is quite likely that many applicants with good but not outstanding scores and B+ averages in high school will have worked more diligently than many other applicants with superior academic records.

More generally, selecting a class has much broader purposes than simply rewarding students who are thought to have worked especially hard. The job of the admissions staff is not, in any case, to decide who has earned a "right" to a place in the class, since we do not think that admission to a selective university is a right possessed by anyone. What admissions officers must decide is which set of applicants, *considered individually and collectively,* will take fullest advantage of what the college has to offer, contribute most to the educational process in college, and be most successful in using what they have learned for the benefit of the larger society. Admissions processes should, of course, be "fair," but "fairness" has to be understood to mean only that each individual is to be judged according to a consistent set of criteria that reflect the objectives of the college or university. Fairness should not be misinterpreted to mean that a particular criterion has to apply—that, for example, grades and test scores must always be considered more important than other qualities and characteristics so that no student with a B average can be accepted as long as some students with As are being turned down.

Nor does fairness imply that each candidate should be judged in isolation from all others. It may be perfectly "fair" to reject an applicant because the college has already enrolled many other students very much like him or her. . . .

To admit "on the merits," then, is to admit by following complex rules derived from the institution's own mission and based on its own experiences educating students with different talents and backgrounds. These "rules" should not be thought of as abstract propositions to be deduced through contemplation in a Platonic cave. Nor are they rigid formulas that can be applied in a mechanical fashion. Rather, they should have the status of rough guidelines established in large part through empirical examination of the actual results achieved as a result of long experience. . . .

Above all, merit must be defined in light of what educational institutions are trying to accomplish. In our view, race is relevant in determining which candidates "merit" admission because taking account of race helps institutions achieve three objectives central to their mission—identifying individuals of high potential, permitting students to benefit educationally from diversity on campus, and addressing long-term societal needs.

IDENTIFYING INDIVIDUALS OF HIGH POTENTIAL

An individual's race may reveal something about how that person arrived at where he or she is today —what barriers were overcome, and what the individual's prospects are for further growth. Not every member of a minority group will have had to surmount substantial obstacles. Moreover, other circumstances besides race can cause "disadvantage." Thus colleges and universities should and do give special consideration to the hard-working son of a family in Appalachia or the daughter of a recent immigrant from Russia who, while obviously bright, is still struggling with the English language. But race is an important factor in its own right, given this nation's history and the evidence presented in many studies of the continuing effects of discrimination and prejudice.[2] Wishing it were otherwise does not make it otherwise. It would seem to us to be ironic indeed—and wrong—if admissions officers were permitted to consider all other factors that help them identify individuals of high potential who have had to overcome obstacles, but were proscribed from looking at an applicant's race.

BENEFITING EDUCATIONALLY FROM DIVERSITY ON THE CAMPUS

Race almost always affects an individual's life experiences and perspectives, and thus the person's capacity to contribute to the kinds of learning through diversity that occur on campuses. This form of learning will be even more important going forward than it has been in the past. Both the grow-

2. One of the most compelling findings of this study is that racial gaps of all kinds remain after we have tried to control for the influences of other variables that might be expected to account for "surface" differences associated with race. We have described and discussed black-white gaps in SAT scores, socioeconomic status, high school grades, college graduation rates, college rank in class, attainment of graduate and professional degrees, labor force participation, average earnings, job satisfaction, marital status, household income, civic participation, life satisfaction, and attitudes toward the importance of diversity itself. In short, on an "other things equal" basis, race is a statistically significant predictor of a wide variety of attributes, attitudes, and outcomes. People will debate long and hard, as they should, whether particular gaps reflect unmeasured differences in preparation and previous opportunity, patterns of continuing discrimination, failures of one kind or another in the educational system itself, aspects of the culture of campuses and universities, individual strengths and weaknesses, and so on. But no one can deny that race continues to matter.

ing diversity of American society and the increasing interaction with other cultures worldwide make it evident that going to school only with "the likes of oneself" will be increasingly anachronistic. The advantages of being able to understand how others think and function, to cope across racial divides, and to lead groups composed of diverse individuals are certain to increase.

To be sure, not all members of a minority group may succeed in expanding the racial understanding of other students, any more than all those who grew up on a farm or came from a remote region of the United States can be expected to convey a special rural perspective. What does seem clear, however, is that a student body containing many different backgrounds, talents, and experiences will be a richer environment in which to develop. In this respect, minority students of all kinds can have something to offer their classmates. The black student with high grades from Andover may challenge the stereotypes of many classmates just as much as the black student from the South Bronx.

Until now, there has been little hard evidence to confirm the belief of educators in the value of diversity. Our survey data throw new light on the extent of interaction occurring on campuses today and of how positively the great majority of students regard opportunities to learn from those with different points of view, backgrounds, and experiences. Admission "on the merits" would be short-sighted if admissions officers were precluded from crediting this potential contribution to the education of all students.

Imposition of a race-neutral standard would produce very troubling results from this perspective: such a policy would reduce dramatically the proportion of black students on campus—probably shrinking their number to less than 2 percent of all matriculants at the most selective colleges and professional schools. Moreover, our examination of the application and admissions files indicates that such substantial reductions in the number of black matriculants, with attendant losses in educational opportunity for all students, would occur without leading to any appreciable improvement in the academic credentials of the remaining black students and would lead to only a modest change in the overall academic profile of the institutions.

ADDRESSING LONG-TERM SOCIETAL NEEDS

Virtually all colleges and universities seek to educate students who seem likely to become leaders and contributing members of society. Identifying such students is another essential aspect of admitting "on the merits," and here again race is clearly relevant. There is widespread agreement that our country continues to need the help of its colleges and universities in building a society in which access to positions of leadership and responsibility is less limited by an individual's race than it is today.

The success of C&B colleges and universities in meeting this objective has been documented extensively in this study. In this final chapter, it is helpful to "look back up the river" from a slightly different vantage point. Some of the consequences of mandating a race-neutral standard of admission can be better understood by constructing a rough profile of the approximately 700 black matriculants in the '76 entering cohort at the C&B schools whom we estimate would have been rejected had such a standard been in effect. Our analysis suggests that:

Over 225 members of this group of retrospectively rejected black matriculants went on to attain professional degrees or doctorates.

About 70 are now doctors, and roughly 60 are lawyers.

Nearly 125 are business executives.

Well over 300 are leaders of civic activities.

The average earnings of the individuals in the group exceeds $71,000.

Almost two-thirds of the group (65 percent) were *very* satisfied with their undergraduate experience.

Many of these students would have done well no matter where they went to school, and we cannot know in any precise way how their careers would have been affected as a result. But we do know that there is a statistically significant association, on an "other things equal" basis, between attendance at the most selective schools within the C&B universe and a variety of accomplishments during college and in later life. Generally speaking, the more selective the school, the more the student achieved subsequently. Also, we saw that C&B students as a group earned appreciably more money than did the subgroup of students in our national control with mostly As, which suggests that going to a C&B school conferred a considerable premium on all C&B students, and probably an especially high premium on black students. Black C&B students were also more likely than black college graduates in general to become leaders of community and social service organizations. These findings suggest that reducing the number of black matriculants at the C&B schools would almost certainly have had a decidedly negative effect on the subsequent careers of many of these students and on their contributions to civic life as well.

Even more severe effects would result from insisting on race-neutral admissions policies in professional schools. In law and medicine, all schools are selective. As a consequence, the effect of barring any consideration of race would be the exclusion of more than half of the existing minority student population from these professions. Race-neutral admissions policies would reduce the number of black students in the most selective schools of law and medicine to less than 1 percent of all students. Since major law firms and medical centers often limit their recruitment to the most selective schools, this outcome would deal a heavy blow to efforts to prepare future black leaders for the professions. . . .

American society needs the high-achieving black graduates who will provide leadership in every walk of life. This is the position of many top officials concerned with filling key positions in government, of CEOs who affirm that they would continue their minority recruitment programs whether or not there were a legal requirement to do so, and of bar associations, medical associations, and other professional organizations that have repeatedly stressed the importance of attracting more minority members into their fields. In view of these needs, we are not indifferent to which student gets the graduate fellowship.

Neither of the authors of this study has any sympathy with quotas or any belief in mandating the proportional representation of groups of people, defined by race or any other criterion, in positions of authority. Nor do we include ourselves among those who support race-sensitive admissions as compensation for a legacy of racial discrimination.[3] We agree emphatically with the sentiment expressed by Mamphela Ramphele, vice chancellor of the university of Cape Town in South Africa, when she said: "Everyone deserves opportunity; no one deserves success." But we remain persuaded that present racial disparities in outcomes are dismayingly disproportionate. At the minimum, this country needs to maintain the progress now being made in educating larger numbers of black professionals and black leaders. . . .

If, at the end of the day, the question is whether the most selective colleges and universities have succeeded in educating sizable numbers of minority students who have already achieved considerable success and seem likely in time to occupy positions of leadership throughout society, we have no problem in answering the question. Absolutely.

We commented earlier on the need to make clear choices. Here is perhaps the clearest choice. Let us suppose that rejecting, on race-neutral grounds, more than half of the black students who otherwise would attend these institutions would raise the probability of acceptance for another white student from 25 percent to, say, 27 percent at the most selective colleges and universities. Would we, as a society, be better off? Considering both the educational benefits of diversity and the need to include far larger numbers of black graduates in the top ranks of the business, professional, governmental, and not-for-profit institutions that shape our society, we do not think so.[4]

How one responds to such questions depends very much, of course, on how important one thinks it is that progress continues to be made in narrowing black-white gaps in earnings and in representation in top-level positions. . . . This goal of greater inclusiveness is important for reasons, both moral and practical, that offer all Americans the prospect of living in a society marked by more equality and racial harmony than one might otherwise anticipate.

We recognize that many opponents of race-sensitive admissions will . . . argue that there are better ways of promoting inclusiveness. There is everything to be said, in our view, for addressing the underlying problems in families, neighborhoods, and primary and secondary schools that many have identified so clearly. But this is desperately difficult work, which will, at best, produce results only over a very long period of time. Meanwhile, it is important, in our view, to do what can be done to make a difference at each educational level, including colleges and graduate and professional schools. The alternative seems to us both stark and unworthy of our country's ideals. Turning aside from efforts to help larger numbers of well-qualified blacks gain the educational advantages they will need to move steadily and confidently into the mainstream of American life could have extremely serious consequences. . . . Leon Higginbotham spoke from the heart when, commenting on the aftermath of the *Hopwood* decision, he said, "I sometimes feel as if I am watching justice die." To engender such feelings, and a consequent loss of hope on the part of

---

3. Justice Thurgood Marshall made such an argument in the *Bakke* case in urging his colleagues on the Supreme Court to uphold the racial quotas provided by the University of California, Davis, Medical School; in his view, such programs were simply a way "to remedy the effects of centuries of unequal treatment. . . . I do not believe that anyone can truly look into America's past and still find that a remedy for the effects of that past is impermissible" (438 U.S. at p. 402). Understandable as this argument may seem against a historical background of slavery and segregation, it did not prevail because the remedy is not precise enough to be entirely just in its application. Not every minority student who is admitted will have suffered from substantial discrimination, and the excluded white and Asian applicants are rarely responsible for the racial injustices of the past and have sometimes had to struggle against considerable handicaps of their own. For these reasons, a majority of justices in the *Bakke* case rejected Marshall's reasoning, although similar arguments continue to be heard.

4. This emphasis on the consequences of rejecting race-neutral policies will seem misplaced to some of the most thoughtful critics of affirmative action, who will argue that their objection to race-based policies is an objection in principle: in their view, no one's opportunities should be narrowed, even by an iota, by reference to the individual's race. We respect this line of argument. However, we do not agree, "in principle," that colleges and universities should ignore the practical effects of one set of decisions or another when making difficult decisions about who "merits" a place in the class. The clash here is principle versus principle, not principle versus expediency. As we argued earlier in the chapter, in making admissions decisions, what is right in principle depends on how one defines the mission of the educational institution involved. For us, the missions of colleges and universities have strong educational and public policy aspects and do not consist solely of conferring benefits on particular individuals.

many who have not attained Judge Higginbotham's status, seems a high price to pay for a tiny increase in the probability of admission for white applicants to academically selective colleges and universities.

THE IMPORTANCE OF INSTITUTIONAL AUTONOMY

Who should decide how much consideration to give to race in the admission process? One of the great advantages of the American system of higher education is that it is highly decentralized, allowing a great deal of experimentation and adaptation to suit the varying needs of society, students, and the marketplace. . . .

As a society, we should think very carefully before reducing the authority of these institutions to make their own determinations (and occasionally their own mistakes) in an area of decision-making so closely bound up with their missions, values, and views of how best to educate students. An important reason why American higher education has become preeminent in the world is the greater willingness of the government to respect the autonomy of colleges and universities and to refrain from imposing its own judgments on what justice Felix Frankfurter once described as "the four essential freedoms of a university—to determine for itself on academic grounds who may teach, what may be taught, how it should be taught, and who may be admitted to study."

Diversification of Higher Education: Latino Americans

21. *El Plan de Santa Barbara: A Chicano Plan for Higher Education,* 1969

The beginnings of a statewide and ultimately nationwide movement for Chicano studies programs came from a conference of Chicano leaders in California. The Santa Barbara plan of 1969, reprinted in part here, voiced the desires and demands of Latinos for higher education to meet their needs. The voice was militant, instructive, and deeply felt. Three decades later there were about eight hundred thousand Central Americans in California, for whom Chicano studies programs were still not satisfactory due to their increasingly diverse geographic origins. By the year 2000, the proposals announced in this document, though not fully met, had evolved into more than fifty Chicano studies programs in California colleges, which graduated influential Latino leaders in many walks of life.

The word *Chicano* carried ambiguity. It began as a political label describing the descendants of Mexican people who occupied their mythical ancestral homeland, called Aztlán. Chicano joined the Aztec word *Mexica* (pronounced "mecheeka") with the Spanish word *Mexicano* (pronounced "meheekano"): they both mean Mexican. Still, with their growing numbers from Central America, some Latinos have looked for a more inclusive name when one is needed.

Chicano Coordinating Council on Higher Education, *El Plan de Santa Barbara: A Chicano Plan for Higher Education: Analyses and Positions* (Oakland, 1969): 9–11, 55, 59–60. Reprinted with permission. Further Reading: Patricia Gándara, California Policy Seminar Report, *Choosing Higher Education: The Educational Mobility of Chicano Students* (Berkeley, 1993); Gándara, *Over the Ivy Walls: The Educational Mobility of Low-Income Chicanos* (Albany, NY, 1995); Felix M. Padilla, *The Struggle of Latino/a University Students: In Search of a Liberating Education* (New York, 1997); and American Council on Education, *Annual Status Report on Minorities in Higher Education* (Washington, ongoing).

EL PLAN DE SANTA BARBARA

Manifesto

For all peoples, as with individuals, the time comes when they must reckon with their history. For the Chicano the present is a time of renaissance, of renacimiento. Our people and our community, el barrio and la colonia, are expressing a new consciousness and a new resolve. Recognizing the historical tasks confronting our people and fully aware of the cost of human progress, we pledge our will to move. We will move forward toward our destiny as a people. We will move against those forces which has denied us freedom of expression and human dignity. Throughout history the quest for cultural expression and freedom has taken the form of a struggle. Our struggle tempered by the lessons of the American past, is an historical reality.

For decades Mexican people in the United States struggled to realize the "American Dream." And some, a few, have. But the cost, the ultimate cost of assimilation, required turning away from el barrio and la colonia. In the meantime, due to the racist structure of this society, to our essentially different life style, and to the socio-economic functions assigned to our community by Anglo-American society—as suppliers of cheap labor and dumping ground for the small-time capitalist entrepreneur—the barrio and colonia remained exploited, impoverished, and marginal.

As a result, the self-determination of our community is now the only acceptable mandate for social and political action; it is the essence of Chicano commitment. Culturally, the word Chicano, in the past a pejorative and class-bound adjective, has now become the root idea of a new cultural identity for our people. It also reveals a growing solidarity and the development of a common social praxis. The widespread use of the term Chicano today signals a rebirth of pride and confidence. Chicanismo simply embodies and ancient truth: that a person is never closer to his/her true self as when he/she is close to his/her community.

Chicanismo draws its faith and strength from two main sources: from the just struggle of our people and from an objective analysis of our community's strategic needs. We recognize that without a strategic use of education, an education that places value on what we value, we will not realize our destiny. Chicanos recognize the central importance of institutions of higher learning to modern progress, in this case, to the development of our community. But we go further: we believe that higher education must contribute to the information of a complete person who truly values life and freedom. . . .

The destiny of our people will be fulfilled. To that end, we pledge our efforts and take as our credo what Jose Vasconcelos once said at a time of crisis and hope: "At this moment we do not come to work for the university, but to demand that the university work for our people." . . .

Function of M.E.Ch.A.—To the Student

To socialize and politicize Chicano students of their particular campus to the ideals of the movement. It is important that every Chicano student on campus be made to feel that he has a place on the campus and that he/she has a feeling of familia with his/her Chicano brothers, and sisters. Therefore, the organization in its flurry of activities and projects must not forget or overlook the human factor of friendship, understanding, trust, etc. As well as stimulating hermanidad, this approach can also be looked at in more pragmatic terms. If enough trust, friendship, and understanding are generated, then the loyalty and support can be relied upon when a crisis faces the group or community. This attitude must not merely provide a social club atmosphere but the strengths, weaknesses, and talents of each member should be known so that they may be utilized to the greatest advantage. Know one another. Part of the reason that students will come to the organization is in search of self-fulfillment. Give that individual the opportunity to show what he/she can do. Although the Movement stresses collective behavior, it is important that the individual be recognized and given credit for his/her efforts. When people who work in close association know one another well, it is more conductive to self-criticism and re-evaluation, and this every M.E.Ch.A. person must be willing to submit to. Periodic self-criticism often eliminates static cycles of unproductive behavior. It is an opportunity for fresh approaches to old problems to be surfaces and aired; it gives new leadership a chance to emerge; and must be recognized as a vital part of M.E.Ch.A. M.E.Ch.A. can be considered a training ground for leadership, and as such no one member or group of members should dominate the leadership positions for long periods of time. This tends to take care of itself considering the transitory nature of students. . . .

Function of M.E.Ch.A.—Education

It is a fact that the Chicano has not often enough written his/her own history, his/her own anthropology, his/her own sociology, his/her own literature. He/she must do this if he is to survive as a cultural entity in this melting pot society, which seeks to dilute varied cultures into a gray upon gray

pseudo-culture of technology and materialism. The Chicano student is doing most of the work in the establishment of study programs, centers, curriculum development, entrance programs to get more Chicanos into college. This is good and must continue, but students must be careful not to be co-opted in their fervor for establishing relevance on the campus. Much of what is being offered by college systems and administrators is too little too late. M.E.Ch.A. must not compromise programs and curriculum which are essential for the total education of the Chicano for the sake of expediency. The students must not become so engrossed in programs and centers created along establishes academic guidelines that they forget the needs of the people which these institutions are meant to serve. To this end, barrio input must always be given full and open hearing when designing these programs, when creating them and in running them. The jobs created by these projects must be filled by competent Chicanos, not only the Chicano who has the traditional credentials required for the position, but one who has the credentials of the Raza. Too often in the past the dedicated pushed for a program only to have a vendido sharp-talker come in and take over and start working for his Anglo administrator. Therefore, students must demand a say in the recruitment and selection of all directors and assistant directors of student-initiated programs. To further insure strong if not complete control of the direction and running of programs, all advisory and steering committees should have both student and community components as well as sympathetic Chicano faculty as members.

Tying the campus to the Barrio. The colleges and universities in the past have existed in an aura of omnipotence and infallibility. It is time that they be made responsible and responsive to the communities in which they are located or whose member they serve. As has already been mentioned, community members should serve on all program related to Chicano interests. In addition to this, all attempts must be made to take the college and university to the Barrio, whether it be in form of classes giving college credit or community centers financed by the school for the use of community organizations and groups. Also, the Barrio must be brought to the campus, whether it be for special programs or ongoing services which the school provides for the people of the Barrio. The idea must be made clear to the people of the Barrio that they own the schools and the schools and all their resources are at their disposal. The student group must utilize the resources open to the school for the benefit of the barrio at every opportunity. This can be done by hiring more Chicanos to work as academic and non-academic personnel on the campus; this often requires exposure of racist hiring practices now in operation in may college and universities. When functions, social, or otherwise, are held in the barrio under the sponsorship of the college and university, monies should be spent in the Barrio. This applies to hiring Chicano contractors to build on campus, etc. Many colleges and universities have publishing operations which could be forced to accept Barrio works for publication. Many other things could be considered in using the resources of the school to the Barrio. There are possibilities for using the physical plant and facilities not mentioned here, but this is an area which has great potential. . . .

22. Gloria Cuádraz, "Meritocracy (Un)Challenged," 1993

By 2003, the Latino/Hispanic population formed by a slight margin the largest minority in the United States, yet was handicapped by the smallest percentage of college-bound or -graduated young people. The scarcity of narratives by student Hispanic/Latinos or Chicano/as from which a telling document could here be included only underscored a national educational and social need. No literary work matched Richard Rodriguez's autobiographical *Hunger of Memory* (New York, 1982), the memoir of a brilliant graduate student who by choice passed over an academic career to find a wider audience through writing and journalism. To picture the educational motives and ambitions awakened among Chicano/as, Gloria Cuádraz's doctoral dissertation (the only dissertation excerpted in this volume) carried the words of young people from families of poor or modest means who came to higher education and on into graduate study. Various inquiries had pursued this topic statistically with some interviews, but none had examined personal motivations so clearly. Cuádraz studied forty Chicano/a students who from 1967 to 1979 attended the University of California, Berkeley, a campus that produced more Latino/Hispanic doctorates than any other in the land. Its record was of course impelled by affirmative action, yet it was the students themselves who found different ways into the newly opened doors and, once equipped with a bachelor's degree, stepped farther into graduate work. By 1993, thirty-four of these interviewed students held tenure-track or administrative positions in academic life. Reprinted here are brief pseudonymous quotations from some of the students whom Cuádraz described as pre-college "average" or "high" achievers. Cuádraz is a professor of Language, Culture, and History at Arizona State New College of Arts and Sciences. She is faculty director of the Ethnic Studies Program there and serves on the Reserve Advisory Board of the American Association of University Women while also participating in the Human Relations Commission for the City of Phoenix.

Gloria Holguin Cuádraz, "Meritocracy (Un)Challenged: The Making of a Chicano and Chicana Professoriate and Professional Class," Ph.D. dissertation, University of California Berkeley, 1993, 128–30, 133–35, 144–46, 150, 152, 172–74. Reprinted with the kind permission of the author under her copyright. Brief identities, rephrased here from the author's description, are bracketed. Further reading: Cuádraz, *Telling to Live: Latina Feminist Testimonios* (Durham, NC, 2001); Ruben Navarrette, *A Darker Shade of Crimson: Odyssey of a Harvard Chicano* (New York, 1993); Frances Esquibel Tywoniak and Mario García, *Migrant Daughter: Coming of Age as a Mexican American Woman* (Berkeley, 2000), an earlier oral history from Berkeley; Carlos Munoz Jr., *Youth, Identity, Power: The Chicano Movement* (London and New York, 1989); Patricia Gándara, *Choosing Higher Education: The Educational Mobility of Chicano Students* (Berkeley, California Policy Seminar, 1993) and *Over the Ivy Walls: The Educational Mobility of Low-Income Chicanos* (Albany, NY, 1995); Felix M. Padilla, *The Struggle of Latino/a University Students: In Search of a Liberating Education* (New York and London, 1997); Vicki L. Ruiz, *From Out of the Shadows: Mexican Women in Twentieth-Century America* (New York, 1998); Michael A. Olivas, ed., *Latino College Students* (New York, 1986); Stephen Cole and Elinor Barber, *Increasing Faculty Diversity: The Occupational Choices of High-Achieving Minority Students* (Cambridge, MA, 2003); and II, 21.

[From Teofilo whose father was "heavyhanded and authoritarian":]

I didn't pick enough crops fast enough, whatever. Picking up cotton or whatever. And I seemed to be the worst in my family. I was beaten up probably in a semi-serious to serious fashion probably at least fifty times a week. . . . I would be literally flogged in front of people with a "rama" (branch) . . . or a piece of whipping cotton . . . or the rope from the scales that you weighted your cotton. They whipped me with it. Whatever they got hold of.

[Although punishment was "common" in his family, Teofilo declared:]

. . . my family is the only positive thing that I had. The state would change. The schools would change. The teachers would change. The classmates and peer groups would change. Everything was changing. The only thing that remains constant and stable was just my family. That's all I really had to rely on. . . .

As far as the intellectual upbringing or what not in my family, it was very low. My parents read. They were both literate. They read and wrote, but they did very little of it. It was just sending a letter to a friend, or just writing down the number of sacks of onions or the number of pounds you picked of cotton, or documenting something. But never sitting down and reading the newspaper or something like that. As a consequence, I grew up reading basically comic books.

[From Victor, an average student, the son of farm-working parents with fifteen children—whose mother spoke no English, and the father some English:]

They didn't give us money or anything like that. They fed us. People ask, "How did you get encouraged to go to college and the university?" I say, "Well, my parents fed me; they clothed me, and beyond that, they didn't know much about school." They were proud of me, but they didn't know if I was doing well or not. I could lie if I wanted to, and once in a while, I did lie. They wouldn't know. I wrote all my notes if I was absent or whatever.

[From Alicia, brought up in a middle class home:]

My father, I remember my father reading to us every night. He would read a chapter from something. He went through all the children's classics, and things like that, and he also . . . we would tell stories. That was one of my favorite family activities. . . . My father was a wonderful storyteller; he had a great way with words. I think that that had a lot to do with, not only learning how to speak correctly and quickly, even though I spoke only Spanish in the beginning, but also the fact that I did well in school. . . .

[Also from Alicia a high-achiever who had dropped out of high school:]

the reason I got my education had more to do with my political leanings than anything else. If I were to credit one thing with my being who I am, it's the politics of the times—and my anger at the injustices, and my anger at the racism. And, anger can be very motivating, in my opinion. And my father had a great deal to do with that anger because he exposed me to the realities of the FBI, and the CIA, and Latin American politics. My first exposure came from him. And, it was steady all through my life. I never was able to value it as a child because I was still with the horrors of being Chicana, but as an adult, those experiences are still there. As an adult, they all sort of came to fruition. And the times, it was a major factor.

[From Sandra, an average-achiever who went to community college in California where she worked in the Dean's Office, dated a "blondhair, blue-eyed guy," and encountered Chicano pintos (convicts) from Soledad:]

So they discovered me. They treated me with respect, but they started rapping to me about politics. They started talking about racial and cultural oppression. And they started telling me that I should read this book and that book. And they started telling me about Cesar Chavez and the movement, and the farmworkers' struggle. And they started telling me about the struggles of men in the joint. And they started telling me about our Chicano community struggles. They politicized me. Everything they said was not difficult for me to understand. Because, mind you, I had already come from this childhood that was full of racial and cultural oppression, and *I had lived it* (my emphasis). . . . "I am a Chicana. Oh, is that what I am?" Because I wasn't anything then. I was Mexican, but I was Sandra. It was like they were describing my life, my history, my personal struggle, and I said, "Yes, yes, yes." I was so excited.

[From Maya, a high achiever:]

It was at the community college I discovered the Chicano Movement and developed a political consciousness. I knew absolutely nothing about Chicano history, about politics, about organizing. I drove past striking farmworkers and never asked. I remember at one point early in my first year of college, asking one of my friends, "what's a huelga?" I also didn't know Spanish. They all laughed and made all these jokes about how naive I was. Then they started to tell me what it was . . . I remember, at

the same time, going through the process of saying to a friend—my then boyfriend—saying, "I'm not a Mexican-American. I'm a Chicana." It was really exhilarating to discover that. It was a discovery.

[From Michael, a high achiever, who helped produce the first Chicano journal on a university campus, *El Grito*:]

The truth of the matter was that we didn't really want so much a revolution as we wanted to have recognition and the ability to enter and participate along with every[body] else. That was the real dichotomy. That was the paradox of the whole movement. All we wanted were teaching positions, faculty positions, money to go to school. To be honest, it was very, very goal oriented—very middle class goals. But everybody kept saying, "No, we want revolution."

[From Carlos, an average-achiever, who after time in the Army, spent eight years getting a community college A.A. degree, and described Berkeley when he entered graduate school:]

See, all these professors that were the untenured faculty—they were all the Marxists and the Fanonists. Somehow, when my class came in, they wrestled control of the admissions committee. Somehow they had a majority of the votes on the admissions committee. So they gave as a priority for my class that they wanted activists. Now you had to have a minimum scholarship to get into graduate school, but that wasn't their top priority. It was their activism. So into my class came a Black Panther, a longshore organizer, a Socialist feminist organizer, a radical radio station producer, three Socialist feminists, a couple of Black power militants, everybody in my whole class had some kind of a history of being a leader of activism. So we were a kick ass group. I was a lightweight in that group. There were some heavies. We made that place even more radical, and we weren't going to let it backtrack to what it used to be.

[From Armando:]

The only thing that attracted me about Berkeley was that I heard they were recruiting Chicanos. This faculty member told me about it, and I heard they were offering fellowships to minority students. It was part of their whole affirmative action effort, and I was fortunate enough to have been able to have benefited from that. It was not anything I did that got me into Berkeley; it was the whole climate in the country—the civil rights movement and everything else. It was just an accident that I even went to college and totally accidental that I went to grad school.

[From Rosemary, a "completer":]

One of the patriarchs of the program, he was on leave when I first came, so the second year, he said, "Oh, you don't look Latin to me." And I said, "Why?" He said, "You're not wearing braids." That's the level of comments that would be made. He'd say, "I saw you with your husband. He looks just like Pancho Villa." It was that kind of stuff that was so out there.

[From Caridad, a "completer," from a social science department, on first being interviewed by a senior professor who said, "You know, we're taking a chance on you." When she asked him why, he answered, "because you're very young, you're a woman, and you're Mexican."]

> I took offense to the Mexican part; [I said], "what do you mean? What does my being Mexican have to do anything?" This is my freshman, my first semester in graduate school. Then he says, "well, we know that Mexican women, when they get married . . ." And I wasn't married, he didn't have any idea that I was going to get married, but that was in their mind. He said, "soon as they get married, their husbands don't let them come to school. They like them barefoot and pregnant." I said, "you know what? Our people left the caves the same time as white people did. And they don't drag us around by the hair anymore than you guys drag the white woman around by the hair. So it really is not even an issue." Oh, we went at it until we had a big argument.

[From Juanita a high achiever with a schoolteacher mother:]

> One of my earliest memories in fact when I was probably like 4 was being in the University . . . [My mother] was picking up some books and looking over and seeing a whole bunch of students sitting very quietly. . . . It was getting to be dark and the lights were on in their carrels. I remember asking her what that was, and she said that those were carrels for the graduate students, and someday when you're working on a Ph.D. you'll have one of those carrels. I remember thinking that I didn't know what a carrel was and I didn't know what a Ph.D. was, but somehow it looked important. I remember making that connection in my head.

[Again from Juanita a high achiever from a social science department, in an exchange with a faculty member of "New England blue blood" on the first day of the quarter who asked her how long her family had been in this country:]

> I was trying to figure out this answer and he was lighting his pipe. He had just filled it with this incredibly expensive tobacco. I could tell it was expensive because it smelled so incredibly good, real sweet. I said, "Well, which side of my family?" "Well, either side." He was just totally impatient. He just sort of wanted to get me out of there. Then I said, "Well, you know, on my father's side, I guess they've been here 450 years, and on my mother's side, 20 or 25,000 years." And I mean his face just like, and then he threw out the tobacco that he hadn't even lit. He refilled the pipe. He threw that out without lighting it. He refilled it again. I remember looking at him and thinking, "Oh, my God." And then it was like there was nothing more to say, and I walked out of there, and I didn't do well in that seminar.

23. Ilan Stavans, "The Challenges Facing Spanish Departments," 2005

The fortunes of college Spanish instruction since the nineteenth century are briefly traced here. Ilan Stavans (1961–) points out the changes incurred by the immense increase of Latino peoples in the United States since the mid–twentieth century, relating these changes as much to waning "peninsular" Spanish literary interests as to a new cultural impetus from Latino newcomers and South American literary currents. He urges a globalized view on the teaching of Spanish culture and a receptivity to the experiences of first- and second-generation Latino students.

Stavans is guided not only by the many directions in Octavio Paz's works, but by the changes of language among Latinos, even including serious attention to "Spanglish." His own background is as colorful and varied in employment as some of the writers he has studied. Born the son of a Jewish actor in Mexico, he came to the United States in 1985, took his doctorate at Columbia and taught for three years at Baruch College before going to Amherst College. His books and articles far exceed in number those of most academic people his age. He is recognized as a guiding star to those who seek breadth and imagination in modern Latin-American Studies. "Being Hispanic," he says, "doesn't mean having brown skin or having the last name Rodriguez. We are Spaniards and Asians and Jews and Muslims."

Ilan Stavans, "The Challenges Facing Spanish Departments," *Chronicle of Higher Education,* July 29, 2005, B6–7. Reprinted with the permission of the author; copyright © 2005. Further reading: Ilan Stavans, "How Elite Universities Fail Latino Students," *Chronicle of Higher Education,* January 20, 2006, B20, and Ilan Stavans, *On Borrowed Words: A Memoir of Language* (New York, 2001); Scott Heller, " 'Living in the Hyphen' between Latin and American," *Chronicle of Higher Education,* January 9, 1998, A17; and Young May Cha, "Ilan Stavans Publishes Two 'Essential' Books," *The Amherst Student,* October 18, 2000, 24.

Spanish today is the most widely taught foreign language on American college campuses, with enrollments at some institutions surpassing the combined number of students in the next-largest fields of French, German, Italian, American Sign Language, Japanese, Chinese, and Latin. Increasingly popular over the last 35 years, the language and the study of its culture became even more so in the 1990s, spurred by such factors as free-trade agreements, immigration, and the growing number of Latinos in the United States.

Unfortunately, Spanish departments are ill equipped to respond to the demand. Too often faculty members, to a surprisingly large extent, are poorly trained to teach the actual language, many having been conscripted into class from their studies of Spanish civilization. Too often they seem unaware of the ethnic changes in the American population—holding fast to the mantle of Cervantes and rejecting the newer Latino sense of self that has emerged north of the Rio Grande.

And too often, the result is internecine struggles within departments that end up wasting enormous amounts of energy. Nor do administrators seem to care: Their mostly uninformed, unengaged attitude toward Spanish reflects the haphazard, even racist, way that the subject was first added to the curriculum, almost as an afterthought.

The ones paying the bills, of course, are the students, and they surely aren't getting their money's worth.

But the future of Spanish departments should concern us all. In 2003 the U.S. Census Bureau declared Latinos to be the largest minority group in the United States, surpassing black people and reaching 40 million, which constitutes more than 10 percent of the whole Spanish-speaking world. By the end of the 21st century, their impact on American life will be enormous (as will their cultural, political, and economic influence south of the border).

Indeed to describe Spanish as a "foreign" language in the United States is increasingly problematic. Is a form of communication so intimately related to the fabric of our nation's life, spoken by millions, really alien to our collective identity? Is the language, history, and culture of a region—Latin America—that commerce and the consolidation of democratic capitalism have made so much the focus of the rest of the world really something to be taught as an afterthought? Surely how we teach Spanish and its cultural heritage in the classroom matters to everyone. It's time for Spanish departments, and the rest of academe (which, in general, has been slow to react to the growth of the Latino population), to wake up and pay attention. . . .

As a language of instruction, Spanish crept back into American consciousness after World War II, part of the package of Romance languages that gained new attention as the United States became more involved in Europe and the wider world. This could be called the "foundation period," when Spanish departments were established, often under the umbrella of "modern languages." Teaching Spanish as part of that group, however, emphasized its philological origins. It stressed the language's past, not its present.

The fact that philologists who joined Spanish departments came from Europe, many of them refugees from the Spanish Civil War, reinforced the old-world emphasis. Even as exiles fleeing the Cuban Revolution or Latin American dictatorships joined them on campuses, the focus tended to stay on older linguistic traditions. In part that was because many Latin American intellectuals had been heavily influenced by European thought. In part it was because, while they welcomed the security of tenured jobs, they tended to view the United States as an imperial force meddling in the issues of the Southern hemisphere: In an odd dynamic, they saw Latinos born in America as the internal byproduct of the same imperialism they detested overseas.

The postwar period built on earlier pedagogical efforts, as Spanish departments devoted growing attention not only to teaching the language but to showcasing the cultural manifestations of the Iberian peninsula and its American satellites. But the focus was still on continuity with the past. How were the leitmotifs of Spanish culture in Europe replicated, and then transformed, on the other side of the Atlantic? What were the connections among the Golden Age luminaries . . . and the literary generation of 1898 . . . ? Where does the art and literature of the Spanish Civil War, chiefly the *oeuvre* of Federico García Lorca, fit in the tradition? What were the forces behind the early Latin American novels of José Joaquín Fernández de Lizardi?

Drawing on the works of the former colonies, courses sprang up on the Modernista movement (José Martí, Rubén Darío), on the indigenous novels of the 19th century (like the works of Alcides Arguedas, Ciro Alegría, and Clorinda Matto de Turner), and on the literature of the Mexican Revolution (Mariano Azuela and Martín Luis Guzmán). Later the work of authors like Julio Cortázar, Gabriel García Márquez, and Mario Vargas Llosa, known collectively as the generation of *El Boom,* refreshed the canon by offering a different lens through which to understand the Americas. That literature revolutionized our perception of the region: "Magical Realism" (a term that, for various reasons, is much contested) showcased what was exciting and distinct in what was once thought to be merely primitive.

The 1960s, however, brought change. As revolutionary movements spread in Latin America, the Chicano movement on American campuses made Spanish the language of the indigent farmworkers in the Southwest. But the quest was for political pride, not for verbal competency. And so when programs focusing on Mexicans and Puerto Ricans were established in academe, Spanish often wasn't part of the package. That resulted in a rivalry between new ethnic-studies courses and Spanish departments, whose members felt alienated. They expressed their alienation by looking down on Chicano activism and studies as a lowbrow activity—and on the increasing number of Latino students who began to make it to the campuses as affirmative-action tokens.

Meanwhile, by the 1980s, two opposing sides had emerged in Spanish departments: the *peninsularistas,* as faculty members known for teaching topics exclusive to Spain were called, and their nemeses, the *latinoamericanistas,* devoted to material from the region encompassing the Pampas and the Caribbean Basin to the U.S.-Mexican border. The tension was, in truth, a matter of pride. At the heart of Hispanic civilization, above all when studied vis-à-vis the Anglo-Saxon tradition, was that inferiority complex traceable back to the defeat of the Armada. It kept academics busy battling for a morsel of prestige. Had the Americas usurped Iberian cultural stature? Was Europe no longer the center of the world? Time and again, that apprehension manifested itself in tenure cases.

Then came the fall of the Berlin Wall. During the cold war, Russian and other Slavic languages had begun to attract students interested in international relations. But the collapse of Communism in the Soviet Union radically changed the zeitgeist. Shortly after, the White House began to look at Latin America as a potential business partner in the new world order. Immigration from Spanish-speaking countries swelled, as did the *vida loca,* a mercantile bonanza of things Hispanic at the forefront of American culture. Music, gastronomy, dance, radio, and TV—Spanish was *en todas partes,* everywhere.

The transformation of Spanish from peripheral player to protagonist on the American scene happened too fast for Spanish departments. Mired in vicious internal fights, themselves the result of colonial fractures, they have been slow to respond. How slow can be seen in the type of Spanish taught in courses until the late 1980s. Castilian, the syntactical form used in central Spain, was considered to be the standard. . . . Some teachers quietly dismissed that approach, but, in general, classes focused on the Iberian peninsula. That meant that American students used *vosotros,* a second-person plural conjugation, in spite of the fact that, in four-fifths of the Spanish-speaking world, people never employed the form.

Nor did Spanish departments adapt quickly to the changing composition of students they began to attract. For years the bulk of students enrolling in Spanish classes had been Anglos. Since the 1990s they have been joined by Latino students, black students, Asians—a far more multicultural group that is interested in Spain, Latin America, and Latino life in the United States in equal measure. . . .

The classroom is a space in which to expand students' minds, to push them to question what they know, and to know what they don't. Canonical Spanish language and texts should be taught. *How* is where innovation is required.

Why continue to compartmentalize the material by geographical areas? Why can't Iberian, Peruvian, and Dominican novels, for example, appear on the same syllabus? Students traveling abroad to Spain are mesmerized by how immigration from Africa and the Americas is changing that country. Why can't such exchanges be explored in the classroom? Students are interested in discovering Hispanic civilization in full. Why can't topics like the Islamic and Jewish legacies in Hispanic civilization be analyzed more attentively? Ethnic, gender, border, and translation studies are all prisms, tools to help understand Hispanic culture and language. So are colonial studies, postmodern studies, and a variety of other approaches. We need an interdisciplinary analysis to deal with the current complexity of the Hispanic world.

Happily, the old guard is retiring, and a new group of faculty members—many of them Latinos from states like Florida, California, Texas, and New York—is taking its place, bringing a kaleidoscopic interest in the diversity of Hispanic civilization. Things are beginning to change.

Courses on Latinos north of the Rio Grande, for example, have trickled into Spanish-department catalogs (although in many colleges they are still taught in English and American studies). They are including topics like ghetto life, crime, domestic violence, and assimilation. The literature and culture of a post–Magical Realist Latin America, including writers like Zoe Valés, Alberto Fuguet, Mayra Montero, and Edmundo Paz Soldán and the so-called McOndo and crack music, are also showing up in classes devoted to drugs, rock 'n' roll, and urban life today. Non-Spanish forms of culture in Latin America are being addressed, including those produced by the Nahuatl, Otomí, Taino, Mapuche, and Quechua people.

By far the most visible change is in language instruction. In the 1990s, an array of fresh textbooks was published under the editorship of scholars less focused on the Iberian peninsula. The recognition of varieties of Spanish aside from Castilian is tangible in them. These resources value the so-called *autonomías* in Spain, suggesting that Catalan, Galician, Basque, and other regional tongues are worthy of attention. Obviously the textbooks still endorse the "standard" form of Cervantes' language, but that standard is more flexible, less suffocating than it ever was before.

Some textbooks are also citing Spanglish, the hybrid vehicle of communication mixing English and Spanish, as an object of study—or at least, of worthy debate. I've come across a rising number of examples of materials for Spanish courses that make reference to verbal expressions ("Wáchale!" "el sandwich en la lonchera") that one was once likely to hear mainly in East Los Angeles or the Lower East Side, but that now have become ubiquitous. The newer material reinvigorates classroom discussions and signals how much Hispanic civilization is in a state of transformation.

Language instruction can't be an improvised activity any more. Once taught by scholars interested in other topics (or even by faculty wives), now it is a field of its own. . . .

If Spanish is no longer a foreign language in the United States, we need to talk more about how and how much we can combine language and ethnic studies; how we can break down all those disciplinary boundaries.

Those questions need to be asked with commitment at the departmental level; and they need to be recognized by top administrators. I sometimes sense that many deans, chancellors, and presidents still harbor a tacit xenophobia, a sense that the rowdy are knocking at the door—they know they need to pay attention to Latino students, but how much do they have to do?

In any case, curricular planning can no longer be

piece-meal. Old divisions like those between *peninsularistas* and *latinoamericanistas* must give way to an approach that allows geographical and chronological periods to relate to each other in an agile, continuing manner.

If the classroom isn't the place where the depth and complexity of the Spanish language and culture is addressed, where will it be?

Open Admissions

24. Jerome Karabel, "Open Admissions," 1972

The years of social and political pressures for civil rights saw a variety of responses in American higher education. The most structured and sometimes dramatic institutional response came in developing a policy of open admissions to students at some urban public universities, a development that recalled the early struggles of community colleges. Like those junior institutions, universities seeking to offer admission to all high school graduates were in effect facing the implicit program of an established, well-educated meritocracy ever broadening its ranks. Setting the social results of public higher education in this context occasioned heated argument throughout the 1960s. Jerome Karabel (1950–) augmented this theme in an article that stands out among several wide-ranging discussions that came to grips with the egalitarian issues involved.

Karabel is a sociologist at Berkeley and also a Senior Fellow at the Rockridge Institute.

Jerome Karabel, "Open Admissions: Toward Meritocracy or Democracy?" *Change* (May 1972): 38–43. Reprinted with permission of the Helen Dwight Reid Educational Foundation. Published by Heldref Publications, 1319 Eighteenth St. NW, Washington, D.C. 20036-1802 Copyright © 1980. Further reading: Jerome Karabel, *The Chosen: The Hidden History of Admission and Exclusion at Harvard, Yale, and Princeton* (New York, 2005); Jerome Karabel with Steven Brint, *The Diverted Dream: Community Colleges and the Promise of Educational Opportunity in America, 1900–1985* (New York, 1989); Hugh Davis Graham, *The Strange Convergence of Affirmative Action and Immigration Policy in America* (New York, 2003); and II, 24–25.

In a now-famous speech on open admissions delivered in the spring of 1970 in Des Moines, Spiro Agnew raised the specter of "bargain basement diplomas" and predicted that the City University of New York (CUNY) would soon be transformed into a "four-year community college" devoid of academic distinction. Several months later, Rowland Evans and Robert Novak, in an article entitled "The Wrecking of a College," described CUNY's open admissions program as "egalitarianism run wild." And Irving Kristol, at a forum sponsored by the Council for Basic Education, said flatly that the promise of open admissions "is fraudulent" and expressed astonishment that "anyone who knows anything about education could really believe for a moment that it would work."

Unquestionably, the controversy over open admissions has been an embittered one. Yet, on the face of it, the outcry seems excessive; after all, what could be a better expression of the American belief in equality of opportunity than giving everyone a chance to go to college? It is difficult to believe that such issues as academic standards, dropout rates, learning capacities and the like—problems which are of concern primarily to professional educators— could stir up such violent feelings and such impassioned public controversy. Something else must be at stake in the battle over open admissions besides the educational questions around which the debate has ostensibly revolved.

Open admissions has been criticized on the grounds that it was not an outgrowth of purely educational considerations. In Irving Kristol's words, "open admissions had precious little to do with education itself, and almost everything to do with ethnic and racial politics." Implicit in this statement is the belief that open admissions represents an unwanted intrusion of politics into the educational process. The underlying image is of the academic institution as an ivory tower, consecrated to intellectual excellence and suddenly defiled by the crude political demands of people unfit to pass through its gates.

But the decision as to who shall be given access to college is not made in a social vacuum. The higher education system virtually determines entry into middle- and upper-level positions in the occupational hierarchy and is thus a key distributor of privilege in contemporary America. The way in which a society distributes its rewards is a profoundly political matter, and as long as the occupational structure remains linked to the educational system, the admissions process is inherently political. The open admissions movement, though indeed political, cannot, therefore, be called an intrusion.

College attendance has traditionally been related to social class, and the situation has not changed as much as some of us might like to think. Census Bureau figures from 1969 indicated that families with incomes of over $15,000 were four times as likely to send their children to college as were families with incomes of under $3,000. One could argue that these figures reflect differences in ability but the evidence indicates otherwise. A massive national study of high school seniors, Project TALENT, found that, even when measured ability was controlled statistically, high socioeconomic status continued to be closely correlated with college enrollment. William Sewell, in a study of Wisconsin high school seniors, found that wealthy students in the bottom ability quartile were six times as likely to enter college as were disadvantaged students of equal ability and over one and a half times as likely to enter college as were disadvantaged students in the top ability quartile.

The economic benefits of attending college are well known. Census Bureau figures for 1968 show that a college graduate can expect to earn $184,000 more during his lifetime than a high school graduate can. Again, one could argue that these figures reflect ability differences be the two groups, but again the evidence fails to support the argument. W. Lee Hansen, for example, reports that, even after adjusting for ability differences, higher education explains about three-fourths of the difference in earnings.

In short, higher education is inextricably linked to the transmission of inequality from generation to generation. Wealthy students are more likely to attend college than are equally able students from low-income backgrounds, and a college degree, in turn, confers economic benefits which extend above and beyond measured ability differences. The entire process helps ensure that the already affluent receive an education which enables them to retain their privilege and position.

Nonetheless, the educational system continues to be viewed as an equalizing force, although the process of selective admissions, even if applied on a purely meritocratic basis, serves to accentuate existing differences. Imagine, for the sake of argument, a system of higher education which admits only the able, regardless of background. Ability is measured in grade 12, and those in the top half of the distribution are allowed to go on to college while those in the bottom half immediately enter the world of work. There is no gainsaying that some people are more able than others; the point is that selecting only the able for further education would cause the already existing gap to become a chasm.

In addition, the meritocratic model of higher education results in an ingrained elitism that unquestioningly accepts the expenditure of disproportionate sums on the most able. Edward Denison reports that we spend $5,811 of public funds for the higher education of the white high school graduate who made at least an A− average but only $666 for the high school graduate with an average below C−. Such differentials in expenditures per student can only serve to increase inequalities in later income. A genuinely equalizing approach to higher education would decree that we spend more rather than less money on the less able; indeed, the simple expedient of spending an *equal* amount on all students would help to reduce the current exaggeration of background and ability differences. Yet we retain a system of colleges and universities that does precisely the opposite, a system so widely accepted that it has rarely been subjected to scrutiny.

The system of higher education does more than just distribute privilege and magnify class and ability differences. At the same time that it allocates people to slots in the occupational hierarchy, it also provides the ideological justification for this placement. Those who succeed in the system see themselves—and are seen—as the deserving, whereas those who are less successful tend to blame themselves rather than the system for their "failure." Not coincidentally, it is generally the students from

fairly affluent backgrounds who are most successful, in part because their family milieu provides the cultural opportunities and values that encourage high academic aspirations and achievements. Hence, status is transmitted intergenerationally not through the explicit mechanism of inheritance but rather through achievement in a supposedly neutral educational system. . . .

Beneath all the rhetoric about standards lies a recognition that open admissions challenges both the process by which American society distributes its rewards and the legitimacy of that process. Like "busing," "academic standards" has become a term connoting far more than its literal meaning. Just as "busing" signifies not a mode of transportation but rather racial and class integration of the school system, so "academic standards" represents a particular mode of distributing privilege.

The ideology of academic standards brilliantly reconciles two conflicting American values: equality and equality of opportunity. Through the system of public education, everyone is exposed to academic standards, yet only those who succeed in meeting them advance in our competitive system. Everyone enters the educational contest, and the rules are usually applied without conscious bias. But since the affluent tend to be the most successful, the net result of the game is to perpetuate intergenerational inequality. Thus academic standards help make acceptable something which runs against the American grain: the inheritance of status.

There was a time when the application of uniform academic standards was decidedly progressive. Immigrant groups excluded from higher education through quota systems regarded such merit criteria as test scores and grades as the primary channel of mobility in an ascriptive society. Now that many members of these groups have themselves achieved success, they view with horror the abolition of merit criteria, particularly for college entry. After all, it was the meritocratic system of higher education that bestowed upon them their privileges, and it is the ideology of merit that will enable them to transmit their status to their children. Open admissions threatens these people (and, more widely, the "haves" of American society) precisely because it challenges the legitimacy of the principle that justifies their position.

Were college admissions based solely on educational considerations, surely those individuals who are least distinguished academically are the very persons who need further education. The higher education system should concern itself with maximizing the educational growth of the student, whatever his level at entrance. The critical variable is the "value added" by college attendance; a truly successful institution would change a student's performance level rather than insure its own prestige by "picking winners" through a stringent selection process. . . .

The central problem is that, in a meritocracy, not

only does increased equality have no priority as a goal, but it is studiously avoided lest incentives be lost. The credo of meritocracy is mobility, the more the better, since everyone must rise (or sink) to his appropriate station in life. Indeed, the response of the meritocrat to the problems caused by the towering social edifice of stratification is to grease the elevators rather than to change the structure of the building. And, as Michael Young first pointed out in *The Rise of the Meritocracy,* insofar as intelligence is genetically determined, a meritocracy tends to take on the very hereditary character it was designed to combat.

Moreover, its social costs are considerable, the competition more frenetic and unrelenting than that of an openly class-based society, and the toll exacted from both losers and winners a harsh one. Failure in a class society is tolerable in that it can be attributed to the "system," but failure in a meritocracy can be blamed only on oneself. Inevitably, this damages the self-esteem of the losers. The winners in a meritocratic society are marked not only by the scars acquired in the competitive battle but also by a tendency to be self-righteous about the elite status which they "earned." Though presenting itself as dynamic, a meritocracy actually tends toward stasis in that it deprives the lower classes of the talent, both in leaders and in the rank and file, necessary if they are to challenge the system. Further, insofar as merit criteria and mobility provide the ultimate justification for inequality, a meritocracy is unlikely to make any move to distribute its resources more equitably.

A meritocratic society is also a credentialist society; it requires certification in the form of grades, diplomas, test scores and the like. However well these credentials reflect cognitive achievement, and however appropriate to advancement through the educational system, they are often poor predictors of job performance, particularly in areas other than the natural sciences. . . .

The tension that now exists between open admissions and the meritocracy derives, of course, from open admissions' abandonment of merit criteria in college entry. At the same time, however, most of the oratory accompanying open admissions has emphasized equality of opportunity, not equality. Whether open admissions will serve to undermine the meritocracy or to make it more efficient is one of the key questions facing higher education today.

In a sense, the issue of open admissions is already dead. Long before CUNY opened its doors, high school graduates in California and elsewhere had been guaranteed admission to college. Now, with the nationwide proliferation of community colleges, we are close to achieving universal access to some form of postsecondary education. What made open admissions at CUNY such an explosive issue was that campuses that were previously very selective, particularly City, Brooklyn, Queens and Hunter, were forced to relax their admissions standards. As long as open admissions was confined to unprestigious two-year colleges, there was little controversy. The real issue all along has not been whether every high school graduate will have a chance to go to college but rather which institutions will be open to him.

Open admissions is by no means incompatible with the meritocracy; what is essential is that the system of higher education retain its social selection function. Under pressure both from the poor wanting access to higher education and from business and industry needing more highly trained workers as jobs become increasingly complex, the meritocracy has been quite willing to admit the poor into higher education. Their presence in the nation's colleges in no way interferes with the sorting function. A hierarchy of institutions can be every bit as effective as exclusion in sorting people, and it has the added advantage of giving credibility to the myth of equal opportunity. Moreover, the abolition of admissions standards in no way implies that sorting will not take place *within* an institution after the student has enrolled: hence the real possibility that open admissions may result in nothing beyond a more efficient meritocracy. . . .

Despite its racial and class biases, the hierarchical system of colleges and universities has been justified on grounds that purport to be purely educational: namely, that students develop better academically if they are grouped with other students of similar ability. According to this scheme, elite institutions are designed for the special needs of bright students whereas schools low in the institutional hierarchy are geared to the less able. If this were in fact the case, the hierarchical structure would be diamond-shaped, since extremes of ability, whether low or high, are rare compared with average ability. In reality, however, the institutional hierarchy is shaped like a pyramid: a few highly selective institutions at the top and a large number of undistinguished schools at the bottom. Further, most of the institutions at the bottom do not seek out students of low ability and would be only too happy to attract the kinds of students who generally attend prestigious institutions. What this all suggests, of course, is that the tracking system in higher education does not reflect the conscious application of an educational philosophy but grows out of other factors, most notably the social selection function which the university has assumed. . . .

The first skirmish in the battle for open admissions, the fight to provide a place for all high school graduates at some type of college, is waning, and the egalitarians seem to have won. But their victory may be only Pyrrhic if they do not push on to confront elite institutions with the issues raised by open admissions. The danger is that extreme selectivity at a few colleges may prove as effective as total exclusion in blocking the mobility of the poor and in legitimating the inequalities of American society. Yet proponents of open admissions have apparently failed to realize that a hierarchical system of higher education may merely change the basis of social selection from *whether* one attended college to *where* one attended college. Thus, open admissions may succeed only in further obscuring the class function of higher education and in making the myth of equal opportunity more plausible.

So the next item on the agenda is open admissions at currently selective colleges. The open admissions movement has laid bare the political nature of deciding who shall be educated in a society which distributes its rewards through the educational system and the legitimating function of arguments about academic standards. It has demonstrated that higher education, far from being an equalizing force, accentuates existing differences of background and ability. Finally, it has provided a philosophical basis for countering the ingrained elitism which holds that the higher education system should give special attention to the academically adept and ignore the less able.

25. James Traub, *City on a Hill*, 1994

From the mid-1960s onward, public higher education engaged the issue of enrolling greater numbers of young people from all backgrounds. As an administrative policy matter and a divisive question for political boards of control, open admission to all high school graduates became heatedly controversial in the nation's largest urban centers. This was especially the case in New York City, where its two largest minority groups—African Americans and Puerto Ricans—called increasingly for college admission of all their high school graduates to the multi-campus City University of New York (CUNY). This prospect, ultimately realized (see 26), focused national attention on the City College of New York, founded in 1847 and famed for its distinguished alumni.

Debates there over open admissions in the late 1960s among faculty, students, alumni, and extramural overseers of education heightened public partisanship coaxed by media scrutiny. The controversy, in popular and rather oversimplified terms, was whether the College should adopt as its primary goal "picking winners" from among its best academically qualified applicants or "making winners" from among the many who were admitted with a high school diploma, freely and untested. Or, to use another dichotomy, should college admission rest upon an "egalitarianism" of opportunity or upon an "elitism" of acceptance by tested academic merit.

James Traub, a writer and investigative journalist, considered the turmoil at City College, interviewed many people of varying opinions, and produced a book, here excerpted, that is the best description of the subject.

From City on a Hill: Testing the American Dream at City College by James Traub. (Cambridge, Mass., 1994): 4–5, 9, 13, 18, 69, 78–80, 204–5. Copyright © 1994 by James Traub. Reprinted by permission of Perseus Books PLC, a member of Perseus Books, L.L.C. Further reading: Leonard Kriegal, *Working Through: A Teacher's Journey in the Urban University* (New York, 1972); Robert E. Marshak, *Academic Renewal in the 1970s* (Washington, D.C., 1982); Mina Shaughnessy, *Errors and Expectations* (New York, 1977); and Jack E. Rossman, Helen S. Astin, Alexander W. Astin, and Elaine H. El-Khawas, *Open Admissions at City University of New York: An Analysis of the First Year* (Englewood Cliffs, NJ, 1975); and II, 24, 26.

No nation has created so large a middle class, and so prosperous a one, as we have. The forging of a middle-class nation from the ranks of unlettered immigrants and dirt farmers and the millions in the ghettos, generation after generation, is arguably America's greatest achievement, and the crowning glory of industrial capitalism. Our political stability, and the social equilibrium that has brewed in our melting pot, depend on the confidence of each new generation of the poor that they, too, will be inducted into an ever-expanding middle class—the faith that the American promise applies to them as much as to those who came before.

Plainly, something has gone wrong with this great process of assimilation. Poverty has become persistent, and apparently self-reinforcing, for millions of city dwellers, most of them black or Hispanic. The growth and endurance of this "underclass," despite thirty years of antipoverty efforts, are corroding our sense of shared purpose and shared interest, and exposing the bombast in our everlasting sense of moral superiority. . . . The failure to lift the poor into the middle class is thus a far graver national problem than the erosion of middle-class standards and expectations with which we are now so preoccupied. The market may rescue the middle class; it is clearly not rescuing the poor. And so we look, with increasing desperation, toward the institutions that have fostered social mobility in the past. . . .

In our heavily privatized, free-market society, the schools have been the public institutions we count on most for the great task of transformation. . . . We expect the public schools to compensate for the lottery of birth by offering to everyone the basic skills required for middle-class life. But that's not happening. . . .

As the public schools' task is set by the shortcomings and failures of the world around them, so City College's task is set by those disadvantages *and* the failures of the public schools to overcome them. The stakes are very high; but that uphill climb is extremely steep. . . .

It's impossible, at City College, not to look back. City is perhaps the longest-running radical social experiment in American history. Founded in 1847, City was America's first urban college, and it became one of the great democratizing institutions of an emerging urban culture. Tuition was free, and admission was open to anyone who qualified. And it wasn't second-rate goods, as the poor were accustomed to. A City College education was something fine. And a City College degree was a talisman, a magic key to the good life available in America. For the tens of thousands who went there, and the millions who knew of it, City College was a living emblem of the American Dream. . . .

City was, against all odds, one of America's great colleges. Between 1920 and 1970 more of its graduates went on to receive Ph.D. degrees than those of any other college except Berkeley, despite the fact that City had no graduate program of its own, no research facilities, nor even a very distinguished faculty. Eight graduates received the Nobel Prize, a record for a public institution. Of the cadre of New York Jewish intellectuals who grew up just before World War II, a remarkable fraction did their undergraduate studies at City College—not only Irving Howe but Irving Kristol, Daniel Bell, Seymour Martin Lipset, Alfred Kazin. Vast numbers of New York's accountants, and physicists, and teachers, attended City. And these graduates still speak of their college days with reverence.

What distinguished City from every other college at its level was its transformative mission. City did not reproduce privilege, as the Ivy League schools did. It gave poor, talented boys (women were not regularly accepted until after World War II) the opportunity to make it into the middle class; it compressed into a few years a process that otherwise took a few generations. City was the most meritocratic of institutions; and because the idea that a man should get ahead according to his abilities, rather than the accident of birth or background, was the core principle of America's free-market society, City had a moral status that no elite college could claim. . . .

But that promise was challenged by new realities. By the 1960s City's rigorous standards had come to seem like a perpetuation of privilege for the well educated, rather than a commitment to egalitarianism. The civil rights movement advanced the idea that blacks and other disadvantaged groups were being denied the right to develop the abilities that would allow them to compete in the marketplace. That was why the great forces of social mobility were failing for this generation of the poor. And City was an almost helplessly faithful register of the world around it: just as the college had symbolized for generations the meritocratic values of a new urban culture, and of America itself, so now it came to stand for the new principle of "equal opportunity," or, in the more contentious phrasing, "affirmative action." In 1969 black and Puerto Rican students shut down the campus to demand vastly greater access for minority students. There were marches and fires and fistfights, and an irrevocable taking of sides. It was a single moment that defined, in a burst of harsh light, the crisis that liberalism itself was undergoing. The racial challenge could not be either repudiated or accommodated without sacrificing cherished beliefs. Liberalism—the self-confident faith fueled by the engines of assimilation and progress—could not survive this shock. It was no wonder that many of those who viewed City as the incarnation of the American Dream reacted to the uprising as if a holy site had been desecrated.

The students won. City's admissions standards were lowered to open the college to those who had formerly been excluded. "Open admissions" shattered City's history into two parts, "before" and "after." But it also arguably represented continuity, or even consummation, for City was engaged once again in a radical social experiment and in the deeply American labor of transformation. The European immigrants didn't need City anymore; it was the black and Puerto Rican citizens of Harlem, the people who for years had looked up the hill at the remote campus, who needed it now. Because of its history, its before and after, City forced a comparison and a question: Could the forces of social mobility work on the new poor as they had on previous generations? . . .

City has a strange, hodgepodge academic identity that comes of this process of simultaneous accumulation and displacement. In certain respects City is very much a traditional liberal arts / professional college. Every student must pass through an extensive core curriculum, including courses such as World Humanities 101. City has a large and fairly accomplished English faculty, a wide variety of history electives, and several hundred students eager to read good books. The majority of students graduate in one of four professional schools—Engineering, Education, Nursing, and Architecture. City has a number of highly sophisticated programs in the sciences, including the Sophie Davis School of Medicine, an elite five-year program that enrolls 200 undergraduate students. At the same time, in recent decades City, like many other undergraduate colleges, has ramified upward into a quasi-university. Now there are 3,000 graduate students as well as 11,500 undergraduates. And doctoral programs in clinical psychology, physics, engineering, and several other fields are located on the City campus, though in fact they serve all students in the City University of New York, of which City College is a part.

But all of this is only the aboveground portion of the great massif that is City College. Hidden from view, and extending far downward, is City's vast remedial underworld. Three-quarters of City's entering freshmen are assigned to at least one remedial class, in language, math, or "college skills." These classes have hierarchies of their own. Students who hope to be engineers or architects may have to take, and of course pass, four remedial math courses. About a third of entering freshmen are admitted through what is known as the SEEK program, which offers access to senior college to students who cannot meet admissions standards and whose family income falls below a poverty threshold. Most of these students take remedial classes in all three fields. And City's English as a Second Language (ESL) program constitutes an entirely separate track, delicately known as "developmental" rather than "remedial." Another third of entering students begin in the ESL program, though owing to overlap the combined ESL/SEEK population is about half of any given freshman class. These students may spend years trudging upward toward the blue sky of the regular curriculum; many leave City College before even reaching core classes like Grazina Drabik's World Humanities 101. The students I saw there, in other words, represented a culled sample of City's entering class. One large body of students stretches below the core; another stretches above. It's only a slight exaggeration to say that City is really two colleges, a liberal arts / professional institution and a remedial / open admissions one....

My sixties liberalism may have been giving way around the edges, but it was still the basic shaping influence of my beliefs. I had grown up with the civil rights movement and the war on poverty; and their shortcomings or bad endings scarcely discredited the efforts themselves in my eyes. I believed in government activism, and I took it as a premise that a humane society focuses an important part of its energy on bringing the poor into the mainstream. I believed in the old-fashioned meritocratic principle that City College had arguably abandoned with open admissions, but I was also committed to the ideal of equal opportunity. It was troubling that in City College's history the two ideals seemed to rise and fall like the ends of a seesaw. But the zero-sum equation didn't seem inescapable, and in any case the sacrifice seemed small enough, and the gain great enough, to justify the bargain....

In the fall of 1970, open admissions hit the City College campus like the D-day landing. The previous fall 1,752 new students had registered for class; now the figure was 2,742, an increase of almost 60 percent. The freshman class would peak in 1971 at 3,216, and then fall off, for the simple reason that City College was not built for the volume of students considered normal in the Big Ten. Chaos reigned: Students stood in line for hours, sometimes for an entire day, just to register. The college rented space in a building down the hill at 134th Street to accommodate overflow classes. Great Hall, the cavernous space in Shepherd where grand and bitter debates had been staged for sixty years, was divided by partitions into a dozen classrooms. City had always been bulging at the edges and out at the elbows; but now the school felt like a rushing, bellowing madhouse. If the Board of Higher Education had decided to punish City for its impertinence, it had succeeded admirably....

In the early 1970s open admissions was a burning, bitter issue for policy intellectuals, fraught with symbolic overtones. Like school desegregation, the other great issue of the day, it represented a massive attempt by the state to transform the lives of the poor by giving them access to a good enjoyed by the middle class. In fact open admissions was often posed as the means to desegregate higher education. For people on the Left, open admissions represented the commitment, begun in the civil rights era, to confer full citizenship on black Americans. For conservatives it represented the vanity of social

engineering and the breakdown of the liberal state in the face of impossible demands. And this was especially true for the neoconservatives who considered themselves the heirs of an abandoned tradition of postwar liberalism. Many of the neoconservatives were City College alumni like Irving Kristol and Seymour Martin Lipset. For them, City College's demise was of a piece with what they saw as the collapse of national values in the 1960s.

In 1972 the Council for Basic Education, a Washington-based think tank, sponsored a symposium on open admissions in which Kristol was one of half a dozen panelists. Kristol denounced open admissions as "a fraud." And it was, he continued, a fraud with a critically important moral: "To think that you can take large numbers of students from a poor socio-economic background, who do badly in high school, who do badly on all your standardized tests . . . who show no promise, and who do not show much motivation—to think you can take large numbers of such students and somehow make them benefit from a college education instead of merely wasting their time and their money, I say that this is demonstrably false. . . . Schools just cannot do that much and colleges simply cannot accomplish this mission." Kristol conceded that his skepticism about the power of institutions "runs against the grain of our American ideology—by now an American instinct—which asserts that it is always in man's power to abolish injustice and inequity, if only the will to justice and equity is strong enough." But, he said, "that proposition, quintessentially American though it be, happens to be false."

This was too much for Kenneth Clark, the black psychologist whose research had been instrumental in shaping the Supreme Court's decision in *Brown v. Board of Education.* Clark had taught at City College for decades, and he insisted that Kristol and others were gilding City's past with retrospective glory in order to discredit the present. Like so many other supporters of open admissions, Clark asserted that higher education had never performed the intellectual function that the neoconservatives were now urging on it. He had, he said, "given up" trying to infuse scholarly values into higher education, "because I think a more concrete and immediate battle is to open up higher education in America on what I consider questionable values . . . to a larger proportion of the American people." Here was the argument for credentialism in pure form—open admissions without illusions.

But Clark had devoted his entire career to proving that disadvantaged children were victims of their environment, and to arguing for reform of that environment. If he was cynical about the values of the academy, he was deeply idealistic about the human capacity for change and growth—about potential. "Institutions, and particularly schools, do perform miracles," Clark retorted to Kristol. "And one of the miracles which I think he is ignoring is the miracle of taking a precious human being and dehumanizing him. . . . A kind of amoral cynicism permits this miracle to continue when it actually could be remedied and solved, and I think those of us who believe that institutions are important in affecting lives of human beings cannot permit ourselves to be seduced by your perspective."

Open admissions was one of those fundamental questions about which, finally, you had to make an almost existential choice. Realism said: It doesn't work. Idealism said: It *must*. . . .

CUNY's record, and City's, is not as poor as it is because the institutions discriminate against the students they enroll, but because the students themselves are so heavily disadvantaged both socially and academically; every study of retention vindicates that conclusion. The figures actually show that City and CUNY are doing a relatively good job in overwhelmingly adverse conditions. But in absolute terms, a college dropout rate of 55 percent is still stunning (so is the national rate of 40 percent). What is to be done to solve this massive problem of "fit"? It wont help to *raise* standards, since City already loses students because of its standards. The premise behind proposals to raise standards in the high schools, such as the College Preparatory Initiative, is that it is the student, and not the institution, that must change. The dropout problem might well be eased by *lowering* standards, however, as in various ways the partisans of the new student have proposed.

Why insist, as with the CPI, that the student rise to the level of the institution, rather than having the institution sink to the level of the student? Why not make it easier to get a degree, when a degree means so very much? There can be only one answer: Because if you do, you will no longer have a college. You will have a job-training institute, a social-service agency, a passport-stamping office. Higher education's overwhelming economic importance leads it into precisely these roles. But the intellectual values that have traditionally informed college life pull it in the opposite direction, toward engagement with ideas rather than with students' disabilities.

City College lives at the intersection of these two principles. It cannot fully satisfy both. The only way to ensure that it flourishes as a fine professional and liberal arts institution, as it once did, is to recognize the limits of its social mission. City, and any other college that aspires to high academic standards, cannot be asked to educate large numbers of deeply, disadvantaged students. . . . It's not unreasonable to ask that students who complete high school without the academic credits detailed in the College Preparatory Initiative complete them elsewhere, presumably in a community college. . . . And City cannot allow its commitment to remedy disadvantage to lead to the sort of "social promotion" that has such a demoralizing impact on the high schools. City must accept students who have a decent chance of succeeding, ply them with help, and then insist that they satisfy not only high expectations but high standards.

26. Benno C. Schmidt,
CUNY: An Institution Adrift, 1999

The egalitarian ideal of opening college classes to all high school graduates (22, 23) met its major test at the City University of New York (CUNY). By the mid-1960s, two of the largest minority groups in New York City, African Americans and Puerto Ricans, became increasingly insistent on seeing their path to higher education widened. In compliance with the federal Civil Rights Act of 1964, the first official ethnic survey of students at the multicampus CUNY in 1967 found that African-American and Puerto Rican enrollment had increased "significantly" to 15,500, or 13 percent of the student body of 121,000. Throughout the next year Chancellor Albert Bowker (1919–2005) kept pushing for more university enrollment and planning to have a 1969 freshman class of 26 percent African Americans and Puerto Ricans that would capture the top one hundred graduates from the city's sixty-six academic high schools, including those in disadvantaged areas. The Higher Education Board of CUNY unanimously went with Bowker's plan in November 1966, and the New York State Regents likewise endorsed CUNY's request for open admissions to all high school graduates—this while several faculty groups and various city and statewide officeholders were charging that the policy would lower academic standards. When in September 1970 CUNY began classes with the open enrollment plan, 33 percent of the freshmen were African-American or Puerto Rican. Upon testing 80 percent of these students, over one-half of them were shown to be in varying need of remedial help in reading, math, or both. For two decades CUNY had struggled with the academic handicap of remediation, accompanied by underfunding, lack of common guidelines for its many campuses, and falling faculty morale.

Mayor Rudolph Giuliani made "open admissions" and the weakness of the CUNY four-year colleges a political issue. Thereupon he appointed a mayoral task force chaired by Benno Schmidt (1942–), who at that time headed Edison Schools, Inc. Earlier Schmidt had clerked for Earl Warren at the U.S. Supreme Court (1966–67), had worked briefly at the Justice Department, and then had gone on to the Harlan Fiske Stone Professorship of Law at Columbia (1969–86). Thereafter he returned to his alma mater, Yale (B.A. 1963; J.D. 1966), as professor of law and president (1986–92). Later in 2003 Schmidt was appointed chair of the CUNY Board of Trustees, and at year's end he boasted that CUNY had become "the pride of the city," having made "stunning" progress over five years. He noted a rise of 100 points in SAT scores of students admitted to CUNY's five senior colleges; he mentioned the rising number of black, Hispanic, and Asian entrants; he claimed a 50 percent increase in grants and contracts; and he emphasized the addition of 625 full-time faculty to make a total faculty body of 5600.

The Schmidt Report, here excerpted, was a lengthy, detailed, and sharp indictment. It brought wide publicity and some significant though gradual changes at CUNY. It stressed that the major obstacle to reaching the ideal college experience for all high school graduates in order to shape an informed democratic citizenry was the shocking lack of preparation among so many incoming students. Attention to remediation took away more time and resources from an overburdened faculty than effective teaching could withstand without common guidelines. It bluntly laid responsibility for this situation at the door of the city's public schools and their administration. The report insisted that this disgrace did not belong to the students', no matter what their economic or social disadvantages, but to their schooling.

Benno C. Schmidt Jr., "The City University of New York: An Institution Adrift," *Report of the Mayor's Advisory Task Force on the City University of New York*, June 7, 1999, Chairman. Mayor's Office, New York City, New York, pp. 11, 13, 19, 21–22, 25, 31, and 37–38. Further reading: *New York Times*, December 17, 2003; and II, 23–24.

The City University of New York is adrift. Its graduation rates are low, and the relatively small number of students who succeed take longer to earn degrees than in other public universities. At a time when the public schools and most other public universities are increasing enrollment, most CUNY senior colleges are losing enrollment. Accountability is largely ignored in its governance processes, and there is little strategy or planning in the way it allocates its resources. Academic standards are loose and confused, and CUNY lacks the basic information necessary to make sound judgments about what works and what doesn't. It is inundated by graduates of the New York City Public Schools who lack basic academic skills, but it has not made a strong effort to get the public schools to raise their standards. It conducts remediation on a massive scale, but lacks objective information about the effectiveness of its remediation efforts. Its full-time faculty is shrinking, aging and losing ground. Part-time faculty has increased by leaps and bounds and now delivers the majority of CUNY's teaching, which almost guarantees institutional anomie. An institution of critical importance to New York and the nation, potentially a model of excellence and educational opportunity to public universities throughout the world, CUNY currently is in a spiral of decline.

CUNY has never really come to grips with what it means to be a university system. Its very constitution, its system architecture, remains to be drawn out of the inertia of the past. To illustrate, CUNY is unique among public universities anywhere of size, in having not a single four-year college that is in the top-tier of public institutions nationwide in the academic quality of its entering students. Every other system of size has multiple campuses in this category. The State University of New York ("SUNY") has ten. California, nine. Florida has five public institutions that are top tier. Wisconsin, five. CUNY has never articulated a strategy that New Yorkers are less in need of top-tier public institutions, among the range of higher education opportunities provided, than are the citizens served by other large public university systems in the country. Nor could it. It just happened. Institutional outcomes of such

fundamental importance should be the result of thoughtful planning not drift. This is only one symptom of CUNY's failure, in contrast to other public university systems, to embrace mission differentiation among its various institutions.

This downward spiral can be and must be reversed. CUNY can be and should be a model for the nation of urban higher public education. The improvement of public education at all levels, kindergarten through college, and especially in our cities, is America's most important public policy objective. Nothing is more important to the future well-being of New York City. At the eve of a new century, the United States urgently needs a model of the urban public university. CUNY can and should be this model. The creation of first-rate urban higher education opportunities is as crucial to our nation in the 21st century as was the creation of the great land-grant universities in the 19th century.

At the outset, the Task Force wishes to emphasize its absolute commitment to CUNY's historic institutional mission: to provide access to first-rate college and graduate-degree opportunities for all New Yorkers ready and able to take advantage of community and senior college education in the liberal arts, sciences, and the professions. The Task Force applauds CUNY's special commitment to students who, by reason of jobs, family responsibilities, or lack of financial means, must struggle to avail themselves of higher education opportunities. We believe this mission embraces a special openness to New York's immigrant population and to adults who wish to resume their education after some years in other pursuits.

This is not casual rhetoric. . . . We have considered whether other institutions, public or private, could perhaps better serve CUNY's purposes. We have asked ourselves whether CUNY might be better off as part of SUNY, or whether it should be disintegrated, leaving its constituent campuses to go their own way. Our response is clear.

CUNY's historic mission has never been more critical to the well being of New York and the nation; access to higher education of quality will become more and more important as time goes on. For individuals living in the age of information and the global economy, a college education is the essential foundation for a life of opportunity. For cities, states, and nations, the educational capacity of their citizenry will be more and more the decisive factor in prosperity and the quality of life. This is especially the case for New York City.

The cty is gaining population, and gains are especially large among young people who need a first-rate education. During the 1990's, NYCPS enrollment increased by over 100,000 students, an increase of 12.5%. More than one-third of New York City's graduating high school seniors will look to CUNY for their opportunity for higher education.

The ethnic composition of New York City is undergoing dramatic change. During the 1990's, the white population of New York City declined by 19.3%, while the black, Hispanic and Asian populations have risen by 5.2%, 19.3%, and 53.5%, respectively. These trends are projected to continue into the next century. For the past three decades, blacks, Hispanics, and Asians have been over-represented among CUNY students, relative to their levels in the labor force. New York City must improve the educational opportunities available to all its citizens, but this is most urgently the case regarding disadvantaged students and blacks, Hispanics and immigrants. Because so many low-income and minority students look to CUNY for their college opportunities these demographic shifts and existing patterns of educational deprivation mean that CUNY will be even more vital to the City's well-being in the future than it has been in the past. . . .

The Trustees have insisted on phasing out remediation at the senior colleges, and some of the senior colleges, in particular Baruch and Queens, have been moving independently in this direction. This move by the Trustees does more than simply deal with remediation. It sends a clear message that CUNY must embrace a sensible differentiation of academic mission as between the senior and community colleges and that the senior colleges must be colleges rather than the passive receiving ends of eroded standards and failed policies of social promotion in the public schools. The Trustees deserve praise for insisting on their positions, despite the predictable furor raised by defenders of the status quo. . . .

We wish to stress the limits of our capacity and our wisdom. CUNY is an extremely large, diverse, and confusing agglomeration of individual institutions shaped over many decades and by local and often parochial interests. Its information systems are poor. The data necessary to make informed judgments about quality and productivity are often lacking or inconsistent. . . . We suspect that we have been more successful in identifying problems that need urgent attention than in fashioning particular solutions. Moreover, we are acutely aware that the issues we address—how to reconcile access and excellence in higher education, how to create effective governance in public universities, how to bring accountability to higher education, how to manifest high standards in urban public education, how to assure that education serves rather than frustrates equal opportunity—are among the most daunting and controversial questions facing our society. Accordingly, the Task Force has tried to approach its work with an appropriate humility and what Learned Hand liked to call "the spirit of liberty—the spirit that is not too sure it is right."

But an appropriate humility in the face of issues of profound importance must not lead to continued drift. It is time for action. CUNY is in peril. . . . Clear, rigorous standards of academic achievement must be the foundation of CUNY's commitment to educational opportunity. In view of the critical importance of CUNY to New York City, the State, and the Nation, we must follow the wisdom of another great American, Louis D. Brandeis: "If we would guide by the light of reason, we must let our minds be bold." The time is ripe.

When open admissions was inaugurated three decades ago, CUNY recognized that many students entering CUNY were not prepared for college work at either the baccalaureate or the associate degree level, and it resolved that the University should undertake to help those students succeed. The Task Force believes that remediation is still an appropriate and valuable endeavor for CUNY community colleges to undertake. We salute CUNY's willingness to step into the breach for high school graduates whom the schools have failed, immigrants, and returning adults.

While CUNY's commitment to providing remediation is laudable, we believe that in many important respects the way CUNY goes about remediation is flawed. Indeed, the whole remediation enterprise seems slapdash and symptomatic of the acute problems in CUNY's governance. In the first place, CUNY has failed to do its part in reducing the need for postsecondary remediation. . . . In addition, the Task Force has identified the following problem areas, which we discuss below:

- the extensive remedial needs of CUNY's incoming freshmen;
- problems with CUNY's student assessment testing program;
- CUNY's failure to institute systematic, objective remedial exit standards;
- CUNY's failure to ensure that remediation is effective;
- the relationship between financial aid and remediation; and
- the costs of remediation at CUNY.

The fact that significant numbers of CUNY students are underprepared may not be surprising. Indeed, the poor performance of the City's public schools, in combination with CUNY's failure to institute clear, objective admissions standards, effectively guarantees this unfortunate circumstance. But the Task Force has been shocked by both the scale and the depth of CUNY students' remediation needs. Because 60% of CUNY's incoming freshmen are NYCPS graduates, our description of CUNY's incoming students is largely a description of the public school system's graduates. The data points to an urgent need to help the City's public school students acquire verbal and math skills long before they arrive at CUNY. . . .

CUNY does not fulfill its access mission merely by opening its doors and giving needy New Yorkers a "shot" at a college education. Providing meaningful access requires ensuring that the open door does not become a revolving door.

While the educational level of CUNY's incoming freshmen constitutes a baseline against which one might assess the value added by a CUNY education, and while it may help to explain why CUNY's graduation rates are so much lower than national and state averages, it should not be construed as providing excuses for the system's failure—over the course of three decades—to provide effective programs or demonstrate positive student outcomes.

CUNY conducts remediation on a huge scale. Nationally, about 40% of public community college freshmen take one or more remedial courses, compared with the 87% of CUNY's community college freshmen who failed one or more of CUNY's remedial placement tests. About 22% of the freshmen attending public four-year colleges take one or more remedial courses, compared with the 72% of CUNY senior college freshmen who failed one or more placement tests. At public institutions with high minority student populations, about 43% of freshmen take remedial courses; the percentage of CUNY freshmen who failed one or more placement tests is almost double that. This means more than 9,000 entering community college students and more than 10,000 entering senior college students go into remediation each year at CUNY. In sum, remedial activity at CUNY is roughly three times the national norm for public colleges and universities.

Perhaps even more disturbing is the fact that 55% of CUNY freshmen fail more than one remediation test. Fully half of all entering CUNY students (61% at community colleges, 43% at senior colleges) are deficient in reading, the most basic of the basic skills. Thus, it is the depth of CUNY students' remediation needs, as well as the absolute scale of remediation activity at CUNY that reveals the appalling educational deprivation of so many entering CUNY students.

It is very troubling that most of the entering students requiring such heavy remediation are recent graduates of New York City public high schools. The scale and depth of remediation at CUNY should be a call to arms for the City's public schools. . . .

There is a widespread impression that CUNY's extraordinarily high levels of remediation, as well as other features such as longer time to degree and low graduation rates, are a result of certain unique characteristics of the CUNY student body: that it is "nontraditional" in being much older (many more adults and parents with family responsibilities), that it includes many working students, that the students are disproportionately poor, that there are higher percentages of immigrants for whom English is not their native language, and that there are higher percentages of racial minorities. There is some truth to these points, but the characteristics of CUNY's students do not explain CUNY's problems.

The Task Force does not dispute the incredible diversity of CUNY's student body. But in the thirty years since open admissions was established, CUNY has done far too little to tailor the traditional college model to its "nontraditional" student body.

Black and Hispanic students each make up just under one-third of CUNY freshmen, whites make up one-quarter, and Asian students one-eighth. Thirty percent of CUNY students reported that they are or have been married, and almost as many say they are supporting children. Half of CUNY's freshmen are foreign-born, though only 16% report that they are most comfortable in a language other than English.

The high average age of CUNY's undergraduates . . . is due in large part to the fact that both NYCPS and CUNY students take much longer than average to graduate. It is also interesting to note that CUNY's older students require remediation at slightly lower rates than the younger students. . . .

CUNY's different campuses each employ a wide variety of remedial approaches. For example, some campuses believe in immersion and strict time limits, while others believe remediation works best over longer periods of time if students work on basic skills while they are taking substantive, college courses. Moreover, CUNY's remediation instructors are largely free to design the courses they teach. There is nothing wrong with a system of institutions such as CUNY approaching remediation in different ways. A healthy competition among approaches will produce innovation, efficiency, and choice. But this only happens if there is an effort to measure what works and useful information about outcomes is made available.

Given the large scale and variety of its remediation efforts, CUNY ought to be the world's leading repository of knowledge about
- the cognitive needs of different types of remediation students;
- which instructional methods are most effective;
- which professors with what kind of training are most effective; and
- which institutions are best able to focus their energy and skills on remediation programs that work. . . .

Curiously, CUNY as a system appears to be agnostic about these questions. CUNY has made little effort to determine which approaches work well or badly for particular student populations. Neither we nor CUNY knows whether and how many remediation students are in fact mastering basic academic skills sufficient for college readiness. Moreover, there has been little analysis to determine which of CUNY's various institutions and programs are best suited to provide which types of remediation. . . .

Degree programs in senior and community colleges have extremely important work to do with very limited resources of money and time. Any baccalaureate program worthy of the name must educate students broadly in the humanities, the natural sciences and the social sciences; encourage a critical independence of intellect and judgment; enable lucid writing and speaking; and require in-depth study of at least one major academic discipline. Students who cannot read or write at college levels, or lack mathematical understanding necessary to study the natural sciences, economics, or political science, will not only be frustrated in their own efforts, but will undermine the ability of other students and faculty to pursue their work. If they are awarded degrees, their degrees will lose their value as educational credentials. . . .

Admissions standards should be different for community college associate's degree programs, but are no less essential. Associate's degree programs prepare students for critically important careers in which success absolutely depends on certain basic academic skills. To paraphrase John Gardner, a first-rate nurse is infinitely more valuable to society than a second-rate philosopher. Nurses, x-ray technicians, real estate brokers, bookkeepers, computer programmers, and secretaries all need to know how to read, to handle numbers, to manage technical documents, to communicate effectively orally and in writing. The academic skills may be less than those required for baccalaureate programs for accountants, financial analysts, teachers or those preparing for graduate study, but it is equally critical that standards be clear, be assessed, and be satisfied.

Accordingly, one of the most constructive steps that CUNY can take to renew itself and to help NYCPS raise standards is to promulgate a spectrum of clear, objective admission requirements, keyed to the academic preparation required for different types of institutions and programs. . . .

CUNY must recognize remediation for what it is. Remediation at CUNY may be necessary and legitimate to keep open the doors of opportunity. But in the case of high school graduates coming directly to college, remediation is an unfortunate necessity, thrust upon the colleges by the failure of the schools, and a distraction from the main business of the University.

It is too obvious for argument that the best time and place for students to learn to read and write and to understand math is in school. Primary and secondary schools that fail to equip their students with these basic academic skills are not only failing to prepare them for college, but denying them an elementary education as well. Students who arrive at college unable to read, write or compute have already wasted much of their opportunity for learning. The fact that CUNY should not abandon such students does not diminish the tragic failure of educational opportunity such students have already suffered.

By the same token, every hour and every dollar spent by CUNY teaching recent high school graduates what they should have learned in school is time and money diverted from CUNY's central mission. CUNY was not conceived to be a second-chance high school. The City and the State have invested CUNY with a different mandate: to offer first-rate college-level programs to those who are prepared to succeed. Accordingly, remediation should exist in due proportion to the central work of the University.

Lifelong Learning

27. John Sawhill, "Lifelong Learning," 1979

A modern Princetonian (A.B. 1958) in the nation's service, John Crittenden Sawhill (1936–2000) received his doctorate at New York University (1963) while also a dean at the School of Business Administration. Following employment with business firms, he served the federal government in various capacities until he returned to New York University as president (1975–79). His membership in President Carter's cabinet as secretary of energy was short-lived (1979–81). From 1990 until his death he was president of the Nature Conservancy, which became the world's largest private conservation group and the nation's fourteenth largest nonprofit institution.

John C. Sawhill, "Lifelong Learning: Scandal of the Next Decade?" *Change* 10 (December–January 1978–79): 7, 80. Reprinted with permission of the Helen Dwight Reid Educational Foundation. Published by Heldref Publications, 1319 Eighteenth St. NW, Washington, D.C. 20036-1802 Copyright © 1980. Further reading: Ron Chernow, "John Sawhill: Academe's Crisis Manager," *Change* 11 (May–June 1979): 32–41, 70; and Verne A. Stadtman, *Academic Adaptations: Higher Education Prepares for the 1980's and 1990's* (San Francisco, 1980), 151–67.

Higher education is approaching the territory of lifelong learning with standards, forethought, and a sense of dignity reminiscent of the California Gold Rush. Now that many young people are already being kept in school until their mid- or even late twenties, the rest of the adult population looks like the last frontier for educators, and institutions are eager to stake their claims. This drive for the high noon of the life cycle has brought some new vigor to our colleges and universities, but the competition for students has also produced a cornucopia of dubious offerings. At a university in Ohio, for example, students now are able to earn two hours of academic credit by riding roller coasters and writing about their experiences, at a cost of $65 tuition plus $10 for the rides (see "From What We Gather," *Change*, September 1978). The classic example of basket weaving looks almost philosophical compared with what has followed it. Can we name any human experience, no matter how recreational, private, or trivial, and be certain today that some institution of higher learning is not offering credit for it?

At the same time, competition for students has contributed to the practice of giving credit even for life experiences outside the academic purview. Originally, this type of special credit was awarded as advanced standing to adults who, having engaged in years of work or reading, had satisfied the substance of certain requirements. Unfortunately, some institutions have abused this admirable system by their willingness to offer credit for experience that does not have a normal academic parallel. After all, a college degree is not a certificate for years of successful living. When adults can demonstrate that certain of their experiences are comparable to existing courses at an institution, the practice of awarding credit is appropriate and respectable. When credits are simply dangled in a bid for student dollars, without a firm academic basis, the practice is disreputable.

The quest for lifelong learning, or at least for offering and earning credits in adulthood, has arisen from several sources. On the side of supply, institutions have responded to the decline in the pool of traditional applicants by casting about for new clienteles. On the demand side, adults have been deeply affected by the psychology of self-development, by the women's movement, by rapid shifts in the job market, by recertification requirements in certain professions, and by a combination of leisure time and discretionary income. Perhaps most deeply, adults are influenced by the widespread feeling that one is never too old to learn.

In response to motives such as these, colleges and universities have of course brought forth not only the sort of questionable programs already mentioned, but a wide range of extraordinary opportunities for adults. The prima ballerina in the Danish ballet, an editor of *Time*, the commissioner of business and finance in the Carey administration, a publishing tycoon's wife, an internationally known Chinese chef, and the president of the world's largest public relations firm probably have only one thing in common: They are all in the process of earning bachelor's degrees at New York University. What do these accomplished adults want from higher education? I do not believe that, on the whole, they are seeking an amusement park ride. I think, for example, of a *New York Times* article featuring a retired grandfather who decided to earn a college degree after a prosperous career in business. He selected one of the most demanding programs available, because, as he told the reporter, "I did not want a school that offered the educational equivalent of baby food—mashed, strained, predigested courses specially designed for 'mature' students . . . I wanted to be taught, marked, judged by the same standards applicable to all new college students. I wanted to be bound by the same course requirements and discipline."

As president of a large and diverse university, with a long tradition in the field of educating adults, I believe that we face a twin challenge as higher education moves into an era of lifelong learning. On the one hand, we must live up to the expectations of adults like this grandfather who arrive in our classrooms not as seniors just out of high school but as citizens with decades of experience as professionals and perhaps parents. On the other hand, we have to keep in mind that not all adults are as disciplined as the one I have quoted, not as self-confident, not as well informed nor as able to discriminate among the vast array of courses and programs available. To these potential learners we owe a duty that goes well beyond the cynical motto *caveat emptor*, which allows us to abdicate our prime responsibility as educators. . . .

Historically, adult education has suffered second-class status in many institutions, in part because the vocational needs of mature students were disdained by many professors, in part because certain subjects cannot be properly appreciated by students dipping back briefly into formal education, and in part perhaps because some faculty may have felt more comfortable with young students than with people with an experience of the world which an academic could not always match. In any case, adult students came to be viewed as less malleable, less worthy of academic ministrations than students of traditional age. Often the adults were kept segregated in special programs tolerated by the university as money makers.

Disdain for a group of clients is a danger sign in any profession, and perhaps especially in teaching. . . .

In a period when adults (and other "nontraditional" students) will play a much larger role in higher education, we need to assure a first-class experience for them, not only in order to appeal effectively over the long term but also in order to maintain the standards and integrity of our own institutions and the degrees we offer. . . .

According to federal projections, 11 million people over the age of 35 will be studying for bachelor's degrees by 1980. Millions more will be enrolled in continuing education courses, certificate programs, and advanced degree programs. If we respond adroitly to the real needs of these diverse learners, higher education can profit not only financially but in the quality of its whole internal environment. If we seek this clientele but fail to serve them adequately, lifelong learning could be the scandal of the next decade.

The Soul of the University

28. Arthur Levine, "The Soul of the University," 2000

Following his bachelor's work in biology at Brandeis (1970) and a doctorate at SUNY-Buffalo (1976), Arthur Elliott Levine (1948–) became an invigorating and imaginative presence in higher education. First associated with the Carnegie Foundation in its Policy Studies in Higher Education, Berkeley (1975–80), and its Washington Center (1980–82), he went on to serve as president of Bradford College (1982–89), chair the Institute for Educational Management at Harvard (1989–94); he became president of Teacher's College, Columbia in 1994. In 2006 he assumed the presidency of the Woodrow Wilson National Fellowship Foundation. Among his articles, books, and opinion pieces appeared this essay in the *New York Times*.

Arthur Levine, "The Soul of the University," *New York Times*, March 13, 2000, A21. Reprinted with permission of the *New York Times*; Copyright © 2000. Further reading: Levine, *Quest for Common Learning* (Washington, D.C., 1982), *Shaping Higher Education's Future* (San Francisco, 1989), and *Higher Learning in America* (Baltimore, 1993).

In "The Education of Henry Adams," describing his college experience under a curriculum that had not changed in several decades, Adams said he had received an 18th century education when the world was plunging toward the 20th. In a space of just a few years, education had fallen 200 years behind the times.

Today's pace of economic, social and, above all, technological change has put higher education in danger of falling behind again. And this time, pressures from outside are likely to force those of us who shape the academy not only to adapt our institutions, but to transform them.

In the decades after World War II, higher education was a growth industry. Governments around the world, eager for better educated populations, supported it with few questions asked. Today it is a mature industry, and in return for continuing support, through direct funding, grants and student aid, government is asking a good many questions. How much should faculty teach? What's the appropriate balance between teaching and research?

How much should it cost to educate a student? Should we have lifetime appointments for faculty? Why aren't graduation rates higher? Why does it take students so long to graduate?

Once higher education could simply add new activities to the old, but the current wisdom is that it must do more with less. We in academia must figure out what is really critical to us and what we are willing to give up.

Not all of these choices will be ours alone. Our students, as well as our governments, have changing expectations. Information economies require higher levels of education and more frequent education. More of the new student body may be part time, working and older.

I asked some students in this new breed what relationship they wanted with their colleges. They told me that it should be like the relationship with a utility company, supermarket or bank—their emphasis was on convenience, service, quality and affordability. This group is going to gravitate toward online instruction, with education at home or in the workplace.

The rise of online education and other new technologies has enormous implications for all of us. Textbooks are dying. We're moving to learning materials that can be customized for the students who are in our classes. There won't be any excuse for those of us who are still using yellowed notes to teach our courses year after year.

An article in an airline magazine last year said that travel agencies of the future will show customers virtual trips, letting them see, by computer, the hotel room they'll stay in, walk the beaches, see the restaurants. The time is coming when colleges and universities will do something similar: instead of telling students about 15th-century Paris, for example, we will take them there. And when a student can smell the smells—which must have been putrid,

walk the cobblestones, go into the buildings, how will a stand-up lecture compete?

It is possible right now for a professor to give a lecture in Cairo, for me to attend that lecture at Teachers College and for another student to attend it in Tokyo. It's possible for all of us to feel we're sitting in the same classroom. It's possible for me to nudge (via e-mail) the student from Tokyo and say, " 'I missed the professor's last comment. What was it?' "; have my question translated into Japanese; have the answer back in English in seconds. It's possible for the professor to point to me and my Japanese colleague and say, " 'I want you to prepare a project for next week's class.' " If we can do all of that, and the demographics of higher education are changing so greatly, why do we need the physical plant called the college?

Many countries built systems of higher education based on propinquity, trying to build a campus in easy proximity of every citizen. How long will it be before nations ask why they have so many campuses? How long before they ask higher education to request new technologies, not new buildings? This is where growth of the private sector in higher education comes in.

In the United States alone, higher education is an industry with revenues of $225 billion, and that is causing the private sector to look at postsecondary education as a potential target for investment.

One corporate entrepreneur recently told me: "You know, you're in an industry which is worth hundreds of billions of dollars, and you have a reputation for low productivity, high cost, bad management and no use of technology. You're going to be the next health care: a poorly managed nonprofit industry which was overtaken by the profit-making sector."

An amazing phenomenon is the for-profit University of Phoenix, which has all the appropriate accreditation and is traded on the stock exchange. It would like to reach 200,000 students within the next decade and is already online with more than 6,000. It has thrown out most of what higher education does traditionally, using mostly part-time faculty. Class syllabuses are uniform and prepared every few years with help from industry professionals and academics in the field.

Phoenix is the nation's largest proprietary institution, and entrepreneurs around the world are watching its example. Investment firms are developing higher education practices. Venture capital groups are starting to put money into higher education enterprises. I recently saw a list 30 pages long, single-spaced, of for-profit firms that have entered higher education internationally.

Not long ago a questioner at a conference asked what my biggest fear was. I answered: "I think in the next few years we're going to see some firm begin to hire well-known faculty at our most prestigious campuses and offer an all-star degree over the Internet. So they'll take the best faculty from Columbia,

Oxford and Tokyo University and offer a program at a lower cost than we can."

A top-notch professor on our campus touches a couple of hundred students a year. The lower-paid online professor may touch thousands. The economics is not in our favor.

After the speech, a fellow came up to me and said, "Who told you?" I said, "What do you mean, 'Who told me?' This isn't rocket science." He said: "We're doing this. Who leaked?" The simple fact is that we're going to see an increasing number of these enterprises.

The biggest danger is that higher education may be the next railroad industry, which built bigger and better railroads decade after decade because that's the business it thought it was in. The reality was that it was in the transportation industry, and it was nearly put out of business by airplanes. Colleges and universities are not in the campus business, but the education business.

The trend is a convergence in knowledge-producing organizations: publishers, television networks, libraries, museums, universities. The head of technology at a large publisher told me recently, "We're not in the book business anymore." When I asked what business he was in, he answered: "We're in the knowledge business. Our big focus now is teacher education. We're using television and we're using computers, and we're in thousands of schools. We want to put our brand name on professional development for teachers."

The "content people," he went on, "are on staff, not at universities." As for credits and degrees, "we're working on that," he said.

In the years ahead, every knowledge-producing organization will begin to produce similar kinds of products. Those of us in higher education have a small amount of time to stop and think. What is the purpose of higher education? How shall we continue to accomplish it? Not to answer these questions is to make a profound decision, by default, about our own prospects for the future.

Part III   Liberal Arts

The liberal arts education derives from the humanist education of the Renaissance, constituting the *trivium* and the *quadrivium,* to prepare men for public life. That ideal of liberal learning endured for centuries, and for most of that time the content and even the sequence was fixed, as was its masculinity. In the nineteenth and especially the twentieth century, public life became more inclusive, and so did the logic of liberal education. Indeed, for some, the rubric "general education" was substituted for liberal education to distinguish its modern form from its aristocratic and male inheritance. The expansion of academic knowledge, encouraging and encouraged by specialization, pointed toward the proliferation of fields, courses, and course election, beginning with the introduction of electives at Harvard in 1869 (1–2). Pluralization of the curriculum transformed the meaning and the structure of a liberal education. Since then the discussion of the liberal arts has been discussed as the relation of a "core" to "specialized" work, and the curricular challenge has been to determine their relative importance and relations. Finding the proper balance or proportions involved the structure of the academy as well as considerations of content. As the academy grew, epistemic pluralism was inevitable, making discussions of general content quite difficult. There was, in addition, a tension built into the definition of the modern humanities between the work of preserving and passing on culture and the work of nourishing critical thought among free persons in a free society (3).

The baseline for postwar discussions of curricula was Harvard's Red Book, but by the late 1960s and 1970s there was a general move toward reconsideration of the liberal arts, at Harvard (5) as well as elsewhere. The spectrum of approaches ranged from the bold and synthetic, as in Daniel Bell's proposal *The Reforming of General Education at Columbia* (1966), to the neotraditional teaching of the classics of western thought largely independent of historical context (4, 6). The political and academic turmoil of the 1960s and 1970s also raised the question of whether the sharp focus upon—some might say defense of—western culture was parochial. This issue produced deep cultural divisions, both inside and outside the academy, and the controversy came to be called the "culture wars" (7–10). The debates

were rarely edifying, as is evident in the transcript of a televised confrontation between the pugnacious William Bennett, former chair of the National Endowment of the Humanities and secretary of education, and Donald Kennedy, the president of Stanford University, where, according to Bennett, curricular reform had "trashed" western civilization (7, but cf. 11). More impressive was Sidney Hook's engagement with Allan Bloom, a fellow conservative, who had blasted higher education, particularly for its alleged lapse into relativism (8–9). Most significant of all, however, was the shifting of the debate from lists of books and courses to a consideration of just what qualities of mind and character constitute the aim of a liberal arts education, which implicitly made the point that there is no fixed or eternal content to being liberally educated. A liberal education in this framing is a curriculum that enables one to explore and fulfill one's humanity. The only constant of liberal education, according to William Cronon (13), lies in acquiring a capacity to make connections between talking and listening, between different bodies of analytical and aesthetic knowledge, between oneself and one's community and other individuals and societies marked by cultural difference.

For all the writing and talking and teaching about the liberal arts in the half century since 1945, study of the arts and sciences, the home of liberal education, declined, slowly but noticeably. After the war nearly 50 percent of students pursued liberal arts degrees, but by the end of the century the percentage had fallen to no more than a quarter, with the humanities dropping to about 5 percent (14; IV, 4). It was not that the number of liberal arts majors had dropped (although statistics are imperfect) but rather that newer, more vocational fields absorbed the expansion of higher education while the liberal arts, not keeping pace, looked more and more like a periphery than a "core." Aside from very selective private universities and colleges, it became difficult to claim that the arts and sciences constitute the soul of higher education in the United States (II, 28). Yet one should note how distinctive to the United States and Britain are the concern for the tradition of the liberal arts curriculum and the constant discussion of its fate.

Retrospect and Prospect

1. Hugh Hawkins, "Curricular Reform in Historical Perspective," 1986

Exemplifying the publishing scholar and teacher at a small college, Hugh Hawkins (1929–) has been one of the few American historians whose writings have been devoted to higher education. He has published significant works on Charles William Eliot, the founding of the Johns Hopkins University, and on the beginnings of national associations of higher education. Following a doctoral degree at Johns Hopkins, Hawkins taught for a year at the University of North Carolina, then went to his long membership and chair in the Amherst College faculty (1957–2000). He comments here on the alternating cycles in the chronology of liberal arts studies over the last century.

Hugh Hawkins, "Curricular Reform in Historical Perspective," *Perspectives: American Historical Association Newsletter* 24, no. 1 (January 1986): 21–23. Reprinted with permission. Further reading: Hugh Hawkins, "The University," in *Encyclopedia of the United States in the Twentieth Century*, ed. Stanley I. Kutler, vol. 4 (New York, 1996): 1819–39; Hawkins, *Banding Together: The Rise of National Associations in American Higher Education, 1887–1950* (Baltimore, 1992); Frederick Rudolph, *Curriculum: A History of the American Undergraduate Course of Study since 1636* (San Francisco, 1977); Arthur Levine and Ernest Boyer, *A Quest for Common Learning: The Aims of General Education* (Princeton, NJ, 1981); and III, 2, 4–7.

The history of American higher education during the mid-nineteenth century consists largely of the undermining of the position of the Yale Report. Utilitarian pressures led to a parallel course that downplayed the ancient languages. A partial course allowed students to direct their studies toward career interests rather than the degree. Some faculty yearned to teach more advanced courses that drew, perhaps, on their doctoral training in Germany. They wanted space in the curriculum, release from required elementary work, and the stimulus of students who were studying with them voluntarily. Although the antebellum pattern allowed for gradual additions of new subjects such as chemistry and history, these were crowded into an already full curriculum. The resulting shallowness undercut long-held claims of mental discipline.

An important, if unspoken, argument on behalf of the set curriculum had been that it did not cost much, and colleges were poor. With post–Civil War fortunes available and philanthropy on the rise, it was easier to admit new specialties into the curriculum, deleting requirements to make room. Finally, as academic departments emerged, these new communal centers of power within the institution pressed to depose the curricular monarchs of the old regime.

This saga of the rise of electivism and its fruit in the creation of the American university is generally familiar. Its historical presentation has usually been either heroic or . . . progressive. In contrast, the current intensified interest in curricular reform has linked the rise of electives to a number of evils in today's colleges and universities. The gentler term that is used in various reports and news stories is "disarray." Sometimes the rhetoric intensifies, and we hear about "chaos." . . .

A very respectable history of twentieth-century American higher education could center on efforts to counteract the elective system. It would include the new rules requiring concentration and distribution, the emergence of general education courses, sometimes called a "core," and the effort to enhance student community through having them share required courses. Prerequisites, sequences, honors programs, and comprehensive examinations complicated college catalogs and students' lives. Harvard, Columbia, Swarthmore, and Chicago were conspicuous in such efforts, but many less renowned institutions were also establishing new structures. These efforts climaxed in the wake of World War II, drawing on wartime reassessment of national purpose and Cold War challenges.

But this retreat of electivism was not to go unchallenged. For various reasons, student choice set the tone of curricular change in the late 1960s and early 1970s. The colleges, having struggled to widen the class and ethnic range of their student bodies, found that some of the new students bluntly objected to requirements that lacked relevance to their career intentions or social concerns. On the other hand, students prepared in the most advanced secondary schools criticized general education requirements as tediously repetitive of work already done, and they too had social concerns that they expected to find reflected in the classroom. The worst prepared and the best prepared both asked to be freed from curricular trammels. The spirit of the times was with them. With new generational self-consciousness, anything that smacked of *in loco parentis* was suspect. The same force that ended parietal hours in dormitories eroded required course requirements. It was a time to "Do what the spirit says do," to "Question authority," and to "Off the establishment."

Making common cause with the students, some teachers complained about being dragooned into general education courses. They taught better, many said, in courses within their own specialties. The old academic political deals of "I'll vote to require your course, if you vote to require mine" began to operate in reverse. If the science requirement went, could foreign languages be far behind? Sometimes curricular structure, like the fabled feudalism at the hands of the French Estates-General, was abolished all in one night. . . .

The recent litany of academic flaws has grown familiar. Students are taking easy courses. They are over-concentrating on academic work they hope is job-related. The major has crowded out other interests. The new possessors of bachelor's degrees are often the most sophomoric of specialists. Faculty are withdrawing from broad institutional concerns into the work of their disciplines, a move allowed by the open curriculum and encouraged by the tight job market. Administrators are preoccupied with economic resources and inter-institutional coordination. Nobody cares about the curriculum as a whole.

Although the country's three thousand institutions of higher education do not fit a single pattern, there has been enough general truth to the foregoing worst case to help get a reform movement started, a movement now apparently near its climax. Much of the story occurs within institutions. In 1973 at Harvard, Dean Henry Rosovsky issued a twenty-two-page letter to the faculty urging serious reconsideration of the undergraduate program. His annual report for 1975–76 intensified the call. The long process of restructuring at Harvard can be traced in Phyllis Keller's delightfully frank *Getting at the Core: Curricular Reform at Harvard* (Cambridge, MA, 1982). At Amherst in 1975 the faculty refused to accept a report justifying a free-electivist status quo and voted to appoint a select committee to develop a plan for more curricular structure. The outcome, though still highly electivist, instituted required Introduction to Liberal Studies courses, first offered in 1978. At Gustavus Adolphus in 1981 faculty members were required to submit all their courses to a quo warranto proceeding. They must either offer a new rationale for their established courses, or—the preferred alternative—redesign them and explain why. A required core has now been established there.

The most consequential educational history probably lies in multiple local efforts like these, many unsung beyond an institution's immediate constituency. But it is press coverage of reports by national bodies that stirs public excitement. Beginning in the mid-1970s, independent foundations showed new interest in the college curriculum. Partly through its Council on Policy Studies in Higher Education, the Carnegie Foundation issued between 1977 and 1981 a series of curricular studies, notable for their breadth of view and freedom from axe-grinding.

In these reports it was granted that the curriculum is not the most important element in the education an institution gives, since it is less significant than faculty quality. Generally moderate in tone, they did label general education "an idea in distress" or even "a disaster area." That concern has been central to some of the more urgently expressed recent reports by other bodies.

Besides foundations, organs of the federal government have taken an increasing role in viewing higher education with alarm and calling for change. The National Institute of Education's contribution, *Involvement in Learning,* disavowed any intention "to define the 'knowledge most worth having,'" being chiefly concerned with whether or not students learn what courses purport to teach. . . .

The institutional associations, most of them headquartered in Washington, have never been known for shying away from committees and reports. In this phase of curricular reconsideration, the leading example is the Association of American Colleges with its *Integrity in the College Curriculum: A Report to the Academic Community* (Washington, D.C., 1985). It opens with a historical account that passes harsh judgment on the elective system. It maintains that with the "collapse of structure and control in the course of study," programs of ephemeral knowledge have been introduced and the curriculum has become "a supermarket where students are shoppers and professors are merchants of learning. Fads and fashions, the demands of popularity and success, enter where wisdom and experience should prevail." It recognizes that it is part of a chorus of reports and helpfully summarizes the others in an appendix. It calls for a minimum required curriculum, but contrary to the impression given in some newspaper stories, this is not the same as calling for required courses. . . .

While reports are appearing, headlines being printed, and panels at conventions holding forth, it seems worth remembering that "reform" is a very slippery concept. Who is really likely to benefit from the changes proposed? Are there special interests being served? Without claiming to prove the case or exhaust the possible candidates, let me name three groups that have self-interest reasons for embracing the suggested turn against electivism. Conservative and neoconservative politicians can see this as a new way to appeal to their supporters' fundamentalist, back-to-basics attitudes. College trustees and financial officers may see it as a way of saving money, since requirements tend to limit course proliferation, and the humanities are temptingly inexpensive to teach. Also, faculty members within the humanities are drawn to these programs to counteract recent steep enrollment declines in English, foreign languages, philosophy, and history. Self-interest we have always with us, and an idea, say anti-electivism, is not necessarily bad because it serves other interests besides the declared one of better education. But faculties considering curricular change should beware of shallow or self-serving educational nostrums.

2. Stanley N. Katz, "Possibilities for Remaking Liberal Education," 1995

A keen participant and national figure in the cause of the liberal arts, Stanley N. Katz (1934–) contributed to an important symposium of scholars in the humanities examining the condition of liberal education. He was then serving as president of the American Council of Learned Societies. Earlier, he had received all his degrees at Harvard (Ph.D. 1961), then taught there for four years and from there went to the University of Wisconsin (1965–71). He was professor of legal history at the University of Chicago (1971–78) and was then chair in the history of American law and history at Princeton (1978–86). Among his trusteeships and other offices in scholarly and legal organizations was the presidency of the Organization of American Historians (1987–88).

Stanley N. Katz, "Possibilities for Remaking Liberal Education at the Century's End," in *The Condition of American Liberal Education*, ed. Robert Orrill (New York, 1995), 127–33. Footnotes omitted. Copyright © 1995. Reprinted with the kind permission of the College Entrance Examination Board. Author's references in the document are: Bruce A. Kimball, *Orators and Philosophers: A History of the Idea of Liberal Education*, expanded ed. (New York, 1995); and Francis Oakley, "Against Nostalgia: Reflections on Our Present Discontents in American Higher Education," in *The Politics of Liberal Education*, ed. Darryl J. Gless and Barbara Herrnstein Smith (Durham, NC, 1992), 267–89. Further reading: Stanley N. Katz, "The Pathbreaking, Fractionalized, Uncertain World of Knowledge," *Chronicle of Higher Education*, September 20, 2002, B7–9; and W. B. Carnochan, *The Battleground of the Curriculum: Liberal Education and American Experience* (Stanford, CA, 1993).

Liberal, or general, education is widely acknowledged to be one of the central tasks of almost all institutions of higher education. Why then should we worry about the situation of liberal education in our colleges, and universities . . . as I do, about the fundamental (or at least comparative) health of higher education in this country? I believe the answer is . . . that liberal education has evolved to serve specific goals throughout modern history. In the United States, the most recent iteration of this development was the general education movement. That took root after World War I. It was designed to give the new American elite (largely white, male, and European in origin) a broad and shared cultural experience prior to entering the increasingly requisite graduate professional training.

General education was revivified after World War II in the more democratic circumstances of the postwar era. The underlying theory of the new approach was nowhere better articulated than in James Bryant Conant's Introduction to the Harvard Red Book. . . .

But the tradition has by now weakened at most institutions and disappeared at some. There are no doubt many reasons for this phenomenon, ranging from a lack of a sense of novelty to rejection of liberal education in favor of vocationalism. Over the past decade, however, even the postwar version of liberal education has increasingly been rejected by significant numbers of faculty and students as being anti-democratic in its pro-Western, intellectually elitist assumptions. The vanguard of this attack has been led by those who describe themselves as multiculturalists, those who believe that undergraduate curricula must more nearly reflect the newly pluralistic character of faculty and undergraduates. I think, however that most multiculturalists still share many of the objectives of liberal education, including the notion that education for citizenship in contemporary democracy requires a common core of intellectual experience. But the multiculturalists define that core entirely differently than did the founders of contemporary Civilization at Columbia, the General Education program at Harvard, or Integrated Liberal Studies at the University of Wisconsin.

Kimball's powerful argument that Deweyan pragmatism forms the underlying rationale for a contemporary liberal education in the United States gives hope that there is a core of common understanding that may form the basis for a reconsideration and reformulation of a liberal education in these last years of the century.

I, for one, share John Dewey's views on the relationship of education to democracy. But I am less sure than Kimball that a consensus on the meaning of liberal education is emerging. For I see few signs of awareness among education leaders that a clear vision of the goals of education is feasible or desirable. . . .

Diversity is one of the glories of U.S. higher education, but this very diversity has made it difficult to think about higher education in large parts, much less as a whole. And that is one of the principal reasons why there is so little writing about "education" by education leaders.

Another reason for the absence of intellectual debate about liberal education is that "higher ed" does not attract scholarly attention. We no longer have persuasive paradigmatic frameworks in which to situate our thinking about the reform of postsecondary education. And, alas, academic contempt for schools of education and writing on education serves as a continuing disincentive to informed speculation about education. Small wonder, then, that the critics of higher education have had a field day for more than a decade. Much of their writing, and that most frequently rehearsed in the popular media, is factually inaccurate, but at least the ideological conservatives among the critics have had the great advantage of building their negative analyses on a logically structured view of the world.

The leaders of our universities (less so the presidents of our colleges) have been unwilling or unable to respond, in part because they no longer seem to have an intellectually coherent view of the enterprises they purport to lead. We may today reject the pronouncements of Robert Maynard Hutchins and Conant as simplistic and out-of-date, but we do not have anything with which to replace them. We thus live in a state of educational anomie, and, for the moment, I fear that we shall simply have to make the best of it. That, in my judgment, requires at least that each institution (and each component segment) undertake the task of self-analysis to articulate its own goals and values. Perhaps induction will work when deduction is no longer feasible. . . .

Hostile critics of higher education have made much of the trend toward overemphasizing research and graduate education, the tendency to overbuild plants, and the consequent financial dependency of our universities, contrasting these with a half-imagined golden age of close faculty-student relations, institutional symmetry, and parsimony. The critics are not all wrong, of course, but they fail to see the powerful reasons (scientific as well as economic) for building research capacity, although most defenders of the multiversity justify their efforts in just such terms. We have done less well in responding to the charges of undergraduate neglect, probably because we have little to say on the subject. The universities were able to explain how they served liberal education in the 1940s and 1950s, but they have seldom troubled themselves to do so over the last generation. It will not do to say that liberal education is simply one element of undergraduate education, because *it is the essence of educational liberality that it must be the organizing principle of education.*

Is it still possible . . . to aspire to organize undergraduate education according to the principles of liberal education? I am not as sure as Kimball that it is. It seems to me that the competing pressures of vocationalism on the one hand, and disciplinarity on the other make it difficult for general education to compete as an operational theory. The context of higher education has changed so dramatically from that which confronted the authors of the Red Book in 1945 that it is inappropriate to apply old education strategies to the conduct of contemporary liberal education, at least at the research universities. I have already indicated that I concur with Oakley's optimism about the resilience of our institutions of higher education, but my optimism is based on the university's success in coping with changed material circumstances, not on its pedagogical vitality.

I am less optimistic about our capacity to rise to the challenge of adapting liberal education to the intellectual circumstances of the late twentieth century. Here the principal obstacles are the knowledge explosion, the breakdown of the nineteenth- and early twentieth-century sociology of knowledge, and the new pluralism (which is how I interpret multiculturalism). We have learned so much in every field of thought, especially in the sciences, since the end of World War II that it is less and less clear how to represent all this new knowledge in our universities, much less how to present it to undergraduate students. New knowledge is not only the result of conceptual and experimental breakthroughs, however. It is also the result of the dramatic growth in the number of trained researchers and, correspondingly, in the enlargement of the detail in which we understand relatively familiar subjects. The power of the microscope lenses in all fields has geometrically increased. The result is that we can examine subject matters in infinite detail and in so doing perceive patterns and activities that were previously shielded from our sight. As a matter of *Wissenschaft* this is enormously exciting, but we do not know how to handle our newfound power pedagogically.

The rapidly expanding quantity of knowledge causes problems enough, but these are in turn exacerbated by our inability to reorganize the structure of the university to cope with the intellectual challenge of new knowledge. I have in mind here the departmental structure, based on disciplinary departments founded on the sociology of knowledge that predominated during the first half of this century. While the traditional disciplines continue to have analytical and methodological power, they no longer constitute the organizing principles for much cutting-edge research. Similarly, they no longer constitute the divisions of thought most important for drawing undergraduates into the excitement of the new knowledge. We have responded to this problem with the creation of off-budget units ("centers" and "programs"), but these are precisely the parts of the university most likely to fall to the budgetary axe in this period of financial stringency and "downsizing."

The new pluralism intersects with the expansion of knowledge and the need to reorganize the taxonomy of knowledge. We are now aware of the global context of knowledge in all fields, especially in the humanities and social sciences. It is less feasible these days to focus almost exclusively on the European and North American situation, both from the point of view of student (and faculty) demand and from that of intellectual rigor. The world is smaller and our need for global understanding is greater. The demands of multiculturalism create an urgent need for both new bodies of evidence and new modes of understanding, and these needs arise in the context of an ever-expanding universe of knowledge and an increasingly rigid intellectual organization of the university. . . .

Thus, the pessimist in me is discouraged by the absence of discussion, much less action, in the direction of structural reform. The optimist in me, however, believes that there is hope for the continued centrality of liberal education. I agree with Kimball that John Dewey's emphases on the relationship between learning and experience, sense and sensibility, fact and value, democracy and education offer a promising basis for the organization of undergraduate education. I also agree with Kimball that liberal education cannot prosper as a backward-looking set of principles, but must constantly adapt itself to social change. What could be more pragmatic? But the question remains—are university faculty and administrators up to the challenge?

The Humanities in Wartime

3. George Boas, "The Humanities and Defense," 1951

George Boas (1891–1980) settled into a long professorship at the Johns Hopkins University (1921–57) after undergraduate studies at Brown and a Ph.D. at Berkeley (1917) with Jacob Loewenberg. He served in both world wars, first as an army officer in Europe and later as a navy officer at General Eisenhower's headquarters. At Hopkins Boas joined his senior colleagues Arthur O. Lovejoy and Gilbert Chinard in founding the History of Ideas Club in 1923. His prolific scholarship dealt not only with the history of philosophy but also with art history, criticism, and aesthetics. This essay was written shortly after he had become involved in organizing a legal defense for Owen Lattimore, another Hopkins professor, who was mercilessly and unjustifiably attacked as "a Communist agent" by Senator Joseph McCarthy.

George Boas, "The Humanities and Defense: The Importance of the Dissenter," *Journal of Higher Education* 22, no. 5 (May 1951): 229–35. Reprinted with the kind permission of George Boas. Copyright © 1951 by the Ohio State University Press. Further reading: E. H. Gombrich, "In Memory of George Boas," *Journal of the History of Ideas* 42 (April–June 1981): 335–54. Lattimore's experiences are described in his *Ordeal by Slander* (Boston, 1950). See also Stanley I. Kutler, *The American Inquisition: Justice and Injustice in the Cold War* (New York, 1982), ch. 7; Robert P. Newman, *Owen Lattimore and the "Loss" of China* (Berkeley, 1992); Ellen Schrecker, *No Ivory Tower: McCarthyism and the Universities* (New York, 1986); David H. Price, *Threatening Anthropology: McCarthyism and the FBI's Surveillance of Activist Anthropologists* (Durham, NC, 2004); and *Academe* 89 (May–June 2003).

Those men and women nowadays who are engaged in humanistic research are usually identified with those who study philosophy and its branches, the various literatures and languages, and history. That these subjects are more important to humanity than mathematics and physics depends on what is meant by important. But one thing could be said about them which might give them greater importance and that is that they are what makes a civilization civilized rather than barbarous, for they seem to be the things for which the other studies exist. This statement is unfair and needs qualification. When all is said and done, however, it is the philosophy and poetry and architecture and sculpture of, for instance, the Hellenic world which have survived as dynamic forces, and not the mathematics nor physics nor astronomy nor zoology.

A lot of nonsense is, I admit, talked about this, about the eternal values of art and the oneness which we feel with Homer. But one has only to think of a civilization, without the various arts and philosophy, a civilization which would rival the anthill or beehive in its perfect efficiency, to have a nightmare which the thickest compound of repressions could not release.

If one wished to indulge in a bit of sentimentality, one could say that the truths of science become obsolete, outdated, and rejected, but that the truth of the arts is everlasting. I personally should hesitate to talk in this fashion because philosophers like to have one meaning for one word and the word *truth* in this context is ambiguous. Nevertheless, it cannot be denied that the drawings in the caves of Les Eyzies or Altamira are just as good drawings as those made in 1951, and that certain scenes in *Iliad* are just as good poetry, most people would admit, as any that has been written since. But there is no reason why the everlasting should be any better than the momentary. Superstition is as enduring as truth. The fact is, however, that the arts express the complexity of human nature, the unexpected, the deviant, the original, the personal, even when they most persistently attempt to be traditional; and I suspect that those of us who spend our time studying them find in them a compensation for the awful regularity of the sciences.

Whether that is so or not, I have no way of knowing. But one thing is certain, that man seen by a sociologist or an economist or a biologist must perforce be man-in-general and not man as he is in time and space, with all his recalcitrancy, his pathetic resistance to law, his fantastic hopes and ambitions, his perpetual refusal to be discouraged by the failures of his ancestors, his inability to learn from the experience of others, his sense of his own individuality and difference. If a man were to reconcile himself to being what used to be called the economic man, dominated only by his economic wants, a routine would take the place of what we call civilization. But man as he actually is always feels that he can go against his economic interests, can even persuade large groups of his fellows to do likewise. It is in vain that social scientists point to what they think are the general trends, the waves of the future, the inevitable forces of history, there are always some people who stubbornly say, "But we are different . . ." And when it comes down to matters of fact, they are. The fact that they are does not in any way contradict the laws, assuming now that the laws are true. For the laws can only be true on the whole: true of the group, not of the individual; true of large masses, not of the units which make up those masses. Laws, when carefully phrased, whether in physics or in sociology, always include the equivalent of the words, "other things being equal." But among the things which have to be equal are the individual differences in human beings. The individual isolated from all other things in the universe is a law unto himself; it is only in those respects in which he is not an individual that he exemplifies the law. . . .

I could stop at this point, but no good American brought up in the Puritan tradition could stop without pointing a moral. We are in a national situation where millions are being spent daily on studies the results of which will be weapons. The more deadly the weapons, the better. Pure science is tolerated because it is suspected that it may contain implications useful for warfare. Psychology and economics are permitted because it is hoped that the former may teach us how to beguile the enemy successfully into treason or cowardice, the latter because it may teach us how to capture or destroy the materials vital to the enemy's defense. But the historian, the student of language and literature, and especially that human gadfly the philosopher, are not encouraged. They are not essential to defense. They are merely essential to civilization. . . .

One could always, of course, have official poets and official painters who would go through the motions of artistic creation and who would be turning out patriotic hymns to order and didactic poems and posters technically proficient but repeating the slogans of whatever administration happened to be in power. The routine of the beehive would not prevent the queen bee from ordering music which the workers could hum. Both Hitler and Stalin have had armies of skilled versifiers and painters and architects. But their works were cut out after a pattern prescribed by the state and not by the artist's sincere insight. The people of such a state would not necessarily be unhappy; men are happy even in the Army, some men. There is nothing in conformity to make all men miserable, and the few original types who might find such a regime a bit hard could easily be liquidated, as unco-operative professors are sometimes told that they would be happier in some unspecified elsewhere. The task of the artist would be the endless repetition of the norm, and all deviation from the norm would be severely punished. Is that not what has happened in Russia?

Unfortunately, man lives in time, and, as time passes on, new and unforeseen occurrences put obstacles in the way of success. A civilization which does not encourage people to adjust themselves to novelty, does not encourage people to look for the accidental which may create a problem, is a civilization which clearly is doomed. Not merely is it doomed to sterility, it is doomed to extinction. As teachers you all know how easy it is for knowledge to become stereotyped—you have all used textbooks. What is needed is a kind of teaching which will prevent petrification and ritualization, and will give the premium to the nonconformist who has an eye for the odd, the peculiar, the exception. He must be balanced, to be sure, by the scientist who has an eye for regularities, but, as Henry Allen Moe recently said, "It is the lonely thinker, not the administrator, who makes discoveries, and the lonely thinker by definition is the thinker who is not regimented." . . .

Against what are we defending ourselves? If it is the Russians, we can turn into Russians and thus beat them to the goal. We shall then have a world modeled on that of Orwell's *1984*. But if we are defending ourselves against ignorance, superstition, and cultural death, we are just as necessary to defense as the physicist, for only we can defend the physicist. It was that great soldier, General Foch, who said that the art of war lay in improvisation. The vanquished are usually vanquished by their own paralysis, not by the enemy. The same could be said of a civilization. As soon as it leans in the direction of ritualization, it is safe only so far as the ritual works. But once let the situation change, the ritual will fail and the gift of improvisation will have to be called into play. That gift lies in the hands not of the regimented, the slaves of authority and tradition, but in those of the free spirits whom we are doing our utmost to exterminate.

Revising the Curricula

4. Daniel Bell,
The Reforming of General Education, 1966

Born in New York City and educated at the College of the City of New York (B.S. 1938) and Columbia (Ph.D. 1960), Daniel Bell (1919–) entered his academic career in sociology at the University of Chicago (1945–48) and in 1953 moved to Columbia, where he remained for seventeen years. He also worked in journalism as labor editor of *Fortune* (1948–58) and later became a founder and for some years coeditor of *The Public Interest*. In 1969 he became professor of sociology at Harvard.

Daniel Bell, *The Reforming of General Education: The Columbia College Experience in its National Setting* (New York, 1966), 274–78, 289–95. Reprinted with permission from the author. Copyright © 1966 by Columbia University Press. Further reading: Daniel Bell, *The Winding Passage: Essays and Sociological Journeys* (New York, 1980); John William Ward, *Red, White, and Blue: Men, Books, and Ideas in American Culture* (New York, 1969), 330–48; Henry David Aiken, *Predicament of the University* (Bloomington, IN, 1971), ch. 8; Ron Chernow, "The Cultural Contradictions of Daniel Bell," *Change* 11 (March 1979): 12–17; "Daniel Bell and Lawrence Veysey on Contemporary America: A Symposium," *American Quarterly* 34 (Spring 1982): 49–94; William Theodore deBary, "A Program of General and Continuing Education in the Humanities," *Columbia Reports* 7 (April 1973): 3–7; Robert L. Belknap and Richard Kuhns, *Tradition and Innovation* (New York, 1977); and Gilbert Allardyce, "The Rise and Fall of the Western Civilization Course," *American Historical Review* 87 (June 1982): 695–725.

This book is entitled *The Reforming of General Education*. The work *reforming*, in this context, may have an awkward sound. Why not simply *reform*? Why the gerund? Because education is not just a set of new structures, but a continuing experience that reworks the thought of the past and is a self-conscious scrutiny of one's own practice. The reforms proposed here, apart from their particular application to Columbia College, are not meant as a new enlightenment or new general truths. They build upon a tradition and are intended to adapt that tradition to fresh circumstances—and also to bend some of those circumstances to the necessary needs of a continuing tradition.

What is, then, new and distinctive about the present that has called the old practices into question? For the purposes of this reprise, I shall identify briefly some of those elements.

1. The college is no longer the place of the elect. Today about 40 percent of the eighteen to twenty-one age group (as a total figure, although not all proceed ahead immediately) attend college; at present, even though only little more than half these

students complete the four-year course and obtain a degree. The rapid growth of the two-year junior and community college has tended to blur the once distinct "break" between secondary school and college, and this fact, along with the failure of many students to complete their work for a bachelor's degree, is creating new social and intellectual distinctions—not, as before, between those who have attended college and those who have not, but between the graduates of "elite" colleges and those of "mass" or of "second-rank" colleges.

2. The pressure for admission to the elite colleges will probably increase. But the number of talented young people has not risen in proportion to the number now seeking admission to college. . . .

3. The graduate school has become central within the university. In 1936, when Robert Maynard Hutchins first proposed his plan for general education at Chicago, and less than a decade later, when the Harvard proposals were set forth in the Redbook, it was assumed that only a small proportion of undergraduates would proceed to graduate school. The reverse is true today. The graduate school has tended to enhance research rather than teaching within the university. It has encouraged the trend toward intensive specialization in the undergraduate colleges. It has drained away teachers from the colleges and reinforced a status distinction between those who teach in the graduate school and those who teach only in the college. Because relatively few students are admitted to the elite graduate schools, the competition for superior grades in the colleges has increased, as has the undergraduates' sense of pressure about the future.

4. The scope of the college as a place for intellectual exploration, or, in Erik Erikson's phrase, as a "psycho-social moratorium" for testing one's interests or finding oneself, has shrunk. This loss becomes expressed, in the voiced and unvoiced dissatisfactions of the students, as a protest against the impersonality of a university, its rushed and dispersive quality, and the lack of "encounter" between student and faculty—not just personally, but in a moral and intellectual sense. The student comes to a college and expects to find a "community." Instead he finds a "society."

5. Education in the United States today takes place within a radical new political, economic, and intellectual setting. The fact of war and the state of protracted ideological conflict have given a new mold to American society in the past twenty-five years. The new role of the United States as the great power in the world, along with the extension of our political commitments around the globe, has made us sharply aware of non-Western societies and cultures. The emergence of half a hundred new states has enlarged our area of political and intellectual inquiry and created a vast new "laboratory" for the comparative study of nation-building, economic and political development, rapid social and psychological change, and the like.

The conditions of the cold war have created a new "mobilized polity." For the first time we have developed a large-scale permanent military establishment. For the first time, too, the federal government has begun to spend huge sums of money on research and development, and to give systematic support to science and research. Large new laboratories and research centers in the physical sciences, life sciences (biology and medicine), and social sciences (particularly "area studies") have been built with government support. The relationship between the government and the intellectuals is now, clearly, permanent.

6. The growth of knowledge and the process of "branching," whereby new discoveries give rise to distinct new sub-specializations and fields, have multiplied the number of subjects a university is now called upon to teach. . . .

7. The university now occupies a central position in the society. Formerly its chief function was that of conserving and transmitting the intellectual traditions and cultural values of society. Now the university serves more as the center for research and innovation. Though the university once reflected the status system of the society, it now determines status. Its ties with government have become more complex. The university is the training center for specialists; the best of the professors now move easily in and out of policy-making and advisory positions in the government.

More so than ever before in American life, the university has become a public service institution, its resources increasingly used by government, industry, and the local communities. At the same time, because of its vastly increased financial needs, the university has itself become a "constituency," a significant claimant on the monetary powers of government. The scientific, technical, and literary intelligentsia, most of whom are now housed in the university, has become a significant social stratum, amounting almost to a new class of society.

Traditionally, the university has been a collegium; it is now becoming a bureaucracy. A complex administrative superstructure is built above the academic, research, and business parts of the university. Functions once inseparable from a school's identity (admissions, for example) have been taken over by specialized and professional personnel without faculty status and often outside faculty control. The activity of teaching—the heart of the tradition of the university as a free community of self-governing scholars—has been diminished as a function of the university.

The intellectual direction and emphasis of the university—the elements that define its character—are influenced more and more by outside forces. Thus a university's expansion into new fields is often less the product of a long-range intellectual plan than it is a response to pressures from the foundations and the government, both of which have taken over in considerable measure the defining of the society's needs in relation to new intellectual, social, and political areas. The multiplication of nonteaching research centers, institutes, and laboratories, each with its own hierarchy and professional employees, not all of whom have faculty status, brings more strain and stress into the university. To work out new structural forms appropriate to its tasks, and still maintain its self-directing and self-governing autonomy in intellectual affairs, will be one of the great problems of the university in the years ahead. . . .

Writing a curriculum, like cooking, can be the prototype of the complete moral act. There is perfect free will. One can put in whatever one wishes, in whatever combination. Yet in order to know what one has, one has to taste the consequences. And as in all such acts, there is an ambiguity for evil, in that others who did not share in the original pleasures may have to taste the consequences. In sum, it is the moral of a cautionary tale.

Every argument has its key terms within a master structure. To the extent that a structure has been articulated for the present argument, the key terms would, I think, be *conceptualization* and *coherence*. Yet such nouns make the approach sound unduly abstract, and this would be far from my intention. The curriculum presented here is organized along a number of dimensions, of which the emphasis on the centrality of method is but one. Other equally important aims are to reduce the intellectual provincialism bred by specialization and to demonstrate the philosophical presuppositions and values that underlie all inquiry. The emphasis on history and the humanities is as integral to these proposals as the concern with conceptual innovation. The unity of the scheme derives from the efforts to link the necessary historical and humanities sequences with training in a discipline, and to relate one's own discipline not only to a number of other subjects but to broader intellectual problems as well.

To recapitulate the proposals:

1. The Contemporary Civilization A course would be reorganized and extended to a year and a half instead of the year it is now allotted. All students would be required to take the three-term sequence. . . .

2. Following the year and a half work in history, each student would be required to take a one-term course in one of the following: economics, sociology, government, anthropology, or geography. These courses would be organized not as Contemporary Civilization courses, but as introductions to disciplines, so that students would acquire a competent understanding of at least one social science subject. Ideally, each course would have two tracks—one for a student beginning his major in that subject, the other for students who would prefer to study the discipline in a broader social science context.

If the three-term introductory historical sequence should prove to be impractical, and the present requirement of two years' work in Contemporary Civilization is retained, I would propose, in place of the present second year (paralleling my proposed math-physics, math-biology requirement), an economics-government, economics-sociology sequence. More and more, it seems to me, that economics is becoming the central discipline of the social sciences. Not only does it have a more complete intellectual structure than the other social sciences, but its subject matter is crucial in contemporary society. Each student, to be an adequately informed citizen, should have some knowledge of economics; equally significant is the fact that many of the basic analytical concepts and techniques of economics (optimizing, programming, rationality, utility preference) are permeating the other social sciences. Given these developments, I would argue that economics can be linked most fruitfully with a course in government or a course in sociology, to provide a coherent unit for the study of contemporary society.

3. The Humanities course is organized on the principle of having a student confront a literary or philosophical masterpiece directly, so that his reading will be as fresh an experience as possible. The Humanities staff has for this reason consistently opposed the use of secondary or critical writing about the work that is being read. While one may want the individual student to experience a "shock of recognition," I have argued that it is faulty esthetic or social reasoning to assume that a wholly naive approach is possible. As E. H. Gombrich has said, "the innocent eye sees nothing." Esthetic experience is in great measure conventional; it can be understood only within the specific context of the tradition that produced it and the historically available alternatives open to the original artists working from that tradition. I have proposed that the Humanities course add more critical and historical reading in order to give the student a sense of how an imaginative work relates to its own time and how its enduring qualities transcend that time.

I have also proposed that a third term be added to the Humanities year; it would introduce modern and contemporary art into the course in order to extend the student's sense of the historical continuity of literature.

4. The music and fine arts Humanities courses, even more than the first-year course, are organized on the premise that a student is best initiated in esthetic experience by confronting him with masterpieces from our cultural heritage. I have suggested that because students in the secondary schools are now so greatly exposed to culture both in school and through the mass media, these Humanities courses should be examined with a view to devoting more attention to the nature of visual forms in the arts and new forms of sound in music. It was proposed further that since some freshmen can be expected to show proficiency in music or art, those who could be exempted from, say, the music course be allowed to devote a year to the visual arts, and a student exempted from fine arts to spend a year in music.

5. The English composition course has come to

be more and more of a financial and organizational strain on the College. To staff this course, the English department has increasingly had to rely on preceptors, who then become employed in teaching the humanities courses as well. I have suggested that Columbia College, in conjunction with the other Ivy League colleges, take steps to eliminate such courses by requiring applicants to demonstrate competence in English composition as a prerequisite for entrance. Students lacking such proficiency would be required to have made up for it, on their own, by the start of the second year.

6. The present distribution requirement in science seems unsatisfactory. I have proposed that all students be required to take a two-year mathematics-physics or mathematics-biology sequence, for these reasons: mathematics is a necessary tool (as well as a style of thought) for work in almost all fields except the humanities; and physics and biology, by virtue of their successive logical "paradigms," can best exemplify the conceptual order of science.

7. The system of majors, which has become increasingly important in Columbia College, should be reexamined with two problems in mind: first, the possibility of creating a "double track" in each major as a whole (not just in the introductory courses); second, being more specific about the necessary, "related courses" for each major. . . .

8. A third-tier scheme is proposed wherein each student in his senior year would take a number of courses that would "brake" the drive toward specialization by trying to generalize his experiences in his discipline. There would be, in principle, four kinds of third-tier courses: one in the historical foundations of the intellectual disciplines in a common field; one in the methodological and philosophical presuppositions of the disciplines in a common field; another in the application of several disciplines to common problems; and still another in comparative studies, particularly of non-Western cultures. The kind of course would differ with different fields—the social sciences, the humanities, and the sciences would each have third-tier courses appropriate to its particular problems. By exploring interrelationships, by aiming at philosophical sophistication about the foundations of a field, and by pointing out the possible value problems that might be encountered in applying a discipline, such courses would make a distinctive contribution to general education.

Two final points are in order about the subject of curriculum. First, the emphasis on conceptual inquiry that has been raised so often in this book comes from the conviction that learning is not simply a matter of empiricism or of conditioning but a skill that derives from our unique ability to deal with the world symbolically. It is dependent on a rational faculty, of mind. . . .

Second, I have attempted to repair a serious deficiency, for in the excessive preoccupation with the cognitive elements of thought (concepts, paradigms, intellectual structures) one neglects the esthetic element that is present for some people in the elegance of intellectual solutions, the fidelity to intellectual craftsmanship, and the pleasure, even the sensuous beauty, of a well-wrought theory, as in the contemplation of a Grecian urn. Intellectual work has, or should have, its esthetic, as well as its practical, satisfactions, and a curriculum must take them into account.

5. Harvard Curriculum Report, 1979

Appointed Dean of the Faculty of Arts and Sciences at Harvard University by President Derek Bok in 1973, Henry Rosovsky (1927–) began an examination of the educational goals of Harvard College. In a letter to the faculty in October 1974, he reminded everyone that since the General Education Report of 1945 (I, 1), the Harvard undergraduate curriculum had been undergoing piecemeal and unsystematic change. With considerable faculty and student support, Rosovsky went on to appoint faculty task forces on the curriculum and, by November 1976, to report on "the possibility of common discourse among educated people" in a university enrolling a far broader constituency than it had in 1945. By the spring of 1978, substantive course requirements in five areas, replacing the older general-education requirement, plus requirements in expository writing, mathematics, and foreign languages were approved by a faculty vote, 182 to 65. Final revisions of the new core curriculum, drawn up by Rosovsky and eighteen principal "contributors" from the faculty, were adopted in May 1979 and put fully into operation by the 1982–83 academic year.

Faculty of Arts and Sciences, Harvard University, *Report On The Core Curriculum, Revised, May 1979* (Cambridge, MA, 1979), 3–16. Reprinted with the kind permission of Dean Henry Rosovsky. Further reading: Phyllis Keller, *Getting at the Core: Curricular Reform at Harvard* (Cambridge, MA, 1982), reviewed by Richard A. Katz, *Academe* 69 (May–June 1983): 77–78; Ongoing critical comment includes *Chronicle of Higher Education*, May 8, 1978, 1, 12; April 20, 1981, 1, 13; and May 30, 1984, 15–16; *Harvard Magazine*, May–June 1978, 74–76; Susan Schiefelbein, "Confusion at Harvard," *Saturday Review*, April 1, 1978, 12–20; [*Change* magazine], *The Great Core Curriculum Debate* (New Rochelle, NY, 1979); John F. A. Taylor, *The Public Commission of the University: The Role of the Community of Scholars in an Industrial, Urban, and Corporate Society* (New York, 1982); and James W. Hall and Barbara L. Kevles, *In Opposition to Core Curriculum: Alternative Models for Undergraduate Education* (Westport, CT, 1982); and III, 1–3.

I. PURPOSE OF THE CORE CURRICULUM

In his Annual Report for 1975–76, Dean Rosovsky attempted to state what it means to be an educated person in the latter part of the twentieth century. The standard that he outlined provided the context for the review of undergraduate education at Harvard, including the development of the Core Curriculum. The elements of this standard, which broadly outline the educational goals of the College, were as follows.

1. An educated person must be able to think and write clearly and effectively.

2. An educated person should have achieved depth in some field of knowledge. Cumulative learning is an effective way to develop a student's powers of reasoning and analysis, and for our undergraduates this is the principal role of concentrations.

3. An educated person should have a critical appreciation of the ways in which we gain and apply knowledge and understanding of the universe, of society and of ourselves. Specifically, he or she should have an informed acquaintance with the aesthetic and intellectual experience of literature and the arts; with history as a mode of understanding present problems and the processes of human affairs; with the concepts and analytic techniques of modern social science; and with the mathematical and experimental methods of the physical and biological sciences.

4. An educated person is expected to have some understanding of, and experience in thinking about, moral and ethical problems. It may well be that the most significant quality in educated persons is the informed judgment which enables them to make discriminating moral choices.

5. Finally, an educated American, in the last third of this century, cannot be provincial in the sense of being ignorant of other cultures and other times. It is no longer possible to conduct our lives without reference to the wider world within which we live. A crucial difference between the educated and the uneducated is the extent to which one's life experience is viewed in wider contexts.

The first goal, that our students learn to communicate with precision, cogency, and force, is addressed by the requirement in Expository Writing, and reinforced throughout the curriculum. The second goal, depth of knowledge in a particular field, is accomplished through the requirement that students concentrate a substantial portion of their work in a single subject. The importance and value of concentration was reaffirmed by both the Task Force on the Core Curriculum and the Task Force on Concentrations.

The third, fourth, and fifth goals are met specifically through the Core Curriculum. Its purpose is to assure that all students, regardless of their special field of concentration, acquire the knowledge, skills, and habits of thought that the Faculty believes to be of general and lasting intellectual significance. Broadly stated, the goal of the Core is to encourage a critical appreciation of the major approaches to knowledge, so that students may acquire an understanding of what kinds of knowledge exist in certain important areas, how such knowledge is created, how it is used, and what it might mean to them personally. We seek, in other words, to have students acquire basic literacy in major forms of intellectual discourse. . . .

To this end we have established requirements in five areas. Requirements in Literature and Arts will acquaint students with important literary and artistic achievements and will aim to develop a critical understanding of how man gives artistic expression to his experience of the world. History requirements will focus on major aspects of the present world viewed in historical perspective and will attempt to lead students to an understanding of the complexity of human affairs in specific situations in the past. Requirements in Social Analysis and Moral Reasoning introduce central concepts and ideas in these intellectual realms and will develop students' abilities to think systematically about fundamental aspects of individual and social life in contemporary society. Science requirements will acquaint students with basic principles of the physical, biological, and behavioral sciences and with science as a way of looking at man and the world. Finally, a Foreign Cultures requirement is designed to expand tie student's range of cultural experience and to provide fresh perspectives of his or her own cultural assumptions and traditions. This aim may be achieved through appropriate Core courses in Literature and the Arts, History, or Social Analysis or in special courses in Foreign Cultures. The intention here is not only to avoid an exclusive focus on Western traditions, but to expose students to the essential and distinctive features of foreign cultures, whether Western or non-Western.

These different areas of the Core Curriculum are linked by a common question: how do we gain and apply knowledge and understanding of the universe, of society, and of ourselves? The underlying purpose of the Core is to set a minimum standard of intellectual breadth for our students. Yet the Core is not meant to stand alone. Fulfilling Core requirements will consume the equivalent of about one academic year, as did the previous General Education requirement. Concentration requirements will continue to involve the equivalent of about two years of academic work. Students will retain the equivalent of one academic year for electives, within which they can express their own priorities by initiating or advancing selected aspects of their intellectual development. Conjoined with these electives and work in the field of concentration, the Core will provide a solid and shared base of general and liberal education for all of our students.

It is also important to note what is *not* intended in the Core Curriculum. We have not established an identical set of courses for all students, or an even-handed introduction to all fields of knowledge. The proliferation of knowledge and the diversity of our students make both of these goals impractical. We do not think there is a single set of Great Books that every educated person must master, and we do not think an inevitably thin survey of the traditional subject areas—humanities, social sciences, and natural sciences—is any longer useful. Nor do we think a loose distribution requirement among departmental courses can accomplish the educational priorities that we have identified. Finally, the Core Curriculum is not intended as a model for higher education in general. We do not believe all colleges should perform the same function or offer the same curriculum; indeed, we are dismayed by the uniformity that has come to characterize much of higher education. Our purpose is to provide the best possible education for our own students. If we are successful, others may benefit as well, but this is a secondary consideration.

II. THE CORE REQUIREMENT

The Core Program establishes requirements in five areas. Detailed guidelines for the courses in each area are as follows:

Area 1: Literature and the Arts

Characteristics of the Courses: The common aim of these courses is to foster a critical understanding of how man gives artistic expression to his experience of the world. Through the examination of selected major works, students will be expected to develop and refine skills of reading, seeing, and hearing; to apprehend the possibilities and limitations of the artist's chosen medium and the means available for expression; to understand the complex interplay between individual talent, artistic tradition, and historical context. In the requirement for this area the written word takes precedence over other forms of artistic expression to the extent that the study of literature is required of all students, while a choice is offered between music and fine arts. . . .

Area 2: Historical Study

Characteristics of the Courses: These courses seek to accomplish two aims: A) to orient students historically to some of the major concerns of the contemporary world; and B) to help them acquire a measure of understanding of the complexity of human affairs in specific situations in the past and the process by which important changes have taken place. . . .

Area 3: Social Analysis and Moral Reasoning

Characteristics of the Courses: The common aim of these courses is to introduce students to the central concepts and ideas of social science and moral and political philosophy, and to develop their analytic skills in understanding the fundamental social institutions and concerns of contemporary society. Courses will be organized around selected topics or themes chosen for their effectiveness in demonstrating how social scientists and philosophers think about social and moral issues. Courses will focus primarily, but not exclusively, on one of the following: A) the application of a formal body of theory and of empirical data to an understanding of some fundamental aspect of individual or social life in contemporary society; or B) the investigation of significant and recurrent questions of choice and value which arise in ordinary political and moral experience, drawing on writings of political and social theorists. Courses may include an historical or comparative dimension. They need not attempt comprehensive coverage of the work currently going on in any single discipline. . . .

A—Social Analysis: The object of these courses is to familiarize students with some of the central approaches of the social sciences and to do so in a way that gives students a sense of how those approaches can enhance their understanding of human behavior in the context of contemporary society. The courses offered to meet this part of the Core requirement will provide coherent formal theories or analytical approaches that are tested or illuminated by empirical data. A Core course in economics, for example, would explain the nature, assumptions, and consequences of rational choice in the context of scarce resources. A Core course in anthropology might explain the meaning of culture and how it affects ways of perceiving, valuing and acting in a social context. A Core course in psychology might take as its central concept personality, motivation or intelligence, whereas one in sociology might focus on the nature, causes and implications of social stratification. A Core course in government might explore the nature of power in governmental decision-making.

In addition to exposing students to the Core approaches or theories of various disciplines, courses will also expose students to the empirical data (statistical or other) used by disciplines in testing or elucidating key theories or propositions. Consideration will be given to the limitations as well as to the uses of social science data. Wherever possible, courses will explore the implicit values and assumptions underlying the analysis.

The key criteria for acceptance into the Core for all courses will be whether such courses give students a systematic introduction to some major social science field and to its theoretical and empirical foundations. Introductory courses that place primary emphasis on current policy issues without explicit and substantial use of formal theories or approaches will not be eligible for inclusion.

B—Moral Reasoning: These courses will serve a multiple purpose: to introduce students to important traditions of thought, to make them aware of the intricacies of ethical argument, and to bring them to grips with particular questions of choice and value. They are to learn that it is possible to think systematically about such issues as justice, obligation, personal responsibility, citizenship, and friendship. The emphasis in this part of the Core will be on Western traditions of thought and their relationship to political institutions and moral practice.

Courses will focus on ethics, law, and politics. Three different approaches to these subjects ought to be reflected in each year's Core listings. First, the historical approach, involving the study of major texts organized around one, or a very few, central themes, or examining in detail moral values and beliefs at some critical period of Western history; examples might be Greek Ethics, or Citizenship in Historical Perspective. Second, a disciplinary approach stressing those concepts and issues that underlie the study of moral, political, and legal choice: determinism and responsibility, utilitarianism, the theory of rights, law and morals, legitimacy, and so on. Third, an approach in terms of concrete problems such as distributive justice, obligations, civil rights, or medical ethics, emphasizing particular moral and political controversies, legal cases, and historical examples.

Area 4: Science

Characteristics of the Courses: The common aim of these courses is to help students increase their scientific literacy and their capacity to approach scientific material intelligently. A further purpose is to convey a general understanding of science as a way of looking at man and the world.

The wealth of important and fundamental scientific knowledge is immense and rapidly growing. So is the need to understand increasingly complex interrelations between science and human affairs. The Core science requirement is intended to ensure that every student acquires some appreciation of this vast and fundamental intellectual activity. In addition to the two half-courses required, there is a mathematics prerequisite (discussed in section IV) which will permit the Core courses to assume some mathematical preparation on the part of all students.

Observations of the physical and biological world have led scientists to formulate principles that provide universal explanations of diverse phenomena. These include the laws that govern classical dynamics, thermodynamics, radiation and the microscopic structure of matter, and the basic principles that underlie chemistry, molecular and cellular biology, biological evolution and behavior. The Core will contain courses that treat such basic scientific concepts and findings in some depth.

Every undergraduate should learn how scientists go about understanding the world through examples that illustrate these fundamental concepts and principles. The courses should consider not only what scientists believe is true in some domain, but how they have developed and validated their laws and principles. The critical role of observation and experiment in this process should be exhibited.

Core courses need not be limited to, nor provide broad and full coverage of, a single discipline. It is hoped that a number of the courses created or adapted for the Core will be interdisciplinary in nature. Some may bring historical or social perspectives to bear, describing, for example, how commonly held views have been overturned by certain major scientific discoveries, and some of the methods and motivations of the discoverers. Several Core courses should have no prerequisite other than some knowledge of mathematics (see section IV). The skills necessary to attack selected problems should be developed along the way. A number of courses, particularly in the physical sciences, may have a considerable mathematical component.

Many entering students already have a good background in the sciences. To serve these students, as well as those who wish to pursue their scientific education beyond the minimum requirement, some courses that presuppose an understanding of certain basic concepts and theories should also be offered. These courses might focus on the major principles and findings in areas of contemporary scientific research. . . .

Area 5: Foreign Cultures

Characteristics of the Courses: The common aim of all the courses is to expand the student's range of cultural experience and to provide fresh perspectives on the student's own cultural assumptions and traditions. Courses may well emphasize language as a means of entry into another culture; but proficiency should not be considered enough in itself for this purpose.

Courses need not attempt comprehensive coverage, but rather will penetrate deeply into selected aspects of the culture being studied. They may be problem-oriented, and should include consideration of the historical background and contemporary aspects of the culture under study. As much as possible, they will devote attention to religious and ethical values, social systems, intellectual trends, and literary and artistic achievements. Whether the primary emphasis is on the analysis of key texts and works of art, on historical orientation and perspective, or on fundamental aspects of individual or social life, these courses will seek to identify the distinctive patterns of thought, belief, and action that account for the particular configuration or ethos of another culture.

The foreign cultures studied in Core courses will, primarily but not exclusively, be living cultures and represent major cultural traditions. For these purposes, foreign cultures may be divided into two groups, with the principle that the less "foreign" a culture, the more advanced should be its study. The area subcommittee will determine the boundaries between the two groups on a case by case basis.

6. St. John's College, "List of Great Books," 1979

Stringfellow Barr (1897–1982) and Scott Buchanan (1895–1968) were the founding fathers of the modern St. John's College in Annapolis, Maryland. They were philosophers at the University of Virginia in 1937 when Robert M. Hutchins called them to the University of Chicago. Within a year they were offered the opportunity to completely reorganize a decrepit college in Annapolis. Taking with them much of the curricular spirit of Hutchins's Chicago in the 1930s, they initiated a curriculum that has become renowned for its steadfast concentration upon the "great books" and works of music in Western culture. Their purpose was not to return to a nineteenth-century American college curriculum but rather to employ a modern equivalent of the even older *trivium* and *quadrivium,* offered to all students over four years. Since 1937 the faculty has replaced about two-thirds of the original list of books with new titles and added five short works of twentieth-century fiction. In 1964 a second campus was established at Santa Fe, New Mexico.

St. John's College: Statement of St. John's Program, 1979–81 (Annapolis, MD, 1979), 23–25, 27. Reprinted with the kind permission of St. John's College. Copyright © 1979 by St. John's College. Further reading: J. Winfree Smith, *A Search for the Liberal College: The Beginning of the St. John's Program* (Annapolis, MD, 1984); Russell Thomas, *The Search for a Common Learning: General Education, 1800–1960* (New York, 1962), 230–43; Gerald Grant and David Riesman, *The Perpetual Dream: Reform and Experiment in the American College* (Chicago, 1978), ch. 3; and Amy Apfel Kass, "Radical Conservatives for Liberal Education," Ph.D. dissertation, Johns Hopkins University, 1973.

The books that serve as the core of the curriculum were chosen over a period of nearly forty years, first at Columbia College, at the University of Chicago, at the University of Virginia, and, since 1937, at St. John's College. The distribution of the books over the four years is significant. Something over two thousand years of intellectual history form the background of the first two years; about three hundred years of history form the background for almost twice as many authors in the last two years.

The first year is devoted to Greek authors and their pioneering understanding of the liberal arts; the second year contains books from the Roman, medieval and Renaissance periods; the third year has books of the seventeenth and eighteenth centuries, most of which were written in modern languages; the fourth year brings the reading into the nineteenth and twentieth centuries.

The chronological order in which the books are read is primarily a matter of convenience and intelligibility; it does not imply an historical approach to the subject matter. The St. John's curriculum seeks to convey to the student an understanding of fundamental problems that man has to face today and at all times. In doing that it may help the student to discover a new kind of historical perspective and perceive through all the historical shifts and changes the permanence and ever present gravity of human issues.

The list of books which constitute the core of the St. John's program is subject to review and revision by the Instruction Committee of the faculty. Those listed here are read at one or both campuses. Books read only in part are indicated by an asterisk.

FRESHMAN YEAR

Homer:	*Iliad, Odyssey*
Aeschylus:	*Agamemnon, Choephoroe, Eumenides, Prometheus Bound*
Sophocles:	*Oedipus Rex, Oedipus at Colonus, Antigone, Philoctetes*
Thucydides:	*Peloponnesian War*
Euripides:	*Hippolytus, Medea, Bacchae*
Herodotus:	*Histories**
Aristophanes:	*Clouds, Birds*
Plato:	*Ion, Meno, Gorgias, Republic, Apology, Crito, Phaedo, Symposium, Parmenides, Theaetetus, Sophist, Timaeus, Phaedrus*
Aristotle:	*Poetics, Physics*, Metaphysics*, Nicomachean Ethics*, On Generation and Corruption*, The Politics*, Parts of Animals*, Generation of Animals**
Euclid:	*Elements**
Lucretius:	*On the Nature of Things*
Plutarch:	*Pericles, Alcibiades*
Nicomachus:	*Arithmetic**
Lavoisier:	*Elements of Chemistry**
Essays by:	Archimedes, Torricelli, Pascal, Fahrenheit, Black, Avogadro, Dalton, Wollaston, Gay-Lussac, Cannizzaro, Proust, Berthollet, Richter, T. Thomson, Berzelius, Dulong
Galen:	*On the Natural Faculties**
Harvey:	*Motion of the Heart and Blood*
Lamarck:	*Philosophical Zoology*

SOPHOMORE YEAR
The Bible*

Aristotle:	*De Anima, On Interpretation*, Posterior Analytics*, Categories**
Apollonius:	*Conics**
Marcus Aurelius:	*Meditations**
Virgil:	*Aeneid*
Plutarch:	*Lives**
Epictetus:	*Discourses, Manual*
Tacitus:	*Annals*
Ptolemy:	*Almagest**
Plotinus:	*The Enneads**
Augustine:	*Confessions, On the Teacher**
Anselm:	*Proslogium*
Aquinas:	*Summa Theologica*, Summa Contra Gentiles**
Dante:	*Divine Comedy*
Chaucer:	*Canterbury Tales**
Des Prez:	*Mass*
Machiavelli:	*The Prince, Discourses**
Copernicus:	*On the Revolutions of the Spheres**
Luther:	*The Freedom of a Christian, Secular Authority*
Rabelais:	*Gargantua**
Palestrina:	*Missa Papae Marcelli*

Montaigne: *Essays**

Viète: *Introduction to the Analytical Art*

Bacon: *Novum Organum**

Shakespeare: *Richard II, Henry IV, Henry V, The Tempest, As You Like It, Twelfth Night, Hamlet, Othello, Macbeth, King Lear, Sonnets**

Poems by: Marvell, Donne, and other 16th and 17th century poets

Descartes: *Rules for the Direction of the Mind, Geometry**

Pascal: *Generation of Conic Sections*

Bach: *St. Matthew Passion, Inventions*

Haydn: Selected Works

Mozart: Selected Operas

Beethoven: Selected Sonatas

Schubert: Selected Songs

Stravinsky: *Symphony of Psalms*

Webern: Selected Works

JUNIOR YEAR

Cervantes: *Don Quixote*

Galileo: *Two New Sciences**

Hobbes: *Leviathan**

Descartes: *Discourse on Method, Meditations, Rules for the Direction of the Mind*, The World**

Milton: *Paradise Lost*, Samson Agonistes*

La Rochefoucauld: *Maximes**

La Fontaine: *Fables**

Pascal: *Pensées**

Huygens: *Treatise on Light*, On the Movement of Bodies by Impact*

Spinoza: *Theologico-Political Treatise*

Locke: *Second Treatise of Government, Essay Concerning Human Understanding*

Racine: *Phèdre*

Newton: *Principia Mathematica**

Kepler: *Epitome IV*

Leibniz: *Monadology, Discourse on Metaphysics, What is Nature? Essay on Dynamics*

Swift: *Gulliver's Travels*

Berkeley: *Principles of Human Knowledge*

Hume: *Treatise of Human Nature*, Dialogues Concerning Natural Religion, Enquiry Concerning Human Understanding*

Rousseau: *Social Contract, The Origin of Inequality*

Adam Smith: *Wealth of Nations**

Kant: *Critique of Pure Reason*, Fundamental Principles of Metaphysics of Morals, Critique of Practical Reason**

Mozart: *Don Giovanni*

Jane Austen: *Pride and Prejudice, Emma*

Wordsworth: *"Ode on Intimations of Immortality"*

Hamilton, Jay, and Madison: *The Federalist*

Melville: *Billy Budd, Benito Cereno*

Dedekind: *Essay On the Theory of Numbers*

Tocqueville: *Democracy in America**

Essays by: Young, Maxwell, S. Carnot, L. Carnot, Mayer, Kelvin, Taylor, Euler, D. Bernoulli

SENIOR YEAR

Moliere: *The Misanthrope, Tartuffe*

Goethe: *Faust**

Mendel: *Experiments In Plant Hybridization*

Darwin: *Origin of Species, Descent of Man*

Hegel: *Introduction to the History of Philosophy, Preface to the Phenomenology, Logic* (from the Encyclopedia), *Philosophy of History*, Philosophy of Right**

Lobachevsky: *Theory of Parallels**

Tocqueville: *Democracy in America**

Lincoln: Selected Speeches

Kierkegaard: *Philosophical Fragments, Fear and Trembling*

Wagner: *Tristan and Isolde*

Marx: *Communist Manifesto, Capital*, Political and Economic Manuscripts of 1844**

Dostoevski: *Brothers Karamazov, The Possessed*

Tolstoy: *War and Peace*

Mark Twain: *The Adventures of Huckleberry Finn*

William James: *Psychology, Briefer Course*

Nietzsche: *Birth of Tragedy, Thus Spake Zarathustra*, Beyond Good and Evil*

Freud: *General Introduction to Psychoanalysis, Civilization and Its Discontents, Beyond the Pleasure Principle*

Valéry: Selected Poems

Kafka: *The Trial*

Heisenberg: *The Physical Principles of the Quantum Theory**

Supreme Court: *Opinions**

Millikan: *The Electron**

Wittgenstein: *Philosophical Investigations**

Keynes: *General Theory*

Joyce: *The Dead*

Poems by: Yeats, T. S. Eliot, Wallace Stevens, Baudelaire, Rimbaud, and others

Essays by: Faraday, Lorenz, J. J. Thomson, Whitehead, Minkowski, Rutherford, Einstein, Davisson, Bohr, Schrödinger, Maxwell, Bernard, Weismann, Millikan, de Broglier, Heisenberg, John Maynard Smith, Dreisch, Boveri, Mendel, Teilhard de Chardin

7. Proposals to Change the Program at Stanford University, 1989

A front-page story in the *New York Times* in August 1988 alerted readers to a seeming calamity at Stanford University. The program in Western Culture was under consideration for revision to a program called "Cultures, Ideas, and Values." Criticism of the proposed change had already come from the U.S. secretary of education, William Bennett, in a speech to the American Council on Education in Washington. He asked: "Has the Western culture all of a sudden collapsed because the great thinkers of the West all of the sudden became stupid? No, it's not for that reason; it's not for any academic reason. There is no intellectual or academic defense for such a thing; it just seems that what's going on is that a very vocal minority is attempting to overpower a less vocal majority." This publicity followed lengthy committee and academic council deliberations at Stanford, none of which was seen there as a radical departure. Exhibiting the power of televised news media seizing upon slow academic deliberations, the *MacNeil/Lehrer NewsHour* on April 19 was host to Secretary Bennett and President Donald Kennedy of Stanford. Peter Graumann of KQED San Francisco furnished a background for the interview. Substantial portions of their exchange are reprinted here.

E.S. [Edward Shils], "The Discussion about Proposals to Change the Western Culture Program at Stanford University," *Minerva* 27 (Summer–Autumn 1989): 223–411, *MacNeil/Lehrer NewsHour* excerpt, April 19, 1998, 406–11. Reprinted with kind permission of Springer Science and Business Media. Copyright © 1989 by Springer. Further reading: I, 9–10, 13–14; III, 8–10.

Peter Graumann: After months of intense debate a compromise was reached last month to replace the Western culture class with a new course called Cultures, Ideas and Values. While retaining a shortened list of classics, the new course will also examine non-Western ideas and the role of race, sex, and class in ideology. As the debate at Stanford has unfolded, Education Secretary William Bennett has been following the controversy. Last night he came to the Stanford campus to express his displeasure with the results, charging that liberal and minority students used intimidation to get their way.

William Bennett: Stanford's decision of 31 March to alter its Western culture program was not a product of enlightened debate, but rather, an unfortunate capitulation to a campaign of pressure politics and intimidation.

Does anyone really doubt that selecting works based on the ethnicity or gender of their authors trivializes the academic enterprise? Does anyone really doubt the political agenda underlying these provisions?

Events of the past two years at Stanford, therefore, in my mind strike as an example of what Allan Bloom has called the "closing of the American mind." In the name of opening minds and promoting diversity, we have seen in this instance, the closing of the Stanford mind. The loudest voices have won—not through force of argument, but through

bullying and threatening and name-calling. That's not the way a university should work.

Peter Graumann: While Bennett's remarks drew applause at last night's forum, which was sponsored by the Stanford Republican Club, among others, his charge of intimidation is rejected by most of those involved at Stanford. Craig Heller is a biology professor who chaired the faculty committee deliberating the issue.

Craig Heller: The only intimidation that I see was the intimidation coming from outside the university of people making false accusations.

Peter Graumann: Did you feel intimidated at any point?

Heller: At no time. The students would come to meetings and wish to be heard, they were invited in, and they would state in very rational terms what their opinions were, and they would let the committee go about its work and eagerly anticipate the results, and it was a very democratic process.

MacNeil: And now to Secretary Bennett and President Kennedy. President Kennedy, how do you react to Secretary Bennett's charge that this change was made as a result of pressure politics and intimidation?

Kennedy: In the first place I want to thank the secretary for going to Stanford. I'm sorry I couldn't be there to welcome him myself. I think that the speech he made and the reception it got added constructively to the discussion we're having.

As to the discussion itself and the outcome to which it led, I disagree with Secretary Bennett's assessment on two grounds; the first is process, the second is outcome. He doesn't like the outcome, which we viewed as a very marginal change in what is predominantly a Western culture course and still will be, and he criticizes the process, claiming that it involved intimidation. No one who participated in it, including those who took the status quo side in the beginning, can be found who will say that they were intimidated. The decision-makers really operated in a very free and a very rational and very constructive environment.

MacNeil: The decision-makers being members of the faculty?

Kennedy: Members of the Academic Senate.

MacNeil: Mr. Secretary, what is the basis for your use of the word intimidation, then?

Bennett: Last night I said—one student responded much the way President Kennedy has just responded and said, I don't think there was any intimidation (this was a student who was in favor of pushing these changes through)—I said, well, was there any intimidation? Did anyone sense any intimidation? And voices started coming out in the audience, "I did," "I did," "I did," "I did," until we had a very loud chorus.

In terms of the faculty, afterward I spoke to several faculty members. One faculty member from the French Department said to me, "It was like Vichy France here. If you stood up and challenged the reformers, you were called racist and sexist." Now that's not the way a university should behave.

Kennedy: Those of us who were around in the late '60s and passed through that difficult passage really did experience some intimidation. I think we know what it's like and I just don't see any resemblance between what went on at Stanford and what any reasonable person could call intimidation.

I'm not surprised that Secretary Bennett got that reaction last night . . .

MacNeil: Why does that not surprise you?

Kennedy: Well, the occasion was constructed by the Young Republican Club; those who were assenting to that view I think wanted very much to please him. I would still like to know the identity of any member of the Faculty Senate who participated in the process that brought about this change who felt intimidated. Prof. Kenneth Arrow, who was one of those who disagreed with the outcome and said why, says he did not feel intimidated.

Bennett: He said, exactly, that he did not feel physical intimidation. I never argued that it was physical intimidation, but it was quite clear that if you disagreed with the proposal being pushed, you would be called a racist, and that's a matter of public record, President Kennedy. That's in your newspaper, not in a Republican newspaper, it's in the *Stanford Daily,* it's in the San Francisco press. I will give you the name of the faculty member—I will not give it to you on television—provided you promise nothing will happen to that faculty member because there was a lot of this last night and it was quite distressing to hear.

But there are other parts of the record. There was an occupation of your office, there was an occupation of the provost's office, there were quotes from student leaders in the public record saying, "The faculty was getting a little timid, so we thought we ought to put a little pressure on them." At the last meeting, on 31 March, as you know, 300 students were waiting outside and, as the press reported, they said if the faculty was going the wrong way they were going to march in.

Kennedy: Two corrections of that record: First, the University news service didn't even report the students outside and the faculty inside never heard them, were unaware of their presence until they greeted them with polite, scattered applause on their exit, but there was nothing like 300 people there. And the sit-in last spring, which lasted four hours and did not outstay the time at which they could legally be present in the reception area, was about 10 issues, one of which was this one, and it was never discussed and was plainly low priority at the time. So I just think that mischaracterizes the climate as it actually existed during this conversation.

Bennett: Well, again, there is a substantial press record. You may want to turn this frog into a prince, but you can't. A frog is a frog. The press accounts are there, all one has to do is go back and examine the record. The people I talked to last night certainly

were at Stanford every bit as much and felt that this was intimidation.

MacNeil: Let me turn the frog and the prince in any order you all want to identify them.

Bennett: Don't you do that.

MacNeil: OK, sorry . . . into the substance of what the debate was all about. The secretary said, Dr. Kennedy, that this trivializes the academic enterprise.

Kennedy: Well we spent five full meetings of the Academic Senate, at two hours-plus each, in really the most thoughtful debate that you can imagine. I don't think that's trivializing anything. Indeed, the entire campus was swept up into a concern about what I think the secretary and I agree is the most important thing that can take place in an academic setting, and that is a discussion of what ought to be the common intellectual property of educated men and women.

The outcome is not to junk Western culture. The tracks in the course now called Culture, Ideas and Values will still consist of most of the same materials, but there will be added to it significant work from other cultures and from other kinds of authors. I don't think anything has been thrown overboard. I think what we have has been enriched.

MacNeil: I want to get the secretary's response on that. Just to make sure I understand your position, Dr. Kennedy, you did not vote on this issue, right?

Kennedy: No, I'm not allowed.

MacNeil: OK. If you had voted, would you have voted with the majority? Do you believe this is a just and right decision?

Kennedy: Plainly.

MacNeil: All right. Mr. Secretary, how does this trivialize the academic enterprise, and what's the harm of what Stanford has decided to do?

Bennett: Well, again, I think that the means in here is in the ends. Right from the beginning this was an assault on Western culture and Western civilization and if you look at these Stanford newspaper editorials and other things you will see that over this period of time there were many editorials saying Western culture is sexist, racist, imperialistic, and so on, all sorts of things written out of ignorance, which demonstrated the need for students to study Western culture so they would understand that it is Western culture which taught the rest of the world how to overcome many of these things.

But the process, of course, was the problem. But so was the end. This was no trifling change. There were 15 books in the original course.

MacNeil: Let's make sure we understand; that was the core course, the Western civilization course, and there were 15 core books.

Bennett: The so-called modest change dropped nine of those books. That's pretty substantial. Dropping Homer and dropping Dante and dropping Freud, and dropping Darwin and Luther and Thomas More, I think is pretty significant.

Kennedy: And to be replaced by . . .

Bennett: Well that's to be decided by a group of the faculty each year. This year they've decided to keep six of the books, but next year they could drop them all if they wanted to. Now, I think that students at Stanford should study non-Western culture. When I was chairman of the National Endowment for the Humanities, I gave Stanford a grant to develop a course in non-Western culture.

You don't make the case for studying non-Western culture by trashing Western culture. And you don't know non-Western culture any better by knowing Western culture less.

Kennedy: I promise everybody that we didn't trash Western culture . . .

Bennett: Check the record.

Kennedy: . . . that Secretary Bennett's grant was and is very much appreciated, and that we do have a separate non-Western culture requirement, and finally that the enrichment of this course retains 90 percent of what was there, that. . . .

MacNeil: Is he wrong when he says 15 books, nine of them were cut?

Kennedy: It is correct that we cut the core list a bit more than in half: That absolutely required list, which must be included in all of the so-called tracks. There's a whole additional list of strongly recommended works that our faculty have always drawn on, including now the ones that were deleted from the absolutely required list. The faculty teaching that course actually asked for a marginal increase in the flexibility because, for example, philosophers interested in exploring the history of the relationship between state and citizen wanted a little more freedom to assign Locke and Hobbes and Rousseau, which were not on the original, absolutely required list.

So this was the Stanford faculty deciding how it best could teach.

MacNeil: Mr. Secretary, what about the basic complaint that has been made about your position and that the Western civilization core as it existed before Stanford changed it; which was that it is basically a European, white male civilization?

Bennett: Well, yes, as one of the editorials said, "We're tired of reading books by dead white guys." The problem is, a lot of dead white guys wrote very important books. They wrote very important books which all of our students should study. The fact that they were white is irrelevant, as is the fact that they're dead. If the books are important, they should be read. Should books about other societies and cultures be read? Of course they should. But, again, it's like saying we should study French or we should study a foreign language. I believe in that. But I don't make the case for studying French by saying we shouldn't study English. We should study both.

Again, the whole temper of the debate, and the conclusion, was that the West, really, has *too* important a place, when, in fact, I think you could argue that it doesn't have an important *enough* place, and that this whole thing was a process of trashing Western culture and putting something else in its place.

MacNeil: Is he right when he says that it's irrelevant that these are in fact men and that they are white and that they are dead?

Kennedy: I pretty much agree with that; I don't think there's any reason for us to trash Western culture and that's why we haven't. That buzzword just doesn't make a case. All it does is to reflect the secretary's annoyance at an outcome that I think is actually much less of a change then he has perceived it to be.

Let there be no mistake about it, we do believe that the study of even Western culture considered by itself will be made more valuable by the introduction of some of these other strands, more meaningful to our students, and that it will make this kind of study more exciting and spread it more broadly, and I hope that the whole debate at Stanford will be made available to a wider audience and that people can judge that for themselves.

MacNeil: Is it your position, Mr. Secretary, that books by, say, women writers and black writers, to use two examples, were chosen just because they were written by women and blacks and not because they were of the quality that should be included in a Western civilization course?

Bennett: Sure; well, that's what it says, that's what the new guideline says: that books will be selected based on the ethnicity and race and gender of the authors. That's not a sound criterion. Now, to teach a good course on Western civilization you will have books by women. But you will have books by women because they are great books, and that should be the criterion. And you don't go around saying—as the new requirement says—we're going to pick them by race, ethnicity, and gender, and the second part, we will be sure to pay attention to the issues of class and race and gender.

I think that any academic looking at this knows what this is; this is a political agenda. This is not an intellectual agenda, it is a political agenda.

MacNeil: Dr. Kennedy? Serious charge.

Kennedy: I respectfully disagree with that. I think the agenda really is one that seeks to grapple with some of the complexity and the diversity of contemporary American culture and values, and I furthermore think it is possible to enrich this course by the careful and thoughtful selection of works that the Stanford faculty believes are there and can be selected to make this a stronger curriculum.

Bennett: Wait a minute. Let's just talk about "enrich" for a second, because when you enrich and start by removing nine of 15, you've got to make up for an awful lot once you've eliminated that nine. As I said last night to the students, if the study of non-Western cultures, for example, is important at Stanford, then increase the one-quarter requirement in non-Western culture. But don't do it at the expense of studying people like Homer and Dante and Luther and More. There are important reasons for studying these people, and again they deserve better than the treatment they got during this debate.

Kennedy: Those authors are on the strongly recommended list. Their works and their contributions are deeply respected in this debate, but we think they'll be made more meaningful, and that the course of which they are a part will be more meaningful by the introduction of what you must admit, realistically, are strands that are non-Western that contribute significantly to the way our institutions are now and the way they've evolved from those traditions of which you speak.

Bennett: Fine. I am for inclusion, not exclusion. But when you start by cutting the number of books and people to be read, I think that's a mistake.

MacNeil: We'll have to leave it there. Dr. Kennedy, Secretary Bennett thank you both for being with us tonight.

The Mind of the University

8. Allan Bloom,
The Closing of the American Mind, 1987

After a bachelor's degree (1949) and a doctorate (1955) under the influence of Leo Strauss at the University of Chicago, Allan Bloom (1930–92) lectured there for five years, visited Yale as an assistant professor for a year, then went to Cornell to teach government and political theory (1963–70). Confronted with armed student protesters, disrupted teaching, and what he, a lonely but outspoken defender of a neoclassical liberal arts curriculum, saw as administrative and faculty spinelessness, he left Cornell for the University of Toronto (1970–79). Thereafter he returned to Chicago for the rest of his life as a member of the distinguished interdisciplinary Committee on Social Thought and co-director of the John M. Olin Center of Inquiry into the Theory and Practice of Democracy.

Bloom's Cornell experience put a sharp edge on the blade he would swing against the new academic models of the 1960s and 1970s and against American culture generally. That blade was forged from an ardent commitment to seminal minds in western philosophy, particularly Aristotle, Plato, and Rousseau; he edited writings by the latter two. The weapon of ideas became a passionate and personal book, *The Closing of the American Mind,* extensively reprinted here. Surprisingly to many academic people and to Bloom himself, this book gained a huge readership. It appealed to Americans perplexed by the changing condition of higher education; it sold over one million copies and was first in the *New York Times* bestseller list for ten weeks.

From *The Closing of the American Mind* by Allan Bloom (New York, 1987): 29–31, 34–35, 37–39, 135–36, 178, 251–54, 256, 315, 319–20, 322–23, 325. Copyright © 1987 by Allan Bloom. Abridged by permission of Simon and Schuster Adult Publishing Group. Further reading: Ann T. Keene, "Allan Bloom," in *American National Biography,* ed. John A. Garraty and Mark C. Carnes, vol. 3 (New York, 2000), 44; Donald Alexander Downs, *Cornell '69: Liberalism and the Crisis of the American University*

(Ithaca, NY, 1999); Jim Sleeper, "Allan Bloom and the Conservative Mind," *New York Times Book Review,* September 4, 2005, 27; and I, 20; III, 9–10.

Liberalism without natural rights, the kind that we knew from John Stuart Mill and John Dewey, taught us that the only danger confronting us is being closed to the emergent, the new, the manifestations of progress. No attention had to be paid to the fundamental principles or the moral virtues that inclined men to live according to them. To use language now popular, civic culture was neglected. And this turn in liberalism is what prepared us for cultural relativism and the fact-value distinction, which seemed to carry that viewpoint further and give it greater intellectual weight.

History and social science are used in a variety of ways to overcome prejudice. We should not be ethnocentric, a term drawn from anthropology, which tells us more about the meaning of openness. We should not think our way is better than others. The intention is not so much to teach the students about other times and places as to make them aware of the fact that their preferences are only that—accidents of their time and place. Their beliefs do not entitle them as individuals, or collectively as a nation, to think they are superior to anyone else. John Rawls is almost a parody of this tendency, writing hundreds of pages to persuade men, and proposing a scheme of government that would force them, not to despise anyone. In *A Theory of Justice,* he writes that the physicist or the poet should not look down on the man who spends his life counting blades of grass or performing any other frivolous or corrupt activity. Indeed, he should be esteemed, since esteem from others, as opposed to self-esteem, is a basic need of all men. So indiscriminateness is a moral imperative because its opposite is discrimination. This folly means that men are not permitted to seek for the natural human good and admire it when found, for such discovery is coeval with the discovery of the bad and contempt for it. Instinct and intellect must be suppressed by education. The natural soul is to be replaced with an artificial one.

At the root of this change in morals was the presence in the United States of men and women of a great variety of nations, religions, and races, and the fact that many were badly treated because they belonged to these groups. Franklin Roosevelt declared that we want "a society which leaves no one out." Although the natural rights inherent in our regimes are perfectly adequate to the solution of this problem, provided these outsiders adhere to them (i.e., they become insiders by adhering to them), this did not satisfy the thinkers who influenced our educators, for the right to vote and the other political rights did not produce social acceptance. The equal protection of the laws did not protect the man from contempt and hatred as a Jew, Italian, or a Black.

The reaction to this problem was, in the first

place, resistance to the notion that outsiders had to give up their "cultural" individuality and make themselves into that universal, abstract being who participates in natural rights or else be doomed to an existence on the fringe; in the second place, anger at the majority who imposed a "cultural" life on the nation to which the Constitution is indifferent. Openness was designed to provide a respectable place for these "groups" or "minorities"—to wrest respect from those who were not disposed to give it—and to weaken the sense of superiority of the dominant majority (more recently dubbed WASPs, a name the success of which shows something of the success of sociology in reinterpreting the national consciousness). That dominant majority gave the country a dominant culture with its traditions, its literature, its tastes, its special claim to know and supervise the language, and its Protestant religions. Much of the intellectual machinery of twentieth-century American political thought and social science was constructed for the purposes of making an assault on that majority. It treated the founding principles as impediments and tried to overcome the other strand of our political heritage, majoritarianism, in favor of a nation of minorities and groups each following its own beliefs and inclinations. In particular, the intellectual minority expected to enhance its status, presenting itself as the defender and spokesman of all the others. . . .

Actually openness results in American conformism—out there in the rest of the world is a drab diversity that teaches only that values are relative, whereas here we can create all the life-styles we want. Our openness means we do not need others. Thus what is advertised as a great opening is a great closing. No longer is there a hope that there are great wise men in other places and times who can reveal the truth about life—except for the few remaining young people who look for a quick fix from a guru. Gone is the real historical sense of a Machiavelli who wrested a few hours from each busy day in which "to don regal and courtly garments, enter the courts of the ancients and speak with them."

None of this concerns those who promote the new curriculum. The point is to propagandize acceptance of different ways, and indifference to their real content is as good a means as any. It was not necessarily the best of times in America when Catholics and Protestants were suspicious of and hated one another; but at least they were taking their beliefs seriously, and the more or less satisfactory accommodations they worked out were not simply the result of apathy about the state of their souls. Practically all that young Americans have today is an insubstantial awareness that there are many cultures, accompanied by a saccharine moral drawn from that awareness: We should all get along. Why fight? . . .

The reason for the non-Western closedness, or ethnocentrism, is clear. Men must love and be loyal to their families and their peoples in order to preserve them. Only if they think their own things are good can they rest content with them. A father must prefer his child to other children, a citizen his country to others. That is why there are myths—to justify these attachments. And a man needs a place and opinions by which to orient himself. This is strongly asserted by those who talk about the importance of roots. The problem of getting along with outsiders is secondary to, and sometimes in conflict with, having an inside, a people, a culture, a way of life. A very great narrowness is not incompatible with the health of an individual or a people, whereas with great openness it is hard to avoid decomposition. The firm binding of the good with one's own, the refusal to see a distinction between the two, a vision of the cosmos that has a special place for one's people, seem to be conditions of culture. This is what really follows from the study of non-Western cultures proposed for undergraduates. It points them back to passionate attachment to their own and away from the science which liberates them from it. Science now appears as a threat to culture and a dangerous uprooting charm. In short, they are lost in a no-man's land between the goodness of knowing and the goodness of culture, where they have been placed by their teachers who no longer have the resources to guide them. Help must be sought elsewhere. . . .

This is the sound motive contained, along with many other less sound ones, in openness as we understand it. Men cannot remain content with what is given them by their culture if they are to be fully human. This is what Plato meant to show by the image of the cave in the *Republic* and by representing us as prisoners in it. A culture is a cave. He did not suggest going around to other cultures as a solution to the limitations of the cave. Nature should be the standard by which we judge our own lives and the lives of peoples. That is why philosophy, not history or anthropology, is the most important human science. Only dogmatic assurance that thought is culture-bound, that there is no nature, is what makes our educators so certain that the only way to escape the limitations of our time and place is to study other cultures. History and anthropology were understood by the Greeks to be useful only in discovering what the past and other peoples had to contribute to the discovery of nature. Historians and anthropologists were to put peoples and their conventions to the test, as Socrates did individuals, and go beyond them. These scientists were superior to their subjects because they saw a problem where others refused to see one, and they were engaged in the quest to solve it. They wanted to be able to evaluate themselves and others.

This point of view, particularly the need to know nature in order to have a standard, is uncomfortably buried beneath our human sciences, whether they like it or not, and accounts for the ambiguities and contradictions I have been pointing out. They want to make us culture-beings with the instruments that were invented to liberate us from culture. Openness used to be the virtue that permitted us to seek the good by using reason. It now means accepting everything and denying reason's power. The unrestrained and thoughtless pursuit of openness, without recognizing the inherent political, social, or cultural problem of openness as the goal of nature, has rendered openness meaningless. Cultural relativism destroys both one's own and the good. What is most characteristic of the West is science, particularly understood as the quest to know nature and the consequent denigration of convention—i.e., culture or the West understood as a culture—in favor of what is accessible to all men as men through their common and distinctive faculty, reason. Science's latest attempts to grasp the human situation—cultural relativism, historicism, the fact-value distinction—are the suicide of science. Culture, hence closedness, reigns supreme. Openness to closedness is what we teach. . . .

A significant number of students used to arrive at the university physically and spiritually virginal, expecting to lose their innocence there. Their lust was mixed into everything they thought and did. They were painfully aware that they wanted something but were not quite sure exactly what it was, what form it would take and what it all meant. The range of satisfactions intimated by their desire moved from prostitutes to Plato, and back, from the criminal to the sublime. Above all they looked for instruction. Practically everything they read in the humanities and social sciences might be a source of learning about their pain, and a path to its healing. This powerful tension, this literal lust for knowledge, was what a teacher could see in the eyes of those who flattered him by giving such evidence of their need for him. His own satisfaction was promised by having something with which to feed their hunger, an overflow to bestow on their emptiness. His joy was in hearing the ecstatic "Oh, yes!" as he dished up Shakespeare and Hegel to minister to their need. Pimp and midwife really described him well. The itch for what appeared to be only sexual intercourse was the material manifestation of the Delphic oracle's command, which is but a reminder of the most fundamental human desire, to "know thyself."

Sated with easy, clinical and sterile satisfactions of body and soul, the students arriving at the university today hardly walk on the enchanted ground they once did. They pass by the ruins without imagining what was once there. Spiritually detumescent, they do not seek wholeness in the university. These most productive years of learning, the time when Alcibiades was growing his first beard, are wasted because of artificial precociousness and a sophistic wisdom acquired in high school. The real moment for sexual education goes by, and hardly anybody has an idea of what it would be. . . .

For us the most revealing and delightful dis-tinction—because it is so unconscious of its wickedness—is between inner-directed and other-directed, with the former taken to be unqualifiedly good. Of course, we are told, the healthy inner-directed person will *really* care for others. To which I can only respond: If you can believe that, you can believe anything. Rousseau knew much better. . . .

Much of the theoretical reflection that flourishes in modern democracy could be interpreted as egalitarian resentment against the higher type represented by Pascal, denigrating it, deforming it and interpreting it out of existence. Marxism and Freudianism reduce his motives to those all men have. Historicism denies him access to eternity. Value theory makes his reasoning irrelevant. If he were to appear, our eyes would be blind to his superiority, and we would be spared the discomfort it would cause us.

It is to prevent or cure this peculiar democratic blindness that the university may be said to exist in a democracy, not for the sake of establishing an aristocracy but for the sake of democracy and for the sake of preserving the freedom of the mind—certainly one of the most important freedoms—for some individuals within it. The successful university is the proof that a society can be devoted to the well-being of all, without stunting human potential or imprisoning the mind to the goals of the regime. The deepest intellectual weakness of democracy is its lack of taste or gift for the theoretical life. All our Nobel prizes and the like do nothing to gainsay Tocqueville's appraisal in this regard. The issue is not whether we possess intelligence but whether we are adept at reflection of the broadest and deepest kind. We need constant reminders of our deficiency, now more than in the past. The great European universities used to act as our intellectual conscience, but with their decline, we are on our own. . . .

The university's task is thus well defined, if not easy to carry out or even keep in mind. It is, in the first place, always to maintain the permanent questions front and center. This it does primarily by preserving—by keeping alive—the works of those who best addressed these questions. . . . Reason transformed into prejudice is the worst form of prejudice, because reason is the only instrument for liberation from prejudice. The most important function of the university in an age of reason is to protect reason from itself, by being the model of true openness. . . .

The university as an institution must compensate for what individuals lack in a democracy and must encourage its members to participate in its spirit. As the repository of the regime's own highest faculty and principle, it must have a strong sense of its importance outside the system of equal individuality. It must be contemptuous of public opinion because it has within it the source of autonomy—the quest for and even discovery of the truth according to nature. It must concentrate on philosophy, theology, the literary classics, and on those scientists like Newton, Descartes, and Leibniz who have the most comprehensive scientific vision and a sense of the relation of what they do to the order of the whole of things. These must help preserve what is most likely to be neglected in a democracy. They are not dogmatisms but precisely the opposite: what is necessary to fight dogmatism. The university must resist the temptation to try to do everything for society. The university is only one interest among many and must always keep its eye on that interest for fear of compromising it in the desire to be more useful, more relevant, more popular. . . .

To sum up, there is one simple rule for the university's activity: it need not concern itself with providing its students with experiences that are available in democratic society. They will have them in any event. It must provide them with experiences they cannot have there. Tocqueville did not believe that the old writers were perfect, but he believed that they could best make us aware of our imperfections, which is what counts for us.

The universities never performed this function very well. Now they have practically ceased trying. . . .

At Cornell and elsewhere in the United States, it was farce because—whatever the long-range future of our polity—the mass of the country (there really was no mass but a citizenry) was at that moment unusually respectful of the universities, regarded them as resources for the improvement of Americans, and accepted the notion that scholarship should be left undisturbed and was likely to produce a great range of views that should be treated seriously and with tolerance. The nation was not ready for great changes and believed about universities the things professors professed to believe about them. A few students discovered that pompous teachers who catechized them about academic freedom could, with a little shove, be made into dancing bears. . . .

There were two results of the campus disruptions. The university was incorporated much more firmly into the system of democratic public opinion, and the condition of cavelike darkness amidst prosperity feared by Tocqueville was brought painfully near. When the dust settled it could be seen that the very distinction between educated and uneducated in America had been leveled, that even the pitiful remnant of it expressed in the opposition between highbrow and lowbrow had been annihilated. . . . The very ideas of truly different goals and motives of action that we can really take seriously, incarnated not only in systems of thought but in real and poetic models, began to disappear. . . .

About the sixties it is now fashionable to say that although there were indeed excesses, many good things resulted. But, so far as universities are concerned, I know of nothing positive coming from that period; it was an unmitigated disaster for them. I hear that the good things were "greater openness," "less rigidity," "freedom from authority," etc.—but these have no content and express no view of what is wanted from a university education. . . .

The fact is that the fifties were one of the great periods of the American university, taking into account, of course, the eternal disproportion between the ideal and the real. Even the figures most seminal for "the movement," like Marcuse, Arendt and Mills, did what serious work they did prior to 1960. From 1933 on the American universities profited from the arrival of many of Europe's greatest scholars and scientists as well as a number of clever intellectuals of a sophistication beyond that known to their American counterparts. They were, for the most part, heirs of the German university tradition, which . . . was the greatest expression of the publicly supported and approved version of the theoretical life. All were steeped in the general vision of humane education inspired by Kant and Goethe, whose thought and talents were of world historical significance and who intransigently and without compromise looked to the highest moral and artistic fulfillments within the new democratic order of things. They initiated us into a tradition that was living, and that penetrated the tastes and standards of society at large. Those who received this tradition had experience of the vast scholarship accumulated since its inception, as well as the advanced ideas that clustered around its inspiration. . . .

In short, in the fifties a goodly portion of the professors still held the views about freedom of thought put forward by Bacon, Milton, Locke and John Stuart Mill (this was just prior to the success in America of the Continental critique of these); another portion, were of the Left, and they had a personal interest in the protection afforded them by those views. When the former lost their confidence, and the latter gained theirs, the strength of academic freedom declined drastically. . . .

9. Sidney Hook, Review of
The Closing of the American Mind, 1989

Sidney Hook's review of Allan Bloom's book (III, 8) epitomized the pragmatic or instrumentalist method of philosophical inquiry that Hook (1902–89) pursued since his days as John Dewey's doctoral student (1927) at Columbia, where in 1960 he also was awarded the L.H.D. Throughout his long career as professor of philosophy at New York University (1927–69) and later as a research fellow at the Hoover Institution on War, Revolution, and Peace (1973–89), Hook was a scholarly activist and writer on public affairs. A keen interest in Karl Marx led him early into the American Communist party, which he left in 1933 while he developed the position that Marx must be distinguished from Marxism. He was the first to introduce the study of Marx to the academic classroom, and by 1939 he was leading intellectuals in opposing Russian and German totalitarianism, then a new word. Steadfast in his advocacy of social justice, civil liberties, and academic freedom (excepting Communists), he shunned the label of liberal or conservative and proclaimed intellectual independence. The author of more than sixteen books, Hook was honored in his last decade by delivering the Jefferson Lecture for the N.E.H. in 1984 and by receiving the Presidential Medal of Freedom in 1985.

Sidney Hook, "The Closing of the American Mind, An Intellectual Best-Seller Revisited," *The American Scholar* (Winter, 1989): 123, 126–28, 130–32, 135. Reprinted, with permission of Ernest Hook, from *The American Scholar*; Copyright © 1989. Further reading: Sidney Hook, *Out of Step: An Unquiet Life in the Twentieth Century* (New York, 1987); Matthew J. Cotter, ed., *Sidney Hook Reconsidered* (New York, 2004); and Nicholas Capaldi, "Sidney Hook," in *American National Biography*, ed. John A. Garraty and Mark C. Carnes, vol. 11 (New York, 2000), 125–28.

Allan Bloom is convinced that he knows the reason for the failure of American education, particularly higher education—the headwaters of the system— whose products make their influence felt on all subordinate levels of instruction. He attributes the deficiencies and troubles of higher education to its failure to grasp the central philosophical truths about human nature, and a consequent failure to devise a proper, ordered curriculum of studies that would transmit the perennial truths, problems, and aspirations of (in a term he often uses) "the human soul."

Any realistic conception of social causation would find rather naive Bloom's assumption that the social evils impinging on the school systems can be profoundly modified by curricular change or reorganization. On the other hand, given that the schools by themselves can neither reconstruct nor revolutionize society, it still remains true that they can gradually have *some* influence in modifying the attitudes and behavior of their students. They can do this not so much by the information they impart as by the values of appropriate conduct they stress, and especially the habits of mind (or mindlessness) they teach their students. Although Bloom himself sometimes gives the impression that, as a seeker after the truth, he is indifferent to whether he influences or affects anyone or anything, like all educators from Plato to the present he really is trying to improve society or prevent it from going to the dogs. He certainly cannot be faulted on this score.

Before assessing the validity of Bloom's analysis of the current educational scene and his proposals for improving it, I must credit him with two indisputable achievements. The first is to have evoked the astonishing spectacle of the intellectual bankruptcy of the so-called political and cultural left in its response to the positions he has developed in his book. . . .

The second and greater distinction is his sober, brilliant, and really quite devastating accounts of the barbarous attack on American universities in the sixties—an attack from whose consequences they are still suffering. Bloom is not the first to draw the parallel between the riotous American students in the sixties and the behavior of the Nazi-infected students in German universities after Hitler came to power. Those who are too young to remember or

who have tried to forget will find Bloom's account of what occurred at Cornell—which mutatis mutandis is what occurred at Harvard, NYU, Buffalo, San Francisco State, Berkeley, and other institutions—so galvanizing that it will overcome their initial incredulity. They will also find it shocking that he does not hold the riotous students themselves solely or even primarily responsible for the collapse of academic freedom and integrity during this period, but the faculties—their teachers. Students, Bloom writes, "discovered that the pompous teachers who catechized them about academic freedom, could, with a little shove, be made into dancing bears." Most of the time only the threat of a shove sufficed. . . .

Much can be forgiven Bloom because of the story he tells, as distinct from his proposed remedy, all the more so because the memory of those violent days and the lessons that can be drawn from them have been largely ignored. It is striking that of the hundreds of millions of dollars expended on research projects by the great liberal educational foundations, not a single study can be found of the stormy period that transformed so many American universities into political battlefields. Someone has suggested that in part this can be explained by the fact that a considerable number of the university administrators of that era subsequently moved into positions of influence in the foundations as officers and board members. . . .

Despite my fundamental differences with Allan Bloom—and we are separated by an abyss—and despite the easy and frequent charges of his critics that his views would lead to the curtailment of academic freedom, I have much more confidence that my academic freedom is safer in an institution governed by him and his Straussian colleagues than in one governed by his critics.

Bloom indicts American students of the current generation for many things: a lack of understanding of the perennial ideals of Western civilization, an absence of coherent intellectual outlook on the world, an addiction to novelties in cultural life, a hypersensitivity to mind-numbing modern music, the pursuit of sex as a kind of organized sport, a glorification of freedom and an openness of mind whose consequences in fact close the student's mind to moral, metaphysical, and religious truths which constitute the true legacy of liberal civilization. It would not be unfair to ask him for empirical evidence of actual changes over the years in the basic beliefs of the American student body. Certain student practices, of course, are new and different— the vogue of new music, drugs, the flaunting of sexual promiscuity. But what seems to outrage Bloom most is what he calls the students' moral and historical relativism. Sometimes he calls it "cultural relativism," sometimes "relativity," sometimes the belief that "truth is relative." His opening sentence reads: "There is one thing a professor can be absolutely certain of: almost every student entering the university believes, or says he believes, that truth is relative." Students, he writes, "are unified only in their relativism and in their allegiance to equality." Here we focus on his views about relativity and disregard the fact that he is talking about students in our elite universities and not the vast numbers still enrolled in religious and church-related institutions.

It may be hard to believe, but Bloom's whole discussion of the theme from the first page to the last is vitiated by a fundamental blunder. He confuses subjectivism with moral relativity. He seems to be unaware of the difference between saying (1) all truth is relative, meaning nothing is true or false, good or bad, but that our saying so or feeling so makes it so, and saying (2) all truth is relational, depending upon a complex of things that determine its validity or objectivity. To Bloom the opposite of relational is absolute, not subjective. The subjectivist judgment is arbitrary: it does not call for reasons or evidence to buttress its claims. It does not make a cognitive claim at all. It merely declares a state of feeling. A relational or relativistic judgment, on the other hand, can be challenged to justify itself. Bloom seems not to have heard of the notion of objective relativism. Sometimes what a proposition is relational to is simple: "Milk is a nourishing food," in relation to the digestive systems of organisms of type y. No subjectivism here, only more specification. Bloom would recognize the point at once if someone were to ask him: "How far is Chicago?"

Often what makes a statement true or false, good or bad is much more complex, especially moral statements, since for the problem in hand they are related not only to facts but to shared values in that situation. The complexity of our moral statements depends on certain historical conditions and on the plurality of values always involved in a genuine moral problem. "What shall we do?" may be a technical problem merely concerning the best or most effective means to achieve a given end. But when it is a *moral* question, it always presupposes a conflict of ends that must be resolved here and now. No important policy issue is merely a technical problem of means. Bloom assumes that there exists one underlying good that can be grasped if we understand "the nature of man," and from which all moral judgments of good or bad can be ultimately derived in all situations. He also holds that there are a number of self-evident natural rights sufficient to answer all our questions of right and wrong.

Not only is this position false, but demonstrably false. He does not realize that our moral economy is one in which good often conflicts with good, and right with right. No matter what the particular good or right may be which we seek to absolutize, it may be overridden in the light of the possible consequences of our actions on other goods or rights to which we are committed in the particular historical situation we find ourselves. . . .

The difference between Bloom and the objective relativists whose position he distorts is that, for

him, good is good and right is right—and that's the end of it. To the objective relativist, however, morals are related to human weal and woe, to human and social needs, and to the feasible alternatives of action open to mankind at any historic time. . . .

The conception of cultural and ethical relativism in American thought, as Bloom interprets it, leads to the view that "anything goes." The true conception, however, leads instead to a better understanding of the causes and conditions of the values and practices different groups hold, and the likely consequences of alternative policies in dealing with the conflicts that arise from such differences in order to discover the more reasonable and better way of preserving our democratic society. Bloom rejects this approach as "liberalism without natural rights"—rights, that is, enshrined in the Declaration of Independence and the Constitution, ultimately derivable from God and Nature. He makes no attempt to show how they can be derived from these theological and metaphysical notions. And he seems unaccountably indifferent to the obvious fact that the rights to life, liberty, and happiness in the Declaration are not always compatible with each other, and that the rights enumerated in the Constitution are often in direct conflict with each other. The right to due process and a fair trial may be threatened by the exercise of free speech. This makes it incoherent to regard all of them as inalienable, indefeasible, or absolute. The compulsions of an ordered and orderly democratic society may make it necessary to override for a limited time any of the enumerated rights; hence none can be regarded as absolute. Only the use of intelligence or reason in making the decision can be deemed absolute.

To hold this view, Bloom is compelled to flagrantly distort history and to interpret the right to freedom of religion as belonging to the realm of knowledge rather than to practice. He must ignore also the fact that the practice is far from absolute, since a religion that practiced human sacrifice, or sacred prostitution, polygamy, or any other currently illegal action would not be tolerated under the constitutional right of freedom and religion. To cover up the glaring gaps in his argument—or rather the absence of argument—he charges that ethical relativism entails the lunatic doctrine that freedom, conceived as the right to do anything one pleases in the name of democracy, is absolute. . . .

The difficulty with Bloom's position is that, like Leo Strauss, he has not emancipated himself from the Greek notion that the cosmos is also an ethos, and that what is good and bad, right and wrong for man is essentially related to the cosmic order rather than to the reflective choices of men and women confronted by problems of what to do. Bloom speaks of "the rational quest for the good life according to nature." He tells us that "nature should be the standard by which we judge our own lives and the lives of people," but he does not tell us where we must go to find it. He certainly does not mean nature "red in tooth and claw" as a standard. Nor can the metaphysical or theological order be of any more help. We may hold that all men are biological brothers or brothers under the fatherhood of God. But this conviction does not clarify in the slightest why we believe it is wrong to act like Cain toward his brother Abel but right to act like Jonathan to David, who was not his brother. . . .

Implicit in Bloom's analysis, and more explicit in the writings of his mentors, is his denial of the autonomy of the moral experience. Without reference to the existence of God or to some metaphysical "order of the whole of things," we cannot, according to him, intelligibly determine what is right or wrong or rationally defend a belief in human rights conceived in Jeffersonian fashion as reasonable rights, not literally as natural rights. Bloom offers not a single plausible argument to defend his position but, to reassert it, falls back on pages upon pages about Nietzsche and relativity. He is strikingly and strangely sympathetic to Nietzsche under the twofold delusion that Nietzsche's declaration that "God is dead" left man not only bereft or in anguish but in terror without any compass to direct his life; and that the development of reason itself must lead to the rejection of reason.

All this is absurd. Hume long ago showed that there is no such thing as pure reason, that it always acts in the context of interest and passion. Thereafter a whole brigade of thinkers, including both Dewey and Freud (one of the few things they have in common) showed that the cultivation of reason or intelligence, by establishing new behavior or habit patterns, can modify and reorder the interests and passions to avoid self- and socially destructive consequences. Utopian fools believe that this can be done easily. It is just as foolish to believe that it is altogether impossible, that nothing can be done by intelligent nurture and education. Those who talk of "the bankruptcy of reason" or of science in virtue of the consequences of its development—which generates, of course, new problems and challenges—exhibit failure not only of nerve but of intelligence.

Let us finally return to the issue dividing Bloom from the pack of frenzied detractors of his book (among the latter, I note, are some of his ideological kinsmen, doubtless envious of his success)—that is, the issue of what the curriculum of a liberal arts college should be today. Bloom's approach rests upon the grasp and application of certain metaphysical truths about the nature of man and society. More comprehensive in its claim, and yet more detailed in its application, was the similar approach to higher education taken before him by Mortimer Adler and Robert Hutchins with an occasional assist from Alexander Meiklejohn as a justification of the curriculum of St. John's College. . . .

The specific details of any college curriculum are, of course, never fixed. They are affected by contingencies of national crises as well as by slow changes in the encompassing society of which the educational system is always a part. But it is possible to develop on empirical grounds, regardless of differences on first or last things, broad outlines for certain required areas of study appropriate for the liberal education of men and women in our time. . . .

Although I reject Allan Bloom's analysis of what is wrong with higher education in our day, and therefore I reject as well his remedies, I nonetheless wish to pay tribute to his good will and intellectual effort, which has succeeded in arousing the country to the necessity, at long last, of a serious debate on what a serious education for modern men and women should be. His noble failure will do more to enrich and uphold the quality of higher education in the United States than the recent vaunted reforms of curricular offerings that in the name of an unlimited, and therefore educationally meaningless, diversity seek to politicize our universities.

10. Lawrence Levine,
The Opening of the American Mind, 1996

Nine years after Allan Bloom published his bestselling book, Lawrence Levine (1933–2006) responded to Bloom and similar critics of American higher education with his book proclaiming the "opening" of the American mind. His rejoinder was as pointed and personal as Bloom's indictment. In contrast to Sidney Hook's philosophical disagreement with Bloom, Levine wrote as a cultural historian with broad interests in the recent American past.

After completing his doctoral dissertation (1962) at Columbia with Richard Hofstadter, Levine became an instructor at Princeton for a year and then went to a long tenure (1962–94) in the history department at Berkeley. Thereafter he joined the faculty of George Mason University. He was awarded a MacArthur Fellowship in 1983, and presided over the Organization of America Historians in 1992–93.

The Opening of the American Mind: Canons, Culture, and History by Lawrence W. Levine © 1996 by Lawrence W. Levine. Reprinted by permission of Beacon Press, Boston, pp. 18–21, 28–33. Footnotes omitted. Further Reading: III, 8–9.

These developments . . . trouble so many of the critics whose lament is less about politics in the classroom than about the cultural changes that have taken place in the university. The advocacy they complain about most vigorously is cultural rather than political in nature. It is the *openness* of the contemporary university that is so threatening and the complexity of the education available to students today that is so disturbing to the university's most vigorous detractors. The title of Bloom's *The Closing of the American Mind* was paradoxical. His real target was what he called "the recent education of openness." He characterized the contemporary university as "open to all kinds of men, all kinds of lifestyles, all ideologies," and thus "closed" to the absolute truths of the classical writings and great books that alone constitute true education. Bloom identified the real villain as cultural relativism which he defined as the conviction that all societies and values are "as good" as all others. Bloom's anxiety was not relieved by the fact that what cultural relativism commonly taught students is not to make a simple-minded equation between everything as equal, but rather to be open to the reality that all peoples in societies have cultures which we have to respect to the extent that we take the trouble to understand how they operate and what they believe. Bloom found this perspective no less dangerous since it opens students to the possibility that *their* culture is not necessarily superior and potentially weakens the conviction that Western culture and "Civilization" are synonymous. He condemned contemporary education for "destroying the West's universal or intellectually imperialistic claims, leaving it to be just another culture." Bloom insisted that the permanent and natural state between cultures is one of Darwinian competition. Values, he argued, "can only be asserted or posited by overcoming others, not by reasoning with them. Cultures have different *perceptions,* which determine what the world is. They cannot come to terms. There is no communication about the highest things. . . . Culture means a war against chaos *and* a war against other cultures." . . .

The "traditional" curriculum that prevailed so widely in the decades between the World Wars, and whose decline is lamented with such fervor by the conservative critics, ignored most of the groups that compose the American population whether they were from Africa, Europe, Asia, Central and South America, or from indigenous North American peoples. The primary and often exclusive focus was upon a narrow stratum of those who came from a few Northern and Western European countries whose cultures and mores supposedly became the archetype for those of all Americans in spite of the fact that in reality American culture was forged out of a much larger and more diverse complex of peoples and societies. In addition, this curriculum did not merely teach Western ideas and culture, it taught the *superiority* of Western ideas and culture; it equated Western ways and thought with "Civilization" itself. This tendency is still being championed by contemporary critics of the university. "Is it Eurocentric to believe the life of liberty is superior to the life of the bee hive?" Charles Krauthammer inquired in his justification of the European conquest of the Americas. Without pretending to have studied the cultures of Asia and Africa in any depth, Secretary of Education William Bennett did not hesitate to inform the faculty and students of Stanford University that "the West is a source of *incomparable* intellectual complexity and diversity and depth."

To say that a curriculum that questions these parochial assumptions is somehow anti-Western or anti-intellectual is to misunderstand the aims of education. If in fact the traditions of Western science and humanities mean what they say, modern universities are performing precisely the functions institutions of higher learning should perform: to stretch the boundaries of our understanding; to teach the young to value our intellectual heritage not by rote but through comprehension and examination; to continually and perpetually subject the "wisdom" of our society to thorough and thoughtful scrutiny while making the "wisdom" of other societies and other cultures accessible and subject to comparable scrutiny; to refuse to simplify our culture beyond recognition by limiting our focus to only one segment of American society and instead to open up the *entire* society to thoughtful examination.

To require more careful study and more convincing documentation for the charges against the university is not to be pedantic or picayune; it is to hold the critics of the university to the same scholarly standards and the same humanistic values they claim the university itself has abandoned. The irony is that the critics of the contemporary university too often have become parodies of the very thing they're criticizing: ideologues whose research is shallow and whose findings are widely and deeply flawed by exaggerated claims, vituperative attacks, defective evidence, and inadequate knowledge of the history of the university in the United States and of the process by which canons and curricula have been formed and reformed since the beginning American higher education. . . .

It surely was much simpler when the university community was a homogeneous one, not because there was more freedom but because homogeneity ensured that there was more unanimity about what constituted acceptable ideas and behavior; because, that is, there was *more,* not less, of what today is called political correctness. When Allan Bloom blamed the radical students of the 1960s for opening the university to the "vulgarities present in society at large," he conveniently ignored the truth that long before the student movements universities had hardly transcended the larger society's "vulgarities" but had in fact mirrored its often prejudiced, repressive, and "politically correct" attitudes toward gender, race, and ethnicity in their admissions policies, their hiring practices, and their curricula.

But the American university no longer is and never again will be homogeneous, and much of what we have seen recently in terms of speech codes and the like are a stumbling attempt to adapt to this new heterogeneity. The major consequence of the new heterogeneity on campuses, however, has not been repression but the very opposite—a flowering of ideas and scholarly innovation unmatched in our history. . . .

The British historian Sir Lewis Namier observed that "the crowning attainment of historical study is a historical sense—an intuitive understanding of how things do not happen." It is exactly this understanding of how things do *not* happen that the leading critics of the contemporary university lack. Thus they freely spin their facile theories of how the survivors of the New Left lost the political wars but won their ultimate triumph by capturing the university and transforming it from an institution of culture and learning to a high-handed and inflexible purveyor of Political Correctness. The problem with such notions-aside from the fact that they are promulgated, to borrow Carl Becker's memorable phrase, without fear and without research-is that they are telling examples of how things do not happen. Universities in the United States are not transformed by small cabals of political and social radicals who somehow (the process is never revealed) capture venerable private and public institutions of higher learning, convert them to their own agendas, overwhelm and silence the majority of their colleagues while boards of regents and trustees benignly look on, and mislead generations of gullible and passive college youth who are robbed of their true heritage thus compelled to stumble forth into the larger world as undereducated and uncultured dupes mouthing the platitudes taught them by the band of radical mesmerists posing as college professors. "I have never fully understood the notion that faculty could brainwash me into believing whatever they wanted me to," a Stanford undergraduate testified. "Reading Hitler did not make me a fascist; reading Sartre did not make me an existentialist. Both simply enabled me to think about those philosophies in ways I hadn't previously." It should not take a great deal of reflection to realize that neither college students nor college faculties nor college administrations operate in the manner posited by the apocalyptic and conspiratorial views of the contemporary university. This is not how things happen in the American university and to comprehend why some people are convinced that they do we might ponder Richard Hofstadter's notions of the "paranoid style" in American politics.

In no sense did Hofstadter equate what he called the paranoid style with psychological pathology. He argued that while clinical paranoia describes an individual who is convinced of the existence of a hostile and conspiratorial world "directed specifically *against him*," the paranoid style involves belief in a conspiracy "directed against a nation, a culture, a way of life." Hofstadter found this style recurring throughout American history in the anti-Masonic and anti-Catholic crusades, and in such manifestations of anti-Communism as McCarthyism and the John Birch Society. But there is nothing particularly retrograde about the style; one can find it in aspects of abolitionism, of Populism, and of antiwar movements as well. It is less tied to particular political goals than to a way of seeing the world, a way of understanding how things work by invoking the process of conspiracy. "The paranoid spokesman," according to Hofstadter, "sees the fate of this conspiracy in apocalyptic terms. . . . He is always manning barricades of civilization. He constantly lives at a turning point: is now or never in organizing resistance to conspiracy. Time is forever just running

out. . . . The apocalypticism of the paranoid style runs dangerously near to hopeless pessimism, but usually stops just short of it."

I would argue that this manner of envisioning reality has frequently characterized those who resisted the changes taking place in American higher education, and never more so than during the past several decades. Perhaps the most unfortunate aspect of this mode of analysis is not merely that it's incorrect but that it's so simple and pat and that we learn little, if anything, from it. "We are all sufferers from history," Hofstadter concluded, "but the paranoid is a double sufferer, since he is afflicted not only by the real world, with the rest of us, but by his fantasies as well."

What is wrong with the dominant critiques is not that they are mistaken in every instance, nor that there aren't things to criticize in contemporary universities. Of course there are. We need to integrate learning more fully and to have more sequential courses that build on one another. We need to minimize the use inaccessible jargon wherever possible, particularly in those where jargon has become a way of life. We need to make a greater effort to communicate with colleagues in other disciplines, with students, and with the general public. We need to ensure that teaching ability is considered seriously in all faculty personnel decisions. We need to learn how to respond to the considerable challenge of teaching the most wide-ranging and heterogeneous body of students in the history of American higher education. The problem is that the charges against the university are so hyperbolic, so angry, so conspiracy-minded, and so one-sided, they can find almost nothing positive to say. They see little if any good coming out of the new research and teaching on race and gender, the multifaceted study of American culture, the attempts to more completely understand the world and its peoples and cultures, the exciting development of a student body and faculty that are increasingly becoming more representative of the nation's population.

There *is* fragmentation in the United States; there *is* distrust; there *is* deep anger-and much of this is reflected in and acted out in universities, but none of it is *caused* by universities or by professors or by young people. Nevertheless, all three are easy scapegoats for the problems of the larger society. The many changes taking place in the nation's universities have created awkward moments pregnant with the possibilities of progress but also containing an abundance of room for egregious mistakes, and universities have had their share of both. But to collect dozens of anecdotes illustrating the stumbling of many universities in the face of new pressures and challenges—while ignoring all of their many successful adjustments and innovations—and to parade these stories forth as indicative of the great problem we face is mistaken. Those who do so disregard the fact that the real fragmentation confronting this society has nothing to do with the university, which is one of the more successfully integrated and heterogeneous institutions in the United States, and everything to do with the reality that forms of fragmentation—social, ethnic, racial, religious, regional, economic—have been endemic in the United States from the outset. In our own time this historic fragmentation has been exacerbated because a significant part of our population has been removed from the economy and turned into a permanent underclass with no ladders leading out of its predicament and consequently little hope.

Americans' complicated and ambivalent attitudes toward the university have created the myth that universities are not part of the "real" world, and many professors, pleased at the notion that they were apart from and therefore more "objective" about the surrounding society, have been willing to go along with this illusion and to varying extents have even come to believe it. In truth, as this study will illustrate again and again, universities are never far removed from the larger society. To have a literature of crisis built upon the university and the young as *the* enemy, as *the* creators of fragmentation, discontent, and social turmoil, is so bizarre as to almost, but not quite, defy understanding. Rather than face the complex of reasons for our present state of unease, it is easier and certainly much more comforting to locate the source of our dilemma in an institution—the university—that has always been deeply suspect in the United States, in a group—professors—who have always been something of an anomaly in a theoretically egalitarian land, and in a generation—college youth—who have always made us nervous because they never *seem* to be our exact replicas.

The trouble with the widespread apocalyptic view of the sudden takeover of the university by forces essentially alien to its basic spirit is that this vision removes the American university from the context of its own extended history and transforms long-term processes of change and development into short-term accidents. . . . To understand where the university is we have to understand where it has been and how its present state was constructed. There is no quicker or easier way to proceed; to fathom today requires some awareness of yesterday. In the process we will learn not only about higher education, we will discover truths about our culture, and hopefully, about ourselves as well.

Teaching the Connection

11. Gerald Graff, "How to Save 'Dover Beach,'" 1992

Controversies among ancients and moderns lie at the center of intellectual life. In the second half of the twentieth century, partisanship between traditionalists and revisionists disrupted some humanities and social science departments by the introduction of ethnic and gender studies. Through this well-known essay set in a faculty lounge, Gerald Graff (1937–) illustrated such a contro-

versy by endorsing "teaching the conflicts" in an English department. He extended his picture into a description of how theory can evolve out of a modern humanities dispute. In all, his first concern here and in other essays from this book was the classroom. How can students from diverse backgrounds and levels of preparation be awakened to the vitality of literature?

Educated at the University of Chicago (B.A. 1959), and at Stanford (Ph.D. 1963), Graff taught for three years at the University of New Mexico (1963–66) before joining the Northwestern University faculty as John C. Shaffer Professor of English and Humanities (1980–91). He went on to the University of Chicago as George M. Pullman Distinguished Service Professor of English and Education (1991–2000). In 2000 he moved to the College of Liberal Arts and Sciences at the University of Illinois at Chicago.

Gerald Graff, "How to Save 'Dover Beach,'" in Gerald Graff, *Beyond the Culture Wars, How Teaching the Conflicts Can Revitalize American Education* (New York, W.W. Norton, 1992): 37–52 abridged. Copyright © 1992 Gerald Graff. Reprinted with the kind permission of the author. Further reading: III, 12, 13.

The scene: the English department faculty lounge at Middle America University. An older professor enters, draws a cup of coffee, and remarks that he has just come from teaching Matthew Arnold's famous Victorian poem "Dover Beach" and was appalled to discover that his students found the poem virtually incomprehensible. Here is another sorry illustration, he sighs wearily, of the deplorably ill-prepared state of our students today. Why—can you believe it?—says the older male professor (I'll call him OMP for short), these students hardly knew what to make of the famous concluding lines, which he recites with slightly self-mocking grandiloquence:

> Ah, love, let us be true
> To one another! for the world, which seems To lie
>   before us like a land of dreams,
> So various, so beautiful, so new,
> Hath really neither joy, nor love, nor light, Nor
>   certitude, nor peace, nor help for pain; And we
>   are here as on a darkling plain
> Swept with confused alarms of struggle and flight,
> Where ignorant armies clash by night.

One of his colleagues who happens to be in the lounge, a young woman who teaches courses in literature by women (let's call her YFP), replies that she can appreciate the students' reaction. She recalls that being forced to study "Dover Beach" in high school caused her to form a dislike for poetry that it had taken her years to overcome.

OMP (furiously stirring his Coffee-mate): In *my* humble opinion—reactionary though I suppose it now is—"Dover Beach" is one of the great masterpieces of the Western tradition, a work that, until recently at least, every seriously educated person took for granted as part of the cultural heritage.

YFP: Perhaps, but is that altogether to the credit of the cultural heritage? Take those lines addressed to the woman: "Ah, love, let us be true to one another . . ." and so forth. In other words, protect and console me, my dear—as it's the function of your naturally more spiritual sex to do—from the "struggle and flight" of politics and history that we men have been assigned the regrettable duty of dealing with. It's a good example of how women have been defined by our culture as naturally private and domestic and therefore justly disqualified from sharing male power.

OMP: So much for teaching "Dover Beach," then . . .

YFP: On the contrary, we *should* teach "Dover Beach." But we should teach it as the example of phallocentric discourse that it is.

OMP: That's the trouble with you people; you seem to treat "Dover Beach" as if it were a piece of political propaganda rather than a work of art. To take Arnold's poem as if it were an instance of "phallocentric discourse," whatever that is, misses the whole point of poetry, which is to rise above such transitory issues by transmuting them into universal human experience. To read poems as if they were statements about gender politics replaces the universal concerns of art with the gripes of a special-interest group. "Dover Beach" is no more about gender politics than Macbeth is about the Stuart monarchical succession.

YFP: But Macbeth *is* about the Stuart monarchical succession, among other things—or at least its original audience may well have thought so. It's about gender politics, too: Why does Lady Macbeth have to "unsex" herself to qualify to commit murder? Not to mention the business about men born of woman and from their mothers' womb untimely ripped. It's not that "Dover Beach" and Macbeth are "statements about gender politics" but that these texts assume definitions of men's and women's "natures" that still shape our behavior and that we blind ourselves to if we read them as accounts of universal experience.

What you take to be the universal human experience in Arnold and Shakespeare, Professor OMP, is male experience presented as if it were universal. You don't notice the presence of politics in literature —or in sexual relations, for that matter—because for you patriarchy is simply the normal state of affairs and therefore as invisible as the air you breathe. My reading of "Dover Beach" seems to you to reflect a "special-interest" agenda, but to me yours does, too. You can afford to "transmute" the sexual politics of literature onto a universal plane, but that's a luxury I don't enjoy.

At this point other colleagues passing through the lounge begin to jump in. An old-fashioned formalist close reader asks YFP where, in "Dover Beach," there is any indication that the speaker and addressee are respectively male and female. Might not Arnold have avoided specifying the genders, he asks, precisely to stress the universal nature of the experience? "Don't you concede that all of us at times, women and men both, have felt fed up with politics

as a clash of ignorant armies? Then, too, the mutuality of the experience seems to be stressed—'let us be true *to one another*. . . .' It's an equal partnership."

OMP (beaming): Precisely, precisely.

YFP: Honestly now, have you ever encountered anyone who read "Dover Beach" as spoken by a woman to a man? I know I haven't. Could any woman in Victorian England—even Victoria herself —have spoken with such a voice? It's true that the impulse to escape into private experience is felt by everyone, but that's my point. Women are no more naturally "private" than men, but historically that's the role they've been assigned. Because of this difference in our histories, "let us be true to one another" says something different to me from what it says to you. But suppose you're right. Suppose that we read the poem as spoken by a woman to a man (or, for that matter, two people of the same sex) and that the speaker assumes a more equal relation between the parties than I see. This would not make the poem any less political; it would simply make it a *different* politics, a better politics, but still a politics. . . .

Another feminist chimes in, saying, "Yes, I'm glad you acknowledge the possibility of a more complex politics in the poem than a straightforward 'phallocentric discourse.' As you know, feminist criticism long ago moved away from attacking white male authors for sexism. I think most current feminists would see a conflict of attitudes toward love in the poem—on the one hand, a desire for utopian equality between the sexes; on the other, the man doing all the talking and reveling in melodramatic self-pity. . . ."

A more up-to-date close reader enters the fray. "If I take that further, it seems to me that both of you, OMP and YFP, are partly right and that something like your conflict remains unresolved in 'Dover Beach' itself. Arnold tries to do what you see it as doing, OMP, to assert the transcendence of love and the great art and religions of the past, which are invoked earlier in the poem, over the 'ignorant armies' of contemporary history and politics. But in recognizing those ignorant armies, he is forced to acknowledge the pull of history and social conflict that challenges the universals he wants to reaffirm. Arnold is not aware of the gender conflicts you're concerned with, YFP (which is your point), but the turbulence of nineteenth-century social upheaval is surely there in the reference to 'struggle and flight. . . .'"

Predictably, this interpretation only provoked further objections. The discussion continued. . . .

COMMON CULTURE OR COMMON DEBATE?

When one considers the enormous diversity of American universities, it seems strangely self-defeating to think of disagreement as an impasse. For many decades now ambitious universities have been systematically recruiting faculties that would represent the increasing multiplicity of human knowledge and culture. It is this intellectual and cultural richness that has made American higher education the envy of the world. A college president who did not find deep conflicts of principle on his or her faculty would have far more reason to worry than one who found such conflicts frequently. A state of peace and quiet would indicate that major perspectives had been excluded, the sure sign of a second-rate institution. Yet having programmed the inevitability of ideological contention into our system, we seem shocked to discover there is so much ideological contention around. . . .

We are right to seek a clear vision of what educated people should know, but we have been looking for that vision in the wrong place. We have been seeking it in a consensus that has become increasingly less attainable as American education has become increasingly less culturally and philosophically homogeneous. A really clear vision would see that when what educated persons should know is deeply disputed, the dispute itself becomes part of what educated persons should know. Once the cultural status of "Dover Beach" has become controversial, that controversy becomes part of the study of literature.

Even if [William] Bennett is right that there is more consensus than we recognize on the important thinkers, ideas, and books, deep differences remain in the way these books are interpreted and taught. "Dover Beach" as taught by OMP will seem so different a poem from "Dover Beach" as taught by YFP that it may hardly look like the same work to a student who takes courses from both. For this reason, agreement could be reached tomorrow on a core list of texts and little of the current contention would abate.

Does this mean, then, that the very idea of a common culture must be scrapped? It depends what is meant by that too loosely used term "common culture." What is troubling about those who invoke the idea of common culture against teachers like YFP is their habit of speaking as if the content of that culture were already settled—as if there were no question about what the common culture will include and who will have a voice in defining it. . . .

There is always a background of agreement that makes disagreement possible, and through debate that area of agreement can be widened. We need to distinguish between a shared body of national beliefs, which democracies can do nicely without, and a common national debate about our many differences, which we now need more than ever. . . .

What most multiculturalists and feminists question is not the ideal of a common culture but the assumption that this ideal is already a realized fact, excusing us to return to educational business as usual after adding a few token minority texts to the syllabus. The quarrel of these groups is not with the idea of shared cultural experience but with the use of that idea as an excuse for inequality and injustice, as if to say, So what if there is a huge and widening gulf in the United States between rich and poor,

white and black, majority and minority cultures? We're all part of the common culture, aren't we? . . .

But we won't strengthen fragile "bonds of cohesion" by attacking others for being divisive. . . . To tell those who have been forcibly excluded from the benefits of the melting pot that their complaints are too "divisive" is a good way to drive them into permanent opposition.

The current attack on "divisiveness," "Balkanization," and so forth is really an attack on the unpleasant fact of social conflict itself while fobbing off the responsibility for it on somebody else. It represents an essentially defensive and frightened way of responding to conflict, one that prevents us from seeing that it is precisely in divisive disagreements like that between OMP and YFP that the starting point for a common cultural discussion might be found.

WHAT IS GOOD FOR "DOVER BEACH"?

In fact, in a country where literature has not exactly been high on the list of national priorities, there is something a bit bizarre about the belief that the eruption of a passionate quarrel over literature is bad for it. What would truly be bad for "Dover Beach" is if no such quarrel existed, something that would imply that we do not care enough about such works to bother going to battle over them. The classics, I suggest, have less to fear from newfangled ideological hostility than from old-fashioned indifference. . . .

What has really been disastrous for classics like "Dover Beach" is the belief that we honor such classics by protecting them from disrespect. Though this protective attitude postures as a form of reverence for Western culture, it really betrays a lack of confidence in that culture, whose monuments we evidently fear cannot stand up to criticism. It is Western insecurity, not Western self-confidence, that one senses beneath the chest-thumping exhortations heard today to stop acting like wimps, whiners, and victim lovers and to stand up for the superiority of the West. In fact, the West-Is-Besters are doing precisely what they denounce others for: reveling in self-pity, presenting themselves as helpless victims, and using the curriculum to prop up a flagging self-esteem. Anybody who was really confident of the West's accomplishments would welcome strong criticism of them. . . .

One might think traditionalists would be encouraged by the revival of their own favorite questions about the civic role of the arts, but of course, the new ways of reviving the question of value are not what traditionalists had in mind. Evaluating literature has come to be thought of as a process in which we efface our particular social circumstances and become a kind of neutral everyman. If a work is good, it is good in itself apart from whoever happens to be reading it under whatever circumstances. YFP's argument seems shocking because she rejects this universal contract and refuses to forget who she is and where she came from when she reads "Dover Beach." In asserting that she does not have the luxury to forget she is a woman, YFP says, in effect, that because women have historically been treated differently from men, something different can be at stake for them even in something so seemingly harmless as how a woman is addressed in a love poem. (YFP is not the first to have noticed a certain male pomposity in "Dover Beach"; Anthony Hecht has satirized this very quality in his widely anthologized poem "The Dover Bitch" [". . . To have been brought / all the way down from London, and then be addressed / As a sort of mournful cosmic last resort / Is really tough on a girl].). . . .

I am suggesting that what is threatened by the debate in the faculty lounge is not "Dover Beach" but OMP's conception of "Dover Beach" as a repository of universal values that stand above controversy, above politics, above who we are as readers and the different backgrounds and interests we bring to our reading. Whereas this conflict-free idea of culture once held a privileged place in humanistic education as something that went without saying, it has now become one theory among others, something that you have to argue for against competing theories. This is what most bothers OMP: that the literary canon, once seen as an accepted heritage to be noiselessly passed from one generation to the next, has become a conflict of theories.

THEORY HAS BROKEN OUT

One way to describe the conflict in the faculty lounge, then, is to say that theory has broken out. "Theory," by my definition anyway, is what erupts when what was once silently agreed to in a community becomes disputed, forcing its members to formulate and defend assumptions that they previously did not even have to be aware of. As soon as OMP and YFP discover they hold conflicting assumptions about poetry in general, they have no choice but to have a dispute about theoretical questions: What is poetry? Should students study it and why, and how should it be taught? How do we know what a poem like "Dover Beach" or a play like Macbeth is about?

Teachers like OMP tend to see this kind of discussion as a lamentable diversion of our attention from literary works—as if what we mean by "literature" should not need to be disputed. Others, as we have seen, view it as a case of the professors bickering among themselves and losing sight of their object of study, as if those who make this objection were not implicated in the "bickering." Literature is not being left behind in the dispute between OMP and YFP, however, but rather is being discussed in the more theoretically conscious way that becomes necessary when we no longer agree on the nature and function of literature. . . .

A variant of this objection holds that while theoretical debate is all well and good in its place, in the usual undergraduate teaching situation there isn't time for it. Had we but world enough and time, this objection runs, debates on the politics of poetry like the one engaged in by OMP, YFP, and their colleagues might be valuable to explore. But considering the inevitable constraints, especially with students who may be taking their sole literature class in college, the teacher's primary responsibility must be to teach "Dover Beach" itself. After all, how can undergraduates be expected to fathom such theoretical debates if they cannot yet make out the prose sense of "Dover Beach"—and probably do not even know where Dover Beach is?

I try to show in my next chapter how disastrous for the teaching of literature has been the seemingly commonsensical view that critical and theoretical talk about literature *competes* with reading "literature itself." Suffice it to say here that OMP (or any other teacher) is *already* implicitly teaching his theories when he teaches "Dover Beach." Teaching theory is not a question of adding something to one's analysis of the poem itself but of explaining what one is doing and why one is doing it that way and not another. In an important sense OMP and YFP are already teaching their theoretical debate even if they never mention their assumptions to their classes. Teachers who claim there is not enough time for theory remind me of the politician who reportedly asked, "How can you expect me to be concerned about ethics when there are all these other things I have to do?" . . .

The very word "theory" is misleadingly bloodless and off-putting, with its connotations of a specialized, esoteric discourse that is over the head of the layperson. Few who react violently against "theory" would object to the proposition that we inevitably have general ideas about such practices as writing and reading or that when disagreement erupts over these practices, it is often necessary and useful to debate our principles. The critics have every right to dislike the kinds of "theory" that are popular in today's academy, but to attack theory as such is equivalent to attacking thinking. . . .

We do not usually reflect on our assumptions and practices unless something forces us to, however, and what usually provides that stimulus is conflict, some challenge to premises that previously seemed so obvious that we did not have to be aware of them as such. "Theory" is a name for the kind of self-consciousness that results when a community ceases to agree on these heretofore seemingly obvious, "normal" assumptions—like the assumption that women are domestic by nature, or that a classic tragedy and a TV sitcom have no significant features in common, or that a slave narrative has no literary qualities that might make it worth teaching, or that politics and literature do not mix. This habit of questioning what seems like common sense is what makes theorists a nuisance, forcing us to give reasons for assumptions that we once could take for granted, as Socrates irritated his fellow Athenians by insisting that the unexamined life is not worth living.

The recent spread of theory as a sort of common currency across the cultural disciplines coincides with the erosion of consensus on the meaning of such central concepts as "literature," "literary value," "author," "reading," "politics," "tradition," "universality," and "culture," as these and many other concepts are thrown into the arena of theoretical discussion. Though this development stimulates arcane kinds of speculation, it only parallels what has been happening in society at large, as challenges to traditional sexual definitions, for example, force us into theoretical debates about the meanings of terms like "male" and "female." Theoretical controversy is not the monopoly of faddish literati. It is instanced in debates on abortion and gun control, occurs in lunchtime conversations, letters to the editor, and talk shows, and is everywhere else in the news.

In my sense of the term, then, OMP is as much a "theorist" as YFP, having been forced by her disagreement to articulate his traditional view of literature as a theory, something he would not have had to do a few decades ago. Though most contemporary theory is critical of traditional ideas of culture, there is nothing intrinsically antitraditional about theory. On the contrary, it is perfectly possible to defend the infusion of theory into the curriculum on traditional grounds-namely, that students have a right to understand the rationale underlying what they are being taught, to know why they should do what they are being asked to do. In this respect the real enemy of tradition is the kind of "traditional" teaching that is content to hand on received tastes and values without investigating the assumptions behind them.

12. Arthur Levine and Jeanette Cureton, "The Quiet Revolution," 1992

Although the introduction of ethnic and gender studies in the 1970s and 1980s occasioned excitement and academic partisanship, new multicultural courses were not quite as widespread or numerous as was then commonly thought. Yet these authors demonstrate that their increasing presence nevertheless amounted to a "quiet revolution." Their conclusion was based upon 196 responses to a questionnaire sent to 270 public and private colleges and universities, including two- and four-year institutions. Although the questionnaire did not define *multiculturalism* or *diversity,* respondents based their replies on definitions used at their campuses. For Arthur Levine, see II, 28. Jeanette Cureton was then director of a *Change* multicultural study at the Harvard Graduate School of Education.

Arthur Levine and Jeanette Cureton, "The Quiet Revolution: Eleven Facts about Multiculturalism and the Curriculum," *Change,* pp. 25–29, January–February, 1992. Reprinted with permission of the Helen Dwight Ried Educational Foundation. Published by Heldref Publications, 1319 Eighteenth St. NW, Washington, D.C. 20036-1802 Copyright © 1980.

The competing claims about multiculturalism boom loudly today. Some say the college curriculum has been largely impermeable to multiculturalism: that it remains unalterably "Eurocentric," ignoring—or, at best, marginalizing—diversity concerns. Others counter that higher education has sold its soul in the name of multiculturalism: that the academy currently is purging the curriculum of its historic Western canon and replacing it willynilly with non-Western, ethnic, and gender studies.

This article is an attempt to go beyond that rhetoric. It is a report on actual curriculum practices today in higher education—a snapshot of the condition of multiculturalism on campus that is based on a first-of-its-kind study of 196 colleges and universities stratified by Carnegie type to be representative of American higher education. . . . Surprisingly, the survey findings present a picture that does not reflect either of these two perceptions about multiculturalism and the curriculum. Instead, they show:

1) More than a third (34 percent) of all colleges and universities have a multicultural general education requirement. That's where the similarities end. Some focus on domestic diversity (12 percent), more emphasize global multiculturalism (29 percent), and most include both (57 percent).

The programs vary in structure, too. An eighth (13 percent) might be called core curricula, meaning all students take the same courses. Another two-thirds (68 percent) could be described as prescribed distributions, in which students are permitted to choose from a relatively short list of approved courses. And the remainder (19 percent) include every variation of general education known to humankind.

2) At least a third of all colleges and universities offer coursework in ethnic and gender studies. Departments and programs in these areas still tend to be rare in higher education, but courses in ethnic and gender studies aren't. More than a third of all colleges and universities offer classes in women's studies, African-American studies, Hispanic-American studies, Native American studies, and Asian-American studies. Courses in gay and lesbian studies lag far, far behind. . . .

3) More than half (54 percent) of all colleges and universities have introduced multiculturalism into their departmental course offerings. It's not happening in every department. The leaders by far are English, history, and an assortment of social sciences. But when multiculturalism does enter the disciplines, the clear way of doing so is by adding new materials to existing courses. Far less common is mounting new courses, or even indulging in new multicultural scholarship. . . .

4) A majority of colleges and universities are seeking to increase faculty multiculturalism. Recruitment is the chief mechanism. More than one-third (36 percent) of all institutions have an active program to attract underrepresented populations to

the campus. Nearly a quarter more (22 percent) report passive initiatives. There is enormous variation in the ways schools are going about this agenda, including target-of-opportunity appointments, broad-scale advertising, reduced course loads for minorities, accelerated salary scales, grow-your-own policies, recruiting ABD minorities on probationary status, visiting appointments, loan cancellation policies, administrators with oversight responsibility for recruitment, faculty mentor programs to support minorities, numerical guidelines and triggers, and mandatory review of appointment processes failing to turn up minorities.

The other device for enhancing diversity is faculty development. More than two out of every five institutions (42 percent) have a program specifically targeted at multiculturalism, supporting some combination of research, study leaves, course development, and campus workshops. Another fifth (22 percent) include multiculturalism as one of a variety of possibilities within their more general faculty development portfolios.

5) Half of all colleges and universities have multicultural advising programs. The range is enormous. There are programs for African-Americans, Native Americans, Hispanics, Asians, women, international students, gays, and a variety of other groups and subgroups. They focus on personal, social, financial, academic, and career advising. They make use of the services of faculty, professional counselors, peers, members of the external community, and every conceivable combination thereof. And they take place on campus and off campus, during orientation, and in freshman seminars, residence halls, workshops, classes, and campus media of all types and descriptions.

6) More than a third (35 percent) of all colleges and universities have multicultural centers and institutes. They include a grab bag of activities. The institutions surveyed reported 124 different centers and institutes ranging across ethnicity, race, geography, religion, sexual preference, and gender. One school alone had 11 centers. In the main, the institutes and centers have two distinct and separate purposes—providing support for multicultural students and homes for faculty research.

7) Four-year colleges are more active than two-year schools in putting multiculturalism into the curriculum. Despite the far greater diversity of the student bodies at two-year colleges, four-year institutions are ahead in every area of cultural diversity examined in this study-general education, ethnic and gender studies, the disciplines, the faculty, advising, and centers and institutes. . . .

8) Among four-year institutions, research universities lead the rest in their multicultural efforts. Despite the fact that the research university is thought of as the branch of higher education least interested in teaching and undergraduate education, these schools outdistance all other four-year institutions

in adding multiculturalism to their programs, except in the areas of general education, faculty development, and supplementing existing courses. . . .

9) In the main, public institutions have surpassed private colleges in their multicultural efforts. Despite the greater freedom of action and autonomy from public opinion of the private sector, public institutions are doing more about multiculturalism than their private counterparts, except in the areas of promoting new scholarship, adding multicultural material to existing courses, and establishing Asian-American studies programs. (One caveat is noted: neither publics nor privates are offering programs focusing on sexual preference). . . .

10) Multicultural programming exists in every region of the country. The middle Atlantic states and the West seem to be developing diversity initiatives most quickly, and the South and Northwest more slowly, but there is no region of the nation not significantly affected. . . .

11) Multiculturalism in the curriculum is a major topic of concern on campuses across the country. More than seven out of ten of the vice presidents and deans surveyed (72 percent) at four-year schools, and four out of ten at two-year colleges said they talk about multiculturalism frequently or continually. This seems extreme, but they said it.

What can we conclude from this study? One thing is clear: the picture that emerges from our data doesn't look like either of today's popular perceptions of multiculturalism and the curriculum. The sheer quantity of multicultural activity identified in the study belies the belief that the traditional curriculum has been largely impermeable to, or has simply marginalized, diversity. And the character of the change—principally add-ons to, rather than substitutes for, existing practice—makes untenable the notion that multiculturalism is replacing the historic canon.

Put simply, what it adds up to is this: multiculturalism today touches in varying degrees a majority of the nation's colleges and universities. These schools are located in every region of the country and include every type of institution of higher education-two-year and four-year colleges, public and private schools.

The inescapable conclusion is that multiculturalism is widespread in higher education today. There has been a quiet revolution of sorts, perhaps more in a quantitative than a qualitative sense. But the activity has not been systematic or well defined. It has occurred more by accretion than design. It is uneven, affecting some sectors of higher education far more than others—public institutions more than private, four-year schools more than two-year schools, research universities more than other types of colleges, and middle Atlantic and western schools more than southern and northwestern institutions.

The very real remaining question is about effect. What is the impact of the grab bag of current multiculturalism initiatives on the curriculum? What differences, if any, do they make for students? Is the whole any greater than the sum of its many parts?

Regardless of how these questions are answered, there are at least two certainties today. The first, as indicated by the level of concern reported by administrators, is that all that has occurred so far is only a beginning of what is likely to be a very long process. The second certainty is that there has been a major shift in the way the academy is thinking about multiculturalism and the curriculum. If our earlier question was whether there ought to be a relationship between the two, the sheer level of current multicultural activity shows the question has changed. Now we must ask what form this relationship should take.

13. William Cronon, "Only Connect . . . ," 1998

William Cronon (1954–) briefly distilled his teaching experience in this widely known essay to describe how one recognizes liberally educated people. What others have mulled over elsewhere, he outlined succinctly by taking as his key E. M. Forster's counsel: "Only Connect."

Cronon grew up in an academic household in Madison, Wisconsin, where he took his bachelor's degree at the University (1976). After study as a Rhodes scholar he returned to earn a masters and doctorate (1979, 1990) at Yale. Within two decades he became prominent in American academic life and in the popular advocacy of environmental causes, along the way receiving a D. Phil. in British history from Oxford (1981) and a MacArthur Foundation Fellowship (1985–90). He taught in the Yale history department (1981–92) and finally went to occupy the Frederick Jackson Turner Chair in History, Geography, and Environmental Studies at the University of Wisconsin, Madison (1992). His first book, *Changes in the Land* (New York, 1983), received the Francis Parkman Prize, and *Nature's Metropolis* (New York, 1991) won the Bancroft Prize. At Madison he founded the Chadbourne Residential College (1997–).

William Cronon, " 'Only Connect . . .' The Goals of a Liberal Education," *The American Scholar* 67 (Autumn 1998): 73–80. Reprinted, with the permission of William Cronon, from *The American Scholar*; Copyright © 1998. Further reading: Vartan Gregorian, "Colleges Must Reconstruct the Unity of Knowledge," *Chronicle of Higher Education*, June 4, 2004, B12–14; and I, 9–10, 12–14.

What does it mean to be a liberally educated person? It seems such a simple question, especially given the frequency with which colleges and universities genuflect toward this well-worn phrase as the central icon of their institutional missions. Mantra-like, the words are endlessly repeated, starting in the glossy admissions brochures that high school students receive by the hundreds in their mailboxes and continuing right down to the last tired invocations they hear on commencement day. It would be surprising indeed if the phrase did not begin to sound at least a little empty after so much repetition, and surely undergraduates can be forgiven if they eventually regard liberal education as either a marketing ploy or a shibboleth. Yet many of us continue to place great stock in these words, believing them to describe one of the ultimate goods that a college or university should serve. So what exactly do we mean by liberal education, and why do we care so much about it?

In speaking of "liberal" education, we certainly do not mean an education that indoctrinates students in the values of political liberalism, at least not in the most obvious sense of the latter phrase. Rather, we use these words to describe an educational tradition that celebrates and nurtures human freedom. These days liberal and liberty have become words so mired in controversy, embraced and reviled as they have been by the far ends of the political spectrum, that we scarcely know how to use them without turning them into slogans—but they can hardly be separated from this educational tradition. Liberal derives from the Latin liberalis, meaning "of or relating to the liberal arts," which in turn derives from the Latin word liber, meaning "free." But the word actually has much deeper roots, being akin to the Old English word leodan, meaning "to grow," and leod, meaning "people." It is also related to the Greek word eleutheros, meaning "free," and goes all the way back to the Sanskrit word rodhati, meaning "one climbs," "one grows." *Freedom* and *growth*: here, surely, are values that lie at the very core of what we mean when we speak of a liberal education.

Liberal education is built on these values: it aspires to nurture the growth of human talent in the service of human freedom. So one very simple answer to my question is that liberally educated people have been liberated by their education to explore and fulfill the promise of their own highest talents. But what might an education for human freedom actually look like? There's the rub. Our current culture wars, our struggles over educational standards are all ultimately about the concrete embodiment of abstract values like "freedom" and "growth" in actual courses and textbooks and curricular requirements. Should students be forced to take courses in American history, and if so, what should those courses contain? Should they be forced to learn a foreign language, encounter a laboratory science, master calculus, study grammar at the expense of creative writing (or the reverse), read Plato or Shakespeare or Marx or Darwin? Should they be required to take courses that foster ethnic and racial tolerance? Even if we agree about the importance of freedom and growth, we can still disagree quite a lot about which curriculum will best promote these values. That is why, when we argue about education, we usually spend less time talking about core values than about formal standards: what are the subjects that all young people should take to help them become educated adults?

This is not an easy question. Maybe that is why—in the spirit of E. D. Hirsch's *Cultural Literacy* and a thousand college course catalogs our answers to it often take the form of lists: lists of mandatory courses, lists of required readings, lists of essential facts, lists of the hundred best novels written in English in the twentieth century, and so on and on. This impulse toward list making has in fact been part of liberal education for a very long time. In their original medieval incarnation, the "liberal arts" were required courses, more or less, that every student was supposed to learn before attaining the status of a "free man." There was nothing vague about the *artes liberalis*. They were a very concrete list of seven subjects: the *trivium*, which consisted of grammar, logic, and rhetoric; and the *quadrivium*, which consisted of arithmetic, geometry, astronomy, and music. Together, these were the forms of knowledge worthy of a free man. We should remember the powerful class and gender biases that were built into this vision of freedom. The "free men" who studied the liberal arts were male aristocrats; these specialized bodies of knowledge were status markers that set them apart from "unfree" serfs and peasants, as well as from the members of other vulgar and ignoble classes. Our modern sense of liberal education has expanded from this medieval foundation to include a greater range of human talents and a much more inclusive number of human beings, holding out at least the dream that *everyone* might someday be liberated by an education that stands in the service of human freedom. . . .

One problem, I think, is that it is much easier to itemize the requirements of a curriculum than to describe the qualities of the human beings we would like that curriculum to produce. All the required courses in the world will fail to give us a liberal education if, in the act of requiring them, we forget that their purpose is to nurture human freedom and growth.

I would therefore like to return to my opening question and try to answer it (since I too find lists irresistible) with a list of my own. My list consists not of required courses but of personal qualities: the ten qualities I most admire in the people I know who seem to embody the values of a liberal education. How does one recognize liberally educated people?

1. *They listen and they hear.*

This is so simple that it may not seem worth saying, but in our distracted and over-busy age, I think it's worth declaring that educated people know how to pay attention—to others and to the world around them. They work hard to hear what other people say. They can follow an argument, track logical reasoning, detect illogic, hear the emotions that lie behind both the logic and the illogic, and ultimately empathize with the person who is feeling those emotions.

2. *They read and they understand.*

This too is ridiculously simple to say but very difficult to achieve, since there are so many ways of reading in our world. Educated people can appreciate not only the front page of the *New York Times* but also the arts section, the sports section, the business section, the science section, and the editorials. They can gain insight from not only THE AMERICAN SCHOLAR and the *New York Review of Books* but also from *Scientific American*, the *Economist*, the *National Enquirer*, *Vogue*, and *Reader's Digest*. They can enjoy John Milton and John Grisham. But skilled readers know how to read far more than just words. They are moved by what they see in a great art museum and what they hear in a concert hall. They recognize extraordinary athletic achievements; they are engaged by classic and contemporary works of theater and cinema; they find in television a valuable window on popular culture. When they wander through a forest or a wetland or a desert, they can identify the wildlife and interpret the lay of the land. They can glance at a farmer's field and tell the difference between soy beans and alfalfa. They recognize fine craftsmanship, whether by a cabinetmaker or an auto mechanic. And they can surf the World Wide Web. All of these are ways in which the eyes and the ears are attuned to the wonders that make up the human and the natural worlds. None of us can possibly master all these forms of "reading," but educated people should be competent in many of them and curious about all of them.

3. *They can talk with anyone.*

Educated people know how to talk. They can give a speech, ask thoughtful questions, and make people laugh. They can hold a conversation with a high school dropout or a Nobel laureate, a child or a nursing home resident, a factory worker or a corporate president. Moreover, they participate in such conversations not because they like to talk about themselves but because they are genuinely interested in others. A friend of mine says one of the most important things his father ever told him was that whenever he had a conversation, his job was "to figure out what's so neat about what the other person does." I cannot imagine a more succinct description of this critically important quality.

4. *They can write clearly and persuasively and movingly.*

What goes for talking goes for writing as well: educated people know the craft of putting words on paper. I'm not talking about parsing a sentence or composing a paragraph, but about expressing what is in their minds and hearts so as to teach, persuade, and move the person who reads their words. I am talking about writing as a form of touching, akin to the touching that happens in an exhilarating conversation.

5. *They can solve a wide variety of puzzles and problems.*

The ability to solve puzzles requires many skills, including a basic comfort with numbers, a familiarity with computers, and the recognition that many problems that appear to turn on questions of quality can in fact be reinterpreted as subtle problems of quantity. These are the skills of the analyst, the manager, the engineer, the critic: the ability to look at a complicated reality, break it into pieces, and figure out how it works in order to do practical things in the real world. Part of the challenge in this, of course, is the ability to put reality back together again after having broken it into pieces—for only by so doing can we accomplish practical goals without violating the integrity of the world we are trying to change.

6. *They respect rigor not so much for its own sake but as a way of seeking truth.*

Truly educated people love learning, but they love wisdom more. They can appreciate a closely reasoned argument without being unduly impressed by mere logic. They understand that knowledge serves values, and they strive to put these two—knowledge and values—into constant dialogue with each other. The ability to recognize true rigor is one of the most important achievements in any education, but it is worthless, even dangerous, if it is not placed in the service of some larger vision that also renders it humane.

7. *They practice humility, tolerance, and self-criticism.*

This is another way of saying that they can understand the power of other people's dreams and nightmares as well as their own. They have the intellectual range and emotional generosity to step outside their own experiences and prejudices, thereby opening themselves to perspectives different from their own. From this commitment to tolerance flow all those aspects of a liberal education that oppose parochialism and celebrate the wider world: studying foreign languages, learning about the cultures of distant peoples, exploring the history of long-ago times, discovering the many ways in which men and women have known the sacred and given names to their gods. Without such encounters, we cannot learn how much people differ—and how much they have in common.

8. *They understand how to get things done in the world.*

In describing the goal of his Rhodes Scholarships, Cecil Rhodes spoke of trying to identify young people who would spend their lives engaged in what he called "the world's fight," by which he meant the struggle to leave the world a better place than they had found it. Learning how to get things done in the world in order to leave it a better place is surely one of the most practical and important lessons we can take from our education. It is fraught with peril because the power to act in the world can so easily be abused—but we fool ourselves if we think we can avoid acting, avoid exercising power, avoid joining the world's fight. And so we study power and struggle to use it wisely and well.

9. *They nurture and empower the people around them.*

Nothing is more important in tempering the exercise of power and shaping right action than the recognition that no one ever acts alone. Liberally educated people understand that they belong to a community whose prosperity and well-being are crucial to their own, and they help that community flourish by making the success of others possible. If we speak of education for freedom, then one of the crucial insights of a liberal education must be that the freedom of the individual is possible only in a free community, and vice versa. It is the community that empowers the free individual, just as it is free individuals who lead and empower the community. The fulfillment of high talent, the just exercise of power, the celebration of human diversity: nothing so redeems these things as the recognition that what seem like personal triumphs are in fact the achievements of our common humanity.

10. *They follow E. M. Forster's injunction from Howard's End: "Only connect. . . ."*

More than anything else, being an educated person means being able to see connections that allow one to make sense of the world and act within it in creative ways. Every one of the qualities I have described here—listening, reading, talking, writing, puzzle solving, truth seeking, seeing through other people's eyes, leading, working in a community—is finally about connecting. A liberal education is about gaining the power and the wisdom, the generosity and the freedom to connect.

I believe we should measure our educational system—whether we speak of grade schools or universities—by how well we succeed in training children and young adults to aspire to these ten qualities. I believe we should judge ourselves and our communities by how well we succeed in fostering and celebrating these qualities in each of us.

But I must offer two caveats. The first is that my original question—"What does it mean to be a liberally educated person?"—is misleading, deeply so, because it suggests that one can somehow take a group of courses, or accumulate a certain number of credits, or undergo an obligatory set of learning experiences, and emerge liberally educated at the end of the process. Nothing could be further from the truth. A liberal education is not something any of us ever *achieve*; it is not a *state*. Rather, it is a way of living in the face of our own ignorance, a way of groping toward wisdom in full recognition of our own folly, a way of educating ourselves without any illusion that our educations will ever be complete.

My second caveat has to do with individualism. It is no accident that an educational philosophy described as "liberal" is almost always articulated in terms of the individuals who are supposed to benefit from its teachings. I have similarly implied that the ten qualities on my list belong to individual people. I have asserted that liberal education in particular is about nurturing human freedom—helping young people discover and hone their talents—and this too sounds as if education exists for the benefit of individuals.

All this is fair enough, and yet it too is deeply misleading in one crucial way. Education for human freedom is also education for human community. The two cannot exist without each other. Each of the qualities I have described is a craft or a skill or a way of being in the world that frees us to act with greater knowledge or power. But each of these qualities also makes us ever more aware of the connections we have with other people and the rest of creation, and so they remind us of the obligations we have to use our knowledge and power responsibly. If I am right that all these qualities are finally about connecting, then we need to confront one further paradox about liberal education. In the act of making us free, it also binds us to the communities that gave us our freedom in the first place; it makes us responsible to those communities in ways that limit our freedom. In the end, it turns out that liberty is not about thinking or saying or doing whatever we want. It is about exercising our freedom in such a way as to make a difference in the world and make a difference for more than just ourselves.

And so I keep returning to those two words of E. M. Forster's: "Only connect." I have said that they are as good an answer as any I know to the question of what it means to be a liberally educated person; but they are also an equally fine description of that most powerful and generous form of human connection we call love. I do not mean romantic or passionate love, but the love that lies at the heart of all the great religious faiths: not eros, but agape. Liberal education nurtures human freedom in the service of human community, which is to say that in the end it celebrates love. Whether we speak of our schools or our universities or ourselves, I hope we will hold fast to this as our constant practice, in the full depth and richness of its many meanings: *Only connect.*

The Arts and Sciences in Decline

14. Sarah H. Turner and William G. Bowen, "The Flight from the Arts and Sciences," 1990

Among the many research contributions from the Andrew W. Mellon Foundation to higher education, this study by Sarah Turner (1968–) and William Bowen (1933–), then president of the foundation, examined graduation rates in the humanities and the various sciences from the 1950s to 1986. Turner was associated with the Mellon Foundation at this writing and later went to the national Bureau of Economic Research. Bowen earlier had a distinguished tenure as an economist and president of Princeton University.

Reprinted with permission from Sarah E. Turner and William G. Bowen, "The Flight from the Arts and Sciences: Trends in Degrees Conferred," *Science,* October 26, 1990, 517–20. Copyright © 1990 AAAS. Further reading: Francis Oakley, "Against Nostalgia: Reflections on Our Present Discontents in American Higher Education," in *The Politics of Liberal Education,* ed. Darryl J. Gless and Barbara Herrnstein Smith (Durham, NC, 1992): 280–81; Thomas Bartlett, "What's Wrong with Harvard," *Chronicle of Higher Education,* May 7, 2004, A14–16; and II, 21; IV, 4.

In this country, undergraduates are free to elect (and change) the fields of study in which they major. Their choices directly affect the demand for teaching hours in the academic disciplines and the preparation that graduating classes take with them as they enter job markets, pursue further education, and participate in civic activities. The shifting popularity of fields of study tells a great deal about a society's evolving philosophy of education—and its values.

The distribution of degrees conferred has changed greatly in recent years, and there is evidence of a dramatic flight from the arts and sciences. Between 1968 and 1986, the number of BA degrees awarded to students who concentrated in one of the fields within the arts and sciences (humanities, social sciences, mathematics, physical sciences, biological sciences, and psychology) plummeted from 47% of all BA degrees to about 26%. This rapid decline followed a steady increase in the arts and sciences share (AS share) during the earlier post–World War II (hereafter postwar) years. The increase in the AS share occurred simultaneously with the most rapid expansion of higher education in the nation's history.

Some students elect fields of study for reasons that are strictly intellectual; others may be influenced by job prospects, broad social and political trends, family background and parental pressures, and the curricular options made available by colleges and universities. An exhaustive analysis would require examination of all variables influencing the perceived returns (noneconomic as well as economic) related to investments by students and educational institutions of time and other resources in various fields of study.

The analytical framework used here is less comprehensive. We first consider the implications of broad developments in higher education, both demographic and curricular. Then we concentrate on an explanatory key of considerable power: the role of gender and the factors associated with the changing curricular choices made by men and women.

DEMOGRAPHIC CHANGES

During the 1960s, the traditional college-age population increased by slightly more than 50% as a result of the baby boom. The sectors of higher education that grew most rapidly (state colleges and large comprehensive institutions) were not the sectors that traditionally emphasized the arts and sciences (such as liberal arts colleges). Thus, these population-driven increases in enrollment should have reduced the AS share at the very time that it increased significantly.

A second demographic factor also raised enrollments during the 1960s: sharply higher age-specific enrollment rates. The percentage of the 18 to 24 age group enrolled in college increased from 15.9% in 1960 to 23.9% in 1970. Normally, a rapid increase in enrollment rates would be expected to lead to a decline in the AS share of degrees conferred because new college entrants, representing a wider socioeconomic spectrum and a broader range of aptitudes, are likely to come disproportionately from families inclined to emphasize training for the job market rather than the more general values associated with an arts and sciences curriculum. Nonetheless, the AS share rose significantly between 1952 and 1969; it was only during the last years of the expansion (1969 to 1974) that it started to decline. Moreover, the most pronounced decline in the AS share occurred in those years (1974 to 1984) when enrollment rates and degrees conferred were roughly constant.

In short, the principal demographic variables (excluding gender) not only fail to explain the observed changes in AS shares, but they push in the wrong direction, putting more burden on other variables.

INSTITUTIONAL AND CURRICULAR CHANGES

Colleges are much more than passive actors in determining AS shares. They establish the curricular options open to students, based on institutional aspirations and other considerations such as the costs of entering (and leaving) various disciplines.

Hefferlin's examination of curricular change between 1962 and 1966 is helpful in explaining why the AS share rose so rapidly during the 1960s, a time of widespread reform and curricular expansion in higher education.[1] Within vocational fields, departments dropped service offerings and adopted a more academic focus; at the same time, the arts and sciences became more inclusive. Some of the increase in the AS share may have reflected developments of this kind. There was also a movement away from preprofessional programs and toward greater emphasis on basic disciplines.

When the supply of students was increasing rapidly, "many formerly struggling institutions . . . [had] the opportunity . . . to move toward academic respectability. . . . Former vocational colleges . . . at last embraced general education."[2] Favorable labor market conditions and the general mood of optimism that characterized much of the 1960s facilitated these curricular changes by encouraging students to assume that they could study whatever they liked, without having to worry about whether they would be able to get a job after graduation.

A reverse process took place in the 1970s. When the supply of students stopped rising, colleges had to compete vigorously to fill their classes and dormitories, and they were much less able to insist on their own academic priorities. The advent of more difficult economic conditions caused students to worry about their vocational prospects, and institutions that had moved aggressively to bolster their offerings in the arts and sciences now became more inclined to emphasize preprofessional and job-related offerings. Whereas educational institutions have considerable leeway to shape academic programs when the demand for education is rising (the 1960s), student preferences can be expected to have more impact on college curricula when demand is weaker and there is strong pressure on institutions to maintain enrollment (the 1970s). . . .

Thus, the overall increase in the AS share during the 1960s was associated with a fundamental change in the character of many state colleges and comprehensive institutions. It was at these rapidly growing schools, which had been heavily oriented toward professional and preprofessional programs in the immediate postwar years, that the sharpest increases in AS shares occurred. Subsequently, the flight from the arts and sciences was most pronounced at these same institutions, even though it also occurred at many research universities.

CHOICES OF MAJORS BY MEN AND WOMEN

For the arts and sciences as a whole, the pattern of year to year changes in shares is remarkably similar for men and women: each time that the AS share for men rose (or fell), so too did the share for women. Between 1954 and the mid-1980s, the AS share for men was consistently higher than the AS share for women; but this gender gap finally closed, and in 1986 the shares were precisely the same.

Taken field by field, however, male and female choices have diverged significantly. In the case of the humanities the differences by gender are especially striking: for men, the humanities share declined steadily from 1954 to 1986; but for women, the humanities share increased sharply only between 1954 and 1966, before falling to about 5%.

The social sciences enjoyed the greatest surge in popularity during the 1960s, when fields such as sociology were perceived by many as the source of answers to the societal problems that were so high on the national agenda. But this boom was short-lived, and the appeal of these subjects soon declined along with interest in the humanities.

The launching of Sputnik in 1957 evoked a wave of concern about the nation's standing in mathematics and the related sciences, which was followed by a substantial rise in the proportion of undergraduates majoring in mathematics, especially among men. Degrees conferred in the physical sciences also responded to the events of the mid-1950s, but in less dramatic fashion. We suspect that increased numbers of students majored in mathematics because it was perceived as a pathway into many applied fields, including engineering and computer science. Interest in both fields peaked between 1962 and 1964, and then declined steadily until new plateaus were reached—with, however, very different ratios of male to female students majoring in these subjects

---

1. J. B. Lon Hefferlin, *Dynamics of Academic Reform* (San Francisco, 1971: Especially ch. 3).

2. *Ibid.*, 67.

(about 1 to 1 in mathematics versus 2.5 to 1 in the physical sciences, respectively).

Historically, men have been more heavily represented than women in the biological sciences; however, this differential has narrowed markedly, perhaps partly as a consequence of increased participation by women in the field of medicine, and hardly any difference by gender remains. Psychology is the only field in which differences by gender have widened. Between 1954 and 1970, the psychology shares for men and women were nearly the same; by 1986, women were more than twice as likely as men to major in this field.

GENDER-RELATED COMPONENTS OF CHANGES IN SHARES

Because men and women choose fields in different proportions, any change in the relative number of men or women in the student population will itself affect overall shares, even in the absence of changes by males and females in their choices of majors. In the postwar period there has been a marked increase in the relative number of BA degrees awarded to women. In 1954, women earned 39% of all BA degrees; by 1986, they earned 51%. For this reason, the male-female ratio must be considered along with male and female choices of majors in seeking to explain overall changes in shares of degrees conferred. . . .

Contrary to what one might have expected to find, changes in the male/female ratio never accounted for a significant part of the total change in the AS share; the changing choices of fields by both men and women were far more important.

Extending this analysis to individual fields of study leads to an important finding: male choices have been more important than female choices in determining movements in shares in five of the six fields of study within the arts and sciences—in every field but the humanities. . . .

Why should male choices so consistently explain more of the change in shares than female choices, both when shares were rising and when they were falling? We have a simple hypothesis: as a rule, men have had more occupational options than women. Thus, when general economic conditions have changed, or when job opportunities have become more attractive in one sector and less attractive in another, men have had an easier time adapting.

In the humanities alone, the changing curricular choices of women have dominated the other determinants of changes in shares. As we saw earlier, men began moving away from the humanities as early as 1962, and continued to do so (more or less regularly) since then. Women, on the other hand, increasingly chose to major in the humanities between 1954 and 1970, and these changes were so powerful that they caused the overall humanities share to rise between these years in spite of the declining interest of men in these fields. Then, be-

tween 1970 and 1986, the declining participation of women accounted for more than three times the loss in share attributable to reduced interest in the humanities among men. This pattern can be understood only by examining developments outside the arts and sciences.

EDUCATION AND BUSINESS

Education and business are the largest fields of study outside the arts and sciences, and the changing appeal of these fields has also had the greatest impact on other curricular choices made by women. The increasing demand for teachers caused by the baby boom resulted in more women entering the field of education in the early and mid-1950s. By 1958, nearly half of all BA degrees awarded to women were conferred in education. Ever since, however, there has been an unrelenting decline, and by 1986, only 13% of all BA degrees earned by women were in education. Revolutionary changes occurred at institutions such as Ball State, which once were primarily teachers colleges and have since diversified their offerings. In 1954, over 90% of all degrees awarded to women at Ball State were in education; that figure tell to 64% in 1970 and to 18% in 1986.

Between 1958 and 1966, a large share of the women who might have gone into education migrated to the humanities. Other women, in relatively smaller numbers, elected to study the social sciences. These shifts are consistent with the educational backgrounds of most women at this time. It was easier for many of them—who, in earlier times, might have chosen to major in education—to choose these subjects than it would have been for them to major in fields that required radically different kinds of preparation, especially in mathematics.

The years from 1966 to 1974 can be thought of as a period of transition: women in increasing numbers decided not to major in education and determined that the humanities were not the best alternative. Some of them turned to fields such as biology and psychology. There was also a modest increase in interest in mathematics and the physical sciences, but the absolute numbers of women in these fields continued to be small.

By far the most significant developments took place in the field of business. Beginning in the early 1970s, there was an extraordinary increase in the relative number of women majoring in business as a direct consequence, presumably, of the marked improvement in professional employment opportunities for women in related occupations. The business share of all degrees earned by women rose from 2.8% in 1970 to 21.7% in 1986. Whereas the business share of degrees earned by men also rose during these years, the rate of change was much more modest. In both business and education, then, the shifting patterns of degrees conferred have been dominated by the movements of women into and out of these fields with pronounced effects on interest in the humanities.

IMPLICATIONS

Fields of concentration chosen by men and women have converged substantially, and gender-related variables may have less influence on the pattern of degrees conferred in the future. It is unlikely, in our view, that men's choices of majors will dominate changes in shares within the arts and sciences, as they have over the past three decades.

The overall AS share of degrees conferred is likely to be more stable over the next few decades than it has been during 1954 to 1986. Some of the main factors responsible (in at least a proximate sense) for recent trends have run their course. In particular, greatly increased opportunities for women in fields outside the arts and sciences, such as business, have removed certain culturally imposed constraints that in the past induced comparatively large numbers of women to major in areas such as the humanities. We do not expect the flight from the arts and sciences to continue, and one implication is that the demand for faculty in these fields may be greater in the years ahead than recent projections suggest.

Perhaps the most significant developments will occur within the arts and sciences, since there is certainly no current equilibrium between men and women in their choices of majors such as physics. If more progress can be made in removing cultural barriers and in improving teaching and learning at the primary and secondary levels of schooling, women may participate much more fully in the math-intensive subjects. Marked changes have occurred in other fields, and these changes should encourage efforts designed to address what seems to us to be the most serious anomaly in the present pattern of degrees conferred.

Part IV   Graduate Studies

Between 1940 and 1960, the number of institutions granting Ph.D. degrees doubled, and in the 1960s more new faculty members were hired than had been hired in the first three centuries of higher education in America. This expansion of higher education and particularly the professoriate, driven by the Cold War and prosperity, stalled in the 1970s. Since then—as a result of financial constraint, especially at public institutions—the academic profession, at least the market for new Ph.D.'s, fell into a prolonged slump. The number of doctoral students, nevertheless, continued to climb, producing by the 1990s grim job prospects in all disciplines, hovering somewhere near a 50 percent employment rate, with some variation by discipline. With such a surplus labor pool and increasing undergraduate enrollments, part-time employment dramatically increased, resulting in the emergence of a two-tier class system, called a "caste system" by Lynn Hunt (7).

It was a dramatic turnaround. The first quarter-century following World War II was preoccupied with the expansion of the faculty; the big worry was how to produce enough Ph.D.'s without diluting quality (1), while in the final quarter of the century the issue was the oversupply of Ph.D.'s. To put the matter differently and more accurately, there were more Ph.D.'s than academe had the financial resources to hire into regular positions, resorting instead to larger classes and ill-paid part-time labor. In fact, in 1966 the leaders of higher education had been warned that there was going to be a flip from a shortage of supply to a surplus, but no one seemed to take seriously the accurate projections of Alan Cartter (2). Nor were they sufficiently worried, as he and Bernard Berenson were, about the signs of an increasing number of weak doctoral programs being established in non-flagship public institutions for purposes of local prestige or better funding formulas (1–3).

In the 1980s, the persistence of poor job prospects discouraged enough potential doctoral students, especially in history and the humanities, to begin to move the vectors representing the production of jobs and of Ph.D.'s closer together over time. At decade's end, William Bowen and his co-researcher published a hugely influential report foreseeing a "substantial" shortage of Ph.D.'s, beginning in 1992 and accelerating dramatically in 1997 (4). President of the Mellon Foundation at the time, Bowen went on to sponsor or coauthor statistical and highly regarded reports (II, 20; III, 14), but this one was distressingly flawed. Here they predicted that in the humanities there would be only "seven candidates for every ten positions." Students flocked into the field, only to find a glutted market that has yet to

find an equilibrium of supply and demand. These developments cast a pall over graduate education. There were many proposals for reform and reinvigoration, all seeking to reduce the isolation of increasingly specialized and esoteric research (and jargon) from the common life of Americans (8–11). Might the highly educated be more adaptable, able to contribute as professionals in institutions and occupations other than university professorships? On top of all this, a growing chorus insisted that those who found academic employment needed to be more fully prepared as teachers and faculty colleagues as well as researchers (10–11).

At the same time, perhaps paradoxically, there were important movements toward the democratization of the next generation of academics. Or, to resolve the paradox, there might be a perverse explanation: the increase of women and other underrepresented groups was less the fulfillment of the ideals of democracy than a case of declining professional prestige resulting in choices by white males to opt out for occupations with greater standing and financial reward. Either way, did greater inclusion or diversity weaken professional claims on social resources (7)? Whatever the larger meaning, professional associations established committees and commissions devoted to increasing the representation of women and underrepresented minorities (6). After a striking but limited increase in minority members on university faculties, the recruitment curve flattened, leaving them significantly underrepresented (5). However, the proportion of women among new Ph.D.'s and, gradually, within faculties continued to climb and to move toward parity in some humanities disciplines and even beyond. The same trend was evident in the social sciences. Economics and philosophy experienced distinctively less demographic change, and the same was true of the natural sciences.

Along with this growing inclusion of women, there remained significant stratification among graduate students and in their later career paths. If in the immediate postwar years, many of the new Ph.D.'s were awarded to students of working-class backgrounds (mostly from Jewish immigrant families in which the father had only a high school education or less), by the end of the century the socioeconomic status of new Ph.D.'s, as measured by father's education, came from backgrounds marked by more education and family resources (1, 7). And though the proportion of women increased, at the top-tier universities in the 1990s the senior ranks tended to remain a bastion of white males. Many humanities professors assumed that bringing multicultural perspectives into their disciplines and classrooms would attract minority students, but whatever impact these changes had on the students, they did not draw significant numbers into graduate schools and the professions (7). Meeting the continuing challenge of diversifying liberal education would depend on engaging students from ever more diverse backgrounds.

Graduate Surveys and Prospects

1. Bernard Berelson, *Graduate Education in the United States,* 1960

Bernard Berelson (1912–79) produced the primary study of American graduate programs in the post–World War II decades. Beyond his report of conditions then current in American graduate life, Berelson prescribed rather strong medicine for what he considered to be the major ailments of American graduate programs. Among his recommendations were (1) enforcement of the four-year norm for a doctorate; (2) more specific and more closely directed doctoral training; (3) shorter dissertations; (4) more flexible foreign language and final oral examinations; (5) teaching experience within their programs for all candidates; and (6) experimentation with a two-year intermediate doctorate for college teachers only. Thirty-five years after Berelson's book, Margaret Rossiter, in her canvass of American women scientists, signaled changing perspectives about the role of women in academic life when she pointed to Berelson's omissions or oversights. She noted that his sources were exclusively male administrators, that his statistics were faulty, and that the report could "only infuriate."

Bernard Berelson was a specialist in communication and public opinion. His degrees came from Whitman College (A.B. 1934), the University of Washington (M.A. 1937), and the University of Chicago (Ph.D. 1941). At Chicago he became dean of the Graduate Library School and chairman of the Committee on Communications in 1947. He served at the Ford Foundation from 1951 until 1957 when he returned to Chicago for two years while preparing this book under a grant from the Carnegie Corporation. He next went to Columbia University as director of the Bureau of Applied Social Research and then moved to the directorship of the communication research program and ultimately the presidency of the Population Council (1968–74).

Bernard Berelson, *Graduate Education in the United States* (New York, 1960), pp. 19–20, 35–36, 93–95, 97, 109–11, 113, 130–31, 133–35, 143. Further reading: Margaret W. Rossiter, *Women Scientists in America before Affirmative Action, 1940–1972* (Baltimore, 1995): 66–67, 542; for a brief history of American graduate schooling, see John S. Brubacher and Willis Rudy, *Higher Education in Transition,* 3rd ed. (New York, 1976), ch. 9 and references. The issue of graduate student recruitment was addressed in Robert H. Knapp and Joseph J. Greenbaum, *The Younger American Scholar: His Collegiate Origins* (Chicago, 1953); Robert H. Knapp and H. B. Goodrich, *The Origins of American Scientists* (Chicago, 1953), and Robert H. Knapp, *The Origins of American Humanistic Scholars* (Englewood Cliffs, NJ, 1964).

The recurrent character of the debate over graduate study can perhaps best be summarized by the frequent pleas for someone to settle the question of what the doctorate was *for*—as though another definition or statement of objective would suddenly clarify the entire enterprise. To anticipate somewhat, every decade provides a few examples:

1912 Dean Woodbridge, at the AAU: "Since the degree is conferred in Sanskrit and in animal husbandry, in philosophy and highway engineering, for what does it essentially stand?"

1928 Dean Heller, at the AAU: "Since the end of the 16th century it has been copiously written about . . . this stupendously unentertaining literature (inquiring into the when, why, whence, wherefore, and particularly the 'whomfor' of the Doctor's degree). . . . Nearly all those treatises attempted to settle the still somewhat open opinion—What does the degree really mean?"

1939 The advisory committee on the Isaiah Bowman report, in its introduction: "One of the most important problems . . . was the development of a clear statement of the functions of the graduate school." . . .

1957 The report of the Committee on Policies in Graduate Education of the AGS: "This critical degree . . . now seems to offer nearly as many services as the A.B. itself. Current pressure forces us to examine our myth-enveloped Ph.D. with candor. What we see makes us look away with shock. . . . The basic flaw is: we have never clearly *defined* this protean degree."

What always seems to be wanted is not so much acceptance of *a* definition as acceptance of one's own! . . .

During the post-war period, one reason for the increase [in graduate studies] stemmed directly from that basic ingredient of educational growth: money. Graduate study received increasing support in this period from the Federal government—directly in fellowship funds and through the GI Bill, indirectly in research grants, housing loans, and other funds. The whole enterprise could not have prospered as it has without that support. Here it is necessary only to point out a simple but crucial fact: namely, that such funds were forthcoming because the graduate school had become a highly important institution from the standpoint of the national security.

As we shall see, this growth was handled not only by the traditional universities but by the newer entrants into graduate work. In 1940, about 100 institutions gave the doctorate and about 300 the Master's; in 1958 the figures were 175 and 569. There are a number of reasons for this development: the pressure of enrollments; the certification and promotional policies in the public school systems that encourage or even "force" teachers into graduate programs; the colonization of the underdeveloped institutions by ambitious products of the developed ones who then seek to make the colony a competitor of the mother university; the need to have graduate students as research and teaching assistants, partly in order to get and hold senior staff; the vanity, pride, and legitimate aspirations of institutions.

Once a university undertakes doctoral work seriously, it does not give it up again: the only dropouts in this century have been the colleges giving cheap doctorates in the very first years. Just as the way for the academic man to get ahead was to earn the doctorate, the way for an institution to get ahead was to offer it. "There is no man who does not need to climb." Neither, apparently, are there many institutions—and in our educational system, climbing means getting into the big league of graduate, and especially doctoral, study.

Besides the increases in number of students and of institutions there was also an increase in the number of fields in which doctoral training was offered, thus reflecting further the expansion and proliferation of knowledge. If every distinctive name for the field of award is counted, there are now well over 550 fields in which the doctorate is awarded by one or another institution (but only one institution in almost 400 of them). This figure is directly comparable to the 149 fields in 1916 to 1918. Actually, of course, the number of "real" fields is much smaller: depending on how a "field" is defined, one gets between 60 and 80—all the others are variants, offshoots, or combinations.

The central fields in the arts and sciences are much the same as forty years ago: chemistry (doctorates now offered in about 110 institutions as against 20 in 1916 to 1918); physics (90); psychology, mathematics, history, and English (75 to 85 each); economics (65); philosophy (50); and so on. Similarly, the fields offered by particular institutions doubled in these decades: from an average of about 25 to 30 in the major institutions to about 55 to 60 in each of them.

The fields changed in complexion as well. Perhaps most notably, the professionalization of graduate study continued to grow. As for the Master's degree, even in this single decade, the tide of educational degrees became stronger. Ten years ago, 38% of the degrees were awarded in the arts and sciences as against only 28% in 1957–1958 and education is up by over half again, from 30% to nearly half of all Master's degrees.

The situation at the doctoral level is not so extreme, but there is a clear movement over the long run toward professional fields. From the early years of the century there has been a constant increase in the proportion of professional doctorates. According to present figures, over a third of all the doctoral degrees are in professional fields, and most of this relative growth has come at the expense of the historical center of higher education, the humanities, which have fallen from one-quarter of the total to about one-tenth. . . .

Historically, the national system of higher education has depended on a relatively few institutions to carry the load of graduate training. However, we are now in a long trend of decentralization in graduate work, a trend that has pretty well run its course for

the Master's degree but is still active in the case of the doctorate. The story is suggested by these simple figures:

Up to the mid-1920's, the five most productive institutions (Columbia, Chicago, Harvard, Johns Hopkins, Yale) awarded about half the doctorates in this country.

In the 1930's, the five most productive (Columbia, Chicago, Harvard, Wisconsin, Cornell) awarded about a third of the doctorates.

In the 1950's, the five most productive (Columbia, Wisconsin, California, Harvard, Illinois) awarded well under a quarter of the doctorates. . . .

The growth of the system is the story of the rise of particular universities on the national scene. If we consider "genuine entry" into graduate study to mean the conferral of about 1% or more of the doctorates annually, here are the dates of entry (with the number of doctorates awarded in 1957–1958, the latest available year):

By 1900	By 1925	By 1940
Chicago (233)	Cal Tech (54)	North Carolina (73)
Columbia (538)	Catholic (107)	Penn State (126)
Cornell (188)	Iowa (158)	Purdue (216)
Harvard (371)	Iowa State (133)	Southern California (147)
Johns Hopkins (82)	Michigan (268)	Texas (138)
Pennsylvania (155)	Minnesota (221)	
Yale (185)	NYU (296)	**By 1950**
	Ohio State (261)	Indiana (199)
	Princeton (105)	UCLA (164)
By 1920	Stanford (187)	
California (312)		**By 1955**
Illinois (351)	**By 1930**	Boston (89)
Wisconsin (303)	MIT (153)	Maryland (102)
	Northwestern (107)	Michigan State (131)
	Pittsburgh (96)	Syracuse (80)
		Washington, Seattle (115) . . .

The institutional picture has been changing in important ways. To start with, the traditional monopoly or near-monopoly of doctoral work has gradually worn away under the challenge of the newer entrants. It has been customary to say, and it still is, that despite the large numbers of institutions engaged in doctoral work, the overwhelming majority of degrees is granted by a handful of the great universities. Such universities still figure prominently in the conferral of doctoral degrees, of course, but not nearly so prominently as they did only a short time ago. In 1900, the 14 institutions in the AAU gave almost 90% of the doctorates; in 1958, the 39 institutions in the AAU gave only 70%. The top 10 in size gave 86% of the doctorates in 1900, and less than half that in 1958.

As the system has grown, the *relative* concentration has stayed about the same—a fourth of the institutions awarding doctorates gave about three-fourths the degrees in 1908, 1928, and 1958—but *which* institutions they are have changed. A year or so ago, Purdue gave almost as many doctorates as Chicago, Southern California about as many as Pennsylvania, Penn State more than Princeton, Indiana more than Cornell, Michigan State far more than Johns Hopkins or Cal Tech.

This trend has meant a movement of doctoral study not only toward the newer entrants but, concomitantly, of two other kinds. The first has been the gradual shift in the load of doctoral study from the private to the public universities. The numerical dominance of the private universities, so strong at the start, finally gave way only a few years ago to the long-run trend: more doctorates are now being given by the public universities. The private universities got to doctoral study first and it took some time for the public institutions to catch up. But now they have caught up, and since they are sure to grow faster in the years ahead than their private counterparts, it is not unlikely that a decade hence the private universities will be awarding not many more than two out of every five doctorates in the country. . . .

The dominance of the better universities, an historic feature of the national system of higher education, has gone down under the expansion and decentralization of the system. In earlier times, the best universities also happened to be the leading producers of doctorates. Today, as doctoral study has spread out to more and more institutions, that is less clearly the case. In short, the concentration of doctoral study, especially in the "great private universities," has been greatly lessened and the trend has not yet run its course. This does not mean that the day of the great private university is over—far from it. Their quality is holding up, but their production is falling off relative to the system as a whole. . . .

The graduate school is one of the most important distributors of talent in American life. It is a critical rung in the academic career ladder—in some ways, *the* critical one.

What the sociologist would call social stratification, complete with social mobility, exists within the system of higher education at the doctoral level, on the basis of the differences in (perceived) institutional quality. Just as a person's eventual position in society depends on the class he was born into as well as on his own talent, so his eventual position in higher education depends on the standing of the (parental) institution where he took his doctorate as well as on his scientific or scholarly capabilities. In each case, a good deal depends on what step of the ladder you start from. This is not to say that "class" is everything and talent nothing, any more than that is the case in other departments of life. But it does matter. . . .

To begin with, the winners of the national fellowship programs end up largely at the top graduate schools. In fall 1959, for example, about 60% of the Woodrow Wilson Fellows and nearly 75% of the National Science Foundation Fellows went to the top 12 universities, which have only about 35% of the total doctoral enrollment. Such concentration has been a matter of great controversy in recent years, so much so in fact that both agencies have taken countermeasures. . . .

The better schools have a better chance to select the better students; they have more applicants and generally the first choice among them. But at the same time, precisely because they are the *national* graduate schools, they register fewer of those admitted. . . . The better students apply to several of the better schools, are admitted to a few of them, but then can register at only one. The lesser institutions are more regionally based: they admit large proportions of their applicants in order to have graduate students, and large proportions of their applicants actually register since they have applied to only the admitting institution or perhaps one other. Thus the problem of multiple applications is a problem only at the very top of the pyramid, and as more and more students apply for graduate study in the years ahead, the rich will get richer in the sense that the top universities will have even more of the top talent to select from. . . .

The odds are clear: the chances of taking one's doctorate at the top universities are two out of three if the baccalaureate is taken there; about two in five if it is taken from the best colleges; and about one in four from anywhere else. In-breeding by quality of institution is also evident; that is, those who took their Bachelor's degrees from the second layer of universities tend to take their doctoral degree there, and similarly for the third layer. Moreover, in every case, there is more movement up the academic hierarchy, from Bachelor's to Doctor's, than there is down.

Why does it matter where people take the doctorate? Leaving aside anything else, it matters because the institution where a person gets the doctorate has a determining effect on where he ends up. The higher the institutional level of the doctorate, the higher the subsequent post in academic life. . . .

Institutionally, the graduate universities get only about 15 to 20% of their doctoral students from their own undergraduate colleges. Where, then, do they come from? In the first place, most graduate students come from a relatively few institutions. In their well-known study, *The Younger American Scholar*, Robert Knapp and Joseph Greenbaum remark on "the concentration of scholarly creativity among a surprisingly small group of institutions" (roughly 50 out of 800), and they conclude that this leaves "undeveloped and unproductive large segments of the American system of higher education. We strongly suspect that under proper circumstances, effective recruitment of younger scholars could be accomplished from many institutions now virtually barren of productivity." The median undergraduate college sends 10 to 15% of its graduates on to graduate school in the arts and sciences, but the range is from less than 5% to well over 40%.

Now Knapp and Greenbaum, and these college figures, deal with rates. But rates do not staff graduate schools; gross numbers do. So far as numbers are concerned, especially of doctoral students, it is the universities that mainly supply the graduate schools. Even in Knapp and Greenbaum's figures, for example, about two-thirds of the "young scholars" (recipients of the doctorate or certain fellowships) took their baccalaureate degrees at universities. According to the NRC study of the baccalaureate origins of all doctorates conferred from 1936 to 1956, concentration at that level is even greater than at the doctoral level itself: less than 10% of the institutions produced nearly 75% of those who went on to the doctorate.

What are the leading producers of baccalaureates who complete their doctorates? With the exceptions of CCNY and Brooklyn (both high because of their attendance by bright Jewish students of New York), all of the top 20 institutions are large universities. Oberlin is the first liberal arts college, and it is 25th; Dartmouth is next, and it is 40th; then Swarthmore (54th), Hunter (59th, again New York City), Amherst (71st), Wesleyan (80th), Reed (81st), and College of Wooster (84th)—and that is all in the top 95 institutions responsible for 74% of all baccalaureates who achieved the doctorate from 1936 to 1956. These eight liberal arts colleges, the top producers in their class, account for less than 4% of the students who went on to the doctorate in that period. . . .

Hence the majority of doctoral candidates, and even more of recipients, come from the universities. In *rate* of production, the liberal arts colleges may be equally high, but in *numbers* of students they are not. . . .

Certainly, graduate students have become more heterogeneous in background and social origin. That was almost a natural accompaniment of the increase in numbers—there simply were too few of the "elite" variety to support such a growth. Now, the recipients of the doctorates come from a range of social backgrounds. . . .

Here again we see the importance of the graduate school as a giant step in the career mobility of young people from what can fairly be described as lower-middle-class homes. Well over half the recent recipients come from families where the father had only a high school education or less—and more often less—or held a job low in the occupational hierarchy. Thus Sartre's cynical comment that the Ph.D. was given in America as a reward for having a wealthy father and no opinions is at least half wrong (in fact, that is much more likely to be true abroad, I am told). By comparison, students of law and medicine come more from the top occupational groups: two-thirds to three-fourths come from professional, managerial, or proprietary families as against less than half the doctoral recipients. Thus scholarship has come to be more the preserve of less-than-upper-class people, as against professional practice, and the criterion of intellectual capability

has made a social selection as well as the one it was directly intended for.

It pleases some observers to see in this, as the jargon puts it, a dangerous tendency toward the alienation of the intelligentsia from the managers of the society, but on the whole I find them more nearly in tune now—partly because of what I earlier referred to as the professionalization of doctoral training. In any case, it is hard to overstate the importance of the graduate school to students of high talent but low origin—and especially to those from an ethnic minority traditionally devoted to learning, like the Jews, who are strongly over-represented in the graduate population—or its contribution in this respect to the American dream.

Another important change in the student body has changed the whole environment of graduate study. Graduate students these days are usually married. Of the 1957 recipients of the doctorate, over half were married when they began doctoral study and three-fourths when they finished. Of those married, over half had children when they started, and almost three-fourths when they finished.

This makes a difference to graduate work in several ways. One is financial: families must be supported, not just the student. This has required the graduate schools or national fellowship programs to add dependency allowances to their stipends. (Graduate students with wives but no children are in the optimal position: they are supported by the working wives. As the saying goes, they get through graduate school by the sweat of their fraus.) Another is social: graduate students live a more normal social life—the wives are even organized on some campuses—and institutions now have the problem of providing housing for married students along with the usual dormitory space. Another is intellectual: the monastic dedication to graduate study is lessened or gone. Graduate students have families to be dedicated to as well as their studies, and some deans feel that this has had a big and undesirable effect on graduate work in distracting the students' attention from what should be intensive devotion to a subject.

So much is being said these days about the possibility of solving the "college teacher shortage" with women Ph.D.'s that it is perhaps worth noting that they constituted 10% of the doctorates in 1910 and not quite 11% last year. Except for the war years, they have never accounted for a much larger segment than that. . . .

2. Allan M. Cartter, "The Supply of and Demand for College Teachers," 1966

Allan M. Cartter (1922–76), economist and statistician, was the first to offer a critical measurement of the fluctuating numbers and the placement of doctoral graduates nationally during the 1950s and 1960s. In so doing, he cautiously challenged the optimistic forecast of academic administrators and federal statisticians. Cartter did his undergraduate work at Colgate (1946) and received his doctorate at Yale (1952). He taught at Duke (1952–57), where he became dean of the graduate school (1959–62). Thereafter he was vice president of the American Council on Education (1963–66), next chancellor of New York University (1966–72), a senior research fellow of the Carnegie Commission on Higher Education (1972–74), and finally director of the laboratory for research on higher education at UCLA (1974–76). During his administrative career he was a member of a number of various presidential and state advisory and survey groups.

Allan M. Cartter, "The Supply of and Demand for College Teachers," in *The Journal of Human Resources: Education, Manpower and Welfare Policies* I, no. 1 (Summer 1966): 22–38. Copyright © 1966. Reprinted by permission of the University of Wisconsin Press. Further reading: IV, 3.

Considering the importance of the problem to higher education, and the many hundreds of millions of dollars appropriated by the federal government for the expansion of graduate education over the last few years, it is rather astonishing that we know so little about the present and probable supply and demand of college teachers. The consensus today, as expressed by several federal agencies, the National Education Association, and many college and university presidents and graduate deans, seems to be summed up in the following three propositions: (a) persons trained at the doctoral level are in increasingly short supply; (b) the quality of faculty (as measured by highest degree attained) in the nation's colleges and universities is deteriorating; and (c) the situation will worsen over the coming decade as a consequence of burgeoning undergraduate enrollments. Over the last few years various distinguished educational spokesmen have used such terms as "disastrous shortage," "serious crisis," the nation's standing "virtually paralyzed," "frightening figures," and "a major national scandal" to describe the supply of college teachers and have called for "heroic efforts," "crash programs," and new degrees short of the doctorate to stem the tide.

At the risk of flying in the face of commonly held opinion, I wish to argue the reverse of the above propositions: namely that (a) the "sellers market" in academic personnel is likely to disappear over the coming decade; (b) the quality of faculty in the nation's colleges and universities has improved, not deteriorated, over the last ten years; and (c) the situation is moderately well in hand now and will improve dramatically in the 1970's. In an attempt to support these views, the paper will first summarize events of the last ten years and then present a growth model helpful in projecting supply and demand conditions ahead to 1985.

THE LAST DECADE

The belief that things are getting worse rather than better is largely attributable to the biennial research bulletins issued since 1955 by the National Education Association on "Teacher Supply and Demand in Universities, Colleges and Junior Colleges." The first report presented a distribution of total staff by highest degree for 637 reporting institutions in 1953–54. Successive reports, however, have only inquired as to highest degree of *new* teachers. The figures . . . taken from the various NEA reports, have led some readers to believe that a rapid deterioration in faculty quality was in fact occurring. . . .

One further factor . . . is also favorable to the view that the quality of faculty (as measured by highest degrees attained) has not deteriorated. *A priori* one would assume that teachers with the doctorate are more likely to make a lifetime career of teaching than those without a doctorate. It would be reasonable to assume that there is a differential net transfer rate for the two groups. A recent Office of Education study, to be published later this year, indicates that for 1962–63 the rate of those leaving college teaching for reasons other than death or retirement was 3.1 percent for doctorates and 7.1 percent for nondoctorates. Other data . . . further indicate that the net transfer rate of doctorates into and out of teaching has been approximately zero in recent years. . . .

FACULTY FORECASTING MODELS

Projections of the demand for college teachers made over the last decade have varied widely, and most have been such poor predictors of actual developments as to call for careful scrutiny of the basis on which the projections were made. The best known model is that . . . in the 1959 NEA report, and now used by the Office of Education. . . . The result of this model, when applied to Office of Education enrollment projections, is to predict an aggregate need for some 556,000 new college teachers over the next ten years. Assuming constant quality of faculty, the Office of Education predicts a probable "deficit" of more than 120,000 doctorates by 1973/74.

There are a number of aspects of the current OE model which I believe lead to a considerable exaggeration of future faculty needs. First, the projected student/staff ratio (18:1, based on total instructional staff) is lower than the experience of the last decade would indicate. . . . It has averaged 19.3:1 and there is no clear trend upward or downward. On reflection, this does not seem an unusually high marginal ratio, for a number of reasons. First, junior colleges, where the average ratio is 20:1 or greater, represent a larger portion of increments in enrollment than they do of the current total (nearly 30 percent of the annual increases, as compared to less than 15 percent of the total). Second, enrollment in public institutions, where the ratio is moderately high, is expanding more rapidly than in private colleges and universities. Third, much of the expansion is occurring in already existing institutions, and one would expect there to be some manpower economies of scale associated with such growth. Finally, modest changes in technology (language laboratories, educational television, independent study, etc.) presumably work to increase the ratio despite enrollment expansion. A continuing *marginal* ratio of nearly 20:1 would mean that the *average* ratio will rise from 15.3:1 today to 17.3:1 by 1985. The Office of Education choice of an 18:1 ratio, therefore, appears to overstate the expansion needs by nearly 10 percent.

A second, and more major, criticism is the use of a 6 percent replacement rate for faculty, for I believe it overstates replacement needs by a factor of three, for the following reason. If one applied this model to the last decade, beginning with 1953/54, then we should have experienced a decline in the percentage of doctorates on teaching faculties from about 40 percent to 30 percent; instead . . . it has risen by seven to ten percentage points for four-year institutions. As I have indicated in another paper, the actual experience of the last ten years is consistent with a replacement rate of *slightly less than 2 percent*. . . .

A third objection to the OE model is that included in full-time equivalent staff are personnel for administrative services (few of whom, below the level of academic deans, would be expected to have the doctorate), junior instructional staff (who by definition are teaching assistants without the doctorate), and a large number for "research." Since research personnel needs are determined by factors largely independent of the purely educational function, and doctorates are probably not a large fraction of the other two categories, it seems much more appropriate to concentrate just on the needs for teaching faculty. As a corollary, this requires counting only new doctorates who enter teaching as a component of supply, rather than the number who enter higher education in all of its various facets. . . .

CONCLUSIONS

The preceding analysis suggests that educators have been much too pessimistic about the adequacy of both the present and future supply of college teachers. We seem to have learned little from the experience of the 1950's, when the National Education Association and most public school officials were maintaining that there was a critical shortage of school teachers, only to find by the end of the decade that both the number and quality (as measured by formal preparation) of teachers had been steadily rising. Similarly, the despairing cries about the rapidly deteriorating situation on the college level have now proved to be in error, and the future looks bright beyond the next three to five years.

If the projections of total college enrollment and of doctorates to be awarded are even approximately correct, the sellers' market for college faculty will quickly disappear in the early 1970's. This has many implications for public policy and for the nation's colleges.

Given the time lag between entrance to graduate school and completion of doctorate, it is conceivable that graduate education facilities might be expanded too rapidly by basing decisions on degrees awarded in the recent past. The *present* faculty and facilities, at their current level of utilization, would

turn out about 20,000 doctorates a year in a stable system. That is to say, because we are rapidly expanding, we occasionally forget that the fifteen thousand doctorates awarded this year reflect the teaching capacity of the graduate schools about 1960. If, as the model suggests, the demand for new doctorates in teaching will stabilize or even decline after 1968, as a consequence of the declining rate of growth of the total system, then a serious question of public policy may be whether or not it is desirable to encourage many new institutions to enter the doctoral field. Four-fifths of the nearly 250 universities presently awarding the Ph.D. are too small to be educationally or economically efficient. We might well ask whether public policy would be better served by consolidating and strengthening our existing graduate schools, rather than by encouraging another ten or twelve new doctoral-granting institutions to join the university ranks each year, as is now occurring.

The model also has serious implications for the future level of academic salaries. For the next three years, the market will remain fairly tight, and the succeeding several years may be needed to regain temporarily lost ground. The 1970's, however, may usher in a "buyers' market," and academicians may experience again a decline in their *relative income* position. The model above assumed that the replacement rate remained constant over the next twenty years, but this is unlikely in a market where supply is relatively abundant. There may develop a trend for colleges to lower mandatory retirement ages . . . and the transfer rate of senior staff . . . will probably rise a few percentage points. . . .

If I were to hazard a guess fifteen or so years ahead, I would predict a fairly constant marginal faculty coefficient, a gradually diminishing percentage of new Ph.D.'s entering teaching after 1970, a continuing modest improvement in the percentage of faculty with the doctorate, a positive net outtransfer rate, and a slowing down in the upward drift of academic salaries, becoming noticeable in the early 1970's. It may well be that the real challenge to Committee Z of the American Association of University Professors will come in the 1970's, when in all probability market forces will oppose rather than uphold efforts to improve the relative income position of college teachers.

The discussion above has ignored field-by-field differences, partly in the interests of brevity and partly because the aggregate data are better than that for individual disciplines. There are wide variations in the values of each of the coefficients from field to field, but the demarcations between fields are too fuzzy to permit the application of such a model with any degree of precision to individual disciplines. Certainly, shortages in many fields will continue beyond 1970, but the general outlook appears to be favorable for the continued expansion and improved quality of higher education in the United States.

3. Horace W. Magoun,
"The Cartter Report on Quality," 1966

A few months after Allan Cartter's report on graduate school quality, Horace Winchell Magoun (1907–91) presented Cartter's findings graphically, an act that brought a much wider readership to that work. Unlike earlier ratings of graduate schools made by Raymond M. Hughes (1925) and Hayward Keniston (1959), Magoun published tables of institutional rankings. This work began the ratings of undergraduate as well as graduate studies in American colleges and universities that would be so visible in national magazines in the decades to come. Graduate schools were later ranked in K. D. Roose and C. J. Andersen, *A Rating of Graduate Programs* (Washington, 1970) and, most comprehensively in five volumes, in Lyle V. Jones, Gardner Lindzey, and Porter E. Coggeshall, *An Assessment of Research-Doctorate Programs in the United States,* (Washington, 1982–83).

Magoun received degrees at University of Rhode Island (B.S. 1929), Syracuse (M.S. 1931), and at Northwestern (Ph.D. 1934), where he remained on the staff of the medical school in neuroanatomy until 1962. Later he was dean of the graduate division at UCLA (1962–72), where he was also professor of psychiatry in the school of medicine.

H. W. Magoun, "The Cartter Report on Quality in Graduate Education: Institutional and Divisional Standings Compiled from the Report," *Journal of Higher Education* 38 (December 1966): 481–92. Reprinted with the permission of The Ohio State University Press. Further reading: A. H. Bowker, "Quality and Quantity in Higher Education," *Journal of the American Statistical Association* 60 (March 1965): 1–15, institutional ranking within broad fields of inquiry and according to fellowship awardees choosing each school; Rebecca Zames Margulies and Peter M. Blau, "The Pecking Order of the Elite: America's Leading Professional Schools," *Change* 5 (November 1973): 21–27; "The Cartter Report on the Leading Schools of Education, Law, and Business," *Change* 9 (February 1977): 44–48, a critical study; Lewis C. Solmon and Alexander W. Astin, "Departments without Distinguished Graduate Programs," *Change* 13 (September 1981): 23–28; J. Gourman, *The Gourman Report: A Rating of Undergraduate Programs in American and International Universities* (Los Angeles, 1977); J. D. Lawrence and K. C. Green, "A Question of Quality: The Higher Education Ratings Game," *AAHE-ERIC Higher Education Research Report* 5 (Washington, D.C., 1980); David S. Webster, "America's Highest Ranked Graduate Schools, 1925–1982," *Change* 15 (May/June 1983): 14–24; and IV, 2.

There is little need for further expression of the widespread interest and general approbation that have been evoked by the recent publication of the Cartter Report, *An Assessment of Quality in Graduate Education.*[1] Its detailed evaluation of the quality of graduate faculty and the attractiveness of graduate programs at more than a hundred institutions throughout the United States brings up to date (1964), and provides comparisons with the earlier

---

1. Allan M. Cartter (Washington, D.C.: American Council on Education, 1966).

assessments of Raymond M. Hughes[2] and Hayward Keniston.[3] The Cartter Report is considerably more extensive than its predecessors, and has gone to elaborate lengths to establish the validity of its evaluations. . . .

The fifty-seven-page heart of the Cartter Report consists of detailed tabular expositions of departmental ratings in almost thirty academic disciplines, ranging through the fields of graduate specialization from classics to mechanical engineering. It is followed by a chapter devoted to "generalizations about quality programs . . . considering the university as a whole." This chapter opens with the surprising statement, "At the outset of the study, it was decided not to aggregate scores to arrive at university-wide ratings," and ends with the conclusion, " . . . We leave to the reader the task of drawing generalizations from the detailed presentations . . ."[4]

The Report is somewhat more amenable to the consideration of divisional standings. It points out that "most academicians feel that . . . strength in one field of study requires the presence of strong departments in other closely allied disciplines," and indicates that the "study lends moderate support to the view that good departments in closely allied fields cluster together." Table 37 of the Report, *The Leading Universities, by General Areas of Study, as Measured by Quality of Faculty, 1964,* presents the over-all standings of five to nine of the highest-rated universities in each of the four divisions of letters and science and in engineering, with the comment, California, Berkeley, appears in the leading group in all five divisions, a finding which supports the claim that it is the best balanced distinguished university in the country. Harvard and Stanford appear in four divisions; Columbia, Illinois, Yale, Princeton,

---

2. *A Study of the Graduate Schools of America* (Oxford, Ohio: Miami University, 1925). (Copy prepared by the Miami University Library and kindly made available by H. Bunker Wright, dean of the Graduate School.)

3. "Appendix: Standing of American Graduate Departments in the Arts and Sciences," *Graduate Study and Research in the Arts and Sciences at the University of Pennsylvania* (Philadelphia: University of Pennsylvania Press, 1959), pp. 115–50.

4. The Cartter Report's objection to over-all standings obtained by summating scores rests on the presumptive ground that this might imply an equation of the importance of the subject-fields involved. Additionally, it is proposed, summation would penalize an institution which did not offer work in each of the fields under review. In contrary opinion, the qualities of faculty and programs, which the Report has assessed, are or should be just as important for graduate study in one field as in another. In the present article, the assessment of these qualities is considered to be quite independent of the comparative merits of the different fields. Moreover, in so far as could be determined from available catalogues, the over-all standing of each institution is based on the assessment of these qualities only in fields in which graduate study was offered.

Michigan, and Cal. Tech. in three; and M.I.T., Chicago, and Wisconsin in two. . . .

In addition to the usefulness of aggregate standings in providing a developmental view of higher education and provoking concern on the part of central administrative officers for the improvement of their universities, such syntheses are of value today because of the extent to which activities related to graduate education have come to determine the intellectual and economic well-being of the communities and regions in which graduate schools are situated. In our contemporary society, many extramural groups and agencies are interested in the over-all standings of universities and their divisions.

For the reasons given, as well as to reduce the reader's task, tables have been compiled from data in the Cartter Report to show, for the top twenty-five universities (Group A), the comprehensive institutional standings in letters and science and the divisional standings in the humanities, social sciences, life sciences, and physical sciences, as well as those in engineering.[5] In every case except engineering, analogous standings from the Hughes and Keniston reports are presented for comparison (Tables I–V [see pp. 213–16]). . . .

The data presented in the Cartter Report, under the individual departmental ratings of "strong, good, and adequate plus," form an outstanding collection of current information on this subject. From the aggregate of this detailed information, tables have been compiled to show, for the second twenty-five institutions in the country (Group B), the comprehensive institutional standings in letters and science and the divisional standings in the humanities, social sciences, life sciences, and physical sciences, as well as those in engineering (Table VI [see p. 217]).[6]

In each of these categories, the upper clusters of institutions are the most clearly differentiable. In the inclusive list for letters and science, the upper cluster comprises the University of Iowa, Michigan State, Rochester, and Pittsburgh; in the humanities, Bryn Mawr, Pittsburgh, the University of Iowa, and Tulane; in the social sciences, Michigan State, Syracuse, the University of Iowa, and Oregon; in the life sciences, U.C., Davis, the University of Iowa, Western Reserve, Rochester, Michigan State, Kansas, Rutgers, Yeshiva, and Pittsburgh; in the physical sciences, Rice, Colorado, Rochester, Brandeis, and Michigan State. Collectively, the institutions in the upper clusters of each of the divisions listed make up approximately the upper half of the inclusive list for letters and science. In engineering, the upper cluster includes Illinois Institute of Technology, Iowa State, Pennsylvania State, Lehigh, Yale, Rice, Syracuse, and Michigan State (Table VII [see p. 218]).

These remarks of Lloyd Berkner may be relevant for a number of the institutions in both Groups A and B above:

Since the new society will require at least one great graduate institution in each of the hundred metropolitan cores of our nation, we face the problem of developing new institutions at the true graduate-university level in each core where one is now lacking. The failure to develop such institutions after the 1930 era stems from a variety of forces, all acting to discourage such ventures.

The very existence of the top 20 or 25 makes it well-nigh impossible to attract scholars to what should be new centers of learning. Thus, rising to graduate status today, in the face of the distinction of the Yales, Harvards, and Princetons, the MITs, or the Berkeleys and Wisconsins, is a completely different problem [from that which] those universities had to cope with in their adolescence.[7]

4. William G. Bowen and Julie Ann Sosa, *Prospect for Faculty in the Arts and Sciences*, 1989

This widely used statistical book, with information on the enrollment by field, the number of graduate students in the arts and sciences, and population trends and age distribution of faculties, was compiled and written in 1989 by William G. Bowen and Julie Ann Sosa. Although cautious at the outset in its conceptions and clear that it was making projections and not predictions, the book

---

5. In the compilation of the divisional standings in Group A, each institution's scores in subject-fields in that division were added, and the sum divided by the number of fields in which graduate programs were offered. The institutional standing in letters and science was determined by adding the divisional scores and dividing by four.

In determining institutional standings based on quality of graduate faculty, the "all respondents score" (ranging from 5.00–3.00) was used as given in the Report; listings of "good" and "adequate plus" (for which no score was included in the Report) were scored 2.00 and 1.00 respectively; 0.50 was scored when an institution was not included in any rating but offered a graduate program in the subject-field.

Standings in attractiveness of graduate program were determined similarly: the "all respondent score" (ranging from 3.00 to 1.50) was used as given in the Report; a listing of "acceptable plus" (for which no score was included in the Report) was scored 1.00; 0.50 was scored when an institution was not included in any rating but offered a graduate program in the subject-field.

6. In compiling divisional standings in Group B, each institution's scores in subject-fields in that division were added, and the total was used as the institution's aggregate score. The over-all standing in letters and science

was determined by adding the divisional scores and dividing by four.

In determining standings of quality of graduate faculty, the "all respondents score" (ranging from 5.00–3.00) was used when given, and listings of "good" and "adequate plus" (with which no score was included in the Report) were scored 2.00 and 1.00 respectively.

This method of ranking, which differed from that for Group A institutions, was intended to identify areas of existing strength.

7. Lloyd Berkner, "Government Support for Academic Science," *Educational Record*, XLVII (Spring, 1966), 44, 46.

Table I
Institutional Standing in Letters and Sciences of Universities in Group A*

| Hughes Report† (1925) (1) | Keniston Report‡ (1957) (2) | Cartter Report (1964) | |
		Faculty (3)	Program (4)
1. Chicago	1. Harvard	1. Harvard	1. Harvard
2. Harvard	2. U.C., Berkeley	2. U.C., Berkeley	2. U.C., Berkeley
3. Columbia	3. Columbia	3. Yale	3. Yale
4. Wisconsin	4. Yale	4. Princeton	4. Princeton
5. Yale	5. Michigan	5. Chicago	5. Stanford
6. Princeton	6. Chicago	6. Stanford	6. Wisconsin
7. Johns Hopkins	7. Princeton	7. Michigan	7. Michigan
8. Michigan	8. Wisconsin	8. Wisconsin	8. Chicago
9. U.C., Berkeley	9. Cornell	9. Columbia	9. Columbia
10. Cornell	10. Illinois	10. U.C.L.A.	10. Cornell
11. Illinois	11. Pennsylvania	11. Johns Hopkins	10. Johns Hopkins
12. Pennsylvania	12. Minnesota	12. Cornell	11. Illinois
13. Minnesota	13. Stanford	13. Illinois	12. U.C.L.A.
14. Stanford	14. U.C.L.A.	14. Pennsylvania	13. Pennsylvania
15. Ohio State	15. Indiana	15. Minnesota	14. Minnesota
16. Iowa	16. Johns Hopkins	16. Indiana	15. U. of Washington
17. Northwestern	17. Northwestern	17. Northwestern	16. Northwestern
18. North Carolina	18. Ohio State	18. U. of Washington	17. North Carolina
19. Indiana	19. N.Y.U.	19. Texas	18. Texas
	20. U. of Washington	20. North Carolina	19. Indiana
		21. Brown	20. Duke
		22. N.Y.U.	21. Brown
		23. Ohio State	22. Ohio State
		24. Washington U.	23. N.Y.U.
		25. Duke	24. Washington U.

*In Tables I–VI, Group A refers to the highest-rated twenty-five universities in the United States, and in Table VII Group B refers to the next twenty-five, as compiled from Allan M. Cartter, *An Assessment of Quality in Graduate Education* (Washington, D.C.: American Council on Education, 1966). Abbreviations of the names of universities in the tables generally follow those used in the Cartter Report (Appendix E, pp. 129–31). In all tables in which ties appear, the institutions are given the same numbers and are arranged alphabetically. The comparative divisional standings of a number of additional institutions with concentrations of emphasis or areas of special strength are listed in footnotes to the tables.
†Raymond M. Hughes, *14 Study of the Graduate Schools of America* (Oxford, Ohio: Miami University, 1925).
‡Hayward Keniston, "Standing of American Graduate Departments in the Arts and Sciences (1957)" *Graduate Study and Research in the Arts and Sciences at the University of Pennsylvania* (Philadelphia: University of Pennsylvania Press, 1959), pp. 115–50.

was too optimistic about the supply and demand for faculties over the next quarter-century. Its circulation among academic administrators, made more hopeful by its findings, caused considerable dismay over the next decade. Changing national, international, economic, and demographic conditions accentuated the risk inherent in projections of this kind. The authors did, however, emphasize that their findings were in part dependent upon the supply and especially the demand for academic "labor," which over the years did not meet their expectations. When Bowen left the presidency of Princeton to preside over the Andrew W. Mellon Foundation, he was accompanied by Julie Ann Sosa, who had been a prominent Princeton undergraduate, to assist in this study.

William G. Bowen and Julie Ann Sosa, *Prospects for Faculty in the Arts and Sciences: A Study of Factors Affecting Demand and Supply, 1987–2012* © 1998 Princeton University Press. Reprinted by permission of Princeton University Press: 12–14. Further reading: II, 21; III, 15.

In thinking about education, many of us are autobiographical. We tend to make judgments about the

future on the basis of our own experiences and the experiences of friends, which makes it difficult to anticipate changes in circumstances. This is a particularly serious problem in planning for higher education because of the exceptionally long lead time involved in moving from recognition of a problem to effective action.

Our analysis leads us to believe that the next decades will be different in important respects from both the postwar period of expansion and the more recent period of sluggish labor markets for academics in most fields. No new baby boom is anticipated; nor do we expect significant increases in enrollment rates. The rapid expansion of the 1960s, which had such profound effects on American higher education, will not be replicated.

Population changes will produce some increases (as well as some decreases) in enrollments. However, any significant increases in enrollment *rates* would seem to us to require major changes in public policy and in the quality of elementary and secondary

Table II
Divisional Standing in the Humanities of Universities in Group A

Hughes Report (1925) (1)	Keniston Report (1957) (2)	Cartter Report (1964) Faculty (3)	Cartter Report (1964) Program (4)
1. Harvard	1. Harvard	1. Harvard	1. Yale
2. Chicago	2. Yale	2. U.C., Berkeley	2. Harvard
3. Columbia	3. Columbia	3. Yale	3. U.C., Berkeley
4. Yale	4. U.C., Berkeley	4. Princeton	4. Princeton
5. Princeton	5. Michigan	5. Columbia	5. Michigan
6. Johns Hopkins	6. Princeton	6. Michigan	6. Columbia
7. U.C., Berkeley	7. Chicago	7. Chicago	7. Chicago
8. Cornell	8. Pennsylvania	8. Johns Hopkins	8. Cornell
8. Wisconsin	9. Cornell	8. Wisconsin	9. Pennsylvania
9. Pennsylvania	10. Wisconsin	9. Pennsylvania	10. Wisconsin
10. Michigan	11. Illinois	10. Cornell	11. Johns Hopkins
11. Illinois	12. Indiana	11. Stanford	12. Stanford
12. Bryn Mawr	13. Johns Hopkins	12. U.C.L.A.	13. North Carolina
13. Minnesota	14. N.Y.U.	13. Illinois	14. Illinois
14. Stanford	15. North Carolina	14. Texas	14. U.C.L.A.
15. Ohio State	16. U.C.L.A.	15. North Carolina	15. Indiana
16. Northwestern	17. Minnesota	16. Indiana	16. Texas
17. Iowa	18. Washington	17. Brown	17. Brown
18. North Carolina	19. Northwestern	18. N.Y.U.	18. Northwestern
19. Indiana	20. Texas	19. Minnesota	19. Minnesota
		20. U. of Washington	19. U. of Washington
		21. Northwestern	20. Ohio State
		22. Ohio State	21. N.Y.U.
		23. Washington U.	22. Duke
		24. Duke	23. Washington U.

Table III
Divisional Standing in the Social Sciences of Universities in Group A

Hughes Report (1925) (1)	Keniston Report (1957) (2)	Cartter Report (1964) Faculty (3)	Cartter Report (1964) Program (4)
1. Columbia	1. Harvard	1. Harvard	1. Yale
2. Chicago	2. Chicago	2. U.C., Berkeley	2. Harvard
3. Harvard	3. Columbia	3. Chicago	3. U.C., Berkeley
4. Wisconsin	4. U.C., Berkeley	4. Yale	4. Princeton
5. Michigan	5. Yale	5. Princeton	5. Michigan
6. Minnesota	6. Michigan	6. Wisconsin	6. Columbia
7. Johns Hopkins	7. Minnesota	7. Michigan	7. Chicago
8. Cornell	8. Stanford	7. Stanford	8. Cornell
9. Illinois	9. Cornell	8. Columbia	9. Pennsylvania
10. Yale	10. Wisconsin	9. U.C.L.A.	10. Wisconsin
11. Princeton	11. Princeton	10. Cornell	11. Johns Hopkins
12. Pennsylvania	12. U.C.L.A.	11. Northwestern	12. Stanford
13. Iowa	13. Illinois	12. Minnesota	13. North Carolina
14. Stanford	14. Pennsylvania	13. Pennsylvania	14. Illinois
15. Ohio State	15. Northwestern	14. Johns Hopkins	14. U.C.L.A.
16. U.C., Berkeley	16. Johns Hopkins	15. U. of Washington	15. Indiana
17. North Carolina	17. U. of Washington	16. Indiana	16. Texas
18. Northwestern	18. Indiana	17. North Carolina	17. Brown
	19. North Carolina	18. Illinois	18. Northwestern
		19. Washington U.	19. Minnesota
		20. Duke	19. U. of Washington
		21. N.Y.U.	20. Ohio State
		22. Texas	21. N.Y.U.
		23. Ohio State	22. Duke
		24. Brown	23. Washington U.

Table IV
Divisional Standing in the Life Sciences of Universities in Group A

Hughes Report (1925) (1)	Keniston Report (1957) (2)	Cartter Report (1964) Faculty* (3)	Cartter Report (1964) Program† (4)
1. Chicago	1. Harvard	1. U.C., Berkeley	1. U.C., Berkeley
2. Columbia	2. U.C., Berkeley	2. Harvard	2. Harvard
3. Harvard	3. Wisconsin	3. Stanford	3. Stanford
4. Wisconsin	4. Michigan	4. Michigan	4. Michigan
5. Johns Hopkins	5. Indiana	5. Illinois	5. Wisconsin
6. Cornell	6. Cornell	6. Wisconsin	5. Yale
7. Michigan	7. Yale	6. Yale	6. Illinois
8. Yale	8. Columbia	7. Pennsylvania	7. Minnesota
9. Illinois	9. U.C.L.A.	8. Cornell	8. Johns Hopkins
10. U.C., Berkeley	10. Pennsylvania	8. Johns Hopkins	9. Pennsylvania
11. Minnesota	11. Illinois	9. Princeton	10. Cornell
12. Princeton	12. Johns Hopkins	10. Chicago	11. U.C.L.A.
12. Stanford	13. Stanford	10. Minnesota	11. U. of Washington
13. Ohio State	14. Chicago	11. U.C.L.A.	12. Princeton
14. Missouri	15. Duke	12. Columbia	13. Indiana
15. Bryn Mawr	15. Princeton	13. U. of Washington	14. Chicago
16. Indiana	16. Minnesota	14. Indiana	15. Duke
17. Pennsylvania	17. Ohio State	15. Duke	16. Columbia
	18. Texas	16. Washington U.	17. Texas
	19. N.Y.U.	17. Northwestern	18. Northwestern
		18. Texas	19. Brown
		19. Brown	20. North Carolina
		20. North Carolina	21. Ohio State
		21. N.Y.U.	22. N.Y.U.
		22. Ohio State	23. Washington U.

*Rockefeller and Cal. Tech. fall between 2 and 3, and Purdue ties with 19.
†Rockefeller and Cal. Tech. fall between 2 and 3, and Purdue falls between 17 and 18.

education. Such changes could be stimulated by the growing complexity of the economy and an attendant increase in the demand for better-educated employees, but it is far from certain that this will occur.

The fluctuations in enrollment that can be projected will, nonetheless, have important effects. Enrollment-driven changes in the number of new positions will have greater influence on period-to-period *variations* in demand for faculty than will other factors—such as the number of retirements.

Contrary to what is often said, the replacement component of demand will not, we believe, fluctuate appreciably over the next twenty-five years. We foresee no cataclysmic bunching of exits from academia; instead, our analysis suggests a relatively smooth (but steady) pattern of departures. Replacement demand will, however, be the dominant determinant of the *level* of demand for faculty. Overall, we estimate that perhaps 90 percent of all openings will be attributable to vacancies. In this respect, the years ahead will be dramatically different from the 1960s.

Our enrollment projections depend heavily on assumptions about student interests, and another theme of this study is the importance of the flight from the arts and sciences that has been so pronounced in recent years. We were surprised—and concerned—to learn that between 1971 and 1985 the

arts-and-sciences share of degrees conferred fell from 40 percent to 25 percent. In 1985, less than 5 percent of all degrees were awarded in the humanities. This level is *so* low that any further decline is unlikely; indeed, some evidence suggests that there is already a very modest recovery of interest in the humanities underway.

The increasing concentration of arts-and-sciences enrollments in certain sectors of higher education is a related concern. The research universities and the selective liberal arts institutions have become responsible for larger and larger fractions of the teaching in these fields, and especially in the humanities and social sciences. At the same time, the general trend toward pre-professional and job-related courses of study has been especially pronounced in other sectors. The resulting bifurcation of functions within higher education has implications that reach beyond faculty staffing.

The fall-off in student interest in the arts and sciences between 1977 and 1987 was not matched by a comparable decrease in faculty positions. As a result, student/faculty ratios actually declined, and this development buffered what otherwise would have been a precipitous drop in the number of faculty members teaching in the arts and sciences. In projecting the number of faculty positions, we have assumed that these key ratios are likely either to

Table V
Divisional Standing in the Physical Sciences of Universities in Group A

Hughes Report† (1925) (1)	Keniston Report‡ (1957) (2)	Cartter Report (1964)	
		Faculty (3)	Program (4)
1. Chicago	1. U.C., Berkeley	1. Harvard	1. Harvard
2. Harvard	2. Harvard	2. U.C., Berkeley	2. Stanford
3. Yale	3. Chicago	3. Princeton	2. U.C., Berkeley
4. U.C., Berkeley	4. Princeton	4. Stanford	3. Princeton
5. Princeton	5. Columbia	5. Chicago	4. Wisconsin
6. Columbia	6. Wisconsin	6. Yale	5. Yale
7. Wisconsin	7. Michigan	7. Columbia	6. Chicago
8. Michigan	8. Yale	8. Wisconsin	7. Columbia
9. Johns Hopkins	9. Illinois	9. Michigan	8. Michigan
10. Cornell	10. Stanford	10. Johns Hopkins	9. Johns Hopkins
11. Illinois	11. Cornell	11. U.C.L.A.	10. Cornell
12. Minnesota	12. Minnesota	12. Illinois	11. Illinois
13. Stanford	13. U.C.L.A.	13. Minnesota	12. U.C.L.A.
14. Iowa	14. Ohio State	14. Cornell	13. U. of Washington
15. Pennsylvania	15. Northwestern	15. Northwestern	14. Minnesota
16. Ohio State	16. Indiana	16. Ohio State	15. Northwestern
17. Northwestern	17. Johns Hopkins	17. Indiana	16. Indiana
		18. U. of Washington	17. N.Y.U.
		19. Brown	18. Texas
		20. N.Y.U.	19. Brown
		20. Pennsylvania	20. Ohio State
		21. Texas	21. Pennsylvania
		22. Duke	22. Duke
		23. North Carolina	22. Washington U.
		24. Washington U.	23. North Carolina

*Cal. Tech. and M.I.T. fall between 2 and 3; Purdue, between 12 and 13; and Rice, between 14 and 15.
†Cal. Tech. precedes 1; M.I.T. falls between 4 and 5; Rice, between 13 and 14; Purdue, between 16 and 17; and Case and Brooklyn Polytech., between 22 and 23.

remain constant or to decline much more modestly. We have also made projections that allow for the possibility that student/faculty ratios could rise if there were to be a significant recovery in arts-and-sciences enrollments.

Labor market conditions in the 1970s made it difficult for young people in many areas of the arts and sciences to find suitable academic employment, and the drop in the number of new Ph.D.'s was more pronounced than people such as Cartter had assumed. At the same time, a larger number of the Ph.D.'s that were awarded went to nonresidents, and a larger fraction of all recipients of Ph.D.'s chose to pursue non-academic careers. The consequent decline in the pool of candidates for academic appointment—especially when we take account of qualitative considerations—is another source of considerable concern.

When we combine projections of supply with projections of demand, we find no compelling reason to expect major changes in academic labor markets within the next few years. But we do project some significant increase in demand relative to supply as early as 1992–97—and then far more dramatic changes beginning in 1997–2002. All of our models project demand to exceed supply by *substantial* amounts from that point on. A surprising conclu-

sion is that the projected imbalances are particularly severe for the humanities and social sciences. For at least a decade, beginning in 1997, three of our four models imply that there will be only seven candidates for every ten positions in these fields.

As always, adjustments of various kinds will take place, correcting some of the potential imbalances. In general, however, we do not believe that adjustments on the demand side of the equation will be very large. The supply of new doctorates is likely to be much more responsive to improved labor market conditions. We expect supply-side adjustments to take two principal forms: larger numbers of candidates for doctorates in the arts and sciences and (we hope) some shortening of the average time spent obtaining a degree.

Another potential supply-side adjustment, retirement, is the subject of a great deal of discussion these days; we have concluded, however, that even extreme changes in retirement patterns would have little effect on projected supply/demand ratios. Retirement decisions are, of course, very important to individuals and institutions, but primarily for other reasons.

Policy decisions are potentially at least as important as any of the market-driven forms of adjustment. Universities can strengthen their graduate

Table VI
Institutional Standing in Engineering of Universities in Group A

Cartter Report (1964)	
Faculty (1)	Program (2)
1. M.I.T.	1. U.C., Berkeley
2. U.C., Berkeley	2. M.I.T.
3. Stanford	3. Stanford
4. Cal. Tech.	4. Illinois
5. Illinois	5. Cal. Tech.
6. Michigan	6. Michigan
7. Harvard	7. Princeton
7. Minnesota	8. Wisconsin
8. Wisconsin	9. Purdue
9. Purdue	10. Cornell
10. Princeton	11. Harvard
11. Northwestern	12. Johns Hopkins
12. Columbia	12. U. of Washington
12. Cornell	13. Carnegie Tech.
13. Carnegie Tech.	14. Northwestern
14. Johns Hopkins	15. Texas
15. Texas	16. Minnesota
16. Ohio State	17. Brooklyn Polytech.
17. U.C.L.A.	18. Case
17. U. of Washington	19. Columbia
18. Brooklyn Polytech.	19. N.Y.U.
19. N.Y.U.	19. Ohio State
20. Rensselaer	19. Pennsylvania
21. Case	19. Rensselaer
22. Pennsylvania	20. U.C.L.A.

programs while simultaneously reducing the time that it takes a student to earn a doctorate. A particularly strong case can be made for beginning now to establish the incentives that will attract a larger number of excellent candidates to graduate study and then to academic careers. Although both private and public support is needed, we believe that the federal government must take a leadership role in providing the amounts and forms of student aid that will be required.

5. Denise K. Magner,
"Decline in Doctorates Earned by
Black and White Men Persists," 1989

The supply of minority doctoral students in all academic fields, but particularly in the arts and sciences, remained a continuing problem in the decades following affirmative action. Optimism in the early 1970s gave way to declining numbers of Ph.D. recipients among black and Native American students. By the mid-1980s, there was some cause for hope that academic ranks would be broadened because of rising numbers in doctorates awarded to Asian and Hispanic students. Denise K. Magner, a senior editor and frequent contributor to *The Chronicle of Higher Education,* reported on the alarming decline in anticipated degrees given to the largest minority group, African-American students. Magner earned a journalism degree at Michigan State (1985) and was first employed at *The Chronicle* in 1988.

Denise K. Magner, "Decline in Doctorates Earned by Black and White Men Persists, Study Finds; Foreign Stu-

dents and U.S. Women Fill Gaps," *Chronicle of Higher Education,* March 1, 1989, A11. Copyright 1989, *The Chronicle of Higher Education.* Reprinted with permission.

Black American men earned slightly fewer doctoral degrees in 1987 than in the year before, sustaining a decade-long decline that saw the number of doctorates awarded to them fall by 54 per cent.

A new survey of doctoral recipients at U. S. institutions shows that the number of degrees awarded to American men, overall, fell by 28 per cent from 1977 to 1987, the most recent year for which statistics are available. . . .

The greatest proportional drop occurred among U.S. black men, who earned 317 doctorates in 1987, compared to 684 in 1977. The number of white American men receiving doctoral degrees also dropped significantly—from 17,011 in 1977 to 12,116 in 1987. Research doctorates earned by American men with Asian, Hispanic, or American Indian backgrounds increased, although their numbers remained low.

While fewer American men earned Ph.D.s, the total number of students receiving doctorates at the nation's universities increased by about 500 students, to 32,278 in 1987.

Foreign students and American women filled the gaps created by the decline in American men earning, doctorates, said Lori Thurgood, research associate at the National Research Council.

Students with temporary or permanent visas earned 22.2 percent of the doctorates awarded in 1987, compared to 15.2 cent in 1977. During that time, the share of doctorates earned by U.S. citizens fell from 82.4 to 70.8 per cent.

The total number of women earning doctorates rose by one-third, to 11,370 in 1987. A greater proportion of those receiving doctoral degrees were women—up from 25 percent in 1977 to 35 per cent in 1987.

Ms. Thurgood noted, however, that the proportion of doctorates earned by women has stalled at about 35 per cent since 1984. While the number of white American women receiving doctorates rose 36 per cent from 1977 to 1987, the number of black American women getting doctorates grew only 4 per cent, and actually declined in 1986 and 1987.

Many of the statistics come as little surprise to university leaders, and serve only to reinforce trends to which they have been alerted in recent years.

Several explanations are offered for the decline in doctorates earned by American men, and blacks in particular, including deficiencies in earlier education and market trends that offer higher salaries for jobs outside higher education.

Said Charles U. Smith, dean of graduate studies at Florida A&M University: "The black male appears to be in a dangerous state of decline" in both academe and society at large. He laid part of the blame on the Reagan Administration for cutbacks

Table VII
Divisional and Institutional Standing of Graduate Faculty of Universities in Group B as Compiled from the Cartter Report

Institutional Standing	Divisional Standing				Institutional Standing
Letters and Science (1)	Humanities* (2)	Social Sciences (3)	Life Sciences I (4)	Physical Sciences (5)	Engineering (6)
1. U. of Iowa	1. Bryn Mawr	1. Michigan State	1. U.C., Davis	1. Rice	1. Ill. Inst. of Tech.
2. Michigan State	2. Pittsburgh	2. Syracuse	2. U. of Iowa	2. Colorado	1. Iowa State
3. Rochester	3. U. of Iowa	3. U. of Iowa	3. Western Reserve	3. Rochester	1. Penn. State
4. Pittsburgh	4. Tulane	3. Oregon	4. Rochester	4. Brandeis	2. Lehigh
5. U. of Kansas	5. Colorado	4. Pittsburgh	5. Michigan State	5. Maryland	3. Yale
6. U. of Oregon	5. Rice	4. Vanderbilt	6. U. of Kansas	6. Michigan State	4. Rice
7. Rutgers	5. Rochester	4. Virginia	7. Rutgers	7. Iowa State	5. Syracuse
8. Western Reserve	5. Syracuse	5. Penn. State	7. Yeshiva	8. Penn. State	6. Michigan State
9. Syracuse	5. U.S.C.	5. Rochester	8. Pittsburgh	8. Virginia	7. Delaware
10. U.C., Davis	6. Brandeis	6. U. of Kansas	9. Iowa State	9. U. of Iowa	8. Georgia Tech.
11. Iowa State	6. U. of Kansas	6. Rutgers	10. Oregon	9. U. of Kansas	9. U. of Florida
11. Penn. State	6. Michigan State	7. Brandeis	10. Utah	9. Oregon	9. Maryland
12. Brandeis	6. Rutgers	7. Bryn Mawr	11. Oregon State	9. U.S.C.	9. No. Carolina State
13. Colorado	6. Virginia	7. Emory	11. Penn. State	10. Pittsburgh	9. Oklahoma State
13. Rice	6. Western Reserve	7. Iowa State	11. Vanderbilt	11. Rutgers	10. Colorado
14. U.S.C.	7. Emory	8. Colorado	12. Emory	11.Syracuse	10. Oregon State
14. Tulane	7. U. of Florida	8. Maryland	13. U. of Florida	11. Utah	10. Pittsburgh
15. Vanderbilt	7. Oregon	8. Rice	13. Tulane	12. U.C., Davis	10. U.S.C.
16. Maryland	7. Penn. State	8. U.S.C.	14. Brandeis	12. U. of Florida	10. Washington U.
17. Yeshiva	7. Vanderbilt	8. Tulane	15. Maryland	12. Tulane	11. U. of Arizona
18. Virginia		8. Western Reserve	15. U.S.C.	13.Oregon State	11. Cincinnati
19. Utah			15. Syracuse	13.Vanderbilt	11. U. of Iowa
20. Emory			16. Colorado	13.Western Reserve	11. U. of Kansas
21. U. of Florida			17. Rice	13.Yeshiva	11. Missouri
22. Bryn Mawr			18. Virginia		11. New Mexico
22. Oregon State			18. Bryn Mawr		11. U. of Oklahoma
					11. Tennessee
					11. Texas A. and M.
					11. Utah

*Catholic falls between 4 and 5, and Fordham ties with 5.
†Louisiana State falls between 3 and 4, Claremont ties with 5, and U. of Arizona and New School tie with 6.
‡Tufts falls between 10 and 11, Washington State ties with 13, and Buffalo falls between 13 and 14. Notre Dame ties with 10,
    Wayne State with 11, and U. of Arizona and Louisiana State with 12.

in financial aid for graduate education and efforts to dismantle affirmative-action advances.

Others said universities had done a poor job of selling the advantages of a career in teaching and research to American students. "A tremendous number of our brightest young people are now being attracted to master's in business administration or to professional degrees," said Robert L. Ringel, vice-president and dean of the graduate school at Purdue University. "Many professional schools have done an excellent job of marketing these careers. I don't think universities have done enough to show what a fantastic career opportunity is available by joining the faculty of an institution."

Whatever the reason for the decline, several educators said the statistics reinforced the need for state and federal governments to finance more fellowships.

Robert M. Rosenzweig, president of the Association of American Universities, said fellowships offer practical and symbolic support to students by showing that society values professors and research.

A common misperception is that foreign students are displacing American students in graduate schools, but that is not the case, according to several officials. "Every time people ask me about the 'foreign-student problem,' I tell them that it's not the foreign-student problem, it's the U. S.-student problem," said Frank E. Perkins, dean of the graduate school at the Massachusetts Institute of Technology.

"With the declining interest among U. S. citizens in research doctorate programs, colleges have to keep the programs going so they fill them up with foreign applicants. There is certainly no shortage of foreign applicants."

Foreign students are classified in two categories in the research council's survey—those with temporary and those with permanent visas. The survey found that 75 per cent of those with permanent visas planned to seek employment or do postdoctoral work in the United States once they finished doctoral work. Meanwhile, about 48 per cent of those with temporary visas planned to remain in this country after earning their doctorate.

"We are getting the benefit of a large pool of labor that we don't have to educate from grade one through high school." Mr. Rosenzweig said. "I don't see that as a problem."

Dozens of universities have announced programs to increase the recruitment of minorities at the undergraduate level and to attract more of them to the teaching profession. M.I.T., for instance, offers a summer science program for undergraduates from the nation's black colleges.

Florida A&M sends the names of top black students to graduate schools and asks the schools to reserve financial-aid packages for them. But most officials said it would be several years before they could assess whether the programs had resulted in more research doctorates for members of minority groups.

Graduate schools need to correct misunderstandings about doctoral work, said Clara Sue Kidwell, dean-in-residence at the Council of Graduate Schools and a professor of American Indian studies at the University of California at Berkeley. One misperception, she said, is that all graduate students are struggling to repay huge college costs in the face of low salaries. While students at professional schools may face a high debt burden once they graduate, most of those seeking doctorates finance their education through teaching and research positions, fellowships, and a limited number of federal grants, she said.

According to the survey, 54 per cent of the doctorate recipients said they faced no debt burden upon graduation. Of the 46 per cent who did, the average debt was about $7,000, which officials said is manageable.

"I think that where we really need to start grooming people for graduate school is at the high school level," said Ms. Kidwell. "Going to graduate school is a state of mind. You go because the subject excites you and you find out someone will pay you for studying it. We have to sell students early that learning can be fun and provide exciting opportunities."

Improving the Status of Academic Women

6. AHA Committee on the Status of Women in the Profession (the Rose Report), 1970

Responding to the women's movement of the 1960s, a committee of the American Historical Association chaired by Willie Lee Rose (1927–78) delivered one of the first reports from any academic organization on the status of its women members. It became a model for similar studies from other academic societies. Rose had won distinction for her pathbreaking study *Rehearsal for Reconstruction* (1964). That book came from a prize-winning dissertation under the direction of C. Vann Woodward and began an unfortunately short-lived career studying American slavery and American legal history. But before her death she had held the Commonwealth Professorship at the University of Virginia (1971–73), where she had taught since 1965. She then returned to her doctoral home, Johns Hopkins. She held the Harmsworth Professorship of American History at Oxford University (1977–78).

American Historical Association, Committee on the Status of Women, Report, November 9, 1970, 1–5, 11–13. Reprinted with the kind permission of the American Historical Association. Among the few then current surveys of academic working women in American society were Helen S. Astin, *The Woman Doctorate in America: Origins, Career, and Family* (New York, 1969); R. J. Simon, S. M. Clark, and K. Galway, "The Woman Ph.D.: A Recent Profile," *Social Problems* (Fall 1967); and Lawrence A. Simpson, "A Study of Employing Agents' Attitudes toward Academic Women in Higher Education," doctoral dissertation, Pennsylvania State University, 1969. The influence of the Rose Report can be seen in U.S. Council of Graduate Schools, "Alternate Approaches to Graduate Education" (1973), among others. The Committee on the Status of Women in the Economics Profession stated in 2005 that of all Ph.D.'s in economics for the 2004–2005 academic year, 29.5 percent were women, up from 23.7 percent in 1994–95. Further reading: II, 10–15; V, 9–12.

The Committee is well aware of the extent to which the broad question of the teaching, placement, and career development of women in professional history is a part of the even broader question of women's role in contemporary society. Identifying those aspects of both questions that may be met by action on the part of a professional association has not always been easy, but the Committee is convinced that there is for the AHA a very significant area of responsibility and opportunity. Our profession will be strengthened to the extent that its practices are recognized as equitable, based on merit, and designed to encourage and develop the best talent available within our ranks. Believing that our professional practices are not effectively meeting these objectives, the Committee is recommending certain institutional arrangements and policies to secure greater equity for women as prospective students and teachers of history.

Our study has convinced us that many, though not all, of the problems of women in academic life are reflections of general problems affecting men as well as women, and it is our belief that most of our recommendations would serve to provide a more liberal, encouraging, and progressive atmosphere for all students and teachers of history. . . .

PART ONE: *RECOMMENDED RESOLUTIONS*

The present demand for social justice for women coincides with the permanent interest of the historical profession. To increase the opportunities open to women in the field of history is to advance the quality of the profession itself. Both objectives dictate the necessity of vigorous steps to remove existing disabilities and to establish a genuine parity for women historians. The American Historical Association has a responsibility for developing professional criteria and administrative practices that will contribute to the achievement of these ends. Accordingly we propose that the Association adopt the following basic positions, policies, and institutional measures:

I *Positions*

1) The American Historical Association expresses its formal disapproval of discrimination against women in graduate school admissions, grants, awarding of degrees; and in faculty recruitment, salary, promotions and conditions of employment.

2) The American Historical Association pledges itself to work actively toward enlarging the numbers of women in the profession by enhancing the opportunities available to them, acting both through its own resources as an organization and through the cooperation which departments of history may be expected to give it.

II *Policies*

The American Historical Association commits itself to the following policies in four areas which it regards as crucial to significant progress in the foreseeable future:

1) Continuing surveillance of institutional policy and practice in the training, recruitment, and academic promotion of qualified women.

2) Assistance to individual women in the development of their scholarly and teaching careers.

3) Involvement of greater numbers of women in the formal activities of the Association.

4) Development of means for rectifying grievances resulting from discriminating practices.

III *Institutional measures*

. . .

2) The American Historical Association will act together with committees on the status of women and on academic freedom that exist in other professional organizations to develop effective mechanisms for dealing with individual cases of alleged discrimination against women. The Association will also support actively any positive steps in this direction undertaken by the AAUP's recently reactivated committee established for this purpose.

3) The American Historical Association will secure greater representation of women on the programs of its meetings, on its standing committees, and on the Executive Council.

4) The American Historical Association will seek to enlist the active collaboration of departments of history in:

a) Working for the elimination of nepotism rules, written or unwritten.

b) Developing a greater flexibility with regard to part-time employment. The Association urges that part-time positions carry full academic status and proportionate compensation at all levels, including the tenured ranks.

c) Encouraging a greater flexibility in the administration of graduate degree requirements by adapting these to the needs and capacities of individual students. The Association encourages graduate departments to work for greater flexibility in permitting the transfer of graduate course work from one institution to another.

d) Encouraging the adoption of a policy of maternity leaves for women graduate students and women faculty. For graduate students, the period of leave (whether it takes the form of full-time leave, reduced work load, or extension of the schedule within which requirements have to be fulfilled) should not be counted against the number of years that precede consideration for promotion. . . .

Part Three: *Summary of Findings*

The proportion of women receiving doctorates in all fields has never been high, but it has been lower in the 1950's and 1960's than it was in 1920, 1930, or 1940. Most recent figures show about eleven percent of doctorates going to women, down from the earlier high of sixteen percent in the twenties and thirties. The percents in history run a little higher than the overall figures. During the last ten years the ten leading graduate departments of history (based on the 1966 American Council on Education evaluation) have been granting about fifteen percent of their Ph.D.'s to women. The proportion of women receiving M.A.'s in history from these universities is nearly double those receiving Ph.D.'s.

Although women receive Ph.D.'s in history from leading graduate departments, they are not appointed to these faculties in significant numbers. . . . These departments employed between 98 and 99 percent men on their faculties, the women serving primarily in the lower ranks. Five of these leading ten departments appointed no woman to any of the three professorial ranks. In the first three of these years none of the departments had a woman full professor, and only three of the ten departments had a woman full professor at any time during this period.

Women constitute about ten percent of the history department members of ten excellent coeducational liberal arts colleges. For the graduate departments the figure is less than two percent. Most startling, however, is the progressive deterioration in the status of women in the departments of coeducational colleges. In 1959–60 sixteen percent of the full professors were women, but in 1968–69 only one woman full professor remained, and she retired the following year. The decline is undoubtedly largely attributable to the retirement of the generation of women historians trained in the twenties and thirties combined with the tendency to hire men in the post-war years. A decline is also noticeable in the proportion of women associate professors; only among the assistant professors is any increase perceptible. Seven of the ten women's colleges surveyed follow the pattern customarily associated with them of having had a high proportion of women in their history faculties during the first half of the century followed by a decline in the last decade.

One factor militating against the advancement of women Ph.D.'s is the widely-held assumption that women prefer to marry and devote themselves to domestic life. This assumption is belied by the evidence offered by Helen S. Astin in *The Woman Doctorate in America*. She shows that 91 percent of the women receiving doctorates in all fields in the mid-fifties were employed in some type of work seven years later. Moreover, married women Ph.D.'s who are employed full-time show a higher publication rate than either unmarried women Ph.D.'s or men Ph.D.'s, according to the studies of Rita Simon, Shirley Merritt Clark, and Kathleen Galway. The discrepancy between women's professional status and performance is thus not grounded in any lack of commitment to the life of learning. Lawrence Simpson's ingenious investigations have thrown new light on the problem. He has shown that those who practice discrimination against women in academic employment also hold general views concerning female inferiority. Prejudiced attitudes are strongest among men who have been in teaching and/or administration for a period of from five to twenty years. This age group may be assumed to constitute the majority of decision makers in almost any department. The least prejudiced attitudes toward women are found in those under 30 and over 60 years of age.

In history as in other academic areas, our sample of thirty institutions indicates women are employed primarily in non-tenured ranks. Moreover, far from abandoning their professions for pure domesticity, their very eagerness to work has made women vulnerable to exploitation. Their readiness—and sometimes their need—to accept irregular and part-time positions has led to their exclusion from participation in the main stream of academic rewards and preferment. Opening regular career lines to partially employed women emerges from our findings as an urgent need. Faculties and students stand to benefit no less than the women whose services are presently not adequately utilized and recognized.

Finally, the Association should take note of the fact that it has no better record than the colleges and universities we have surveyed in engaging the participation of women in its central activities.

Consequences of Democratization

7. Lynn Hunt,
"Democratization and Decline?" 1997

A historian whose wide scholarly pursuits led to her election to the presidency of the American Historical Association (2002–3), Lynn Hunt (1945–) described the dilemma of the humanities amid the increasingly democratic conditions of academic life at the close of the twentieth century. In her paper, she reduced important data from the *Digest of Education Statistics* and other sources to bolster her theme. Her career has engaged modern European history with special studies of the French past as well as other notable historiographical essays. After graduating from Carleton College (1967) and taking her doctorate at Stanford (1973), she taught at Berkeley (1974–87) and at Pennsylvania (1987–98) before taking the Eugen Weber Professorship of Modern European History at UCLA in 1999. Hunt's diverse interests are exemplified in her coauthorship of *Beyond the Cultural Turn* (1999) and *Telling the Truth About History* (1994).

Lynn Hunt, "Democratization and Decline? The Consequences of Demographic Change in the Humanities," in *What's Happened to The Humanities?* ed. Alvin Kernan © 1997 Princeton University Press, 17–31. Reprinted by permission of Princeton University Press. Further reading: the rest of the Kernan book; appendix includes total bachelors and doctoral degrees in all institutions, 1966–93; Jeffrey F. Milem and Helen S. Astin, "The Changing Composition of the Faculty: What Does It Really Mean for Diversity?" *Change* 25 (March–April 1993): 22, 25.

Teaching and research in the humanities are shaped by various factors, not all of which are immediately evident either to the public or to humanities scholars themselves. This essay examines the role of some of those silently acting but nonetheless effective agents in remaking the world of higher education. The focus will be on the intersection of two major structural trends: the ever-progressing democratization of higher education and the less certain but nonetheless potentially momentous decline in the status of the humanities. How are these trends connected to each other? More generally, what are the likely consequences of demographic changes in and for the humanities sector of higher education? I do not argue that economic and demographic changes will determine all the social and intellectual outcomes, but it does seem likely that they will shape those developments in significant ways.

My basic lines of argument can be briefly summarized: (1) Scholars in the humanities must meet the demographic and cultural challenge of an ever more multiethnic and feminine student population in an era of declining resources and perhaps declining prestige, especially for their field. (2) All faculty, but perhaps especially those in the humanities, face the potentially divisive social side effects of age cohorts that have different sex and minority ratios and different professional experiences and expectations —effects that could be exacerbated by the rise of the two-earner partnership and uncertainties about the retirement of the senior faculty. (3) Intellectual trends in the humanities will inevitably be affected by declining prestige, dwindling resources, and internal social divisions. I do not mean to paint a bleak portrait of our future, for in many ways higher education has never been more successful anywhere in the world than it is now in the United States. But a reminder of an old definition of the difference between optimism and pessimism might come in handy: the optimist proclaims that we live in the best of all possible worlds, while the pessimist fears this is true.

American higher education has been undergoing an ever-accelerating process of democratization since the 1870s. In 1870 52,000 students enrolled in American universities and colleges; twenty years later their number had more than doubled to 157,000, and by 1910 the total had reached 355,000. The number of students leapt to over 2 million after World War II and rapidly increased to 15 million by 1994. According to projections published in the September 1, 1995, almanac issue of the *Chronicle of Higher Education,* college enrollment will remain static until 1998 when it will recommence its inexorable climb, reaching 16 million by 2005. In recent decades this growth has been due largely to an increase in the proportion of high school graduates going on to college. In 1983 32.5 percent of high school, graduates went on to college; in 1992 the figure reached 41.9 percent. However, in 1993 the percentage declined slightly to 41.4 percent. If the percentage of high school graduates going on to college continues to stagnate or decline, the process of democratization might also stagnate or decline, thus reversing or at least halting a century-long development.

Democratization of higher education is probably more advanced in the United States than anywhere else in the world; in the 1980s, only Canada and Sweden even came close to sending as many young people on to higher education, and Australia, France, the USSR, and West Germany sent only about half as many of their nineteen- to twenty-four-year-olds to university (in the United Kingdom the proportion was even lower). In North America the percentage of the *total* population studying at the "third level" (which includes all institutions of higher education) has climbed from 4 percent in 1970 to 5.3 percent in 1991 (a 32 percent increase in just twenty years). In Europe the comparable figures are 1.4 percent in 1970 and 2.1 percent in 1991 (a 50 percent increase); in Africa, 0.1 percent in 1970 and 0.4 percent in 1991 (a 300 percent increase, albeit from a much lower level). In many other countries (indeed in most of the world, but especially in Europe), government policy has shifted in the direction of admitting more students to university-level study, which may mean that these countries will face social and intellectual tensions similar to those that Americans have confronted on campuses over the last decades.

If the worldwide trend toward expanding higher education does continue, it will generate pressures on the physical plants and faculties of universities and colleges, since the number of institutions is not increasing by much if at all, schools are expanding their plants only very slowly, and the size of faculties may not continue to expand as it has in the past. In the United States, the total number of institutions offering higher education nearly doubled between 1870 and 1920, doubled again between 1920 and 1960, increased by 57 percent between 1960 and 1980, and even increased by 12 percent between 1980 and 1990, but the rate of growth in our institutions has now tapered off to about 1 percent a year. Worldwide, the faculty/student ratio at the third level has remained virtually stagnant, declining slightly from a ratio of 13.22 students per faculty member in 1970 to 13.46 in 1980 and 13.67 in 1991.

Although higher education has become more available to almost every kind of social group in the United States, women have made the most spectacular gains. In the 1980s alone, for example, the number of bachelor's degrees awarded to men increased by 7 percent while the number of those awarded to women rose 27 percent. Women now make up 55 percent of the student population, and the number of women among the faculty is increasing too, albeit at a slower pace. In 1987, 27 percent of full-time college professors were women. By 1992, this had risen to 33.5 percent. The humanities have one of the highest proportions of women faculty: 33 percent in 1987. . . , compared to 2 percent women faculty in engineering, 17 percent women faculty in natural sciences, and 22 percent in the social sciences. Only health and home economics had a higher percentage of women faculty in 1987.

The entrance of women into the academy has been particularly apparent in the humanities at the doctoral level; the proportion of doctoral degrees conferred on women in all disciplines increased from one in ten in 1966 to over one in three by 1993, while the proportion of humanities doctorates conferred on women grew from about one in five to virtually one in two in the same time period. Women have long taken B.A. degrees in the humanities, and at this level there has been less change. While overall the proportion of B.A. degrees conferred on women rose from about one-third in 1966 to nearly one-half in 1993, the proportion of women gaining B.A.s in the humanities remained remarkably steady, ranging between 50 and 60 percent in the research universities and 55 and 65 percent in the liberal arts colleges. . . . At the B.A. level, then, women have maintained their traditional interest in the humanities, but the real increase has come in non-humanities fields.

Accompanying (but not exactly paralleling) the increase in women students has been the less dramatic but still significant increase in the numbers and percentages of minority students. In 1993 minority students made up 22.6 percent of college and university students; in 1992 13.2 percent of the faculty were minorities. (In the humanities 11 percent of the faculty were minorities in 1987. This figure put them in the middle of all fields, which ranged from 13 percent minorities in engineering [almost entirely Asians] to 6 percent in agriculture and home economics.) Changes in immigration patterns may well raise the number of minority students coming to colleges and universities. Between 1931 and 1960, Europeans made up 58 percent of immigrants to the United States, Canadians 21 percent, Latin Americans 15 percent, and Asians only 5 percent. Between 1980 and 1984, in contrast, Europeans made up only 12 percent of the immigrants and Canadians just 2 percent, while Latin Americans comprised 35 percent and Asians 48 percent. But the consequences of this change for the humanities are not yet clear, for unlike white women, minority students do not gravitate toward the humanities for their majors or doctorates.

Minority students take fewer B.A.s and fewer doctorates in the humanities than whites. It is worth noting that only education and the social sciences produced proportionately more women Ph.D.s than the humanities in 1993, whereas all other fields—including the natural sciences—produced more minority Ph.D.s in 1993 than the humanities. Thus, though demographic changes might put feminism and multiculturalism inevitably on the intellectual agenda, their impact on the humanities should be viewed as less than self-evident. Perhaps a paradox is at work here: the humanities have responded most vehemently in intellectual terms to the changes within the student body, but they have not shared equally in all those changes; humanities faculty teach their subjects somewhat differently because of changes in the student body, but they have not actually attracted those different students to serious study of the humanities. It is possible that minority students have been especially alert to the potential decline in status of the humanities or that they have felt that the humanities are inherently more elitist and white in subject matter because the humanities are more closely tied to Western culture than the social or natural sciences.

A DECLINE IN STATUS?

The increasing "feminization" of the humanities (and to some extent of higher education more generally) raises serious questions about long-term consequences, for the feminization of work almost always has led to a decline in skill status in other occupations in the past. One measure of the relative status of the humanities can be found in comparative pay scales. In a national faculty salary survey of 1993–1994, researchers found that the average salary (all ranks included) for foreign languages and literature was $41,038, for English $41,346, for philosophy and religion $43,489, and for history $45,337. During the period 1966–1993, history and philosophy and religion had much lower proportions of women receiving doctorates than foreign languages or English. . . . Similarly, nonhumanities fields were generally characterized by higher average salaries than the humanities: biology $44,390, mathematics $45,000, physics $52,660, economics $52,755, and engineering $62,280. There is a correlation between relative pay and the proportion of women in a field:

faculty in those academic fields that have attracted a relatively high proportion of women are paid less on average than those in fields that have not attracted women in the same numbers.

The potential for a decline in status has become more likely with the increased use of part-time positions for teaching. Already in 1989, before the effects of economic recession and stagnation became apparent, one quarter of four-year-college faculties were part-time and fully one-half of those teaching at two-year colleges were part-time. Women comprise 42 percent of the part-time faculty, and 43.2 percent of women faculty members work on a part-time basis as compared to 30 percent of the male faculty. As more and more positions go part-time or temporary and more and more teaching is done by lecturers and adjuncts, the social structure of the university faculty is likely to become proletarianized at the bottom. There are intellectual consequences as well. A recent study of *full-time* but non-tenure-track faculty has shown that compared to untenured faculty on a tenure track they had less interest and engagement in research; less of a sense that they could influence matters in their department, and more of a sense that they had made the wrong career choice and might soon leave academia.

The size of the faculty has been increasing, by 30 percent between 1976 and 1989, when the number of students increased 25 percent, but the teaching environment has been subtly transformed even for full-time, tenure-track faculty. The number of teaching and research assistants has increased hardly at all, by only 2 percent between 1976 and 1989. The number of administrators and nonteaching professionals employed by the university has increased most of all, by 43 percent for administrators and by 123 percent for "nonfaculty professionals" (many of whom we would probably consider administrators). The university staff as a whole is getting bigger, but the relative presence of faculty, secretaries, and janitors is actually declining. By 1991, the percentage of faculty within the total staff of institutions of higher education had declined from 34 percent in 1976 to 32.5 percent, the percentage of nonprofessional (janitorial, secretarial) staff had declined from 42.4 percent to 37.3 percent, and the percentage of instruction and research assistants had declined from 8.6 percent to 7.8 percent, while the presence of nonfaculty professional staff had increased from 9.6 percent to 16.8 percent. As the university becomes increasingly bureaucratized to meet financial pressures, the humanities—preeminently a teaching sector—are unlikely to prosper.

If the humanities are perceived as especially "soft" because they have become "feminized" (admitting more women to their ranks as students, B.A.s, doctoral candidates, and faculty), and especially contentious because they "man" the forward trenches of the "culture wars," they may suffer disproportionately from decreases in funding, declines in faculty size, or increases in adjunct and part-time teaching. Such a trend would exaggerate a decline in status. This decline may already have been registered in comparative numbers of doctoral degrees, which in the humanities have declined from a high of 14.8 percent of all doctoral degrees in 1973 to a low of 8.4 percent in 1988–1989 (rising marginally to 9.2 percent in 1992), compared to a more steady state in the social sciences (rising from a low of 14.6 percent in 1966 to a high of 18.8 percent in 1977). The natural sciences had long dominated (32.3 percent of doctorates in 1966), but they have also declined somewhat (to 23.7 percent in 1993), though no doubt for different reasons (many of the students in the natural sciences, especially at the doctoral level, are now foreign-born, reflecting declining interest in the natural sciences among native-born students). At the B.A. level, both the humanities and the natural sciences seem to be suffering from a long-term malaise; as the number of B.A. degrees overall has more than doubled (from 1966 to 1993), the proportion in the humanities has steadily dropped from just over 20 percent in the late 1960s to a low of about 10 percent in the mid-1980s, increasing only to 12 percent in the early 1990s. Similarly, the proportion in natural sciences has dropped steadily from 11 percent in the late 1960s to under 7 percent in the early 1990s. At the B.A. level, as at the doctoral level, the social sciences have achieved more of a steady state, claiming 15 to 17 percent of the B.A.'s in the late 1960s, then rising slightly, then declining slightly, only to end again at 15 percent in the early 1990s.

The now seemingly permanent stagnation or slow growth of Western economies and the consequent cuts in national and state-level funding for higher education will exacerbate the effects of these trends, encouraging university administrations to downsize faculties, keep the lid on faculty salaries, hire more part-timers with lesser or no benefits, and devote more and more university time and personnel to the raising of funds. This atmosphere of constraint has unpredictable but momentous effects on scholarly life, that is, on the social and intellectual structures that shape the humanities.

One potential effect, already evident in some universities, is the demand that faculty teach more students, either in bigger classes or in more classes per faculty member. In general this means teaching more with fewer resources. This requirement will eventually influence the kind of teaching that is performed: less face-to-face interaction with students, more multiple-choice tests, bigger and fewer discussion sections, fewer papers, and so on. Some of the public universities seem to be pointing in just this direction.

SOCIAL PRESSURES

Economic constraints, feminization, and the turn toward part-time employment are creating a kind of class or caste system within the universities, with proletarianized part-time or non-tenure-track lecturers and adjuncts at the bottom and junior faculty with uncertain or temporary positions on the next highest rung; followed by regular ladder faculty with tenure who have no prospects of outside offers or much inside advancement; topped off by a relatively small group of "stars" who have secure positions, high salaries, a steady stream of graduate students, and the prospect of continual advancement. This new hierarchy, is already reflected in severe salary compression in the assistant, associate, and even full professor ranks; economic stagnation will only make these effects more prevalent and more divisive. This trend seems to affect all the disciplines alike: the average salary of a new assistant professor in English is only about $9,000 less than the salary of an average associate professor and the range is similar in other fields (biology $8,000; mathematics $9,000; economics less than $7,000).

The entrance of new groups into the faculty has distinctly changed the social dynamics within the university in just the last twenty to thirty years. In the 1960s Jews finally gained full admission to faculty positions, followed by women in the 1970s and ethnic minorities in the 1980s. Reactions to these changes cannot be measured precisely, but it seems that resistance and obstruction have been correlated largely with recentness of entry to the profession: Jews are on the whole accepted (with many exceptions), women are somewhat accepted, and minorities still meet greater resistance. In any case, the atmosphere of a club of gentleman scholars has largely disappeared, or at least begun to dissipate.

The pace of change should not be exaggerated, however. Between 1972 and 1989 the proportion of women faculty in all institutions of higher education rose only from 21.4 percent to 28.3 percent. The proportion of nonwhite faculty grew from just 5 percent to 9.1 percent (figures for women and minorities vary from study to study depending on the institutional base included). But these averages mask significant differences between types of schools: private universities averaged only 20.3 percent women on their faculties in 1989 as opposed to 21.3 percent in public universities, 27.1 percent in public four-year colleges, 30.8 in private four-year colleges, and 39.2 percent in public two-year colleges. (Once again, the lower the status, the higher the proportion of women; the converse is also true.) The variation in minorities, however, was less pronounced: from 6.7 percent in private four-year colleges to 10.6 percent in public two-year colleges in 1989.

Change has been more marked in recent hires. In 1989 38.6 percent of the new hires were women (compared to 24.4 percent of the current faculty) and 13.8 percent of the new hires were minorities (compared to 9.8 percent of the current faculty). The figures for 1972 were much lower for women: 24.1 percent of the new hires in that year (20.5 percent of the current faculty in 1972 were women, so the increase in percentage of women faculty was not great). In 1972 only 8.3 percent of the new hires were minorities (5.6 percent of the current faculty were minorities in the same year).

The remaking of the university has not come without a struggle. The statistics show that changes in the faculty have not followed automatically from changes in the student body or in the pool of doctoral candidates. The statistics cannot explain this discrepancy, but other kinds of evidence have been uncovered (for those who have not experienced it firsthand). Peter Novick has demonstrated how history professors resisted the democratization of their profession. One secretary of the American Historical Association wrote in the early twentieth century, "One has it [the aesthetic sense] by inheritance or by long training. . . . It is more apt to be found in persons who are born of and trained in families of long standing in the upper classes of society than in persons who have sprung from the class that is accustomed to the plainer ways and thinking of the world. The leading historians of the past, for the most part, belonged to this class." This original prejudice against scholars from the lower classes translated in the twentieth century into anti-Semitism and discrimination against women and minorities. . . .

If there is a continuing correlation between the pool of applicants and the faculty chosen (and there is such a correlation, however imperfect in the past), the proportion of women faculty in the humanities will continue. . . . The same does not hold, unfortunately, for minorities; in 1993 only 10.9 percent of the new Ph.D.'s came from minority groups (whereas minorities comprised 11 percent of the humanities faculty in 1987). The disparity between women and minorities should be cause for alarm: at every level, the humanities attract women candidates in greater numbers than minorities. Although this is true to some extent in every field of study, the discrepancy is greatest in the humanities; it is among the most successful in attracting women faculty and among the least successful in attracting minority faculty. In 1987, for example, the ratio of women to minority faculty in the humanities was 3:1 whereas in both the social sciences and the natural sciences it was 2:1 (in large part, admittedly, because there were fewer women in those fields).

The diversification of the faculty has created an unprecedented social situation in which the rules of interaction are less than clear. The confusion about social codes has been aggravated by social differences between age cohorts within higher education, the vagaries of the job market, the rise in two-earner partnerships, and the continuing wave of early retirements. The potential for social conflict within the academy has been on the rise, while the factors that might mitigate it have been in decline. . . .

Changes in the economy and in customs have encouraged the rise of two-earner partnerships, which have had an impact on the university along with other sectors of society. Wives now work, many of them within the university. No one sex is assigned the invariable role of social facilitator in the couple. Since everyone works all day, no one has the energy to organize the dinner parties of old with eight, ten, or twelve colleagues sharing a festive meal laboriously prepared by a dutiful (and unemployed outside the home) wife. As a result, socializing and social life in general have almost disappeared in favor of official functions and much more informal interaction (but generally, I would argue, simply less interaction). Junior faculty feel left out, even though there is no "in" that is clearly identifiable. The result is that there is not much of a mechanism for smoothing over the tensions already cited. Just at the moment when economic pressures create the potential for internal strife, social bonding within the university has weakened. Esprit de corps rests only tenuously on common interests, especially in disciplines that are increasingly fragmented by specialization (as most are).

Uncertainty about retirement might exacerbate these developments. Early retirement schemes remove the stratum of the university population that has traditionally played the role of arbiter, mediator, and facilitator. Ironically, the apparent resistance to retirement in schools without early retirement schemes could increase social tensions for the opposite reason; if senior faculty are perceived as staying beyond the point of productivity and thereby blocking progress by younger scholars, their very presence would generate tensions between the age groups. In either case, the older faculty will be unable to exercise the role of sage elders, mitigating conflict in the interest of the community. In either case, the social environment is in danger of deterioration. . . .

I do not mean to paint a nostalgic picture of the past, when a gentleman's club often functioned through various forms of prejudice and unspoken exploitation. But I do mean to suggest that present-day faculty and administrators should think about the social conditions of their employment as much as the economic ones. This is especially true in the humanities, which by their disciplinary nature have been connected in some fashion with notions of a life worth living.

INTELLECTUAL CONSEQUENCES

I have placed considerable emphasis on the economic and social conditions within the university because I believe that they may fundamentally transform the intellectual options facing us. The rise of new fields of knowledge on the backs of multiculturalism and postmodernism (ethnic, gay and lesbian, women's, and postcolonial studies among others), increasing interdisciplinarity, and the attractions of cultural studies—to name some of the important trends in my part of the humanities—all take on a different meaning when looked at in the light of faculty downsizing, feminization of the work force, the rise of part-time employment, perennial budget crisis, and the disappearance of mechanisms for resolving social conflict within the academy. New fields appear now not in an atmosphere of buoyant expansion as in the 1960s, but in a fiercely contested zero-sum game in which new positions must displace older ones.

Although new forms of knowledge are not a symptom of decline but rather of the robust growth of higher education for so many decades, they may well coexist now with certain forms of decline in status, prestige, and power for the humanities as a sector. As higher education has expanded, the humanities have not grown apace (and neither have the natural sciences); new fields have attracted many of the new students and therefore an important share of the funding. The humanities have become the site of political and academic contention just when they have become more vulnerable within the university, i.e., as their relatively older faculties retire without replacements, have become markedly more feminized than other faculties, and attract relatively fewer undergraduates and doctoral students compared to faculties in other fields. (Needless to say, I am not arguing that the humanities should purge women from their ranks in order to improve their status!) . . .

In short, the decline of old intellectual models has its potential costs as well as benefits. Intellectual change cannot be made to depend on a cost-benefit analysis, but the negotiation of economic and social tensions might be enhanced by a broader understanding of the trends that are shaping our decisions.

The only intellectual trends that seem to follow inexorably from the changing demography of higher education are feminism and multiculturalism, if these are taken as broad affiliations rather than fixed ideological positions. The rise in number of women and minority students, the increase in number of women and minority faculty (but especially women faculty), and the expansion of education to previously excluded social classes must exert some pressure on the structure of knowledge, especially in the humanities and social sciences, whose subject matter is sensitive in one way or another to social configurations. The increasing emphasis on the social construction of knowledge and identity probably stems from these same changes, for previously excluded groups are especially sensitive to the ways in which social structures and social meanings have shaped their lives (if only because such influences worked to exclude people like them from higher education in the past). Even if affirmative action admission and hiring policies were to be effectively dismantled tomorrow, the process of change in values would most likely continue apace because it is rooted in the democratization of the university (both the student body and the faculty), which has proceeded, however fitfully and con-

testedly, since at least 1870, that is, since the days when the modern university first took shape.

Moreover, feminism and multiculturalism in the curriculum depend not only on changes in the consumers and producers of knowledge but also on changes in world politics; in humanities courses this means that as Europe has receded from world dominance in favor first of the superpower rivalry of the United States and the former Soviet Union and now of a more even free-for-all in which the Pacific Rim carries increasing weight, so too the emphasis will shift in at least some measure from a seemingly automatic Eurocentrism to a more diverse world perspective. It is not just the identity of the students in the class that forces change, but also the realities of geopolitics today. We may and no doubt will still teach the common values that shaped Western civilization because we still share them with Europeans, but we will also have to make an effort to understand how the new world we live in has come to be.

Understanding that world also includes understanding the forces that shape the American university as a place for acquiring and transmitting knowledge and values. This essay has been an exercise in a particular kind of self-reflexivity. Rather than look at the intellectual trends themselves, I have shifted focus to consider structural changes in the size and composition of the student body and the size and composition of the faculty in the humanities. We do not always clearly see these structural changes, though we live every day with their consequences as some colleagues retire, new ones are hired, positions are lost, and sometimes others of a different sort are gained. It might be helpful to keep those broader, silent forces in mind as we prepare for education in the next century.

Rethinking the Ph.D.

8. Louis Menand, "How to Make a Ph.D. Matter," 1996

The merit and utility of the doctoral degree have been questioned in academic life ever since William James's memorable essay, "The Ph.D. Octopus" (1903). A shrinking job market for newly minted Ph.D.'s, tightened institutional budgets, and a surplus of new teachers, especially in the humanities, were all circumstances of the late twentieth century that brought James to the minds of graduate school teachers. Here Louis Menand (1952–) suggests relief, if not a remedy, for this recurring problem. Menand achieved prominence as a literary critic and winner of the Pulitzer Prize in 2001 for his study *The Metaphysical Club*. His writings appeared frequently in *The New Yorker* and to *The New York Review of Books*. After a bachelor's degree at Pomona College (1973) he took his doctorate at Columbia (1980) and then began teaching English at Princeton. Following a stint at the University of Virginia Law School, he became Distinguished Professor of English in the Graduate Center of the City University of New York, then went to a professorship at Harvard (2003–). His commitment to the heart of academic life can be seen in his editing *The Future of Academic Freedom* (1998).

The debate over the present and future condition of the American university is consistently reduced to a debate over ideology. The troubled relations between academics and the rest of the society get explained as the consequence of political and philosophical differences: if professors weren't so left-wing or multiculturalist or theoretical, if they could only start to think like the rest of us, the university's social standing would be restored. This manner of posing the issue is good for polemicists, but it is not much good for anyone else. For the real problem has nothing to do with politics and philosophy and everything to do with economics and structure.

Of the many symptoms of the current distress, the most telling is the dismal job market for new professors. The typical person who receives a Ph.D. in English spends eight years in graduate school, accumulates $10,000 worth of debt and is unable to find a job. Since 1989, the number of advertised job openings for people with Ph.D.'s in English has dropped by nearly 50 percent, and many of the positions that are advertised are withdrawn later after schools revise their budgets. The placement rate for new Ph.D.'s in English is about 45 percent. But the number of doctorates awarded in English goes up almost every year.

The typical person with a new Ph.D. in history is 35 years old, has spent more than eight and a half years as a graduate student and faces a less than 50 percent chance of getting an academic job. Still, in 1994 the number of new Ph.D.'s in history rose 10 percent from the previous year; there are now more employable people with Ph.D.'s in history than ever before. The examples go on. More than 14 percent of new mathematics Ph.D.'s are unemployed. A report on the job-market experiences of chemists who had earned their doctorates between 1988 and 1994 found that a third of them are either engaged in postdoctoral study or are holding teaching positions that are only temporary.

The collapse of the job market for new professors has, in short, not been selective. Virtually every field of study has been affected. Since 1989, the number of academic job openings advertised in the field of history has dropped by 11 percent; in art and art history, 26 percent; in foreign languages, 35 percent; in political science, 37 percent. And every year universities give out more Ph.D.'s than they did the year before. Somehow, the supply curve has completely lost sight of the demand curve in American academic life.

This is not just a problem of inefficient social expenditure, of overinvestment in a product—people with brand-new doctorates—nobody wants to buy. It's a problem that can be measured in less quantifiable terms as well. Resentment generated by unmet expectations is up; average intellectual quality is down. Driven by anxiety about the competition for employment, more people are publishing more articles of less scholarly value at a younger age than ever before. A new academic class system is becoming established, in which younger, part-time and non-tenure-track college teachers live in a different economic universe from older, tenured and tenure-track professors. And as the value of professional publications and scholarly expertise rises, the intellectual scope of the American university grows narrower and narrower—and the gap between the culture of people in the academy and the culture of everyone else gets wider and wider.

The lesson of the story the numbers tell seems straightforward enough: if there are fewer jobs for people with Ph.D.'s, then universities should stop giving so many people Ph.D.'s. But this is the wrong solution, because the story told by the numbers is not the most important story. The most important story is the less quantifiable one—of resentment, of the academic generation gap and of the intellectual marginalization of the university. This story has a different lesson. It points, I think, to precisely the opposite solution—which is that there should be a lot more Ph.D.'s awarded and that they should be a lot easier to get.

How did the American university reach a state in which it seems no longer able to reproduce itself efficiently? The ready assumption would be that if there are fewer jobs for professors, it must be because there are fewer students to teach, but this is not the case. In 1988, at the beginning of the current downward spiral in the job market for professors, there were 13.5 million students enrolled in American institutions of higher learning. Today, there are more than 15 million students. And these are not just part-timers: the number of bachelor's degrees awarded between 1988 and 1993 rose by more than 17 percent. It is expected that 10 years from now, the total enrollment in American colleges and universities will exceed 16 million. The bodies (with minds, presumably, attached) are there.

The academic employment crisis didn't begin yesterday. Like certain other industries, the university was a great beneficiary of the cold war. It was, for many years after 1945, the pet institution of the expanding national Government, which pumped research dollars into its programs and helped to subsidize the educations of millions of people who would otherwise have had no access to higher learning. Between 1940 and 1990, Government funds for academic research grew by a factor of 25 and enrollments increased by a factor of 10. The percentage of college-age Americans actually attending college rose from 16 percent to more than 40 percent, with half of all Americans now enjoying some exposure to higher education at some point in their lives.

The most intense period in this 50-year expansion was the 1960's. In that decade alone, enrollment increased by more than 120 percent, and more faculty positions were created than had existed in the entire 360-year history of American higher education to that point. But this enormous surge in the number of professors had an immediately depressing effect on the market for the following classes of Ph.D.'s. The recent erosion in the academic job market is not even a decline from relative prosperity: that market, particularly in the humanities, has been depressed since the early 1970's.

Many people expected that the generation of professors who entered the academic economy in the 1960's would be due for professional expiration in the 1990's—another reason why the actual employment scene in 1996 is so discouraging. The 1990's was supposed to be the time of demographic transition in the university. But the generation of professors who got in when universities were flush is getting out when funds are evaporating. They are leaving, but their budget lines are leaving with them.

For the most striking fact about the expansion of the university since 1960, the decade in which all those professors now due to retire got their jobs, is that it took place overwhelmingly in the public sector. Between 1960 and 1980, the number of public institutions of higher education in America more than doubled—from 700 to 1,600. And although there are today 1.5 million more students enrolled in private colleges and universities than there were in 1960, there are 8 million more students enrolled in public institutions.

And this is therefore where the crunch is being felt. With less reason to pour money into research and development now that the cold war is over, and with more pressure to lower taxes and reduce spending, the Federal Government and many state governments are reducing subsidies to public higher education. State appropriation to public higher education in California, which has the largest system in the country, was cut 29 percent between 1991–92 and 1993–94. In the same period, state expenditures on higher education nationally have decreased by 4 percent. (State expenditures on corrections, though, have increased by 40 percent. If prison guards were required to hold doctorates, the academic placement rate could be reversed overnight.)

This was not the ideal time for an internal crisis of confidence to arise. But academic uncertainty about the purpose and the wisdom of isolating intellectual work within universities has never been greater. "We live in a state of educational anomie," says Stanley N. Katz, the president of the American Council of Learned Societies, in "The Condition of American Liberal Education," a book published last year by the College Board.

Academic professionalism has never been more intense, but the point of all the "rigor" is less and less self-evident. In a recent survey of the condition of the social sciences, titled "Visions of the Sociological Tradition," Donald Levine concludes that the established disciplines in social science "no longer fulfill the function of providing orienting frameworks for intellectual communities." The Modern Language Association's annual conventions now feature panels with titles like "Paradigms Lost." What is it exactly, these panels ask, that requires English professors to be locked up in this airborne Giant Peach of professional journals, presses and conferences, making refinements on theoretical arguments few people outside the field can make sense of? Why, as Levine's book implies, should there be separate departments of sociology, anthropology, history and political science, each with its own theories and methods and its own solar system of academic stars and black holes? What makes these disciplines useful ways of carving up the world for inquiry, and what pedagogical or social good is the inquiry doing?

This reconsideration of the intellectual basis of academic work would be stimulating if it did not have the misfortune of coinciding with those other malign portents—the end of the cold war, the reduction in state support and the wider public criticism of academic thought. Academic self-doubt is only adding to the sense of general uncertainty. So why, in circumstances of unraveling conviction and commitment, is creating more Ph.D.'s a good idea?

The key statistic in the profile of the typical new Ph.D. is the extraordinary amount of time he or she has spent acquiring the thing. As the old question asks, how many graduate students does it take to screw in a light bulb? One is the answer; but it takes him seven years. The median elapsed time between the B.A. and the Ph.D. is now 10.5 years, of which 7.1 are spent as a registered student trying to get the bulb in the socket. The median age of those graduating this year with a Ph.D. is slightly over 34.

This is not a function of the difficulty of the research. Students in the humanities are among those who take the longest—11.9 years between degrees, 8.3 of them as registered students. William G. Bowen and Neil L. Rudenstine suggest in their landmark study, "In Pursuit of the Ph.D.," that this is because it is in the humanities that the paradigms for scholarship have become the most unclear. But whatever the reason, getting a doctorate is now an enormous investment in training for a profession that offers, in many fields, a less than 50 percent chance of employment.

Money would help, of course. But there are a few things the American academy needs even more than money. One is greater intellectual freshness and sense of purpose. Another is a higher degree of interchange with the world of art and ideas outside the university. Indifference, and even hostility, to academic writing is not restricted to conservatives who regard the university as a refuge of left-wing thought. It is shared by many liberal nonacademic intellectuals as well. I can't think of a single person I know who entered college around the time I did, in 1969, and who did not go on to become a professor, who has the slightest sympathy with or interest in (except, occasionally, a negative one) what goes on within university humanities departments. And many of these people are themselves producers and consumers of art and ideas.

One thing that has cut American cultural life in two in this way is the wall of credentialism that has arisen between academic intellectuals and everyone else. Graduate students looking for work sometimes complain that their credential is not transferable—that despite their enhanced literacy skills, they are actually considered less rather than more employable by people in nonacademic fields like publishing or advertising or business. But transferability is a two-way street. If a publisher suddenly decided to take up a career as a professor and proposed to walk into a college department and start to teach, academics would be outraged. Where is the credential? David Damrosch, a professor of English and comparative literature at Columbia who last year published a book critical of the culture of the university, "We Scholars," points out that in 1969 fully one-third of the nation's faculty members did not have a Ph.D. But during the 1970's, he says, the doctorate became mandatory for academic employment.

When the market tightened, professionalism grew and credentialism became wildly overvalued. And the more the academy walled itself off by specialization and credentialism, the more it exacerbated its division from the rest of the educated world. The division is destructive on both sides. The nonacademic world would be enriched if more people in it had had exposure to academic research and teaching, thereby acquiring a little understanding of the issues that bugaboos like "critical theory" and "the multicultural curriculum" are attempts to deal with. And the academic world would be enlivened if it conceived of its purpose as something larger and more various than mere professional reproduction.

Three things make graduate education so time-consuming: the lack of intellectual focus in many fields, the time spent working as a part-time instructor and the dissertation. If all Ph.D. programs were three-year programs, with no teaching and no dissertation—if getting a doctorate were like getting a law degree—graduate education would immediately acquire focus and efficiency. It would attract more of the many students who, after completing college, yearn for deeper immersion in academic study but who cannot imagine spending seven years struggling through a graduate program only to find themselves virtually disqualified for anything but a teaching career they can no longer count on having.

The intellectual gain would be an increase in diversity within the academy. More students would be entering graduate school without having a commitment to academia and would thus be likely to be more skeptical of the reigning scholarly paradigms in their fields. But when these students do graduate and go on to careers outside the university, they would bring with them an understanding of those paradigms, which might lead to a greater commonality between professors and other people who work with art and ideas. The gain in efficiency would come from providing graduate-level education to people who can emerge from school in their mid-20's, rather than in their mid-30's, and still contemplate a number of career options. And the gain in focus would come from reconceiving higher learning in a field as a sequence of courses—much as law schools require basic courses in contracts, property, torts and civil procedure along with various electives—rather than as the present potpourri of specialized classes reflecting the particular research interests of the professors who happen to be teaching in a given semester.

The objection that a longer apprenticeship is necessary to produce qualified college teachers is specious, since many first- and second-year graduate students now teach college classes without training or supervision. In a bad economy, this teaching can even become a source of exploitation, as graduate students work, year after year, at unlivably low rates while searching for full-time employment. If universities had to hire people who already had degrees and did not feel like indentured servants, the academic employment scene would be a lot healthier. Doctoral programs could even require one course in pedagogy, which would be one more course in pedagogy than most professors have ever had in their lives.

The case against the dissertation requirement is partly an old one, which is that there is no correlation between the ability to write a dissertation and the ability to teach, and partly a more recent one (made by, among others, Professor Damrosch), which is that many scholarly books today are just journal articles on steroids. Few dissertations, the majority of which are written in conditions of poverty and overwork, are publishable in any case without substantial rewriting. The production of a single publishable article for each student graduated would be a net plus for American scholarship.

Shortening and intensifying graduate education in this way might seem to make less sense for the natural sciences, but in fact the idea has already been broached in that area. Last March, Anne C. Petersen, then the deputy director of the National Science Foundation, argued in The Chronicle of Higher Education that "the Ph.D. should be construed in our society more like the law degree. A lot of people go to law school with no plans to practice law." And Jesse H. Ausubel of Rockefeller University and the Alfred P. Sloan Foundation has suggested "valorizing the master's degree" in the sciences—making the M.S. a viable employment credential. If this makes sense for biologists, it ought to make sense for literary critics and historians.

Since the 1960's, the American academy has profited by a huge increase in the number of Americans demanding higher education and the benefits it can bring. And it has profited, even during bad patches in national economic prosperity, from continued public investment and support. But it has been damaged by an increasing and increasingly pointless emphasis on credentialism. Now the expansion seems to have halted. It's a good time to take another look at the kind of good universities can do.

9. Robert Weisbuch,
"Six Proposals to Revive the Humanities," 1999

Robert Weisbuch (1946–) brought an innovative presidency to the Woodrow Wilson National Fellowship Foundation (1997–2005). Fellowship offerings were broadened to attract young women and minority students, and grants were offered to undergraduate scholars aiming at public service. His occasional essays in *The Chronicle of Higher Education* and elsewhere suggested new ways of approaching academic issues, especially those at the graduate level. As an Emily Dickinson scholar he came to a professorship in English and later deanship in graduate studies at the University of Michigan (1972–1996) after a B.A. at Wesleyan (1968) and a Ph.D. at Yale (1972). He moved to the presidency of Drew University in 2005.

Robert Weisbuch, "Six Proposals to Revive the Humanities," *Chronicle of Higher Education,* March 26, 1999, B4. Reprinted with the kind permission of Robert Weisbuch, President, Drew University. Further reading: Catharine R. Stimpson, "General Education for Graduate Education," *Chronicle of Higher Education,* November 1, 2002, B7–10; Michael T. Nettles and Catherine M. Millett, *Three Magic Letters, Getting to Ph.D.* (Baltimore, 2006); and IV, 11.

Today's consensus about the state of the humanities —it's bad, it's getting worse, and no one is doing much about it—is supported by dismal facts. The percentage of undergraduates majoring in humanities fields has been halved over the past three decades. Financing for faculty research has decreased. The salary gap between full-time scholars in the humanities and in other fields has widened, and more and more humanists are employed part time and paid ridiculously low salaries. The "job crisis" has existed for over a quarter of a century—no crisis, then, but a semi-permanent depression. As doctoral programs in the humanities proliferate irresponsibly, turning out more and more graduates who cannot find jobs, the waste of human talent becomes enormous, intolerable.

More broadly, the humanities, like the liberal arts generally, appear far less surely at the center of higher education than they once did. We have lost the respect of our colleagues in other fields, as well as the attention of an intelligent public: The action is elsewhere. We are living through a time when outrage with the newfangled in the humanities— with deconstruction or Marxism or whatever—has

become plain lack of interest. No one's even angry with us now, just bored.

Our collective responsibility as humanists is to face those facts. But it is also to refuse fatalism.

Why not the following for a future? Graduates of our doctoral programs not merely well and fully employed, but fought over by universities, businesses, and public agencies. Children of any age, not just those between 18 and 21, taught to learn by experts. Cultural and educational institutions cooperating to such a degree that humanists go back and forth between sectors, and the publicly acting intellectual becomes the norm. A widespread adoption among citizens of a once-popular assumption: that the humanities uniquely provide a hard-won wisdom, gleaned from the total experience of humankind. The humanities holding sway, profoundly influencing decisions large and small.

That future, I insist, need not wait on the powers that be to experience an epiphany (or suffer a breakdown). But to achieve it, we must question why we have fallen so far. Who's to blame? In a recent essay in Harvard's alumni magazine, the literary scholars James Engel and Anthony Dangerfield name their chief villain in the title: "The Market-Model University." Certainly, there is fault in a society that spends billions on the health of the nation's body and chump-change on its soul. But that crazy imbalance, after all, measures not only others' coarseness, but also our own failure. After spending much time haranguing educational capitalism and a new administrative crassness—we administrators are crass, but that's not new, nor is the power of money— Engel and Dangerfield acknowledge that humanists might share the responsibility for their own plight. Arguing "more and more only with themselves" in "unedifying disputes," the two authors say, faculty members in the humanities suffer from "endemic pettiness, bad faith, and guilt by association."

One simple reason for the decline of the humanities is that they have stopped being fun—for faculty members and students and for the public beyond academe. Coinciding with an emphasis on the sciences and with increasingly narrow career training, the culture wars might have chosen better timing. Like never.

But the nastiness—and there appears to be a record number of dysfunctional humanities departments now—is not limited to intellectual matters. In Richard Russo's novel *Straight Man,* the English-department chairman at a small college asks a colleague how things are going in other fields, such as French, Spanish, German, Italian, and classics. "Silly, small, mean-spirited, lame," his colleague answers. "Same as English."

The abusive pettiness that Russo satirizes is a climate. It is the weather of failure. The evil lies not in our cost-recovery stars, dear Brutus, but in ourselves. It lies in the defeatism of humanities departments; and insularity is its fearful twin.

I became aware of such defeatism when I spent a year recently as an interim graduate dean. I began to notice my reactions to the day's schedule. If a group of scientists made an appointment, I knew that I should lock the safe or get my checkbook ready for compelling and expensive proposals. If I saw that my colleagues in the humanities were coming by, I would reach instead for a tissue. The president of a major research university told me that, when he offered his faculty members funds for new proposals, he received more than 50 ideas from scientists, 30 from social scientists, and nothing from humanists except requests to put more money into existing programs.

That's the problem. We sometimes confuse selling our disciplines with selling out, and wholesale distrust of our own institutions inspires neither us to ask nor the institution to give. Beyond that, we are not problem solvers. An engineer takes a problem and fixes it. A humanist takes a problem and celebrates its complexity. That is fine until we ourselves are the problem.

The current generation of humanities graduate students is not quietly accepting a losers' culture. That is laudable, even critical. But the complaining tone of the graduate-student caucus at last December's meeting of the Modern Language Association imitates the very voice of the mentors that the students chastised for not doing enough to ease the job shortage. And their reported opposition to a new emphasis on meaningful careers beyond academe also imitates their elders' myopia. Maximizing academic employment and populating the frontiers beyond the academy do not constitute alternatives. Those are not either/or solutions. They are interdependent.

Our insularity is a political and intellectual failure as well as an economic one. We have become increasingly interested in the world examined by the humanities, but we have never had less actually to do with that world. We have debated canons and taught Toni Morrison, but we have not engaged with urban schools and community groups. As a result, the percentage of African-American and Hispanic graduates of our doctoral programs remains dismally low.

In all, too much posturing and too few ideas headed toward action contribute to a culture of edgy despair and fretful infighting in the humanities.

Lest I repeat the faults that I name (and I have been guilty of every one of them myself), I want to offer six proposals:

Act on fact. Humanists tend to substitute rhetoric for data, just as social scientists often substitute data for thought. What departments and programs do not know about their own graduates is stunning. I worry that we humanists often do not collect information—about, for example, where our graduates get jobs—because we do not want to know what it will tell us. And the universities that gather data on their departments too often behave in the fashion of Dickens's Chancery, collecting mounds of statistics but using them only to fill storage rooms with paper. While the merely quantitative can be misleading, it also can spur dialogue.

Practice doctoral birth control. It is astonishing that there are now more than 140 doctoral-degree programs in English, when only about one-third of their graduates get tenure-track jobs in their first year on the market. Of course we must reduce enrollments and programs. I don't know how to discourage status-conscious universities from maintaining worse-than-useless doctoral programs other than by the kind of public disapprobation they are already beginning to attract.

Those departments that do want to be responsible might consider either of two rules of thumb in admitting students. First, any department should accept only 1.3 times the number of incoming students as the number of graduates in the previous year who found truly significant jobs—positions that they chose, not jobs that they accepted out of economic necessity. The extra 0.3 allows conservatively for attrition. That rule might lead to many fewer students—or it might encourage faculty members and students to collaborate to enlarge the range of meaningful careers. Alternatively, let any department admit as many new doctoral students as it can assuredly support through fellowships and teaching for every term of a five-year Ph.D. program. Less-than-full support prevents full-time education and encourages a lethargic approach to earning a degree. It's exploitative, an anti-luxury that no one can afford.

Reclaim the curriculum. In the near term, reducing enrollments is vital, but doing so is not free of the taint of defeatism: It is based on an assumption of a continuing shortage of opportunities for humanists. Humanists have the power to increase the number of dignified faculty positions: The key is to put new value on all courses being taught. How? Have the regular faculty members at large universities resume teaching those courses that many have shunned—chiefly freshman writing and language instruction. If students don't want to take a particular course, and the faculty members don't want to teach it, better redesign the course. Redesign, then reassign—not to exploited adjuncts or part-timers, but to newly created tenurable positions (at best) or postdoctoral fellowships that (at least) constitute a carefully considered career step. If full-time faculty members teach the entire curriculum, then universities might combine adjunct lines into additional tenurable positions.

The humanities have always held two advantages over other fields: First, we attract a cohort that teaches wonderfully; second, our scholarship and teaching often have far more to do with each other than holds true in other fields. Shockingly, we've lost the lead in curricular innovation to the sciences during the past decade—perhaps out of fear that our emphasis on teaching is a result of how little our scholarship is valued. If that is the case, we must immediately lose our resentment and re-establish our pedagogical eminence.

Unleash the humanities from the insularity of academe. Even generating additional faculty positions will not get us to where we need to be. The math just won't compute. In my own department of English, at the University of Michigan, after two years of trying to persuade faculty members to teach more first-year courses and administrators to allow us to convert lecturer slots into assistant professorships, we created three new positions in a department of 75, an increase of only 4 per cent. Clearly, the economic status of the humanities within the academy will not change until there is a major improvement in job prospects for humanists beyond the academy—which will provide the kind of competition that universities face for scientists, engineers, lawyers, and even social scientists. . . .

There is evidence that the world beyond academe is not hostile to humanists, and may even be welcoming. We have been swamped with e-mail offers of assistance and internships from a wide range of employers. . . .

Redesign graduate programs. Most graduates of our programs who do achieve academic positions will be taking them at institutions of learning very different from their own, ones that stress teaching far more than research. That is why the Preparing Future Faculty program, sponsored by the Association of American Colleges and Universities, the Council of Graduate Schools, and the Pew Charitable Trusts, matters so greatly: It sends students from research universities to other kinds of higher-education institutions to learn about other kinds of academic lives. . . .

I am not saying that our graduate programs must change wholesale. Disciplines do have their own integrity, and that integrity should be guarded with religious intensity. But I would make a distinction between the scholarly aspect of programs and the surrounding activities of professional development. We need internships, carefully staged and guided development of pedagogical abilities, even degrees that combine a humanities discipline with necessary knowledge in, say, new technology or journalism.

Embrace contradiction. While we must insist on learning for its own human sake, we also must connect the humanities to the immediate challenges in our culture. To make the world safe for private scholarship that is deliberately, grandly, rightly unconcerned with consequence, we need to become newly public. That means requiring students to learn how to explain their work to non-humanists. And it means that all of us must speak up. We must make the case for the value of a liberal-arts education, and for the sense that the humanities make possible the thinking about values and creativity that no technology can produce—and without

which any democracy will fail. Someone must have convinced us that sermonizing was out or that the song was tired—but when I state the value of the humanities to public groups, it is as if many in the audience are hearing the goldenest oldie imaginable, a song they loved, still love, and have not heard for too long.

Without that music, a culture dies. Triumph for the humanities? Just imagine the consequences of defeat.

10. AAU Report on Graduate Education, 1998

Stirred by increasingly critical voices from some quarters of academe and from the public, the Association of American Universities formed a committee to reevaluate national graduate programs. The resulting report in 1998 was the most extensive survey of this subject since Bernard Berelson's study (1). The committee comprised fifteen people from presidencies and provostships in American universities, chaired by William H. Danforth of Washington University in St. Louis.

Association of American Universities, Committee on Graduate Education, "Report and Recommendations" (Washington, D.C., 1998), 1–5. Reprinted with the kind permission of the Association of American Universities. Further reading: national studies of graduate programs in various fields have been sparse, while slightly more have appeared in the humanities than in the sciences; a recent model is Thomas Bender, Philip M. Katz, Colin Palmer, and the Committee on Graduate Education of the American Historical Association, *The Education of Historians for the Twenty-first Century* (Urbana, IL, 2004) and its selected bibliography. For the sciences, see "The American Astronomical Society's Examination of Graduate Education in Astronomy," *Bulletin of the American Astronomical Society* 29, no. 5 (1997): 1426–65; and Committee on Science, Engineering, and Public Policy, *Reshaping the Graduate Education of Scientists and Engineers* (Washington, D.C., 1995).

Graduate education in the United States is widely recognized as the best in the world, yet it is far from perfect and will remain in a leadership position only by continual self-examination and improvement. Criticisms commonly heard today include overproduction of Ph.D.s; narrow training; emphasis on research over teaching; use of students to meet institutional needs at the expense of sound education; and insufficient mentoring, career advising, and job placement assistance.

Taking these criticisms seriously, the Association of American Universities (AAU) formed the Committee on Graduate Education to evaluate the conduct of graduate education on its member campuses. The Committee examined the institutional perspectives on graduate education, surveyed its institutions about their graduate programs, and developed guidelines on best practices for graduate education policies and programs. The Committee concentrated on Ph.D. or doctoral education, the focus of the national debate on graduate education.

THE NATIONAL PERSPECTIVE

Graduate education prepares the scientists and engineers needed by industry, government, and universities to conduct the nation's research and development; educates the scholars in the humanities, social sciences, and the arts who preserve and enlarge our understanding of human thought and the human condition; and develops the scholars in all disciplines who become the faculties of the nation's colleges and universities.

Following World War II through the early 1970s, graduate education experienced unprecedented growth. This growth leveled off during the late 1970s and the first half of the 1980s, but it has increased steadily for the last decade. In 1995, the number of Ph.D. recipients reached an all-time high of 41,610. The growth in Ph.D. recipients has been accompanied by increased participation of women, minorities, and foreign students.

Over the last decade, the number of Ph.D.s awarded by U.S. universities to foreign students has increased at more than twice the rate of Ph.D.s awarded to U.S. citizens, reaching 32 percent of all doctorate recipients in 1995. Concern has been expressed about the impact of foreign Ph.D.s on the domestic employment market, but several factors suggest that the impact is small. Moreover, those foreign students who remain in the U.S. enrich the nation's talent pool.

Employment data indicate that Ph.D. recipients have low unemployment rates upon completion of their graduate work and throughout their careers. However, an increasing number of Ph.D. recipients are still seeking postgraduate commitments upon completion of their doctoral programs, and a growing number of commitments that are secured at Ph.D. completion are for postdoctoral appointments. Understanding the implications of these trends will require additional information.

THE INSTITUTIONAL PERSPECTIVE

Although graduate education makes important contributions to the education and research missions of universities, its overriding purpose must be the education of graduate students. Apprenticeship teaching and research activities that, under faculty mentorship, provide progressively increasing levels of responsibility are effective ways to teach graduate students how to teach and conduct independent research. However, subsuming the interests of students to conflicting institutional or faculty interests can undermine the educational benefits of these apprenticeship arrangements.

Student interests should also be paramount in designing a graduate curriculum that prepares students for a broad array of careers, and in building a diverse student body that enriches the educational environment and that prepares students to work effectively in a global environment.

The policies governing federal support of research assistantships through the federal research project grant system run counter to sound educational policy. Graduate students involved in teaching and research are students, not employees; the principal purpose for their teaching and research activities is to learn how to teach and conduct research. But Office of Management and Budget (OMB) Circular A-21 stipulates that federal agencies can support graduate students as research assistants on federally funded research grants only to the extent that "a bona fide employer-employee relationship" exists between a graduate student and faculty investigator. Federal policy should be changed to eliminate the employer-employee stipulation and encourage the dual benefits to research and education of graduate students serving as research assistants.

Universities need to track the placement of their Ph.D. students at least to their first professional employment. Institutions also should maintain program performance and student evaluation information. Such information is needed for both internal evaluation of programs and external accountability for them.

Many universities have examined their graduate programs in light of concerns discussed in a number of national forums and have responded with a wide range of creative programs to meet evolving student and societal needs. Among other initiatives, universities and their academic departments have improved teacher preparation programs, reduced enrollments and improved student financial support, instituted interdisciplinary opportunities, and improved faculty mentoring and career advising.

RECOMMENDATIONS FOR BEST PRACTICES IN GRADUATE EDUCATION

The Committee encourages each university and each department within an institution to examine the size, scope, and performance of its graduate programs to determine whether these programs are meeting the interests of students in preparing them for the diversity of careers to which they may aspire, and to take appropriate actions where they do not. The Committee has sought to identify common elements in recent institutional changes and adaptations in developing the following recommendations or guidelines for best practices.

RECRUITMENT AND ADMISSIONS

Admissions decisions should be made with the goal of maintaining and improving the quality of programs.

Departmental recruitment and admissions policies should include provisions designed to increase the participation of talented students from groups underrepresented in their graduate programs. To make significant progress, universities will need to work with undergraduate institutions and K–12 schools to reach minority students as early as possible in their educational lives and encourage them to prepare for and pursue graduate study.

Universities should encourage enrollment of exceptional foreign students while continuing efforts to develop the U.S. domestic talent pool.

FINANCIAL SUPPORT

All admitted students should be given accurate information about the costs they will incur and realistic assessments of future prospects for financial support.

Financial support should be designed to assist students in their progress to a degree; financial support through work that draws students away from their graduate programs should be avoided.

GRADUATE CURRICULUM

Institutions should evaluate the graduate curriculum to assure that it equips students with the knowledge and skills needed for a broad array of postdoctoral careers that they might wish to pursue.

The graduate curriculum should balance breadth and depth with the need to minimize time-to-degree.

FACULTY MENTORING

Faculty mentors should confer with students frequently to assess students' progress, and should provide the department with periodic assessments on progress to the degree.

Institutions and departments should clearly affirm the importance of faculty mentoring through policy guidelines and incentives.

DATA FOR INSTITUTIONAL POLICYMAKING, PROGRAM EVALUATION, AND STUDENT ADVISING

Institutions should maintain data on completion rates, time-to-degree, and placement to the first professional employment, as well as conduct exit surveys for all Ph.D. recipients. Institutions should provide such program performance data to student applicants.

Institutions should provide job placement assistance for students who request it.

PROGRAM EVALUATION

Institutions should evaluate the quality of and justification for their doctoral programs through self-study, on-site evaluation by external reviewers, or both.

Institutions should terminate programs that cannot maintain the infrastructure and student financial support necessary for acceptable program quality.

Institutions should not begin new programs absent a regional or national need and sustainable support.

POLICY IMPLEMENTATION AND MAINTENANCE

Institutions should ask departments to provide descriptions of their goals and expectations for their graduate programs, and should periodically compare these against departmental program performance data.

The AAU should assist institutions in developing common definitions and reporting procedures that will permit cross-institutional comparisons of program performance.

EXTERNAL SUPPORT FOR GRADUATE EDUCATION

Support for graduate education from a number of external sectors plays a critical role in sustaining the quality of graduate education:

The federal government provides valuable support for graduate education through competitively funded fellowship and traineeship programs, research assistantships funded through the federal research project grant system, and student loans that augment and fill gaps in other sources of financial support. These forms of support meet important needs in graduate education; all should be continued.

Given the importance of federal support, recent cutbacks in federal fellowship programs and proposals to reduce or eliminate the subsidized components of federal student loans for graduate and professional students raise serious concerns. Financial support is critical for graduate students, who are young adults forgoing employment to pursue additional education. Moreover, graduate education benefits the nation, and federal support of graduate education advances the national interest.

States support graduate education primarily through teaching and research assistantships at resident public universities. States also support graduate education indirectly through research and development investments and graduate fellowship programs, which may be available to students attending both public and private institutions.

Private foundations enable universities to embark on new and continuing initiatives that are otherwise difficult to sustain. Industry support provides financial assistance to students and graduate programs while fostering university-industry research connections and exposing students to industrial career opportunities.

Future Faculty

11. James Duderstadt, "Preparing Future Faculty for Future Universities," 2001

Rising through ranks of administration to the presidency of the University of Michigan (1988–96), James Duderstadt (1942–) gathered keen insight into the workings of American universities and their needs for the future. He became particularly concerned that graduate education become more sensitive to public needs and to unprecedented economic, technological, and social forces. He initiated the Michigan Mandate, which soon resulted in doubling the university's minority student population. Graduate programs as well as institutions, he stressed, should become learner-centered rather than faculty-centered. Trained as an engineer at Yale (1964) and at the

California Institute of Technology (Ph.D. 1965), he started his Michigan career in 1969, staying there until his retirement as president emeritus and University Professor of Science and Engineering in 1996. Beyond his service to the state of Michigan, he chaired the National Science Board (1991–94), was named National Engineer of the Year in 1991, and received the E. O. Lawrence Award from the U.S. Department of Energy in 1986.

James J. Duderstadt, "Preparing Future Faculty for Future Universities," *Liberal Education* 87 (Spring 2001): 24–31. Reprinted with permission from *Liberal Education*, Spring 2001. Copyright held by the Association of American Colleges and Universities. Further reading: Michael T. Nettles and Catherine M. Millett, *Three Magic Letters: Getting to Ph.D.* (Baltimore, 2006); and I, 16–21.

The current highly specialized form of research-dominated graduate education may no longer respond to the needs both of our students and our society. The attrition in many graduate programs has risen to unacceptable levels, with more than 50 percent of those who enroll in Ph.D. programs failing to graduate (compared to attrition rates in law and medicine of less than 5 percent). The increasing trend toward unionization of graduate student assistants on many of our larger university campuses suggests we may need to reconsider their broader role in supporting our university teaching and research. . . .

During the past decade we have seen a number of important efforts to better prepare graduate students for the reality of academic careers. . . . There is a growing effort to approach pedagogy as scholarship and to develop graduate programs better aligned with faculty roles in academic institutions that stress teaching over research. . . .

Here I will touch upon several familiar issues including the mismatch between the way we prepare doctoral students and the nature of the contemporary academic career. I wish to add yet another theme. It is my belief that higher education has entered a period of very rapid change. While current efforts such as the Preparing Future Faculty program are valuable, we must take care not to prepare graduate students for the world of higher education as we understand it today (or, in some cases, remember it nostalgically from the past). The real challenge is to prepare future faculty for the future colleges and universities that will characterize their careers.

CURRENT PARADIGM OF GRADUATE EDUCATION

There is general agreement that graduate education in America's research universities represents the world's leading effort for producing the next generation of researchers. For decades, the conventional wisdom has been that research and teaching were mutually reinforcing and should be conducted together, at the same institutions by the same people. . . .

Our current paradigm of graduate education is based on an important, yet fragile, relationship between the graduate student and the faculty that evolves from mentorship into collegiality. Graduate students are expected to attach themselves early and tightly to individual professors. In fact, since many are supported by research grants, they are required to work on problems relevant to their faculty advisor's research grant with little opportunity to broaden their studies or their interests. As a result, graduate education is almost entirely one-dimensional, focused on producing the next generation of researchers largely as clones of their dissertation advisors. We really don't "teach" graduate students how to teach but rather expect them to learn the trade from their own experience as students. Furthermore, our current approach to preparing students for the academic careers is unique among professional programs in the absence of formal training in ethics and values. Physicians, engineers, and lawyers all must understand and commit themselves to following well-prescribed codes of ethics and behavior to be a member of their profession. Yet university professors, responsible not only for the education of the young but as well for the integrity of one of civilization's most important and enduring social institutions, the university, have no such preparation or ethical code of conduct.

Of course, graduate education does not end with the Ph.D. In many fields, an appointment as a postdoctoral fellow has become not only commonplace but also effectively a requirement for a later academic position. Unlike graduate students, postdocs have the sophistication to be highly productive in the laboratory or in a research group of senior scientists. They are highly motivated and work extremely hard, since they realize that their performance as a postdoc may be critical in attaining the faculty references necessary for further employment. And they are cheap, typically working at only a small fraction (20 to 30 percent) of the salary of a faculty member or research scientist.

Hence, it is not surprising that in many fields, the postdoctoral student has become the backbone of the research enterprise. In fact, one might even cynically regard postdocs as the migrant workers of the research industry, since they are sometimes forced to shift from project to project, postdoc to postdoc appointment, even institution to institution, before they find a permanent position (National Academy of Sciences 2000).

SOME REALITIES OF TODAY'S ACADEMY

Many tend to think of the faculty as a homogeneous group, all engaged in similar activities of teaching and research, and all experiencing similar stresses of publish or perish, tenure or out. Yet, there is as much diversity among faculty and their roles as across any other aspect of contemporary society. All are valued members of the university faculty, but their activities, their perspectives, their needs, and their concerns are remarkably diverse.

So, too, the role and activities of a faculty member change considerably over the course of a career. Most faculty members concentrate early in their careers on building scholarly momentum and reputation and developing teaching skills. Once the early hurdles of tenure and promotion have been achieved, professors become more involved in service both within and external to the university. Some become involved in deeper games where they use their intellectual power to shape their field of scholarship. Others assume important roles as advisors or consultants to government or industry. Still others become campus politicians, representing their colleagues in faculty governance. Still others take on administrative roles as chairs, deans, or perhaps even university presidents. Yet, despite this extraordinary diversity of faculty across fields and careers, there is a tendency both in perception and in policy to regard all faculty members the same, as if all were assistant professors in history or economics.

Perhaps the greatest source of variation in the academy is due to the great diversity in the nature of colleges and universities. The majority of faculty members work in two-year or four-year public colleges and universities where teaching is the primary role. In sharp contrast, faculty members in research universities enjoy the opportunity to participate in teaching, research, service, and administrative activities on a far more balanced basis. Yet, with the freedom and opportunity to undertake broader roles than simply classroom teaching comes an additional responsibility: Research university faculty members are expected to generate a significant fraction of the resources necessary to support their activities. That is, most faculty members at research universities are expected to be entrepreneurs as well as teachers and scholars.

Although many colleges and universities operate with unionized faculties and negotiated compensation systems, the very best institutions function as meritocracies. The academy is usually both rigorous and demanding in its evaluation of the abilities of its members, not only in promotion and tenure decisions, but also in determining compensation. The promotion ladder is relatively short, consisting primarily of the three levels of assistant professor, associate professor, and professor. The faculty reward culture is unusually one-dimensional, based primarily upon salary. Hence that faculty reward structure creates a highly competitive environment that extends beyond a single institution as a national or even global marketplace for the very best faculty talent.

Increasingly, the entry-level academic positions in a university available to recent graduates are part-time in nature. New Ph.D.s serve in a variety of roles, from postdoctoral fellowships to clinical faculty, lecturers, instructors, research scientists or even as technical staff. None of these roles is "tenure-track," in the sense that they lead to permanent faculty positions. There are also an increasing number of affiliated faculty positions such as adjunct professors or professors of practice, accommodating individuals whose full-time position is outside the university, for example, in industry or government, but who provide instructional or research services to the institution.

In theory, policies, procedures, and practices characterizing the appointment, role, reward, and responsibilities of the faculty should be consistent with the overall goals of the institution and the changing environment in which it finds itself. In practice, these decisions tend to be made at the level of individual disciplinary departments with relatively little consideration given to broader institutional concerns or long-range implications. Most departments will tend to replace departing or retiring faculty members with similar colleagues if not identical clones. And in so doing, the academy, just as our doctoral programs, tends to cling tightly to the practices and perspectives of the past rather than recognizing the extraordinary challenge of change that will characterize higher education in the future.

PREPARING FOR THE UNIVERSITY OF THE FUTURE

A century ago, a high school diploma was viewed as a ticket to a well-paying job and a meaningful life. Today, a college degree has become a necessity for most careers, and graduate education desirable for an increasing number. A growing population will necessitate some growth in higher education to accommodate the projected increases in the number of traditional college age students. But even more growth and adaptation will be needed to respond to the educational needs of adults as they seek to adapt to the needs of the high performance workplace. Some estimate this adult need for higher education will become far larger than that represented by traditional eighteen to twenty-two year old students. Furthermore, such educational needs will be magnified many times on a global scale, posing both a significant opportunity and major responsibility to American higher education. There is growing concern about whether our existing institutions have the capacity to serve these changing and growing social needs—indeed, even whether they will be able to survive in the face of the extraordinary changes occurring in our world. . . .

The increased blurring of the various stages of learning throughout one's lifetime—K–12, undergraduate, graduate, professional, job training, career shifting, lifelong enrichment—will require a far greater coordination and perhaps even a merger of various elements of our national educational infrastructure.

The weakening influence of traditional regulations and the emergence of new competitive forces, driven by changing societal needs, economic realities, and technology, are likely to drive a massive restructuring of the higher education enterprise. From our experience with other restructured sectors of the economy such as health care, transportation, communications, and energy, we could expect to see a significant reorganization of higher education, complete with the mergers, acquisitions, new competitors, and new products and services that have characterized other economic transformations. More generally, we may well be seeing the early stages of the appearance of a global knowledge and learning industry, in which the activities of traditional academic institutions converge with other knowledge-intensive organizations such as telecommunications, entertainment, and information service companies. . . .

Information technology eliminates the barriers of space and time and new competitive forces such as virtual universities and for-profit education providers enter the marketplace to challenge credentialing.

This perspective of a market-driven restructuring of higher education as an industry, while perhaps both alien and distasteful to the academy, is nevertheless an important framework for considering the future of the university. While the postsecondary education market may have complex cross-subsidies and numerous public misconceptions, it is nevertheless very real and demanding, with the capacity to reward those who can respond to rapid change and punish those who cannot. Universities will have to learn to cope with the competitive pressures of this marketplace while preserving the most important of their traditional values and character. Yet, if markets are allowed to dominate and reshape the higher education enterprise, we could well find ourselves facing a brave, new world in which some of the most important values and traditions of the university fall by the wayside.

A contrasting and far brighter future is provided by the concept of a society of learning, in which universal or ubiquitous educational opportunities are provided to meet the broad and growing learning needs of our society. Today, educated people and the knowledge they produce and utilize have become the keys to the economic prosperity and well-being of our society. Furthermore, one's education, knowledge, and skills have become primary determinants of one's personal standard of living, the quality of one's life. Today it has become the responsibility of democratic societies to provide their citizens with the education and training they need, throughout their lives, whenever, wherever, and however they desire it, of high quality and at an affordable cost. So what would be the nature of a university of the twenty-first century capable of creating and sustaining a society of learning? It would be impractical and foolhardy to suggest one particular model. The great and ever-increasing diversity characterizing higher education in America makes it clear that there will be many forms, many types of institutions serving our society. But there are a number of themes that will almost certainly factor into at least some part of the higher education enterprise.

UNIVERSITY OF THE FUTURE

Just as other social institutions, our universities must become more focused on those we serve. We must transform ourselves from faculty-centered to learner-centered institutions, becoming more responsive to what our students need to learn rather than simply what our faculties wish to teach. Society will also demand that we become far more affordable, providing educational opportunities within the resources of all citizens. . . .

Already we see new forms of pedagogy: asynchronous (anytime, anyplace) learning that utilizes emerging information technology to break the constraints of time and space, making learning opportunities more compatible with lifestyles and career needs; and interactive and collaborative learning appropriate for the digital age, the plug-and-play generation. The great diversity characterizing higher education in America will continue, as it must, to serve an increasingly diverse population with diverse needs and goals.

In a society of learning, people would be continually surrounded by, immersed in, and absorbed in learning experiences. Information technology has now provided us with a means to create learning environments throughout one's life. These environments are able not only to transcend the constraints of space and time, but using artificial intelligence and genetic algorithms they, like us, are capable as well of learning and evolving to serve our changing educational needs.

CONCLUSION

Is today's form of graduate education preparing the future faculty for this vision of a twenty-first century "society of learning"? I think not. The mismatch between the one-dimensional goal of preparing the next generation of researchers and the broader needs of higher education tend to moor graduate education rigidly to the past rather than addressing the future needs of our colleges and universities. . . .

What we need is a Flexner Report (1910) for graduate education, akin to the Carnegie Foundation report which transformed medical education a century ago. Clearly we need to rethink the graduate experience, recognizing that the current paradigm is ill-suited to prepare the faculty of the future university. . . .

We need a more concerted effort to restructure the education for academic careers as that for a true learned profession, based firmly on an accepted set of values, ethics, and practices currently absent or at least unstated in academic life.

Part V

Disciplines and Interdisciplinarity

The teaching activities of colleges and universities are organized in departments based on disciplines driven by and guided by research agendas. The way disciplines manage intellectual production and reward excellence is thus central not only to the content but also to the administration of universities. Local teaching responsibilities are significantly shaped by the directions taken by the disciplines, which are oriented to global research communities rather than the college curriculum. Work in the various academic units depends upon the stability of the disciplines, but too much disciplinary stability can stifle the vitality of academic culture. By the 1920s the management of universities had taken a more or less standard form, organized into schools or divisions and disciplinary departments, and beyond the local institution the disciplines were formed into national and even international professional organizations. This arrangement has remained in place ever since.

Despite considerable organizational persistence, the content of the disciplines has been repeatedly transformed over the decades. Change was driven by the inherent volatility of research agendas marked by shifting scholarly interests, whether the result of developments intrinsic to disciplinary practice or of public concerns urged upon academe. At play, too, were the tensions of disciplinary paradigms (policing mechanisms) and movement into new domains or modes of inquiry. And still another issue came to bear upon this complex balance as well. To the degree that the reward structure of the disciplines honors those who push knowledge forward within a discipline, there was always the question of whether the most advanced disciplinary thinking addressed the varied challenges of our common life on this planet, which typically extended beyond the scope of any single discipline. In order to grapple with the life of a cell, for example, to say nothing of a whole organism, the life sciences turned to interdisciplinary methods, whether by linking established disciplines, as in biochemistry, or by bringing in methods of analysis developed in other disciplines, such as computational sciences. Similar issues emerged in the social sciences and humanities (12).

Foundations have repeatedly urged such interdisciplinary work, using the argument that both natural phenomena and social life sometimes demand a more holistic approach than can be captured in a single discipline (VIII, 11). After World War II, however, with the notable exception of the foundation-supported move toward an interdisciplinary behavioral science and area studies, the social science and humanities tended to move in a different direction, seeking disciplinary autonomy, favoring rigor over reach (3, 5; VIII, 12). Social and academic turmoil of the 1970s produced a double movement in academe: some scholars, mostly in the harder social sciences and philosophy, withdrew from public discourse and moved into highly technical work, while many in the humanities reached out to fill the vacuum, incorporating concern with a variety of social problems into humanistic research and teaching (4).

The language and concepts central to nearly all considerations of the disciplines from the 1960s onward were largely drawn from one small book, *The Structure of Scientific Revolutions,* published in 1962 by Thomas Kuhn (1). His historicist understanding of science was taken to legitimate the historical disciplines (or humanities) more generally. He also described the discipline as a community of peers, thus indicating that the maintenance of a disciplinary "paradigm," the basis for truth-making and validation in "normal" science, was at least in part a social process, which undermined the more extravagant claims of disciplinary autonomy and objectivity. Other more radical scholars, taking his ideas in directions he would not have taken, drew on his work to argue a strong position on the social construction of knowledge. Given the centrality of Kuhn's work across the disciplines, challenges to his framing of the process of scientific innovation and the validation of knowledge had important implications for discussions of academic knowledge as a whole (2).

The Cold War need for greater knowledge of other parts of the world and pressing domestic social issues prompted the development of interdisciplinary, problem-focused academic structures. The earliest of these in the 1940s were Army area studies programs that brought selected soldiers and teachers together on the basis of a wartime need to know about the language and culture of a particular enemy region. Their aim was not disciplinary affiliation, yet these bounded areas too often became another form of intellectual enclosure (12).

Later, the several movements associated with the "rights revolution" of the 1960s and 1970s pressed universities to establish interdisciplinary centers that would address issues of race, ethnicity, and gender (6–11). Other disappointments with the "normal" practices of the disciplines and their withdrawal from pressing public issues prompted many humanities scholars and some social scientists to turn to a variety of theories, mostly identified with France, that went by a variety of rubrics, including "poststructuralism," "postmodernism," or, more generally, "culture studies" (11). This development energized many teachers and scholars, but it also produced considerable uneasiness among other academics and intellectuals, mostly self-described liberals unfairly lumped together in the "culture wars" with conservatives (III, 7–10, 12). The result was a decade or so of exaggerated rhetoric that formed an important axis of the culture wars that is cooled down in the supple prose of Marjorie Garber's *Academic Instincts* (14) and in Gerald Graff's strategy of overcoming division by teaching it (13; III, 11).

The Work of Disciplines

1. Thomas S. Kuhn,
The Structure of Scientific Revolutions, 1962

Trained at Harvard University in physics (B.A. 1943, M.A. 1946, and Ph.D. 1949), Thomas S. Kuhn (1922–96) developed an interest in the history of science as a way to integrate science into general education. Beginning with a series of lectures at Boston's Lowell Institute while a member of the Society of Fellows at Harvard, he shifted his research from physics to history. His first major work was *The Copernican Revolution* (1957), but his next book, *The Structure of Scientific Revolutions*, published in 1962, extended his reputation and readership far beyond the field of the history and philosophy of science. That book pressed a historicist understanding of science and explored the sociological and psychological aspects of scientific discovery and validation. This brief but dense book, which sold nearly a million copies, was both widely celebrated across academe and criticized by his fellow philosophers of science. He introduced into the discussion of disciplinary practice the controversial but often used term *paradigm*. Equally important, his book was deeply informed by a sociological sense, arguing that truth was established by the consent of disciplinary communities that shared a paradigm. What he called "normal" science was practiced within a disciplinary paradigm, which suggested experiments and supplied predictive theory. Most science was normal science, but episodically cumulative experimental findings weaken the paradigm, producing anomalies and thus a crisis. These crises are resolved by a "scientific revolution," like the Copernican, which produces a new paradigm. Unlike work within a paradigm, there are no clear rules for selecting a new paradigm, which, in Kuhn's telling, allowed for the play of a complex of values, ideas, and even aesthetic preferences and emotions in the selection of a successor paradigm.

This opened science up, making it historical, rather than something outside of culture and history. Such an understanding of scientific knowledge-making weakened the sharp distinction between the natural sciences and the human sciences, acknowledging the historicity of them all.

Kuhn's book was debated by philosophers of science and historians of science, but more important for higher education generally was the wider discussion of scholarly disciplines that it invited. More than a hundred books and articles have been written about this book, and in many cases Kuhn's ideas were pulled in directions—particularly toward notions of the politics of knowledge and challenges to referential theories of knowledge—that Kuhn himself strongly rejected. The most notable and influential example of such extension was Richard Rorty's important book challenging the dominant postwar direction of academic philosophy in the United States, *Philosophy and the Mirror of Nature* (1979).

Kuhn taught at the University of California, Berkeley, from 1958 to 1962, when he moved to Princeton (through 1978), where he and Rorty were colleagues, and he finished his career at MIT, retiring in 1992.

The Structure of Scientific Revolutions (Chicago, 1962; enlarged ed. 1970), 1–7, 10–11, 19–21, 23–25, 37–38, 52–55, 84–85, 108–10, 148–54, 157–58. Reprinted with permission of University of Chicago Press, Copyright © 1962. Further reading: Kuhn himself contributed to the literature surrounding the book in his collection of essays, *The Essential Tension* (Chicago, 1977). The best introduction to the implications of Kuhn's work beyond science is David A. Hollinger, "T. S. Kuhn's Theory of Science and Its Implications for History," *American Historical Review* 78 (1973), 370–93. Kuhn is located within a cluster of other leading scholars in the human sciences, mostly poststructuralists, with whom Kuhn's work was often associated but with which he would not identify, in Quentin Skinner, ed., *The Return of Grand Theory in the Human Sciences* (New York, 1985). The more sociological aspects of Kuhn's work are explored and extended in Barry Barnes, *T. S. Kuhn and Social Science* (London, 1982). The debate over paradigms can be followed in Gary Gutting, ed., *Paradigms and Revolutions* (Notre Dame, IN, 1980).

If science is the constellation of facts, theories, and methods collected in current texts, then scientists are the men who, successfully or not, have striven to contribute one or another element to that particular constellation. Scientific development becomes the piecemeal process by which these items have been added, singly and in combination, to the ever growing stockpile that constitutes scientific technique and knowledge. And history of science becomes the discipline that chronicles both these successive increments and the obstacles that have inhibited their accumulation. . . .

In recent years, however, a few historians of science have been finding it more and more difficult to fulfill the functions that the concept of development-by-accumulation assigns to them. As chroniclers of an incremental process, they discover that additional research makes it harder, not easier, to answer questions like: When was oxygen discovered? Who first conceived of energy conservation? Increasingly, a few of them suspect that these are simply the wrong sorts of questions to ask. Perhaps science does not develop by the accumulation of individual discoveries and inventions. Simultaneously, these same historians confront growing difficulties in distinguishing the "scientific" component of past observation and belief from what their predecessors had readily labeled "error" and "superstition." The more carefully they study, say, Aristotelian dynamics, phlogistic chemistry, or caloric thermodynamics, the more certain they feel that those once current views of nature were, as a whole, neither less scientific nor more the product of human idiosyncrasy than those current today. If these out-of-date beliefs are to be called myths, then myths can be produced by the same sorts of methods and held for the same sorts of reasons that now lead to scientific knowledge. If, on the other hand, they are to be called science, then science has included bodies of belief quite incompatible with the ones we hold today. . . .

The result of all these doubts and difficulties is a historiographic revolution in the study of science, though one that is still in its early stages. Gradually, and often without entirely realizing they are doing so, historians of science have begun to ask new sorts of questions and to trace different, and often less than cumulative, developmental lines for the sciences. Rather than seeking the permanent contributions of an older science to our present vantage, they attempt to display the historical integrity of that science in its own time. They ask, for example, not about the relation of Galileo's views to those of modern science, but rather about the relationship between his views and those of his group, i.e., his teachers, contemporaries, and immediate successors in the sciences. . . .

What aspects of science will emerge to prominence in the course of this effort? First, at least in order of presentation, is the insufficiency of methodological directives, by themselves, to dictate a unique substantive conclusion to many sorts of scientific questions. Instructed to examine electrical or chemical phenomena, the man who is ignorant of these fields but who knows what it is to be scientific may legitimately reach any one of a number of incompatible conclusions. Among those legitimate possibilities, the particular conclusions he does arrive at are probably determined by his prior experience in other fields, by the accidents of his investigation, and by his own individual makeup. . . . [T]he early developmental stages of most sciences have been characterized by continual competition between a number of distinct views of nature, each partially derived from, and all roughly compatible with, the dictates of scientific observation and method. What differentiated these various schools was not one or another failure of method—they were all "scientific"—but what we shall come to call their incommensurable ways of seeing the world and of practicing science in it. Observation and experience can and must drastically restrict the range of admissible scientific belief, else there would be no science. But they cannot alone determine a particular body of such belief. An apparently arbitrary element, compounded of personal and historical accident, is always a formative ingredient of the beliefs espoused by a given scientific community at a given time. . . .

Normal science, the activity in which most scientists inevitably spend almost all their time, is predicated on the assumption that the scientific community knows what the world is like. Much of the success of the enterprise derives from the community's willingness to defend that assumption, if necessary at considerable cost. Normal science, for example, often suppresses fundamental novelties because they are necessarily subversive of its basic commitments. Nevertheless, so long as those commitments retain an element of the arbitrary, the very nature of normal research ensures that novelty shall not be suppressed for very long. Sometimes a normal problem, one that ought to be solvable by known rules and procedures, resists the reiter-

ated onslaught of the ablest members of the group within whose competence it falls. On other occasions a piece of equipment designed and constructed for the purpose of normal research fails to perform in the anticipated manner, revealing an anomaly that cannot, despite repeated effort, be aligned with professional expectation. In these and other ways besides, normal science repeatedly goes astray. And when it does—when, that is, the profession can no longer evade anomalies that subvert the existing tradition of scientific practice—then begin the extraordinary investigations that lead the profession at last to a new set of commitments, a new basis for the practice of science. The extraordinary episodes in which that shift of professional commitments occurs are the ones known in this essay as scientific revolutions. They are the tradition-shattering complements to the tradition-bound activity of normal science.

The most obvious examples of scientific revolutions are those famous episodes in scientific development that have often been labeled revolutions before. . . . Each produced a consequent shift in the problems available for scientific scrutiny and in the standards by which the profession determined what should count as an admissible problem or as a legitimate problem-solution. And each transformed the scientific imagination in ways that we shall ultimately need to describe as a transformation of the world within which scientific work was done. Such changes, together with the controversies that almost always accompany them, are the defining characteristics of scientific revolutions.

These characteristics emerge with particular clarity from a study of, say, the Newtonian or the chemical revolution. It is, however, a fundamental thesis of this essay that they can also be retrieved from the study of many other episodes that were not so obviously revolutionary. For the far smaller professional group affected by them, Maxwell's equations were as revolutionary as Einstein's, and they were resisted accordingly. The invention of other new theories regularly, and appropriately, evokes the same response from some of the specialists on whose area of special competence they impinge. For these men the new theory implies a change in the rules governing the prior practice of normal science. Inevitably, therefore, it reflects upon much scientific work they have already successfully completed. That is why a new theory, however special its range of application, is seldom or never just an increment to what is already known. Its assimilation requires the reconstruction of prior theory and the re-evaluation of prior fact, an intrinsically revolutionary process that is seldom completed by a single man and never overnight. No wonder historians have had difficulty in dating precisely this extended process that their vocabulary impels them to view as an isolated event.

Nor are new inventions of theory the only scientific events that have revolutionary impact upon the specialists in whose domain they occur. The commitments that govern normal science specify not only what sorts of entities the universe does contain, but also, by implication, those that it does not. It follows, though the point will require extended discussion, that a discovery like that of oxygen or X-rays does not simply add one more item to the population of the scientist's world. Ultimately it has that effect, but not until the professional community has re-evaluated traditional experimental procedures, altered its conception of entities with which it has long been familiar, and, in the process, shifted the network of theory through which it deals with the world. Scientific fact and theory are not categorically separable, except perhaps within a single tradition of normal-scientific practice. That is why the unexpected discovery is not simply factual in its import and why the scientist's world is qualitatively transformed as well as quantitatively enriched by fundamental novelties of either fact or theory. . . .

"Normal science" means research firmly based upon one or more past scientific achievements, achievements that some particular scientific community acknowledges for a time as supplying the foundation for its further practice. Today such achievements are recounted, though seldom in their original form, by science textbooks, elementary and advanced. These textbooks expound the body of accepted theory, illustrate many or all of its successful applications, and compare these applications with exemplary observations and experiments. Before such books became popular early in the nineteenth century (and until even more recently in the newly matured sciences), many of the famous classics of science fulfilled a similar function. Aristotle's *Physica*, Ptolemy's *Almagest*, Newton's *Principia* and *Opticks*, Franklin's *Electricity*, Lavoisier's *Chemistry*, and Lyell's *Geology*—these and many other works served for a time implicitly to define the legitimate problems and methods of a research field for succeeding generations of practitioners. They were able to do so because they shared two essential characteristics. Their achievement was sufficiently unprecedented to attract an enduring group of adherents away from competing modes of scientific activity. Simultaneously, it was sufficiently open-ended to leave all sorts of problems for the redefined group of practitioners to resolve.

Achievements that share these two characteristics I shall henceforth refer to as 'paradigms,' a term that relates closely to 'normal science.' By choosing it, I mean to suggest that some accepted examples of actual scientific practice—examples which include law, theory, application, and instrumentation together—provide models from which spring particular coherent traditions of scientific research. These are the traditions which the historian describes under such rubrics as 'Ptolemaic astronomy' (or 'Copernican'), 'Aristotelian dynamics' (or 'Newtonian'), 'corpuscular optics' (or 'wave optics'), and so on. The study of paradigms, including many that

are far more specialized than those named illustratively above, is what mainly prepares the student for membership in the particular scientific community with which he will later practice. Because he there joins men who learned the bases of their field from the same concrete models, his subsequent practice will seldom evoke overt disagreement over fundamentals. Men whose research is based on shared paradigms are committed to the same rules and standards for scientific practice. That commitment and the apparent consensus it produces are prerequisites for normal science, i.e., for the genesis and continuation of a particular research tradition. . . .

When the individual scientist can take a paradigm for granted, he need no longer, in his major works, attempt to build his field anew, starting from first principles and justifying the use of each concept introduced. That can be left to the writer of textbooks. Given a textbook, however, the creative scientist can begin his research where it leaves off and thus concentrate exclusively upon the subtlest and most esoteric aspects of the natural phenomena that concern his group. And as he does this, his research communiqués will begin to change in ways whose evolution has been too little studied but whose modern end products are obvious to all and oppressive to many. No longer will his researches usually be embodied in books addressed, like Franklin's *Experiments . . . on Electricity* or Darwin's *Origin of Species* to anyone who might be interested in the subject matter of the field. Instead they will usually appear as brief articles addressed only to professional colleagues, the men whose knowledge of a shared paradigm can be assumed and who prove to be the only ones able to read the papers addressed to them.

Today in the sciences, books are usually either texts or retrospective reflections upon one aspect or another of the scientific life. The scientist who writes one is more likely to find his professional reputation impaired than enhanced. Only in the earlier, pre-paradigm, stages of the development of the various sciences did the book ordinarily possess the same relation to professional achievement that it still retains in other creative fields. And only in those fields that still retain the book, with or without the article, as a vehicle for research communication are the lines of professionalization still so loosely drawn that the layman may hope to follow progress by reading the practitioners' original reports. Both in mathematics and astronomy, research reports had ceased already in antiquity to be intelligible to a generally educated audience. In dynamics, research became similarly esoteric in the later Middle Ages, and it recaptured general intelligibility only briefly during the early seventeenth century when a new paradigm replaced the one that had guided medieval research. Electrical research began to require translation for the layman before the end of the eighteenth century, and most other fields of physical science ceased to be generally accessible in the nineteenth. During the same two centuries similar transitions can be isolated in the various parts of the biological sciences. In parts of the social sciences they may well be occurring today. Although it has become customary, and is surely proper, to deplore the widening gulf that separates the professional scientist from his colleagues in other fields, too little attention is paid to the essential relationship between that gulf and the mechanisms intrinsic to scientific advance. . . .

In a science . . . a paradigm is rarely an object for replication. Instead, like an accepted judicial decision in the common law, it is an object for further articulation and specification under new or more stringent conditions.

To see how this can be so, we must recognize how very limited in both scope and precision a paradigm can be at the time of its first appearance. Paradigms gain their status because they are more successful than their competitors in solving a few problems that the group of practitioners has come to recognize as acute. To be more successful is not, however, to be either completely successful with a single problem or notably successful with any large number. The success of a paradigm—whether Aristotle's analysis of motion, Ptolemy's computations of planetary position, Lavoisier's application of the balance, or Maxwell's mathematization of the electromagnetic field—is at the start largely a promise of success discoverable in selected and still incomplete examples. Normal science consists in the actualization of that promise, an actualization achieved by extending the knowledge of those facts that the paradigm displays as particularly revealing, by increasing the extent of the match between those facts and the paradigm's predictions, and by further articulation of the paradigm itself.

Few people who are not actually practitioners of a mature science realize how much mop-up work of this sort a paradigm leaves to be done or quite how fascinating such work can prove in the execution. And these points need to be understood. Mopping-up operations are what engage most scientists throughout their careers. They constitute what I am here calling normal science. . . .

Perhaps these are defects. The areas investigated by normal science are, of course, minuscule; the enterprise now under discussion has drastically restricted vision. But those restrictions, born from confidence in a paradigm, turn out to be essential to the development of science. By focusing attention upon a small range of relatively esoteric problems, the paradigm forces scientists to investigate some part of nature in a detail and depth that would otherwise be unimaginable. And normal science possesses a built-in mechanism that ensures the relaxation of the restrictions that bound research whenever the paradigm from which they derive ceases to function effectively. At that point scientists begin to behave differently, and the nature of their

research problems changes. In the interim, however, during the period when the paradigm is successful, the profession will have solved problems that its members could scarcely have imagined and would never have undertaken without commitment to the paradigm. And at least part of that achievement always proves to be permanent. . . .

One of the things a scientific community acquires with a paradigm is a criterion for choosing problems that, while the paradigm is taken for granted, can be assumed to have solutions. To a great extent these are the only problems that the community will admit as scientific or encourage its members to undertake. Other problems, including many that had previously been standard, are rejected as metaphysical, as the concern of another discipline, or sometimes as just too problematic to be worth the time. A paradigm can, for that matter, even insulate the community from those socially important problems that are not reducible to the puzzle form, because they cannot be stated in terms of the conceptual and instrumental tools the paradigm supplies. Such problems can be a distraction, a lesson brilliantly illustrated by several facets of seventeenth-century Baconianism and by some of the contemporary social sciences. One of the reasons why normal science seems to progress so rapidly is that its practitioners concentrate on problems that only their own lack of ingenuity should keep them from solving.

If, however, the problems of normal science are puzzles in this sense, we need no longer ask why scientists attack them with such passion and devotion. A man may be attracted to science for all sorts of reasons. Among them are the desire to be useful, the excitement of exploring new territory, the hope of finding order, and the drive to test established knowledge. These motives and others besides also help to determine the particular problems that will later engage him. Furthermore, though the result is occasional frustration, there is good reason why motives like these should first attract him and then lead him on. The scientific enterprise as a whole does from time to time prove useful, open up new territory, display order, and test long-accepted belief. Nevertheless, *the individual* engaged on a normal research problem *is almost never doing any one of these things*. Once engaged, his motivation is of a rather different sort. What then challenges him is the conviction that, if only he is skillful enough, he will succeed in solving a puzzle that no one before has solved or solved so well. . . .

VI. ANOMALY AND THE EMERGENCE OF SCIENTIFIC DISCOVERIES

Normal science, the puzzle-solving activity we have just examined is a highly cumulative enterprise, eminently successful in its aim, the steady extension of the scope and precision of scientific knowledge. In all these respects it fits with great precision the most usual image of scientific work. Yet one standard product of the scientific enterprise is missing. Normal science does not aim at novelties of fact or theory and, when successful, finds none. New and unsuspected phenomena are, however, repeatedly uncovered by scientific research, and radical new theories have again and again been invented by scientists. History even suggests that the scientific enterprise has developed a uniquely powerful technique for producing surprises of this sort. If this characteristic of science is to be reconciled with what has already been said, then research under a paradigm must be a particularly effective way of inducing paradigm change. That is what fundamental novelties of fact and theory do. Produced inadvertently by a game played under one set of rules, their assimilation requires the elaboration of another set. After they have become parts of science, the enterprise, at least of those specialists in whose particular field the novelties lie, is never quite the same again.

We must now ask how changes of this sort can come about, considering first discoveries, or novelties of fact, and then inventions, or novelties of theory. That distinction between discovery and invention or between fact and theory will, however, immediately prove to be exceedingly artificial. Its artificiality is an important clue to several of this essay's main theses. Examining selected discoveries in the rest of this section, we shall quickly find that they are not isolated events but extended episodes with a regularly recurrent structure. Discovery commences with the awareness of anomaly, i.e., with the recognition that nature has somehow violated the paradigm-induced expectations that govern normal science. It then continues with a more or less extended exploration of the area of anomaly. And it closes only when the paradigm theory has been adjusted so that the anomalous has become the expected. Assimilating a new sort of fact demands a more than additive adjustment of theory, and until that adjustment is completed—until the scientist has learned to see nature in a different way—the new fact is not quite a scientific fact at all.

To see how closely factual and theoretical novelty are intertwined in scientific discovery examine a particularly famous example, the discovery of oxygen. At least three different men have a legitimate claim to it, and several other chemists must, in the early 1770's, have had enriched air in a laboratory vessel without knowing it. The progress of normal science, in this case of pneumatic chemistry, prepared the way to a breakthrough quite thoroughly. The earliest of the claimants to prepare a relatively pure sample of the gas was the Swedish apothecary, C. W. Scheele. We may, however, ignore his work since it was not published until oxygen's discovery had repeatedly been announced elsewhere and thus had no effect upon the historical pattern that most concerns us here. The second in time to establish a claim was the British scientist and divine, Joseph Priestley, who collected the gas released by heated

red oxide of mercury as one item in a prolonged normal investigation of the "airs" evolved by a large number of solid substances. In 1774 he identified the gas thus produced as nitrous oxide and in 1775, led by further tests, as common air with less than its usual quantity of phlogiston. The third claimant, Lavoisier, started the work that led him to oxygen after Priestley's experiments of 1774 and possibly as the result of a hint from Priestley. Early in 1775 Lavoisier reported that the gas obtained by heating the red oxide of mercury was "air itself entire without alteration [except that] . . . it comes out more pure, more respirable." By 1777, probably with the assistance of a second hint from Priestley, Lavoisier had concluded that the gas was a distinct species, one of the two main constituents of the atmosphere, a conclusion that Priestley was never able to accept.

This pattern of discovery raises a question that can be asked about every novel phenomenon that has ever entered the consciousness of scientists. Was it Priestley or Lavoisier, if either, who first discovered oxygen? In any case, when was oxygen discovered? In that form the question could be asked even if only one claimant had existed. As a ruling about priority and date, an answer does not at all concern us. Nevertheless, an attempt to produce one will illuminate the nature of discovery, because there is no answer of the kind that is sought. Discovery is not the sort of process about which the question is appropriately asked. The fact that it is asked—the priority for oxygen has repeatedly been contested since the 1780's—is a symptom of something askew in the image of science that gives discovery so fundamental a role. Look once more at our example. Priestley's claim to the discovery of oxygen is based upon his priority in isolating a gas that was later recognized as a distinct species. But Priestley's sample was not pure, and, if holding impure oxygen in one's hands is to discover it, that had been done by everyone who ever bottled atmospheric air. Besides, if Priestley was the discoverer, when was the discovery made? In 1774 he thought he had obtained nitrous oxide, a species he already knew; in 1775 he saw the gas as dephlogisticated air, which is still not oxygen or even, for phlogistic chemists, a quite unexpected sort of gas. Lavoisier's claim may be stronger, but it presents the same problems. If we refuse the palm to Priestley, we cannot award it to Lavoisier for the work of 1775 which led him to identify the gas as the "air itself entire." Presumably we wait for the work of 1776 and 1777 which led Lavoisier to see not merely the gas but what the gas was. Yet even this award could be questioned, for in 1777 and to the end of his life Lavoisier insisted that oxygen was an atomic "principle of acidity" and that oxygen gas was formed only when that "principle" united with caloric, the matter of heat. Shall we therefore say that oxygen had not yet been discovered in 1777? Some may be tempted to do so. But the principle of acidity was not banished from chemistry until after 1810, and caloric lingered until the 1860's. Oxygen had become a standard chemical substance before either of those dates. . . .

The transition from a paradigm in crisis to a new one from which a new tradition of normal science can emerge is far from a cumulative process, one achieved by an articulation or extension of the old paradigm. Rather it is a reconstruction of the field from new fundamentals, a reconstruction that changes some of the field's most elementary theoretical generalizations as well as many of its paradigm methods and applications. During the transition period there will be a large but never complete overlap between the problems that can be solved by the old and by the new paradigm. But there will also be a decisive difference in the modes of solution. When the transition is complete, the profession will have changed its view of the field, its methods, and its goals. One perceptive historian [Herbert Butterfield], viewing a classic case of a science's reorientation by paradigm change, recently described it as "picking up the other end of the stick," a process that involves "handling the same bundle of data as before, but placing them in a new system of relations with one another by giving them a different framework." Others who have noted this aspect of scientific advance have emphasized its similarity to a change in visual gestalt: the marks on paper that were first seen as a bird are now seen as an antelope, or vice versa. That parallel can be misleading. Scientists do not see something *as* something else; instead, they simply see it. We have already examined some of the problems created by saying that Priestley saw oxygen as dephlogisticated air. In addition, the scientist does not preserve the gestalt subject's freedom to switch back and forth between ways of seeing. Nevertheless, the switch of gestalt, particularly because it is today so familiar, is a useful elementary prototype for what occurs in full-scale paradigm shift. . . .

The characteristic shifts in the scientific community's conception of its legitimate problems and standards would have less significance to this essay's thesis if one could suppose that they always occurred from some methodologically lower to some higher type. In that case their effects, too, would seem cumulative. No wonder that some historians have argued that the history of science records a continuing increase in the maturity and refinement of man's conception of the nature of science. Yet the case for cumulative development of science's problems and standards is even harder to make than the case for cumulation of theories. The attempt to explain gravity, though fruitfully abandoned by most eighteenth-century scientists, was not directed to an intrinsically illegitimate problem; the objections to innate forces were neither inherently unscientific nor metaphysical in some pejorative sense. There are no external standards to permit a judgment of that sort. What occurred was neither a decline nor a raising of standards, but simply a change demanded by the adoption of a new paradigm. Furthermore,

that change has since been reversed and could be again. In the twentieth century Einstein succeeded in explaining gravitational attractions, and that explanation has returned science to a set of canons and problems that are, in this particular respect, more like those of Newton's predecessors than of his successors. . . .

By shifting emphasis from the cognitive to the normative functions of paradigms [we] enlarge our understanding of the ways in which paradigms give form to the scientific life. Previously, we had principally examined the paradigm's role as a vehicle for scientific theory. In that role it functions by telling the scientist about the entities that nature does and does not contain and about the ways in which those entities behave. That information provides a map whose details are elucidated by mature scientific research. And since nature is too complex and varied to be explored at random, that map is as essential as observation and experiment to science's continuing development. Through the theories they embody, paradigms prove to be constitutive of the research activity. They are also, however, constitutive of science in other respects, and that is now the point. In particular, our most recent examples show that paradigms provide scientists not only with a map but also with some of the directions essential for map-making. In learning a paradigm the scientist acquires theory, methods, and standards together, usually in an inextricable mixture. Therefore, when paradigms change, there are usually significant shifts in the criteria determining the legitimacy both of problems and of proposed solutions. . . .

To the extent, as significant as it is incomplete, that two scientific schools disagree about what is a problem and what is a solution, they will inevitably talk through each other when debating the relative merits of their respective paradigms. In the partially circular arguments that regularly result, each paradigm will be shown to satisfy more or less the criteria that it dictates for itself and to fall short of a few of those dictated by its opponent. . . .

But, in fact, these conditions are never met completely. The proponents of competing paradigms are always at least slightly at cross-purposes. Neither side will grant all the non-empirical. assumptions that the other needs in order to make its case. Like Proust and Berthollet arguing about the composition of chemical compounds, they are bound partly to talk through each other. Though each may hope to convert the other to his way of seeing his science and its problems, neither may hope to prove his case. The competition between paradigms is not the sort of battle that can be resolved by proofs.

We have already seen several reasons why the proponents of competing paradigms must fail to make complete contact with each other's viewpoints. Collectively these reasons have been described as the incommensurability of the pre- and postrevolutionary normal-scientific traditions, and we need only recapitulate them briefly here. In the first place, the proponents of competing paradigms will often disagree about the list of problems that any candidate for paradigm must resolve. Their standards or their definitions of science are not the same. Must a theory of motion explain the cause of the attractive forces between particles of matter or may it simply note the existence of such forces? Newton's dynamics was widely rejected because, unlike both Aristotle's and Descartes's theories, it implied the latter answer to the question. When Newton's theory had been accepted, a question was therefore banished from science. That question, however, was one that general relativity may proudly claim to have solved. Or again, as disseminated in the nineteenth century, Lavoisier's chemical theory inhibited chemists from asking why the metals were so much alike, a question that phlogistic chemistry had both asked and answered. The transition to Lavoisier's paradigm had, like the transition to Newton's, meant a loss not only of a permissible question but of an achieved solution. That loss was not, however, permanent either. In the twentieth century questions about the qualities of chemical substances have entered science again, together with some answers to them.

More is involved, however, than the incommensurability of standards. Since new paradigms are born from old ones, they ordinarily incorporate much of the vocabulary and apparatus, both conceptual and manipulative, that the traditional paradigm had previously employed. But they seldom employ these borrowed elements in quite the traditional way. Within the new paradigm, old terms, concepts, and experiments fall into new relationships one with the other. The inevitable result is what we must call, though the term is not quite right, a misunderstanding between the two competing schools. The laymen who scoffed at Einstein's general theory of relativity because space could not be "curved"—it was not that sort of thing—were not simply wrong or mistaken. Nor were the mathematicians, physicists, and philosophers who tried to develop a Euclidean version of Einstein's theory. What had previously been meant by space was necessarily flat, homogeneous, isotropic, and unaffected by the presence of matter. If it had not been, Newtonian physics would not have worked. To make the transition to Einstein's universe, the whole conceptual web whose strands are space, time, matter, force, and so on, had to be shifted and laid down again on nature whole. Only men who had together undergone or failed to undergo that transformation would be able to discover precisely what they agreed or disagreed about. Communication across the revolutionary divide is inevitably partial. Consider, for another example, the men who called Copernicus mad because he proclaimed that the earth moved. They were not either just wrong or quite wrong. Part of what they meant by "earth" was fixed position. Their earth, at least, could not be moved. Correspondingly, Copernicus'

innovation was not simply to move the earth. Rather, it was a whole new way of regarding the problems of physics and astronomy, one that necessarily changed the meaning of both "earth" and "motion." Without those changes the concept of a moving earth was mad. On the other hand, once they had been made and understood, both Descartes and Huygens could realize that the earth's motion was a question with no content for science.

These examples point to the third and most fundamental aspect of the incommensurability of competing paradigms. In a sense that I am unable to explicate further, the proponents of competing paradigms practice their trades in different worlds. One contains constrained bodies that fall slowly, the other pendulums that repeat their motions again and again. In one, solutions are compounds, in the other mixtures. One is embedded in a flat, the other in a curved, matrix of space. Practicing in different worlds, the two groups of scientists see different things when they look from the same point in the same direction. Again, that is not to say that they can see anything they please. Both are looking at the world, and what they look at has not changed. But in some areas they see different things, and they see them in different relations one to the other. That is why a law that cannot even be demonstrated to one group of scientists may occasionally seem intuitively obvious to another. Equally, it is why, before they can hope to communicate fully, one group or the other must experience the conversion that we have been calling a paradigm shift. Just because it is a transition between incommensurables, the transition between competing paradigms cannot be made a step at a time, forced by logic and neutral experience. Like the gestalt switch, it must occur all at once (though not necessarily in an instant) or not at all.

How, then, are scientists brought to make this transposition? Part of the answer is that they are very often not. Copernicanism made few converts for almost a century after Copernicus' death. Newton's work was not generally accepted, particularly on the Continent, for more than half a century after the *Principia* appeared. Priestley never accepted the oxygen theory, nor Lord Kelvin the electromagnetic theory, and so on. The difficulties of conversion have often been noted by scientists themselves. Darwin, in a particularly perceptive passage at the end of his *Origin of Species*, wrote: "Although I am fully convinced of the truth of the views given in this volume . . . , I by no means expect to convince experienced naturalists whose minds are stocked with a multitude of facts all viewed, during a long course of years, from a point of view directly opposite to mine. . . . [B]ut I look with confidence to the future,—to young and rising naturalists, who will be able to view both sides of the question with impartiality." And Max Planck, surveying his own career in his *Scientific Autobiography*, sadly remarked that "a new scientific truth does not triumph by convincing its opponents and making them see the light, but rather because its opponents eventually die, and a new generation grows up that is familiar with it."

These facts and others like them are too commonly known to need further emphasis. But they do need re-evaluation. In the past they have most often been taken to indicate that scientists, being only human, cannot always admit their errors, even when confronted with strict proof. I would argue, rather, that in these matters neither proof nor error is at issue. The transfer of allegiance from paradigm to paradigm is a conversion experience that cannot be forced. Lifelong resistance, particularly from those whose productive careers have committed them to an older tradition of normal science, is not a violation of scientific standards but an index to the nature of scientific research itself. The source of resistance is the assurance that the older paradigm will ultimately solve all its problems, that nature can be shoved into the box the paradigm provides. Inevitably, at times of revolution, that assurance seems stubborn and pigheaded as indeed it sometimes becomes. But it is also something more. That same assurance is what makes normal or puzzle-solving science possible. And it is only through normal science that the professional community of scientists succeeds, first, in exploiting the potential scope and precision of the older paradigm and, then, in isolating the difficulty through the study of which a new paradigm may emerge.

Still, to say that resistance is inevitable and legitimate, that paradigm change cannot be justified by proof, is not to say that no arguments are relevant or that scientists cannot be persuaded to change their minds. Though a generation is sometimes required to effect the change, scientific communities have again and again been converted to new paradigms. Furthermore, these conversions occur not despite the fact that scientists are human but because they are. Though some scientists, particularly the older and more experienced ones, may resist indefinitely, most of them can be reached in one way or another. Conversions will occur a few at a time until, after the last hold-outs have died, the whole profession will again be practicing under a single, but now a different, paradigm. We must therefore ask how conversion is induced and how resisted.

What sort of answer to that question may we expect? Just because it is asked about techniques of persuasion, or about argument and counterargument in a situation in which there can be no proof, our question is a new one, demanding a sort of study that has not previously been undertaken. We shall have to settle for a very partial and impressionistic survey. In addition, what has already been said combines with the result of that survey to suggest that, when asked about persuasion rather than proof, the question of the nature of scientific argument has no single or uniform answer. Individual scientists embrace a new paradigm for all sorts of reasons and usually for several at once. Some of these reasons—for example, the sun worship that helped make Kepler a Copernican—lie outside the apparent sphere of science entirely. Others must depend upon idiosyncrasies of autobiography and personality. Even the nationality or the prior reputation of the innovator and his teachers can sometimes play a significant role. Ultimately, therefore, we must learn to ask this question differently. Our concern will not then be with the arguments that in fact convert one or another individual, but rather with the sort of community that always sooner or later re-forms as a single group. . . .

Probably the single most prevalent claim advanced by the proponents of a new paradigm is that they can solve the problems that have led the old one to a crisis. When it can legitimately be made, this claim is often the most effective one possible. In the area for which it is advanced the paradigm is known to be in trouble. That trouble has repeatedly been explored, and attempts to remove it have again and again proved vain. "Crucial experiments"— those able to discriminate particularly sharply between the two paradigms—have been recognized and attested before the new paradigm was even invented. Copernicus thus claimed that he had solved the long-vexing problem of the length of the calendar year, Newton that he had reconciled terrestrial and celestial mechanics, Lavoisier that he had solved the problems of gas-identity and of weight relations, and Einstein that he had made electrodynamics compatible with a revised science of motion.

Claims of this sort are particularly likely to succeed if the new paradigm displays a quantitative precision strikingly better than its older competitor. . . .

The claim to have solved the crisis-provoking problems is, however, rarely sufficient by itself. Nor can it always legitimately be made. In fact, Copernicus' theory was not more accurate than Ptolemy's and did not lead directly to any improvement in the calendar. Or again, the wave theory of light was not, for some years after it was first announced, even as successful as its corpuscular rival in resolving the polarization effects that were a principal cause of the optical crisis. Sometimes the looser practice that characterizes extraordinary research will produce a candidate for paradigm that initially helps not at all with the problems that have evoked crisis. When that occurs, evidence must be drawn from other parts of the field as it often is anyway. In those other areas particularly persuasive arguments can be developed if the new paradigm permits the prediction of phenomena that had been entirely unsuspected while the old one prevailed. . . .

But paradigm debates are not really about relative problem-solving ability, though for good reasons they are usually couched in those terms. Instead, the issue is which paradigm should in the future guide research on problems many of which neither competitor can yet claim to resolve completely. A decision between alternate ways of practicing science is called for, and in the circumstances that decision must be based less on past achievement than on future promise. The man who embraces a new paradigm at an early stage must often do so in defiance of the evidence provided by problem-solving. He must, that is, have faith that the new paradigm will succeed with the many large problems that confront it, knowing only that the older paradigm has failed with a few. A decision of that kind can only be made on faith.

2. Peter Galison, *How Experiments End,* 1987

How do scientists proceed? Does theory precede experiment? Is their understanding of experimental data shaped by a preexisting paradigm that undergirds scientific inquiry? Or does theory follow the filtering processes of experiment? Thomas Kuhn's famous work *The Structure of Scientific Revolutions* (1) reasoned that normal science works within paradigms; here Peter Galison (1955–) maintains that instrumentation and observation play an equally important, if not entirely independent, role. From his ordering and assessment of scattered notes and memo exchanges left by teams of high-energy particle physicists he produced a more complex explanation. This historiographical issue within the history of science bears significantly upon the understanding of academic culture. For a generation, Kuhn's notion of the relation of paradigms and communities of peers was taken by practitioners in most of the social science and in some of the humanities disciplines to define the way they work. There is a certain conservatism or even determinism in Kuhn's notion, while Galison's account suggests a greater degree or a different kind of contingency in scientific discovery.

Galison asserted that scientists have stopped short in their understanding of human interactions with nature by setting up idea or presupposition against machine or instrument. Though respectful of theory, he posited that it is a presupposition to be examined with "autonomous experimentation." Images in microphysics are received from machines in such a variety of ways by a variety of observers in laboratories of high-speed computers, bubble chambers, and Monte Carlo simulations. Teams of research people create fluid social situations. Theory and experiment are not there joined "in lockstep." Even though Galison's thinking applied to the physical sciences, it raised questions about the circumstances and provenance of evidence and its images to scholars considering processes of change in other disciplines. The questions became unavoidable in a global, interconnected electronic age. What do investigators from different fields in different parts of the world need to do to understand one another and, setting aside theory, to come to common accord upon the meanings of evidence? Galison's insistence on an international scientific vocabulary, or lingua franca, found concurrence among widely dispersed searchers in different fields. He later expanded this idea in his weighty book *Image and Logic* (1997).

Peter Galison took his bachelor and doctoral degrees at Harvard (1983) and his M. Phil. from Cambridge University (1978); at Stanford (1983–92) he rose through the academic ranks to become professor of philosophy and physics and then went to chair the history of science department at Harvard, taking the Mallinckrodt Professorship in the History of Science and Physics in 1994. He was a MacArthur Foundation fellow (1997–2002) and was awarded the Max Planck Prize in 1999. He is currently Pellegrino University Professor at Harvard.

Peter Galison, *How Experiments End* (Chicago, 1987): ix–x, 1–10, 251–52, 256, 276–77. Reprinted with permission of University of Chicago Press, Copyright © 1987. Further reading: Brian Pippard, reviewing Peter Galison, *How Experiments End,* in *Minerva* 27, no. 1 (Spring 1989): 126–31; Peter Galison, *Image and Logic: A Material Culture of Microphysics* (Chicago, 1997): 830–38; Freeman Dyson, "Clockwork Science," *New York Review of Books,* November 6, 2003, 42–44; Peter Galison, "Objectivity is Romantic," in *The Humanities and the Sciences,* ed. Jerome Friedman, Peter Galison, and Susan Haack, ACLS Occasional Paper, no. 47 (Washington, D.C., 1999): 15–43; Donald E. Stokes, *Pasteur's Quadrant: Basic Science and Technological Innovation* (Washington, D.C., 1997); and V, 1.

Despite the slogan that science advances through experiments, virtually the entire literature of the history of science concerns theory. Whether scholars have looked to the seventeenth-century scientific revolution, to nineteenth-century field theory, or to twentieth-century relativity and quantum mechanics, the histories they write highlight the evolution of concepts, not laboratory practice. Paraphrasing Einstein, there seems to be an asymmetry in historical analysis not present in the events themselves.

This book is addressed to readers interested in how arguments emerge from the modern physical laboratory. It is neither an overview of particle physics nor a collection of the results of "great experiments" summarized to teach physics. Instead, the book is written for those intrigued by the history, philosophy, and sociology of laboratory science, as well as for working physicists. Motivating the book are several questions: What bits of theory shape experimentalists' faith in a microphysical effect? Which piece of apparatus can they trust? How does the overwhelming historical expansion of the laboratory from bench to factory affect the building of a persuasive argument?

The following differs from most accounts of the development of physics, not only by its focus on the laboratory, but by its treatment of the twentieth century beyond 1926. For too long the history of physics has been mired in special relativity and non-relativistic quantum mechanics. Can one imagine a political history of the twentieth century without World War II? Certainly the invention of quantum mechanics was an epochal accomplishment, but it is the beginning, not the end, of this century's physics. Our task is not to point in awe at the costliness of big accelerators but to look *inside* the laboratory to understand how teams of physicists mount a case for the existence of a process that takes place in a hundred-millionth of a second and looks like ten other processes.

To portray the big experiment, the historian needs documents. Some of that need is fulfilled by notebooks, letters, or published papers. . . .

The most important type of evidence, however, stems from the inextricable social component of scientific teamwork. Team members have to work together. They argue through meetings, and they summarize these in photocopied minutes; they make proposals and counterproposals through technical memoranda circulated only within the group; they put forward claims and refutations as the data begin to bubble up through the many-layered filters of analysis. Papers like these compose a new form of scientific literature that physicists have created in response to the explosive growth of collaborative experiments. For the historian, such novel artifacts are a boon not only because they track the day-to-day interactions among the scientists, but because teams produce them in multiples: if one participant discarded a copy, another often retained it. Since the memoranda frequently refer to one another, I could identify holes in the record, and over the course of the last seven years, I have pieced together a nearly complete set of several hundred. Together they form the documentary record that made a large section of this book possible. . . .

From a historical perspective the question of how experiments end commands our interest because it directs attention to that fascinating moment in the activities of the laboratory when instrumentation, experience, theory, calculation, and sociology meet. To understand how endings are constructed, we must narrow our historical gaze in order to identify the arguments, evidence, skills, and hardware that drive the investigators themselves to feel confident that they have gold in their pans, not pyrite. For any experimentalist, much is invested in the decision to terminate an experimental study, and the choice to end a project will always carry a risk. Researchers' reputations will hinge on their judgment of when they have adduced adequate evidence. In late twentieth-century particle physics the ante is further raised by the vast resources committed to an experimental inquiry: from planning to publication, such enterprises take between five and ten years, involve tens of millions of dollars and tens, even hundreds, of collaborators. And as soon as a collaboration releases results, the pressure rises. The theorists next door will begin struggling to understand the new numbers; other teams will begin to reconsider their own experimental agendas.

For philosophical reasons, as well as historical ones, the endings of experimental endeavors are significant. Experimentalists' demonstrations of the reality—or artificiality—of an effect or particle will never have the closed form of a deductive argument. Philosophers have long argued that no finite set of facts will ever suffice to *prove* a general assertion; others, including Duhem, Quine, and Putnam, have emphasized that experiments confront no single hypothesis, but a web of interrelated beliefs. Worse yet, that web includes not just our explicitly held beliefs but also an infinite number of auxiliary hypotheses. . . .

Although the exhaustive enumeration of all hypotheses is impossible, the researcher can and does invoke prior or parallel studies to show that specific mimicking or "background" effects are negligible. . . .

Nonetheless . . . all experimental physicists, biologists, chemists, geologists, and their corresponding members of other disciplines *do* come to view evidence as persuasive, even, occasionally, when it disagrees with their expectations. Between first suspicion and final argument there is a many-layered process through which belief is progressively reinforced. These intermediate stages in the construction of a demonstration belie the radical dichotomy between a "psychologistic logic of discovery"— where arguments are no more than the arbitrary, completely idiosyncratic prejudices of the discoverer—and the formal, fully persuasive "logic of justification" that finds its way to print. Amidst the varied tests and arguments of any experimental enterprise, experimentalists must decide, implicitly or explicitly, that their conclusions stand *ceteris paribus*: all other factors being equal. And they must do so despite the fact that the end of an experimental demonstration is not, and cannot be, based purely on a closed set of procedures.

For all these reasons, the decision to end an investigation draws on the full set of skills, strategies, beliefs, and instruments at the experimentalists' disposal. How else could they proceed? *Theoretical presuppositions* serve to carve out a piece of the phenomenal world as interesting; they shape the measurement procedures and the interpretative techniques. As we will see in detail below, without *experimental presuppositions* of some sort even the gross properties of matter would be in doubt. The relevance and applicability of certain *types* of instruments would be in question at the same time as the detailed performance of a *particular* apparatus. Such commitments cannot *all* be optional, nor can they be treated as if they were distorting "biases." Rather they are the sine qua non of beginning an experiment—as well as ending it.

Somewhere, something has to hold firm or no experimentalist could ever rely on any set of results. Certain manipulations of apparatus, calculations, assumptions, and arguments give confidence to the experimentalist: what are they? This is a pressing question for the experimentalist. For, like Shakespeare's Gaunt, experimentalists know that they will be remembered for what they say last. When do experimentalists stake their claim on the reality of an effect? When do they assert that the counter's pulse or the spike in a graph is more than an artifact of the apparatus or environment? In short: How do experiments end? . . .

Historians of science, principally those interested in the development of *ideas*, have often insisted that any historical reconstruction that ignores what seems in retrospect to be erroneous will be an inadequate account. . . .

When historians such as Koyré and Kuhn refer to historically held beliefs as "mistaken," it is not for the purpose of judging past theories anachronistically. On the contrary, they seek to identify theoretical problems and solutions that are no longer accepted but which can serve as guides to precepts that, in their time, were held to be of central importance. In the process of delineating the historically relevant problem set, we can come to appreciate those forgotten frames of mind in their own terms. Similarly, in discussing experiments we look for historical "mistakes" just as geologists search for indicator minerals: in both cases as clues suggesting deeper-lying forces.

There is a second reason for studying those experiments that did not progress in a textbook fashion toward a now-accepted result. When an experiment proceeded as expected or was quickly confirmed elsewhere, it may appear both to us and to the experimentalists' contemporaries as the inevitable recognition of something present in nature. Attending only to successful results casts the doubts, tests, and arguments of experimental demonstrations into the background. When a result bearing on fundamental physical questions is challenged by contemporaries, however, it drives the community's attention back to earlier stages of the experiment where crucial beliefs and practices have been partially buried. Such questioning may occur when a dearly held theory is at risk, when a new conjecture is strikingly confirmed, or, even in the absence of any particular model, when a surprising new experimental effect is observed. At such controversial moments it becomes apparent that the decision to end an experiment is not inescapable.

During these times of controversy the experimentalists themselves are forced to ask explicitly which of their data ought to be kept and which discarded. In the course of understanding how, in these circumstances, certain "aberrant" results were handled, we can force to the surface the hidden presuppositions (theoretical and experimental) that were also present in the production of now-accepted results. Developing a more discriminating vocabulary to distinguish among the different kinds of presuppositions will aid the cause of understanding how experiments can become persuasive without being strictly deductive.

When experimentalists construct their arguments, the persuasive force of their demonstrations typically depends, at least in part, on theoretical and experimental knowledge imported from the past. What kinds of presuppositions are there? How do they affect experimental demonstrations?

Though at first such problems may appear to be of purely philosophical interest, their resolutions have direct historiographical consequences. For example, suppose historians were to adopt the view that experimental facts reflect a publicly available, more or less unproblematic, experience. The history of experimentation would then have a very limited scope: the task of historical writing would be to explicate the technical requirements needed to make an experiment and then to recount the theoretical uses to which the empirical results were applied.

Conversely, it is possible to write about physics as if experimental outcomes have *no* autonomy from theory. The burden of such a historical account would be quite different: a history of experimentation would focus almost exclusively on the conceptual framework in which experiments were performed. In short, judgments about the scope of experimental autonomy are intimately tied to decisions about which historical factors need to be taken into an account of experimentation. . . .

It is ironic that the very philosophers who called themselves logical empiricists had virtually no interest in the *conduct* of experiments. . . . Missing from the positivist account is the arena of argument situated between perception and the establishment of "facts." In the laboratory lies all the interest, for that is where experimentalists muster arguments, rearrange equipment, test apparatus, and modify interpretive skills. . . .

When the inevitable reaction against logical empiricism came, it was powerful and widespread. And of the traditional positivists' tenets, the placement of observation *before* theory was a primary target. In his 1962 work, *The Structure of Scientific Revolutions,* Thomas Kuhn assailed the universal adjudicating power of experiments, and therefore their independence from theory. Instead of arguing that observation must precede theory, Kuhn contended that theory has to precede observation. The history of science, for Kuhn, amply demonstrated the essential role theory plays in the conduct of experimentation, in the interpretation of data, and in the definition of "relevant" phenomena. As long as the celestial object later called Uranus was considered to be a star, Kuhn observes, its motion was not noticed. Only when astronomers threw its identity in question could people "see" it move. Similarly, when discussing the revolution in chemistry, Kuhn repeatedly refers to what Lavoisier and Priestley could, or could not, *see*; where Priestley *saw* a deficiency of phlogiston, Lavoisier *saw* oxygen.

To capture the role of expectations in organizing perception, both Kuhn and Norwood Russell Hanson invoked the striking results of perceptual psychology as a model of the relation of theory to experiment. Both authors referred to reversible Gestalt images such as the one that can be seen alternately as a duck or a rabbit. Images of this type have lines and curves that take on completely different significance under two different "theoretical presuppositions." Above all, the Gestalt metaphor suggests the difficulty of seeing a certain line element as anything other than that given by its place in the scheme one has in mind: the viewer can see either a duck or a rabbit, but never both. Considerations like these, which Kuhn takes as deeper-going than mere metaphors, evoke a picture of science in which change comes slowly against a stabilizing theoretical framework that eventually collapses all in a piece. There are several problems with such a monolithic image of scientific practice. . . .

Kuhn elaborates on the inertia of belief by invoking another psychological experiment, in which the experimenter flashes a sequence of playing cards, all of one suit, before a subject. If a different suit is quickly flashed among the others, the subject, expecting the pattern to continue, simply *sees* the odd card as one of the majority. In this way prior expectations can lock the experimenter into a particular way of viewing the world of empirical phenomena. Similarly, a researcher looking at a group of experimental results *before* a radical theoretical change sees a very different state of affairs from the scientist looking at the same results *afterward*.

In these psychological models Kuhn stresses how theoretical expectations profoundly shape what is observed and when. However, beyond alluding to the perceptual psychology experiments, he does not pursue the mechanisms of that influence. . . .

Some sociologists of science carry Kuhn's claim that theories (or theoretically grounded "paradigms") are prior to observation much further. In particular, they recast the vocabulary of "prior beliefs" into the language of sociology: every scientific belief or commitment should be explained as the satisfaction of earlier sociological "interests." Such interests may range from class or religious interests to narrowly defined professional ones. In the case of narrow professional interests, the argument is that after investing years in the acquisition of particular skills, practicing scientists' interest in the future applicability of their hard-won skills is so great that they accept or reject new scientific work on that basis. . . .

Just as there are programmatic theoretical commitments, there are programmatic laboratory practices. The experimentalist may well believe that *in general* microscopes, telescopes, spark chambers, or geiger counters are valid instruments for the investigation of some part of the phenomenal world. Still open is the question of trusting *this* microscope or *that* spark chamber. Physicists frequently make such decisions using calibration tests such as Stewart employed or comparative responses to identical probes such as the tests employed on the spark

chambers to be used in E1A. [Galison is here referring to an American group of physicists researching "neutral currents" through spark-chamber and calorimeter experiments.—Eds.] Once the instrument was tested against other instruments and against calculations of its performance, the device came to have a reliability of its own.

While machines can certify results without constant reference to theory, they can also import assumptions *built into the apparatus itself*. We might do well to call these hardwired assumptions "technological presuppositions" to remind ourselves that machines are not neutral. . . .

Too little is known about the ways in which scientific beliefs re-create themselves in instrument design. What is needed is something quite orthogonal to the antiquarian history of instruments that glorifies pure technique. The history of instruments that we need must be an archaeology that uses the material culture of science to unearth buried theoretical assumptions and experimental practices.

Finally, the design and interpretation of experiments can be shaped by particular theories and models, constraints loosely analogous to Braudel's "individual time." Several different theoretical models may be compatible with the broad constraints of any given program. But precisely because these models lead to definite quantitative predictions, they are notoriously effective in restraining the experimentalists' decision to end an experiment. . . .

For both epistemological and historiographical reasons, we must recognize that experimental and theoretical training, skills, and judgments are not necessarily coextensive. In the future, as other branches of natural science undergo the schism between theory and experiment, we will need a better qualitative picture of the relation of theorists to experimenters. It will have to capture the partial autonomy of each, without implying that they never interact. One model for this relation might come from cultural history, where historians must regularly grapple with multiple subcultures within a single society. Carlo Ginzburg's brilliant study of a sixteenth-century miller's cosmology illustrates the problems. Ginzburg shows how his miller took fragments of developed Christian theology and embedded them in a concrete, materialist context, likening creation itself to the spontaneous generation of worms in cheese. By exploring the internal coherence of the peasants' world view, Ginzburg depicts a peasant "low" culture that is not just a "distortion" of high culture, nor totally independent of it. Each culture necessarily borrows from the other, transforming the borrowed material and incorporating it into its central concerns. Renaissance society embraced both high and low cultures. Similarly, we can consider the larger discipline of physics as encompassing a culture of experimenters and one of theorists, each with its own standards of demonstration, commitments to methods, and programmatic goals. The distinction between the two cultures has existed for most of the twentieth century, but the scale and complexity of high-energy physics has widened the gap.

Each of these broad classes of constraints helps restrict the laboratory moves and verbal conclusions that appear reasonable to the working experimentalist. Each helps to isolate phenomena and to divide them into classes. It is the progressive imposition or acceptance of these constraints that constitutes the separation of signal from background.

Michelangelo was once asked how he had carved his marble masterpiece. The sculptor apocryphally responded that nothing could be simpler; all one needed was to remove everything that was not *David*. In this respect the laboratory is not so different from the studio. As the artistic tale suggests, the task of removing the background is not ancillary to identifying the foreground—*the two tasks are one and the same*. Precisely for this reason, discussion of the analysis and debates over background figures prominently in the preceding pages. The magnetic field, the turbulence in the cloud chamber, the neutron collisions: these were the issues on which the case for a demonstration was lost or won. When the background could not be properly circumscribed, the demonstration had to remain incomplete, like Michelangelo's *St. Matthew*, in which the artist was unable to "liberate" his sculpture from its "marble prison."

In physics the analogous process of "liberation" of an effect from the background is linked to theory on the many levels discussed above. Each of the different levels of theory, by articulating assumptions about what kind of things exist and what things are grouped together, can encourage—or preclude—an investigation. An experimentalist often will design an apparatus precisely to exclude a background and, just as in the choice of where to look, may exclude phenomena later considered vital. During the "runs" of the apparatus, a further selection takes place, in modern experiments often electronically, before phenomena are ever recorded. Once recorded, data selection again cuts between the foreground and background as "good" events are split from "bad." The "bad" can be discarded on the basis of quite general principles—as when energy is apparently not conserved, or on the grounds of the details of phenomenological models describing the process or the apparatus. Sometimes an event can be thrown out simply because it does not look right.

Though the concern with background may not be uppermost in theorists' minds, for experimentalists it is the central concern. . . .

Throughout this book, the spotlight has been on the procedures to gain stability and directness that *experimentalists* use in their decision to class phenomena as real or artifactual. It is not surprising that this historical approach must periodically yield results that clash with the criteria put forward by theorists, historians, sociologists, or philosophers who may have their own criteria of when experimentalists "ought" to accept an entity. . . .

Physics goals demand an increasing size, but that augmentation creates an increasing delay between proposal and publication that makes it possible that physics goals will change during the course of the experiment. Yet once they have built an instrument, experimenters have no choice as time goes on but to pursue their new problems within the material constraints of the aging apparatus.

One way to recapture the lost ability to manipulate the big machines has been to simulate their behavior on a computer. In a sense the computer simulation allows the experimentalist to see, at least through the eye of the central processor, what would happen if a larger spark chamber were on the floor, if a shield were thicker, or if the multiton concrete walls were removed.

The Monte Carlo program can do even more. It can simulate situations that *could never exist in nature*. What would the signal look like if electricity and magnetism did not exist? Such altered universes do work for the experimentalist. . . .

In some respects the Monte Carlo programs function as theoretical calculations, in others like experiments. Like a calculation, physicists write their Monte Carlo simulations in terms of equations and mathematical manipulations—not by attaching cables or soldering circuit boards. Yet, unlike a calculation, it is impossible to follow a typical simulation from beginning to end analytically because it is simply too complex. Instead, as we saw in both the Gargamelle case and in E1A, the experimentalists will compare the outputs of different programs much the way experimentalists compare the results of related experiments. Or, as in an experiment, the Monte Carlo writer can vary the inputs to see that the corresponding output is well behaved. Recall the importance of Fry and Haidt's demonstration that their simulation indicated that cascading neutrons could not account for the number of neutral-current candidates even when they significantly varied the input parameters. Here, then, is a search for a new kind of stability, one not found in varying the apparatus. Instead stability emerges upon comparing an old with a new Monte Carlo, running an old one with new parameters, or even cutting the data in a novel fashion. . . .

As the computer simulations acquire new significance, it is natural that they should generate their own controversies; after all, they too have both theoretical and experimental assumptions embedded in them. Where does a muon distribution come from? What idealization of the geometry of the concrete shielding should be used? What kind of beam should be assumed? Which approximations should be used in the passage of particles through the apparatus? All these questions arise because physicists use simulations to explore the characteristics of both the effect being sought and the background effects that might imitate it. In the case of neutral currents, as in so many modern particle-physics experiments, the computer is not an optional time-saving device used to collate data. Electronic data processing was both a response to and a source of the increasing scale of experimentation. By the late 1960s it had become an inextricable part of the end of an experiment. Maxwell's three-part division—source of energy, means of delivery, and mode of detection—must be supplemented by the fourth stage, data analysis, now elevated from the calculation of error bars to a major commitment of material and human resources. . . .

To capture the process by which consensus develops within the community, I spoke earlier of an expanding circle of belief. In retrospect it is apparent that there were in fact several expanding circles. . . . In fits and starts, in one place with the suddenness of the single-electron discovery, elsewhere with the incremental development of the Monte Carlos, evidence is transformed from the oddities of a new machine, through a period in which the evidence points to a "probable cause," and finally to one of the empirical pillars of the new physics.

The introjection of competition, meetings, autonomous investigations, hierarchy, publication, and complementary arguments into one overarching experiment signals the creation of a new kind of activity. Each of these facets of scientific life, previously occurring in the experimental community as a whole, now finds its locus in a single experiment. In biology a venerable doctrine is captured in Haeckel's famous dictum that "ontogeny recapitulates phylogeny," that many features of the evolutionary history of the species are repeated in the embryological growth of the individual. In the history of modern experimentation, the individual experiment recapitulates the dynamics of the experimental community writ large. *Within* the development of a single large-scale experiment one finds the internal analogue of familiar processes previously found in the interaction *between* experiments. Now there are internal competition, internal conferences, internal publication, internal critiques of method, internal theoretical assumptions, and internal model building.

By the aggregation, refinement, criticism, and synthesis of arguments the decision to end was reached. The answer to the question, Was this process a *social* one? is a resounding yes. Sociological influences on the conduct of experimentation are visible everywhere, from planning to reception. Competition shapes strategies, forces choices, and can shape the decision to stop now rather than later. Most importantly, though, the social aspect of large-scale experimentation is reflected in the division of analytical labor because that is where the sociological and demonstrative structures of the experiment overlap. Who is concerned about which backgrounds? Which *kind* of evidence will persuade them? What does it take to make a particular subgroup of an experiment give up a certain belief? But

insisting on the overlaid structures of working groups and demonstrations does not force one to take a radically relativist stance toward experimental conclusions.

The whole thrust of this book is to communicate that experiments are about the assembly of persuasive arguments, ones that will "stand up in court" by their exploration of the many articulated branches of the trees of background causal relations. That exploration progresses by constraining results in two broad senses: by improving the directness of an experiment and by rendering the results more stable. And it is in that period of reinforcement of belief that the content of experimentation takes form. By describing science as if it could be divided into an often capricious context of discovery and a rule-governed context of justification, philosophers have obscured the only truly interesting context for laboratory science, the context of real laboratory life that is neither one nor the other.

In denying the old Reichenbachian division between capricious discovery and rule-governed justification, our task is neither to produce rational rules for discovery—a favorite philosophical pastime—nor to reduce the arguments of physics to surface waves over the ocean of professional interests. The task at hand is to capture the building up of a persuasive argument about the world around us, even in the absence of the logician's certainty.

Experiments begin and end in a matrix of beliefs. Some are metaphysical, others programmatic, and yet others no more general than a formal or visualizable model. But laboratory work also exists amid practical constraints that may have little in the way of theory to support them: beliefs in instrument types, in programs of experimental inquiry, in the trained, individual judgments about very local behavior of pieces of apparatus or the tracks, pulses, and counts recorded every day. Unraveling these factors is essentially a historical enterprise, one that follows no fixed set of rules. . . .

3. Carl E. Schorske, "The New Rigorism in the 1940s and 1950s," 1997

Widely acclaimed and internationally honored for his humanistic scholarship, Carl E. Schorske (1915–) was acutely reflexive, examining the ways his own and allied disciplines developed, the ways that they frame intellectual work, and their implicit politics and ethical implications. The author of a classic of modern historical writing, *Fin de Siècle Vienna: Politics and Culture* (1980), he also collected his essays reflecting on the discipline in *Thinking with History: Explorations in the Passage to Modernism* (1998). His teaching and research were particularly skillful in locating cultural productions in both temporal and synchronic fields, something made possible by his remarkable command of other areas, both in the arts and academic disciplines. The essay reprinted here was originally published in a special issue of *Daedalus*, the publication of the American Academy of Arts and Sciences, on "American Academic Culture in Transformation," for which he was one of the two guest editors. He received his B.A. at Columbia University (1936) and his doctorate at Harvard University in 1950 after service in the OSS during World War II. His teaching career began at Wesleyan University in 1946. He moved to Berkeley in 1960, and in 1969 he took a position at Princeton, where he became the Dayton-Stockton Professor until his retirement in 1980. He was in the first group of scholars and artists named MacArthur ("Genius") Fellows.

Carl E. Schorske, "The New Rigorism in the 1940s and 1950s," *Daedalus* 126 (Winter 1997): 289–309. © 1971 by the American Academy of Arts and Sciences, abridged with permission. (Reprinted hardcover, Princeton, NJ, 1998). Further Reading: Thomas Bender and Carl Schorske, eds. *American Academic Culture in Transformation: Four Disciplines / Fifty Years* (Princeton 1998); Julie A. Reuben, *The Making of the Modern University: Intellectual Transformation and the Marginalization of Morality* (Chicago, 1996); David Easton and Corrine S. Schelling, eds., *Divided Knowledge: Across Disciplines, Across Cultures* (Newbury Park, CA, 1991); Marjorie Garber, *Academic Instincts* (Princeton, NJ, 2001); George Steinmetz, ed., *The Politics of Method in the Human Sciences: Positivism and its Epistemological Others* (Durham, NC, 2005).

"My generation was drawn to economics," Robert Solow told the participants at a conference in Pasadena in the voice of his generational culture, "by the depression and to a lesser extent by the war; by the desire to fix things, to do good. Today economists are drawn more by the appeal of scientism; this contributes to the appeal of Gerard Debreu [the mathematical economic theorist]." Is there not a historical connection between these phases? The depression provided not merely a stimulus to critical social thought, but also, through the New Deal, an opportunity for action, a chance "to fix things." Paradoxically, the engagement of university social scientists in the reforming work of the New Deal—a logical extension of their previous academic roles as independent social analysts and critics—began their transformation into technical experts for whom mathematics and statistics were of the highest usefulness. The war, with its expanded demand for purely operational, applied scholarship in the service of relatively uncontested policy goals, likewise increased the imperative for scientific reliability. The original political motivation for the university's intellectuals entering public employment, born of social and international crisis, could easily be transmuted to a career motivation in which the neutral application of technical skills assumed primacy over some normative public-service imperative.

Further encouragement and support for the development of a more astringent and scientific scholarship came to economics from the business community. One of the most fertile research centers for the development of economic theory refined by mathematics and statistics was the Cowles Commission. Its founder, Alfred Cowles, was an investment counselor who, after the crash of 1929, sought ways to improve the sadly deficient means of economic forecasting. After the war, the Cowles Commission became a vital center for new approaches to general economic theory and econometrics. The perfection of forecasting techniques and the fine-tuning of economic policy decisions became the vehicle for a closer involvement of professional economists with business as well as government elites. Central to the pursuit of such expanded social roles was the concentration of the discipline on mathematical model-building and statistical-empirical analysis. The intellectual quest for scientific objectivity and the professional advantages of a value-free neutrality reinforced each other in the establishment of a new methodological consensus as the basis of the discipline. This in turn affected the character of graduate training and increased the mathematical qualifications in student selection. Thanks to a combination of rigorous standards and strict gate control, economics has, from the 1950s until the present, become the strongest of the four disciplines in its intellectual identity and internal cohesion. It has also become the most closely identified with the American elite in government and business.

In political science, the behavioralists, new protagonists of the scientific method, did not achieve as full a victory as did their colleagues in economics. Four subfields that have long characterized political science remained intact and resistant: political theory in the philosophic tradition, international politics, public administration, and American politics. The behavioralists swept only the last field, that of American politics. . . .

For behavioralists, . . . a dual commitment to science as a method and to the democratic system created a problem. The very nature of the scientific method is to affirm the given, the reality it aims to analyze. As Sheldon Wolin has observed, the natural scientist does not criticize nature. If nature fails to conform to his theory, it is his theory that is at fault and must be changed. Traditional political theory, anchored in pre-analytic philosophy, posits a different relation between theory and reality. Such theory, including as it does norms of moral and political judgment, analyzes reality not only for its inner workings but also in its relation to those norms. In the dissonance between the political reality and the claims of the traditional theorist, it is the given reality that must be corrected, not necessarily—or, as in the case of science, not only—the theory by which it is understood. . . .

In the late 1950s and early 1960s the emergence of new political agents, essentially unrepresented in the political structure and its normal electoral processes, triggered a crisis of particular gravity for the behavioralists. The civil rights movement, the anti-war protests, the student rebellion, the explosion of the cities—these historical upheavals of the alienated, all of which were unanticipated under the scientific method, revealed how much the new political science in the 1940s and 1950s had fallen victim to what [Charles] Lindblom calls "Pollyannaism." It had given "benign interpretations" to democratic political systems, defining political parties by reference only to their useful functions, ignoring racial exclusions and exploitation in the governmental and institutional processes. . . .

Behavioralism, while it suffered a loss of the prestige (not to say the primacy) it enjoyed and the enthusiastic élan it generated in the 1960s, continued as a major strand in the discipline. Like economics, it was sustained by the expansion of policy studies in and outside the government, with their stress on technical analytic skills. It also found a new link to economics, whose psychological assumptions and analytic methods were put to work in rational-choice theory. For the pursuit of the increasingly pressing issues of domination, community dysfunction, and racism that had been marginalized by the behavioralists' agenda of systemic affirmation, other less value-neutral approaches to the discipline proved more useable.

Philosophy must share with economics the double distinction of having both recast its intellectual foundations and successfully unified itself as a professional discipline on the basis of that achievement. Epistemological reliability became a primary focus of philosophical work. Once again, as in our social disciplines, science provided the model for the redefinition of the mission and methods of a field of learning. The émigré logical positivists, whose intellectual antecedents in nineteenth-century Central Europe were as much philosophically concerned scientists and mathematicians as scientifically engaged philosophers, gave a powerful impulse to the new movement in America. They were largely Austrians who shared in the English empirical tradition that informed that country's liberal tradition. Their vigorous anti-metaphysical and anti-idealist orientations found ready echoes among American philosophers seeking an autonomous *locus standi* amid the value-laden and ideological forces that had characterized their field.

The same combination (sometimes accompanied by tension) of formal mathematical theory and empirical constituents of scientific thinking that informed and inspired the model-building culture of the new economics appeared in philosophy. The same consequence attended it: the subject matter was reduced to topics that were securely verifiable. The analytic philosophers purged or marginalized traditional areas of concern where values and feelings played a decisive role. Ethics, aesthetics, metaphysics, and politics were all for a time equally excluded as the source of pseudo-problems that could not be formulated or addressed with the rigorous canons of epistemological reliability developed by and out of science. . . .

The second branch of the analytic movement, ordinary-language philosophy, did not center its concerns so completely on the language and logic of science. Yet it too pursued conceptual analysis as its basic aim. Like the logical positivists, its practitioners defined their task as analyzing not the nature of the world but the meanings and validity of the concepts that others used to explore or understand it. With respect to the realm of value that had been so prominent a constituent in traditional philosophy, they held that the philosopher could not tell us what "the good" or "the beautiful" was. Such terms are too emotion-laden to be meaningful. The philosopher could, however, analyze the consistency and logical relations of terms and concepts used in evaluative or "emotive" discourse. . . .

In its New Critical movement, English literature shared the quest for analytic precision with the other three fields examined here. But how different from them is its trajectory of transformation since the 1960s! . . . They have . . . assaulted the very cultural system of European humanism that bound the 1950s scholars—whatever their differences in their critique of their fathers' scholarship—to the past, to each other, and to the academic culture as a whole. In view of the deep and radical break represented by the advent of deconstruction and the culture wars after the 1960s, their own critical turn of the 1940s and 1950s, so fundamental to the other fields, recedes into comparative insignificance.

Should one then speak at all of a turn in early postwar literary scholarship that is the intellectual and historical equivalent of the new centering of economics, political behavioralism, and philosophy on science and its empirical methods? Surely, the New Criticism had some similar characteristics. If so, why did the literary disciplines as redefined under its suzerainty not survive the shocks of the cultural revolutions of the 1960s and 1970s? Why, when economics and philosophy maintained their hegemonies of method by modest adaptations to meet the challenges of new value claims against the given, was the New Criticism, ahistorical though it was, swept away as a quintessential part of the history from which the postmodernists in literature were making a decisive break? . . .

At its most astringent, [this] . . . formalistic kind of criticism freed the literary object from its non-aesthetic context—historical, moral, and psychological. As the literary work of art was distinguished from other kinds of language use by the special techniques that removed it from everyday reality, so the critic's task became a technical one. He would devise formal and structural analytic procedures to illuminate the particularity and protect the autonomy of the literary work. Here *l'art pour l'art*, an originary premise of modernism in art itself when its avant-garde protagonists freed it from social relationships, found its scholarly analogue in a modernist criticism.

As the text was separated from its context in this extreme object-centered form of criticism, so could the critic separate himself from other fields with which literary study had been associated. In this respect, the New Critic pursued for literature the same purging function that the analytic philosopher accomplished by extruding metaphysics and other areas not susceptible to his logical method, or that the economic model builder achieved in shutting out sociological and historical approaches from his discipline. In all cases, the clarification of method brought with it the reduction of the discipline's agenda.

In its purest, formalist variety, the New Criticism also provided the profession with a timely methodological shield of neutrality against the danger of ideological contamination in the era of McCarthy and the Cold War. Even though its genealogy included both English and southern American strains of anti-industrial and anti-democratic conservatism, the New Criticism found in its ahistorical and amoral analytic technique the equivalent to the value-freedom that the social sciences of the 1950s had justified by their adherence to the scientific method and its fidelity to the given.

In its narrow sense, the analytic of the New Criticism that sought to lift the literary artifact clear of all historical and moral imbrication did not succeed in achieving in English departments the clear dominance that was won by the new rigorist approaches in economics and philosophy. Like behavioralism in political science, it succeeded only partly. Within faculties of English the competing viewpoints were too strong for a methodological New Critical victory. The most critical of these countervailing tendencies was a new form of historicism. . . . A series of pathbreaking studies in the new historical vein . . . combined critical analysis of literary works with the configurative perspective and interpretive techniques of the rapidly developing field of intellectual history. Such contextual literary study naturally ran counter to the solipsistic aesthetic practice of hard-core New Criticism. It also resisted the effort of the New Criticism to separate literature from the other disciplines. . . .

The protest movements of America in the 1960s and 1970s struck hard in the universities. Academic culture as a whole had to confront the revolution in values in each of its three dimensions—social, political, and cultural. Within the university an activated and socially expanded student body became a conspicuous protagonist for moral and social claims raised outside it. As the society moved away from the defensive consensual passivity of the first two Cold War decades to open up divisive issues of racial justice, war, sexual freedom, and women's liberation, the university, as befitted its traditional if not usually intended social function of intellectualizing the tensions and conflicts of society, was called upon—not to say pressed—from within and without to address them.

Needless to say, the relevance of the new issues to our four disciplines varied with their subject matter and self-definition. Their responses varied accordingly, yet all had a common problem. All had rebuilt their foundations and postwar professional identities on analytic methods, if to differing degrees. To do so, they had shrunk, marginalized, or extruded some of the value concerns of their traditional subject matter. Now the world of value, an ancient concern of university culture, rose in a "return of the repressed" to raise in new forms normative claims against the expanded dominion of science (or, in English, aesthetic formalism) in the study of man and the fields of social power with which it had, to varying degrees, become associated.

The transformation of the disciplines since the 1970s lies beyond the scope of this essay. But let me offer a few comparative observations on the relation of the disciplines to each other and their adaptation of the shared intellectual platform of the 1950s to the new cultural situation.

The polarity in the human sciences as a whole reveals itself most drastically in the fields of economics and English. No discipline stood its ground more securely through the storm than economics; none was more totally fractured by it than English literature. Economics, in its prewar, descriptive aspect often a center of social criticism, had left that function behind in the analytic consolidation of the 1950s. In a strange reversal of roles, however, younger members of literature departments, abandoning their aesthetic detachment, took up social-critical functions when the New Critical umbrella was shredded by the storm.

The shift in the disciplinary locus of engaged criticism from economics to literature, however limited, was appropriate enough. In the 1930s the discontents were strongly social and economic; in the 1960s, they were social and cultural. In fact, none of the 1960s movements—minority, feminist, or sexual —challenged the economic system. Like the economists themselves, the protest movements recognized, however tacitly, the capitalist free market as part of the factual order of things. The new claimants—women and African-Americans, to name only two—wished not to reshape that order but to gain access to its positions and its bounty. Why should there be a critical economics when the protesters themselves had little interest in economic criticism? . . .

As the most technical of social-scientific disciplines, economics centers its educational function on graduate and professional training and its social function on instrumental service to the elite. English, perhaps the most value-sensitive of the humanistic disciplines, has its principal educational mission in undergraduate education. In the cultural revolution, it has assumed (along with history and anthropology) a new social function: to study and fortify the culture of previously excluded minorities, as until now it has studied and fortified the high culture of Europe and the United States. The university-encouraged demographic change in the student body has created constituencies to support, in effect, a professional diaspora of literary scholars into cultural studies programs. Whether defined by ethnicity, race, or gender, the mission to the underprivileged and excluded weakens the walls that the New Critics built to separate the literary profession from others. . . .

Why should literature departments be a principal locus of the university's attempt to absorb the problem? (History is another such locus, yet that discipline, defined by configurational thinking rather than subject matter or conceptual principles, can absorb value conflict readily.) Literature departments have remained, despite the efforts of aesthetic purists, guardians of cultural values *par excellence* in the age of analysis. . . .

Of all the humanistic disciplines, philosophy had, in its analytic incarnation, most systematically distanced itself from the problems of culture. A preoccupation with epistemological and conceptual problems had led it to abandon the synoptic position it still maintained, based on Dewey's pragmatism, for a place with science at the "hard" end of the spectrum of disciplines. Analytic philosophy had basically disarmed itself to respond to the culture challenges of the 1960s. It could, however, still draw on its Lockean liberal heritage to reactivate its concern for ethics and politics. Opening new relations with the social sciences, analytic philosophers addressed again marginalized areas of value germane to the new claims for political participation, equality, and social justice. John Rawls's pathbreaking *A Theory of Justice* appeared in 1971, the same year that Marshall Cohen and his colleagues founded *Philosophy and Public Affairs,* a significant vehicle for expanding philosophy's public mission. . . .

The polarization of the human sciences today follows, however roughly, the line of division between Anglo-Saxon and continental philosophic cultures. Quite aside from the problems arising from the incorporation of new social groups and non-Western cultures, the legacy of the 1950s was to separate the Anglo-Saxon empirical-scientific strand in American intellectual culture from the continental, value-oriented, and existential strands that were also strong in it. The marginalization of historical and descriptive approaches in economics, of philosophic theory in political science, of historical and psychological interpretation in the New Criticism—all these were cognates of the extrusion of non-Lockean values and existential problems within analytic philosophy. Most of the academic culture in the disciplines we have considered, along with the liberalism in which it was embedded, fell back in the 1950s on its Anglo-Saxon heritage and built, almost unwittingly, a kind of Atlantic wall against continental thought. . . .

For the academy to address the problems of difference, both social and intellectual, that have entered its body, it will have to find some equivalent for the more capacious, less rigoristic disciplinary culture with which this account began.

4. David A. Hollinger, "The Disciplines and the Identity Debates," 1997

It is difficult to gain sufficient historical perspective to write a history of one's own time, but in a regular flow of essays on contemporary intellectual history David Hollinger (1941–) did just that. His work particularly addressed in the American context issues of scientific values, religion, ethnicity, and, as in the case of this essay, the lines of development in the academic disciplines. Many of these essays have been collected in book form, most notably *Science, Jews, and Secular Culture: Studies in Mid–Twentieth Century American Intellectual History* (1996). Hollinger received his B.A. at La Verne College (1963) and his doctorate at Berkeley (1970). He taught at SUNY-Buffalo (1969–77) and the University of Michigan (1977–92) before returning to Berkeley, where he is the Preston Hotchkiss Professor of American History. He has garnered many academic honors and fellowships, including a Guggenheim Fellowship, the Harmsworth Professorship at the University of Oxford, and election to the American Academy of Arts and Sciences.

David A. Hollinger, "The Disciplines and the Identity Debates," *Daedalus* 126 (Winter 1997): 333–51. © 1971 by the American Academy of Arts and Sciences, abridged with permission. (Reprinted hardcover, Princeton, NJ, 1998.) Further Reading: David Hollinger, ed., *The Humanities and the Dynamics of Inclusion* (Baltimore, 2006); and Victoria Bonnell and Lynn Hunt, eds., *Beyond the Cultural Turn* (Berkeley, CA, 1999).

In 1992 *Critical Inquiry* published a special issue on "Identities." In that same year another transdisciplinary journal, *October*, ran a special issue on "The Identity Question." The simultaneous appearance of these special issues is an emblem for two prominent features of American academic history of the last quarter-century. One is the emergence of a robust discourse about "theory" that focused increasingly on the problem of "identity." The second is the proliferation of transdisciplinary forums designed to facilitate and institutionalize this discourse across the lines separating the various social scientific and humanistic disciplines whose members were eager to talk "theory" and "identity." Social scientists and humanists managed to bring the theory wars and identity debates into their disciplinary forums, too, and they continued to perform work that was remote from these wars and debates. But anyone scrutinizing the social sciences and the humanities as a whole during the period from 1970 to 1995 will not get far without confronting these two, closely related developments.

Critical Inquiry is perhaps the most complete embodiment of the basic type of transdisciplinary "professional" journal that has proliferated in the last generation. This Chicago-based quarterly, founded in 1974, draws contributions from philosophers, historians, art historians, musicologists, and film critics as well as from the literary scholars at the journal's center. It is heavily footnoted and is decidedly not afraid of "jargon." *Raritan*, begun at Rutgers in 1980, represents a slightly different variation. It breaks the standard pattern by eschewing footnotes, as does its older and more intellectually conservative counterpart, *The American Scholar*. Prominent among *Raritan*'s editorial advisors and contributors are political scientists and anthropologists as well as humanists from several disciplines. Although neither *Critical Inquiry* nor *Raritan* limit their scope with any particular, topical specialty, many of the transdisciplinary academic journals focus on a narrow cluster of inquiries. Among the most widely appreciated journals with a topical specialty are *American Quarterly*, *Public Culture*, *Diaspora*, and *Modernism/Modernity*. Some of the transdisciplinary academic journals tilt toward the social scientific side of the academy. These include *Social Research*, *Contention*, and *Society*. But the bulk of them can be accurately described as humanities journals, with a largely literary base, that reach out to the most humanistic elements within political science, anthropology, sociology, history, and geography. This description applies to *October*, *Common Knowledge*, *Representations*, *Salmagundi*, and *Social Text*.

The increased role that transdisciplinary journals play in the professional work of members of many humanistic and social scientific disciplines is, in itself, an indicator of the much-noted weakening of disciplinary boundaries and loyalties. Nowhere did the theory wars and the identity debates proceed more fiercely than where academics confronted each other across disciplinary lines. These journals manifest a striking blend of wissenschaftliche and essayistic styles. Indeed, the transdisciplinary journals need to be distinguished from two other kinds of periodicals to which social scientists and humanists regularly contribute.

One is the disciplinary professional journal, of which *Journal of Philosophy*, *American Political Science Review*, *American Economic Review*, and *Proceedings of the Modern Language Association* are widely recognized examples of long-standing. The other is the more "journalistic" periodical that, while also read and written largely by professors, is ostensibly directed toward a wider public. These include *Commentary*, *Harpers*, *The Atlantic*, *The Nation*, *The New Republic*, and, somewhat more academic, *The American Prospect*, *Public Interest*, and *Dissent*, as well as, arguably, even academia's most popular "nonprofessional" periodical, *The New York Review of Books*. These "general circulation" periodicals are distinguished from the trans disciplinary "professional" journals in several crucial respects: they are less controlled by predominantly academic boards, they have fewer footnotes, they are more welcoming of frank political advocacy, and they are much less likely to be counted as "peer reviewed" when deans examine a faculty member's publication record.

Genuinely transdisciplinary academic journals were rare in the 1950s, although literary quarterlies with some pretense to transdisciplinarity were scattered widely around the country. By the 1980s, however, scholars with strong reputations within their own disciplinary communities proved eager to publish their work in the pages of Critical Inquiry and its analogues. And there were oodles of opportunities. . . . *Partisan Review* was an exceptionally important forum from the 1930s through the 1960s, but it prided itself on its nonacademic past. Only gradually did it become what it is today: a not-quite-professional journal written mostly by and for professors, especially of English. Yet *Partisan Review*'s decline in relative significance is partly a consequence of its success and the prodigious increase in competition. This once-great quarterly was originally designed for "writers" and exemplified in the pre-1970 era one of two modes integrated in the plethora of journals founded after 1970. To write for Clement Greenberg's and Lionel Trilling's *Partisan Review* of old was to be "an intellectual," and this, for a great many humanistic and social scientific scholars of the 1970s, 1980s, and 1990s, was an idea not always supported by their disciplinary communities. The second mode was exemplified in the 1950s and 1960s by *American Quarterly*; contributing to it made one a "scholar," though this distinction was not to be limited by any of the traditional disciplines in which the cultural life of the United States was sometimes studied. This journal, founded in 1949, was always self-consciously academic, but its academic ambitions were long caught up in a struggle to make American studies into a full-fledged discipline. *American Quarterly* later outgrew this preoccupation and now functions as a "cultural studies" journal, very much like those whose transcending of any discipline-specific mission is a major point of their existence.

What actually went on the pages of the transdisciplinary journals between 1970 and 1995 is more various and extensive than I will attempt to describe here. But the desire to blend the essayist and wissenschaftliche modes was obviously bound up with a desire to retain something of what Carl Schorske calls the "rigorism" of the academic culture of the 1950s while addressing the normative dimensions of life that "rigorists" in the various disciplines were felt to have slighted. Humanists and social scientists of the post-1970 era proved reluctant to renounce a generically academic ethos but were determined, at the same time, to engage basic theoretical issues about society and culture that belonged exclusively to no discipline. Among these issues, none proved more deeply engaging to more scholars from more disciplines than the issues that came to be flagged with the term "identity."

Central to the identity debates was a drive to come to grips cognitively, and to some extent politically, with a set of enclosures the discovery of which was generally said to be a contribution of the 1960s. These enclosures, felt to have been ignored by the universalist, rationalist, and individualist biases of the previous generation, included the human body, language, class, gender, and, above all, the solidarities and confinements associated with ethnicity and race. Academic intellectuals of the 1940s, 1950s, and even the 1960s were felt by many of their immediate successors to have been incapable of appreciating the enabling function of groups and the diversity and particularity of the life sustained by groups. This incapacity was part of a larger failure to gauge the extent to which human lives were structured by race, class, and gender. The generation that flourished in the mid-century decades had dealt with identity as a matter of individual psychology rather than of collective experience and consciousness. That well-meaning but naive generation—this critique continued—had fallen victim to the conceit of a "God's-eye-view" of the world, and had thus failed to understand that even the most warranted of ideas owed much to the historical circumstances under which they had achieved their legitimacy. Knowledge, like the men and women who made it, needed to be "situated."

These blind spots of the previous generation were being corrected in the early and mid-1970s, often in a spirit of great confidence and conviction. An enhanced appreciation for groups, for particularity, for diversity, and for the power of historical circumstances was enthusiastically registered. Yet this appreciation, as it was developed and specifically applied, ran up against the Enlightenment conscience of many of its own partisans, who were unwilling to renounce altogether the old vision of the epistemic and moral unity of a humankind consisting of intrinsically valuable individual selves. Hence there followed, especially in the 1990s, a flurry of "neo-Enlightenment" attempts to prevent the hermeneutics and politics of identity from obscuring the agency of individuals, the epistemic authority actually earned by scientific communities, the emancipatory potential of intersubjective reason, and the legitimacy and value of civic and moral communities of broad scope transcending ethnoracial lines.

It is "disheartening," noted philosopher John Rajchman while introducing October's special issue on the "identity question," that the rejection of Eurocentric models has sometimes, in its extremity, "reproduced some of the worst aspects of the organicist romantic conception of identity that flourished in Europe in the last century and that was to have catastrophic consequences in this one." The popular notion of "cultural identity" as a replacement for "race" was actually a betrayal of antiracist commitments, argued literary critic Walter Benn Michaels in Critical Inquiry's special issue. This notion served to perpetuate "racial thought," amounting to the self-contradictory "rescue of racism from racists." In a special issue of Social Research in 1994, a group of political scientists embraced what one of their colleagues, Rogers M. Smith, described as "the proper

task for liberals": to refuse the fashionable assertion of "the Enlightenment's demise," and to "see how the liberal project of enhancing human freedom and dignity can be strengthened and extended." Two law professors brought out an anthology entitled After Identity; Michael Dyson, a prominent figure in African-American cultural studies, proclaimed the need for a "post-multiculturalism" designed to respect "the integrity of particularity" while seeking "race-transcending grounds of common embrace"; and my own book, entitled Postethnic America: Beyond Multiculturalism, criticized from a historian's perspective multiculturalism's implicit assigning of cultural identity to individuals on the basis of the physical marks of descent, calling attention to the historical specificity of the ethnoracial categories by which ideas and individuals had come to be "situated." All this casting about for a more critical approach to identity bespeaks a frustration with a discourse in which the "context" for just about everything has turned out to be the salient ethnoracial and gender identities. Hence we may speak of a dynamic of "identity and its discontents," according to which the drive to come to grips with previously ignored or undervalued enclosures came up against residual universalist, rationalist, and individualistic values. . . .

The early and mid-1970s established a unique frame for the engagement of humanistic and social scientific scholars. . . . [We must look at] the simultaneous, often synergistic action of four discrete intellectual forces during exactly these years.

We can call these four movements "Kuhn," antiracism, feminism, and "Foucault." The salient result of their far-from-harmonious commingling was an imperative to "situate" ideas and to recognize the "identity" of people, and to do so in light of certain assumptions about the constituent parts of situations and identities. Each of the four movements had taken on some of its shape during the vaunted decade of the 1960s. It makes some sense to treat these forces as "legacies of the sixties," but today's image of the sixties as a cultural and political monolith—fully as misleading as it is inescapable—risks homogenizing distinctive impulses that were then connected only episodically. Innumerable forces affected academic culture in the early and mid-1970s, including some that had defined themselves in the 1960s. Yet the coming together of these four, I want to suggest, created an intellectual setting decisive for the unfolding of the dynamic before us: the exploring of identity and the discovering of its limits. My point is not to pretend to do justice to these movements, but only to indicate how and when the most prominent features of these movements came into the position that enabled them to contribute to this particular effect. I speak in the tentative voice appropriate to any attempt to analyze the experiences of one's own generation.

By invoking "Kuhn" I intend to refer to the broadly based acceptance, of which Thomas S.

Kuhn's *Structure of Scientific Revolutions* was by far the most influential example, of the dependence of knowledge on the workings of contingent, historically specific human communities. . . .

The intellectual movement to historicize knowledge and the processes of its creation clearly predated the antiestablishment movements of the late 1960s. It was originally rooted in the supremely confident scientific culture of the 1950s of which Kuhn's book of 1962 was a relatively complacent product. Kuhn's protean work was put to service in numerous and scattered causes even during the 1960s, including some associated with the New Left. Eventually, the notion that learned communities had developed paradigms oblivious to the experiences of women and ethnoracial minorities became a common component of critiques of sexism and racism in the scholarly establishment. The additional idea that subaltern subjectivities possess their own ways of "knowing" could also be justified in Kuhnian terms. But we will misunderstand recent history if we forget that a project of situating truth in the historically particular experience of human communities had a formidable trajectory of its own, energized by a largely uncritical respect for the procedures and achievements of existing scientific communities. Only in the 1970s did the "strong program" of the Edinburgh school of sociologists take "science studies" in more "constructivist" directions, and only in that decade did this trajectory become extensively entangled with the trajectories of antiracism, feminism, and Foucault.

Antiracism was a more direct and obvious extension of commitments declared and acted upon with unique intensity in the previous decade. Early in the new decade, antiracism fostered the expansion of affirmative action programs and inspired the proliferation of ethnic and minority studies. It also deepened sensitivity to the ways in which ethnoracial exclusions and inclusions had affected the destiny of individuals and of many ostensibly universalist endeavors, including some fields of scholarly inquiry. In so doing, the antiracism of academic intellectuals, developed in close alliance with national priorities in social policy and with popular interest in the special circumstances of black Americans. . . .

Prevailing senses of what these distinctions meant underwent a change in the early and mid-1970s. The "color-blind" ideologies, according to which ethnoracial distinctions were largely barriers to a viable common life, gave way increasingly to competing ideologies of "color-consciousness." The latter gained credibility partly in response to the failure of empowered whites to act to integrate American society. Affirmations of ethnoracial identity also defended the particularity of cultural initiatives taken within minority ethnoracial communities. Color-blindness threatened to erase historic achievements attained under the ordinance of the color line, however invidiously drawn and manipulated. But color-consciousness increased also in relation to a quest for more aggressive antidiscrimination remedies. No incident in this quest looms larger, in retrospect, than the decision of the Office of Management and Budget in 1977 to instruct the. federal census to count Americans by what amounted to the five classic color categories: black, white, red (American Indian), yellow (Asian or Pacific Islander), and brown (Hispanic white). The official consolidation of an ethnoracial pentagon was designed, of course, to facilitate the enforcement of voting rights and laws against employment discrimination. But this physically-based system of classification was easily conflated with culture at a time when educators were developing programs designed to teach and study cultural diversity. The panorama of cultural diversity could be conveniently reduced to the five parts of the pentagon, which came eventually to be denoted as African-American, Asian-American, European-American, Latino, and Indigenous. The "essentialism" that made culture a function of biology was widely criticized by many, including "minority" scholars. But the use of the ethnoracial pentagon as a basis for organizing the appreciation of cultural diversity proved hard to resist. It had a profound effect on colleges and universities and was reflected in the structure and title or a great expanse of new academic units. A person of Chinese, Japanese, Korean, or Cambodian descent, whatever his or her self-perception, discovered that he or she actually possessed an "Asian-American identity."

Identity by "gender" also proved to be a matter of intense discussion, going well beyond traditional talk of "roles" for men and women. Attention to gender expanded rapidly in the wake of the feminist movement, giving additional structure to efforts to clarify identity and to determine just what kinds of location were implied when one asked where somebody—especially a maker of ostensibly universal truth-claims—was "situated." Although feminist struggles against sexism derived some inspiration from antiracism and gained some popular support through the analogy between racism and sexism, feminism is a much more distinctly "seventies" phenomenon. Feminism owed much to events of the 1960s, including the publication of Betty Friedan's *The Feminine Mystique* (1963) and the founding of the National Organization for Women (1966), but the bulk of feminism's crucial political and theoretical articulations date from the following decade. *Ms.* magazine was founded in 1972. There emerged in the early and mid-1970s a succession of popular feminist works of increasing theoretical ambition and sophistication, ranging from Kate Millett's *Sexual Politics* (1970) to Adrienne Rich's *Of Woman Born* (1976). Most of these works were produced outside academia, but the founding of *Signs* in 1975—yet another transdisciplinary academic journal dating from this period—is a helpful marker of the emergence of feminism as an academic presence.

The meaning of the gender distinction was debated in terms that overlapped to some extent with the simultaneous discussion of ethnoracial distinctions. Differences between the world of men and the world of women could be construed as derived ultimately from biology, enormous in magnitude, and destined to remain in place even after women were liberated from the oppression that men had visited upon them. Or, the essential difference between male and female could be understood as not extending beyond sexual reproduction, in which case most of what passed for "masculine" and "feminine" were cultural constructions, at best, and, at worst, barriers serving to keep women from living lives as full as those routinely available to men. Disputes between what were crudely called "difference feminists" and "sameness feminists" were given a focal point in 1982 by Carol Gilligan's *In a Different Voice*, which argued that deeply structural differences between men and women could be discerned even in the moral reasoning characteristic of boys and girls. As feminism came to be informed by poststructuralism, these controversies took the form of more pointed debates over the nature and sustaining conditions of the female "subject" (and of the male). A point of these debates, as Judith Butler described it, is to ponder "what happens to the subject and to the stability of gender categories when the epistemic regime of presumptive heterosexuality is unmasked as that which produces and reifies these ostensible categories of ontology?"

Butler spoke self-consciously in the idiom of Michel Foucault, which brings into play the fourth of our synergistic elements. In using "Foucault" to indicate the fourth of these trajectories, I intend simply to allude to the poststructuralist ideas developed by French theorists that were widely disseminated in the United States. The impact of the abortive Paris revolution of 1968 on Foucault and his comrades enables one to construe this trajectory, too, as a "legacy of the sixties." But the peculiar Frenchness of the political dynamics of poststructuralism—entailing a reaction against varieties of Marxism less deeply rooted in the American intelligentsia—renders this "sixties connection" less vital to any account of the generational pushes and pulls of American academic culture. The sudden and commanding influence of the French theorists in the United States is one of the most chronologically concentrated of the events that now enable us to see the early and mid-1970s as a distinctive historical moment. Some of the earliest works by American scholars advancing these ideas were, like literary critic Paul de Man's *Blindness and Insight* (1971), absorbed primarily by a narrowly defined disciplinary constituency, but the French texts translated into English during these years were widely perceived to be prodigious in their implications for an enormous swath of social scientific and humanistic endeavors. This was especially so in the case of Foucault himself. . . .

Foucault and his coworkers accelerated the movement Kuhn had stimulated from "objectivist" to "constructivist" theories of knowledge. Any piece of knowledge was for Foucault not only a construction, but the embodiment of a certain dispersion of power. He spoke not of knowledge in relation to power, but of a single formation, "power/knowledge." Intersubjective reason, long regarded as a means of human liberation, was, for Foucault, a frequent instrument of domination. He declared, in a much-quoted aphorism, that "knowledge is not made for understanding; it is made for cutting." A second relevant consequence of French theory was to undercut the faith in human autonomy and individual agency that many American intellectuals had sustained through the 1960s. Individuals achieve their "subjectivity" in their capacity as sites for the operation of categories of language that act prior to an individual's will. . . .

Foucault, feminism, antiracism, and Kuhn thus together fostered the exploration of identity that "problematized" (as it was often put, to the horror of those valuing "good English") a number of ideas that the previous generation rarely felt obliged to defend. The ensuing debates drew heavily on the energies of historians, anthropologists, and sociologists, among others. . . .

One could write an exceedingly detailed history of this entire episode without mentioning a single economist. This exclusion applies even to those economists who sometimes write about large and hard-to-solve problems for transdisciplinary audiences, such as Robert Heilbroner, Albert Hirschman, and Amartya Sen. This is neither to disparage economists nor to congratulate them. The clarity of disciplinary boundaries is sharper in the case of economics than in any other of the social sciences and humanities. . . .

English is at the other extreme. In no other major discipline, including even sociology, anthropology, and history, did transdisciplinary journals play remotely as large a role in a "peer-reviewed" discourse as they did in English. Repeatedly, it was professors of English who founded, edited, and supervised these projects, and it was they who did most of the writing. It was professors of English, moreover, who dominated the proliferating humanities institutes of which the transdisciplinary journals were the textual counterpart. Literary scholars took the lead in affirming the importance of gender and ethnoracial minority cultures as matrices for the production of literature, and they took no less of a lead in the demonstration of the constructed character of any and all identities. . . .

What enabled literary critics to talk "professionally" about almost anything they pleased—to be "real intellectuals" while colleagues in other disciplines risked becoming "mere technicians"—was the textualization of the world. As more and more objects of inquiry were said to be "discursively constructed," the more sense it made for an expanding panorama of objects to be studied by specialists in discourse. "The special analytical skills" of literary scholars, as Gallagher puts it, were felt "applicable to all cultural phenomena, and only unadventurous critics would confine themselves to conventional literary texts." . . .

From this dilemma political scientists were free, at least when it came to the identity debates. The discipline of political science had, among its classic fields, political theory. For political theorists, the identity debates were a standard professional activity. Hence the writings of Seyla Benhabib, William Connelly, Bonnie Honig, George Kateb, Judith Shklar, Michael Walzer, and Bernard Yack, among others, were able to speak to an audience beyond their own discipline even as they evaluated the competing claims of "communitarianism" and "liberalism." Unlike their counterparts in English, however, most of the political theorists operated within a relatively narrow, canonical frame. . . . The political theorists were a distinctive and often isolated subgroup within the discipline of political science. They did not . . . constitute the core of the discipline. During exactly the years in which the dynamic of identity and its discontents was being played out, the attention of the discipline was more often captured, as Smith points out, by another of the discipline's most sharply defined subgroups, the rational-choice theorists.

The rational-choice segment of political science has been as far removed from the identity debates as have been the model-building economists. Arguments about the merits and drawbacks of both fall into similar patterns. Critics accuse the rational choicers of failing to illuminate anything of genuine significance to the study of politics, just as model-building economists are sometimes accused . . . of avoiding the complexities of the real world. . . .

Political science thus presents two antithetical faces to the identity debates. It has successfully professionalized these debates in a way that has proved difficult for English. On the other hand, political science has altogether avoided these debates, in the manner of economics. Neither of these persona can be credibly attributed to philosophy.

Philosophy presents a paradox more striking than any presented by the other . . . disciplines considered here. It polices its borders much more vigilantly than do most of the humanities and social sciences and maintains an image of great austerity. The vast majority of its practitioners remain aloof from transdisciplinary chit-chat and are prone, in private moments, to make exceedingly uncharitable comments about their colleagues in other disciplines. . . .

It was the fastidious disciplinary culture of philosophy that served up, in [Richard] Rorty, one of the most loquacious and listened-to voices in the identity debates. Yet the more central Rorty became to the theoretical conversations of non-philosophers, the more he voluntarily separated himself from most philosophers and the more the latter were glad to return the favor. While the author of *Contingency, Irony, and Solidarity* (1989) now strikes many philosophers as good stock gone to seed—having transformed himself from a respectable analytical philosopher into just another literary essayist who could quote Continental thinkers—Rorty's extensive constituency throughout the humanities and the social sciences has welcomed the discipline-honed clarity he has brought to conversations bedeviled by pretentious obscurity. In his eagerness to distance himself from an epistemological tradition he thinks bankrupt, Rorty may underestimate the intellectual capital he has inherited from a rigorous disciplinary tradition.

Rorty's case can be instructively contrasted to that of Thomas Kuhn, perhaps the most influential single thinker in the entire debate over the character and boundaries of epistemic enclosures. But was Kuhn, news of whose death arrives as I write these lines, "a philosopher?" Kuhn began as a historian (although trained, before that, as a physicist) and was gradually, if at first grudgingly, welcomed into philosophy while Rorty was finding, and being shown, the exit. Kuhn fled from the transdisciplinary discussion of his own work and in the process identified himself less as a historian and more as a philosopher. Analytic philosophers embarrassed by Rorty's frequent indiscretions could trust Kuhn to behave. Yet Kuhn's most creative work was accomplished when he was straddling the line between philosophy and history, building on the intellectual capital he had derived from his work as a historian, taking chances of the sort he later eschewed. . . .

Area Studies

5. William Nelson Fenton,
Area Studies in American Universities, 1947

Area studies entered the liberal arts curricula as interdisciplinary programs during the Cold War era. They were introduced as responses to real or anticipated threats to national security. Although academic efforts to increase knowledge about Russia preceded the Cold War, rising tensions with Soviet Russia and perceived dangers from Fidel Castro's Cuba brought substantial foundation and federal funding for Russian and Latin American studies. The Vietnam War brought South Asian studies, with African and Middle Eastern programs to follow. Important lobbying in Washington for higher education produced largess, resulting in the growth of coordinating agencies and associations on Dupont Circle in Washington, D.C. Faculty members with relevant interest and expertise joined the new interdisciplinary projects, many eagerly sensing a new departure for academic inquiry. In contrast to earlier interdepartmental courses with a central idea or theme in the humanities, such as Western Civilization in the 1920s at Columbia or the postwar Princeton Humanities 101–02 on human freedom, area studies were geographically centered and called upon faculty participants from many fields in the social sciences, the humanities, and the biological sciences.

The forerunner and in some ways prototype for area

studies was introduced during World War II by the United States Army. To meet the need for soldiers trained in a foreign language and acquainted with the culture of enemy or occupied territory, the Army Specialized Training Program was established. The program began in early 1943 and was closed down in February 1944 because of unforeseen manpower shortages that necessitated more ground troops. At its peak, the courses on 227 campuses enrolled upwards of 140,000 soldiers. After the war the impact of area studies was strong enough to leave some faculty hoping for more of the same. But attempts to perpetuate these broad cultural inquiries met with considerable faculty and administrative opposition.

This appraisal of area programs was conducted by William Nelson Fenton (1908–2005). His review emphasized the obstacles met by postwar area studies proponents and former ASTP faculty, which presaged the difficulties met by area studies initiatives in the late 1950s and 1960s. One may note the contrast between the difficult implementation of area studies and the relative ease and necessity of interdisciplinary inquiries in the physical and natural sciences.

Fenton was a Dartmouth graduate with a doctorate from Yale and an esteemed anthropologist of Native American culture. During World War II he was connected with the Smithsonian War Committee and with the National Research Council. He closed his career as Distinguished Professor Emeritus at SUNY-Albany.

William Nelson Fenton, *Area Studies in American Universities* (Washington, 1947), 80–82, 86–88. Reprinted with permission from the American Council on Education, © 1947. Further reading: Louis E. Keefer, *Scholars in Foxholes: The Story of the Army Specialized Training Program in World War II* (Jefferson, NC, 1988); Henry L. Stimson and McGeorge Bundy, *On Active Service in Peace and War* (New York, 1948): 458–61; Robert R. Palmer, Bell I. Wiley, and William R. Keast, *United States Army and World War II, The Army Ground Forces, Procurement and Training of Ground Combat Troops* (Washington, 1948): 28–39, 76, 88, 117–19, 200, 475–76. An important description of later developments in area studies is David L. Szanton, "The Origin, Nature, and Challenges of Area Studies in the United States," in *The Politics of Knowledge: Area Studies and the Disciplines,* ed. David L. Szanton, University of California Press / University of California International and Area Studies Digital Collection, Edited vol. 3, 2003, available at http://repositories.cdlib.org/uciaspubs/edited volumes/3/1.

In its ultimate effects upon the organization and conduct of instruction in the social sciences and related disciplines in American colleges and schools, the idea of integrating the study of all pertinent aspects of the culture of a given geographic area, as attempted during the war in one segment of the Army Specialized Training Program and in the Army's Civil Affairs Training Program, may be of great significance. . . .

The Army Specialized Training Program, established in 1943 and eventually installed in 227 universities and colleges, was for enlisted men of substantial intellectual ability and academic attainment who volunteered for it, and might consist of one or several successive three-month terms of instruction. . . .

IMPLICATIONS FOR FUTURE AREA STUDIES

The sudden demise of ASTP in the winter of 1944, which closed European programs but allowed Far Eastern programs to linger through another session, and the prolongation of Far Eastern CATS projected the university faculties into a dither of postwar planning. The thinking anent area studies relates to a general foment for reform in the curriculum of liberal colleges. It touches the question of the aims of general education, and it interposes the triangle of liberal-professional-vocational education, raising the spectre of training versus education. When ASTP withdrew from the colleges, the faculties of some institutions returned to old loyalties, revealing that ASTP was to them just something to keep the college open during the war; but in other places the permanent faculty of area-study programs favored carrying over the better features of the wartime training programs and improving less successful aspects for future education.

Committees on area studies were in being at many institutions. Ordinarily they included prominent members of the wartime area staff but support came from other quarters—from members of previous committees to reform the curriculum, from members of "Council" committees on integration of social sciences, on the humanities, and on American studies, from professors of international relations, and often enough from a liberal president. The great enthusiasm of temporary appointees, who were brought in for the program, may be discounted, but we noted that the more successful teachers were retained as research associates to prepare teaching materials toward future area studies or were appointed to permanent positions in some departments.

Committees on postwar planning existed at all levels of education. Several universities had a committee in the arts college, another in the graduate school, and sometimes an over-all committee on postwar education. All of these groups were in some way concerned with area studies. The most powerful committee, and in some ways the most conservative, is the committee on educational policy, which sits to hear the case for integrated area studies. It is sometimes called the curriculum committee or the committee on the course of study, and often enough is dominated by guardians of existing academic organizations—the dean, heads of departments, and senior members of the faculty. These men have a stake in fields and in their organizations, and they are justifiably concerned over further fragmentation of their staff to new experiments. The deans are skeptical of new fads and fear superficiality, but they are often open to new ideas and are interested in what the other colleges are doing.

AREA AS AN INTEGRATING CONCEPT

Integrated area study threatens the regular departmental organization of the university since by its very nature it calls for a realignment of subject-matter fields and methodologies in order to concentrate them on the total civilization of a region. It joins language learning to a cultural core which imparts new meanings to unconscious behavior patterns. By pointing to overlaps in the existing curriculum of concurrent courses and by revealing lacunae that exist between the disciplines, integrated area study accelerates the trend toward fewer courses in the liberal college. All threats to the reduction of the staff and the number of courses with a resultant drop in enrollments, loss of book fees, and decline in budget are resisted by heads of departments.

The very methodology of integrated area study constitutes a challenge. In taking a functional view of contemporary civilizations, it jeopardizes the strong position which the historical method holds in academic thinking, as evidenced by course organization and sequences; it offers concentration on the present situation with its latent historicity in place of long developmental curricula running from Aristotle to modern times, and it calls on the method of the culture historian to develop the major themes in the civilization, delving deep enough into the past only to make the present understandable. Besides relying heavily on the methods of the functional disciplines, integrated area study utilizes the comparative method, continually drawing contrasts between the culture under study and our own. The development of an intercultural viewpoint contributes to objectivity in either direction. Finally, in first focusing the study of society on the local group and then branching out to the regional culture, integrated area study follows the method of ethnography which assumes that concentration on the community will produce the deep understanding of culture that makes the spatial extensions of culture comprehensible. Culture is the central concept of anthropology, the study of man, as region is the central concept of geography. These combine in area study. Integrated area study, then, may be defined as the focusing of all the disciplinary competences (geography, history, economics, language, and literature, philosophy, political science, and the like) upon a cultural area for the purpose of obtaining a total picture of that culture. A discipline must have a methodology and a body of knowledge. The latter is assured, and the former derives from the methodologies of participating competences which they do not possess uniquely. Certainly meeting a foreign culture through the offices of several branches of learning is a broader educational experience than via any one of them, and does not preclude concentration in any single discipline at the graduate level. Whatever bent the scholar follows, he will share with his fellow students of a major cultural area a common interest which previously has existed informally outside the university in organizations of Americanists, Hispanists, and Orientalists. Let the future answer the question: Does integrated area study qualify as a discipline? . . .

STAFF

Administrations have been awaiting the return of their staffs from wartime assignments and from Washington before taking the next step in area studies. In four years away from the universities the prodigals have become something else; a few have flown to better jobs, and many have returned with new ideas. Field experience is an important qualification in an area teacher and so is knowledge of the language; but yet training in a discipline enabled the academic to outstrip the untrained native of the area.

However, the value of having a representative of the culture at hand, especially if he also possesses academic competence, was demonstrated time and again when academic methods failed to extract from existing literature realia of the culture. In approaching new areas the academic will find informants of great usefulness for research, especially if they are unsophisticated, while a more articulate person will be wanted for teaching purposes. But no academic will be willing to try area teaching without assurance about his status. He will want relief from teaching load during peak periods in the area schedule, and he will need credit toward promotions for the greater effort required in preparation and conduct of area seminars. Time for reflective study and travel abroad will enable him to master the area materials in more than one discipline and to write the necessary books; periodic field work will help him to bring the living society into the classroom. Clearly this is a program for younger men who are free of past commitments.

The problem of staffing differs between areas. Our universities have developed scholars of distinctive attainment in all fields relating to Euro-American culture, but as yet scholars have to be developed in sufficient numbers for the Far East. There are some now available for the Soviet Union. Until scholars are developed for little known areas, programs must be postponed to the graduate research level.

INTEGRATION

It is doubtful that the enthusiasm for faculty cooperation will persist. Yet, as the Cornell Russian experiment demonstrated, the integration that is necessary to the broad view in the area approach can be effected by combining concurrent courses and personnel typical of departmental disciplines within the undergraduate college. A program of concurrent courses puts the least strain on the college. It has the advantage of several points of view and continuity of personnel. With careful planning the schedules may be made to dovetail. The weaknesses are duplications, separatism, and leaving integration to the student. It omits all the fields that lie between the disciplines.

Between concurrent courses and a sequence of courses there is little choice. While not given in a single year, the sequence disturbs less the normal proportions of courses in the college, allowing two courses in the junior year and three the senior year, following on certain foundation courses at lower class levels. It has the same weaknesses as the program of concurrent courses in a single year plus one other. While it may be expected that students have mastered certain disciplines, say geography of the area, experience in ASTP showed that students forget and fail to relate separable units of a sequence.

The single integrated course, given as a "jumbo" or double course in the junior and senior years, capped by a senior seminar and an essay, seems best adapted for capturing the better features of wartime cooperation and joint teaching. Whether it is better for a single individual to carry the course clear through at the introductory level or introduce a series of lectures, with attendant difficulties of accommodation, remains for future experiment. Many academics are opposed to the principle of briefing another man to present an unfamiliar field. Men of broad methodological background have carried whole courses on the less-complicated civilizations. But where several viewpoints are present in the staff the method of taking their discussions to the classroom seems better suited to presenting a major area. Cultures differ as to their integration and possibly as to level of difficulty, and no single outline of cultural materials will do for all. The single integrated course seeks the pattern in the particular regional culture and then works out a method of teaching it.

Certain points of view and certain competences seem basic to area studies: anthropology's concept of culture, geography's concept of region, social relations, human organization for economic enterprise, government, communication, literature, and relations with the supernatural, and withal a keen sense of how these things came to be. Clearly these are but facets of a single whole. The language and the culture go together. . . .

Black Studies

6. Martin Kilson, "Reflections on Structure and Content in Black Studies," 1973

Martin Kilson (1931–) was one of the first academic people to diagram or analyze the structure and purposes of black studies in the college curriculum. He not only discussed the proportion of African-American students in white colleges who may major in black studies but also compared black studies with other ethnic programs. Kilson was a professor of government at Harvard (1967–2000), where he was the first tenured African American and became the Frank G. Thomson Professor of Government.

Martin Kilson, "Reflections on Structure and Content in Black Studies," *Journal of Black Studies* (March 1973): 297, 300–301, 303–10, 312–13. Copyright © 1973. Reprinted by permission of Sage Publications Inc. Further reading: *The Journal of Blacks in Higher Education,* especially the Autumn 2004 issue.

Perhaps the first thing to note with regard to the nature of Black Studies is that those concerned with these studies today stand squarely on the shoulders of the precursors in the field of Black Studies. Nothing is more untrue than the notion of militant students and teachers involved in Black Studies thinking that what they began to call "Black Studies" several years ago was something they invented.

In truth, there is virtually no area, field, or subject related to the history, sociology, culture, politics, and anthropology of either Old World—Africa—or New World—America and other Western Hemisphere—black peoples that has not received major scholarly and intellectual attention between the late nineteenth century and the end of World War II. Numerous scholars of highest skill and sensitive humanity, both white and black scholars, contributed to the study of these facets of black peoples and societies during this period. . . .

One notable feature of the black and white precursors of Black Studies . . . is that they were all well-trained scholars. They all pursued graduate studies and doctorates. None of these precursors was a charlatan or a dilettante. Nor was any of them an ideologue, or a politician sporting intellectual garb. They all were, to a man, either liberal or progressive, and a few were radical. But they knew that the scholarly study of blacks required special skills and a uniquely disciplined frame of mind—an outlook that enabled the scholar, white or black, to surmount his own prejudices and ideological proclivities in behalf of disciplined knowledge. One of these precursors, W.E.B. DuBois, was indeed a very political man; yet he recognized the need to keep politics in its proper place when he sought the scholarly study of social and historical problems of Afro-Americans.

These attributes associated with the pioneers in the study of blacks must be the basis of the organization of Black Studies curricula today. Thus, only persons of tested scholarly abilities and training should be involved in the organization and administration of Black Studies curricula. This means, of course, that placing undergraduate students on the governing bodies, committees or departments, concerned with Black Studies curricula is out of order. A number of colleges and universities—including Harvard University—have allowed undergraduate executive roles in administering Black Studies curricula. Quite frankly, this is utter nonsense. With rare exceptions, no undergraduate is ready to exercise scholarly authority in any field—he would not be a student if he were—and certainly not in as complex an interdisciplinary field as Black Studies. . . .

I am not myself opposed to black militancy—let me make this clear: it has its place in a racist society like ours, which has been cruel and vulgar in its social and political relationships with blacks; in this society, militant pressures are required to help change behavior and institutions in more progressive and humane directions. But once militancy has made its point, it should, so to speak, mind its business. What I am saying, in short, is that once militant students helped modify the limitations in college curricula with regard to the study of blacks, these militant students should return to being students. . . .

What I mean to suggest . . . is that the best approach to a field of such interdisciplinary complexity as Black Studies is through one of the established academic and technical disciplines like economics, anthropology, sociology, psychology, and so on. I would suggest that no interdisciplinary subject like Asian Studies, African Studies, Middle Eastern Studies, American Studies, and Black Studies (each of which intersects all major academic and technical disciplines) can evolve into a scholarly and intellectually viable field without the curricular control of an established discipline. Thus, if students are allowed to approach an intrinsically interdisciplinary subject like Black Studies without the curricular control of a discipline like economics, psychology, and so on, these students will be academically and technically diffuse and disoriented. They will be jack-of-all-disciplines, so to speak, but master of none. In a word, they will be dilettantes at best, and charlatans at worst.

Indeed, it would be tragic for the current generation of Afro-American students, nearly seventy-five percent of whom are now in white colleges, to have them become victims of academically and technically diffuse Black Studies curricula or programs. To allow students in Black Studies programs to pick, for example, in a hit-and-miss fashion among two black economic courses, two black sociology, two literature, one philosophy, one anthropology, two political science, two history, and so on, and then to graduate these students at the bachelor degree level as presumably qualified to apply social science analysis or to apply to graduate schools in history, economics, sociology, and the like is to perpetrate a cruel hoax on the black students. Unfortunately, this situation is now widespread in colleges with Black Studies curricula. But in view of the present small skill pool of professionally and technically trained Afro-Americans, the black community simply cannot afford this mode of organizing a Black Studies curriculum. . . .

Now let me be more concrete about how the interdisciplinary subject of Black Studies should be controlled by the established disciplines when shaping a curriculum. First, the principles underlying my view of the proper curriculum: The principle I employ is that of tracking; a student majoring in Black Studies should be "tracked" through an established discipline like, say, economics, in such a fashion that he would be in effect fulfilling two majors or concentrations. One major, dealing with the established discipline of economics, would require the student to meet at least the basic set of courses required of all economics majors. . . . The second major, dealing with Black Studies, would require the student to take courses which apply economic analysis to problems related to blacks—like welfare economics, labor economics, urban investment policies, economics of urban education, and related courses. Thus, with this mode of organizing a major in Black Studies, you can ensure against producing dilettantes and students ill-prepared for graduate studies; even if they do not pursue graduate studies, they would at least have a technical basis of some worth in a given discipline, rather than the diffuse set of "skills" provided by the catch-as-catch-can type of Black Studies curriculum I referred to above, which is far too prevalent today.

Of course, what is primary to the type of Black Studies curriculum I am proposing is that a student must decide first of all in favor of a particular discipline. He must be required to decide after his first year whether he wishes to be a sociologist, economist, political scientist, or whatever, and on the basis of this choice he has his curriculum in Black Studies "tracked" through an established discipline. To take another concrete example of tracking a student through a discipline within an overall Black Studies curriculum or program, let us say a student decides to be a sociologist. This student should first be required to fulfill at least the basic prerequisites required of sociology majors: thus, he should take statistics, social theory (e.g., Pareto, Parsons, Weber, Durkheim, Marx, Simmel, Merton, and so on), political sociology, social structure (e.g., kinship, formal organization, and the like), and demography. Solid grounding in these or other basic sociological subjects would be a prerequisite for the courses that apply sociology to the study of blacks. Once this is obtained—and some of these prerequisites could be taken simultaneously with courses specifically related to blacks—the student pursues a range of courses, available both in the Black Studies program or department and in other departments that relate to blacks. These courses might include demography of the ghetto, urbanization in the ghetto, Afro-American family structures, sociology of Afro-American health, deviant behavior among Afro-Americans, Afro-American leadership patterns, Afro-American voluntary organizations, and so on. . . .

I consider it much more desirable intellectually and academically that the scholars who teach in the Black Studies curriculum be represented in all the established departments like classics, comparative literature, philosophy, and economics, and that to the extent there is a Black Studies department at all, it will be a composite body of those scholars who are in the established departments but teach a Black Studies curriculum. Perhaps the best way to realize this is to adopt the policy of joint academic appointments for scholars in the established departments who teach in the Black Studies curriculum. This is quite feasible at the wealthier colleges or universities, though again at the average college what is called the Black Studies department will be in effect a committee of scholars who teach in the established departments but also participate in the Black Studies curriculum.

But, of course, the important matter is not whether the Black Studies curriculum is housed in a department of its own, realized through coordination of existing departments and divisions or through some other means. The significant issue is to guarantee that students—especially those marked for graduate schools and professional schools—who pursue Black Studies are simultaneously grounded in an established academic and technical discipline. A Black Studies curriculum, like other interdisciplinary curricula (American Studies, Asian Studies) cannot stand alone: it must, so to speak, be clothed in the tested scholarly and technical garment of an established discipline.

WHO SHOULD MAJOR IN BLACK STUDIES?

First of all, there should be no political or other extraneous qualification for majoring in Black Studies. Efforts by authoritarian and xenophobic militant black students to discourage white students from pursuing Black Studies—which occurs at some colleges—must be criticized and opposed. Although some black militants prefer the fantasy world on which their political style thrives, it is clear that blacks and whites in American society have a profound interconnection, and neither white racist nor black racist ideology can alter this. Happily, this is already becoming more apparent to some militant black students at white colleges who several years ago shed associations with white peers, but today are restoring these relationships, which, of course, are fundamental to the black students' efforts to gain the optimum benefit from white colleges. This trend, however, is far from complete, and currently there are many black students who persist in imposing a separatist pattern upon their education at white colleges, and especially upon Black Studies departments or programs. But this must be openly and firmly opposed by all scholars who take the life of the mind seriously. . . .

Another aspect of who should take Black Studies is the issue of what proportion of black students in white colleges should major in this curriculum. Some militants among Negro students and teachers appear to support the majority of black students concentrating in Black Studies. This would be an enormous error, I think. We now have the majority

of blacks in college attending white institutions, and this situation will persist. The opportunity this affords Afro-Americans at first-class institutions . . . to major in the scientific and technological fields like chemistry, engineering, architecture, computer sciences, and biology should not be lost because of some ideological and psychological proclivity toward Black Studies. As Professor Arthur Lewis . . . has pointed out . . . the road to the top and middle jobs in American society is through the sciences and technologies, not through the humanities and social sciences, of which Black Studies is, of course, a part. Professor Lewis also noted that today Afro-Americans, while twelve percent of the American population, hold only two percent of the top or elite jobs in the society and only one percent of the middle-level jobs, but some sixty percent of the lower-level jobs. The black community can change this weak position in the structure of jobs (and thus of power) in American society only by entering in much larger numbers the technological and scientific fields. No amount of psychological, therapeutic, or symbolic dependence upon Black Studies should be permitted to prevent this development; if it does, the road to group suicide awaits us, for in the coming decades American society will be more, not less, dependent upon scientific and technological skills. . . .

Thus, one might ask me who, then, should major in Black Studies, since I have excluded a sizable chunk of Afro-American students from this major. My reply is that those special students, black and white, who have a serious appreciation of and good aptitude for the social sciences and the humanities are the ones who should major in Black Studies. . . .

Indeed, at numerous colleges and universities white faculty and administrators have been far too ready to accept the most outrageous demands from militant black students and teachers with regard to Black Studies. This behavior by white faculty must be seen, in fact, as blatantly patronizing, comparable to one's tolerance of the antics of a child. What is equally disturbing, the black militant students and teachers in white colleges quickly accept the concessions granted by white faculty. Militant blacks at white institutions have, it seems, a pathetic dependence upon the psychologically satisfying but academically disastrous concessions they wrench from white faculty and administrators. I would like to conclude with a warning, if I may. Unless this psychological immaturity, nearly endemic to the militants in the Black Studies movement, soon ceases, a large section of blacks who seek intellectual status will be relegated to the backwaters or the trash-heap of American academic and intellectual life. Perhaps, alas, this is the unconscious wish—a kind of death wish—of large segments of militant black students and intellectuals. Lacking the stamina and special stuff required of first-class students and scholars, these militant black students and teachers sport a fashionable and psychologically gratifying militant style in order to achieve a protected and segregated (but academically undemanding and inferior) educational niche called a Black Studies program.

7. Manning Marable, "We Need New and Critical Study of Race and Ethnicity," 2000

Manning Marable (1950–) began his teaching and writing during the maturing and embedding of black studies in college curricula. By 2000 he was aware of the program's limitations, especially its rather self-protective or distant relationship to other minority studies, which themselves were equally distanced by their specialized concerns. In this broad review Marable invited a new century of scholars from different curricular compass points to reexamine their premises. Consider, he asks, issues of ethnicity being studied advantageously in tandem with the older problems of race. He takes up the phrase "racial ethnicity" and exhibits persuasive immigration and demographic statistics to frame his theme. Are there intersecting roles or common social purposes to be studied by scholars of racial minority groups and of younger cultural or ethnic minority groups? Such questions have not been easily approached, let alone answered. Marable stresses the multiple dimensions of his proposal, their inescapable complexities, and their reach into issues of class and gender. Still, his working idea of "racial ethnicity" invited colleagues from all of the social sciences to enter into interdisciplinary conversations.

After a bachelor's degree at Earlham College (1971) and his Ph.D. at the University of Maryland (1976), Marable taught at several institutions where he chaired sociology or black studies departments including at Fisk, Colgate, Ohio State, and Colorado at Boulder. In 1993 he assumed a professorship and founding directorship of the Institute for African-American Studies at Columbia.

Manning Marable, "We Need New and Critical Study of Race and Ethnicity," *Chronicle of Higher Education,* February 25, 2000, B4–7. Reprinted with kind permission from the author. Marable's most recent book is *Living Black History* (New York, 2006). Further reading: his *Dispatches from the Ebony Tower: Intellectuals Confront the African American Experience* (New York, 2000), from which this essay was adapted; *Race, Reform, and Rebellion* (Jackson, MS, 1984), *Black American Politics* (New York, 1985), *W. E. B. Du Bois, Black Radical Democrat* (Boston, 1986). See also V, 6.

When Nelson Mandela was elected president of a newly democratic South Africa in 1994, an entire period of racial history came dramatically to an end. Since the 1960's, the United States has witnessed the rise of an affluent African-American middle class and the dismantling of the last vestiges of legal segregation. In Europe, growing numbers of ethnic and racial minorities have had an impact on governments and political parties on both the left and the right. Such recent historical events illustrate how the meaning of race and the way it is expressed through political power are being rapidly transformed across the world. But while a great deal of scholarly attention has gone into studying both race

and ethnicity, too often the discussion has been mired in old debates and definitions. To understand the changes around us, we need a new and critical study of the increasingly complicated relationship between race and ethnicity.

Part of today's confusion stems from the fact that the concepts of race and ethnicity have evolved very differently. Race is a dynamic social construct that has its roots in the transatlantic slave trade, the establishment of plantation economies based on enslaved labor, and the ideological justification for the vast extermination of millions of indigenous Americans. White Americans have thought of themselves in terms of racial categories for several centuries.

By contrast, ethnicity is a relatively recent concept. There are no references to ethnicity per se in the social-science literature of the 19th and early 20th centuries. Ethnicity surfaced as an important category of analysis in the writings of sociologists during the Great Depression, as a means to describe the diverse immigrant populations that came largely from Southern and Eastern Europe. Later, ethnicity was used to describe the development of modern European nationalism and the conflicts developing among various communities defined by their cultural and social traditions.

Because of the hegemony of race and racism in the social development of the United States, European immigrants who arrived here quickly learned that the key to their advancement and power was to claim the status of being white. In other words, during the 19th century race was much more powerful than what we might today call ethnicity in determining the lives of most new immigrants.

The Irish experienced severe discrimination upon their arrival. But within several generations, they had become "white." They had assimilated the values of privilege and the language and behavior of white domination that permitted them to claim status within the social hierarchy. Conversely, immigrants from Latin America and Asia were frequently "racialized" by both legislative means and de facto segregation. After the U.S.-Mexican War of 1846–48, the United States incorporated roughly half of Mexico's entire territory into its own legal boundaries. Slavery, which had previously been abolished by the Mexican government, was re-established. Only Mexicans who were defined as Spanish or white could claim U.S. citizenship; American Indians, peasants, and mestizos were treated as inferior groups.

Small wonder that there are currently major academic disagreements over the meanings and materiality of both race and ethnicity. For example, should race be subsumed under ethnicity as a subcategory? Or is race an exceptional social category in its own right, because of its peculiar historical development, discourses, relations with culture, etc., which set it apart from ethnicity? To what extent, if at all, should race be measured by biological, genetic, or cultural differences among groups? Can ethnic minority groups who are at least partly defined by their legal racial categories, such as African-Americans, be guilty of "racism" themselves? And what of the complex relationships among racialized ethnicities—Asian-Americans, American Indians, Latinos, and African-Americans?

Many different theoretical approaches have been proposed to address such questions. . . .

Therefore, it is not surprising that a national conversation around issues of race and social diversity, such as the 1997–98 President's Race Initiative, is so difficult to carry out. The discourse about race continues to be politically charged, both in public policy and on our campuses, and people generally talk past each other—precisely because there is no consensus, in abstract theory or in the real world, on what is meant by race and ethnicity.

As a field of scholarship, the study of race and ethnicity is the intellectual product of vast historical and social changes within U.S. society. The field is still in the process of evolving, but its essential character was forged in the demographic, political, and cultural transformations of 20th-century American society that occurred in response to protests about white indifference.

At the dawn of the 20th century, American universities rarely focused on racial groups except to explore them as communities with "problems"—as in "the Negro problem." Black higher education was confined to about 100 academic institutions that had been constructed in the decades after the Civil War, and it was at those underfinanced but proud colleges that the black intellectual tradition of scholarship was first nurtured. Then, as Northern industrial and manufacturing jobs became available to black people around the turn of the century, millions trekked out of the South in the Great Migration. Later, in the 1940's and 1950's, several million people from Mexico crossed the border to work in the Southwest. By the 1960's, every major city in the United States had substantial numbers of people from ethnic minority groups whose identity was defined, at least in part, by their race. As those people arrived on white campuses, they demanded changes in the curriculum that reflected their own experiences and intellectual traditions. African-American studies came first, to be followed by Chicano studies and Asian-American studies.

The development of Native American studies was different. For years, the study of American Indian cultures and societies had been dominated by white, frequently ethnocentric and even racist, anthropologists. American Indians, who usually thought of themselves in terms of their tribal identities, did not begin to develop a pan-Indian cultural identity until the 1950's, when the federal government began to expel more than 100 tribes from lands promised them by historic treaties. The militancy that such policies provoked finally came together in the 1980's in a demand for Native American studies.

As a result, that field today has two very different types of institutional structures: many traditional programs initiated and led by white scholars at predominantly white universities, which focus on anthropological, linguistic, historical, and folkloric themes, and the more radical Indian-studies programs, frequently connected with the network of tribal colleges. (The second group often defines its research outside the boundaries of ethnic studies, saying that Indian Americans are the only "indigenous" people in the United States.)

For the most part, African-American studies, as a field, was at first only marginally affected by the emergence of those newer programs. The racialized discourse and framing of inquiry along the boundaries of the black experience limited the development of comparative studies. Similarly, the male-dominated hierarchies and paradigms in African-American studies on many campuses limited interaction with the emerging interdisciplinary programs in women's, gender, and queer studies.

Ethnic-studies programs that explicitly examined the interactions, comparisons, and contacts among racialized minorities came later. The first of the major ethnic-studies departments to develop was, not surprisingly, in ethnically diverse California. The department of ethnic studies at the University of California at Berkeley was founded in 1969, at the height of the antiwar and Black Power movements, and was originally conceived of as an umbrella-like structure, with four interdependent programs operating within one department. Four separate majors and curricula were established, in Native American studies, Chicano studies, Asian-American studies, and Afro-American studies.

Within several years, serious problems had developed in the program. Because each major focused on a single racial ethnicity, students and faculty members alike tended to function only in their narrow area of scholarly interest. Few undertook comparative research. Moreover, there was internal competition for resources, and cooperation among the divisions sometimes broke down completely. Nevertheless, for nearly 20 years Berkeley's model prevailed in the dozens of ethnic-studies programs that developed. Then, as significant numbers of Asian-American students enrolled in elite universities throughout the country, their presence on campuses helped to promote a new approach to teaching ethnic studies, with a broader comparative and global focus.

The department of ethnic studies at the University of California at San Diego, founded in 1991, was representative of the new directions in the field. Courses previously taught under separate academic menus of Asian-American, Chicano, American Indian, and African-American studies were integrated in one rigorous, comparative core curriculum. Faculty members were recruited largely on their academic interest in comparative ethnic research. The department has also recently begun the process of creating graduate programs.

As of 1996, there were nearly 100 ethnic-studies programs throughout the United States, and approximately 30 of them were full departments. The most successful share several characteristics. First, and perhaps foremost, they offer courses that fulfill undergraduate core-curriculum or general-distribution requirements. Second, and related, they avoid racialization and ghettoization, refusing to limit the study of race and ethnicity to Latino, Asian-American, American Indian, and African-American students and scholars. Successful programs nearly always also have the authority to initiate appointments and recruit and retain their own faculty members, who are well-grounded in a traditional academic discipline and who define their primary field of research in broadly interdisciplinary and comparative terms.

To be sure, that can create tensions. At a number of programs, by the mid-1980's some older faculty members—hired in the initial wave of institutionalization, often without scholarly credentials—had ceased to function as intellectuals beyond their normal responsibilities as classroom instructors. At times, they developed a siege mentality, admonishing junior faculty members never to work with traditional departments or other interdisciplinary programs like women's studies. But much of the most innovative and creative scholarship is produced at the borders, the intellectual spaces between old disciplines. At its best, ethnic studies expands inquiry and provides innovative ways of thinking about traditional ideas.

Nevertheless, the central recurring dilemmas of scholarship in ethnic studies continue to be the twin problems of cultural amalgamation and racial essentialism. I say "twin problems" because those two different tendencies nevertheless have a subterranean unity.

First, look at cultural amalgamationists. As I've noted above, many people who study race and ethnicity tend to homogenize groups into a broad political construct: "people of color." That concept has tremendous utility in highlighting the commonalities of oppression and resistance that racialized ethnic groups have experienced; our voices and visions cannot properly be understood or interpreted in isolation from one another. But to argue that all people of color are therefore equally oppressed and share a common politics is dubious at best.

The opposite tendency—essentialism ("identitarianism," in the literary critic and activist Gayatri Spivak's term) encapsulates our respective racialized groups within the narrow terrain of our own experiences. In our own separate languages, from the vantage point of our respective grievances, we trust only in ourselves, cursing the possibility that others unlike ourselves might share a similar destiny.

Most scholars of ethnic studies today don't fall into either trap. We recognize both the profound divergences *and* the parallels in the social construction of ethnicity. Different ethnic groups retain their own unique stories, insights and reflections, triumphs and tragedies from their sojourns through American life. None of that can take away from the deep structural parallels, especially in the processes of racial oppression, in struggles for survival and resistance, and in efforts to maintain cultural and social integrity and identity. Those create the dynamic social framework that brings us together.

But let us take seriously the dynamic, dialectical characteristics of social change that define the framework of American race and ethnicity. Most scholars agree that racialization is a social and historical process—that "races" are not fixed categories. They are permeated by the changing contours of class, gender, nationality, and sexual orientation. If that is true, then we must also recognize that an "oppressed race" in one historical epoch, such as the Irish or the Ashkenazi Jews, can be incorporated into the privileged strata of whiteness. Racial designations of identical cultural groups may differ from country to country and in diverse places and times.

The general tendency of most people in the United States is to think about race and racism parochially, solely within a North American context and within our current moment in history. A much richer perspective about race can be obtained from a comparative approach. In South Africa, for example, a racialized society very different from that in the United States developed, with a "coloured" group forming something of a buffer between black and white groups. Under the former regime of apartheid, certain Asian nationalities, such as the Japanese, could be classified as white, while others, like the Chinese, were relegated to the lower status of coloureds. Even today, African-Americans traveling to South Africa are usually racially "coded" by their appearance as coloured, but generally have a political orientation and cultural consciousness that is defined as black in local terms. South Africa, thus, highlights how fluid racial categories can be.

In colonial Brazil, the importation of more than four million enslaved Africans was the foundation for the construction of a distinctive racialized society. Color and phenotype were important criteria for placing an individual within the racial hierarchy. But social class, education, family background, and other elements were also extremely important in interpreting racial distinctions. For more than a century, Brazilians have used the expression "Money lightens the skin," which suggests how a minority of Brazilian blacks have been able to scale the hierarchy of whiteness through the acquisition of material wealth and cultural capital. Until recently, that was rarely the case in the United States. But the situation is changing.

Moreover, the state always has a vested interest in the management of diversity. The U.S. government's decision in 1971 to create a new "ethnic, but not racial" category of "Hispanic" on its census form is the best recent example of state manipulation of the politics of difference. The designation

"Hispanic" was imposed on more than fifteen million citizens and resident aliens who had very different nationalities, racial-ethnic identities, cultures, social organizations, and political histories.

The Puerto Rican people had been in every respect a "nation" incorporated into the political system of the United States, in much the same way that Mexicans in the Southwest had been brought into the country. Both groups were racialized national minorities within the hierarchy of American race relations. By contrast, most Cuban-Americans who had fled to the United States following the Cuban revolution of 1959 were immediately granted the status of whiteness. To this day, their legal status and access to material resources from the U.S. government is strikingly different from that of black Hispanics from the Dominican Republic or Panama.

The Hispanic category on the census encompasses both Puerto Rican-Americans and Cuban-Americans, as well as such extraordinarily different groups as: upper middle-class immigrants from Argentina, Uruguay, and Chile, who are phenotypically white and culturally European; black working-class Panamanians and Dominicans; the anti-Castro Cuban exiles of 1959–61 who now form much of Florida's ruling political elite and professional class; and Mexican-American farm workers in California's agricultural districts. Which of those distinct nationalities and cultural groups will largely set the standards for what the Hispanic legal and social construct may become?

The central driving force today behind the configuration of the U.S. racial formation is immigration, and it is creating a host of new problems for our understanding of race and ethnicity. Nationwide, about a third of the total growth rate of the U.S. labor force comes from legal and illegal immigration. According to an Urban Institute study, more than 90 percent of the new immigrant population settles in urban areas where there are high concentrations of black Americans. That means that native-born black workers increasingly find themselves in sharp competition with foreign-born nonwhites.

In some cities, black workers complain that they have been fired or have lost low-wage jobs because they are not fluent in Spanish. Increasingly, some Latino and Asian-American groups are using laws against discrimination achieved by the civil-rights movement to attack what many African-Americans see as hard-won gains. For instance, in late 1994 Tirso del Junco, the only Latino on the Board of Governors of the U.S. Postal Service, charged that African-Americans were "overrepresented" within the Postal Service work force.

In the area of education, the gains achieved by African-Americans during the 1960's and 1970's are also being reversed. The percentage of graduating black seniors who went on to college leveled off in the 1980's and started to descend. By contrast, 51 percent of all 1980 Asian-American high-school se-

niors had enrolled in four-year colleges by February 1982, compared with 37 percent of all white seniors, 33 percent of African-American seniors, and 20 percent of Hispanic seniors. In terms of business development, the Census Bureau estimated in 1987 that about 6 percent of all Asian-Americans owned businesses, compared with 6.5 percent of all white people, 2 percent of Hispanics, 1.5 percent of African-Americans, and 1 percent of American Indians.

Those and other striking differences in opportunities and upward mobility of racialized ethnics set the context for increasing social and legal conflicts, from the black and Latino violence in 1992 in Los Angeles, which was aimed squarely against Korean establishments, to the debate two years later in California over Proposition 187, which denied undocumented immigrants access to education and health-care services. Asian-Americans voted overwhelmingly for the initiative; most black voters rejected it, but by a narrow margin of 53 percent opposed and 47 percent in favor. With the initiative's passing, black-Latino conflicts intensified in poor urban communities such as Compton, where underfinanced schools, public-health facilities, and social services had already reached a crisis.

Conflicts among America's racialized ethnic groups are also exacerbated by the significant differences based on social class, nationality, language, and religion—that subdivide each grouping. The Asian-American category includes Japanese-Americans, who have higher median family incomes than whites, and the Hmong of southeast Asia, who are one of the poorest U.S. population groups. There is significant class stratification and polarization within the Chinese community, with a growing professional and corporate group facing tens of thousands of working poor people. Moreover, the attempt to construct a pan-ethnic Asian-American identity and cultural/political consciousness is historically a very recent phenomenon and remains extremely contested.

All of that means that ethnic studies must both have a broad perspective—and at the same time be careful to make distinctions. Much of the focus in Asian-American studies, for example, has concentrated largely on the experiences of Japanese and Chinese immigrants. But as Indians, Pakistanis, Indonesians, Vietnamese, Arabs, Cambodians, and others increasingly enter the discussion regarding the definition of what the Asian-American category should mean, the conversation will become even more complicated.

Ethnic studies will also have to contend with the continuing attempt to differentiate some "model" minority groups from other minority groups. In today's period of globalization, corporate capital requires a multicultural, multinational management and labor force. Racialized ethnic consumer markets in the United States represent hundreds of billions of dollars; African-Americans alone spend more than $350-billion annually. To better exploit those vast consumer markets, capital has developed a strategy of manipulating cultural diversity to maximize profit.

In terms of the governmental, financial, and corporate interests, certain ethnic minorities are seen as being connected with powerful geopolitical countries such as China and Japan. At a symbolic level, the prestige or power of a nation-state's economy in the global marketplace is inevitably translated in the United States and Western industrialized countries into public policies, which in turn impact the representation and treatment of different groups. Ideologically and culturally, the so-called backward peoples who have been historically identified with Africa, the Caribbean, and much of Latin America and southern Asia are at a distinct disadvantage in racist Western societies.

A century ago, W.E.B. Du Bois predicted that the problem of the 20th century would be "the problem of the color-line." Although many Americans still think about race in largely biological and socially static terms, in a paradigm of black versus white, that historical color line is now being transformed. A new racial formation is evolving rapidly in the United States, with a new configuration of racialized ethnicity, class, and gender stratification and divisions. Increasingly the phenotypical, color-based categories of difference that only a generation ago appeared rigid and fixed are being restructured and reconfigured against the background of globalized capitalism and neoliberal government policies worldwide.

In a curious way, William Julius Wilson was both right and wrong when he predicted the "declining significance of race" nearly two decades ago. Traditional white racism is certainly declining. But its place is being taken by a qualitatively new color line of spiraling class inequality and extreme income stratifications, mediated or filtered through old discourses and cultural patterns more closely coded by physical appearance, legal and racial classification, and language.

What the critical study of racialized ethnicities can bring into focus is how and why such domestic and global processes are currently unfolding, and what can be done to challenge them.

Women's Studies

8. Nancy F. Cott, "The Women's Studies Program: Yale University," 1984

The introduction to women's studies at Yale was led by Nancy Cott (1945–). After a B.A. (1967) from Cornell and a Ph.D. (1974) from Brandeis, she started her professorial career at Yale (1975–2001). Thereafter she moved to a professorship of history and director of the Schlesinger Library at Harvard. Her several books substantiated the role of women in the social and political matters of the early nation. A stream of articles, reviews, and edited books placed her at the forefront of historians in this field, and her scholarly reputation was underscored by fellowships from Rockefeller, Guggenheim, and the Charles Warren Center at Harvard. This report on starting up women's studies at Yale was a prototype for similar programs elsewhere.

Nancy F. Cott, "The Women's Studies Program: Yale University," in *Toward a Balanced Curriculum: A Sourcebook for Initiating Gender Integration Projects,* ed. Bonnie Spanier et al. (Cambridge, MA, 1984), 91–97. Reprinted with the permission of Schenkman Books, Inc., © 1984. Further reading: Cott, *The Grounding of Modern Feminism* (New Haven, 1987), and Marilyn Jacoby Boxer, *When Women Ask the Questions: Creating Women's Studies in America* (Baltimore, 1998).

For more than 250 years, Yale College offered degrees only to men. In 1969, it opened its doors for the first time to women: now women comprise approximately 40.7 percent of the undergraduate student body of 5,100. The institution has strongly supported and skillfully assimilated its new population, yet women at Yale (like men at Yale) live in the context of a powerful male tradition. The ideals of academic excellence which control curricular development have been largely evolved from principles of male education: the values that dominate the university are predominantly male values.

Many undergraduates at Yale, and for that matter, many graduate students and faculty members, would not understand the meaning of terms like "male education" and "male values", since they have become accustomed to think male norms and human norms identical. The principles for distribution of courses formulated in the college catalogue articulate the necessity for overcoming "geographical provincialism" (by studying foreign languages) and "temporal provincialism" (by studying history), but only under the aegis of the recently created Women's Studies Program is the provincialism of gender addressed. Established in 1979, the Women's Studies Program incorporates the new scholarship on women which has emerged in the past two decades in response to two pressing intellectual needs: one, for more information about women's lives and contributions; two, for revision of existing theory which, although it supposedly elucidates human behavior or culture, makes sense of men's part only. Across the disciplines, the new scholarship is based on the premise that gender *matters* in social and cultural study: that women and men may perceive or experience differently the same event or situation, in ways that must be investigated if we are to understand humanity fully. Another shared premise is that inequality between the sexes, as a human construction rather than a divine or natural ordinance, forms a proper—in fact, a necessary—subject for social, cultural, and historical analysis. Introducing the critical perspective of women's studies means reconsidering present concepts, methods, and data in light of women's experience, conducting new empirical research bearing on women, and formulating paradigms which will include both sexes.

Both the need and the opportunity for a strong and vital Women's Studies Program at Yale have been great because of the academic excellence of the institution. The authority and subtlety of the teaching that Yale undergraduates obtain tend to indicate to the student that what has been taught is what exists to be known; the student will not necessarily recognize how much is missing from most conventional courses, will not necessarily see how academic disciplines routinely perpetuate the equation of "human" to "male." Both male and female students suffer from the convention of ignoring women's contributions to culture and society and women's intellectual perspectives. Yet because Yale has outstanding resources in its faculty and libraries, because distinguished scholars at Yale have already begun to focus their imaginations and intellects on the problems of broadening curricular preoccupations to include women, the possibility exists for women's studies courses to be taught at a high level of conceptualization and substance.

In 1980 the Women's Studies Program applied for and in 1981 received NEH pilot grant funds to build the Program sufficiently to support a major. The principal activities under the pilot grant were (a) a Faculty Development Seminar, (b) four new courses, (c) lectures by outside speakers and (d) publicity about the Program.

The Faculty Development Seminar, during the spring of 1981, evoked unanimous enthusiasm and appreciation from its participants and a strong awareness of women's studies among other members of the academic community. Five faculty members received released time (one course each) for participating, and six other faculty, as well as one acting instructor, one librarian and research associate, also participated (fourteen in all). The structure that was adopted (somewhat different from the original plan proposed, but, as was generally felt, more useful) was to meet weekly to share readings and discussion of central texts, themes, and questions in women's studies. The seminar required its members to think about curricular offerings and about the intellectual foundations of women's studies. Members read intensively and developed bibliographies in areas of most interest to them. The group investigated the relation of women's studies to the standard disciplines; it generated unusual opportunities for academics to communicate the rationale and perceptions of their own disciplines to those committed to other modes of thinking. Thus the seminar fostered intellectual awareness and helped its members to enlarge as well as to communicate their own insights. It provided, in other words, an opportunity for high-level teaching as well as a forum for discussing teaching. It supplied a supportive environment for testing ideas, an opportunity for exchange, a mode of commitment to women's studies. Its stated aims—to stimulate the research and the teaching of its members, to articulate goals and procedures for the undergraduate

program, to aid members in the planning of new courses, and to improve and solidify the design of the women's studies advanced seminar for seniors—were all realized. . . .

In November [1981], the Yale faculty approved the interdisciplinary major in women's studies to comprise fourteen term courses, seven of which constitute the women's studies core, and seven electives in an area of concentration ordinarily defined with a standard department. This significant milestone attracted national publicity. The amount of attention given to the Yale women's studies major in the national press suggests the great potential impact of strengthening women's studies at Yale. Because of the University's prestige and its reputation for traditional academic excellence, Yale's acceptance of innovative interdisciplinary curricula carries particular weight in the academic world at large. Indeed, letters have been received from women's studies directors at colleges and universities across the nation applauding the decision on the major at Yale and affirming its importance as a national model. . . .

Our approach to the development of a women's studies curriculum focuses on two objectives: We hope both to introduce new courses with a specific focus on women and to help standard courses incorporate women's studies material and perspectives. The coherent core of courses within the Women's Studies Program, together with the courses on women originating in other departments and cross-listed in Women's Studies, are now in place, and we are eager to add to this curriculum. Approximately half of the courses to be revised or designed will therefore be specifically incorporated within the Women's Studies Program. We consider it equally important, however, to encourage the inclusion of the new scholarship on women within the traditional curriculum. Through this double strategy, women's studies at Yale will be able to grow in two mutually supportive directions: women's studies will increase in strength and fullness as a program, and it will make a significant and transformative impact on the Yale curriculum at large.

The proposed courses, which bring several innovations into the Yale curriculum, can be distinguished in several ways. Of eleven new courses planned to focus on women, four originate in departments which heretofore have had no women's studies listings. The presence of these courses in departments which did not until now address the issue of gender will make it possible for more varied students and faculty to become acquainted with the new scholarship on women. Four other new courses focusing on women in literature are planned, three originating in the English Department and one in Spanish. Additional new courses focusing on women will be offered in American studies, anthropology and sociology.

A major part of women's studies' expansion in

the Yale curriculum is the revision of key lecture courses to include women's experiences and perspectives. . . .

The profile of faculty developing courses differs significantly from faculty earlier associated with women's studies. Of twenty-one faculty participating only four had already been involved in women's studies, either through teaching or membership in the Faculty Development Seminar. The women's studies faculty have until now been predominantly untenured and female, but the grant activities include twelve senior faculty (eleven male, one female) and nine junior faculty (three male, six female). The new profile marks a significant addition of male and tenured faculty, a fact which should have an impact on the kind of audience women's studies will be able to reach.

The potential impact of the proposed group of new and expanded courses can hardly be overestimated. Because influential and distinguished faculty members will participate, thus tacitly endorsing the enterprise of women's studies at Yale, the Program will automatically acquire a kind of status and prestige it has previously not had. Because the lecture courses, which include some of the University's most popular offerings, will reach a very large audience of undergraduates, awareness of the implications of women's studies will greatly increase in the student body as a whole.

9. Florence Howe,
Myths of Coeducation, 1984

Florence Howe (1929–) delivered this lecture in various forms at more than a dozen colleges and universities in the 1970s; this is the version presented at Yale. It served as a chartering history and inspiration for the modern women's movement in higher education. Howe (Hunter College, B.A. 1950; Smith College, M.A. 1951), while an assistant professor at Goucher College (1960–71), had taught at a summertime Mississippi Freedom School (1964). Convinced that education is the basis for bringing about social reforms, she thereafter spoke forcefully for civil rights. Insistently she urged reforms in higher education that address the "male bias" of the social science and humanities curricula. She taught humanities and American studies at Old Westbury College of the State University of New York (1971–87), English at City College of the City of New York (1987–) and at CUNY's Graduate Center. She held visiting professorships at home and abroad, founded and still publishes the Feminist Press (1970–), and was president of the Modern Language Association (1973), which awarded her its Mina P. Shaughnessy Medal (1982–83).

Florence Howe, "Myths of Coeducation" in *Myths of Coeducation: Selected Essays, 1964–1983* (Bloomington, 1984): 206–20, abridged. Copyright © 1984, Florence Howe. Reprinted with the permission of the author. Further reading: her other essays in the same volume; *Contemporary Authors* 124 (1988): 221–25; and Howe, ed., *The Politics of Women's Studies: Testimony from Thirty Founding Mothers* (New York, 2000).

Myths are and are not true. The single most famous myths relevant to the subject of coeducation concerns the creation of woman. Eve out of Adam's rib or Athena springing full grown from the head of Zeus—we who understand biology know these as mythic explanations of another reality; not the biological but the social, not the rude facts of life but the complex systems of belief that code and codify the social world. Myths provide meaning and structure to the flux of daily life, to the seemingly disordered behavior of men, women, and children.

Thus, Western myths about the creation of woman by man are representations of social order; of the patriarchy under which, at least in recorded time, we have been living. The mythic narratives establish the creative power of men and the position of woman as social extension of man's wisdom and justice, or as man's chattel, his wifely support, bone of his bone, flesh of his flesh.

Myths about coeducation spring from the same source, or at least the pattern is reminiscent of the creation myths. The prefix "co" allows women to join with men in an educational enterprise, sometimes a college. Coeducation. The education of women with men. Is that its meaning? Of course, coeds are not men. When a man goes to college, he gets an education; when a woman goes, she gets a coeducation. If a man says, "I go to a coeducational college," he means there are women in it. If a woman says, "I go to a coeducational college," she means she does not go to Wellesley or some other women's college. But what is coeducation? What emblem appears, what narrative captures its essence? . . .

Coeducation—in elementary schools or in colleges—functions within the patriarchal limits of the society in which it exists. In mythic terms, coeducation opened doors to women. And so it did. But those doors were—and to a significant extent still are—different from those open to men.

The principal myth is Oberlin itself: the first coeducational college in the nation. True and not true. True if we understand that coeducation meant the admission of women to a male-initiated, male-centered, male-controlled institution. For the brave experiment was just that. Its participants had no models: they came from male seminaries and colleges or from female seminaries. Their task through Oberlin's formative years was to chart, without detailed instructions from the founder, institutional and social arrangements under which the two sexes could be educated, although with clearly differentiated rights and duties for each. Oberlin was an effort to found not only a college, but a model society. . . . The one model available to Oberlin's pioneers was the family. And so the students sat opposite each other in the dining hall. And so women had their domestic chores, men their field work, and it was perfectly understandable in those terms that women were paid half or less than half the hourly wages of men. Indeed, when one considers that most housework is unpaid labor, Oberlin women were well-off.

But if we are looking for a coeducational institution that is a model of equality between the sexes, if we are looking for a coeducational curriculum, a coeducational faculty, coeducational assumptions about the rights of both sexes to work at the same jobs and for equal pay, even coeducational assumptions about the rights of men and women to a share in the drudgeries and the joys of family life: we will not find any of this in Oberlin's history. Nor will we find it anywhere, except perhaps in our dreams of a more perfect future society. . . .

I want to talk further about the myths of coeducation in the nineteenth century and today. And I want to place these myths against the history of women's education, especially in the light of its two major patterns: education separate and different from men's; education modeled precisely on men's education. Both of these patterns flourish today. What we call women's studies is a new departure. Its patterns and purposes . . . bear heavily on the future of coeducation. . . .

The basic idea behind . . . early nineteenth-century visions of women's higher education was that women were biologically different from men and that this difference was closely related to women's child-bearing function. Thus, even the most militant of the women's leaders, who argued for the establishment of . . . early schools for women— in the 1820s and 1830s—and who raised money in nickels and dimes for them, believed that women's education had to be as different from men's as their biology was different.

These biological beliefs were a product of the understanding by the medical professional of physiological functions. Scientific belief held not only that the brains of women were smaller than those of men, but also that brain size was directly related to intelligence, and that hence women were less capable than men of academic learning. More important, however, was the medical assumption that only one bodily organ functioned optimally at any one time. Thus, if women used their brains during adolescence, their uterine development would be disturbed and their childbearing abilities impaired, perhaps so severely as to cause the production of malformed or dead infants. Indeed, higher education might in and of itself sterilize women. . . . For the female scholar, intense study directly inhibited her ability to bear children, or to bear healthy normal ones, capable of surviving past infancy.

And so it is not difficult to appreciate the enormous step taken in the 1820s and 1830s to establish educational institutions for women. It is also understandable that the women interested in female education did not challenge the assumptions of their day. It is easy to dismiss them as reactionary, and even to see them as direct antecedents of today's ERA opponents. Certainly, as a group, they were opposed to most of the political reforms espoused

by many of their students, Elizabeth Cady Stanton included. But these early reformers took the first necessary steps. They introduced into women's education what had always been essential for men's education: a vocational goal, teaching. They wanted to educate teachers, they said, not only because women needed a profession, especially if they did not or could not marry; they were also hopeful that women as a group would care more for the education of other women than men had. Hence, the education of teachers would in itself promote the education of women across the land. And this work would, because of the alleged nature of women, raise the quality of the nation's moral character. . . .

The second wave of feminism is the one we usually associate with the term "feminism" itself. This idea is expressed most simply by the statement, "I can do anything that you can do," spoken by a woman with her eye on a man. It assumes the model of maleness, of maleness as normality, of women as coming up to the male level of normality. It eliminates theorizing about or ignores biological functions. It is also, of course, the mainstream view of the nineteenth-century women's movement. If one is looking for a date and an ideological statement, 1848 and the Seneca Falls Declaration of Sentiments are key. Elizabeth Cady Stanton, one of the first students to attend Emma Willard's Troy Seminary, was an organizer of the Seneca Falls meeting and one of the writers of that document. (It is important to mention, given what I have said about biology, that Stanton was already, at the time of the Seneca Falls Convention, the mother of three healthy normal children under the age of six.) . . .

The Seneca Falls Declaration lists nearly a score of injustices against women and makes recommendations for change. Suffrage was only one of these, and the least acceptable at the time, but the only one known to most Americans. The seventy-two-year history of the fight for suffrage parallels the movement for women's access to higher education equal to their brothers'.

In the 1870s major universities began to open their doors to women; in the same decade, women's colleges were opened that provided an education comparable to that offered men. More and more women wanted to attend colleges, especially if they were the daughters of the burgeoning middle class. And even some male colleges—Miami University in Ohio and Wesleyan University in Connecticut, for example—opened their doors to women in times of economic strain.

Coeducation had been tried earlier in the century by a few colleges in Ohio and elsewhere, but it was far from acceptable on such prestigious campuses as the universities of Wisconsin and Michigan. Not surprisingly, those few university campuses that already admitted women, did so through the doors to the Normal School of course: that is, through teacher education, which fast became the chief sex-segregated educational area for women. . . .

The risks of opening doors to women can be summarized quickly, since a vigorous debate about the merits of coeducation continued through the rest of the nineteenth century, indeed continues to this day, although some of the old myths have been replaced by new ones. First, there was the myth that coeducation would lower the intellectual standing of a college among other top colleges in the nation, since coeducation, critics argued, would lower the general standards of excellence: women as a group, it was said openly at first, and then in muted fashion later, were not as intelligent or capable as men. . . .

A second myth about coeducation really concerned extracurricular life on campus. Opponents of coeducation alleged that it causes a "moral decline" among undergraduates. Not only do women keep men from concentrating on their studies, but the presence of women encourages immorality. . . .

Two myths focused on the woman student herself: as already noted, the delicate health of women could be harmed by hard study. As if in preparation for the possibility that that myth might not be acceptable for long (although it actually was), there was a counter-myth: coeducation would cause "the decline of feminine charm." That is, women in the presence of men would become as "coarse" as they. On college campuses, one might see women drinking, cursing, smoking, asking questions, and speaking out in "promiscuous assemblies," that is, in groups of males and females. In short, women who studied on coeducational campuses might get ideas about independence, might attempt to imitate male models of achievement.

Still another myth focused on male students: the advocates of coeducation claimed that it would help tame the savage beasts. Male students would even eat in a more civilized fashion if women were present in the dining hall. And a pair of myths emerge from this one: coeducation would produce more manly men and more womanly women; finally, coeducation would prove "conducive to mating." Probably these last two myths are more "true" than any of the others. Certainly college students married each other, and perhaps they were more manly men and more womanly women. It is true enough that for coeducational colleges as a whole, such indices of achievement as the Ph.D. function for men only and not for coeds. . . .

The great coeducational universities of the land, responsible for the majority of graduate and professional degrees—and for the development of the natural resources of the nation—became institutions that admitted both women and men, but encouraged their segregated study: women to teaching, then later to home economics, library school, social work, and nursing; men to agriculture, engineering, forestry, marine science, law, medicine, business, and other specialized areas too numerous to mention.

On the other hand, that great fountainhead of assumptions and mythologies, the liberal arts curriculum, was indeed open to both sexes. Whether they sat side by side in classrooms at Oberlin or Kansas, or whether they separately attended Williams or Wellesley, they studied "the men's curriculum." Indeed, after the 1920s, even if they were black women and men in sex-segregated or coeducational colleges of the south, they studied the (white) "men's curriculum." I doubt that this is a novel idea today, but it was a novel idea to feminists only a little more than a decade ago. The discovery has been of some consequence, but it has also made its discoverers feel understandably foolish: for why had it taken so long to see what was utterly visible and obvious?

What is this men's curriculum that we have long since gained the right to study? Indeed, in 1981, eleven years after the term "women's studies" was first coined, some of us think that the men's curriculum is not fit for either men or women.

The men's curriculum educated me from the day I entered kindergarten in 1934 to the day I left graduate school in 1954. In kindergarten and through elementary school, the men's curriculum told me that when I grew up I would be a mommy, married to a daddy who would go to work each day while I cleaned the house, shopped, cooked, sent my two children—an older son, a younger daughter—to school, and waited for everyone to come home so that I could make life truly pleasant and comfortable for them. Because I was the daughter of working-class immigrant Jews, I was taught at home that I was also to become a teacher, an elementary school teacher. That lesson was not overtly part of the men's curriculum, for I never met a woman teacher in my text books, but of course there was an example for me to observe every day in the classroom.

All through my school days and at Hunter College High School and Hunter College and Smith College—all schools only for women—I studied the men's curriculum. That is, I learned the history of the fathers of this country, the laws they passed, the wars they fought, the land they pioneered. I accepted without a blink phrases like "the pioneer and his wife," and I never asked whether women had always been able to vote or whether any woman had ever run for president. I simply accepted that boys and men could do more interesting things than girls or women could. . . . In high school, I loved the study of biology, but I never dreamed of being a biologist or making a medical discovery. Rather, I thought I might become a biology teacher. That is what the curriculum—and the presence of a female biology teacher—had taught me.

In college and graduate school I studied literature and art history. I also studied sociology and anthropology. My teachers at Hunter taught me about race prejudice and the biological fallacies about race people still believed in; they taught me about the significance of environment and culture, and they also taught me respect for the varieties of human culture, the different peoples who inhabited the planet. But there was never a mention of gender, of men and women, of the fallacies people still believed about them. At the University of Wisconsin where I studied art history as well as literature, I saw no women painters, although of course men painted women, often nude, and certainly more often than they painted nude men. Similarly, although there were no British women poets before Elizabeth Barrett Browning (and we were told that she was really not very good) male poets seemed to write mainly about their love for women. I certainly got the idea early in my academic career that women could teach literature but they could not produce it.

When I began to teach in 1951, you know what I taught: the "men's curriculum." How could I teach anything else? It was all I knew. The best I could say about women was that, if one worked exceptionally hard to learn the "men's curriculum," she could become a superior woman—a special case—a woman who worked in a man's world.

Please understand: I was not conscious of teaching the "men's curriculum." I was not conscious at all. I was teaching what I thought was true. . . .

Never before our own time has a group of women questioned the "men's curriculum." If you are surprised, at least one logical explanation may help. It is difficult to criticize adversely an institution you want access to. It is difficult also to criticize an institution you have access to but want equality in. At least as the nineteenth century women's movement understood the issue of equality, it came to mean the ignoring of gender. One was not a woman in the university; one was some other species of being. It was an unreal position, and of course it had clearly begun to break down by the time our own feminist movement touched the campus about a decade ago.

For more than ten years across the land feminists, according to Elizabeth Janeway, have begun the exploration of social mythology. That is her way of describing women's studies, the contemporary feminist movement for change on university campuses. Slowly but firmly during the past decade, women's studies has inched its way into the educational establishment. As a program, women's studies exists on more than 450 campuses. As discrete courses, on more than 1,500, perhaps on all campuses—I have not surveyed the larger scene since 1974. There is now a national professional association, a number of consequential journals, and an annual convention each June that hosts between 1,500 and 2,000 participants.

But if women's studies is a response to the effort to gain for women the right to the men's curriculum, it may also be a reactionary move—back to the separate curriculum for women. Early in the seventies, women's studies began as a compensatory curriculum that would raise the consciousness of women to their place in this world. But knowledge moved hand-in-hand with consciousness, and the

result is very different than our first few simple glimpses of the future. For it is impossible in most areas of knowledge to simply add women to the curriculum. . . .

Women in history; men in history. If you find this distressing—why can't we simply talk about people? We simply can't. That is not the way the world has ever been, nor are brothers and sisters, even if they are twins today, simply "people." But why is this so important? Why must you hear that sometimes unnerving sound of urgency in a feminist's voice? For two reasons. First, there is the matter of truth, of knowledge that is accurate and honest, which omits no essentials—like the history of half the human race in making a judgment about an age and civilization. Second, there is the purpose of truth and knowledge: to affect the lives we live, the opportunities we have. I am deadly serious about the fact that the liberal arts curriculum shapes our assumptions, forms the mythologies of women and men that allow them to live or die. What you learn in school is not a joking matter. It forms an invisible network of belief—interfaced by the networks of church and family and now the media—that may blind us or may free us to see.

I promised a concluding vision, and there are a few signs in sight to support my dreams: that within the next decades whole colleges will consider essential for the well-being of its students and for its allegiance to knowledge and truth the development of a new curriculum. I hesitate to call this curriculum coeducational, given my explorations of that word.

But it will be something beyond both the men's curriculum and women's studies as we know it today. This is not the end of the vision, but the beginning. For it is not simply for its own sake that we will, in this new curriculum, study the social mythology that has separated the sexes in unnatural ways. Rather, and I say this with the consciousness of the purposes of the original Oberlin Collegiate Institute: such study will move us to action, to plan for and organize a more equitable society. So I dream of a new form of coeducation in which the curriculum considers all the inhabitants of the planet. And I expect all of you, faculty, students, administrators to begin now the dynamic process . . . *to be, every one of you, reformers,* part of the process of change.

10. Ellen DuBois et al., *Feminist Scholarship*, 1985

Five women collaborated to produce one of the earliest surveys of feminist scholarship down to the mid-1980s. In keeping with the ethos of "sisterhood," no single author was identified; all shared responsibility for the text. They surveyed the impact of the women's liberation movement on five disciplinary settings: anthropology, education, history, literature, and philosophy. After an incisive introduction about the overall trend in feminist scholarship to that time, they concluded their book by surveying the issues of interdisciplinary scholarship in its relation to feminist writings.

Four of these authors, Ellen DuBois (now at UCLA), Gail Kelly, Elizabeth Kennedy, and Carolyn Korsmeyer were on the faculty of the State University of New York–Buffalo at the time, while Lillian Robinson was affiliated with the Stanford University Center for Research on Women.

Ellen Carol DuBois, Gail Paradise Kelly, Elizabeth Lapovsky Kennedy, Carolyn W. Korsmeyer, and Lillian S. Robinson, *Feminist Scholarship: Kindling in the Groves of Academe* (Urbana, IL, 1985): 1–5, 7–8, 197–202. Reprinted with kind permission from the authors, © 1985. Further reading: Gerda Lerner, *The Majority Finds Its Past: Placing Women in History* (New York, 1979); Linda K. Kerber and Jane D. Mathew, eds., *Women's America: Refocusing the Past* (New York, 1982); Ellen Messer-Davidow, *Disciplining Feminism: How Women's Studies Transformed the Academy and Was Transformed By It* (Durham, 2002); and 8, 9.

The subject of this book is feminist scholarship and its development within and outside the academic disciplines. Our goal is to understand how feminist scholarship both challenges and is shaped by disciplinary inquiry; to present its emergence as a body of research in its own right; to assess its promise for influencing the future conduct of academic research; and finally to explore the implications of all of this for the nature of feminist scholarship.

The work we explore in this book is relatively new, having its source in the general ferment of the 1960s and early 1970s. That period was one of social and political change in the United States and in many other parts of the world. The continuing movement for civil rights among black Americans, protest against the war in Southeast Asia, the women's liberation movement, and somewhat later the gay movement were principal events that called into question the authority and many of the accepted values of American social institutions. Since a significant segment of the participants in these movements were students and faculty at universities, the educational establishment itself was especially subject to scrutiny and challenge, and the political excitement that marked American campuses in that period had an impact on the direction and methods of intellectual inquiry. There were charges that scientific and technological research ultimately served the military rather than the progress of human knowledge, and scholarship in the social sciences and humanities was criticized for its neglect of urgent social issues, the working class, minority groups, and—of most importance for our present study—women.

The criticisms of the American university that emerged from the feminist movement of the late 1960s and 1970s were directed at both the structure of educational institutions and the conduct and content of scholarly research. University administrations and faculties, and in some fields student bodies as well, were increasingly recognized as places that excluded women, and as a part of their struggle for equal opportunity women demanded an end to overt and covert discriminatory practices. When it came to the research conducted within the academy, the assessments and challenges of feminists became more complex, varying with the subjects and methods of each field. It was a uniform complaint, however, that as a subject for research women were being neglected, overlooked, or distorted by existing scholarship. From this criticism flowed a body of new research about, and mostly by, women in a wide-range of disciplines. From this criticism also arose a struggle to restructure the academic establishment in ways that more readily permitted the study of women. Women's studies programs were started in many colleges and universities, separate programs where the distorting lenses of traditional study might be corrected. . . .

In this study we explore a series of relationships that we believe obtain between "the academy" and "feminist scholarship": that between the goals of feminist scholars to formulate a complete body of research about women and the methodological perspectives of each discipline; between scholarship on women guided by disciplinary and nondisciplinary political frameworks; and between the writings of academic and nonacademic feminists. These relationships are complex and often fraught with tension, but they are an essential part of the creation and development of feminist scholarship.

Some of this tension derives from the peculiar position of women in the university. Many feminist academics are also active in the women's movement and conceive of their scholarship as a part of that activity. Thus a source of mutual antagonism is the negative stance that institutions of higher education tend to take toward research that candidly serves political or social ends. That most academic fields have been and still remain almost entirely controlled by men is related to this tension. As the women's liberation movement arose and consciousness of women's secondary status in society spread, many women in the academy became acutely aware that they constituted a small minority in their professions and that, by and large, they occupied positions of lesser rank and influence than their male colleagues. With the growing recognition that inequality between the sexes was both unjust and remediable, women academics—faculty members, graduate students, and those without institutional affiliation—began to group together to share experiences, combat their isolation, and remedy their professional situations. Feminist subgroups within national academic organizations were formed to exert pressure on governing boards, convention program committees, and the like to include more women in the activities sponsored within the professions. In the process, these feminist groups fostered critical perspectives on the scholarship conducted within their disciplines and became places from which challenges to the treatment of women as subjects for research were launched. Thus within particular academic professions there arose dialogue, and often heated debate, over the character of disciplinary inquiry.

However, perhaps the most complex source of tension between feminist scholarship and the academy stems from feminist scholarship itself, particularly that branch associated with "women's studies." In the United States at least, the creation of women's studies programs was an important aspect of the women's liberation movement. Many feminists active in women's liberation in the late 1960s were also active in the student movements, and the drive toward creating women's studies programs was primarily student led. The critical perspective that would later lead scholars to challenge disciplinary research methods began in criticism and rejection of the standard classroom curriculum, where the neglect of women was suddenly obvious.

Of most significance as background for our study is the conception of an alternative way to learn about women that attended the move to establish women's studies programs. In most instances their creation involved a criticism of the traditional organization of knowledge by discipline. No discipline treated women adequately, it was argued, and, further, women's lives and all that affects them could not be contained within the confines of any single field. Thus women's studies programs were from the outset conceived as "interdisciplinary," as programs for study where the boundaries that separate disciplines might be broken down, fostering a broader and more complete approach to the understanding of women. Similar thinking contributed to the later formation of a number of journals devoted expressly to publishing work on women. Multidisciplinary journals such as *Signs, Feminist Studies,* and *Women's Studies* have been milestones in the development of feminist scholarship. In many cases this interdisciplinary conception was an implicit criticism of the whole structure of higher education itself. The women's movement gave rise to many of the landmark works of feminist scholarship, and studies produced outside the academy continue to be an important source of feminist research. Such work challenges the academy and its pretense to monopoly over scholarly endeavors.

Yet, while women's studies has often seen itself in opposition to the academic establishment and to the organization of knowledge by discipline, it also builds upon those disciplines, being as much shaped by them as by the transdisciplinary political interests of feminism. Its dual nature is reflected in the offerings of women's studies programs, which typically include both courses from single disciplines and courses that assume a topical, interdisciplinary approach. Similarly, women's studies journals publish research from disciplinary as well as interdisciplinary perspectives. . . .

The reader will have noticed that we have been using terms such as "feminist research" and "scholarship on women" interchangeably. Clearly the two are not synonymous, for there is work on women that is sexist or even misogynist as well. Nonetheless the looseness of the terminology we adopt is intentional, for we generally found that the concepts guiding feminist work vary so importantly from subject to subject that there is no useful way to use the term in a restricted sense while discussing scholarship as a whole. . . .

At the outset of our project we were interested in making a distinction between "feminist scholarship"—that is scholarship with a recognizably feminist analytical perspective on the oppression and liberation of women—and work "just on the subject of women." One of our underlying goals was to defend the intellectual integrity of the former, which we believed was often suspect in academia because of its explicitly political character. It was not our concern to engage in the debate on the impossibility of value-free scholarship, a debate that extends far beyond feminist scholarship and has been fully explored by others. However, we believed—we still believe—that the connection to a political movement is the lifeblood of feminist scholarship, not its tragic flaw, and we wanted to demonstrate this by example. Yet when we tried to apply political criteria to scholarship on women, we found it impossible to make the distinction we were seeking. Part of the problem obviously lay in the differences among our disciplines. For instance, definitions that emphasized contemporary political issues, such as equality and abortion rights, were somewhat helpful in distinguishing feminist from nonfeminist work in education and philosophy, but useless in literature. The problem with translating a set of political injunctions into a set of scholarly criteria is that the result is a definition of feminism as an ideal type, in comparison to which almost all scholarship falls short, if only because of limitations of subject matter. Eventually we came to understand that there were many feminist perspectives among scholars, none of which we wished to exclude and that at this stage in the growth of the field, even work "just on women," if it tells us something we did not know before, can be seen as feminist, if that term is broadly conceived.

The problems with feminist versus nonfeminist as a typology for contemporary scholarship on women led us to reconceptualize feminism less as a subcategory of research on women than as the context within which virtually all scholarship on women is currently being developed. . . .

At the most we might say that all feminist analyses begin with the concepts of oppression and liberation, but even these basic ideas cannot be used rigidly to distinguish feminist from nonfeminist scholarship. The prior conduct of scholarship itself has been identified as oppressive, and the very act of accumulating knowledge on women has been extremely liberating. Once feminists had criticized the disciplines for denying or distorting information about women, much of their effort concentrated on gathering knowledge to fill the void left by the sexist practices of the disciplines. While we have seen that some of the new research on women explicitly addresses the questions of liberation and oppression, it does not all do so, and it would be counterproductive to use that as a criterion to distinguish feminist from nonfeminist work. However, although we acknowledge that some contemporary feminist scholarship simply studies women and does not explicitly explore the concepts of oppression and liberation, this is not to say that the mere accumulation of information on women is the point of the entire field. Over time scholarship "just on women" promises less and less if it is not synthesized and meshed with basic analytic concepts and feminist debates. Research on women becomes part of feminist scholarship by relating itself to the field as a whole and to the dialogue that it encompasses.

Finally . . . research on women must be evaluated in relation to its disciplinary context. What we learn about women through individual disciplines derives from different traditions of learning, making it hard to find common criteria to determine what counts as feminist scholarship across the various fields. It is our conclusion that feminism within the world of scholarship is best conceived as a progression of ideas proceeding from certain perspectives, rather than a precisely delimited body of material. At the heart of feminist scholarship in all fields of study is an awareness of the problem of women's oppression and of the ways in which academic inquiry has subtly subsidized it, a sense of the possibilities for liberation, and a commitment to make scholarship work on women's behalf. The critiques that ensue from such a stance act, figuratively, as stones dropped in a pool of water. The waves they produce clear space for a multiplicity of ideas and investigations about women and other relevant, new topics. . . .

THE IDEAL OF INTERDISCIPLINARY STUDY

Since the beginning of the feminist revival in the academy, it has been a goal of many scholars to transcend the inhibiting boundaries that divide disciplines from one another and to achieve a fuller, more integrated approach to the study of women. The pioneer journals, that fostered the growth of research on women saw their role, in part, as providing a forum for exchange of ideas from many fields and analytical perspectives. For some time, it was a commonplace that research on women would eventually coalesce into an interdisciplinary field. But more recently feminist scholars have begun to consider the complexities of doing interdisciplinary research and to debate the virtues of integrating work from many disciplines versus conceiving of women's studies as a discipline in itself. As of now, there is no generally accepted understanding of what interdisciplinary research means in women's studies. In our discussion we have, at different

points, used the terms "multidisciplinary," "interdisciplinary," and "transdisciplinary" to emphasize different aspects of the effort to integrate scholarship from many fields. . . .

Let us start with an appreciation for the factors that have enhanced the ability of feminist scholarship to achieve so much toward becoming an interdisciplinary field. Perhaps first and foremost, the connection to the women's liberation movement has provided a foundation for shared perspectives and ideas. From the very beginning the analytic concepts of oppression and liberation have been especially important as organizing principles for the feminist scholar. These are, of course, fundamentally political ideas, imported into the academy from the feminist movement, and they contribute a dimension of intellectual coherence to feminist studies not available to all interdisciplinary efforts. While fields like American or urban studies, for example, amalgamate scholarship from several disciplines around a set of shared topics, it is not just the subject of women that unifies feminist scholarship. Rather, the politics of modern feminism provides women's studies with an additional way to bring together diverse scholarship into a unified endeavor.

Second, many of the central works of feminist scholarship draw from methods of inquiry that do not fit into any one of the standard academic compartments but have flourished outside of the contemporary American university. These perspective include Marxism, psychoanalysis, and most recently structuralism. While these are all intellectual traditions that precede feminism, have been marked by a decided male bias, and were subject to feminist critiques very much like those directed at the academic traditions, they have contributed to the interdisciplinary character of feminist scholarship because they themselves draw on research from many academic fields: Marxism from history, economics, and political theory; psychoanalysis from psychology, literature, and philosophy. . . .

Within more standard academic fields certain disciplinary boundaries have proved particularly permeable, as combined research perspectives have generated new ideas and insights. For instance, studies of the social and cultural milieu of nineteenth-century British and American middle-class women have drawn so evenly on the perspectives of history and literature that it makes sense to talk about one body of scholarship spanning both fields. The same may be said of research on the effects of modernization on women in the Third World, because it integrates concepts and methods of economics, anthropology, political science, sociology, and education to the point that an individual researcher's disciplinary orientation is not always immediately apparent. Still, it is worth observing that not all disciplines have proved equally amenable to merger, and feminist scholarship is also notable for likely disciplines that have remained apart, such as history and philosophy. In fact, interdisciplinary trends are striking precisely because so much feminist scholarship retains a strongly disciplinary character. This fact directs our attention to the shape the disciplines impose on scholarship and how deep their continuing imprint is.

Often, especially with respect to a subject like women, the differences between disciplines appear to be those of research focus: literature studies writings by and about women, history investigates women of the past, anthropology studies women in other cultures, and so on. This view would suggest that different disciplines provide information on particular sectors of women's existence that can be brought together into a whole. It is as if knowledge about women were a jigsaw puzzle and the different disciplines were the pieces that would fit together into a complete picture, if only we persevere in their arrangement. The jigsaw model neglects the fact that the deepest distinctions among disciplines are not topical but methodological, which is why the research that comes from them may be both disparate and incommensurable. We have found there is no one picture, no single integration of the disciplines to be discovered in the realities of women's lives. In the writing of this book, for example, an organization employing topics that appear to follow aspects of women's reality, like work, daily life, family and so forth, did not permit the full incorporation of even our five fields. Far from being exhaustive, such topics import an inevitable analytical construction that in this case consistently underrepresents the contributions of some fields, such as philosophy and literature, and overrepresents others, notably the social sciences.

Our efforts to integrate the research on women from many different fields has not only come up against impervious methodological barriers, it has also demonstrated how much feminists continue to learn from the varieties of traditional discourse. In short, the disciplines are not solely nefarious boundary builders that prevent us from seeing the unitary condition of women. They afford different ways of knowing, and it is this that makes their integration so difficult and their power to shape scholarship so strong.

From the start and to the present, feminist scholars have exhibited a profound conflict over the attitude they adopt toward the disciplines. At one extreme there is the urge to reject them altogether as hopelessly male-biased, establishing in their stead a body of knowledge specific to women and unified by that fact. On the other hand, there is the recognition that knowledge cannot develop without research tools, that one cannot usefully start from scratch to develop new research on women, and that we have all been trained in particular disciplines. There is the desire to be incorporated into the curriculum of the disciplines, as well as the fear of being compromised, absorbed, and diluted. . . .

The intellectual tasks of feminist scholarship require us to work both inside traditional disciplines

and independent of them. Feminist scholarship has generated a body of knowledge that is rigorous and provocative; it suggests ways of thinking and imagining that promise a new understanding of the world. The entirety has a coherence that cannot be forced into existing disciplinary frameworks. From the beginning, it has required independent sites for development—journals, conferences, and departments—to continue. At the same time feminist scholarship continues to respond to the imperative that knowledge for and about women must not be made into a special interest. This book began with an investigation of the ways in which the disciplines were distorted by what they did not know about women; it ended with a study of the disciplines' minimal response, to date, about all that we have learned about women. The impulse to transform the disciplines is as important to feminist scholarship as its independent development as a field, and this is the most challenging of the goals of integration.

11. *Lynn v. Regents of the University of California,* 1981

This is the first federal court case confirming the equal place of women's studies in the offerings of a public university. Therese Ballet Lynn, an assistant professor at the University of California, Irvine, who had been refused merit increases and tenure, was denied due process by the lower court. Her case was heard on appeal because, undisclosed to her, the lower court had used her confidential tenure review file as evidence to determine whether its contents were privileged. The final reasoning of the appellate court stated that for this breach of confidentiality the plaintiff had been denied constitutional due process applied to the equal opportunity provisions of Title VII of the Civil Rights Act of 1964 (as amended in 1972). This ruling was upheld in subsequent federal court proceedings. Justice Stephen R. Reinhardt (1931–) here brought the issue of admitting women's studies to equal standing in the university. His argument shifted from the technicality of confidential tenure review to the existence of a "discriminatory attitude" at Lynn's institution, fully supported by statistics. Within twenty years the Lynn case elicited 106 citing decisions.

A related or "substantially identical" case at the same campus, *LaBorde v. Regents of University of California,* 686 F.2d 715 (1982), put the issue of "inadequate scholarship" to the fore, notwithstanding the establishment of prima facie sex discrimination. There a tenured professor seeking full professorship brought an employment discrimination suit. Her case was lost.

Therese Ballet Lynn v. The Regents of the University of California, 656 F.2d 1337 (1981). Further reading: Mary Gray, "Academic Freedom and Nondiscrimination: Enemies or Allies?" *Texas Law Review* 66 (June 1988): 1593. The later history of legal "academic privilege" affording confidentiality issues relating to the disclosure of tenure material in Title VII cases is traced in Laura I. Weintraub, "Academic Privilege and Title VII: The Birth, Death, and Possible Rebirth of An Evidentiary Privilege," *Columbia Journal of Law and Social Problems* 33 (Spring 2000): 313–41; see also Barbara A. Lee, "Balancing Confidentiality and Disclosure in Faculty Peer Review: Impact of Title

VII Litigation," *Journal of College and University Law* 9 (1982–83): 279–314; George R. LaNoue and Barbara A. Lee, *Academics in Court: The Consequences of Faculty Discrimination Litigation* (Ann Arbor, MI, 1987). A broad examination of social and legal barriers impeding women's professional opportunities (including the academy) can be found in Deborah L. Rhode, "Perspectives on Professional Women," *Stanford Law Review* 40 (May 1988): 1163–1207.

The district court clearly erred in concluding that Lynn failed to establish a *prima facie* case of discrimination based on sex. "The burden of establishing a *prima facie* case is not onerous." *Texas Dept. of Community Affairs v. Burdine*, 450 U.S. 248, 253. . . . In addition to testimony and documentary evidence, Lynn submitted two types of statistical data; the first, which we refer to as "specific statistical data," tended to show that she met the objective criteria for tenure, and the second, which we refer to as "general statistical data," tended to show a general pattern of discrimination by the University in favor of men.

Lynn's specific statistical data, relating to the objective criteria for tenure, provided evidence that she had the same education, experience and number of published works as others who had been granted tenure. For purposes of deciding whether Lynn has established a *prima facie* case we find the specific statistical data submitted to be highly persuasive. It supports Lynn's contentions that she "was qualified for the position or rank sought," . . . and that "others (*i.e.*, males) with similar qualifications achieved the rank or position." . . .

The general statistical data submitted by Lynn, as mentioned, provides evidence of a pattern of academic sex discrimination by the University. The district court described the University's past practices as follows:

> Over the years University administrators have shown a lack of concern for the need for minority and female faculty members, and such indifference persists. Even though the University of California at Irvine maintains an Affirmative Action Program, statistical summaries still display an under utilization of these groups.

Later in its memorandum, the district court noted "since its founding, Irvine has granted tenure to 26 men and only two women—the last woman tenured was in 1972."

The Supreme Court has stated that general statistical data is helpful in individual employment discrimination cases. *McDonnell Douglas*, 411 U.S. at 805. . . . It is particularly helpful in the academic context, where the tenure decision is highly subjective.[1] . . . Proof of a general pattern of sex discrimination is, in any event, evidence which tends to establish that it is "more likely than not" that a University's decision to deny tenure was based on sex, "a discriminatory criterion under the Act.". . .

In addition, testimony at trial revealed that the University's evaluation of Lynn's scholarship was due, in part, to its view that women's studies is not a substantial topic for scholarly work.[2] The district court stated:

> The criticism leveled at her work by scholars and administration officials appears to reflect their disdain of this [women's studies] as a topic of substance in a scholarly work. I find their lack of enthusiasm for her effort may stem from their belief that women's [sic] studies was an unworthy topic to pursue.

The district court concluded, however, that the University's lack of enthusiasm towards women's studies was not evidence of discrimination because the University would have had the same objection if a man concentrated his studies on women's issues. We do not agree. A disdain for women's issues, and a diminished opinion of those who concentrate on those issues, is evidence of a discriminatory attitude

---

1. Reliance on statistical proof at the *prima facie* case stage is not only practical, but also represents sound policy. The ultimate issue in a case like the one before us is whether the tenure decision was made on the basis of merit or on the basis of sex. Often, there is little direct evidence that plaintiffs can obtain when attempting to show that the decision was based on sex, *i.e.*, that there was discrimination in an individual hiring decision. Despite such problems of proof, Congress entrusted to the courts the responsibility of providing a forum for the litigation of claims of discrimination in universities and other institutions of higher learning. *Powell v. Syracuse University*, 580 F.2d 1150, 1154 (2d Cir. 1978); The Equal Employment Opportunity Act of 1972, 86 Stat. 103, sec. 3 (1972). Although statistical data does not provide direct evidence of discrimination in the individual hiring decision, use of such data is an effective method of proof, and, accordingly allows us to discharge our responsibility under Title VII. Moreover, its use has another substantial benefit. Statistical evidence does not deal with the merits of the university's tenure decision, which necessarily involves academic judgments. Its use thus allows us "to steer a careful course between excessive intervention in the affairs of the university and the unwarranted tolerance of unlawful behavior" proscribed by Title VII. *Powell*, 580 F.2d at 1154.

We do not suggest that avoiding review of internal university processes is an overriding policy. To the contrary, by amending Title VII to cover educational institutions, Congress "evidenced particular concern for the problem of employment bias in an academic setting," *Powell*, 580 F.2d at 1154, and thereby made the decision that the broad societal interest in eliminating discrimination should be of overriding concern in Title VII cases in the academic context. We note only that the use of statistical data minimizes the possibility that courts will substitute their judgments for those of university personnel while providing courts with an effective tool with which to enforce Title VII.

2. Lynn's study of French literature concentrated heavily on women's issues, *e.g.*, the influence of women on the development of French literature.

towards women.[3] The existence of a discriminatory attitude, like general statistical data, tends to establish that it is more likely than not that the University's decision was based on an impermissible criterion, and therefore tends to establish Lynn's *prima facie* case.

After consideration of both types of statistical proof, and the other evidence submitted at trial, we believe it is clear that the district court's finding that Lynn failed to satisfy her initial burden of establishing a *prima facie* case was erroneous. . . .

Since, as we concluded *ante*, the district court properly found that the University "articulated [a] legitimate, non-discriminatory reason," we would ordinarily next determine if the reason "articulated" by the University was "a pretext or discriminatory in its application." However, we do not decide that issue here.

Throughout the proceedings below, Lynn was denied access to her tenure review file. The materials contained in the file were those upon which the tenure review committee claims that it based its denial of tenure, and, as such, are highly relevant to the issues in this case. At the discovery stage, when Lynn requested that the University produce the file, the district court issued a protective order. At trial, the University submitted the file to the court; the

court reviewed it *in camera* but refused to disclose the contents of the file to Lynn. Lynn asserts that the file was submitted by the University, and used by the district court, as evidence, rather than for the purpose of determining whether the contents of the file were privileged. Thus, Lynn contends that the refusal to disclose the contents of the file violated due process. We agree. . . .

The record leaves little doubt that the University submitted the tenure review file to counterbalance the effect of the minority report and that the district court acceded to this use of the file.

The receipt and review by the district court of the tenure review file for the purpose of assisting it to make factual determinations or to evaluate other evidence violated principles of due process upon which our judicial system depends to resolve disputes fairly and accurately. The system functions properly and leads to fair and accurate resolutions, only when vigorous and informed argument is possible. Such argument is not possible, however, without disclosure to the parties of the evidence submitted to the court. Thus, the district court's receipt and review of the file, without disclosure of its contents to Lynn, requires reversal of the order of the district court.

Interdisciplinarity

12. SSRC, "Negotiating a Passage between Disciplinary Boundaries," 2000

Discovering a confluence of concepts, methods, and findings from related themes in various fields of study that feed into a broader or sharper body of meaning has been an ongoing challenge in the age of proliferating academic specializations. The core of a discipline must be protected, many agree, while its borders are permeable for rewarding interdisciplinary conversations. For the sciences, E. O. Wilson promoted "consilience," a neologism of his creation that he defines as "the jumping together of knowledge" across disciplines "to create a common groundwork of explanation." For the humanities and social sciences, where individual effort rather than the team projects of the sciences is customary, the discipline itself can become an impediment. Can dedication to evidentiary rigor and commitment to department-bureaucratic habit become in effect "doing a sum" that Oliver Wendell Holmes Jr. rejected in preference to viewing life as "painting a picture"?

Ken Wissoker, editor in chief of Duke University Press, wrote this essay in 2000. Later that year the Social Science Research Council, which has a claim on initiating the idea of "interdisciplinarity," reprinted the essay in *Items*. Since Wissoker emphasizes cultural studies and the humanities, the SSRC invited responses from people in the social sciences. Included here are the comments of Arjun Appadurai, then Samuel N. Harper Professor in anthropology and South Asian languages and civilizations at the University of Chicago and now the John Dewey Professor of Social Sciences at the New School for Social Research, and Thomas Bender, professor of history and University Professor of the Humanities at New York University.

---

3. While we might not have made the statement in the text which accompanies this note a number of years ago, today its truth seems self-evident. The history of our nation reflects the evolution of our understanding of the nature of man (in the generic sense of the word) and the legitimate aspirations and rights of the individual. Attitudes which seemed benign at one time are now understood to be discriminatory. *Compare Brown v. Board of Education of Topeka*, 347 U.S. 483, 74 S.Ct. 686, 98 L.Ed. 873 (1954) *with Plessy v. Ferguson*, 163 U.S. 537, 16 S.Ct. 1138, 41 L.Ed. 256 (1896). The beliefs that women should not have the right to vote, practice law, or serve on the United States Supreme Court, were once reflective of the majority view, and the law. We now understand, somewhat belatedly, that these concepts reflect a discriminatory attitude. Today any person is free to hold to such concepts, but such concepts may not serve as the basis for job-related decisions in employment covered by Title VII. Other concepts reflect a discriminatory attitude more subtly; the subtlety does not, however, make the impact less significant or less unlawful. It serves only to make the courts' task of scrutinizing attitudes and motivation, in order to determine the true reason for employment decisions, more exacting. We are sensitive to the problems related to judicial examination of issues like the importance of women's studies, and to the need for courts to refrain from substituting their judgment for that of educators in areas affecting the content of curricula. Accordingly, the view we express is a narrow one. We are saying only what Title VII commands: when plaintiffs establish that decisions regarding academic employment are motivated by discriminatory attitudes relating to race or sex, or are rooted in concepts which reflect such discriminatory attitudes, however subtly, courts are obligated to afford the relief provided by Title VII.

Ken Wissoker, "Negotiating a Passage between Disciplinary Borders," *Chronicle of Higher Education,* April 14, 2000, B4; reprinted as adapted from Social Science Research Council, *Items and Issues* 1 (Fall 2000): 1, 5–7; the responses by Arjun Appadurai and Thomas Bender appeared in the same issue. Reprinted with the kind permission of Ken Wissoker, © 2000. Further reading: references in Diana Rhoten, "Interdisciplinary Research: Trend or Transition," *Items and Issues* 5 (Spring/Summer 2004): 6–11; Stephanie L. Pfirman, James P. Collins, Susan Lowes, and Anthony F. Michaels, "Collaborative Efforts: Promoting Interdisciplinary Scholars," *Chronicle of Higher Education,* February 11, 2005, B15; Leila Zenderland, "Constructing American Studies: Culture, Identity, and the Expansion of the Humanities," in *The Humanities and the Dynamics of Inclusion Since World War II,* ed. David A. Hollinger (Baltimore, 2006): ch. 10; Julie Thompson Klein, *Humanities, Culture, and Interdisciplinarity: The Changing American Academy* (Albany, NY, 2005) contains an excellent bibliography; E. O. Wilson, *Consilience: The Unity of Science* (New York, 1998): 8; D. Hicks and J. Katz, "Where is Science Going?" *Science, Technology and Human Values* 21 (1996): 379–406; and I, 17–18; V, 5, 13.

How interdisciplinary is interdisciplinarity? Is the literary critic who analyzes five novels and a film to understand the rise of consumer culture doing interdisciplinary work? Is the environmental scientist who borrows a model from game theory? We might ask about both: Is their work interdisciplinary, or are they simply expanding the tool kit of their own disciplines? Perhaps we have now reached a time to pause and consider what interdisciplinary work is, and what it is not.

By now, we know a good deal about the intellectual and institutional histories of academic disciplines and even subdisciplines. But we've given far less thought to understanding the histories and sociologies of interdisciplinary work. What do we mean by interdisciplinarity, anyway? Is it an attribute of the author? The work? The audience? If an art historian employs theories from philosophy and psychology in a study of Impressionism, are the methods recognizable to readers in those disciplines? Must they be, for the work to be considered interdisciplinary? Is this "inter" a bridge connecting two ways of working? Or is it some third way, one that is beyond them?

We tend to talk about interdisciplinarity as if it always has the same meaning. From my vantage point as an editor, however, I see different fields taking recognizably different approaches. Interdisciplinary work by an art historian looks markedly different from that by a sociologist of art. Sometimes the differences are glaring, sometimes subtle. They are traces that reflect choices made along the way: how to frame a question, or what weight to give various forms of evidence.

Indeed, I believe it is nearly impossible to produce work that does not bear the marks of the discipline of its origin. The literary critic Donald E.

Pease speaks of a "disciplinary unconscious" that frames our thinking. Far from being surprised, I consider that an anthropological insight, one that takes seriously the cultures, categories, and valuations of particular disciplines. Intention is no more the guarantor of "escaping" one's discipline than it is of escaping one's race or gender. While some causes of disciplinary power are structural and exterior to a scholar—such as departmental pressures and expectations—many others result from internalizing the standards and values of normal scholarly practices.

Let's examine how interdisciplinary work is produced. When one writes for an interdisciplinary audience, one is trying to please readers both outside and inside one's own discipline. Sometimes those outside are real readers, a group of colleagues from other departments who share an intellectual quest. A sociologist working on the civil-rights movement, for example, might be a member of a reading group composed of historians, political scientists, and literary critics studying the same topic.

Sometimes the outsiders are phantasmatic: what a sociologist anticipates a historian or critical-race theorist would expect to see. . . . Scholars balance such expectations from other fields with familiar rules, needs, practices and understandings of their own discipline. After all, they want their cohort, as well as outsiders, to appreciate their work.

That relates to the exterior pressures. . . . Scholars have to worry about how their work will be seen in professional, career contexts. . . .

Interdisciplinary work, then needs to be seen as a compromise, a hybrid between disciplinary forces and the desire to use concepts and methods from—or to speak to—other disciplines. . . .

It is not hard for scholars engaged in interdisciplinary projects to remember that their own work must balance disciplinary and interdisciplinary impulses, and they can usually recognize similar trade-offs in work in their own field. They recognize when an author is pushing boundaries and when he or she is staying within disciplinary conventions. However, when scholars go to evaluate interdisciplinary work from another field, they often forget the forces that helped structure that work, and read it as if it were a direct representation of the author's beliefs. . . .

I have come to see how . . . a failure of understanding operates to distinguish scholars as interdisciplinary writers from scholars as interdisciplinary readers, especially when they read something that crosses into their own disciplinary practice or subject area. As writers, many scholars inclined to interdisciplinary work are happy *bricoleurs,* trawling other disciplines for useful theories, methods, and information. They are pleased to enrich their own work by using those practices in their own *bricolage,* picking up bits and pieces as needed. Generally, they have a reasonable degree of trust in their own ability to use tools and practices for good purposes. Far from being sloppy, that is seen as doing the extra work that creative scholarship requires.

However, a whole different set of responses comes into play when the same scholars read work from another discipline that uses theory or practice from their own discipline badly (and isn't it always bad?) . . .

The work is often seen as careless, using tools from the discipline without understanding their attendant histories, contexts and shortcomings. Scholars turn out to have great affective attachments to their methods of their own fields, even if they spend much of their academic lives grumbling about them or picking them apart. Do they ever wonder why people in their own discipline are so much better at creating hybrid methods? Why they always make better choices than people in other disciplines?

There is something about academic training that makes people insistent that one disciplinary approach must be right and others wrong, or, at best, misguided. . . .

Territoriality is often redoubled when interdisciplinary spaces are at stake. Perhaps that is because such spaces are new, with boundaries less clear and less ritualized than in traditional disciplines. Take the case of cultural studies. Like many other such areas, it was set up as a place for interdisciplinary work, but it is often attacked by people in a variety of other fields as if it were a marauding discipline. I realize that cultural studies is a very particular example, but hope that an analysis of how such a relatively visible area has been embraced and attacked will be helpful in the consideration of interdisciplinary projects in general.

Cultural studies is organized around some common themes, questions, and politics—what the connections are among cultural forms, and between culture and politics, or how culture is produced, circulated, consumed. It boasts e-mail lists, book series, and journals. Cultural studies is not a discipline; it has no organization, no annual meeting and very few departments. Most of the departments that do exist are renamed versions of other disciplines. Most of the practitioners—those who would say "I do cultural studies"—in some discipline: communications, literature, film studies, anthropology. For the most part, cultural studies is not an institutional or professional space; it is an interdisciplinary one, an intellectual one. What cultural studies has become is a space for work between disciplines.

Yet most anthropologists see cultural studies as replacing ethnographic studies with textual readings, replacing studies of actual others with theories about the "other"—in short, they fault it for becoming less anthropological and more like literary criticism. Many literary critics, on the other hand, see cultural studies as replacing text-based studies with historically or culturally based ones, and replacing

aesthetic judgments with political ones. In other words, they see cultural studies as replacing literary criticism with anthropology (and/or history and sociology).

To borrow the jargon of each discipline, we might ask whether the cultural studies "othered" by anthropologists is the same as the cultural studies "othered" by literary critics. The answer, clearly, is no. But so few scholars realize that. My point here is that, rather than seeing cultural studies as an intellectual project composed of scholars from their own and other disciplines, many people see it only from their own perspective: as a competing discipline trying to take over their academic space.

In some ways, cultural studies has come to be used interchangeably with postmodernism (which, by now, is almost an epithet; seemingly, it has no adherents) or some other sign of the looming apocalypse. Generally, much of this loose talk turns out to have little to do with cultural studies itself, and instead serves primarily to reinforce the disciplinary solidarity of the complainers.

I've dealt with cultural studies at some length here, because I think the responses to the field—which are sometimes both positive and negative from the same people—have much to teach us about the prospects of interdisciplinary spaces in general. If scholars are unable or unwilling to learn how to read work that draws on other disciplines—to become aware of their own disciplinary biases, and to hold them in check—all the talk of interdisciplinarity will be just that.

We must acknowledge that interdisciplinary spaces are hard to construct and hard to maintain. It is relatively easy to produce disciplinary versions of purportedly interdisciplinary spaces: literary cultural studies, sociological cultural studies, etc. Those do nothing but reshape the boundaries and methods of the existing disciplines. The real challenge is to find a way to hold the interdisciplinary and the disciplinary in view, not only as authors, but as readers, listeners, and participants in academic institutions. Only then will truly interdisciplinary work flourish.

ARJUN APPADURAI'S RESPONSE

The very idea of disciplines has a short history, connected with the evolution of the modern research university, of professional specialization and of the growing vocationalization of the professoriate in the West. Within this short history, specific disciplines grew and grew distinct, and in the European university framework, certain fault lines—as between the natural sciences and the human sciences, and between the humanities and the social sciences—became especially important. No modern discipline in Europe and North America is much more than 150 years old. Many are much younger.

This double historicity—that of disciplinarity and that of disciplines—produces an embarrassment, namely that boundaries of short duration are difficult to defend strongly. When in the 60s and 70s, the ideas of Karl Popper, Thomas Kuhn and others had their greatest impact, it became accepted wisdom that all forms of conjecture thrived on the possibility of refutation. This obviously was relevant to the boundaries between disciplines, which could hardly claim eternal verity if all substantive truths were potentially—and even virtuously—refutable. So there are some who easily concede the historicity of the idea of disciplinarity but become true believers when it comes to disciplines—especially their own. The inverse case is rarer, when scholars find the boundaries of this or that field entirely artifactual but the idea of disciplinarity valuable.

The second position is the one that I regard as the source of a healthy approach to interdisciplinarity. The idea of disciplinarity is good, if for no other reason than its managerial or triage function in an era of exploding knowledge and imploding specialization. Simple efficiency calls for sub-fields that can guarantee their own good health. But the specific shape of this or that discipline is quite another matter, since it can come to reflect contingency in its more sclerotic, self-interested forms. The defense of specific disciplinary boundaries is often connected with funds, careers, power and institutional fiefdoms. Ideas rarely suffer from propinquity or promiscuity. Individuals and careers often do.

As far as specific disciplines go, there is one other point to be made. It may be well for us to worry more about disciplinary cores, nodes, or centers rather than their edges, boundaries or frontiers. The latter are a natural place for traffic, mutation, invention and sheer chance. The boundary is the province of invention. The center, on the other hand, is well worth defense, for in it lies the hard work of choosing between good ideas, of training (discipline in its linked, secondary sense) and of curricular ordering and systematicity, without which transmission and teaching would become impossible. The center of a discipline must also be open to change, but it is appropriate that it be more conservative than its boundary.

Thus, where interdisciplinarity is concerned, let us worry about the center—the key texts, the core ideas, the persistent preoccupations, the formative thinkers, the durable histories—and the boundaries will take care of themselves. Today, in an academic world driven by the contradictions of high costs, intense competition for the global student dollar, and intense passions for rankings of every type, we worry too much about what happens at the boundaries between fields and mistakenly leave disciplinary centers to take care of themselves. This is the road to trench warfare over funds and power, rather than over ideas. If we think about the centers of our fields, we are still obliged to reflect on our fields as essentially historical artifacts, but we are likely to have something worthwhile to traffic in. Otherwise, we will have no disciplinarity with which to be inter—or interesting.

THOMAS BENDER'S RESPONSE

Are academic disciplines (collectively or singly) intended to describe and explain the world, or is their work to develop working paradigms (to use a now outmoded phrasing) that allow disciplinary practitioners to keep at work creating new knowledge and new disciplinary problems to solve?

The incorporation of theories or methods from other disciplines to advance one's own does not in these terms amount to interdisciplinary work, though it may be enormously fruitful. Indeed, one can argue that most of the important disciplinary innovations of the past century, and especially the past half-century, derive from the incorporation of concepts or methods from other disciplines. That is a powerful argument against disciplinary parochialism, or, to put it more positively, a call to a disciplinary cosmopolitanism that allows and encourages serious participation in a more general intellectual culture. But it is not necessarily a call for interdisciplinarity as I am defining it.

The disciplines rule. Tenure committees seldom ask whether the candidate's work effectively describes the world (to say nothing of whether it is "true"). Rather they ask whether the methods and theories are original, innovative within the discipline and likely to stimulate further work in the discipline. . . . Interdisciplinarity, understood as intellectual engagement with the world we share with our nonacademic neighbors, is a means, however crude, of counterbalancing this endgame of professional insularity.

If we accept Ken Wissoker's argument for cultural studies—"space for work between disciplines" —one has a contemporary version of the founding idea of the SSRC. He rightly points out that many who today fly under the banner of cultural studies are addressing issues they consider to be (and surely are) of social significance. These concerns do not, however, seem to fit in any adequate way into the protocols of the established disciplines. Cultural studies provide a space for such inquiries, and that is doubtless the explanation for strong foundation support of the field.

Yet interdisciplinary scholarship is as problematic as it is essential. How is one to judge its validity? Who is to judge its merit? It is true that the past two decades have witnessed the proliferation of interdisciplinary journals. None, however, claims a role equivalent to the traditional disciplinary journals. As newcomers to the academic marketplace and aware of the competition for resources, these journals and their editors are often as concerned with promoting the "field" and building "networks" as with judgment.

Although there is much evidence that the established disciplines are not so effective as their founders might have hoped in keeping the market and its values at bay, interdisciplinary studies are even more vulnerable to the perverse forms the market assumes in academe today. The individualism of the marketplace is transformed in academe into a kind of expressive individualism that values the performance of difference. To some extent, the disciplines can moderate this. But interdisciplinary fields, partly because of their defining virtues, exhibit some of the worst aspects of contemporary academic culture. Far from C. S. Peirce's or even John Dewey's weaker vision of a "community of inquirers" cumulatively enriching a common knowledge base, reputation and advancement derive from solo performances of originality and differentiation.

More serious yet is the question of training. Pioneers in an interdisciplinary field are often granted licenses to proceed with a fairly thin knowledge of the second or third or fourth disciplines being drawn upon. Since these scholars were trained in a discipline, quite visible traces of that discipline inform their work and provide a way of evaluating it— both for promotions and for its credibility. More is (rightly) expected of participants in the second and third waves, many of whom begin with a commitment to cultural studies and thus may not have even the benefit of the originating discipline that sustained the work of their mentors. Yet they are expected to have much fuller grounding in the various bodies of scholarship upon which they draw. How is this to be done?

If we locate cultural studies, as I have, within the context [of] the public concerns that framed the establishment of the SSRC, there is a further complexity—or irony. It turns out to be more difficult than anticipated to return to the public with scholarly findings in the language of the public rather than as academic jargon.

It is all very worrisome, even discouraging. Yet if we wish to keep addressing the issues of contemporary life and if we wish to maintain intellectual vitality in the disciplines, we must keep advocating and doing interdisciplinarity, however impossible.

13. Marian Cleeves Diamond, "A New Alliance for Science Curriculum," 1983

Laboratory biologists in the 1970s were increasingly employing sophisticated computers to advance their research. The consequent proliferation of specialized sub-fields led them by the 1980s to anticipate or form integrated departments to meet their need for understanding and teaching widening curricula. Marian Diamond (1926–) described here her excitement in joining newly integrated biological disciplines at the University of California in the early 1980s. Hers was a remarkable professorship in anatomy at the University of California, Berkeley (1962–95). She earned degrees there (B.A. 1948, Ph.D. 1953), followed by appointments at Harvard (1952–54), Cornell (1954–58), and at University of California at San Francisco (1959–62), before joining the Berkeley faculty as the first woman professor in the sciences, later becoming professor of integrated biology. In 1990 she entered a five-year directorship of the Lawrence Hall of Science. Rejecting retirement, she was in 2005 still lecturing

to large classes of students. Many research, publication, and teaching awards testify to her statewide and national distinction.

Marian Cleeves Diamond, "Hearts, Brains, And Education: A New Alliance for Science Curriculum," in *Higher Learning in America, 1980–2000*, ed. Arthur Levine (Baltimore, 1983): 279–82. Copyright © 1983 Reprinted with kind permission from the author and from The Johns Hopkins University Press. Further reading: V, 4, 12, 14.

In the 1980s, both internal and external review committees met to make recommendations for the reorganization of the biology departments on the Berkeley campus. Since the biological sciences were undergoing a remarkable revolution, it was essential to reexamine the present and future directions for this branch of science. Which disciplines were advancing in an explosive manner? Molecular genetics and cell biology emerged as separate disciplines. Biochemistry had demonstrated the underlying similarities in the chemistry of all living things. Utilizing model computer techniques, population biologists were able to integrate concepts that infused new life into the fields of systematics, evolution, and ecology. At the same time that these individual fields were emerging, it was essential to keep in mind that quantitative biological science has a substructure of overlapping disciplines with broad general applications. A study of all organisms includes their biochemistry, genetics, cell biology, ecology, and population dynamics. With the many advances in medicine that have benefited from new knowledge in modern biology, biotechnology companies have been formed to take advantage of the recent discoveries. Pharmaceutical, chemical, agricultural, and energy industrial firms are investing actively in the various applications of biological technology.

Universities now have the obligation to adjust their teaching and research programs to meet the demands of preparing their students for entrance into the work force in these diverse yet interrelated biological fields. Not only do the teaching and training programs have to be revised, but the building facilities need remodeling as well. The report of the external review committee in April 1981 summarized the direction of the biological sciences quite clearly. "The biological sciences constitute a gathering force that will affect every aspect of our society, a force which may have even greater impact than those of chemistry and physics in the past. Those institutions that play a leading role in the development of this force and its application to the great problems of society will benefit greatly, both within themselves and the society they serve" (p. 7).

The Berkeley undergraduate biology curriculum was considered to have unnecessary duplication, fragmentation, and specialization because of the disconnected departmental structure. Such problems could no doubt be rectified with considerable reorganization. Utilizing the information from all of the review committee reports, three new departments were established after dismantling the existing ones. The new departments include Integrative Biology, Plant Biology, and Molecular and Cell Biology. The subdepartments within these new departments are the following:

- *Integrative Biology*: Track 1: Morphology, Physiology, and Development. Track 2: Behavioral Biology. Track 3: Systematic Biology, Paleontology, Genetics, and Evolution. Track 4: Ecology. Track 5: Integrative Human Biology
- *Plant Biology*: none
- *Molecular and Cell Biology*: Biochemistry and Molecular Biology; Cell and Departmental Biology; Cell Physiology and Biophysics; Genetics, Immunology and Tumor Biology; and Neurobiology

It was amazing to see how well the faculty in general adopted their new departments and carried on business in their new environment. Several reasons were undoubtedly responsible for the ease of this transition. During the reorganization, faculty had the opportunity to form affinity groups as well as choose space in close proximity to former colleagues either from their home department or from others within the campus. In most cases the course content was not modified significantly, with the exception of a few new courses that took advantage of the reorganization. Because the professors continued to teach essentially the same course but in a new department, the stress of becoming established in a new department was not unusually severe. Perhaps the need for reorganized course material will come in the future.

What do I find of value in my new department after having worked in my original one—Physiology-Anatomy—for over thirty years? First, it might help to note which departments were recombined to form the new Integrative Biology Department. These included Physiology-Anatomy, Botany, Genetics, Zoology, and Paleontology. From this new mix, the faculty works surprisingly well together on both general university business and departmental matters. Faculty meetings are obviously more heterogeneous in nature, and faculty seminars cover a much broader spectrum of topics than when the original departments existed.

This subject bears some expansion to illustrate specifically what I have found of value with my new department. At one seminar, I sat next to a botanist who was attempting to understand the role of the protein calmodulin in plants. I asked if he was familiar with the role of calmodulin in the animal nervous system. After learning from me that calmodulin interacts with calcium to assist the movement of vesicles in the nerve fibers toward their terminals, he wondered if the same function was true in plants. Now one reads that a proposed mechanism for a plant's growth pattern may be due to increased calcium in the cytoplasm. One of the genes that has recently been isolated in plant codes for calmodulin has been shown to combine with calcium ions. The calcium-calmodulin complex redirects the axis of the cell dimension by rearranging the ingredients of the internal skeleton of the cell. Is it possible that this is happening in the nerve fiber as well, resulting in a rearrangement of the cytoskeleton to direct the vesicles toward the terminal nerve membrane?

Why was it important to present this conversation is such detail? To illustrate that it is refreshing to integrate knowledge from a completely new source in a departmental seminar setting. To me it is a very exciting event to learn that common mechanisms are occurring in both plants and the mammalian nervous system. If my department had not reorganized at this time, such integration of biological systems might have remained unknown to me. Such material can be of greater use because eventually it becomes integrated into lectures in the classroom.

With such beneficial outcomes after reorganization, one wonders if other tightly disciplined departments might consider dismantling and regrouping. If parts of physics, chemistry, and biology risked integrating, what new combination of efforts might emerge? Traditional science departments might find that not only would their particular research disciplines benefit, but also the teaching curriculum would gain new directions. This kind of integrative action might be more beneficial for the older members of the faculty who have their basics well established and could more easily combine the subject matter.

To risk reorganization takes a good deal of courage. The feeling of instability is not only painful but frustrating at first. It is as if one's whole academic carpet had been pulled out from under. But now that the process has been successfully attempted at one large, major university, others might follow in even more bold directions. The time commitment to develop new integrated scientific lectures would be great, but the results have exciting potential.

14. Marjorie Garber, "Coveting Your Neighbor's Discipline," 2001

A lively critic of American arts and letters as well as a noted Shakespearean scholar, Marjorie Garber's interests led her to play upon and sketch many approaches to interdisciplinarity. This brief statement is taken from her vigorous essays in a short book on academic culture. Garber (1944–) is William R. Kenan Jr. Professor of English at Harvard and Director of its Humanities Center in the faculty of Arts and Sciences. She took her bachelor's degree at Swarthmore (1966) and her doctorate at Yale (1969).

Marjorie Garber, "Coveting Your Neighbor's Discipline," *Chronicle of Higher Education*, January 12, 2001, B7–9, and critical letters, *Chronicle of Higher Education*, February 23, 2001, B20–21; adapted from her *Academic Instincts* (Princeton, NJ, 2001): 72–96. Copyright © Marjorie Garber, 2001. Reprinted with the permission of Marjorie Garber. Further reading: Marjorie Garber and Nancy J. Vickers, eds., *The Medusa Reader* (New York, 2003); Marjorie Garber, *Symptoms of Culture* (New York, 1998); and V, 7, 9, 12.

One response to envy is to try to have it all, which in disciplinary terms means interdisciplinarity.

"*Interdisciplinary* studies, of which we hear so much," writes one of my favorite critics, "do not merely confront already constituted disciplines (none of which, as a matter of fact, consents to *leave off*). In order to do interdisciplinary work, it is not enough to take a 'subject' (a theme) and to arrange two or three sciences around it. Interdisciplinary study consists in creating a new object, which belongs to no one." The critic was Roland Barthes. The year was 1972—almost thirty years ago.

We still hear much, perhaps too much, about interdisciplinary studies: their desirability, their impossibility, their inevitability, their courtship of imposture.

In fact, *interdisciplinary* is a word as much misunderstood these days as *multiculturalism*, and for similar reasons. Both words seem to their detractors to break down boundaries and hierarchies, to level differences rather than discriminate among them, to invite an absence of rigor, and to threaten—somehow—to erase or destroy the root term (*culture, discipline*).

Does interdisciplinarity trump the disciplines? Here's a practical example. I chaired a search committee, called "the Wild Card Committee," for my department. Our charge was to think of exciting scholars who didn't fit any traditional search category: people who worked in several fields or periods or who were cross- or interdisciplinary. Once the department accepted a recommendation from us, my job was to help the chairman redescribe the candidate as at the heart of a recognizable "field," a field which was on more than one occasion configured around the chosen scholar. He, or she, then "fit" the search description perfectly, of course. To my colleagues I reiterated the range of meanings that *wild* could carry, from untamed and undomesticated to enthusiastic and versatile. But if and when these scholars joined the department, they would become professors of English—not of Interdisciplinarity. The "discipline" would impose its own discipline upon them.

The impetus to cross or link the disciplines does not come only from scholars or authors; it also comes from publishers and bookstores. Have a look at the books on your shelf to see how the publisher wants them classified and shelved. On the back cover, usually on the top left corner, you'll find instructions. Pierre Bourdieu's book *On Television* is labeled "Sociology / Media Studies"; James Elkins's *The Poetics of Perspective* is "Art History / Aesthetics"; Foucault's *Discipline and Punish* is "Philosophy/Criminology"; my book *Dog Love* is "Psychol-

ogy/Pets." It makes sense that the vendors should want more than one placement for their wares. The result, though, is a continuing sense of the restlessness or ambivalence of intellectual projects, their unwillingness to stay at home, where they belong.

In a testy op-ed piece on the trivialization of the Holocaust, Gabriel Schoenfeld, the senior editor of *Commentary*, took the opportunity to decry, in depressingly familiar terms, "the culture of victimhood, visible in our society at large but particularly ensconced in the universities." For Schoenfeld, the Holocaust, "the ultimate in victimization," was "simply assuming pride of place in a field that also comprises women's studies, gay and lesbian studies, disability studies, and all the other victim disciplines that today constitute the cutting edge of the academic world."

Schoenfeld's position, when examined without the emotion that the particularity of the Holocaust so naturally produces, is fundamentally an anti-intellectual one. Some things are too important, too painful, too historic, too terrible, to be analyzed. Schoenfeld implicitly assigns the Holocaust to the realm of the *predisciplinary*. "Holocaust studies" as a discipline, the "academicization" (his jargon word, not mine) of the subject, is itself to be avoided.

So on the one hand there are things that are too important to become mere disciplines, like the Holocaust, and on the other hand there are things that are too *un*important to become disciplines, like gay and lesbian studies and disability studies.

Notice that the word *studies* here has become in a way a suspect piece of jargon. Yet it has had, until recently, a respectable history. In fact *studies* as a term has itself shifted over the last several decades from geographical regions and historical eras to cultural groups. It is perhaps most familiar from the concept of "area studies," where it identified a region (Latin American studies, South Asian studies, Middle Eastern studies) and a complex of scholarly interests and approaches. "Studies" were precisely *not* disciplines; they were interdisciplines, nexes of overlapping interest. As far as I can gather, this is a postwar (and a Cold War) coinage, a sign of the increasing interest in non-European or non-Western regions of the world. At the same time, of course, departments of and programs in "American studies" were appearing on the academic scene.

We should add to this geographical notion of "studies" another, parallel development that was historical rather than specifically, or explicitly, regional: "medieval studies" and "Renaissance studies," for example. These "studies" were *temporal*, rather than *regional*. (Initially, the lack of a specified region indicated that they were primarily concerned with Western Europe.) In terms of academic prestige, both kinds of studies, after their initial "cutting edge" moment, were sometimes regarded as slightly "soft," because they were accretions rather than theoretical interventions. They did not shift paradigms but rather enshrined them. They were nothing if not respectable. But women's studies, Afro-American studies, and ethnic studies were something else. The very word *studies* had begun to take on a suspect "political" tinge, as if from the beginning "area studies"—founded on Cold War counterphobia—had not had intrinsic, and often manifest, political designs.

While the proliferation of "studies" in the humanities galls some commentators, few are exercised at the permutations of departments and programs in the natural sciences. I've seen no outrage at the founding of a Center for Genomics and Proteomics, nor any public outcry against such bastardizations as "biophysics," "neuroscience," or "environmental science and public policy," all relatively new entries in the course catalog.

In the wake of "studies" that were anti- or cross- or interdisciplinary by design, the traditional disciplines have in some cases begun renaming themselves as "studies": English studies, literary studies, Romance studies. And these new "studies" include issues like culture, history, language, cartography, gender, and sexuality in the range of courses they offer. The cluster model more and more obtains, with or without the "studies" designation. To make a long story short, the once outside has become the new inside. Or, to take a longer historical view, that which was once considered collectively (in the grand old days of unified knowledge: the trivium and quadrivium) and was later individualized, categorized, classified, and assorted into "departments" is now again being viewed as a collectivity. With a difference. Whether we call this poaching, cultural imperialism, hegemony, interdisciplinarity, or the end of the intellectual world as we know it will depend upon where we're coming from, where we think we're going, and in what company.

CONTEXT

By the end of the twentieth century, the most important fact about the academic profession in a historical sense was its diversity—of backgrounds, of work environments, and of professional activities (18). The identities of the people who became professors changed in the decades after World War II. The rise of fascism and the advent of war sent hundreds of European academics to the United States, many of whom were international leaders in their fields. They established new disciplines (most notably art history and musicology) in American universities, they brought new methodologies and gave historical and philosophical depth to the social sciences, and they played a vital role in the postwar rise of American science (1). The decades after 1960 saw greater demographic change: the children and grandchildren of immigrants entered academe, African Americans and scholars from other underrepresented groups, including Catholics, achieved careers in the academic mainstream. Women were the largest new group to join the professoriate. This pluralizing of academic culture was the product of broad social changes—and it forced further change.

Generalization about the profession is impossible, and perhaps for that reason the discussion of the profession almost always finds its modal type at institutions situated at the top of the hierarchy in American higher education. Notions of the ivory tower academic and the much-loved campus Mr. Chips figure continued into the postwar period, but that was becoming nostalgia rather than description. To the extent that the creation and transmission of knowledge, the "university's invisible product" in the phrase of Clark Kerr, became central to modern American life, the university could not be separated from society, making necessary another round of discussion: Is the American university too utilitarian in curriculum and research, or not enough so? Was academe too much at ease with dominant values, or too far from them (14)?

The image of the ivory tower professor disconnected from the world around him does not explain the actual history of the professoriate. Scientists after World War II could not ignore the larger implications of their work, nor were they ignored by government and business—with the Vietnam War, critics of the government began to notice them as well (3). A professional practice that enabled an academic to locate his mental life most of the time in the seventeenth century may have been possible at the beginning of this period, with its relatively homogeneous campus (male, white, mostly from comfortable classes), while families accepted a gender-based division of responsibilities for the tasks of everyday life (2). By the 1960s, however, the work of managing the increasingly typical two-career aca-

demic family greatly complicated the relation of the professional and the private aspects of academic lives. Discussion about flexible faculty work schedules notwithstanding, the disparate tasks and vaguely defined obligations produced both practical and psychological challenges (11). One relevant sign for bureaucratized campus duties was the appearance in 1993 of an easy guide to collegiate behavior in the universal faculty committee meeting (16). But efforts to improve the quality of undergraduate education by rethinking its connections to professional practices had little impact. Under pressure, a comprehensive professional model that would still bear upon teaching seemed to be elusive (17).

Feeling powerless within the established structures of governance, which by the end of the century had become increasingly corporate in form and style even if these were still recognizably distinct from those in the business world (11), faculty and even graduate assistants turned to unionization. The question of whether faculty or graduate assistants are "labor" is thus a crucial issue. Is a university professor in a unique employment category, demanding unique employment policies (9)? At many public universities there are now faculty unions, something facilitated by state labor codes. Such codes do not apply to private institutions. If their faculty or graduate students were to be determined by the National Labor Relations Board to be labor, not management or student, their right to unionize would be protected. But not otherwise (12).

Minority faculty remained in short supply; women became more numerous, but they were employed at lower ranks for lower pay and at institutions of lower prestige (8). The social issues of the larger society became part of the academy as new groups socially marked by categories of race, gender, and socioeconomic status increasingly populated higher institutions. Many teachers who identified with these groups, often themselves similarly labeled, radically rethought teaching methods and aims (5–7).

Diversity brought conflicts in values and, for that matter, lifestyles. Were not universities teaching values, many asked. What these increasingly worried voices meant was: Isn't it the obligation of the university to imbue the new students with the traditional values of the Eurocentric intellectual tradition and the white male academic culture of 1940? Not, some answered, if the critical intellect is the aim of modern education. A university, as Donald Kennedy pointed out, does not impose values as one might rules of conduct on campus. Values invite inquiry, understanding, and judgment (15).

The Intellectual Migration

1. Laura Fermi,
Illustrious Immigrants, 1971

Born and educated in Rome and married in 1928 to Enrico Fermi, Laura Capon Fermi (1907–77) came to the United States in 1939. She and her husband, renowned for his early work in atomic fission at the University of Chicago, were two of the hundreds of gifted scientists, artists, writers, and academic people who fled from totalitarianism to the United States and thereby immensely enriched American intellectual life. Laura Fermi's acquaintances within the wide community of migrant intellectuals were many, which has helped to make hers the most empathetic and comprehensive study of the cultural migration of the 1930s.

Laura Fermi, *Illustrious Immigrants: The Intellectual Migration from Europe, 1930–41*, 2nd ed. (1961; repr. Chicago, 1971), 74, 76, 93, 95–99, 101, 386–87. Reprinted with permission of University of Chicago Press, Copyright © 1971. Further reading: Donald P. Kent, *The Refugee Intellectual: The Americanization of the Immigrants of 1939–1941* (New York, 1953); Donald Fleming and Bernard Bailyn, eds., *The Intellectual Migration: Europe and America 1930–1960* (Cambridge, MA, 1969); and Lewis A. Coser, *Refugee Scholars in America: Their Impact and Their Experiences* (New Haven, 1984).

Alvin Johnson, a liberal man of wide vision, was a founder of the New School for Social Research, in New York City, and its director from 1921 until his retirement in 1945. Like Abraham Flexner, he had traveled extensively in Germany and was personally acquainted with many academics. In the course of his work for the *Encyclopedia of the Social Sciences,* of which he was a founder and editor, he had corresponded with most of the social and political scientists who were later dismissed by Hitler. Like Flexner, he was in Germany in 1932 and was deeply disturbed by what he saw and heard there. . . .

Over the years the New School made room for an incredible number of refugees and hired them to lecture in regular or special programs, sometimes on a permanent basis, more often on a temporary appointment. Thus countless scholars, scientists, artists, and musicians went through the doors of the New School in their early contacts with American education. Many Europeans owe their lives to Alvin Johnson. On the occasion of Johnson's ninetieth birthday, on December 17, 1964, the president of the Federal Republic of Germany, Heinrich Luebke, sent him a congratulatory message to express the gratitude of the German people for his "devoted help and support . . . to the German scientists and artists persecuted under Nazi terrorism. . . ."

By one road or another the intellectuals from continental Europe kept streaming to America from 1930 through 1941, until the war put a virtual end to their coming. . . .

The national composition of the wave varied in time. The Germans, who were the largest national group, representing about 44 per cent of the total, reached the highest percentage in the years 1933–34, when they constituted almost two-thirds of the intellectuals of all nationalities. This fact mirrors both the sudden outburst of widespread persecutions in Germany and the deafness of other countries to the warning. The ratio of Germans remained nearly as high in the period from 1935–37, before the great expansion of Hitler's sphere of influence, but it began to fall after the Nazis moved to the conquest of Europe and refugees from many countries left for America. The German percentage was at its lowest in the years 1940–41, when the Germans were only about one-third of the intellectuals coming here.

The Austrians were the second largest national group in the cultural migration, representing about 20 per cent of the total. Almost one-half of all Austrians in the wave came to this country in the period 1938–39, driven out of their homes by the *Anschluss* and Nazi rule in Austria. In those two years they formed about 29 per cent of all nationalities, the highest percentage they reached. The lowest was in 1933–34, when they were only a little over 11 per cent of the total.

Like the Austrian wave, the waves of Hungarians, Czechoslovakians, and Italians reached their peaks in the period 1938–39; the French, Polish and Russians showed their highest percentage in 1940–41. (Other national groups seem too small for statistical consideration.) . . .

If inertia had been the only force acting on the newcomers, all those who arrived in New York would have remained there. Instead, individual initiative and the spirit of adventure, and the efforts of organized assistance, pushed many from New York and resulted in a wide geographical distribution. Many places come to mind as I quickly review where I have met European intellectuals in the United States or where those of whom I know have been. Most are large universities and colleges that over the years have hired many emigres, but others are smaller institutions. At Sweet Briar, in Virginia, a German woman, Hilde Stücklen, was the chairman of the physics department for thirteen years; in Winston-Salem, North Carolina, the distinguished Italian biologist Camillo Artom has engaged in research since 1939; the Austrian composer Ernst Kanitz taught at Winthrop College at Rock Hill, and Erskine College at Due West, both in South Carolina; the German psychiatrist Rudolph Kieve has practiced for many years in Santa Fe, New Mexico; and Los Alamos saw in wartime the highest density of European talent ever assembled in the United States. No state of the Union has been entirely without intellectual immigrants.

By and large, this pattern of distribution of European intellectuals is similar to that of American culture in general. It shows the highest concentration on a strip along the central part of the East

Coast, the second highest on the West Coast, and the lowest in the vast spaces in between, with denser islands in such cities as Chicago. . . .

Until recently, the department of astronomy at the University of Chicago was one of the most "European" departments of astronomy in the United States. Also at the University of Chicago, the Oriental Institute has been much favored by Assyriologists from Europe and other experts in civilizations of the Near East. Art historians flocked to New York University, and so did an outstanding group of mathematicians; other mathematical talent gathered in Princeton, New Jersey, and at Brown University in Providence, Rhode Island. Composer Darius Milhaud wrote about Mills College, whose faculty he joined in 1940: "I believe that Mills College is the only school in the United States to engage a French writer for the summer session every year . . . the 1941 summer school was placed resolutely under the sign of French culture, through the engagement of Fernand Leger, Andre Maurois, and me." And Black Mountain College in North Carolina was remarkable in so many respects that it deserves some comment.

I had never heard of Black Mountain College until I started to examine the biographical data of European-born intellectuals and noticed that many teachers, artists, and musicians had spent considerable time there. Not believing in coincidence, I sought an explanation, and to my confusion found that a coincidence was indeed at the heart of the matter. Black Mountain College was opened in the fall of 1933, just a few months after the first victims of Hitler's policies had begun to arrive in the United States. It was founded as an educational experiment by a splinter group of teachers and students from Rollins College, Florida. "Without the Europeans it could not have functioned," said the German-born musicologist Edward Lowinsky, who was a member of its music department from 1942 until 1947. Set at an altitude of 2,400 feet among green, wooded hills cut by swiftly running brooks and with its own little lake, the college strongly resembled many summer resorts on the slopes of the Alps. . . . But the Europeans were attracted also, I dare say mainly, by other features: the great stress that Black Mountain College placed on the arts, its communal life, self-government, and student teacher relations. When the college opened in the fall of 1933, the painter Josef Albers and his wife Anni, a weaver, lecturer, and writer, were on the faculty. Josef Albers had been a member of the German Bauhaus until a few months earlier, when Hitler dissolved it. At Black Mountain he established a similar school, on a smaller scale but with the same emphasis on the reconciliation of the fine arts and the applied arts, of the medieval type of instruction in the crafts and the need for industrial design in the machine age.

Albers and his wife stayed at Black Mountain College from 1933 until 1949, at which time its rapid decline had begun. The Dutch painter Willem de Kooning, who came to the United States in 1926, joined its faculty in 1948, and several other European artists were invited to teach at special summer institutes, among them the famous German architect Walter Gropius, founder of the original Bauhaus in Weimar; sculptors Jose de Creeft and Ossip Zadkine, one from Spain, the other from Russia; the Spanish architect Jose Luis Sert; the French painter Amedee Ozenfant; and Lyonel Feininger, who was born in the United States but lived in Germany from the age of sixteen until Hitler drove him out.

The music department was also European. Several Germans besides Lowinsky were on its faculty at various times: conductors Heinrich Jalowetz and Fred Cohen (with their wives, singer and voice teacher Johanna Jalowetz and dancer and choreographer Elsa Cohen); composer Stefan Wolpe; harpsichordist Erwin Bodky; and violist and violinist Gretel Lowinsky. Among the musical celebrities teaching or performing at the college during summer institutes were German musicologist Alfred Einstein; Hungarian violist Marcel Dick; Russian cellist Nikolai Graudan; and three Austrians: Hugo Kauder, composer, Ernst Krenek, musicologist and composer, and Yella Pessl, harpsichordist. Although the largest number of European-born were in the arts and music, there were some in other departments. I've mentioned Anna Moellenhoff, who taught biology. Her husband Fritz taught psychology for two years and was succeeded by another German psychiatrist, Erwin Straus (whose wife is a violinist). Physicist Peter Bergmann, mathematician Max Dehn, and anthropologist Paul Leser were also German. Frances de Graaff, an expert in Russian literature, came from Holland. The Czech economist Karl Niebyl joined the faculty for one year, and another Czech, the eminent scholar and writer Erich Kahler, visited the college for long periods.

As an example of the advanced ideas prevailing at Black Mountain College, Edward Lowinsky recalled that it had attempted integration ten years before the decision of the Supreme Court. Lowinsky, charged with the execution of the plan, succeeded in recruiting Negro students and faculty. He persuaded the Negro tenor Roland Hayes to visit the college with his wife and daughter Africa for three weeks during the summer institute of 1945. And in the summer, the music department gave weekly concerts attended by the people of Asheville. Hayes sang for an overflow audience with perhaps 10 percent Negroes, who were not seated separately by decision of the college. "The times have changed, haven't they?" an old woman in the audience reportedly commented to a neighbor. And that was all; there were no disturbances. At the height of the integration program the small college, with its ratio of twenty teachers to sixty to eighty students, had six Negro students and one Negro faculty member (the latter changing every semester).

Black Mountain College was held together by its spirit rather than by its finances or any benefits to its faculty. After the war it could not stand the competition of institutions of larger means and lost many faculty members. Their later careers are an indication of its excellence. Albers and de Kooning went to Yale and Bodky to Brandeis. Lowinsky was first at Queens College, then at the University of California at Berkeley, and finally at Chicago. Cohen went to the Juilliard School of Music; Erwin Straus became head of psychiatry at the Veterans' Hospital in Lexington, Kentucky, and Fritz Moellenhoff, after some wandering, became a member of the staff of the Chicago Institute for Psychoanalysis. Others scattered to various colleges, universities, and related institutions. . . .

Once in this country, the Germans were surprised at the high academic level of their American colleagues. Most Germans were swiftly won over by the friendliness, benevolence, and tolerance of those with whom they came in contact, teachers and students alike. At the same time, they could not help missing the high status and distinction granted professors in Germany. Even as spiritual a man as Paul Tillich once remarked that in the change from a German to an American university he had, so to speak, "come down seven steps on the social ladder." But in the end they accepted this demotion with good grace. They had one common mission: to fight Nazi propaganda in the United States, urge Americans to make a distinction between Germany and the Nazi regime, and persuade Americans that there was popular opposition to Hitler in Germany. Each also had an individual mission: theoretical physicists felt they had to bring theory into American laboratories and explain its role; applied mathematicians devoted themselves to the task of removing American mathematics from the isolation of its abstractness and promoting interdisciplinary contacts with physics, mechanics, and technology; lawyers considered it their duty to acquaint Americans with European law; historians offered the solid background of experience that Germany had acquired during its process of maturation to help America strengthen itself. In general, the Germans rapidly recognized the good features of the American cultural patrimony and did not try to supplant American methods and ideas with their own but strove to fuse them, promoting understanding between the two traditions. . . .

It seems almost trite to say that freedom of thought and freedom from fear are essential conditions for productive exercise of the mind and to recall that the many who came to America from totalitarian countries had been deprived of these freedoms for periods that in some instances were of two decades (the youngest in the cultural wave had forgotten the taste of life in a democracy). But the factor of the greatest practical value, one that gave countless Europeans the chance to resume their intellectual careers in this country, may well have been the flexibility of American institutions of higher learning. A small minority of Europeans was obliged to resettle in non-intellectual occupations; but without the flexibility of American institutions the proportion would have been much higher. In contrast to the rigid European systems, American colleges and universities could select the teachers they wanted, appoint foreigners, and create new posts if funds were available. Throughout the thirties, foreigners were indeed appointed and many positions were created for them. American generosity provided the funds. After the war, in the increased demand for education, more foreigners obtained appointments in American schools and more positions were created, but no longer was there need for the citizens' generosity: educational programs were either self-supporting or received government grants. This same flexibility existed in art and music schools, in hospitals and clinics and other institutions; all were able to make room for the arriving intellectuals.

At Work in the Academy

2. J. H. Hexter, "The Historian and His Day," 1961

Jack Hexter's sketch of the humanist-scholar's frame of mind during his working day endures as a recollection of a scholarly, if not monastic, clock. Written at a time when academic people, then the majority males, were increasingly on the go, his essay by contrast fairly described, where many failed to define, the professorial "ivory tower" often envied or misunderstood by lay people. Hexter (1910–96) is remembered for his challenging studies in modern historiography and English history. Born in Tennessee and trained in history at Harvard (Ph.D. 1937), he taught at Queen's College, New York (1939–45), Washington University (1945–64, 1978–), and at Yale (1964–78).

J. H. Hexter, "The Historian and His Day," *Reappraisals in History* (Evanston, IL, 1961): 6–9. Further reading: J. H. Hexter, "Call Me Ishmael: Or a Rose by Any Other Name," *American Scholar* 52 (Summer 1983): 339–53; and Robert M. MacIver, *As a Tale That Is Told: The Autobiography of R. M. MacIver* (Chicago, 1968), ch. 19.

I rise early and have breakfast. While eating, I glance through the morning paper and read the editorial page. I then go to the college that employs me and teach for two to four hours five days a week.[1] Most of the time the subject matter I deal with in class is cobwebbed with age. Three fourths of it dates back from a century and a quarter to three millennia; all of it happened at least thirty years ago. Then comes lunch with a few of my colleagues. Conversation at lunch ranges widely through professional shoptalk, politics, high and ghostly matters like religion, the nature of art or the universe, and the problems of

---

1. A change in place of employment since the above sentence was written has resulted in a reduction of the number of hours I spend in teaching.

child rearing, and finally academic scuttlebutt. At present there is considerable discussion of the peculiar incongruence between the social importance of the academic and his economic reward. This topic has the merit of revealing the profound likemindedness, transcending all occasional conflicts, of our little community. From lunch to bedtime my day is grimly uniform. There are of course occasional and casual variations—preparation of the ancient material above mentioned for the next day's classes, a ride in the country with the family, a committee meeting at college, a movie, a play, a novel, or a book by some self-anointed Deep Thinker. Still by and large from one in the afternoon to midnight, with time out for dinner and domestic matters, I read things written between 1450 and 1650 or books written by historians on the basis of things written between 1450 and 1650. I vary the routine on certain days by writing about what I have read on the other days. On Saturdays and in the summer I start my reading or writing at nine instead of noon. It is only fair to add that most days I turn on a news broadcast or two at dinnertime, and that I spend an hour or two with the Sunday paper.

Now I am sure that many people will consider so many days so spent to be a frightful waste of precious time; and indeed, as most of the days of most men, it does seem a bit trivial. Be that as it may, it remains one historian's own day. It is his own day in the only sense in which that phrase can be used without its being pretentious, pompous and meaningless. For a man's own days are not everything that happens in the world while he lives and breathes. As I write, portentous and momentous things are no doubt being done in Peiping, Teheran, Bonn, and Jakarta. But these things are no part of my day; they are outside of my experience, and though one or two of them may faintly impinge on my consciousness tomorrow via the headlines in the morning paper, that is probably as far as they will get. At best they are likely to remain fluttering fragments on the fringe of my experience, not well-ordered parts of it. I must insist emphatically that the history I write is, as the present-minded say, intimately connected with my own day and inextricably linked with my own experience; but I must insist with even stronger emphasis that my day is not someone else's day, or the ideal Day of Contemporary Man; it is just the way I happen to dispose of twenty-four hours. By the same token the experience that is inextricably linked to any history I may happen to write is not the ideal Experience of Twentieth-Century Man in World Chaos, but just the way I happen to put in my time over the series of my days.

Now it may seem immodest or perhaps simply fantastic to take days spent as are mine—days so little attuned to the great harmonies, discords and issues of the present—and hold them up for contemplation. Yet I will dare to suggest that in this historian's own humdrum days there is one peculiarity that merits thought. The peculiarity lies in the curious relation that days so squandered seem to establish between the present and a rather remote sector of the past. I do not pretend that I am wholly unconcerned by the larger public issues and catastrophes of the present; nor am I without opinions on a large number of contemporary issues. On some of them I am vigorously dogmatic as, indeed, are most of the historians I know. Yet my knowledge about such issues, although occasionally fairly extensive, tends to be haphazard, vague, unsystematic and disorderly. And the brute fact of the matter is that even if I had the inclination, I do not have the time to straighten that knowledge out except at the cost of alterations in the ordering of my days that I am not in the least inclined to undertake.

So for a small part of my day I live under a comfortable rule of bland intellectual irresponsibility vis-à-vis the Great Issues of the Contemporary World, a rule that permits me to go off half-cocked with only slight and occasional compunction. But during most of my day—that portion of it that I spend in dealing with the Great and Not-So-Great Issues of the World between 1450 and 1650—I live under an altogether different rule. The commandments of that rule are:

1. Do not go off half-cocked.
2. Get the story straight.
3. Keep prejudices about present-day issues out of this area.

The commandments are counsels of perfection, but they are not merely that; they are enforced by sanctions, both external and internal. The serried array of historical trade journals equipped with extensive book-review columns provides the most powerful external sanction. . . .

The reviewing host seems largely to have lined up with the history-minded. This seems to be a consequence of their training. Whatever the theoretical biases of their individual members, the better departments of graduate study in history do not encourage those undergoing their novitiate to resolve research problems by reference to current ideological conflicts. Consequently most of us have been conditioned to feel that it is not quite proper to characterize John Pym as a liberal, or Thomas More as a socialist, or Niccolò Machiavelli as a proto-Fascist, and we tend to regard this sort of characterization as at best a risky pedagogic device. Not only the characterization but the thought process that leads to it lie under a psychological ban; and thus to the external sanction of the review columns is added the internal sanction of the still small voice that keeps saying, 'One really shouldn't do it that way.'[2]

---

2. I do not for a moment intend to imply that current dilemmas have not suggested *problems* for historical investigation. It is obvious that such dilemmas are among the numerous and entirely legitimate points of origin of historical study. The actual issue, however, has nothing to do with the point of origin of historical studies, but with the mode of treatment of historical problems.

The austere rule we live under as historians has some curious consequences. In my case one of the consequences is that my knowledge of the period around the sixteenth century in Europe is of a rather different order than my knowledge about current happenings. Those preponderant segments of my own day spent in the discussion, investigation and contemplation of that remote era may not be profitably spent but at least they are spent in an orderly, systematic, purposeful way. The contrast can be pointed up by a few details. I have never read the Social Security Act, but I have read the Elizabethan Poor Law in all its successive versions and moreover I have made some study of its application. I have never read the work of a single existentialist but I have read Calvin's *Institutes of the Christian Religion* from cover to cover. I know practically nothing for sure about the relation of the institutions of higher education in America to the social structure, but I know a fair bit about the relation between the two in France, England and the Netherlands in the fifteenth and sixteenth centuries. I have never studied the Economic Reports to the President that would enable me to appraise the state of the American nation in the 1950s, but I have studied closely the *Discourse of the Commonwealth of England* and derived from it some reasonably coherent notions about the condition of England in the 1550s. Now the consequence of all this is inevitable. Instead of the passions, prejudices, assumptions and prepossessions, the events, crises and tensions of the present dominating my view of the past, *it is the other way about*. The passions, prejudices, assumptions and prepossessions, the events, crises and tensions of early modern Europe to a very considerable extent lend precision to my rather haphazard notions about the present. I make sense of present-day welfare-state policy by thinking of it in connection with the 'commonwealth' policies of Elizabeth. I do the like with respect to the contemporary struggle for power and conflict of ideologies by throwing on them such light as I find in the Catholic-Calvinist struggle of the sixteenth century....

3. Steven Weinberg, "Reflections of a Working Scientist," 1974

Steven Weinberg (1933–) became a leading theoretical physicist in 1967 by successfully applying hidden symmetry to low-energy meson phenomena. By 1979 he and two other physicists shared a Nobel Prize for independently developing a model that became the standard theory of the electroweak interaction of elementary particles. Their work brought physicists closer to a unified theory of the nongravitational forces operating in nature. Weinberg graduated from Cornell University (1954), received his Ph.D. in physics at Princeton (1957), and spent his early academic career at the University of California, Berkeley (1959–69). He went on to the Massachusetts Institute of Technology (1969–73), to Harvard University as Higgins Professor of Physics (1973–82), and finally to the University of Texas. His essay is one of the few personal and suc-

cinct defenses of the working theoretical scientist written in the 1970's.

Steven Weinberg, "Reflections of a Working Scientist," *Daedalus* 103 (Summer 1974): 22–45. © 1971 by the American Academy of Arts and Sciences, abridged with permission. Further reading: Weinberg, *The Discovery of Subatomic Particles*, rev. ed. (New York, 2003); Harriet Zuckerman, *The Scientific Elite* (New York, 1977); Warren G. Hagstrom, *The Scientific Community* (New York, 1965); and V, 1.

I once heard the period from 1900 to the present described as "this slum of a century." Certainly the case could be made that the twentieth century fails to come up to the nineteenth in the grand arts—in music, in literature, or in painting. Yet the twentieth century does stand among the heroic periods of human civilization in one aspect of its cultural life—in science. We have radically revised our perceptions of space, time, and causation; we have learned the basic principles which govern the behavior of matter on all scales from the atomic to the galactic; we now understand pretty well how continents form and how the genetic mechanism works; we may be on the verge of finding out the over-all space-time geometry of the universe; and with any luck we will learn by the end of the century how the brain is able to think. It seems strange to me that of all the enterprises of our century, it should be science that has come under attack, and indeed from just those who seem most in tune with our times, with contemporary arts and ways of life.

I take it that my role . . . is not so much to defend science . . . but rather to serve as an exhibit of the "genuine article," the unreformed working scientist. I will therefore simply list three of what I take to be the common current challenges to science, and react to each in turn.

These reflections arise from my own experiences as a theoretical physicist specializing in the theory of elementary particles, and I am not really certain how far they would apply to other areas of science. I intend most of my remarks to apply to the whole range of natural nonbehavioral pure sciences, but some of them may have a more limited validity. On the other hand, I explicitly do not intend my remarks to apply to the social or psychological sciences, which seem to me to face challenges of a special and different sort.

THE SCIENTIST AS DR. FRANKENSTEIN

1. *Scientists pursue their research, without taking due account of the harm that may be done by practical application of their work.*

This is in some degree true. There are even some scientists, though I think not many, who argue that it is their business to pursue knowledge wherever it leads them, leaving the question of practical application to businessmen, statesmen, and generals whose responsibility it is to worry about such matters. For example, many critics point to the nuclear weapon as the ugliest product of "pure" research. But this charge overestimates the degree to which the scientist can look into the future. The nuclear physicists who discovered fission at the end of the 1930's were not so much indifferent to the danger of nuclear weapons as they were unaware of it. . . . Later, of course, nuclear weapons were developed in the United States and elsewhere by scientists who knew perfectly well what they were doing, but this was no longer for the sake of pure research, but in the hope of helping to win World War II.

I do not see how my present work on elementary particles and cosmology could possibly have any applications, good or evil, for at least twenty years. But how can I be sure? One can think of many dangers that might arise from present pure research, especially research on genetics and the human mind, and I hope that the researchers will be able to hold back the most dangerous lines of research, but they will not have an easy time of it. For a scientist unilaterally to cut off progress along certain lines because he calculates that more harm than good will come out of it requires a faith in the accuracy of his calculations more often found among businessmen, statesmen, and generals than among natural scientists. And do the critics of science really want the scientist and not the public to make these decisions?

2. *In order to gain material support for their "pure" research or for themselves, scientists prostitute themselves to industry or government by working directly on harmful technological developments.*

Again, scientists being human, this charge is, in some measure, true. One has only to think of Leonardo's letter to the Duke of Milan offering his services in the construction of ingenious instruments of war. It seems strange to me, however, to single out scientists to bear the burden of this charge. Returning to the unavoidable example of nuclear weapons, Oppenheimer, Fermi, and the others who developed the nuclear fission bomb in World War II did so because it seemed to them that otherwise Germany would develop the bomb first and would use it to enslave the world. Since World War II a large fraction of the physicists whom I know personally have washed their hands of any involvement, part-time or full-time, in military research and development. I know of no other group, certainly not workers or businessmen, who have shown a similar moral discrimination. And what of those scientists who have not washed their hands? Admittedly; there are some who work on defense problems for money, power, or fun. There are a few others who are convinced on political grounds that any weapon that adds to military strength should be developed. However, most of the "pure" scientists in the U.S. who have been involved in military work have tried to draw a line at one point or another, and to work only on a limited class of problems where, rightly or wrongly, they felt that more good than harm could be done. . . .

I would like to be able to argue that academic scientists have had a humane and restraining influence on military policy, but looking back, it is hard to find evidence that I, or even those much more active and influential than myself, have had any influence at all. However, I am convinced at least that the world would not be better off if we had kept our hands out.

3. *Scientific research of all types is oppressive, because it increases the power of the developed nations relative to the underdeveloped, and increases the power of the ruling classes relative to the ruled.*

This charge rests on such far-ranging political and historical assumptions that I cannot begin to do it justice. I am not convinced that new technology tends to support old power structures more than it tends to shake them up and put power in new hands. I am also not convinced that one should always support underdeveloped nations in conflict with more modern ones. . . .

Furthermore, this argument for stopping scientific research logically requires a permanent general strike by everyone whose work helps to keep modern industrialized society going, not just by scientists. . . .

I would agree, however, that certain special kinds of technology are particularly liable to be used in an oppressive way, especially the modern computer with its capacity for keeping track of enormous quantities of detailed information. I would be in favor of cutting off specific kinds of research where specific dangers clearly present themselves, but decisions in this realm are always very hard to make. Usually, as in the case of computer technology, it is not possible, by closing off lines of research, to ward off the dangers of technology without at the same time giving up its opportunities.

4. *Scientific research tends to produce technological changes which destroy human culture and the natural order of life.*

I am more sympathetic to this charge than to most of the others. Even apart from what has been done with new weapons of war, a terrible ugliness seems to have been brought into the world since the industrial revolution through the practical applications of science. As an American, I naturally think of what I see from my car window: the great superhighways cutting cross the countryside, the suburban strips with their motels and gas stations, and the glittering lifelessness of Park Avenue.

I am not sure why this should have happened. Earlier new technology, such as the pointed arch and the windmill, created more beauty than ugliness. Perhaps it is a question of scale; so many people now have cars and electric appliances that the impact of highways, factories, and power stations is too great to be absorbed into the natural background—unlike an occasional windmill or cathedral. . . .

5. *While serious human needs go unfulfilled, scientists spend large sums on accelerators, telescopes, etc.,*

which serve no purpose other than the gratification of their own curiosity.

There is no doubt that a great deal of scientific work is carried out without any expectation of practical benefit, and indeed would be carried out even if it were certain that no practical benefit would result. It is also true that some of this work is very expensive, for the simple reason that in any given field the experiments that can be done with string and sealing wax tend to have been done already.

I suppose that if one takes the strictly utilitarian view that the only standard of value is integrated public happiness, then scientists ought to be blamed for doing any research not motivated by calculations of how much it would contribute to public welfare. By the same reasoning, no one ought to support the ballet, write honest history, or protect the blue whale, unless it can be shown that this will maximize public happiness. However, anyone who believes that knowledge of the universe is, like beauty or honesty, a good thing in itself, will not condemn the scientist for seeking the support he needs to carry out his work. . . .

THE SCIENTIST AS MANDARIN

There is a widespread suspicion that science operates as a closed shop, closed to unorthodox ideas or uncomfortable data, especially if these originate outside a small circle of established leaders. . . .

1. *How open is science to new ideas from the young, unestablished scientist?*

Of course, there is a scientific *cursus honorum,* and those who are just starting are less influential than their seniors. The fact is, however, the system of communication in science, probably more than that in any other area of our society, allows the newcomer a chance at influencing his field.

In physics, my own field, the preeminent journal is the *Physical Review.* Almost all physicists at least scan the abstracts of the articles in their own specialties in each issue. The *Physical Review* has a panel of over a thousand reviewers who referee submitted papers, but in fact about 80 percent of all papers are accepted, and of the others a good proportion are rejected only because they are unoriginal. The *Physical Review* is an expensive operation, supported by subscriptions and page charges paid by the authors' institutions, but if in author cannot arrange to have the page charge paid, the paper is published anyway (though admittedly with a few months' delay).

There is also a more exclusive journal, *Physical Review Letters,* which publishes only short papers judged to contain material of special importance. As might be expected there is a crush of authors trying to get their papers published in *Physical Review Letters,* and every year sees several editorials in which the editor wrings his hands over the difficulty of making selections. Nevertheless, *Physical Review Letters* does a good job of judging the paper rather than the author. (In 1959, when I was an unknown research associate, I had several papers accepted by *Physical Review Letters*; in 1971, as a reasonably well-known professor at M.I.T., I had one rejected.)

In addition to the *Physical Review* and *Physical Review Letters,* there are a great number of other physics journals in which it is even easier to publish. So well does this system work that it has become quite common for a physics department chairman who needs advice on the work of a young physicist in his own department to solicit comments from senior physicists in other universities who have never even met the young physicist, on the assumption that they will of course be familiar with his or her published work.

Of course, the humanities and social sciences also have widely circulated journals, but I have the impression that they do not provide anywhere near so effective a channel of communication for the young or unestablished scholar as do the natural science journals. The reason is that the natural sciences have more objective (though not necessarily more reliable) standards for judging the value of a piece of work. A young physicist who succeeds in calculating the fine-structure constant from first principles, or in solving any one of dozens of other outstanding problems, is sure of a hearing. . . .

I suspect that a graduate student in history who has revolutionary ideas about the fall of the Roman Empire might have a harder time getting a hearing.

The less academic professions such as law, medicine, business, the military, and the church, are even less open. In these, a young person's work is, I believe, directed to a small circle of superiors rather than to an international community, and it is natural for their judgment of his ideas to be colored by subjective factors, such as the degree to which he accommodates himself to their preconceptions. Only a few, after getting over these hurdles, reach a level from which they can communicate to their whole profession.

None of this reflects any moral superiority in the scientists themselves. It is a natural outgrowth of the fact that they work in specialties small enough that a beginner has a chance to communicate with the whole international community of specialists, and with standards objective enough that they all can recognize the value of a piece of important research. However, it does seem peculiarly inappropriate to charge the sciences with being closed to new ideas from the young and unestablished.

For the sake of fairness, I should add here that these observations are strongly colored by my own experience as a theoretical physicist who works alone at his desk or at a blackboard with one or two colleagues. I concede that the scientific enterprise may look very different to experimental scientists, and most especially to those experimentalists in high energy nuclear physics who work in large research teams.

For instance, a recent paper reporting the discovery of an important new class of neutrino interaction had no less than fifty-five authors from seven different institutions. I do not know to what extent a junior member of such a team can really get a hearing for an idea of his own.

2. *How open is science to new ideas from the outside?*

What about the prophet in the wilderness, the truly original genius outside the scientific community whose ideas cannot be understood by the pedants in university science departments?

I submit that there is no such person. I do not know of any piece of work in physics in this century which was originally generally regarded as crackpot—as opposed to merely wrong—which subsequently turned out to be of value....

3. *How open is science to truly revolutionary ideas?*

Even granting that the scientific communication system works as well as it ought to, are not scientists' minds closed to ideas, from whatever source, which challenge orthodox scientific dogma? ... Many laymen and some scientists seem to believe that any number of scientific revolutions would immediately become possible if only scientists would give up some of their preconceptions.

I believe that this is a mistake, and arises from a misconception as to the nature of scientific advance. The scientific principles which at any given moment are accepted as fundamental are like structural timbers which support a great superstructure of successful predictions. It is easy to imagine knocking down any of these timbers, but very hard to imagine what would then keep the roof from falling on our heads.

For a major scientific advance to occur, it must become clear not only that fundamental changes are necessary, but also how the successes of the previous theory can be saved....

What the scientist needs is not a wide open mind, but a mind that is open just enough, and in just the right direction.

4. *How open is science to uncomfortable new data?*

One often reads in popular histories of science that "So and so's data showed clearly that this and that were false, but no one at the time was willing to believe him." Again, this impression that scientists wantonly reject uncomfortable data is based on a misapprehension as to the way scientific research is carried on.

The fact is that a scientist in any active field of research is continually bombarded with new data, much of which eventually turns out to be either misleading or just plain wrong. (I speak here on the basis of my experience in elementary particle physics and astrophysics, but I presume that the same is true in other fields as well.) When a new datum appears which contradicts our expectations, the likelihood of its being correct and relevant must be measured against the total mass of previously successful theory which might have to be abandoned if it were accepted....

Above all, in judging the openness of science, one should remember its unique capacity for discovering its own mistakes. Most natural scientists have the experience several times in their lives of being forced by new data or mathematical demonstrations to recognize that they have been seriously wrong about some important issue.... On a larger scale, the physics community has many times been forced by new data to scrap large bodies of existing theory. If this takes away from our reputation for infallibility, it should also take away the impression that our minds are closed.

THE SCIENTIST AS ADDING MACHINE

The most profound challenge to science is presented by those, such as Laing and Roszak, who reject its coldness, its objectivity, its nonhumanity, in favor of other modes of knowledge that are more human, more direct, more rapturous. I have tried to understand these critics by looking through some of their writings, and have found a good deal that is pertinent, and even moving. I especially share their distrust of those, from David Ricardo to the Club of Rome, who too confidently apply the methods of the natural sciences to human affairs. But in the end I am puzzled. What is it that they want *me* to do? Do they merely want the natural scientist to respect and participate in other modes of knowledge as well as the scientific? Or do they want science to change in some fundamental way to incorporate these other modes? Or do they want science simply to be abandoned? These three possible demands run together confusingly in the writings of the critics of science, with arguments for one demand often being made for another, or for all three....

My answer is that science cannot change in this way without destroying itself, because however much human values are involved in the scientific process or are affected by the results of scientific research, there is an essential element in science that is cold, objective, and nonhuman.

At the center of the scientific method is a free commitment to a standard of truth. The scientist may let his imagination range freely over all conceivable world systems, orderly or chaotic, cold or rhapsodic, moral or value-free. However, he commits himself to work out the consequences of his system and to test them against experiment, and he agrees in advance to discard whatever does not agree with observation. In return for accepting this discipline, he enters into a relationship with nature, as a pupil with a teacher, and gradually learns its underlying laws. At the same time, he learns the boundaries of science, marking the class of phenomena which must be approached scientifically, not morally, aesthetically, or religiously.

One of the lessons we have been taught in this way is that the laws of nature are as impersonal and free of human values as the rules of arithmetic. We didn't want it to come out this way, but it did. . . .

But there are compensations. Precisely at the most abstract level, furthest removed from human experience, we find harmony and order. . . .

The order we find in astronomy on the largest scale is only a small part of a much grander intellectual picture, in which all the systematic features of nature revealed by experiment flow deductively from a few simple general laws. The search for these laws forces us to turn away from the ordinary world of human perception, and this may seem to the outsider to be a needless specialization and dehumanization of experience, but it is nature that dictates the direction of our search. . . .

When we spend millions today to study the behavior of particles that exist nowhere in the universe except in our accelerators, we do so not out of a perverse desire to escape ordinary life, but because this is the best way we know right now to approach the underlying laws of nature. It is fashionable these days to emphasize the social and political influences upon scientific research, but my reading of history and my own experience in physics convince me that society provides only the *opportunity* for scientific research, and that the *direction* of this research is what it is to an overwhelming degree because the universe is the way it is. . . .

3. *If science cannot be reformed, it should be abandoned.*

Suppose for the sake of argument that the case could be made that we would be happier if science were driven into some obscure utilitarian corner of our consciousness. Should we let this happen?

In the end, the choice is a moral, or even a religious, one. Having once committed ourselves to look at nature on its own terms, it is something like a point of honor not to flinch at what we see. For me, and perhaps for others, the helplessness of man in the face of pain and death also gives a certain bitter satisfaction to the attempt to master the objective world, if only in the mind. Roszak and Laing point out what they see as the moral dangers of objectivity, fearing that it is likely to leave the scientist himself as cold and value free as an adding machine. I do not see this happening to my colleagues in science. But, in gurus and flower-children, I do see the danger of subjectivity, that the rejection of an external standard of truth can leave a person as solipsistic and self-satisfied as a baby.

Finally, I must emphasize again that the "coldness" I have referred to above only characterizes the discovered *content* of science, and has nothing to do with the wonderfully satisfying *process* of scientific research. . . . Even though scientific research may not fill us with the rapture suggested by a Van Gogh, the mood of science has its own, beauty—clear, austere, and reflective, like the art of Vermeer. Or to use a different simile: if you accept the cliché that hearing a Bach fugue is like working out a mathematical theorem, then you ought also to realize that working out a mathematical theorem is like hearing a Bach fugue.

4. David W. Wolfe [on Carl Woese], *Tales from the Underground*, 2001

In contrast to the group efforts of Big Science (VIII, 10), one persevering student of nature can still offer astonishing results to the modern world. Carl Woese (1928–) is such a twentieth-century inquirer, whose identification of ancient subterranean bacteria, named Archaea, produced a revised picture of "the tree of life." Woese's slowly recognized and ultimately acclaimed findings resulted from his working out a way to classify microbial life forms by comparing their basic building block, rRNA. Assisted by Ralph S. Wolfe, he was guided by his belief that, like physics, "biology's 'subatomic' (subcellular) level is rich in information, rich in understanding, and rich in beauty."

After a bachelor's degree at Amherst College and graduate degree in biophysics at Yale (1953), Woese worked for a few years at the Louis Pasteur Institute in Paris, then at General Electric, before entering his long professorship in microbiology at the University of Illinois in 1964. He took over the Stanley Ikenberry Chair there in 1996. Awards came to him with increasing acceptance of his theory: a MacArthur Fellowship in 1984, the rarely bestowed Leeuwenhoek Medal for microbiology in 1990, the National Medal of Science in 2000, and the Crafoord Prize (complement to the Nobel Prize) from the Royal Swedish Academy of Science in 2003. The best account of his work to date is this portion of a book by David Wolfe, a professor of ecology at Cornell.

From *Tales from the Underground: A Natural History of Subterranean Life* by David W. Wolfe (Cambridge, MA, 2001): 53–55, 57–60, 62–70. ISBN: 0738201286. Copyright © 2001 by David W. Wolfe. Reprinted by permission of Basic Books, a member of Perseus Books, L.L.C. Further reading: Woese, "Archaebacteria," *Science* 244 (1981): 98–122; Virginia Morell, "Microbiology's Scarred Revolutionary," *Science* 276 (1997), 699–702; *Amherst* (Fall 2002): 13–17; the citations to the Woese–Ernst Mayr debate in Wolfe, *Tales from the Underground*, 195; and Woese's comment on the beauty of his findings in Robert Crease, *The Prism and the Pendulum: The Ten Most Beautiful Experiments in Science* (New York, 2003).

Late one evening about a quarter-century ago, in a dimly lit laboratory in Urbana, Illinois, a middle-aged scientist sat crouched over a lightbox that illuminated a large sheet of translucent photographic film. Imprinted on the film were rows of dark bands that represented the nucleotide sequence of genetic material that had been isolated from several microbes. . . .

The bar code–like pattern exposed on the photographic film was the culmination of many days of tedious preparatory work. Each row represented RNA fragments from a different organism, and by quantifying the similarity in the location and width of the bands in each row, he could estimate the genetic similarity between the organisms. In fact, he was repeating an analysis he had performed some days earlier. . . . He had checked and double-checked his work during all aspects of the procedure. This was not some experimental artifact caused by a mix-up in the chemicals used, an accidental switching of samples, or some other error. The results, if they could be confirmed by additional tests, could mean only one thing—this would be one of the most important discoveries of the twentieth century. He had identified not just a new microbial species but an entire new kingdom, or superkingdom, of organisms!

The scientist was Dr. Carl Woese (pronounced "woes") of the University of Illinois, and the year was 1976. In reality, the discovery unfolded over many days, nights, and weeks. The microbe that shook his world, and eventually initiated controversy and revolution in biology, was considered at the time to be nothing more than an obscure type of bacteria known as a methanogen. . . . Methanogens get their name from the fact that they produce methane, or natural gas, as a by-product of their metabolism. It was not known when Woese first studied them, but it is now believed that most of the natural gas deposits buried within the upper mile or two of the Earth's crust have been produced by methanogens. They are also the soil organisms that produce the combustible marsh gas that sometimes hovers over wetlands, rice paddies, and other vegetated areas with waterlogged and oxygen-depleted soils.

What Carl Woese conclusively established in 1976 was that, although the methanogens look like common bacteria under a microscope, genetically they are as distinct from bacteria as bacteria are from plants or animals. In fact, on a genetic basis, the methanogens have less in common with the other bacteria than a redwood tree or fungus has with you or me. If plants, animals, and bacteria are to be considered separate kingdoms, then so must the methanogens.

As Woese expanded his analyses, he soon found that not only the methanogens but many other supposed bacteria were also in the unique genetic category he had discovered. He began referring to the new category as a "domain" and gave it the name Archaebacteria, for "ancient bacteria." Later the name would be changed to simply Archaea to indicate more clearly the uniqueness of methanogens from bacteria and other forms of life. Woese recognized that these findings would shake our concept of the evolutionary "tree of life" down to its roots. What he could not foresee at the time were the personal and professional battles he would have to fight to gain acceptance and understanding of his revolutionary discovery. . . .

From the beginning, Woese's major interest has been the origin and evolution of life's most important molecules—the DNA (deoxyribose nucleic acid) and RNA (ribose nucleic acid) that make up the genetic code. The double-helix DNA provides the master copy of an organism's genes, and RNA, a single-stranded version of DNA, translates the genetic code into life's essential processes, beginning with the synthesis of the protein-enzymes that catalyze life's biochemistry. He recognized that an essential first step would be to build a more complete and accurate tree of life, one that encompasses the early evolution of the incredibly diverse microbial world. By identifying the present-day microbes that are the most direct descendants of our most ancient ancestors, he was bound to gain insight into the mother of all cells and the origin of the genetic code itself. It was clear to Woese that the existing tree, emphasizing plants and animals, was artificially skewed toward large, recently evolved surface organisms like ourselves, and so was of little use to him. Shaking the tree of life was just a means to an end, although, as we shall see, it led him to serendipitous discovery, controversy, and career jeopardy. . . .

Woese and just a handful of others at the time were convinced that within every living cell, at a level beyond the view of microscopes, are clues to our evolutionary past, tucked away in the structure of long, chainlike molecules such as proteins and genes. This approach could not even have been imagined earlier because scientists did not have the techniques for examining the structure of proteins or genes in detail. Woese's plan was to use the newly emerging tools of molecular biology to reach back in time beyond the oldest fossils, to the period when all life was microbial and our most ancient ancestors roamed the planet. Woese would not need to travel to exotic lands to seek out our past; he would do all of his digging in a modest laboratory in Urbana, Illinois.

Woese decided that a small subunit of a type of RNA called ribosomal RNA (rRNA) would be the best molecular clock for his purposes. Ribosomal RNA gets its name from the fact that it is associated with cellular structures called ribosomes that are part of the protein-building machinery of every cell. The particular subunit Woese selected is involved in the synthesis of protein-enzymes that no organism can do without. Thus, it is found in all creatures, from bacteria to begonias, from mushrooms to humans. Using rRNA would allow Woese and others to compare all of Earth's genetic diversity on the same terms and construct a truly universal tree of life. Similar to the changes in the amino acid sequence of the proteins studied by Pauling and Zuckerkandl, the rRNA undergoes random neutral changes in nucleotide sequence that serve as a reliable counting mechanism—the "tic-toc" of evolutionary time.

In the early days, Woese worked in almost total anonymity, ignored by most of the scientific community. Many of those who did pay attention considered him a crackpot who was using an excruciatingly tedious technique that could never answer the big questions he claimed to be interested in. His first step was to isolate the rRNA subunit from cells. Today, with rapid automated equipment, an entire

1,500–1,800 nucleotide rRNA subunit can be sequenced in a couple of days, but when Woese began in the late 1960s, doing so took half a year or more. . . .

Woese was able to compare analogous fragments of rRNA from any two organisms and to quantify their relative evolutionary age and degree of relatedness based on the proportion of nucleotides that matched up in sequence. From this he was able to construct simple dendograms, or "trees," and determine which organisms belonged on the same branch or twig and where the important branching points were located. For the first time, the "invisible" microbes, which so dominate the underground world and embody much of the genetic diversity and living biomass on our planet, were on an equal footing with multicellular creatures on the tree of life.

Woese labored away in near isolation from the 1960s through the 1980s, while his laboratory shelves became jammed with boxes of the large film sheets containing genetic information for hundreds of organisms. Woese was one of the few scientists in the world who was capable of interpreting these films as "bar codes" representing nucleotide sequences and evolutionary relationships. Gradually, a new universal tree of life began to emerge. It was filled with surprises, some of them small, and others revolutionary. . . .

Prior to the "Woesian Revolution" our tree of life was essentially an eye-of-the-beholder version of reality: it was based primarily on what creatures look like, and what we could guess their ancestors looked like from the fossil record. Our evolutionary tree had advanced surprisingly little from the time of the ancient Greeks. . . .

By [1970] the detailed comparisons of organisms made with powerful scanning electron microscopes had revealed that all of Earth's life forms could be grouped into two "superkingdoms" based on cellular structure: The eukaryotes, which have cells with a well-formed nucleus, and prokaryotes, whose cells lack a nucleus. Within the five-kingdom scheme, all multicellular plants, animals (including humans), fungi, and the single-celled protozoa are within the superkingdom of eukaryotes; only the bacteria are prokaryotes.

This is where things stood when Woese arrived on the scene. Woese was not satisfied with the five-kingdom tree. He knew that the prokaryotes, the bacterial branch, represented most of the evolutionary history of life on the planet, and that their living members had the metabolic diversity to survive in a wider range of ecological niches than the other four branches. Bacteria and their relatives have been evolving for at least three and a half billion years, while the multicellular creatures emphasized in the five-kingdom tree have been around for less than one billion years.

A tree based primarily on visual characteristics would never do justice to the genetic diversity of the prokaryotes or the unicellular organisms that were at the base of the other branches. . . .

So Woese pursued his molecular approach. One by one, he isolated the rRNA of individual bacterial strains and compared fragments for distinctions in nucleotide arrangement. During his first ten years of research at the University of Illinois, Woese gathered enough rRNA data on about sixty types of bacteria to begin publishing their genealogies—that is, the shape of the prokaryote branch. Occasionally he would dabble with the members of the other four branches of the five-kingdom tree, the eukaryotes. . . .

Not much was known about the methanogens at the time, except that they appeared to be bacteria, they often inhabited subsurface soils, waters, and other places deficient in oxygen, and they produced methane gas as a by-product of their metabolism. . . . Woese put the methanogen sample through his rRNA sequencing mill. As described earlier, when he examined the film that resulted, the sequences for methanogens did not match up with anything he or anyone else had ever seen for a bacteria. And the sequences were also distinct from those of all the eukaryotes—the protozoa, fungi, plants, and animals. For Woese, one of the few who could interpret and fully appreciate the rRNA sequence data, it was as startling as stepping into the backyard and seeing a new bizarre creature that was clearly neither plant nor animal.

Any scientist would be thrilled at discovering a new species to add to our understanding of Earth's biodiversity, but Woese had unexpectedly dredged up an entire continent of new life forms, a new superkingdom. . . .

Day by day the evidence accumulated, and soon it was abundantly clear to Woese that all life on Earth could be divided into three primary superkingdoms, or "domains" as they are now referred to: Bacteria, Archaea, and Eukarya. (The Eukarya domain encompasses the former kingdoms of plants, animals, fungi, and protozoa.) These domains have unique "signature" nucleotide sequences in certain parts of their rRNA subunit to establish that they represent the deepest, most fundamental, branches in the universal tree of life.

Within a year of the initial discovery, Woese and Wolfe published their results in the *Proceedings of the National Academy of Sciences*. Their discovery of the archaea did not go unnoticed by the popular press, and in November 1977, it was front-page news not only in Woese's hometown paper, the *Urbana News Gazette*, but even in the *New York Times*. . . .

What shocks the socks off most people almost immediately is that the visible diversity of life we see all around us, the multicellular plants and animals, is represented by only two small twigs on one branch, the eukaryotic branch, of the new universal tree. It clarifies how our overreliance on visual evidence has for thousands of years warped our perspective on the evolution of life on our planet. Most high school and introductory college textbooks on biology today continue to perpetuate this thinking by emphasizing the plant and animal kingdoms. The rRNA analyses tell us that within each of the three domains of life are dozens of other kingdoms. And most of those kingdoms, most of Earth's genetic diversity, is microbial.

The prokaryotes, previously thought to be a single branch of primitive creatures within a five-kingdom tree dominated by large multicellular life forms, are now recognized as representing fully two-thirds of Earth's genetic diversity—the Archaea and Bacteria domains. There is greater diversity and evolutionary distance, by several orders of magnitude, within the new domain of Archaea discovered by Carl Woese than exists among the plants, animals, and fungi combined. . . .

Carl Woese brought the study of evolution into the molecular age and, in so doing, brought the microbes of the underground into the Darwinian fold. In 1977, when Woese first went public with his findings about the methanogens, he knew he had made a contribution that most scientists can only fantasize about. He had, after all, discovered a third domain of life! But what happened next—or rather, what did *not* happen—was discouraging.

After the initial few weeks of attention and newspaper reports, the requests for interviews quickly dwindled. As the months passed, the struggle to find funding to continue his work did not improve, and there was no flood of eager graduate students clamoring for a post in Woese's laboratory. The worst part of that period, according to Woese, was that most microbiologists simply ignored the mountain of evidence for a three-domain tree of life that he had so painstakingly put together. They refused to believe that this scientist, working on his own for years examining tiny bits of bacterial rRNA, was really on to something. Some openly criticized Woese's work, scoffed at his conclusions, and warned his supporters that they were jeopardizing their own careers by associating with him. . . .

Fortunately, Woese's credentials and scientific methods were impeccable, and a slow but steady stream of his publications made it through the peer review process. He gained a handful of well-respected and influential supporters. . . . This small support group stood by him, often putting their own reputations on the line.

The cold shoulder from the scientific community did little to dissuade Woese. Stubborn and self-confident by nature, he dug in his heels. He read Thomas Kuhn's *The Structure of Scientific Revolutions* and gained some comfort from the fact that his struggle was not unique in the history of scientific advance. . . .

Gradually, during the 1980s, the tables slowly turned, and the number of microbiologists who belittled Woese's efforts began to dwindle. The rRNA of several hundred organisms, representing all three of the major domains, was characterized. By the end of the decade, most scientists had at least come to accept that archaea are a unique life form, although many continued to dispute that the archaea deserve their own branch on the evolutionary tree. Woese, once shunned by many microbiologists, had become one of their leaders, even hailed as a hero by some. Woese's universal tree of life is now considered dogma among microbiologists, and the number of skeptics in other fields is dwindling as well. Virtually all of the scientific community now acknowledges the genetic uniqueness of the archaea, and most would agree that rRNA analysis has become an important tool for clarifying evolutionary relationships. . . .

5. Adrienne Rich, "Taking Women Students Seriously," 1979

Adrienne Rich (1929–) lent her resolute voice as a writer and poet to the feminist and, later, lesbian equal rights movements of the 1960s and 1970s. Her challenges to gendered social complacencies in what she viewed as a patriarchal culture were directed increasingly to curricular experimentation and the acceptance of women's studies. She had broad experience with college teaching. Her early years were at City College of the City of New York (1968–75) and next at Douglass College, Rutgers (1976–78), where she wrote this talk. She went on to the Andrew Dickson White Professorship-at-Large at Cornell University (1982–85), next to the faculty at San Jose State University (1984–86), and then to Stanford University (1986–92). Wooster, Harvard, Swarthmore, and C.C.N.Y. awarded her Honorary Litt.D.'s. National recognition of her gifts came from poetry and literary societies and by the National Institute of Arts and Letters award for poetry (1961), the National Book Award (1974), the National Medal of Arts (declined, 1977), a MacArthur Foundation Fellowship (1994), and the Lannan Foundation Lifetime Achievement Award (1999).

Excerpts from "Taking Women Students Seriously," from *On Lies, Secrets, and Silence: Selected Prose 1966–1978* by Adrienne Rich (New York, 1979): 237–45. Copyright © 1979 by W.W. Norton & Company, Inc.; used by permission of the author and W.W. Norton & Company, Inc. Further reading: for her full bibliography, see *Contemporary Authors: New Revision Series 74* (Detroit): 338–42. See also Craig Hansen Werner, *Adrienne Rich: The Poet and Her Critics* (Chicago, 1988); Cheri Colby Langdell, *Adrienne Rich: The Moment of Change* (New York, 2004); Linda Eisenmann, *Higher Education for Women in Postwar America, 1945–1965* (Baltimore, 2006); and VI, 6–7.

When I went to teach at Douglass, a women's college, it was with a particular background which I would like briefly to describe to you. I had graduated from an all-girls' school in the 1940s, where the head and the majority of the faculty were independent, unmarried women. One or two held doctorates, but had been forced by the Depression (and by the fact that they were women) to take secondary school teaching jobs. These women cared a great deal about the life of the mind, and they gave a great deal of time and energy—beyond any limit of teaching hours—to those of us who showed special intellectual interest or ability. We were taken to libraries, art museums, lectures at neighboring colleges, set to work on extra research projects, given extra French or Latin reading. Although we sometimes felt "pushed" by them, we held those women in a kind of respect which even then we dimly perceived was not generally accorded to women in the world at large. They were vital individuals, defined not by their relationships but by their personalities; and although under the pressure of the culture we were all certain we wanted to get married, their lives did not appear empty or dreary to us. In a kind of cognitive dissonance, we knew they were "old maids" and therefore supposed to be bitter and lonely; yet we saw them vigorously involved with life. But despite their existence as alternate models of women, the *content* of the education they gave us in no way prepared us to survive as women in a world organized by and for men.

From that school, I went on to Radcliffe, congratulating myself that now I would have great men as my teachers. From 1947 to 1951, when I graduated, I never saw a single woman on a lecture platform, or in front of a class, except when a woman graduate student gave a paper on a special topic. The "great men" talked of other "great men," of the nature of Man, the history of Mankind, the future of Man; and never again was I to experience, from a teacher, the kind of prodding, the insistence that my best could be even better, that I had known in high school. Women students were simply not taken very seriously. Harvard's message to women was an elite mystification: we were, of course, part of Mankind; we were special, achieving women, or we would not have been there; but of course our real goal was to marry—if possible, a Harvard graduate.

In the late sixties, I began teaching at the City College of New York—a crowded, public, urban, multiracial institution as far removed from Harvard as possible. I went there to teach writing in the SEEK Program, which predated Open Admissions and which was then a kind of model for programs designed to open up higher education to poor, black, and Third World students. Although during the next few years we were to see the original concept of SEEK diluted, then violently attacked and betrayed, it was for a short time an extraordinary and intense teaching and learning environment. The characteristics of this environment were a deep commitment on the part of teachers to the minds of their students; a constant, active effort to create or discover the conditions for learning, and to educate ourselves to meet the needs of the new college population; a philosophical attitude based on open discussion of racism, oppression, and the politics of literature and language; and a belief that learning in the classroom could not be isolated from the student's experience as a member of an urban minority group in white America. . . .

When I went to teach at Douglass College in 1976, and in teaching women's writing workshops elsewhere, I came to perceive stunning parallels to the questions I had first encountered in teaching the so-called disadvantaged students at City. . . .

In teaching women, we have two choices: to lend our weight to the forces that indoctrinate women to passivity, self-depreciation, and a sense of powerlessness, in which case the issue of "taking women students seriously" is a moot one; or to consider what we have to work against, as well as with, in ourselves, in our students, in the content of the curriculum, in the structure of the institution, in the society at large. And this means, first of all, taking ourselves seriously: Recognizing that central responsibility of a woman to herself, without which we remain always the Other, the defined, the object, the victim; believing that there is a unique quality of validation, affirmation, challenge, support, that one woman can offer another. Believing in the value and significance of women's experience, traditions, perceptions. Thinking of ourselves seriously, not as one of the boys, not as neuters, or androgynes, but *as women*.

Suppose we were to ask ourselves, simply: What does a woman need to know? Does she not, as a self-conscious, self-defining human being, need a knowledge of her own history, her much-politicized biology, an awareness of the creative work of women of the past, the skills and crafts and techniques and powers exercised by women in different times and cultures, a knowledge of women's rebellions and organized movements against our oppression and how they have been routed or diminished? Without such knowledge women live and have lived without context, vulnerable to the projections of male fantasy, male prescriptions for us, estranged from our own experience because our education has not reflected or echoed it. I would suggest that not biology, but ignorance of our selves, has been the key to our powerlessness.

But the university curriculum, the high-school curriculum, do not provide this kind of knowledge for women, the knowledge of Womankind, whose experience has been so profoundly different from that of Mankind. Only in the precariously budgeted, much-condescended-to area of women's studies is such knowledge available to women students. Only there can they learn about the lives and work of women other than the few select women who are included in the "mainstream" texts, usually misrepresented even when they do appear. Some students, at some institutions, manage to take a majority of courses in women's studies, but the message from on high is that this is self-indulgence, soft-core education: the "real" learning is the study of Mankind.

If there is any misleading concept, it is that of "coeducation": that because women and men are sitting in the same classrooms, hearing the same lectures, reading the same books, performing the same laboratory experiments, they are receiving an equal education. They are not, first because the content of education itself validates men even as it invalidates women. Its very message is that men have been the shapers and thinkers of the world, and that this is only natural. The bias of higher education, including the so-called sciences, is white and male, racist and sexist; and this bias is expressed in both subtle and blatant ways. I have mentioned already the exclusiveness of grammar itself: "The student should test himself on the above questions"; "The poet is representative. He stands among partial men for the complete man." Despite a few half-hearted departures from custom, what the linguist Wendy Martyna has named "He-Man" grammar prevails throughout the culture. The efforts of feminists to reveal the profound ontological implications of sexist grammar are routinely ridiculed by academicians and journalists, including the professedly liberal *Times* columnist, Tom Wicker, and the professed Humanist, Jacques Barzun. Sexist grammar burns into the brains of little girls and young women a message that the male is the norm, the standard, the central figure beside which we are the deviants, the marginal, the dependent variables. It lays the foundation for androcentric thinking, and leaves men safe in their solipsistic tunnel-vision.

Women and men do not receive an equal education because outside the classroom women are perceived not as sovereign beings but as prey. The growing incidence of rape on and off the campus may or may not be fed by the proliferations of pornographic magazines and X-rated films available to young males in fraternities and student unions; but it is certainly occurring in a context of widespread images of sexual violence against women, on billboards and in so-called high art. More subtle, more daily than rape is the verbal abuse experienced by the woman student on in many campuses—Rutgers for example—where, traversing a street lined with fraternity houses, she must run a gauntlet of male commentary and verbal assault. The undermining of self, of a woman's sense of her right to occupy space and walk freely in the world, is deeply relevant to education. The capacity to think independently, to take intellectual risks, to assert ourselves mentally, is inseparable from our physical way of being in the world, our feelings of personal integrity. If it is dangerous for me to walk home late of an evening from the library, *because I am a woman and can be raped,* how self-possessed, how exuberant can I feel as I sit working in that library? how much of my working energy is drained by the subliminal knowledge that, as a woman, I test my physical right to exist each time I go out alone? . . .

Finally, rape of the mind. Women students are more and more often now reporting sexual overtures by male professors—one part of our overall growing consciousness of sexual harassment in the workplace. At Yale a legal suit has been brought against the university by a group of women demanding an explicit policy against sexual advances toward female students by male professors. Most young women experience a profound mixture of humiliation and intellectual self-doubt over seductive gestures by men who have the power to award grades, open doors to grants and graduate school, or extend special knowledge and training. Even if turned aside, such gestures constitute mental rape, destructive to a woman's ego. They are acts of domination, as despicable as the molestation of the daughter by the father. . . .

Look at a classroom: look at the many kinds of women's faces, postures, expressions. Listen to the women's voices. Listen to the silences, the unasked questions, the blanks. Listen to the small, soft voices, often courageously trying to speak up, voices of women taught early that tones of confidence, challenge, anger, or assertiveness, are strident and unfeminine. Listen to the voices of the women and the voices of the men; observe the space men allow themselves, physically and verbally, the male assumption that people will listen, even when the majority of the group is female. Look at the faces of the silent, and of those who speak. Listen to a woman groping for language in which to express what is on her mind, sensing that the terms of academic discourse are not her language, trying to cut down her thought to the dimensions of a discourse not intended for her *(for it is not fitting that a woman speak in public);* or reading her paper aloud at breakneck speed, throwing her words away, deprecating her own work by a reflex prejudgment: *I do not deserve to take up time and space.*

As women teachers, we can either deny the importance of this context in which women students think, write, read, study, project their own futures; or try to work with it. We can either teach passively, accepting these conditions, or actively, helping our students identify and resist them.

One important thing we can do is *discuss* the context. And this need not happen only in a women's studies course; it can happen anywhere. We can refuse to accept passive, obedient learning and insist upon critical thinking. We can become harder on our women students, giving them the kinds of "cultural prodding" that men receive, but on different terms and in a different style. Most young women need to have their intellectual lives, their work, legitimized against the claims of family, relationships, the old message that a woman is always available for service to others. We need to keep our standards very high, not to accept a woman's preconceived sense of her limitations; we need to be hard to please, while supportive of risk-taking, because self-respect often comes only when exacting standards have been met. At a time when adult literacy is generally low, we need to demand more, not less, of women, both for the sake of their futures as thinking beings, and because historically women have always had to be better than men to do half as well. A romantic sloppiness, an inspired lack of rigor, a self-indulgent incoherence, are symptoms of female self-depreciation. We should help our women students to look very critically at such symptoms, and to understand where they are rooted.

Nor does this mean we should be training women students to "think like men." Men in general think badly: in disjuncture from their personal lives, claiming objectivity where the most irrational passions seethe, losing, as Virginia Woolf observed, their senses in the pursuit of professionalism. It is not easy to think like a woman in a man's world, in the world of the professions; yet the capacity to do that is a strength which we can try to help our students develop. To think like a woman in a man's world means thinking critically, refusing to accept the givens, making connections between facts and ideas which men have left unconnected. It means remembering that every mind resides in a body; remaining accountable to the female bodies in which we live; constantly retesting given hypotheses against lived experience. It means a constant critique of language, for as Wittgenstein (no feminist) observed, "The limits of my language are the limits of my world." And it means that most difficult thing of all: listening and watching in art and literature, in the social sciences, in all the descriptions we are given of the world, for the silences, the absences, the nameless, the unspoken, the encoded—for there we will find the true knowledge of women. And in breaking those silences, naming our selves, uncovering the hidden, making ourselves present, we begin to define a reality which resonates to *us*, which affirms *our* being, which allows the woman teacher and the woman student alike to take ourselves, and each other, seriously: meaning, to begin taking charge of our lives.

6. Carolyn Heilbrun, "The Politics of Mind," 1988

Lionel Trilling's celebration of Mind in 1974 (I, 9) was later qualified by his Columbia colleague Carolyn Heilbrun (1926–2004). Her critical studies on women's themes proposed new questions about women's intellectual lives, pioneering what was later called gender analysis. After graduation from Wellesley College (1947), Heilbrun began her long and distinguished career at Columbia (M.A. 1951, Ph.D. 1959) from 1960 until her retirement as Avalon Foundation Professor of Humanities in 1993. Her scholarly honors were many, capped by presidency of the Modern Language Association (1984). Publishing mystery novels under the name Amanda Cross, she won the Nero Wolfe award in 1981. These novels showed the sorrier aspects of academic life while her professor-detective heroine was similarly learned, witty, and sharp.

Carolyn Heilbrun, "The Politics of Mind: Women, Tradition, and the University," *PLL* 24, no. 3 (Summer 1988). Copyright © 1988 by Carolyn Heilbrun and reprinted with the kind permission of Emily Heilbrun and family. Further reading: Heilbrun, *Toward a Recognition of Androgyny* (New York, 1973), *Reinventing Womanhood* (New York, 1979), and *Writing a Woman's Life* (New York, 1988).

I have been a member of the Columbia University community for more than thirty-five years, and I cannot but consider myself to be speaking as what Lionel Trilling called an opposing self, opposed to culture—in this case the culture of the university. Lionel Trilling was the most powerful and honored presence during most of my years at Columbia; as much as anyone, he defined, both for his department and for the wider community beyond it, what he honored as the life of the mind. But history has moved, times have changed, the politics inherent in that phrase "the life of the mind" have emerged. We have come to recognize the degree to which the life of the mind is organized to reflect the politics of mind, particularly the politics of a wholly male-centered culture and university. The numbers of women in universities today, and the whole question of the canon, has come under a scrutiny which Trilling could scarcely have foreseen. It is unfortunate that the very phrase "the life of the mind," which has for so long represented all that was desired from education and all that women, excluded from education, had come to cherish as an ideal, what Virginia Woolf called "the strange bright fruits of art and knowledge," has become a kind of "buzz word" for something disembodied, unconnected with gender or race or the differing cultures and aspirations in our rapidly changing world. . . .

My thesis, then, is that women particularly have a great deal to contribute to the life of the mind in the University but that they have been prevented from doing so because much of what passes for the life of the mind is, in fact, no more than the politics of mind. The life of the mind is a synonym for what is referred to as the universal—treated, revered, accepted as though it had been engraved somewhere as eternal and unchanging truth. But we must ask what is lost to this "life of the mind"—to the mind itself, to colleges and universities, to that proud contemplation of texts and culture to which Lionel Trilling devoted his life—when women are excluded from taking their full part?

There are additional reasons for considering at this time the importance of women to the essential life of a university, to its life of the mind in the most creative and vital sense. One is the extraordinary fact that there are almost no all-male colleges or universities left in the United States or, for that matter, in England. (That all the original, all-male, colleges at Oxford now have women undergraduates is a phenomenon little noticed or commented upon in this country. The loss to these colleges has not been to the life of the mind but to the life of the playing fields. The athletic, hearty, and rather mindless young men who made up about a third of these famous colleges are no longer there, their absence fundamentally affecting the quality of undergraduate life, though probably not the quality of the life of the mind.) Many women, on the other hand, for reasons faculties of coeducational institutions ought to take more seriously than they do, still prefer to attend all-women colleges. This has a great deal to do with the life of the mind.

Feminism has now reached a retrospective stage. We are very far from the early years when rather unsophisticated methods started feminist literary critics on the heady road toward reinterpretation. Feminism itself has developed new critical strategies for reading literature and has elaborated theoretical models which place literature and cultural forms within a complex set of ideological and social arrangements. Despite this, often the most sophisticated male readers of cultural texts, even those who in their own work underscore the material and symbolic conditions that produce a politics of mind, resist the broader implications of feminist theory. Thus we discover these words from a prominent male scholar—my colleague, Edward Said: "Nearly everyone producing literary or cultural studies makes no allowance for the truth that all intellectual or cultural work occurs somewhere, at some time, on some very precisely mapped-out and permissible terrain, which is ultimately contained by the State. Feminist critics have opened this question part of the way, but they have not gone the whole distance." Women, it seems, are likely to be condemned both if they do go all the way, and if they don't.

We must recognize the unique force of feminist criticism in revising the assumptions and deflating the platitudes of our cultural and literary life, in or out of universities, but particularly within them. More than a few male academics, however, remain fearful of what they conceive to be a feminist threat. That is, I think, most unfortunate, for men in the university have everything to gain and little to lose from feminist criticism. Of course, they must put aside the fear of feminization in a profession that has always risked appearing effete and in which the codes and flourishes of masculinity have long been fetishistically clung to.

Why are men so afraid? "I think the answer to this question," Christine Froula, a young feminist critic, writes, "has to do with the fact that woman's voice threatens to discredit that masculinist culture upon which [men have] modeled their identity." Many works of the canon have constructed their "speech on the bedrock of woman's silence." "Men very commonly express the fear that feminist criticism will invert that hierarchy in which they have invested so much—will, in other words, silence *them* as patriarchal discourse has silenced women. . . . But woman speaking does not reverse the conditions of her own silencing. She does not demand that men be silent; she only asks that men cease speaking in such a way as to silence her." . . .

Feminist criticism is another way of knowing. Uniquely, it addresses the longest established binarism of our culture, a binarism seen as most in need of protection by those who fear change, new ideas, and the loss of power and control. It is no accident that the new Right, here and around the world, and

the religious fundamentalists with whom they are almost coextensive, are driven first of all by the need to return women to their traditional place of powerlessness in society. . . .

All women who have ever read a classic or undertaken an intellectual pursuit have imagined themselves as men. What alternative was there? Women in universities and outside of them have always "read with a double consciousness—both as women and as the masculine reader they have been taught to be." Might not men gain now by learning to read, not with a double consciousness but consciously as men in relation to women? The male establishment at universities might consider that the discomfort they feel before women's texts is the discomfort women have long lived with and have never quite learned to take for granted, though some have been more thoroughly trained to this, as to restrictive clothing, than others. In literature and out, femininity has existed only as a representation of masculine desire: "Men appear unwilling to address the issues placed on the critical agenda by women unless those issues have first been neutralized . . . to the already known, the already written. . . ." Women challenge the degree to which all male modern texts are narratives of mastery; women may suggest other narratives, other modes of relationship.

Yet we live in a time when the already read and the already written are being hailed as revitalizing our "legacy," when men like Secretary of Education William Bennett and retired Yale President A. Bartlett Giamatti bemoan the loss of some fetishized tradition. We may notice that men in fundamentalist societies fear the loss of virginity in unmarried women: sexual experience for women, like the not-already-read books written by women or with women as their protagonists, seem horribly to threaten the male claim on paternity and authorship. Virgins are held sacred, and terribly fragile; and female writings are declared ephemeral, charming, but altogether too sensitive for the manly business of literary authority. . . . These gentlemen express with clarity the phallocentric values of our universities—a set of assumptions which we have not sufficiently debated and which Bennett and Giamatti would have us take for granted, marking all debate as destructive.

"What characterizes good teaching in the humanities?" Bennett asks, and triumphantly answers himself: "First, and foremost, a teacher must have achieved mastery of the material." Bennett does not mean only that the teacher should have read the material but that he should have incorporated it into his conception of the universe. More importantly, mastery means that one knows what questions to ask and, more important still, what questions not to ask. Giamatti is in no doubt about this last criterion. He says that today "students of literature are increasingly talking only to ourselves and no one else is paying any attention." We are hardly surprised to learn that the two villains are feminism and theory, which are largely to blame for the failure of the many eager students of literature to come properly to love what has, by theorists, feminists, and their ilk, been snatched from them. It does not occur to either of these gentlemen that what marks the immortality of the literature we all love and cherish is precisely that it continues to require new questions. We love what we are in dialogue with; the rest we endure, or protect out of fear. Universities are not, or should not be, merely museums for the display of culture. They ought to be theaters for its ongoing creation and re-creation. . . .

Women within the university need not only to pass from the margin to the center of intellectual life, they need help from the university in confronting the problems of being female in our culture and especially in the culture of the university at this time. There is a sign in my local newspaper store reading: "By the time you know all the rules you're too old to play the game." Men in today's university might well complain that, by the time they know the rules, women have changed the game. But rules always change with time, and women, like men, need help from one another as these rules inevitably change.

Women need help in the university in other ways besides challenging the canon or daring to see our heritage as other than male centered (or other than racist or classist, since it also comes to that). The woman student faces special problems. As likely as her male counterpart—perhaps likelier—to have mixed feelings about a female authority figure, she is at the same time eager to show herself worthy of the club she has been allowed to join. Deliberately or not, women are raised to be untroublesome, and to many women, young and old, it seems profoundly boorish to question the nice gentlemen who have let them into their university. As E.M. Forster put it, it is hard, after accepting six cups of tea from your hostess, to throw the seventh in her face. Women fought for a century or more to gain a university education, and they are slow to realize that they are no longer pounding on the doors but, on the contrary, finding that the door they lean on gives way so readily that they collapse across the threshold. There is, furthermore, a tendency for an accomplished woman to think of herself as a special case, not as a member of a group called "women"—a situation intensified by the unfortunate fact that, in any revolution, those who fight are seldom those who win. The young women who now receive the rewards scarcely understand what the struggle was all about. How could they, for they will never find themselves so equal as they seem in college. Unfortunately that makes it difficult for the college to prepare them to cope with the inevitable inequalities of work, marriage, childrearing, and aging. If the men who teach them refuse to bring openly into discussion the place of females in our culture, the young women will rest in an attitude of gracious appreciation, bathed in the comforts of male authority, marvelously unprepared for the life that awaits them, including the life of the mind. To this might be added that young men themselves would benefit from knowing what the female destiny has been and may be, and from questioning not so much their attitude toward women as their attitude toward themselves and the presumptions of their maleness. . . .

7. Lani Guinier, "Becoming Gentlemen," 1994

Lani Guinier (1950–) headed toward a legal career by way of Radcliffe College (B.A. 1971), Yale Law School (J.D. 1974), and a district court clerkship (1974–76). After a year as a juvenile court referee she served at the civil rights division of the U.S. Department of Justice (1977–81) and next with the NAACP Legal Defense Fund (1981–88). Her professorial experience began with an adjunct professorship at New York University (1985–89), then a law professorship at the University of Pennsylvania (1988–97), and finally appointment to the Harvard Law School in 1998 as its first African-American woman professor. Both Pennsylvania and Harvard have given her distinguished teaching awards, and she has been honored by various legal and legislative organizations.

Lani Guinier, "Becoming Gentlemen: Women's Experiences at One Ivy League Law School," *University of Pennsylvania Law Review* 143 (November 1, 1994). Copyright © 1994. Reprinted with the permission of William S. Hein and Company, Inc. and the kind permission of University of Pennsylvania Law Review. Further reading: Guinier, *Lift Every Voice: Turning a Civil Rights Setback into a New Vision of Social Justice* (New York, 1998) and *The Miner's Canary: Enlisting Race, Resisting Power, Transforming Democracy* (Cambridge, MA, 2001).

In the conventional sense of the term, I function not only as a teacher but as a symbol for certain student voices and aspirations. I bear witness as a trophy of achievement. My conspicuous presence may rebut assumptions of group inferiority that undermine student confidence and performance. My example not only legitimizes the competence of matriculating minority students; my visibility helps lure future minority and female students into the profession. Role models provide psychological uplift, affirming the status of black women as law school citizens who can participate fully in the educational process. By confirming black and female advancement, black women role models may also be seen as living symbols of the equal opportunity process.

I do not object to being a role model, even if I had a choice about the matter, which I probably do not. Indeed, I do feel special responsibilities as a black woman law professor. But in my own eyes, I am a mentor more than a role model. I hold my students to high expectations of *themselves*, not of me. I facilitate their learning, not my being. I view teaching as a reciprocal, interactive relationship that is primarily about *their* education.

I do not view myself in my teaching role as the purveyor of an image but as a mentor who takes from the margin to facilitate student reflection, insight, and professional responsibility. Indeed, repercussions from a recent public call for more black women role models prompt me to explore the uneasiness I have with a role model rationale as a justification of my presence in legal education.

I resist the term "role model" in part because I worry about the way the role model argument is often used to diminish the actual role outsiders play, one that benefits insiders, not just other outsiders. I question the way the concept measures successful outsiders by an insider yardstick. In addition, I take issue with the idea that someone of a given person's own gender and racial or ethnic group is necessarily a model or representative for that person. Role models may grant a passport to power or status to people who then take no account of how they arrived at their destination.

The first problem with the role model argument is that it trivializes the important contribution that outsiders play in diversifying a faculty. Presenting women of color law professors primarily as role models ignores their role as scholars and intellectual leaders whose presence on a faculty might alter the institution's character, introducing a different prism and perspective. Women of color legal scholars may influence their white male colleagues to perform their own roles better.

In other words, women of color law professors symbolize more than their own singular achievement. They can be templates for how the role itself might be performed differently. For example, some black women may draw on the outsider consciousness of being a minority group advocate and member. From this vantage point, they can see that many women and students of color, already wary because of their status, respond less enthusiastically to learning by individual intimidation than to other emotional stimulants such as peer encouragement and sorority of intellectual views.

Indeed, as teachers, they may learn to use an interactive, communicative process—what Iris Marion Young calls a *communicative discourse*—to change the educational conversation. A communicative, rooted discourse requires "careful listening, questioning for clarification, the willingness to express oneself many different ways, to engage in struggle and conflict without walking away." Such a discourse rejects as the exclusive mode of participation a dominating, theatrical style of expression that often operates to silence and disadvantage members of some groups. Reciprocity, trust, and interest in "others" are valued instead. Giving a marginal perspective credibility in everyone's eyes does not require emotional detachment or rigid argumentation but many different forms of communication, including personal narrative.

A professor who engages students using Iris Young's communicative style of teaching refocuses attention away from the professor. She or he provides opportunity for student-initiated learning projects, encourages peer interaction where it provides intellectual stimulation, acknowledges where appropriate the relevance of race or gender, and makes explicit the value of listening carefully and of paraphrasing rather than parodying. He or she reinforces skilled argument, acknowledges sophisticated perceptions, and points out constantly the nuances, the implications, the complexity of voice, of analysis, of legal rules, of policy alternatives.

Like most law teachers, I was trained that the tension of the Socratic dialogue motivates learning. But though I try hard not to silence or intimidate, I still find that many women and people of color are reluctant partners in the Socratic exchange. Performance-oriented questioning, even by a "compassionate" black woman, may diminish self-esteem, and may insult students' privacy and dignity. To reach women and people of color in particular, I encourage all students to prepare for class in teams, to talk through their ideas first in less formal settings. Students who have otherwise been silent are often more likely to share their points of view openly with their classmates in such a context. And many women and men of all colors thrive once they have a chance to hear themselves think aloud, alone with their peers.

A genuinely interactive perspective on legal education does not mean lack of rigor. The big difference, it seems, is the establishment of an atmosphere of respect in which the students can safely challenge each other. "There is a different feeling in the classroom when students go after each other than when a professor goes after them; the fear is gone and people aren't afraid to have personal viewpoints." . . .

An interactive, communicative discourse may help awaken the classroom participation of some students, and subsequently enhance their learning. For others, a discourse that legitimizes alternative forms of participation, respects listening before speaking, and broadens the educational dialogue may make them better advocates by deepening their knowledge of the world around them, as well as increasing their understanding of the implications of their claims. Law students trained in a communicative discourse may become better advocates in a pluralistic society, even outside a civil rights or social change context.

Some women of color law professors also bring a sense of social responsibility to their scholarship. They can teach their colleagues how to be "organic intellectual[s] with affiliations not restricted to the walls of the academic institution." They can produce law review articles and engage in educational instruction not in isolation but in solidarity with other like-minded scholars. Speaking in their own voices connects them to the richness of their own experience and empowers them to overcome silencing by even well-intentioned white male colleagues. Their stories enrich the reality of majority group members. And their efforts to connect with others are both a means of psychic self-preservation and a lessening of their own subordination.

As women of color, we may contribute to legal education not merely through our physical presence but by pulling from the richness and rootedness of our experience, by continuously reaching for the transformative possibilities of our role. In this way, we are often less role models than teachers, educators who empower through feedback, guidance, and sharing rather than commanding through example, visibility, or physical stature.

Working in Universities / Working in Business

8. Judith Glazer-Raymo, "Academia's Equality Myth," 2001

In contrast to the personal voices in VI, 5, 6, and 7, Judith Glazer-Raymo drew together demographic and egalitarian arguments for advancing women's higher education. After graduation from Smith College (1953) and taking her doctorate in higher education at New York University, Glazer-Raymo became a dean in the School of Education at St. John's University and then went on to a professorship of education at the C.W. Post campus of Long Island University. Upon retirement there, she became adjunct professor of higher and postsecondary education at Teachers College.

Judith Glazer-Raymo, "Academia's Equality Myth," *Smith Alumnae Quarterly* (Spring 2001), drawn from her book, *Shattering the Myths: Women in Academe* (Baltimore, 1999). Reprinted with kind permission. Further reading: Linda Eisenmann, *Higher Education for Women in Postwar America, 1945–1965* (Baltimore, 2006).

Colleges and universities may advertise themselves as "equal opportunity employers," but the current political and economic climate is challenging that ideal. Higher education has become big business and the effect on academic institutions has been dramatic. The viability of many campuses is often dependent on the whims of corporate entities, market forces, and profit margins. Trustees and presidents have diverted their energies away from the university as an academic enterprise and instead spend much of their time cultivating new sources of funding and political influence. The higher education system itself has become stratified, with large multi-campus institutions setting the policy agenda for smaller ones whose main hope for success derives from their ability to identify niche markets such as study abroad, distance learning, access to consortia, or single-sex education. In effect, academic life is being redefined by economic and political forces external to our institutions—and over which we have little if any control.

For minorities and women, who are now entering the academy in higher numbers than ever, these changes have resulted in fewer opportunities for career success in academia. Indeed, the gendered consequences of four interrelated trends—the retreat from tenure, the hiring of faculty off the tenure track, the lag in academic salary-setting, and the impermeability of the glass ceiling—reveal the severity of the problems now confronting women faculty and cast doubts on the viability of the American professoriate. Here is a brief overview of the effect of these trends on women faculty and professional staff.

Economists predict tenure's demise within the next two decades. A review of data shows that institutions are less committed to recruiting full-time tenure-track faculty and instead are relying more on low-paid part-time and non-tenure-track faculty. By the 1990s, such tenure alternatives as post-tenure reviews, renewable contracts, and revenue-generating clinical appointments became increasingly commonplace in professional schools and public universities. . . .

This occurs at a time when the United States is awarding 42 percent of Ph.D.s to women. Women now receive the majority of Ph.D.s in four out of 10 academic fields: area/ethnic studies, foreign languages, letters, and psychology; and in five out of sixteen professional fields: education, health sciences, home economics, library/archival sciences, and public affairs. As well, women now earn a majority of degrees in the status professions of veterinary medicine (66.6%), pharmacy (64.5%), and optometry (53.2%), and are reaching parity in medicine (41.4%) and law (43.7%).

For women faculty the glass is half full, but when they can expect to reach equity with male colleagues in hiring, promotion, and tenure is unclear. In its 1999–2000 report on the economic status of the professoriate, Committee Z of the American Association of University Professors (AAUP), which represents 2,200 institutions, finds "striking evidence of a distorted gender distribution by rank" as well as within the ranks of full professors. Although some disparities can be attributed to disciplinary field, a disproportionate number of women faculty are tenured at the associate professor rank (35.2%) than at the rank of full professor (19.3%). For women science and engineering faculty, the gender imbalance is even greater: they are only 16.3 percent of tenured science and engineering faculty and 35 percent of untenured faculty (Babca, 2000). Overall, the National Center for Educational Statistics (NCES) reports that white males comprise 53 percent of all faculty compared to white females, who account for 35 percent, and people of color, who account for 13 percent (5% African American, 4% Asian/Pacific, 3% Latino, and .4% Native American). It also reports a 20 percent gender gap between tenured men (72%) and tenured women (52%) (Snyder & Hoffman, 2000). Hiring freezes that began more than a decade ago have contributed to a Ph.D. glut. Fewer faculty lines mean diminished opportunities to pursue academic careers. As a result, universities are diverting resources from high-cost doctoral programs into professional schools, distance learning, and tuition-generating undergraduate programs taught largely by part-time faculty and teaching assistants.

In its report, "The Vanishing Professor," the American Federation of Teachers notes that between 1973 and 1998 the ranks of part-time faculty have grown by 266 percent, term appointments by 28 percent, and non-tenure-track faculty by 51 percent (Gold &Robinson 1998); however, in those 25 years full-time, tenure-track faculty have grown by only 49 percent. More alarming, the AFT forecasts more downsizing through early retirement buyouts, differentiated staffing, and the replacement of full-time tenured faculty with part-time adjuncts and teaching assistants, all based on economic criteria having little to do with academic excellence. Linda Bell, the AAUP's chief economist, observes: "We worry that we are losing ground in relative terms to the many professionals who are cashing in on talents not dissimilar to our own in private sector; nonacademic jobs. This concern is not only personal; it may also affect the future of quality higher education in this country" (Committee Z, 2000). According to the AAUP's Committee W on the Status of Women in the Academic Profession, women now outnumber men at the lowest ranks of lecturer (55.6%) and instructor (58.6%), in most cases teaching off the tenure track with little assurance of either benefits or employment from year to year. They also spend more time teaching and less time doing research, predominantly in community colleges and less selective universities where emphasis is placed on teaching rather than on rates of publication (still the main route for achieving national recognition and remunerative rewards). The result is a dual employment system that reinforces hierarchies in which deans and department chairs set policy with the acquiescence of full-time tenured faculty. In contrast, the voices of those teaching off the tenure track, either as part-time adjuncts or non-tenure-track faculty, are rarely heard in campus governance and decision-making forums. The recent mobilization of graduate assistants to form unions at such prestigious institutions as the University of California and New York University indicates the depth of their frustration with their roles as quasi-faculty existing on modest stipends with meager prospects for academic employment beyond graduation.

The dissatisfaction among women faculty regarding persistent salary inequities in their fields mirrors American women's general disappointment with public inattention to their professional concerns. . . .

In 1986, the *Wall Street Journal* coined the phrase "glass ceiling" to suggest why so few women, despite their credentials and achievements, move up the career ladder as rapidly or successfully as men. In higher education, this phenomenon has manifested itself in the fact that women's ability to earn full professorships, major grants, named chairs, presidencies, and other forms of recognition and status remain largely dependent on men in positions of power. By 1999, according to a survey of 3,124 university and college presidents, women comprised 19 percent of the total, mainly in community colleges, women's colleges, denominational colleges, and public four-year colleges. For example, 50 of the 71 women's colleges in the United States boast women presidents. What's more, the country's 3,885 accredited colleges and universities have been organized into a hierarchy dominated by research and doctoral-granting universities. As a result, status accrues to those who lead and teach in the upper tier of research universities. For most women, leadership at that level is an elusive goal.

Another way of assessing women's progress in professional administration is to review their status as deans, one of the primary gatekeeping roles at research institutions. Alas, data from professional associations present a dismal picture. Women deans are in the minority in business, law, medicine, engineering, pharmacy, dentistry, and even education, one of the most highly feminized professions. One promising sign, however, is the increase of women as provosts. Fifteen women now hold this title at Ivy League, Big Ten, and University of California institutions, leading some to speculate that these women eventually may break through the glass ceiling into presidencies of research universities. The appointment of Ruth Simmons as president of Brown University sends a salutary message to the search committees of Harvard, Princeton, and other universities now seeking new leadership.

What are women doing to remove the barriers that impede their progress? On some campuses, they are capitalizing on student activism to gain greater equity for research and teaching assistants who do the bulk of undergraduate teaching. At some cost to themselves, they also use the courts to challenge discriminatory policies. Through their professional groups, they speak out against unfair and inequitable practices that diminish their professional prerogatives. However, despite public perceptions, some might say myths, that women have achieved parity with men, the data show emphatically that this is not the case. In systems dominated by corporate boards of trustees, political officials, and business managers, economic considerations too often preempt academic ones.

For women, it has been argued that merit, not race or gender, should be the sole criterion for admissions and employment. The weakening of affirmative action and equal opportunity offices does not augur well for enforcement of sexual harassment, hostile environment, and equal opportunity policies. Making gender the basis for either-or arguments raises questions about women's qualifications, commitment, and motivation.

Opportunities now exist for women that could not have been dreamed of when I graduated from Smith in 1953. In fact, women students at coeducational institutions have been in the majority (55.6 percent of all students and the majority of undergraduates and graduate students within each racial/ethnic group) for almost two decades. But in our efforts to diversify and continually "reinvent" ourselves, we run the risk of disregarding the fact that women are the majority of students and in some fields are gaining a greater share of professional and academic credentials. The next generation of students should benefit from access to full-time faculty (many of whom will be women) whose salaries become more competitive with other professions.

If real progress is to be achieved, though, coeducational institutions need to make commitments to women's career ambitions by providing adequate child care and parental leave policies, mentoring women into leadership positions, and creating organizational cultures that view women as catalysts for change. Ultimately, we need to mobilize the intellectual capital of feminists, including those who have been diverted from grassroots advocacy in support of fundamental women's issues by their preoccupation with more theoretical concerns. Only then can we expect to remove the barriers that thwart women's efforts to bring about sustained institutional change.

9. Michael McPherson and Gordon Winston, "The Economics of Academic Tenure," 1983

Unlike most essays covering academic tenure for the professoriate, this one bypasses the major issue of protecting academic freedom. Instead it compares the economic efficiency of tenure in academic institutions to practices in business corporations without tenure. Written by two eminent economists with long academic experience, the essay does not engage all the ramifications of the tenure debate, but its unique and specific approach to the issue has made theirs a memorable piece.

Michael McPherson (1947–) taught and was a dean at Williams College (1974–96). He became president of Macalester College in 1996 and later headed the Spencer Foundation. His writings have concerned the economics and finance of higher education as well as studies on economics and philosophy. Gordon C. Winston (1929–) has also worked in the economics department at Williams College (1971–). His writings have dealt with education, production, and organizations.

Michael S. McPherson and Gordon C. Winston, "The Economics of Academic Tenure: A Relational Perspective," *Journal of Economic Behavior and Organization* 4 (1983): 163–78. Further reading: the complex issue of tenure does not have another entry in this volume, but it is discussed briefly in the selections by Donald Kennedy (VI, 13), James Carlin (VI, 18), Walter Metzger (X, 12), and AAUP (x, 1).

The main argument advanced in favor of the institution of tenure is the protection it provides for academic freedom. Defenders of tenure seem ready to concede its economic inefficiency, but see it as a necessary price to pay to protect scholarly independence. Those who question the value of academic freedom, or see other ways to protect it, then see

little to recommend the institution of tenure. Indeed, in one of the few economic articles on tenure, Armen Alchian explained its existence cynically as an expensive and wasteful luxury indulged in by a professoriate freed through the non-profit status of colleges and universities from the rigors of the competitive economy.

Such a negative view of the economic role and consequences of tenure seems to us one-sided and importantly misleading. The implicit assumption that the world outside the academy provides most workers with little effective job security is false, and the idea that colleges and universities could function efficiently by operating on the basis of personnel policies analogous to the longshoreman's shape-up is mistaken. Indeed, some of the most interesting empirical work in labor economics of late has emphasized what Robert Hall (1982) calls, in the title of one of his papers, 'The Importance of Lifetime Jobs in the U.S. Economy'. And much of the most exciting recent work in analytical labor economics, and in macroeconomics as well, has aimed at understanding the mutual interest workers and firms have in sustaining stable long-term employment relations, and in protecting each other from the vagaries of the market.

Academic tenure, of course, differs importantly from the kind of job protection seniority affords to production workers or (more to the point for comparison with academics) the kind that corporate employment policies provide to middle level managers. But, we suggest, the difference lies less in the degree of job security afforded than in the nature of the job guarantee and, surprisingly, in the explicit and risky probation that precedes obtaining the guarantee. To put the latter point somewhat polemically: the striking thing about the university, compared to a typical corporation, is not the number of college graduates employed there with secure jobs, but the number of high-level employees who don't expect to be allowed to stay. This point is closely related to our first point, the nature of the job guarantee. For academic employees are assured not only continued employment with the 'firm', but continued employment in a highly specific and well-defined position: teaching, for instance, eighteenth century French literature. The system of rigorous probation followed by tenure is a reasonable way of solving the peculiar personnel problems that arise in employing expensively trained and narrowly specialized people to spend their lifetimes at well-defined and narrowly specialized tasks. The character of this problem, and of this solution, moreover, helps to explain a good deal about academic employment.

It is these themes that we shall develop. They will show that the tenure institution has some desirable efficiency properties that are often overlooked. This, of course, does not prove that tenure should not be reformed or abolished, especially in light of an emerging situation which may raise some of the costs of tenure. Neither does it suggest that we dismiss arguments for tenure based on academic freedom; we merely put them to one side. But we do suggest that any serious proposal for the reform of tenure has to show how alternative arrangements would solve the personnel problems tenure solves; both theory and experience suggest that the implicit alternative of providing faculty with no job guarantee does not solve these problems. Our major aim, in any event, is not to evaluate alternative policies, but to contribute to understanding how tenure actually works in the context of the university. . . .

In academic employment there is very little of this internal job mobility: it is a crucial fact that people who are hired to the faculty either stay on the faculty or are dismissed: they do not move to alternative employment within the institution, except for the relatively few who move into academic administration. And, of course, non-academic employees are hardly ever promoted to the faculty. Reasons for this crucial fact will be discussed shortly, but first it is important to note that it radically reshapes the structure of the employment problem that colleges and universities face, compared to that of large corporations. . . .

Academic employers have thus settled on . . . more intensive initial screening as a central element of their personnel policies. This takes the form both of more intensive pre-employment screening than corporations undertake for entry level positions and of intensive on-the-job screening concentrated in the first few years of employment. These considerations help account for several of the key features of academic employment policy.

First, and most centrally, we can understand why such 'a big deal' is made out of promotion and tenure decisions. The decision to employ a person permanently in a well-defined position is momentous both for the worker and the firm: the worker gets not merely employment security but something close to a guarantee of status and lifetime income prospects; the firm is locked into not only a stream of future wage payments, but a stream of future productivity from the worker over which it will have very little control. It follows therefore that firms will invest quite heavily in the scrutiny of their non-tenured employees, and that workers will attach great importance to perceived fairness of the institutions for making tenure and promotion decisions. The result is a concentration of everyone's energy and attention on that single point in the career, which is quite the opposite of the more diffuse but more sustained attention to worker performance in the corporation.

The obverse of close attention to the academic worker's performance prior to tenure is the marked inattention to performance after tenure. This too can be seen as a rational response to the academic employment situation. In the corporation, with its flexible job assignment policies, a principal role for the continual monitoring of employee performance is the making of continual marginal adjustments in workers' job assignments: increasing the productivity of the existing labor force by reallocating tasks among workers. But in the university, where the tasks are final once the employment guarantee is made, monitoring performance has little value, for there is little to do with the information. To be sure, information about tenured faculty can influence the rate of wage advance to some degree and can serve as a basis for moral suasion, but the central use to which such information is put in the corporation, to shape the path of the worker's career advance, is markedly less available within an academic institution.

These considerations also help account for the existence in academia of a sharply defined 'nodal point' by which time a decision of 'up-or-out' on tenure must be made. Personnel decisions in the corporation are almost always taken at the margin: to hasten or delay promotion; to expand or contract the range of responsibility. In academics, the possible decisions at any time are two: the marginal one of continuing employment for another year or the dramatically non-marginal one of terminating employment. If the former decision is always available, there will be an almost inevitable tendency to evade the latter one, which is bound to be difficult and unpleasant. To force a decision by a fixed moment serves both to legitimize the harsh decision to let someone go—the option of another chance just isn't available—and provide an incentive to gather the large amounts of costly information needed to make such a weighty decision responsibly.

These remarks show the fundamental differences between the personnel problems of the academic institution and the corporation that follow from the narrowness and specificity of the academic job commitment. Much more remains to be said in elaboration of the implications of these points for the operation of colleges and universities. But it is time now to examine with care the reasons for this crucial structural difference between the university and the corporation: why do universities not offer—and why do faculty not seek—the wide range of career paths offered within a typical corporation?

The fact that individuals are hired to do quite narrowly defined and rigidly specified jobs is central to the economics of tenure, and describes the major structural contrast between university and corporate employment. The sources of this difference lie on both the production and demand sides of the market. The 'organizational technology' of the university is such that it attaches relatively little value to preserving its freedom to change the job assignments of particular workers. At the same time, worker preferences are such that a faculty member would typically prefer to continue his occupation (say, teaching physics) at another institution than to stay with the 'firm' in a different job. Behind these differences in organizational technology and preferences lies an important difference between the corporation and the university in the kinds of 'knowledge capital' workers acquire to do their jobs. In the university, this knowledge is predominantly tied to the worker's academic subject: it is specific to the *occupation* and not to the firm. In the corporation, there is likely to be a greater premium on *firm-specific* human capital: knowledge of the particular codes, practices, and procedures of *that* corporation as opposed to others. . . .

This contrast is reflected in the differences in training patterns for corporate and university work. In academic employment, training is for a specific academic discipline and not for a specific employment or firm. Academic training is an extreme case of the classic 'non-appropriability' of worker training—the fact that firms are reluctant to invest their resources in the training of their employees and more so the less specific is that training to that firm—the more generally valuable it is in other firms. Training for university employment is so extreme a case of non-appropriability that the firm—the hiring university—refuses to provide any training and, instead, hires its employees with virtually their full complement of training (the PhD) secured elsewhere and at someone else's expense. This is underscored by the curious, if familiar, fact that the new academic employee does the same thing—teaches the same sorts of classes in the same way and writes the same sorts of articles and books—as the thirty year veteran. Quality, it is hoped, improves with maturity, but the duties of faculty members remain remarkably the same.

Again, the corporation presents the antithesis in its widespread employment of individuals trained as generalists who are subsequently put through a highly firm-specific training followed by a career of additional training in different, again firm-specific, activities. The multiplicity of suitable corporate jobs with their often differentiated internal training requirements and the individual worker's multiple job assignments, *seriatim*, over his career are aspects of the high degree of substitutability among those jobs. An important reason for the substitutability appears to be the absence of high levels of requisite prior training; conversely, the absence of much prior training before workers enter the firm tends to make all jobs similar for the generally-talented but not specifically trained individual.

This difference in training and human capital accumulation patterns naturally shapes worker interests in the character of the job guarantee they will seek. Individual academics will typically prefer to substitute one employer for another while retaining their occupations rather than to scrap their costly training in favor of taking a different job at the same institution. Moreover, it is reasonable to expect that only workers with a relatively strong prior commitment to the occupation will undertake training in the first place, so that the commitment to the profession is a result of preferences as well as the opportunity cost of the specialized investment in training.

The academic worker will thus put little value on a guarantee of employment which is not specific about the kind of employment guaranteed. The new corporate employee, on the other hand, with less investment in occupation-specific training, and less knowledge about where his skills and interests lie, will care more about job security as such, and may put positive value on the corporation's implicit offer to match his job assignment to his aptitudes, as information about those aptitudes emerges.

The tendency to job rigidity in the university is compounded by its objectives of doing its job of education and research (producing its product) at reasonable cost. An important aspect of the technology of university production, the result of the specialized human capital possessed by academics, is that it is rarely as easy to substitute employees among jobs as it is to hire new employees from outside for those particular jobs. If the university has an opening for a worker to teach and do research in particle physics, the productivity in that job of a professor of French Literature currently employed by the university is unlikely to be nearly as high as that of a new employee trained specifically in particle physics—someone currently in graduate school or employed in the physics department of another university. The occasional Renaissance Man, of course, is the exception that proves the rule. It will similarly be unlikely that the best person for a non-academic job opening will be a faculty member—in many cases it seems true that intense academic training does as much to *dis*qualify as to prepare people for other kinds of work. So on pure productivity grounds, too, the university will accommodate these sharp technological differences in productivity among individuals and will hire French scholars to teach French and Physicists to teach Physics.

The corporation, of course, shows that this employment pattern is far from inevitable. It hires the liberal arts graduate—often a History or English major—for a broadly defined 'management' training program from which he or she may be assigned to a specific job in production management or financial management or sales. . . . And even a cursory examination of corporate management careers makes it clear that once assigned to sales or production or finance, the corporate employee will often be reassigned to quite different sorts of managerial employment throughout his career with the firm. Indeed, even employees (like engineers) who may be hired for their specific skills will often, if successful, 'graduate' into jobs that do not depend on those skills.

So both sides of the market lead to narrowness and rigidity of academic employment: the technology of production sharply reduces flexibility in inter-job substitution at the same time that the preferences of workers sharply reduce their willingness to change fields rather than changing firms. Neither appears dominant.

It is understandable, then, in light of the important differences in the interests at work in the academic and corporate employment settings that the form of the agreements ensuring job security will differ. . . . The contract governing any employment relation will be importantly 'incomplete', with the worker ceding an important amount of discretionary authority to the firm about exactly what activities he must undertake. In the corporate setting, the firm's authority generally extends to granting the firm considerable freedom to determine what position in the firm the worker will fill, not only to begin with but through the career. The *quid pro quo* is an implicit commitment by the firm to retain the employee in some capacity, barring markedly unusual circumstances. But in the university, the faculty member cedes much less authority to the 'firm' to determine the content of his job. Indeed, it can be argued that this is one of the most attractive features of academic employment—the fact the workers are, to a remarkable extent, asked to do very little they don't choose to do. They get paid for reading, thinking, talking and writing about those things that they find interesting and rewarding. The result, of course, is that the university has little authority to re-assign workers to different work; it may make offers and suggestions, but the presumption is that an academic worker always has the right to stick to his job. An offer of tenure ensures this security in a specific job permanently. The *quid pro quo* is, however, a little different than in the corporate world: job security comes only following a lengthy and rigorous period of probation. . . .

The university . . . essentially *knows* what its people are going to do and, if it is to attract good employees, it cannot allow itself very much discretion about how much it will pay people to do it. Its problem then is to ensure that it gets good quality workers into the 'firm' and to ensure that they stay motivated in the absence of sensitive marginal incentives. The probation-tenure system is a reasonable response to this distinctive employment problem. . . .

It is not necessary to this analysis to assert that corporate productive activities are any easier to measure than those of academia. What counts for the present analysis in differentiating the two organizations and their labor markets is, simply, that the university combines measurement difficulties *and* job-specific employment while the corporation combines its measurement difficulties with job-flexible employment: the corporation can second-guess and the university cannot. . . .

THE TENURE DECISION

While it is useful in some contexts to speak of the 'university' as making decisions on tenure and job security, in fact specific individuals within the institution are charged with making them. The arrangements in the university are quite different from typical corporate arrangements, and these dif-

ferences can be at least partly understood in terms of the analysis developed here.

In the corporation, decisions about promotions are typically made in a hierarchical manner, with those at higher levels in the hierarchy deciding on those lower down, and with a well articulated structure of levels shaping the whole. In the university, however, while Deans and Presidents may be involved in decisions, most of the weight of the tenure decision is typically borne by those members of the discipline who have already been given tenure: peer review is the order of the day. . . .

The rationale for peer, rather than hierarchical, authority is clearly linked to the specialized nature of academic job assignments: judgment of an employee's performance during the probationary period must be made by those who are competent in his field since his main productive activities are specific to that field. Just as the university cannot usually hire a French professor to teach particle physics, so it cannot rely on a French professor (or a dean or president trained for that role) to judge the performance of a particle physicist. Of course, formally the role of peers may only be advisory to those with hierarchical authority, but Higher-ups will rarely have grounds to overrule strong recommendations from departments, and, if such recommendations are often overruled, the Higher-ups will undermine the incentive for departments to put much effort into evaluations. . . .

Last is the question why non-tenured people are typically excluded from the group of peers who decide on tenure. One obvious reason is the potential conflict of interest in evaluating a potential competitor—or conversely the potential conspiracy on the part of candidates to support one another's interests. Indeed, the need for objective evaluations has been cited by some observers (we think wrongly) as the key rationale for the institution of tenure itself: without job security, faculty would be motivated to resist retaining workers superior to themselves. A separate reason for excluding non-tenured personnel from tenure decisions is the relatively brief time over which they can expect to be associated with the institution, which may lead them to give undue weight to the short-term interests of the institution in making decisions. . . .

The institution of tenure is not simply a constraint imposed on universities, whether to protect faculty jobs or to ensure academic freedom, but an integral part of the way universities function. The tenure/probation system is a reasonable response to the highly specialized nature of academic work and to the long training such work requires. An intelligent understanding of the operation of universities and a constructive approach to the reform of their personnel policies needs to take these realities into account.

This conclusion need not be so complacent as it may sound. One could, for example, question whether academic training needs necessarily to be so specialized as it has become. It is also true that our analysis presents a somewhat idealized picture of how tenure and promotion decisions are made, and there is room for argument about how close to these ideals various colleges and universities come in practice. Our point, however, is that criticism of the tenure system and proposals for reform must come to grips with the quite real and special academic personnel problems the tenure system responds to. Much existing criticism, by failing to understand the economic functions of tenure, fails to do that.

A further step away from complacency may be taken by recalling some of the special pressures that may arise for the tenure system in the near future. Our analysis incorporates two key assumptions about the workings of the academic labor market: one, that the typical individual will enter the academic career with a stronger commitment to the occupation than to a particular institution; the other, that the granting of tenure amounts to a lifetime employment guarantee in practice. Both these have for the most part been true over the fifty years or so that the institution of tenure has been in full force in America. But of course tenure is always granted subject to financial exigency for the institution, and people can only pursue a lifetime commitment to academic employment if jobs are available. . . .

10. American Historical Association, "Who Is Teaching in U.S. College Classrooms?" 2000, and "Breakthrough for Part-Timers," 2005

The high cost of maintaining and increasing academic facilities to meet increasing enrollments on many campuses in the last quarter of the twentieth century pinched institutional resources. Downswings in the national economy turned college administrators repeatedly toward employing part-time, nontenured instructors. Traditional paths of entry into tenured positions for new Ph.D.'s became increasingly narrow and slippery. In 1975 43 percent of faculty members in all degree-granting institutions were contingent faculty, meaning part- and full-time non–tenure-track instructors. By 2002–3 their numbers amounted to 65 percent of the national totals. The title "adjunct," long given to senior visiting professors or lay specialists, became a label for (soon-aging) junior part-timers. The Coalition on the Academic Workforce, representing twenty-five academic societies, took the measure of this situation in 1999, as reported here by the American Historical Association. A study in 2005 describing a mediating if not successful outcome of a part-time faculty strike at the New School is added here. There both teachers and administrators hailed this resolution as a possible model for easing the national employment crisis for college teachers.

American Historical Association, "Who Is Teaching in U.S. College Classrooms?" *AHA Perspectives,* November 22, 2000; *Inside Higher Ed News* Online Journal, "Breakthrough for Part-Timers," November 1, 2005. Reprinted with permission from the American Historical Association, available at www.historians.org/caw/press release.htm. Further reading: *Academe* (July–August 2005): 5; AAUP, *Faculty Matters* (Fall 2005): 1, 3; and U.S.

Department of Education, "Background Characteristics, Work Activities, Compensation of Instructional Faculty and Staff: Fall 2003," (Washington, D.C., 2003).

WHO IS TEACHING IN U.S. COLLEGE CLASSROOMS?

Permanent full-time faculty members are now a minority in many academic departments, according to data collected on nine disciplines in the humanities and social sciences. The disciplinary associations that collected the data are part of the Coalition on the Academic Workforce, a group of 25 academic societies. The growing use of part-time faculty in higher education has been well documented, but the consequences of the trend for higher education and the students it serves are less well understood. The report also provides solid evidence of the second-class status of the part-time and adjunct teachers who are replacing the vanishing traditional faculty members.

In seven of the nine disciplines surveyed in the Fall 1999 study, traditional full-time tenured and tenure-track faculty accounted for less than half of the instructional staff in the responding departments and programs. According to Julia Haig Gaisser, Professor of Humanities at Bryn Mawr College and President of the American Philological Association (classics), "The present practice jeopardizes the next generation of teachers and scholars. It also shortchanges undergraduates, especially in the first two years, since often the faculty with whom they have the greatest contact are both transient and without a place or voice in the institution."

Composition programs and English departments, which teach large numbers of required introductory writing courses, have the smallest proportion of full-time tenured and tenure-track faculty members. Freestanding composition programs (those outside of English departments) report that only 14.6 percent of their teaching staff is full-time tenured and tenure-track, while English departments report that 36.3% of the faculty is full-time tenured and tenure-track. In foreign language programs just over a third of their instructional staff were in this category. Anthropology, history, and philosophy departments indicated that full-time tenured and tenure-track faculty members comprise just slightly more than half of the instructional staff.

While faculty members who hold traditional, full-time appointments still teach slightly more than half of the introductory courses in several disciplines, in some core humanities fields that is no longer the case. The student signing up for an introductory course in composition has a less than one in four chance of landing a spot in a classroom with a full-time tenured and tenure-track faculty member. For the beginning foreign language student, the odds are only marginally better.

At a time when access to a college education is widely recognized as important for most if not all high school graduates, the disappearance of a critical mass of permanent, full-time teacher-scholars raises questions about the ability of colleges and universities to deliver the kind of education previous generations of students received. "For the past decade, higher education's investment in a stable, full-time faculty has been declining. As larger numbers of undergraduates seek a college education in the years ahead, the effects of these employment decisions will have to be faced," says Linda Hutcheon, president of the Modern Language Association and Professor of English at the University of Toronto. Will the current shortage of schoolteachers soon be matched by a shortage of experienced teacher scholars, whose classes and research made U.S. Higher Education the envy of the world?

Full-time faculty are being replaced by lower paid part-time teachers attractive to higher education administrators, who are under pressure to keep costs down. In addition to receiving few if any benefits, most of these faculty members receive less than $3,000 per course. . . . Nearly one third of them earn $2,000, or less per course. In fields like English and history nearly half of the part-timers are in this category. At this rate of pay, part-time teachers—almost all of whom have the masters degree and many of whom have the PhD—would have to teach five courses to earn between $12,000 to $15,000 a year. They could earn comparable salaries as fast food workers, baggage porters, or theater lobby attendants. "One does not need a PhD in mathematics to calculate how many classes such a historian would have to teach to earn a decent living, or to realize that it is impossible for most adjuncts to function as research scholars or keep up with historical literature under these conditions," observed Eric Foner, President of the American Historical Association and Professor of History at Columbia University.

Surprisingly, graduate students comprised 15 to 25% of the instructional staff in the majority of the disciplines examined. Colleges and universities have been hiring part-time faculty members and graduate student teaching assistants because they are irresistibly cost-effective. But the terms and conditions of their appointments are often inadequate to support responsible teaching and research. Moreover, with fewer tenured and tenure-track faculty members available to plan and evaluate programs and courses, liberal arts departments are increasingly hard-pressed to give attention to administrative matters that depend on the knowledge and sustained commitment of experienced permanent faculty members. "It would be entirely wrong to stigmatize part-time historians as second-class teachers and scholars," cautions AHA President Foner. "The point is that the conditions under which they work often make it impossible for them to act effectively as educators. In the long run, excessive reliance on part-time teachers compromises the nature of higher education."

Roper Starch Worldwide conducted the survey of staffing arrangements in higher education in fall 1999. . . . Six groups—anthropology, cinema studies, folklore, linguistics, English, foreign languages, and philology—surveyed all departments in their fields. Three other groups—history, philosophy, and freestanding composition programs—surveyed a sample of departments. Most disciplines received response rates of between 40 and 45 percent. The surveys asked departments about who is teaching their classes, and what they provide their part-time and adjunct faculty in the way of support, benefits, and salaries.

The 1999 survey grew out of an earlier conference on the growing use of part-time and adjunct faculty, which was held in Washington, DC, in September 1997. Its purpose was to address a growing concern on the part of many in higher education that excessive or inappropriate reliance on part-time faculty members by colleges and universities can weaken an institution's capacity to provide essential educational experiences.

BREAKTHROUGH FOR PART-TIMERS

In the wee hours of Monday morning, a part-time faculty strike at the New School was averted when the university reached an agreement with negotiators for Academics Come Together, a United Auto Workers local representing nearly 2,000 part-timers. Both university officials and union members are hailing the pact as significant because it will provide benefits and job security of the sort that adjuncts nationally have not been able to achieve to date. . . .

Gregory Tewksbury, a union negotiator, said that the agreement provides job security for part-time employees who have been with the university for 10 semesters or more. "This is a sizable improvement," he said. "Given that this is our first contract, I feel like we did the best we could without a strike."

The deal followed three years of often tense negotiations between the union and the university. The UAW appealed to academics and politicians throughout the process to put pressure on the New School, which has strong progressive roots, but lacks the deep pockets to match its historic idealism.

"What's most unique about this contract is that it offers faculty continued employment not just on a course by course basis," said Julie Kushner, a UAW negotiator who has been working with faculty members since they started organizing in 2002. "If a course doesn't run because of a curriculum change or insufficient enrollment, the university must look to replace that course for a faculty member. They have an obligation to do that under this agreement."

Calling the agreement "a tremendous boost for part-time faculty nationally," Kushner added that the agreement also requires the university to begin to pay some of the costs of family coverage for health care and to offer paid academic leave for adjunct faculty members who have been with the institution for specified periods of time.

"We've looked at a lot of part-time contracts across the nation in recent weeks and months," said Joel Schlemowitz, president of the local chapter and an adjunct film instructor at the university. "And we believe that adjunct unions will be looking at this agreement for years to come as a milestone in the part-time labor equity movement."

New School's lawyer, Ned Bassen, concurred with that assessment, indicating that administrators were "delighted and proud" to have come to an agreement. "This is the first time that a private university has agreed to give job security to part-time faculty," he said Monday evening. "It took a great deal of work and creativity." . . .

In terms of wages, the agreement calls for an across the board retroactive increase of $10 per hour for each part-timer as of September 1, according to Tewksbury. He said that there's a large variation in the hourly pay of different part-time faculty at New School. On the low end, instructors currently receive about $25 per hour. Schlemowitz, who has taught at the New School for nine years, said that he makes about $2,400 in total pay per three-credit class he teaches each semester.

"Folks on the lowest end of pay will also automatically get [a new] minimum base salary, which is about $35 plus the $10 raise," said Tewksbury.

Additional wage increases—up to a maximum of $15 per hour—would be offered based on semesters of service to the university.

Schlemowitz noted that by the end of the contract—which would last four years if it is ultimately agreed to by a majority of the union, as expected—part-time faculty would receive the same percentage of contributions toward retirement as full-time faculty.

"We are confident that we're going to be able to demonstrate that these kinds of agreements are beneficial to both the institution and individual faculty members," said Kushner. "I think this is really something to build on. . . . I hope that we are setting standards for other institutions."

Experts not connected to the New School or UAW agreed. "This is an amazing contract," Richard Boris, director of the National Center for the Study of Collective Bargaining in Higher Education and the Professions, at the City University of New York's Hunter College, said upon reviewing highlights of the accord. "This agreement might well serve as a template for contingent faculty throughout the country."

11. Lotte Bailyn, *Breaking the Mold,* 1993

The structure of modern American universities was increasingly likened by its critical inhabitants to what Alvin Kernan termed "the typical successful social organization of our time and place: the multinational corporation." In her study of this "new corporate world," Lotte Bailyn, since 1970 a Sloan professor at the Massachusetts Institute of Technology, here qualifies the contention that the personal lives of academic and corporate people are similar. "The unbounded nature of the academic career" determines its unique character in the modern workplace.

Lotte Bailyn, *Breaking the Mold: Redesigning Work for Productive and Satisfying Lives* (1993; repr. Ithaca, NY, 2006): 42–47. Copyright © 2006 by Cornell University. First edition copyright © 1993 by The Free Press. Used by permission of the Publisher, Cornell University Press. Further reading: Alvin B. Kernan, "A High-Priced Product: The Managerial University as Multinational Corporation," reviewing Morton and Phyllis Keller, *Making Harvard Modern: The Rise of America's University* (New York, 2001), in *Harvard Magazine* 104 (September–October 2001): 22–31; and VI, 10–11, 16.

In contradistinction to these corporate careers, what can be said about the effect of a professorial role on one's private life? Generally the psychological demands on professors are embedded in the distinctive characteristics of academic life. First, the university setting differs from that of industry in that the expectation of a lifelong technical career is fulfillable (even expected), and a managerial role is not considered to be the most successful career path (often, in fact, the least successful). Second, universities have rigid timetables. The seven-year up-or-out tenure rule sharply divides one's career into two segments: the years before tenure with one clearly specified goal and the much longer period after tenure, in which standards and guidelines are assumed to be internalized. In the latter period the academic career has fewer milestones and fewer checkpoints than most other professional career paths. It also has fewer clearly specified requirements; often the only time one's presence is essential is during classes, which typically do not occupy much more than six hours a week. In addition, one has a long summer vacation.

These characteristics seem to make the academic career ideal for individual satisfaction and for linking one's employment to the needs of one's private life. It seemingly has all the flexibility that employees are currently asking for. Unfortunately the evidence proves the opposite, which is why an analysis of this career is critical as one considers changing the shape of work in the corporate world.

The lack of external requirements or specific career goals intensifies the internal pressures of the academic role. Comparisons tend to be made with those few signs of achievement that do exist in the system: named university chairs, Nobel Prizes, and the like. Since these affect only the exceptional few, the great majority are doomed, to some degree, to feelings of inadequacy and lack of appreciation. It is the very lack of formal signals of achievement that contributes to the frenetic quality of academic life.

People in academic careers also face a multiplicity of demands. Rewards tend to come from scholarly research, an activity that creates a great deal of mental overload. Research is a long-range activity and needs constant attention; successful books cannot be written in small fragments. Thus, in an academic career, there is much input but relatively little and long-delayed output. On top of this, professors must prepare and teach their classes, serve on administrative committees, and interact with outside professional, governmental, and industrial organizations. The combination of a multiplicity of demands and the mental overload from the activities that produce new knowledge profoundly affects the ability of professors to combine work with satisfying and meaningful personal lives. Academics work long hours and, despite their general satisfaction with their careers, express extreme dissatisfaction with the workload it demands.

Neither the character of the activities involved in being a professor nor the conditions surrounding the career make a balance between work and private life easily attainable. In fact, professors have an unusually difficult time integrating work and family. Despite the seeming flexibility of their working lives, their occupations are highly absorptive, primarily because they are subject to a complex set of demands. Moreover, their work activities offer little help. Academic occupational norms (like those of doctors and lawyers) assume that each incumbent is an expert in his or her own right. Both as scholars and as teachers, professors present themselves as sources of truth and knowledge and models for what is deemed appropriate and right.

These problems are exacerbated by the fact that professors, more than managers or independent contributors, are likely to have partners who themselves are professionals, and hence they are subject to the compelling demands for commitment to the private sphere characteristic of dual-career families. Given the structure of academic careers, these conflicting demands are more likely to lead to strain than to any accommodation to one's family. For example, professors far along in their careers tend to be less accommodative to family and more involved with career success than are their junior colleagues—the opposite of the pattern for independent contributors.

The academic career is paradoxical. Despite its advantages of independence and flexibility, it is psychologically difficult. The lack of ability to limit work, the tendency to compare oneself primarily to the exceptional giants in one's field, and the high incidence of overload make it particularly difficult for academics to find a satisfactory integration of work with private life. It is important to remember these difficulties as we consider shifting corporate careers from structured moves up hierarchical ladders to livelihoods built on normative involvement with loosely defined missions and goals.

Moreover, though the demand of academic life for full emotional and cognitive involvement—its absorptiveness—affects all people in it, it seems especially to create strain for women. We know, for example, that women faculty are much less likely to have children, or to expect ever to have children, than is the case for their male colleagues. Data from a 2004 survey of professors at a large research university showed an average workweek of sixty hours. Further, 71 percent agreed that it was difficult to combine a successful faculty career with significant personal responsibilities (28 percent strongly agreed). Women faculty felt this more strongly (83 percent agreement compared to 68 percent for men). As might be expected, untenured men and faculty with children under eighteen years of age agreed with this more strongly than their tenured male colleagues or those with only older children. Surprisingly, though, for women faculty there was no difference by tenure or by presence of children. It was just hard under all conditions.

Most faculty members are satisfied with their jobs and acknowledge a fair degree of control over the scheduling of their work hours. But the total amount of time seen as necessary for promotion, tenure, and distinctive accomplishment supersedes the advantages of control and creates significant stress. This personal dilemma is vividly described by one university professor:

> I cannot ask for more flexibility; it is the total amount of work that does me in. I love my family and value the time I spend with them. I also love my work and the time I spend in the lab. It is the great conflict of my life. I have not achieved a satisfactory solution. Most of the anger that I ever carry is due to this friction.

It is the unbounded nature of the academic career that is the heart of the problem. Time is critical for professors because there is not enough of it to do all the things their job requires: teaching, research, and institutional and professional service. Hence it is impossible for faculty members to protect other aspects of their lives, and work tends to dominate. These comments by two senior male professors are by no means unique:

> The existing pattern of time demands on a faculty member degrades the quality of life to an unacceptable degree in my case. The problem is not time pressure per se; rather it is the number of separate factors that are able to make independent and uncontrollable demands on my time. . . . I am not living with a partner largely because I cannot command the hours/week that any reasonable relationship demands. . . . Early retirement is a serious option if I cannot effect a substantial improvement in my situation.
>
> Since marriage, my time has been essentially devoted to my profession (student to professor), e.g., 7 days/week throughout the year. My wife was responsible for raising four children and now cares for our grandchildren. About five years ago we did start to have a family vacation. I would like to live a more normal life, but pressure keeps increasing to

increase my productivity. I am looking forward to partial retirement ASAP (say, a 40–50-hour week).

The academic experience suggests one must be careful not to change corporate careers by increasing apparent flexibility while at the same time increasing the unboundedness of expectations. And one must not impose on women the additional demands that are often evident in university life. Faculty women are frequently asked to carry—or perhaps they set for themselves—a heavy agenda of involvements with committees; students, and women's affairs. They are on call from administrations seeking to ensure the participation of women in decision making, but since there are still relatively few of them, their load is heavier than that of their male colleagues. Also, students may find it easier to "burden" female teachers with their concerns. Though time-consuming, some of these roles take place behind the scenes, and the women involved may get no official credit. This enhances the tendency of women to be invisible, to be valued less than their male colleagues. Though seemingly contradictory, both extremes of women's roles—their overinvolvement and their invisibility—make it more difficult for them to meet the traditional requirements for promotion and tenure.

CONCLUDING NOTE

Each of the occupational roles discussed in this chapter—despite similarities in the extent of initial training required and in the standard of living provided—entails different psychological demands and different satisfactions and rewards, which have profound effects on the lives of those involved. For managers, there seems to be a complementarity between the activities and skills needed on the job and those required off it. But the organizational demands require that the family be subservient to the primary career, particularly during the early years. In contrast, for many independent contributors (whose spheres of activities may not in themselves be complementary), the organizational tendency to decrease the challenge of the job is likely to create the opportunity for an easier integration between work and personal life. Paradoxically, the psychologically most difficult situation seems to be that of professors, despite the flexibility of their time schedules. This is caused by overload, the nature of the work, and the lack of terminal points and limits to ambition.

We tend to think of occupations only in terms of whether they match our talents, our knowledge, and our experiences and ignore the fact that they also differ profoundly in terms of the types of lives they allow us to lead. Even people educated in similar ways and with a core of common interests find themselves in occupational roles and organizational settings that represent unexpectedly complicated sets of psychological demands. Hence both individuals and organizations must be aware of these demands and recognize the effect they have on people's lives.

Teachers as Labor and Management

12. *NLRB v. Yeshiva University,* 1980

This finding by the U.S. Supreme Court for Yeshiva University reached to the core administrative issue facing the American professoriate in a corporate and bureaucratized institutional setting. Are professors in fact primarily managers of university affairs or are they principally professional employees subject to managerial administrators? The opinion of the Court was written by Associate Justice Lewis F. Powell Jr. (1907–98), joined by Chief Justice Burger and Associate Justices Stewart, Rehnquist, and Stevens; the dissent was written by Associate Justice William Brennan Jr., joined by Associate Justices White, Marshall, and Blackmun. Both opinions share a respect for professorial purposes and also for the authority of the National Labor Relations Board, whose decisions favoring the professors' employee status, thus permitting them to engage in unionized collective bargaining, caused the university to bring on these proceedings. The Court's five-four majority favored Yeshiva. It held that for all practical purposes professors act as managers because their professional interests, even though exercised "as independent judgment primarily in their own interests," together with their collaborative work with administrators, effectively run the university. In his dissent Justice Brennan held that "the mere connection of interests on many issues has never been thought to abrogate the right to collective bargaining."

444 U.S. *NLRB v. Yeshiva University* (1979): 672–706. Further reading: William A. Kaplin, *The Law of Higher Education: Legal Implications of Administrative Decision Making* (San Francisco, 1983), 95–108; Joel M. Douglas, "Faculty Collective Bargaining in the Aftermath of Yeshiva," *Change* 13 (March 1981): 36–43; Lee Modjeska, *NRLB Practice* (Rochester, NY, and San Francisco, 1983), 42–46; Donald Kennedy, *Academic Duty* (Cambridge, MA, 1997), 118–24; Howard B. Means and Philip W. Semas, *Faculty Collective Bargaining*, 2nd ed. (Washington, 1976), 137–45, bibliography; Jeffrey J. Williams, "The Post–Welfare State University," *American Literary History* 18 (Spring 2006): 190–216, valuably summarizes a growing critical literature on institutional control, support, and the situation of academic workers within "academic capitalism" entering the twenty-first century; and *National Center for the Study of Collective Bargaining in Higher Education and The Professions* (New York, 1973–present): no. 10 and annual bibliographies.

Mr. Justice Powell delivered
the opinion of the Court.

Supervisors and managerial employees are excluded from the categories of employees entitled to the benefits of collective bargaining under the National Labor Relations Act. The question presented is whether the full-time faculty of Yeshiva University fall within those exclusions. . . .

A three-member panel of the Board granted the Union's petition in December 1975, and directed an election in a bargaining unit consisting of all full-time faculty members at the affected schools. . . . The unit included Assistant Deans, senior professors, and department chairmen, as well as associate professors, assistant professors, and instructors. Deans and Directors were excluded. The Board summarily rejected the University's contention that its entire faculty are managerial, viewing the claim as a request for reconsideration of previous Board decisions on the issue. Instead of making findings of fact as to Yeshiva, the Board referred generally to the record and found no "significan[t]" difference between this faculty and others it had considered. The Board concluded that the faculty are professional employees entitled to the protection of the Act because "faculty participation in collegial decision making is on a collective rather than individual basis, it is exercised in the faculty's own interest rather than 'in the interest of the employer,' and final authority rests with the board of trustees."

The Union won the election and was certified by the Board. The University refused to bargain, reasserting its view that the faculty are managerial. In the subsequent unfair labor practice proceeding, the Board refused to reconsider its holding in the representation proceeding and ordered the University to bargain with the Union. . . . When the University still refused to sit down at the negotiating table, the Board sought enforcement in the Court of Appeals for the Second Circuit, which denied the petition.

Since the Board had made no findings of fact, the court examined the record and related the circumstances in considerable detail. It agreed that the faculty are professional employees under 2 (12) of the Act. . . . But the court found that the Board had ignored "the extensive control of Yeshiva's faculty" over academic and personnel decisions as well as the "crucial role of the full-time faculty in determining other central policies of the institution." . . . The court concluded that such power is not an exercise of individual professional expertise. Rather, the faculty are, "in effect, substantially and pervasively operating the enterprise." Accordingly, the court held that the faculty are endowed with "managerial status" sufficient to remove them from the coverage of the Act. We granted certiorari, 440 U.S. 906 (1979), and now affirm.

The Board does not contend that the Yeshiva faculty's decisionmaking is too insignificant to be deemed managerial. Nor does it suggest that the role of the faculty is merely advisory and thus not managerial. Instead, it contends that the managerial exclusion cannot be applied in a straightforward fashion to professional employees because those employees often appear to be exercising managerial authority when they are merely performing routine job duties. The status of such employees, in the Board's view, must be determined by reference to the "alignment with management" criterion. The Board argues that the Yeshiva faculty are not aligned with management because they are expected to exercise "independent professional judgment" while

participating in academic governance, and because they are neither "expected to conform to management policies [nor] judged according to their effectiveness in carrying out those policies." Because of this independence, the Board contends there is no danger of divided loyalty and no need for the managerial exclusion. In its view, union pressure cannot divert the faculty from adhering to the interests of the university, because the university itself expects its faculty to pursue professional values rather than institutional interests. The Board concludes that application of the managerial exclusion to such employees would frustrate the national labor policy in favor of collective bargaining.

This "independent professional judgment" test was not applied in the decision we are asked to uphold. The Board's opinion relies exclusively on its previous faculty decisions for both legal and factual analysis. . . . But those decisions only dimly foreshadow the reasoning now proffered to the Court. Without explanation, the Board initially announced two different rationales for faculty cases, then quickly transformed them into a litany to be repeated in case after case: (i) faculty authority is collective, (ii) it is exercised in the faculty's own interest rather than in the interest of the university, and (iii) final authority rests with the board of trustees. . . . In their arguments in this case, the Board's lawyers have abandoned the first and third branches of this analysis, which in any event were flatly inconsistent with its precedents, and have transformed the second into a theory that does not appear clearly in any Board opinion.

The controlling consideration in this case is that the faculty of Yeshiva University exercise authority which in any other context unquestionably would be managerial. Their authority in academic matters is absolute. They decide what courses will be offered, when they will be scheduled, and to whom they will be taught. They debate and determine teaching methods, grading policies, and matriculation standards. They effectively decide which students will be admitted, retained, and graduated. On occasion their views have determined the size of the student body, the tuition to be charged, and the location of a school. When one considers the function of a university, it is difficult to imagine decisions more managerial than these. To the extent the industrial analogy applies, the faculty determines within each school the product to be produced, the terms upon which it will be offered, and the customers who will be served.

The Board nevertheless insists that these decisions are not managerial because they require the exercise of independent professional judgment. We are not persuaded by this argument. . . .

In arguing that a faculty member exercising independent judgment acts primarily in his own interest and therefore does not represent the interest of his employer, the Board assumes that the professional interests of the faculty and the interests of the institution are distinct, separable entities with which a faculty member could not simultaneously be aligned. The Court of Appeals found no justification for this distinction, and we perceive none. In fact, the faculty's professional interests—as applied to governance at a university like Yeshiva—cannot be separated from those of the institution.

In such a university, the predominant policy normally is to operate a quality institution of higher learning that will accomplish broadly defined educational goals within the limits of its financial resources. The "business" of a university is education, and its vitality ultimately must depend on academic policies that largely are formulated and generally are implemented by faculty governance decisions. See K. Mortimer & T. McConnell, *Sharing Authority Effectively* 23–24 (1978). Faculty members enhance their own standing and fulfill their professional mission by ensuring that the university's objectives are met. But there can be no doubt that the quest for academic excellence and institutional distinction is a "policy" to which the administration expects the faculty to adhere, whether it be defined as a professional or an institutional goal. It is fruitless to ask whether an employee is "expected to conform" to one goal or another when the two are essentially the same. . . .

The university requires faculty participation in governance because professional expertise is indispensable to the formulation and implementation of academic policy.[1] It may appear, as the Board contends, that the professor performing governance functions is less "accountable" for departures from institutional policy than a middle-level industrial manager whose discretion is more confined. Moreover, traditional systems of collegiality and tenure insulate the professor from some of the sanctions applied to an industrial manager who fails to adhere to company policy. But the analogy of the university to industry need not, and indeed cannot, be complete. It is clear that Yeshiva and like universities must rely on their faculties to participate in the making and implementation of their policies.[2] The large measure of independence enjoyed by faculty members can only increase the danger that divided loyalty will lead to those harms that the Board traditionally has sought to prevent. . . .

Finally, the Board contends that the deference due its expertise in these matters requires us to reverse the decision of the Court of Appeals. The

1. The extent to which Yeshiva faculty recommendations are implemented is no "mere coincidence," as Mr. Justice Brennan's dissent suggests. . . . Rather this is an inevitable characteristic of the governance structure adopted by universities like Yeshiva.

2. The dissent concludes, citing several secondary authorities, that the modern university has undergone changes that have shifted "the task of operating the university enterprise" from faculty to administration. . . . The shift, if it exists, is neither universal nor complete.

question we decide today is a mixed one of fact and law. But the Board's opinion may be searched in vain for relevant findings of fact. The absence of factual analysis apparently reflects the Board's view that the managerial status of particular faculties may be decided on the basis of conclusory rationales rather than examination of the facts of each case. The Court of Appeals took a different view, and determined that the faculty of Yeshiva University, "in effect, substantially and pervasively operat[e] the enterprise." 582 F.2d, at 698. We find no reason to reject this conclusion. As our decisions consistently show, we accord great respect to the expertise of the Board when its conclusions are rationally based on articulated facts and consistent with the Act. . . . In this case, we hold that the Board's decision satisfies neither criterion.

AFFIRMED.

Mr. Justice Brennan, with whom Mr. Justice White, Mr. Justice Marshall, and Mr. Justice Blackmun join, dissenting.

In holding that the full-time faculty members of Yeshiva University are not covered employees under the National Labor Relations Act, but instead fall within the exclusion for supervisors and managerial employees, the Court disagrees with the determination of the National Labor Relations Board. Because I believe that the Board's decision was neither irrational nor inconsistent with the Act, I respectfully dissent. . . .

In any event, I believe the Board reached the correct result in determining that Yeshiva's full-time faculty is covered under the NLRA. The Court does not dispute that the faculty members are "professional employees" for the purposes of collective bargaining under 2 (12), but nevertheless finds them excluded from coverage under the implied exclusion for "managerial employees." The Court explains that "[t]he controlling consideration in this case is that the faculty of Yeshiva University exercise authority which in any other context unquestionably would be managerial." *Ante*, at 686. But the academic community is simply not "any other context." The Court purports to recognize that there are fundamental differences between the authority structures of the typical industrial and academic institutions which preclude the blind transplanting of principles developed in one arena onto the other; yet it nevertheless ignores those very differences in concluding that Yeshiva's faculty is excluded from the Act's coverage. . . .

The touchstone of managerial status is thus an alliance with management, and the pivotal inquiry is whether the employee in performing his duties represents his own interests or those of his employer. If his actions are undertaken for the purpose of implementing the employer's policies, then he is accountable to management and may be subject to conflicting loyalties. But if the employee is acting only on his own behalf and in his own interest, he is covered under the Act and is entitled to the benefits of collective bargaining. . . .

Unlike the purely hierarchical decisionmaking structure that prevails in the typical industrial organization, the bureaucratic foundation of most "mature" universities is characterized by dual authority systems. The primary decisional network is hierarchical in nature: Authority is lodged in the administration, and a formal chain of command runs from a lay governing board down through university officers to individual faculty members and students. At the same time, there exists a parallel professional network, in which formal mechanisms have been created to bring the expertise of the faculty into the decisionmaking process. . . .

What the Board realized—and what the Court fails to apprehend—is that whatever influence the faculty wields in university decisionmaking is attributable solely to its collective expertise as professional educators, and not to any managerial or supervisory prerogatives. Although the administration may look to the faculty for advice on matters of professional and academic concern, the faculty offers its recommendations in order to serve its own independent interest in creating the most effective environment for learning, teaching, and scholarship.[3] And while the administration may attempt to defer to the faculty's competence whenever possible, it must and does apply its own distinct perspective to those recommendations, a perspective that is based on fiscal and other managerial policies which the faculty has no part in developing. The University always retains the ultimate decisionmaking authority, . . . and the administration gives what weight and import to the faculty's collective judgment as it chooses and deems consistent with its own perception of the institution's needs and objectives. . . .

Yeshiva's faculty, however, is not accountable to the administration in its governance function, nor is any individual faculty member subject to personal sanction or control based on the administration's assessment of the worth of his recommendations. When the faculty, through the schools' advisory committees, participates in university decisionmaking on subjects of academic policy, it does not serve as the "representative of management." Unlike industrial supervisors and managers, university professors are not hired to "make operative" the policies and decisions of their employer. Nor are they retained on the condition that their interests will correspond to those of the university administration. Indeed, the notion that a faculty member's professional competence could depend on his undivided loyalty to management is antithetical to the whole concept of academic freedom. Faculty members are judged by their employer on the quality of their teaching and scholarship, not on the compatibility of their advice with administration policy. . . .

It is no answer to say, as does the Court, that Yeshiva's faculty and administration are one and the same because their interests tend to coincide. In the first place, the National Labor Relations Act does not condition its coverage on an antagonism of interests between the employer and the employee. The mere coincidence of interests on many issues has never been thought to abrogate the right to collective bargaining on those topics as to which that coincidence is absent. Ultimately, the performance of an employee's duties will always further the interests of the employer, for in no institution do the interests of labor and management totally diverge. Both desire to maintain stable and profitable operations, and both are committed to creating the best possible product within existing financial constraints. Differences of opinion and emphasis may develop, however, on exactly how to devote the institution's resources to achieve those goals. When these disagreements surface, the national labor laws contemplate their resolution through the peaceful process of collective bargaining. And in this regard, Yeshiva University stands on the same footing as any other employer.

Moreover, the congruence of interests in this case ought not to be exaggerated. The university administration has certain economic and fiduciary responsibilities that are not shared by the faculty, whose primary concerns are academic and relate solely to its own professional reputation. The record evinces numerous instances in which the faculty's recommendations have been rejected by the administration on account of fiscal constraints or other managerial policies. Disputes have arisen between Yeshiva's faculty and administration on such fundamental issues as the hiring, tenure, promotion, retirement, and dismissal of faculty members, academic standards and credits, departmental budgets, and even the faculty's choice of its own departmental representative. The very fact that Yeshiva's faculty has voted for the Union to serve as its representative in future negotiations with the administration indicates that the faculty does not perceive its interests to be aligned with those of management. Indeed, on the precise topics which are specified as mandatory subjects of collective bargaining—wages, hours, and other terms and conditions of employment—the interests of teacher and administrator are often diametrically opposed.

Finally, the Court's perception of the Yeshiva faculty's status is distorted by the rose-colored lens through which it views the governance structure of the modern-day university. The Court's conclusion that the faculty's professional interests are indis-

---

3. As the Board has recognized, due to the unique nature of their work, professional employees will often make recommendations on matters that are of great importance to management. But their desire to exert influence in these areas stems from the need to maintain their own professional standards, and this factor—common to all professionals—should not, by itself, preclude their inclusion in a bargaining unit.

tinguishable from those of the administration is bottomed on an idealized model of collegial decisionmaking that is a vestige of the great medieval university. But the university of today bears little resemblance to the "community of scholars" of yesteryear. Education has become "big business," and the task of operating the university enterprise has been transferred from the faculty to an autonomous administration, which faces the same pressures to cut costs and increase efficiencies that confront any large industrial organization. The past decade of budgetary cutbacks, declining enrollments, reductions in faculty appointments, curtailment of academic programs, and increasing calls for accountability to alumni and other special interest groups has only added to the erosion of the faculty's role in the institution's decisionmaking process.

These economic exigencies have also exacerbated the tensions in university labor relations, as the faculty and administration more and more frequently find themselves advocating conflicting positions not only on issues of compensation, job security, and working conditions, but even on subjects formerly thought to be the faculty's prerogative. In response to this friction, and in an attempt to avoid the strikes and work stoppages that have disrupted several major universities in recent years, many faculties have entered into collective-bargaining relationships with their administrations and governing boards.[4] An even greater number of schools—Yeshiva among them—have endeavored to negotiate and compromise their differences informally, by establishing avenues for faculty input into university decisions on matters of professional concern.

Today's decision, however, threatens to eliminate much of the administration's incentive to resolve its disputes with the faculty through open discussion and mutual agreement. By its overbroad and unwarranted interpretation of the managerial exclusion, the Court denies the faculty the protections of the NLRA and, in so doing, removes whatever de-

---

4. As of January 1979, 80 private and 302 public institutions of higher education had engaged in collective bargaining with their faculties, and over 130,000 academic personnel had been unionized. . . . Although the NLRA is not applicable to any public employer, . . . as of 1976, 22 States had enacted legislation granting faculties at public institutions the right to unionize and requiring public employers to bargain with duly constituted bargaining agents.

The upsurge in the incidence in collective bargaining has generally been attributed to the faculty's desire to use the process as a countervailing force against increased administrative power and to ensure that the ideals of the academic community are actually practiced. As the Carnegie Commission found, "[u]nionization for [faculty] is more a protective than an aggressive act, more an effort to preserve the status quo than to achieve a new position of influence and affluence. . . ." Carnegie Commission on Higher Education, Governance of Higher Education 40 (1973).

terrent value the Act's availability may offer against unreasonable administrative conduct. Rather than promoting the Act's objective of funneling dissension between employers and employees into collective bargaining, the Court's decision undermines that goal and contributes to the possibility that "recurring disputes [will] fester outside the negotiation process until strikes or other forms of economic warfare occur."

In sum, the Board analyzed both the essential purposes underlying the supervisory and managerial exclusions and the nature of the governance structure at Yeshiva University. Relying on three factors that attempt to encapsulate the fine distinction between those professional employees who are entitled to the NLRA's protections and those whose managerial responsibilities require their exclusion, the Board concluded that Yeshiva's full-time faculty qualify as the former rather than the latter. I believe the Board made the correct determination. But even were I to have reservations about the specific result reached by the Board on the facts of this case, I would certainly have to conclude that the Board applied a proper mode of analysis to arrive at a decision well within the zone of reasonableness. Accordingly, in light of the deference due the Board's determination in this complex area, I would reverse the judgment of the Court of Appeals.

13. *Brown University,*
342 National Labor Relations Board, 2004

Are paid graduate students assisting in part-time teaching or research to be regarded as students learning a profession or employees? This question increasingly touched fundamental issues of graduate education when undergraduate class enrollments in large institutions rose sharply after 1970. Graduate assistants became unionized at some major state universities on the basis of law. Those at private universities were not covered by such laws: they fell instead within the guidelines of the National Labor Relations Board, which declined for many years to categorize them as labor. By the 1990s, graduate students, concerned about their working conditions and worried about future employment, began to form unions at major private research universities. The movement began and was most intense at Yale, but victory came at New York University. The UAW and AFL-CIO on behalf of the students petitioned the regional director of the National Labor Relations Board, seeking a vote on unionization and recognition at NYU. The director ruled in favor of the petitioners, but New York University appealed to the National Board, which affirmed the regional director's decision in October 2000. The university, supported by *amici curiae* from several other private research universities, had argued that graduate assistants are students, not employees. The NLRB agreed with the regional director, holding that "there is no basis to deny collective-bargaining rights to statutory employees merely because they are employed by an educational institution in which they are enrolled as students." An election followed, the students voted to unionize, and a contract was negotiated; it went into effect in the 2001–2 academic year.

But in 2004, in the document included here, the NLRB ruled 3–2 that teaching assistants at Brown University, another private institution, are primarily students not with an economic but with a "mentoring relationship" to the faculty and are not covered by federal labor law, thus reversing its finding in the NYU case. (On this basis of this ruling, NYU subsequently refused to negotiate a renewal of its earlier contract.) The dissenting members of the board stated that graduate students would continue to organize unions and that federal law should encourage collective bargaining to avoid labor disputes.

Brown University and International Union, United Automobile, Aerospace and Agricultural Implement Workers of America, UAW AFL-CIO, Petitioner (July 13, 2004) 342 NLRB No. 42. Further reading: *NYU* 332 NLRB 1205 (2000); Douglas Sorrelle Streitz and Jennifer Allyson Hunkler, "Teaching or Learning: Are Teaching Assistants Students or Employees?" *Journal of College and University Law* 24 (Fall 1997): 349–75; Grant M. Hayden, " 'The University Works Because We Do': Collective Bargaining Rights for Graduate Assistants," *Fordham Law Review* 69 (March 2001): 1233–64; Daniel J. Julius and Patricia J. Gumport, "Graduate Student Unionization: Catalysts and Consequences," *Review of Higher Education* 26 (2003): 187–216; and Neal H. and Melissa B. Hutchens, "Catching the Union Bug: Graduate Student Employees and Unionization," *Gonzaga Law Review* 39 (2003/04): 105–30.

DECISION ON REVIEW AND ORDER BY CHAIRMAN BATTISTA AND MEMBERS LIEBMAN, SCHAUMBER, WALSH, AND MEISBURG

On November 16, 2001, the Regional Director for Region 1 issued a Decision and Direction of Election in which she applied New York University, 332 NLRB 1205 (2000) (*NYU*), to find that teaching assistants, research assistants, and proctors are employees within the meaning of Section 2(3) of the Act and constitute an appropriate unit for collective bargaining. Thereafter, in accordance with Section 102.67 of the Board's Rules and Regulations, Brown University (Brown) filed a timely request for review, urging the Board, inter alia, to reconsider *NYU*. . . .

The case presents the issue of whether graduate student assistants who are admitted into, not hired by, a university, and for whom supervised teaching or research is an integral component of their academic development, must be treated as employees for purposes of collective bargaining under Section 2(3) of the Act, The Board in *NYU* concluded that graduate student assistants are employees under Section 2(3) of the Act and therefore are to be extended the right to engage in collective bargaining. That decision reversed more than 25 years of Board precedent. That precedent was never successfully challenged in court or in Congress. In our decision today, we return to the Board's pre-*NYU* precedent that graduate student assistants are not statutory employees.

Until *NYU*, the Board's principle was that gradu-ate student assistants are primarily students and not statutory employees. See *Leland Stanford Junior University*, 214 NLRB 621 (1974). The Board concluded that graduate student assistants, who perform services at a university in connection with their studies, have a predominately academic, rather than economic, relationship with their school. Accordingly, the Board held that they were not employees within the intendment of the Act.

This longstanding approach towards graduate student assistants changed abruptly with *NYU*. The Board decided that graduate student assistants meet the test establishing a conventional master-servant relationship with a university, and that they are statutory employees who necessarily have "statutory rights to organize and bargain with their employer."

After carefully considering the record herein, and the briefs of the parties and amici, and for the reasons detailed in this decision, we reconsider *NYU* and conclude that the 25-year precedent was correct, and that *NYU* was wrongly decided and should be overruled.

The Petitioner sought to represent a unit of approximately 450 graduate students employed as teaching assistants (TAs), research assistants (RAs) in certain social sciences and humanities departments, and proctors. The Petitioner, relying on *NYU*, supra, contended to the Regional Director that the petitioned-for TAs, RAs, and proctors are employees within the meaning of Section 2(3) and that they constitute an appropriate unit for collective bargaining.

Brown contended to the Regional Director that the petitioned-for individuals are not statutory employees because this case is factually distinguishable from *NYU*. Brown asserted that, unlike *NYU*, where only a few departments required students to serve as a TA or RA to receive a degree, most university departments at Brown require a student to serve as a TA or RA to obtain a degree. Brown contended that these degree requirements demonstrate that the petitioned-for students have only an educational relationship and not an employment relationship with Brown. Brown also argued that the TA, RA, and proctor awards constitute financial aid to students, emphasizing that students receive the same stipend, regardless of whether they "work" for those funds as a TA, RA, or proctor, or whether they receive funding for a fellowship, which does not require any work. Finally, Brown argued that even assuming the petitioned-for individuals are statutory employees, they are temporary employees who do not have sufficient interest in their ongoing employment to entitle them to collectively bargain.

The Regional Director, applying *NYU*, rejected Brown's arguments. She also concluded that the petitioned-for unit was appropriate, and she directed an election.

The election was conducted on December 6, 2001, and the ballots were impounded pending the disposition of this request for review. . . .

1. Brown

In its Brief on Review, Brown argues that *New York University*, 332 NLRB 1205 (2000), was wrongly decided, contending that it reversed 25 years of precedent "without paying adequate attention to the Board's role in making sensible policy decisions that effectuate the purposes of the Act." Brown contends that the Board "did not adequately consider that the relationship between a research university and its graduate students is not fundamentally an *economic* one but an *educational* one." Further, Brown contends that the support to students is part of a financial aid program that pays graduate students the same amount, regardless of work, and regardless of the value of those services if purchased on the open market (i.e., hiring a fully-vetted Ph.D.). Brown also emphasizes that "[c]ommon sense dictates that students who teach and perform research as part of their academic curriculum cannot properly be considered employees without entangling the . . . Act into the intricacies of graduate education." Brown also incorporates arguments made in its request for review that, at a minimum, *NYU*, supra, is distinguishable from this case because of the extent that teaching and research are required for a graduate degree, and because the graduate assistants are temporary employees.

2. Petitioner

The Petitioner argues that the Regional Director correctly followed the Board's decision in *NYU*, and that *NYU* must be upheld. The Petitioner contends that the petitioned-for employees clearly meet the statutory definition of "employee" because they meet the common law test. The Petitioner disputes Brown's contention that TA and RA stipends, like fellowship stipends, are "financial aid." The Petitioner argues that Brown's contention that TAs or RAs lose their status as employees because the TAs and RAs are academically required to work is based on the false notion that there is no way to distinguish between a graduate student's academic requirements and the "work appointments" of the TAs or RAs. Further, even assuming that these individuals usually are satisfying an academic requirement, this is not determinative of employee status.

With regard to the RAs in the life and physical sciences that the Regional Director excluded, the Petitioner now asserts that these individuals should be included in the unit because they provide a service to Brown and are compensated for such service in a manner consistent with a finding that they are employees within the meaning of the Act.

Finally, the Petitioner contends that the petitioned-for individuals are not temporary employees. . . .

The evidence demonstrates that the relationship between Brown's graduate student assistants and Brown is primarily educational. As indicated, the first prerequisite to becoming a graduate student assistant is being a student. Being a student, of course, is synonymous with learning, education, and academic pursuits. At Brown, most graduate students are pursuing a Ph.D. which, as described by the Brown's University Bulletin, is primarily a research degree with teaching being an important component of most graduate programs. The educational core of the degree, research, and teaching, reflects the essence of what Brown offers to students: "the advantage of a small teaching college and large research university." At least 21 of the 32 departments that offer Ph.D. degrees require teaching as a condition of getting that degree. Sixty-nine percent of all graduate students are enrolled in these departments. Thus, for a substantial majority of graduate students, teaching is so integral to their education that they will not get the degree until they satisfy that requirement. Graduate student assistant positions are, therefore, directly related to the core elements of the Ph.D. degree and the educational reasons that students attend Brown. The relationship between being a graduate student assistant and the pursuit of the Ph.D. is inextricably linked, and thus, that relationship is clearly educational.

We recognize that a given graduate student may be a teacher, researcher, or proctor for only a portion of his or her tenure as a student. However, as described above, that task is an integral part of being a graduate student, and cannot be divorced from the other functions of being a graduate student.

Because the role of teaching assistant and research assistant is integral to the education of the graduate student, Brown's faculty oversees graduate student assistants in their role as a research or teaching assistant. Although the duties and responsibilities of graduate student assistants vary among departments and faculty, most perform under the direction and control of faculty members from their particular department. TAs generally do not teach independently, and even teaching fellows who have some greater responsibilities follow faculty-established courses. RAs performing research do so under grants applied for by faculty members, who often serve as the RA's dissertation adviser. In addition, these faculty members are often the same faculty that teach or advise the graduate assistant student in their coursework or dissertation preparation.

Besides the purely academic dimension to this relationship is the financial support provided to graduate student assistants because they are students. Attendance at Brown is quite expensive. Brown recognizes the need for financial support to meet the costs of a graduate education. This assistance, however, is provided only to students and only for the period during which they are enrolled as students. Further, the vast majority of students receive funding. Thus, in the last academic year, 85 percent of continuing students and 75 percent of incoming students received assistance from Brown. In addition, as noted above, the amounts received by graduate student assistants generally are the same or similar to the amounts received by students who receive funds for a fellowship, which do not require any assistance in teaching and research. Moreover, a significant segment of the funds received by both graduate student assistants and fellows is for full tuition. Further, the funds for students largely come from Brown's financial aid budget rather than its instructional budget.

Thus, in light of the status of graduate student assistants as students, the role of graduate student assistantships in graduate education, the graduate student assistants' relationship with the faculty, and the financial support they receive to attend Brown, we conclude that the overall relationship between the graduate student assistants and Brown is primarily an educational one, rather than an economic one. . . .

Even if graduate student assistants are statutory employees, a proposition with which we disagree, it simply does not effectuate the national labor policy to accord them collective bargaining rights, because they are primarily students. In this regard, the Board has the discretion to determine whether it would effectuate national labor policy to extend collective bargaining rights to such a category of employees. Indeed, the Board has previously exercised that discretion with respect to medical residents and interns. See *St. Clare's Hospital & Health Center,* 229 NLRB 1000 (1977). Thus, assuming arguendo that the petitioned-for individuals are employees under Section 2(3), the Board is not compelled to include them in a bargaining unit if the Board determines it would not effectuate the purposes and policies of the Act to do so.

We also reject the dissent's contention that our policy is unsound because we "minimize the economic relationship between graduate student assistants and their universities." Contrary to the dissent, the "academic reality" for graduate student assistants has not changed, in relevant respects, since our decisions over 25 years ago. See, e.g., the description of graduate assistants in *Adelphi University,* 195 NLRB at 640. As the Board explained in *St. Clare's,* the conclusion that these graduate student assistants are primarily students "connotes nothing more than the simple fact that when an individual is providing services at the educational institution itself as part and parcel of his or her educational development the individual's interest in rendering such services is more academic than economic." 229 NLRB at 1003. That is the essence of the relationship between a university and graduate student assistants, and why we decline to accord collective bargaining rights to them.

Although the dissent theorizes how the changing financial and corporate structure of universities may have given rise to graduate student organizing, these theories do not contradict the following facts demonstrating that the relationship between Brown and its graduate student assistants is primarily academic: (1) the petitioned-for individuals are *students*; (2) working as a TA, RA, or proctor, and receipt of a stipend and tuition remission, depends on continued enrollment as a *student*; (3) the principal time commitment at Brown is focused on obtaining a degree, and, thus, being a *student*; and (4) serving as a TA, RA, or proctor, is part and parcel of the core elements of the Ph.D. degree, which are teaching and research. Although the structure of universities, like other institutions, may have changed, these facts illustrate that the basic relationship between graduate students and their university has not. . . .

Finally, our colleagues suggest that we have concluded that "there [is] no room in the ivory tower for a sweatshop." Although the phrase is a catchy one, it does nothing to further the analysis of this case. Our decision does not turn on whether our nation's universities are ivory towers or sweatshops (although we do not believe that either has been shown). Rather, our decision turns on our fundamental belief that the imposition of collective bargaining on graduate students would improperly intrude into the educational process and would be inconsistent with the purposes and policies of the Act.

For the reasons we have outlined in this opinion, there is a significant risk, and indeed a strong likelihood, that the collective-bargaining process will be detrimental to the educational process. Although the dissent dismisses our concerns about collective bargaining and academic freedom at private universities as pure speculation, their confidence in the process in turn relies on speculation about the risks of imposing collective bargaining on the student-university relationship. We decline to take these risks with our nation's excellent private educational system. Although under a variety of state laws, some states permit collective bargaining at public universities, we choose to interpret and apply a single federal law differently to the large numbers of private universities under our jurisdiction. Consistent with long standing Board precedent, and for the reasons set forth in this decision, we declare the federal law to be that graduate student assistants are not employees within the meaning of Section 2(3) of the Act.

The Regional Director's Decision and Direction of Election is reversed, and the petition is dismissed. Dated, Washington, D.C., July 13, 2004.

Robert J. Battista, Chairman, Peter C. Schaumber, Member, Ronald Meisburg, Member.

Members Liebman and Walsh, dissenting.

Protocols and Ethics

14. Edward Shils,
"The Academic Ethic," 1982

These brief paragraphs can hardly do justice to a scholar's scholar whose printed bibliography ran to almost 25 pages. Still, they touch the heart of what Shils (1910–95) considered a university and its people to be and to mean in society. Shils, born in Springfield, Massachusetts, took his B.A. at the University of Pennsylvania (1931), then went to the University of Chicago to study sociology, with which he would be associated throughout his life. His most enduring book is *Tradition,* a word he honored in his writings and activities. His affinity for British higher education took him to posts at the London School of Economics and Cambridge University. Always active in international academic affairs, he also began in 1962 to edit the periodical *Minerva, A Review of Science, Learning, and Policy* and continued as its editor until his death. From its pages emerged his belief that the "worldwide community" of science is "the closest thing to the ideal of a body bound together by a universal devotion to a common set of standards derived from a common tradition."

Edward Shils, "The Academic Ethic," *Minerva* 20 (Spring–Summer 1982): 121–23, 178. Copyright © 1982 by Springer. Reprinted with the kind permission of Springer Science and Business Media. Further reading: Shils, *Tradition* (Chicago, 1981); H. R. Trevor-Roper, "In Memoriam: Edward Shils, 1910–1995," *The New Criterion* 14, no. 2 (October 1995); Joseph Epstein, "My Friend Edward," *American Scholar* 64 (Summer 1995): 371–94; Clark Kerr, "The Academic Ethic and University Teachers: A 'Disintegrating Profession,' " *Minerva* 27 (Summer–Autumn 1989): 139–56; and Derek Bok, *Universities in the Marketplace: The Commercialization of Higher Education* (Princeton, NJ, 2003), chs. 9–10.

The Service-University: Universities have always been integrated into the practical life of their societies. They have always included among their functions the training of lawyers and physicians; later, they introduced courses for civil servants and advanced secondary school teachers as well, and later still, courses for engineers and scientists who worked in government, agriculture and industry. In the present century, they have continued to do all these things as well as to educate their own succession in science and scholarship and the practitioners of many occupations, such as journalism, librarianship and social work, which did not exist in their present form until quite recently; nursing education has also become in some places a responsibility accepted by universities. For quite a long time in American and British universities, they have also provided training for the management of private business firms.

Despite these perfectly obvious facts, the charge that universities are ivory towers has been a common one throughout the present century. The charge has been made by narrow-minded political zealots who resented the studious detachment of universities in the pursuit of truth in numerous fields of intellectual work and the training of their students to face the facts of life, without dogmatism or rigid prejudice and to apply the best established knowledge in their professional careers. It has also been made by social reformers and radicals who thought that their causes—sometimes good causes, sometimes pernicious ones—could not wait any longer for their realisation, and who required that everyone throw himself into the battle without regard for balanced judgment based on carefully assessed knowledge. Similar criticism of universities used to be made from the quite different standpoint of the "practical man", usually the businessman, who could not see the point of intellectual activities which did not show a profit or which did not contribute directly to industrial and agricultural production. The criticism of the university as an "ivory tower" has greatly diminished in recent years. Both businessmen and humanitarian reformers, both civil servants and politicians have accepted that the university is not in fact an "ivory tower".

Similarly the universities have practically ceased to be criticised for being too "utilitarian". This was a common view especially in the United States in the early part of this century but such criticism has nearly disappeared. The universities are now regarded by academics, both in principle and by their own individual engagement in practical activities as rightly serving the intellectual-practical demands of their societies. There is a general consensus inside and outside the universities that they should be and are involved in the practical concerns of their societies in so far as these activities have a substantial intellectual—above all scientific—content.

Universities are now regarded as indispensable to more practical activities than were ever conceived before as requiring systematic knowledge, and hence, higher education for the acquisition of that knowledge. There is general agreement about this between most academics on the one hand and the leaders in practical affairs on the other. Local and state governments and national governments in almost all Western countries, private business firms and civic organisations now think that the knowledge which universities produce is necessary to them. They do not think that it is sufficient for them just to appoint the graduates of universities who have had these necessary kinds of fundamental knowledge imparted to them as students before taking up their appointments and who have learned at universities how to acquire the fresh knowledge which their tasks will require.

The prospective "users" of the knowledge and of the techniques of gaining new knowledge which their employees have acquired in universities have however begun to demand something more immediately practical. The first steps were taken about a century and a half ago when enterprisers in chemical industries began to solicit individual academic chemists to do research on problems which were of practical importance to the chemical industry. They began to invite academics to do research designed for immediate practical use, alongside or instead of concentrating on the advancement of fundamental knowledge. More recently they have wanted universities to offer special training courses for already employed persons in order to provide them with very particular kinds of knowledge which have been created since those persons had been trained as regular students. Academics, for their part, began to offer advisory services to help governments or business enterprises to deal with highly specific current problems. These expectations and the positive responses of academics became very common after the Second World War.

Also after the Second World War governments became persuaded that the well-being of their societies, or of particular parts of their societies, would in the future depend on having sufficient numbers of persons with the necessary higher educational qualifications; the "planning of high-level manpower" in one form or another was widely recommended and taken seriously. The universities came to be regarded more specifically than ever before as the places where immediately usable scientific research was and could be performed and where the scientists and other persons could acquire the scientific and technical knowledge which was to be immediately applied in the technology and management of the affairs of industrial and commercial firms and governments. This belief was one of the major reasons for the greatly increased financial support for universities. Although this was not a sharp disjunction from what had been developing over the preceding century, the specificity and insistence of the demands for these practical services in research and education have become much more prominent elements in the conception of the tasks of the university. . . .

The idea of being useful to society is being badly misinterpreted at present. Some reformers think that being useful to society means that universities should give up their concern with fundamental knowledge and with the rationale of evidence, experience and tradition and should concentrate on the training of young and middle-aged persons for the performance of the specific skilled operations which their society is willing to employ and pay for. These are, of course, perfectly legitimate educational activities, but not all of them must be taught in universities and they are certainly not all that universities should teach. Burdening universities with tasks which should be performed by other institutions, hampers the universities in their performance of those tasks which are necessary for society and which the universities alone can perform. It has the consequence too that the young are trained only for occupations which exist here and now. In a rapidly changing society, such an education can easily produce future unemployables, quite incapable of adjusting to new techniques.

The enlightenment of the wider public through "extension" courses presented away from the campus or of lectures open to the public but delivered on the campus is a very desirable activity but it does not fall directly within the circle of the primary obligation of university teachers. The main achievement of the university in the furtherance of public enlightenment should be sought through the education of the university's students in the substance and methods of thought of the various academic disciplines and through arousing and maintaining in them intellectual curiosity and sensibility which will persist in their life long after they have completed their studies and which they will diffuse through its presence in their professional activities.

15. Donald Kennedy,
Academic Duty, 1997

In his broad canvas of recurring scenes in academic institutions Donald Kennedy (1931–) draws largely upon his own experiences at Stanford University (1980–92). As one of a half-dozen books by prominent university administrators to come out at the end of the twentieth century, his is exceptionally comprehensive. Here he discusses a perennial question raised about undergraduate teaching and incidentally illustrates how far removed from their nineteenth-century predecessors modern presidents are in their public pronouncements.

Harvard trained Kennedy (B.A. 1952, Ph.D. 1956) came to Stanford in 1965 as a professor of biological sciences. He filled successively the posts of departmental chair, provost, and president, while also serving government offices in the 1970s.

Reprinted by permission of the publisher from *Academic Duty* by Donald Kennedy, pp. 65–67, Cambridge, Mass.: Harvard University Press, Copyright © 1997. Further reading: Kennedy's views on other subjects are found at VII, 10; XII, 6; and Neil W. Hamilton, *Academic Ethics: Problems and Materials on Professional Conduct and Shared Governance* (Westport, CT, 2002).

The question of what to teach is as controversial as how much to teach. Higher education in the United States has always been perplexed about whether the university should "teach values." Recent pronouncements, especially from the political Right, have taken the academy to task for what is often called "moral relativism"—a refusal to take clear stands on what are seen as the fundamental values of our society. This charge actually sweeps up a netful of concerns about the modern university environment: it is too pluralistic (for example, in its failure to require courses in the Great Works of Western culture); it is too soft and permissive (in its campus rules about drugs and sex); it too readily gives in to the demands of minority students (or women, or gays) to have their "communities" recognized or honored.

This debate is unlikely to end very soon. Indeed, there is some reason to hope that it won't. It has put into play strong and conflicting views about the purposes of higher education and the role of university faculties, and through its challenges it has encouraged their resolution on campus and their recognition off campus. The controversy is heightened by—in fact, would probably not exist without—the enormous changes in the student bodies of our most selective colleges and universities. It was hard not to notice, at the time of my wife's twenty-fifth reunion at Stanford in the spring of 1993, that ethnic minorities constituted only a tiny percentage of her class. In fact, six African-Americans graduated in that year of Martin Luther King's assassination. But in the freshman class that enrolled during her reunion year, only about half the students were "nonminority!"

Such environments are conducive to clashes over values, because everybody brings different ones to the campus. Differences surface all the time without much encouragement, generating one "teachable moment" after another. But with all this struggling and sorting out going on in the community, what is the faculty member's role? Those who don't try to figure that out are going to be spectators in one of the most vital growth zones to be found anywhere in the university.

Clearly, if we are to prepare students for leadership we are required to give them more than knowledge, and even more than the ability to think. Values are important as well—and here I mean the beliefs we hold about what is important, how we ought to act toward one another, and how our society ought to be composed and governed. Although values form and direct conduct, they are not the same thing. Conduct is a description of actual behavior; in the case of the college or university, it is the way in which the campus community is structured and the way people act in and toward it.

Many critics of the university also believe in the centrality of values. Often they inquire as to whether we "teach values," when in fact they mean something quite different. For example, in response to a thoughtful talk by Derek Bok, then the president of Harvard, on the subject of teaching values, Secretary of Education William Bennett said that what he thought was important in this area was getting the drugs off campus. His statement was not about the teaching of values but about the regulation of conduct. To be sure, rules of conduct reflect an institution's views about values. If they display respect for due process and for the openness that is critical to an academic community, that is an important signal. But regulating conduct is not the same as teaching about values.

Indeed, the troubling question, and a source of much confusion, is whether we teach values or teach *about* them. For example, one of the great value questions for contemporary American culture and institutions is this: What balance should be struck between the individual freedom to pursue self-interested ends and the individual's obligation to the larger society? Some would have us preselect an answer to this question and "teach" it as though it had normative status. Of course, such advocates have different opinions about which is the correct value. Libertarians would place great weight on the side of individual freedom, whereas Socialists would place it on the side of service to the state. Most Americans take some intermediate position in which freedom and responsibility, liberty and duty coexist in a delicate, sometimes tense balance.

To offer courses that simply advance a particular position would be bad policy and bad pedagogy. There has, after all, been a history of the development of these ideas. There is also a record of social experiment. We have access to both, and they are the raw material for serious academic study. To analyze the ideas of Locke, Hobbes, Mill, and Rousseau, to compare societies with varying commitments to freedom and obligation—that is the way to form one's own values securely. They can't be short-ordered; they aren't McThoughts. Rather, they have to be formed through laborious analysis, through the intellectual equivalent of gourmet cooking.

Letting students work this out for themselves requires almost exquisite restraint on the part of the teacher/scholar—a careful curb on the natural desire to display one's own convictions. A central purpose of teaching, as of scholarship, is to help students acquire that kind of detachment. Plainly, one of its enemies is too much passion for a particular point of view. That does not mean, of course, that personal belief is out of bounds. Personal and even passionate commitment to the subject is an important source of resonance between a teacher and students. But as to analysis and to the development of theory, some distance is essential.

Another argument for restraint in advocacy has to do with fairness. In this context as in others, the teacher brings formidable powers to the teacher-student relationship. It is almost too easy for a professor to persuade, to impose personal views on those whose state of expectation and relative lack of experience may make them vulnerable. The charismatic but careless professor, with a gaggle of adoring but uncritical followers, is a fairly uncommon but nonetheless troubling campus landmark. In the late 1960s it was both more common and more troubling.

16. Neil Smelser, *Effective Committee Service,* 1993

Committee discussions and findings are central to the life of modern organizations. In higher education they have given faculty members a voice in guiding administrative affairs. The degree to which this voice is heeded by campus officers and boards of control has often been the measure of success toward achieving educational purposes. At their best, cooperative relations between faculty and administrative committees have resulted in a beneficial shared governance or guidance of their institution.

Faculty committees spend time that generally is removed from their immediate commitments to teaching and research. Beyond regarding committee time as a necessary interruption or distraction, members know that their voluntary service, though presumably a credit in their record, may be viewed as only minimally rewarding for their rise up an academic ladder. Thus they come to committee deliberations with varying motives, attitudes, and expressions of interest.

This candid guide to committee behavior by Neil Smelser (1930–) is unique. It comes from more than four decades of academic and associational experiences, during which he became a committeeman extraordinaire with a strong basis for his highly regarded studies of group behavior. An eminent sociologist at Berkeley (1958–94), Smelser held key campus and university-wide committee posts and was appointed in 1972 as a system-wide University Professor. He served more extramural committees as a trustee or director of the Social Science Research Council, the Russell Sage Foundation, and the Center for Advanced Study in the Behavioral Sciences where he was director (1994–2000), and as president of the American Sociological Association.

Neil J. Smelser, *Effective Committee Service* (Newbury Park, CA, 1993), viii–xi, 49–51, 57–58, 61, 68–69. Copyright © 1993. Reprinted by permission of Sage Publications Inc. and the kind permission of Neil J. Smelser. Further reading: Neil J. Smelser and Dean R. Gerstein, eds., *Behavioral and Social Science: Fifty Years of Discovery* (Washington, D.C., 1986); and Robert F. Bales, *Interaction Process Analysis: A Method for the Study of Small Groups* (Cambridge, MA, 1950).

No organization runs without committees. If we scan the landscape of contemporary organizational life, we find them to be omnipresent creatures. Academic organizations are no exception. In fact, they are probably honeycombed with more committees than their counterparts in other institutional spheres—business firms, hospitals, civil service bureaucracies, and military units, for example. There is a good reason for this. The main currency of colleges and universities is collegial influence, not the exercise of power and authority. It might even be said that if an order has to be issued in academia, that is a sure sign of organizational failure. Committees, moreover, are generators and peddlers of influence. They gather information, reflect, make recommendations, and advise—in short, they influence—as academic organizations move through their eternal cycles of routine functioning, problem solving, crisis meeting, and decision making.

One does not have to be a card-carrying functional analyst to observe that, being omnipresent, committees serve a great variety of both manifest and latent functions in academic and other organizations. . . . At the same time, our feelings about the committee often resemble our feelings about a spouse in a neurotic marriage: We need and are dependent on it and may even love it sometimes, but we also detest it and wish in vain that we could shake free from it. This ambivalence is reflected in familiar bits of cynical humor.

Forming a committee is thought to be a sub-stitute for decisive action: "When in doubt, form a committee." Committee work is felt to be a boring and useless chore. Committees engage in "make work." And committees are believed to produce vague, wishy-washy, lowest-common-denominator results: "A camel is a horse drawn by a committee." Yet, as in a neurotic marriage, we keep falling back and relying on the committee as a tried and true organizational mechanism.

Every one of us in academia has served on some kind of committee or committeelike group. Even when a department chair asks a couple of colleagues to sit down, think about an issue or problem, and come up with some ideas, an informal committee is at work. In my own academic career, which is now approaching four decades, I sometimes feel as though I have served on every committee in and around academia. That is false, of course, but there have been very many. . . .

This book contains both analysis of and advice about committee work. In offering the latter, I do not intend to suggest that all of you should behave as I have behaved on committees. Everyone develops his or her own style in groups, and many different styles can be effective. Nevertheless, some rules of thumb can be articulated, and I present these as general guidelines, always with the caution that you should read them as such and not as eternal principles. . . .

THE EXPRESSIVE SIDE OF COMMITTEE LIFE

The term *expressive* refers to the fact that a group—in our case, a committee—has to spend part of its energy in safeguarding its own integrity. A committee must have rules or understandings about who talks when, when it gets into a state of unfocused discourse, when and how it comes to decisions, and how it affirms those decisions (e.g., by informal consensus; by majority vote). More generally, groups—including committees—are forever in danger of bogging down in their work through lack of direction, frustration, loss of interest, low morale, alienation of members, and internal conflict. Many groups do break down and fail in their work for these "expressive" reasons, and those that do not have to devote some of their time and energy—sometimes consciously, sometimes unconsciously—to seeing that they do not.

Most committees, especially when they are small, proceed with a minimum of procedural rules. A committee of three or five that is arranging the details of a graduation ceremony, for example, does not need many rules beyond those understandings of conversational civility—understandings about not talking too much or too little, not shouting or insulting, not interrupting incessantly, and so on. It is only in moments of excited talk or conflict that the chair will have to make explicit the familiar rule that people will talk in the order that he or she recognizes them. Small, informal committees of this sort also do not need elaborate procedures for coming to decisions. Decisions may be made when someone asks, "Are we agreed that. . . ." or suggests "Let's decide that. . . ." and assent is given.

As groups grow larger, more formal procedures come into play. If 12 to 15 people are discussing whether a statistics requirement ought to be included in an undergraduate social-science major, almost everybody will have something to say and disagreements of educational philosophy and pedagogical strategy will inevitably arise. At the very least the chair of such a group has to maintain order by recognizing people in order, setting limits on how long a given topic should be discussed, and guiding the discussion to some kind of conclusion, even if that conclusion should be deciding not to decide.

The most formal expression of procedural order for meetings, including committee meetings, is found in books such as *Robert's Rules of Order*. These are extremely complex documents that specify, for example, when the chair of a group may silence someone ("You are out of order"), when someone can interrupt without being recognized ("Point of order!"), when things can and cannot be discussed (for example, if an amendment is made to a motion, the amendment must be discussed before the motion is discussed), and how meetings begin ("calling to order") and end ("rules of adjournment"). Books of this sort are akin to rule books for games like baseball. They aim to specify *every* possible situational contingency that may arise in a game or a meeting and to specify a corresponding rule that covers it. Rules of order, like rules of the game, are designed to minimize uncertainty and ambiguity. Such an objective can never be fully attained, of course. Baseball games need umpires to make calls and invoke rules and deliberative bodies need chairs and sometimes parliamentarians to decide what kind of situation is at hand and what rules apply. Both games and meetings thus have a residue of judgment and arbitrariness, but the rules of order attempt to minimize these and even contain procedures for reducing arbitrariness (for example, appealing an umpire's decision to the league office; overruling the chair's decision).

Many committees, then, are shrouded in rules and procedures. However, it might be suggested that if a chair, a parliamentarian, or a member of a deliberative group is forced to consult the rule book, it is a sign that the group is in trouble. To invoke a rule is often a sign that informal civility has broken down.

When groups work themselves into a paralysis through *procedural* or parliamentary wrangling, that signifies, to me at least, that they are probably paralyzed by substantive conflict. Prolonged procedural discussions often mean that groups are either finding refuge in elaborate procedural discussions as a way of working their way out of the thickets of conflict or that some people in the group are attempting to score *substantive* victories by prevailing on procedural points. Elaborate rules of order serve best when they are an unused reservoir. By that I mean that the committees that work best are those that rely on informal understandings of civility and cooperativeness, move toward consensus in easy ways, and settle issues and decisions without actually invoking rules and voting. . . .

THE EVOLUTION OF A COMMITTEE CULTURE

Every committee experiences the development of a "committee culture"—or had better do so if it is going to work together.

How does this culture develop? It involves first of all the building of a committee memory. People are continuously remembering things that were said and points that were made in past meetings, and identifying those things with other committee members. It involves some benign and some not-so-benign stereotyping. Members come to assume roles in committees by taking a particular line, and these roles are solidified by typing them, by labeling them, by joking about them. Other, scapegoated members come to symbolize what the committee culture does not stand for: incivility, disagreeableness, stubbornness, and the like. The committee culture is also built through the development of rules and understandings about how to proceed: some from the book, some imported from members' experience on other committees, some generated through the give-and-take of the committee's own work.

Through all this there develops a sense of the committee as a definite entity set off from the rest of the world at least temporarily, which is also an essential aspect of a culture. And finally, there develops a feeling on the part of committee members that they are somehow special, even though this "specialness" may be experienced in a modest way. And, having developed this committee culture, committees proceed further to develop their own little world of rituals, "in jokes," and immodest self-congratulation, as well as an implicit and sometimes explicit hostility to outsiders who are not part of the culture. All this is to say that a committee is no different from any other type of group, and if a committee is to maintain any integrity and any capacity to function, it must necessarily develop a common culture of which its members feel they are a part. . . .

Learning on committees is done almost entirely by doing, and seldom is one told how he or she is doing. It is something like college or university teaching; there is a tacit assumption that simply because one has gained a higher degree, he or she knows how to teach. . . .

One does learn, however, even though much of the learning is unconscious and never articulated. Even a very experienced committee member believes that he or she is simply "being oneself" on a committee and does not think, much less plot, very much in terms of strategies and tactics. For this reason, the following abstracted rules of thumb for behaving as a committee member are just that: abstracted from many years of experience and reflection, not carried around in my head as so many strategies every time I go into a committee meeting. That being said, let me specify several principles that seem to foster effectiveness and influence in committee work. . . .

RELYING ON HUMOR

The advantages of timely use of humor in a committee cannot be exaggerated. It is difficult to speak of guidelines in this respect, because a person's sense of humor is a kind of "given" and one cannot be coached into having one. Notwithstanding, its advantages are numerous. To reveal a sense of humor is a way of communicating that one maintains a certain distance from the proceedings, and it implies that one has neither defensive nor aggrandizing intent. Humor also constitutes a way of attacking an idea or another person without being openly discrediting.

I can recall one incident at a meeting of a committee of the systemwide Academic Senate when we were discussing, somewhat wearily, the subject of "mandatory matriculation," an arcane aspect of transferring from community colleges to the University of California. Almost nobody understood or was interested in the subject, and nobody seems to know what we were supposed to do about it. At a given moment, I observed, quite spontaneously, that "mandatory matriculation" sounded to me like an obscure form of sexual malfunctioning. Though I had not consciously intended the remark to have this effect, it brought forward loud laughter and effectively killed the discussion—which, I might add modestly, was well on its way to dying a natural death, anyway.

Humor, finally, is a way of simultaneously expressing hostility, releasing tension, and, oddly, becoming the object of other members' affection. I cannot say that I understand the dynamics of this, but I have often found myself and seen others being drawn to the committee wag who knows how and when to joke in good taste, how to attack without seeming to attack, and how to expose without revealing an intention to expose. I have also experienced this effect when I have taken on that role.

AVOIDING EXTREMES AND SELF-SCAPEGOATING

I do not know how to make the last point without seeming banal, but it is so important that it must be mentioned. It has to do with avoiding all kinds of extremes in committee work. The effective committee member must talk but not become verbose, be humorous but not biting, be serious but not funereal, be conscientious but not compulsive, be knowledgeable but not arrogant, be prepared to defend what he or she has said without being defensive, be cooperative but not submissive, and be a good citizen without overconforming. If one attacks another point of view or argument that one finds stupid or otherwise unacceptable, it ought to be done carefully, in a measured way, and in the context of venturing other comments that grant *general* legitimacy to the person being attacked.

These several "golden mean" observations add up to the truth that moderation and tact are two of the most valuable assets in the committee setting. There are a couple of reasons for this. First, these characteristics are normally highly valued in the code of civility that constitutes the committee culture. Second, if one moves toward any extremes of behavior in this kind of group setting, one invites being typecast and being scapegoated. (Actually, the tactful committee member *also* runs the risk of being Mr. or Ms. Moderate if he or she is caricatured in the expression of moderation.) And if typecast or scapegoated, the committee member then runs the risk of losing flexibility and influence, because his or her conduct is discounted as showing predictability.

So much for a set of guidelines that have proven helpful in committee work over the years. I think they have some general validity in the committee context. I should end with a final bit of qualifying advice: *Do not follow these rules to the point of becoming a phony.* Insofar as what I have outlined involves the expression of a personal style of my own, you should discount that appropriately, because your personal style is your own and difficult to alter. If you consciously attempt to alter it, moreover, you are likely to be seen for what you are: unauthentic. And the quality of unauthenticity is certainly not an asset in the committee setting.

17. Ernest Boyer, *Scholarship Reconsidered,* 1990

Along with Clark Kerr, Ernest L. Boyer (1928–95) occupied a central role in higher education throughout the 1970s and 1980s. As president of the Carnegie Foundation for the Advancement of Teaching (1979–95), preceded by wide experience in administration at the State University of New York (1970–77) and as U.S. commissioner of education (1977–79), Boyer turned out studies of American and international colleges and universities. His writing tended to be directed more to the academic content of institutions and to the professional activities of their members than to purely administrative descriptions. Out of long experience, he here briefly defined ways in which faculty may respond to their mandates of teaching and scholarship.

Boyer received his M.A. and Ph.D. degrees (1955, 1957) from the University of Southern California, and he would eventually amass nearly 140 honorary degrees. He also received honorary awards from a variety of groups, both national and professional, and *U.S. News and World Report* named him an outstanding leader in American education in 1978 and 1990.

Ernest L. Boyer, *Scholarship Reconsidered: Priorities of the Professoriate* (Princeton, NJ, 1990), 16–25. Copyright © Carnegie Foundation for the Advancement of Teaching, 1990. Reprinted with permission of John Wiley & Sons, Inc. Further reading: III, 13.

How then should we proceed? Is it possible to define the work of faculty in ways that reflect more realistically the full range of academic and civic mandates? We believe the time has come to move beyond the tired old "teaching versus research" debate and give the familiar and honorable term "scholarship" a broader, more capacious meaning, one that brings legitimacy to the full scope of academic work. Surely, scholarship means engaging in original research. But the work of the scholar also means stepping back from one's investigation, looking for connections, building bridges between theory and practice, and communicating one's knowledge effectively to students. Specifically, we conclude that the work of the professoriate might be thought of as having four separate, yet overlapping, functions. These are: the scholarship of *discovery;* the scholarship of *integration;* the scholarship of *application;* and the scholarship of *teaching.*

The first and most familiar element in our model, the *scholarship of discovery,* comes closest to what is meant when academics speak of "research." No tenets in the academy are held in higher regard than the commitment to knowledge for its own sake, to freedom of inquiry and to following, in a disciplined fashion, an investigation wherever it may lead. Research is central to the work of higher learning, but our study here, which inquires into the meaning of scholarship, is rooted in the conviction that disciplined, investigative efforts within the academy should be strengthened, not diminished.

The *scholarship of discovery,* at its best, contributes not only to the stock of human knowledge but also to the intellectual climate of a college or university. Not just the outcomes, but the process, and especially the passion, give meaning to the effort. The advancement of knowledge can generate an almost palpable excitement in the life of an educational institution. . . .

When the research records of higher learning are compared, the United States is the pacesetter. If we take as our measure of accomplishment the number of Nobel Prizes awarded since 1945, United States scientists received 56 percent of the awards in physics, 42 percent in chemistry, and 60 percent in medicine. Prior to the outbreak of the Second World War, American scientists, including those who fled Hitler's Europe, had received only 18 of the 129 prizes in these three areas. With regard to physics, for example, a recent report by the National Research Council states: "Before World War II, physics was essentially a European activity, but by the war's end, the center of physics had moved to the United States." The Council goes on to review the advances in fields ranging from elementary particle physics to cosmology.

The research contribution of universities is particularly evident in medicine. Investigations in the late nineteenth century on bacteria and viruses paid off in the 1930s with the development of immunizations for diphtheria, tetanus, lobar pneumonia, and other bacterial infections. On the basis of painstaking research, a taxonomy of infectious diseases has emerged, making possible streptomycin and other antibiotics. In commenting on these breakthroughs, physician and medical writer Lewis Thomas observes: "It was basic science of a very high order, storing up a great mass of interesting knowledge for its own sake, creating, so to speak, a bank of information, ready for drawing on when the time for intelligent use arrived."

Thus, the probing mind of the researcher is an incalculably vital asset to the academy and the world. Scholarly investigation, in all the disciplines, is at the very heart of academic life, and the pursuit of knowledge must be assiduously cultivated and defended. The intellectual excitement fueled by this quest enlivens faculty and invigorates higher learning institutions, and in our complicated, vulnerable world, the discovery of new knowledge is absolutely crucial.

THE SCHOLARSHIP OF INTEGRATION

In proposing the *scholarship of integration,* we underscore the need for scholars who give meaning to isolated facts, putting them in perspective. By integration, we mean making connections across the disciplines, placing the specialties in larger context, illuminating data in a revealing way, often educating nonspecialists, too. In calling for a scholarship of integration, we do not suggest returning to the "gentleman scholar" of an earlier time, nor do we have in mind the dilettante. Rather, what we mean is serious, disciplined work that seeks to interpret, draw together, and bring new insight to bear on original research.

This more integrated view of knowledge was expressed eloquently by Mark Van Doren nearly thirty years ago when he wrote: "The connectedness of things is what the educator contemplates to the limit of his capacity. No human capacity is great enough to permit a vision of the world as simple, but if the educator does not aim at the vision no one else will, and the consequences are dire when no one does." It is through "connectedness" that research ultimately is made authentic.

The scholarship of integration is, of course, closely related to discovery. It involves, first, doing research at the boundaries where fields converge, and it reveals itself in what philosopher-physicist Michael Polanyi calls "overlapping [academic] neighborhoods." Such work is, in fact, increasingly important as traditional disciplinary categories prove confining, forcing new topologies of knowledge. Many of today's professors understand this. . . .

The scholarship of integration also means interpretation, fitting one's own research—or the research of others—into larger intellectual patterns. Such efforts are increasingly essential since specialization, without broader perspective, risks pedantry. The distinction we are drawing here between "discovery" and "integration" can be best understood, perhaps, by the questions posed. Those engaged in discovery ask, "What is to be known, what is yet to be found?" Those engaged in integration ask, "What do the findings *mean*? Is it possible to interpret what's been discovered in ways that provide a larger, more comprehensive understanding?" Questions such as these call for the power of critical analysis and interpretation. They have a legitimacy of their own and if carefully pursued can lead the scholar from information to knowledge and even, perhaps, to wisdom. . . .

Today, more than at any time in recent memory, researchers feel the need to move beyond traditional disciplinary boundaries, communicate with colleagues in other fields, and discover patterns that connect. Anthropologist Clifford Geertz, of the Institute for Advanced Study in Princeton, has gone so far as to describe these shifts as a fundamental "refiguration, . . . a phenomenon general enough and distinctive enough to suggest that what we are seeing is not just another redrawing of the cultural map—the moving of a few disputed borders, the marking of some more picturesque mountain lakes —but an alteration of the principles of mapping. Something is happening," Geertz says, "to the way we think about the way we think.". . .

These examples illustrate a variety of scholarly trends—*interdisciplinary, interpretive, integrative.* But we present them here as evidence that an intellectual sea change may be occurring, one that is perhaps as momentous as the nineteenth-century shift in the hierarchy of knowledge, when philosophy gave way more firmly to science. Today, interdisciplinary *and* integrative studies, long on the edges of academic life, are moving toward the center, responding both to new intellectual questions and to pressing human problems. As the boundaries of human knowledge are being dramatically reshaped, the academy surely must give increased attention to the *scholarship of integration.*

THE SCHOLARSHIP OF APPLICATION

The first two kinds of scholarship—discovery and integration of knowledge—reflect the investigative and synthesizing traditions of academic life. The third element, the *application* of knowledge, moves toward engagement as the scholar asks, "How can knowledge be responsibly applied to consequential problems? How can it be helpful to individuals as well as institutions?" And further, "Can social problems *themselves* define an agenda for scholarly investigation?" . . .

Colleges and universities have recently rejected service as serious scholarship partly because its meaning is so vague and often disconnected from serious intellectual work. As used today, service in the academy covers an almost endless number of campus activities—sitting on committees, advising student clubs, or performing departmental chores. The definition blurs still more as activities beyond the campus are included—participation in town councils, youth clubs, and the like. It is not unusual for almost any worthy project to be dumped into the amorphous category called "service."

Clearly, a sharp distinction must be drawn between *citizenship* activities and projects that relate to scholarship itself. To be sure, there are meritorious social and civic functions to be performed, and faculty should be appropriately recognized for such work. But all too frequently, service means not doing scholarship but doing good. To be considered *scholarship,* service activities must be tied directly to one's special field of knowledge and relate to, and flow directly out of, this professional activity. Such service is serious, demanding work, requiring the rigor—and the accountability—traditionally associated with research activities.

The *scholarship of application,* as we define it her, is not a one-way street. Indeed, the term itself may be misleading if it suggests that knowledge is first "discovered" and then "applied." The process we have in mind is far more dynamic. New intellectual understandings can arise out of the very act of application—whether in medical diagnosis, serving clients in psychotherapy, shaping public policy, creating an architectural design, or working with the public schools. In activities such as these, theory and practice vitally interact, and one renews the other. . . .

THE SCHOLARSHIP OF TEACHING

Finally, we come to the *scholarship of teaching.* The work of the professor becomes consequential only as it is understood by others. Yet, today, teaching is often viewed as a routine function, tacked on, something almost anyone can do. When defined as *scholarship,* however, teaching both educates and entices future scholars. Indeed, as Aristotle said, "Teaching is the highest form of understanding."

As a *scholarly* enterprise, teaching begins with what the teacher knows. Those who teach must, above all, be well informed, and steeped in the knowledge of their fields. Teaching can be well regarded only as professors are widely read and intellectually engaged. One reason legislators, trustees, and the general public often fail to understand why ten or twelve hours in the classroom each week can be a heavy load is their lack of awareness of the hard work and the serious study that undergirds good teaching.

Teaching is also a dynamic endeavor involving all the analogies, metaphors, and images that build bridges between the teacher's understanding and the student's learning. Pedagogical procedures must be carefully planned, continuously examined, and relate directly to the subject taught. . . .

Further, good teaching means that faculty, as scholars, are also learners. All too often, teachers transmit information that students are expected to memorize and then, perhaps, recall. While well-prepared lectures surely have a place, teaching, at its best, means not only transmitting knowledge, but *transforming* and *extending* it as well. Through reading, through classroom discussion, and surely through comments and questions posed by students, professors themselves will be pushed in creative new directions.

In the end, inspired teaching keeps the flame of scholarship alive. Almost all successful academics give credit to creative teachers—those mentors who defined their work so compellingly that it became, for them, a lifetime challenge. Without the teaching function, the continuity of knowledge will be broken and the store of human knowledge dangerously diminished. . . .

Here, then, is our conclusion. What we urgently need today is a more inclusive view of what it means to be a scholar—a recognition that knowledge is acquired through research, through synthesis, through practice, and through teaching. We acknowledge that these four categories—the scholarship of discovery, of integration, of application, and of teaching—divide intellectual functions that are tied inseparably to each other. Still, there is value, we believe, in analyzing the various kinds of academic work, while also acknowledging that they dynamically interact, forming an interdependent whole. Such a vision of scholarship, one that recognizes the great diversity of talent within the professoriate, also may prove especially useful to faculty as they reflect on the meaning and direction of their professional lives.

18. Burton R. Clark, "Small Worlds, Different Worlds," 1997

Burton Clark (1921–) brought a sociologist's perspective to bear upon the varieties of specialized institutional lives in American higher education. A longtime student of academic ways abroad as well as at home, Clark offered stimulating comparative explanations. He came to the study of sociology at UCLA (B.A. 1949, Ph.D. 1954) and then served appointments at Berkeley (1958–66) and at Yale (1966–80), where he chaired the Department of Sociology. He returned to UCLA as Allan M. Cartter Professor of Higher Education (1980–91).

Burton R. Clark, "Small Worlds, Different Worlds: The Uniqueness and Troubles of American Academic Professions," *Daedalus* 126 (Fall 1997): 21–42. © 1971 by the American Academy of Arts and Sciences, abridged with permission. Further reading: Clark, *Academic Power in the United States* (Los Angeles, 1978), *The Academic Life* (San Francisco, 1987), *The Academic Profession* (Los Angeles, 1987), and "Faculty: Differentiation and Dispersion," in *Higher Learning in America, 1980–2000*, ed. Arthur Levine (Baltimore, 1983), ch. 10.

The academic profession is a multitude of academic tribes and territories. As in days of old, it is law, medicine, and theology. It is now also high-energy physics, molecular biology, Renaissance literature, childhood learning, and computer science. Built upon a widening array of disciplines and specialties, it hosts subcultures that speak in the strange tongues of econometrics, biochemistry, ethnomethodology, and deconstructionism. Driven by a research imperative that rewards specialization, its fragmentation is slowed, though not fully arrested, by limited resources to fund all the new and old lines of effort in which academics would like to engage. Already very great, knowledge growth builds in a self-amplifying fashion. . . . As subjects fragment, so does the academic profession, turning it evermore into a profession of professions.

No less important in the differentiation of the academic profession in America is the dispersion of faculty among institutions in a system that, when viewed internationally, must be seen as inordinately large, radically decentralized, extremely diversified, uniquely competitive, and uncommonly entrepreneurial. A high degree of institutional dispersion positions American faculty in many varied sectors of a national "system" that totaled 3,600 institutions in the mid-1990s: a hundred-plus "research universities" of high research intensity; another hundred "doctoral-granting" universities that grant only a few doctorates and operate off of a small research base; five hundred and more "master's colleges and universities," a catch-all category of private and public institutions that have graduate as well as undergraduate programs, offering master's degrees but not doctorates; still another six hundred "baccalaureate colleges," heavily private and varying greatly in quality and in degree of concentration on the liberal arts; a huge array of over 1,400 two-year colleges, 95 percent public in enrollment, whose individual comprehensiveness includes college-transfer programs, short-term vocational offerings, and adult education; and finally a leftover miscellany of some seven hundred "specialized institutions" that do not fit into the above basic categories.

These major categories in turn contain much institutional diversity. Buried within them are historically black colleges, Catholic universities, women's colleges, fundamentalist religious universities and colleges, and such distinctive institutions as the Julliard School (of Music), the Bank Street College of Education, and Rockefeller University. The American faculty is distributed institutionally all over the map, located in the educational equivalents of the farm and the big city, the ghetto and the suburbs, the darkened ravine located next to a coal mine and the sunny hill overlooking a lovely valley.

Disciplinary and institutional locations together compose the primary matrix of induced and enforced differences among American academics. These two internal features of the system itself are more important than such background characteristics of academics as class, race, religion, and gender in determining work-centered thought and behavior. These primary dimensions convert simple statements about "the professor" in "the college" or "the university" into stereotypes. We deceive ourselves every time we speak of *the* college professor, a common habit among popular critics of the professoriate who fail to talk to academics in their varied locations and to listen to what they say. Simple summary figures and averages extracted from surveys, e.g., "68 percent of American professors like their mothers" or "On the average, American professors teach eight and a half hours a week," also should be avoided. Understanding begins with a willingness to pursue diversity.

DIFFERENT WORLDS, SMALL WORLDS

The disciplinary creation of different academic worlds becomes more striking with each passing year. In the leading universities, the clinical professor of medicine is as much a part of the basic work force as the professor of English. The medical academic might be found in a cancer ward, interacting intensively with other doctors, nurses, orderlies, laboratory assistants, a few students perhaps, and many patients in a round of tightly scheduled activities that can begin at six in the morning and extend into the evenings and weekends. Such academics are often under considerable pressure to generate income from patient-care revenues; their faculty groups negotiate with third-party medical plans and need a sizeable administrative staff to handle patient billing. Salaries may well depend on group income, which fluctuates from year to year and is directly affected by changes in the health-care industry and the competitive position of a particular medical school-hospital complex. Even in a tenured post, salary may not be guaranteed. Sizeable research grants must be actively and repetitively pursued; those who do not raise funds from research grants will find themselves encumbered with more clinical duties.

The humanities professor in the leading universities operates in a totally different environment. To begin with, teaching "loads" are in the range of four to six hours a week, office hours are at one's discretion, and administrative assignments vary considerably with one's willingness to cooperate. The humanities academic typically interacts with large numbers of beginning students in introductory classes in lecture halls; with small numbers of juniors and seniors in specialized upper-division courses; and with a few graduate students in seminars and dissertation supervision around such highly specialized topics as Elizabethan lyric and Icelandic legend. Much valuable work time can be spent at home, away from the "distractions" of the university office. . . .

Disciplines exhibit discernible differences in individual behavior and group action, notably between "hard" and "soft" subjects and "pure" and "applied" fields: in a simple fourfold classification, between hard-pure (physics), hard-applied (engineering), soft-pure (history), and soft-applied (social work). Across the many fields of the physical sciences, the biological sciences, the social sciences, the humanities, and the arts, face-to-face research reveals varied work assignments, symbols of identity, modes of authority, career lines, and associational linkages. Great differences in the academic life often appear between letters and science departments and the many professional-school domains in which a concern for the ways and needs of an outside profession must necessarily be combined with the pursuit of science and truth for its own sake. The popular images of Mr. Chips chatting up undergraduates and Einsteinian, white-haired, remote scholars dreaming up esoteric mathematical equations are a far cry from the realities of academic work that helps prepare schoolteachers, librarians, social workers, engineers, computer experts, architects, nurses, pharmacists, business managers, lawyers, and doctors—and, in some academic locales, also morticians, military personnel, auto mechanics, airport technicians, secretaries, lathe operators, and cosmetologists. For over a century, American higher education has been generous to a fault in admitting former outside fields, and new occupations, into the academy—a point made by historians of higher education and of the professions.

Because research is the first priority of leading universities, the disciplinary differentiation of every modern system of higher education is self-amplifying. The American system is currently the extreme case of this phenomenon. . . . Throughout the twentieth century and especially in the last fifty years, the reward system of promoting academics on the grounds of research and published scholarship has become more deeply rooted in the universities (and would-be universities and leading four-year colleges) with almost every passing decade. The many proliferating specialties of the knowledge-producing disciplines are like tributaries flowing into a mammoth river of the research imperative.

The most serious operational obstacles to this research-driven amplification are the limitations of funding and the institutional need to teach undergraduates and beginning graduate students the codified introductory knowledge of the various fields. There also remains in American higher education the long-standing belief in the importance of liberal or general education—a task, we may note, that Europeans largely assign to secondary schools. The saving remnant of academics who uphold the banner of liberal and general education are able to sally forth in full cry periodically—the 1920s, the late 1940s, the 1990s—to group some specialties into more general courses, narrow the options in distribution requirements from, say, four hundred to one hundred courses, insist that teaching take priority over research, and in general raise a ruckus about the dangers of the specialized mind. Meanwhile, promotion committees on campus continue their steady scrutiny of individual records of research-based scholarship. Central administrators work to build an institutional culture of first-rateness, as it is defined competitively across the nation and the world according to the reputations of noted scholars and departments. Sophisticated general educators and liberal-arts proponents in the universities recognize the primacy of the substantive impulse and learn how to work incrementally within its limits.

INSTITUTIONAL DIFFERENTIATION

As powerful as self-amplifying disciplinary differences have become in dividing the American professoriate, institutional diversity now plays an even more important role. This axis of differentiation places approximately two-thirds of American academics in settings other than that of doctoral-granting universities. We find about a fourth of the total faculty in the colleges and universities that offer degree work as far as the master's; a small share, about 7 percent, in the liberal-arts colleges; and a major bloc of a third or so (over 250,000) in the nearly 1,500 community colleges. In student numbers in 1994, the universities had just 26 percent of the total enrollment; the master's level institutions, 21 percent; the baccalaureate colleges, 7 percent; the specialized institutions, 4 percent; and the community colleges, 43 percent—by far the largest share. The two-year colleges admit over 50 percent of entering students. There is no secret that academics in this latter section do an enormous amount of the work of the system at large.

These major locales exhibit vast differences in the very basis of academic life, namely, the balance of effort between undergraduate teaching and advanced research and research training. Teaching loads in the leading universities come in at around four to six hours a week, occasionally tapering down to two to three hours—a class a week, a seminar a week—while sometimes, especially in the humanities, rising above six. The flip side is that faculty commonly expect to spend at least half their time in research, alone or in the company of graduate students, other faculty, and research staff. We need not stray very far among the institutional types, however, before we encounter teaching loads that are 50, 100, and 200 percent higher. The "doctoral-granting universities" that are not well supported to do research often exact teaching loads of nine to twelve hours, as do the liberal-arts colleges, especially those outside the top fifty. In master's colleges, loads of twelve hours a week in the classroom are common. In the community colleges, the standard climbs to fifteen hours and loads of eighteen and twenty-one hours are not unknown. Notably, as we move from the research

universities through the middle types to the two-year, institutions, faculty involvement shifts from advanced students to beginning students; from highly selected students to an open-door clientele; from young students in the traditional college age-group to a mix of students of all ages in short-term vocational programs as well as in course work leading toward a bachelor's degree. In the community colleges, students in the college-transfer track are numerically overshadowed by students in terminal vocational programs, and both are frequently outnumbered by nonmatriculated adults who turn the "college" into a "community center."

The burdens of remedial education are also much heavier as we move from the most to the least prestigious institutions. The open-door approach, standard in two-year colleges and also operational in tuition-dependent four-year colleges that take virtually all comers, means that college teachers are confronted with many underprepared students. Those who work in the less selective settings also more frequently work part-time. During the last, two decades, the ranks of the part-timers have swollen to over 40 percent of the total academic work force, with heavy concentrations in the less prestigious colleges and especially in the community colleges, where over half the faculty operate on a part-time schedule. At the extreme opposite end of the institutional prestige hierarchy from those who serve primarily in graduate schools and graduate-level professional schools in the major universities we find the full-time and, especially, part-time teachers of English and mathematics in downtown community colleges, who teach introductory and subintroductory courses over and over again—the rudiments of English composition, the basic courses in mathematics—to high-school graduates who need remediation and to adults struggling with basic literacy.

With the nature of work varying enormously across the many types of institutions that make up American postsecondary education, other aspects of the academic life run on a parallel course. If we examine the cultures of institutions by discussing with faculty members their basic academic beliefs, we find different worlds. Among the leading research universities, the discipline is front and center, the institution is prized for its reputation of scholarship and research, and peers are the primary reference group. . . . Academics in this favored site have much with which to identify. They are proud of the quality they believe surrounds them, experiencing it directly in their own and neighboring departments and inferring it indirectly from institutional reputation. The strong symbolic thrust of the institution incorporates the combined strengths of the departments that in turn represent the disciplines. Thus, for faculty, disciplinary and institutional cultures converge, creating a happy state indeed.

The leading private liberal-arts colleges provide a second favored site. Here, professors often waxed lyrical in interviews about the small-college environment tailored to undergraduate teaching. . . . These institutions retain the capacity to appear as academic communities, not bureaucracies, in their overall integration and symbolic unity.

But soon we encounter sites where faculty members are troubled by inchoate institutional character and worried about the quality of their environment. In the lesser universities, and especially in the comprehensive colleges that have evolved out of a teachers-college background, at the second, third, and fourth levels of the institutional prestige hierarchy, . . . the overall institutional culture is weaker and less satisfying for many faculty members at the same time that disciplinary identifications are weakened as heavy teaching loads suppress research and its rewards.

In these middle-level institutions, professors often spoke of their relationship with students as the thing they value most. Students begin to replace peers as the audience of first resort. That shift is completed in the community colleges, with the identifications of faculty reaching a high point of student-centeredness. In a setting that is distinctly opposed to disciplinary definitions of quality and excellence, pleasures and rewards have to lie in the task of working with poorly prepared students who pour in through the open door. . . . In the community colleges, the equity values of open door and open access have some payoff as anchoring points in the faculty culture. But in the overall institutional hierarchy, where the dominant values emphasize quality, selection, and advanced work, the community-college ideology can play only a subsidiary role. The limitations cannot be missed: "It would be nice to be able to teach upper-division classes."

As go work and culture, so go authority, careers, and associational life. To sum up the story on authority: in the leading universities faculty influence is relatively strong. Many individuals have personal bargaining power; departments and professional schools are semiautonomous units; and all-campus faculty bodies such as senates have primacy in personnel and curricular decisions. University presidents speak lovingly of the faculty as the core of the institution and walk gently around entrenched faculty prerogatives. But as we move to other types of institutions, faculty authority weakens and managerialism increases. Top-down command is noticeably stronger in public master's colleges, especially when they have evolved out of a teachers-college background. The two-year colleges, operating under local trustees much like K–12 schools, are quite managerial. Faculty in these places often feel powerless, even severely put upon. Their answer (where possible under state law) has been to band together by means of unionization. The further down the general hierarchy of institutional prestige, the more widespread the unions become, especially among public-sector institutions.

To sum up the associational life of faculty: in the leading universities, faculty interact with one another across institutional boundaries in an extensive network of disciplinary linkages—formal and informal; large and small; visible and invisible; local, regional, national, and international. When university specialists find national "monster meetings" not to their liking, they go anyway to participate in a smaller division or section that best represents their specific interests, or they find kindred souls in small, autonomous meetings of several dozen people. In the other sectors, however, involvement in the mainline disciplinary associations declines; there is less to learn that is relevant to one's everyday life, and travel money is scarce in the institutional budget. Academics then go to national meetings when they are held in their part of the country. They look for special sessions on teaching; they break away to form associations (and journals) appropriate to their sector. Community-college teachers have developed associations in such broad areas as the social sciences and the humanities, e.g., the Community College Humanities Association, and in such special fields as mathematics and biology, e.g., the American Mathematics Association for Two-Year Colleges.

Different worlds, small worlds. Institutional differentiation interacts with disciplinary differentiation in a bewildering fashion that steadily widens and deepens the matrix of differences that separate American academics from each other. . . .

The complaint that professors do too much research and too little teaching has been prevalent for almost a hundred years. . . . The protest of too much research has been a perennial battle cry of the American reformer seeking more emphasis on undergraduate programs and on their general or liberal education components in particular. The 1980s and early 1990s have seen a strong resurgence of this point of view inside and outside the academy. Careful critics beamed their messages at research universities, would-be universities, and even four-year private and public colleges that have opened their faculty reward systems to the research imperative. They understand that professors teach when they supervise students in the preparation of master's and doctoral theses. They are sometimes aware that in the best private liberal-arts colleges professors involve their undergraduate students in research as an effective way to teach and to learn. But the critical comment overall has turned into a generalized charge that "professors" should do less research and more teaching, meaning undergraduate teaching. In the popular press, and even in the academic press, careful targeting is forgone. In the extreme, a minimization of teaching by professors is portrayed as part of a "scam."

But across the dispersed American professoriate, the reality is the reverse: more academics teach too much than teach too little. Fifteen hours of classroom teaching each week is far too much for the maintenance of a scholarly life; even twelve hours is excessive. But as noted earlier, most institutional sectors present such loads, specifying assignments that are two to three times greater than that of professors in research-based institutions. Twelve and fifteen hours a week in the classroom at the college level tend to push professors out of their disciplines. A sense of being a scholar is reduced as the "physicist" becomes entirely a "teacher of physics," the "political scientist" a "teacher of political science"— and then mainly as teachers of introductory courses only. Interest flags in what is going on in the revision of advanced topics; command of the literature weakens. Excessive teaching loads apparently are now becoming a source of academic burnout, importing into higher education the teacher burnout long noted as a problem in the K–12 system. . . .

Command structures are not unheard of in American colleges and universities. Professors in research universities and leading private four-year colleges certainly encounter trustee and administrator influence. Their professional position is also increasingly challenged by the professionalization of administrative occupations clustered around central management. . . . But academics in these favored sites generally have strong countervailing power of a professional kind that is rooted in their personal and collective expertise. Department by department, professional school by professional school, they exercise much internal control. They expect to dominate in choosing who to add to the faculty and what courses should be taught. They expect to be consulted in many matters rather than to receive orders from those in nominally superior positions. But in public and private comprehensive colleges, and especially in community colleges, the foundations of authority change. Subject expertise becomes more diffuse, occasionally amounting only to sufficient knowledge in the discipline to teach the introductory course to poorly prepared students, while at the same time the role of trustees and administrators is strengthened, sometimes approaching the top-down supervision found in local school districts. Such managerialism is particularly evident in public-sector institutions, especially when they are exposed to state assertions of accountability.

Adding greatly to the vulnerability of academic professionals to political and administrative dictate is the marginal position of part-time faculty. In all institutional sectors, part-timers have long been with us: witness the traditional use and abuse of faculty spouses in part-time work in foreign language departments of research universities. But the use of part-timers grew greatly during the last two decades as a form of mobile and inexpensive labor. It unfortunately turns out that floating student "clienteles" require dispensable academic staff, hence the deteriorating situation for staff in community colleges where a majority of faculty now serve part-time. The part-timers themselves have only marginal influence, and their large numbers weaken the influence of full-time faculty vis-à-vis trustees and administrative staff. A relatively powerless proletariat exists in American academic life, centered in employment that is part-time and poorly paid. . . .

All-encompassing academic values are increasingly hard to find in American academic life. The claims frequently made by reformers that academics must somehow find their way back to agreement on core values and assume an overarching common framework become less realistic with each passing year. Different contexts, especially institutional ones, promote different values. Even common terms assume different meanings. "Academic freedom" in one context means mainly the right to do as one pleases in pursuing new ideas; in another, not to have an administrator dictate the teaching syllabus one uses; in another, the right to teach evolution in a college where the local board of trustees is dominated by creationists; in yet another, the right to join an extremist political group. Promotion criteria vary from an all-out emphasis on research productivity to weight put solely on undergraduate instruction, from complicated mixtures of teaching and research and several forms of "service" to heavy weighting of years on the job and seniority rights. . . . Professional schools must value their connection to outside professions as well as to other parts of their universities, thereby balancing themselves between two sets of values in a way not required in the letters and science departments. The grounds for advancement then become particularly contentious. All such differences in outlook among academics widen as differentiation of academic work continues.

Under all the strengths and weaknesses of American academic life, we find the persistent problem of the professional calling. When academic work becomes just a job and a routine career, then such material rewards as salary are placed front and center. Academics stay at their work or leave for other pursuits according to how much they are paid. They come to work "on time" because they must (it is nailed down in the union contract); they leave on time because satisfaction is found after work is concluded. But when academic work is still a calling, it . . . transmutes narrow self-interest into other-regarding and ideal-regarding interests: one is linked to peers and to a version of a larger common good. The calling has moral content; it contributes to civic virtue. . . .

19. James F. Carlin, "Restoring Sanity to an Academic World Gone Mad," 1999

This confident indictment of American higher education by James F. Carlin includes a statement of his high achievements in business and his substantial service to the state of Massachusetts. His unique position gave him an exceptional vantage point to observe a state system. The essay follows a decade or more of conservative criticism of higher education, its administrators, the faculties and the tenure that gives them security of employment.

James F. Carlin, "Restoring Sanity to an Academic World Gone Mad," *Chronicle of Higher Education,* November 5, 1999: Reprinted with the kind permission of James Carlin, Vice Chair / Trustee, University of Massachusetts 1983–1990, Chair, Massachusetts Board of Higher Education 1995–1999. Further reading: Francis Oakley, I, 15, contains a lengthy bibliographical footnote listing books that variously play on the themes in this brief castigation; and Roger L. Geiger, "Research Universities in a New Era: From the 1980s to the 1990s," in *Higher Learning in America, 1980–2000,* ed. Arthur Levine (Baltimore, 1983), ch. 4, esp. 78–82.

If someone had predicted 50 years ago that, in 1999, the primary and secondary schools in the United States would be a mess, and urban public schools an absolute disaster, most Americans would have called that person an alarmist. Today, when anyone dares to suggest that U.S. higher education has serious problems, most listeners give the same response. We have the greatest colleges and universities in the world. But if current trends continue, we will soon face a day of reckoning.

Tuition is so high that the poor are frozen out of higher education, in spite of expanded scholarship programs. Middle-class parents are having a difficult time meeting college expenses. They deplete their savings, remortgage their homes, invade their 401(k) plans, and work two and three jobs to pay their children's college bills. Estimates indicate that about half of graduates leave college with student loans that take years to pay off.

In their zeal to bring in dollars, colleges and universities admit students who can't handle the course work but who may be able to pay the bills. When that happens, everyone suffers—especially the students. But rather than rejecting or expelling those who are ill prepared or lazy, we attempt to remediate them. We make many of our courses too easy, while grade inflation gets students through those that are more difficult. Rigorous core curricula have almost disappeared. Graduation requirements are so relaxed that many employers who seek to fill even entry-level positions just shake their heads in disbelief.

Political correctness and diversity have taken priority in admissions decisions and in classrooms over experience in calculus, foreign languages, physics, chemistry, and Shakespeare. We emphasize the differences in people rather than what they have in common. We keep adding programs and courses to our already bloated curricula in an attempt to be all things to all people.

Meanwhile, faculty members do ever more meaningless research, while spending fewer and fewer hours in the classroom, during an academic year that we have shortened in recent decades.

I have been a businessman for over 35 years, and I was a trustee of the University of Massachusetts and chairman of the Massachusetts Board of Higher Education for a total of 12 years. I am, or have been, a director of eight public corporations, and was chief executive officer of a transit system with an annual budget of $1-billion. I have also founded four businesses, in separate fields, that were recognized by *Inc.* magazine for their rapid growth and success. I think I've learned something about management and controlling costs. Never have I observed anything as unfocused or mismanaged as higher education.

Clearly, the reason tuition is high is that college costs are high. Why are costs high? Nobody is in charge. The trustees occasionally have illusions that they have something to say about the way things work—but, in fact, all that the president, deans, and faculty members generally want trustees to do is to raise money and boost the institution's image.

With very few exceptions, the presidents know that they're not in charge; when John Silber ran Boston University, he was one of the few presidents who had real control over a college or university. The president's primary job, according to John Kenneth Galbraith, is to raise money for the institution. I think Galbraith's job description is a little narrow. It's also the president's job to handle the news media and the politicians, and to try to keep the heat on, the grass cut, and enough parking spaces available. It's the president's job to keep the trustees from asking questions about such matters as teaching loads, tenure, and remedial instruction.

The president is supposed to stay away from academic matters, which are the faculty's turf. That is like telling Louis V. Gerstner, Jr., that—as chairman and chief executive officer of I.B.M.—he's in charge of everything except the design, manufacture, and distribution of his company's computers.

Because presidents rarely are able to take charge, colleges and universities become top-heavy. Academic and administrative staffs have layer after layer of personnel. And, of course, bigger staffs mean higher costs, higher tuitions, and more pressure to raise money for the institution.

Another cause of high costs at colleges and universities is tenure—perhaps once a good idea, but one whose time has passed. In my years as a trustee and chairman of a governing board in higher education, I never spoke to a single individual outside the academy who thought that the tenure system made sense. Tenured and untenured faculty members know it, presidents and administrators know it, trustees know it. Legislators and students and their parents who pay tuition are tired of providing financial support for tenure.

Lifetime job guarantees border on being immoral. What other professions employing hundreds of thousands nationwide offer the equivalent of tenure? Basically, professors want to be accountable to no one.

Faculty members and their unions say, "There are mechanisms in place to terminate a chronically incompetent or non-performing tenured professor." But out of several hundred thousand tenured professors in the United States, you can count on 10 fingers those who have been let go each year because of poor performance or work habits. Tenure rewards the lazy and incompetent. Its costs are enormous.

The argument that we need tenure to protect freedom of speech is bogus. Numerous state and federal statutes, commissions against discrimination, and the vigilant news media protect anyone—in or out of academe—who wants to expound unorthodox beliefs.

Post-tenure review programs are in vogue. But they are usually designed by the faculty, and they are a joke. This year the University of Massachusetts, over my strong objections, put into place a post-tenure-review program that specifically prohibits administrators from using the results of a review for disciplinary purposes. Sponsors of the program are calling it a national model. Please!

The current typical load of six or so hours a week of classroom teaching, for 29 to 32 weeks a year, doesn't cut it. At our major colleges and universities, nine to 12 hours per week should be the norm. If faculty members wanted to earn more money, they could teach more hours. It would be desirable for campuses to hold classes from 7 a.m. to 10 p.m., five days a week—and preferably until noon on Saturdays—for 48 weeks a year. In addition to increasing productivity and lowering costs, more class hours would give students more scheduling options.

We should have two categories of professors: The first would be teachers, who would do only whatever research it took them to be outstanding teachers; they would spend nine to 12 hours per week in the classroom. The second would focus on research; its members might spend three or four hours a week with graduate students or doctoral candidates, and perhaps teach one course a year.

And the courses that professors teach should be much more demanding. At too many colleges and universities today, if students keep paying and attending, they will usually receive a degree. As for-profit institutions, such as the University of Phoenix, offer college credentials in less time, and often

at lower cost, more pressure will be brought to bear on traditional institutions. Throw into the mix the Internet and how it's changing the way society does nearly everything, and you can almost see the academy turning upside down.

We must start making changes now, if we want to keep our educational institutions the best in the world. Trustees and administrators must provide bold, innovative solutions—in spite of faculty members' objections, and even if, in the short term, those changes run contrary to the faculty's economic interests.

The answer to high tuition is not more loan programs. The cost of higher education must come down, and academic standards must go up. If members of the academy don't force change, politicians and taxpayers will—as they are doing with health care and primary and secondary education.

During the past four years, the Massachusetts Board of Higher Education has sought to improve the state's public institutions by setting aside the status quo. . . .

To sum up: During the past four years, system-wide tuition has dropped 17 per cent, state appropriations have increased 36 per cent, and state financial aid to students at public institutions has increased 65 per cent. Applications to the state's public colleges and university are up, acceptance rates are down, and the proportions of accepted students who matriculate are up.

One of the wonderful things about a free society is that what is right usually prevails in time. But that does not happen automatically. We've got a lot of problems in higher education: exorbitant tuition, tenure, foolish research, bloated bureaucracies, low admissions and graduation standards, too much remediation, too many programs, light teaching loads, lack of accountability, narrow-minded faculty unions, and shared governance that leaves nobody in charge. Change will come, as parents, students, taxpayers, and elected officials learn more about what really goes on behind the ivy-covered walls. For right to prevail, good men and women need to act—starting now.

Part VII

Conflicts on and Beyond Campus

CONTEXT

While the incorporation of the university into post–World War II society, even to the center of the knowledge society of the postwar years, brought both resources and influence far beyond anything before the war, it also brought trouble. The university became more like the larger society, and it was more likely to be taxed with responsibility for the failings of the larger society. Its new vulnerabilities concerned the university itself and its relation to society. Like other prominent institutions, it seemed to be driven by organizational imperatives rather than its oft-spoken ideals. Too large, it was likened to a machine filled with interchangeable cogs, and Clark Kerr's brilliant account of the multiversity—the irony of his description was less often missed or was less apparent than it should have been—seemed not only to document that sense of the university but actually to celebrate it as well (I, 11). The university's other liability was a self-indulgent complacency or even, in the eyes of some, hypocrisy. An institution that claimed the moral high ground and made itself the custodian of trained intelligence often seemed disinclined to address the issues of poverty and racism. Much of its research was devoted to the making of weapons of mass destruction and the support of military interventions abroad (6, 13).

The manifesto of Students for a Democratic Society, "The Port Huron Statement," damned the "crust of apathy" and the quiet pursuit of "business as usual" in academe and American society. Tired of "perpetual rehearsals" of preparation, these students were inspired by black students sitting at segregated lunch counters and the civil rights movement in general. They wanted to address poverty and racism, which they saw as the democratic deficit of American political culture. Universities should use their claim upon knowledge, power, and influence for reform, not for a status quo (1, 5).

On the eve of campus conflicts one could see already in 1962 an emerging cultural divide. The conflict over culture had two dimensions, paralleling the double meaning of culture much discussed at the time. The culture (in an anthropological sense) of the everyday life of the educated, which still carried the patina of gentlemen in tweed jackets, was challenged by the rejection of such conventions by the "Beats" and other rebels. And the sacralization of learning and art that was characteristic of the university and the literary and artistic worlds of the 1950s was challenged by both the content, literary form, and personal style of a poet like Allen Ginsberg. If today, Ginsburg, like Whitman, is part of the poetic canon, in 1962 Diana Trilling worried that his vulgarity had no place on a literary platform that had previously welcomed T. S. Eliot (2). Some-

times style is substance, and the first round of campus controversy offers such an instance: for many, the Free Speech Movement at Berkeley was reduced to the issue of "filthy speech" (3).

But in fact the early campus controversies in the troubled 1960s were about academic values. Critics asked for more, not less, intellectual seriousness (4). It was a quest for an intellectual and moral community that was different from the larger society yet still engaged with the troubles of that society. That university, Mario Savio hoped, would be something better and more serious than an exchange of objective tests and letter grades (6). Education without values was challenged, and the responsibility of intellect was emphasized, most notably by Kenneth Clark (14). Others, less persuaded of the validity of this issue, feared that much of the language of reform endangered central meanings of the university (17).

Events at Columbia best revealed the next phase of campus controversy. The existence of the Institute of Defense Analysis on campus linked the university to an increasingly unpopular and disastrous war, while a plan for campus expansion raised the issue of academe's relation to "poorer neighbors and society's treatment of racial ghettoes" (11, 12).

The question of university governance was constantly raised. Students and some faculty certainly understood Paul Goodman's utopian question: How did the "administration" get into the "community of scholars" (4)? The university, many felt, was run by and for the economic elite and their interests, not for students or the broader population, and especially not for those most vulnerable in it. The most extreme statement of that notion was offered by H. Bruce Franklin, whose agitation at Stanford resulted in his being stripped of tenure on the advice of a faculty committee (7, 8, 9). One of two dissenters on that committee, Donald Kennedy, later became president of Stanford. From that position he looked back on the case as important because it sustained the principle of due process (10). A failure to follow due process or even good sense as the campus crises of the 1960s deepened and worsened, including bombing incidents by a small number of protesters, brought on frequent conflicts between police and students, often amid charges of police brutality. With the introduction of the National Guard on campuses, most notably Jackson State College in Mississippi and Kent State in Ohio, campuses were militarized, with consequent tragic student deaths (11, 12).

The controversy, conflict, and apparent chaos on campus soured the public on higher education. The campus turmoil also invigorated a historical American unease with intellectuals and the life of the mind, and universities suffered a consequential loss of public trust that to this day has not been recovered, something especially evident in cutbacks in support for public higher education. Yet in the immediate wake of the most intense moments of crisis, faculty leaders at Columbia and Berkeley offered some exceptionally compelling articulations of the university's calling. These aspirational statements by Richard Hofstadter and William Bouwsma acknowledged the failures of academe and of the larger polity, but they also insisted on the necessity of a distinctive community of teachers and scholars committed to the values of intellectual seriousness, and a plurality of voices, a vision not far off from that sought by Mario Savio and Paul Goodman in 1962.

What Should the University Do?

1. Students for a Democratic Society, *The Port Huron Statement*, 1964

In June 1964, Students for a Democratic Society issued a manifesto from their annual convention at Port Huron, Michigan. This statement became an ideological compass for the student protest movement of the 1960s. It criticized the direction of American life and urged "participatory democracy" for all. The original document, from which a portion dealing with universities is here excerpted, was written by Tom Hayden, cofounder of the SDS with Robert Alan Haber. Hayden (1940–) graduated from the University of Michigan, where he was editor of the University of Michigan *Daily* and was active in student politics. He later advised Columbia students in their rebellion of 1968, was one of the "Chicago Eight" tried for conspiracy to commit a riot during the Democratic Party convention of 1968, acted against the Vietnam War, and became a California state assemblyman.

Students for a Democratic Society, The Student Department of the League for Industrial Democracy, *The Port Huron Statement* (New York, 1964). This statement first appeared in twenty thousand mimeographed copies; its first printing, or second edition, appeared in 1964. Further reading: Tom Hayden, *Rebellion and Repression* (New York, 1969); Tim Findley, "Tom Hayden: *Rolling Stone* Interview," *Rolling Stone*, October 26, 1972, 36–50; Kirkpatrick Sale, *SDS* (New York, 1973); Irwin Unger, *The Movement: A History of the American New Left, 1959–1972* (New York, 1974), ch. 3; Michael Rossman, *The Wedding within the War* (Garden City, NY, 1971) and *On Learning and Social Change* (New York, 1972); Immanuel Wallerstein and Paul Starr, eds., *The University Crisis Reader*, 2 vols. (New York, 1971); and VII, 4–6.

In the last few years, thousands of American students demonstrated that they at least felt the urgency of the times. They moved actively and directly against racial injustices, the threat of war, violations of individual rights of conscience and, less frequently, against economic manipulation. They succeeded in restoring a small measure of controversy to the campuses after the stillness of the McCarthy period. They succeeded, too, in gaining some concessions from the people and institutions they opposed, especially in the fight against racial bigotry.

The significance of these scattered movements lies not in their success or failure in gaining objectives—at least not yet. Nor does the significance lie in the intellectual "competence" or "maturity" of the students involved—as some pedantic elders allege. The significance is in the fact the students are breaking the crust of apathy and overcoming the inner alienation that remain the defining characteristics of American college life.

If student movements for change are still rarities on the campus scene, what is commonplace there? The real campus, the familiar campus, is a place of private people, engaged in their notorious "inner emigration." It is a place of commitment to business-as-usual, getting ahead, playing it cool. It is a place of mass affirmation of the Twist, but mass reluctance toward the controversial public stance. Rules are accepted as "inevitable," bureaucracy as "just circumstances," irrelevance as "scholarship," selflessness as "martyrdom," politics as "just another way to make people, and an unprofitable one, too."

Almost no students value activity as citizens. Passive in public, they are hardly more idealistic in arranging their private lives: Gallup concludes they will settle for "low success, and won't risk high failure." There is not much willingness to take risks (not even in business), no settling of dangerous goals, no real conception of personal identity except one manufactured in the image of others, no real urge for personal fulfillment except to be almost as successful as the very successful people. Attention is being paid to social status (the quality of shirt collars, meeting people, getting wives or husbands, making solid contacts for later on); much, too, is paid to academic status (grades, honors, the med school rat race). But neglected generally is real intellectual status, the personal cultivation of the mind.

"Students don't even give a damn about the apathy," one has said. Apathy toward apathy begets a privately-constructed universe, a place of systematic study schedules, two nights each week for beer, a girl or two, and early marriage; a framework infused with personality, warmth, and under control, no matter how unsatisfying otherwise.

Under these conditions university life loses all relevance to some. Four hundred thousand of our classmates leave college every year.

But apathy is not simply an attitude; it is a product of social institutions, and of the structure and organization of higher education itself. The extracurricular life is ordered according to *in loco parentis* theory, which ratifies the Administration as the moral guardian of the young.

The accompanying "let's pretend" theory of student extracurricular affairs validates student government as a training center for those who want to spend their lives in political pretense, and discourages initiative from the more articulate, honest, and sensitive students. The bounds and style of controversy are delimited before controversy begins. The university "prepares" the student for "citizenship" through perpetual rehearsals and, usually, through emasculation of what creative spirit there is in the individual.

The academic life contains reinforcing counterparts to the way in which extracurricular life is organized. The academic world is founded on a teacher-student relation analogous to the parent-child relation which characterizes *in loco parentis*. Further, academia includes a radical separation of the student from the material of study. That which is studied, the social reality, is "objectified" to sterility, dividing the student from life—just as he is restrained in active involvement by the deans controlling student government. The specialization of function and knowledge, admittedly necessary to our complex technological and social structure, has produced an exaggerated compartmentalization of study and understanding. This has contributed to an overly parochial view, by faculty, of the role of its research and scholarship, to a discontinuous and truncated understanding, by students, of the surrounding social order; and to a loss of personal attachment, by nearly all, to the worth of study as a humanistic enterprise.

There is, finally, the cumbersome academic bureaucracy extending throughout the academic as well as the extracurricular structures, contributing to the sense of outer complexity and inner powerlessness that transforms the honest searching of many students to a ratification of convention and, worse, to a numbness to present and future catastrophes. The size and financing systems of the university enhance the permanent trusteeship of the administrative bureaucracy, their power leading to a shift within the university toward the value standards of business and the administrative mentality. Huge foundations and other private financial interests shape the under-financed colleges and universities, not only making them more commercial, but less disposed to diagnose society critically, less open to dissent. Many social and physical scientists, neglecting the liberating heritage of higher learning, develop "human relations" or "morale-producing" techniques for the corporate economy, while others exercise their intellectual skills to accelerate the arms race.

Tragically, the university could serve as a significant source of social criticism and an initiator of new modes and molders of attitudes. But the actual intellectual effect of the college experience is hardly distinguishable from that of any other communications channel—say, a television set—passing on the stock truths of the day. Students leave college somewhat more "tolerant" than when they arrived, but basically unchallenged in their values and political orientations. With administrators ordering the institution, and faculty the curriculum, the student learns by his isolation to accept elite rule within the university, which prepares him to accept later forms of minority control. The real function of the educational system—as opposed to its more rhetorical function of "searching for truth"—is to impart the key information and styles that will help the student get by, modestly but comfortably, in the big society beyond....

The creation of bridges is made more difficult by the problems left over from the generation of "silence." Middle-class students, still the main actors in the embryonic upsurge, have yet to overcome their ignorance, and even vague hostility, for what they see as "middle class labor" bureaucrats. Students must open the campus to labor through publications, action programs, curricula, while labor opens its house to students through internships, requests

for aid (on the picket-line, with handbills, in the public dialogue), and politics. And the organization of the campus can be a beginning—teachers' unions can be advocated as both socially progressive, and educationally beneficial; university employees can be organized—and thereby an important element in the education of the student radical....

From 1960 to 1962, the campuses experienced a revival of idealism among an active few. Triggered by the impact of the sit-ins, students began to struggle for integration, civil liberties, student rights, peace, and against the fast-rising right-wing "revolt" as well. The liberal students, too, have felt their urgency thwarted by conventional channels: from student governments to Congressional committees. Out of this alienation from existing channels has come the creation of new ones; the most characteristic forms of liberal-radical student organizations are the dozens of campus political parties, political journals, and peace marches and demonstrations. In only a few cases have students built bridges to power: an occasional election campaign, the sit-ins, Freedom Rides, and voter registration activities; in some relatively large Northern demonstrations for peace and civil rights, and infrequently, through the United States National Student Association whose notable work has not been focused on political change....

But the civil rights, peace, and student movements are too poor and socially slighted, and the labor movement too quiescent, to be counted with enthusiasm. From where else can power and vision be summoned? We believe that the universities are an overlooked seat of influence.

First, the university is located in a permanent position of social influence. Its educational function makes it indispensable and automatically makes it a crucial institution in the formation of social attitudes. Second, in an unbelievably complicated world, it is the central institution for organizing, evaluating, and transmitting knowledge. Third, the extent to which academic resources presently are used to buttress immoral social practice is revealed first, by the extent to which defense contracts make the universities engineers of the arms race. Too, the use of modern social science as a manipulative tool reveals itself in the "human relations" consultants to the modern corporations, who introduce trivial sops to give laborers feelings of "participation" or "belonging," while actually deluding them in order to further exploit their labor. And, of course, the use of motivational research is already infamous as a manipulative aspect of American politics. But these social uses of the universities' resources also demonstrate the unchangeable reliance by men of power on the men and storehouses of knowledge: this makes the university functionally tied to society in new ways, revealing new potentialities, new levers for change. Fourth, the university is the only mainstream institution that is open to participation by individuals of nearly any viewpoint.

These, at least, are facts, no matter how dull the teaching, how paternalistic the rules, how irrelevant the research that goes on. Social relevance, the accessibility to knowledge, and internal openness—these together make the university a potential base and agency in a movement of social change. . . .

But we need not indulge in illusions: the university system cannot complete a movement of ordinary people making demands for a better life. From its schools and colleges across the nation, a militant left might awaken its allies, and by beginning the process towards peace, civil rights, and labor struggles, reinsert theory and idealism where too often reign confusion and political barter. The power of students and faculty united is not only potential; it has shown its actuality in the South, and in the reform movements of the North. . . .

To turn these possibilities into realities will involve national efforts at university reform by an alliance of students and faculty. They must wrest control of the educational process from the administrative bureaucracy. They must make fraternal and functional contact with allies in labor, civil rights, and other liberal forces outside the campus. They must import major public issues into the curriculum—research and teaching on problems of war and peace is an outstanding example. They must make debate and controversy, not dull pedantic cant, the common style for educational life. They must consciously build a base for their assault upon the loci of power.

As students for a democratic society, we are committed to stimulating this kind of social movement, this kind of vision and program in campus and community across the country. If we appear to seek the unattainable, as it has been said, then let it be known that we do so to avoid the unimaginable.

2. Diana Trilling, "The Other Night at Columbia," 1962

A poetry reading at Columbia promised to be a confrontation between the "Beats" and the academic establishment, a tussle between ancients and moderns. With police guarding the entrance to McMillan Theater where T. S. Eliot had recently spoken and an audience ready to be disruptive, Trilling (1905–96) witnessed the homecoming of Allen Ginsberg (1926–97), who had once been her husband's student, well known for being obstreperous, eccentric, fiery, and brilliant. She watched the chairman of the English Department preside with a tact and dignity that treated Ginsberg and his friends as the guests they were. Intergenerational ill feelings of the kind that shut down Columbia later in the decade were avoided. Trilling's account reveals as much about herself, her own reading of Ginsberg, and her liberal intellectual friends of the 1950s as it does about this happening.

Diana Trilling's critical essays, reviews, and sharp insights made her one of the famed New York intellectual circle of the 1950s and 1960s. She helped her more famous husband as his stylistic editor but cut her own independent path as a social critic.

Diana Trilling, "The Other Night at Columbia: A Report from the Academy," in her *Claremont Essays* (New York, 1964), 153–73. Copyright © 1974 by Lionel Trilling Estate. Reprinted with the permission of The Wylie Agency, Inc. Further reading: Trilling, *The Beginning of the Journey: The Marriage of Diana and Lionel Trilling* (New York, 1993); Robert Gale, "Diana Trilling," at the *American National Biography* website, www.anb.org; and I, 9.

The "Beats" were to read their poetry at Columbia on Thursday evening and on the spur of the moment three wives from the English department had decided to go to hear them. But for me, one of the three, the spur of the moment was not where the story had begun. It had begun much farther back, some twelve or fourteen years ago, when Allen Ginsberg had been a student of my husband's and I had heard about him much more than I usually hear of students for the simple reason that he got into a great deal of trouble which involved his instructors, and had to be rescued and revived and restored; eventually he had even to be kept out of jail. Of course there was always the question, should this young man be rescued, should he be restored? There was even the question, shouldn't he go to jail? . . .

I now realize that even at this early point in his career I had already accumulated a fund of information about young Ginsberg which accurately forecast his later talent for self-promotion although it was surely disproportionate to the place he commanded in his teacher's mind and quite failed to jibe with the physical impression I had caught in opening the door to him when he came to the apartment. He was middling tall, slight, dark, sallow; his dress suggested shabby gentility, poor brown tweed gone threadbare and yellow. The description would have fitted any number of undergraduates of his or any Columbia generation; it was only the personal story that set him acutely apart. He came from New Jersey, where his father was a schoolteacher, or perhaps a principal, who wrote poetry too—I think for the *Saturday Review*, which would be as good a way as any of defining the separation between father and son. His mother was in a mental institution, and she had been there, off and on, for a long time. This was the central and utterly persuasive fact of the young man's life; I knew this before I was told it in poetry at Columbia the other night, and doubtless it was this knowledge that at least in some part accounted for the edginess to which I responded to so much as the mention of Ginsberg's name. Here was a boy on whom an outrageous unfairness had been perpetrated: his mother had fled from him into madness and now whoever crossed his path became somehow responsible, caught in the impossibility of rectifying what she had done. It was an unjust burden for Ginsberg to put, as he so subtly did, on those who were only later the accidents of his history and it made me defensive instead of charitable with him. . . .

But I remind myself: Ginsberg at Columbia on Thursday night was not Ginsberg at Chicago—according to *Time*, at any rate—or Ginsberg at Hunter either, where Kerouac ran the show, and a dismal show it must have been, with Kerouac drinking on the platform and clapping James Wechsler's hat on his head in a grand parade of contempt—they were two of four panelists gathered to discuss "Is there such a thing as a beat generation?"—and leading Ginsberg out from the wings like a circus donkey. . . . I suppose I have no right to say now, and on such early and little evidence, that Ginsberg had always desperately wanted to be respectable, or respected, like his instructors at Columbia, it is so likely that this is a hindsight which suits my needs. It struck me, though, that this was the most unmistakable and touching message from platform to audience the other night, and as I received it, I felt I had known something like it all along. . . .

Allen Ginsberg, with his poems in which there was never quite enough talent or hard work, and with his ambiguous need to tell his teacher exactly what new flagrancy had opened to his imagination as he talked about Gide with his friends at the West End Café, had at any rate the distinction of being more crudely justified in his emotional disturbance than most. He also had the distinction of carrying mental unbalance in the direction of criminality, a territory one preferred to leave unclaimed by student or friend. . . .

Well, the "beats" weren't lucky enough to be born except when they were born. Ginsberg says he lives in Harlem, but it's not the Harlem of the Scottsboro boys and W. C. Handy and the benign insanity of trying to proletarianize Striver's Row; their comrades are not the comrades of the Stewart Cafeteria nor yet of the road, as Kerouac would disingenuously have it, but pick-ups on dark morning streets. But they have their connection with us who were young in the thirties, their intimate political connection, which we deny at risk of missing what it is that makes the "beat" phenomenon something to think about. As they used to say on Fourteenth Street, it is no accident, comrades, it is decidedly no accident that today in the fifties our single overt manifestation of protest takes the wholly nonpolitical form of a group of panic-stricken kids in blue jeans, many of them publicly homosexual, talking about or taking drugs, assuring us that they are out of their minds, not responsible, while the liberal intellectual is convinced that he has no power to control the political future, the future of the free world, and that therefore he must submit to what he defines as political necessity. Though of course the various aspects of a culture must be granted their own autonomous source and character, the connection between "beat" and respectable liberal intellectual exists and is not hard to locate: the common need to deny free will, divest oneself of responsibility and yet stay alive. The typical liberal intellectual of the fifties, whether he is a writer or a sociolo-

gist or a law-school professor, explains his evolution over the last two decades—specifically, his current attitudes in foreign affairs—by telling us that he has been forced to accept the unhappy reality of Soviet strength in an atomic world, and that there is no alternative to capitulation—not that he calls it that—except the extinction of nuclear war. Even the diplomacy he invokes is not so much flexible, which he would like to think it is, as disarmed, an instrument of his impulse to surrender rather than of any wish to win or even hold the line. Similarly docile to culture, the "beat" also contrives a fate by predicating a fate. Like the respectable established intellectual—or the organization man, or the suburban matron—against whom he makes his play of protest, he conceives of himself as incapable of exerting any substantive influence against the forces that condition him. He is made by society, he cannot make society. He can only stay alive as best he can for as long as is permitted him. Is it any wonder, then, that *Time* and *Life* write as they do about the "beats"—with such a conspicuous show of superiority, and no hint of fear? . . .

I would simply point to the similarities which are masked by the real differences between the "beats" and those intellectuals who most overtly scorn them. Taste or style dictates that most intellectuals behave decorously, earn a regular living, disguise instead of flaunt any private digressions from the conduct society considers desirable; when they seek support for the poetical impulse or ask for light on their self-doubt and fears, they don't make the naked boast that they are crazy like daisies but they elaborate a new belief in the indispensability of neurosis to art, or beat the bushes for some new deviant psychoanalysis which will generalize their despair though of course without curing it. And these differences of style are undeniably important, at least for the moment. It is from the long-range view of our present-day cultural situation, which bears so closely upon our continuing national crisis, that the moral difference between a respectable and a disreputable acceptance of defeat seems to me to constitute little more than a cultural footnote to history.

But perhaps I wander too far from the other night at Columbia. There was enough in the evening that was humanly immediate to divert one from this kind of ultimate concern. . . .

It was not an official university occasion. The "beats" appeared at Columbia on the invitation of a student club-interestingly enough, the John Dewey Society. . . . The advance warnings turned out to be exaggerated. It was nevertheless disconcerting that Fred Dupee of the English Department had consented, at the request of the John Dewey Society, to be moderator, chairman, introducer of Ginsberg and his fellow-poets, for while it provided the wives of his colleagues with the assurance of seats in a section of the hall reserved for faculty, it was not without its uncomfortable reminder that Ginsberg had, in a sense, got his way; he was appearing on the same Columbia platform from which T. S. Eliot had last year read his poetry; he was being presented by, and was thus bound to be thought under the sponsorship of, a distinguished member of the academic and literary community who was also one's long-time friend. And indeed it was as Dupee's friend that one took a first canvass of the scene: the line of policemen before the entrance to the theater; the air of suppressed excitement in the lobbies and one's own rather contemptible self-consciousness about being a participant in the much-publicized occasion; the shoddiness of an audience in which it was virtually impossible to distinguish between student and camp-follower; . . . It was distressing to think that Dupee was going to be "faculty" to such an incoherent assembly, that at this moment he was backstage with Ginsberg's group, formulating a deportment which would check the excess of which one knew it to be capable, even or especially in public, without doing violence to his own large tolerance. . . .

But Dupee's proper manners, that's something else again: what could I have been worrying about, when had Dupee ever failed to meet an occasion, or missed the right style? I don't suppose one could witness a better performance than his on Thursday evening: its rightness was apparent the moment he walked onto the stage, his troupe in tow and himself just close enough and yet enough removed to indicate the balance in which he held the situation. Had there been a hint of betrayal in his deportment; of either himself or his guests—naturally, he had made them his guests—the whole evening might have been different: for instance, a few minutes later when the overflow attendance outside the door began to bang and shout for admission, might not the audience have caught the contagion and become unruly too? Or would Ginsberg have stayed with his picture of himself as poet serious and triumphant instead of succumbing to what must have been the greatest temptation to spoil his opportunity? "The last time I was in this theater," Dupee began quietly, "it was also to hear a poet read his works. That was T. S. Eliot." A slight alteration of inflection, from irony to mockery, from wit to condescension, and it might well have been a signal for near-riot, boos and catcalls and whistlings; the evening would have been lost to the "beats," Dupee and Columbia would have been defeated. Dupee transformed a circus into a classroom. He himself, he said, welcomed the chance to hear these poets read their works—he never once in his remarks gave them their name of "beats" nor alluded even to San Francisco—because in all poetry it was important to study the spoken accent; he himself didn't happen especially to admire those of their works that he knew; still, he would draw our attention to their skillful use of a certain kind of American imagery which, deriving from Whitman, yet passed Whitman's use of it or even Hart Crane's. . . . It was Dupee speaking for the Academy, claiming for it its place in life, and the

performers were inevitably captive to his dignity and self-assurance. Rather than Ginsberg and his friends, it was a photographer from *Life*, exploding his flashbulbs in everybody's face, mounting a ladder at the back of the stage the more effectively to shoot his angles, who came to represent vulgarity and disruption and disrespect; . . . One could feel nothing but pity for Ginsberg and his friends that their front of disreputableness and rebellion should be this vulnerable to the seductions of a clever host. With Dupee's introduction, the whole of their armor had been penetrated at the very outset. . . .

A dozen years ago, when Ginsberg had been a student and I had taxed Lionel with the duty to forbid him to misbehave, he had answered me that he wasn't the boy's father, and of course he was right. Neither was Mark Van Doren the boy's father; a teacher is not a father to his students, and he must never try to be. Besides, Ginsberg had a father of his own who couldn't be replaced at will: he was in the audience the other night. One of the things Ginsberg read was part of a long poem to his mother, who, he told us, had died three years ago, and as he read it, he choked and cried; but no one in the auditorium tittered or showed embarrassment at this public display of emotion, and I doubt whether there was a young Existentialist in the audience who thought, "See he has existence: he can cry, he can feel." Nor did anyone seem very curious when he went on to explain, later in the evening, that the reason he had cried was because his father was in the theater. . . .

I don't remember how the question was put to Ginsberg—but I'm sure it was put neutrally: no one was inclined to embarrass the guests—which led him into a discussion of prosody; perhaps it was the question about what Ginsberg as a poet had learned at Columbia; but anyway, here, at last, Ginsberg had a real classroom subject: he could be a teacher who wed outrageousness to authority in the time-honored way of the young and lively, no-pedant-he performer of the classroom, and suddenly Ginsberg announced firmly that no one at Columbia knew anything about prosody; the English department was stuck in the nineteenth century, sensible of no meter other than the old iambic pentameter, whereas the thing about him and his friends was their concern with a poetic line which moved in the rhythm of ordinary speech; they were poetic innovators, carrying things forward the logical next step from William Carlos Williams. And now all at once the thing about Ginsberg and his friends was not their social protest and existentialism, their whackiness and beat-upness: suddenly it had become their energy of poetic impulse that earned them their right to be heard in the university, their studious devotion to their art: Ginsberg was seeing to that. . . . And thus did one measure, finally, the full tug of something close to respectability in Ginsberg's life . . . and thus, too, was the soundness of Dupee's reminder, that there is always something to learn from hearing a poet read his poems aloud, borne in on one. For the fact was that Ginsberg, reading his verse, had naturally given it the iambic beat: after all, it is the traditional beat of English poetry where it deals with serious subjects, as Ginsberg's poems so often do. A poet, one thought—and it was a poignant thought because it came so immediately and humanly rather than as an abstraction—may choose to walk whatever zany path in his life as a man; but when it comes to mourning and mothers and such, he will be drawn into the line of tradition; at least in this far he is always drawn toward "respectability." . . .

There was a meeting going on at home of the pleasant professional sort which, like the comfortable living room in which it usually takes place, at a certain point in a successful modern literary career confirms the writer in his sense of disciplined achievement and well-earned reward. . . . Auden, alone of the eight men in the room not dressed in a proper suit but wearing a battered old brown leather jacket, was first to inquire about my experience. I told him I had been moved; he answered gently that he was ashamed of me. In a dim suffocated effort of necessary correction, I said, "It's different when it's human beings and not just a sociological phenomenon," and I can only guess, and hope, he took what I meant. Yet as I prepared to get out of the room so that the men could sit down again with their drinks, I felt there was something more I had to add—it was so far from enough to leave the "beats" as no more than human beings—and so I said, "Allen Ginsberg read a love poem to you, Lionel. I liked it very much." It was an awkward thing to say in the circumstances, perhaps even a little foolish as an attempt to bridge the unfathomable gap that was all so quickly and meaningfully opening up between the evening that had been and the evening that was now so surely reclaiming me. But I'm certain that Ginsberg's old teacher knew what I was saying, and why I was impelled to say it.

Campus Free Speech

3. *Goldberg v. The Regents of the University of California*, 1967

On March 4, 1965, during the "filthy speech" protests at the University of California, Berkeley, Arthur L. Goldberg led a student rally from the steps of Sproul Hall, the administration building, to protest the March 3 arrest of a nonstudent who had displayed on campus a sign reading "Fuck! Verb." Moderating and addressing the rally, Goldberg repeatedly used this word "in its various declensions." He and others were arrested and charged with violating the obscenity statutes and disturbing the peace. The next day at a rally on the steps of the Student Union Building he used an expanded vocabulary with other taboo words. On April 20, after notice and hearings, he, two other graduate students, and one undergraduate were suspended and dismissed from the university. These four then sued the university, claiming a violation of their constitutional right to freedom of speech. Ruling

that the university's disciplinary action was a proper exercise of its inherent power to maintain order, the Court of Appeal of California, First Appellate District declared here that protest itself was not the cause for dismissal but rather the repeated, loud, and public use of certain improper terms, unacceptable to the academic and broader social communities.

Wakefield Taylor (1912–2005), who issued this decision, served on the appellate bench from 1963 until retirement in 1982. He received both his B.A. (1934) and LL.B. (1937) from Berkeley and was president of the Associated Students in his senior year.

Goldberg v. The Regents of the University of California, 57 Cal. Rptr, 468–73, 476 (1967). Further reading: "Symposium: Student Rights and Campus Rules," *California Law Review* 54 (March 1966): 177–78; Robert Post, "Legal and Constitutional Issues," in *The Free Speech Movement: Reflections on Berkeley in the 1960s*, ed. Robert Cohen and Reginald E. Zelnik (Berkeley, 2002), 401–45; Gerard J. De Groot, "Ronald Reagan and Student Unrest, 1966–1970," *Pacific Historical Review* 65 (February 1996): 107–29; and VII, 7–10; XI.

February 28, 1967
Taylor, Associate Justice.

Article IX, section 9 of the state Constitution, provides that the University of California shall constitute a public trust to be administered by the existing corporation known as The Regents of the University, with full powers of organization and government, subject only to such legislative control as may be necessary to insure compliance with the terms of the endowment of the University and the security of its funds. Accordingly, the University is a constitutional department or function of the state government. . . . The Regents have the general rule-making or policy-making power in regard to the University . . . and are (with exceptions not material here) fully empowered with respect to the organization and government of the University . . . , including the authority to maintain order and decorum on the campus and the enforcement of the same by all appropriate means, including suspension or dismissal from the University. . . .

The more recent federal cases stress the importance of education to the individual and conclude that attendance in a state university is no longer considered a privilege as in Hamilton v. Regents of University of California (1934) . . . but is now regarded as an important benefit (Dixon v. Alabama State Board of Education) (1961). . . .

For constitutional purposes, the better approach, as indicated in Dixon, recognizes that state universities should no longer stand in loco parentis in relation to their students. Rather, attendance at publicly financed institutions of higher education should be regarded a benefit somewhat analogous to that of public employment. Accordingly, we deal with the question here presented within the same constitutional framework as that applied in the recent public employment cases. . . . The test is whether conditions annexed to the benefit reasonably tend to further the purposes sought by conferment of that benefit and whether the utility of imposing the conditions manifestly outweighs any resulting impairment of constitutional rights. . . .

Broadly stated, the function of the University is to impart learning and to advance the boundaries of knowledge. This carries with it the administrative responsibility to control and regulate that conduct and behavior of the students which tends to impede, obstruct or threaten the achievements of its educational goals. Thus, the University has the power to formulate and enforce rules of student conduct that are appropriate and necessary to the maintenance of order and propriety, considering the accepted norms of social behavior in the community, where such rules are reasonably necessary to further the University's educational goals.

Unquestionably, the achievement of the University's educational goals would preclude regulations unduly restricting the freedom of students to express themselves. As stated in *Edwards v. South Carolina*: . . ."[A] function of free speech under our system of government is to invite dispute. It may indeed best serve its high purpose when it induces a condition of unrest, creates dissatisfaction with conditions as they are, or even stirs people to anger. Speech is often provocative and challenging. It may strike at prejudices and preconceptions and have profound unsettling effects as it presses for acceptance of an idea."

Historically, the academic community has been unique in having its own standards, rewards and punishments. Its members have been allowed to go about their business of teaching and learning largely free of outside interference. To compel such a community to recognize and enforce precisely the same standards and penalties that prevail in the broader social community would serve neither the special needs and interests of the educational institutions, nor the ultimate advantages that society derives therefrom. Thus, in an academic community, greater freedoms and greater restriction may prevail than in society at large, and the subtle fixing of these limits should, in a large measure, be left to the education institution itself.

The question here is whether the University's requirement that plaintiffs conform to the community's accepted norms of propriety with respect to the loud, repeated public use of certain terms was reasonably necessary in furthering the University's educational goals. We note that plaintiffs were not disciplined for protesting the arrest of Thomson, but for doing so in a particular manner. The qualification imposed was simply that plaintiffs refrain from repeatedly, loudly and publicly using certain terms which, when so used, clearly infringed on the minimum standard of propriety and the accepted norm of public behavior of both the academic community and the broader social community. Plaintiffs' contention that the words were used only in the context of their demonstration is not borne out

by the record which indicates that the terms were used repeatedly, and often out of context, or when used in context given undue emphasis. The conduct of plaintiffs thus amounted to coercion rather than persuasion.

The association with an educational institution as a student requires certain minimum standards of propriety in conduct to insure that the educational functions of the institution can be pursued in an orderly and reasonable manner. The limitation here imposed was necessary for the orderly conduct of demonstrations, not unlike reasonable restrictions on the use of loudspeakers. . . . The irresponsible activity of plaintiffs seriously interfered with the University's interest in preserving proper decorum in campus assemblages. . . . Conduct involving rowdiness, rioting, the destruction of property, the reckless display of impropriety or any unjustifiable disturbance of the public order on or off campus is indefensible whether it is incident to an athletic event, the advent of spring, or devotion, however sincere, to some cause or ideal.

We hold that in this case, the University's disciplinary action was a proper exercise of its inherent general powers to maintain order on the campus and to exclude therefrom those who are detrimental to its well being. . . . Thus, for the purposes of this appeal, it is not necessary to discuss plaintiffs' contention that any particular regulation was unconstitutionally vague. . . .

As we have previously indicated, the University, as an academic community, can formulate its own standards, rewards and punishments to achieve its educational objectives. In this context, violations of certain rules of the outside community (parking, for example) are of little significance to the University's functions and objectives. Similarly, certain conduct that violates no laws of the external community, such as cheating on an examination, is properly proscribed by and disciplined by the University as it interferes with the University's basic educational purpose. Thus, except for the applicable constitutional limitations, the relationship between appropriate University rules and laws of the outside community is entirely coincidental. The validity of one does not establish the validity of the other. . . .

We conclude, upon the application of all pertinent constitutional requirements, that plaintiffs' complaint does not state a cause of action on any theory.

The answer is stricken from the record and the judgment is affirmed.

A Learning Community

4. Paul Goodman,
The Community of Scholars, 1962

Though calling his book "a little treatise on anarchist theory," Paul Goodman (1911–72) infused this consideration of the community of scholars with something of the spirit of an older American radicalism and social utopianism. His sentences may be read as an educational coda to the major work *Communitas* he wrote with his brother Percival Goodman in 1947. Goodman was a popular lecturer in the 1960s on many campuses and was widely considered to be the guru to a generation that boasted it would trust no one over thirty. His major theme was that education should be more than a training ground for the demands of one's society.

After graduating from City College in New York (1931), Goodman became a novelist and social critic. Along his way he earned a Ph.D. at Chicago (1954), held relatively brief academic appointments at Chicago, New York University, and Black Mountain College, and was associated for some years with the Institute for Gestalt Therapy in New York City.

Paul Goodman, *The Community of Scholars* (New York, 1962), pp. ix–xi, 3–10. Reprinted with the permission of Random House, Inc., Copyright © 1962, and the kind permission of Sally Goodman. All rights reserved. Further reading: Goodman, *Growing Up Absurd* (New York, 1960) and *Compulsory Mis-Education* (New York, 1964); Kingsley Widmer, *Paul Goodman* (Boston, 1980); a critical analysis by Richard King, *The Party of Eros: Radical Social Thought and the Realm of Freedom* (Chapel Hill, NC, 1972), ch. 3; and *Contemporary Authors New Revision Series*, vol. 34 (1991), 170–73.

It is impossible to consider our universities in America without being powerfully persuaded of the principle of anarchy, that the most useful arrangement is free association and federation rather than top-down management and administration. Nowhere else can one see so clearly the opportunities for real achievement so immediately available—for the work is teaching-and-learning and *there* in the school are the teachers and students themselves—and yet so much obstruction, prevention, extraneous regulation and taxation, by management and the goals of management. All the philosophical critics see this and say this—for instance, Veblen, Hutchins, or Taylor—but they have other things in mind: they are interested in higher learning, curriculum, individual development. But I am here interested in the naked constitutional question itself: Is this the most efficient setup? how has it come to be organized this way? how should it be done? how could it be done?

Naturally the schools are tightly involved with the performance, and even more with the style, of the dominant system of society. Any significant reform of them would involve a threat to that dominant system. But that also is very well. . . .

My concern is liberal education, the education of the sons of the free, to be free and exercise initiative in the world they inherit. Many readers will no doubt, then, be surprised at how little mention there is of the liberal-arts curriculum, of the well-rounded course of studies as opposed to specialization, the intellectual as opposed to the practical. These are the usual topics, but I do not think that they are important. Curriculum is always given; it is the sciences, mores, and institutions of our civilization. In every part of it, it is possible to find

spirit, for it was created by spirit—how else is anything created? The problem of education is how the scholars are to confront that civilization and make it freely their own. I propose an ancient but neglected invention, the community of scholars. Given it, it does not matter much about the syllabus. Without it, nothing will be learned, though many may get degrees.

This book may seem a little preachy and over-earnest. Yes, I am a loyal university man, and I fear—this also is historically familiar—that our culture is in danger of extinction, etc. My fear is exaggerated.

Nevertheless, there is a serious issue. Harold Rosenberg has said that the most important service that we can perform at present is to expose the scandal of the intellectuals, in the schools, the press, the government, etc., playing along with the forces that are senseless. He is right. When, in writing this book, I copy out the Enlightenment sentences of Kant—that the faculty of philosophy is a watchdog, that the young are educated according to the possible future of mankind—I feel a thrill of pride, in him, and satisfaction that I too urge these sentences the best I can.

Besides, just humanly speaking, these days when so many are going off to college and trying to get into college, it is sad to see so much waste of effort, and even unnecessary torture, of both students and the teachers. We—or *they*—must hit on some way for them to get more out of it than they do. . . .

The 1,900 colleges and universities are the only important face-to-face self-governing communities still active in our modern society. Two-thirds of them have fewer than 75 teachers and 1,000 students, who live with one another, interact, and continually decide on all kinds of business by their statutes, customs, and social pressures. The rural town-meetings that are left are not so close-knit, and perform only rudimentary functions. The congregational churches have come to play only a supportive Sunday role, not much different from fraternal lodges or clubs. Almost all the other face-to-face self-governing associations that once made up nearly all society—the municipalities, craft guilds, and joint-stock companies—have long since succumbed to centralization, with distant management.

In this book on the colleges, I want to stress that they are communities, really small *cities*, for they have a heterogeneous population and are cut off from their environments as if walled. At present there is a great expansion of education—at least of the number going to schools—and so there have been many new books about colleges; but I do not know one that concentrates on their community. Yet it is remarkable. . . .

Our university cities comprise teachers and students—and administrators. I separate the administrators from the scholars because their presence raises the first question I want to ask: What are administrators doing there? how did they get in? In any community there must be a certain number of caretakers and functionaries. But the community of scholars is, or could be, quite moderate in size; historically, except in exceptional cases, the number has hovered between 500 and 1,000, and sometimes we shall be speaking of celebrated universities that numbered 100 people! (It is hard for Americans to grasp this.) Such a community seems to require only a handful of unpretentious administrators—a rector unwillingly elevated from the faculty for a short term, a typist, and a couple of janitors. Instead, in the American colleges, the Administration is a vast army and its President is almost regarded as the college itself. How is this?

Another question—closely related, as we shall see—is: If the universities are as if walled, what are the transactions between such walled cities and the rest of society that has a different organization? The wall itself, the separateness, is inevitable—until society itself becomes an international city of peace. For the culture of the scholars is inevitably foreign: it is international and comprises the past, present, and future. The language, even though the scholars speak English instead of Latin, has different rules of truth and evidence that cannot be disregarded when it happens to be convenient. The scholars come from all parts and do not easily abide the local prejudices. They cannot always fly the national flag.

In my opinion, it is finally this foreignness, this humanism, that makes a university; it is not the level of the studies, the higher learning, the emphasis on theory, or anything like that. . . .

Put it this way: there are 1,900 colleges and universities; at least several hundred of these have managed to collect faculties that include many learned and creative adults who are free to teach what they please; all 1,900 are centers of lively and promising youth. Yet one could not name ten that strongly stand for anything peculiar to themselves, peculiarly wise, radical, experimental, or even peculiarly dangerous, stupid, or licentious. It is astounding! that there should be so many self-governing communities, yet so much conformity to the national norm. How is it possible?

Or consider it this way: at present, the organization of American society is an interlocking system of semi-monopolies notoriously venal, an electorate notoriously unenlightened, misled by mass media notoriously phony, and a baroque State waging cold war against another baroque State. The colleges, on their part, are powerful and importantly independent. Between such forces one would expect a continual and electric clash. Instead, there is harmony. It looks like harmony but is really a clinch. The scholars are not acting, not being men; and therefore *within* the communities of scholars, there is very little education or growing up.

It is my thesis that the agent of this clinch is administration and the spread of the administrative mentality among the teachers and even the students. It is the genius of administration to enforce a false harmony in a situation that should be rife with conflict. Historically, the communities of scholars have perennially been invaded by administrators from the outside, by Visitors of king, bishop, despotic majority, or whatever is the power in society that wants to quarantine the virulence of youth, the dialogue of persons, the push of inquiry, the accusing testimony of scholarship. But today Administration and the administrative mentality are entrenched in the community of scholars itself; they fragment it and paralyze it. Therefore we see the paradox that, with so many centers of possible intellectual criticism and intellectual initiative, there is so much inane conformity, and the universities are little models of the Organized System itself. . . .

Obviously, these are biased sentences. I am a partisan of the scholars and we are losing badly. But I do not think I am unfair. Administrators, administration-minded faculty, and conformist students are of course inevitable products of a long history and the kind of society we have. On the average, I should not be surprised if the universities are better run than the average graft-ridden municipality or big business firm. Nevertheless, it *is* the case that college administrators have a considerable leeway and freedom of choice, more than ward politicians or corporation executives. And—granting their own mythology—they are professional "educators," not merely politicians or businessmen; they have authority to tell their employers what is best, and not to act like hired hands or members of the wolf pack. Unhappily, what is best is usually for them to reduce themselves to a fairly modest function, and I suppose that this is against human nature.

But in this chapter, let me invite the reader—perhaps a student or a young instructor at a great state university—to imagine the community of scholars as if it were new, before there were any administrators at all, but only students and teachers, they themselves. Ask, what is it that essentially occurs in teaching and learning at the college level? And imagine the relations of the persons in your community if the community were stripped to the essential.

5. Charles Muscatine, *Education at Berkeley*, 1966

On the heels of the free speech protests at the University of California, Berkeley, a select committee on education of the academic senate was appointed by Acting Chancellor Martin Meyerson in March 1965 to consider "a pluralistic approach to education." Charles Muscatine, professor of English, was chairman of this committee whose report surveyed the many proposals for curricular change and accommodation to undergraduate needs put forward over the preceding months on a huge campus. The report was henceforth known as the Muscatine Report. It made forty-two recommendations for academic reform and was greeted enthusiastically by advocates for change at Berkeley and by the nation at large. The report began with a description of the different types of students then at Berkeley, a portrait which in its brief and authentic depiction of the nonconforming student is unmatched in a large literature. Charles Muscatine (1920–), a noted Chaucerian scholar, earned degrees at Yale (B.A. 1941; Ph.D. 1948) and went to teach at Berkeley in 1948.

University of California, Berkeley, Academic Senate, *Education at Berkeley: Report on the Select Committee on Education* (Berkeley, 1966): 27–31, 33–35. Reprinted with permission from the Berkeley Division of the Academic Senate, University of California. Copyright © 1966 by the Regents of the University of California. Further reading: Joseph Tussman, *Experiment at Berkeley* (New York, 1969); Neil J. Smelser, "Berkeley in Crisis and Change," in *Academic Transformation: Seven Institutions Under Pressure*, ed. David Riesman and Verne A. Stadtman (New York, 1973); Nevitt Sanford, ed., *The American College: A Psychological and Social Interpretation of the Higher Learning* (New York, 1962) and Kenneth Keniston, "The Faces in the Lecture Room," in *The Contemporary University: U.S.A.*, ed. Robert S. Morison (Boston, 1966), 315–49, probe student culture of the 1950s; Kenneth Keniston, *Young Radicals: Notes on Committed Youth* (New York, 1968), on student lifestyles of the 1960s; Mark Gerzon, *The Whole World is Watching: A Young Man Looks at Youth's Dissent* (New York, 1969); Julian Foster and Durward Long, eds., *Protest! Student Activism in America* (Boston, 1970); Irving Louis Horowitz and William H. Friedland, *The Knowledge Factory: Student Power and Academic Politics in America* (Chicago, 1970); Seymour M. Lipset and Gerald M. Schaflander, *Passion and Politics: Student Activism in America* (Boston, 1971), ch. 3; and Kenneth Keniston, *Radicals and Militants: An Annotated Bibliography of Empirical Research on Campus Unrest* (Lexington, MA, 1973).

We need to understand the mentality of these intelligent non-conformist students. . . .

Our description is more impressionistic than scientific and more simple than the description of a highly complex phenomenon should be. But we offer it in the belief that even in its broad outlines it may help to dispel some of the confusion and misunderstanding that has gathered about a group of our students.

The most obvious feature of their outlook, which every observer notes immediately, is their outright rejection of many aspects of present-day America. They find much to fear and condemn and, overtly at least, little to praise. Essentially, they see our society as controlled by a group which has abandoned the common welfare in its own self-interest and has resorted to many techniques to disguise its activities and to manipulate the general public. As these students see it, while the dominant group claims to champion freedom, religion, patriotism, and morality, it produces and condones slums, racial segregation, migrant farm laborers, false advertising, American economic imperialism, and the bomb. In private life, moreover, the students find as much immorality and injustice as in public life. They

commonly explain it as the product of an all-pervasive hypocrisy.

To succeed in this society, they believe, you must mask your real feelings and become an organization man, wear what you're expected to wear, say what you're expected to say, and praise the product of your company when you know it has been built to wear out. It's all a game, playing a role; and these young people find that Americans in this other-directed age have been conditioned to accept without a thought or a murmur their own falsity. They accuse Americans of sacrificing conscience to the quest for status. In this society, they say, those who claim to be moral are really immoral and those who claim to be sane are truly insane.

All this these students condemn. What terrifies them is their conviction that the failure of the individual sense of responsibility, in combination with technology and cybernation, is producing a bureaucratized, machine-run society. They find themselves in danger of losing both their freedom and their humanity to IBM machines and to those who use them. They say that a man must fight hypocrisy to live in a moral world, but he will have to halt the computers if he is to remain a man at all. The fear of 1984, common in the Forties and Fifties, of the totalitarian state based on ubiquitous terror, has reverted among the present generation of radical students to a fear of the scientifically conditioned Brave New World. In the student mind, the dominant group takes the form of the "organized system" that Paul Goodman decries, or the "power structure" opposed by civil rights organizations, or simply "the establishment." "You can't trust anyone over thirty" expresses a vague but pervasive belief that their elders have been corrupted past salvation by the system. Commonly, the students, taking an existentialist position of belief in individual responsibility, seek individuals to blame for the evil actions of society—men who through fear, weak character, or dishonesty have abdicated their moral responsibility. Student radicals find, for example, McGeorge Bundy, Robert McNamara, and ultimately President Johnson responsible for what they see as American aggression in Vietnam.

For a significant number of young people the older generation is represented most clearly by their parents, who have accepted the system and made their way in it. If the parents remain faithful to religious practices and teachings, the child may be further alienated, since he is likely to be religiously skeptical or atheistic. What most exasperates members of the new generation is their belief that their elders do not take them seriously. "How many roads must a man walk down before you call him a man?" the popular protest singer Bob Dylan asks in a song adopted by the FSM.

Ultimately the students find their society decadent and the dominant group intellectually sterile. For them, American art is created by folk singers,

Negro musicians, and bohemian artists and writers. In their most pessimistic moments, America, and indeed the whole West, no longer appears to have any message for the world. Zen Buddhism offers more hope for humanity than does Christianity.

The revolt turns against the traditional ideals of America which the older generation holds up for admiration: the puritan ethic, individualism, and old-fashioned patriotism. Against the puritan ethic non-conformist students flaunt sexual and emotional freedom. They find individualism in the form of private property evil when it justifies exorbitant wealth, dishonest products, and segregated housing. The past history of America becomes for them a sordid tale of the exploitation of non-Anglo-Saxon cultures and races at home and of innocent countries abroad. They see patriotic appeals to the ideals of life, liberty, and pursuit of happiness as trappings to cover sham and hypocrisy.

Before 1960 the usual reaction of the few young people who held this view of our world was to withdraw from society, as did the uncommitted youths studied by Keniston at Harvard. They "went beat" and demonstrated their rejection of the system in their personal life and dress. Since then, this type of reaction has become much more widespread. Beards, long hair, and bare feet protest the conspicuous waste and conformity of the status-conscious society. Instead of the whiskey of their parents, many of these students prefer to use marijuana. Revolt also takes other forms which an outsider can view only as self-destructive; some students can explain laziness, procrastination, and irresponsibility as rejection of the puritan ethic of hard work. Thus many young people clothe in a quasi-moral garb the traditional student difficulty of buckling down to work. This attitude can lead brilliant students to fall behind and eventually drop out.

Another disturbing and ironic development of the new generation is its commitment to form. It has lost respect for the public-relations mentality of "the system," but it has its own admiration for style. In personal relations the highest mark of style is being "cool." Originally the praiseworthy quality of not losing one's head in a crisis, in the Fifties being cool came to mean not opening oneself up, not revealing one's weaknesses, having love affairs without becoming emotionally involved. Keeping cool involves as much role-playing as does the hypocrisy the student finds in the scorned minion of the system.

The search for style is in fact a manifestation of the internal conflict and ambiguity that plagues many of these young men and women. Freed from traditional inhibitions, they find that their new role-playing, their "cool," deprives them of the satisfying personal relationships that more traditional patterns used to foster. Paradoxically, old-fashioned romantic love remains their ideal. Some attempt pathetically to simulate love at first sight. Through the exchange of intense confidences, they seek to "communicate" completely and to "build meaningful relationships." To little avail. Instant love proves exhausting and empty.

The search for genuine experience leads also to experimenting with non-addictive hallucinatory drugs. The student hopes through them to free his mind from the shackles of reason and logic, to apprehend the ineffable truths about himself and his surroundings, and to become truly creative. This desire for instant poetry, instant psychoanalysis, and instant mysticism is a further form of escape from hard work, a translation to intellectual and emotional spheres of the American cult of the labor-saving device. The belief that experience through drugs provides more insight than hard rational thought cannot but affect the attitude of young people toward formal education.

These ways of rejecting society in one's private life are outgrowths of the patterns of the earlier "beat" or non-committed generation. At Berkeley the non-conformist has always had another avenue of protest against society: in preference to ironic withdrawal, some have chosen alienated commitment. Since 1960 the radical students of Berkeley have been at the forefront of a wave of student activism that has spread throughout the country.

The activists often reject formal ideologies as a suspect heritage from their elders and attack instead specific policies that they find evil: atomic testing, racial segregation, and, lately, American involvement in Vietnam. Admitting their admiration for anarchism and existentialism, these students assert that the individual must oppose evil directly no matter how strong the system that protects it; for to condemn without acting, as did the Germans who submitted to Hitler, is to share in the guilt. Yet they seldom act as individuals; instead they form groups to organize public acts of protest—petitions, marches, vigils, and, ultimately, sit-ins and civil disobedience. Besides giving strength to their voices, organizations with a high purpose can serve to compensate for a lack of rewarding relationships in their private lives. To join a cause is part of the anxious search for a new "sense of viable community" that makes this generation seem hardly less other-directed than its elders.

There is a similar ambiguity in their expectations. On the surface they display a quiet determination and optimism: "we shall overcome." At times, they seem to believe that a solution to society's ills is at hand if only their demands are met: "Freedom now!" Except in moments of exhilaration, however, as during the height of the Free Speech Movement, this confident appearance masks an underlying pessimism. They are not very hopeful of achieving instant freedom and instant reform. Their acts of defiance are often also acts of despair. . . .

The University takes pride in its devotion to finding and teaching truth and knowledge. Accepting it on these terms, the potentially alienated student expects to find within its walls idealism silencing cant and hypocrisy. Disillusioned with his elders, he comes to the faculty seeking a "prophet" or a "wise man" (the terms are quoted from students). Here he expects to fill his need for a community in which he can participate, find satisfactory communication with adults, and enlist their support in his struggle to right the wrongs of society. With such high, if unformulated, expectations, this kind of student is bound to be disappointed. Communication with the older generation often fails to materialize in large lecture courses. Few if any of his teachers even know his name. He comes to believe that his worth is measured in answers to mass examinations, not in personal assessment of his work and ideas. He learns to play a game within the University, to select his courses according to the grade he is likely to receive, to write ritual papers, and to second-guess the instructor. He decides that the University is too busy conforming to the needs of the establishment to produce men capable of opposing its evils.

In the critical student's eyes, the professors turn out to have their own system and play their own game. He sees their research as a means for their own advancement rather than as a search for truth. They turn out to be neither prophets nor wise men, only specialists in one area with all their prejudices in other areas intact.

We have seen that students who have this outlook on life are more likely to be in the humanities and social sciences than in the natural sciences or professional schools. Some of these students soon become convinced that even in the humanities and social sciences the professor's command of his specialty and fame through publication count for more than teaching the elements of a subject to beginning students. They decide that the only refuge may be outside. But while they prefer creativity in art and literature to its exegesis, the reforming of society to its analysis, most realize that they must still work to live, and in their disillusion end up playing the game.

In sum, the dissatisfied student finds the University to be just another part of the established order. His alienation from society turns into an alienation from his University. His distrust of the older generation makes it difficult for him to appreciate traditional methods of instruction or the faculty's idea of a good education, especially when some professors do in fact display insouciance in their teaching. The student's view of the University is molded to a large extent by the same unwillingness to accept human imperfection that molds his general views of our social system.

This explanation of the attitudes of alienated students collapses into simple logical sequence what is in fact a complex evolution. The potentially alienated freshman or transfer student comes with no clear idea of what to expect in the University, and with inchoate, largely traditional views of society. His images of American society and of the ideal university take shape simultaneously as a result of what he sees and hears after he arrives.

To say that the students reject the University because they regard it as an extension of the organized system is hardly a novel insight; it is a charge that has often been repeated by student leaders. There is a further, less obvious connection between the students' general outlook and their reaction to the University. Those who believe that there can be short cuts to social reform, mysticism, and love cannot conceive that there are no short cuts to learning. Difficult courses that make them pore over facts and theorems can seem a tedious waste of time concocted by unimaginative professors. There must be instant knowledge—if only the faculty would become attuned to the modern world. To overcome this attitude the University must discover how to impart once more the truth that there is no royal road to mathematics.

The anti-rational aspects of student thought contribute to this attitude. Students who hold unreflectingly the belief that feeling is a surer guide to truth than reason, cannot readily appreciate the University's commitment to rational investigation. If they believe that Western culture is decadent, they cannot appreciate the University's devotion to its preservation and transmission.

Commitment to social action also prevents students from accepting as valuable an autonomous world of ideas. They find it hard to conceive that the purpose of the University can be to seek and preserve pure knowledge. They feel that impartiality cannot exist in the social sciences, or for that matter in any subject that deals with man and his culture. Instead of praising the impartiality of the teacher who does not relate his lessons to immediate problems, they accuse him of moral irresponsibility.

There is a contradiction in this criticism that betrays the anti-intellectual stance of the nonconformist students. They condemn the University because it is a factory that turns out the products demanded by society and trains students in the rules of the game; yet they want their education to be related to present-day life and to their personal needs, not to the abstract concerns of the humanities and sciences. They see the University as an agent of the power structure, and they want it to become instead an agent of their moral revolution. A major task of the University is to convince the students of the value of free and independent inquiry, of the need of the University for autonomy from all quarters if it is properly to serve society.

6. Mario Savio, "The Uncertain Future of the Multiversity," 1966

As a twenty-two-year-old undergraduate philosophy major at Berkeley in the fall of 1964, Mario Savio (1942–96) sprang overnight to campus and national prominence as the impassioned voice of the Free Speech Movement. Two years later in one of his few published pieces, abridged here, he responded to the Muscatine Report from the Berkeley Academic Senate (5). Savio's life thereafter was spent chiefly as a teacher; he died of heart failure at the age of 53. But he is affectionately remembered by his friends and colleagues from those tempestuous years. An inscribed tablet on the steps of the Berkeley administration building was dedicated to him, as was the large volume *The Free Speech Movement, Reflections on Berkeley in the 1960s*, ed. Robert H. Cohen and Reginald E. Zelnik (Berkeley, 2000).

Mario Savio, "The Uncertain Future of the Multiversity," *Harper's Magazine* 233 (October 1966): 88–90, 93–94. Copyright © 1966 by *Harper's Magazine*. All rights reserved. Reproduced from the October issue by special permission. Further reading: Mario Savio, "The University Has Become a Factory," *Life*, February 26, 1965, 100–101; Oliver Johns, obituary, available at www.physics.sfsu.edu/savio-obit.html; Eric Pace, obituary, *New York Times*, November 8, 1996; Irwin Unger, *The Movement: A History of the American New Left, 1959–1972* (New York, 1974), ch. 3; W. J. Rorabaugh, *Berkeley at War, the 1960s* (New York, 1989), ch. 1; Jo Freeman, *At Berkeley in the '60s: The Education of an Activist, 1961–1965* (Bloomington, IN, 2004); and VII, 4–5, 7.

The Berkeley Free Speech Movement in the fall of 1964 brought into focus the deepest conflicts dividing American society. It especially cast in relief the distorted education which Berkeley undergraduates endure. It made clear how destructive of human values any educational institution must be when it is run by and in the economic interests of the millionaires who sit on the University Board of Regents.

In the spring following the crisis several Berkeley students (among them some who had taken prominent roles in the Free Speech Movement) participated in meetings with then Acting Chancellor Martin Meyerson. In those meetings we and Meyerson exchanged views on the need for comprehensive reforms at Berkeley. We discussed specific proposals for the improvement of Berkeley education, and we considered ways to facilitate the acceptance of these proposals. The most important of the measures we discussed was the creation of a commission, with the highest authority, to study the present state of Berkeley education and make specific recommendations for its improvement. Chancellor Meyerson proposed a faculty commission for this purpose; the Academic Senate approved Meyerson's proposal and nine faculty members were appointed to the Select Committee on Education—better known as the Muscatine Committee, after its Chairman, Professor of English Charles Muscatine. Of these nine, not more than two—by their public support of student demands during FSM—could be said to have won the trust of those students most interested in university reform.

Those of us who participated in those early meetings with Chancellor Meyerson expressed grave doubts that any commission which did not include

students as voting members would take the evils of the existing educational system very seriously. We had just come through an enlightening semester. We had learned that even on the far less complex civil-liberties questions with which the Free Speech Movement was mostly concerned, only an invasion of the campus by several hundred police could move the Academic Senate to declare itself opposed to the administration's regulation of the *content* of speech! After a semester of watching the Academic Senate—an unwieldy body whose meetings vary in size from one hundred to twelve hundred—bungle through their simple legislative procedures, we were scarcely eager to trust the faculty with advancing student interests in complicated questions of university reform—especially when those student interests were clearly in conflict with powerful interests on the faculty.

We wanted an end to the system of lecture courses, grades, and course units, to be replaced by instruction in small seminars and tutorials, with the quality of students' work evaluated at length in writing rather than by the assignment of a numerical or letter grade. All of us were familiar with the regular use of grades as an escape from careful, detailed individual evaluation of a student's progress. But this evil sprang in good measure from the widespread practice of lecturing to large classes (up to as many as one thousand students). Instructors in these mammoth classes simply did not have enough time to get to know more than a tiny fraction of "their" students. They could therefore treat them all equally only by treating none fairly. They had to make do with "objective" examinations geared to what the mythical average student should have learned, a practice which coerced students into passive acceptance of a pat version of what they *should* know. The resulting conformity would be rewarded with the all-important grade.

The California legislature's niggardly appropriations are the reason for these large lectures. Within its modest budget, the University is simply unable to recruit a large enough faculty without lowering its standards. Given these economic facts of life, each faculty member must choose to be primarily a teacher or primarily a researcher; there is not enough time to do both jobs adequately. Thus external economic pressures on the University force many faculty members to regard the educational needs of undergraduates as something of a threat to their personal research interests. And this cleavage is accentuated by the astronomical sums of money for research and professional education being poured into the University by government and big business, both of which are well-represented on the University Board of Regents.

But the present disproportionate emphasis on specialized education and research is apparently not bad enough. Clark Kerr, members of the Board of Regents, members of the legislature, and others who inhabit the stratosphere of educational high finance have been attempting to force on the state university and on the state colleges and junior colleges a "Master Plan" for long-range development of the California system of higher education. This arrangement would divide responsibility for different "levels" of higher education among the many state colleges and universities. Under the Plan Berkeley will undertake a major responsibility for graduate education and research, which will be accompanied by a further loss of emphasis (in time and money) on undergraduate teaching. Indeed, some legislators reportedly favor dropping undergraduate instruction at Berkeley altogether. If this Plan is not stopped soon (some opposition is developing among the more independent state college faculties through the Association of California State College Professors), the great enthusiasm for reform generated by the Free Speech Movement will be lost.

Little wonder Berkeley ranks among the nation's top graduate schools, while its undergraduate colleges have suffered such serious neglect. The Muscatine Report was supposed to have been concerned primarily with redressing this imbalance. Any serious reform of undergraduate education must be based on a clear understanding of the limitations of the present system; unfortunately, the Report's analysis of the University's offerings is not only superficial; it shows no deep understanding of the aims of higher education. . . .

There have been a multitude of small experiments involving radical innovation in college curricula on American campuses. These experiments (such as the present "Tussman Program" at Berkeley) have shown that with sufficient reliance on tutorials and small seminars, it is possible to do away with the coercive aspects of the present system of large classes and letter grades. These experiments have been designed for from less than fifty students to a few hundred. Precisely what is needed at this time is an experiment in *mass*, noncoercive higher education. The very problems which would be most pressing in any program for reform of Berkeley as a whole—therefore the problems we are most in need of solving—will not even appear in an experiment involving less than a thousand students. . . .

By "small undergraduate class" the Muscatine Committee means a class at least one and a half times as large as the *average* graduate class (10.3 students in 1970)! By "small" I understand "tutorial" or "small seminar"—six students or fewer. And in any case, after the harassment of three classes of 180 students each, only the exceptional student will be able to take full advantage of the modest benefits of a "small" class of twenty. The Report assures us: *"The Committee would favor an eventual reduction in class size by gradual expansion of the faculty while student enrollment holds constant."* This single sentence is the only clear indication in the entire Report that the Muscatine Committee even considered

what is after all the only adequate remedy. Perhaps it was italicized so we shouldn't miss it in too rapid reading. It is no more than a pious wish. "Optimum teaching effectiveness within the existing budgetary constraints" means in fact that far from being reduced, the average undergraduate class size will be increased.

The Berkeley faculty declared itself clearly opposed to the quarter system of year-round operation. (The quarter system too is part of the Master Plan.) Nevertheless, despite the expressed will of the faculty, in the interests of economic efficiency the campus is going off the traditional semester system beginning this fall. The Committee clearly accepts as normal a student's program of *four or even five courses* per quarter. Yet in persuading the Berkeley faculty to accept the quarter system, administration spokesmen had argued that its adoption would result in students being less coerced, more able to pursue their studies with greater leisure and in greater depth, since they could then attend only three courses each quarter rather than the five courses per semester as at present.

The Muscatine Committee was appointed largely in response to severe student criticisms of the University, yet it failed to deal in any meaningful way with these criticisms. The Report says: "In sum, the dissatisfied student finds the University to be just another part of the established order. His alienation from society turns into alienation from his university." Nowhere does the Committee begin to consider whether it is *in fact* reasonable to regard the University as largely "just another part of the established order." The clear concern here is to discover not what is wrong with the University, but what is wrong with the students.

The two questions are, of course, inseparable. But standing the matter thus on its head, the way is cleared for a psychological rather than a political or economic explanation:

> The antirational aspects of student thought contribute to this attitude. Students who hold unreflectingly the belief that feeling is a surer guide to truth than is reason, cannot readily appreciate the University's commitment to rational investigation. If they believe that Western culture is decadent, they cannot appreciate the University's devotion to its preservation and transmission.

After this caricature of "student thought," the Committee has the reader well prepared to dismiss the students' indictment of the submission of the University to the growing influences of government and industry. This indictment is portrayed as a logical contradiction, resulting from the know-nothing antirationalism of the students. . . .

How much less convincing this rhetoric would have been had the Committee taken the trouble to point out that the thesis they attribute to the students was originally obtained by them from Clark Kerr himself. This sad thesis is a central theme of Kerr's now-legendary Godkin Lectures on the "Multiversity." And what of the supposed contradiction? To be a "factory that turns out the products demanded by society and trains students in the rules of the game" is manifestly incompatible with the ideal of a free and independent University; but to be an "agent of the students' moral revolution" requires nothing more—nor less—than a declaration of independence and "autonomy from all quarters." A major task of the University is to be itself convinced of "the value of free and independent inquiry." . . .

The history of the adoption of the Master Plan and a careful study of the Muscatine Report show that faculty members and students are consistently excluded from those groups of legislators, bureaucrats, and businessmen which make the most far-reaching decisions concerning the development and reform of the University. Those of us whose lives are directly involved are denied any effective voice in these decisions which structure and pervert our immediate, daily environment. What has become of the "consent of the governed"? . . .

The Franklin Affair

7. John Howard and H. Bruce Franklin, *Who Should Run the Universities?* 1969

Among the leaders of campus student protests who attained national prominence in the 1960s, H. Bruce Franklin (1934–) was exceptional. He was a tenured faculty member and an avowed Marxist. His intellectual position was not conceived until 1966, after he had helped to lead efforts to stop the manufacture of Napalm-B at the United Technology Center near Stanford, where he was an associate professor of English. His stance became more fully developed during the next academic year when, on leave at Stanford-in-France, he became committed to Marxist studies and conferred with French and North Vietnamese communists. Supporting his increasingly doctrinaire views were memories of summer jobs during his Amherst College years, when he experienced the degrading conditions of workers in a Brooklyn manufacturing sweatshop and unequal divisions of pay and labor among tug boatmen in New York harbor. A term after college as navigator on a SAC KC-97 Arctic refueling tanker and as squadron intelligence officer made him acutely aware of the often disorganized, chancy, and nearly catastrophic actions of American and Russian military during the Cold War.

Franklin's indictment of the American university, reminiscent to some of Thorstein Veblen's *Higher Learning in America*, and his charge against the American "capitalist empire" were set forth in a debating paper he presented to the American Enterprise Institute in 1969, excerpted here. Added here are shorter paragraphs from his co-panelist at this debate, John A. Howard (1921–), who was president of Rockford College (1960–77), recipient of a Ph.D. from Northwestern (1962), and a decorated World War II veteran.

John A. Howard and H. Bruce Franklin, *Who Should Run the Universities?* (Washington, 1969): 24–27, 31–32, 37–45, 53–58, 62–63, 66–68, 239–40. Reprinted with the permission of The American Enterprise Institute for Public Policy Research, Washington, D.C. Further reading: VI, 8–10.

I would like to distinguish three stages in the history of the university; the medieval or feudal university; the university of the bourgeoisie; and the future university of the working people. Each of the first two stages has contained the preconditions of the emerging subsequent stage. That is, what we are now witnessing is an institution in the process of transcending itself, being revolutionized, turning into its opposite at the very moment it is developing to its own extreme.

In the medieval university, student and faculty power was total and devotion to the humanities was complete. It was a feudal institution, unequivocally servicing the church and the aristocracy. The medieval university bequeathed to its successor a legacy at once rich and reactionary, precious and dangerous. The ideal of contemplation outside the struggle of society; the fraternity of scholars; the quest for philosophic, as opposed to practical, truth; the purity of the academy—all these are still present to some degree in the university. And, strange as it may seem, the university is the last stronghold of that central medieval concept—so completely shattered by the Renaissance, the rise of capitalism, and modern science—the ideal of timelessness. The medieval university still exists in the minds of many academics, who occasionally resent the intrusions of the war machine almost as much as they resent the protest demonstrations against it. Periodically, from Cardinal Newman's 1852 glorification of a dead institution, "The Idea of the University," to S. I. Hayakawa's recent wistful claim that "in another time I would have been a priest," that ideal is resurrected to serve as a shield against the dynamic forces reshaping a far different university. . . .

Changes came with the depression and World War II, when the federal government became increasingly involved in the universities; this represented part of the process of the collapse of private enterprise capitalism and its replacement by monopoly and state capitalism. In World War II the university was recruited directly into war research, and the cold war, together with the increasing demands of monopoly capitalism at home and abroad, has fused what is now commonly called the military-industrial-educational complex, which may be understood as an early stage of state capitalism.

In this stage the medieval university, a cosmos fused by a single purpose, has become completely transformed into its opposite, what Clark Kerr has aptly named the multiversity, where the central value is the bourgeois ethic of competition. Competition reigns supreme at all levels and in all activities. The community of scholars has been replaced by the academic marketplace; grades and class standings determine the course of life, and for many young men, whether they will live at all;

departments and schools are pitted against each other; the faculty, student body, administration, and board of trustees struggle against each other and against their counterparts in other universities; the competitiveness of football teams, fraternities, and departmental hiring committees is only an outward manifestation of the battles for money relentlessly waged in, through, and by every segment of the multiversity structure. For, as Clark Kerr has put it, the multiversity is "a mechanism held together by administrative rules and powered by money." . . .

This multiversity, comparable to a small nation, is only one of the giants, even within California. Surely nobody would argue with Kerr's contention that the multiversity "has become a prime instrument of national purpose." And when we realize that "six universities received 57% of federal research funds in a recent year, and twenty universities received 79%," that the knowledge industry as a whole constitutes 29 percent of the gross national product and is growing at a rate twice that of the rest of the economy, when we realize all this, we must recognize that the slogans "Student Power" and "Faculty Power" are, to say the least, inadequate. The only adequate slogan for control over an institution this central to our society is "Power to the people."

The multiversity is at one and the same time the highest form of the university of the bourgeoisie and the developing form of the university of the masses of the people. Like the other economic institutions of overdeveloped capitalist society, it is in the process of shifting from control by private enterprise through control by monopoly capital to control by the state. Though this state calls itself a public state, it is in fact an instrument of monopoly capital, safely under the control of the corporate rich. Its internal contradictions, however, do indeed prepare the way for a true government of the people. The multiversity presents the contradictions of this stage of development in striking form. Of all the major institutions in the society, it perpetuates the most frankly elitist values; yet it does so behind a totally egalitarian facade. It is the wellspring of articulate bourgeois liberalism and the seedbed of the most outspoken radicalism. Its virtually all-white and overwhelmingly male faculties profess the most democratic of bourgeois ideals to a student body now one-third female, becoming racially mixed, and rapidly widening in class origin. It is an essential bulwark of the status quo and a source of fundamental social, economic, and political changes. And the question Who should run the universities? is seriously debated at a time when it should be perfectly clear that no group can control the universities without controlling society as a whole.

Who now actually does run the universities? As far as ultimate power, the answer is very simple: the owning class runs the universities, much as they run the rest of society. . . .

The actual work of capitalist society is not done by the owning class, and the working class knows this, dimly in prosperous times, acutely in periods of economic stress. Work, as well as ownership, is at least a potential source of power, and the working class recognizes this in practice: its main effective tactic is withdrawing its labor. By challenging the legitimacy of the, power of the owning class, the working class makes possible a challenge of the source of that power—private property.

In the university, useful labor is performed by students, faculty, administrators, and non-teaching workers, both blue- and white-collar. Some of the tools are physical, such as books, classroom buildings, equipment, etc.; these are made by the interdependent labor of intellectuals and industrial workers, both directly and by using capital created by other workers. The main tool and the main product is knowledge, which in its totality is nothing less than the most important product of all previous humanity. There are at least three distinct kinds of knowledge used and produced in the university. First is useful knowledge or "know how," which creates, among other things, factories, industries, power, and empires. This kind of knowledge can be owned, at least temporarily, a fact attested to by the patent office, by the laws governing ownership of industrial research, and by the security classifications of the Department of Defense. The other two kinds may be called ideological knowledge and cultural knowledge; these belong to the class that produced them and serve the interests of that class. Ultimate power and legal control over all the physical tools and products of the university lie in the hands of the corporate elite, both directly, through their total occupation of the boards of trustees and regents, and indirectly, through the political apparatus they control. The same is true for the useful knowledge, which becomes the property of either corporations or the state. And by having ultimate control over the procedures and principles of hiring, the trustees and regents so far have been able to make sure that only the culture and ideology of their own class and of previous ruling classes can be propagated in their universities. . . .

The agents of the trustees' and regents' power are the administrations of the various universities. Of course their role is a good deal more complicated than that. University administrators are rather Janus-headed figures, with one face that looks like a corporate industrial manager and another that resembles the pure academician.

In the most typical nineteenth century industrial enterprises, there was no question who ran the show. The owner was the boss. He either ran things directly or hired managers to transmit his directives. As we all know, that typical enterprise evolved into a joint-stock company, then into a huge complex corporation, and now into a labyrinthine structure of many corporations, interlocked with each other and with the state. The corporate conglomerate is, like the multiversity, a characteristic form of the military-industrial-educational complex of developing state capitalism. As this evolution has taken place, the role of owner and the role of manager have become redefined. The managerial function has gained increasingly independent power, while, at the same time, it has become increasingly dependent on complicated objective conditions. It is not the owner who tells the manager what to do; both of them take their orders from the internal dynamics of the bureaucratic and mechanical labyrinths they "run." And although some large and important decisions are still made by the owners, the day-to-day operating decisions are made by the managers. Does this group constitute, as some have argued, a distinct new class, the managerial class, having fundamental contradictions with the owning class? Clearly this is not so in corporations, where the big managers get to be, as a condition of their employment, part owners. In the university, this does not totally apply. Is there then a class distinction—and therefore a fundamental contradiction—between the administration and the board of regents or trustees? I think not. First of all, though the administration runs the university in the sense of managing or administering it, that is, making the day-to-day operating decisions, it is thereby implementing purposes over which it has no control. In practice the administration cannot question the premises of the multiversity, and to do so would be—quite literally—unthinkable for most administrators. They draw their identity, like the salary, from the class they serve and into which they merge. They are not merely the surrogates of the owning class, for as nineteenth century private enterprise capitalism evolves through corporate capitalism into state capitalism, the owning class as such becomes superfluous. Managing increasingly becomes the effective equivalent of owning and finally substitutes for it.

No contradiction between present managers or administrators and owners or trustees is a class contradiction, any more than contradictions between the management of Ford and General Motors are class contradictions, or, for that matter, any more than contradictions between the state capitalist managers of the Soviet Union and those of the United States are class contradictions. The class enemies of all these are their own working class and the peoples of the Third World. This is why the administrators of the American multiversity are as eager as their boards of trustees and regents to throw the full might of their institutions against the forces of what they call instability in the world and at home.

But the administration has limits placed upon it from other directions. Caught between the trustees or regents and the forces in rebellion against that very class, it often finds itself in the position of attempted mediator or buffer in class struggle. This is complicated by the fact that most administrators have their immediate origin in the faculty, a group itself torn by internal contradictions.

The faculty of the multiversity includes powerful businessmen, professional military officers, would-be medieval humanist scholars, scientists with independent contracts and dependent research teams, doctors, lawyers, and bohemian writers. According to some New Left theorists, the faculty belongs to the "new working class," but surely this might be true of only parts of the faculty, relatively small parts at the so-called "top" universities. Even those that do belong to the working class represent one of its most privileged and highest paid strata, and the other end of the spectrum shades off into the managerial and owning class, particularly in the schools of engineering and business. The salaries of professors are directly proportional to their contribution to production, to profit, and to the ideological and material defense of monopoly capitalism. But even professors of the humanities are now well paid in comparison to most of the working class; in the San Francisco Bay Area, in fact, their starting salary is almost as high as that of a policeman. (After doing my graduate work and teaching at Stanford for five years, my own take-home pay equalled what it had been as a lieutenant in the Air Force.) Extremely few faculty members at the prestige universities consider themselves members of the working class, but in the state colleges and junior colleges there is often a substantial minority who do so identify themselves, as evidenced by the rapid growth of trade unions among them.

Most professors, however, are both objectively and subjectively members of the middle and petty bourgeoisie. As such, they share a very common idea of their class—that class struggle, if it exists at all, involves other people and springs from their irrationality. Hence the liberal idea that conflict comes from people not communicating well enough. As a sub-class, professors fervently cling to the belief that they, perhaps alone of all groups, are above that sordid field of confused struggle. This belief justifies their very reason for existence, for they believe that they alone can offer a neutral, objective, classless, more or less *truth*ful view of the other classes, of the history of their struggles, and of the culture which springs from this history and gives it comprehensible form. Their pursuit of such pure truth incidentally commits them to lives where they associate only with other members of the middle and petty bourgeoisie, particularly other "professional" people. Though they may advocate integrated schools and housing, they live in all-white ghettoes and send their children to tokenly integrated schools. Though they may be sympathetic to workers in the abstract, they probably do not know a single blue-collar worker personally, and therefore lament that the industrial working class is "content with their car and TV sets."

Only inside the university do the professors act on what they understand as class relationships, their relationships to the students and, sometimes, to the administration. Toward the upper level of the internal university hierarchy, professors are in a somewhat ambiguous position. There is a good deal of mobility from the faculty into the administration. In many universities administrative *labor* is spread out among the faculty. Professors do not generally question the premises of the university, and therefore do not often object to having little or no say about fundamental decisions. There is commonly a simmering resentment against administrative control over salaries, but the faculty gets more upset with the administration when it permits their security and privileges to be exposed to the onslaught of the unwashed masses, the students. For one thing all faculty members have in common, whether they sit in the highest councils of Washington or whether they are struggling humanist scholars straight out of graduate school: they have more direct power over more people's lives than exists almost anywhere in our society, with the possible exception of the military. . . .

The demands of advanced capitalism for a highly educated labor force, the population explosion within the generation reaching college in the sixties, and the vastly expanded financial support from foundations, industry, state and federal government have all combined to change the internal class composition of the faculty. There has been wide recruiting of young people who before could not have been able to afford degrees, much less been able to penetrate the country club faculties. The wider class basis of the younger faculty creates new contradictions. Why, many of us do not even consider ourselves gentlemen. And some of us are beginning to identify clearly and openly not only with the American working class but with all the peoples of the world most oppressed and exploited by American imperialism. On the surface this looks like a generational gap. Last month at the annual convention of the Modern Language Association, which consists of college and university teachers of all the modern languages and literatures, a serious rebellion took place. It was a rebellion against the establishment, against tradition, against the prevailing ideas of what a professor should be, and against American imperialism. . . . All those who think that this conflict is primarily between age groups and that we will outgrow our present ideologies overlook two things—the past and the future. For such a rebellion is without precedent, and the forces behind it are growing each year. I do not support "faculty power" because it is abstractly legitimate, but only because and only insofar as it represents the power of the exploited and oppressed. . . .

Advanced monopoly capitalism, by making huge quantitative changes, increases the role of students qualitatively. Its demands for highly skilled manpower, and virtually only highly skilled manpower, force it to educate unprecedented numbers of students to unheard-of levels of proficiency in understanding and manipulating abstract knowledge. And the demands of managing and rationalizing a worldwide empire create even greater needs. In all previous societies, university students were a chosen elect, the sons of the ruling class plus the most able sons of the professional and middle classes. Now university students are the sons and *daughters* of all classes except the lowest, which in the United States means racial minorities. And at this moment, of course, even the sons and daughters of blacks, Chicanos, and Indians are beginning to move into the universities. When we are talking about "students" we are now talking about a significant portion of the entire population. The number of college students now approximately equals the country's total armed forces plus its three largest unions (Teamsters, UAW, and United Steelworkers).

The widening class background of the younger faculty is amplified several times over among the students. So the most significant development now taking place among the student left is the rapid rise of a working-class orientation. . . .

On the campus there exists another group, rarely if ever thought of as a possible co-ruler of the university—the nonteaching employees. The lower strata of this group—janitors, gardeners, maintenance men, kitchen workers, maids, clerks, typists—include a far higher proportion of racial minorities, live in neighborhoods removed from the faculty and administration but often shared with students, particularly graduate students, and are the most direct representatives of the super-exploited. Generally these people are looked upon by all other groups within the university—administration, faculty, and students—as not being a part of the university. In fact, they come close to being invisible. As they organize, one demand that they will raise is that the educational facilities of the university be made available not only to their children but to them. If they were to win this demand, the effects would be extremely radical. Their presence in an economics class or a history class would *force* a change in the content of the course. . . .

In the final analysis, there can be only one radical position: the overwhelming majority of people, that is, the working class, must run the universities. . . .

JOHN HOWARD

It is my judgment that it must be the president who runs the university. I believe it is essential that the man who holds that office be a highly capable scholar whose particular academic capacity is as a comprehensivist. . . .

There are numerous pressures and demands in higher education today which not only direct the time and the energy of the president away from the genuine business of academic statesmanship, but which seem to be changing the concept of the presidential office from that of educational philosopher to that of professional manager. This is, I believe, a vicious circle. The less time the president devotes directly to the educational mission of his own institution, the more the problems multiply which demand his time on other matters.

The primary and consuming work of the university president should be as first scholar of the faculty, doing his creative work in understanding how his university can best serve mankind, in analyzing and anticipating the changes in society so that the educational services will be dealing with what is and will be, rather than what was.

The president also has heavy teaching assignments. It is his continual responsibility to teach his colleagues in the faculty, student body, and administration the concepts that underlie university policy and think through with those colleagues how their large decisions relate to those policies and how they can best be implemented. He also bears a critically important teaching task in his relationship to the trustees. If their decisions are to strengthen the university, then he must have helped them to understand what is at issue.

It may be that some university presidents suppose that they should not only be the principal agent between trustees and campus personnel, but should also be a buffer to keep the two groups as far apart as possible and filter out those thoughts and comments from the one side that would be abrasive to the other. On the contrary, I think the president has an obligation to inform the trustees fully and candidly of the whole range of complications with which he must deal. To his trustee "classes" he should bring "guest speakers" from the student body and faculty who can articulate the differing views on the issues before the board. The continuing education of the trustees is in the hands of the president.

The president also is the teacher of the general public. It is he who must explain what the university is doing, why it is valid, why it is important, and why the services provided by his institution deserve ever-increasing financial support. He must not only be clear and persuasive on the theory of his university but must be armed with illustrations from the classroom and laboratory and student programs to support his case.

I wish to suggest that present difficulties and dilemmas faced by universities may, in large part, be the result of the transition from the philosopher-president to the campus-troubleshooter-and-all-purpose-advisor-and-distinguished-director-of-distant-enterprises president. . . .

No committee or group can make the judgments which are required every day to keep a university running. No committee or group can keep itself sufficiently informed about the interactions and frictions among university personnel or be familiar enough with the relative importance of their requests to know when to say, "Yes," and when to say, "No," and when to ask for more information in order to keep the whole system working together. And no committee can maintain the consistency of decisions which has to prevail in a human agency.

To summarize, it is the president who must run the university. He is subordinate to the trustees and must work within the limits and toward the objectives they prescribe. But, if he is a competent president, their prescriptions will most often be what he has recommended.

To the faculty will be delegated that authority which is properly theirs. The president will do his utmost to support them in their work according to their judgments, but when their actions conflict with university policy, or when faculty interests are at odds with the interests of students, or security guards, or other university personnel, it is the president who is the last echelon of mediation or judgment.

In running the university, the president's preeminent roles are as theorist, interpreter, implementer and judge of the purposes of the institution.

BRUCE FRANKLIN'S RESPONSE TO JOHN HOWARD

Given the fact that I think most people here, as Dr. Howard very frankly says, are not conversant with Marxism, I would like to make something very clear. Marxists do not say "capitalism is bad; communism is good." They say capitalism is good up to a point, that it is capitalism which, through competition, yes, has released the productive resources that enable man to meet his material needs, that we had to go through capitalism. It produced a technology which was fantastic. Marx described capitalism's constant revolutionizing of production, which remains very important. Marxism is not for some static utopia. But when capitalism develops to a certain point its internal contradictions make it increasingly irrational.

I further would argue that the bourgeois university is good insofar as it has developed, insofar as it has been able to meet some real human needs on a large scale. I am not for going back to some primal, beautiful university that never existed. As a Marxist, I see my obligation to give an analysis of the processes of change that are going on within that university itself; my argument was pointed to certain actual basic changes. One, you have vastly increased and increasing enrollment, which means a widening class basis for the student body and also a widening class basis for the younger faculty. Then you have—and this is not reversible—an increasing inter-penetration of the giant university, the multiversity, with the other major economic and political and social institutions of the society.

At the same time you have a rapidly generating technology within that university. Another change which is a product of this is that you have rapidly increasing demands being made on the university, demands of widening numbers of people to be serviced by the university, and to participate in the university as students but also as people who make decisions about what that university should be doing.

My answer to the question: Who should run the university? is that analysis of the actual processes that I see going on. (Applause.)

8. H. Bruce Franklin,
Back Where You Came From, 1975

Following his return from France in the fall of 1967, Franklin's outspoken and unflagging public criticism of Stanford's "direct involvement in the Indochina War" antagonized university administrators, trustees, and many faculty members, although his own English department almost unanimously (one abstention) voted his promotion to full professor in the fall of 1969. The administration "vetoed" that recommendation. He was viewed as a kingpin in anti-CIA demonstrations, in the demonstrators' siege of the Stanford Research Institute Center for Counterinsurgency in Southeast Asia, and in a "disruption" of a speech by Henry Cabot Lodge, when sitting silently with his son on his lap caused offense.

Franklin's account of the immediate cause for his firing is reprinted here, including an additional quotation from the decision of the faculty board advisory to the president that recommended his dismissal.

Pages 3–4, 31–33 from *Back Where You Came From: A Life in the Death of the Empire* by H. Bruce Franklin, Copyright © 1975 by H. Bruce Franklin. Reprinted by permission of HarperCollins Publishers. Further reading: VI, 1, 9–10.

For my role in the protest against the university's direct involvement in the Indochina War, I was suspended and banished by injunction from the campus for seven months prior to any hearing. The hearing itself lasted six weeks and generated five thousand pages of transcript. It was held before the Advisory Board, whose function was to "advise" the president, who had brought the charges.

I was unanimously convicted on only one charge —making a speech on February 10, 1971, advocating a "strike," or rather "a voluntary boycott," "to shut down the most obvious machinery of war" at Stanford, beginning with the computer. The speech was declared to have "urged and incited" people "towards disruption of University functions and shut down of the Computation Center." It was ruled irrelevant whether these were legitimate functions of the university or whether, even according to Stanford's own rules, the Computation Center ought to be temporarily shut down.

No laws were broken by the demonstrators at the Computation Center. In fact, they did not even break any Stanford regulations. None of the demonstrators was ever prosecuted by Stanford or in court. But the administration called a hundred-man police riot unit to the campus to break up the peaceful, noncoercive, lawful demonstration that took place inside the Computation Center. The demonstrators left the building before the police entered, and then stood around talking to other people on the lawns outside. The police illegally declared all people in the two-block area of the computer to constitute an unlawful assembly, threatened everybody with immediate arrest, and poised to charge. My unsuccessful efforts to get two official faculty observers to stay on the scene and to convince the police not to attack were defined as urging

and inciting people not to disperse, a charge upheld by a 5-2 vote, with even the chairman of the Advisory Board and one other member acknowledging that I was merely exerting legal rights and attempting to prevent violence by the police.

Finally, I was charged for making a speech at a rally that night which allegedly "urged and incited students and other persons present to engage in conduct calculated to disrupt activities of the University and of members of the University community and which threatened injury to individuals and property." It was never specified what "conduct" I "urged and incited," what "activities" this conduct was calculated to disrupt, or how that conduct threatened injury to anybody or anything. The faculty board found me guilty anyhow, again by a 5-2 vote, this time basing their decision primarily on an earlier speech that the administration had officially declared to be "not contended by the University to be inciteful at all." The majority of the faculty board admitted that this speech was an effort to persuade people new to the movement to vote for the demand "Free All Political Prisoners," but found it criminal anyhow because "his way of undertaking this persuasion was itself inflammatory": "He made assertions of such hostile content in such an angry manner regarding the University and the police that . . .they must surely have intensified the resentment of many persons favorable to the 'movement' and thereby raised the probability of violent actions later." Earlier that day Stanford University had brought in over a hundred riot police in order to protect its ability to plan an invasion of North Vietnam. These police, according to uncontested testimony at the hearing, had indiscriminately beaten students, professors, and workers. A professor who stated those facts that night in an "angry" or "hostile" manner must be thrown out of the university.

The five-man majority of the Advisory Board had summed up the case in these terms:

> Professor Franklin asserts that the university's actual function is to serve as a training and research center for the maintenance of an imperialistic hegemony over the "Pacific Basin Empire"; yet to most of his colleagues, that is a bizarre mischaracterization. Thus the basis of a pattern of conduct is itself subject to conflicting interpretations, depending upon the perception of reality from which it is being described.

Agreed. And, as the science of Marxism demonstrates, perception of reality is determined primarily by class relations to the means of production. Two members of the seven-man board voted not to fire me. I do not think it a coincidence that these were the only two not primarily dependent on government and corporation financing of their work. The only humanist of the seven—and the most innocent—was Robert McAfee Brown, Professor of Religion, whose definition of the business of the university is a mere anachronism (as out of date as Cardinal Newman's 1852 "The Idea of the University"):

> I believe very strongly that, however much I and many of my colleagues may disagree with what Professor Franklin says or how he says it, Stanford University will be less a true university without him and more of a true university with him. I fear that we may do untold harm to ourselves and to the cause of higher education unless, by imposing a penalty short of dismissal, we seek to keep him as a very uncomfortable but very important part of what this University, or any university, is meant to be.

When the president's advisory board arrived at this decision to fire me from my tenured associate professorship at Stanford because I was not a suitable case for "rehabilitation," they explained that the cause of my incurability lay in my "perception of reality." (It is worth noting that one of the five gentlemen who wrote this decision was then chairman of the Department of Psychiatry.) With sadness for me and concern for the security of Stanford, they pointed out that my "perception of reality . . .differs drastically from the consensus in the university." Then they went on to outline this "perception of reality," which they elsewhere characterized as "bizarre":

> In his opening argument Professor Franklin proclaimed deep convictions about the evils of American foreign and domestic policy and about the inevitable influences of our socio-economic system in shaping that policy. Essential to this perception is a mistrust of the allegedly intricate interrelationship between the economic power of America's "ruling class" and the maintenance of policies that are imperialistic abroad and oppressive at home. Of crucial importance in the present case is his expressed view that the university, run by and for this ruling class, possesses a substantial institutional guilt for the ongoing prosecution of those policies. . . .

9. Franklin v. Leland Stanford University, 1985

Not until the last day of 1985 would the Franklin affair finally be settled, at least for Stanford, when the California Supreme Court denied a hearing on the decision by the California Court of Appeals three months earlier. The Appeals Court had upheld the trial court's verdict that Franklin not be reinstated at Stanford. The suit against Stanford was first entered on Bruce Franklin's behalf by the Northern California American Civil Liberties Union on First Amendment grounds. In examining this case, the appellate judges visited many First Amendment federal court precedents, mainly omitted here from this abbreviated reprinting.

Meanwhile, Franklin, having been turned down by the Regents of the University of Colorado for a position there, secured a tenured post at Rutgers University, Newark, where he became The John Cotton Dana Professor of English and American Studies.

Franklin v. Leland Stanford Junior University, 172 Cal. App. 3d 322: 218 Cal. Rptr. 228 [September 1985]: 322, 328, 341–43, 346–50. Further reading: VI, 7–8, 10.

September 20, 1985
OPINION BY: AGLIANO, J.

This appeal by plaintiff H. Bruce Franklin challenges the judgment of the trial court upholding plaintiff's dismissal by his former employer, Leland Stanford Junior University (University). The underlying dispute dates back to a time of protest against the Vietnam war. More specifically, it concerns plaintiff's conduct on February 10, 1971. He was then, as he described himself, a leader of the local antiwar movement, his stature deriving partly from his tenured position as an associate professor of English. This action, filed August 15, 1972, challenges his dismissal from that position. Plaintiff's major contentions are that his conduct was protected by the First Amendment and the University regulations authorizing his discharge were unconstitutionally vague. We reject these contentions and the others discussed below. . . .

It is clear that the constitutional freedom to speak does not license a teacher to substantially disrupt and interfere with the normal operations of his or her employer, whether they be instruction, research, or administration. Expressive conduct which may not justify criminal or civil liability may be the subject of employer discipline. (*Franklin* v. *Atkins*, 409 F.Supp. 439, 451; see *Mabey* v. *Reagan*, 537 F.2d 1036, 1046.)

Plaintiff's expressive conduct in our view was well out of constitutional bounds. Speech which results in disruption, which materially interferes with school activities, or impairs discipline is not constitutionally protected against an employer's response. (See *Adcock* v. *Board of Education*, 10 Cal.3d 60, 65, 68–69.) That description fits plaintiff's White Plaza speech and his interference with the police dispersal order at the Computation Center.

Turning first to the latter incident—the occupation of a university building by demonstrators itself was a disruption of normal research operations. Plaintiff perceived a potential for violence in the ensuing face-off between the police and the protestors. His loud, emotional disagreement with the police dispersal order, particularly in light of his acknowledged leadership role in protest activities, could only serve to prolong the existing state of campus disorder. His example caused some members of the crowd to disregard the order. His aggressive, challenging conduct was a material interference with an attempt to restore normalcy to the campus. . . .

Plaintiff makes other arguments about the Computation Center incident which simply miss the point of *Pickering* and *Tinker* and fail to appreciate the obligations of his status as a university professor. . . .

We turn next to the White Plaza speech. The expressive behavior was more purely speech and it occurred in "a forum for free and open discussion of the problems vitally affecting the institution and its members." (*Adcock* v. *Board of Education*, 10 Cal.3d

60, 68.) The speech alone did not materially disrupt the University's operations. However, we find it to be significantly different from the type of criticism of school policies found protected in cases like *Adcock*. There, no showing was made that the teacher's "speeches disrupted classrooms, teaching efficiency, or in any way led to a potentially dangerous situation at the school." (*Id.*, at p. 69.)

We need not, as plaintiff suggests, engage in a meticulous textual analysis of his speech to understand it. It contained more than abstract disagreement with school policies; it was an exhortation to disruptive action. He challenged the students to assume a leadership role in the antiwar protest movement, describing the impact of a student strike on working people the previous year. He ridiculed a student strike as a "fake" in which they risked nothing, but asked them to set an example. Plaintiff, a leader in the antiwar protest movement, called for a strike to shut down some of the University's activities, specifically the Computation Center. He now characterizes his identification of the Computation Center as a target as "an afterthought," but this revisionism is a distortion we reject.

Plaintiff's advocacy of a shut down of the Computation Center in this context was directed to and likely to incite immediate material disruption of the University's work and consequently was entitled to no constitutional protection against his employer's response. . . .

Plaintiff argues he was dismissed for his "perception of reality," not merely for his unprotected expressive conduct. The 1972 faculty advisory board acknowledged an awareness of the difference between plaintiff's set of perceptions and those of the majority of Stanford faculty members. They took into account his different perception of reality as it explained his pattern of conduct in considering what sanction to impose. The Board stated, however: "The real issue in these hearings is Professor Franklin's behavior on the offenses charged, not his political views." The 1980 faculty advisory board echoed these concerns. They considered his "point of view" insofar as it included "encouragement of violent or coercive tactics against the members of the university community."

Healy v. *James*, 408 U.S. 169 . . . , validates these considerations by the faculty board. The court held that a student group could not be denied recognition simply because the university president found its philosophy abhorrent. . . . On the other hand, if the group announced its unwillingness to be bound by reasonable school rules governing conduct, nonrecognition might be justified. . . . Similarly, nonrecognition could be justified if there were support for the conclusion that the group "posed a substantial threat of material disruption." . . .

The faculty board thus was entitled to consider plaintiff's viewpoint insofar as it promised a repetition of disruption. Severing the employment relationship was determined necessary to preserve

campus order. Plaintiff does not challenge the severity of the discipline, but only its basis. . . .

Having independently reviewed the record, we conclude plaintiff has not established defendants terminated him for any constitutionally impermissible reasons. . . .

School regulations need not be spelled out with the precision of a criminal code. . . . We find the Stanford regulations at issue constitutionally clear as interpreted by the faculty advisory board to apply to plaintiff's conduct.

The judgment is affirmed.

10. Donald Kennedy, *Academic Duty,* 1997

The painstaking and protracted hearings over Bruce Franklin's dismissal from Stanford were conducted by the seven-member faculty board advisory to President Richard Lyman. The proceedings were chaired by Donald Kennedy (1931–), a professor of biological sciences who later would serve in federal agencies and become provost at Stanford (1979–80) and then president of the university (1980–92). Kennedy was one of two on the advisory board who voted against dismissal. Beyond the following brief account, Kennedy noted elsewhere in his book that these public hearings dealt mostly with the rights of faculty members while faculty responsibilities, "though not pertinent to the specific charges," were "largely ignored." Franklin's seminar course on Melville "often met at the site of various political 'actions,' and . . . the subject matter often had no detectable relationship to Melville." Thus Franklin did not meet Kennedy's "germaneness test" for a faculty member who expresses personal views in the classroom (*Academic Duty,* 67–69).

Reprinted by permission of the publisher from *Academic Duty* by Donald Kennedy, 131–34, Cambridge, Mass.: Harvard University Press, Copyright © 1997. Further reading: Rebecca S. Lowen, *Creating the Cold War University: The Transformation of Stanford* (Berkeley, 1997); and VI, 7–9.

In the late 1960s new challenges to the principles of tenure protection appeared. Institutions were faced not just with the occasional instance of professorial incompetence or moral turpitude, but with faculty members who joined with students to challenge the values and sometimes the rules of those institutions.

In a case at Stanford in 1971–72, President Richard Lyman proposed to fire a tenured professor of English, H. Bruce Franklin, on the basis of four specific charges. The most serious alleged that he had led a student occupation of the university's computer center, subsequently urged a crowd outside the building to ignore a police order to disperse, and later made a speech in which he incited students and others to make "people's war" against the university.

Because this was a celebrated case that drew heavy media attention, and because it was so controversial inside Stanford, the huge investment of effort made to resolve it fairly was probably a good one. But in fact that investment was required by the level of due process guaranteed under the university's rules, which, like those in most institutions, afford extensive protections to faculty defendants. At Stanford the rules require that the president present formal charges to the faculty member accused, and propose a penalty that could range from formal censure through fines or restrictive conditions to discharge. If the faculty member accepts the penalty, that is the end of it. But if he or she does not, then the Advisory Board—a seven-person faculty committee elected from across the university to evaluate appointments and promotions—hears the case and makes its recommendation to the president. The faculty member may elect to have the hearing public or private.

In the Franklin case the president proposed dismissal. Franklin, a self-proclaimed revolutionary with an active campus movement behind him, elected to have the hearing public—and promised to use it as an occasion for making his views and those of his followers widely known. A large classroom was converted to a hearing room capable of holding more than two hundred people, and at least in the beginning it was always full. Both the university and Professor Franklin were represented by counsel, the university by a patient litigator from the Los Angeles law firm of Tuttle and Taylor, and Franklin by a changing cast that initially included the well-known defense attorney Michael Kennedy and, for a time, Professor Alan Dershowitz of Harvard Law School (who withdrew promptly upon seeing a picture of Stalin above the defense table but invited himself back in as an *amicus* near the end). There were also a number of talented amateur volunteer lawyers! The hearings lasted six hours a day, six days a week, for six weeks; The Advisory Board heard from more than a hundred witnesses between disruptions and guerrilla theater, and after it was over had to sort through a million words of testimony. As the chairman of the Advisory Board at the time, I presided over the hearings. I learned that being a judge isn't easy—especially when you have neither bailiffs nor a sergeant at arms.

The Advisory Board consisted of unusually busy and committed scholars. One was the director of the world's largest linear accelerator. Two went on to become presidents of major foundations or universities. Three were department chairmen at the time. It seems almost inconceivable now that an academic community would invest such resources in so trying and unpleasant a task. But to all of us then it seemed as though the very fabric of academic life was under unbearable stress, and that cases such as this one would decide whether the great universities of this country could remain livable places.

The three main charges, having to do with the computer center occupation and its aftermath, all involved incitement. Because this was widely seen as a "speech case," the Advisory Board had to decide whether it would adopt the applicable Constitutional interpretations, as though Stanford were a state institution, or claim private status. We decided on the former course. Professor Franklin then argued that what he did—advocating occupation of the computer center, trying to get people not to disperse following a police order, and urging various actions against the university—was in fact constitutionally protected speech. The Advisory Board held to the contrary, finding that under the most liberal Supreme Court standard Professor Franklin's speech constituted incitement in that it increased the risk of imminent lawless action and injury to others. The board held that Professor Franklin's pattern of conduct in these incidents violated not only the Policy on Campus Disruptions but the general conditions regarding faculty conduct set out in Stanford's tenure policy. By a vote of five to two, the board recommended dismissal. The dissenters (I was one) did not differ with the majority on the basic speech issues, but believed that the university failed to sustain its burden of proof on two of the charges. They recommended serious penalties short of dismissal.

The American Civil Liberties Union (ACLU) of Northern California was persuaded to take Franklin's case into the courts, where it was argued that he had been dismissed for constitutionally protected speech. After a tortuous eight years of decision and appeal, during which every ruling went against the ACLU, the case was finally decided in the university's favor. Several years after the Advisory Board's decision, I was asked how I felt about my own investment of time and energy in the case. I replied that I thought I had wasted half a year of my life. That was in the late 1970s; peace had returned to the nation's campuses, and in some ways it seemed hard to recall what all the fuss had been about. Since then I have spent nearly three years in government and more than a dozen in university administration, and I have a different view of the matter. At Stanford, the Franklin case was influential in reshaping the faculty's view of its own role, leading to a new Statement on Faculty Discipline, adopted in 1972, in which more precise definitions of sanctionable activities are provided. More important, I now believe that this case and others like it proved that faculties can take hold of the values of their institutions, defend them successfully, and make a reality of the vision of the academy under even the most stressful challenges. The Franklin verdict, whether one agrees with it or not, represented a real triumph of due process. Thus it spoke volumes about the capacity of the faculty to fuse the different versions of university governance, reinforcing the communitarian vision while guaranteeing the institution's survival into the future. At this vital moment the faculty *were* the university.

Inquiries

11. Archibald Cox et al., *Crisis at Columbia*, 1968

Archibald Cox (1912–2004) was called to Columbia University in May 1968 to lead a committee of inquiry into the chronology and underlying causes of the "disturbances" that had wracked the university in the previous month. Serving with Cox on the commission were a sociologist, a physician, an attorney who had been a judge, and another professor of law, all from outside Columbia. The commission held its hearings for twenty-one days and heard seventy-nine witnesses. Its transcript covers 3,790 pages.

Long associated with Harvard University as student (A.B. 1934, LL.B. 1937) and professor at the law school (1946–76), Cox was also a prominent public servant as solicitor general in the U.S. Department of Justice (1961–65) and director of the Watergate Special Prosecution Force (1973). He was also chairman of Common Cause (1980–92). Among his several books on judicial matters were *The Warren Court* (Cambridge, MA, 1968), *Freedom of Expression* (Cambridge, MA, 1981), and *The Court and the Constitution* (Boston, 1987).

Archibald Cox et al., *Crisis at Columbia: Report of the Fact-Finding Commission Appointed to Investigate the Disturbance at Columbia University in April and May 1968* (New York, 1968), 189–99. Copyright © 1968 by Random House, Inc. All rights reserved. Abridged with the permission of Random House, Inc. Further reading: Ken Gormley, *Archibald Cox: Conscience of a Nation* (Reading, MA, 1997); Jerry L. Avorn et al., *Up against the Ivy Wall: A History of the Columbia Crisis* (New York, 1969); Roger Kahn, *The Battle for Morningside Heights: Why Students Rebel* (New York, 1970); Robert Liebert, *Radical and Militant Youth: A Psychoanalytic Inquiry* (New York, 1971); Walter P. Metzger, "The Crisis of Academic Authority," *Daedalus* 99 (Summer 1970): 568–608; Irwin Unger, *The Movement: A History of the American New Left, 1959–1972* (New York, 1974), ch. 4; I, 9; and VII, 2, 12, 14.

The April uprising started and grew haphazardly. As it developed to the final academic cataclysm, its entire character was altered.

The long series of turbulent demonstrations beginning in 1965, which were tolerated by most of the University community, leave a tragic sense of the inevitability of the final escalation. Packing the lobby of Hamilton Hall—even the somewhat ambiguous obstruction of Dean Coleman's liberty—was scarcely different from the earlier confrontation in John Jay Hall or the sit-in following the CIA demonstration. SAS's decision to evict the whites and barricade the doors in a demonstration of black student power—one of the key turning points—was a response to an occasion thrust upon the black students. With each successive day the uprising gathered its own physical and emotional momentum.

We reject the view that ascribes the April and May disturbances primarily to a conspiracy of student revolutionaries. That demonology is no less false than the naive radical doctrine that attributes all wars, racial injustices, and poverty to the machinations of a capitalist and militarist "Establishment." Student revolutionists within SDS planned turbulent confrontations and revolutionary tactics. They manipulated facts in ways that created distrust and bred unwarranted antagonism. There apparently was occasional talk of wider revolution to overthrow the present political system. A very few revolutionists may have been in dead earnest. More, we suspect, were half in dreamland, feverishly discussing romantic tactics but hardly contemplating realistic execution. Part of the responsibility for the disturbances rests upon the revolutionaries consciously seeking to subvert and destroy the University but their total number was small—much less than the full SDS membership—and their activities were only the catalyst that precipitated a deeper movement.

By its final days the revolt enjoyed both wide and deep support among the students and junior faculty and in lesser degree among the senior professors. The grievances of the rebels were felt equally by a still larger number, probably a majority, of the students. The trauma of the violence that followed police intervention intensified emotions but support for the demonstrators rested upon broad discontent and widespread sympathy for their position.

The record contains ample proof of this conclusion. The very number of students arrested in the buildings—524 Columbia students in the first police action—is convincing. Many more had been in the buildings earlier. Some of the latter were doubtless curiosity seekers. For others in both groups the affair probably had many of the elements of the once-traditional spring riots and subsequent "panty raids." But even after discount is made for those elements, the extent of active participation in violent and unlawful protest is significant.

The existence of broad underlying unrest is also shown by the progress of the seizures. The action of the black students in Hamilton Hall was entirely independent of SDS. The seizure of Avery Hall by architectural students was their own movement. The occupation of Fayerweather Hall, in which a large part of graduate study in the social sciences is centered, was apparently spontaneous; no evidence of an SDS connection has come to our attention.

Outside the buildings the militants enjoyed visible support in the form of the thousands who watched from various points on campus, most conspicuously at the Sundial. A campus poll reportedly boycotted by those in the buildings showed that 74 percent of the participants favored "end gym construction," 66 percent favored severing ties with IDA [Institute for Defense Analyses], and 37 percent even favored amnesty for all students involved in the demonstrations.

The events after the police "bust" point to the same conclusion. The emotions excited by the brutality must have polarized opinion. There would be a tendency to put unjust blame upon those who called for police intervention rather than those—chiefly from SDS—whose deliberate efforts to provoke disruptive turbulence made it almost inevitable that police action would he required. Despite these complex cross-currents, the extent and persistence of the ultimate reaction against the University Administration is adequately explained only by the presence of strong but latent dissatisfaction quickened by the violence of events.

For the future it is equally important to note that the support for the activists has come from the portions of the student body who are most energetically concerned with university and community affairs.

The avowed objectives of the April demonstrations, stripped of their context and symbolism, were inadequate causes for an uprising.

The University's IDA affiliation had little practical importance. It was being reviewed by the Henkin Committee as part of a larger study of Columbia's relations to outside agencies. There was not the slightest reason to doubt that the normal academic procedures could produce a reasoned and fair-minded decision upon the merits. The disruptive potential of the IDA affiliation at Columbia, as at other universities, was that it enabled the large part of the intellectual community, especially students, to transfer to the campus their intense moral indignation against the Vietnam war.

The gymnasium issue was more complex, but it too was a symbolic issue. At least some black students freely acknowledge not only that the issue was oversimplified but that the public gymnasium to be built by Columbia would be more beneficial to the community than the 2.1 acres of rocky parkland, *if* the project could be judged upon that aspect alone. But the project could not be judged out of the context of Columbia's relations with its poorer neighbors and society's treatment of racial ghettos.

The third issue, the discipline of the six IDA demonstrators, had somewhat greater substance. Although most students would probably have agreed that the disruptive manner of conducting SDS demonstrations was becoming intolerable, many students were antagonized by the manner in which the "no indoor demonstration" rule was promulgated, and the discipline was administered.

Since the rule came close to the area of free expression staunchly guarded by Columbia's liberal tradition, it was of intense concern to the entire University community. Nevertheless, the prohibition was promulgated by President Kirk without consultation with students, and apparently without prior discussion with faculty members. In fact, the rule ran contrary to the unanimous recommendation of a tripartite committee whose report the President withheld.

The rule, which was an obvious target for militants, was formulated in terms that hampered consistent administration and invited provocation.

Out of the 100 students who engaged in the March IDA demonstration, six SDS leaders were selected for punishment. It was difficult to persuade students that this was not a discriminatory selection even though the Dean's office explained that these six and no others were recognized.

The six IDA demonstrators were refused a public hearing and peremptorily punished. Although the older paternalistic procedures probably gave much greater protection to most student offenders, there is wide and justified campus support for the principles (1) that a student is no less entitled to due process of law than one charged with a public offense and (2) that students should share in disciplinary procedures as part of the right of participation in decisions affecting their interests.

Three among the purely internal causes of unrest especially impressed us.

1. At a time when the spirit of self-determination is running strongly, the administration of Columbia's affairs too often conveyed an attitude of authoritarianism and invited distrust. In part, the appearance resulted from style: for example, it gave affront to read that an influential University official was no more interested in student opinion on matters of intense concern to students than he was in their taste for strawberries. In part, the appearance reflected the true state of affairs. The machinery of student government had been allowed to deteriorate to a point where Columbia College had no student government. The Report on Student Life was not released for seven months until CUSC members threatened publication. The President was unwilling to surrender absolute disciplinary powers. In addition, government by improvisation seems to have been not an exception, but the rule.

2. The quality of student life was inferior in living conditions and personal association.

3. Columbia, like other universities, has scarcely faced the extraordinary difficulties that face black students in the transition from a society permeated by racial injustice to one of true equality of opportunity. We recognize, of course, the difficulty of immediately remedying such deficiencies as the paucity of black teaching and administrative personnel and of appropriate courses and counseling for all students, but the indisputable fact of alienation of our black students, with all that that fact entails, makes a more active and creative search for solutions particularly urgent.

The fabric of Columbia was twisted and torn by the forces of political and social revolution outside the University. Columbia's geographic situation symbolizes the relation between white and black, affluence and poverty, youthful reform and established order. The University's need for physical expansion in an urban center creates inescapable tensions but its relations with the community had further deteriorated because of its apparent indifference to the needs and aspirations of its poorer neighbors. The handling of the gymnasium controversy thus came, even somewhat unfairly, to epitomize the conflict between the spirit of the civil rights movement and the attack on poverty, on the one hand, and, on the other, the ways of an *ancien régime*. Energetic and idealistic students, alienated from the older generation by an extraordinarily wide gulf in manners and interests and offended by the plethora of human suffering, were drawn to the side of change. Where they were frustrated by the

massive anonymity of the government and the un-
manageability of the social system, they could strike
out at the more vulnerable University.

In like fashion, the University became the surro-
gate for all the tensions and frustrations of United
States policy in Vietnam.

The desire for student power, while scarcely articulated as a cause for seizing the campus buildings,
was a powerful element of the explosion. Discussion
since the uprising has focused upon the methods by
which students may exert more influence upon the
government of an institution of which they are vital
and integral parts. Participation in self-government
is a natural human desire that today's students feel
with greater urgency, particularly at institutions
with highly selective admissions policies because
they are much better educated than their predecessors, more sophisticated, in many respects more
mature, and more interested in social problems
than seeking out conventional careers. (Unfortunately, they are also much less disciplined.)

The hurricane of social unrest struck Columbia at a time when the University was deficient in
the cement that binds an institution into a cohesive unit.

Again, geography is a factor. The competing attractions of the exciting metropolitan area, coupled
with the housing problems that induce a majority of
the faculty to live outside Manhattan, operate as
centrifugal forces. Yet the dispirited quality of student life outside the classroom is not beyond the
University's power of influence.

The formal organization of both the administrative offices and the faculties apparently tends to discourage the cohesiveness that comes from shared
responsibility in matters of university concern. We
were struck by the constant recital of an apposition
between the Administration and the faculty as rival
bodies with separate interests, for it would seem to
us that on educational questions the two should be
essentially one. The lack of a University Senate and
the division of the professors and other teachers
into three or four faculties—quite apart from the
professional schools—where other universities have
a single Faculty of Arts and Sciences, apparently
discourages faculty participation in the formulation
of University policy and the improvement of student life. The central Administration to which the
full burden of the quality of student life is left is
not equipped for the duty. Far too few members
of the University family are closely involved, outside the classroom, in the constant informal enterprises and discussions by which the values of an
academic community are constantly reexamined
and those which stand the test are passed on to the
next generation.

Institutional coherence is also affected by the
presence or lack of a spirit of institutional self-confidence. Unhappily, despite her inherent strengths,
the spring crisis struck Columbia when her self-
confidence was shaken by the decline in relative

position in AAUP rankings of graduate departments, the exclusion from a Ford Foundation grant
for improvement of graduate studies, the resig-
nations of a number of senior professors, and the
Strickman filter incident.

The scale of the disturbances was greatly enlarged
in numbers, intensity and violence by the delay in
calling the police—from Thursday night until Monday night—which the Ad Hoc Faculty Group forced
upon the University officials. Although perhaps the
effort had to be made, there was never a significant
chance that the Group could negotiate a peaceful
withdrawal from the buildings. Forcing the delay,
by threats of physical interposition, increased the
likelihood of violence and magnified the reaction by
lending an air of legitimacy to use of the tactics of
physical disruption as means of forcing one view of
policy upon those who held another.

Our next five observations must be taken as a
unit. Language requires stating them one at a time,
but none can survive unless joined with the others.

A.

A university is essentially a free community of
scholars dedicated to the pursuit of truth and
knowledge solely through reason and civility.

A privately-endowed university depends upon
the experienced guidance of wise counselors and
managers both inside and outside academic ranks,
and also upon the financial and moral support of a
large, organized body of alumni and friends. Put
their vital contribution must never obscure the essential quality of the institution: the university is
a community of scholars, both teachers and students. Any tendency to treat a university as business
enterprise with faculty as employees and students
as customers diminishes its vitality and communal
cohesion.

B.

Resort to violence or physical harassment or obstruction is never an acceptable tactic for influencing decisions in a university. This principle does not
require notions of property or legality to sustain it.
It derives from three considerations.

First, force, harassment, and physical obstruction contradict the essential postulate that the university is dedicated to the search for truth by reason
and civility.

Second, resort to such physical coercion tends to
set in motion an uncontrollable escalation of violence. This is the plainest lesson of the rising cycle
of violence that began at Columbia with the Naval
ROTC demonstration in 1965 and culminated in the
brutality of April 30 and May 22. The sequence of
steps was not inevitable but each was the readily
predictable consequence of those that went before.

Third, the survival—literally the survival—of the
free university depends upon the entire community's active rejection of disruptive demonstrations.
Any sizeable group, left to pursue such tactics, can

destroy either the university by repeatedly disrupting its normal activities or the university's freedom by compelling the authorities to invoke overwhelming force in order that its activities may continue. The only alternative is for the entire community to reject the tactics of physical disruption with such overwhelming moral disapproval as to make them self-defeating.

This vital decision rests with the liberal and reform-minded students. They can save or destroy the institution.

C.

The acceptability of the foregoing principle depends upon organization of the scholarly community in ways that produce both loyalty and the relief of grievances. The government of a university depends, even more than that of a political community, upon the consent of all the governed to accept decisions reached by its constitutional processes. The consent of the dissenters depends partly upon their knowing that their views effectively entered into the process of consensus, even though they did not prevail. They must also be convinced that the opportunities for change are open and the goals and stance of the enterprise are sufficiently right for it to deserve their loyalty despite specific points of disagreement. Administrative intractability and resistance to change contribute to the breakdown of law and order.

D.

The student body is a mature and essential part of the community of scholars. This principle has more validity today than ever before in history. It is felt more keenly by a wider number of students, perhaps because of the increasing democratization of human institutions. As with all human activities, the wise division of functions and responsibilities must take into account the special skills or limitations of particular groups, as well as efficiency of operation. The process of drawing students into more vital participation in the governance of the university is infinitely complex. It cannot be resolved by either abstractions or tables of organization. It does not mean that issues must be settled by referenda. *We are convinced, however, that ways must be found, beginning now, by which students can meaningfully influence the education afforded them and other aspects of the university activities.*

The activist supporters of reform who voiced the grievances pressed by the rebels included many of the natural leaders among students—both political and intellectual leaders. They were deeply hurt by statements treating them merely as disloyal troublemakers aligned with a small band of rebels. While their own releases, for reasons of student politics, contributed to the polarization of opinion by their lack of civility, we have not the slightest doubt that the survival of Columbia as a leading university depends upon finding ways of drawing this very large and constructive segment of the student body, which supported the strike, back into the stream of university life where it can share in the process of rebuilding.

With participation, students will surely acquire a more sophisticated understanding of the universities' difficulties and complexities and of the necessary functions of the faculty and administration, the alumni, and the governing body. In the same process, the latter would come to an understanding they cannot otherwise acquire of the true needs and aspirations of students and values and shortcomings of current educational measures.

E.

We add only that the success of those who must follow this difficult course will depend in no small measure upon the willingness of parents, alumni, and friends to recognize that the April crisis is thus being converted into a creative source of renewal.

12. William Scranton et al., *Report of the President's Commission on Campus Unrest*, 1970

Established by President Richard Nixon on June 13, 1970, the President's Commission on Campus Unrest held thirteen days of public hearings, traveled widely for interviews, met fifteen times in executive session, and submitted its 231-page report on September 26, 1970. William W. Scranton (1917–   ), a graduate of Yale College and Law School and a former governor of Pennsylvania, was chairman of the commission. The other commissioners were the chief of police of New Haven, Connecticut, the editor of the *Christian Science Monitor*, the president of Howard University, a retired air force lieutenant general, an associate professor at Boston College, the dean of the Stanford Law School, a New Orleans attorney, and a junior fellow from Harvard. The commission's staff numbered over 125 people. Some of the academic members of the editorial staff or consultants who had already studied and written on student behavior in the 1960s were Nathan Glazer, Kenneth Keniston, Seymour M. Lipset, Martin Trow, and James Q. Wilson.

In its main report, the commission chiefly discussed national student protest, but it also took up the black student movement, considerations of university law enforcement, and government responses to protest. It later issued a full bibliography and special reports on the tragic episodes at Kent State University, Ohio, on May 4, 1970, and at Jackson State College, Mississippi, on May 13–14, 1970. All three reports were subsequently published as one volume. In view of the political atmosphere of the time and the short time in which its assignment was completed, the Scranton report in later years appears remarkably comprehensive.

William Scranton et al., *The Report of the President's Commission on Campus Unrest* (Washington, D.C., 1970), pp. 2–23, 27–30, 32–41, 43–47, 104–7. Further reading: Rebecca Jackson, *The 1960s: An Annotated Bibliography of Social and Political Movements in the United States* (Westport, CT, 1992); Thomas D. Clark, *Indiana University, Midwestern Pioneer*, vol. 3, *Years of Fulfillment* (Bloomington, IN, 1977): chs. 10, 11, chronicles one midwestern state university's difficulties with provincial and national excitement over sex research (Alfred Kinsey) and "un-americanism" in the McCarthy Era; Ernest L. Boyer, "Campus Climate in the 1980s and 1990s: Decades of Apathy and Renewal," in *Higher Learning in America, 1980–2000,* ed. Arthur Levine (Baltimore, 1983), ch. 19, examines contrasting decades after the 1970s; Arthur Marwick, *The Sixties: Cultural Revolution in Britain, France, Italy, and the United States, 1958–1974* (New York, 1998); and VII, 5, 11, 15–16.

THE BACKGROUND OF STUDENT PROTEST

Student discontent in America did not begin at Berkeley in 1964, or with the civil rights movement in the early 1960's. The history of American colleges during the early 19th century is filled with incidents of disorder, turmoil, and riot. These disturbances generally arose over poor food, primitive living conditions, and harsh regulations. Even today, such traditional complaints still spark many more campus protests than is generally realized. But though 19th century campus turbulence occasionally reflected a rebellion against the dominant Puritan religious ethic of the colleges of the time, student discontent here, unlike that in Europe, was largely apolitical.

This pattern began to change during the early years of the 20th century, when the first important radical political movement among American college students—the Intercollegiate Socialist Society—emerged. When the ISS flourished, it had more members, measured as a proportion of the total student population, than the Students for a Democratic Society (SDS) had in the late 1960's. During the 1920's, there were campus protests against ROTC, denunciations of the curriculum for its alleged support of the established system, and attacks on America's "imperialistic" foreign policy. During the Depression, there was still greater student discontent. Polls taken during the 1930's showed that a quarter of college students were sympathetic to socialism and that almost 40 per cent said they would refuse to take part in war. There were many student strikes against war, a few disruptions, and some expulsions.

Thus, it is not so much the unrest of the past half-dozen years that is exceptional as it is the quiet of the 20 years which preceded them. From the early 1940's to the early 1960's, American colleges and universities were uncharacteristically calm, radical student movements were almost non-existent, and disruptions were rare. The existence of this "silent generation" was in part a reflection of the Cold War. But as the tensions of the Cold War lessened, students felt less obliged to defend Western democracy and more free to take a critical look at their own society. Once again the American campus became a center of protest.

In its early phases, this reemerging campus activism was reformist in its aims and nonviolent in its tactics and pursued its goals by means of moral and political persuasion. But it did not persist in this form. For in the autumn of 1964, a critical series of events at the University of California at Berkeley transformed campus activism into the complex, changing phenomenon it is today.

The Berkeley revolt did not explode in a vacuum. It was preceded by a chain of developments during the late 1950's and early 1960's which helped to revive campus activism.

The most important of these was the civil rights movement. Since protest by black students has many unique features of its own, the distinctive character of black student protest is reviewed separately and at greater length elsewhere in this report. Here we need only emphasize that throughout the sixties, black college students played a central role in the civil rights movement. After four black students from North Carolina Agricultural and Technical College staged an historic sit-in at a segregated lunchcounter in Greensboro, North Carolina, in February 1960, the spread of sit-ins and other civil rights activities aroused the conscience of the nation and encouraged many students to express their support for civil rights through nonviolent direct action.

The peace movement, founded on an abhorrence of nuclear weapons, added another important element to the background of student activism. And in 1962, in Port Huron, Michigan, the Students for a Democratic Society reorganized itself with a statement that called on students to work for a society where all men would more fully control their own lives and social institutions. Under the banner of "participatory democracy," the SDS launched its early efforts to organize slum dwellers in northern cities.

Local events in the San Francisco Bay Area further prepared the way for the Berkeley revolt. In 1960 there had been a tumultuous demonstration, in which Berkeley students took part, against the House Un-American Activities Committee. Later, University of California students participated in a series of sit-ins, sleep-ins, shop-ins, and other actions to persuade Bay Area employers to hire Blacks. Like the HUAC demonstration, many of these involved off-campus confrontations with the police. And on campus, growing student and faculty dissatisfaction with higher education led to a movement to reform the university curriculum.

Thus by the autumn of 1964, there was growing student concern on the Berkeley campus that expressed itself both in protest demonstrations and in community service. Its focus was on the unresolved issues of war and peace, on civil rights, on the quality of education, and on the plight of the poor. Within this context of opinion and activity the Berkeley revolt broke out.

THE BERKELEY INVENTION

What happened at Berkeley was more than the sum of its parts. The events on that campus in the autumn of 1964 defined an authentic political invention—a new and complex mixture of issues, tactics, emotions, and setting—that became the prototype for student protest throughout the decade. Nothing quite like it had ever before appeared in America, and it is with the nature and evolution of this long-lived invention, in all its variations, that this Commission is concerned. . . .

Perhaps the most distinctive aspect of the Berkeley invention was its success in combining two impulses that previously had been separate in student disruption. The high spirits and defiance of authority that had characterized the traditional school riot were now joined to youthful idealism and to social objectives of the highest importance. This combination moved the participants to intense feeling and vigorous political activism and provoked from state or university officials reactions and overreactions that promised to keep the whole movement alive.

THE BERKELEY INVENTION EXPANDS

The mass media gave intensive coverage to the Berkeley events, and Americans were exposed for the first time to a new sort of news story—the tumultuous campus disruption. It was news in a traditional sense because it involved conflict and controversy. It was especially suitable for television because it was colorful and visually interesting. Night after night, television film of events on one campus carried the methods and spirit of protest to every other campus in the country.

Most student protestors, like advocates of all ages and points of view, welcomed television coverage. Many of them grew sophisticated in inviting it, and some of them undoubtedly played to it. Television news crews obliged them occasionally in an irresponsible fashion. But of far greater importance was the selective nature of the television medium itself, with its tendency to emphasize the most emotionally and visually exciting aspects of stories. Again and again, the cameras focused on whatever was most bizarre, dramatic, active, or violent. Few television or radio and newspaper reporters had the time or knowledge to explore the causes and complexity of campus protests.

The public reacted to Berkeley with concern and anger. In California and throughout the nation, campus events because controversial political issues. Many citizens believed the students had no reason to protest. Many were deeply opposed to the protestors' disruptive tactics. Many also criticized the faculty and administration for not taking a sufficiently "hard line." As student protest spread to more campuses and as its tactics became more disruptive or violent, citizens and political leaders called for action to prevent further campus disturbances.

Even in 1964–65, the year of the Berkeley disturbance, there was much more turmoil on campus than the media reported or the public knew of. Of 849 four-year colleges responding to a national survey that year, the great majority reported some kind of protest. But almost all of these protests were of the pre-Berkeley variety—traditional, single-issue protests, many of them conducted off-campus. More than a third of the campuses reported off-campus civil rights activities, and just over one fifth had on-campus protests against the Vietnam War. A variety of other issues stimulated protests on campus, including the quality of food, dress requirements, dormitory regulations, controversies over faculty members, censorship of publications, rules about campus speakers, and the desire for more student participation in university governance.

This early pattern of campus protest, then, reflected a high level of concern and activism diffused among a large number and broad range of distinct issues, which students rarely lumped together in criticisms of "the system." The university usually was subject to protest only over matters that were within its own control.

After 1964–65, however, this pattern began to change, and students increasingly related campus issues to broader political and social issues, and these broader issues to one another. As they did, the Berkeley invention began to spread to other campuses.

The growing frequency with which campus protest reflected the Berkeley scenario was largely the result of the emergence and development of three issues: American involvement in the war in Southeast Asia, the slow progress of American society toward racial equality, and charges of "unresponsiveness" against the federal government and the university and against their "repressive" reaction to student demands. These three issues gave campus protests their unifying theme. They were defined by protesting students as fundamentally moral issues, and this definition gave a tone of passion, fervor, and impatience to student protest.

The rapid escalation of American military efforts in Vietnam in 1965 made the Vietnam War one of the bitterest issues of the decade. This issue gave student activists an ever-increasing self-assurance and solidarity, for growing public concern over the constant escalation of the war seemed to legitimate the activists' early opposition. They redoubled their efforts; the Vietnam issue came to dominate their thoughts; and the previously scattered pattern of campus protest began to alter accordingly. . . .

As the escalation of the war in Vietnam proceeded and as a radical analysis of the wider society evolved, few campus issues were seen as *not* related to the basic problems of the nation.

Anger and despair over persistent racial injustice in American society provided a second and equally important focus for student protest. Racial prejudice—especially against Blacks but in some parts of the country equally cruel in its effect upon Mexican-Americans, Puerto Ricans, and other minorities—became increasingly unacceptable to many students. For many young Blacks in the mid-1960's the drive for equality and justice took a new form, symbolized by the concepts of Black power and Black pride. Young whites, even those who feared Black separatism, could not deny the justice of demands for equality.

Just as the Vietnam War was escalating, the civil rights movement underwent a fundamental change. The summer of 1964 was the last in which black and white students, liberals and radicals, worked together in a spirit of cooperation and nonviolence. But urban riots in Harlem, in Rochester, and in Watts divided many white liberals and moderates from those white and black militants who considered the riots legitimate rebellions. In 1965, Stokely Carmichael helped establish an all-black political party in Lowndes County, Alabama. During the next spring, he led those who were no longer committed to nonviolence in taking control of the Student Nonviolent Coordinating Committee. Subsequently, whites were expelled from the organization. In the summer of 1966, the cry of "Black Power" was first heard, and Huey Newton and Bobby Seale founded the Black Panther Party in Oakland, California.

These events marked a rapid erosion of the commitment by civil rights activists to nonviolence and to interracial political action—and had important consequences for campus protest. Militancy on southern black campuses increased during 1966 and 1967. In May 1967, students at Jackson State College in Mississippi fought with police for two nights. The National Guard was called out, and one person was killed. Militant actions by students at Howard University established a pattern that was to be repeated at black colleges and would spread to northern campuses as well.

Whereas earlier civil rights activism had generally attacked off-campus targets, the protests of black militants now were usually directed against the university itself. The university, they claimed, had helped to perpetuate black oppression through its admissions policies, its "white-oriented" curriculum, and its overwhelmingly white teaching staff. Black students found their cultural heritage slighted or ignored altogether. Their critique of the university intensified in the late 1960's, as predominantly white institutions began to admit black students in larger numbers. At Harvard, at San Francisco State, and elsewhere, black students organized groups dedicated to serving the larger black community. Their aim was to establish for Blacks an equal place in all parts of the university. Their attention thus focused not only on curriculum, faculty appointments, and student living conditions, but also on nonacademic matters like the university's hiring practices and its impact on local housing conditions. . . .

In addition to war and racism, a third issue—the issue of "repression"—began to emerge. The charge that the American system is basically "repressive" originated with radicals. But moderates began to give it credence as student protest encountered official force. Many students were "radicalized" by excessive police reactions to disorderly demonstra-

tions. Although major property damage in campus disruptions between 1960 and 1970 was almost entirely perpetrated by students, and although injuries to students occurred largely during confrontations which they themselves had provoked, students suffered more deaths than their adversaries. A growing number of students came to see themselves as "victimized" by law enforcement officials.

Events at the Democratic National Convention in 1968 had a particularly strong impact. Student protest at the convention was often disruptive, provocative, and violent, and it was met by a police reaction so brutal that the Walker Report called it a "police riot." Some students perceive "repression" also in the harassment of young persons with distinctive clothing or long hair and in police enforcement, which they believe to be selective, of the laws against marijuana and other drugs. . . .

COLUMBIA: THE BERKELEY INVENTION REVISED

At Columbia University in the spring of 1968, students participated in a tumultuous series of demonstrations, sit-ins, and disruptions. The Columbia revolt was important because it illustrated the spread of the Berkeley invention and the rising tide of student opposition to war and racial injustice. It was important also because the differences between it and the Berkeley revolt four years earlier indicated the growing disillusionment of many American students with the possibilities of change within the existing political system, their diminishing commitment to nondisruptive forms of protest, and the consequent evolution of the Berkeley scenario. . . .

The Berkeley invention, then, was substantially modified at Columbia and after. In its new form, it involved:

Destruction of property, papers, and records. At Columbia, university officials estimated that the 1968 incidents resulted in hundreds of thousands of dollars of property damage. On a number of campuses, ROTC buildings became popular targets for arson. Threats were made to destroy other university facilities unless the radicals' demands were met. At Columbia, the notes of an historian, the result of years of work, were destroyed by a fire that some alleged was maliciously set by student protestors. The rifling and copying of files became a more common occurrence in student-occupied buildings.

Counterviolence against protesting students by law enforcement officers. There were charges of police brutality at Columbia, and many of them had a basis in fact. Both before and after Columbia, every police bust gave rise to brutality charges. Far too often, they were true.

University unpreparedness. In spite of the increase in the number and intensity of student protests since Berkeley, university administrators rarely had formulated plans to deal with them. Convinced that their own campuses were immune to disruptive or violent protests, administrators were unprepared to cope with them when they occurred. In the midst of a crisis, some administrators believed that their only options were to do nothing or to call in the police. If they did nothing, they would allow the extremists to take over the campus; if they called in the police, they could not be sure the police would act properly.

Threats against university officials. In April 1968, black students at Trinity College in Hartford, Connecticut, held the school's trustees captive until their demands were accepted. In November 1968, students at San Fernando Valley State College in Los Angeles held officials at knife point. Anonymous threats against university officials and faculty members critical of student activities became more frequent.

Acts of terrorism. In February 1969, a secretary at Pomona College in California was severely injured by a bomb. In March 1969, a student at San Francisco State College was critically injured while attempting to place a bomb in a classroom building. On another occasion, a bomb was placed near the office of a liberal faculty member who opposed the "Third World" strike there. Later that year, a custodian at the University of California at Santa Barbara was killed by a bomb in the faculty club. The underground press proclaimed that the bombing in Madison, Wisconsin, on August 24, 1970, was part of a terrorist strategy. Earlier this summer, Assistant Secretary of the Treasury Eugene T. Rossides reported that, between January 1, 1969, and April 15, 1970, almost 41,000 bombings, attempted bombings, and bomb threats were recorded in the nation as a whole. Most could not be attributed to any specific cause. Of those that could be attributed to some cause, more than half—over 8,200—were attributable to "campus disturbances and student unrest."

University disciplinary action. Faced with increasingly disruptive or violent demonstrations, university officials began to take stronger disciplinary actions against disruptive and violent students. In 1969, for example, one study of disciplinary measures at 28 campuses reported that more than 900 students had been expelled or suspended, while more than 850 others were given reprimands. In a statement to this Commission, J. Edgar Hoover reported that disruptive and violent protests resulted in over 4,000 arrests during the 1968–69 academic year and about 7,200 arrests during 1969–70. At the University of Chicago, Harvard, and elsewhere, students were expelled from the university because of their involvement in building occupations. Others were suspended or placed on probation.

The influence of a new youth culture. Student unrest was increasingly reinforced by a youthful "counterculture" that expressed itself in new kinds of art and music, in the use of drugs, and in unorthodox dress and personal relations. Students were receptive to this culture's accent on authenticity and alienation. Many university communities began to attract nonstudents who also participated in the new youth culture. These "street people" in turn played a prominent part in some student demonstrations, violence, and riots, and complicated responses to campus unrest.

The growth of militancy and of political and cultural self-consciousness among minority group students other than Blacks, particularly among Puerto Ricans in the East and among Chicanos in the West and Southwest. Chicano and Puerto Rican student activists increasingly formed cohesive groups dedicated to asserting the claims of their communities upon the resources, curriculum, admissions policies, and concern of the university. While maintaining its separate identity, the movement of Spanish-speaking students sometimes made common cause with black and other minority students in a "Third World" coalition, as at San Francisco State and elsewhere.

Public backlash against campus unrest. The great majority of Americans were outraged by violence on American campuses. Such reactions against campus unrest were often intensified by a more general revulsion against the distinctive dress, life style, behavior, or speech adopted by some young people. Concerned over what they saw as an erosion of standards, a loss of morality, and a turn toward violence, many Americans came to believe that only harsh measures could quell campus disturbances. Many failed to distinguish between peaceful dissent and violent protest and called for the elimination of all campus unrest. Such public backlash made events on campus—in particular, protests, disruptions, and violence—a major political issue, both rationally discussed and irresponsibly exploited.

Legislative action. As a major political issue, campus unrest has been the subject of much legislation, most of it punitive. By mid-1970, over 30 states had enacted a total of nearly 80 laws dealing with campus unrest. Some laws require expulsion or withdrawal of financial aid from students committing crimes or violating campus rules; others require dismissal or suspension of faculty members for similar offenses. Criminal statutes passed in 12 states so far authorize jail sentences and fines for anyone who willfully denies free use of university property and facilities to members of the university community. The federal Higher Education Act of 1968 and a number of federal acts passed since 1968 bar federal financial aid to students who disrupt campus activities.

Indirect legislative reactions also became increasingly common. In some states, appropriations for higher education were delayed or denied; in others, funds were diverted from major universities and colleges to community colleges where there have been fewer protests. Public officials, regents, and trustees intervened far more actively in university decisions on curriculum and faculty appointments.

In the years since Berkeley and Columbia, an ongoing escalation of rhetoric and tactics has taken place. On the students' side, the incidence of violence, destruction of property, and disruption has risen steadily. On the part of civil authorities, the response to student protest has become harsher and at times violent. Some segments of the public also have become increasingly disenchanted with student protests of all kinds—and even with higher education itself. . . .

There are more than seven million college students in America today. Of these, only a handful practice terrorism. Indeed, some of the violence for which students are blamed is in fact perpetrated by nonstudents. Yet despite their small number, those students who have adopted violence as a tactic have caused much destruction and have evoked considerable sympathy from other students. In a few major campus areas—the San Francisco Bay Area, Madison, and Cambridge—they have done great damage. At Stanford, in April 1970, bands of "guerrillas" systematically terrorized the campus over a period of several nights, throwing rocks, breaking windows, and setting fire to buildings. After the August 1970 explosion at the University of Wisconsin, which killed a postdoctoral researcher and did $6 million worth of damage, underground newspapers all over the country gleefully reported that another blow had been struck against the "pig nation." Students at Madison expressed regret at the death of the young researcher—but some refused to condemn the bombing of the Army Mathematics Center which caused it.

Increasingly, the argument was heard that the use of violence is justified, whether to promote social change or to suppress campus unrest. Many Americans, confused and indignant over student unrest, concluded that only harsh and punitive measures could control students. Some Americans openly applauded police violence against students, arguing that they had only themselves to blame if they were killed by police during disruptive or violent protests. Such public attitudes clearly encouraged violent responses by civil authorities.

Violent and terroristic incidents naturally received wide publicity, whereas the peaceful protests and constructive efforts of the majority of student activists have received less exposure. College and university disciplinary actions against disruptive or violent protestors have not been publicized. The appearance of a group of nonviolent students, liberals and radicals, who have actively countered the violent style of the tactical extremists has also received little public attention.

A central theme, then, in the current history of student activism is the emergence of an ever larger and more active group of students who, reacting against the extremist tactics of other students, were moved to press for change—which they insisted must come through peaceful, nonviolent means.

An example of the new role of moderates occurred on May 1, 1970, when 12,000 people gathered on the New Haven Green in support of a group of Black Panthers on trial for murder. The precautions of police officials, the cooperation of Yale University administrators, and the careful plans of Yale students and faculty helped prevent all but minor disturbances. Moderates retained control, too, of the 1969 April and October moratoriums against the Vietnam War. Indeed, on many campuses, these events were the perfect expression of the moderates' style and strength.

The moderates had also brought this style to the campaign for Eugene McCarthy's presidential candidacy in 1968, to a number of marches on Washington—and, above all, to the spontaneous demonstrations for peace in May 1970.

Most of the activities during the student strike in May 1970 were peaceful, although there were some cases of disruption and violence. In many cases, state authorities took measures to avert violence. In California, Governor Ronald Reagan shut down for four days all 28 campuses of the University and State College systems. Guardsmen were sent onto the campuses of the Universities of Kentucky, South Carolina, Illinois at Urbana, and Wisconsin at Madison. There was trouble at Stanford, Berkeley, the University of Maryland at College Park, and other places. At Fresno State College in California a firebomb destroyed a million-dollar computer center.

But overall, violence by protestors was limited. University opposition to the combined issues of Cambodia, Kent State, and Jackson State had become so widespread that moderate protestors far outnumbered extremists, and the vast majority of protests remained peaceful. While nearly 30 per cent of U.S. campuses were involved in some degree of strike activity, only 5 per cent experienced violence.

The main reason for the general nonviolence is again to be found in the paradox of tactics: the massive number of moderates who had joined the protest, partly because of violent acts against students, then guaranteed by their involvement that the protests would be largely nonviolent. In part, moderates were able to do this because they outnumbered extremists. But more important were their decisions: on campus after campus, students, faculty, and administrators set up programs of action designed to provide politically viable alternatives to violent action.

Princeton University, for example, decided to reschedule its fall classes to allow students to work in political campaigns for the two weeks before election day. The Movement for a New Congress, an effort to elect antiwar candidates, spread from Princeton to other campuses. At scores of colleges, academic requirements were changed to give students time for political activities. These students canvassed homes, churches, and service clubs to present their views and gather signatures on antiwar petitions.

On May 9, 1970, more than 60,000 people, most of them students, assembled on the Ellipse in Washington for a peaceful antiwar demonstration. Thousands more went to Washington to lobby Congressmen, Senators, Cabinet officers, and even the President himself. For example, on May 11, over a thousand students and faculty members from Yale, led by President Kingman Brewster, Jr., talked with more than three hundred members of Congress or their aides.

Large delegations headed for the Capitol from Brandeis, from the University of North Carolina, from Haverford College, and from many other colleges.

Although all this nonviolent political activity indicated that the moderates had generally prevailed over extremists on the question of tactics, it is clear in retrospect that, on the question of ends, it was the radicals who were victorious. For years, radicals had been working to politicize universities, and in May 1970 entire universities were, in effect, mobilized against the policies of the present national administration. Students, faculty members, and administrators united to turn their attention away from scholarship to what seemed to them the far more urgent demands of politics and of keeping protest activities nonviolent. In May 1970, students did not strike against their universities; they succeeded in making their universities strike against national policy.

Furthermore, the May 1970 strike movement revealed how much the meaning of tactical "moderation" had changed since the events at Berkeley in 1964. In the early 1960's, few moderates would have imagined themselves participating in a student strike, much less in a disruptive sit-in. But as extremist tactics became more extreme and violent, moderate tactics became less moderate and began to include strikes and disruptions. Thus, in May 1970, moderate students and faculty members at hundreds of colleges and universities interrupted their normal academic activity—in some cases, with official university sanction—in order to devote their time and effort to political work against the war. In some places, university property was used for political activity and classes and exams were postponed or cancelled.

For the most part, violence was avoided. But some universities had been politicized for at least a few weeks; and, perhaps most important in the long run, there was growing public concern, anger, indignation, and outrage at the spread of campus unrest. . . .

THE STATUS OF BLACKS IN HIGHER EDUCATION

Education, and especially higher education, has served as an instrument of social mobility for every American ethnic group—except for black Americans and other similarly disadvantaged minorities.

Despite the nation's growing commitment to universal access to college education, and the openness of the American system of higher education, the socioeconomic status and inferior schooling of America's Blacks have prevented many Blacks from attending college. As in other areas of American life, the status of Blacks in higher education remains one of inequity and disprivilege. . . .

The *Time*–Louis Harris survey conducted in April 1970 revealed that 97 per cent of young Blacks planned to complete high school and 67 per cent expected to go to college.

Despite the strong faith in education and the extraordinary desire or expectation of young Blacks to attend college, current data indicate that only 58 per cent of black school children complete the eighth grade while 73 per cent of white school children do so. Only about 40 per cent of black teenagers complete high school, compared to 62 per cent of white teenagers; and only 22 per cent of black young people of college age are enrolled in college, compared to 38 per cent of white youth of college age.

Although black college enrollment has doubled since 1964, the proportion of Blacks among college students has not significantly increased: in 1964, black students constituted approximately 5 per cent of the total national enrollment; by 1969, the proportion of black students had grown to 6 per cent. And from 1940 through 1969, the percentage of black men and women in the age group 25–34 with four or more years of college increased less than the percentage of whites of the same age group. The gap between the level of higher education for Blacks and whites, so wide at the beginning of the thirty-year period, has grown even wider. That fact is more significant than the numerical increase in black college enrollment. . . .

We also cannot overlook the fact that in spite of the overwhelming desire and expectation of black youth to attend college, the end result is not equity and parity, but further disprivilege and disparity. In 1968, a black high school graduate earned less on the average ($5,801) than a white male who had completed only grade school ($6,452), and a Black who had completed four or more years of college earned less than a white who had completed only high school.

In sum, the status of Blacks in higher education adds up to one of the most glaring inequities in American life: an inequality of quantity as well as an inequality of quality.

Academic Commitment in Crisis Times

13. Sheldon Wolin, "Remembering Berkeley," 1974

Sheldon Wolin (1922–) was a professor of political science at Berkeley for seventeen years (1954–71). He became active in faculty efforts to have the right of free expression extended to students. Although his memory here of the Berkeley protests is written a decade later, it retains a tone of critical social thinking with an enlarged point of view. Wolin earned his degrees at Oberlin (B.A. 1946) and Harvard (Ph.D. 1950). In 1971 he became a professor of politics at Princeton and was later a professor of history, comparative literature, and political science at the Graduate Center of the City University of New York.

Sheldon W. Wolin, "Remembering Berkeley," *Chronicle of Higher Education*, December 23, 1974, 20. Reprinted with kind permission from the author. Copyright © 1974 by *The Daily Princetonian*. Further reading: Sheldon S. Wolin and John H. Schaar, *The Berkeley Rebellion and Beyond: Essays on Politics and Education in the Technological Society* (New York, 1970); Seymour Martin Lipset and Sheldon S. Wolin, eds., *The Berkeley Student Revolt: Facts and Interpretations* (Garden City, NY, 1965); W. J. Rorabaugh, *Berkeley at War: The 1960s* (New York, 1989); Gerard J. De Groot, "Ronald Reagan and Student Unrest in California, 1966–1970," *Pacific Historical Review* 65 (February 1996): 107–29; Nathan Glazer, *Remembering the Answers: Essays on the American Student Revolt* (New York, 1970); Hal Draper, *Berkeley: The New Student Revolt* (New York, 1965); Philip G. Altbach, *A Select Bibliography on Students, Politics, and Higher Education* (Cambridge, MA, 1967); Seymour M. Lipset and Philip G. Altbach, eds., *Students in Revolt* (Boston, 1969); Walter P. Metzger, "The Crisis of Academic Authority," *Daedalus* 99 (Summer 1970): 568–608; and VII, 3, 5–6, 14.

Berkeley is where it all began—so runs the common view of the campus upheavals of the 1960's. But, folklore to the contrary, the events which took place on the Berkeley campus in the fall of 1964 did not begin a causal chain which disrupted campuses throughout the United States and Western Europe; nor did the Berkeley Free Speech Movement, which was the organized expression of student action, represent a radical, still less a revolutionary, force. What did begin at Berkeley was the first substantial political challenge to campus authority, the first politics of mass student protest. The events are worth remembering not as a cause of other events but as signifying features of a more general condition.

The original objectives of the Free Speech Movement were limited and classically liberal. They concerned University restrictions on free speech and political activity. As the conflict intensified, its effect—as the protesters saw it—was to expose the nature of the university, revealing it to be both a microcosm of the larger society and an extension of the power of the dominant interests. There was ample evidence to support this view: from the composition of the board of regents, which epitomized the structure of power and wealth in California, to the form and structure of the university itself.

Berkeley was the model of a large-scale public institution, designed to educate large numbers of students by furnishing scientific and professional training to those who had made their career choice and by offering courses in the humanities and social sciences to those who had not. Berkeley was also designed as a "service" institution for distributing the benefits of technical knowledge: to special economic interests (through the schools of agriculture, mining, business, law, engineering, and others), to American society in general (through close collaboration, for example, between Berkeley science departments and nearby atomic laboratories), and to the world (through "exchange" programs which brought foreign students to the campus and sent Berkeley faculty members to "underdeveloped" nations).

The university came to be the mirror-image of liberal social values: a growth economy, competitive, progressive, expanding, upwardly mobile and academically imperialistic, rich with opportunities and resources; at the same time, a dynamic society of conflicting interests and ambitions, "a mechanism," as its chief designer, Clark Kerr, put it, "held together by administrative rules and powered by money." Like the corporate and governmental structures of the larger society, the structure of the university was bureaucratic and hierarchical. Publicly it professed an ideology of political neutrality whose justification was that "the university shall be established entirely independent of all political or sectarian influence. . . ." In practice the university followed a bureaucratic version of liberal politics. Politics consisted of the adjudication of interest-conflicts and the establishment of priorities within a system of rules laid down by the authorities. Berkeley's great reputation was a tribute to its distinctively modern achievement, the rationalization of liberal values in a bureaucratic form.

The history of political theory reminds us that one of the founders of modern liberalism, John Locke, had asserted that the political order comes into existence in order to protect property and that the rights of private property should, therefore, set the proper limits to politics. It was fitting that the events which shook the university had a Lockean beginning in a dispute over private property and that the university's first strategy was to deny student politics by asserting a right of ownership.

A small strip of pavement adjoining the campus had been used by students for assorted political activities, such as speech-making, fund-raising, and recruiting for various causes. It was widely assumed that the land belonged to the City of Berkeley. But in September, 1964, university administrators suddenly announced that it was university property and hence subject to a constitutional prohibition against political activity on campus. During the next few months the controversy was defined in classical liberal terms of free speech, political rights, due process for students charged with rule violations, and student participation in rule-making processes.

Eventually, on Dec. 8, 1964, the Berkeley faculty overwhelmingly passed a series of resolutions that recognized the rights of students to free speech and to political activity on campus, but only after the entire campus had undergone an intense and unprecedented political experience—of mass demonstrations and rallies, political organization and action, strikes, the collapse of campus authority, and intervention by police, the governor, and the state legislature. However, the "victory" of student and faculty members did not usher in an era of peace, but of instability, fretful conflict, and violence (including the "occupation" of the campus and city by the National Guard in 1969) which served to deepen the alienation of students and widen the polarization of the faculty.

Why instead of a new beginning did the events of 1964 produce six years of intermittent conflict? A satisfactory explanation would have to examine a wide variety of local circumstances and causes, but there was one cause worth examining because of its more general bearing. As we have pointed out, the politics of the campus took shape around traditional liberal definitions of free speech, political activity, due process, and participation. It remained transfixed in this form, but meanwhile, student culture was significantly changing, from the simple political activism inspired by the civil rights movement of the early '60's into a complex mix of political, aesthetic, erotic elements. There were new modes of dress, language, living arrangements; new economies of handicrafts and small shops; new life-rhythms; new music. This new culture, which increasingly defined the actual existence of students, could not be accommodated to the liberal-bureaucratic categories which determined the politics of the university.

But the task of creating new political forms that could give coherence and staying power to the new culture proved too difficult. The forms and modes of student action succeeded in changing the existing structure but not in redefining it. The students' politics of confrontation and non-negotiable demands were ultimately self-defeating and empty; their idea of participatory democracy had promise, but it required a commitment to duration, to politics extended over time that ran contrary to the student impulse to a politics of spontaneity and climax.

Instead of creating a new form which could connect their culture to a politics of the long pull, students accepted a solution which produced short-run instability and long-run despair. Whenever they thought that the occasion demanded it, they fell back on confrontation. This led to turmoil but not to durable results.

In the intervals between confrontations students attempted to work within the system, agreeing to abide by the conventions of bureaucratic politics in return for a "piece of the action." This meant accepting the institution's conception of controversy and its definition of a problem. Fundamentally it meant accepting the notion that controversies about education, student existence, and politics were really about interests and that university problems were essentially problems of rules. Accordingly, students agreed to argue about rules for political activity, speech, personal conduct, and discipline; to debate the rules for determining what was a rule and which rules should govern the interpretation of other rules.

Pettifoggery nearly became a recognized major, much to the relief of campus administrators and many faculty members. For while all bureaucrats live off rules, educational bureaucracies are specially advantaged because the subjects of their rules have initially agreed to follow regulations and fulfill requirements in exchange for the privilege of certification. So students adjusted their complaints to the specifications of a rules-culture and adapted their notions of participation to fit the "decision-making process." Since bureaucracy instinctively settles participation into the routines of a hierarchical structure, the fate of student participation was predictable. If faculty members and administrators were patient, the boredom of committee routines would do their work. Then word could be passed around that students were apathetic toward the opportunities for participation.

The fate of student participation was symptomatic of a deeper problem which never succeeded in getting articulated. The original aim of the Free Speech Movement had been to establish the rights of students to use campus facilities for political purposes. What began as a contest over political "space" quickly became a struggle over "time." A large-scale university—27,000 students and more than 1,000 faculty members—must impose a conception of time suitable to its structure and purposes. Education has to be conceived as a "process" in which time is "scheduled." The literal definition of a faculty member at Berkeley was as an "F.T.E." (Full Time Equivalent). For the student, time took the form of courses which had to be completed during a prescribed period; the reward for each course completed was a certain number of "units" and "grade points." Thus student time was scheduled and routinized, and student education was rendered abstract.

In a half-conscious way, student protests were about bureaucratic time: they dropped out or took "time off" or, occasionally, exploded collectively in an irruptive moment. Despite the negativity of these forms of protest, they pointed to a real problem. The pace of academic life left little time for thoughtful participation in the common affairs of the university. Students and professors alike were driven to a frenzied existence as they sought both to be civic members and to prepare their assignments, fulfill their "obligations," and complete their "work." Needless to say, exhaustion and guilt made everyone eager to return to their accustomed routines. The possibilities of a new integration of education, politics, and culture went unfulfilled. The faculty resumed its role as producer, and the student's became consumers once more.

14. Kenneth B. Clark, "Intelligence, the University, and Society," 1967

Best known for his support of appellants' briefs before the Supreme Court in the case of *Brown v. Board of Education*, Kenneth Clark (1914–2005) carried on a distinguished professorship in psychology at the City College of New York (1942–75). His writings were applied to civil rights, desegregation, and equality of educational opportunity. His tempered appraisal of the unrest in American colleges of the 1960s stands in contrast to writers on the left and the right. Clark took his Ph.D. at Columbia (1940) after an undergraduate degree from Howard University in 1935. In later years he became a member of the Board of Regents of the State of New York, a trustee of the University of Chicago, and president of the American Psychological Association. Among many honors he was awarded the Franklin Delano Roosevelt Four Freedoms Award (1985) and the National Medal for Liberty (1986).

Kenneth B. Clark, "Intelligence, the University, and Society," *The American Scholar* 36 (Winter 1966–67): 28–32. Reprinted with the kind permission of Hilton B. Clark. Further reading: his *Desegregation: An Appraisal of the Evidence* (New York, 1953), *Prejudice and Your Child* (Boston, 1955), and *How Relevant is Education in America Today?* (Washington, D.C., 1970).

Intellectual detachment and scientific objectivity can be most insidious and dangerous forms of moral irresponsibility. Indifference, equivocation and expediency avoid the risks engendered by the use of human intelligence for the attainment of social justice and human progress. When our colleges and universities become havens from value, when our teachers become defenders of such transparent escapes, they abdicate their responsibilities for moral leadership and they contribute to, if not help to create, the profound tragedy of the moral erosion and emptiness of those who have the intellectual gifts that might make human advancement and survival possible.

The persistent protests of a small number of our college students extensively reported in the newspapers beginning with the first sit-ins of Negro college students, followed by the Berkeley rebellion, and the Vietnam protests can be seen as symptomatic of the deep undercurrent of moral uneasiness of sensitive young people. They are demanding of their colleges and the universities some demonstration of humanity. They are demanding honesty. They are demanding evidence of concern with justice. They are demanding that colleges and universities be socially and morally relevant. They are few, and they are anguished and confused; but they are concerned—and they assume the risks of the concerned.

So far our colleges and universities and the men who control and run them have not yet answered these young people affirmatively. Perhaps they do not understand them. It is probably that the years of moral denial and studied blindness to flagrant problems of social injustice that were deemed essential to the efficient financing and administration of a large and complex educational institution have made it difficult and impractical to listen to pleas for dialogue and for resolution of fundamental moral issues. Our colleges and universities have a long history of default on important moral issues. They have frequently tried to make a virtue of isolation from the problems of the marketplace and from the anguished yearnings of the deprived and powerless people of our society. They have thrown in their lot with the powerful in government, business and industry. . . .

An attempt at a somewhat balanced appraisal of the role of American universities requires one to mention some exceptions to these severe charges. Probably the chief exception would be found in the research and teaching in the medical and public health schools of our universities, which are directly tied to human need and human welfare. Their findings must be directly or indirectly relevant. They cannot be pompously trivial. But even they are more concerned with individual cure than with the prevention of the conditions of poverty and degradation that lead to disease.

There are many specific and relevant areas in which American colleges and universities have defaulted in providing morally sensitive intellectual leadership for our society:

— They have watched silently, and facilitated, the process whereby education from the primary grades on has become ruthlessly competitive and anxiety-producing—in which the possibility of empathy, concern for one's classmate and the use of superior intelligence as a social trust are precluded, as our children are required to learn by their experiences in the classroom, by the demands of their teachers and the insistence of their parents, that education is competition and that intelligence is a device to obtain superior status and economic advantage over others.

— Under the guise of efficiency, the demands of mass education and the pressure of limited facilities in colleges, they have facilitated the reduction of the educational process to the level of content retention required for the necessary score on the College Boards and the Graduate Record Examinations at the price of reflective and critical thought.

— They have permitted our elementary and secondary schools to become contaminated by and organized in terms of the educationally irrelevant factors of race and economic status.

— They have watched without sustained protests the erosion of the quality of education provided for minority group children and other lower-status children—erosion to the point of criminal inefficiency and dehumanization.

— They have watched in silence the creeping blight of our cities and the spawning of Negro ghettos, concerned only when the pathologies associated with the ghetto come too close to the walls of the university. Only then do they seek to protect themselves, sometimes through a ruthless and callous dispossessing of the unwanted lower-status people.

— They have abdicated any sustained, forthright moral leadership in America's attempt to resolve the anguish of its pervasive racial problem. Leadership in the civil rights struggle has come from civil rights organizations, from the federal courts, and more recently from the executive and legislative branches of the federal and some state governments; and from the Catholic, Protestant and Jewish churches and synagogues. Despite the commitment of some of their faculty, American colleges and universities have, as institutions, remained detached and nonrelevant to this major domestic issue of our times. Indeed colleges and universities are major bastions of a subtle and persistent form of white supremacy.

In summary, the major charge that must now be made against American colleges and universities is that they have not fulfilled their responsibility and obligation to develop and train human beings with a morally relevant and socially responsible intelligence. They have operated as if it were possible for a detached, amoral intelligence to be adaptive. They have not provided their students with the moral guidelines essential for the effective, creative and adaptive use of superior intelligence. They have not provided their faculties with the stimulation or protection for a socially responsible use of their own critical intelligence. And above all they have not provided the moral leadership for society—they have not alerted the public to the urgency of finding moral and democratic solutions to critical domestic and international problem.

Given these real and chronic deficiencies, how can one hope that American colleges and universities can become morally relevant in time to make any difference in the destiny of man? One can hope because one must. The deficiencies in our educational system are remediable. The first step in any attempt at remedying a problem is the courage to recognize it as a problem—followed by the commitment to change. . . .

American higher education need not continue to subordinate itself to the goals of efficiency, expediency, power, status and success. Young people can be trained in our schools, colleges and universities to value critical and independent thought above conformity and packaged opinions; to value evidence of concern, commitment and social sensitivity above personal acceptance and mere social success. Once they understand the stakes and the nature of the challenge, it will be possible for our colleges and universities to produce totally educated persons.

A truly educated person is trained to mesh his intelligence with his feelings in a disciplined whole. He cannot deny or subordinate either his brain or his heart because each is essential to the effective functioning of the other. Our colleges must provide the opportunities for students to test their courage to stand alone—to accept the risks of alienation and aloneness that come with the anguish and the torture of the search for moral commitment and disciplined, intelligent action. Colleges must be the place where human beings are prepared to bolster in-

telligence with compassion, courage and increasing wisdom. . . .

15. Richard Hofstadter, "Columbia University Commencement Address," 1968

Soon after receiving a bachelor's degree from the University of Buffalo (1937) in his native city, Richard Hofstadter (1916–70) began his long attachment to Columbia University, broken only by four years of teaching at the University of Maryland (1942–46). He took his Columbia doctorate in 1942, joined the faculty in 1946, and became DeWitt Clinton Professor of American History in 1959. This address, in the troubled spring of 1968, was the first commencement talk given by a Columbia faculty member. Hofstadter's works, which twice won the Pulitzer Prize, continue to seize the interest of those who value broad and imaginative perspectives on the American past.

Richard Hofstadter, "Columbia University Commencement Address for the 214th Academic Year," *The American Scholar* 37 (Autumn 1968): 583–89. Copyright © 1968 by the United Chapters of Phi Beta Kappa. Reprinted with the kind permission of *The American Scholar* and Beatrice Hofstadter. Further reading: relevant to the themes of higher education are his *Social Darwinism in American Thought, 1860–1915* (Philadelphia, 1945); with Walter P. Metzger, *The Development of Academic Freedom in the United States* (New York, 1955); *Anti-Intellectualism in American Life* (New York, 1963); edited with Wilson Smith, *American Higher Education: A Documentary History*, 2 vols. (Chicago, 1961). More generally, see Stanley Elkins and Eric McKitrick, "Richard Hofstadter: A Progress," in *The Hofstadter Aegis,* ed. Elkins and McKitrick (New York, 1973): 300–367; Thomas Bender, "Richard Hofstadter," in *American National Biography,* ed. John Garraty and Mark C. Carnes, vol. 14 (New York, 2002), 1–4; Peter Gay, "Richard Hofstadter," in *International Encyclopedia of the Social Sciences,* vol. 18 (1979), 310–12; Arthur Schlesinger Jr., "Richard Hofstadter," in *Pastmasters,* ed. Marcus Cunliffe and Robin Winks (New York, 1969): 278–315; and Susan Stout Baker, *Radical Beginnings: Richard Hofstadter and the 1930s* (Westport, CT, 1985).

For a long time, Columbia University has been part of my life. I came here as a graduate student in 1937, returned as a member of the faculty in 1946, and have since remained. In these years, I have had at this University many admired and cherished colleagues, and many able students. In this respect, I am but one of a large company of faculty members who, differing as they do on many matters, are alike in their sense of the greatness of this institution and in their affection for it. In this hour of its most terrible trial, it could surely have found a great many of us willing to speak. Quite frankly I have never been very much interested in Commencements, although I recognize their important symbolic function. But it seems to me entirely appropriate, and also symbolic, that on this unusual occasion a member of the faculty should have been asked to speak. Trustees, administrators and students tend to agree that in ultimate reality the members of the faculty *are* the university, and we of the faculty have not been disposed to deny it.

Yet while I hope I am speaking in the interest of my university, it would be wrong to suggest that I am precisely speaking for it. It is in fact of the very essence of the conception of the modern university that I wish to put before you that no one is authorized to speak for it. A university is firmly committed to certain basic values of freedom, rationality, inquiry, discussion; and to its own internal order; but it does not have corporate views of public questions. Administrators and trustees are, of course, compelled by practical necessity to take actions that involve some assumptions about the course and meaning of public affairs; but they know that in so doing they are not expressing a corporate university judgment or committing other minds. Members of the faculties often express themselves vigorously on public issues, but they acknowledge the obligation to make it clear that they are not speaking in the name of their university. This fact of our all speaking separately is in itself a thing of great consequence, because in this age of rather overwhelming organizations and collectivities, the university is singular in being a collectivity that serves as a citadel of intellectual individualism.

Although I mean to say a few things about our prospects at Columbia, let me first suggest to you how I think the modern university as such ought to be regarded.

A university is a community, but it is a community of a special kind—a community devoted to inquiry. It exists so that its members may inquire into truths of all sorts. Its presence marks our commitment to the idea that somewhere in society there must be an organization in which anything can be studied or questioned—not merely safe and established things but difficult and inflammatory things, the most troublesome questions of politics and war, of sex and morals, of property and national loyalty. It is governed by the ideal of academic freedom, applicable both to faculty and students. The ideal of academic freedom does indeed put extraordinary demands upon human restraint and upon our capacity for disinterested thought. Yet these demands are really of the same general order as those we regard as essential to any advanced civilization. The very possibility of civilized human discourse rests upon the willingness of people to consider that they may be mistaken. The possibility of modern democracy rests upon the willingness of governments to accept the existence of a loyal opposition, organized to reverse some of their policies and to replace them in office. Similarly, the possibility of the modern free university rests upon the willingness of society to support and sustain institutions part of whose business it is to examine, critically and without stint, the assumptions that prevail in that society. Professors are hired to teach and students are sent to learn with the quite explicit understanding

that they are not required to agree with those who hire or send them.

Underlying these remarkable commitments is the belief that in the long run the university will best minister to society's needs not alone through its mundane services but through the far more important office of becoming an intellectual and spiritual balance wheel. This is a very demanding idea, an idea of tremendous sophistication, and it is hardly surprising that we have some trouble in getting it fully accepted by society or in living up to it ourselves. But just because it is demanding we should never grow tired of explaining or trying to realize it. Nor should we too quickly become impatient with those who do not immediately grasp it.

We are very much impressed now not simply by the special character of the free university but also by its fragility. The delicate thing about freedom is that while it requires restraints, it also requires that these restraints normally be self-imposed, and not forced from outside. The delicate thing about the university is that it has a mixed character, that it is suspended between its position in the external world, with all its corruption and evils and cruelties, and the splendid world of our imagination. The university does in fact perform certain mundane services of instruction and information to society—and there are those who think it should aspire to nothing more. It does in fact constitute a kind of free forum—and there are those who want to convert it primarily into a center of political action. But above these aspects of its existence stands its essential character as a center of free inquiry and criticism—a thing not to be sacrificed for anything else. A university is not a service station. Neither is it a political society, nor a meeting place for political societies. With all its limitations and failures, and they are invariably many, it is the best and most benign side of our society insofar as that society aims to cherish the human mind. To realize its essential character, the university has to be dependent upon something less precarious than the momentary balance of forces in society. It has to pin its faith on something that is not hard-boiled or self-regarding. It has to call not merely upon critical intelligence but upon self-criticism and self-restraint. There is no group of professors or administrators, of alumni or students, there is no class or interest in our society that should consider itself exempt from exercising the self-restraint or displaying the generosity that is necessary for the university's support.

Some people argue that because the modern university, whether public or private, is supported by and is part of the larger society, it therefore shares in all the evils of society, and must be quite ruthlessly revolutionized as a necessary step in social reform, or even in social revolution. That universities do share in, and may even at some times and in some respects propagate, certain ills of our society seems to me undeniable. But to imagine that the best way to change a social order is to start by assaulting its most accessible centers of thought and study and criticism is not only to show a complete disregard for the intrinsic character of the university but also to develop a curiously self-destructive strategy for social change. If an attempt is made to politicize completely our primary centers of free argument and inquiry, they will only in the end be forced to lose their character and be reduced to centers of vocational training, nothing more. Total and pure neutrality for the university is in fact impossible, but neutrality should continue to define our aim, and we should resist the demand that the university espouse the political commitments of any of its members. This means, too, that the university should be extraordinarily chary of relationships that even suggest such a political commitment.

The university is the only great organization in modern society that considers itself obliged not just to tolerate but even to give facilities and protection to the very persons who are challenging its own rules, procedures and policies. To subvert such a fragile structure is all too easy, as we now know. That is why it requires, far more than does our political society, a scrupulous and continued dedication to the conditions of orderly and peaceable discussion. The technique of the forcible occupation and closure of a university's buildings with the intention of bringing its activities to a halt is no ordinary bargaining device—it is a thrust at the vitals of university life. It is a powerful device for control by a determined minority, and its continued use would be fatal to any university. In the next few years the universities of this country will have to find the effective strategy to cope with it, and to distinguish it sharply and permanently from the many devices of legitimate student petition, demonstration and protest.

This brings me to our own problem. Our history and situation, our own mistakes, have done a great deal to create this problem; but it must not be regarded as an isolated incident, since it is only the most severe, among American universities, of a number of such incidents. We are at a crisis point in the history of American education and probably in that of the Western world. Not only in New York and Berkeley, but in Madrid and Paris, in Belgrade and Oxford, in Rome, Berlin and London, and on many college and university campuses throughout this country, students are disaffected, restive and rebellious.

I cannot pretend to offer a theory that will pull together all these events in a single coherent pattern. Nothing could be more dissimilar, for example, than the intramural situation of students at Columbia and students at the Sorbonne—nor, for that matter, than the response of the community to their actions—and yet the common bond of dissatisfaction is obvious. It is easier to account for the general rise in activism on American campuses, for all our students are troubled today by two facts of the most fundamental consequence for all of us—the persis-

tence at home of poverty and racial injustice, and abroad of the war in Vietnam. It is the first of these that we will have to live with the longer and address ourselves to much more fully, imaginatively and generously than we have so far done. But in the short run the escalation of this cruel and misconceived venture in Vietnam has done more than any other thing to inflame our students, to undermine their belief in the legitimacy of our normal political processes, and to convince them that violence is the order of the day. I share their horror at this war, and I consider that the deep alienation it has inflicted on young Americans who would otherwise be well disposed toward their country is one of the staggering uncountable costs of the Vietnam undertaking. This war has already toppled a President; but its full effects on our national life have not yet been reckoned.

Here at Columbia, we have suffered a disaster whose precise dimensions it is impossible to state, because the story is not yet finished, and the measure of our loss still depends upon what we do. For every crisis, for every disaster, there has to be some constructive response. At Columbia the constructive response has been a call for university reform. I have spoken to no one who does not believe in its desirability, and I believe that the idea of reform commands an extraordinarily wide positive response in all bodies from trustees to students, although when we come to discussing particulars, we will surely differ sharply about them. Our foundation dates from the eighteenth century, and although we have made elaborate and ingenious improvisations upon it through the generations, we have never had a decisive, concerted moment of thorough and imaginative reconsideration of our procedures. Powers need to be redistributed. Some new organs of decision and communication need to be created. A greater participation of students in university decisions seems to me to be bound to come here and elsewhere. Some students call for student power—others shrink from the term because they have some sense of the arduous work, the sheer tedium, the high responsibilities that are always a part of administrative power. I would suggest that, except for certain areas in which student decision has proved workable, what students need and should have is influence, not power; but they also need formal channels to assure them that their influence is in fact effective.

About university reform certain guiding principles ought to be observed. Columbia has been a distinguished university these many decades because it has been doing *some* things right. Plans for the future should be based upon an evolution from existing structures and arrangements, not upon a utopian scheme for a perfect university. The business of reforming a university takes time, requires a certain willingness to experiment and to retreat from experiment when it does not work, and indeed a willingness not to undertake too many interlocking experiments all at once. As reform demands time, it demands peace of mind, the ability to exchange views and proposals in a calm and deliberative spirit. It cannot be carried out, although it can be begun, in a moment of crisis. It cannot be carried out under duress.

What we need then is stability, peace, mutual confidence. The time will soon come when the first halting gestures toward conciliation can be multiplied and strengthened, when we can move more rapidly toward the reconstruction of the frame of trust.

Friends outside the university who know how serious is the damage we have suffered have asked me: How can Columbia go on after this terrible wound? I can only answer: How can it not go on? The question is not whether it will continue but in what form. Will it fall into a decline and become a third- or fourth-rate institution, will it be as distinguished as it has been for generations past, or will it somehow be made even more distinguished? Columbia is a great and—in the way Americans must reckon time—an ancient university. In this immense, rich country, we have only a limited number of institutions of comparable quality. We are living through a period in which the need for teaching and research—for the services a university performs and the things it stands for—is greater than it ever was before. What kind of a people would we be if we allowed this center of our culture and our hope to languish and fail? That is the question I must leave with you.

16. William Bouwsma, "Learning and the Problem of Undergraduate Education," 1970

A scholar of the Italian Renaissance, William James Bouwsma (1922–2005) served as vice chancellor for academic affairs at Berkeley (1967–69) during the height of campus and city violence. Before going to Berkeley he had earned degrees at Harvard (A.B. 1943, Ph.D. 1950) and had taught history at the University of Illinois (1950–57). After his administrative post at Berkeley he went back to Harvard for two years (1969–71) and then returned to Berkeley as Sather Professor (1971–91). Bouwsma was president of the American Historical Association (1978).

William J. Bouwsma, "Learning and the Problem of Undergraduate Education," in *Confrontation and Learned Societies*, ed. John Voss and Paul L. Ward (New York, 1970), 79–103. Reprinted by permission of New York University Press, Copyright © 1970 by New York University. Further reading: VII, 5, 14, 17; the Commonwealth Club address by then Governor Ronald Reagan, to which Bouwsma refers, was reported in *San Francisco Chronicle*, June 14, 1969, 1, 12.

Higher education, it seems to me, is experiencing a crisis of the most fundamental and dangerous kind —a crisis of public confidence that involves all elements in our diverse constituencies and threatens private and public universities alike. In spite of the conviction of scholars that learning in its various forms has never been more important and more urgently required in the modern world, in spite of the ease with which we can all demonstrate this and the frequency with which it is asserted, universities have never been so unpopular or under such broad attack.

Let me emphasize that criticism of us comes from every direction, some of it from places where we would least have expected it. Thus even our best students often insist that we are "irrelevant"; and if they frequently seem vague about the meaning of the word, this only suggests that it expresses discontents almost too deep and general for articulation. We all know how many students stick to their academic tasks grudgingly or with an uneasy sense of copping out, because they can think of nothing better to do, or because the alternative may be Viet Nam; many others drop out altogether. Even in the graduate schools a high proportion of students, admitted with the best possible credentials, give the impression of being still chiefly unsatisfied seekers; and they too, disappointed once again, often simply disappear. Under these conditions I suspect that we would be unwise to count on our students' eventually thinking better of us as alumni and thus helping to improve the unfavorable balance of opinion about us among older groups. Meanwhile our present alumni increasingly baffle us by their general apathy to our glowing accounts of the triumphs of scholarship and their skepticism or indifference when we describe imaginative new courses and promising educational reforms. Minority groups and the poor are angry with us because we do so little for them, although it is often unclear what they seek from us that is legitimately ours to bestow. And men in public office, or eager to attain it, have discovered that few gestures are more popular with the electorate than an attack on higher education.

There are doubtless various reasons why this is so, but I think we would be dangerously wrong to attribute fundamental importance to public indignation over campus disorder and political militancy, and to count on a restoration of public confidence with a change in the political climate. The reaction against campus radicalism by a profoundly frightened society is closely related to the basic problem, and it has also focused attention on higher education and accelerated a more general kind of public discontent, which might otherwise have developed more gradually. But even more serious forces have been at work, and to get at these I should like to stress the remarkable unanimity of our various critics. In their distrust and disapproval of us, if on little else, old and young, politicians and students, Right and Left, are in basic agreement. Not enough has yet been made, I think, of this fact and of the strange alliances it has produced. The real problem stems from the general assumption of our public that the primary task of the university is the education of the young who are entrusted to us as undergraduates, and the widespread and growing conviction that we are presently failing badly with this essential responsibility. And I am inclined to believe not only that this indictment is largely valid, but also that the cause of our failure lies in an unhealthy relationship, the product of several decades of development, between learning and education, especially undergraduate education, in the university. This is the deeper lesson to which the apparently "political" criticism of higher education should direct our attention. And, if I am right about this, learned societies indeed have particular cause for concern.

A speech by Governor Ronald Reagan to the Commonwealth Club of San Francisco on June 13, 1969, supplies an unusually useful illustration of this analysis. Much of the Governor's talk was in defense of police tactics (i.e., the use of shotguns and gas) against Berkeley demonstrators during the altercation over the People's Park the previous month, and this part of his speech was received, predictably enough, with applause, and two standing ovations. But Reagan went on from here to present a remarkable explanation of Berkeley's endemic political troubles. They were the natural expression, he suggested, of "the disappointment and resentment of an entire college generation—a generation that is justifiably resentful of being fed into a knowledge factory with no regard to their individuality, aspirations or their dreams." Although the voice was the voice of Ronald Reagan, the words were remarkably those of the Free Speech Movement, which would thus appear to have made a notable convert. And the Governor went on to offer himself as an ally of discontented students. "The challenge to us," he declared, "is to establish contact with these frustrated young people and join in finding answers before they fall to the mob by default."

He did not identify very clearly the questions to which he sought answers; and in view of his suspicions about the influence of professors on the young, his own "answers" seemed somewhat inappropriate, and in any case hardly adequate to the greatness of the challenge. His crucial point, nevertheless, seemed to be that professors should spend more time with their students. He said that teachers should be persuaded to teach, and it was evident that he believed they are not presently doing so. To this end he proposed that research should be subordinated to teaching and that it should cease to be the primary standard by which a university measures its quality. He also suggested that professors might work harder (in context this evidently meant that they might do more teaching) if they did not have tenure. He clearly wanted education to be restored to the university from which he believed it had largely disappeared, and he also called on education itself to become relevant. His conception of relevance was made explicit in his conclusion:

"The few subversives on our campuses will be much easier to handle if the so-called silent majority has inner convictions, beliefs, and confidence in our society and in us as adults." . . .

I would argue, indeed, that however crude the form of the criticism to which we are being subjected, it makes a point with which even those of us whose interests are well served by the present focus of the university are in at least partial agreement, and which has obscurely troubled our consciences. For it reflects a serious conception of education, one that is rather different from what most of us now represent as academic men but one that happens nevertheless to be the traditional view of education, as opposed to mere training, in Western society. This is, of course, the idea of education as *paideia*, as the transmission of the deepest insights, attitudes, and values of a society, the most precious legacy it can pass on to succeeding generations. Education, in this conception, should convey a society's general beliefs about the meaning and purpose of life, its perceptions about the coherence of experience, its concern with social duty and the relation between the needs of life in society and the development of the individual personality. This is what education has consistently meant for those men in the past who have thought most deeply, and with the steadiest and most pervasive influence, about education. This is what education meant to the Greeks and to the pedagogical theorists of the Renaissance and the Enlightenment, and it survived in the classical curricula and the denominational colleges of the last century. (I do not mean to idealize these last in all respects, but at least they had a sense of purpose, a *paideia* to communicate.) And much of our present crisis is a consequence of the persistence into our own time, if only half consciously, of the idea of *paideia* as the model governing our sense of what education ought to be, while at the same time it has been largely disappearing from our universities. Higher education is now under judgment by this standard, and it has been found utterly and profoundly wanting.

Let us take a brief look at ourselves with the idea of *paideia* in mind. As we all know, today's university has been largely shaped by what Jencks and Riesman have called "the academic revolution," i.e., in their own words, "the rise to power of the academic profession." This development has been understandably satisfying to the profession itself, and it has also been useful for meeting many of the specialized needs of modern society. It is admirably suited to the training of specialists and the preparation of various sorts of professional men. But it happens also to be very badly adapted to the needs of undergraduate education, which has been persistently regarded—except perhaps in the university itself—as our primary obligation. It is very little concerned with the transmission of values, except for such values (I do not minimize them) as may be inherent in or necessary to specialized training; with general ideals, except indirectly and incidentally; or with the meaning of human experience and the purpose of life, even as questions requiring perennial discussion. It is thus about as indifferent to education as *paideia*, unless there is a specific *paideia* of scholarship itself, as one can possibly imagine.

Above all the academic revolution, though made possible by the increasing practical importance of some academic groups to society, has resulted paradoxically in a peculiar kind of detachment from society. The academic profession, strong in the sense of its new importance, has come to regard the university as largely its own possession, as an essentially autonomous entity with a moral obligation to resist the pressures and demands of the society that brought it into existence, although this obligation is of course generally rationalized as somehow in the ultimate interest of society itself. The professor has come to see his natural community not as the local society from which his university draws its support but rather as the national or international community of scholars, and the university itself as the agency through which that larger community operates. Within the university the academic profession therefore insists (with general success) on the right of the faculty to make decisions about courses and curricula, in accordance with its professional interests, somewhat in the manner of a priesthood, the keepers of mysteries too sacred to be treated by the multitudes. It has been almost equally successful in asserting the right of the faculty to select other faculty, and so its priorities are effectively perpetuated. And it has also sought the right to determine who should be admitted as students, with the frequent result in practice—highly satisfactory for our disciplines but less obviously sound from the standpoint of society as a whole—that we devote most of our attention and our resources to the best students: i.e., to precisely those students who would appear to need them least. Finally, the academic revolution has been largely responsible for our emphasis on research even in our teaching; although I reject the ease with which the distinction between research and teaching is often made, it is nevertheless true that they are often coordinated chiefly by converting the classroom into an opportunity for reporting research. Again I should emphasize that these developments have produced important benefits and met important needs. I want only to point out that these needs have been served at a heavy cost: namely, the sacrifice of education as *paideia*.

For what the academic revolution has meant is, in effect, the triumph of learning over education, the laissez-faire pursuit of the specialized interests of learned men over the general formation of the young. Absorbed in the search for truth, we have given a minimum of attention to the coherence of the entire intellectual enterprise of the university, to problems of meaning and value, and to our deeper

social role. Seeing knowledge as an end in itself, we have lost sight of its broader human purpose; and professors have tended increasingly to operate on the assumption that education consisted essentially in the scholar's training his successors. In this light the university may well appear as the last stronghold of nineteenth-century liberalism, and in this respect not the most advanced but the most inert of institutions. It has operated on the vague assumption that if each scholar does his thing, all will somehow work out mysteriously for the best; through random exposure students will somehow emerge as educated men, and society should be content. The assumption has turned out to be dreadfully wrong.

At the same time I do not want to convert these remarks into just another attack on higher education. It is characteristically American to blame the schools when things go wrong, out of an apparently unshakable confidence, one of our more awkward legacies from the Enlightenment, that education can cure all ills. Universities are therefore likely to serve as a convenient scapegoat in time of crisis; this is the negative corollary of the importance we ourselves have attributed to them. The problem of the modern university cannot, however, be dealt with so simply; the failure of universities to educate is only a symptom of deeper difficulties. For universities, however we should prefer them, are not divinely set apart from the rest of our society, in a position to act on it and to solve its problems, so to speak, from the outside. They are rather, however remotely, agents of society and bearers of its assumptions, and they are therefore hardly capable of supplying by themselves what has been lacking in our culture as a whole. I am inclined, therefore, to take the attack on higher education as a sign of profound discontent with the general quality of modern life. If the universities now produce so much anger because they appear to lack a coherent educational ideal and a clear sense of purpose, one has only to look at the world that has produced them to discover the true cause: a world that is itself fragmented, specialized, mechanistic, incoherent, and lacking in clear and generally accepted values. By the same token, if this kind of world now provokes widespread discontent, we may be in the presence of a far deeper set of cultural changes than we have yet supposed.

Under these conditions, I must confess that most proposals for university reform seem to me remarkable chiefly for their superficiality, and even when most likely to prove effective, calculated rather to intensify the educational problem than to solve it. Little can be expected, as I have suggested, from university administrators. Even if they were not too busy fending off political militants on one side and the outraged public on the other, or trying to mediate among the numerous special interests that each demand a piece of the multiversity, they are virtually powerless in the realm of educational policy too suspect among both individualistic faculty and angry students to exert significant influence on the educational process. Put even under the most favorable conditions I am not persuaded that administrators really know what to do. Their common receptiveness to innovation and experiment in undergraduate education (and I hasten to add that I do not exclude myself from this indictment) strikes me less as a virtue than as a confession of educational bankruptcy, and more likely to subvert the tasks the university presently performs well than to benefit students. The faculty, meanwhile, has a vested interest in a status quo which has worked so well from its standpoint; and most administrators have found professors, on the whole, depressingly reluctant to abandon their disciplinary commitments in order to engage in novel pedagogical schemes that seem to them, with some reason, of doubtful promise. The only innovations that appear to have much attraction for professors are those calculated to improve teaching in their own subjects, for example freshman seminars that introduce students at the earliest possible moment to the problems and the spirit of modern scholarship. I think it important to observe that most faculty members are, in my experience, intensely serious about their teaching and very good at it; the point is that their goals as teachers are largely disciplinary goals.

Nor do I see much reason to flatter students for their insights into what is needed in the way of educational reform, though I think we should take their discontents very seriously indeed. Student proposals for educational change seem to me no less timid and confused than those coming from other sources. This is in part, I think, because of a contradiction between the need for coherence, meaning, and value, which seems to me the real significance of the demand for a "relevant" education and which points in one direction, and the natural desire of the young, which points in the opposite direction, for more freedom and even fewer prescriptions than are now to be found in most undergraduate curricula. In addition the constraints of an unsatisfactory education have encouraged students to believe that the problem lies in constraint itself and thus that its solution lies in greater freedom. In any event, student proposals for change have either seemed trivial or tended to reinforce existing weaknesses, for example the elimination of grades, the abolition of language requirements, or the introduction of courses dealing with contemporary problems, courses that would merely add another set of specialized inquiries to our already disjointed instructional program. The educational proposals of students give the impression rather of shifting about on a bed of pain than of a movement toward health; and I find the most significant hints of the needs of students not in their curricular suggestions but in such phenomena as their growing interest in the occult, which I interpret as a sign of longing for a kind of meaning and coherence they have been seeking vainly in more respectable quarters. The al-

leged radicalism of students makes many of our fellow citizens uneasy; I would suggest, on the contrary, that students, like the rest of us, have not been in a true sense nearly radical enough about education, the values it should serve, and the ways it could be made to serve them. On the other hand, I have never quite understood why we should expect, as some of my colleagues appear to expect, greater wisdom about education from the youngest members of the academic community than from the rest of it. There are, however, many romantic assumptions about that that deserve closer scrutiny.

Another conception of relevance has also been frequently proposed, from outside as well as inside the university, as the principle for desirable changes in higher education: that the university should focus far more of its attention on immediate social problems and needs. This may well be desirable and even necessary in some cases, but it should be clear that it has to do primarily with the role of the university in the training of specialists; it offers no solution to the problems of undergraduate education, which it would compound rather than ameliorate. For it should be obvious that this kind of educational relevance merely opens the way to an even higher degree of conformity than at present to the practical requirements of a fragmented and aimless society. . . . If the university is to retain its general usefulness, as I hope it can, it must not constantly transform itself to solve particular and passing problems. Far from making the university truly relevant, this would only insure its irrelevance for the future.

If my analysis of the problem of the university is valid, we would thus appear to be in a fearful dilemma: we crave a true *paideia* as the heart of the undergraduate curriculum, yet the quality of our culture, whatever the discontents that may be gathering, seems to exclude it. And if the problem is ultimately cultural rather than educational, there would seem to be little that we could do to attack it. Yet . . . I am not altogether without hope. For if I noted the valuelessness and incoherence of contemporary culture, I emphasized also the gathering of a movement in the opposite direction, a movement, it may be added, of the kind that has usually become already irresistible by the time it attracts general notice. And I see a few signs that the conservatism of the academic profession (its own revolution accomplished) and our general blindness to the nature of the dissatisfaction with higher education that now surrounds us may be giving way in one of those mysterious, uncalculated cultural adjustments that even universities cannot permanently resist.

Thus I would point to the emergence at Berkeley of several new undergraduate programs which appear on first inspection utterly different but on a deeper level reveal, it seems to me, common characteristics that may be of considerable significance. The oldest and most highly developed of these is Professor Joseph Tussman's lower division college, recently described in his book *Experiment at Berkeley* (New York: Oxford University Press, 1969); the second is a new residential program in modern history and literature within the College of Letters and Science; the third is a program, or more precisely a series of programs, dealing with the historical experience, the culture, and the present predicament of minority groups: Afro-American studies, Mexican-American studies, Asian-American studies, and American Indian (or native American) studies.

Since the first two have had difficulty in obtaining faculty support and the third is only now being developed, I can hardly make any large claims yet for the success of these programs, and they certainly do not demonstrate that Berkeley is about to change its basic character. Nevertheless they are alike in several interesting respects, and in their similarities I suspect that there may lurk some hint of the more general adaptation required of us. All three are undergraduate programs, conceived outside the traditional departments, interdisciplinary in structure, which aspire to make use of the learning available through the established disciplines for educational goals that have been formulated with relative clarity. Professor Tussman is concerned to deepen a student's values and his understanding of himself in relation to society by examining the ethical and social thought of other periods of historical crisis; the program in history and literature aims to help students "locate" themselves in relation to their own culture (and might be described as a WASP identity study); the aim of ethnic studies is to deepen our understanding of minority groups and perhaps also (for students from minority backgrounds) the individual's sense of relationship to his community. In pursuit of these goals, furthermore, all three programs are far more highly organized and prescriptive than most other undergraduate curricula. All three are also evidently concerned with values, and based quite directly on a conviction of their central importance for undergraduate education. And finally, in each case, this primary concern is expressed through a study of the experiences, the collective wisdom, attitudes and insights, and the tradition of some community, whether the larger cultural community of the West or the particular community of a ghettoized ethnic group.

But this, I submit, is very close to the general meaning of *paideia;* and in the emergence of these and other similar programs (I have no doubt that they are now also appearing in many universities) we may perhaps discover an important lesson for the times. One of our difficulties would appear to be not so much that our society is lacking in *paideia,* but that it is peculiarly pluralistic. What is therefore missing is chiefly consensus about the content of *paideia,* and the solution to our problem may well lie in the frank recognition of diversity, in a clear perception that our society is characterized by a number of *paideiai* each of which may be appropri-ate to explore, in the interest of a genuine undergraduate education that will provide students with some sense that they inhabit a universe of serious values and dependable relationships. Indeed, each of the *paideiai* among us may need exploration in the interest of an ultimate social unity, since an awareness of differences must come before we can recognize what we have in common. . . .

17. John Bunzel, "Six New Threats to the Academy," 1974

As a faculty member in political science at California State University, San Francisco (1963–70), John Harvey Bunzel (1924–) witnessed the strife that closed that institution in late 1968. He was a Princeton graduate (1948) with a doctorate from Berkeley (1954), who served as president of California State University at San Jose (1970–78), where he issued these comments. Later he became a senior research fellow at the Hoover Institution (1978–83); in the latter year he was appointed to the United States Civil Rights Commission. In 1990 he received the Hubert Humphrey Award from the American Political Science Association for his years of service as "an outstanding public policy practitioner."

John H. Bunzel, "Six New Threats to the Academy," *Chronicle of Higher Education,* January 14, 1974, 24. Copyright © 1974 by *The Chronicle of Higher Education.* Further reading: VII, 11–12.

Both the time and the need are at hand for the higher-education community to turn its attention to some of the more novel challenges to academic freedom that have arisen since the last most conspicuous university crisis. . . .

Most of us are persuaded, I think, that the experiences of the middle and late 1960's have left their mark in an indelible way. It is not merely a question of a bruise or two. We will just never be the same. While the principles and values of those of us committed to the defense of academic freedom have remained constant, the university and its cultural climate have not.

I encounter almost every day much mischievous advice about how best to deal with these concerns. Some of that advice is the usual dreary stuff and comes from false counselors, those whom Dante quite properly placed way down toward the bottom of the Abyss in the eighth level of the eighth circle. Those we will always have with us.

But there is also the bad advice offered by those who seem to have difficulty perceiving what is harmful to the university. They are unable or unwilling to see how maledictions are currently disguised as benedictions. These maledictions constitute the new threats to academic freedom.

1. **The revival of communalism disguised as pluralism.** At their worst, many ethnic-studies and affirmative-action programs have encouraged the growth of an infatuation with ethnicity that is socially divisive, frequently bewildering in its actual demands on institutions, and harmful to the com-

mitment of the university to the principle of reward based on individual merit.

We are witnessing in our day a powerful and necessary upsurge in the movement for social justice for which many of us have fought for decades and towards which the country has struggled for over 200 years. We are also simultaneously witnessing a rebirth of communal ties of all sorts, much of it sound and affirmative in character but some of it, unhappily, expressing its harmful factionalist spirit.

The movement within the academic world which expresses this spirit frequently seems intent on dividing the university into special groupings based on ruse or ethnic origins (or, indeed, on sex), which amounts to nothing less than a regressive sundering of the unity and objective character of knowledge. It revives criteria for appointment and advancement which are irrelevant to the search for truth. It is a movement sustained by the argument that tribalism is really indistinguishable from pluralism, and that affirmation of the democratic desire for diversity means acceptance of a group mentality indifferent to recognition based on personal merit.

2. **The reappearance of populism disguised as egalitarianism.** This malediction might also be characterized as "the exaltation of the ordinary disguised as democracy." There are simplistic views of democracy that assume or allege that the existence of any differences constitutes *prima facie* evidence of inequality—and since in a democracy "all men are created equal," these differences are presumed to be a self-evident indictment of democracy. Advocates of such pseudo-egalitarianism may be found in many quarters, including faculties and legislatures, attacking "elitist education." I have heard such arguments from faculty members who insist on their right to award only A's and B's.

The antidote to such confusion and illogic might perhaps begin with a rereading of the founding fathers and de Tocqueville.

3. **The rise of vulgarity disguised as freedom.** I refer here to intellectual and aesthetic vulgarity, to aggressive coarseness in speech and manners, to contempt for grammar and indifference to logic, to sloganeering as a substitute for thought, to hatred of culture, antipathy to history, and release into fashionable nihilism. All these are paraded as the sweet, necessary, and inevitable fruit of liberty. More accurately, they represent a betrayal of freedom and of the life of the mind, both of which are essential to the very idea of the university.

4. **The worship of relevance disguised as realism.** The arguments in support of the modish and the jazzy are all too familiar. We are sometimes told that realism requires us to endorse the search for immediate gratification, that it is folly to deal with people except with reference to "where they are" at that moment.

Such a view is in part a tautology and in part a non sequitur. Obviously, people must be encountered where they are, since that is the only place they can be found. But it is far from obvious—indeed, it is a serious error to suppose—that this requires us to define where they are or where they should be exclusively in terms of the current catch-words. For almost a decade in higher education, "relevance" has been used as a rallying cry for legitimating the immediate and for wrongly equating the transitory with the more enduring.

We would do well to remember that it is the essence of university life to struggle for objectivity and personal knowledge by skeptical testing of the immediate and the known and the continuous exploration of the unknown. Intoxication with relevance blunts this vital activity, since it tends to confine the examination of reality to the immediately relevant.

5. **The recourse to litigation disguised as equity.** Everybody, it appears, wants to sue in the interest of justice. Matters never brought to litigation before, i.e., tenure, promotion, the making of professional judgments (which can do someone an "injury" and hence open you to a lawsuit), are now increasingly headed for the courts.

It is not the appeal to law that is necessarily bad. It is the scale of these appeals and the degree to which normal university procedures are being pushed from the center of university life to another center of gravity. In short, academic due process is giving way to the legal adversarial process.

6. **The appeal to subjectivism disguised as individualism.** This is the "do your own thing" disease. Too often it is a form of anarchy or eccentricity disguised as the right of the individual to express himself without hindrance.

In one of the state universities in California, an established scholar with 20 years of academic experience was recently charged by a student with infringing on her constitutional and individual rights because he made critical comments on her research paper. Sometimes such a charge is supported by a belief that "objective knowledge" is impossible to achieve. It presumably follows that in the absence of authoritative judgments, anything—or almost anything—is legitimate. Such an irresponsible view is tantamount to social illiteracy. It obscures the real character of individual rights, reducing them entirely to personal whim and neglecting entirely their meaning within a nexus of social relationships. University life is one of those social relationships where it is essential to recognize the reality of differences in knowledge and authority without regarding these differences as adversarial in character or menacing to the human rights of the individual.

These are but some of the maledictions that are the legacy of the 1960's. Each has been with us to some degree in the past. They have now gained new credibility because in the last ten years our cultural values have shifted, and with that has come, inevitably, a shift in university standards and norms.

It would be comforting if there were some potent wizardry to cope with these maledictions. What is available to us instead are the arts of persuasion and civility, the principles of logic and argumentation, respect for the rule of law and due process, and the processes of science and scholarship broadly conceived as involving a commitment to rational and fair public discourse and scrupulous concern for the assessment of evidence.

Part VIII

Government, Foundations, Corporations

CONTEXT

The postwar years witnessed the entry of the government as a powerful agent of external influence shaping higher education in the United States. Government thus joined foundations, some of which—Carnegie and Rockefeller—had been active and effective since early in the twentieth century, particularly in promoting innovative research in the natural and social sciences (11). But when the estates of Henry and Edsel Ford were settled in 1949, the Ford Foundation suddenly became the world's richest philanthropy, and it had the resources to create whole new domains of research and teaching, most notably in the "behavioral sciences" and area studies (12). And the Fulbright Act made higher education in the United States more cosmopolitan (2).

Intervention by government went beyond investment in research, important as that was in the age of big science (8–10; I, 2–3). Beginning with the G.I. Bill, federal programs and policies transformed the social characteristics of college students and graduates, thus contributing to the expansion and diversification of an American middle class. It is true that the main beneficiaries of the G.I. Bill were white males, but later judicial, legislative, and executive actions of the 1950s and 1960s worked in favor of women, African Americans, and other underrepresented groups (1; II, 16, 20; V, 11; IX, 1–5). The National Defense Education Act, passed in response to the Soviet Union's successful launch of its *Sputnik* earth satellite, served to expand and diversify the professoriate and the American research establishment. The N.D.E.A. legislation recognized, moreover, that undue expansion of the science and engineering divisions of universities, the areas most likely to contribute directly to national defense, put disciplinary balance and important ideals of liberal education at risk. Such distortion was a matter of considerable concern to higher education administrators, and the N.D.E.A. legislation wisely supported doctoral education in the humanities and social sciences as well (4). There were other worries about the impact of government engagement, including the relation of research to teaching and fear of undue regulations and bureaucracy (3, 5, 6, 8). And there was nervousness, in some measure justified, that government-funded research oriented toward national security might corrupt academe, making science and scholarship the servant of power rather than the independent pursuit of knowledge (7).

By the end of the century, the scale of higher education and the research establishment especially in the sciences, meant that philanthropy, save in highly specific and restricted areas, could no longer have either a transforming or sustaining impact. That made government funding even more important for big science, which required huge investments in equipment, such as a nuclear accelerator, and in the biological sciences, which replaced physics after about 1975 as the most widely discussed frontier of discovery. When government funding failed to keep up with the seemingly insatiable needs of researchers, corporations, especially in the agricultural sciences and pharmaceuticals, stepped in. That caused a whole new set of worries about distorting the core principles of the university. The commercialization of university research was seen by many academic people as a threat to the basic value of open access to findings and to peer-reviewed determination of promotions and tenure (13, 14). At the same time, opinion polls revealed that a majority of Americans doubted the scientific merit of the theory of evolution that underlay modern biology, favoring instead "creationism" or "intelligent design." Scientists, already worried by this apparently religious-based revolt against science, were further shaken when the president of the United States banned the use of federal funds for any research that depends upon stem cells derived from human embryos (10). One could not help but wonder whether the grand vision of science as the "endless frontier" might be at risk (10; I, 2–3, 5).

Government

1. The Servicemen's Readjustment Act, Public Law 346 (The G.I. Bill of Rights), 1944

The G.I. Bill brought wider access to higher education in a democracy and became a milestone in twentieth-century American social history. For educational importance, it ranks with the egalitarian judicial and legislative civil rights federal directives of the decades to follow. Yet the gap between the much-noted postwar educational impact of the act and the prewar shortsightedness toward its educational possibilities even among its sponsors—as well as outright opposition among leading university presidents—makes for a rich historical irony. During a radio fireside chat in the summer of 1943, President Franklin D. Roosevelt, recalling the unrewarded and unemployed position of many veterans after World War I and echoing commanders of the American Legion, emphasized that this time returning military "must not be demobilized into . . . a place on a bread line or on a corner selling apples." From Harvard, however, James B. Conant warned against indiscriminately admitting academically unproven veterans to his institution. Robert M. Hutchins, often colorful in his opinions, declared that too generous an educational bill for veterans would be only a device for "coping with mass unemployment" and would convert colleges and universities "into educational hobo jungles." Various versions of a bill were lengthily debated throughout 1944—all suggested or supported by veteran groups and all agreeing with FDR's general sentiment. Early on, publicists from the American Legion and other veterans' organizations had conceived the legislation to be a G.I. Bill of Rights. The name stuck. An army enlisted person was a GI, standing for "Government Issue," but in the early thirties the letters had meant galvanized iron military equipment, particularly the common trash can with which all soldiers on KP ("kitchen police") duty were familiar. The final bill, whose relevant educational parts are reprinted here, passed through Congress unopposed as the Servicemen's Readjustment Act (Public Law 346) and followed wording drafted by American Legion Commander Henry Colmery. It offered economic and educational help to over fifteen million honorably discharged servicemen and women who had served at least ninety days.

The effects of Public Law 346 were quite the opposite of what many had feared. By 1951 some eight million veterans had taken advantage of the various parts of the program. Government-guaranteed loans were made toward the purchase of homes, farms, and small businesses. Three and a half million veterans attended vocational schools under the G.I. Bill; 1.5 million took on-the-job training; almost seven hundred thousand used their entitlement for farm training. The G.I. Bill supported over 2.2 million veterans at two- and four-year colleges and universities. Public postsecondary institutions especially were swamped with maturing, purposeful, and hardworking students confronting inadequate teaching facilities and housing shortages.

The nation was in turn well rewarded. An educated and industrious economic middle class grew to dim the record of prewar years. Taxes from these one-time citizen soldiers helped to fund public projects and services.

By 1964 the Veterans Administration reported that G.I. Bill veterans had entered the professions in the following numbers: 243,000 accountants, 36,000 clergymen, 180,000 doctors, dentists, and nurses, 450,000 engineers, 360,000 school teachers, and 150,000 scientists. College gates formerly closed to the children of immigrants, Catholics, and Jews, were opened.

The G.I. Bill nevertheless had its limitations. Though not certifying veterans' intentions, the Veterans Administration conceded that out of the total number of G.I. college students, perhaps only 20 percent comprised those who would not have attended college without the G.I. Bill. Of 350,000 women veterans, only about 64,000 used the G.I. Bill for college, many not having been informed of their eligibility; some found college-required job openings going only to returning males; many followed the historical postwar tendency to return to motherhood and homemaking. Discrimination toward black soldiers that had poisoned race relations in the war zones was reflected by the still-segregated historically black colleges of the South, which did increase their black G.I. enrollments but lacked facilities to take all who were eligible. Six decades later, the record shows significant discrimination against black veterans until the mid-1960s by limiting or denying them any of the broad range of economic, educational, or employment benefits of the G.I. Bill.

Similar though not identical congressional acts for the education of Korean and Vietnam War veterans passed in 1952, 1966, and 1967. Like the first G.I. Bill, these rewards to military people initiated the hope and expectation of a college education in the next generations.

Public Law 346, 78th Congress, 2nd Session, June 24, 1944. An Act to provide Federal Government aid for the readjustment in civilian life of returning World War II veterans. Further reading: The G.I. Bill awaits a large and comprehensive chronicle. Until one appears, see Keith W. Olson, *The G.I. Bill, the Veterans, and the Colleges* (Lexington, KY, 1974); Americo D. Lappati, *Education and the Federal Government: A Historical Record* (New York, 1975), 60–61; Davis R. B. Ross, *Preparing for Ulysses: Politics and Veterans during World War II* (New York, 1969); Michael J. Bennett, *When Dreams Come True: The G.I. Bill and the Making of Modern America* (New York, 1996); John R. Thelin, *A History of American Higher Education* (Baltimore, 2004): 262–68; Ira Katznelson, *When Affirmative Action Was White: An Untold History of Racial Inequality in Twentieth-Century America* (New York, 2005); Daniel A. Clark, " 'The Two Joes Meet—Joe College, Joe Veteran': The G.I. Bill, College Education, and Postwar American Culture," *History of Education Quarterly* 38 (Summer 1998): 165–89; Milton Greenberg, "How the G.I. Bill Changed Education," *Chronicle of Higher Education*, June 18, 2004, B9–11, the best brief description of the GI Bill's influence; Suzanne Mettler, *Soldiers to Citizens: The G.I. Bill and the Making of the Greatest Generation* (New York, 2005)—beyond the treatments of the foregoing titles, Mettler surveys, with abundant statistics, the life histories of G.I. Bill veterans who came to "civic consciousness" through actions of the federal government before World War II and held that disposition, reinforced by their military service, to carry them into active civic lives throughout the 1950s and 1960s. Quoted here: Samuel J. Rosenman, ed., *The Public Papers and Addresses of*

Franklin D. Roosevelt (New York, 1950), 1943 volume: 333–34; James B. Conant, "Annual Report of the President of the University," *Harvard Alumni Bulletin*, January 22, 1944, 244 (also Olson, *The G.I. Bill*, 123); Robert M. Hutchins, "The Threat to American Education," *Collier's*, December 30, 1944, 20–21.

PART VIII

1. Any person who served in the active military or naval service on or after September 16, 1940, and prior to the termination of the present war, and who shall have been discharged or released therefrom under conditions other than dishonorable, and whose education or training was impeded, delayed, interrupted, or interfered with by reason of his entrance into the service, or who desires a refresher or retraining course, and who either shall have served ninety days or more, exclusive of any period he was assigned for a course of education or training under the Army specialized training program or the Navy college training program, which course was a continuation of his civilian course and was pursued to completion, or as a cadet or midshipman at one of the service academies, or shall have been discharged or released from active service by reason of an actual service-incurred injury or disability, shall be eligible for and entitled to receive education or training under this part: *Provided,* That such course shall be initiated not later than two years after either the date of his discharge or the termination of the present war, whichever is the later: *Provided further,* That no such education or training shall be afforded beyond seven years after the termination of the present war: *And provided further,* That any such person who was not over 25 years of age at the time he entered the service shall be deemed to have had his education or training impeded, delayed, interrupted, or interfered with.

2. Any such eligible person shall be entitled to education or training, or a refresher or retraining course, at an approved educational or training institution, for a period of one year (or the equivalent thereof in continuous part-time study), or for such lesser time as may be required for the course of instruction chosen by him. Upon satisfactory completion of such course of education or training, according to the regularly prescribed standards and practices of the institutions, except a refresher or retraining course, such person shall be entitled to an additional period or periods of education or training, not to exceed the time such person was in the active service on or after September 16, 1940, and before the termination of the war, exclusive of any period he was assigned for a course of education or training under the Army specialized training program or the Navy college training program, which course was a continuation of his civilian course and was pursued to completion, or as a cadet or midshipman at one of the service academies, but in no event shall the total period of education or training exceed four years: *Provided,* That his work continues to be satisfactory throughout the period, according to the regularly prescribed standards and practices of the institution: *Provided, however,* That wherever the additional period of instruction ends during a quarter or semester and after a major part of such quarter or semester has expired, such period of instruction shall be extended to the termination of such unexpired quarter or semester.

3. Such person shall be eligible for and entitled to such course of education or training as he may elect, and at any approved educational or training institution at which he chooses to enroll, whether or not located in the State in which he resides, which will accept or retain him as a student or trainee in any field or branch of knowledge which such institution finds him qualified to undertake or pursue: *Provided,* That, for reasons satisfactory to the Administrator, he may change a course of instruction: *And provided further,* That any such course of education or training may be discontinued at any time, if it is found by the Administrator that, according to the regularly prescribed standards and practices of the institution, the conduct or progress of such person is unsatisfactory. . . .

5. The Administrator shall pay to the educational or training institution, for each person enrolled in full time or part time course of education or training, the customary cost of tuition, and such laboratory, library, health, infirmary, and other similar fees as are customarily charged, and may pay for books, supplies, equipment, and other necessary expenses, exclusive of board, lodging, other living expenses, and travel, as are generally required for the successful pursuit and completion of the course by other students in the institution: *Provided,* That in no event shall such payments, with respect to any person, exceed $500 for an ordinary school year: *Provided further,* That no payments shall be made to institutions, business or other establishments furnishing apprentice training on the job. . . .

6. While enrolled in and pursuing a course under this part, such person, upon application to the Administrator, shall be paid a subsistence allowance of $50 per month, if without a dependent or dependents, or $75 per month, if he has a dependent or dependents, including regular holidays and leave not exceeding thirty days in a calendar year. . . .

11. As used in this part, the term "educational or training institutions" shall include all public or private elementary, secondary, and other schools furnishing education for adults, business schools and colleges, scientific and technical institutions, colleges, vocational schools, junior colleges, teachers colleges, normal schools, professional schools, universities, and other educational institutions, and shall also include business or other establishments providing apprentice or other training on the job,

including those under the supervision of an approved college or university or any State department of education, or any State apprenticeship agency or State board of vocational education, or any State apprenticeship council or the Federal Apprentice Training Service, . . . or any agency in the executive branch of the Federal Government authorized under other laws to supervise such training.

2. The Mutual Educational and Cultural Exchange Act (Hays-Fulbright Act), 1961

College courses on the ways of other countries and regions gained a foothold in more institutions after World War II, and foreign studies soon escalated amid Cold War tensions. One government program did more to enable graduate students and faculty members to have firsthand experience in international studies than any other institutional arrangement. It was the brainchild of J. William Fulbright (1905–95). He was a Missourian and a conservative Democrat who, after a Rhodes scholarship, went on to become president of the University of Arkansas (1939–41) and was then elected to the U.S. Senate (1945–74). As an internationally minded idealist, he was convinced that comity among nations would be enhanced by personal relationships and academic interchanges. Beginning in 1945, he skillfully and slyly, at times and locations where opposing senators would be scarce, maneuvered his design to fund the international exchange of college students and faculty. Monies for this program were to come from the sale of postwar surplus American property overseas. Fulbright's plan passed unopposed as a rider to another bill (A Bill to Amend the Surplus Property Act of 1944, The Fulbright Act, Public Law 584, 1946). Fifteen years later, Senator Fulbright joined with Congressman Wayne Hays to sponsor the Hays-Fulbright Act, known also as the Cultural Exchange Act; its early portions are reprinted here. The revision consolidated several federal exchange programs, including the original Fulbright Act.

By 2004 the program had engaged more than two hundred thousand Americans abroad, the majority having done advanced research, lectured, or taught in elementary and secondary schools. Additionally, 42,200 international scholars came to do research and teaching in the United States as Fulbright Visiting Scholars. The presence of Fulbright programs encouraged the growth of American undergraduate studies in foreign countries, often termed "junior years abroad," established independently by many colleges and universities. Senator Fulbright's one-time tutor at Oxford once called the senator's program "the largest and most significant movement of scholars across the earth since the fall of Constantinople in 1453." John F. Kennedy called the program "the classic modern example of beating swords into plowshares." In his later years, Fulbright wrote simply that his idea had "a globe-trotting career."

Public Law 87-256, 87th Congress, H. R. 8666, September 21, 1961. Further reading: Americo D. Lapati, *Education and the Federal Government: A Historical Record* (New York, 1975); Randall Bennett Woods, *Fulbright, A Biography* (New York, 1995), quotation 136; Walter Johnson and Francis J. Colligan, *The Fulbright Program: A History* (Chicago, 1965); Haynes Johnson and Bernard M. Gwertzman, *Fulbright, the Dissenter* (New York, 1968), quotation 108.

The Secretary of State is authorized to enter an executive agreement or agreements with any foreign government for the use of currencies, or credits for currencies, of such government held or available for expenditure by the United States or any agency thereof . . . for the purpose of providing, by the formation of foundations or otherwise, for (A) financing studies, research, instruction, and other educational activities of or for American citizens in schools and institutions of higher learning located in such foreign country, or of the citizens of such foreign country in American schools and institutions of higher learning located outside the continental United States, Hawaii, Alaska (including the Aleutian Islands), Puerto Rico, and the Virgin Islands, including payment for transportation, tuition, maintenance, and other expenses incident to scholastic activities; or (B) furnishing transportation for citizens of such foreign country who desire to attend American schools and institutions of higher learning in the continental United States, Hawaii, Alaska (including the Aleutian Islands), Puerto Rico, and the Virgin Islands, and whose attendance will not deprive citizens of the United States of an opportunity to attend such schools and institutions: *Provided, however,* That no such agreement or agreements shall provide for the use of an aggregate amount of the currencies, or credits for currencies, of any one country in excess of $20,000,000 or for the expenditure of the currencies, or credits for currencies, of any one foreign country in excess of $1,000,000 annually at the official rate of exchange for such currencies, unless otherwise authorized by Congress, nor shall any such agreement relate to any subject other than the use and expenditure of such currencies or credits for currencies for the purposes herein set forth: *Provided further,* That for the purpose of selecting students and educational institutions qualified to participate in this program, and to supervise the exchange program authorized herein, the President of the United States is hereby authorized to appoint a Board of Foreign Scholarships, consisting of ten members, who shall serve without compensation, composed of representatives of cultural, educational, student and war veterans groups, and including representatives of the United States Office of Education, the United States Veterans' Administration, State educational institutions, and privately endowed educational institutions: *And provided further,* That in the selection of American citizens for study in foreign countries under this paragraph preference shall be given to applicants who shall have served in the military or naval forces of the United States during World War I or World War II, and due consideration shall be given to applicants from all geographical areas of the United States.

3. American Council on Education, *Sponsored Research Policy of Colleges and Universities*, 1954

Committees from both the National Science Foundation and the American Council on Education in 1954 were inquiring into the manifold problems of government-university relations that had been troubling all academic people concerned with federally funded contracts since World War II. A committee from the ACE here suggests how academic institutions should respond to the grant of federal monies and contracts. Other reports out of Washington in the 1950s and 1960s described the national condition of academic bureaucracies proliferating to supervise, disperse, coordinate, and manage federal largess that mirrored the same activities in their even larger governmental counterparts. Some of the issues in this report have not yet been fully resolved.

The American Council on Education, founded in 1918, describes itself as "the nation's major coordinating body for postsecondary education." By the 1970s its president and the heads of thirteen other academic associations in Washington, D.C., were called the "Washington Higher Education Secretariat" and by one critic the "academic Vatican."

American Council on Education, Committee on Institutional Research, *Sponsored Research Policy of Colleges and Universities* (Washington, D.C., 1954): 4, 11–21. Reprinted with permission from ACE Publications, Copyright © 1954 by American Council on Education. Further reading: George W. Bonham, "The Wrong Move at the Wrong Time," *Change* 3 (Summer 1971): 11–13; Sanford A. Lakoff, ed., *Knowledge and Power: Essays on Science and Government* (New York, 1966), pt. 3, on university contract grants under federal funding; and Alvin M. Weinberg, *Reflections on Big Science* (Cambridge, MA, 1967), pt. 4.

No educational institution should seek or accept funds for emergency research or development unless it has special advantages of men, experience, and facilities which make it clear that the institution can undertake the work better than some other agency. Even under these conditions, the institution might appropriately refuse the work unless it should become compellingly clear that it has a responsibility to help the government meet an emergency objective.

Except for emergency projects, sponsored research should be closely related to the normal program and recognized objectives of the institution. It should involve only work which can be carried out with enthusiasm by the staff, and it specifically should not be work which the staff would undertake with reluctance and which would be unrelated to their educational and professional programs. A member of a faculty should never be assigned to contract research against his will. Normally, no project should be accepted unless it is open to qualified students.

Imposition of restrictions on publication of research results, either for secrecy or patent reasons, is incompatible with the basic concept of an educational institution as a source and distributor of knowledge and is difficult to reconcile with the other basic aims of such an institution. Such restrictions, especially long-term or permanent restrictions, should be undertaken only for exceptional or emergency reasons; otherwise, no arrangement should be permitted which could inhibit free and effective scholarship, freely disseminated.

The college or university should maintain a proper balance between the sponsored research it undertakes with short-term financing and its normal program, in order to avoid the hazards enumerated above. No institution should permit itself to become so dependent upon sponsored research that the cancellation of this research would seriously damage it.

The educational institution should carefully determine the entire cost to it of sponsored research, and if it accepts contracts or grants that do not cover both direct and indirect costs, the institution should do so with the full recognition that it is itself making a contribution to the cost of the work. The Committee believes that this is a part of a larger problem facing our colleges and universities, involving the acceptance of grants-in-aid from those foundations and other sources which at present do not pay the full cost of the projects they support. The Committee recognizes that "full-cost" arrangements may be modified when appropriate by provisions regarding disposition of equipment.

Institutions should define their academic and fiscal policies and thus avoid differences and conflicts within their own organizations. To avoid disagreements about costs properly chargeable to contracts, they should follow clear accounting procedures themselves and should insist on unambiguous and equitable contracts.

Educational institutions should invite all research-sponsoring agencies, whether governmental, foundational, or industrial, to give more careful consideration to the advantages of institutional research grants over the specific project type; and in their dealings with these agencies they should exert their utmost influence toward a wider application of the principle of institutional rather than project support of research, recognizing at the same time that there are research problems that can be attacked only on a project basis.

The institution should make a continuous effort to see that its own faculty members are provided with sufficient information on over-all costs and financial problems so as to minimize internal misconceptions over "diversion" of part of contract or grant funds to meet indirect costs.

RESEARCH UNDERTAKEN WITH GOVERNMENT SUPPORT

Both the government and the institutions should be aware of and should guard against the danger that these large-scale projects may, under the exigencies of government sponsorship, take on more of the aspects of competitive business than befits an educational institution. One way to accomplish this is to insist insofar as practicable that investigations undertaken are fundamental in character. . . .

In the event that further large-scale defense research projects become necessary, the Committee suggests that the government should give consideration to the desirability of establishing additional central laboratories involving the multiple participation of institutions. A good geographical distribution of such facilities by which the special abilities of institutions and their staffs can be utilized may provide one of the most satisfactory ways for meeting the government's needs while at the same time meeting the special requirements of colleges and universities. . . .

No single government agency should have responsibility for managing all the government's general-purpose research in educational institutions. The establishment of the National Science Foundation has been welcomed by educational institutions, but occasional efforts to transfer to the foundation all general-purpose research funds in the government are viewed with apprehension. The Committee recommends that the government not concentrate its general-purpose research funds in any single government agency, since such concentration might result in creating a powerful bureaucracy, which could exert too much control of education and which might lose the great advantages in research management of diversity in method and objectives. No single government agency, however ably managed, could have all the "right" policies and methods.

Although no one agency could be expected to have enough wisdom to manage the government's entire program of general-purpose research, every effort should be made by all government agencies to achieve uniformity in contractual procedures and provisions.

The effectiveness of government-supported research in universities and colleges would be greatly increased if the government were to stabilize its support, both in funds and management. Sharp or capricious reductions, even when followed by later increases, cause disruptions to institutions and damage to the research programs. Grants or contracts should be planned and awarded on the basis of at least a three-year commitment.

4. The National Defense Education Act, 1958

Signed by President Eisenhower on September 2, 1958, this bill was the American educational response to the launching, one year earlier, of the Russian space vehicle, *Sputnik.* Widespread concern over Russian superiority in missile development put the thrust of this bill behind scientific programs and modern foreign language instruction in colleges. Inadequate financing of schools for the post–World War II Baby Boom added impetus for the bill in a time when proposals for federal school funding had continuously been resisted by state rights proponents and religious groups who wanted federal support of parochial schools. Leaders in higher education vigorously

opposed the Communist disclaimer in Title X, which remnant of the McCarthy period was repealed in 1962.

The NDEA demonstrated a gathering consensus over federal aid at least to college students. By 1964 student loans were no longer awarded only in the critical "defense" fields and were extended to curricula in English, history, reading, and geography. By 1968 the country had spent $3 billion on fifteen thousand NDEA graduate fellowships and on loans to 1.5 million undergraduates, support of institutes for 122,000 teachers, training for 44,000 guidance counselors, modernization of teaching procedures, and foreign language and area study centers.

Public Law 85–864, 85th Congress, 2nd Session, September 2, 1958. Further reading: Barbara Barksdale Clowse, *Brainpower for the Cold War: The Sputnik Crisis and National Defense Act of 1958* (Westport, CT, 1981); Americo D. Lapati, *Education and the Federal Government: A Historical Record* (New York, 1975), 72–88; A. Whitney Griswold, *Liberal Education and the Democratic Ideal and Other Essays,* new enlarged ed. (New Haven, 1962), ch. 16; and Edward P. St. John and Michael D. Parsons, *Public Funding of Higher Education: Changing Contexts and New Rationales* (Baltimore, 2006).

TITLE I—GENERAL PROVISIONS

Findings and Declaration of Policy

SEC. 101. The Congress hereby finds and declares that the security of the Nation requires the fullest development of the mental resources and technical skills of its young men and women. The present emergency demands that additional and more adequate educational opportunities be made available. The defense of this Nation depends upon the mastery of modern techniques developed from complex scientific principles. It depends as well upon the discovery and development of new principles, new techniques, and new knowledge.

We must increase our efforts to identify and educate more of the talent of our Nation. This requires programs that will give assurance that no student of ability will be denied an opportunity for higher education because of financial need; will correct as rapidly as possible the existing imbalances in our educational programs which have led to an insufficient proportion of our population educated in science, mathematics, and modern foreign languages and trained in technology.

The Congress reaffirms the principle and declares that the States and local communities have and must retain control over and primary responsibility for public education. The national interest requires, however, that the Federal Government give assistance to education for programs which are important to our defense.

To meet the present educational emergency requires additional effort at all levels of government. It is therefore the purpose of this Act to provide substantial assistance in various forms to individuals, and to States and their subdivisions, in order to insure trained manpower of sufficient quality and quantity to meet the national defense needs of the United States.

Federal Control of Education Prohibited

SEC. 102. Nothing contained in this Act shall be construed to authorize any department, agency, officer, or employee of the United States to exercise any direction, supervision, or control over the curriculum, program of instruction, administration, or personnel of any educational institution or school system. . . .

Condition of Agreements

SEC. 204. An agreement with any institution of higher education for Federal capital contributions by the Commissioner under this title, shall—

provide for establishment of a student loan fund by such institution . . .

provide that in the selection of students to receive loans from such student loan fund special consideration shall be given to (A) students with a superior academic background who express a desire to teach in elementary or secondary schools, and (B) students whose academic background indicates a superior capacity or preparation in science, mathematics, engineering, or a modern foreign language. . . .

TITLE IV—NATIONAL DEFENSE FELLOWSHIPS

Appropriations Authorized

SEC. 401. There are hereby authorized to be appropriated such sums as may be necessary to carry out the provisions of this title.

Number of Fellowships

SEC. 402. During the fiscal year ending June 30, 1959, the Commissioner is authorized to award one thousand fellowships under the provisions of this title, and during each of the three succeeding fiscal years he is authorized to award one thousand five hundred such fellowships. Such fellowships shall be for periods of study not in excess of three academic years. . . .

Fellowship Stipends

SEC. 404. (a) Each person awarded a fellowship under the provisions of this title shall receive a stipend of $2,000 for the first academic year of study after the baccalaureate degree, $2,200 for the second such year, and $2,400 for the third such year, plus an additional amount of $400 for each such year on account of each of his dependents.

(b) In addition to the amounts paid to persons pursuant to subsection (a) there shall be paid to the institution of higher education at which each such person is pursuing his course of study such amount, not more than $2,500 per academic year, as is determined by the Commissioner to constitute that portion of the cost of the new graduate program or of the expansion in an existing graduate program in which such person is pursuing his course of study, which is reasonably attributable to him. . . .

TITLE VI—LANGUAGE DEVELOPMENT

Part A—Centers and Research and Studies Language and Area Centers

SEC. 601. (a) The Commissioner is authorized to arrange through contracts with institutions of higher education for the establishment and operation by them, during the period beginning July 1, 1958, and ending with the close of June 30, 1962, of centers for the teaching of any modern foreign language with respect to which the Commissioner determines (1) that individuals trained in such language are needed by the Federal Government or by business, industry, or education in the United States, and (2) that adequate instruction in such language is not readily available in the United States. Any such contract may provide for instruction not only in such modern foreign language but also in other fields needed to provide a full understanding of the areas, regions, or countries in which such language is commonly used, to the extent adequate instruction in such fields is not readily available, including fields such as history, political science, linguistics, economics, sociology, geography, and anthropology. . . .

TITLE X

Miscellaneous Provisions

. . . (f) No part of any funds appropriated or otherwise made available for expenditure under authority of this Act shall be used to make payments or loans to any individual unless such individual (1) has executed and filed with the Commissioner an affidavit that he does not believe in, and is not a member of and does not support any organization that believes in or teaches, the overthrow of the United States Government by force or violence or by any illegal or unconstitutional methods, and (2) has taken and subscribed to an oath or affirmation in the following form: "I do solemnly swear (or affirm) that I will bear true faith and allegiance to the United States of America and will support and defend the Constitution and laws of the United States against all its enemies, foreign and domestic." The provisions of section 1001 of title 18, United States Code, shall be applicable with respect to such affidavits. . . .

5. Daniel S. Cheever, *Harvard and the Federal Government*, 1961

This report on two decades of federal funding at Harvard reveals the growth, internal changes, and problems, unforeseen before 1939, commonly experienced by most American universities enjoying federal support. The principal author of the report was Daniel S. Cheever (1916–), with his B.A. from Harvard (1939) and his Ph.D. (1948). He was a specialist in government and international affairs who in 1961 assisted the president of Harvard and later became a professor at the University of Pittsburgh (1961–82) and then a professor of international relations at Boston University.

Daniel S. Cheever, *Harvard and the Federal Government: A Report to the Faculties and Governing Boards of Harvard University,* September 1961 (Cambridge, MA, 1961), 3–10, 13–14, 19–20. Further reading: Nathaniel Pusey, *Report of the President of Harvard University* (1960–61).

Harvard is by no means unique in its new relationship with Government. At least 80% of the institutions of higher education in the United States now receive Federal funds, and Harvard is one of those heavily involved in Federal programs. It is difficult to obtain precise totals but a sampling of seventeen institutions with large Federal programs showed Harvard in ninth place both in the amount received and in the relation Federal money bore to the total university budget.

Government funds tend to concentrate in the relatively few institutions with strong graduate and professional programs in the natural sciences because of the heavy national emphasis on research. A recent study of Federal expenditures for research in 287 institutions showed that 5 institutions received 57% of the total, while 20 institutions received 79% and 66 received 92%. . . .

While the use of Federal funds at Harvard has, up to the present, served the interests of both public policy and the advancement of knowledge, there are enough potential difficulties in the relationship to warrant taking a careful look at where we are and where we seem to be going.

With the First Morrill Act of 1862, the Congress turned from the idea of a national university that had intrigued a number of the Founding Fathers and adopted two policies that have persisted as the basis of Federal programs in higher education. It decided to give land grants to both private and state institutions, and to this day Federal grant programs do not discriminate between them. At the same time it decided to give support not to the general purposes of education, but to the improvement of the "agricultural and mechanic arts," and Federal support is still granted not for "education" but rather to further the specific purposes of particular Federal departments and agencies. But this leads inevitably into it a complicated situation. For example, the national programs in which universities are now involved are not confined to the field of defense; they are also growing, wherever the advancement of knowledge may make a contribution to the solution of social problems or the advancement of human welfare. For instance, Congress has multiplied by ten times in eight years the resources of the National Institutes of Health whose grants have done so much to support research, and provide research facilities, at Harvard.

Federal support is most conspicuous in the research portions of the University's budget. . . .

During 1959–60, Harvard received more than $18 million from the Government of which $11,860,000 was solely for research purposes. This total included $6,512,000 from the Department of Health, Education and Welfare, of which $5,495,000 came from the various National Institutes of Health for research toward the cure of specific diseases, $826,000 from the Division of General Medical Science, and $132,000 from The Office of Education. The other major sources were The National Science Foundation, established to foster basic research, which provided $1,155,000, and the Office of Naval Research which provided $1,704,500.

The several Facilities of the University obviously did not share equally in Federal support for research. The principal benefactors . . . were the three schools in the Medical area and the Faculty of Arts and Sciences. Moreover there are variations among the departments within the Faculty of Arts and Sciences, with the chief research support going to departments in the Natural Sciences, including the Division of Engineering and Applied Physics, and to the museums. But small amounts do come to the Russian Research Center and the Laboratory of Social Relations, and programs in mental health are beginning to bring some support to the social sciences.

The Federal Government has been even more generous, in certain specialized fields, in the construction and operation of research facilities. The Cambridge Electron Accelerator will be completed in 1962 at an estimated cost of $11,630,000. This sum will have come from the Atomic Energy Commission. While the Commission will retain title to this facility for 25 years, Harvard and M.I.T. will operate it jointly so as to provide new research opportunities not only for their own Faculties, but for an additional research staff. The work made possible by this new facility is of such importance that the Atomic Energy Commission will support additional research staff and the entire operating costs, which are expected to total approximately $5 million annually by 1963–64.

Here clearly is a wholly new dimension in higher education. Advance in nuclear physics requires expenditures beyond the capacity of private donors. In the main, Federal backing does not in this case involve financial cost to the University nor does it impose limitations on freedom of inquiry or the right to publish. The scientific community in Harvard, in M.I.T., and in the Government agreed that a facility of this sort should be built. Its presence near the Harvard Yard is eloquent testimony to the joint concern of the university world and the Federal Government for the advancement of nuclear physics. . . .

While it might seem the Federal Government makes an arbitrary distinction in favor of research and against instruction, there are exceptions. The School of Public Health received from the Public Health Service in 1959–60 almost $154,000 to support its general instructional programs. Furthermore, support for instructional programs in certain foreign languages was provided by the Office of Education. Under the National Defense Education Act, that office paid out over $80,000 for instruction in Far Eastern and Middle Eastern languages, on condition that this be matched in equal amounts by the University. The three Armed Services contributed nearly $130,000 toward the ROTC program. The School of Public Health participated in a program, aided by a $23,000 grant from the International Cooperation Administration for teachers of preventive medicine and public health. The Atomic Energy Commission and the National Science Foundation sought to promote the training of science teachers by furnishing the School of Education and the Faculty of Arts and Sciences something over $283,000.

In addition the Federal Government has turned to universities for specific advice on important issues. In the summer of 1960, for example, the Senate Foreign Relations Committee asked the Harvard Center for International Affairs to prepare studies on certain problems in American foreign policy at a cost of approximately $20,000 to the Government.

Far more often, however, the Government turns to individual Faculty members, through consulting arrangements which may benefit both the Government and the University. So long as a Faculty member is able to carry out his academic responsibilities, he is free to consult as much as he wishes. Practice varies from Faculty to Faculty. . . . When Departments are considered as a whole, the average number of days of off-campus consulting per month per Faculty member is surprisingly small. In the Faculty of Arts and Sciences, it was exceptional to find that the average number of days per member spent on Government business exceeded a day a month. It is true that the University continues to pay fringe benefits and salaries to Faculty members while they are consulting in Washington or elsewhere. Unreimbursed costs of this kind were estimated to amount to $211,310 for the academic year 1959–60. Such an amount, however, cannot properly be considered an unreimbursed cost in the sense that reimbursement should be expected or desired. Nor is such Faculty consulting without benefit to the University or to the faculty member. The figure is simply a measure of the University's involvement with the Federal Government through consultation by Faculty members on an individual basis. . . .

In addition to those who received Training Grants through the University, hundreds of graduate and post-doctoral students came to Harvard either on Federal fellowships, or under some Federal program for the advanced training of its Military, Foreign, or Civil Service, notably in the Graduate School of Public Administration. The University, of course, retains the right to accept or reject these students. The list of agencies awarding fellowships is a long one. The natural science departments in the Faculty of Arts and Sciences have had a considerable share of the total available National Science Foundation Fellowships. A number of National Defense Foreign Language Fellowships encourage study of Far Eastern and Near Eastern languages. By bringing able professional men and women, including government officials, to many parts of the University, these programs have contributed heavily to our academic life.

There is very little Federal assistance for undergraduates. . . .

Harvard has found it impossible to participate in the loan program of the National Defense Education Act (Title 2) on account of the objectionable disclaimer affidavit requirement. It is a source of concern to us that the Congress has completely failed to understand the position of Harvard and the Association of American Universities in the matter. There is a danger signal here. . . .

By 1960 Harvard was participating in at least thirty-four categories of programs managed by two score of Federal agencies, under the general oversight of a dozen Congressional Committees. Since all the Faculties were involved, though in widely varying degrees, Harvard's relationship with Washington was clearly managed on a highly decentralized basis.

While this decentralized pattern, with its heavy emphasis on particular fields and specific activities, has brought about a great many difficult problems, it has probably made it easier to maintain the essential academic freedom of the University. The Federal Government has clearly not interfered in the direction of Harvard's research projects. It has certainly sought to encourage, in fields colored by a national interest, research which our Faculty members wished to undertake. The variety of sources of support helps make it possible for a distinguished scientist in a respected institution to obtain backing for his research on terms acceptable to him and his university. The image of a coercive government dictating what shall and shall not be done in university laboratories and libraries simply does not fit Harvard's experience with Washington. . . .

The availability of Federal grants for project research tends in any university to divide the responsibility of the faculty, and to weaken the influence of the president and the deans, in planning the content, emphasis, and direction of research and teaching. Individual faculty members tend to be influenced less by their colleagues and the needs of their faculty or department as a whole than by the interests they discover can be implemented through their channels of communication with Government agencies. Is it possible to get the tremendous advantages of Federal support and at the same time to maintain a proper balance among the several interests of the University?

Harvard seems to have done so, but it may nevertheless be useful to review our problems as well as our opportunities.

One of the most serious of questions in Federal programs is that of unreimbursed indirect costs on grants. Most spectacular in 1959–60 were the unreimbursed costs arising from research grants, which made satisfactory allowance for direct, but not for indirect costs. While spending $11,860,836 of Federal funds for project research, the University incurred $687,500 in unreimbursed indirect costs.

What a university thinks about the issue of indirect costs depends a great deal on the size of the grants. If a faculty looks to Washington for little of its support, indirect costs are negligible and may in fact be difficult to identify. In sufficient magnitudes, however, Federal grants can make a university poorer rather than richer by building up unreimbursed costs. More than one Faculty at Harvard has found it necessary to limit its participation in desirable programs lest their indirect costs drain away its unrestricted income. . . .

The Federal policy of encouraging construction and modernization of research facilities by a "matching fund" formula, with the University and the Government sharing costs on a dollar for dollar basis, also presents a complex of opportunities and difficulties. A lack of space in some areas of the University has forced the postponement of important research and instruction. Meanwhile, unreimbursed costs of Government-sponsored research have delayed the accumulation of funds that could be used to match the Federal contributions for construction.

The matching fund formula has, of course, long been used by private donors. Whether used by them or the Government, the formula tends to channel funds to the stronger institutions with adequate financial and research resources for facilities which they are fully equipped to support. The matching requirement also helps to prevent universities from becoming dependent on any one source of financial support, thus protecting their freedom of scientific investigation. At present, the matching requirement seems most feasible in construction grants for research facilities, in which private corporations and foundations seem also to be primarily interested. Matching funds for teaching facilities from private sources are manifestly more difficult to obtain. . . .

While all Harvard professors are expected to engage in research, the University community, as a result of Federal funds, now includes a large and growing proportion of research workers who are not members of the teaching Faculty. In view of the type of work they do, Harvard may now have to adjust some of the rules that were designed to maintain the proper balance between those Faculty members with, and those without, permanent tenure.

The problem arises especially in connection with the growing numbers, in many Departments, of Research Assistants, Research Associates, and Research Fellows. These staff members, most of whom are scientists, are recognized as important members of the University community. Most of them (with the exception of the Research Assistants who are primarily students) have corporation appointments,

and receive the same fringe benefits as regular Faculty members. The quantity of Federal funds for research has greatly increased the numbers of such staff members, and thus intensified the perennial problem that a great many more able scholars are attracted to Harvard by temporary positions than can possibly be given tenure appointments. The temptation is very great to use the short-term Federal funds to keep at Harvard scientists for whom there is no prospect of a permanent position being available, to an age when their opportunities elsewhere diminish.

To protect against this danger, we have a general rule that non-tenure appointments for Faculty or research personnel shall not be extended beyond a total of eight years (eleven in the Medical area) or beyond a total of three years for those 35 years of age or older. . . .

6. Harold Orlans, *The Effects of Federal Programs on Higher Education*, 1962

From the 1950s onward, the welcome to government research funds by academic institutions in one respect troubled enough university people to result in this study by Harold Orlans (1921–) sponsored by the Brookings Institution. Did federal research grants indirectly affect teaching because of the needs and importance of faculty research time? Based on his interviews with 400 administrators and the completed results of 3,500 mailed questionnaires, Orlans concluded that federal generosity indeed impinged upon and weakened teaching. His report caused academic leaders to think twice about federal financial assistance. Although his widely read book was taken by some to be a blanket indictment of federal aid, Orlans carefully stated that American culture itself, together with massive academic enrollments, shared responsibility for the "attenuation" of teaching.

Orlans pursued a career of research and writing for the Brookings Institution and the National Science Foundation. He contributed to *Change* and published a biography of T. E. Lawrence.

Harold Orlans, *The Effects of Federal Programs on Higher Education: A Study of 36 Universities and Colleges* (Washington, D.C., 1962), 44, 53–54, 56–57, 64–67, 219–20, 293–94. Further reading: Alice Rivlin, *The Role of the Federal Government in Financing Higher Education* (Washington, D.C., 1961); John C. Honey and Terry W. Hartle, *Federal-State Institutional Relationships in Postsecondary Education* (Syracuse, NY, 1975); Americo D. Lapati, *Education and the Federal Government: A Historical Record* (New York, 1975); Chester E. Finn Jr., *Scholars, Dollars, and Bureaucrats* (Washington, D.C., 1978); Derek C. Bok, "The Federal Government and the University," in *In the Public Interest: The Governmental Role in Academic Institutions*, ed. George Bonham (New Rochelle, NY, 1979), 80–101; and VIII, 3, 5, 10.

It is our thesis that federal research programs, acting in concert with other educational forces, have reduced the time that senior university faculty devote to undergraduates and informal faculty contacts with students, and, in general, have attenuated the personal aspects of undergraduate education at the great universities. Among the other causes of these trends are the increase in both undergraduate and graduate enrollment, the reduced prestige of undergraduate education and teaching, the enhanced prestige of graduate education and research, and the growth in professorial administrative responsibilities. . . .

We have described the diminution of faculty contact with undergraduates at some length without reference to the federal government to emphasize that the government is not the only villain in the piece. The enormous increase in enrollment is the principal cause. But government research programs which devalue undergraduate teaching and reduce the time faculty need devote to it are an important contributory factor.

That, outside of the independent liberal arts college, undergraduate teaching is devalued these days can hardly be disputed. An elder statesman at a private university, recalling the days in the 1920's when things were different, said with feeling, "There's not a university in the country—not Princeton or Harvard—where as much attention is given to undergraduate instruction as to graduate these days." . . .

It appears that the teacher at the good liberal arts college is more widely respected in educational circles than the permanent teacher at the undergraduate college of a great university. The former is at least in an environment of his peers; the latter has to be judged against the standard set by the eminences in his graduate school.

The staff that teaches solely in the undergraduate college of the great universities seems to consist mainly of young men awaiting advancement, older professors surviving from days when undergraduate teaching was more esteemed, women, foreigners, able but doctorless souls, mediocrities with doctorates, and others who, for one reason or another, belong to the legion of the academically disenfranchised. Perhaps most useful and respected are the good teachers who enjoy associating with and influencing undergraduates, but have never quite made the grade in the merciless world of independent scholarship. The cases in which influential and productive men like David Riesman or C. Wright Mills have lodged for many years in the undergraduate college of a great university are so rare as to prove the rule (and it was not a coincidence that both are such unorthodox members of their profession). . . .

Let us repeat, therefore: the problem was *not* created by government research programs. It *has* been exacerbated by them. . . .

REDUCED TEACHING LOADS

BEFORE: There were some reductions in teaching loads at the best universities to encourage research. . . .

NOW: Teaching loads have been reduced so drastically at some institutions that they can hardly get much lower (in 1960–61, scientists at Group I universities taught an average of 6 hours a week; at three universities, their average load was down to 3.9, 4.5 and 4.9 hours respectively); the reductions are more widespread; and the government is reimbursing institutions for the time faculty members devote to federally-financed research during the academic year—in short, the government is paying scientists to teach less. "We have a leaky bucket," said one science dean discussing his teaching problems, "and more and more people are punching holes in it."

BEFORE: Scientists often had a heavier teaching load than humanists . . . .

NOW: The situation is reversed at the universities, and although scientists still carry a heavier load at colleges, the gap between them and the humanists has probably been narrowed. The present study has found a mean teaching load of 6 classroom hours in the sciences and 8.3 in the humanities at Group I universities, compared with 12.7 hours in the sciences and 11.2 in the humanities at twelve liberal arts colleges. . . .

SOME REMEDIES

It is easy to rattle off a string of recommendations as to what universities and the government should do to remedy the reduction of meaningful contact between undergraduates and faculty; but it is not so easy to come up with practical recommendations. We have been at some pains to point out that the loss in contact is not due simply to government research programs; it is a long-standing trend, aggravated by increases in enrollments. For more and more youth today, a college education is serving the function of a high school education a generation ago, and, as college education becomes more common, many of the social values and professional benefits formerly attached to it are increasingly being transferred to graduate and even postdoctoral education.

There is no substitute for smallness. There may be no loss of educational content as enrollment increases—very likely, the content improves, if more money becomes available to pay for better teachers and equipment, and if teachers prepare more carefully for large lectures than they do for smaller discussion sections. But largeness brings with it a reduction particularly in the more informal and spontaneous exchanges between undergraduates and faculty, and probably also a certain narrowing of intellectual horizons to departmental lines.

We are, therefore, all for smallness, where it can be maintained. But it is not going to be maintained at many universities. Any widespread solution to the problem of impersonality must, therefore, be undertaken with the resources and conditions generally found at large universities. One of these resources . . . is the large number of full-time research personnel not presently fully utilized in educational activities.

A more fundamental resource is the time of good

teachers which is misused in second-rate research, because the government and universities have made second-rate research more rewarding than first-rate teaching. Nothing is more essential to intellectual vitality, social progress, and national strength than a high level of high-quality research in all fields. Second-rate research is another matter. Were the optimal balance between research and teaching to be defined, not by the money, but by the talent available for each, there would be much more encouragement of research in the colleges, the humanities, and social sciences, and more encouragement of undergraduate teaching at the big universities. . . .

Institutions have tended to increase the size of undergraduate lecture classes, in order to handle enrollment increases economically while maintaining low teaching hours. The result of these and other developments has been to diminish personal contacts particularly between senior university faculty and lower division students.

Federal programs have had a powerful but indirect influence on these trends because their emphasis on research has served to reduce teaching hours and to strengthen long-established tendencies to devalue undergraduate teaching at the great universities. It can be shown statistically that, in every major field and type of institution, a high degree of involvement in research is accompanied by a reduction in the time spent teaching undergraduates.

While no ready and certainly no cheap way to improve this situation is feasible, the general direction to be taken is clear: (1) a strengthening of those smaller institutions that still preserve meaningful personal contacts between faculty and undergraduates; (2) a greater effort to increase such contacts at larger institutions; and (3) a better balance of federal expenditures between aid to research and teaching.

The distance that higher education, or science education, has gone toward federal subsidization of faculty salaries is astonishing. It is hard to believe that a dozen years ago a committee at the Massachusetts Institute of Technology, which has been in the vanguard of so many innovations in federal-university relations, condemned the practice of providing *summer* salaries on federal research projects— . . . or that, in 1952, the Director of the National Science Foundation stated that it is "a serious thing" for the government to pay the salaries of tenured faculty, "because after all the permanent officers of an institution are the board of directors educationally and it may very well be questionable for the government to be paying their salaries directly or indirectly."

Within a given federal budget for research and development at universities, if more money is allocated to one purpose such as faculty salaries, clearly, less will be available for other purposes such as graduate students, research associates, and equipment. But universities don't look at it that way, assuming rather that federal research appropriations will continue to rise; and each institution, of course, hopes to maximize its *own* immediate income.

Our conclusion will not be popular in many university quarters, but we believe that universities are making a mistake when, in effect, they put their faculty on the federal payroll. (The mistake might be remedied if the present practice were only a way station to some broader form of federal aid to educational institutions.) To be sure, those schools which first capitalize on a new government cost policy will get a bigger initial piece of the pie. Immediately, they stand to gain; but over the long run, it may be feared, they stand to lose two important assets: the ability to pay their faculty from independent sources of income, and, thereby, their ability to say "no" to the government. And the ability to say "no" is as fair a test of virtue in a university as in a woman.

CONCLUSION

This inquiry commenced with three questions:

1. What have been the effects of federal programs upon the quality of higher education, particularly at the undergraduate level?

2. To what extent can or should fuller use be made of institutions not heavily involved in present federal programs?

3. What has been the experience of institutions with the administration of current federal programs?

The text has elaborated the complexity of these questions, and the difficulties of giving simple answers to them. Nevertheless, our answers may be summarized as follows:

1. The direct effects of federal programs have been profound and beneficial in the sciences, noticeable but more imbalanced in the social sciences, and negligible in the humanities. Federal programs have *not* notably affected the relative proportion or quality of faculty or students going into the sciences, but *have* concentrated a large number of faculty and many of the best students at a few leading institutions. While improving the content of instruction by enlarging our knowledge in the sciences, their emphasis upon graduate research and education has depreciated the status of undergraduate teaching and reduced personal contact between senior faculty and lower classmen, especially at large universities. Nor has the quality of undergraduate science education been advanced by the deflection of the best graduate students from teaching assistantships to federal fellowships and research assistantships. The government (and vaster historical forces) has divided the liberal arts faculty into a contingent of relatively young scientists and social scientists with lighter teaching loads, higher income, substantial research support, and other pre-

requisites, and another contingent of older humanists, with heavier teaching loads, lower incomes, and little research support.

2. The heavy concentration of federal research and development funds at a few major installations should be continued; but a greater effort is warranted to extend other programs of scientific research and education to more institutions below the doctoral level which do not now participate extensively in them. The desirability of dispersing more broadly among doctoral level institutions funds now heavily concentrated at a few leading universities must be determined by the degree to which this advances the objectives of individual programs. High priority should be given to strengthening scientific research and education at leading state universities.

3. Government programs have developed along two administrative lines: the project system, in which funds are controlled by individual faculty for designated purposes; and various forms of aid for broader purposes, in which funds are controlled by alliances of faculty or by higher administrative officers. Both methods of support are needed: the project system is vital to the maintenance of high professional standards and the freedom of the individual investigator; broader forms of support are desirable to strengthen neglected scientific and educational areas. In both systems, it is important to emphasize criteria of quality and to resist pressures to distribute money on the basis of a mathematical formula.

To alleviate demands on their own unrestricted income, universities are requesting and receiving from the government increasing sums for the salaries of both junior and tenured faculty for that portion of their time which they devote to federally sponsored research; and they are also seeking reimbursement of the full indirect costs of this research in government grants as well as contracts. We fear that the former policy, especially, is short-sighted, for it reduces the institution's ability to say "No" to the government. Broader forms of aid in which faculty salaries are not tied to specific research undertakings would be preferable; but institutions must remain alert to the dangers of control inherent in any form of large-scale aid. These dangers are not merely past or prospective; they are always present.

7. Robert A. Nisbet, *Project Camelot,* 1966

Project Camelot (1964–65) became a scandal that tested the scholarly propriety and integrity of the social sciences collaborating in peacetime with the American military. Over thirty eminent American scholars signed on for a project with the Special Operations Research Office at American University, funded by the United States Army Office of Research and Development. They represented sociology, social psychology, anthropology, and related behavioral disciplines. All assumed that their overseas inquiries into the national, cultural, and political ways of developing countries could be "indicators and causes of potential internal conflicts" and would be received as impartial, objective observation. In the Cold War climate, several nations were to be studied, but it was Chile, not the primary country for research, that would become the scene of scandal and fiasco. When the identity of the American army as the actual employer of the researchers was mistakenly revealed, Chilean academic people, the citizenry at large, and the Chamber of Deputies were shocked and angered. The project was viewed as an unwarranted invasion into their nation's domestic affairs, tantamount to espionage. Back in 1919 Franz Boas, the father figure of American anthropology, had warned his colleagues against being seen by their overseas subjects as spies. The government's embarrassment in its delicate relations with a sovereign Latin American state caused the secretary of defense to cancel the project in July 1965.

Robert Nisbet (1913–96) wrote one of the first assessments of the project. His was exceptional in emphasizing the reactions in Chile. Nisbet earned his degrees and taught sociology at the University of California (1939–72), then went to Columbia as Albert Schweitzer Professor of the Humanities (1974–78).

Robert A. Nisbet, "Project Camelot: An Autopsy," *The Public Interest* 5 (Fall 1966): 45, 48–55. Reprinted with the kind permission of the author, copyright © 1966 by Robert A. Nisbet. Further reading: *American Psychologist* 21 (May 1966): 441–54, an issue that included Irving Louis Horowitz's detailed narrative of the episode and a reprinting of the hearings in the Subcommittee on International Organizations and Movements of the House Committee on Foreign Affairs; Ellen Herman, "Project Camelot and the Career of Cold War Psychology," in *Universities and Empire: Money and Politics in the Social Sciences During the Cold War,* ed. Christopher Simpson (New York, 1988): 97–133, also reprinting Franz Boas, "Scientists as Spies" [letter to *The Nation*, December 20, 1919], 1–2; Seymour J. Deitchman's autobiographical *The Best-Laid Schemes: A Tale of Social Research and Bureaucracy* (Cambridge, MA, 1967); and David Engerman, "Rethinking Cold War Universities: Some Recent Histories," *Journal of Cold War Studies* 5 (Summer 2003): 80–95. The contrasting positions that Project Camelot revealed between traditional behaviorists and newer rational choice practitioners and their relevance to Kuhnian paradigm shifts in the social sciences are set forth in Ron Robin, *The Making of the Cold War Enemy: Culture and Politics in the Military-Intellectual Complex* (Princeton, NJ, 2001): 206–25.

Project Camelot may well have been the worst single scientific project since King Canute dealt with the tides: the worst conceived, worst advised, worst designed, and worst executed. But this much has to be said for it. Never has one project in the social sciences aroused interest so broad, so diverse, and in such high places of the national government. More important, never has one project produced, or at least stimulated, results so momentous (and possibly beneficial) in the long run to government policy with respect to the social sciences.

What was Project Camelot, and why the fuss? Reading through the multitude of reactions and comments aroused by Project Camelot one is reminded irresistibly of the ancient tale of the three blind men and their individual descriptions of an elephant. . . .

One of the Camelot consultants, an assistant professor of anthropology, of Chilean birth but American citizenship, who was on his way to Chile for the summer on personal business, offered—for a fee, of course—to sound out Chilean social scientists on their possible enthusiasm for a project in which the United States Army, working through behavioral scientists, would undertake—in a strictly basic science sort of way, naturally, and with only the highest of motives—to investigate the conditions of social unrest, of insurgency, and means of counterinsurgency, in foreign countries; not necessarily in Chile, understand, but in other Latin American and foreign countries. This seemed like a dandy idea to the Chief Camelotians in Washington, and off went the, if not very first, the very last of Camelot's Intrepids.

The rest is history. Chilean social scientists, for some reason, did not take kindly to the thought of their country or any other being investigated by behavioral scientists who, however pure in heart and in methodological design, and however many echelons removed from tanks and flamethrowers, were nevertheless inescapably acting as agents of the United States Army on foreign ground. We are informed in the Chilean Select Committee Report to the Chamber of Deputies that the initial slight interest of a few Chilean social scientists in the project came from their having been assured in writing that such study as Camelot envisaged was sponsored by private or civil agencies and that it was not until they began reflecting on the implications of the use of a code name and, even more revealing, had received a full and documentary account of what Project Camelot was in fact from another of its consultants—a man of pacifist inclination unable to bear longer the weight of guilt—that they were able to respond in ways appropriate to the occasion. . . . Domestic uproar was predictably immediate and substantial, reaching the Chamber of Deputies. . . . All things considered, the Chilean report is remarkable for its temperateness, but it spares few details of Camelot, its operating structure, personnel, contacts with Chileans, and so on. In these respects it is a more useful document than the report on Camelot of our own House Subcommittee on International Organizations and Movements which protects the identity of Camelot scientists and the nature of all the details of the project—in a way that would probably not have been allowed had Camelot involved business or government figures rather than academics.

But if the Chilean Select Committee report was relatively moderate in temper, public and governmental opinion was not. The backlash produced by Camelot caught at least one American social scientist that I know of, leading to his summary eviction from Chile, with months of important research left dangling. He was indeed a victim, hardly qualifying as a bystander, for he was not only unconnected in any way with Camelot but totally ignorant of its existence. . . .

It was not, however, Chilean but Washington reaction to Camelot that proved decisive and of great long run significance to the behavioral sciences. Our Ambassador to Chile, Ralph Dungan, stung by his ignorance of something that (given U.S. Army sponsorship) understandably seemed part of his proper business, sent a sharp cable to Rusk after reading the details of Camelot in Chilean newspapers. Rusk went to LBJ, LBJ went to McNamara, McNamara went down gracefully (and gratefully, no doubt), and out of it—in one of the fastest actions ever recorded in official Washington—came a Presidential directive prohibiting Government-sponsored foreign area research that in the opinion of the Secretary of State would adversely affect United States foreign relations. Without the loss of measurable instant, Defense put Camelot to rest; or, to stay within the lovely imagery of it all, sentenced its inhabitants to return to the world of reality.

And the saddest of all the sad little ironies in the whole story is that, as one of the principals was to say, almost plaintively, Chile had not even been marked for Camelot study, had not been brainstormed, programmed, coded or punched! Of such, alas, is the city of man.

But Camelot's memory lingers on. Its real importance in the history of the social sciences begins indeed with its death. . . . From the hearing conducted on Camelot by the House Subcommittee on International Organizations and Movements came a report, and I can think of nothing more edifying for social scientists than a reading of this two-hundred-page document; edifying and flattering. If any further medicine is needed to wash away the minority-group syndrome that still characterizes the self-evaluation of so many of us in the social sciences, that still leads us to feel despised, discriminated against, and disliked by society and government, it is to be found, free, in this report. Let it be trumpeted far and wide: the Federal government, starting with the Subcommittee whose job it was to look into Camelot's coffin, and going all the way across town to Secretaries Rusk and McNamara, loves the behavioral sciences.

In fact, one discovers, as he reads through the text of the Report, that the behavioral sciences are miraculously found free of sin. The Military's *use* of the behavioral sciences is not free of sin, but that . . . is a different story. . . .

Reading the Report one finds himself, as a social scientist, almost literally holding his breath as he progresses through the testimony, for if ever a single behavioral science project lay exposed—in professional judgment, in design, in execution, quite apart from heavy expenditure of money (several hundred thousands of dollars had already gone into it)— to the possibility of merciless caricature by a Congressional committee, it was Project Camelot. But, far from caricature or hostility, there is only respect, courtesy, and seriousness of interest in the contributions of the behavioral sciences and in their proper status in the Federal government. After all, where else in a Congressional document (or professional document, for that matter) can one find the behavioral sciences characterized as "one of the vital tools in the arsenal of the free societies," with concluding recommendation made that funds for their subvention be greatly increased and their official status honored by inclusion in the Executive Office of the President as well as in a national foundation?

Not once in the Subcommittee hearing was the matter of professional ethics raised with respect to the behavioral scientist participants of Project Camelot. It was, however, in Chile, where apparently a different standard of conduct is expected of academic scholars. Reading the Chilean Select Committee report and some of the expressions of opinion in Chilean newspapers, one finds little if any of the censure of the American military that our own Subcommittee confined itself to, for in Chile, as in Latin America generally, nothing but the worst is usually expected from the military. What bothered, and still bothers, Chilean social scientists is, first, the fact that American academics could have allowed themselves to become involved in something like Camelot and, second, that no acts of censure toward Camelot social scientists have been taken, or even voiced, by American social science organizations. From a Chilean perspective it seemed incredible that social scientists could have given themselves, in the first instance, to a project under the auspices of the United States Army involving research into "the most intimate details" of Latin American institutions and personal lives; equally incredible that in their earliest communication with Chilean social scientists American social scientists had camouflaged Army sponsorship by referring vaguely to private foundation and National Science Foundation support. To this day there are Chilean and other Latin American social scientists who believe it the responsibility of American academic professional organizations to render apology in some form; even to register censure for the conduct of the Americans. But anyone who knows the reluctance of American professions, medical, legal, or academic, to voice censure of their own kind knows that the Chileans will wait a long time. . . .

But what cannot be overlooked is the fact that a group of American social scientists, acting as social scientists, allowed the American military to believe there was nothing *scientifically* wrong in an American social science project, under American Army sponsorship, entering the historically sensitive areas of Latin America for the express purpose of discovering, through every possible penetration of culture and mind, the conditions of social unrest, conflict, and insurgency.

Here is a cross-cultural consideration that one might justifiably assume to be understood by every sophomore in an introductory sociology or anthropology course, one that might occur to any lay American who has been reading the news over the past decade or two. Was there no one in the administrative organization of SORO, no one among the social scientists who were appointed as *professional* men, not as simple technicians, to say in effect to Lt. General William Dick, Chief of Research and Development, Army: "Your objective is your business and no doubt admirable from the point of view of the Army; as behavioral scientists we desire to be of such help as we can; *but everything we know as behavioral scientists suggests the monumental, possibly catastrophic, unwisdom of such a project."* . . .

But if the behavioral scientists and the Military never saw the underlying, constitutive question, the members of the House subcommittee assuredly did. Over and over during the hearing, the question was raised by one or another member as to the wisdom of the Military undertaking the kind of research contained in Camelot's objective. No one asked the question more tersely and pointedly than Representative Roybal: "Wouldn't the mere fact that the Army was heading the Project itself create a problem in many countries?" That is indeed the question: How does the military get into this act? . . .

It was not a behavioral scientist connected with Camelot but, once again, Congressman Fraser who uttered the following words. . . :

> [T]here is throughout your whole presentation a kind of—an implicit attitude or relationship that this country bears to the rest of the world which, if I were not an American, I would find perhaps most highly offensive, but it suggests somehow we are the ones to find out the dynamisms that are at work in these countries for the benefit of our Military Establishment. If I were a Latin American, I wouldn't find this a particularly happy arrangement. . . .

Despite the myth of Immaculate Conception that obtains among American behavioral scientists—under which the most aggressively intimate forays into human privacy are held miraculously pure—the rape of national dignity by American academic enterprise is as repugnant to foreign feeling as rape by American business or government. The Chilean Select Committee Report makes this very plain indeed! On a hot day one can chill himself by reflecting on what might have happened in Chile—or any of the countries marked by Camelot for invasion—had the project had "good" luck; had it been "successful"; had unforeseen exposure not led to premature death. Several regiments of Marines would have been necessary to salvage American research capital and protect American researchers' lives. . . .

To talk serenely about the holy ground of science in the aftermath of Camelot, a project that, above anything that has ever happened, has weakened the confidence of Latin American intellectuals *in the*

American academic and scholarly community, is a little like talking about the rights of free private enterprise in the predatory contexts of dollar diplomacy.

As I indicated above, the members of the Chilean Select Committee were unmoved by the "scientific" objectives of Camelot. It is useful to quote the words of the Committee report: "We wish to say that this foreign intervention in our internal affairs may not be defended on the pretext that the social investigation which was proposed has a scientific character." . . .

More important, however, to the future of American foreign-area research than type of research project and question is its potential volume. Here we have something that can, not inexactly, be put in Malthusian terms. The number of foreign research areas will increase (through dropping of barriers) *arithmetically*, but the population of American behavioral scientists with questions to ask of foreign areas will increase *geometrically*. Where once American foreign area research was confined to a tiny handful of anthropologists and geographers who learned, the hard way, the exceeding importance of tact, trust, honesty, and limits to questions when dealing with foreign peoples, and who went in as individuals, not as members of formidable projects, such research now, as we know, engulfs all the behavioral sciences. . . . Given all this, it could hardly be a matter for wonder if more and more foreign governments (and also foreign academic communities) began to take the hostile stance toward American social scientists that was once reserved for American businessmen. The bland and righteous belief among American academics that any degree of invasion of privacy, any degree of public exposure of the human psyche, is justified so long as it is in the name of science rather than, say, the TV industry, is no more likely to win popularity in the long run than did the medieval Inquisition when it defended its invasions in the name of piety and protection of the faithful. To assume that all will be well if only investigation of natives abroad is done by an American NSSF or a university is, I fear, naive.

8. Don K. Price,
"The Scientific Establishment," 1962

For many years, Don K. Price (1910–95) studied and participated in the processes and agencies that connect academic life, independent research organizations, and federal executive offices. His experiences informed and sharpened scholarly publications that deal with urban government, American foreign policy, and the rise since World War II of the federal-academic scientific establishment he described here. A Kentuckian with long attachments to Vanderbilt University (B.A. 1931, trustee 1964–78) and Nashville, where he began as a newspaper editor (1930–32) before accepting a Rhodes scholarship, Price served various government commissions and the Social Science Research Council in the 1930s. Before and after service in the Coast Guard (1943–45) he worked for the Public Administration Clearing House, then moved to

the Bureau of the Budget, to the research and development staff of the Department of Defense, to the Ford Foundation, and finally to the deanship of the Kennedy School of Government at Harvard (1958–77).

Don K. Price, "The Scientific Establishment," *Proceedings of the American Philosophical Society* 106 (June 1962): 235–45. Many of the author's priceless (pun intended) footnotes are included. Reprinted with kind permission from the American Philosophical Society, copyright © 1962. Further reading: Price, *Government and Science* (New York, 1954), *The Scientific Estate* (Cambridge, MA, 1965), and the autobiographical comments in *America's Unwritten Constitution: Science, Religion, and Political Responsibility* (Baton Rouge, LA, 1983), 153–93; and I, 1, 8.

Now that the federal government is spending more money on research and development than its total budget before Pearl Harbor, American scientists find it hard to figure out their new role in society. They used to assume that democracy would never be a patron of the sciences, and even after the Second World War the Executive had to urge the support of research on a skeptical Congress. But even though the last administration started to cut back on expenditures for science, it ended by quadrupling them. And this was by no means for defense alone; over those eight years the Congress multiplied the budget of the National Institutes of Health more than ninefold, giving them each year more than the President recommended. It is almost enough to make one try to apply to politics the theory of Henry Adams that science, as it becomes more abstract, increases in geometrical progression the power that it produces.[1]

In his farewell message President Eisenhower warned the nation against the danger that "public policy could itself become the captive of a scientific-technological elite." Even though he quickly explained that he was not talking about science in general, but only those parts allied with military and industrial power, this was a shock to the scientists.[2] To one who believes that science has helped to

---

1. Adams predicted that "the future of Thought, and therefore of History, lies in the hands of physicists . . . ," and went on to speculate that a rapid acceleration of thought in the direction of the abstract sciences might "reduce the forces of the molecule, the atom, and the electron to that costless servitude to which it has reduced the old elements of earth and air, fire and water. . . ." His prediction was uncanny, except for the term "costless" (*The degradation of the democratic dogma*, 277, 303, New York, 1958; first published in 1919).

2. Quoted in *New York Times*, 22 January, 1961, p. 4E. See also the authorized interpretation of this statement by the President's Special Assistant for Science and Technology, Dr. George B. Kistiakowsky, in *Science* 133: 355, 1961. As Chief of Staff, General Eisenhower had told the Army in 1946 that "The future security of the nation demands that all those civilian resources which by conversion or redirection constitute our main support in time of emergency be associated closely with the activities of

liberate man from ancient tyrannies—who in short still takes his political faith from Franklin and Jefferson and the Age of the Enlightenment—it is disconcerting to be told that he is a member of a new priesthood allied with military power.

Yet the plain fact is that science has become the major Establishment in the American political system: the only set of institutions for which tax funds are appropriated almost on faith, and under concordats which protect the autonomy, if not the cloistered calm, of the laboratory. The intellectual problems involved in this new status are likely to trouble scientists almost as much as the fears of the apocalyptic uses to which their discoveries may be put by the politicians. . . .

This faith of the Enlightenment tended to persist in the political thinking of American scientists, even in the period between the two World Wars, when it came to seem naive to their colleagues abroad. Even to this day they have shown singularly little interest in the conservative political theorists who have been telling them that science cannot deal with basic values or solve the major human problems, and the radical theorists who tell them that science can, if it will only join in a political system that will give it real power over society.[3] The conservative theorists have usually supported the conventional views of those in the European parliamentary tradition who believed that major political issues should be dealt with by party leaders and career administrators, with scientists speaking on such matters only when spoken to. And the most important radicals have been the Marxists, who proposed to let science, as they defined it, determine all human values through a disciplined system that would leave no room for the disorder of liberal democracy.

If American scientists generally ignored both the conservative and radical critics of the Enlightenment, it was probably, in the main, because they were simply not interested in political theory, or even in politics. But it may have been also because neither theoretical position seemed very relevant to their practical experience. In disregard of the conservative and conventional theory, American scientists have come to have a much more direct role

in high administration and in the making of policy than their counterparts in the parliamentary systems of Western Europe. (This is not to say that they had a more satisfactory role in the performance of scientific functions in the government.) And the more influence the scientists acquire, the more they now seem to work toward the dispersal of government organization and the decentralization of decisions, a trend impossible to explain to technocrats or the theorists of Marxism. . . .

Our Jacksonian revolution indeed destroyed the hopes of John Quincy Adams for a continuation of the Jeffersonian alliance between science and republicanism. At the same time, by wiping out the beginnings of a career system, it prevented the development of an elite administrative corps and thus cleared the channels of promotion for the scientists who, decades later, were to begin to move up in the civil service. The frontier radicalism of the day distrusted all forms of Establishment; this was the era in which state constitutions forbade ministers to hold public office and prohibited educational qualifications for admission to the bar. But as the business of government got more complicated, the frontier had to admit that certain skills were necessary. Its essentially pragmatic temper insisted, as it became necessary to hire civil servants for merit rather than patronage, that the requirements be defined in terms of the needs of the specific jobs, rather than by general educational status. It was easiest to prove the need for special skills, of course, in technical fields, partly on account of the objective nature of the problem, partly because scientific societies were determined to raise and maintain their professional standards in the civil service as well as in private practice.[4]

As a result, it was to the scientific and professional fields that the career civil service system was first pushed up to the higher ranks. As we developed our top civil service, we made it something quite different from a career Administrative Class; most of its members are not only nonpolitical, but nonadministrative as well, and they are not career officials in the same sense as a U.S. Navy officer or a British Civil Servant.

In recent years, scientists and engineers, while

the Army in time of peace," and advised the Army to contract extensively for scientific and industrial services (Memorandum for . . . General and Special Staff Divisions, etc., "Scientific and Technological Resources as Military Assets;" 30 April, 1946).

3. Maritain, Unamuno, and Ortega y Gasset represent the conservative critics of the Enlightenment; J. D. Bernal may be taken as a sample on the Socialist side. Judith N. Shklar, whose *After Utopia* begins with the observation that "nothing is quite so dead today as the spirit of optimism that the very word Enlightenment evokes," goes on (p. 3) to admit that "The less reflective public, certainly until 1914, remained cheerfully indifferent to the intellectual currents of despair. . . ." In this optimistic category, I would include most American scientists, and bring the date up to the present.

4. As A. Lawrence Lowell put it, "The great professions, which have secured general recognition in the community, have been strong enough to insist that strictly professional work must not be entrusted to men who have had no professional training or experience" (*Public opinion and popular government,* 274, New York, 1926). Detailed illustrations for specifically scientific fields may be found in the series of "Service Monographs of the United States Government" published by the Institute for Government Research, notably those on the Steamboat Inspection Service, the Office of Experiment Stations, the General Land Office, and the Public Health Service. See also Lewis Mayers, *The federal service,* Institute for Government Research, 21, 1922, and Lewis Meriam, *Public personnel problems,* 317.

certainly rare among those in high political office, have done reasonably well in the civil service. The positions of administrative continuity and bureaucratic power in Washington are, in the civil service departments, the bureau chiefs. A study in 1958 of the 63 bureau chiefs showed that 9 of them had advanced degrees in the natural sciences, and 17 others had been trained in lesser ways as engineers or technicians. By comparison with these 26 from various branches of technology, there were 9 economists and only 8 lawyers, and 20 from miscellaneous administrative or business careers.[5] Aside from the positions of bureau chief, the top career positions are the so-called "super-grades," which were added above the regular civil service grades to let the government compete for scarce talent.[6] The favorite justification for these positions is the need to employ capable scientists and engineers, notably in the technical branches of the Defense Department and the National Aeronautics and Space Agency. Administrators have ridden along to higher salaries on the political coattails of scientists.

Scientists who become bureau chiefs are, of course, no longer practicing scientists; they are doing work that in the United Kingdom would be done by a member of the Administrative Class educated in history or the classics. But when they are good at their jobs, as some of them are, it is for a reason that would have appealed to Macaulay, who used to argue that he wanted to recruit university graduates in the classics not because they had been studying the classics, but because the classics attracted the best minds, which could adapt themselves to anything.[7] And the American scientist who turns administrator is the equal of his English humanist counterpart in at least one respect: his lack of interest in management as a science, or sometimes at all. . . .

The land grant colleges and the associations of various kinds of agricultural scientists maintained an important influence on the Department of Agriculture, supplied most of its career personnel, and generally provided the intellectual leadership for national agricultural policy. They thus in effect greatly weakened the old constitutional distinction between state and federal functions, but without subjecting the field of agriculture to the control of a centralized bureaucracy.

The pattern of grants in aid, with its new set of administrative relationships, met two cardinal

needs: to provide money, as well as national policy direction, from Washington, and to maintain the autonomy of the states. It accordingly became the basis on which new programs were developed—highways, public health, social security, welfare, housing, and others. This was what political scientists came to call the "New Federalism," which has given the scientists and specialists in each field of policy a chance to work out programs without too much constraint by any party doctrine.

An elite administrative corps may look on scientists as properly subordinate, and science as a way of thinking that should deal with the means to support a policy, a tradition, or an ideology, rather than an end in itself. We can understand this relationship in other countries if we recall how until recent years our military services thought that civilian scientists in military laboratories should conduct their research only pursuant to "requirements" defined by military staff work. This notion was exploded as it became apparent that what scientists discovered by unrestricted research might be of greater military importance than the things the military officers thought they wanted—in short, that the means might determine the ends. . . .

It is easy to guess why large groups among American scientists—especially in the agricultural sciences—were less pessimistic in the period after the First World War than their European colleagues with respect to the role of science in democratic politics. In two very practical ways their situation was entirely different; in civil service, their advancement was not blocked by a career bureaucracy, and the constitutional system gave them a chance to advocate policies in comparative freedom from administrative or political discipline. It was no wonder that they had not lost faith in the political approach of the Enlightenment, for they had made it work.

Nevertheless, by the time of the Great Depression this naive faith was least prevalent in the most important universities and the most advanced fields of science. In them, science was supported more by private corporations and foundations than by government, and its leaders in newer fields like nuclear physics and biochemistry had closer intellectual ties with their European counterparts than with the agronomists or engineers of the land-grant colleges. For the loose American constitutional system had worked best in those aspects of public affairs in which the power of government and the power of the great industrial corporations were not in rivalry. The scientists in institutions that derived their support from industrial wealth and were interested in problems of the industrial urban economy saw the constitutional model in a different political perspective. Among them, accordingly, were to be found both those conservative scientists who were most distrustful of government, and those radicals who tended to take a Marxist view of the role of science in society. . . .

5. Smith, Michael E., Bureau chiefs in the federal government, 1958, in *Public Policy*, the Yearbook of the Graduate School of Public Administration, Harvard University 10: 62, 1960.

6. United States Civil Service Commission, *The federal top salary network*, Washington, 1960.

7. He put it more pointedly in 1833: "If astrology were taught at our universities, the young man who cast nativities best would generally turn out a superior man." Royal Commission on The Civil Service, *Fourth report*, Cd. 7338, 1914.

Private universities as well as the land-grant colleges were drawn into public service functions, partly because they were, in the absence of a career bureaucracy, the main reservoir of expertise on which politicians could draw for advice, and partly in response to the influence of the philanthropic foundations.

By the 1920's, some of the major foundations had lost interest in the charitable alleviation of social problems, and began to hope that science might solve them. This idea led to a strategy of supporting both scientific research and demonstration projects to test the application of such research, which could then be extended by the greater resources of government. Their aid to scientific education and research is a familiar story, in almost every branch of science. But equally important, they went on to help strengthen the professional organizations of scientists,[8] and to pay for the efforts of governments to improve their organization and administration, and to make use of research and research institutions as they did so. By the time of the Second World War, the leading scientists knew that a grantmaking agency like a foundation could initiate nationwide programs by working with independent universities and governmental agencies, as the stories of hookworm control, the foundation of public libraries, and the reform of medical education all suggested. And political leaders were inclined to turn to private funds to help them explore future policy opportunities, or experiment with them, as when President Hoover sought foundation financing for his Committee on Social Trends and for a National Science Fund, and the Public Administration Clearing House provided the initial administrative costs for President Roosevelt's Science Advisory Board.[9]

As scientists learned that the organization of government was something that could be influenced from the outside, and that universities and foundations could have a substantial influence on public policy, they were in effect freeing themselves from the assumption that government and private institutions were sharply different in nature. They were accordingly ready, at the outset of the Second World War, to work out a thoroughly pragmatic set of arrangements for the conduct of weapons research. The approach that they adopted was simply to enlist institutions rather than individuals in the two great scientific programs of the war: the Office of Scientific Research and Development (OSRD), and the Manhattan Project of the Army Engineers.

To those who expect wartime crises and military authority to produce a centralization of authority, this approach must have been as surprising as if the Army had used the war as an excuse to increase, rather than decrease, its reliance on the state militias. But in the hands of Vannevar Bush, James B. Conant, and Karl T. Compton, the government contract became a new type of federalism. Under the OSRD, the Massachusetts Institute of Technology took on the responsibility for developing radar, and California Institute of Technology rockets, and under the Manhattan District, the University of Chicago set up the first sustained nuclear reaction and the University of California fabricated the first atomic bomb, while du Pont, General Electric, Union Carbide, and other industrial giants built the facilities to produce the fissionable materials.[10]

The postwar sequel is a well-known story. Through a continuation of this system of administering research and development programs by grant or contract, the Atomic Energy Commission, which was hailed by the draftsmen of the Atomic Energy Act as a triumph of socialism,[11] supports a program in which some nine-tenths of the employees work for private corporations. The adamant argument of many scientific leaders of the 1930's against federal support of science now seem as ancient and irrelevant as debates over infra- or supra-lapsarianism; no major university today could carry on its research program without federal money. The Massachusetts Institute of Technology, California Institute of Technology, Chicago, and Johns Hopkins, of course, all administer special military or atomic energy programs and consequently draw from three-fifths to five-sixths of their budgets from government, while Harvard, Yale, and Princeton now get a larger proportion of their operating revenues from federal funds than do land-grant colleges like Illinois, Kentucky, and Maryland. . . .

American scientists, who had tended to be a little disillusioned about their relationship with politicians ever since the Jacksonian period, are now entitled to look with somewhat greater satisfaction on the domestic Establishment that they have helped set up. For to some small extent science has helped the political system of the United States develop along lines quite different from the classic patterns

---

8. The National Research Council, created by President Wilson to do in the First World War (in a rudimentary way) what the Office of Scientific Research and Development did in the Second, was supported not by appropriations but by the Rockefeller and Carnegie foundations (Axt, Richard G., *The federal government and financing higher education*, 78, New York, 1952).

9. *Report of the Science Advisory Board*, 15, Washington, D.C., Sept. 20, 1934.

10. See the first volume of the forthcoming official history of the Atomic Energy Commission, Hewlett, Richard G., and Oscar E. Anderson, Jr., *The new world*, to be published in 1962.

11. "The field of atomic energy is made an island of socialism in the midst of a free enterprise economy" (Newman, James R., and Byron S. Miller, *The control of atomic energy*, 4, New York, 1948). Mr. Newman, writing a preface to this book a year after the text was completed, noted that "Only one major policy formulation, the decision by the Atomic Energy Commission not to conduct research in its own laboratories, departs sharply from the interpretations of the Act set forth in these pages" (p. xi).

of either parliamentary government and laissez-faire economics on the one hand, or socialism and one-party rule on the other. Among its essential institutional features are universities that are concerned with applied as well as basic sciences, and continuously exchange personnel with the government at all age levels; a personnel system which puts up no barrier against the administrative promotion of men with scientific training; and grants-in-aid and contracts through which federal agencies may influence or guide the policies, but not direct the detailed management, of certain aspects of local governments, business corporations, and universities. Among these institutions, the connecting links are strongest in scientific and technical fields. And the peculiar looseness of the constitutional system enables the scientists in each field to take the initiative in developing policies—just as their innovations are providing the greatest impetus to industrial enterprise. Most important, science is not restrained in its impact on policy by any rigid distinction between ends and means, imposed by institutionalized systems of traditional or ideological values. The key to this is the freedom to influence or determine the organization and procedures of government from the outside, not conceding control over them to professional administrators or party leaders.

But there are some good reasons why scientists should not be too self-satisfied about their new status. A good many of them already think that science has been corrupted by this new system, and the wealth that it has brought.[12] They tend to look back on pre-war science as the Reformers looked back to the Primitive Church: a period of austere purity, an era in which no vows were needed to guarantee the poverty of the professor, no scientist was seduced by a government contract, and teaching fellows were obedient. One may well be a little skeptical about this point of view, and, suspect that poverty probably brought its distractions no less troublesome than those of riches. But even if we discount such dangers so far, the worst may be yet to come. The public and members of Appropriations Committees are being led to think of science in terms of spectacular results like a space satellite or a cancer cure, and the political pressure to pass miracles may lead to some major distortions in our national policy, and put some uncomfortable pressures on the independence of scientific institutions. We probably have less reason to fear that major governmental decisions involving science will be secret than that they will be popular.

For while our new system of administration by contract temporarily avoids the political problems that come with the growth of bureaucracy, it encounters them again in more subtle and difficult

forms. We do well to recognize that a government bureau is tempted to be more concerned with its own status and power than with the purposes of national policy. But if we entrust those purposes to industrialists or even scientists, we do not sterilize that political temptation. We only let it begin to work directly on the industrialists and scientists. If public ownership is no guarantee of unselfishness, neither is private ownership. And it is ironic, in view of the general public image of his political ideas, that it was President Eisenhower who presented most forcefully to the country the danger that, having hired private corporations to further specific public ends, we will see them use the public means for private profit, or even in political efforts to control the policy decisions of the government.

Government policy, like science itself, needs to be conceived and pursued with some regard for its totality as well as its parts. By giving priority to the parts—by turning over the administration of public functions to private institutions—we have strengthened our ability to do a great many separate things, but not our ability to give integrity and discipline and direction to our total effort. Indeed, by relying too much on the contracting method we have probably weakened the quality of the scientists within the civil service, whose help is needed by the executive who seeks to manage our scientific programs as a coherent system.[13]

In the dimensions of its financial support and in the breadth of its influence, science has indeed become a national Establishment. Politicians are more likely to abuse it by calling on it to advance their special causes than they are to ignore it. In this predicament, scientists cannot protect their essential interests in government by setting themselves apart in a separate status or separate department. They used to be content with the control of particular bureaus or programs. Today, in the White House Office or the lobbies of the Capitol, they are obliged by the nature of the system they helped create to play a responsible role in all aspects of national policy, and in the development of a new pattern of relationships between public and private institutions in our society.

9. W. K. H. Panovsky, "SLAC and Big Science," 1992

Within a decade after World War II, the federal government began to sponsor, prod, and finance American higher education on an unprecedented scale. The G.I. Bill (1) greatly expanded and democratized the student population, and the Supreme Court through *Brown v. Board of Education* (IX, 3) opened college and university doors wider to all young people. The third action of enduring significance was government funding of academic scien-

12. Tuve, Merle A., Basic research in private research institutes, in Dael Wolfle, Ed., *Symposium on basic research*, 178, Washington, 1959.

13. Brown, Harold, *Research and engineering in the defense laboratories* (An address by the Director of Defense Research and Engineering), Washington, October 19, 1961.

tific research. Before the war, federal funds had augmented private foundation money for some academic research in the physical sciences, creating what is now seen as the early stage of big science. During World War II, Congress secretly funded the Manhattan Project that employed the talents of many academic physicists. Challenged by Soviet Russia's successful space venture with *Sputnik* in 1957 and by the intense rivalry of the Cold War, Congress then openly legislated increasingly larger expenditures for research and development in the physical sciences. Several universities—notably Berkeley, Brookhaven (later SUNY-Brookhaven), Chicago, and Stanford—turned their physicists to exciting work in high energy or elementary particle physics. The name "Big Science" became indelibly stamped upon these workplaces. The name meant the use of large numbers of specialized and hierarchically arranged laboratory people working with concentrated resources at a limited number of research centers where equipment and instrumentation ran easily into the millions of dollars. Guiding these projects was usually a government-initiated, utilitarian "mission" for protecting and advancing national interests, which did not preclude inquiries into the fundamental actions of nature. These efforts were designed with the necessary expertise of academic scientists acting as consultants or advisors to sponsoring government agencies (See I, 2–3). Big Science defined a remarkable change from prewar, small-scale academic research in physics.

Wolfgang Kurt Herman "Pief" Panovsky (1919–2007) witnessed and participated in, almost from its inception, government-university relationships in nuclear physics during the postwar era. After receiving his bachelor's degree at Princeton and doctorate at the California Institute of Technology, Panovsky was a consultant to the Manhattan Project (1943–45), became a member of the physics faculty and laboratory at Berkeley (1945–51), and then went to four decades of work in elementary particle physics at Stanford, where he directed the Stanford Linear Accelerator Center (SLAC, 1961–89). A member or consultant to numerous scientific boards and recipient of awards in high energy physics, he sat on the Presidential Science Advisory Committee (1958–64) in decisive years for American scientific research. His memoir and chronology here summarize the issues and intricacies within government-funded big science affecting all levels of a university from the vantage point of a physicist administrator.

W. K. H. Panovsky, "SLAC and Big Science: Stanford University," From Peter Galison and Bruce Hevly, eds. *Big Science: The Growth of Large-Scale Research* (Stanford, CA, 1992): 130–46. Copyright © 1992 by the Board of Trustees of the Leland Stanford Jr. University. Further reading: Galison and Hevly, "Introduction," *Big Science.* An anthropologist's report on the facilities, personnel, and work patterns at SLAC, contrasting these with arrangements at a Japanese facility, can be found in Sharon Traweek, *Beamtimes and Lifetimes* (Cambridge, MA, 1988); the changes brought on by Big Science to Stanford and the kinds of new knowledge it created are examined in Rebecca S. Lowen, *Creating the Cold War University: The Transformation of Stanford* (Berkeley, CA, 1997). See also Helen Kragh, *Quantum Generations: A History of Physics in the Twentieth Century* (Princeton, NJ, 1999), preceded by Daniel J. Kevles's classic *The Physicists: The History of a Scientific Community in Modern America* (New York,

1978); and Peter J. Westwick, *The National Labs: Science in an American System* (Cambridge, MA, 2002).

Today, physics at Stanford University has evolved into a highly diverse activity, spreading over many departments and academic units. It spans a very large range in scale from traditional small laboratory experiments to the Stanford Linear Accelerator Center (SLAC) and the precessing gyroscope testing general relativity in space.

The progressive changes in physics have raised many profound issues relating to the role of Stanford University. Among these are the conflict, on the one hand, or symbiosis, on the other, between research and teaching; the extent to which large science enterprises permit the creative participation of graduate students and junior faculty; and the issue of proper recognition of the work of individuals when scientific papers require one page of a journal just to list the authors. Above all, we are facing tensions between the sponsor's quest for accountability, and even control, and the traditional academic freedoms to publish, to choose one's work, and to choose the academic staff within the university.

One must recognize that none of these issues is at all new and that in spite of all the changes that have taken place there remains a unifying spirit throughout the physics enterprise at Stanford. This spirit is an attempt to understand inanimate nature in its most fundamental aspects and to communicate this understanding to future generations.

SLAC did not represent a sudden transition to big science but was a step in an evolutionary pattern of growth that was initiated at Stanford during the Korean War. At that time a deliberate decision was made . . . that the university should expand its involvement in government-supported scientific and technical activities. A primary motive for doing so at that time was the fear that during the Korean War the technical faculty would leave Stanford, following the pattern that occurred during World War II.

The evolution at Stanford from the Mark I to the Mark III and Mark II linear accelerators . . . is well documented. . . .

Mark II and particularly Mark III were not "small science." Budgets each year were in the multi-million-dollar range (when a million dollars was still a million dollars!). Professional operating technician crews were necessary, and the beam of the Mark III accelerator was shared among a multitude of users. With few exceptions these users were, however, "in-house," that is, Stanford faculty, students, and staff. Most of the work was done collaboratively, but these groups were small by today's standards in high-energy physics and in general a member of the Stanford faculty directed each collaboration. The lab was the responsibility of a director who was not necessarily a member of the regular faculty. He, in turn, was advised or controlled—it never was totally clear which—by a committee whose majority were members of the regular professoriate.

THE BIRTH OF SLAC

Mark III was a great success, leading to many important discoveries in particle physics including the Nobel Prize–winning work on the size and shape of the proton and neutron. This lent encouragement to studies that eventually culminated in a proposal for the construction of the two-mile linear accelerator, a laboratory that came to be called SLAC after some search for alternative acronyms.

The proposal to construct SLAC originated first from suggestions by Professor Robert Hofstadter, born from his desire to extend his Nobel Prize–winning studies on the structure of the proton and neutron to higher energies. Meetings were then held at my home and that of Professor Ginzton, leading subsequently to an informal study group encompassing most of the active staff members of the High-Energy Physics Laboratory and some members of the Microwave Laboratory. This group met informally "after hours," wrote extensive technical memoranda, and finally in April 1957 produced a proposal of about 100 pages. The civil engineering analysis that was part of the proposal was contributed by an outside corporation volunteering its services. It is interesting to compare this process with the vastly more extensive documentation now required to initiate a big-science construction project, illustrated by the superconducting supercollider (SSC). The studies leading to the SSC proposal involved up to 100 paid individuals, major experimental work on superconducting magnets carried out at three or four participating laboratories, innumerable reviews of cost and research and development, and the full-blown environmental impact statement process. The actual cost of writing the SSC proposal came close to a million dollars, in response to the government-required format.

The Stanford proposal to construct SLAC was submitted simultaneously to the Department of Defense, the National Science Foundation, and the Atomic Energy Commission. It would be impossible to conceive that an identical proposal could be submitted to three different government agencies today, since each agency requires its own detailed format for proposal submission. In contrast a single agency, the Department of Energy, issued a request for proposal to build the SSC and only one proponent—the Universities Research Association, Inc., then a consortium of 66 universities—responded. In summary, whereas in 1957 the SLAC proposal was a search for *support* of work to be directed by the proponents, in 1988 the SSC proposal was straightjacketed into the format of a government *acquisition,* with the work to be performed by the most qualified performer.

Let us return to the fate of the SLAC proposal. After many discussions and after review by an *ad hoc* panel appointed by the General Advisory Committee of the Atomic Energy Commission and the President's Science Advisory Committee (PSAC),

President Eisenhower recommended that SLAC be given the "green light"; Congress authorized the project in 1961 after a one-year delay.

Some remarks on PSAC might be in order. That institution was created by President Eisenhower after Sputnik signaled that American science was not all it was expected to be. The work of PSAC was in essence divided into two categories: science in policy, and policy in science. The former dealt with providing informed scientific input to policy decisions in many areas of concern to the U.S. government. In the modern age hardly any field of governmental activity is unaffected by science, be it national defense, agriculture, foreign relations, health, or housing. It became clear that the president needed for his policy decisions scientific input that was not filtered through the programmatic or policy objectives of the various government departments and agencies.

The second category had to do with government support of science. Traditionally, a large number of government agencies support both basic and applied science. It is noteworthy that the one agency specifically created to support basic science, the National Science Foundation, actually provides funds for only about 20% of the total governmental contributions; the balance is supplied by the so-called mission agencies such as the Defense Department, what used to be the Department of Health, Education, and Welfare (in the health sciences), and the Atomic Energy Commission, now the Department of Energy (in nuclear and high-energy physics). While the role of PSAC in giving advice on "science in policy" has in retrospect been very successful, this cannot be said with equal conviction in respect to "policy in science." It is extremely difficult, if not impossible, for scientists active in a variety of disciplines to agree on scientific priorities when they are constituted into advisory bodies; this is perhaps neither unexpected or unhealthy. If major projects such as SLAC are under consideration, the most knowledgeable individuals are those directly affected by the discussions and therefore have to disqualify themselves from the deliberations. This is precisely what I did in respect to SLAC. In essence I served only as a witness before PSAC; in no way did I participate in its deliberations on whether the construction of SLAC should or should not be authorized.

Support of science by the federal government is an extremely complex and extensive undertaking. A presidential committee cannot possibly review even a small fraction of the proposals before government agencies, and it can hardly deal with the division of responsibility among different agencies. To do so would require a very large supporting staff and would essentially establish a group like PSAC as another layer in governmental bureaucracy, thereby impeding even further the speed of governmental decisions. Thus, as a practical matter, PSAC dealt only with some selected major decisions in this area, in particular when big-ticket items such as SLAC were involved. Ground for SLAC was broken in 1962, five years after the proposal was submitted, and the first beam was generated in 1966. Thus the interval between proposal submission and the first beam was about nine years, divided roughly evenly between the political process of securing authorization and the physical process of building the machine. . . .

A noteworthy fact about these time scales is that the construction time of "frontier" accelerators, from the electrostatic machines of the 1930's through SLAC and Fermilab of the 1960's, has hardly changed from the norm of four to six years, notwithstanding the increase in energy by five orders of magnitude. Somehow the effort brought to bear on constructing frontier high-energy accelerators has grown to make possible construction in the same period. In other words, the ratio of inertia to muscle needed to accomplish the task has remained roughly constant; the reader will recognize that this is the same reason why a flea and an elephant can jump roughly to the same height. Of course such a compression of construction time is desirable both from the point of view of efficiency and to accommodate both participation in construction and participation in research within one academic career.

SLAC AND THE ASSOCIATED COMMUNITY

1. SLAC was the largest accelerator proposed at the time and remained the most expensive single installation in high-energy physics until the construction of the National Accelerator Laboratory, now Fermilab.

2. The community of physicists was not enthusiastic about the creation of SLAC. At the time of its creation the mainstream of high-energy physics used protons as the bombarding particle, and the wisdom of switching to the use of an electron beam with bad duty cycle was widely doubted. Yet because at the time of the SLAC proposal science budgets were growing at roughly 15% per year there was no feeling of competition or threat from the new facility to the programs of other sciences. The type of divisive debate that we are seeing today with respect to the SSC was absent.

3. Interestingly enough, although no other scientists opposed SLAC from fear that it might take priority over their own aspirations, there was opposition from one senior statesman of science. Professor Eugene Wigner testified before Congress that he opposed the construction of SLAC because it would usurp so much scientific and technical manpower that it would interfere with the military efforts of the United States. In retrospect concerns about insufficient manpower to carry out big science have been largely unfounded both with respect to SLAC and other projects. Big science projects such as SLAC themselves contribute greatly to the training of scientists and engineers.

It has been true throughout the history of particle physics that the number of proponents qualified for the experimental use of such facilities has exceeded available opportunities. It is largely for this reason that research groups tend to be larger than they really have to be. The only area where there is indeed a shortage of qualified performers is the construction and technology of accelerators, rather than the use of accelerators for physics. Qualified accelerator specialists have been and are now in great demand. A major reason for this is not so much the growth of new facilities for research but the burgeoning applications of accelerator technology to such areas as synchrotron radiation, cancer therapy, industrial radiography, and various defense-related problems.

The High-Energy Physics Lab was a facility of Stanford University, although it was operated outside the regular departmental framework. When SLAC was initiated there was a debate within the Stanford physics community whether SLAC should be operated like the High-Energy Physics Lab, described somewhat simplistically as an arm of the regular Stanford physics department, or should become more national in character. The decision was made and accepted by the government that SLAC should be a "national facility," meaning not quite a national laboratory. The meaning of this term evolved to signify that SLAC should be available equitably to scientists throughout the world, with judgment on priorities to be based on scientific merit and demonstrable ability to carry out the proposed program.

A committee structure was established for SLAC including a Scientific Policy Committee composed of scientists from outside Stanford, advising the president of the university and designed primarily to safeguard the rights of the outside users. . . . Yet the line responsibility for running SLAC was strictly within Stanford. It devolved from the Stanford board of trustees to the president to the director to the line organization of the laboratory. This pattern is unique. Other high-energy physics laboratories in this country and abroad have become what Leon Lederman, the past director of Fermilab, has characterized as "truly national laboratories." This means that the legal responsibility for the laboratory is vested in a board composed of members from many universities or other entities. At the same time other large accelerators, notably that at Cornell, have remained proprietary.

With the benefit of hindsight I consider much of the debate about national laboratory, national facility, and even proprietary campus machines to be a tempest in a teapot, as long as the installations require a major professional presence for their design, maintenance, and operation. As a practical matter, the social interactions between the accelerator professionals, the inside users, and the outside participants are controlled much more by the state of the science and technical circumstances than they are by the formal arrangements for allocating use. The decision-making process, the mechanisms for review by outside committees, and the relationship to government oversight are all remarkably similar.

This conclusion that the decision-making process allocating research time is not greatly dependent on the nature of the official laboratory "constitution" does not mean that allocation of running time and other resources is without controversy. Possibly the most profound disagreements swirl around the question whether allocations are to be made *ad hominem* or on the demonstrable merit of each proposal. There always have been and will continue to be members of the scientific community with a not inconsiderable ego who feel that the "powers that be" should allocate facilities and running time to them on the basis of their reputation and past performance rather than on the merit of what they are proposing to do. During the history of SLAC and other laboratories several senior members of the scientific community have withdrawn their requests for running time in a huff, maintaining that they should not be subjected to the degrading level of review that the peer program committee reporting to the director generally exacts. Paradoxically, few members of the scientific community object to peer review of their proposals when such review groups advise government agencies. However, when such detailed accountability is due a laboratory director, or as far as that goes, a department head in a university, some senior members of the scientific community take offense. In other words, there is some objection in the academic community to detailed accountability to their immediate academic or scientific peers but much less objection if that accountability is focused on a more remote decision-making body.

When SLAC was created the matter of "national facility" vs. "proprietary physics department lab" was resolved by establishing SLAC as a national facility but having its own faculty. The need for a faculty was deemed necessary because traditionally the regular faculty members are the first-class citizens on a university campus, and therefore the use of the title was believed to be essential to attract the intellectual leadership so essential to the success of SLAC. In hindsight this decision proved to be amply justified by the results obtained. Yet the university paid a price for this choice in controversy. Moreover, the size of the faculty at SLAC was determined by the central university administration, and SLAC chose to accept such limits whether they did or did not match the needs of SLAC's program. Again the balance of values involved here might be resolved differently under different circumstances.

Then there is the relationship to the outside users. When SLAC was inaugurated, as mentioned above, the interest of the particle physics community at large was mainly focused on proton machines. Initially, therefore, the interest of outside users in spending a large amount of time and intellectual effort at SLAC was limited. For technical rea-

sons associated with the characteristics of the SLAC electron beam, most experiments at SLAC were expected to be "facility centered," that is, to require the construction of large particle detectors that could then be used for a variety of experiments. Experiments in which a small user group assembles a single experiment from "building blocks" are rare and difficult at SLAC.

There are a variety of general technical reasons why SLAC's experiments are more likely to require large particle detectors. Experiments consist of recording the particles produced from primary collisions, registering in which direction the particles travel, determining their energy, and identifying their charge, mass, and possibly other characteristics. This task is accomplished by determining where particles go in space and in time, under the influence of external agents such as magnetic fields or interposed materials. For processes produced by SLAC's electron beam discrimination in time is very difficult, because the beam comes in bursts of less than one microsecond, repeated up to 360 times per second. Thus within the short time of the beam pulse it is very difficult, even with modern electronic devices, to untangle the time sequence of events. Thus all particles from the primary target must be first sorted out by direction and energy before their arrival can be timed; this takes complex equipment.

There are other technical reasons as well, increasing the complexity of detecting systems. SLAC's beam is very intense, but only a small fraction of the electrons produce events of interest. Thus the final detectors designed to tag the selected interesting phenomena have to be heavily shielded and separated from the primary target. Large and complex detectors are also a necessity for use with SLAC's colliding-beam storage rings; here the rates of interesting events are so slow that one cannot afford to throw anything away; thus the detectors have to surround the interaction point fully and identify each track as well as possible. Again this means complex detectors and associated facilities.

The design and construction of complex facilities requires the participation of first-rate particle physicists. However, in the initial absence of a strong outside interest, most of these instruments had to be built under the direction of SLAC faculty and staff, and this was done successfully. Thus the lab endured some criticism for allegedly "excluding" users from its program and thus not really living up to its charter as a "national facility." Yet again this was an unavoidable consequence of the technical situation with respect to electrons and the distribution of users' interests during the 1960's.

The situation changed dramatically when some of the techniques that had proven successful for proton accelerators were imported to SLAC. The most noted example is the transfer of the large 82-inch bubble chamber from Berkeley to SLAC. This device accumulates data in the form of pictorial images on film, which can be scanned at many university laboratories. The transfer of the instrument, together with the construction at SLAC of a special bubble chamber recording data at a high rate, suddenly transformed the laboratory to the world's most prolific producer of bubble-chamber film for a wide outside community. These examples illustrate that it is frequently a technical circumstance rather than an administrative fiat that controls the degree and kind of user participation.

A fundamental problem besetting all big-science high-energy physics facilities is the extent to which the lab should deviate from its primary goal of maximizing short-range physics output from its facilities in the interest of assuring the widest practical participation of university users. Frequently short-range productivity is impaired by the complexity and the realities of outside academic participation. Yet the very existence of high-energy physics depends in the long run on the creative input of university scientists and on the training of a new generation of students. Again, this is an issue that requires a middle course but should not be a source of major conflict.

All these controversies, quite prevalent earlier in the history of SLAC, have now largely run their course, and the practice of having a local program advisory committee advise the director is fully accepted. This practice has become a necessity if younger, less prominent proponents are to be permitted the opportunity to have their proposals considered on their merits. Large detectors have become the rule rather than the exception at all high-energy physics laboratories worldwide.

THE CONSTRUCTION OF BIG SCIENCE FACILITIES AND ACADEME

The advent of big science has raised a series of profound questions concerning the role of academic institutions in the management of big science laboratories. Dealing with these issues requires administrative inventiveness. Blind insistence on preserving academic practices no longer applicable is counterproductive, yet exclusive emphasis on administrative efficiency, financial accountability, etc., in disregard of academic values is even more destructive.

Academic institutions have become involved in big science laboratories as managers and operators of the facilities as well as through the participation of their faculties, students, and staff in the design and research work. But these roles involve challenges to traditional practices.

As the size of government-supported big science facilities has grown, the question of whether academic institutions are the proper agents to construct, manage, and operate such facilities keeps recurring. Superficially, construction of big science facilities has become a major undertaking akin to many space and military projects. Thus cost control is a prominent issue. Is it really appropriate to give contractual responsibility for the construction of such major multibillion-dollar installations as the SSC to academic institutions rather than to contract such construction out to "experienced industry" and then "turn the key over" to the "long-hairs and eggheads" to carry out their academic researches? This issue has substance. The construction of a laboratory like SLAC is indeed an activity quite dissimilar from the usual on-campus construction projects at a university. However, there are three main reasons militating against the "turn-key" approach where industry builds and academe uses:

1. The record of academic bodies, both individual universities and university consortia, in building big science installations costing nearly $1 billion within projected expenses, within schedule, and within advertised performance has been excellent. In fact, the record is much superior to that of projects for space, military systems, or commercial reactors.

2. Creation of a major accelerator or other big science facility involves a great deal more than constructing a major technical tool to within specified costs, schedule, and performance. Rather, what is involved is the creation of a vibrant institution that can support the research using the new facility, that can upgrade that facility as scientific needs change, and that provides the general infrastructure and intellectual atmosphere necessary for continued scientific vigor. This ambience must be created during the construction period.

3. In small science, responsibility for carrying out a proposed project rests with the "principal investigator," who is a member of the academic staff of the university. He or she works with students and young research associates. If the principal investigator leaves or loses interest in the project, then the activity disappears. In contrast, when a university (or consortium of universities) proposes a big science activity the responsibility for both the construction of the facility and putting it to proper scientific use rests with the university and transcends the availability of a particular project leader or laboratory director. Thus, should a project head depart, the university is obligated to conduct an expeditious search for a qualified successor. In turn, the implication of this process is that there is continuity from construction to utilization of the new facility, since the basic objective of the facility is intellectual rather than economic. This process, then, has to be consistent with the basic premise that construction of a new facility is not a construction project in the usual sense but a creation of an integrated organizational entity whose success will be judged by its intellectual products.

Note that, for these reasons, nuclear and high-energy physics laboratories have generally been built in America under contract with academic institutions. . . .

RESEARCH IN BIG SCIENCE

Research in big science involves collaborative efforts by large groups. However, the dynamics of this collaboration has frequently been misunderstood. Indeed, the construction of an accelerator is a major collaborative effort, and frequently the potential users get involved in many phases of such construction. The potential users participate in workshops determining the fundamental design parameters of the machine, they maintain contact with the builders to make sure that provisions for future experiments are adequate, and they frequently get involved in the commissioning of the machine both to accelerate its completion and to become acquainted with its detailed operating characteristics.

Design and construction of particle detectors also tend to be major cooperative enterprises, involving in recent times frequently over 100 physicists from many institutions. Yet individual inventiveness and skill remain absolutely essential to the successful creation of a modern particle detector system. Data-taking with such a facility again involves many physicists because the machine usually runs 24 hours per day and the computer software needed to analyze the data is enormously complex.

Note that in big science of this type far more data are recorded than are required for the experiment's specifically identified primary goals. The real scientific exploitation of the data consists of "mining the tapes." It is during this later phase of data analysis that individual ingenuity becomes paramount. Frequently, important physics discoveries have been made years after the primary data were taken. . . .

THE RELATION OF BIG SCIENCE TO ACADEMIC PRACTICE

It should be noted that throughout this process of big science at SLAC the motivation of the academic physicist participants remained exactly the same as it had been in smaller endeavors, that is, to uncover new basic facts of inanimate nature. However, because of the way in which the work must be carried out, there are indeed conflicts with traditional academic practices that must be resolved. Among these are

1. *Recognition of individual contributors.* Because most but not all of the participation by physicists is in the form of group activities, individual contributions cannot be easily traced through the publication record alone. Therefore, during faculty searches and promotion inquiries reference must be made to personal contacts, with bibliographical data being used for backup only. At SLAC we make a major effort to draw the speakers at major national and international physics conferences from the younger members of a large research collaboration.

2. *The tenure clock.* Attainment of a truly significant scientific result may require a time span not under the control of the young physicist participating in the work. At the same time the "up or out" practices on the academic ladder require documentable accomplishment during a fixed time. The question is whether the "tenure clock" can be

stopped while the individual participates in, say, the construction of a major detector.

3. *Thesis standards.* Ph.D. theses are expected to be "independent" pieces of work. As a practical matter this standard is frequently violated in many fields of natural science—big or small. Because "big science" research is carried out in groups and is frequently conditioned by the available facilities, true independence is hard to come by. At the same time, the graduate student may indeed make major and independent contributions to the instrumental part of his or her activity. However, departments are loath to recognize contributions to the design of instruments as a significant component of a thesis, even if they are intellectually highly challenging. This should be changed.

4. *Absenteeism.* The participation by the research physicist in experiments at SLAC is frequently controlled by the vagaries of the machine, the governmental financial support pattern, and other factors not under laboratory control. Thus a faculty member and his students may have to absent themselves from their teaching duties on a schedule difficult to predict, with consequent burdens on their colleagues. In most users' institutions this matter requires multiple teaching loads when the researchers return to campus. Universities will have to define the price they are willing to pay for participation in big science in greater flexibility in assignment of teaching duties.

5. *Quality of local facilities.* It is clearly desirable from the academic point of view that absences from campus of faculty and students collaborating in big science at other institutions be minimized. This would maximize the interaction of these individuals with their fellow academic colleagues and their contributions to academic life at the home institution. However, to make this practical the home institution cannot be permitted to let its supporting facilities—shops, computers, technical staff assistance—deteriorate; if that happens the academic people involved have no choice but to carry out an even larger part of their work at the big science lab. Recently the quality of support facilities at universities has slipped unacceptably. The fault for this is divided between the sources of government support and the academics themselves: financial support by the government has not grown as fast as most people hoped, but at the same time the principal investigators at most academic institutions have been less than responsible, using available funds for augmenting their academic personnel excessively, to the detriment of adequately building up the supporting structure.

All these points imply serious problems but none that cannot be solved by some flexibility and inventiveness.

Tensions between big science and the universities have arisen over the question of whether there should be a university or a branch of a university located in a big science facility. This is, of course, not an issue at SLAC, because Stanford University is in the fortunate position of being able to accommodate a two-mile accelerator on its seventeen-square-mile campus. Note, however, that when the University of Chicago attempted to establish a branch campus on the site of the Argonne National Laboratory a great howl arose from many other midwestern universities. They claimed that the University of Chicago was trying to take unfair advantage, relative to its sister academic institutions in the Midwest, of Argonne's resources. At the same time there is criticism, some merited, that the intellectual atmosphere at some big science facilities could be greatly improved if the relationship to universities were more intimate. Attempts in this direction have been made, for instance, at the branch of the State University of New York at Stony Brook, just outside the gates of Brookhaven National Laboratory.

BIG SCIENCE AND "ACADEMIC FREEDOM"

Much has been said and written on whether the advent of big science upsets the traditional values generally listed under the heading of academic freedom. Often expressed is the worry that as big science funds are expended in support of science, "who pays the piper calls the tune." In other words, there is concern that the sponsor, in this case the government, will unduly influence the conduct of the work, affect the selection of the principal personnel, and force the introduction of extraneous criteria into various program decisions. This is a problem a university faces irrespective of whether the science is big or small. A university such as Stanford continually confronts the issue of whether to accept a gift or grant from a donor or sponsor if there are too many "strings" attached. While totally unrestricted gifts to the university are highly desirable, most contributions are earmarked for a specific purpose. Yet when that purpose is defined in terms too narrow, the university can be and often is forced to reject the donation. . . .

The relationship between Stanford University and the U.S. government . . . is governed by a contract between the U.S. Department of Energy and the trustees of the university that is renewable every five years. Under that contract the government supports the work at a financial level it chooses in response to annual program submittals by the university, but the university is not obligated to follow the technical and scientific conduct of these proposals except in the most general terms once funding is received. Under the contract the government has a right to approve the director and deputy director of the laboratory when they are first appointed, but it has no right to ask for their removal; the government has no authority to influence the selection of any other personnel or to control the participation by foreign nationals. Decisions about program are made by the laboratory director on the advice of a program advisory committee that passes on the scientific merit of each proposal for use of the SLAC facilities and on the projected capability of the proponents to carry out the work. Publications may not be held up for either national security or commercial considerations; patent review proceeds in parallel with submission of a manuscript to the publishers. In the remote eventuality that the government wishes to use the facilities it owns at SLAC for classified work, then the university has no obligation to carry out such activities. In summary, from the point of view of preserving the traditional academic values, these arrangements for government support of big science compare well with the prewar pattern of industrial support of small science.

IS THERE A CHOICE BETWEEN "BIG" AND "SMALL" SCIENCE?

One should not lose sight of the fact that the motivation of big science and small science remains the same; the expansion to big science is brought on by technical necessity, not by delusions of grandeur of the scientific community. We simply do not know how to obtain information on the most minute structure of matter (high-energy physics), on the grandest scale of the universe (astronomy and cosmology), or on statistically elusive results (systematic genetics) without large efforts and large tools. The evolution of technical and scientific fact has driven the changes, not a change in motivation or ethics of the scientific leaders.

Yet "big science bashing" has become popular. For instance, a recent article in *Issues in Science and Technology* attributed recent instances of scientific fraud to a decrease in morality brought on by big science, notwithstanding the fact that those instances occurred in "small" medical research and fraud is in fact virtually impossible within the large cooperative efforts of big science.

There is no conflict between big and small science as such, and in fact there is a continuum of scale among the different activities. There is no difference in motivation between the practitioners of big and small science. Much of the apparent but intellectually not real conflict between big and small science is simply caused by a perceived competition for resources. Critics point out with some merit that the cost per Ph.D. produced, the cost per scientific publication in refereed journals, the cost per Nobel Prize, or whatever other measures in cost vs. effectiveness the critic may choose, "big science" may not fare well. Yet that is not really the issue. First, this competition for funds need in fact not be real as long as support in basic science remains a very small fraction of the total national product, or even a small fraction of federally supported research and development. Historically, funding for big and funding for small science have risen or fallen together, not one at the expense of the other. Moreover, one should not demand comparable cost effectiveness of the multitude of scientific endeavors: If certain answers crucial to man's understanding of nature can be obtained only by large effort, is that sufficient reason for not seeking such answers?

10. George W. Bush, "Remarks by the President on Stem Cell Research," 2001

President George W. Bush (1946–) stated his position on stem cell research to the media from his ranch in Crawford, Texas on August 9, 2001.

"Text of President Bush's Speech," *Washington Post,* August 10, 2001, A12. Text of speech also available at "Remarks by the President on Stem Cell Research," www.whitehouse.gov, news section, August 9, 2001. Further reading: Jeffrey Brainard, "Stem-Cell Research Moves Forward," *Chronicle of Higher Education,* October 1, 2004, A22, and "California Universities Start Preparing for Windfall in Stem-Cell Research," *Chronicle of Higher Education,* November 12, 2004, A15; letter from Steven Clark, *Chronicle of Higher Education,* November 19, 2004, A55. See also Alison Thomson and Jim McWhir, eds., *Gene Targeting and Embryonic Stem Cells* (London and New York, 2004); President's Council on Bioethics, *Monitoring Stem Cell Research: The Ethical Debates Reviewed* (Washington, D.C., 2003) and *The Administration's Human Embryonic Stem Cell Research Funding Policy: Moral and Political Foundations* (Washington, D.C., 2003); Kirk C. Lo, Weber W. Chuang, and Dolores J. Lamb, "Stem Cell Research: The Facts, the Myths, and the Promises," *Journal of Urology* 170 (December 2003): 2453–58; and New York Times Current File at http://proquest.umi.com/.

TEXT OF PRESIDENT BUSH'S SPEECH

The issue of research involving stem cells derived from human embryos is increasingly the subject of a national debate and dinner table discussions. The issue is confronted every day in laboratories as scientists ponder the ethical ramifications of their work. It is agonized over by parents and many couples as they try to have children or to save children already born. The issue is debated within the church, with people of different faiths—even many of the same faith—coming to different conclusions.

Many people are finding that the more they know about stem cell research, the less certain they are about the right ethical and moral conclusions.

My administration must decide whether to allow federal funds, your tax dollars, to be used for scientific research on stem cells derived from human embryos.

A large number of these embryos already exist. They are the product of a process called in vitro fertilization, which helps so many couples conceive children. When doctors match sperm and egg to create life outside the womb, they usually produce more embryos than are implanted in the mother.

Once a couple successfully has children, or if they are unsuccessful, the additional embryos remain frozen in laboratories. Some will not survive during long storage; others are destroyed. A number have been donated to science and used to create privately funded stem cell lines. And a few have been implanted in an adoptive mother, and born, and are today healthy children.

Based on preliminary work that has been privately funded, scientists believe further research using stem cells offers great promise that could help improve the lives of those who suffer from many terrible diseases, from juvenile diabetes to Alzheimer's, from Parkinson's to spinal cord injuries. And while scientists admit they are not yet certain, they believe stem cells derived from embryos have unique potential.

You should also know that stem cells can be derived from sources other than embryos: from adult cells, from umbilical cords that are discarded after babies are born, from human placentas. And many scientists feel research on these types of stem cells is also promising. Many patients suffering from a range of diseases are already being helped with treatments developed from adult stem cells.

However, most scientists, at least today, believe that research on embryonic stem cells offers the most promise because these cells have the potential to develop in all of the tissues in the body.

Scientists further believe that rapid progress in this research will come only with federal funds. Federal dollars help attract the best and brightest scientists. They ensure new discoveries are widely shared at the largest number of research facilities, and that the research is directed toward the greatest public good.

The United States has a long and proud record of leading the world toward advances in science and medicine that improve human life, and the United States has a long and proud record of upholding the highest standards of ethics as we expand the limits of science and knowledge.

Research on embryonic stem cells raises profound ethical questions, because extracting the stem cell destroys the embryo and thus destroys its potential for life.

Like a snowflake, each of these embryos is unique, with the unique genetic potential of an individual human being.

As I thought through this issue, I kept returning to two fundamental questions. First, are these frozen embryos human life and, therefore, something precious to be protected? And second, if they're going to be destroyed anyway, shouldn't they be used for a greater good, for research that has the potential to save and improve other lives?

I've asked those questions and others of scientists, scholars, bioethicists, religious leaders, doctors, researchers, members of Congress, my Cabinet and my friends. I have read heartfelt letters from many Americans. I have given this issue a great deal of thought, prayer and considerable reflection, and I have found widespread disagreement.

On the first issue, are these embryos human life?

Well, one researcher told me he believes this five-day-old cluster of cells is not an embryo, not yet an individual, but a pre-embryo. He argued that it has the potential for life, but it is not a life because it cannot develop on its own.

An ethicist dismissed that as a callous attempt at rationalization. "Make no mistake," he told me, "that cluster of cells is the same way you and I, and all the rest of us, started our lives. One goes with a heavy heart if we use these," he said, "because we are dealing with the seeds of the next generation."

And to the other crucial question—if these are going to be destroyed anyway, why not use them for good purpose?—I also found different answers.

Many of these embryos are byproducts of a process that helps create life, and we should allow couples to donate them to science so they can be used for good purpose instead of wasting their potential.

Others will argue there is no such thing as excess life, and the fact that a living being is going to die does not justify experimenting on it or exploiting it as a natural resource.

At its core, this issue forces us to confront fundamental questions about the beginnings of life and the ends of science. It lives at a difficult moral intersection, juxtaposing the need to protect life in all its phases with the prospect of saving and improving life in all its stages.

As the discoveries of modern science create tremendous hope, they also lay vast ethical mine fields.

As the genius of science extends the horizons of what we can do, we increasingly confront complex questions about what we should do. We have arrived at that "Brave New World" that seemed so distant in 1932 when Aldous Huxley wrote about human beings created in test tubes in what he called a hatchery.

In recent weeks, we learned that scientists have created human embryos in test tubes solely to experiment on them. This is deeply troubling and a warning sign that should prompt all of us to think through these issues very carefully.

Embryonic stem cell research is at the leading edge of a series of moral hazards. The initial stem cell researcher was at first reluctant to begin his research, fearing it might be used for human cloning. Scientists have already cloned a sheep. Researchers are telling us the next step could be to clone human beings to create individual designer stem cells, essentially to grow another you, to be available in case you need another heart or lung or liver.

I strongly oppose human cloning, as do most Americans. We recoil at the idea of growing human beings for spare body parts or creating life for our convenience.

And while we must devote enormous energy to conquering disease, it is equally important that we pay attention to the moral concerns raised by the new frontier of human embryo stem cell research. Even the most noble ends do not justify any means.

My position on these issues is shaped by deeply held beliefs. I'm a strong supporter of science and technology, and believe they have the potential for incredible good—to improve lives, to save life, to conquer disease. Research offers hope that millions of our loved ones may be cured of a disease and rid of their suffering. I have friends whose children suffer from juvenile diabetes. Nancy Reagan has written me about President Reagan's struggle with Alzheimer's. My own family has confronted the tragedy of childhood leukemia. And like all Americans, I have great hope for cures.

I also believe human life is a sacred gift from our creator. I worry about a culture that devalues life, and believe as your president I have an important obligation to foster and encourage respect for life in America and throughout the world.

And while we're all hopeful about the potential of this research, no one can be certain that the science will live up to the hope it has generated.

Eight years ago, scientists believed fetal tissue research offered great hope for cures and treatments, yet the progress to date has not lived up to its initial expectations. Embryonic stem cell research offers both great promise and great peril, so I have decided we must proceed with great care.

As a result of private research, more than 60 genetically diverse stem cell lines already exist. They were created from embryos that have already been destroyed, and they have the ability to regenerate themselves indefinitely, creating ongoing opportunities for research.

I have concluded that we should allow federal funds to be used for research on these existing stem cell lines, where the life-and-death decision has already been made. . . .

I also believe that great scientific progress can be made through aggressive federal funding of research on umbilical cord, placenta, adult and animal stem cells, which do not involve the same moral dilemma. This year your government will spend $250 million on this important research.

I will also name a president's council to monitor stem cell research, to recommend appropriate guidelines and regulations, and to consider all of the medical and ethical ramifications of biomedical innovation.

This council will consist of leading scientists, doctors, ethicists, lawyers, theologians and others and will be chaired by Dr. Leon Kass, a leading biomedical ethicist from the University of Chicago.

This council will keep us apprised of new developments and give our nation a forum to continue to discuss and evaluate these important issues.

As we go forward, I hope we will always be guided by both intellect and heart, by both our capabilities and our conscience.

I have made this decision with great care, and I pray it is the right one.

Foundations

11. Warren Weaver,
U.S. Philanthropic Foundations, 1967

Warren Weaver (1894–1978) was one of the first private foundation executives to engage in an assessment of their overall record. He defended their good judgment as donors, denied any invasiveness of university autonomy, and insisted upon imagination in their activities. Wisconsin-born and -educated, Weaver taught mathematics for several years at Cal Tech and at Wisconsin, after which he went to the Rockefeller Foundation in New York City to become director of various divisions and finally vice president (1932–59). Thereafter, he presided over the Alfred P. Sloan Foundation (1959–64). For his work with governmental research projects during World War II and for his writings in applied and mathematical sciences, he received many awards, among them the United States Medal of Merit in 1948.

pp. 153–4, 160–2 from *U.S. Philanthropic Foundations: Their History, Structure, Management, and Record* by Warren Weaver, Copyright © 1967 by the American Academy of Arts and Science. Reprinted by permission of HarperCollins Publishers. Further reading: his autobiography, *Scene of Change* (New York, 1970); Merle E. Curti and Roderick Nash, *Philanthropy in the Shaping of American Higher Education* (New Brunswick, NJ, 1965), chs. 8–12; the critical study by Waldemar A. Nielsen, *The Big Foundations* (New York, 1972); Ellen Condliffe Lagemann, *Private Power for the Public Good: A History of the Carnegie Foundation for the Advancement of Teaching* (New York, 1983); and Noliwe M. Rooks, *White Money Black Power: The Surprising History of African American Studies and the Crisis of Race in Higher Education* (Boston, 2006).

If . . . it *were* to be conceded that foundations have invaded the autonomy of universities, luring them financially into doing things they did not really want to do, if a university *were* to accept an almost wholly unwelcome grant in order to avoid offending the potential source of a later, larger, and wholly welcome grant—would such projects hurt the universities?

I myself know of no clear and significant case of a harmful project forced on a university. Often, in fact, it has been good to crack through the rather conservative and orthodox organizational crust of universities and inject, frankly from the outside, some fresh ideas. R. S. Morison, who combines distinguished careers inside both foundations and universities, suggests several illustrations: the Flexner reform of medical education, the General Education Board reform of admission standards and of college and university accounting practices, the Rockefeller Foundation-sponsored development of psychiatry in medical schools, the early emphasis on the behavioral sciences by the Laura Spelman Rockefeller Memorial, the role of foundations in introducing area studies and the study of exotic languages.

For a quite different reason, the possible invasion of university autonomy by philanthropic foundations would today no longer be a serious threat even if foundations were less thoughtful and sensitive than they are. For foundation support of universities does not comparatively bulk nearly as large as it used to.

There was a time, nearly fifty years ago, when the Carnegie Corporation and the General Education Board were making annual grants amounting to perhaps one-fifth of the total annual income available to all colleges and universities in our country. Thirty years ago the annual grants for research of the Rockefeller Foundation constituted a sizable fraction of the total funds available for academic research in the United States.

At the present time, however, American colleges and universities require about $13 billion a year, and foundations supply only roughly 3 percent of this. The 3 percent is critically important, especially since so much of it is available for innovation; but if one scales down the 3 percent so as to include only ideas originating with foundations as contrasted with ideas which wholly represent the universities' own enthusiasms, and then scales down again to include only poor foundation ideas, he would wind up with so small a fraction of one percent of university support that the integrity of the university structure could not thereby be importantly threatened. . . .

There are three basic reasons why foundations *must* have ideas. First, the relationship between universities (and here we must broaden the category to include *all* the persons with whom foundations deal) simply cannot be one of integrity unless this relationship is based upon mutual respect. If scientists, scholars, and artists accept money from a source whose personnel they cannot meet on equal terms, then the relationship must degenerate to a level at which the recipients become nothing better than fawning mendicants. The discussions must be carried out on each side by persons who understand the issues, who are competent in the subject matter involved, who not only have ideas but who have good ideas. . . .

Having had the advantage of working in scientific fields in which the techniques for recognizing competence are highly developed, I have seen my fellow officers suffer somewhat from the assumption that almost every person considers himself an expert in the social sciences and in education. But I am sure that this assumption is not justified. Study and experience are essential in every field. I even assume, I hope not too optimistically, that it is possible to know something about modern art.

The second basic reason why foundations must have ideas is that creative innovation is imperative in the sector of private philanthropy. If foundations are to continue to be concerned with imaginative activities, if they are to stimulate flexible new ideas in institutions that often tend to be rather conventional, if foundations are, in short, to continue to justify their position as favored social instruments, they must be something more than passive selectors among the assorted ideas brought to them.

A third reason why foundation officers have an important role apart from mere administrative choice among the ideas of others is that a great national resource of information and advice concerning universities, and advice to universities, is formed by the body of philanthropic foundation officers. They travel widely and get to know many, many institutions. They are dependent upon no one of these institutions and thus can have opinions broadly based and little prejudiced. On many occasions university administrators have told me that they knew of almost no place, other than their friends in good foundations, where they could go for information, advice, criticisms, and suggestions which would be really competent and at the same time unbiased. As one academic president has written me, " . . . officers in the large professional foundations are probably the best-informed people in the country with respect to our institutions of higher learning."

12. The Ford Foundation, 1949, 1953, 1999 Reports

Since the founding of Harvard College, American colleges and universities have benefited from private philanthropies. Benefactions increased remarkably with the contributions of the Carnegie, Rockefeller, and Mellon foundations in the late nineteenth and early twentieth century. National prosperity after World War II made possible the creation of many smaller philanthropies, all surpassed in their resources by the Ford Foundation, which expanded in 1950 from a local philanthropy in Michigan to national and international interests. Excerpted here are portions of three reports from the foundation. The first (1949) evokes a neo-Enlightenment faith in the usefulness of knowledge by setting out the goals of the foundation; the second (1953) explains its support for the social or behavioral sciences in founding the Center for the Advanced Study in the Behavioral Sciences at Palo Alto, California; and the third (1999) deals with the foundation's rethinking of area studies, an enterprise that it helped to establish after World War II.

The Ford Foundation, "Report of the Study for the Ford Foundation on Policy and Program" (Detroit, 1949), 19, 22, 93–94, 96–97; "The Ford Foundation Annual Report for 1953" (New York, 1953), 64–67; Toby Alice Volkman, "Crossing Borders: Revitalizing Area Studies" (New York, 1999): ix–xii. Reprinted with permission of the Ford Foundation. Further reading: Robert H. Bremner, *American Philanthropy* (Chicago, 1988); Dwight Macdonald, *The Ford Foundation, The Men and the Millions* (New York, 1955); Richard Magat, *The Ford Foundation at Work, Philanthropic Choices, Methods, and Styles* (New York, 1979); Richard Magat, "In Search of the Ford Foundation," in *Philanthropic Foundations: New Scholarship, New Possibilities*, ed. Ellen Condliffe Lagemann (Bloomington, IN, 1999), 296–317; Lucy Bernholz, "The Future of Foundation History, Suggestions for Research and Practice," in *Philanthropic Foundations*, ed. Lagemann,

359–75; Susan Kastan, "Bibliography: Recent Writings about Foundations in History," in *Philanthropic Foundations*, ed. Lagemann, 377–403; Joseph C. Kiger, *Historiographic Review of Foundation Literature: Motivations and Perceptions* (New York, 1987); *Philanthropy Monthly* (New Milford, CT, 1983–present); *The Chronicle of Philanthropy* (Washington, D.C., 1988–present).

1949

Human Welfare and Democratic Ideals

The Committee's concept of human welfare is closely related to the ideals of democratic peoples— belief in human dignity; in personal freedom; in equality of rights, justice, and opportunity; in freedom of speech, religion, and association; and in self-government as the best form of government. Through the fuller realization of these ideals the life of the individual would become more productive, purposeful, gracious, and secure. In the belief that any successful attempt to improve the lot of mankind must be made on terms compatible with these fundamental principles, the Committee used them as a base in estimating the gravity of human welfare's problems and as a standard in considering programs for their solution.

Democracy does not, of course, consist of the numerical aggregate of these principles or in the exaltation of one at the expense of another. It consists rather in a meaningful relationship among them, resting always on the fundamental conviction of the dignity of man.

These democratic ideals represent for the Committee a particularly significant expression of human welfare since they emphasize man's most crucial problems—the intricate relationships among human beings and social organizations, now so heavily marked by tension and disorder.

While our ultimate concern is with the individual, it is clear that only in society can his full development take place. Modern man cannot forsake society in search of freedom; freedom, for him, exists only within and by means of the social order. Men are no freer than the arrangements and conditions of society enable them to be. In the complex modern world large-scale and complicated arrangements are necessary to provide the social and economic conditions under which freedom can be assured. . . .

The Role of a Foundation

This view of democracy is one of challenge to a modern foundation. By the character of its response the Ford Foundation will determine the degree to which it will help carry toward maturity the modern concept of philanthropy.

The history of philanthropy is the record of a continuously evolving philosophy of giving. At one time the gifts of individuals and benevolent organizations were intended largely to relieve the suffering of "the weak, the poor and the unfortunate." Philanthropy was thought of merely as temporary relief for evil conditions which would always exist and about which nothing fundamental could be done. With the establishment of the modern foundation a much greater concept came into being. The aim is no longer merely to treat symptoms and temporarily to alleviate distress, but rather to eradicate the causes of suffering. Nor is the modern foundation content to concern itself only with man's obvious physical needs; it seeks rather to help man achieve his entire well-being—to satisfy his mental, emotional, and spiritual needs as well as his physical wants. It addresses itself to the whole man and to the well-being of all mankind. . . .

Need for More Basic Knowledge

Our storehouse of verified knowledge of human behavior, however, has a relatively low inventory. Most of our practices in dealing with individual adjustment and social relationships rest on mixtures of scientific data and the fruits of personal experience, including common sense hunches and speculation. If we are to deal adequately with the critical problems of our times our knowledge must be sharpened and expanded.

To stock our storehouse of verified principles of behavior will require intensified and multiplied efforts in research. This must be recognized as a long-range program. The history of science has demonstrated that knowledge for action consists of a slow accumulation of many small bits of knowledge, no one of which is necessarily of practical use until fitted into combination with other bits of data, which themselves may have appeared at first to be equally useless fragments. Because of the established similarity of scientific methods throughout both the natural and behavioral sciences, we must conclude that knowledge is important even if not immediately usable, and that impatient expectation of practical results can be indulged only at the sacrifice of any results and at the expense of scientific progress. . . .

A Foundation Policy for Applied Research

For the reasons stated above, major emphasis should not be placed upon applied or developmental research, or other research designed exclusively to solve particular problems. Unlike natural scientists, however, behavioral scientists can seldom work in closed laboratories and must usually operate in normal life situations. If the objective is basic knowledge rather than immediate solution of practical problems, the selection of topics for scientific study is ordinarily best left to the research worker himself. If a serious problem situation in actual life provides opportunity for research conforming to the accepted standards of scientific work, however, the Committee strongly recommends that it be used as the locus of the appropriate study. Thus, wherever life itself must provide the laboratory for basic research, such research may offer the double prom-

ise of contributing to the solution of a troublesome problem at the same time it adds to the storehouse of knowledge.

Attention is called to a number of stubborn life problems which should be assessed as laboratories for valuable research. One is the problem of minority tensions and race relations. Another is the problem of industrial relations. . . . A third is the problem of old age, only now beginning to receive serious attention. A fourth problem, of somewhat different character, is that of international and intercultural understanding . . . In addition to contributing to scientific knowledge by testing it in the various cultures of mankind, attention to this problem might contribute to the betterment of international relations. . . .

1953

Behavioral Sciences Program

Constructive action to advance human welfare presupposes a broad basis of verified knowledge. The Foundation's Behavioral Sciences Program is designed to contribute to the development of such a body of knowledge through grants for the scientific study of man.

Originally, two objectives were assigned to the program: to increase scientific knowledge of human behavior, and to facilitate the application of such knowledge to human affairs. In order to reach these ends, the Foundation has recognized an intermediate objective, that of supporting the technical development of the behavioral sciences. The Foundation's use of the term "behavioral sciences" is not equivalent to the usual definition of the social sciences as a certain group of academic disciplines. Rather, it denotes those intellectual activities that contribute to the understanding of individual behavior and human relations, no matter where they may be located academically.

Behavioral sciences grants in 1953 covered all three of the program's basic objectives. As in 1952, major emphasis was given to grants for technical development.

Improving the Competence of Behavioral Scientists

The Foundation continued to support efforts to improve the quality and range of training for behavioral scientists. A major element in this support has been the development by the Foundation of an independent Center for Advanced Study in the Behavioral Sciences. By the end of 1953 a director for the Center had been appointed and had taken up his duties, detailed planning was proceeding, and a site was being chosen. Operation of the Center is scheduled to begin in the fall of 1954.

The history of the Center began with preliminary conferences in the fall of 1951 and with a meeting in March, 1952, of an ad hoc group of fourteen behavioral scientists and academic administrators, representing seven disciplines and nine universities, brought together to advise the Foundation on the best means of meeting the problem of advanced training. Their recommendation that a center be organized was followed by the establishment of a planning group which submitted concrete proposals in June, 1952. "What is needed," this group said in its report, "is an institutional innovation to provide a setting in which promising young behavioral scientists can be brought abreast of the highest level of knowledge, insight, research experience, and scholarship available at present, but now unavoidably scattered among the faculties of many universities."

An appropriation for the creation of such an institution was made by the Foundation in July, 1952, providing $3.5 million for one year of planning and five years of operation.

The board of directors of the Center was appointed by the Foundation in the fall of 1952 and met for the first time in January, 1953. Six months later it announced the appointment of Ralph W. Tyler, Dean of the Division of the Social Sciences, University of Chicago, as Director of the Center.

Members of the board of directors are:

Frank Stanton (Chairman), President, Columbia
    Broadcasting System
Paul Buck, former Provost, Harvard University
F. F. Hill, Provost, Cornell University
Clark Kerr, Chancellor, University of California
    (Berkeley)
Robert K. Merton, Chairman, Department of Sociology, Columbia University
Robert R. Sears, Executive Head, Department of
    Psychology, Stanford University
Alan T. Waterman, Director, National Science
    Foundation
Theodore O. Yntema, Vice-President—Finance,
    Ford Motor Company

As stated in the report of the planning group, "the major purpose of the Center is to develop the general field of the behavioral sciences as fully and as richly as possible over a relatively short period of time by concentration upon the advanced study of highly creative and productive behavioral scientists of established reputation and of highly promising young scholars with their professional careers ahead of them. If the level of competence of a considerable number of behavioral scientists can be markedly improved in this way, the program will make a major contribution to the universities, which over the long run must bear the responsibility for developing the behavioral sciences." ...

The objectives of the Center are these: to provide a greater number of highly qualified scholars in the behavioral field for the staffs of the universities where they are now urgently needed; to increase advanced training opportunities for present faculty members; to help in the development of more comprehensive, better-integrated content and methods in the behavioral sciences; to provide new designs and materials for advanced research training.

The Center will consist primarily of two groups: a corps of from ten to fifteen outstanding senior scholars, both American and foreign, on leave from their home institutions for periods normally of one year, and a group of thirty to forty promising junior men, typically at the early post-doctoral level, who will be in residence at the Center for periods of from one to two years. In addition, there will probably be a small group of special members, such as governmental personnel and foreign scholars, in attendance for relatively short periods. Participants will be drawn from the widest range of academic disciplines which contribute to the scientific study of human behavior.

Attracting new talent to the behavioral sciences is another approach to the improvement of personnel, and in 1953 the Foundation continued two projects of this nature. Summer research apprenticeships for college seniors were awarded, under a grant to the Social Science Research Council, to forty-one students out of 325 applicants from more than a hundred colleges. Graduate fellowships for students who had not majored in the behavioral sciences in their undergraduate work were awarded by the Foundation to seventeen out of ninety-one applicants.

The recruitment and training of a larger number of specialists in population problems are needed in areas of growing population pressure, and qualified demographers to direct such training are in short supply. A World Population Conference will be held in Rome in 1954 under the auspices of the International Union for the Scientific Study of Population, and the Foundation has granted $40,000 to help specialists from population pressure areas to attend it.

Improving the Content of the Behavioral Sciences

Of importance to the intellectual development of the behavioral sciences is the problem of improving their relationship with such disciplines as history, social and political philosophy, humanistic studies, and certain phases of economics. Today this relationship is distinguished perhaps as much by recrimination and doctrinal dispute as by scholarly collaboration. In the conviction that valuable contributions to the understanding of man can be made by both sides, the Foundation announced in 1952 and put into effect in 1953 a program of support for interdisciplinary research and study.

TOBY ALICE VOLKMAN, CROSSING BORDERS:
REVITALIZING AREA STUDIES, 1999

Recent developments have challenged some of the premises of area studies itself. The notion, for example, that the world can be divided into knowable, self-contained "areas" has come into question as more attention has been paid to movements between areas. Demographic shifts, diasporas, labor migrations, the movements of global capital and media, and processes of cultural circulation and hybridization have encouraged a more subtle and sensitive reading of areas' identity and composition. The demographics of the area studies community are themselves shifting: students on many campuses are rediscovering their "heritage" languages and cultures, U.S. faculty now compete for academic positions with scholars who are natives of the areas studies, and scholars everywhere work with colleagues who may be situated in quite different disciplinary or institutional locations (an Indian film scholar, for example, in an English department), or who write in different languages.

In recent years, U.S. area studies has been critiqued by some as an outgrowth of European colonialism, and by others who point out its origins as an intellectual support for American foreign policy in the developing world. Area studies has also been profoundly affected by financial retrenchment at many, colleges and universities, as support for intensive language study, extensive field work, and specialized faculty and library resources has become increasingly scarce. . . .

The need for focused cross-disciplinary study of different parts of the world has hardly diminished. Indeed it can be argued that the political complexities of the late twentieth-century world, and the changes brought about by accelerating worldwide trade and communication, make area studies more urgent than ever. To go beyond the facile rhetoric of globalization as homogenization, it is essential to examine how identities and cultures are being formed and re-formed. In this light, it is also essential to analyze the social, cultural, and historical dimensions of such phenomena as global capital flows. Without the kind of interdisciplinary perspective and in-depth knowledge of particular places that area studies fosters, such understanding will not be possible. The commitment to rigorous and detailed knowledge that has characterized area studies at its best must not be abandoned, and must indeed be strengthened.

For this to occur, it is also clear that some of the basic premises and procedures of the field will have to be rethought. This rethinking should occur at all levels of research and pedagogy, from special research institutes and graduate programs to basic undergraduate and graduate curricula. Rethinking may take different forms for area studies subfields; consider, for example, the very different institutional histories, intellectual agendas, and political contexts of African, Russian, Latin American, or Southeast Asian studies. At the same time, a renewed area studies field should strive to make connections among these disparate and typically not connected fields. And it should take into account the potential—as well as the complexities—of new forms of worldwide communication and collaboration that were, until recently, unimaginable.

In 1997, the Foundation launched a multi-year, $25-million initiative, entitled: "Crossing Borders: Revitalizing Area Studies." The goal of this initiative is twofold: first to enhance in-depth study of particular areas, and to activate new, visible, and significant streams of funding; second, to foster innovative approaches to the field's intellectual foundations and practices in light of a dramatically changed, and increasingly interconnected, world.

"Crossing Borders" began in the 1997–98 academic year with thirty grants of $50,000 each to support innovative programs at a wide range of institutions, from major research universities to small liberal arts colleges, from Maine to Hawai'i. The thirty grantees were selected from an initial applicant pool of 205. The pool was created in response to a request for proposals sent to 270 universities and colleges in the United States with area studies programs. The Foundation hopes that the impact of the initial grants will be felt beyond the recipient institutions, as the programs they develop suggest new ways of approaching both the specificity of experience in different parts of the world and patterns of interaction, circulation, and transformation.

The results we hope for from this and future activity are:

- to ensure that knowledge and understanding of particular places continue to be grounded in serious study of culture, language, and history, while finding new ways of conceptualizing "area" so that its study opens up exciting new questions, new approaches, new ways of understanding both history and changes in the contemporary world;
- to create a more truly international area studies in which scholars and practitioners (artists, activists, public intellectuals) from diverse "areas" shape the agenda and formulate, from their own perspectives, important questions about the relationships between regional and global experience;
- to influence the policy climate in the United States in order to generate stronger, sustained support for area studies by government, university administrators, and the donor community. . . .

Corporations

13. Eyal Press and Jennifer Washburn, "The Kept University," 2000

In 1945 Vannevar Bush foresaw the coming of government-funded academic research in science and technology combining with industrial research and productivity to create enduring national benefits (1, 2). His vision became a reality in the next few decades, one that was speeded along in 1980 by the passage of the Bayh-Dole Act. The act permitted universities to patent the results of federally funded research. Academic research institutions thereupon could and did turn to granting licenses from their patents to manufacturing companies, with royalties as their compensation. Early and confident partisans of such partnerships were convinced of the financial benefits to be gained, and they were proven right. Initial skeptics of these arrangements were joined by a growing number of faculty scientists and graduate students. By the 1990s they were calling for free and independent research in public university laboratories and technological workplaces uninfluenced by private corporate financing. They saw the integrity and autonomy of academic science challenged. Tensions between the two positions were widely publicized by this article in *The Atlantic Monthly.* It related an episode at the University of California, Berkeley, where an assistant professor of microbial ecology in April 1999 publicly opposed influential corporate sponsorship. He had once worked for the Swiss agribusiness company Novartis, which was licensed to finance the work of virtually his entire department in return for first rights to commercialize new findings in basic research. To him, corporate support for contracted individual research was proper, but not for an entire department. By late 2003, amid nationwide publicity and considerable faculty support notwithstanding charges of questionable research reporting, he was denied advancement, but finally in May 2005 he was granted tenure by the Berkeley administration.

The authors used this story to begin a critical national survey warning of academic ethics in jeopardy. Jennifer Washburn (1969–) and Eyal Press (1970–) were fellows of the Open Society Institute in New York City; both are freelance writers whose separate writings have appeared in various journals of opinion. Washburn later became a fellow at the New America Foundation in Los Angeles.

Eyal Press and Jennifer Washburn, "The Kept University," *Atlantic Monthly,* March 2000, 39–49, 51–54; reprinted with permission of *The Atlantic Monthly* and the authors; © 2000, Eyal Press and Jennifer Washburn. For corrections to this article and responses by the authors, see vol. 285 (June 2000): 6–7, and vol. 286 (July 2000): 10–11. Further reading: P.L. 96–517 (1980), The Patent and Trademark Law Amendments Act, known as the Bayh-Dole Act, amended in P.L. 98–620 (1984); Jennifer Washburn, *University, Inc.: The Corporate Corruption of Higher Education* (New York, 2005); Goldie Blumenstyk, "A Vilified Corporate Partnership Produces Little Change (Except Better Facilities)," *Chronicle of Higher Education,* June 22, 2001, A24; *The Daily Californian,* May 11–16, June 23, November 7, 2000; February 5, April 5, 9, 2002; April 30, June 27, 2003; June 24, August 2, 2004; Lisa Humes-Schulz, "Professor's Long Fight for Tenure Not Over," December 10, 2004; *San Francisco Chronicle,* December 10, 2004, B5; May 21, 2005, B1, 3; *Wall Street Journal,* December 21, 2004, 1; Arti K. Rai and Rebecca S. Eisenberg, "Bayh-Dole Reform and the Progress of Biomedicine," *Law and Contemporary Problems* (Winter–Spring 2003): 289–315; Eric Gould, *The University in a Corporate Culture* (New Haven, 2004); Sheila Slaughter and Gary Rhoades, *Academic Capitalism and the New Economy: Markets, States, and Higher Education* (Baltimore, 2004); Derek Bok, *Universities in the Marketplace: The Commercialization of Higher Education* (Princeton, NJ, 2003), 151–53; David C. Mowery, Richard R. Nelson, Bhaven N. Sampat, and Arvids A. Ziedonis, "The Effects of the Bayh-Dole Act on U.S. University Research and Technology Transfer," in *Industrializing Knowledge: University-Industry Linkages in Japan and the United States,* ed. Lewis M. Branscomb, Funio Kodama, and Richard Florida (Cambridge, MA, 1999); David C. Mowery, Richard R. Nelson, Bhaven Sampat, and Arvids Ziedonis, *Ivory Tower and Industrial Innovation:*

University-Industry Technology Transfer Before and After the Bayh-Dole Act (Stanford, CA, 2004), revises the historical importance of the Bayh-Dole Act in commercializing university research; Goldie Blumenstyk, "Columbia Patent Battle Winds Down," *Chronicle of Higher Education,* September 16, 2005, A37, summarizes the legal struggle between Columbia and biotechnology companies; Jeffrey J. Williams, "The Post–Welfare State University," *American Literary History* 18 (Spring 2006): 190–216, valuably summarizes a growing critical literature on institutional control, support, and the situation of academic workers within "academic capitalism" entering the twenty-first century; and VIII, 14.

Although our national conversation about higher education remains focused on issues of diversity and affirmative action, nothing provoked more debate on many college campuses last year than the growing ties between universities and business—and nowhere was the debate livelier than at Berkeley.

On the afternoon of April 13, [1999] . . . two dozen faculty members, many of them professors in the College of Natural Resources, had gathered to present the disquieting results of a newly released faculty survey.

The focus of the survey was a controversial agreement that Berkeley had signed in November of 1998 with Novartis, a Swiss pharmaceutical giant and producer of genetically engineered crops. Under the terms of the agreement Novartis will give Berkeley $25 million to fund basic research in the Department of Plant and Microbial Biology, one of four departments within the CNR.

In exchange for the $25 million, Berkeley grants Novartis first right to negotiate licenses on roughly a third of the department's discoveries—including the results of research funded by state and federal sources as well as by Novartis. It also grants the company unprecedented representation—two of five seats—on the department's research committee, which determines how the money is spent.

That the university had the backing of a private company was hardly unusual. That a single corporation would be providing one third of the research budget of an entire department at a public university had sparked an uproar. Shortly after the agreement was signed, a newly formed graduate-student group, Students for Responsible Research, circulated a petition blasting the Novartis deal for standing "in direct conflict with our mission as a public university." . . .

"We are here to discuss the position of the faculty," Ignacio Chapela, a professor of microbial ecology, announced as the April 13 meeting began. Chapela, who was then the chairman of the college's executive committee, a faculty governing body, snapped on an overhead projector to display the results of the survey, and declared that the Novartis deal had left the CNR "deeply divided." While 41 percent of the faculty respondents supported the Novartis agreement as signed, more than

50 percent believed that it would have a "negative" or "strongly negative" effect on academic freedom. Roughly half believed that the agreement would erode Berkeley's commitment to "public good research," and 60 percent feared that it would impede the free exchange of ideas among scientists within the college—one of Chapela's chief concerns. . . . Chapela, like many critics of the deal, is hardly a confirmed opponent of university-industry relations. Before coming to Berkeley, he told us, he spent three years in Switzerland working for none other than Novartis—then named Sandoz—and he continues to have a relationship with the company. "I'm not opposed to individual professors serving as consultants to industry," he said. "If something goes wrong, it's their reputation that's at stake. But this is different. This deal institutionalizes the university's relationship with one company, whose interest is profit. Our role should be to serve the public good."

Gordon Rausser, the chief architect of the Novartis deal, believes that faculty concerns about the alliance reflect ignorance about both the Novartis deal and the changing economic realities of higher education. . . . An economist who served on the President's Council of Economic Advisors in the 1980s, . . . Rausser contends that Berkeley's value is "enhanced, not diminished, when we work creatively in collaboration with other institutions, including private companies." . . .

Rausser's view is more and more the norm, as academic administrators throughout the country turn to the private sector for an increasing percentage of their research dollars, in part because public support for education has been dropping. Although the federal government still supplies most of the funding for academic research (it provided $14.3 billion, or 60 percent in 1997, the latest year for which figures are available), the rate of growth in federal support has fallen steadily over the past twelve years, as the cost of doing research, particularly in the cutting-edge fields of computer engineering and molecular biology, has risen sharply. State spending has also declined. . . . California now supplies just 34 percent of Berkeley's overall budget, as compared with 50 percent twelve years ago. . . .

Meanwhile, corporate giving is on the rise, growing from $850 million in 1985 to $4.25 billion less than a decade later—and increasingly the money comes with strings attached. . . .

In rushing to forge alliances with industry, universities are not just responding to economic necessity—they are also capitalizing on a change in federal law, implemented nearly two decades ago, that laid the foundation for today's academic-industrial complex. In 1980 concerns about declining U.S. productivity and rising competition from Japan propelled Congress to pass the Bayh-Dole Act, which for the first time allowed universities to patent the results of federally funded research. The goal of the legislation was to bring ideas out of the ivory tower and into the marketplace, by offering universities the opportunity to license campus-based inventions to U.S. companies, earning royalties in return. . . . In the years since, Congress has passed numerous other laws to bolster university-industry ties, including generous tax breaks for corporations willing to invest in academic research.

The Bayh-Dole Act was from the beginning controversial. Some in Congress argued that granting private companies the rights to publicly funded research amounted to an enormous giveaway to corporations; others pronounced the act a visionary example of industrial policy that would help America compete in the fast-moving information age. What is undeniable is that Bayh-Dole has revolutionized university-industry relations. From 1980 to 1998 industry funding for academic research expanded at an annual rate of 8.1 percent, reaching $1.9 billion in 1997—nearly eight times the level of twenty years ago. Before Bayh-Dole, universities produced roughly 250 patents a year (many of which were never commercialized); in fiscal year 1998, however, universities generated more than 4,800 patent applications. University-industry collaborations, Rausser argues, have brought important new products—anti-AIDS treatments, cancer drugs—to market, and have spurred America's booming biotech and computing industries. "The University of California alone has issued over five hundred patents since Bayh-Dole," Rausser says.

This is a powerful argument, but a troubling one. In an age when ideas are central to the economy, universities will inevitably play a role in fostering growth. But should we allow commercial forces to determine the university's educational mission and academic ideals? In higher education today corporations not only sponsor a growing amount of research—they frequently dictate the terms under which it is conducted. Professors, their image as unbiased truth-seekers notwithstanding, often own stock in the companies that fund their work. And universities themselves are exhibiting a markedly more commercial bent. Most now operate technology-licensing offices to manage their patent portfolios, often guarding their intellectual property as aggressively as any business would. Schools with limited budgets are pouring money into commercially oriented fields of research, while downsizing humanities departments and curbing expenditures on teaching. . . .

Today scientists who perform industry-sponsored research routinely sign agreements requiring them to keep both the methods and the results of their work secret for a certain period of time. From a company's point of view, confidentiality may be necessary to prevent potential competitors from pilfering ideas. But what constitutes a reasonable period of secrecy? The National Institutes of Health recommends that universities allow corporate sponsors to prohibit publication for no more than one or two months (the amount of time ordinarily necessary to apply for a patent), but lengthier delays are becoming standard. Berkeley's contract with Novartis, for example, allows the company to postpone publication for up to four months. A survey of 210 life-science companies, conducted in 1994 by researchers at Massachusetts General Hospital, found that 58 percent of those sponsoring academic research require delays of more than six months before publication.

"One of the most basic tenets of science is that we share information in an open way," says Steven Rosenberg, of the National Cancer Institute, who is among the country's leading cancer researchers. "As biotech and pharmaceutical companies have become more involved in funding research, there's been a shift toward confidentiality that is severely inhibiting the interchange of information." . . . A 1997 survey of 2,167 university scientists, which appeared in the *Journal of the American Medical Association*, revealed that nearly one in five had delayed publication for more than six months to protect proprietary information—and this was the number that *admitted* to delay. "The ethics of business and the ethics of science do not mix well," Rosenberg says. "This is the real dark side of science." . . .

Mildred Cho, a senior research scholar at Stanford's Center for Biomedical Ethics, . . . in a 1996 study published in the *Annals of Internal Medicine*, found that 98 percent of papers based on industry-sponsored research reflected favorably on the drugs being examined, as compared with 79 percent of papers based on research not funded by industry. . . .

More and more, professors not only accept industry grants to perform research but also hold stock or have other financial ties to the companies funding them. In a study of 800 scientific papers published in a range of academic journals, Sheldon Krimsky, a professor of public policy at Tufts University and a leading authority on conflicts of interest, found that slightly more than a *third* of the authors had a significant financial interest in their reports. Michael McCarthy, an editor at the British medical journal *The Lancet*, says such links are now so common that he "often can't find anyone who doesn't have a financial interest in a drug or therapy the journal would like to review." Although Krimsky doesn't believe that the mere existence of such ties makes an academic study suspect, he advocates full disclosure. Yet in none of the nearly 300 studies in which Krimsky found a conflict of interest were readers informed about it. . . .

Some would argue that such relationships, far from being unseemly, are in keeping with the utilitarian strain that runs through the history of American higher education. Certainly, in comparison with their European counterparts, U.S. universities have always displayed a pragmatic bent. Whereas in Europe universities took pride in pursuing knowledge for its own sake and in remaining aloof from the outside world, in America educators from Thomas Jefferson to John Dewey have argued that universities ought to be engaged in the world, and that

knowledge exists to be put to use. When Congress passed the Morrill Act, in 1862 (which gave rise to America's public land-grant universities, including Berkeley), it specifically instructed the states to establish schools that would teach "agriculture and the mechanical arts . . . in order to promote the liberal and practical education of the industrial classes," rather than the classical curriculum. . . .

World War II, however, ushered in an era of public support for higher education. The role of university scientists in the Manhattan Project and other wartime initiatives—such as the development of penicillin and streptomycin—convinced public officials that academics were uniquely capable of undertaking crucial research initiatives. As corporations slowed their funding of academic research, public money filled the role: from 1953 to 1968 public support grew by 12 to 14 percent annually. Whereas funding for scientific research from all sources totaled $31 million in 1940, federal funding alone reached $3 billion in 1979, much of it dispensed by the National Institutes of Health and other new agencies. This influx of federal dollars reflected a growing appreciation for the basic, undirected research that universities perform. . . .

The Bayh-Dole Act changed this, and not simply by creating incentives for corporations to invest in academic research. What is ultimately most striking about today's academic-industrial complex is not that large amounts of private capital are flowing into universities. It is that universities themselves are beginning to look and behave like for-profit companies. . . .

Traditionally, universities regarded patents as being outside their orbit, generally believing that proprietary claims were fundamentally at odds with their obligation to disseminate knowledge as broadly as possible. Today nearly every research university in the country has a technology-licensing office, and some have gone further. Johns Hopkins Medical School, for example, has established an internal venture-capital fund to bankroll commercially promising lines of research. The University of Chicago, renowned for its classical tradition, has created an affiliated non-profit, the ARCH Development Corporation, whose mission, in part, is to launch start-up companies based on faculty innovations. . . .

No sector of the economy better illustrates the potential benefits of this synergy than biotechnology, a multibillion-dollar industry that grew out of university research labs. Garry Nolan, an assistant professor of molecular pharmacology at Stanford, epitomizes the new generation of professor-entrepreneurs. A few years ago Nolan founded Rigel, a biotech firm based in San Francisco that has pioneered a promising new method for identifying the proteins involved in asthma, allergies, immune disorders, and other health problems. "We've already attracted a hundred and fifty million dollars in investment from various drug companies interested in our work," Nolan says. "There's almost no greater and more immediate feedback than when you find a commercial entity interested in what you're doing." . . .

Is this where the Bayh-Dole Act was supposed to lead? Two summers ago a working group at the National Institutes of Health issued a report to the NIH director, Harold Varmus, warning that changes in the way universities guard their intellectual property are endangering the free exchange of basic research tools—such as gene sequences and reagents—that are crucial to all research. The NIH found that the terms universities impose on their research tools, through their technology-licensing offices, "present just about every type of clause that universities cite as problematic in the [contracts] . . . they receive from industry." These include requirements that universities be allowed to review manuscripts prior to publication and provisions extending their ownership claims to any future discoveries deriving from use of their research materials. Universities, the NIH charges, "have no duty to return value to shareholders, and their principal obligation under the Bayh-Dole Act is to promote utilization, not to maximize financial returns. It hardly seems consistent with the purposes of the Bayh-Dole Act to impose proprietary restrictions on research tools that would be widely utilized if freely disseminated. Technology transfer need not be a revenue source to be successful." Ironically, the proliferation of ownership claims threatens not only to stifle the free exchange of ideas but also to impede economic growth. James Boyle, an expert on intellectual-property law at American University, warns that if current rends continue, "creators will be prevented from creating," as the public domain is "converted into a fallow landscape of walled private plots." . . .

The students at Berkeley were not the only ones protesting the growing corporate influence on university research last spring. In March of 1998 students at dozens of schools, including the University of Wisconsin, Harvard, and Cornell, held a series of teach-ins on the subject. At George Mason University, a state school in Fairfax County, Virginia, another graduation protest erupted as hundreds of students attached bright pink buttons bearing the slogan "Stop Dis-Engaging Our Future" to their caps and gowns. The buttons, which were distributed by Students for Quality Education, were a pointed reference to a recent George Mason mission statement, "Engaging the Future," which calls for increasing investment in information technology and tightening relations between the university and northern Virginia's booming technology industry.

In 1998 James S. Gilmore, the governor of Virginia, promised to increase state funds for GMU by as much as $25 million a year provided that the university better serve the region's high-tech businesses. GMU's president, Alan G. Merten, a computer scientist and a former dean of the business

school at Cornell, hardly needed urging. "We must accept that we have a new mandate, and a new reason for being in existence," he announced at the World Congress on Information Technology, a gathering of industry executives hosted by GMU in the summer of 1998. "The mandate is to be *networked*." By year's end Merten had added degree programs in information technology and computer science, poured money into the 125-acre Prince William campus, whose focus is biosciences, bioinformatics, biotechnology, and computer and information technology, and suggested that all students would be trained to pass a "technology literacy" test. Amid this whirlwind of change, however, other areas fared less well. Degree programs in classics, German, Russian, and several other humanities departments were eliminated.

In defending the changes, Merten speaks as a realist—and, it's impossible not to notice, as someone versed in the language of the business world. "There was a time when universities weren't held accountable for much—people just threw money at them," he says. Today "people with money are more likely to give you money if you have restructured and repositioned yourself, got rid of stuff that you don't need to have. They take a very dim view of giving you money to run an inefficient organization." The process of making GMU more efficient was, he concedes, "a little bloody at times," but there was a logic to it. "We have a commitment to produce people who are employable in today's technology work force," he says. Students at GMU are "good consumers" who want degrees in areas where there are robust job opportunities, and the university has an obligation to cater to that demand.

But should meeting the demand come at the expense of providing a well-rounded education? In response to GMU's cuts in the humanities 1,700 students signed a petition of protest. In addition, 180 professors in the College of Arts and Sciences sent a letter to President Merten arguing that although training students for the job market was a legitimate goal, "precisely in the face of such an emphasis on jobs and technology, it is more necessary than ever to educate students beyond technological proficiency." . . .

Perhaps—but what happened at GMU is clearly part of a national trend. In 1995 the Board of Regents in Ohio assessed how the state's education dollars should be spent. The verdict? Eliminate funding for eight doctoral programs in history. James Engell, a professor at Harvard who has chaired that school's steering committees on degree programs in both history and literature, and Anthony Dangerfield, a former Dartmouth English professor, recently concluded a two-year national study of the state of the humanities. From 1970 to 1994, they found, the number of bachelor's degrees conferred in English, foreign languages, philosophy, and religion all declined, while there was a five- to ten-fold increase in degrees in computer and information sciences. The elite top quarter of Ph.D. programs in English have twenty-nine fewer students per program than they had in 1975. Meanwhile, humanities professors on average earn substantially less than their counterparts in other fields, and the gap has widened over the past twenty years.

"Test what you will—majors, salaries, graduate programs . . . the results come back the same," Engell and Dangerfield write in a lengthy recent article in the Harvard alumni magazine. "Since the late 1960s the humanities have been neglected, downgraded, and forced to retrench, all as other areas of higher education have grown in numbers, wealth, and influence." The authors trace this to what they call the new "Market-Model University," in which subjects that make money, study money, or attract money are given priority. . . .

Surprisingly, such developments have received little attention. Since the early 1980s American culture has obsessively debated the content of the Western canon—whether Shakespeare or Toni Morrison, European history or African history, should be taught to undergraduates. In the decades to come a more pressing question may be whether undergraduates are taught any meaningful literature or history at all. . . .

"It has been the fate of American higher education to develop in a pre-eminently businesslike culture," the historian Richard Hofstadter wrote in 1952. Through the years, Hofstadter acknowledged, America's universities had fostered the nation's technological and economic development. But too often, he lamented, higher education in America was judged on purely pragmatic grounds. "Education is justified apologetically as a useful instrument in attaining *other* ends: it is good for business or professional careers," he wrote. "Rarely, however, does anyone presume to say that it is good for man."

Some would argue that Hofstadter's vision of higher education is an unaffordable luxury. In today's information age ideas have become prized commodities. Still, even on the utilitarian grounds that traditionalists like Hofstadter would scorn, preserving the distinction between higher education and business is vitally important.

For if commercial criteria are allowed to prevail, schools not only risk shrinking their educational mission—they risk ceasing to be centers of technological innovation as well. Paul Berg, a Nobel Prize–winning biochemist we met with at Stanford, tells a story that dramatically illustrates why. Berg, seventy-three, is a seminal figure in the biotech revolution, having laid the groundwork for splicing DNA to make hybrid molecules. (Stanley Cohen and Herbert Boyer built on Berg's work to create the first recombinant DNA clone.) His discovery propelled the billion-dollar industry that is now hailed as a model of university-industry relations. But Berg points to an underlying irony. "The biotech revolu-

tion itself would not have happened had the whole thing been left up to industry," he says. "Venture-capital people steered clear of anything that didn't have obvious commercial value or short-term impact. They didn't fund the basic research that made biotechnology possible." . . .

The freedom of universities from market constraints is precisely what allowed them in the past to nurture the kind of open-ended basic research that led to some of the most important (and least expected) discoveries in history. Today, as the line between basic and applied science dissolves, as professors are encouraged to think more and more like entrepreneurs, a question arises: Will the Paul Bergs of the future have the freedom to explore ideas that have no obvious and immediate commercial value? Only, it seems, if universities cling to their traditional ideals and maintain a degree of independence from the marketplace. This will not be easy in an age of dwindling public support for higher education. But the nation's top-flight universities can lead the way by collectively establishing new guidelines designed to preserve academic freedom in all their interactions with industry. These could include forbidding professors from having direct financial ties to the companies sponsoring their research; banning universities themselves from investing in these companies; prohibiting publication delays of more than thirty to sixty days and any other editorial constraints; and minimizing proprietary restrictions on basic research tools. In addition, universities could do more to make the case for preserving public support for higher education while refusing to tailor either the research agenda or the curriculum to the needs of industry. "The best reason for supporting the college and the university," Hofstadter wrote, "lies not in the services they can perform, vital though such services may be, but in the values they represent. The ultimate criterion of the place of higher learning in America will be the extent to which it is esteemed not as a necessary instrument of external ends, but as an end in itself."

14. Lawrence Busch et al., "External Review of the Collaborative Research Agreement," 2004

Soon after the contract was drawn between Novartis and the Department of Plant and Microbial Biology at Berkeley in 1998, the Berkeley division of the statewide Academic Senate called for an assessment of this arrangement. The purpose was not to inquire into what later became the issue of tenure for an assistant professor in this department (VIII, 12). It was an inquiry into the broader question of academic-industrial contracts at Berkeley. An investigating team from Michigan State University accepted the invitation to review the collaborative research agreement. It comprised six professors, three research members, and an advisor, all from the Institute for Food and Agricultural Standards at Michigan State. Their inquiry took two years and resulted in a report of 188 pages. In late 2003, some months before this review appeared,

Syngenta, the now licensed offspring company of Novartis, ended the partnership with Berkeley. Reproduced here is a portion of the executive summary, including the panel's nine recommendations. The principal investigator in the review was Lawrence Busch, a sociologist and Distinguished University Professor at Michigan State.

Lawrence Busch, Richard Allison, Craig Harris, Alan Rudy, Bradley T. Shaw, Toby Ten Eyck, Dawn Coppin, Jason Konefal, Christopher Oliver, with James Fairweather, *External Review of the Collaborative Research Agreement between Novartis Agricultural Discovery Institute, Inc. and The Regents of the University of California,* East Lansing: Institute for Food and Agricultural Standards, Michigan State University (July 13, 2004), 10–14. Reprinted with the kind permission of the University of California. © 2004 by the authors. Further reading: Council on Governmental Relations, "The Bayh-Dole Act: A Guide to the Law and Implementing Regulations" (Washington, D.C., 1999); Goldie Blumenstyk, "Reviewers Give Thumbs Down to Corporate Deal at Berkeley," *Chronicle of Higher Education,* August 6, 2004, A25; Rex Dalton, "Biotech Funding Deal Judged to be 'A Mistake' for Berkeley," *Nature,* August 5, 2004, 598; and VIII, 12.

There are arguably three principles and associated practices that must stand at the center of any university that is worthy of the title: creativity, autonomy, and diversity. Although occasionally lost sight of, these principles are central to the ethical framework of the university. Perhaps *the* central principle of universities is creativity. Universities can only be successful as organizations to the extent that they foster and cherish creativity among their faculty, students, and staff. But without autonomy, universities soon lose their *raison d'être.* They become bureaucratic entities that perform their tasks in a rote manner. Without substantial autonomy, scholarly work is likely to fail to achieve its objectives. It becomes subject to the political whims of the moment; critical issues are ignored or papered over. Creativity is often constrained by a lack of diversity. The goods that universities provide are nurtured and made more robust through diversity. A diversity of standpoints is essential to the debate and dialogue that must surely be central to a great university. Together, these three principles—creativity, autonomy, and diversity—define what a university is and how it contributes to the common good. Together these three principles enable the university to generate knowledge, inventions, and innovations, to translate and disseminate knowledge in ways that foster the growth and development of people and communities, and to contribute to discourse about social issues. As we show in this report, the agreement between the University of California Berkeley (UCB) and the Novartis Agricultural Discovery Institute (NADI) both promoted and challenged these three principles. This was the case not solely for the research that was the subject of the agreement, but with respect to the educational role of the university

as well. This agreement became an icon for these larger issues. . . .

Lost in the common reading of the controversy as alternative *v.* conventional agriculture, however, is the manner in which the agreement has come to act as a lightning rod for debates, grounded in assumptions rarely made explicit, over the contemporary state and future direction of universities. While the implementation of the agreement has been relatively uncontested and many of the critics' worst fears have not occurred, the fact that the agreement was widely challenged is important on a number of levels. Interviewees offered four broad reasons why the agreement was controversial: (1) the process by which the agreement was created, (2) the substantive content of the agreement, (3) local conditions at UCB and in the Bay Area, and (4) broader issues that reflect the changing character of the university.

On the surface, the terms and conditions of the UCB agreement appear consistent with the behavior of universities adjusting to the emerging norms of university-based economic development. In the late 1990s, the UCB-N agreement was not far from the norm, yet it did have unique characteristics. One key deviation from the norm was the inclusion of nearly an entire academic department in an agreement with a single firm. A second important deviation was the extended capture of intellectual property rights from government-funded research.

The role of the media in the controversy cannot be overlooked, nor should it be overstated. Media coverage made a real impact on the campus, most particularly newspaper and magazine stories crystallized or reified rifts between faculty and administration, between different colleges, between the university and government, between industry and the university, between private citizens and UCB faculty, and so forth. Reporters were widely perceived to sensationalize the agreement and to focus on the negative. This has caused some UCB personnel, particularly within the administration, to think about how things could be done differently in the future.

Faculty members in the Department of Plant and Microbial Biology (PMB) offered three different justifications to explain why their department sought an agreement with an industrial collaborator. The most prevalent idea was that basic science is increasingly expensive and academic units no longer have the resources (financial or material) to keep up with private industry. Thus departments such as PMB require research collaborations with industry as a means for maintaining their cutting edge status. The second justification concerned the expected benefits that would accrue to PMB from the recovery of indirect costs. It was expected that UCB-N would provide significant support for the daily operation of the department in this manner and thus make it easier for faculty members to conduct research. The third justification centered on the benefits of the agreement for PMB's graduate students.

On the whole the PMB faculty viewed the negotiation process as uncontroversial. Faculty were generally satisfied with the extent and degree of their involvement in the negotiations and trusted their department representatives. In comparison to the faculty's view of the negotiation process, many PMB graduate students felt excluded and deliberately kept in the dark about an agreement that was being proposed partly for their putative benefit. This was not a new state of affairs and the general lack of communication and involvement of graduate students in departmental affairs had been a point of contention before UCB-N negotiations were initiated. Post-doctoral researchers in PMB at the time of the UCB-N negotiations also felt that they should have access to and involvement in the information stream. . . .

Many faculty in the department argued that the focus of their research moved more quickly in new and emerging directions than would otherwise have been possible. Almost to a person, the faculty of PMB said that the combination of funds, equipment and information, enabled them to explore research questions that they otherwise would have foregone or postponed. While it was repeatedly emphasized that these shifts in direction were not dictated by Novartis, the faculty clearly acknowledged that many of the changes would not have occurred without UCB-N. . . .

Expectations with respect to the generation of intellectual property by PMB have, to date, remained unfulfilled. Few or no benefits, in terms of patent rights or income, to either UCB or Novartis/Syngenta have emerged from research conducted in the course of the agreement. Of the 51 disclosures made by PMB faculty during the period from November 23, 1998 to November 23, 2003, 20 have been patented. Ten of these patents were on disclosures funded at least in part through UCB-N; NADI expressed interest in six of the patents, though no options to negotiate an exclusive license remain active today.

The most significant consequence of the agreement for PMB graduate students was the increase in cohort size and annual stipend. During the period of UCB-N, PMB doubled the size of its graduate program. Among post-doctoral researchers, salary was deemed to be the greatest benefit of UCB-N. The benefits for PMB undergraduate education are minor, although no one was able to identify any negative effects. However, the publicity surrounding UCB-N appears to have had the temporary effect of depressing the number of undergraduates who chose to major in PMB.

For the academic community, the agreement stood out because it represented significant industrial funding rather than government funding for Berkeley researchers. PMB's financial objective leading to the agreement was to secure a sponsored research agreement from an industrial sponsor of at least $5 million a year over five years. The effort's success at winning industrial patronage of this scale proved unique for UCB. Of the twenty-six awards received in fiscal years 1998 through 2003 of $5 million or more, only four were not from the federal government.

The direct impacts of UCB-N on the university as a whole have been minimal. The agreement has not produced the major changes that many feared it would. However, this is not to say that things have remained the same. First, the agreement brought to the surface a number of long simmering tensions at UCB. Second, the agreement highlighted the crisis-ridden state of contemporary public higher education in California, in Land Grant institutions, and across the country.

Recommendations for consideration by the Berkeley community are as follows. UCB should:

1. Avoid industry agreements that involve complete academic units or large groups of researchers.
2. Reassess in a comprehensive fashion the implications of non-financial and institutional conflicts of interest.
3. Encourage broad debate early in the process of developing new research agendas.
4. Be attentive to the formulation of new goals when motivated by a disruption of patronage or by self-interest.
5. Make organizations associated with UC or supported by institutional resources transparent to the public.
6. Assess institutional obligations and commitments to reliable production and communication of regulatory science.
7. Strive to educate the public on the specific nature of intellectual property, technology transfer, and the nature of institutional accountability.
8. Work to identify and prevent the masking of intended applications of knowledge or potential negative consequences of commercialization with the privileges implied by academic freedom.
9. Begin the difficult task of determining the role a public Land Grant university should play in the twenty-first century by re-examining core commitments.

Part IX

The Courts and Equal Educational Opportunity

CONTEXT

The phrase "affirmative action" came to mean a national effort to overcome past injustices in the lives of women and ethnic minorities, chiefly African Americans, by assuring them of some advantage in employment opportunities and college admissions. The phrase was first used in President John F. Kennedy's Executive Order Number 10925 of March 6, 1961, and was used again in President Lyndon Johnson's Order Number 11246 in September 24, 1965. Directed at business contractors, both orders decreed that all applicants for employment will be treated "without regard to their race, creed, color, or national origin." Johnson amended 11246 as 11375 in October 1967 to include affirmative action for women. The landmark Title VII of the Civil Rights Act (1964) prohibited racial and gender discrimination in any federally financed program (IX, 4). In 1967 the U.S. Commission on Civil Rights, reporting on southern and border state school desegregation in 1966–67, concluded that "freedom of choice" plans at Southern schools could no longer be seen as supporting the "all deliberate speed" policy of *Brown* II (1955). Schools must, it declared, "require affirmative action by both Negro and white parents and pupils before disestablishment [of segregation] can be achieved." From the Supreme Court, Justice William Brennan in *Green v. County School Board of New Kent County* (391 U.S. 440–441, 1968) cited the words of the Civil Rights Commission approvingly. The phrase was now becoming widespread and applied to all levels of education. Beyond legislation, the turbulent decade of the 1960s was also recording Thurgood Marshall at the courts continuing his tireless work with the National Association for the Advancement of Colored People (NAACP) to open equal opportunities to black citizens, Martin Luther King leading nonviolent freedom marches and boycotts, followed by Freedom Riders, the horror of urban riots and burnings, and, not irrelevantly, the national wound of the Vietnam War accompanied by college and university student dissent against campus administrative policies and at times outright rebellion (VII, 11–12). These events spurred affirmative action. And some college administrators were also initiating programs to diversify campuses ethnically.

In a longer view almost two centuries earlier, in a new white republic that included enslaved black people as 18 percent of the population, a vision for affirmative action appeared in Thomas Jefferson's claims for both equality and merit. These two elements of Gunnar Myrdal's modern "American dilemma" still stand counterpoised within the concept of affirmative action for a multiethnic nation. The simple judgment by Chief Justice Earl Warren in *Brown v. Board of Education*, 1954 (3), that separate public schooling is "inherently unequal," invoked the idea of human equality from Jefferson's Declaration of Independence, recalled as colorblind by Abraham Lincoln and remembered by Martin Luther King as "a promise not a reality." Almost a quarter century after *Brown* had emphasized equality, the Supreme Court in *University of California Regents v. Bakke* (4) confronted the Jeffersonian design for recognizing merit or talent through education. Jefferson had advocated educational advancement for all white young men up an increasingly selective and tested ladder or pyramid of academic merit to produce talented republican leaders for an American "aristocracy" of civic leaders. In the 1930s and 1940s James Bryant Conant at Harvard proposed and implemented a similar Jeffersonian meritocracy for higher education drawn from a wide pool of national applicants (II, 5). Thus Justice Lewis F. Powell's opinion for the Court in *Bakke* sought to widen the step on the professional education ladder by admitting the white medical student Allan Bakke, whose academic qualifications were at least equal to those of black applicants, but did not rate higher than the Davis Medical School's admissions quota preferring minority applicants. In his dual judgment Powell nevertheless allowed that an applicant's race could be one criterion for admission among several. The purposes of equality and merit were then presumably satisfied. Over the next twenty-five years, however, shifting public sentiment against affirmative action, together with lower court challenges that *Bakke* was unsatisfactory law, brought affirmative action once again to a head at the Supreme Court in the twin cases from the University of Michigan in 2003 (5).

Throughout the 1970s and 1980s justices on the Supreme Court bench remained reluctant to consider academic policies. After *Brown* word had it that, ironically, the Court was "the national school board." Justices took pains to indicate that this was a misleading characterization, at least in cases of higher education. Justice William O. Douglas in 1973 declared that the "courts are not educators: their expertise is limited" (416 U.S. 344). Justice William Rehnquist, who differed often with Douglas, stated in 1978 that "a school is an academic institution, not a courtroom or administrative hearing room" (435 U.S. 84). In 1985 Justice John P. Stevens, Justice Powell concurring, agreed with the Court's "emphasis on the respect and deference that courts should accord academic [not disciplinary] decisions made by the appropriate university authorities." Stevens added: "When judges are asked to review the substance of a genuinely academic decision . . . they should show great respect for the faculty's professional judgment" (474 U.S. 225).

When the Supreme Court came to grips with the *Gratz* and *Grutter* twin cases at the University of Michigan in 2003 (5), it turned again to affirmative action arguments drawn from the Fourteenth Amendment and Title VII of the Civil Rights Act. "Strictly scrutinizing" the admission policies of a huge public institution, it delved into the arithmetical details of admission quotas—a far cry from Justice Felix Frankfurter's earlier admonition that the fourth freedom of a university faculty is to determine "who may be admitted to study" (X, 7). Since Michigan is a publicly funded institution, Frankfurter's claim was irrelevant. Yet it was still mirrored in the *Grutter* dissent of Chief Justice Rehnquist that the merit of the individual applicant, not his or her membership in a minority group, should here be the desideratum. In effect, he held that affirmative action looks to the civil rights of a group, not to the rights of the individual, and hence it is a policy for equality of result, not equality of opportunity. It remained only for Justice Clarence Thomas, also dissenting in *Grutter,* and the crusade by Ward Connerly (6), with the voters of California supporting him, to insist that African Americans could make their own way successfully without affirmative action. Their view was that merit can be matched with equality. The Jeffersonian question of equality and merit remained an "American dilemma" for higher education.

Toward Racial Equality

1. *Sweatt v. Painter,* 1950

This decision, and its twin (2), written for a unanimous Supreme Court by Chief Justice Fred Vinson (1890–1953), set forth specific guidelines for equality in separate public schools of law. They followed earlier decisions, *Gaines ex rel. Canada v. Missouri* (1938) and *Sipuel v. Oklahoma State Regents* (1948), pointing to the absence of legal education for black students that violated their Fourteenth Amendment equal rights guarantee. In 1950, the two cases here were responses to the prolonged efforts of the National Association for the Advancement of Colored People (NAACP) challenging segregated professional education in public universities. Thurgood Marshall is notable as lead counsel for Heman Marion Sweatt, a Houston, Texas, letter carrier who wanted to become a lawyer. Chief Justice Vinson was a congressman from Kentucky (1924–26, 1930–37), a member of the Circuit Court of Appeals for the District of Columbia (1937–43), and secretary of the treasury (1945–46) under President Harry Truman.

Sweatt v. Painter, 339 U.S. 629 (1950). Further reading: the story of the drive toward equality under the law for black Americans is comprehensively and heartily described in Richard Kluger, *Simple Justice: The History of* Brown v. Board of Education *and Black America's Struggle for Equality* (New York, 1976), ch. 12; Amilcar Shabazz, *Advancing Democracy: African Americans and the Struggle for Access and Equity in Higher Education in Texas* (Chapel Hill, NC, 2004), chs. 3–4; C. Herman Pritchett, *Civil Liberties and the Vinson Court* (New York, 1954); James E. St. Clair and Linda C. Gugin, *Chief Justice Fred M. Vinson of Kentucky, A Political Biography* (Lexington, KY, 2003); Melvin I. Urofsky, "Fred M. Vinson," in *American National Biography,* ed. John A. Garraty and Mark C. Carnes, eds., vol. 22 (New York, 2000), 379–81; and IX, 2.

W. J. Durham and Thurgood Marshall argued the cause for petitioner. . . .

Price Daniel, Attorney General of Texas, and Joe R. Greenhill, First Assistant Attorney General, argued the cause for respondents. . . .

MR. CHIEF JUSTICE VINSON delivered the opinion of the Court.

This case and *McLaurin v. Oklahoma State Regents,* post, p. 637, present different aspects of this general question: To what extent does the Equal Protection Clause of the Fourteenth Amendment limit the power of a state to distinguish between students of different races in professional and graduate education in a state university? Broader issues have been urged for our consideration, but we adhere to the principle of deciding constitutional questions only in the context of the particular case before the Court. . . .

On remand, a hearing was held on the issue of the equality of the educational facilities at the newly established school as compared with the University of Texas Law School. Finding that the new school offered petitioner "privileges, advantages, and opportunities for the study of law substantially equivalent to those offered by the State to white students at the University of Texas," the trial court denied mandamus. The Court of Civil Appeals affirmed. 210 S. W. 2d 442 (1948). Petitioner's application for a writ of error was denied by the Texas Supreme Court. We granted certiorari, 338 U.S. 865 (1949), because of the manifest importance of the constitutional issues involved.

The University of Texas Law School, from which petitioner was excluded, was staffed by a faculty of sixteen full-time and three part-time professors, some of whom are nationally recognized authorities in their field. Its student body numbered 850. The library contained over 65,000 volumes. Among the other facilities available to the students were a law review, moot court facilities, [339 U.S. 629, 633] scholarship funds, and Order of the Coif affiliation. The school's alumni occupy the most distinguished positions in the private practice of the law and in the public life of the State. It may properly be considered one of the nation's ranking law schools.

The law school for Negroes which was to have opened in February, 1947, would have had no independent faculty or library. The teaching was to be carried on by four members of the University of Texas Law School faculty, who were to maintain their offices at the University of Texas while teaching at both institutions. Few of the 10,000 volumes ordered for the library had arrived; nor was there any full-time librarian. The school lacked accreditation.

Since the trial of this case, respondents report the opening of a law school at the Texas State University for Negroes. It is apparently on the road to full accreditation. It has a faculty of five full-time professors; a student body of 23; a library of some 16,500 volumes serviced by a full-time staff; a practice court and legal aid association; and one alumnus who has become a member of the Texas Bar.

Whether the University of Texas Law School is compared with the original or the new law school for Negroes, we cannot find substantial equality in the educational opportunities offered white and Negro law students by the State. In terms of number of the faculty, variety of courses and opportunity for specialization, size of the student body, scope of the library, availability of law [339 U.S. 629, 634] review and similar activities, the University of Texas Law School is superior. What is more important, the University of Texas Law School possesses to a far greater degree those qualities which are incapable of objective measurement but which make for greatness in a law school. Such qualities, to name but a few, include reputation of the faculty, experience of the administration, position and influence of the alumni, standing in the community, traditions and prestige. It is difficult to believe that one who had a free choice between these law schools would consider the question close.

Moreover, although the law is a highly learned profession, we are well aware that it is an intensely practical one. The law school, the proving ground for legal learning and practice, cannot be effective in isolation from the individuals and institutions with which the law interacts. Few students and no one who has practiced law would choose to study in an academic vacuum, removed from the interplay of ideas and the exchange of views with which the law is concerned. The law school to which Texas is willing to admit petitioner excludes from its student body members of the racial groups which number 85% of the population of the State and include most of the lawyers, witnesses, jurors, judges and other officials with whom petitioner will inevitably be dealing when he becomes a member of the Texas Bar. With such a substantial and significant segment of society excluded, we cannot conclude that the education offered petitioner is substantially equal to that which he would receive if admitted to the University of Texas Law School.

It may be argued that excluding petitioner from that school is no different from excluding white students from the new law school. This contention overlooks realities. It is unlikely that a member of a group so decisively in the majority, attending a school with rich traditions and [339 U.S. 629, 635] prestige which only a history of consistently maintained excellence could command, would claim that the opportunities afforded him for legal education were unequal to those held open to petitioner. That such a claim, if made, would be dishonored by the State, is no answer. "Equal protection of the laws is not achieved through indiscriminate imposition of inequalities." . . .

It is fundamental that these cases concern rights which are personal and present. This Court has stated unanimously that "The State must provide [legal education] for [petitioner] in conformity with the equal protection clause of the Fourteenth Amendment and provide it as soon as it does for applicants of any other group." *Sipuel v. Board of Regents*, 332 U.S. 631, 633 (1948). That case "did not present the issue whether a state might not satisfy the equal protection clause of the Fourteenth Amendment by establishing a separate law school for Negroes." *Fisher v. Hurst*, 333 U.S. 147, 150 (1948). In *Missouri ex rel. Gaines v. Canada*, 305 U.S. 337, 351 (1938), the Court, speaking through Chief Justice Hughes, declared that "petitioner's right was a personal one. It was as an individual that he was entitled to the equal protection of the laws, and the State was bound to furnish him within its borders facilities for legal education substantially equal to those which the State there afforded for persons of the white race, whether or not other negroes sought the same opportunity." These are the only cases in this Court which present the issue of the constitutional validity of race distinctions in state-supported graduate and professional education.

In accordance with these cases, petitioner may claim his full constitutional right: legal education equivalent to that offered by the State to students of other races. Such education is not available to him

in a separate law school as offered by the State. We cannot, therefore, [339 U.S. 629, 636] agree with respondents that the doctrine of *Plessy v. Ferguson*, 163 U.S. 537 (1896), requires affirmance of the judgment below. Nor need we reach petitioner's contention that *Plessy v. Ferguson* should be reexamined in the light of contemporary knowledge respecting the purposes of the Fourteenth Amendment and the effects of racial segregation.

We hold that the Equal Protection Clause of the Fourteenth Amendment requires that petitioner be admitted to the University of Texas Law School. The judgment is reversed and the cause is remanded for proceedings not inconsistent with this opinion. Reversed.

2. *McLaurin v. Oklahoma,* 1950

Here Chief Justice Vinson's opinion for the unanimous court described how black students were handicapped by unequal graduate facilities at the University of Oklahoma. He concluded, "The appellant . . . must receive the same treatment at the hands of the State as students of other races." In this case the NAACP Legal Defense Fund, again with Thurgood Marshall leading, supported George W. McLaurin (1887–1968), who was applying to the doctoral program in education at the University of Oklahoma.

McLaurin v. Oklahoma State Regents, 339 U.S. 637 (1950). Further reading: Richard Kluger, *Simple Justice: The History of* Brown v. Board of Education *and Black America's Struggle for Equality* (New York, 1976), ch. 12; and IX, 1.

Robert L. Carter and Amos T. Hall argued the cause for appellant. . . .

Fred Hansen, First Assistant Attorney General of Oklahoma, argued the cause for appellees. . . .

MR. CHIEF JUSTICE VINSON delivered the opinion of the Court.

In this case, we are faced with the question whether a state may, after admitting a student to graduate instruction in its state university, afford him different treatment from other students solely because of his race. We decide only this issue; see *Sweatt v. Painter*.

Appellant is a Negro citizen of Oklahoma. Possessing a Master's Degree, he applied for admission to the University of Oklahoma in order to pursue studies and courses leading to a Doctorate in Education. At that time, his application was denied, solely because of his race. The school authorities were required to exclude him by the Oklahoma statutes, . . . which made it a misdemeanor to maintain or operate, teach or attend a school at which both whites and Negroes are enrolled or taught. Appellant filed a complaint requesting injunctive relief, alleging that the action of the school authorities and the statutes upon which their action was based were unconstitutional and deprived him [339 U.S. 637, 639] of the equal protection of the laws. . . . [A] statutory three-judge District Court held that the State had a Constitutional duty to provide him with the education he sought as soon as it provided that education for applicants of any other group. It further held that to the extent the Oklahoma statutes denied him admission they were unconstitutional and void. On the assumption, however, that the State would follow the constitutional mandate, the court refused to grant the injunction, retaining jurisdiction of the cause with full power to issue any necessary and proper orders to secure McLaurin the equal protection of the laws.

Following this decision, the Oklahoma legislature amended these statutes to permit the admission of Negroes to institutions of higher learning attended by white students, in cases where such institutions offered courses not available in the Negro schools. The amendment provided, however, that in such cases the program of instruction "shall be given at such colleges or institutions of higher education upon a segregated basis." Appellant [339 U.S. 637, 640] was thereupon admitted to the University of Oklahoma Graduate School. In apparent conformity with the amendment, his admission was made subject to "such rules and regulations as to segregation as the President of the University shall consider to afford to Mr. G. W. McLaurin substantially equal educational opportunities as are afforded to other persons seeking the same education in the Graduate College," a condition which does not appear to have been withdrawn. Thus he was required to sit apart at a designated desk in an anteroom adjoining the classroom; to sit at a designated desk on the mezzanine floor of the library, but not to use the desks in the regular reading room; and to sit at a designated table and to eat at a different time from the other students in the school cafeteria. . . .

In the interval between the decision of the court below and the hearing in this Court, the treatment afforded appellant was altered. For some time, the section of the classroom in which appellant sat was surrounded by a rail on which there was a sign stating, "Reserved For Colored," but these have been removed. He is now assigned to a seat in the classroom in a row specified for colored students; he is assigned to a table in the library on the main floor; and he is permitted to eat at the same time in the cafeteria as other students, although here again he is assigned to a special table.

It is said that the separations imposed by the State in this case are in form merely nominal. McLaurin uses the same classroom, library and cafeteria as students of other races; there is no indication that the seats to which he is assigned in these rooms have any disadvantage of location. He may wait in line in the cafeteria and there stand and talk with his fellow students, but while he eats he must remain apart.

These restrictions were obviously imposed in order to comply, as nearly as could be, with the statutory requirements of Oklahoma. But they signify that the State, in administering the facilities it affords for professional and graduate study, sets McLaurin apart from the other students. The result is that appellant is handicapped in his pursuit of effective graduate instruction. Such restrictions impair and inhibit his ability to study, to engage in discussions and exchange views with other students, and, in general, to learn his profession.

Our society grows increasingly complex, and our need for trained leaders increases correspondingly. Appellant's case represents, perhaps, the epitome of that need, for he is attempting to obtain an advanced degree in education, to become, by definition, a leader and trainer of others. Those who will come under his guidance and influence must be directly affected by the education he receives. Their own education and development will necessarily suffer to the extent that his training is unequal to that of his classmates. State-imposed restrictions which produce such inequalities cannot be sustained.

It may be argued that appellant will be in no better position when these restrictions are removed, for he may still be set apart by his fellow students. This we think irrelevant. There is a vast difference—a Constitutional difference—between restrictions imposed by the state which prohibit the intellectual commingling of students, and the refusal of individuals to commingle where the state presents no such bar. . . . The removal of the state restrictions will not necessarily abate individual and group predilections, prejudices and choices. But at the very least, the state will not be depriving appellant of the opportunity to secure acceptance by his fellow students on his own merits.

We conclude that the conditions under which this appellant is required to receive his education deprive him of his personal and present right to the equal protection of the laws. See *Sweatt v. Painter*. We hold that under these circumstances the Fourteenth Amendment precludes differences in treatment by the state based upon race. Appellant, having been admitted to a state-supported graduate school, must receive the same treatment at the hands of the state as students of other races. The judgment is Reversed.

3. *Brown v. Board of Education*, 1954

The three branches of American government began after World War II to address the racism that the Swedish sociologist Gunnar Myrdal in his famous report (1944) called "an American dilemma." At the fore, President Harry Truman in 1948 ordered the armed services desegregated; by the mid-1960s Congress had enacted the Civil Rights Act and the Voting Rights Act. Midway between these developments the United States Supreme Court announced this renowned decision. *Brown* struck down the nearly sixty-year-old ruling in *Plessy v. Ferguson* (1896) that public transportation facilities, and by analogy all public facilities, including public schooling, should be "equal but separate" in their racial "accommodations." Writing for his eight differing brethren whom he had persuaded into unanimity, Chief Justice Earl Warren (1891–1974) stated: "In the field of public education, separate but equal has no place." The Court was building upon its recent rulings in *Sweat* and *McLaurin* that involved professional and graduate public schooling (1–2).

Warren called in the social sciences (later viewed skeptically) to reemphasize the harm that inequality caused black students.

The simple and popular language used by Warren stands in contrast to the complex, controversial, and discouraging history of *Brown* in subsequent years. The decision had prudently avoided instructing lower courts and schools about compliance with its mandate. Within a year of necessity *Brown* v. *Board of Education* II (349 U.S. 294 [1955]) was handed down with the ambiguous order that implementation of *Brown* I should proceed "with all deliberate speed." Although higher education was unmentioned in *Brown* I, the Court confirmed its authority at all levels of public education in *Florida ex. Rel. Hawkins v. Board of Education of Control of Florida*, 350 U.S. 413 (1956). Southern courts continued to lag in their directives to southern schools that were remaining recalcitrant, as also in memorable instances state universities were slow to comply (II, 17). From the 1980s on, the Supreme Court itself as well as a rising conservative sentiment in the nation weakened the commitment to government intervention in behalf of equal rights for African Americans. Nevertheless, *Brown* remains a beacon for justice in American history.

Brown v. Board of Education, 347 U.S. 483 (1954). Further reading: Richard Kluger, *Simple Justice: The History of* Brown v. Board of Education *and Black America's Struggle for Equality* (New York, 1976), a monumental and deeply researched scholarly accomplishment carrying a lively style that enforces its theme; shorter books are J. Harvie Wilkinson III, *From* Brown *to Bakke, The Supreme Court and School Integration: 1954–1978* (New York, 1979), candid and forceful; James T. Patterson, Brown v. Board of Education: *A Civil Rights Milestone and Its Troubled Legacy* (New York, 2001), evenhanded and succinct with an excellent bibliography. For Kenneth B. Clark and Mamie P. Clark's and other studies of pre-school African-American children's racial identifications, cited in the famous Footnote 11 to *Brown*, see Kluger, ch. 14 notes; John P. Jackson Jr., *Social Scientists for Social Justice: Making the Case against Segregation* (New York, 2002). Three law journal essays reveal the legal problems and criticisms raised soon after *Brown*: Herbert Wechsler, "Toward Neutral Principles of Constitutional Law," *Harvard Law Review*, 73, no. 1 (November 1959): 26–35; Louis H. Pollak, "Racial Discrimination and Judicial Integrity: A Reply to Professor Wechsler," *University of Pennsylvania Law Review* (November 1959): 1–34; Charles L. Black Jr., "The Lawfulness of the Segregation Decisions," *Yale Law Journal* 49 (January 1960): 421–30. Biographies of the major figures at Court and their works include Mark V. Tushnet, *The NAACP's Legal Strategy Against Segregated Education, 1925–1950* (Chapel Hill, NC, 1987) and *Making Civil Rights Law: Thurgood Marshall in the Supreme Court, 1936–1961* (New York, 1994); Bernard Schwartz, *Super Chief: Earl Warren and His Supreme Court—A Judicial Biography* (New York, 1983); Schwartz, ed., *The Warren Court: A Retrospective* (New York, 1996); Morton Horwitz, *The Warren Court and the Pursuit of Justice* (New York, 1998). Reevaluations of *Brown*'s historical significance include Mark Tushnet with Katya Levin, "What Really Happened in *Brown v. Board of Education*," *Columbia Law Review* 91 (December 1991): 1867–1930; Gary Orfield and Susan Eaton, *Dismantling Desegregation: The Quiet Reversal of* Brown v. Board

of Education (New York, 1996); Jack M. Balkin, ed., *What* Brown v. Board of Education *Should Have Said: The Nation's Top Legal Experts Rewrite America's Civil Rights Decisions* (New York, 2001); Derrick Bell, *Silent Covenants:* Brown v. Board of Education *and the Unfulfilled Hopes for Racial Reform* (New York, 2004); Kathleen Sullivan, "What Happened to '*Brown*'?" *New York Review of Books*, September 23, 2004, 47–49, 52; Marshall J. Klarman, "From Jim Crow to Civil Rights: The Supreme Court and the Struggle for Racial Equality" (New York, 2004), a far-reaching work that summarizes the national extralegal circumstances that paved the way for and followed *Brown*, including a "different" description of the author's controversial "backlash" theme (Klarman, "How *Brown* Changed Race Relations: The Backlash Thesis," *Journal of American History* 81 (June 1994): 81–118); Randall Kennedy, "Schoolings in Equality: What *Brown* Did and Did Not Accomplish," *New Republic*, July 5, 2004, 29–39, contrasts Kluger's legal and Klarman's extralegal themes; important tracings of *Brown*'s history and outcome are also found in Stephan and Abigail Thernstrom, *America in Black and White: One Nation Indivisible* (New York, 1997); William G. Bowen and Derek Bok, *The Shape of the River* (Princeton, NJ, 1998); and II, 21.

OPINION: MR. CHIEF JUSTICE WARREN delivered the opinion of the Court.

These cases come to us from the States of Kansas, South Carolina, Virginia, and Delaware. They are premised on different facts and different local conditions, but a common legal question justifies their consideration together in this consolidated opinion.

In each of the cases, minors of the Negro race, through their legal representatives, seek the aid of the courts in obtaining admission to the public schools of their community on a nonsegregated basis. In each instance, they have been denied admission to schools attended by white children under laws requiring or permitting segregation according to race. This segregation was alleged to deprive the plaintiffs of the equal protection of the laws under the Fourteenth Amendment. In each of the cases other than the Delaware case, a three-judge federal district court denied relief to the plaintiffs on the so-called "separate but equal" doctrine announced by this Court in *Plessy v. Ferguson*, 163 U.S. 537. Under that doctrine, equality of treatment is accorded when the races are provided substantially equal facilities, even though these facilities be separate. In the Delaware case, the Supreme Court of Delaware adhered to that doctrine, but ordered that the plaintiffs be admitted to the white schools because of their superiority to the Negro schools.

The plaintiffs contend that segregated public schools are not "equal" and cannot be made "equal" and that hence they are deprived of the equal protection of the laws. Because of the obvious importance of the question presented, the Court took jurisdiction. Argument was heard in the 1952 Term, and reargument was heard this Term on certain questions propounded by the Court. . . .

In the first cases in this Court construing the

Fourteenth Amendment, decided shortly after its adoption, the Court interpreted it as proscribing all state-imposed discriminations against the Negro race. The doctrine of "separate but equal" did not make its appearance in this Court until 1896 in the case of *Plessy* v. *Ferguson,* involving not education but transportation. American courts have since labored with the doctrine for over half a century. In this Court, there have been six cases involving the "separate but equal" doctrine in the field of public education. In *Cumming* v. *County Board of Education,* 175 U.S. 528, and *Gong Lum* v. *Rice,* 275 U.S. 78, the validity of the doctrine itself was not challenged. In more recent cases, all on the graduate school level, inequality was found in that specific benefits enjoyed by white students were denied to Negro students of the same educational qualifications. *Missouri ex rel. Gaines* v. *Canada,* 305 U.S. 337; *Sipuel* v. *Oklahoma,* 332 U.S. 631; *Sweatt* v. *Painter,* 339 U.S. 629; *McLaurin* v. *Oklahoma State Regents,* 339 U.S. 637. In none of these cases was it necessary to re-examine the doctrine to grant relief to the Negro plaintiff. And in *Sweatt* v. *Painter, supra,* the Court expressly reserved decision on the question whether *Plessy* v. *Ferguson* should be held inapplicable to public education.

In the instant cases, that question is directly presented. Here, unlike *Sweatt* v. *Painter,* there are findings below that the Negro and white schools involved have been equalized, or are being equalized, with respect to buildings, curricula, qualifications and salaries of teachers, and other "tangible" factors. Our decision, therefore, cannot turn on merely a comparison of these tangible factors in the Negro and white schools involved in each of the cases. We must look instead to the effect of segregation itself on public education.

In approaching this problem, we cannot turn the clock back to 1868 when the Amendment was adopted, or even to 1896 when *Plessy* v. *Ferguson* was written. We must consider public education in the light of its full development and its present place in American life throughout the Nation. Only in this way can it be determined if segregation in public schools deprives these plaintiffs of the equal protection of the laws.

Today, education is perhaps the most important function of state and local governments. Compulsory school attendance laws and the great expenditures for education both demonstrate our recognition of the importance of education to our democratic society. It is required in the performance of our most basic public responsibilities, even service in the armed forces. It is the very foundation of good citizenship. Today it is a principal instrument in awakening the child to cultural values, in preparing him for later professional training, and in helping him to adjust normally to his environment. In these days, it is doubtful that any child may reasonably be expected to succeed in life if he is denied the opportunity of an education. Such an opportunity, where the state has undertaken to provide it, is a right which must be made available to all on equal terms.

We come then to the question presented: Does segregation of children in public schools solely on the basis of race, even though the physical facilities and other "tangible" factors may be equal, deprive the children of the minority group of equal educational opportunities? We believe that it does.

In *Sweatt* v. *Painter,* in finding that a segregated law school for Negroes could not provide them equal educational opportunities, this Court relied in large part on "those qualities which are incapable of objective measurement but which make for greatness in a law school." In *McLaurin* v. *Oklahoma State Regents,* the Court, in requiring that a Negro admitted to a white graduate school be treated like all other students, again resorted to intangible considerations: " . . . his ability to study, to engage in discussions and exchange views with other students, and, in general, to learn his profession." Such considerations apply with added force to children in grade and high schools. To separate them from others of similar age and qualifications solely because of their race generates a feeling of inferiority as to their status in the community that may affect their hearts and minds in a way unlikely ever to be undone. The effect of this separation on their educational opportunities was well stated by a finding in the Kansas case by a court which nevertheless felt compelled to rule against the Negro plaintiffs:

> Segregation of white and colored children in public schools has a detrimental effect upon the colored children. The impact is greater when it has the sanction of the law; for the policy of separating the races is usually interpreted as denoting the inferiority of the negro group. A sense of inferiority affects the motivation of a child to learn. Segregation with the sanction of law, therefore, has a tendency to [retard] the educational and mental development of negro children and to deprive them of some of the benefits they would receive in a racial[ly] integrated school system.[1]

Whatever may have been the extent of psychological knowledge at the time of *Plessy* v. *Ferguson*, this finding is amply supported by modern authority.[2] Any language in *Plessy* v. *Ferguson* contrary to this finding is rejected.

---

1. 87 A. 2d 862, 865.

2. K. B. Clark, *Effect of Prejudice and Discrimination on Personality Development* (Midcentury White House Conference on Children and Youth, 1950); Witmer and Kotinsky, *Personality in the Making* (1952), c. VI; Deutscher and Chein, "The Psychological Effects of Enforced Segregation: A Survey of Social Science Opinion," 26 *J. Psychol.* 259 (1948); Chein, "What are the Psychological Effects of Segregation Under Conditions of Equal Facilities?," 3 *Int. J. Opinion and Attitude Res.* 229 (1949); Brameld, *Educational Costs, in Discrimination and National Welfare* (MacIver, ed., 1949), 44–48; Frazier, *The Negro in the United States* (1949), 674–681. And see generally Myrdal, *An American Dilemma* (1944).

We conclude that in the field of public education the doctrine of "separate but equal" has no place. Separate educational facilities are inherently unequal. Therefore, we hold that the plaintiffs and others similarly situated for whom the actions have been brought are, by reason of the segregation complained of, deprived of the equal protection of the laws guaranteed by the Fourteenth Amendment. This disposition makes unnecessary any discussion whether such segregation also violates the Due Process Clause of the Fourteenth Amendment. . . . It is so ordered.

Affirmative Action

4. *University of California Regents v. Bakke,* 1978

No person in the United States shall, on the ground of race, color, or national origin, be excluded from participation in, or denied the benefits of, or be subjected to discrimination under any program or activity receiving federal financial assistance.

PL 88-352, Title VI, sec. 601
(Civil Rights Act of 1964)

In the second half of the twentieth century, America increasingly confronted the cause of equal rights for all citizens. Progress was slow but moved along by the three branches of the federal government: the executive order to desegregate the armed forces (1948), and two actions directly affecting higher education—judicial dismissal of racially separate public facilities (1954), and congressional legislation (quoted in the epigraph) barring discrimination in federally funded programs or activities (1964). Historians differ on the ultimate power of these federal acts. Did they initiate equitable treatment of African-American and other minority citizens? Or were they secondary agents to a gradual improvement in economic opportunities and cultural or social attitudes urged on by the tumultuous episodes of the 1960s and early 1970s? Whatever the underlying currents of these years, colleges and universities were at the center of this old "American dilemma." The record, while still far from exemplary, showed that from 1960 to 1995 the college graduation rate of young black people aged 25 through 29 rose from 5.4 percent to 15.4 percent. Some institutions were using "set asides" or specific minority quotas to ensure diversity among their matriculants. When white applicants came to view this practice as illegal preferment, litigation arose to test the meaning of the Civil Rights Act of 1964. It came to a head in the case of Alan Bakke. He asked the court: Is the admission policy of a professional school of medicine lawful when it denies admission to a white applicant whose qualifications are equal to an admitted black applicant?

Associate Justice Lewis F. Powell Jr. (1907–98) handed down this majority opinion from the United States Supreme Court (excerpted here without footnotes). At the time it was thought by many to be an extraordinarily skillful statement for mediating among the positions of Powell's eight evenly divided brethren. To Powell "no person" in the Civil Rights Act meant precisely that. For this reason he held the specific admission program at Davis to be unlawful and ordered Bakke admitted. Yet he also held that the race of an applicant can be considered in the admission process as one element among several that can bring advantageous diversity to a student body. He quoted the Harvard College admission policy as a model. Associate Justice William Brennan (1906–97), in his partially dissenting opinion (briefly included here), turned to the weight of contemporary congressional opinion in 1964 and earlier civil rights actions to judge that "no person" in the Civil Rights Act meant no minority person.

Within the next quarter-century Justice Powell's majority opinion, hailed at first by some as Solomon-like, was increasingly challenged by southern state courts. Popular opinion in California led to passage of a statewide proposition barring all affirmative action programs in employment, education, and public contracting, which caused the public universities to revise their admission criteria. And not until 2003 did the University of Michigan win an appeal at the Supreme Court which in effect supported the Bakke decision (V, 6).

University of California Regents v. Bakke, 438 U.S. 205 (1978). Further reading: Alfred A. Slocum, ed., *Allan Bakke versus Regents of the University of California, Yolo County, California, Superior Court, California State Supreme Court,* 6 vols. (Dobbs Ferry, New York, 1978); Herman Belz, "Affirmative Action," in *The Oxford Companion to the Supreme Court of the United States,* ed. Kermit L. Hall (New York, 1992), 18–22, the best though convoluted brief history of affirmative action cases down to 1990; William C. Bowen and Derek Bok, *The Shape of the River: Long-Term Consequences of Considering Race in College and University Admissions* (Princeton, NJ, 1999); Susan Welch and John Gruhl, *Affirmative Action and Minority Enrollments in Medical and Law Schools* (Ann Arbor, MI, 1999); John Gruhl and Susan Welch, "Impact of the *Bakke* Decision on Black and Hispanic Enrollment in Medical and Law Schools," *Social Science Quarterly* 71 (September 1990): 458–73; Timothy J. O'Neill, Bakke *and the Politics of Equality: Friends and Foes in the Classroom of Litigation* (Middletown, CT, 1985); Stephen Thernstrom and Abigail Thernstrom, *America in Black and White: One Nation, Indivisible* (New York, 1997), 412–18; Reynolds Farley, *The New American Reality: Who We Are, How We Got Here, Where We Are Going* (New York, 1996); Michael B. Katz, Mark J. Stern, and Jamie J. Fader, "The New African American Inequality," *Journal of American History* 92 (June 2005): 75–108; Marshall J. Klarman, *From Jim Crow to Civil Rights: The Supreme Court and the Struggle for Racial Equality* (New York, 2004); J. Harvie Wilkinson III, *From Brown to Bakke: The Supreme Court and School Integration, 1954–1978* (New York, 1979); Allan P. Sindler, Bakke, DeFunis *and Minority Admissions: The Quest for Equal Opportunity* (New York, 1978); John C. Jeffries, *Justice Lewis F. Powell, Jr.* (New York, 1994); Howard Ball, *A Defiant Life: Thurgood Marshall and the Persistence of Racism in America* (New York, 1999) and *The Bakke Case: Race, Education, and Affirmative Action* (Lawrence, KS, 2000); and IX, 6.

MR. JUSTICE POWELL ANNOUNCED THE
JUDGMENT OF THE COURT.

For the reasons stated in the following opinion, I believe that so much of the judgment of the California court as holds petitioner's special admissions program unlawful and directs that respondent be admitted to the Medical School must be affirmed.

For the reasons expressed in a separate opinion, my Brothers The Chief Justice, Mr. Justice Stewart, Mr. Justice Rehnquist, and Mr. Justice Stevens concur in this judgment.

After the second rejection, Bakke filed the instant suit in the Superior Court of California. He sought mandatory, injunctive, and declaratory relief compelling his admission to the Medical School. He alleged that the Medical School's special admissions program operated to exclude him from the school on the basis of his race, in violation of his rights under the Equal Protection Clause of the Fourteenth Amendment, Art. I, 21, of the California Constitution, and 601 of Title VI of the Civil Rights Act of 1964, 78 Stat. 252, 42 U.S.C. 2000d. The University cross-complained for a declaration that its special admissions program was lawful. The trial court found that the special program operated as a racial quota, because minority applicants in the special program were rated only against one another, and 16 places in the class of 100 were reserved for them. Id., at 295–296. Declaring that the University could not take race into account in making admissions decisions, the trial court held the challenged program violative of the Federal Constitution, the State Constitution, and Title VI. The court refused to order Bakke's admission, however, holding that he had failed to carry his burden of proving that he would have been admitted but for the existence of the special program.

Bakke appealed from the portion of the trial court judgment denying him admission, and the University appealed from the decision that its special admissions program was unlawful and the order enjoining it from considering race in the processing of applications. The Supreme Court of California transferred the case directly from the trial court, "because of the importance of the issues involved." . . . The California court accepted the findings of the trial court with respect to the University's program. Because the special admissions program involved a racial classification, the Supreme Court held itself bound to apply strict scrutiny. . . . It then turned to the goals the University presented as justifying the special program. Although the court agreed that the goals of integrating the medical profession and increasing the number of physicians willing to serve members of minority groups were compelling state interests, it concluded that the special admissions program was not the least intrusive means of achieving those goals. Without passing on the state constitutional or the federal statutory grounds cited in the trial court's judgment, the California court held that the Equal Protection Clause of the Fourteenth Amendment required that "no applicant may be rejected because of his race, in favor of another who is less qualified, as measured by standards applied without regard to race."

Turning to Bakke's appeal, the court ruled that since Bakke had established that the University had discriminated against him on the basis of his race, the burden of proof shifted to the University to demonstrate that he would not have been admitted even in the absence of the special admissions program. . . .

The special admissions program is undeniably a classification based on race and ethnic background. To the extent that there existed a pool of at least minimally qualified minority applicants to fill the 16 special admissions seats, white applicants could compete only for 84 seats in the entering class, rather than the 100 open to minority applicants. Whether this limitation is described as a quota or a goal, it is a line drawn on the basis of race and ethnic status.

The guarantees of the Fourteenth Amendment extend to all persons. Its language is explicit: "No State shall . . . deny to any person within its jurisdiction the equal protection of the laws." It is settled beyond question that the "rights created by the first section of the Fourteenth Amendment are, by its terms, guaranteed to the individual. The rights established are personal rights." . . . The guarantee of equal protection cannot mean one thing when applied to one individual and something else when applied to a person of another color. If both are not accorded the same protection, then it is not equal.

Nevertheless, petitioner argues that the court below erred in applying strict scrutiny to the special admissions program because white males, such as respondent, are not a "discrete and insular minority" requiring extraordinary protection from the majoritarian political process. . . . This rationale, however, has never been invoked in our decisions as a prerequisite to subjecting racial or ethnic distinctions to strict scrutiny. Nor has this Court held that discreteness and insularity constitute necessary preconditions to a holding that a particular classification is invidious. . . .

In this case . . . there has been no determination by the legislature or a responsible administrative agency that the University engaged in a discriminatory practice requiring remedial efforts. Moreover, the operation of petitioner's special admissions program is quite different from the remedial measures approved in those cases. It prefers the designated minority groups at the expense of other individuals who are totally foreclosed from competition for the 16 special admissions seats in every Medical School class. Because of that foreclosure, some individuals are excluded from enjoyment of a state-provided benefit—admission to the Medical School—they otherwise would receive. When a classification denies an individual opportunities or benefits enjoyed by others solely because of his race or ethnic background, it must be regarded as suspect. . . .

If petitioner's purpose is to assure within its student body some specified percentage of a particular group merely because of its race or ethnic origin, such a preferential purpose must be rejected not as insubstantial but as facially invalid. Preferring members of any one group for no reason other than race or ethnic origin is discrimination for its own sake. . . .

We have never approved a classification that aids persons perceived as members of relatively victimized groups at the expense of other innocent individuals in the absence of judicial, legislative, or administrative findings of constitutional or statutory violations. . . .

The purpose of helping certain groups whom the faculty of the Davis Medical School perceived as victims of "societal discrimination" does not justify a classification that imposes disadvantages upon persons like respondent, who bear no responsibility for whatever harm the beneficiaries of the special admissions program are thought to have suffered. To hold otherwise would be to convert a remedy heretofore reserved for violations of legal rights into a privilege that all institutions throughout the Nation could grant at their pleasure to whatever groups are perceived as victims of societal discrimination. That is a step we have never approved. . . .

The fourth goal asserted by petitioner is the attainment of a diverse student body. This clearly is a constitutionally permissible goal for an institution of higher education. Academic freedom, though not a specifically enumerated constitutional right, long has been viewed as a special concern of the First Amendment. The freedom of a university to make its own judgments as to education includes the selection of its student body. . . .

It may be assumed that the reservation of a specified number of seats in each class for individuals from the preferred ethnic groups would contribute to the attainment of considerable ethnic diversity in the student body. But petitioner's argument that this is the only effective means of serving the interest of diversity is seriously flawed. In a most fundamental sense the argument misconceives the nature of the state interest that would justify consideration of race or ethnic background. It is not an interest in simple ethnic diversity, in which a specified percentage of the student body is in effect guaranteed to be members of selected ethnic groups, with the remaining percentage an undifferentiated aggregation of students. The diversity that furthers a compelling state interest encompasses a far broader array of qualifications and characteristics of which racial or ethnic origin is but a single though important element. Petitioner's special admissions program, focused solely on ethnic diversity, would hinder rather than further attainment of genuine diversity. . . .

The experience of other university admissions programs, which take race into account in achieving the educational diversity valued by the First Amendment, demonstrates that the assignment of a fixed number of places to a minority group is not a necessary means toward that end. An illuminating example is found in the Harvard College program:

In recent years Harvard College has expanded the concept of diversity to include students from disadvantaged economic, racial and ethnic groups. Harvard College now recruits not only Californians or Louisianans but also blacks and Chicanos and other minority students. . . .

In practice, this new definition of diversity has meant that race has been a factor in some admission decisions. When the Committee on Admissions reviews the large middle group of applicants who are "admissible" and deemed capable of doing good work in their courses, the race of an applicant may tip the balance in his favor just as geographic origin or a life spent on a farm may tip the balance in other candidates' cases. A farm boy from Idaho can bring something to Harvard College that a Bostonian cannot offer. Similarly, a black student can usually bring something that a white person cannot offer. . . .

In Harvard College admissions the Committee has not set target-quotas for the number of blacks, or of musicians, football players, physicists or Californians to be admitted in a given year. . . . But that awareness [of the necessity of including more than a token number of black students] does not mean that the Committee sets a minimum number of blacks or of people from west of the Mississippi who are to be admitted. It means only that in choosing among thousands of applicants who are not only "admissible" academically but have other strong qualities, the Committee, with a number of criteria in mind, pays some attention to distribution among many types and categories of students. . . .

In such an admissions program, race or ethnic background may be deemed a "plus" in a particular applicant's file, yet it does not insulate the individual from comparison with all other candidates for the available seats. The file of a particular black applicant may be examined for his potential contribution to diversity without the factor of race being decisive when compared, for example, with that of an applicant identified as an Italian-American if the latter is thought to exhibit qualities more likely to promote beneficial educational pluralism. Such qualities could include exceptional personal talents, unique work or service experience, leadership potential, maturity, demonstrated compassion, a history of overcoming disadvantage, ability to communicate with the poor, or other qualifications deemed important. In short, an admissions program operated in this way is flexible enough to consider all pertinent elements of diversity in light of the particular qualifications of each applicant, and to place them on the same footing for consideration, although not necessarily according them the same weight. Indeed, the weight attributed to a particular quality may vary from year to year depending upon the "mix" both of the student body and the applicants for the incoming class.

This kind of program treats each applicant as an individual in the admissions process. The applicant who loses out on the last available seat to another candidate receiving a "plus" on the basis of ethnic background will not have been foreclosed from all consideration for that seat simply because he was not the right color or had the wrong surname. It would mean only that his combined qualifications, which may have included similar nonobjective factors, did not outweigh those of the other applicant. His qualifications would have been weighed fairly and competitively, and he would have no basis to complain of unequal treatment under the Fourteenth Amendment. . . .

In summary, it is evident that the Davis special admissions program involves the use of an explicit racial classification never before countenanced by this Court. It tells applicants who are not Negro, Asian, or Chicano that they are totally excluded from a specific percentage of the seats in an entering class. No matter how strong their qualifications, quantitative and extracurricular, including their own potential for contribution to educational diversity, they are never afforded the chance to compete with applicants from the preferred groups for the special admissions seats. At the same time, the preferred applicants have the opportunity to compete for every seat in the class.

The fatal flaw in petitioner's preferential program is its disregard of individual rights as guaranteed by the Fourteenth Amendment. . . . Such rights are not absolute. But when a State's distribution of benefits or imposition of burdens hinges on ancestry or the color of a person's skin, that individual is entitled to a demonstration that the challenged classification is necessary to promote a substantial state interest. Petitioner has failed to carry this burden. For this reason, that portion of the California court's judgment holding petitioner's special admissions program invalid under the Fourteenth Amendment must be affirmed.

In enjoining petitioner from ever considering the race of any applicant, however, the courts below failed to recognize that the State has a substantial interest that legitimately may be served by a properly devised admissions program involving the competitive consideration of race and ethnic origin. For this reason, so much of the California court's judgment as enjoins petitioner from any consideration of the race of any applicant must be reversed.

With respect to respondent's entitlement to an injunction directing his admission to the Medical School, petitioner has conceded that it could not carry its burden of proving that, but for the existence of its unlawful special admissions program, respondent still would not have been admitted. Hence, respondent is entitled to the injunction, and that portion of the judgment must be affirmed. . . .

OPINION OF MR. JUSTICE BRENNAN . . .
CONCURRING IN THE JUDGMENT IN PART
AND DISSENTING IN PART.

The Court today, in reversing in part the judgment of the Supreme Court of California, affirms the constitutional power of Federal and State Governments to act affirmatively to achieve equal opportunity for all. The difficulty of the issue presented—whether

government may use race-conscious programs to redress the continuing effects of past discrimination—and the mature consideration which each of our Brethren has brought to it have resulted in many opinions, no single one speaking for the Court. But this should not and must not mask the central meaning of today's opinions: Government may take race into account when it acts not to demean or insult any racial group, but to remedy disadvantages cast on minorities by past racial prejudice, at least when appropriate findings have been made by judicial, legislative, or administrative bodies with competence to act in this area. . . .

In our view, Title VI prohibits only those uses of racial criteria that would violate the Fourteenth Amendment if employed by a State or its agencies; it does not bar the preferential treatment of racial minorities as a means of remedying past societal discrimination to the extent that such action is consistent with the Fourteenth Amendment. The legislative history of Title VI, administrative regulations interpreting the statute, subsequent congressional and executive action, and the prior decisions of this Court compel this conclusion. None of these sources lends support to the proposition that Congress intended to bar all race-conscious efforts to extend the benefits of federally financed programs to minorities who have been historically excluded from the full benefits of American life. . . .

The cryptic nature of the language employed in Title VI merely reflects Congress' concern with the then-prevalent use of racial standards as a means of excluding or disadvantaging Negroes and its determination to prohibit absolutely such discrimination. . . .

Finally, congressional action subsequent to the passage of Title VI eliminates any possible doubt about Congress' views concerning the permissibility of racial preferences for the purpose of assisting disadvantaged racial minorities. It confirms that Congress did not intend to prohibit and does not now believe that Title VI prohibits the consideration of race as part of a remedy for societal discrimination even where there is no showing that the institution extending the preference has been guilty of past discrimination nor any judicial finding that the particular beneficiaries of the racial preference have been adversely affected by societal discrimination. . . .

Davis' articulated purpose of remedying the effects of past societal discrimination is, under our cases, sufficiently important to justify the use of race-conscious admissions programs where there is a sound basis for concluding that minority underrepresentation is substantial and chronic, and that the handicap of past discrimination is impeding access of minorities to the Medical School. . . .

Nothing whatever in the legislative history of either the Fourteenth Amendment or the Civil Rights Acts even remotely suggests that the States are foreclosed from furthering the fundamental purpose of equal opportunity to which the Amendment and those Acts are addressed. Indeed, voluntary initiatives by the States to achieve the national goal of equal opportunity have been recognized to be essential to its attainment. "To use the Fourteenth Amendment as a sword against such State power would stultify that Amendment." . . . We therefore conclude that Davis' goal of admitting minority students disadvantaged by the effects of past discrimination is sufficiently important to justify use of race-conscious admissions criteria. . . .

5. *Gratz v. Bollinger* and *Grutter v. Bollinger*, 2003

Between the *Bakke* decision (4) and the twin cases from the University of Michigan, excerpted here, people in higher education, as well as in business and industries facing affirmative action issues, grew apprehensive about the durability of Justice Lewis Powell's reasoning in *Bakke*. To some jurists Powell's words ended in ambiguity. Significant numbers in the general public were increasingly of the mind that the age of redressing past wrongs and discrimination against African Americans through litigation was passing. This persuasion was reflected in the movement begun by Ward Connerly (6) and the dissent of Justice Thomas included here. Even lower court cases in several states as well as popular voting were chipping away at *Bakke*. The *Grutter* case was received with relief among concurring college and university administrators and with regret by those who held to the doctrine of colorblindness for all applicants. Justice Sandra Day O'Connor's decision in *Grutter*, like Powell's in *Bakke*, was the deciding vote in a split Court. In effect, she upheld *Bakke* on technical constitutional grounds, open always to later legal questions. Aware of the influence her words would have, O'Connor concluded with the hope that in twenty-five years this issue would be no longer before the courts.

Chief Justice Rehnquist's ruling for the Court in *Gratz* stood by his opinions in earlier cases. Absent a compelling government interest, he declared, the Court must place limits on race-conscious college admissions policies. He found unconstitutional the point-based formula that gave preferment to applicants at the College of Literature, Science, and the Arts at Michigan because of their race. The College must, in accord with *Wygant v. Jackson* (1986), practice "strict scrutiny" into all of the qualifications of each applicant. Membership in a minority group alone is not enough. Likewise, his dissent in the *Grutter* case insisted that Michigan Law School's admissions procedure was guided largely by the predetermined preference of group identity and failed to give sufficient weight to the varying merits of each applicant. Rehnquist's position here invites questions of his judicial conservatism. From a judge who usually deferred to academic judgments, was his opinion on admissions here related to Justice Frankfurter's famed quote in *Sweezy* (X, 7), taken from South African scholars, namely that the fourth essential freedom of a university is the freedom "to determine for itself on academic grounds . . . who may be admitted to study"? In her swing vote for the majority, Justice O'Connor, following Justice Powell in *Bakke*, held that "student body diversity is a compelling state interest that can justify the use of race in minority admissions."

Over a year later, a popular referendum in Michigan against affirmative action preferences left this issue unresolved for the university pending a challenge at the highest court to the constitutionality of the referendum.

Gratz v. Bollinger 539 U.S. 244 (2003) and *Grutter v. Bollinger* 539 U.S. 306 (2003). Further reading: *The New York Times*, July 2, 2005, A1, A10–13; William G. Bowen, Martin A. Kurzweil, and Eugene M. Tobin, *Equity and Excellence in American Higher Education* (Charlottesville, VA, 2005); Lawrence White, "Judicial Threats to Academe's 'Four Freedoms,'" *Chronicle of Higher Education*, December 1, 2006, B6–8; and X, 7.

BARBARA GRUTTER, PETITIONER V.
LEE BOLLINGER ET AL.

Justice O'Connor for the majority:

We last addressed the use of race in public higher education over 25 years ago. In the landmark *Bakke* case, we reviewed a racial set-aside program. . . . [F]or the reasons set out below, today we endorse Justice Powell's view that student body diversity is a compelling state interest that can justify the use of race in university admissions. . . .

[W]e turn to the question whether the Law School's use of race is justified by a compelling state interest. Before this Court, as they have throughout this litigation, respondents assert only one justification for their use of race in the admissions process: obtaining "the educational benefits that flow from a diverse student body." . . . In other words, the Law School asks us to recognize, in the context of higher education, a compelling state interest in student body diversity.

We first wish to dispel the notion that the Law School's argument has been foreclosed, either expressly or implicitly, by our affirmative-action cases decided since *Bakke*. It is true that some language in those opinions might be read to suggest that remedying past discrimination is the only permissible justification for race-based governmental action. . . . But we have never held that the only governmental use of race that can survive strict scrutiny is remedying past discrimination. Nor, since Bakke, have we directly addressed the use of race in the context of public higher education. Today, we hold that the Law School has a compelling interest in attaining a diverse student body.

The Law School's educational judgment that such diversity is essential to its educational mission is one to which we defer. The Law School's assessment that diversity will, in fact, yield educational benefits is substantiated by respondents and their amici. Our scrutiny of the interest asserted by the Law School is no less strict for taking into account complex educational judgments in an area that lies primarily within the expertise of the university. Our holding today is in keeping with our tradition of giving a degree of deference to a university's academic decisions, within constitutionally prescribed limits. . . .

We have long recognized that, given the important purpose of public education and the expansive freedoms of speech and thought associated with the university environment, universities occupy a special niche in our constitutional tradition. . . . In announcing the principle of student body diversity as a compelling state interest, Justice Powell invoked our cases recognizing a constitutional dimension, grounded in the First Amendment, of educational autonomy: "The freedom of a university to make its own judgments as to education includes the selection of its student body." . . . From this premise, Justice Powell reasoned that by claiming "the right to select those students who will contribute the most to the 'robust exchange of ideas,' " a university "seek[s] to achieve a goal that is of paramount importance in the fulfillment of its mission." . . . Our conclusion that the Law School has a compelling interest in a diverse student body is informed by our view that attaining a diverse student body is at the heart of the Law School's proper institutional mission, and that "good faith" on the part of a university is "presumed" absent "a showing to the contrary." . . .

As part of its goal of "assembling a class that is both exceptionally academically qualified and broadly diverse," the Law School seeks to "enroll a 'critical mass' of minority students." . . . The Law School's interest is not simply "to assure within its student body some specified percentage of a particular group merely because of its race or ethnic origin." . . . That would amount to outright racial balancing, which is patently unconstitutional. . . . Rather, the Law School's concept of critical mass is defined by reference to the educational benefits that diversity is designed to produce.

These benefits are substantial. As the District Court emphasized, the Law School's admissions policy promotes "cross-racial understanding," helps to break down racial stereotypes, and "enables [students] to better understand persons of different races." . . . These benefits are "important and laudable," because "classroom discussion is livelier, more spirited, and simply more enlightening and interesting" when the students have "the greatest possible variety of backgrounds." . . .

These benefits are not theoretical but real, as major American businesses have made clear that the skills needed in today's increasingly global marketplace can only be developed through exposure to widely diverse people, cultures, ideas, and viewpoints. . . . What is more, high-ranking retired officers and civilian leaders of the United States military assert that, "[b]ased on [their] decades of experience," a "highly qualified, racially diverse officer corps . . . is essential to the military's ability to fulfill its principle mission to provide national security." . . . The primary sources for the Nation's officer corps are the service academies and the Reserve Officers Training Corps (ROTC), the latter comprising students already admitted to participating colleges and universities. . . . At present, "the military cannot achieve an officer corps that is both highly qualified and racially diverse unless the service academies and the ROTC used limited race-conscious recruiting and admissions policies." . . . To fulfill its mission, the military "must be selective in admissions for training and education for the officer corps, and it must train and educate a highly qualified, racially diverse officer corps in a racially diverse setting." . . . We agree that "[i]t requires only a small step from this analysis to conclude that our country's other most selective institutions must remain both diverse and selective." . . .

This Court has long recognized that "education. . . is the very foundation of good citizenship." . . .

Moreover, universities, and in particular, law schools, represent the training ground for a large number of our Nation's leaders. . . . Individuals with law degrees occupy roughly half the state governorships, more than half the seats in the United States Senate, and more than a third of the seats in the United States House of Representatives. . . . The pattern is even more striking when it comes to highly selective law schools. A handful of these schools accounts for 25 of the 100 United States Senators, 74 United States Courts of Appeals judges, and nearly 200 of the more than 600 United States District Court judges. . . .

In order to cultivate a set of leaders with legitimacy in the eyes of the citizenry, it is necessary that the path to leadership be visibly open to talented and qualified individuals of every race and ethnicity. All members of our heterogeneous society must have confidence in the openness and integrity of the educational institutions that provide this training. As we have recognized, law schools "cannot be effective in isolation from the individuals and institutions with which the law interacts." . . . Access to legal education (and thus the legal profession) must be inclusive of talented and qualified individuals of every race and ethnicity, so that all members of our heterogeneous society may participate in the educational institutions that provide the training and education necessary to succeed in America. . . .

Since *Bakke*, we have had no occasion to define the contours of the narrow-tailoring inquiry with respect to race-conscious university admissions programs. That inquiry must be calibrated to fit the distinct issues raised by the use of race to achieve student body diversity in public higher education. Contrary to Justice Kennedy's assertions, we do not "abandon[ ] strict scrutiny," . . . Rather, . . . we adhere to Adarand's teaching that the very purpose of strict scrutiny is to take such "relevant differences into account." . . .

To be narrowly tailored, a race-conscious admissions program cannot use a quota system—it cannot "insulat[e] each category of applicants with certain desired qualifications from competition with all other applicants." . . . Instead, a university may consider race or ethnicity only as a " 'plus' in a particular applicant's file," without "insulat[ing] the individual from comparison with all other candidates for the available seats." . . . In other words, an admissions program must be "flexible enough to consider all pertinent elements of diversity in light of the particular qualifications of each applicant, and to place them on the same footing for consideration, although not necessarily according them the same weight." . . .

We find that the Law School's admissions program bears the hallmarks of a narrowly tailored plan. As Justice Powell made clear in Bakke, truly individualized consideration demands that race be used in a flexible, nonmechanical way. It follows from this mandate that universities cannot establish quotas for members of certain racial groups or put members of those groups on separate admissions tracks. . . . Nor can universities insulate applicants who belong to certain racial or ethnic groups from the competition for admission. . . . Universities can, however, consider race or ethnicity more flexibly as a "plus" factor in the context of individualized consideration of each and every applicant. . . .

We are satisfied that the Law School's admissions program, like the Harvard plan described by Justice Powell, does not operate as a quota. Properly understood, a "quota" is a program in which a certain fixed number or proportion of opportunities are "reserved exclusively for certain minority groups." . . . Quotas "'impose a fixed number or percentage which must be attained, or which cannot be exceeded,'" and "insulate the individual from comparison with all other candidates for the available seats." . . .

[T]he Law School engages in a highly individualized, holistic review of each applicant's file, giving serious consideration to all the ways an applicant might contribute to a diverse educational environment. The Law School affords this individualized consideration to applicants of all races. There is no policy, either de jure or de facto, of automatic acceptance or rejection based on any single "soft" variable. Unlike the program at issue in Gratz v. Bollinger, ante, the Law School awards no mechanical, predetermined diversity "bonuses" based on race or ethnicity. . . . Like the Harvard plan, the Law School's admissions policy "is flexible enough to consider all pertinent elements of diversity in light of the particular qualifications of each applicant, and to place them on the same footing for consideration, although not necessarily according them the same weight." . . .

The Law School does not, however, limit in any way the broad range of qualities and experiences that may be considered valuable contributions to student body diversity. To the contrary, the 1992 policy makes clear "[t]here are many possible bases for diversity admissions," and provides examples of admittees who have lived or traveled widely abroad, are fluent in several languages, have overcome personal adversity and family hardship, have excep-

tional records of extensive community service, and have had successful careers in other fields. . . . The Law School seriously considers each "applicant's promise of making a notable contribution to the class by way of a particular strength, attainment, or characteristic—e.g., an unusual intellectual achievement, employment experience, nonacademic performance, or personal background." . . . All applicants have the opportunity to highlight their own potential diversity contributions through the submission of a personal statement, letters of recommendation, and an essay describing the ways in which the applicant will contribute to the life and diversity of the Law School. . . .

Petitioner and the United States argue that the Law School's plan is not narrowly tailored because race-neutral means exist to obtain the educational benefits of student body diversity that the Law School seeks. We disagree. Narrow tailoring does not require exhaustion of every conceivable race-neutral alternative. Nor does it require a university to choose between maintaining a reputation for excellence or fulfilling a commitment to provide educational opportunities to members of all racial groups. . . . Narrow tailoring does, however, require serious, good faith consideration of workable race-neutral alternatives that will achieve the diversity the university seeks.

The United States advocates "percentage plans," recently adopted by public undergraduate institutions in Texas, Florida, and California to guarantee admission to all students above a certain class-rank threshold in every high school in the State. . . . The United States does not, however, explain how such plans could work for graduate and professional schools. More-over, even assuming such plans are race-neutral, they may preclude the university from conducting the individualized assessments necessary to assemble a student body that is not just racially diverse, but diverse along all the qualities valued by the university. We are satisfied that the Law School adequately considered race-neutral alternatives currently capable of producing a critical mass without forcing the Law School to abandon the academic selectivity that is the cornerstone of its educational mission. . . .

We take the Law School at its word that it would "like nothing better than to find a race-neutral admissions formula" and will terminate its race-conscious admissions program as soon as practicable. . . . It has been 25 years since Justice Powell first approved the use of race to further an interest in student body diversity in the context of public higher education. Since that time, the number of minority applicants with high grades and test scores has indeed increased. . . . We expect that 25 years from now, the use of racial preferences will no longer be necessary to further the interest approved today. . . .

The judgment of the Court of Appeals for the Sixth Circuit, accordingly, is affirmed.

It is so ordered.

Chief Justice Rehnquist, with whom Justice Scalia, Justice Kennedy, and Justice Thomas join, dissenting.

I agree with the Court that, "in the limited circumstance when drawing racial distinctions is permissible," the government must ensure that its means are narrowly tailored to achieve a compelling state interest. . . . I do not believe, however, that the University of Michigan Law School's (Law School) means are narrowly tailored to the interest it asserts. The Law School claims it must take the steps it does to achieve a " 'critical mass' " of underrepresented minority students. . . . But its actual program bears no relation to this asserted goal. Stripped of its "critical mass" veil, the Law School's program is revealed as a naked effort to achieve racial balancing. . . .

Although the Court recites the language of our strict scrutiny analysis, its application of that review is unprecedented in its deference.

Respondents' asserted justification for the Law School's use of race in the admissions process is "obtaining 'the educational benefits that flow from a diverse student body.' " . . . They contend that a "critical mass" of underrepresented minorities is necessary to further that interest. . . . Respondents and school administrators explain generally that "critical mass" means a sufficient number of underrepresented minority students to achieve several objectives: To ensure that these minority students do not feel isolated or like spokespersons for their race; to provide adequate opportunities for the type of interaction upon which the educational benefits of diversity depend; and to challenge all students to think critically and reexamine stereotypes. . . . These objectives indicate that "critical mass" relates to the size of the student body. . . . Respondents further claim that the Law School is achieving "critical mass." . . .

In practice, the Law School's program bears little or no relation to its asserted goal of achieving "critical mass." Respondents explain that the Law School seeks to accumulate a "critical mass" of each underrepresented minority group. . . .

The Court states that the Law School's goal of attaining a "critical mass" of underrepresented minority students is not an interest in merely " 'assur[ing] within its student body some specified percentage of a particular group merely because of its race or ethnic origin.' " . . . The Court recognizes that such an interest "would amount to outright racial balancing, which is patently unconstitutional." . . . The Court concludes, however, that the Law School's use of race in admissions, consistent with Justice Powell's opinion in *Bakke*, only pays " '[s]ome attention to numbers.' " . . .

But the correlation between the percentage of the Law School's pool of applicants who are members of the three minority groups and the percentage of the admitted applicants who are members of these same groups is far too precise to be dismissed as merely the result of the school paying "some attention to [the] numbers." . . .

I do not believe that the Constitution gives the Law School such free rein in the use of race. The Law School has offered no explanation for its actual admissions practices and, unexplained, we are bound to conclude that the Law School has managed its admissions program, not to achieve a "critical mass," but to extend offers of admission to members of selected minority groups in proportion to their statistical representation in the applicant pool. But this is precisely the type of racial balancing that the Court itself calls "patently unconstitutional." . . .

Finally, I believe that the Law School's program fails strict scrutiny because it is devoid of any reasonably precise time limit on the Law School's use of race in admissions. We have emphasized that we will consider "the planned duration of the remedy" in determining whether a race-conscious program is constitutional. . . . Our previous cases have required some limit on the duration of programs such as this because discrimination on the basis of race is invidious. . . .

Justice Thomas Concurring in Part and Dissenting in Part

Like [Frederick] Douglass, I believe blacks can achieve in every avenue of American life without the meddling of university administrators. Because I wish to see all students succeed whatever their color, I share, in some respect, the sympathies of those who sponsor the type of discrimination advanced by the University of Michigan Law School. The Constitution does not, however, tolerate institutional devotion to the status quo in admissions policies when such devotion ripens into racial discrimination. Nor does the Constitution countenance the unprecedented deference the Court gives to the Law School, an approach inconsistent with the very concept of "strict scrutiny." . . .

The law school, of its own choosing, and for its own purposes, maintains an exclusionary admissions system that it knows produces racially disproportionate results. Racial discrimination is not a permissible solution to the self-inflicted wounds of this elitist admissions policy.

The majority upholds the Law School's racial discrimination not by interpreting the people's Constitution, but by responding to a faddish slogan of the cognoscenti. Nevertheless, I concur in part in the Court's opinion. First, I agree with the Court insofar as its decision, which approves of only one racial classification, confirms that further use of race in admissions remains unlawful. Second, I agree with the Court's holding that racial discrimination in higher education admissions will be illegal in 25 years. . . . I respectfully dissent from the remainder of the Court's opinion and the judgment, however, because I believe that the Law School's current use of race violates the Equal Protection Clause and that the Constitution means the same thing today as it will in 300 months.

GRATZ V. BOLLINGER

Chief Justice Rehnquist for the Court:

The current LSA [College of Literature, Science, and the Arts] policy does not provide such individualized consideration. The LSA's policy automatically distributes 20 points to every single applicant from an "underrepresented minority" group, as defined by the University. The only consideration that accompanies this distribution of points is a factual review of an application to determine whether an individual is a member of one of these minority groups. Moreover, unlike Justice Powell's example, where the race of a "particular black applicant" could be considered without being decisive . . . the LSA's automatic distribution of 20 points has the effect of making "the factor of race . . . decisive" for virtually every minimally qualified underrepresented minority applicant. . . .

Respondents contend that "[t]he volume of applications and the presentation of applicant information make it impractical for [LSA] to use the . . . admissions system" upheld by the Court today in *Grutter*. . . . But the fact that the implementation of a program capable of providing individualized consideration might present administrative challenges does not render constitutional an otherwise problematic system.

Affirmative Action Attacked

6. Ward Connerly,
"My Fight against Race Preferences," 2000

Appointed to the University of California Board of Regents by Governor Pete Wilson in 1993, Ward Connerly (1939–) became an increasingly influential opponent of affirmative action. He was a businessman in Sacramento who had earlier worked in state agencies, where he got to know Wilson. On the board, Connerly's attention was turned to statistics that showed whites and Asians being denied admission to the university despite better grades and test scores than black applicants. He proposed abolishing affirmative action in the statewide system and won enough converts to win a regental vote to abolish affirmative action for matriculants in January 1996. Connerly's efforts next led to a successful statewide ballot initiative, Proposition 209, against affirmative action. Thereafter Connerly created the American Civil Rights Initiative on a national basis. That in turn helped a victory to anti–affirmative action voters in the state of Washington, though not in Florida, where Connerly's efforts were rejected by the two political parties. By 2003 he again pushed a ballot measure in California to prohibit state classification of any person by race, ethnicity, color, or national origin, with some exemptions. This proposition lost by over 60 percent of the vote, but in a 2006 ballot initiative, voters in Michigan chose to end affirmative action preferences. Throughout all this Connerly insisted in equality for all before the law and that affirmative action is a form of "reverse racism."

Ward Connerly, "My Fight against Race Preferences: A Quest Toward 'Creating Equal,'" *Chronicle of Higher Education,* March 10, 2000, B6–8. Adapted here from his *Creating Equal: My Fight against Race Preferences* (San Francisco, 2000), Copyright © 2000 by Encounter Books. Further reading: II, 17–21; IX, 1–4, 6.

My life experiences tell me that the question "Who are you?" is the most important one we can ask. And when we focus less on group identity and more on individuals and their individual humanity, we are *creating equal*.

Most people call me a black man. My enemies deny that I am, of course. For them, I'm an "Oreo"— black on the outside and white within. In fact, I'm black in the same way that Tiger Woods and so many other Americans are black—by the "one-drop" rule used by yesterday's segregationists and today's racial ideologues. In my case, the formula has more or less equal elements of French Canadian, Choctaw, African, and Irish American.

But just enumerating racial and ethnic lineages doesn't tell who I am, or who you are. Such a recitation doesn't predict the fears that you have had to face, the obstacles that you have had to overcome, and the strengths that you have discovered along your journey. Nor does it remind you that your "race," whatever it may be, is the least interesting thing about you. . . .

In 1993, California Governor Pete Wilson appointed me to the University of California Board of Regents. I felt that I had been called up to the big leagues of public service. A regent's term is 12 years, but it feels like a lifetime sinecure. You receive no salary, but the perks are world-class.

From the outset, you are made to feel like minor royalty, cosseted by university administrators who look after you in the ritualized way of workers tending a queen bee. The board is steeped in tradition, and your colleagues initiate you into a ceremonial world that seems almost like a secret society. Its plush world of power is second only to the State Supreme Court among such appointed entities in California.

Yet signals are clearly given from the moment you're sworn in that this power is contingent on being a team player. You *will* suppress potentially embarrassing questions; you *will* regard the smooth functioning of the university as the highest good; you *will* avoid comments or controversies that open the board to the prying eye of the media.

The table you sit at may be oval, but it is top-heavy with senior regents at one end. The U.C. Board of Regents is one of those bodies on which you're supposed to serve a season or two being seen and not heard. At least, that was the structure that existed upon my arrival.

I saw all that clearly on the day of my very first meeting. It was at U.C.L.A., and I arrived late because of delays at the Sacramento airport. When I walked in, all of the other regents were already conducting business.

I was introduced as a new member of the board, and they politely applauded. I sat down and tried to keep an intelligent and alert look on my face.

Because one of the agenda items was a possible increase in student fees, a large number of students were in the audience, and the atmosphere was tense. During a discussion of the issue, a couple of hecklers shouted out remarks. . . . [The chairman] suddenly stood up and ordered us to adjourn: "OK, we are leaving now."

As everyone else withdrew, the student regent, a young man named Alex Wong, and I hung back to talk to the angry students. After chatting with them for a while about fee increases and other issues, I walked back to the lounge where the other regents had gathered. When I got there, [the chairman] was waiting. . . .

"When I say we're leaving the room," he said to me, "we leave the room! We all act together!"

"Look, you don't tell me what to do," I interrupted him, "and you don't tell me whom to talk to."

The other regents who were nearby watched us with looks of shocked disbelief. . . .

If the context had been more civil, I would have explained to him that, although I hadn't become a regent to cause controversy, I didn't intend to meekly follow orders. I didn't want to break ranks with the rest of the board, but I wasn't going to be a rubber stamp, either.

And, during my first few months as a regent, when the contentious issue of raising student fees finally came to a vote, I was the only other person on the board who stood against it with the student regent. It seemed to me that the university administration was not serious about cutting costs and wanted students' families to subsidize the self-indulgent status quo. . . .

At that point, affirmative action was a social policy that I generally disagreed with, an annoying intrusion of racial bean-counting into the business world. Based on my limited experience, I believed that it corrupted both the white businesses that called in minority firms to help get contracts and the minority firms that participated in the farce.

But, to the small degree that I thought about it, I regarded affirmative action as a bureaucratic rather than a moral problem, and it concerned me only when it was in my face. I accepted affirmative action as a part of the world in which I lived, a more or less invisible and certainly unchallengeable policy with a life of its own, the white noise of our everyday social transactions.

I know exactly when my attitude toward affirmative action began to change. One morning in 1994, after I'd been on the board for a little over a year . . . Ellen and Jerry Cook from La Jolla . . . had assembled a "report" on how the university was discriminating against Asian and white applicants to our medical schools. . . .

At that juncture, the same university administrators who would later defend preference policies as vitally necessary to build a just society were not even willing to acknowledge the existence of such practices. I believed them when they said that race played a fairly insignificant role in the admissions process, and saw myself as the good soldier whose duty was to defend the institution. . . .

Jerry [Cook] went to the U.C. San Diego campus and got copies of the records of all the students there who had applied to medical school over a period of several years. The records contained no names, but included racial data, test scores, grades, and information about where the students had applied and where they had been accepted. Jerry brought the materials home, sorted out the U.C.S.D. grads that the U.C.S.D. medical school had accepted (to reduce the variables and get an "apple-to-apple" comparison), and then entered the numbers into a computer.

He put the results into a scatterplot—a square field with high grades on the right side and low grades on the left, and high test scores on the top and low ones on the bottom. The accepted students, represented according to race by black circles (for black and Hispanic students) and white circles (for white and Asian students), were placed in the field according to their marks.

When Jerry handed me the scatterplot, the results needed little interpretation. A few black circles appeared in the upper-right part of the square, but most of the circles there were white. The circles in the lower-left part were almost all black. . . .

As I studied the scatterplot, Jerry told me that the preponderance of black circles in the lower-left part of the figure bothered him far more than the white ones clustered in the upper-right corner. He explained that his father had been a sharecropper in Missouri, and that Ellen's father had been a laborer in Kentucky before he went into the Army during World War II. The fact that no white circles appeared in the lower-left part of the square meant that "their people," poor whites who also needed a boost, were never given a break under affirmative action.

Jerry Cook told me later that his heart had fallen when he walked into my office the first time. He hadn't known that I was black. . . .

The last thing I wanted was to become embroiled in racial politics on the Board of Regents. But once I heard the Cooks' story and read the material they gave me, I said to them what I couldn't deny in my heart: "This is wrong."

I told them I would pursue the matter, and that simple decision changed my life. . . .

I have learned a lot from speaking at . . . college campuses, much of it disheartening. However, I still feel hopeful. Invariably, after the radicals have their little drama at those events and people are filing out, a handful of black students will stall until they're almost alone and then come up to talk.

One of the things they always say, although in different ways, is that they are sick of the stereotyping that comes along with preferences, and sick, too, of their elders' coercing them into supporting affirmative action with messages like, "Our generation fought for you to have this," or "Our racist society owes this to you." After those conversations, I always find myself wondering if all the seemingly fanatical support for affirmative action on college campuses is really only skin deep. . . .

When my journey began, the systematic and bureaucratized inequality erroneously referred to as affirmative action was entrenched not only in the University of California, but in institutions at every level of state government. To question it was to be dismissed as quixotic, and to actually challenge it was to risk being stigmatized as a racist.

The stronghold of affirmative action, which we have succeeded in renaming for what it is—a system of race preferences—seemed impregnable those few short years ago. We didn't know then that it was actually a house of cards waiting for a gust of wind to blow it down. That wind, which I know is the wind of freedom, is blowing strongly now—in the electoral and legal arenas, and most of all in the court of public opinion.

A huge added dividend comes with that development. For the first time in 25 years, those minority students now entering the University of California in increasing numbers can hold their heads high and say, *We are here not because of your "help," but because we belong here; we were admitted on our merits.*

What caused this turnaround at the university? It's simple. Administrators who had spent decades trying to get "diversity" on the cheap did what they should have done years earlier. They undertook a massive program of "outreach" initiatives, aimed at creating a competitive pool of minority students. The program stretched not only into high schools, but also into junior highs and even elementary schools, to create a competitive pool of minority students. . . .

We still have much ground to cover before the scar of race fades from the face of America. But it seems to me that in the last few years we have finally reached a clearing after struggling through the tangled undergrowth of racial hostility for three centuries. At last, we can hope to one day see each other as individuals rather than categories.

Part X   Academic Freedom

Academic freedom is at the core of academe. It is, however, a modern and always evolving concept. It emerged with the creation of research universities in nineteenth-century Europe and America that were grounded on the principle, never fully realized, of free inquiry. In the United States this primary idea was formally institutionalized in the "Statement of Principles" written upon the founding of the American Association of University Professors (AAUP) in 1915 and periodically updated (1). The date is important: already, even before the United States had entered World War I, the founders anticipated the pressure that wartime puts on free speech in general. Professors had in the 1890s experienced a different sort of academic freedom cases, which were typically conflicts between trustees and the faculty. The long-term result was a wall (again, not always impermeable) between the trustees and the evaluation of the professional work of the faculty, which came to be lodged within a system of professional disciplines and peer review.

The Cold War, which in some ways had begun in 1917, produced a number of twentieth-century academic freedom cases that resulted from government restraint on the speech and associations of teachers. Academic freedom for teachers is distinct from but related to the First Amendment rights of citizens. Academic freedom is a professional privilege, based upon competence certified by disciplinary peers, while the free speech right protected by the First Amendment is a broad right of citizenship (11). Over the course of time, but certainly not in a straight line, the Supreme Court established academic freedom as a "special concern of the first amendment," in the phrasing of Justice William Brennan (9). The first use of the phrase "academic freedom" in a Supreme Court decision had appeared in a dissent in 1952; by 1967 academic freedom found powerful statement in Brennan's majority opinion (5, 7, 9). Moreover, as Brennan's comment suggests, in the United States academic freedom tends to blend into the more fundamental right of free speech and assembly in a democracy. This is clear in the eloquent statement of Grenville Clark speaking for Harvard, but as he wrote—in the midst of the McCarthy era of repression—the institution found it impossible to live fully up to the ideal (2). Still, Clark rightly argued that universities exist to make possible "the search for truth by a free and uncoerced body of students and teachers. . . . Teachers have rights as citizens to speak and write as men of independence, the students also have rights to be taught by men of independent mind." And this, he adds, is an "American idea" (3). As Justice Brennan later made plain, these basic rights are all the more important in periods when they are most under pressure; it is precisely then that free political discussion is most indispensable, to ordinary citizens no less than to teachers (III, 3).

Three decades after Brennan's opinion, Walter Metzger measured the many uncertain steps taken since the 1950s toward a stronger legal position for academic freedom. His remarkably analytical, heavily documented essay charted for the first time two different and "pivotal" developments: "professional" academic freedom since 1915 and "constitutional" academic freedom shaped by the Supreme and lower courts after World War II (11). Aside from Brennan-like judgments on academic freedom, however, there was on this issue, even in a litigious society, an American space between courts and professors. This "distancing of the courts," Metzger suggested in one of his footnotes, "may be attributed to their natural impulse to refer to their own interpretive traditions in the area of free speech and to the meager edification provided by the AAUP in certain areas, such as freedom of scientific inquiry."[1] On other matters, first and foremost access, the Court showed no such hesitation, being pressed by the civil rights movement and presidential fiats of the 1960s. These movements altered the Court's reluctance to consider contemporary "classroom" cases (IX, Context). Closer attention to civil rights in an unanticipated way promoted the image of a distinct professorial occupation.

Despite their abiding dependence upon legal support for professional academic freedom, scholar-scientists, while they themselves live as citizens under the law, do not live for the law. Their occupational ideal is not above the law, it is essentially beyond it. They attempt to work in a realm of earnest but changeable ideas joining empirical open inquiry. Thus they look to institutional administrators and boards of control to protect their professional freedom and the constitutional-corporate freedom of their institutions. Model presidents of this kind appeared occasionally from the late nineteenth century, but a century later social and economic tides tended to diminish presidential stature and public prestige. For this reason the AAUP in 1970 recognized Father Theodore Hesburgh as an exemplary administrator and public servant who for over thirty-five years had overseen the rise of the University of Notre Dame to a major institution (10). There he protected both professional and constitutional academic freedom and guarded the university's corporate integrity, all the while openly and tactfully retaining its religious connection.

---

1. Walter P. Metzger, "Profession and Constitution: Two Definitions of Academic Freedom in America," *Texas Law Review* 66 (June 1988): 1296n78.

As the twenty-first century began, there were still instances of government action that chilled and even directly limited academic freedom. Moreover, a case can be made, as Joan Scott argued,[2] that the professional peer review system, established as the protector of free inquiry, might itself in subtle and not necessarily intentional ways compromise the ideal of free and uncoerced academic inquiry.

---

2. Joan W. Scott, "Academic Freedom as an Ethical Practice," in *The Future of Academic Freedom,* ed. Louis Menand (Chicago, 1996), 163–80.

Setting the Standard

1. AAUP Statement of Principles, 1940

The AAUP membership of academic teacher-professors has varied throughout the years. Yet all in academic life have been aware of some of the substance of the following document or, failing that, have been made aware through conditions at their own institutions. The entire statement, printed here, contains its own brief headnote, but the document itself followed upon the founders' statement of 1915 in the first issue of their *Bulletin*. (See AAUP Redbook, 291–301, cited below.) By 2001, over 170 learned societies had endorsed these principles.

AAUP, American Association of University Professors, *Policy Documents and Reports* [the Redbook], Ninth Edition (Baltimore, 2001): 3–7. © 2001 AAUP. Further reading: AAUP, *Policy Documents and Reports*, references at 309–10; Ellen Schrecker, *No Ivory Tower: McCarthyism and the Universities* (New York, 1986), ch. 12, on difficulties confronting the AAUP in the McCarthy years; Walter P. Metzger, "The 1940 Statement on Principles of Academic Freedom," *Law and Contemporary Problems* 53, no. 3 (Summer 1990): 3–77.

1940 STATEMENT OF PRINCIPLES ON ACADEMIC FREEDOM AND TENURE

With 1970 Interpretive Comments

In 1940, following a series of joint conferences begun in 1934, representatives of the American Association of University Professors and of the Association of American Colleges (now the Association of American Colleges and Universities) agreed upon a restatement of principles set forth in the 1925 Conference Statement on Academic Freedom and Tenure. *This restatement is known to the profession as the 1940* Statement of Principles on Academic Freedom and Tenure.

The 1940 Statement is printed below, followed by Interpretive Comments as developed by representatives of the American Association of University Professors and the Association of American Colleges in 1969. The governing bodies of the two associations, meeting respectively in November 1989 and January 1990, adopted several changes in language in order to remove gender-specific references from the original text.

The purpose of this statement is to promote public understanding and support of academic freedom and tenure and agreement upon procedures to ensure them in colleges and universities. Institutions of higher education are conducted for the common good and not to further the interest of either the individual teacher [The word "teacher" as used in this document is understood to include the investigator who is attached to an academic institution without teaching duties] or the institution as a whole. The common good depends upon the free search for truth and its free exposition.

Academic freedom is essential to these purposes and applies to both teaching and research. Freedom in research is fundamental to the advancement of truth. Academic freedom in its teaching aspect is fundamental for the protection of the rights of the teacher in teaching and of the student to freedom in learning. It carries with it duties correlative with rights.[1]

Tenure is a means to certain ends; specifically: (1) freedom of teaching and research and of extramural activities, and (2) a sufficient degree of economic security to make the profession attractive to men and women of ability. Freedom and economic security; hence, tenure, are indispensable to the success of an institution in fulfilling its obligations to its students and to society.

Academic Freedom

(a) Teachers are entitled to full freedom in research and in the publication of the results, subject to the adequate performance of their other academic duties; but research for pecuniary return should be based upon an understanding with the authorities of the institution.

(b) Teachers are entitled to freedom in the classroom in discussing their subject, but they should be careful not to introduce into their teaching controversial matter which has no relation to their subject.[2] Limitations of academic freedom because of religious or other aims of the institution should be clearly stated in writing at the time of the appointment.[3]

(c) College and university teachers are citizens, members of a learned profession, and officers of an educational institution. When they speak or write as citizens, they should be free from institutional censorship or discipline, but their special position in the

---

1. The Association of American Colleges and the American Association of University Professors have long recognized that membership in the academic profession carries with it special responsibilities. Both associations either separately or jointly have consistently affirmed these responsibilities in major policy statements, providing guidance to professors in their utterances as citizens, in the exercise of their responsibilities to the institution and to students, and in their conduct when resigning from their institution or when undertaking government-sponsored research. Of particular relevance is the *Statement on Professional Ethics*, adopted in 1966 as Association policy. (A revision, adopted in 1987, may be found in AAUP, *Policy Documents and Reports*, 9th ed. [Washington, D.C., 2001], 133–34.)

2. The intent of this statement is not to discourage what is "controversial." Controversy is at the heart of the free academic inquiry which the entire statement is designed to foster. The passage serves to underscore the need for teachers to avoid persistently intruding material which has no relation to their subject.

3. Most church-related institutions no longer need or desire the departure from the principle of academic freedom implied in the 1940 *Statement*, and we do not now endorse such a departure.

community imposes special obligations. As scholars and educational officers, they should remember that the public may judge their profession and their institution by their utterances. Hence they should at all times be accurate, should exercise appropriate restraint, should show respect for the opinions of others, and should make every effort to indicate that they are not speaking for the institution.[4]

Academic Tenure

After the expiration of a probationary period, teachers or investigators should have permanent or continuous tenure, and their service should be terminated only for adequate cause, except in the case of retirement for age, or under extraordinary circumstances because of financial exigencies.

---

4. This paragraph is the subject of an interpretation adopted by the sponsors of the 1940 *Statement* immediately following its endorsement which reads as follows:

If the administration of a college or university feels that a teacher has not observed the admonitions of paragraph (c) of the section on Academic Freedom and believes that the extramural utterances of the teacher have been such as to raise grave doubts concerning the teacher's fitness for his or her position, it may proceed to file charges under paragraph 4 of the section on Academic Tenure. In pressing such charges, the administration should remember that teachers are citizens and should be accorded the freedom of citizens. In such cases the administration must assume full responsibility, and the American Association of University Professors and the Association of American Colleges are free to make an investigation.

Paragraph (c) of the section on Academic Freedom in the 1940 *Statement* should also be interpreted in keeping with the 1964 "Committee A Statement on Extramural Utterances" (*Policy Documents and Reports*, 32), which states inter alia: "The controlling principle is that a faculty member's expression of opinion as a citizen cannot constitute grounds for dismissal unless it clearly demonstrates the faculty member's unfitness for his or her position. Extramural utterances rarely bear upon the faculty member's fitness for the position. Moreover, a final decision should take into account the faculty member's entire record as a teacher and scholar."

Paragraph 5 of the *Statement on Professional Ethics* also deals with the nature of the "special obligations" of the teacher. The paragraph reads as follows:

As members of their community, professors have the rights and obligations of other citizens. Professors measure the urgency of other obligations in the light of their responsibilities to their subject, to their students, to their profession, and to their institution. When they speak or act as private persons they avoid creating the impression of speaking or acting for their college or university. As citizens engaged in a profession that depends upon freedom for its health and integrity, professors have a particular obligation to promote conditions of free inquiry and to further public understanding of academic freedom.

Both the protection of academic freedom and the requirements of academic responsibility apply not only to the full-time probationary and the tenured teacher, but also to all others, such as part-time faculty and teaching assistants, who exercise teaching responsibilities.

In the interpretation of this principle it is understood that the following represents acceptable academic practice:

1. The precise terms and conditions of every appointment should be stated in writing and be in the possession of both institution and teacher before the appointment is consummated.

2. Beginning with appointment to the rank of full-time instructor or a higher rank,[5] the probationary period should not exceed seven years, including within this period full-time service in all institutions of higher education; but subject to the proviso that when, after a term of probationary service of more than three years in one or more institutions, a teacher is called to another institution, it may be agreed in writing that the new appointment is for a probationary period of not more than four years, even though thereby the person's total probationary period in the academic profession is extended beyond the normal maximum of seven years.[6] Notice should be given at least one year prior to the expiration of the probationary period if the teacher is not to be continued in service after the expiration of that period.[7]

---

5. The concept of "rank of full-time instructor or a higher rank" is intended to include any person who teaches a full-time load regardless of the teacher's specific title.

6. In calling for an agreement "in writing" on the amount of credit given for a faculty member's prior service at other institutions, the Statement furthers the general policy of full understanding by the professor of the terms and conditions of the appointment. It does not necessarily follow that a professor's tenure rights have been violated because of the absence of a written agreement on this matter. Nonetheless, especially because of the variation in permissible institutional practices, a written understanding concerning these matters at the time of appointment is particularly appropriate and advantageous to both the individual and the institution.

7. The effect of this subparagraph is that a decision on tenure, favorable or unfavorable, must be made at least twelve months prior to the completion of the probationary period. If the decision is negative, the appointment for the following year becomes a terminal one. If the decision is affirmative, the provisions in the 1940 *Statement* with respect to the termination of service of teachers or investigators after the expiration of a probationary period should apply from the date when the favorable decision is made.

The general principle of notice contained in this paragraph is developed with greater specificity in the *Standards for Notice of Nonreappointment*, endorsed by the Fiftieth Annual Meeting of the American Association of University Professors (1964). These standards are:

Notice of nonreappointment, or of intention not to recommend reappointment to the governing board, should be given in writing in accordance with the following standards:

(a) *Not later than March 1 of the first academic year of service*, if the appointment expires at the end of that year; or, if a one-year appointment terminates during

3. During the probationary period a teacher should have the academic freedom that all other members of the faculty have.[8]

4. Termination for cause of a continuous appointment, or the dismissal for cause of a teacher previous to the expiration of a term appointment, should, if possible, be considered by both a faculty committee and the governing board of the institution. In all cases where the facts are in dispute, the accused teacher should be informed before the hearing in writing of the charges and should have the opportunity to be heard in his or her own defense by all bodies that pass judgment upon the case. The teacher should be permitted to be accompanied by an advisor of his or her own choosing who may act as counsel. There should be a full stenographic record of the hearing available to the parties concerned. In the hearing of charges of incompetence the testimony should include that of teachers and other scholars, either from the teacher's own or from other institutions. Teachers on continuous appointment who are dismissed for reasons not involving moral turpitude should receive their salaries for at least a year from the date of notification of dismissal whether or not they are continued in their duties at the institution.[9]

---

an academic year, at least three months in advance of its termination.

(b) *Not later than December 15 of the second academic year of service*, if the appointment expires at the end of that year; or, if an initial two-year appointment terminates during an academic year, at least six months in advance of its termination.

(c) At least twelve months before the expiration of an appointment after two or more years in the institution.

Other obligations, both of institutions and of individuals, are described in the *Statement on Recruitment and Resignation of Faculty Members*, as endorsed by the Association of American Colleges and the American Association of University Professors in 1961.

8. The freedom of probationary teachers is enhanced by the establishment of a regular procedure for the periodic evaluation and assessment of the teacher's academic performance during probationary status. Provision should be made for regularized procedures for the consideration of complaints by probationary teachers that their academic freedom has been violated. One suggested procedure to serve these purposes is contained in the *Recommended Institutional Regulations on Academic Freedom and Tenure*, prepared by the American Association of University Professors.

9. A further specification of the academic due process to which the teacher is entitled under this paragraph is contained in the *Statement on Procedural Standards in Faculty Dismissal Proceedings*, jointly approved by the American Association of University Professors and the Association of American Colleges in 1958. This interpretive document deals with the issue of suspension, about which the 1940 *Statement* is silent.

The 1958 *Statement* provides: "Suspension of the faculty member during the proceedings is justified only if immediate harm to the faculty member or others is

5. Termination of a continuous appointment because of financial exigency should be demonstrably bona fide.

1940 Interpretations

At the conference of representatives of the American Association of University Professors and of the Association of American Colleges on November 7–8, 1940, the following interpretations of the 1940 *Statement of Principles on Academic Freedom and Tenure* were agreed upon:

1. That its operation should not be retroactive.

2. That all tenure claims of teachers appointed prior to the endorsement should be determined in accordance with the principles set forth in the 1925 *Conference Statement on Academic Freedom and Tenure*.

3. If the administration of a college or university feels that a teacher has not observed the admonitions of paragraph (c) of the section on Academic Freedom and believes that the extramural utterances of the teacher have been such as to raise grave doubts concerning the teacher's fitness for his or her position, it may proceed to file charges under paragraph 4 of the section on Academic Tenure. In pressing such charges, the administration should remember that teachers are citizens and should be accorded the freedom of citizens. In such cases the administration must assume full responsibility, and the American Association of University Professors and the Association of American Colleges are free to make an investigation.

1970 Interpretive Comments

Following extensive discussions on the 1940 State-ment of Principles on Academic Freedom and Tenure with leading educational associations and with individual faculty members and administrators, a joint committee of the AAUP and the Association of American Colleges met during 1969 to reevaluate this key policy statement. On the basis of the comments received, and the discussions that ensued, the joint committee felt the preferable approach was to formulate interpretations of the Statement in terms of the

---

threatened by the faculty member's continuance. Unless legal considerations forbid, any such suspension should be with pay." A suspension which is not followed by either reinstatement or the opportunity for a hearing is in effect a summary dismissal in violation of academic due process.

The concept of "moral turpitude" identifies the exceptional case in which the professor may be denied a year's teaching or pay in whole or in part. The statement applies to that kind of behavior which goes beyond simply warranting discharge and is so utterly blameworthy as to make it inappropriate to require the offering of a year's teaching or pay. The standard is not that the moral sensibilities of persons in the particular community have been affronted. The standard is behavior that would evoke condemnation by the academic community generally.

experience gained in implementing and applying the Statement for over thirty years and of adapting it to current needs.

The committee submitted to the two associations for their consideration the following "Interpretive Comments. "These interpretations were adopted by the Council of the American Association of University Professors in April 1970 and endorsed by the Fifty-sixth Annual Meeting as Association policy.*

In the thirty years since their promulgation, the principles of the 1940 *Statement of Principles on Academic Freedom and Tenure* have undergone a substantial amount of refinement. This has evolved through a variety of processes, including customary acceptance, understandings mutually arrived at between institutions and professors or their representatives, investigations and reports by the American Association of University Professors, and formulations of statements by that association either alone or in conjunction with the Association of American Colleges. These comments represent the attempt of the two associations, as the original sponsors of the 1940 *Statement*, to formulate the most important of these refinements. Their incorporation here as Interpretive Comments is based upon the premise that the 1940 *Statement* is not a static code but a fundamental document designed to set a framework of norms to guide adaptations to changing times and circumstances.

Also, there have been relevant developments in the law itself reflecting a growing insistence by the courts on due process within the academic community which parallels the essential concepts of the 1940 *Statement*; particularly relevant is the identification by the Supreme Court of academic freedom as a right protected by the First Amendment. As the Supreme Court said in *Keyishian v. Board of Regents*, 385 U.S. 589 (1967), "Our Nation is deeply committed to safeguarding academic freedom, which is of transcendent value to all of us and not merely to the teachers concerned. That freedom is therefore a special concern of the First Amendment, which does not tolerate laws that cast a pall of orthodoxy over the classroom."

The numbers refer to the designated portion of the 1940 *Statement* on which interpretive comment is made.

2. James Bryant Conant, *Education in a Divided World*, 1949

By 1960 James Bryant Conant (1893–1978) earned national eminence. He had been at the center of the wartime Manhattan Project to construct the first atomic weapon, at the time a closely guarded secret; he had been High Commissioner to Germany after the war (1953–55) and then the first American ambassador to the new Federal Republic (1955–57); finally he was an acclaimed leader in reconsidering the democratic role of American public schools (I, 1; II, 5). His earlier presidency of Harvard (1933–53), spanning two decades when the country was beset by depression, global war, and the

Cold War, was neither auspicious nor easy. He came to the job with little experience as an administrator but with a deep commitment to the university from his undergraduate and doctoral years and his distinguished professorship in organic chemistry (1927–33). With a public modesty, a certain Yankee shrewdness and coolness, and a pragmatic approach to issues, he worked to protect the institution and its traditions, keeping to the path of his predecessors, Eliot and Lowell (I, 1). His major achievement to the eyes of recent historians was to turn Harvard toward a "meritocratic" university.

Conant's administration began and ended with intense problems of academic freedom. The Massachusetts legislature passed an oath bill in 1935 requiring teachers to swear their allegiance to the state and federal constitutions. Conant and faculty members testified against this passage, and again the next year, but to no avail. Because it was law, Conant asked his faculty to follow him in signing it. This they did. In his tercentenary address of 1936 Conant struck back by reaffirming A. Lawrence Lowell's notable 1917 wartime support of academic freedom (see Hofstadter and Smith, Vol. II, Part X, Doc. 9). A decade later, with popular anti-Soviet sentiment rising and a Cold War brewing, Harvard faced the seemingly divisive charge of harboring Communist Party professors. The presence of outspoken defenders of absolute academic freedom on the faculty, like the steadfast civil libertarian and Langdell Professor of Law, Zechariah Chafee, together with some faculty members of the national Progressive Party, made the university a target for zealous and suspicious anti-communist politicians and newspapers. Well credentialed by then as defender of academic freedom, but like most university presidents working first to preserve a favorable public image of their institution, Conant found his back against the wall when pressed on the specific matter of card-carrying Communists as faculty members. Since his Manhattan Project duties he had believed privately that Communists were untrustworthy as truthseekers and not only intellectual heretics but also political conspirators. So after the Ober letter (3) he conceded publicly:

> In this period of a cold war, I do not believe the usual rules as to political parties apply to the Communist party. I am convinced that conspiracy and calculated deceit have been and are the characteristic pattern of behavior of regular Communists all over the world. For these reasons, as far as I am concerned, card-holding members of the Communist party are out of bounds as members of the teaching profession.

But for this "single exception" of party membership, he added, his administration was not concerned with the political views or private conduct of a professor, and there surely would be no inquiries into the political views or private behavior of staff members. Four years later, in his final report to the Board of Overseers, he declared that "an investigation aimed at finding a crypto-communist" would do far greater "damage . . . to the spirit of the academic community . . . than any conceivable harm such a person might do." These declarations did not ease the minds of some liberal colleagues like Chafee, who would have supported the appointment of a highly qualified communist professor to a tenured post. They brought his careful biographer to conclude that Conant's sense of responsibility and his caution "led him to actions—or inactions—that vitiated his principled rhetoric." The following document speaks to Conant's broad or administrative view of this whole matter in his determination to uphold the public reputation of Harvard.

Reprinted by permission of the publisher from *Education in a Divided World* by James Bryant Conant, pp. 172–76, 178–80, Cambridge, Mass.: Harvard University Press, Copyright © 1948 by the President and Fellows of Harvard University. Further reading: James Bryant Conant, *My Several Lives: Memoirs of a Social Inventor* (New York, 1970); James G. Hershberg, *James B. Conant* (New York, 1993), quotation 458; Morton Keller and Phyllis Keller, *Making Harvard Modern: The Rise of America's University* (New York, 2001), ch. 1, describes Conant's move toward a "meritocratic" university; Robert M. MacIver, *Academic Freedom in Our Time* (New York, 1955) contains a contemporary bibliography. Critical studies include Ellen W. Schrecker, *No Ivory Tower: McCarthyism and the Universities* (New York, 1986), 111–12, ch. 7; Andrew Schlesinger, *Veritas: Harvard College and the American Experience* (Chicago, 2005); David H. Price, *Threatening Anthropology: McCarthyism and the FBI's Surveillance of Activist Anthropologists* (Durham, NC, 2004); Sigmund Diamond, *Compromised Campus: The Collaboration of Universities with the Intelligence Community, 1945–1955* (New York, 1992); and Robert Bellah, "McCarthyism at Harvard," *New York Review of Books*, February 10, 2005, 42–43. Diamond and Bellah, notable sociologists, described their encounters with the Harvard administration after Conant's presidency while they were graduate fellows with varying connections to the Communist Party.

One condition is essential: freedom of discussion, unmolested inquiry. As in the early days of this century, we must have a spirit of tolerance which allows the expression of a great variety of opinions. On this point there can be no compromise even in days of an armed truce. But we should be completely unrealistic if we failed to recognize the difficulties which arise from the ideological conflict which according to the premise of this book will be with us for years to come. Excited citizens are going to be increasingly alarmed about alleged "communist infiltration" into our schools and colleges. Reactionaries are going to use the tensions inherent in our armed truce as an excuse for attacking a wide group of radical ideas and even some which are in the middle of the road.

How are we to answer the thoughtful and troubled citizen who wonders if our universities are being used as centers for fifth column activities? By emphasizing again the central position in this country of tolerance of diversity of opinion and by expressing confidence that our philosophy is superior to all alien importations. After all, this is but one version of the far wider problem which we encounter at the outset: how are we to win the ideological conflict if it continues on a non-shooting basis? Clearly not by destroying our basic ideas but by strengthening them; clearly not by retreating in fear from the Communist doctrine but by going out vigorously to meet it. Studying a philosophy does not mean endorsing it, much less proclaiming it. We study cancer in order to learn how to defeat it. We must study the Soviet philosophy in our universities for exactly the same reason. No one must be afraid to tackle that explosive subject before a class. If an avowed supporter of the Marx-Lenin-Stalin line can be found, force him into the open and tear his arguments to pieces with counter-arguments. Some of the success of the Communist propaganda in this country before the war was due to the fact that it was like pornographic literature purveyed through an academic black market so to speak. For a certain type of youth this undercover kind of knowledge has a special attraction. And doctrines that are not combated in the classroom but treated merely with silence or contempt may be appealing to the immature.

The first requirement for maintaining a healthy attitude in our universities in these days, therefore, is to get the discussion of modern Marxism out into the open. The second is to recognize that we are not at peace but in a period of an armed truce. That means that the activities which go with war, such as vigorous secret intelligence, sabotage, and even planned disruption of the basic philosophy of a nation may well proceed. We must be on our guard. We must be realistic about the activities of agents of foreign powers, but at the same time be courageous in our support of the basis of our own creed, the maximum of individual freedom. . . . Certain men and women who temperamentally are unsuited for employment by a Federal agency none the less can serve the nation in other ways. They may be entitled to our full respect as citizens though we may disagree with their opinions. For example, a person whose religious beliefs make him a conscientious objector is automatically disqualified from employment by the nation in matters pertaining to the use of force or preparation for the use of force. On the other hand, such a man may be an intellectual and moral leader of the greatest importance for the welfare of our society.

These obvious considerations have bearing on the problems of staffing a university. Universities, however they may be financed or controlled, are neither government bureaus nor private corporations; the professors are not hired employees. The criteria for joining a community of scholars are in some ways unique. They are not to be confused with the requirements of a Federal bureau. For example, I can imagine a naive scientist or a philosopher with strong loyalties to the advancement of civilization and the unity of the world who would be a questionable asset to a government department charged with negotiations with other nations; the same man because of his professional competence might be extremely valuable to a university. Such conclusions are obvious to anyone who takes the trouble to think carefully about the degrees of prudence and sophistication met with in human beings. Such considerations will be self-evident to all who analyze the complex problem of loyalty.

The third condition necessary for maintaining free inquiry within our universities is to ask the scholars themselves to declare their own basic social philosophy. We must then be prepared in our universities to be sure that we have a variety of views represented and that in the classroom our teachers be careful scholars rather than propagandists. But the unpopular view must be protected for we would be quite naive to imagine that there are no reactionaries who would like to drive all liberals from the halls of learning. This issue arises, of course, not in the physical sciences but in connection with the social sciences and sometimes the humanities. . . .

Those who worry about radicalism in our schools and colleges are often either reactionaries who themselves do not bear allegiance to the traditional American principles or defeatists who despair of the success of our own philosophy in an open competition. The first group are consciously or unconsciously aiming at a transformation of this society, perhaps initially not as revolutionary or violent as that which the Soviet agents envisage, but one eventually equally divergent from our historic goals. The others are unduly timid about the outcome of a battle of *ideas;* they lack confidence in our own intellectual armament. (I mean literally the battle of ideas not espionage or sabotage by secret agents.) They often fail to recognize that diversity of opinion within the framework of loyalty to our free society is not only basic to a university but to the entire nation. For in a democracy with our traditions only those reasoned convictions which emerge from diversity of opinion can lead to that unity and national solidarity so essential for the welfare of our country —essential not only for our own security but even more a requisite for intelligent action toward the end we all desire, namely, the conversion of the present armed truce into a firm and lasting peace.

Like all other democratic institutions based on the principles of toleration, individual freedom, and the efficacy of rational methods, the universities are certain to meet with many difficulties as they seek to preserve their integrity during this period of warring ideologies. But we would do well to remember this is not the first time that communities of scholars have been disturbed by doctrinal quarrels so deep-seated as to be in the nature of smoldering wars. The history of Oxford and Cambridge during the Civil Wars of the seventeenth century is interesting reading on this point. At that time the "true friends of learning" rallied to the support of those ancient institutions and protected them against the excesses of both sides. Today, likewise, the friends of learning must recognize the dangers which might threaten the universities if tempers rise as the armed truce lengthens. They must seek to increase the number of citizens who understand the true nature of universities, the vital importance of the tradition of free inquiry, the significance of life tenure for the

older members of each faculty, the fact that violent differences of opinion are essential for education. They must be realistic about the fanatic followers of the Soviet philosophy who seek to infiltrate, control, and disrupt democratic organizations including student clubs. But they must also recognize the threat that comes from those reactionaries who are ready if a wave of hysteria should mount to purge the institutions of all doctrines contrary to their views. In short, our citadels of learning must be guarded by devoted laymen in all walks of life who realize the relation between education and American democracy. So protected, the universities need not worry unduly about infiltration of Marxist subversive elements or intimidation from without. They will remain secure fortresses of our liberties.

3. Grenville Clark, "Freedom at Harvard," 1948

In the spring of 1949, Frank B. Ober (Harvard LL.B. 1913) chaired the Maryland Commission on Subversive Activities, which drafted legislation against communism, which was thereafter enacted into law. He complained in a letter to Conant that the eminent Harvard astronomer Harlow Shapley and a young assistant professor of English Composition, John Ciardi (later a noted poet and editor), had, by their "extracurricular activities" in attending different Progressive Party and peace meetings, used the "prestige" of Harvard University "in a manner hostile to our own country." President Conant briefly acknowledged this letter and asked Grenville Clark (1882–1967), a senior member of the Harvard Corporation, to reply to Ober. This selection is a portion of Clark's letter of May 27, 1949. Clark was class of 1903 at Harvard College and Law School 1906. He was long a member of the New York City bar (1909–46), served in both world wars, and led in the cause of world organization especially through United World Federalists. His membership on the Corporation of Harvard College lasted from 1931 to 1950.

Grenville Clark, "Freedom at Harvard," *Harvard Alumni Bulletin* 51 (June 25, 1949): 732–35, reprinted with the kind permission of *Harvard Alumni Magazine.* Further reading: X, 2.

I repeat that the things you ask for will not and cannot be done at Harvard—at least as long as Harvard retains its basic principles and holds by its tradition. And if the day ever came that such things were done at the physical place on which the Harvard buildings stand or anywhere by the Harvard authorities, it would not be "Harvard" doing them; it would be an institution of an entirely different sort, with wholly different ideas and purposes.

The fundamental reason is that for Harvard to take the course you recommend would be to repudiate the very essence of what Harvard stands for—the search for truth by a free and uncoerced body of students and teachers. And it would be to make a mockery of a long tradition of Harvard freedom for both its students and its faculties.

As to the history of that tradition, while it is much more than eighty years old, it is sufficient, I think, to go back to President Charles W. Eliot's inaugural address in 1869 and follow down from there. . . .

The tradition so expressed was well understood and applied under President Eliot. It was then carried on and emphasized during the more controversial term of President A. Lawrence Lowell from 1909 to 1933.

In his report for 1916–17 (from which Mr. Conant sent you an extract) Mr. Lowell took notice that the war had "brought to the front" questions of academic freedom, especially "liberty of speech on the part of the professor." He then went on to make so discriminating an analysis of the subject that in the opinion of many, including myself, the writing of those few pages was the most lasting public service of his long career. . . .

Doubtless you are familiar with his report and I can only commend a restudy of its closely reasoned pages. The point is that this report, which became famous, stands today as part of the Harvard tradition of freedom of expression, and as a definite guide for Harvard policy.

Coming now to President Conant's term, we find the same basic thought expressed with equal clarity and force. . . .

These declarations of three Harvard presidents are, as you observe, all of a piece. They embody a consistent doctrine that can, I think, be summed up as follows:

(1) *Harvard believes in the "free trade in ideas" of Justice Holmes—a graduate of 1861—which is no more than saying that she believes in the principles of Milton's* Areopagitica *(1644), of Jefferson's First Inaugural (1801), and of Mill's "Essay on Liberty" (1859). She thinks that repression is not wise or workable under our system, that wide latitude for conflicting views affords the best chance for good government, and that in suppression usually lies the greater peril. Harvard is not afraid of freedom, and believes adherence to this principle to be fundamental for our universities and for the integrity of our institutions.*

(2) *She believes that the members of the faculties, in their capacity as citizens, have the same rights to express themselves as other citizens, and that those rights should not be restricted by the University by trying to keep a "watch" on professors or otherwise.*

(3) *She believes that wide limits for free expression by professors are in the interest of her students as well as the teachers. The teachers have rights as citizens to speak and write as men of independence; the students also have their rights to be taught by men of independent mind.*

(4) *Harvard, like any great privately supported university, badly needs money; but Harvard will accept no gift on the condition, express or implied, that it shall compromise its tradition of freedom.*

These beliefs are not a matter of lip service. They have been applied in practice at Harvard for a long time. . . .

It is, I think, unnecessary to go into more detail.

For it is well-established and known that Harvard has a long-declared and, on the whole, well-adhered-to tradition favoring a wide degree of freedom for teacher and student and, therefore, as you must perceive, a tradition utterly at variance with what you recommend.

Mr. Conant mentioned the "significance" as well as the "history" of the tradition.

To my mind, its fundamental significance lies in the thought that the principles back of it are essential to the American Idea—to the workability of our free institutions, and to enabling Americans to live satisfactory lives.

The professor's right to speak his mind and to espouse unpopular causes should not be regarded as something separate and apart from the maintenance of our civil rights in general. I think what is usually called academic freedom is simply part and parcel of American freedom—merely a segment of the whole front.

I believe, however, that it is an especially vital segment because it concerns the students quite as much as the professors. If the professors are censored, constrained, or harassed, it affects not only themselves; it affects also those whom they teach—the future voters and leaders upon whose integrity and independence of mind will depend the institutions by which we live and breathe a free air. For if the professors have always to conform and avoid unpopular views whether in class or out, what kind of men will they be? And where will our young men and women go to hear and weigh new ideas, to consider both sides and acquire balance and integrity? . . .

In that inaugural address of Mr. Eliot's, it is also said: "In the modern world the intelligence of public opinion is the one indispensable condition of social progress." And further: "The student should be made acquainted with all sides of these [philosophical and political] controversies, with the salient points of each system . . . The notion that education consists in the authoritative inculcation of what the teacher deems true may be logical and appropriate in a convent, or a seminary for priests, but it is intolerable in universities and public schools, from primary to professional."

But how can we fulfill the "indispensable condition" of intelligent opinion; and how can we have non-dogmatic and excellent instruction for our leaders if their teachers are coerced or harassed?

It is impossible; and since I believe that the very existence of our free institutions depends on the independence and integrity of our teachers, the main significance for me of the Harvard tradition is that it powerfully helps to sustain those institutions.

No doubt there are other more specialized significances. No doubt the Harvard tradition has significance because, if abandoned, it would make many good people, members of our faculties, very unhappy. No doubt it is significant because its abandonment would force others—administrators and

Governing Boards—either to resign or, against conscience, to engage in work bitterly hateful to them. These things are true and important. But it is enough for me that the tradition is in harmony with and necessary to the maintenance of the free institutions of America, and to the values that make life in our country most worth while.

I cannot help wondering whether you have thought through the implications of what you propose.

Since you wish to discipline professors for taking active part in meetings such as those at which Professors Ciardi and Shapley spoke, would it not be fair to pass in advance on the kind of meetings professors could safely attend? Would this not call for a University licensing board? And would not such a board have an obnoxious and virtually impossible task? . . .

If the University should undertake to decide whether or not a professor, in his capacity as a citizen, could take part in these or other meetings, what Mr. Lowell referred to would necessarily occur. If attendance at the meeting were disapproved, the professor would be deprived, under penalty of discipline, of a right enjoyed by other citizens; while if approved, the University would assume the responsibility for endorsing the meeting.

Moreover, I think you will agree that there would be little sense in censoring attendance at meetings and leaving free from censorship speeches on the radio or writings in the press, magazines, pamphlets, and books. Would not your proposals call for a censorship of all these? . . .

Beyond that, however, how could an effective "closer watch" on "extracurricular activities" be maintained unless the watch extended to conversations and correspondence? And how could that be done without a system of student and other informers—the classic and necessary method of watching for "subversive" utterances?

You may not have realized the full implications of what you ask. But if you will stop to consider what would necessarily be involved if your point of view were accepted, you must agree, I think, that these things are precisely what would be required.

What I have just said applies to the professors. But how about the students? Would it be sensible to have the teachers censored and watched while the students remain at liberty freely to speak and write and to attend such meetings as they choose, subject only to the laws of the land? On your philosophy are you not driven on to restrict, censor, and discipline the students also?

What sort of a place would Harvard be if it went down this road? It would, I think, not require six months to destroy the morale of both our teachers and students, and thereby our usefulness to the country. I think one need do no more than state the necessary implications of what you ask to demonstrate that nothing could be more alien to the principle of free expression that Harvard stands for.

I want to add a comment on your decision not to subscribe to the Law School Fund. As Mr. Conant wrote you, it has happened before that subscriptions have been withheld because of objections to the acts or opinions of professors or because of disapproval of University policy. This is natural and normal, I think; and it is certainly the right of anyone not to aid an institution with which he is as out of harmony as you now seem to be with Harvard. But it is also true, I am sure you will agree, that Harvard cannot be influenced at all to depart from her basic tradition of freedom by any fear that gifts will be withheld. . . .

I think it will always be Harvard policy not to be influenced in any way "to abridge free speech" by the withholding of any subscription. And if $5,000,000 or any sum were offered tomorrow as the price of the removal of Professor Ciardi or Professor Shapley, or of instituting the "closer watch" that you recommend, nothing is more certain than that the Corporation would again reply that it "cannot tolerate" the suggestion. . . .

4. U.C. Loyalty Oath: *Tolman v. Underhill*, 1952

Among 1,780 Academic Senate members at the University of California in 1950, thirty-one refused to sign the loyalty affidavit imposed by the Regents and were dismissed from the university. One of those dismissed, Edward C. Tolman (1886–1959), who had taught psychology at Berkeley for thirty-six years and for whom a building on that campus is named, with seventeen colleagues filed suit at the end of August 1950 against the secretary and treasurer of the Regents of the University of California, Robert M. Underhill, to compel the Regents to continue their appointments at the university. On April 6, 1951, the Third District Court of Appeals unanimously decided in favor of the petitioners (Tolman et al.) that a loyalty oath imposed on the university's faculty that was narrower than that prescribed by the state constitution violated the law and was an abuse of regental discretion. Upon rehearing the case, the California Supreme Court on October 17, 1952, declared in the opinion here reprinted, that the legislature's Levering Oath already applied to all state employees including the faculty and had thus "fully occupied the field," making the Regents' special oath for university personnel improperly redundant. Chief Justice Phil Sheridan Gibson's judgment declined to discuss petitioners' allegation regarding the violation of their civil rights and impairment of their contracts. Thus the loyalty oath at the University of California was struck down and the reappointment of the petitioners was ordered pending their subscription to the Levering Oath (still on the books). The most widely publicized faculty loyalty oath case of the Cold War era ironically did not address the issue, rather it was decided on the technical ground of the legislature's general police powers.

Aside from Tolman, the non-signers included such distinguished scholars as John Caughey, Ludwig Edelstein, Emily Huntington, Ernst Kantorowicz, Hans Lewy, Jacob Loewenberg, Charles Muscatine, and Gian Carlo Wick. Later, the Board of Regents appointed to the university presidency David Saxon, one of the four non-signers at UCLA, at the time still a young assistant professor of physics.

Tolman v. Underhill, 39 C 2d, 709–13 (1952). Further reading: David Pierpont Gardner, *The California Oath Controversy* (Berkeley, 1967), the only detailed scholarly study of the entire episode written by Saxon's successor to the presidency; George R. Stewart, *The Year of the Oath* (Garden City, NY, 1950); Edward L. Barrett Jr., *The Tenney Committee* (Ithaca, NY, 1951); R. M. MacIver, *Academic Freedom in Our Time* (New York, 1955); M. M. Chambers, *The Colleges and the Courts since 1950* (Danville, IL, 1964), ch. 7; and Ellen W. Schrecker, *No Ivory Tower: McCarthyism and the Universities* (New York, 1986), 116–25.

GIBSON, C. J.

Petitioners have taken an oath identical to that prescribed in section 3 of article XX of the state Constitution, as required of all state employees by sections 18150 et seq. of the Government Code. However, when notified of their appointment to their regular position on the faculty for the academic year, petitioners refused to execute letters of acceptance in the form required by the resolution and have brought the present proceeding claiming that the requirement is invalid.

We need not discuss the numerous questions raised by petitioners with regard to alleged violation of their civil rights and impairment of contract because we are satisfied that their application for relief must be granted on the ground that state legislation has fully occupied the field and that university personnel cannot properly be required to execute any other oath or declaration relating to loyalty than that prescribed for all state employees. . . .

Respondents contend that state legislation like sections 1360 et seq. and 18150 et seq. of the Government Code is inapplicable to university personnel because of that portion of section 9 of article IX of the state Constitution which provides that the University of California shall be administered by the regents, "with full powers of organization and government, subject only to such legislative control as may be necessary to insure compliance with the terms of the endowments of the university and the security of its funds." It is well settled, however, that laws passed by the Legislature under its general police power will prevail over regulations made by the regents with regard to matters which are not exclusively university affairs. . . . There can be no question that the loyalty of teachers at the university is not merely a matter involving the internal affairs of that institution but is a subject of general statewide concern. Constitutional limitations upon the Legislature's powers are to be strictly construed, and any doubt as to its paramount authority to require University of California employees to take an oath of loyalty to the state and federal Constitutions will be resolved in favor of its action. . . .

It is immediately apparent, . . . that the loyalty of state employees is not a matter as to which there may reasonably be different standards and different tests but is, without doubt, a subject requiring uniform treatment throughout the state. As we have already seen, the Legislature has enacted a general and detailed scheme requiring all state employees to execute a prescribed oath relating to loyalty and faithful performance of duty, and it could not have intended that they must at the same time remain subject to any such additional loyalty oaths or declarations as the particular agency employing them might see fit to impose. Multiplicity and duplication of oaths and declarations would not only reflect seriously upon the dignity of state employment but would make a travesty of the effort to secure loyal and suitable persons for government service.

We are satisfied that the Legislature intended to occupy this particular field of legislation by enacting Government Code sections 1360 et seq. and 18150 et seq. and that there is no room left for supplementary local regulation. . . . The declaration as to loyalty required by the regents is, accordingly, invalid.

No question is raised as to petitioners' loyalty or as to their qualifications to teach, and they are entitled to a writ directing respondents to issue to each of petitioners a letter of appointment to his post on the faculty of the university upon his taking the oath now required of all public employees by the Levering Act. . . .

Let a writ of mandate issue for the limited purpose above indicated.

Voices of the Supreme Court

5. *Adler v. Board of Education,* 1952

The phrase "academic freedom" was not used in a Supreme Court opinion until 1952. Associate Justice William O. Douglas (1898–1980) emphasized it in a vigorous dissent, Justice Hugo Black concurring. The case of *Adler v. Board of Education of New York* came to the Court during the scare over Communists in public office that had begun in the late 1940s. The appellant had sought a declaratory judgment asking the state courts to hold the New York state legislature's "Feinberg Law" (1949) unconstitutional. The law allowed New York to refuse employment to, or to dismiss after a notice and hearing, teachers in public schools who were members of "subversive" organizations that advocated the overthrow of the government by unlawful means, particularly the Communist Party and affiliated organizations. The Court here found "no constitutional infirmity" in the Feinberg Law. Although Adler was a public school teacher, the Feinberg case applied to teachers at all levels of public-supported institutions. It remained in effect until it was ruled unconstitutional by *Keyishian v. Board of Regents* in 1967 (X, 10). Associate Justice Sherman Minton (1890–1965) wrote the Court's decision in the *Adler* case, expressing a classic or nineteenth-century view of a model public school teacher. Throughout his long career in the Supreme Court (1939–75), Douglas remained a zealous civil libertarian; he was also well-known as an outdoors-man, an environmentalist, and a socially unconventional individualist.

Adler v. Board of Education of New York, 342 U.S. 485 (1952). Further reading: William O. Douglas, *The Court Years, 1939–1975* (New York, 1980); Vernon L. Countryman, *The Judicial Record of Justice William O. Douglas* (New York, 1974); Michael R. Belknap, *Cold War Political Justice: The Smith Act, the Communist Party, and American Civil Liberties* (New York, 1977); Bruce Allen Murphy, *Wild Bill: The Legend and Life of William O. Douglas* (New York, 2003); and X, 11.

MR. JUSTICE MINTON DELIVERED THE OPINION OF THE COURT.

It is first argued that the Feinberg Law and the rules promulgated thereunder constitute an abridgment of the freedom of speech and assembly of persons employed or seeking employment in the public schools of the State of New York. . . .

It is clear that such persons have the right under our law to assemble, speak, think and believe as they will. . . . It is equally clear that they have no right to work for the State in the school system on their own terms. . . . They may work for the school system upon the reasonable terms laid down by the proper authorities of New York. If they do not choose to work on such terms, they are at liberty to retain their beliefs and associations and go elsewhere. Has the State thus deprived them of any right to free speech or assembly? We think not. Such persons are or may be denied, under the statutes in question, the privilege of working for the school system of the State of New York because, first, of their advocacy of the overthrow of the government by force or violence, or, secondly, by unexplained membership in an organization found by the school authorities, after notice and hearing, to teach and advocate the overthrow of the government by force or violence, and known by such persons to have such purpose. . . .

A teacher works in a sensitive area in a schoolroom. There he shapes the attitude of young minds towards the society in which they live. In this, the state has a vital concern. It must preserve the integrity of the schools. That the school authorities have the right and the duty to screen the officials, teachers, and employees as to their fitness to maintain the integrity of the schools as a part of ordered society, cannot be doubted. One's associates, past and present, as well as one's conduct, may properly be considered in determining fitness and loyalty. From time immemorial, one's reputation has been determined in part by the company he keeps. In the employment of officials and teachers of the school system, the state may very properly inquire into the company they keep, and we know of no rule, constitutional or otherwise, that prevents the state, when determining the fitness and loyalty of such persons, from considering the organizations and persons with whom they associate.

If, under the procedure set up in the New York law, a person is found to be unfit and is disqualified from employment in the public school system because of membership in a listed organization, he is not thereby denied the right of free speech and assembly. His freedom of choice between membership in the organization and employment in the school system might be limited, but not his freedom of speech or assembly, except in the remote sense that limitation is inherent in every choice. Certainly such limitation is not one the state may not make in the exercise of its police power to protect the schools from pollution and thereby to defend its own existence. . . .

Membership in a listed organization found to be within the statute and known by the member to be within the statute is a legislative finding that the member by his membership supports the thing the organization stands for, namely, the overthrow of government by unlawful means. We cannot say that such a finding is contrary to fact or that "generality of experience" points to a different conclusion. Disqualification follows therefore as a reasonable presumption from such membership and support. . . .

It is also suggested that the use of the word "subversive" is vague and indefinite. But the word is first used in 1 of the Feinberg Law, which is the preamble to the Act, and not in a definitive part thereof. When used in subdivision 2 of 3022, the word has a very definite meaning, namely, an organization that teaches and advocates the overthrow of government by force or violence.

We find no constitutional infirmity in 12-a of the Civil Service Law of New York or in the Feinberg Law which implemented it, and the judgment is Affirmed.

MR. JUSTICE BLACK, DISSENTING.

This is another of those rapidly multiplying legislative enactments which make it dangerous—this time for school teachers—to think or say anything except what a transient majority happen to approve at the moment. Basically these laws rest on the belief that government should supervise and limit the flow of ideas into the minds of men. The tendency of such governmental policy is to mould people into a common intellectual pattern. Quite a different governmental policy rests on the belief that government should leave the mind and spirit of man absolutely free. Such a governmental policy encourages varied intellectual outlooks in the belief that the best views will prevail. This policy of freedom is in my judgment embodied in the First Amendment and made applicable to the states by the Fourteenth. Because of this policy public officials cannot be constitutionally vested with powers to select the ideas people can think about, censor the public views they can express, or choose the persons or groups people can associate with. Public officials with such powers are not public servants; they are public masters.

I dissent from the Court's judgment sustaining this law which effectively penalizes school teachers for their thoughts and their associates.

MR. JUSTICE DOUGLAS, WITH WHOM MR. JUSTICE BLACK CONCURS, DISSENTING.

I have not been able to accept the recent doctrine that a citizen who enters the public service can be forced to sacrifice his civil rights. I cannot for example find in our constitutional scheme the power of a state to place its employees in the category of second-class citizens by denying them freedom of thought and expression. The Constitution guarantees freedom of thought and expression to everyone in our society. All are entitled to it; and none needs it more than the teacher.

The public school is in most respects the cradle of our democracy. The increasing role of the public school is seized upon by proponents of the type of legislation represented by New York's Feinberg law as proof of the importance and need for keeping the school free of "subversive influences." But that is to misconceive the effect of this type of legislation. Indeed the impact of this kind of censorship on the public school system illustrates the high purpose of the First Amendment in freeing speech and thought from censorship.

The present law proceeds on a principle repugnant to our society—guilt by association. A teacher is disqualified because of her membership in an organization found to be "subversive." The finding as to the "subversive" character of the organization is made in a proceeding to which the teacher is not a party and in which it is not clear that she may even be heard. To be sure, she may have a hearing when charges of disloyalty are leveled against her. But in that hearing the finding as to the "subversive" character of the organization apparently may not be reopened in order to allow her to show the truth of the matter. The irrebuttable charge that the organization is "subversive" therefore hangs as an ominous cloud over her own hearing. The mere fact of membership in the organization raises a prima facie case of her own guilt. She may, it is said, show her innocence. But innocence in this case turns on knowledge; and when the witch hunt is on, one who must rely on ignorance leans on a feeble reed.

The very threat of such a procedure is certain to raise havoc with academic freedom. Youthful indiscretions, mistaken causes, misguided enthusiasms—all long forgotten—become the ghosts of a harrowing present. Any organization committed to a liberal cause, any group organized to revolt against an hysterical trend, any committee launched to sponsor an unpopular program becomes suspect. These are the organizations into which Communists often infiltrate. Their presence infects the whole, even though the project was not conceived in sin. A teacher caught in that mesh is almost certain to stand condemned. Fearing condemnation, she will tend to shrink from any association that stirs controversy. In that manner freedom of expression will be stifled.

But that is only part of it. Once a teacher's connection with a listed organization is shown, her views become subject to scrutiny to determine whether her membership in the organization is innocent or, if she was formerly a member, whether she has bona fide abandoned her membership.

The law inevitably turns the school system into a spying project. Regular loyalty reports on the teachers must be made out. The principals become detectives; the students, the parents, the community become informers. Ears are cocked for tell-tale signs of disloyalty. The prejudices of the community come into play in searching out the disloyal. This is not the usual type of supervision which checks a teacher's competency; it is a system which searches for hidden meanings in a teacher's utterances.

What was the significance of the reference of the art teacher to socialism? Why was the history teacher so openly hostile to Franco Spain? Who heard overtones of revolution in the English teacher's discussion of the *Grapes of Wrath*? What was behind the praise of Soviet progress in metallurgy in the chemistry class? Was it not "subversive" for the teacher to cast doubt on the wisdom of the venture in Korea?

What happens under this law is typical of what happens in a police state. Teachers are under constant surveillance; their pasts are combed for signs of disloyalty; their utterances are watched for clues to dangerous thoughts. A pall is cast over the classrooms. There can be no real academic freedom in that environment. Where suspicion fills the air and holds scholars in line for fear of their jobs, there can be no exercise of the free intellect. Supineness and dogmatism take the place of inquiry. A "party line"—as dangerous as the "party line" of the Communists—lays hold. It is the "party line" of the orthodox view, of the conventional thought, of the accepted approach. A problem can no longer be pursued with impunity to its edges. Fear stalks the classroom. The teacher is no longer a stimulant to adventurous thinking; she becomes instead a pipe line for safe and sound information. A deadening dogma takes the place of free inquiry. Instruction tends to become sterile; pursuit of knowledge is discouraged; discussion often leaves off where it should begin.

This, I think, is what happens when a censor looks over a teacher's shoulder. This system of spying and surveillance with its accompanying reports and trials cannot go hand in hand with academic freedom. It produces standardized thought, not the pursuit of truth. Yet it was the pursuit of truth which the First Amendment was designed to protect. A system which directly or inevitably has that effect is alien to our system and should be struck down. Its survival is a real threat to our way of life. We need be bold and adventuresome in our thinking to survive. A school system producing students trained as robots threatens to rob a generation of the versatility that has been perhaps our greatest distinction. The Framers knew the danger of dogmatism; they also knew the strength that comes when the mind is free, when ideas may be pursued wherever they lead. We forget these teachings of the First Amendment when we sustain this law.

Of course the school systems of the country need not become cells for Communist activities; and the classrooms need not become forums for propagandizing the Marxist creed. But the guilt of the teacher should turn on overt acts. So long as she is a law-abiding citizen, so long as her performance within the public school system meets professional standards, her private life, her political philosophy, her social creed should not be the cause of reprisals against her.

6. *Wieman v. Updegraff*, 1953

Justices Hugo Black (1886–1971) and Felix Frankfurter (1882–1965) delivered memorable concurring opinions, partly reprinted here, on intellectual freedom in teaching. Their views, together with Justice Thomas Clark's majority opinion, did not outlaw disclaimer loyalty oaths but did make them less threatening to academic freedom in public institutions. The case arose out of a taxpayer's suit to enjoin the Board of Regents of Oklahoma Agricultural Colleges from paying the salaries of professors who refused to sign a loyalty oath much like the Levering Oath in California (X, 4). The difference with the Oklahoma oath was that innocent membership alone was a barrier to faculty employment. Lack of knowledge of "subversive" activity by some organization innocently joined could not absolve the oath-taker from guilt by association. In his majority opinion, Justice Clark (1899–1977) rejected the screening of disloyalty by "ideological patterns" and pronounced that the oath "offends due process" because it inhibits innocent persons from freely moving among associations, thus stifling "the flow of democratic expression and controversy." In a similar case against the University of Washington (*Baggett v. Bullitt*, 377 U.S. 360 [1964]), the Supreme Court later declared that such words as "subversive" are by definition so vague as to make statutes incorporating them constitutionally unenforceable. Narrowing further the punishment for perjury in disclaimer oath-taking, Associate Justice Douglas for the Court (*Elbrandt v. Russell*, 384 U.S. 11 [1966]) wrote that a teacher as employee may be punished only for falsely denying a "specific intent" to further the purpose of an unlawful organization.

Wieman v. Updegraff, 344 U.S. 192–96 (1953). Further reading: William W. Van Alstyne, "The Constitutional Rights of Teachers and Professors," *Duke Law Journal* (October 1970): 841–79; Van Alstyne, ed., "Freedom and Tenure in the Academy: The Fiftieth Anniversary of the 1940 Statement of Principles," *Journal of Law and Contemporary Problems* 53 (Summer 1990): 1–418; William P. Murphy, "Educational Freedom in the Courts," *AAUP Bulletin* 49 (December 1963): 309–27; "Developments in the Law: Academic Freedom," *Harvard Law Review* 81, no. 5 (March 1968): 1045–1159; and X, 8.

MR. JUSTICE BLACK, CONCURRING.

I concur in all the Court says in condemnation of Oklahoma's test oath. I agree that the State Act prescribing that test oath is fatally offensive to the due process guarantee of the United States Constitution.

History indicates that individual liberty is intermittently subjected to extraordinary perils. Even countries dedicated to government by the people are not free from such cyclical dangers. The first years of our Republic marked such a period. Enforcement of the Alien and . . . Sedition Laws by zealous patriots who feared ideas made it highly dangerous for people to think, speak, or write critically about government, its agents, or its policies, either foreign or domestic. Our constitutional liberties survived the ordeal of this regrettable period because there were influential men and powerful organized groups bold enough to champion the undiluted right of individuals to publish and argue for their beliefs however unorthodox or loathsome. Today however, few individuals and organizations of power and influence argue that unpopular advocacy has this same wholly unqualified immunity from governmental interference. For this and other reasons the present period of fear seems more ominously dangerous to speech and press than was that of the Alien and Sedition Laws. Suppressive laws and practices are the fashion. The Oklahoma oath statute is but one manifestation of a national network of laws aimed at coercing and controlling the minds of men. Test oaths are notorious tools of tyranny. When used to shackle the mind they are, or at least they should be, unspeakably odious to a free people. Test oaths are made still more dangerous when combined with bills of attainder which like this Oklahoma statute impose pains and penalties for past lawful associations and utterances.

Governments need and have ample power to punish treasonable acts. But it does not follow that they must have a further power to punish thought and speech as distinguished from acts. Our own free society should never forget that laws which stigmatize and penalize thought and speech of the unorthodox have a way of reaching, ensnaring and silencing many more people than at first intended. We must have freedom of speech for all or we will in the long run have it for none but the cringing and the craven. And I cannot too often repeat my belief that the right to speak on matters of public concern must be wholly free or eventually be wholly lost. . . .

MR. JUSTICE FRANKFURTER, WHOM
MR. JUSTICE DOUGLAS JOINS, CONCURRING.

The times being what they are, it is appropriate to add a word by way of emphasis to the Court's opinion, which I join.

The case concerns the power of a State to exact from teachers in one of its colleges an oath that they are not, and for the five years immediately preceding the taking of the oath have not been, members of any organization listed by the Attorney General of the United States, prior to the passage of the statute, as "subversive" or "Communist-front." Since the affiliation which must thus be forsworn may well have been for reasons or for purposes as innocent as membership in a club of . . . one of the established political parties, to require such an oath, on pain of a teacher's loss of his position in case of refusal to take the oath, penalizes a teacher for exercising a right of association peculiarly characteristic of our people. . . . Such joining is an exercise of the rights of free speech and free inquiry. By limiting the power of the States to interfere with freedom of speech and freedom of inquiry and freedom of association, the Fourteenth Amendment protects all persons, no matter what their calling. But, in view of the nature of the teacher's relation to the effective exercise of the rights which are safeguarded by the Bill of Rights and by the Fourteenth Amendment, inhibition of freedom of thought, and of action upon thought, in the case of teachers brings the safeguards of those amendments vividly into operation. Such unwarranted inhibition upon the free spirit of teachers affects not only those who, like the appellants, are immediately before the Court. It has an unmistakable tendency to chill that free play of the spirit which all teachers ought especially to cultivate and practice; it makes for caution and timidity in their associations by potential teachers.

The Constitution of the United States does not render the United States or the States impotent to guard their governments against destruction by enemies from within. It does not preclude measures of self-protection against anticipated overt acts of violence. Solid threats to our kind of government— manifestations of purposes that reject argument and the free ballot as the means for bringing about changes and promoting progress—may be met by preventive measures before such threats reach fruition. However, in considering the constitutionality of legislation like the statute before us it is necessary to . . . keep steadfastly in mind what it is that is to be secured. Only thus will it be evident why the Court has found that the Oklahoma law violates those fundamental principles of liberty "which lie at the base of all our civil and political institutions" and as such are imbedded in the due process of law which no State may offend. . . .

That our democracy ultimately rests on public opinion is a platitude of speech but not a commonplace in action. Public opinion is the ultimate reliance of our society only if it be disciplined and responsible. It can be disciplined and responsible only if habits of open-mindedness and of critical inquiry are acquired in the formative years of our citizens. The process of education has naturally enough been the basis of hope for the perdurance of our democracy on the part of all our great leaders, from Thomas Jefferson onwards.

To regard teachers—in our entire educational system, from the primary grades to the university— as the priests of our democracy is therefore not to indulge in hyperbole. It is the special task of teachers to foster those habits of open-mindedness and critical inquiry which alone make for responsible citizens, who, in turn, make possible an enlightened and effective public opinion. Teachers must fulfill their function by precept and practice, by the very atmosphere which they generate; they must be exemplars of open-mindedness and free inquiry. They cannot carry out their noble task if the conditions for the practice of a responsible and critical mind are denied to them. They must have the freedom of responsible inquiry, by thought and action, into the meaning of social and economic ideas, into the checkered history of social and economic dogma. They must be free to sift evanescent doctrine, qualified by time and circumstance, from that restless, enduring process of extending the bounds of understanding and wisdom, to assure which the freedoms . . . of thought, of speech, of inquiry, of worship are guaranteed by the Constitution of the United States against infraction by National or State government. . . .

7. *Sweezy v. New Hampshire*, 1957

The Supreme Court here moved the concept of academic freedom closer to the First Amendment's protection of speech and association as well as to the Fourteenth Amendment's guarantee of due process. The case came on appeal to the highest court after both the Superior and the Supreme Courts of New Hampshire had found Paul Sweezy in contempt. He refused to answer questions from the New Hampshire attorney general regarding several matters: his guest lecture at the state university, his and his wife's political actions in the Progressive Party, and his "opinions and beliefs." Chief Justice Earl Warren (1891–1974) determined that contents of a classroom lecture are free from governmental inquiry, absent any specific legislative mandate for such information. Warren's judgment reversed the kind of judicial reasoning found in the Bertrand Russell case, *Kay v. Board of Higher Education of City of New York*, 18 N.Y.S. 2d 821 (1940). However, in *Barenblatt v. U.S.*, 360 U.S. 109 (1959) the Court distinguished between First and Fifth Amendment rights, employed the "balancing test," and decided that the congressional power of self-preservation through investigation is superior to a professor's rights under the First Amendment, notwithstanding this *Sweezy* decision.

Justice Frankfurter's concurring opinion is included here for its comprehensive definition of academic freedom on its liberal foundation borrowed from a declaration of South African scholars opposed to apartheid.

Paul M. Sweezy (1910–) was educated at Harvard (B.A. 1931, Ph.D. 1937) and taught economics there (1934– 46). He served in the Office of Strategic Services during World War II. He described himself as a "classical Marxist" and socialist, and he edited *Monthly Review* (1949–).

Sweezy v. New Hampshire, 354 U.S. 234–50 (1957). Further reading: Leonard Boudin, "Academic Freedom and Constitutional Law," in *Regulating the Intellectuals,* ed. Craig Kaplan and Ellen Schrecker (New York, 1983); Robert M. MacIver, *Academic Freedom in Our Time* (New York, 1955), 305–20, a contemporary bibliography; Harry T. Edwards and Virginia Davis Nordin, *Higher Education and The Law* (Cambridge, MA, 1979), ch. 6; "Developments in the Law: Academic Freedom" *Harvard Law Review* 81 (March 1968): 1045–1147; *Texas Law Review* 66 (June 1988): 1247–1649, which features comprehensive legal discussions of academic freedom, including Walter Metzger's essay, reproduced in X, 11; Ellen W. Schrecker, *No Ivory Tower: McCarthyism and the Universities* (New York, 1986), ch. 4; Beshara Doumani, ed., *Academic Freedom after September 11* (Cambridge, MA, 2006); and *Index to Legal Periodicals* (1926–present).

MR. CHIEF JUSTICE WARREN ANNOUNCED THE JUDGMENT OF THE COURT AND DELIVERED AN OPINION, IN WHICH MR. JUSTICE BLACK, MR. JUSTICE DOUGLAS, AND MR. JUSTICE BRENNAN JOIN.

This case . . . brings before us a question concerning the constitutional limits of legislative inquiry. The investigation here was conducted under the aegis of a state legislature, rather than a House of Congress. . . . The ultimate question here is whether the investigation deprived Sweezy of due process of law under the Fourteenth Amendment. For the reasons to be set out in this opinion, we conclude that the record in this case does not sustain the power of the State to compel the disclosures that the witness refused to make. . . .

During the course of the inquiry, petitioner declined to answer several questions. . . . In keeping with . . . this stand, he refused to disclose his knowledge of the Progressive Party in New Hampshire or of persons with . . . whom he was acquainted in that organization. No action was taken by the Attorney General to compel answers to these questions. . . .

The Attorney General lays great stress upon an article which petitioner had co-authored. It deplored the use of violence by the United States and other capitalist countries in attempting to preserve a social order which the writers thought must inevitably fall. This resistance, the article . . . continued, will be met by violence from the oncoming socialism, violence which is to be less condemned morally than that of capitalism since its purpose is to create a "truly human society." Petitioner affirmed that he styled himself a "classical Marxist" and a "socialist" and that the article expressed his continuing opinion. . . .

On March 22, 1954, petitioner had delivered a lecture to a class of 100 students in the humanities course at the University of New Hampshire. This talk was given at the invitation of the faculty teaching that course. Petitioner had addressed the class upon such invitations in the two preceding years as well.

Distinct from the categories of questions about the Progressive Party and the lectures was one question about petitioner's opinions. He was asked: "Do you believe in Communism?" He had already testified that he had never been a member of the Communist Party, but he refused to answer this or any other question concerning opinion or belief.

There is no doubt that legislative investigations, whether on a federal or state level, are capable of encroaching upon the constitutional liberties of individuals. It is particularly important that the exercise of the power of compulsory process be carefully circumscribed when the investigative process tends to impinge upon such highly sensitive areas as freedom of speech or press, freedom of political association, and freedom of communication of ideas, particularly in the academic community. Responsibility for the proper conduct of investigations rests, of course, upon the legislature itself. If that assembly chooses to authorize inquiries on its behalf by a legislatively created committee, that basic responsibility carries forward to include the duty of adequate supervision of the actions of the committee. This safeguard can be nullified when a committee is invested with a broad and ill-defined jurisdiction. . . .

"Subversive persons" are defined in many gradations of conduct. Our interest is in the minimal requirements of that definition since they will outline its reach. According to the statute, a person is a "subversive person" if he, by any means, aids in the commission of any act intended to assist in the alteration of the constitutional form of government by force or violence. The possible remoteness from armed insurrection of conduct that could satisfy these criteria is obvious from the language. The statute goes well beyond those who are engaged in efforts designed to alter the form of government by force or violence. The statute declares, in effect, that the assistant of an assistant is caught up in the definition. This chain of conduct attains increased significance in light of the lack of a necessary element of guilty knowledge in either stage of assistants. . . .

Merely to summon a witness and compel him, against his will, to disclose the nature of his past expressions and associations is a measure of governmental interference in these matters. These are rights which are safeguarded by the Bill of Rights and the Fourteenth Amendment. We believe that there unquestionably was an invasion of petitioner's liberties in the areas of academic freedom and political expression—areas in which government should be extremely reticent to tread.

The essentiality of freedom in the community of American universities is almost self-evident. No one should underestimate the vital role in a democracy that is played by those who guide and train our youth. To impose any strait jacket upon the intellectual leaders in our colleges and universities would imperil the future of our Nation. No field of education is so thoroughly comprehended by man that new discoveries cannot yet be made. Particularly is that true in the social sciences, where few, if any, principles are accepted as absolutes. Scholarship cannot flourish in an atmosphere of suspicion and distrust. Teachers and students must always remain free to inquire, to study and to evaluate, to gain new maturity and understanding; otherwise our civilization will stagnate and die.

Equally manifest as a fundamental principle of a democratic society is political freedom of the individual. Our form of government is built on the premise that every citizen shall have the right to engage in political expression and association. This right was enshrined in the First Amendment of the Bill of Rights. Exercise of these basic freedoms in America has traditionally been through the media of political associations. Any interference with the freedom of a party is simultaneously an interference with the freedom of its adherents. All political . . . ideas cannot and should not be channeled into the programs of our two major parties. History has amply proved the virtue of political activity by minority, dissident groups, who innumerable times have been in the vanguard of democratic thought and whose programs were ultimately accepted. Mere unorthodoxy or dissent from the prevailing mores is not to be condemned. The absence of such voices would be a symptom of grave illness in our society. . . .

The respective roles of the legislature and the investigator thus revealed are of considerable significance to the issue before us. It is eminently clear that the basic discretion of determining the direction of the legislative inquiry has been turned over to the investigative agency. The Attorney General has been given such a sweeping and uncertain mandate that it is his decision which picks out the subjects that will be pursued, what witnesses will be summoned and what questions will be asked. In this circumstance, it cannot be stated authoritatively that the legislature asked the Attorney General to gather the kind of facts comprised in the subjects upon which petitioner was interrogated.

Instead of making known the nature of the data it desired, the legislature has insulated itself from those witnesses whose rights may be vitally affected by the investigation. Incorporating by reference provisions from its subversive activities act, it has told the Attorney General, in effect to screen the citizenry of New Hampshire to bring to light anyone who fits into the expansive definitions. . . .

JUSTICE FRANKFURTER CONCURRING:

When weighed against the grave harm resulting from governmental intrusion into the intellectual life of a university, such justification for compelling a witness to discuss the contents of his lecture appears grossly inadequate. Particularly is this so where the witness has sworn that neither in the lecture nor at any other time did he ever advocate overthrowing the Government by force and violence.

Progress in the natural sciences is not remotely confined to findings made in the laboratory. Insights into the mysteries of nature are born of hypothesis and speculation. The more so is this true in the pursuit of understanding in the groping endeavors of what are called the social sciences, the concern of which is man and society. The problems that are the respective preoccupations of anthropology, economics, law, psychology, sociology and related areas of scholarship are merely departmentalized dealing, by way of manageable division of analysis, with interpenetrating aspects of holistic perplexities. For society's good—if understanding be an essential need of society—inquiries into these problems, speculations about them, stimulation in others of reflection upon them, must be left as unfettered as possible. Political power must abstain from intrusion into this activity of freedom, pursued in the interest of wise government and the people's well-being, except for reasons that are exigent and obviously compelling.

Suffice it to quote the latest expression on this subject. It is also perhaps the most poignant because its plea on behalf of continuing the free spirit of the open universities of South Africa has gone unheeded.

> In a university knowledge is its own end, not merely a means to an end. A university ceases to be true to its own nature if it becomes the tool of Church or State or any sectional interest. A university is characterized by the spirit of free inquiry, its ideal being the ideal of Socrates—"to follow the argument where it leads." This implies the right to examine, question, modify or reject traditional ideas and beliefs. Dogma and hypothesis are incompatible, and the concept of an immutable doctrine is repugnant to the spirit of a university. The concern of its scholars is not merely to add and revise facts in relation to an accepted framework, but to be ever examining and modifying the framework itself. . . .
>
> . . . It is the business of a university to provide that atmosphere which is most conducive to speculation, experiment and creation. It is an atmosphere in which there prevail "the four essential freedoms" of a university—to determine for itself on academic grounds who may teach, what may be taught, how it shall be taught, and who may be admitted to study. (The Open Universities in South Africa, 10–12. A statement of a conference of senior scholars from the University of Cape Town and the University of the Witwatersrand, including A. v. d. S. Centlivres and Richard Feetham, as Chancellors of the respective universities.)

8. *Barenblatt v. United States,* 1959

As a witness who had refused to testify about his beliefs and membership in a Communist club at the University of Michigan, Lloyd Barenblatt was convicted for contempt of Congress. Although he based his refusal upon First Amendment grounds, the Supreme Court, through Justice John Marshall Harlan's 5-4 majority opinion, ruled that the self-preservation of Congress by making inquiries of this kind took precedence over Barenblatt's First Amendment claims. In his strong dissenting opinion, joined by Chief Justice Warren and Justice Douglas, Justice Black put Barenblatt's case on the ground of intellectual freedom and put aside Justice Harlan's "balancing act" with the powers of Congress vis-à-vis that of the individual. Nevertheless, Barenblatt went to Danbury Federal Penitentiary, and the decision bearing his name remains the law of the land.

Barenblatt v. United States, 360 U.S. 109 (1959). Further reading: Dean Alfange Jr., "Congressional Investigations and the Fickle Court," *University of Cincinnati Law Review* (Spring 1961): 113–71; Ellen W. Schrecker, *No Ivory Tower: McCarthyism and the Universities* (New York, 1986), 3–4, bibliography; and X, 5–7, 9.

MR. JUSTICE HARLAN DELIVERED THE OPINION OF THE COURT.

Once more the Court is required to resolve the conflicting constitutional claims of congressional power and of an individual's right to resist its exercise. The congressional power in question concerns the internal process of Congress in moving within its legislative domain; it involves the utilization of its committees to secure "testimony needed to enable it efficiently to exercise a legislative function belonging to it under the Constitution." The power of inquiry has been employed by Congress throughout our history, over the whole range of the national interests concerning which Congress might legislate or decide upon due investigation not to legislate; it has similarly been utilized in determining what to appropriate from the national purse, or whether to appropriate. The scope of the power of inquiry, in short, is as penetrating and far-reaching as the potential power to enact and appropriate under the Constitution.

Broad as it is, the power is not, however, without limitations. Since Congress may only investigate into those areas in which it may potentially legislate or appropriate, it cannot inquire into matters which are within the exclusive province of one of the other branches of the Government. Lacking the judicial power given to the Judiciary, it cannot inquire into matters that are exclusively the concern of the Judiciary. Neither can it supplant the Executive in what exclusively belongs to the Executive. And the Congress, in common with all branches of the Government, must exercise its powers subject to the limitations placed by the Constitution on governmental action, more particularly in the context of this case the relevant limitations of the Bill of Rights.

The congressional power of inquiry, its range and scope, and an individual's duty in relation to it, must be viewed in proper perspective. . . . The power and the right of resistance to it are to be judged in the concrete, not on the basis of abstractions. In the present case congressional efforts to learn the extent of a nation-wide, indeed world-wide, problem have brought one of its investigating committees into the field of education. Of course, broadly viewed, inquiries cannot be made into the teaching that is pursued in any of our educational institutions. When academic teaching-freedom and its corollary learning-freedom, so essential to the well-being of the Nation, are claimed, this Court will always be on the alert against intrusion by Congress into this constitutionally protected domain. But this does not mean that the Congress is precluded from interrogating a witness merely because he is a teacher. An educational institution is not a constitutional sanctuary from inquiry into matters that may otherwise be within the constitutional legislative domain merely for the reason that inquiry is made of someone within its walls.

In the setting of this framework of constitutional history, practice and legal precedents, we turn to the particularities of this case. . . .

The Court's past cases establish sure guides to decision. Undeniably, the First Amendment in some circumstances protects an individual from being compelled to disclose his associational relationships. However, the protections of the First Amendment, unlike a proper claim of the privilege against self-incrimination under the Fifth Amendment, do not afford a witness the right to resist inquiry in all circumstances. Where First Amendment rights are asserted to bar governmental interrogation resolution of the issue always involves a balancing by the courts of the competing private and public interests at stake in the particular circumstances shown. . . .

The first question is whether this investigation was related to a valid legislative purpose, for Congress may not constitutionally require an individual to disclose his political relationships or other private affairs except in relation to such a purpose. . . .

That Congress has wide power to legislate in the field of Communist activity in this Country, and to conduct appropriate investigations in aid thereof, is hardly debatable. The existence of such power has never been questioned by this Court, and it is sufficient to say, without particularization, that Congress has enacted or considered in this field a wide range of legislative measures, not a few of which have stemmed from recommendations of the very Committee whose actions have been drawn in question here. In the last analysis this power rests on the right of self-preservation, "the ultimate value of any society," . . . Justification for its exercise in turn rests on the long and widely accepted view that the tenets of the Communist Party include the ultimate overthrow of the Government of the United States by force and violence, a view which has been given formal expression by the Congress.

On these premises, this Court in its constitutional adjudications has consistently refused to view the Communist Party as an ordinary political party, and has upheld federal legislation aimed at the Communist problem which in a different context would certainly have raised constitutional issues of the gravest character. . . . To suggest that because the Communist Party may also sponsor peaceable political reforms the constitutional issues before us should now be judged as if that Party were just an ordinary political party from the standpoint of national security, is to ask this Court to blind itself to world affairs which have determined the whole course of our national policy since the close of World War II, affairs to which Judge Learned Hand gave vivid expression in his opinion in *United States v. Dennis*, 183 F.2d 201, 213, and to the vast burdens which these conditions have entailed for the entire Nation.

We think that investigatory power in this domain is not to be denied Congress solely because the field of education is involved. Nothing in the prevailing opinions in *Sweezy* v. *New Hampshire*, supra, stands for a contrary view. The vice existing there was that the questioning of Sweezy, who had not been shown ever to have been connected with the Communist Party, as to the contents of a lecture he had given at the University of New Hampshire, and as to his connections with the Progressive Party, then on the ballot as a normal political party in some 26 States, was too far removed from the premises on which the constitutionality of the State's investigation had to depend to withstand attack under the Fourteenth Amendment. . . . This is a very different thing from inquiring into the extent to which the Communist Party has succeeded in infiltrating into our universities, or elsewhere, persons and groups committed to furthering the objective of overthrow. . . . Indeed we do not understand petitioner here to suggest that Congress in no circumstances may inquire into Communist activity in the field of education. Rather, his position is in effect that this particular investigation was aimed not at the revolutionary aspects but at the theoretical classroom discussion of communism.

In our opinion this position rests on a too constricted view of the nature of the investigatory process, and is not supported by a fair assessment of the record before us. An investigation of advocacy of or preparation for overthrow certainly embraces the right to identify a witness as a member of the Communist Party, . . . and to inquire into the various manifestations of the Party's tenets. The strict requirements of a prosecution under the Smith Act . . . are not the measure of the permissible scope of a congressional investigation into "overthrow," for of necessity the investigatory process must proceed step by step. Nor can it fairly be concluded that this investigation was directed at controlling what is being taught at our universities rather than at overthrow. The statement of the Subcommittee Chairman at the opening of the investigation evinces no such intention and so far as this record reveals nothing thereafter transpired which would justify our holding that the thrust of the investigation later changed. The record discloses considerable testimony concerning the foreign domination and revolutionary purposes and efforts of the Communist Party. That there was also testimony on the abstract philosophical level does not detract from the dominant theme of this investigation—Communist infiltration furthering the alleged ultimate purpose of overthrow. And certainly the conclusion would not be justified that the questioning of petitioner would have exceeded permissible bounds had he not shut off the Subcommittee at the threshold. . . .

Affirmed.

MR. JUSTICE BLACK, WITH WHOM THE CHIEF JUSTICE AND MR. JUSTICE DOUGLAS CONCUR, DISSENTING.

The First Amendment says in no equivocal language that Congress shall pass no law abridging freedom of speech, press, assembly or petition. The activities of this Committee, authorized by Congress, do precisely that, through exposure, obloquy and public scorn. . . . The Court does not really deny this fact but relies on a combination of three reasons for permitting the infringement: (A) The notion that despite the First Amendment's command Congress can abridge speech and association if this Court decides that the governmental interest in abridging speech is greater than an individual's interest in exercising that freedom, (B) the Government's right to "preserve itself," (C) the fact that the Committee is only after Communists or suspected Communists in this investigation.

(A) I do not agree that laws directly abridging First Amendment freedoms can be justified by a congressional or judicial balancing process. . . .

To apply the Court's balancing test under such circumstances is to read the First Amendment to say "Congress shall pass no law abridging freedom of speech, press, assembly and petition, unless Congress and the Supreme Court reach the joint conclusion that on balance the interest of the Government in stifling these freedoms is greater than the interest of the people in having them exercised." This is closely akin to the notion that neither the First Amendment nor any other provision of the Bill of Rights should be enforced unless the Court believes it is reasonable to do so. Not only does this violate the genius of our written Constitution, but it runs expressly counter to the injunction to Court and Congress made by Madison when he introduced the Bill of Rights. . . .

But even assuming what I cannot assume, that some balancing is proper in this case, I feel that the Court after stating the test ignores it completely. At most it balances the right of the Government to preserve itself, against Barenblatt's right to refrain from revealing Communist affiliations. Such a balance, however, mistakes the factors to be weighed. In the first place, it completely leaves out the real interest in Barenblatt's silence, the interest of the people as a whole in being able to join organizations, advocate causes and make political "mistakes" without later being subjected to governmental penalties for having dared to think for themselves. It is this right, the right to err politically, which keeps us strong as a Nation. For no number of laws against communism can have as much effect as the personal conviction which comes from having heard its arguments and rejected them, or from having once accepted its tenets and later recognized their worthlessness. Instead, the obloquy which results from investigations such as this not only stifles "mistakes" but prevents all but the most courageous from hazarding any views which might at some later time become disfavored. This result, whose importance cannot be overestimated, is doubly crucial when it affects the universities, on which we must largely rely for the experimentation and development of new ideas essential to our country's welfare. It is these interests of society, rather than Barenblatt's own right to silence, which I think the Court should put on the balance against the demands of the Government, if any balancing process is to be tolerated. Instead they are not mentioned, while on the other side the demands of the Government are vastly overstated and called "self preservation." It is admitted that this Committee can only seek information for the purpose of suggesting laws, and that Congress' power to make laws in the realm of speech and association is quite limited, even on the Court's test. Its interest in making such laws in the field of education, primarily a state function, is clearly narrower still. Yet the Court styles this attenuated interest self-preservation and allows it to overcome the need our country has to let us all think, speak, and associate politically as we like and without fear of reprisal. . . .

(B) Moreover, I cannot agree with the Court's notion that First Amendment freedoms must be abridged in order to "preserve" our country. That notion rests on the unarticulated premise that this Nation's security hangs upon its power to punish people because of what they think, speak or write about, or because of those with whom they associate for political purposes. The Government, in its brief, virtually admits this position when it speaks of the "communication of unlawful ideas." I challenge this premise, and deny that ideas can be proscribed under our Constitution. . . . Our Constitution assumes that the common sense of the people and their attachment to our country will enable them, after free discussion, to withstand ideas that are wrong. To say that our patriotism must be protected against false ideas by means other than these is, I think, to make a baseless charge. . . .

(C) The Court implies, however, that the ordinary rules and requirements of the Constitution do not apply because the Committee is merely after Communists and they do not constitute a political party but only a criminal gang. . . .

No matter how often or how quickly we repeat the claim that the Communist Party is not a political party, we cannot outlaw it, as a group, without endangering the liberty of all of us. The reason is not hard to find, for mixed among those aims of communism which are illegal are perfectly nor-

mal political and social goals. And muddled with its revolutionary tenets is a drive to achieve power through the ballot, if it can be done. These things necessarily make it a political party whatever other, illegal, aims it may have. . . .

The fact is that once we allow any group which has some political aims or ideas to be driven from the ballot and from the battle for men's minds because some of its members are bad and some of its tenets are illegal, no group is safe. . . .

9. *Keyishian v. Board of Regents*, 1967

Four untenured faculty members at the State University of New York, Buffalo, were not reappointed to their positions in 1962 when they refused to sign the "Feinberg Certificate," a declaration that they were not then Communists and that, had they ever been such, they had communicated that fact to the president of the university. They sued the state for having violated their First Amendment rights. In delivering the Supreme Court's opinion, briefly excerpted here, Justice William J. Brennan (1906–97) agreed to the appellants' claim that their First Amendment freedom of association had been violated by the application of vague and overbroad state laws and by an intimidating state bureaucratic machinery of enforcement. His decision overruled *Adler v. Board of Education*, 342 U.S. 485 (1951), which had allowed New York to refuse employment to teachers who were members of listed subversive organizations (X, 5).

Keyishian et al. v. Board of Regents of the University of The State of New York et al., 385 U.S., 602–4 (1966). Further reading: William A. Kaplin, *The Law of Higher Education* (San Francisco, 1983), 141–50; "Developments in the Law: Academic Freedom," *Harvard Law Review* 81 (March 1968): 1045–1159; William W. Van Alstyne, "The Specific Theory of Academic Freedom and the General Issue of Civil Liberties," *Annals of the American Academy of Political and Social Science* 404 (November 1972): 140–56; and X, 5–7.

MR. JUSTICE BRENNAN DELIVERED
THE OPINION OF THE COURT.

There can be no doubt of the legitimacy of New York's interest in protecting its education system from subversion. But "even though the governmental purpose be legitimate and substantial, that purpose cannot be pursued by means that broadly stifle fundamental personal liberties when the end can be more narrowly achieved." . . . The principle is not inapplicable because the legislation is aimed at keeping subversives out of the teaching ranks. In *De Jonge v. Oregon*, 299 U.S. 353, 365, the Court said:

> The greater the importance of safeguarding the community from incitements to the overthrow of our institutions by force and violence, the more imperative is the need to preserve inviolate the constitutional rights of free speech, free press and free assembly in order to maintain the opportunity for free political discussion, to the end that government may be responsive to the will of the people and that

changes, if desired, may be obtained by peaceful means. Therein lies the security of the Republic, the very foundation of constitutional government. . . .

Our Nation is deeply committed to safeguarding academic freedom, which is of transcendent value to all of us and not merely to the teachers concerned. That freedom is therefore a special concern of the First Amendment, which does not tolerate laws that cast a pall of orthodoxy over the classroom. "The vigilant protection of constitutional freedoms is nowhere more vital than in the community of American schools." *Shelton* v. *Tucker*, supra, at 487. The classroom is peculiarly the "marketplace of ideas." The Nation's future depends upon leaders trained through wide exposure to that robust exchange of ideas which discovers truth "out of a multitude of tongues, [rather] than through any kind of authoritative selection." . . .

We emphasize once again that "[p]recision of regulation must be the touchstone in an area so closely touching our most precious freedoms," *N. A. A. C. P.* v. *Button*, "[f]or standards of permissible statutory vagueness are strict in the area of free expression. . . . Because First Amendment freedoms need breathing space to survive, government may regulate in the area only with narrow specificity." Id., at 432–433. New York's complicated and intricate scheme plainly violates that standard. When one must guess what conduct or utterance may lose him his position, one necessarily will "steer far wider of the unlawful zone. . . ." 357 U.S. 513, 526. For "[t]he threat of sanctions may deter . . . almost as potently as the actual application of sanctions." *N. A. A. C. P.* v. *Button*, supra, at 433. The danger of that chilling effect upon the exercise of vital First Amendment rights must be guarded against by sensitive tools which clearly inform teachers what is being proscribed. . . .

The regulatory maze created by New York is wholly lacking in "terms susceptible of objective measurement." *Cramp v. Board of Public Instruction*, 368 U.S. 286. supra, at 286. It has the quality of "extraordinary ambiguity" found to be fatal to the oaths considered in Cramp and *Baggett v. Bullitt*. "[M]en of common intelligence must necessarily guess at its meaning and differ as to its application. . . ." *Baggett* v. *Bullitt*, supra, at 367. Vagueness of wording is aggravated by prolixity and profusion of statutes, regulations, and administrative machinery, and by manifold cross-references to interrelated enactments and rules.

We therefore hold that 3021 of the Education Law . . . of the Civil Service Law as implemented by the machinery created pursuant to 3022 of the Education Law are unconstitutional. . . .

The judgment of the District Court is reversed and the case is remanded for further proceedings consistent with this opinion.

Reversed and remanded.

Voices from Professors

10. Theodore Hesburgh, "The 12th Alexander Meiklejohn Award," 1970

The AAUP in 1970 gave Theodore Martin Hesburgh (1917–), C.S.C., its twelfth annual Alexander Meiklejohn Award. It came for his "sustained and stalwart efforts over the years to restate a role for Catholic higher education which places Catholic Universities squarely in the tradition of academic freedom and uninhibited intellectual inquiry." Reprinted here is a portion of Father Hesburgh's acceptance speech.

President of the University of Notre Dame du Lac for thirty-five years (1952–87), Father Hesburgh guided his institution to national academic prominence. He doubled the size of the student body and tripled the faculty. Annual operating budgets, endowment and scholarships, faculty salaries, and the entire physical plant—all increased impressively. Hesburgh's phenomenal public service brought him renown beyond academic people, alumni, and even beyond Knute Rockne's "subway alumni" football fans. His presidential appointments included membership on the U.S. Commission on Civil Rights (1958–72), the last three years as chair, and ambassadorship to the 1979 U.N. Conference on Science and Technology for Development. He received the Presidential Medal of Freedom in 1964. By 1990 he had received 121 honorary degrees, according to Guinness a record.

"The 12th Alexander Meiklejohn Award," *AAUP Bulletin* 56 (Summer 1970): 151–52. Reprinted with kind permission from the American Association of University Professors. Further reading: Theodore M. Hesburgh, C.S.C., with Jerry Reedy, *God, Country, Notre Dame* (New York, 1990), 237–45; Harold W. Attridge, "Reflections on the Mission of a Catholic University," in *The Challenge and Promise of a Catholic University*, ed. Theodore M. Hesburgh, C.S.C. (Notre Dame and London, 1994), 17–19, 23–25; Zoe Ingalls, "For God, for Country, and for Notre Dame," *Chronicle of Higher Education*, October 13, 1982, 4–7; *Texas Law Review* 66 (June 1988): 1441–80, essays by Charles E. Curran, Douglas Laychock, and Susan Waelbroeck, and Lonnie D. Kliever on academic freedom and church-affiliated universities; Tracy Schier and Cynthia Russett, eds., *Catholic Women's Colleges in America* (Baltimore, 2002); James Nuechterlein, "Athens and Jerusalem in Indiana," *American Scholar* 57 (Summer 1988): 353–68; National Catholic Conference of Bishops, www.nccbuscc.org, Mandatum, 2000, requiring Catholic theologians teaching at Catholic colleges to teach authentic Catholic doctrine; Martha C. Nussbaum, *Cultivating Humanity: A Classic Defense of Reform in Liberal Education* (Cambridge, MA, 1997), ch. 8; Alice Gallin, O.S.U., *American Catholic Higher Education: Essential Documents, 1967–1990* (Notre Dame, IN, 1992); I, 7; and XII, 9.

At the close of Vatican Council II, it seemed important to me—in another capacity as President of the International Federation of Catholic Universities—to have Catholic universities world-wide clarify their commitment to academic freedom. We began by a meeting of North American representatives at Notre Dame's retreat in Northern Wisconsin. This resulted in what has come to be known as the 1967 Land O'Lakes Statement. May I quote three short passages from that statement:

> The Catholic university today must be a university in the full modern sense of the word, with a strong commitment to and concern for academic excellence. To perform its teaching and research functions effectively, the Catholic university must have a true autonomy and academic freedom in the face of authority of whatever kind, lay or clerical, external to the academic community itself. To say this is simply to assert that institutional autonomy and academic freedom are essential conditions of life and growth and indeed of survival for Catholic universities as for all universities.
>
> In a Catholic university all recognized university areas of study are frankly and fully accepted and their internal autonomy affirmed and guaranteed. There must be no theological or philosophical imperialism; all scientific and disciplinary methods, and methodologies, must be given due honor and respect. However, there will necessarily result from the interdisciplinary discussions an awareness that there is a philosophical and theological dimension to most intellectual subjects when they are pursued far enough. Hence, in a Catholic university there will be a special interest in interdisciplinary problems and relationships.
>
> The student must come to a basic understanding of the actual world in which he lives today. This means that the intellectual campus of a Catholic university has no boundaries and no barriers. It draws knowledge and understanding from all the traditions of mankind; it explores the insights and achievements of the great men of every age; it looks to the current frontiers of advancing knowledge and brings all the results to bear relevantly on man's life today. The whole world of knowledge and ideas must be open to the student; there must be no outlawed books or subjects. Thus the student will be able to develop his own capabilities and to fulfill himself by using the intellectual resources presented to him.

Concurrently with our Wisconsin meeting, other regions of the Federation met in Paris, Bogota, and Manila, and the following summer all together for the Eighth General Conference of the Federation at Lovanium University in Kinshasa, Congo. To give you a flavor of this meeting, I shall only cite one paragraph of my presidential address:

> The university, therefore, is the very quintessence of the pilgrim Church in the intellectual order, seeking answers to ultimate questions in concert with men of intelligence and good will, drawing on all knowledges and every way of knowing and, especially, bringing every philosophical and theological insight to bear upon the monumental task at hand, whatever the source of these insights. This is no task for amateurs or dilettantes, nor for second-rate scholars or institutions less than first class. It is not a task that can be done without that intellectual climate of freedom that is the essential atmosphere of a university's research program, especially in theology. It is not something that can be accomplished in the face of arbitrary controls from outside the university's professional community of researchers and scholars.

I would like to add to all these fine words that academic freedom does not live by rhetoric alone. Each year brings its new crisis. When the battle seems newly won, hostilities break out on another front. It is not so much that freedom is fragile as that it must be won daily, and exercised daily and responsibly, by each one of us. . . .

I do not pretend to know the full answers, but I will pose the questions: (1) Are we making the best use of our academic freedom today? and (2) Is the world around us developing a climate in which our freedom within will be increasingly disrespected, threatened, diminished, and, if possible, extinguished from without? I believe that the two questions are not unrelated. In fact, if we answer the first question badly, we almost guarantee a bad answer to the second question.

As to the first, we need often to be reminded that academic freedom is not so much freedom from somebody or something, as freedom to do something, which raises the whole question of what universities should be doing today with their freedom. Alexander Meiklejohn might come back to haunt me if I did not insist here that we use our freedom to do something really creative and imaginative to reform and revivify liberal education which should be at once the guarantee and the crowning achievement of academic freedom. But beyond this urgent and general task that faces us, what of the particular use of our freedom to view our society critically and to exercise our best moral judgment on a whole host of pressing modern topics: The sacredness of human life, the dignity of man, human rights and human equality, the uses of science and technology, war and peace, violence and nonviolence, human as well as physical pollution, the quality, meaning, condition, and effectiveness of academic life, academic commitment, academic protest or protestation or, at times, posturing as we confront these vital issues which sometimes seem more important to our students than they do to us. I am not suggesting the politization of the university, but as a professional class of university men and women, do we effectively bring to our times the wisdom, the insight, the courage, and the moral judgment that should characterize our profession?

As to the second question, I would remind you that as recently as last week a majority of Americans in a CBS News nationwide poll appeared willing to cancel five of the ten guarantees of our Bill of Rights. . . .

The times call for vision and leadership to an extraordinary degree, and hope as well. The French have a saying that "fear is a poor counselor." I suppose that the obverse of that is a call to each of us to use our freedom with courage and, hopefully, with wisdom.

11. Walter Metzger, "Profession and Constitution," 1988

In a pathbreaking essay Walter P. Metzger (1922–) closely examined the emergence of academic freedom as a professional concept in America. It began at a time when universities were coming of age in the early twentieth century. Its agents were the founding members of the American Association of University Professors in 1915. Not until after World War II did a legal or constitutional concept of academic freedom arise out of an uncertain birth in several varying Supreme Court decisions. These two developments Metzger analyzes separately but comparatively. A New Yorker and a City College graduate, Metzger took his doctorate in history from the University of Iowa to return to New York City for a half-century of teaching at Columbia University (1950–2000). His research and writing concerned the history and present condition of academic freedom and tenure as he became the preeminent historian and sociologist of the academic profession in the United States, all the while working closely with committees of the AAUP. With Richard Hofstadter he collaborated on the classic work *The Development of Academic Freedom in the United States* (1955).

Walter P. Metzger, "Profession and Constitution: Two Definitions of Academic Freedom in America," *Texas Law Review* 66 (June 1988): 1265–1322. Reprinted with the permission of Walter P. Metzger and the Texas Law Review Association, which holds the Copyright © 1988. Further reading: William W. Van Alstyne, "The Constitutional Rights of Teachers and Professors," *Duke Law Journal* (1970): 841–48, and "The Specific Theory of Academic Freedom and the General Issue of Civil Liberty," in *The Concept of Academic Freedom,* ed. E. Pincoffs (Austin, TX, 1975), 59–85; Paul D. Carrington, "Freedom and Community in the Academy," *Texas Law Review* 66 (June 1988): 1577–89; David Fellman, "Academic Freedom in American Law," *Wisconsin Law Review* (1961): 3–17, reviews dozens of state cases involving teachers, finding very little on academic freedom; Walter P. Metzger, edited collections of his essays published through Arno Press: *Professors on Guard: The First AAUP Investigations*; *The Constitutional Status of Academic Tenure*; *The American Concept of Academic Freedom in Formation: A Collection of Essays and Reports*; *Reader on the Sociology of the Academic Profession* (all titles New York, 1977); "The Academic Profession in the United States," in *The Academic Profession: National, Disciplinary, and Institutional Settings,* ed. Burton R. Clark (Berkeley, CA, 1987), 123–208; "A Stroll along the New Frontiers of Academic Freedom," in *Unfettered Expression: Freedom In American Intellectual Life,* ed. Peggie J. Hollingsworth (Ann Arbor, MI, 2000), 73–97; and X, 12.

Everyone would agree that freedoms are defined by the manner in which they are defended—by the clarifying factuality of judgments rendered in specific cases that vindicate their claims and assess their limits. But the opposite is no less true: freedoms are defended by the manner in which they are defined—by images in the heads of monitors and judges that identify the persons eligible for protection, the prima facie instances of infringement, and the standards of proof for assigning blame. Convinced that the second causal nexus has not received the attention it deserves, I shall comment on how academic freedom fares solely by pondering on what academic freedom means. . . .

To retrieve those definitions, we need not backtrack very far. Clearly, the martyrology of academic freedom has a much longer history than its seminal formulations. . . . The systematic search for a definition did not effectively begin until after the Civil War and did not bear significant fruit until after the turn of the century. A review of instances in which academics have suffered for freedom's sake ranges over the entire American experience; a reconstruction of major efforts to define academic freedom faces—the less daunting prospect of covering only relatively recent times.

In this country, the quest for definitions had two supremely creative moments: one, just before the outbreak of the First World War, when the American Association of University Professors (AAUP) adapted a foreign paradigm to native professional necessities; and the other, shortly after the Second World War, when the Supreme Court rescued a liberty particular to teachers from the custom of judicial neglect and wrapped it in the protective folds of the Constitution. Each of these ventures brought forth a distinctive definition of academic freedom, and each definition was fated not only to endure but prosper.

The first definition, codified and recodified in pacts worked out by the AAUP and its administrative counterpart, the Association of American Colleges (AAC), was endorsed by most learned societies and widely incorporated into handbooks and by-laws of American colleges and universities. Far more than any other set of credenda, it has become the standard creed of the American academic profession. The second definition, applied by federal courts at every level to all sorts of expressional issues in education, has enjoyed great vitality in its short life; as a term of art or as a hovering presence, this definition of academic freedom has become a fixture in first and fourteenth amendment law. To be sure, neither definition came into being clear as crystal nor weathered the passage of time unchanged. Both require glossarists to uncover their initial meanings and historians to trace their buffetings by events. Nevertheless, each was born with premises that mirrored the distinctive concerns of its institutional progenitor and that to a remarkable degree have survived the give-and-take of negotiation and the twists and turns of adjudication. Moreover, each with its stable inner logic has guided the reasoning of its respective parent and thus has exerted a powerful influence on the results reached by the two foremost defenders of academic freedom in this land—the AAUP and the courts.

I shall call the professional definition "academic freedom (1)," the constitutional definition "academic freedom (2)," and stipulate that these run the gamut of all definitions that have really mattered, if not all that anyone in the past ever dreamed of or that someone in the future may yet invent.

We cannot escape this dual legacy, but this does not mean that we fully understand it. The realization that academic freedom has been handed down to us in two distinguishable versions is, in my opinion, far from common. Among those aware that (1) coexists with (2), some may be hard put to tell wherein they differ or may too readily assume that as time wore on their cradle marks became indistinguishable. In the pages that follow, I shall describe what I take to be the main enduring differences between the professional and the judicial definitions of academic freedom. At the outset, I should make it clear that, though I regard these definitions as seriously incompatible and probably ultimately irreconcilable, I shall not treat either of them as this teacher's pet. I accord the professional version numerical supremacy, not to assert its moral or practical supremacy, but to mark its temporal antecedence. The question of which definition is to be preferred I shall beg by trying to give each of them its due.

II. Academic Freedom (1):
The Professional Definition

An authoritative definition of academic freedom, couched in American terms, did not become crystallized in this country until 1915, when a committee of fifteen distinguished professors, chaired by the Columbia economist E.R.A. Seligman, and led by the Johns Hopkins philosopher Arthur O. Lovejoy, wrote the General Report of the Committee on Academic Freedom and Academic Tenure (1915 Report) for the nascent AAUP. This project was precipitated by the convergence of two counterposed professional developments. One was the remaking of the American academic occupation that had begun in the Gilded Age and had been completed by the high noon of the Progressive Era. This was the period in which the training of American faculty members first became highly specialized, their organization of work first became departmentalized, the pursuit of research first became incorporated into their set of roles and system of rewards. Early in this period, some had imagined that American institutions of higher learning would evolve into a handful of research centers devoted to the pick of the nation's scientists and scholars, and a multitude of undergraduate colleges served by an army of teaching dons. But that division of labor, for reasons rooted in the American academic economy, never came to pass. By the turn of the century it was unalterably decided that American universities would be multitiered and multifunctional, and that members of the American academic work force, professionally speaking, would live double lives. They would belong simultaneously to a profession-across-the-disciplines—the centuries-old entity called a "faculty" charged with institutional tutorial and service duties—and to a profession-in-a-discipline—a new or newly reorganized field of learning such as physics, engineering, or law—that promoted the advancement of knowledge and straddled the academic and nonacademic worlds. An assertive collective consciousness, rare among academics when they had been pedagogues pure and simple, took root among academics as they took on hyphenated loyalties and identities. They became imbued with prides and ambitions they had not felt before: a blossoming sense of class importance founded on the triumphs of modern science; a more insistent demand for intellectual freedom based on the needs of sustained inquiry rather than the quirks of the religious conscience; a strengthened conviction that scholarly competence should be judged only by scholarly experts, fitness to teach only by campus peers....

The Seligman committee did not start from scratch. Between 1870 and 1900, some eight thousand American college graduates had flocked to German universities for advanced instruction in a variety of disciplines,' and many had returned convinced that the Germans' concept of academic freedom held the key to their cynosure achievements and should be transplanted onto American soil....

About half the members of the Seligman committee were alumni of German universities, and those who had gone elsewhere for advanced degrees did not have to be reminded of where the concept of academic freedom, in its most imposing form, had originated. It is true that, after the turn of the century, American academics grew less and less enamored of German culture and less and less convinced that words ending with the suffix "freiheit" held transportable magic cures. But no member of this scholarly generation could write about academic freedom and ignore this memorable gift from Deutschtum. Certainly the members of the Seligman committee did not. To forge a serviceable tool for a profession caught up in a clash between its own heightened self-esteem and resilient social disrespect, they would brandish the venerable heirloom where they could and alter it only where they felt they must.

One alteration was tantamount to an amputation: on the opening page of its report, the members of the Seligman committee announced that they would dispense with the principle of Lernfreiheit.... It is hard to believe that they abandoned the German leave-them-alone philosophy because they believed in natural depravity and feared that permissiveness would let in sin. If anything, these secular social scientists and philosophers with research ambitions were less partial to the time-consuming vigilances required by in loco parentis rules, and less susceptible to the Calvinism imbedded in their culture, than most academics at that time. In all probability, their main reason for abandoning student freedom was not educational or religious but prudential.... Whatever they thought about the merits of leaving students to their own devices, the committee members must have been aware that the heavy investment in dormitories, dining halls, playing fields, social centers, and the like had created a powerful institutional interest in their reputable use and punctilious upkeep, and they may well have calculated that the AAUP had enough exhortative work to do without persuading academic landlords that a student pension did not need a watchful concierge.

Once excised from the profession's concept of academic freedom, Lernfreiheit would never be restored. Consistently, the AAUP would take issue with institutional regulations, such as discriminatory exclusions of outside speakers, that constrained the freedom of faculty and students; occasionally, it would enjoin faculty members to grant students a certain independence as a matter of professional ethics. In the late 1960s, in response to changes in law and student mood, the AAUP joined with other groups in higher education to draft a cautious magna carta of student rights. But the AAUP has never investigated a campus incident in which an alleged violation of student freedom was the sole complaint, and it has always assumed that student freedom is not an integral part of academic freedom, but is something different—and something less. . . .

By 1915, much had caused a parting of the ways: the substitution of national aptitude tests and high school diplomas for substantive college admission examinations, which prompted the retreat of the professoriate from efforts to influence the lower school's curriculum; the centralization and hierarchic reorganization of the public schools, which turned schoolteachers, faster than academics, into members of bureaucratized cadres of white-collar workers; and the formation of the AAUP itself, from its beginning a monument to the distinctness of academic professional concerns. Again, the rejects of 1915 were fated to remain such. The AAUP would gradually enlarge its criteria for membership to take in nonteaching academic professionals and teachers in community colleges on the border between higher and lower education; schoolteachers, through their own organizations, would later press academic freedom claims in court. But the organized profession would always assume that academic freedom meant freedom for the academic, never permissibly less and seldom deservedly more. . . .

Then the AAUP version of Lehrfreiheit took a novel turn. Early in their deliberations, the committee members faced the question of whether they should place academic utterances that do not relate to teaching or research and do not fall in the area of the speaker's acknowledged expertise under the protective umbrella of academic freedom. At first it seemed that the "nays" would have it. Some members, arguing in the German manner, asserted that academic freedom would lose its rationale if it were stretched to protect activities not performed in the course of professional duty. Some members thought that academic freedom could properly extend beyond the classroom and the laboratory to the public forum, but only when academics stuck to topics pertinent to their discipline. The notion that academic freedom should give speech a blanket immunity did not at first sit well with committee members who feared that professors, free to venture beyond their sciences, would be tempted to go beyond their ken. Nor did this broad definition attract those who felt it would be invidious to make academics safer than nonacademics when both were saying the same things. . . .

The final draft of the report labeled as "undesirable" any effort to debar academic scholars "from giving expression to their judgments upon controversial subjects," or to limit their public comments "to questions falling within their specialties," or to deprive them in general of "the political rights vouchsafed to every citizen." The report explicitly incorporated this opinion into the basic morphology of the subject. Academic freedom, it declared, contains not two but three components: not just freedom to teach and to inquire (the German two-part convention), but also "extramural freedom," by which it meant not freedom to speak beyond the walls, but freedom to speak without the warranty of a professional task or an acknowledged expertise. By dividing this Gaul into three main parts, the report provided in effect that academic freedom applied to a certain class of persons, no matter how they chose to express themselves, rather than to certain types of expression found in the repertory of that class. . . .

Lovejoy and company also had a deeper reason for transcending the original limits of Lehrfreiheit, a reason that went to the heart of the difference between the German academic system and their own. Nowhere in the western world was lay authority brought so deeply into the academy, or did there exist so elaborate a machinery of on-site nonacademic control, as in America. In this country, higher education was not monopolized by the state but was shared by a multitude of public and private bodies. Professors were not privileged members of a civil service but employees of the governing boards of numerous discrete enterprises. Administrators were not the chosen instruments of the faculty, but the deputies of the governing board that employed the faculty. An academic administration was not composed of a ceremonial figure called a rector, a number of deans, and a few factotums, but rather of a potentate called a president, to whom governing boards delegated much discretionary power and who had a variously sized but ever-growing bureaucracy largely under his direct command. For Seligman, Lovejoy, and the others, these facts of American academic life formed an ineluctable frame of reference, a focal point for every argument, a source of apprehensions compared with which all others shrank to minor qualms. For them, the question of how, in good logic, academic freedom could be extended across the board was inescapably rolled up in the larger question of how academic freedom in any form could be protected when professors were so far from being masters in their house.

It is instructive to note the answer the Seligman committee rejected. Nowhere in its report did the committee suggest that lay control had to be up-rooted before academic freedom could have a fighting chance. At that time, a syndicalist faction in the Association was campaigning for the reconstruction of academic governance in America along Ox-bridge or German lines. But the AAUP group commissioned to write about academic freedom did not embrace this cause. . . .

Though they remarked on the all-too-pregnable university in an all-too-predatory society, they were conspicuously silent on what might be done in a practical way to protect the one from the other. They urged no change in the financing of higher education (such as the substitution of lump-sum for line-by-line appropriations or of unrestricted for special purpose gifts) that would have put the academy more in command of its resources; they urged no structural reform (such as state constitutional amendments to ensure the operational independence of public colleges or the severance of church ties with private colleges to make them eligible for Carnegie pensions) that might have released the academy from some of its leading strings. Their reason for bypassing these issues is not mysterious: the Seligman committee, to paraphrase an epigram about the leaders of the American Revolution, could not be vitally concerned about home rule knowing what they did about who would rule at home. . . .

The overall effect of these combative images and arguments was to exalt the neutral university at the expense of the autonomous university. Although not presented in so many words in the report, this distinction was nevertheless a crucial one. In the neutral university, the governing board is a fiduciary not for one constituency but for the whole society, and not just for the society-in-being but also for the society-in-prospect a posterity that had as yet no voice. By contrast, in the autonomous university, those who govern may represent groups of like-minded supporters, but they need not (and arguably may not) assume a wider stewardship. The neutral university is obliged not to place a corporate seal of approval or disapproval on a disputed truth-claim; it is enough that the autonomous university should not be the mouthpiece of others when it elects to speak its collective mind. The neutral university may demand a high degree of institutional autonomy; the autonomous university does not require, and is free to resist, a high degree of institutional neutrality.

Accorded a central place in the conceptual defense of academic freedom, the norm of institutional neutrality was destined to have numerous implications for its practical defense as well. . . .

Although the 1915 Report did not give academic boards precise instructions on how best to steer a neutral course, the logic of its arguments showed the way. In later years, the AAUP would take the position that a university can best preserve its neutrality not by deliberately assembling a wide range of views within its faculty (in the manner of an independent newspaper that opens its editorial page to left-wing and right-wing columnists), nor by imposing evenhanded bans on faculty involvement in public controversies (in the manner of a military establishment trying to distance its officers from civilian politics), but simply by making it clear that a faculty speaker is not an institutional spokesman and expresses his own opinions and beliefs. Neutrality by disavowal of responsibility, rather than by representative sampling or nondiscriminatory gagging, would strike the organized profession as the least intrusive and therefore the most palatable approach. . . .

After the section on "principles," which preached a refurbished gospel of academic freedom to America's powerful, backward tribes, the 1915 Report outlined proper dismissal procedures in a set of "practical proposals" designed to prevent camouflaged attacks on academic freedom and to keep governing boards from undergoing merely pro forma conversions. To this end, it recommended that institutions of higher learning award faculty members tenure after a stipulated period of trial; that they dismiss tenured faculty only for adequate cause; that an intramural hearing in which a faculty member may appear in his own defense and answer specific charges precede termination for cause; and that the faculty play a judicial role in these proceedings to insure that the ultimate lay deciders are informed by professional judgments and that a president's word in a trustee's ear is not all there is to academic due process. These were not newfangled ideas: peer-run hearings to assess the suitability of academics had been known to the medieval university, and professorial appointments that continued without being affirmatively renewed had first appeared in the American colonial college. But the deliberate interlinking of the grand axioms of academic freedom with the formal details of tenure policy—a policy destined to grow ever more formalistic and detailed —was an innovation of the New World, not the Old, and was something new under the American academic sun. As time wore on, these practical proposals would spread, though not like wildfire, through the length and breadth of academe.

Thus the AAUP concocted a generically American, profession-centered, multifaceted definition of academic freedom. On these shores, by these lights, academic freedom stood for the freedom of the academic, not for the freedom of the academy. Consequently, a violation of academic freedom was seen as something that happened in a university, not something that happened to a university. In the standard plot of this kind of crime story, a dissident professor was the victim, trustees or regents (and their deputies) were the culprits, the power of dismissal was the favored weapon, the loss of employment was the awful wound. Holding to this criminology, the organized profession grew wise to the ways of the harsh employer, but it lacked a theory and vocabulary to deal with offenses against academic freedom that were not quintessentially inside jobs.

III. Academic Freedom (2): The Constitutional Definition

If my readers are wondering whether a constitutional definition of academic freedom will ever come, they are in good company: most American academics, until fairly recently, wondered too. Before the middle of this century, no American court had ruled that any provision of the federal constitution protected academic freedom. Indeed, no petitioner in any federal court appears to have framed a legal action that required the issue to be settled judicially one way or the other. With one curious exception—the 1940 asseveration of a New York Supreme Court judge that academic freedom was "the freedom to do good and not to teach evil" the term had not even achieved judicial usage or acquired a listing in Words and Phrases. Then, in the late 1940s and 1950s, the government began widespread efforts to root out allegedly subversive teachers, and a judicial response to these efforts at last put academic freedom on the constitutional map.

Why the long-abiding void? It can hardly be attributed to the concept's failure to catch fire in the academic community, for academic freedom had long enjoyed an incandescent reputation. Neither can the courts' silence be explained by a paucity of campus incidents involving academic freedom, for these became numerous with the revival of religious fundamentalism in the 1920s and even more so with the growth of radicalism in the 1930s. Nor can a generally dormant spirit of litigiousness in academe explain the silence, for professors increasingly sought legal redress on other grounds, such as breach of contract. The best explanation, in my view, lies in the lack of a promising legal theory by which to bring a violation of academic freedom, as the profession understood it, under the stern "shall nots" of the Constitution.

The Supreme Court had long before decided that the first and fourteenth amendments laid their prohibitions only against the federal government and the governments of the several states. This state-action doctrine appeared to leave academics in private colleges and universities wholly unprotected. Where the threshold of state action was clearly crossed, as it was in publicly supported institutions of higher learning, other judicially created limits on the reach of the due process clause came into play. Thus, even after the Court finally incorporated provisions of the first amendment into the fourteenth amendment, effective recourse by public employees to the free speech guarantee of the Constitution was blocked for many years by the judicial principle that public employment was not a right, but a privilege, upon which the state could place reasonable conditions, including those that restricted the exercise of constitutional rights. The reasonableness requirement did open the door to judicial review of the constitutionality of public employment practices, but the presumption that job holders held their public jobs as retractable gifts promised an unexacting scrutiny. All in all, so seldom was heard an encouraging word that academics and their attorneys apparently seldom sought and certainly never found a home for academic freedom on these jurisprudential plains. . . .

POTENTIAL WRONGDOERS

The basic truth about the first amendment is that it protects the liberties of citizens solely against actions by the state. This limited protection means that private institutions of higher learning are constitutionally incapable of committing academic freedom crimes (though not of becoming academic freedom victims). The organized profession never has and surely never will write off such a vast potential miscreancy.

In the lineup of potential wrongdoers, the state appears either as a governing power seated in the federal, state, or local lawmaking and law-enforcing institutions of the country, or as an employing authority resident in such bodies as public school boards, academic governing boards, and municipal service departments. In first amendment cases affecting teachers, the Supreme Court has tended to look with particular suspicion on the state as government—the state empowered to compel the testimony of witnesses and punish those who balk, to prescribe loyalty oaths and proscribe subversive activities, to issue commands to public agencies and induce or force private ones to obey its will. Far less has the Court been inclined to mistrust the state as employer—the state that may wrong individuals on its payroll, but cannot issue subpoenas, pass sweeping, repressive legislation, or send anyone to jail. For convenience, the more suspicious character may be called the "prime state," the less suspicious character the "agent state," to which persona may be attached the state as educator and custodian. This selective suspiciousness—call it an inclination to fear possibly coercive governments more than possibly coercive schools—was more likely to be stated as a constitutional formula by judicial conservatives, but it was not limited to one ideological camp on the court. Nor was it exhibited on only one level of the federal judiciary or only in opinions that favored the defending employer against the complaining employee. The tendency to make special allowances for the state in the second of its two guises was a pervasive bias in this field of constitutional law. And it leads to a stark comparison: the lower rank assigned to the agent state on the courts' list of academic freedom suspects not only departs from the professional ordering but inverts.

The Court's selective suspicion of the state was not adventitious, but was rooted in the language and spirit of the Constitution. The Framers of the Bill of Rights had known and sought to check the excesses of central government; the framers of the Civil War amendments had known and sought to counter the vices of state government. But neither had reached for words to thwart the tyrannous potentialities of state employers at a time when staffs for public services were minuscule and the greatest of all services, education, was mostly in private hands.

The provenance of the constitutional text and the Framers' intent were but two of the factors that impelled the Court to give rigorous expressions to its bias against the prime state after World War II. Almost without exception, the first wave of constitutional cases that carried academic freedom beyond the breakwater of judicial neglect involved punitive actions by the prime state using the agent state as its tool. For many members of the Court, these government moves were shudderingly reminiscent of the onset of totalitarianism, still vividly remembered in its Nazi version and still harshly present in its Stalinist and immediate post Stalinist forms. . . .

As it happened, no legal challenge to a faculty dismissal for disloyalty launched and consummated by the agent state wound up on the Court's calendar while it was installing the concept of academic freedom, though campus-initiated dismissals of professors because of their reputed Communist or Communist-front affiliations, or because of their refusal to disclose their affiliations, were far from uncommon occurrences at that time. . . .

By the late 1960s, a second wave of cases, mounting as the first wave subsided, impelled the Court to consider the constitutionality of purely volitional acts by the agent state. It then announced in a series of landmark decisions that, when attacks on first amendment rights are alleged, the public employer acting on its own should not be considered above suspicion. By this time, however, the breakthroughs had already occurred: the privilege-in-employment doctrine had been repudiated; academic freedom had secured a constitutional place. Furthermore, in taking cognizance of the freedom costs of wrongful discharges that did not raise issues of national security, the Court did not surrender its double standard. As we shall see, even in the second wave of purely intramural cases, the Court continued to make special allowances for the agent state. . . .

What credence should be given to the widely held belief that institutional academic freedom has not yet been admitted to the area of constitutional principles? How accurate were the statements in a leading law review that the Supreme Court as of 1982 had never held "academic freedom [to be] an institutional as well as an individual right" and that

"[a]lmost all the cases in which claims of academic freedom have arisen . . . have involved the first amendment rights of individual teachers"? My view is that these are palpable truths that have been given erroneous twists.

It is true that the Supreme Court has never given the norm of institutional neutrality a secure footing in the text of the Constitution. Though not an enumerated right, academic freedom for individuals has been linked by the Court to the freedom of speech and assembly clauses of the first amendment and to the due process clause of the fourteenth amendment. By contrast, and for a number of reasons, the Court has not given academic freedom for institutions a specific constitutional rationale. The Court has never seen fit to extend to non-natural persons the full range of Bill of Rights protections. The claim that public entities such as schools and colleges are protected by the noble bans of the first amendment contains the corollary that the agent state has constitutional rights enforceable against its creator and paymaster, the prime state—an idea that may appeal to legal sentimentalists but that is not an easy one for constitutional logicians to follow or swallow. Current efforts by legal commentators to base institutional autonomy on the pillar of "freedom of association" or on some other inferred or extrapolated collective right seem not to have had significant precursors in the years under discussion. And it may be surmised that a Court which had just engineered a constitutional revolution on behalf of the freedom of public employees had no great enthusiasm to launch another on behalf of public employers. It should be pointed out, however, that a norm without a constitutional plank is not necessarily without constitutional weight. Indeed, the removal of institutional autonomy from the intricate choreography of first amendment argument may have given it a footloose quality that increased its general influence.

Again, it is true that the vast majority of cases dealing with freedom of education and decided on first amendment grounds have concerned the rights of individuals, not institutions. But many cases in this category, though they have been labeled academic freedom cases by legal analysts, were apparently not so considered by the judges who decided them. Only rarely has the Supreme Court or the lower federal courts mentioned academic freedom when they invalidated retaliatory discharges sparked by teacher utterances critical of administrators. To the AAUP, employee-gripe cases in academe belong to the extramural freedom species, which is part of the academic freedom family. To the courts, cases of this type are deemed to belong to the broad first amendment kingdom but not to have—perhaps not to be meaningful enough to deserve—any intermediate link. With some frequency, the lower federal courts have alluded to academic freedom when they affirm the right of teachers in schools or universities to determine their own teaching style or to exert control over the course of study. More often, however, the lower courts do not mention academic freedom in such cases, while the Supreme Court has taken on such cases too infrequently to reveal its mind. All in all, the number of first amendment cases that explicitly mention academic freedom or that are in a line that links them to academic freedom cases is rather small, and of that reduced number, a considerable proportion does define academic freedom in institutional terms.

CONCLUSION

When all the pieces of this puzzle are put together, a major conclusion emerges: after the initiating period, most judges who sought to enhance the freedom of public schoolteachers and academics wielded a bare first amendment in their behalf, but the many more who believed that the values of the first amendment were overweighed by competing values, especially if they curtseyed to academic freedom, wore institutional autonomy in their heart of hearts.

It is here, I believe, that one finds the key to the deepest differences between the professional and constitutional versions of academic freedom. The professional definition subordinates the principle that academic bodies should decide things for themselves to the command that they may never collectively decide what is true or false. In the constitutional definition, institutional-neutrality plays no such commanding role. It has no bearing on private education, where the constitutional immunity of parochial schools from legal bans reinforces the proposition that governing boards are at liberty to sponsor creeds. And in public education, its place, though secure in principle, is circumscribed and fragile in fact. True, in the public sphere, the invitation to institutional partisanship implied by the free exercise of religion clause gives way to a bias against institutional partisanship instinct in the establishment clause. Here, too, the view that no government may "prescribe what shall be orthodox in politics, nationalism, religion, or other matters of opinion" was held to be a "fixed star in our constitu-

tional constellation" by one of the finest rhetoricians on the Court. Nevertheless, in the case-by-case opinionizing that gives flesh to more general rhetoric, the norm of institutional neutrality in the public sphere often barely attains scarecrow strength. In part, this is because lower as well as higher education, students as well as teachers, are in the picture. As long as academic freedom is regarded as an all-tiers, all-status, all-ages concept, the image of an educational institution as an agency of indoctrination is bound to compete powerfully with the image of it as an intellectual experiment station and as a marketplace of ideas. But more than anything else, the notion that a public educational institution should be neutral went against the grain of the principle that it should be autonomous. . . .

More complexities than have been sighted here await the intrepid analyst of the neutral norm in academic freedom law. It must suffice to conclude that the centerpiece in the constitutional definition of academic freedom is not institutional neutrality, the pivot of the professional definition, but institutional autonomy, long seen by the organized profession as a lesser good and potentially as a serious threat.

It would be comforting to believe that the professional and constitutional definitions of academic freedom repair serious shortcomings in one another, and thus jointly contribute to academic freedom's greater glory. To some extent, no doubt they do. Few would deny that academic freedom is better protected today than it was before 1951 and that one reason for this is that it gains protection through legal orders as well as the AAUP's naming-and-shaming techniques. But it would be naive to dismiss the tensions that arise between a basically internal and a basically external defense of academic freedom, or the letdowns that occur when academics bring one definition of academic freedom to a judiciary that strongly holds another. And it would be panglossian to hope that, short of radical changes in the governance of schools and colleges, these tensions and disappointments will ever cease.

Part XI   Rights of Students

The medieval university, the lineal antecedent of the modern university, was self-regulating. Like the church, the university was a sanctuary beyond the reach of civil authorities, where there were special courts for faculty and students, just as there were for the clergy. Something of this tradition persisted into modern times, and the civil authorities left responsibility for proper order to the university, just as families who sent their children off to college implicitly—and sometimes explicitly—asked the institution to assume the right and responsibility of serving *in loco parentis*. It was this lingering sense of the university as a space apart and self-governing that made summoning police onto campus so controversial during the disturbances of the 1960s.

In the second half of the twentieth century, the law has moved in seemingly paradoxical ways in relation to different aspects of privacy. Rights to privacy have been expanded, but at the same time the state has claimed significant rights to invade that realm. For example, privacy in the bedroom has been significantly increased, but so has the power of the state to intervene in family life to protect the vulnerable—abused children, for example. One sees something of the same double movement in the relations of civil society and the university. The rights of parents have been restricted and those of youth have been increased, for example, by the Buckley Amendment of 1974 (3). Yet legislatures and the courts have brought civil concerns onto campus in examining possible discrimination against protected groups, particularly in relation to decisions on admissions and promotions (V, 11; IX, 1–5). Moreover, the rule-making capacity of college authorities has been increasingly subject to judicial review in relation to considerations of First Amendment rights and those of due process (2–4; Parts IX, X). Universities, as we have already seen, have been increasingly subject to government regulations (VIII, 5–6, 8–10).

Directed by the Court and the Congress

1. *Dixon v. Alabama State Board of Education*, 1961

This is the leading case on due process for students in public higher education. During the civil rights protests in Montgomery, Alabama, several black students, who were expelled on March 3, 1960, from Alabama State College for a public lunch grill sit-in and other off-campus demonstrations, sued the Alabama State Board of Education arguing that, under the due process clause of the Fourteenth Amendment, notice and opportunity for hearing must precede dismissal of students for misconduct in a public institution. On appeal, the argument presented by Jack Greenberg and Thurgood Marshall for the National Association for Advancement of Colored People was affirmed. This majority opinion was issued by Judge Richard Taylor Rives (1895–1982) of the Fifth Circuit Court of Appeals, a court that by its repeated interpretations of the Supreme Court's general mandates in the case of *Brown v. Board of Education* (1954) directed the South toward school integration.

Dixon v. Alabama State Board of Education, 294 F. 2nd 150 (1961). Further reading: Jack Bass, *Unlikely Heroes* (New York, 1981); Harvey C. Couch, *A History of the Fifth Circuit, 1891–1981* (Washington, D.C., 1984); Frank T. Read and Lucy S. McGough, *Let Them Be Judged: The Judicial Integration of the Deep South* (Metuchen, NJ, 1978); and Harry T. Edwards and Virginia Davis Nordin, *Higher Education and the Law* (Cambridge, MA, 1979), ch. 10.

RIVES, CIRCUIT JUDGE:

The precise nature of the private interest involved in this case is the right to remain at a public institution of higher learning in which the plaintiffs were students in good standing. It requires no argument to demonstrate that education is vital and, indeed, basic to civilized society. Without sufficient education the plaintiffs would not be able to earn an adequate livelihood, to enjoy life to the fullest, or to fulfill as completely as possible the duties and responsibilities of good citizens.

There was no offer to prove that other colleges are open to the plaintiffs. If so, the plaintiffs would nonetheless be injured by the interruption of their course of studies in mid-term. It is most unlikely that a public college would accept a student expelled from another public college of the same state. Indeed, expulsion may well prejudice the student in completing his education at any other institution. Surely no one can question that the right to remain at the college in which the plaintiffs were students in good standing is an interest of extremely great value.

Turning then to the nature of the governmental power to expel the plaintiffs, it must be conceded, as was held by the district court, that that power is not unlimited and cannot be arbitrarily exercised. Admittedly, there must be some reasonable and constitutional ground for expulsion or the courts would have a duty to require reinstatement. The possibility of arbitrary action is not excluded by the existence of reasonable regulations. There may be arbitrary application of the rule to the facts of a particular case. Indeed, that result is well nigh inevitable when the Board hears only one side of the issue. In the disciplining of college students there are no considerations of immediate danger to the public, or of peril to the national security, which should prevent the Board from exercising at least the fundamental principles of fairness by giving the accused students notice of the charges and an opportunity to be heard in their own defense. Indeed, the example set by the Board in failing so to do, if not corrected by the courts, can well break the spirits of the expelled students and of others familiar with the injustice, and do inestimable harm to their education.

The district court, however, felt that it was governed by precedent, and stated that, "the courts have consistently upheld the validity of regulations that have the effect of reserving to the college the right to dismiss students at any time for any reason without divulging its reason other than its being for the general benefit of the institution." . . . With deference, we must hold that the district court has simply misinterpreted the precedents.

The language above quoted from the district court is based upon language found in 14 C.J.S. Colleges and Universities 26, p. 1360, which, in turn, is paraphrased from *Anthony* v. *Syracuse University*, 224 App.Div. 487, 231 N.Y.S. 435. . . . This case [*Anthony*], however, concerns a private university and follows the well-settled rule that the relations between a student and a private university are a matter of contract. The Anthony case held that the plaintiffs had specifically waived their rights to notice and hearing. . . . We agree with what the annotator himself says: "The cases involving suspension or expulsion of a student from a public college or university all involve the question whether the hearing given to the student was adequate. In every instance the sufficiency of the hearing was upheld." . . .

The appellees rely also upon *Lucy* v. *Adams*, D.C.N.D.Ala.1957, 134 F.Supp. 235, where Autherine Lucy was expelled from the University of Alabama without notice or hearing. That case, however, is not in point. Autherine Lucy did not raise the issue of an absence of notice or hearing. . . .

It [*People ex rel. Bluett* v. *Board of Trustees of University of Illinois*, 10 Ill. App. 2nd. 207] was not a case denying any hearing whatsoever but one passing upon the adequacy of the hearing, which provoked from Professor Warren A. Seavey of Harvard the eloquent comment:

> At this time when many are worried about dismissal from public service, when only because of the overriding need to protect the public safety is the identity of informers kept secret, when we proudly contrast the full hearings before our courts with those in the benighted countries which have no due process protection, when many of our courts are so careful in the protection of those charged with

crimes that they will not permit the use of evidence illegally obtained, our sense of justice should be outraged by denial to students of the normal safeguards. It is shocking that the officials of a state educational institution, which can function properly only if our freedoms are preserved, should not understand the elementary principles of fair play. It is equally shocking to find that a court supports them in denying to a student the protection given to a pickpocket.

Dismissal of Students: "Due Process," Warren A. Seavey, 70 Harvard Law Review 1406, 1407. We are confident that precedent as well as a most fundamental constitutional principle support our holding that due process requires notice and some opportunity for hearing before a student at a tax-supported college is expelled for misconduct.

The case before us requires something more than an informal interview with an administrative authority of the college. By its nature, a charge of misconduct, as opposed to a failure to meet the scholastic standards of the college, depends upon a collection of the facts concerning the charged misconduct, easily colored by the point of view of the witnesses. In such circumstances, a hearing which gives the Board or the administrative authorities of the college an opportunity to hear both sides in considerable detail is best suited to protect the rights of all involved. This is not to imply that a full-dress judicial hearing, with the right to cross-examine witnesses, is required. Such a hearing, with the attending publicity and disturbance of college activities, might be detrimental to the college's educational atmosphere and impractical to carry out. Nevertheless, the rudiments of an adversary proceeding may be preserved without encroaching upon the interests of the college. In the instant case, the student should be given the names of the witnesses against him and an oral or written report on the facts to which each witness testifies. He should also be given the opportunity to present to the Board, or at least to an administrative official of the college, his own defense against the charges and to produce either oral testimony or written affidavits of witnesses in his behalf. If the hearing is not before the Board directly, the results and findings of the hearing should be presented in a report open to the student's inspection. If these rudimentary elements of fair play are followed in a case of misconduct of this particular type, we feel that the requirements of due process of law will have been fulfilled.

The judgment of the district court is reversed and the cause is remanded for further proceedings consistent with this opinion.

Reversed and remanded.

2. *Healy v. James*, 1972

Student petitioners at Connecticut State College sought to form a local chapter of the Students for a Democratic Society (SDS) in September 1969. After the Student Affairs Committee of four students, three professors, and the dean of student affairs had received written statements and held hearings with the SDS students, it voted 6–2 to approve the application. President F. Don James thereupon rejected the committee's recommendation, writing that the local organization held "at least some of the major tenets of the national organization [SDS]" which "openly repudiates" the college's commitment to academic freedom. He feared that a local chapter would adopt the disruptive and violent aims and actions of the national organization, conflicting with this state-supported college's standing regulations on student rights. At the Supreme Court, Associate Justice Lewis F. Powell here ruled once more on "delicate" academic issues and judged the case on First Amendment grounds, yet he balanced a student organization's rights with the authority of their institution.

Healy et al. v. James et al. 408 U.S. 169 (1972). Further reading: William A. Kaplin, *The Law of Higher Education: Legal Implications of Administrative Decision Making* (San Francisco, 1983), 252–61.

MR. JUSTICE POWELL DELIVERED THE OPINION OF THE COURT.

As the case involves delicate issues concerning the academic community, we approach our task with special caution, recognizing the mutual interest of students, faculty members, and administrators in an environment free from disruptive interference with the educational process. We also are mindful of the equally significant interest in the widest latitude for free expression and debate consonant with the maintenance of order. Where these interests appear to compete the First Amendment, made binding on the States by the Fourteenth Amendment, strikes the required balance. . . .

At the outset we note that state colleges and universities are not enclaves immune from the sweep of the First Amendment. "It can hardly be argued that either students or teachers shed their constitutional rights to freedom of speech or expression at the schoolhouse gate." *Tinker v. Des Moines Independent School District*, 393 U.S. 503, 506 (1969). Of course, as Mr. Justice Fortas made clear in Tinker, First Amendment rights must always be applied "in light of the special characteristics of the . . . environment" in the particular case. Ibid. And, where state-operated educational institutions are involved, this Court has long recognized "the need for affirming the comprehensive authority of the States and of school officials, consistent with fundamental constitutional safeguards, to prescribe and control conduct in the schools." Id., at 507. Yet, the precedents of this Court leave no room for the view that, because of the acknowledged need for order, First Amendment protections should apply with less force on college campuses than in the community at large. Quite to the contrary, "[t]he vigilant protection of constitutional freedoms is nowhere more vital than in the community of American schools." *Shelton v. Tucker*, 364 U.S. 479, 487 (1960). The college classroom with its surrounding environs is peculiarly the "marketplace of ideas," and we break no new constitutional ground in reaffirming this Nation's dedication to safeguarding academic freedom. . . .

Among the rights protected by the First Amendment is the right of individuals to associate to further their personal beliefs. While the freedom of association is not explicitly set out in the Amendment, it has long been held to be implicit in the freedoms of speech, assembly, and petition. . . . There can be no doubt that denial of official recognition, without justification, to college organizations burdens or abridges that associational right. The primary impediment to free association flowing from nonrecognition is the denial of use of campus facilities for meetings and other appropriate purposes. The practical effect of nonrecognition was demonstrated in this case when, several days after the [Central Connecticut State College] President's decision was announced, petitioners were not allowed to hold a meeting in the campus coffee shop because they were not an approved group.

Petitioners' associational interests also were circumscribed by the denial of the use of campus bulletin boards and the school newspaper. If an organization is to remain a viable entity in a campus community in which new students enter on a regular basis, it must possess the means of communicating with these students. Moreover, the organization's ability to participate in the intellectual give and take of campus debate, and to pursue its stated purposes, is limited by denial of access to the customary media for communicating with the administration, . . . faculty members, and other students. Such impediments cannot be viewed as insubstantial. . . .

The opinions below also assumed that petitioners had the burden of showing entitlement to recognition by the College. While petitioners have not challenged the procedural requirement that they file an application in conformity with the rules of the College, they do . . . question the view of the courts below that final rejection could rest on their failure to convince the administration that their organization was unaffiliated with the National SDS. For reasons to be stated later in this opinion, we do not consider the issue of affiliation to be a controlling one. . . .

These fundamental errors—discounting the existence of a cognizable First Amendment interest and misplacing the burden of proof—require that the judgments below be reversed. But we are unable to conclude that no basis exists upon which nonrecognition might be appropriate. Indeed, based on a reasonable reading of the ambiguous facts of this case, there appears to be at least one potentially acceptable ground for a denial of recognition. Because of this ambiguous state of the record we conclude that the case should be remanded. . . .

Students for a Democratic Society, as conceded by the College and the lower courts, is loosely organized, having various factions and promoting a number of diverse social and political views, only some of which call for unlawful action. Not only did petitioners proclaim their complete independence from this organization, but they also indicated that they shared only some of the beliefs its leaders have expressed. On this record it is clear that the relationship was not an adequate ground for the denial of recognition. . . .

The mere disagreement of the President with the group's philosophy affords no reason to deny it recognition. As repugnant as these views may have been, especially to one with President James' responsibility, the mere expression of them would not justify the denial of First Amendment rights. Whether petitioners did in fact advocate a philosophy of "destruction" thus becomes immaterial. The College, acting here as the instrumentality of the State, may not restrict speech or association simply because it finds the views expressed by any group to be abhorrent. . . .

The "Student Bill of Rights" at CCSC, upon which great emphasis was placed by the President, draws precisely this distinction between advocacy and action. It purports to impose no limitations on the right of college student organizations "to examine and discuss all questions of interest to them." But it also states that students have no right (1) "to deprive others of the opportunity to speak or be heard," (2) "to invade the privacy of others," (3) "to damage the property of others," (4) "to disrupt the regular and essential operation of the college," or (5) "to interfere with the rights of others." The line between permissible speech and impermissible conduct tracks the constitutional requirement, and if there were an evidential basis to support the conclusion that CCSC-SDS posed a substantial threat of material disruption in violation of that command the President's decision should be affirmed. . . .

The record, however, offers no substantial basis for that conclusion. . . .

The College's Statement of Rights, Freedoms, and Responsibilities of Students contains, as we have seen, an explicit statement with respect to campus disruption. The regulation, carefully differentiating between advocacy and action, is a reasonable one, and petitioners have not questioned it directly. Yet their statements raise considerable question whether they intend to abide by the prohibitions contained therein. . . .

Petitioners may, if they so choose, preach the propriety of amending or even doing away with any or all campus regulations. They may not, however, undertake to flout these rules. . . . Just as in the community at large, reasonable regulations with respect to the time, the place, and the manner in which student groups conduct their speech-related . . . activities must be respected. A college administration may impose a requirement, such as may have been imposed in this case, that a group seeking official recognition affirm in advance its willingness to adhere to reasonable campus law. Such a requirement does not impose an impermissible condition on the students' associational rights. Their freedom to speak out, to assemble, or to petition for changes in school rules is in no sense infringed. It merely constitutes an agreement to conform with reasonable standards respecting conduct. This is a minimal requirement, in the interest of the entire academic community, of any group seeking the privilege of official recognition.

Petitioners have not challenged in this litigation the procedural or substantive aspects of the College's requirements governing applications for official recognition. . . . Since we do not have the terms of a specific prior affirmation rule before us, we are not called on to decide whether any particular formulation would or would not prove constitutionally acceptable. Assuming the existence of a valid rule, however, we do conclude that the benefits of participation in the internal life of the college community may be denied to any . . . group that reserves the right to violate any valid campus rules with which it disagrees.

Because respondents failed to accord due recognition to First Amendment principles, the judgments below approving respondents' denial of recognition must be reversed. Since we cannot conclude from this record that petitioners were willing to abide by reasonable campus rules and regulations, we order the case remanded for reconsideration. We note, in so holding, that the wide latitude accorded by the Constitution to the freedoms of expression and association is not without its costs in terms of the risk to the maintenance of civility and an ordered society. Indeed, this latitude often has resulted, on the campus and elsewhere, in the infringement of the rights of others. Though we deplore the tendency of some to abuse the very constitutional privileges they invoke, and although the infringement of rights of others certainly should not be tolerated, we reaffirm this Court's dedication to the principles of the Bill of Rights upon which our vigorous and free society is founded.

Reversed and remanded.

3. Family Educational Rights and Privacy Act (FERPA), Buckley Amendment, 1974

Known as the Buckley Amendment, this legislation was intended to protect the privacy of students' records and to make those records accessible only to students, the parents of dependent students, and to school employees. It was passed in the Senate as an amendment to the Higher Education Act of 1965 with no significant opposition and without Senate hearings from people in education. It specified that any recorded information created or held by a school or by a person "acting for" a school is a record, rendering null and void confidential evaluations or recommendations unless the student explicitly waives his or her rights. Moreover, requests for release of information about a student to a third party other than parents or school employees without written consent or waiver must be documented by the school, which must

also reveal that such disclosure was declined. The "noble" intention of this legislation, as supporters contended, was to allow a broad interpretation of FERPA allowing "the disciplinary process" to thwart public access to crime information. These general conditions, not specific enough to direct the myriad of American K–12 school bureaucracies, resulted in many state lower court cases and an ongoing parade of congressional amendments to the original legislation. Senator James Buckley (1923–), who sponsored FERPA, was a Yale B.A. (1943) and graduate of its law school (1949) and served one term (1971–77).

The legislation invited bureaucratic havoc in higher education. A former vice president for student affairs at the University of Oregon said, "The current FERPA Regulations are a response to an impossible task. Congress intruded into the affairs of the colleges and universities of this country without even the courtesy of discussion. . . . The uproar created throughout the country . . . is ample evidence that something is awry." Kingman Brewster, former president of Yale, considered the substance of this regulation in 1983 and found that "there appears to be no limit to legislative delegation when compliance is sought by the imposition of conditions rather than by direct regulation. . . . It is fair to say . . . that the potential for covert regulation is far more pervasive than is the incidence of direct regulation." The visible sign of faculty irritation was the posting of student grades by number to preserve privacy, not by name, as was customary. But the most troubling sign was the fate of confidential letters of recommendation from faculty members to extramural institutions or intramural peer-review correspondence. The confidentiality of these documents became suspect on the possible charge that they could harbor unfounded or ungrounded negative personal bias. The need for openness in the expression of academic opinions was held to be preferable to secrecy. Many institutions turned to redacting or blacking out parts of letters of recommendation so that under the law, aggrieved parties could consult some of what was written about them. The monitoring of this situation was left to individual institutions, absent any penalty for contravening the legislation except the withholding of federal funds, which of course were necessary to maintain the functioning of modern educational facilities.

The Family Education Rights and Privacy Act, 20 U.S.C. S.1232g (Supp. IV, 1974). Oregon quotation from Harry T. Edwards and Virginia Davis Nordin, *Higher Education and the Law* (Cambridge, MA, 1979), 760; and Kingman Brewster, "Does the Constitution Care About Coercive Federal Funding?" *Case Western Reserve Law Review* 34, no. 1 (1983): 8. Further reading: Randi M. Rothberg, "Comment," *Cardozo Women's Law Journal* 9 (2002), the best summary of amendments to the Act; *Gonzaga University v. Doe*, No. 01-679, 122 S.Ct. 2268 (June 20, 2002), in which Chief Justice Rehnquist held that "FERPA's nondisclosure provisions contain no rights-creating language, they have an aggregate, not individual focus, and they serve primarily to direct the Secretary of Education's distribution of public funds to educational institutions. They therefore create no rights enforceable under 42 U.S.C. S.1983"; and Lynn M. Daggett, "Bucking Up Buckley," *Catholic University Law Review* 46 (Spring 1997): 617–20.

1232G. FAMILY EDUCATIONAL AND PRIVACY RIGHTS

(1)(A) No funds shall be made available under any applicable program to any educational agency or institution which has a policy of denying, or which effectively prevents, the parents of students who are or have been in attendance at a school of such agency or at such institution, as the case may be, the right to inspect and review the education records of their children. . . .

(B) No funds under any applicable program shall be made available to any State educational agency (whether or not that agency is an educational agency or institution under this section) that has a policy of denying, or effectively prevents, the parents of students the right to inspect and review the education records maintained by the State educational agency on their children who are or have been in attendance at any school of an educational agency or institution that is subject to the provisions of this section.

(C) The first sentence of subparagraph (A) shall not operate to make available to students in institutions of postsecondary education the following materials:

(i) financial records of the parents of the student or any information contained therein;

(ii) confidential letters and statements of recommendation, which were placed in the education records prior to January 1, 1975, if such letters or statements are not used for purposes other than those for which they were specifically intended;

(iii) if the student has signed a waiver of the student's right of access under this subsection in accordance with subparagraph (D), confidential recommendations—

(I) respecting admission to any educational agency or institution,

(II) respecting an application for employment, and

(III) respecting the receipt of an honor or honorary recognition.

(D) A student or a person applying for admission may waive his right of access to confidential statements described in clause (iii) of subparagraph (C), except that such waiver shall apply to recommendations only if (i) the student is, upon request, notified of the names of all persons making confidential recommendations and (ii) such recommendations are used solely for the purpose for which they were specifically intended. Such waivers may not be required as a condition for admission to, receipt of financial aid from, or receipt of any other services or benefits from such agency or institution.

(2) No funds shall be made available under any applicable program to any educational agency or institution unless the parents of students who are or have been in attendance at a school of such agency or at such institution are provided an opportunity for a hearing by such agency or institution, in accordance with regulations of the Secretary, to challenge the content of such student's education records, in order to insure that the records are not inaccurate, misleading, or otherwise in violation of the privacy rights of students, and to provide an opportunity for the correction or deletion of any such inaccurate, misleading or otherwise inappropriate data contained therein and to insert into such records a written explanation of the parents respecting the content of such records.

(3) For the purposes of this section the term "educational agency or institution" means any public or private agency or institution which is the recipient of funds under any applicable program.

(4)(A) For the purposes of this section, the term "education records" means, except as may be provided otherwise in subparagraph (B), those records, files, documents, and other materials which—

(i) contain information directly related to a student; and

(ii) are maintained by an educational agency or institution or by a person acting for such agency or institution.

(B) The term "education records" does not include—

(i) records of instructional, supervisory, and administrative personnel and educational personnel ancillary thereto which are in the sole possession of the maker thereof and which are not accessible or revealed to any other person except a substitute. . . .

(5)(A) For the purposes of this section the term "directory information" relating to a student includes the following: the student's name, address, telephone listing, date and place of birth, major field of study, participation in officially recognized activities and sports, weight and height of members of athletic teams, dates of attendance, degrees and awards received, and the most recent previous educational agency or institution attended by the student.

(B) Any educational agency or institution making public directory information shall give public notice of the categories of information which it has designated as such information with respect to each student attending the institution or agency and shall allow a reasonable period of time after such notice has been given for a parent to inform the institution or agency that any or all of the information designated should not be released without the parent's prior consent.

(6) For the purposes of this section, the term "student" includes any person with respect to whom an educational agency or institution maintains education records or personally identifiable information, but does not include a person who has not been in attendance at such agency or institution. . . .

(2) No funds shall be made available under any applicable program to any educational agency or institution which has a policy or practice of releasing, or providing access to, any personally identifiable information in education records other than

directory information, or as is permitted under paragraph (1) of this subsection, unless—

(A) there is written consent from the student's parents specifying records to be released, the reasons for such release, and to whom, and with a copy of the records to be released to the student's parents and the student if desired by the parents, or

(B) except as provided in paragraph (1)(J), such information is furnished in compliance with judicial order, or pursuant to any lawfully issued subpoena, upon condition that parents and the students are notified of all such orders or subpoenas in advance of the compliance therewith by the educational institution or agency. . . .

(d) **Students' rather than parents' permission or consent**

For the purposes of this section, whenever a student has attained eighteen years of age, or is attending an institution of postsecondary education, the permission or consent required of and the rights accorded to the parents of the student shall thereafter only be required of and accorded to the student.

(e) **Informing parents or students of rights under this section**

No funds shall be made available under any applicable program to any educational agency or institution unless such agency or institution effectively informs the parents of students, or the students, if they are eighteen years of age or older, or are attending an institution of post secondary education, of the rights accorded them by this section. . . .

4. *Board of Regents of the University of Wisconsin System v. Southworth,* 2000

Brought before the Supreme Court by both litigants on First Amendment grounds, this case concerned freedom of expression for student organizations at the University of Wisconsin, Madison. There each student paid a mandatory segregated activity fee set by the university. About one-fifth of the pooled fees were apportioned by the student government to support extracurricular campus student organizations that varied widely in their ideologies and politics. Though administered by the student government, the groups were first registered and approved by the university holding a neutral position toward their purposes. Southworth was one of three respondents who identified themselves as members of conservative student organizations. Their suit against the Regents was entered on the ground that their First Amendment right had been violated when they were subjected to "compelled speech" by paying a mandatory fee that supported groups offensive to their personal beliefs.

Associate Justice Anthony Kennedy (1936–), Stanford B.A. and Harvard Law School graduate and formerly a teacher of constitutional law for over two decades at McGeorge School of Law of the University of the Pacific, delivered the unanimous decision of the Court, abbreviated here. Beyond its close examination of the respondents' First Amendment argument, the Court keyed its decision to the university's position of neutrality and to the retention of its autonomy as the setting "where the State undertakes to stimulate the whole universe of speech and ideas." The lower court's decision upholding the respondents was reversed.

Pertinent to tracing the path of academic freedom in the high court after the 1940s was the concurring opinion written by Associate Justice David Souter (1939–). Although unmentioned by the Court majority, the memorable words of earlier academic freedom cases were briefly noted by Souter. Yet he concluded that these are not controlling precedents: they yield here to a First Amendment analysis wherein they are "an important consideration."

Board of Regents of the University of Wisconsin System, Petitioner v. Scott Harold Southworth et al., 529 U.S. 217 (2000). Further reading: X, 5–10.

JUSTICE KENNEDY DELIVERED THE
OPINION OF THE COURT.

Respondents are a group of students at the University of Wisconsin. They brought a First Amendment challenge to a mandatory student activity fee imposed by petitioner Board of Regents of the University of Wisconsin and used in part by the University to support student organizations engaging in political or ideological speech. Respondents object to the speech and expression of some of the student organizations. Relying upon our precedents which protect members of unions and bar associations from being required to pay fees used for speech the members find objectionable, both the District Court and the Court of Appeals invalidated the University's student fee program. The University contends that its mandatory student activity fee and the speech which it supports are appropriate to further its educational mission.

We reverse. The First Amendment permits a public university to charge its students an activity fee used to fund a program to facilitate extracurricular student speech if the program is viewpoint neutral. . . .

The board of regents classifies the segregated fee into allocable and nonallocable portions. The nonallocable portion approximates 80% of the total fee and covers expenses such as student health services, intramural sports, debt service, and the upkeep and operations of the student union facilities. Respondents did not challenge the purposes to which the University commits the nonallocable portion of the segregated fee.

The allocable portion of the fee supports extracurricular endeavors pursued by the University's registered student organizations or RSO's [Registered Student Organizations]. To qualify for RSO status students must organize as a not-for-profit group, limit membership primarily to students, and agree to undertake activities related to student life on campus. . . . During the 1995–1996 school year, 623 groups had RSO status on the Madison campus. . . . To name but a few, RSO's included the Future Financial Gurus of America; the International Socialist Organization; the College Democrats; the College Republicans; and the American Civil Liberties Union Campus Chapter. As one would expect, the expressive activities undertaken by RSO's are diverse in range and content, from displaying posters and circulating newsletters throughout the campus, to hosting campus debates and guest speakers, and to what can best be described as political lobbying. . . .

In March 1996, respondents, each of whom attended or still attend the University's Madison campus, filed suit in the United States District Court for the Western District of Wisconsin against members of the board of regents. Respondents alleged, inter alia, that imposition of the segregated fee violated their rights of free speech, free association, and free exercise under the First Amendment. They contended the University must grant them the choice not to fund those RSO's that engage in political and ideological expression offensive to their personal beliefs. Respondents requested both injunctive and declaratory relief. On cross-motions for summary judgment, the District Court ruled in their favor, declaring the University's segregated fee program invalid. . . . The District Court decided the fee program compelled students "to support political and ideological activity with which they disagree" in violation of respondents' First Amendment rights to freedom of speech and association. . . . The court did not reach respondents' free exercise claim. The District Court's order enjoined the board of regents from using segregated fees to fund any RSO engaging in political or ideological speech. . . .

As the District Court had done, the Court of Appeals found our compelled speech precedents controlling. After examining the University's fee program, . . . it concluded that the program was not germane to the University's mission, did not further a vital policy of the University, and imposed too much of a burden on respondents' free speech rights. "[L]ike the objecting union members in Abood," the Court of Appeals reasoned, the students here have a First Amendment interest in not being compelled to contribute to an organization whose expressive activities conflict with their own personal beliefs. . . .

The case we decide here, however, does not raise the issue of the government's right, or, to be more specific, the state-controlled University's right, to use its own funds to advance a particular message. The University's whole justification for fostering the challenged expression is that it springs from the initiative of the students, who alone give it purpose and content in the course of their extracurricular endeavors. . . .

The University of Wisconsin exacts the fee at issue for the sole purpose of facilitating the free and open exchange of ideas by, and among, its students. We conclude the objecting students may insist upon certain safeguards with respect to the expressive activities which they are required to support. Our public forum cases are instructive here by close analogy. This is true even though the student activities fund is not a public forum in the traditional sense of the term and despite the circumstance that those cases most often involve a demand for access, not a claim to be exempt from supporting speech. . . . The standard of viewpoint neutrality found in the public forum cases provides the standard we find controlling. We decide that the viewpoint neutrality requirement of the University program is in general sufficient to protect the rights of the objecting students. . . .

We must begin by recognizing that the complaining students are being required to pay fees which are subsidies for speech they find objectionable, even offensive. The *Abood* and *Keller* cases, then, provide the beginning point for our analysis. *Abood* v. *Detroit Bd. of Ed.*, 431 U.S. 209 (1977); *Keller* v. *State Bar of Cal.*, 496 U.S. 1 (1990). While those precedents identify the interests of the protesting students, the means of implementing First Amendment protections adopted in those decisions are neither applicable nor workable in the context of extracurricular student speech at a university. . . .

The proposition that students who attend the University cannot be required to pay subsidies for the speech of other students without some First Amendment protection follows from the *Abood* and *Keller* cases. Students enroll in public universities to seek fulfillment of their personal aspirations and of their own potential. If the University conditions the opportunity to receive a college education, an opportunity comparable in importance to joining a labor union or bar association, on an agreement to support objectionable, extracurricular expression by other students, the rights acknowledged in *Abood* and *Keller* become implicated. It infringes on the speech and beliefs of the individual to be required, by this mandatory student activity fee program, to pay subsidies for the objectionable speech of others without any recognition of the State's corresponding duty to him or her. Yet recognition must be given as well to the important and substantial purposes of the University, which seeks to facilitate a wide range of speech.

In *Abood* and *Keller* the constitutional rule took the form of limiting the required subsidy to speech germane to the purposes of the union or bar association. The standard of germane speech as applied to student speech at a university is unworkable, however, and gives insufficient protection both to the objecting students and to the University program itself. . . . If it is difficult to define germane speech with ease or precision where a union or bar association is the party, the standard becomes all the more unmanageable in the public university setting, particularly where the State undertakes to stimulate the whole universe of speech and ideas.

The speech the University seeks to encourage in the program before us is distinguished not by discernable limits but by its vast, unexplored bounds. To insist upon asking what speech is germane would be contrary to the very goal the University seeks to pursue. It is not for the Court to say what is or is not germane to the ideas to be pursued in an institution of higher learning.

Just as the vast extent of permitted expression makes the test of germane speech inappropriate for intervention, so too does it underscore the high potential for intrusion on the First Amendment rights of the objecting students. It is all but inevitable that the fees will result in subsidies to speech which some students find objectionable and offensive to their personal beliefs. If the standard of germane speech is inapplicable, then, it might be argued the remedy is to allow each student to list those causes which he or she will or will not support. If a university decided that its students' First Amendment interests were better protected by some type of optional or refund system it would be free to do so. We decline to impose a system of that sort as a constitutional requirement, however. The restriction could be so disruptive and expensive that the program to support extracurricular speech would be ineffective. The First Amendment does not require the University to put the program at risk.

The University may determine that its mission is well served if students have the means to engage in dynamic discussions of philosophical, religious, scientific, social, and political subjects in their extracurricular campus life outside the lecture hall. If the University reaches this conclusion, it is entitled to impose a mandatory fee to sustain an open dialogue to these ends.

The University must provide some protection to its students' First Amendment interests, however. The proper measure, and the principal standard of protection for objecting students, we conclude, is the requirement of viewpoint neutrality in the allocation of funding support. . . .

The parties have stipulated that the program the University has developed to stimulate extracurricular student expression respects the principle of viewpoint neutrality. If the stipulation is to continue to control the case, the University's program in its basic structure must be found consistent with the First Amendment.

We make no distinction between campus activities and the off-campus expressive activities of objectionable RSO's. Those activities, respondents tell us, often bear no relationship to the University's reason for imposing the segregated fee in the first instance, to foster vibrant campus debate among students. If the University shares those concerns, it is free to enact viewpoint neutral rules restricting off-campus travel or other expenditures by RSO's, for it may create what is tantamount to a limited public forum if the principles of viewpoint neutrality are respected. . . . We find no principled way, however, to impose upon the University, as a constitutional matter, a requirement to adopt geographic or spatial restrictions as a condition for RSOs' entitlement to reimbursement. Universities possess significant interests in encouraging students to take advantage of the social, civic, cultural, and religious opportunities available in surrounding communities and throughout the country. Universities, like all of society, are finding that traditional conceptions of territorial boundaries are difficult to insist upon in an age marked by revolutionary changes in communications, information transfer, and the means of discourse. If the rule of viewpoint neutrality is respected, our holding affords the University latitude to adjust its extracurricular student speech program to accommodate these advances and opportunities.

Our decision ought not to be taken to imply that in other instances the University, its agents or employees, or—of particular importance—its faculty, are subject to the First Amendment analysis which controls in this case. Where the University speaks, either in its own name through its regents or officers, or in myriad other ways through its diverse faculties, the analysis likely would be altogether different. . . .

The judgment of the Court of Appeals is reversed, and the case is remanded for further proceedings consistent with this opinion. In this Court the parties shall bear their own costs.

It is so ordered.

CONTEXT

Academic leadership is exceptionally complex. Contemporary institutions of higher education are unquestionably hierarchical institutions, yet there is a long history of more democratic institutional governance that cannot be ignored. If corporate styles of management in higher education are increasingly evident, collaboration and participatory decision-making are values strongly held by the key personnel. Indeed, according to rulings of the National Labor Relations Board, the faculty in private universities are considered to be management and thus not labor and not eligible for the protection of the Board, though few faculty at the end of the twentieth century consider themselves so empowered (VI, 12). Universities are unusual institutions in that they employ professionals whose special knowledge is not fully accessible to management, or often even to their closest colleagues—and they are hired for that very reason.

But leading the faculty was only part of the challenge faced by the late twentieth-century college or university president. Leaders have multiple constituencies beyond the faculty—trustees, donors or legislatures, students, parents, alumnae, professional and nonprofessional staff, local civic and business leaders, unions, and more. In addition, most of the subordinate academic administrators with whom they must work—particularly the crucially important department chairs—have no particular training in management. Their training is as scholars, scientists, and teachers. More often than not, the president of a university has a similar background, albeit usually supplemented with fairly long service as a chair, as head of an institute, or as dean or provost. Yet the major research universities they lead are almost always among the largest corporations in their own cities. Even in New York City, the center of the American economy, both New York University and Columbia University are among the five largest private employers (1–3).

Why do men and women take on this challenge? Surely part of it is a strong belief in the importance of the institution and a sense that what happens there is of some larger significance to the local and wider community. There is also the appeal of power, however fractured it may be. There is the satisfaction of having the resources, financial and otherwise, to make something happen, something that enriches the usefulness of the institution to its various constituencies and the general society. University leadership depends upon and requires a sense of responsibility for the institution and for affairs "beyond the ivory tower," to use Derek Bok's phrase (4–8). To some, although less so than in the past, it is a civic platform, a "bully pulpit" (9).

As in other major American institutions, white males have historically held the highest offices in institutions of higher education. And except for a select group of women's colleges, the more distinguished the college or university, the more common that pattern of leadership. By the last decade of the twentieth century, there was a sprinkling of African-American presidents of major interracial colleges and universities, both public and private, and as of this writing, women, one of them African-American, lead four Ivy League institutions. But, as Nannerl Keohane, herself the extremely successful president of a leading research university, notes, "milestones still remain" (10).

Over the course of decades following the generation of James B. Conant at Harvard or Robert Maynard Hutchins at Chicago there arose a chorus of despair about the retreat of such university leaders from civic life. Going back to the era of the Civil War and to Harvard's President Eliot there was a line of university presidents as public figures. Is it a problem that we see no successors to this role among present university presidents? If so, is the issue one of less capable individuals in the positions? Or is it the changed place of the institution in our society? Has public faith in higher education declined—beyond its credentialing role—to the degree that a presidency is not much of a civic platform? Has the job changed in ways that constrain the president who would be inclined to speak out on issues that matter in American civic life and beyond? In fact, the job has indeed changed in ways that reduce the civic presidency of the past. The scale has changed; the president of a major research university manages one of the largest institutions in contemporary America. That generally leaves little time for the expression of compelling insights into the challenges facing the larger society. Related and equally important, the extraordinary and increasing financial needs of these gigantic nonprofit institutions in the past half-century have required constant fundraising. No president can risk antagonizing those to whom he or she must go for those vital funds—whether a state legislature or foundations or private donors. Together, these aspects of their managerial and fundraising responsibilities have taken university presidents away from the very special culture of the community of learners on whose behalf they labor.

In the end, therefore, we have to acknowledge that university presidents as public figures were the products of a specific historical moment, lasting perhaps half a century, that is unlikely to be seen again. Of course, such a view entails the hard work of defining their role for the twenty-first century, no mean challenge (11).

Management

1. Samuel P. Capen, *The Management of Universities,* 1953

Literature on the twentieth-century American college and university presidency is rather large but until the 1960s, with the exception of some notable biographies and autobiographies, it was rather fragmentary. The part of presidential work that was "management" led after World War II to more studies and organizations devoted to educational administration. One of the first books of this type to accent management was a group of essays written by Samuel Paul Capen (1878–1956). Capen was the first director of the American Council of Education (1919–22), a post that led to his becoming chancellor of the University of Buffalo in an exceptional tenure of 28 years (1922–50), marked by strong campus leadership, active participation in civic and regional affairs, and steady commitment to national agencies of higher education.

Though he came of age in the years that initiated managerial "efficiency" in many fields (often tinged with a certain Darwinist ruthlessness), Capen was still a blend of the old-style college president and the newer university administrator. He was the son of a clergyman-president of Tufts College and the husband of the daughter of Carroll D. Wright, first president of Clark University. At Tufts he received his undergraduate and master's degrees (1898) and he got another M.A. at Harvard. His was a college world. He studied at Leipzig (1901–2), earned his Ph.D. at Pennsylvania (1902), and took his first teaching position at Clark (1902–14) in modern languages.

Samuel P. Capen, "Who Should Manage Universities and How?" paper read at the Thursday Club of Buffalo on January 13, 1949, in *The Management of Universities* (Buffalo, NY, 1953), ch. 1. Further reading: Edgar W. Knight, *What College Presidents Say* (Chapel Hill, NC, 1940); John S. Brubacher and Willis Rudy, *Higher Education in Transition,* 3rd ed. (New York, 1976), ch. 17; Walter Crosby Eells and Ernest V. Hollis, "The College Presidency, 1900–1960: An Annotated Bibliography," in *Office of Education Bulletin,* no. 9 (Washington, D.C., 1961); and XII, 2–3.

It should be obvious, it should always have been obvious, that a president cannot make a university and that a board cannot make a university. Either a president or a board can unmake one, however, in a very few months; and many presidents and boards, jointly or severally, have done just that. The only people who can make a university are the professors. But a faculty of cowed professors can only make a rabbit hutch.

In the bright heyday of presidential and board malpractice, it took both constructive wisdom and exceptional courage for a group of the leading professors of the country to band together for the purpose of asserting these self-evident truths. The American Association of University Professors was organized thirty-four years ago this month with the announced objects of promoting the interests of higher education and research, and advancing the standards and ideals of the profession. The first standing committee that the Association created was one on academic freedom and tenure, which included such eminent figures as Seligman of Columbia, Roscoe Pound of Harvard, Ely of Wisconsin, Farnam of Yale and Lovejoy of Johns Hopkins. These gentlemen submitted to the Association a Declaration of Principles culminating in a set of Practical Proposals to Boards of Trustees which is rightly regarded as an educational classic.

But the committee did not stop there. It agreed to investigate the case of any teacher who claimed to have been dismissed because of his opinions or in violation of his legitimate expectations of tenure. The committee's long series of investigations have been for the most part both searching and judicial in character. In case after case its reports have not only exposed to public view the indisputable facts of the unjust treatment of teachers, but have also recommended specific changes in institutional by-laws designed to safeguard freedom of expression and to define tenure rights. Several famous institutions were involved in the earliest of these investigations, to the great embarrassment of their governing authorities. Indeed, a visitation by the emissaries of the Association has been at any time about as welcome to presidents and boards as a plague of locusts. I believe no institution has ever provoked a second call.

In the course of the years, with no other weapons than the high standing of its investigators and the power of the printed word, the Association has succeeded in securing widespread, although unfortunately not universal, acceptance of the principles of freedom and tenure which it has advocated. Other educational associations composed of college and university presidents have twice collaborated with it in formulating joint statements of these principles. The by-laws of scores of institutions have now been amended to incorporate them.

This is truly an epoch-making achievement. As a bulwark of the evolving American university its importance cannot be overestimated. Quietly and slowly a revolution has been wrought in the distribution of prerogatives among the component elements of the university. I do not mean to say that the cause of academic freedom has won a permanent triumph. The price of liberty in this sphere, as in others, is still eternal vigilance. . . .

There are, and there have been for a long time, a number of enlightened boards of trustees. If their practices had been the rule rather than the exception, the organized professors would have had small cause for harping on the need for formal changes in the scheme of management. These boards have recognized that their first and most important function is to conserve and increase the university's property and to make certain that its income is used most wisely for the support and improvement of its educational service. They have recognized that this function will absorb the greater part of the time and thought they can devote to the university's affairs.

They have recognized that they stand in a completely different relation to the teaching staff from that of the directors of a business corporation to its employees; that the teachers are in fact, if not in law, partners in a joint enterprise; that to the teachers should be delegated the entire management of the educational process and that thereafter the delegating body should not interfere in this phase of institutional operations. They have recognized a clear obligation to define by statute the spheres of authority assigned to administrative officers and to faculties, together with all conditions of tenure. They have recognized that although they are the legal custodians of an instrument vital to the public welfare and consequently must finally decide how that instrument shall serve the public, nevertheless, in reaching a decision on any major institutional policy which is not strictly financial, they should seek the advice of their expert associates. Actually these enlightened boards long ago either incorporated in their by-laws or established as accepted institutional traditions most of the specific propositions of the Professors' Association.

Most but not all. Three of the forms of faculty participation in university government which the professors propose have rarely been authorized by any boards, enlightened or unenlightened.

In only a handful of instances has a board allowed an official faculty committee to share in the preparation of the university budget or to participate in any other decision relating to overall financial policy. In my view no board that has ever done so deserves to be called enlightened; and for a very simple reason. No faculty committee can divest itself of a special partisan interest in decisions involving either budgetary allotments or capital expenditures for new developments. Such decisions should be made by persons as nearly neutral to all special interests as possible. On this matter the position of the Professors' Association is untenable, according to any rational standards of administration. Few institutions have set up consulting committees of the faculty authorized to confer directly with the board on matters of general institutional policy. Nevertheless, I believe that this device is generally fruitful and should be much more widely adopted.

Still fewer institutions have ever provided for the attendance of official faculty representatives at board meetings, either as board members or in the guise of watch and ward committees. In my opinion the sole possible gain from such a provision is to allay faculty suspicion of the board, if the faculty happens to cherish suspicion. In every other respect this type of participation in institutional control has been where tried, and would always be, quite meaningless although relatively innocuous.

Suspicion of boards has been, as we know, often justified. But after all it is not boards that faculties now worry about chiefly. In the official pronouncements of the Professors' Association the board, since it has the ultimate power, appears, I believe, as a kind of stalking horse. The president is the actual target aimed at.

How to get a good president; how to keep him in his place once he is acquired; how to get some good out of him, and no damage: these are the really tough problems of current university government. Naturally they bulk larger in the minds of the teachers than in the minds of board members, because of the factor of propinquity, and because teachers are constantly on the receiving end of the president's ministrations.

The spokesmen of the professors object to the conditions now typically surrounding the presidential office and appertaining thereto on these general grounds: Too much power is assigned to it. The incumbent receives too much prominence and unearned public honor. There is no assurance that the incumbent will feel an obligation of loyalty to the faculty as well as to the board. The faculty is too seldom granted a voice in the choice of the incumbent.

Such conditions, they believe, induce certain occupational diseases to which presidents seem rarely to develop immunity. The most serious of these afflictions are several forms of the Jehovah complex: to wit, an indisposition to confer with associates before arriving at decisions, impatience with opposition, the delusion of infallibility, an increasingly virulent dictatorial tendency, ostentation, and a repulsive personal vanity. And these maladies are too often accompanied by another pathetic disability, which should be classed as a congenital defect rather than as an occupational disease, namely, incapacity for genuine educational leadership.

Assuming that the professors are right on these points—and my observation agrees with theirs—what can be done about it? Presidents cannot be abolished, however devoutly one might wish that consummation. They represent not only a natural outgrowth of forces inherent in the structure of universities, but they have come over the years to perform functions necessary to the adaptation of the university organism to its total environment which can be performed by no other agent or agency yet imagined.

These functions are so miscellaneous that no one can perform them all well. There never has been a perfect president, nor one universally acceptable. There have been a few—a very few—great presidents. Practically all of them are dead. In this respect great presidents resemble good Indians.

But if perfection cannot be expected, how may universities get a better break more often? Not I am sure, by any legislation that a board could frame, beyond the kinds of legislation already referred to. Indeed, I can think of only two ways to improve the chances of securing a satisfactory administrative head. First, every board should provide that the nomination of the president shall be entrusted jointly to elected representatives of the faculty and a committee of the trustees. Second, boards should acquire clearer ideas than many of them seem to have of what are the most essential parts of the modern university head's job, and of the qualities of mind and character which these activities demand.

I will confess that I do not know just how these ideas can be spread more widely among the hundreds of American boards of trustees. Faculty committees, if allowed to participate in the selection of the president, may perhaps help to disseminate them. And perhaps more persons who have had an opportunity to study the presidency at close quarters should make more public statements about the chief obligations of that office. If there were enough such statements, the news might get around.

I will close, therefore, by following my own suggestion and will give you in one very long sentence my conception of the proper role of the contemporary university president. To coordinate for the accomplishment of common purposes the efforts of many persons, each more learned in some direction than himself; to be sympathetic toward both people and ideas; to weigh proposals and to bring to bear upon them the critical judgement of many minds; to try to preserve a just balance among the institution's several commitments; to plan, but to submit all plans to democratic ratification; to initiate action, but not to force it until it receives majority consent; to choose, with the advice of academic colleagues, officers of instruction and administration who give promise of growth in wisdom and productivity and power to inspire the young; to be the defender of freedom for teachers and students against all attacks from without or within the institution; to persuade rather than to command; to lead, if God gives him the grace to lead, but never to boss.

Who should manage universities? Boards and presidents and faculties jointly. And how? By both formal and informal cooperation, and in a spirit of mutual confidence and respect.

2. Michael D. Cohen and James G. Marsh, *Leadership and Ambiguity*, 1974

After studying the activities of forty-two college and university presidents, the authors of this widely cited volume concluded that presidents operate in a realm of ambiguities and head institutions that are "organized anarchies." James G. Marsh (1928–) taught at the Carnegie Institute of Technology (1953–64) and at the University of California, Irvine (1964–70) before moving to Stanford as a professor of management, higher education, political science, and sociology. Michael D. Cohen (1945–), his student at Irvine, is a professor of political science at the University of Michigan.

Reprinted by permission of Harvard Business School Press. From *Leadership and Ambiguity: The American College President* by Michael D. Cohen and James G. Marsh. (Boston, MA, 1974): 37–40, 79, 147–49, 151–52. Copyright © 1974 by the Harvard Business School Publishing Corporation; all rights reserved. Further reading: William K. Selden, "How Long is a College President?"

Liberal Education 46 (March 1960): 5–15; Nicholas J. Demerath, Richard W. Stephens, and R. Robb Taylor, *Power, Presidents, and Professors* (New York, 1967); Harold L. Hodgkinson, *College Governance: The Amazing Thing Is that It Works at All* (Washington, D.C., 1971), 12–22, with a useful bibliography on college and university governance; Harold L. Hodgkinson and L. Richard Meeth, eds., *Power and Authority* (San Francisco, 1971); Joseph F. Kauffman, *At the Pleasure of the Board: The Service of the College and University President* (Washington, D.C., 1980); George Keller, *Academic Strategy: The Management Revolution in American Higher Education* (Baltimore, 1983); Judith Block McLaughlin and David Riesman, "The President: A Precarious Perch," in *Higher Learning in America, 1980–2000*, ed. Arthur Levine (Baltimore, 1983), ch. 11; and XII, 3.

It is now commonplace to observe that a president who attempts to run a political system as though it were a bureaucracy is likely to do poorly. Like so many commonplace observations, it is true. It is also true that a president who attempts to run a consensus system or an anarchy as though it were a political system will make a mess of it. Moreover, we think that this latter proposition is closer to what is likely to happen in many contemporary American universities.

The general point, of course, is that the model one has of the system of governance dictates a presidential style. The appropriateness of the style, however, is determined by the adequacy of the model.

Each of our metaphors implicitly prescribes a role for the president of a university:

Metaphor	Presidential role
Competitive market	The college president is an entrepreneur. He may establish any kind of organization he wishes within the constraints imposed by the willingness of students, faculty, donors, and legislators to take their support elsewhere.
Administration	College presidents are appointed by the trustees to pursue the objectives specified by the board and are evaluated in terms of the performance of the organization with respect to those objectives. The major tasks of the president involve controlling the operation to ensure conformity with the objectives, coordinating the several subunits toward that end, assuring consistency within the organization, and avoiding duplication of activities and waste.
Collective bargaining	The college president does two things: First, he attempts to mediate disputes between the interests in the university and help them to find mutually satisfactory agreements. In this activity, he is a facilitator of compromise or invention. Second, he supervises the implementation of the agreements, serving each of the interests to the degree specified by the bargaining outcomes.

Democracy	The college president sees himself as a hypothetical candidate for the office and offers promises of policy action in exchange for promises of support. His objective is to maintain a winning coalition of interest groups by responding to their demands for university policy.
Consensus	The presidential role involves three major activities: the management of the agendas, the public solicitation of consensus, and the implementation of agreements. The president responds to demands by placing them on the agenda for discussion, by inducing a discussion of them, and by implementing them if they survive the discussion.
Anarchy	The president is a catalyst. He gains his influence by understanding the operation of the system and by inventing viable solutions that accomplish his objectives rather than by choosing among conflicting alternatives. "Management" in an anarchy involves the substitution of knowledge and subtle adjustment for the explicit authoritative control of bureaucracy.
Independent judiciary	The college president is not expected to reflect or adjust to the demands of a current set of actors, consumers, constituents, owners, or employees. Rather, he is expected to capture the historic truths of the university as an institution and to reflect those truths during a brief trusteeship.
Plebiscitary autocracy	The president is a decision maker and organizer of opinion. Such consultation or assistance as he uses is simply a convenience to him and imposes no obligation to him to follow the advice. He acts on the objectives as he sees them and subsequently attempts to persuade his constituency that his rule should be continued.

When we survey the leadership roles demanded by the different models, we are struck by some important ways in which the roles associated with familiar metaphors of university governance differ from the roles associated with relatively unfamiliar metaphors. On the whole, the literature of organizations and administration provides a firmer ideological and technical base for the metaphors of administration (manager), democracy (politician), collective bargaining (mediator), and consensus (chairman) than it does for the metaphors of the competitive market (entrepreneur), anarchy (catalyst), independent judiciary (judge), or plebiscitary autocracy (philosopher-king).

What particularly distinguishes these two sets of roles are, we believe, two important things:

1. The extent to which the roles are seen as reactive to demands of others (as in the familiar metaphors) rather than as initiating ideas and structures (as in the unfamiliar metaphors).

2. The extent to which the roles are seen as re-quiring a relatively continuous public posture (as in the familiar metaphors) rather than a somewhat more remote posture (as in the unfamiliar metaphors).

The relationship is not perfect, and one might question the relatively arbitrary attention to organizational-administrative traditions in the literature to the exclusion of the strong entrepreneurial—competitive market traditions of the literature in microeconomics and organizational economics or the strong judicial traditions of the literature in jurisprudence. We believe that the dominant models of organizations likely to affect normatively conventional views of university leadership are those of bureaucratic administration, collective bargaining, consensus formation, and democratic politics. This is particularly true within the academic subculture from which presidents are drawn.

If college presidents accept conventional management wisdom, they will think of universities as systems of administration, collective bargaining, political democracy, consensus formation, or some combination of those metaphors. They will think of themselves as administrators, mediators, political leaders, neighborhood chairmen, or some combination of these roles. Given the processes of movement to the presidency . . . we would be surprised if presidents had substantially unconventional views of organizations and organizational leadership. As we shall see . . . they do not.

If our analysis is correct, however, these conventional views will make university leadership less effective than it might be. The technical requirements for behavior in such roles seem likely to be missing in most colleges and universities much of the time. The logic of bureaucracy is the specification of objectives and technology. The logic of democracy is the organization of consent. The logic of collective bargaining is the discipline of conflict. The realities of higher education seem to be resistant to all three logics. . . .

A perceptive president is likely to be uncomfortable with his own characterization of the role. He is likely to feel that the metaphors of leadership fit the realities of his position rather poorly. Although we can identify processes familiar from markets, bureaucracies, and political democracies in colleges, none of those models seem to capture fully the character of higher educational institutions and their governance. However, uncertainty and discomfort do not necessarily lead to rejection of the conventional models. There is ample room for the ambiguous events of modern university life in almost any set of beliefs that might become accepted among presidents or students of the presidency. There is ample room in the presidential suite for a substantial separation of intellectual constructs from the everyday actions of presidential life. There is ample room in any man's pride for a commitment to heroic role requirements. . . .

These data on the ways college presidents spend their time suggest that the allocation of time on the job is regulated by six major factors:

1. *The size of the school* Presidents in relatively large schools develop a style that is both somewhat more "local" to the college and somewhat less personal. They see their job in somewhat more authoritarian and somewhat more academic terms. Presidents in relatively smaller schools use a style that is oriented less to the internal operation of the school and is somewhat more personal. They see their job in somewhat more mediative and in somewhat less academic terms.

2. *A daily and weekly cycle* Presidents do administration first in the day and first in the week, switch to their external roles later in the day and later in the week, and reserve their time increasingly for "political" activities as the day draws into the evening and the week draws into the weekend.

3. *General expectations within the culture* Presidents work a normal workweek that is approximately the same as that reported by faculty members. The structure of their workweek depends heavily on the initiations of others.

4. *Role expectations of presidents* Presidents expect (and feel that others expect of them) that they will be administrators, politicians, and entrepreneurs. They divide their time more or less equally among the roles. Presidents, and the others around them, expect presidents to perform the royal functions of hearing petitions, granting formal assent, and confirming positions.

5. *The ambiguity of the job* Neither presidents nor the people around them have much idea about the relationship between success and presidential behavior. Unable to point to serious attributes of success, they learn to point to attributes of "effort."

6. *The pleasures of presidents* Presidents generally enjoy and seek out the emotional perquisites and the acknowledgment of office. This phenomenon directly affects the overall pattern of time allocation by the president.

The result of the operation of these factors is a familiarly inextricable combination of "myth" and "reality." The objective situation of presidents is largely built on the beliefs they bring to the job and share with their associates. Those beliefs are not exotic. The utilization of time by presidents is not bizarre. It stems from a series of daily and hourly judgments that are individually unspectacular and mostly unexceptionable. Yet, most presidents and most observers of the presidency are unhappy with the overall allocation of time that results. . . .

In part, the college president has difficulty saying "no" because he has no normatively legitimate basis for substituting his judgment on the way his time should be allocated for the pattern of expectations among his colleagues and contacts. As we have said repeatedly, the university is an organization that does not know what it is doing. Its goals are ambiguous and its technology obscure. As a result, there is no way that a president can demonstrate, either to others or to himself, that an alternative pattern of attention would (or did) result in improved performance.

We believe that the workload and the distribution of that workload among contacts, among styles of activities, and among places reflects the predominately social specifications of the job. Presidents work hard. Many of them are tired. Many of them report the inordinate demands on their time. Few of them ask why they accept the demands. Few of them act decisively to eliminate the demands. They seem to believe that the presidential report card has two components: effort and performance. Performance is largely an act of God or at least not clearly under the control of the president. If the president works hard, he may still face a financial, student, or faculty catastrophe. But if he doesn't work hard, he will be treated as a failure in any event. . . .

The college president is an executive who does not know exactly what he should be doing and does not have much confidence that he can do anything important anyway. His job is the pinnacle of his success, and he has been—by the standards of most of his contemporaries and colleagues—a quite successful person. Consciously or not, presidents organize their time in such a way as to maintain a sense of personal competence and importance in a situation in which that is potentially rather difficult. They make themselves available to a large number of people whose primary claim is simply that they want to see the "president." Counter to most other evidence, such interactions remind the president that he is the boss. Similarly, presidents preside over otherwise largely pointless meetings, for the process of presiding involves a subtle reassertion of primacy.

We also believe that presidents work long hours in large part because they enjoy them. . . . College presidents work long hours because they are successful, not the other way around. . . .

Most presidents would prefer a slightly—even substantially—different world, but not at the cost of undermining their own conceptions of themselves as competent and important individuals. If we wish to change the pattern of activities by presidents, we will need to change the orientation presidents have to their jobs, themselves, and the relationship between the two. We will need to define some reasonable expectations by associates. Without such changes, the time demands on presidents in the future will be as they have been in the past, largely independent of the problems they face or the help they have.

3. Clark Kerr and Marian L. Gade,
The Many Lives of Academic Presidents, 1986

Among the many studies of higher education directed or written by Clark Kerr, this examination with Marian Gade of the American college and university presidency became the foremost study of the subject. It was built around some eight hundred earlier interviews with presidents and their associates that had produced the preceding volume, *Presidents Make a Difference: Strengthening Leadership in Colleges and Universities* (Washington, D.C., 1984). This sequel volume departs from the findings of Cohen and Marsh in 1974 (2). Marian L. Gade was for many years a research associate to Clark Kerr, while Kerr (1911–2003) was the preeminent academic administrator in the last four decades of the twentieth century.

Clark Kerr and Marian L. Gade, *The Many Lives of Academic Presidents* (Washington, D.C., 1986), xiv, 3–5, 28–31, 67–78, 81–83, 118–19, 126, 161–62. © Copyright 1986 Association of Governing Boards of Colleges and Universities. Reprinted with kind permission. All rights reserved. Further reading: Harold L. Hodgkinson, *College Governance: The Amazing Thing Is That It Works at All* (Washington, D.C., 1971): 12–22, with a useful bibliography on college and university governance; Robert Birnbaum, "The Dilemma of Presidential Leadership," in *American Higher Education in the Twenty-First Century*, ed. Robert O. Berdahl, Philip G. Altbach, and Patricia Gumport (Baltimore, 1999), ch. 12; Joseph F. Kauffman, *At the Pleasure of the Board: The Service of the College and University President* (Washington, D.C., 1980); George Keller, *Academic Strategy: The Management Revolution in American Higher Education* (Baltimore, 1983); Derek Bok, "Are Huge Presidential Salaries Bad for Colleges?" *Chronicle of Higher Education*, November 22, 2002, B20; William G. Bowen and Harold Shapiro, eds., *Universities and Their Leadership* (Princeton, NJ, 1998); and rest of pt. XII; I, 11; II, 2.

While this book is about college presidents, much of what is said can be related to city mayors and to city managers, to principals and to superintendents of schools, to hospital administrators, to deans of medical and other professional schools, and to coaches of competitive sports teams—all of whom work in environments of mixed constituencies, of conflicts of interests; of constant time pressures, of evaluations by many persons on the basis of many contrasting tests of performance, of uncertainties about their endurance in the position. These are all positions that test strategies and tactics and skills and character. They belong to that dwindling category of jobs attained and held strictly on merit and performance, not on partial or complete seniority as within the protections of private and public bureaucracies, or on the ownership of property or having a specialization.

The men and women who hold these positions are on the margins of many groups but at the center of an entire social process. They *must* belong in part to many groups but can afford to belong to none of them in whole. Perched on so many peripheries, they inhabit the center all by themselves.

These multiple-constituency leaders are politicians who also administer, administrators who also preach, preachers who also must balance accounts, accountants of finance who must simultaneously balance the books of personal relations, human affairs accountants who must survive today tomorrow, planners of the future whose own careers have an uncertain future. They are the glue that holds their communities together, the grease that reduces friction among the moving parts, and the steering mechanism that guides any forward motion.

All these stressful positions are highly challenging to those who hold them and highly useful to society. To appreciate them in depth, it is necessary to contemplate the many intermixtures of time, of place, and of character that constrain the diverse lives of those who manage these positions, as we seek to do here for academic presidents. . . .

Approximately 5,000 persons will have served as college and university presidents in the 1980s and a similar number in the 1990s—10,000 people by the end of the century. They will have been chosen out of perhaps 50,000 seriously considered persons in each decade who nominated themselves, were nominated by others, or were otherwise considered. Their selections as presidents will have taken place in the midst of intense interest by all trustees, by many faculty members, by a few alumni and students, and by the press. No other campus personnel selections will have drawn such attention.

These presidents will have operated in a multiple series of environments, most marked by a context of confusion about goals, of inconsistent pressures for action and for no action, of substantial constraints, and of opportunities small and great but occasionally nonexistent. The appointed presidents (and often their spouses) will have had their skills tested quite intensely, and their personalities and characters placed under substantial pressures. These 10,000 leaders will have been evaluated, and criticized, and praised to varying degrees by trustees (50,000 in total at any one time), by faculty members (750,000 in total at any one time), and by students, alumni, and community members in the millions. The histories of institutions will be written about the contributions of these presidents as central characters in the ongoing dramas.

Most presidents at the start of each decade will have departed by the end of that decade due to age, to their own choice, or to the choice of others, so that three generations of presidents will have passed by between 1980 and 2000.

Nearly all these presidents will have affected their institutions in some significant manner and occasionally in major ways. Some institutions will have survived because of their presidents while a few will have failed for the same reason; some institutions will have improved marginally while others will have declined, again marginally, due to their efforts. Occasionally an institution will have been moved clearly ahead; and, rarely, some segment of higher education—or even all of higher education—will have been clearly advantaged because of some president's contributions. These are the ultimate tests of performance that very few ever pass.

Overall, the fortunes of higher education institutions will be affected more by the actions of these 10,000 persons, between now and the year 2000, than by any other similar-sized group of individuals within the academic community; and, on balance, the effects will be clearly for the better. To study these presidents and what they do and how they do it is to study higher education more generally, for their positions are central to its development; is to observe changing American society at work on one set of institutions of central importance that has great sensitivity to swirling social currents; and is, also, to see human nature performing under stress.

These 10,000 people are and will be enormously diverse in their abilities, in their characters, in their motivations, in their personalities. They do not and will not conform to any single stereotype—not to Moses leading his people out of the wilderness, not to Mr. Chips beloved by all, not to Mark Hopkins the great friend and teacher sitting on one end of the log with a student on the other, not *The Masters* maneuvering for preferment, not to Dr. Strangelove using fresh knowledge to create a new world or no world at all, not to the Captains of Erudition serving the Captains of Industry, not to the Prince coldly calculating tactics, not to the New Men of Power controlling the masses, not to the Gamesmen getting to the top and trying to stay there. Yet some presidents will conform with each of these models, and nearly all will reflect aspects of two or more.

The 10,000 will have chosen themselves and will have been chosen by others for many reasons and to serve many purposes. They will have come out of the diverse worlds of higher education and the even more diverse worlds of human nature. A universal characteristic of presidents is their diversity. Institutions of higher education are seldom the "lengthened shadow of one man" to the extent they ever were—and some were; yet the president may still cast more of a shadow than anyone else—and most do—and their shadows take many forms. These presidents, in their diversity, will have contributed, in turn, to keeping the world of American higher education safe for the diversity that has marked it throughout its history.

What a governing board and the faculty committee advising it get is not always what they see in advance. What they see in advance is largely credentials—degrees, publications, positions held, plus a surface performance in an artificial situation (the interview). Appointees mostly come from the outside, and reference sources have mixed motives in making their recommendations as well as increasing degrees of caution in making their comments. What they get is a person who must make second and third and repeated impressions (rather than

one alone) and in very diverse roles of executive, salesperson, negotiator-mediator-arbitrator, policymaker, symbol. Nor does the potential president necessarily get what he or she sees in brief acquaintance with the institution.

Both sides gamble. There are no uniform parts to fit uniform slots. Any actual fit is more likely to be roughly biological than precisely mechanical. Yet it is surprising how often the gamble pays off, given how little the parties really know in advance about each other and how various they are in their respective conformations.

Common experiences. Whether expected or not, new presidents frequently come to experience the following:

A sense of loneliness. One called it: "A lonely life in a fishbowl." The president may choose to set himself or herself at a distance from others; some find it a necessity to do so. He or she can confide entirely frankly with few if any persons on campus for fear of gossip or loss of confidential information. Also, "a friend in power is a friend lost," particularly for those who stay on the same campus. Close friends become just friends, friends become acquaintances, acquaintances become critics, critics become enemies, and enemies get new ammunition. The president is a "lonely man," as Harold Stoke has noted.

A sense of being driven. The agenda is never cleared of phone calls not returned, letters not answered, persons not seen. The average president works a 60- to 80-hour week. Much of this work time is spent in the evenings and on weekends.

Presidents complain of a lack of time to read and to think. They now spend from one-third to two-thirds of their time off-campus, and much of it away from home. They mostly fail A. Lawrence Lowell's test: "Never feel hurried."

A sense of being under constant observation— every speech, every letter, every policy decided. The campus community is composed of very bright, very observant, very vocal people as compared with most human institutions. The loss of anonymity can also place a heavy burden on spouse and children.

Concern with how all those evaluations are going and about possible exit is nearly universal. Few presidents know where they might go next. . . .

Tests of performance. Evaluation is not only constant; it is also confusing. Evaluators have so many different standards for evaluation.

Trustees are the ultimate evaluators. They alone can vote a termination. By their own accounts and those of presidents, trustees mostly look for:

Integrity—they want to know the truth about the institution, good and bad.

Competence—the ability to appoint capable staff members, to prepare an agenda and a budget, and to carry out decisions.

Results—a balanced budget each spring and good recruitment results each fall are the most important.

Good external relations—with the alumni in a

residential college, the local community in a community college, the governor and legislators in a state-supported institution.

Effective consultation with the board—early discussion of important issues, adequate information in general, and never any surprises.

Adaptability—the ability to handle the unexpected, the unprogrammed, the undesired.

Tranquility on campus—nothing that hits the media except for winning sports teams. Although, as one said, "I can't hold back the new world."

Most boards look broadly at all these and other tests of performance, but some look much more narrowly. One board chairperson said he set two bottom lines in advance each year: the budget and student enrollments. He added that his policy towards presidents was: "Pay them well. Keep them insecure. Push them hard." Other boards look at how well the interests are being met for those clienteles individual board members believe they represent: the agricultural industry, right-wing citizens, older alumni, and the affiliated church, among others.

Many boards take a long-term look at performance; others react to a single episode. One ex-president said: "In this game, you can strike out only once. I struck out that once but my previous appearance at the plate had been a home run. It did not seem to count."

Faculty members have a different list:
- Acceptance of faculty procedures and advice.
- Support of faculty values, including academic freedom and the personal right to do as they please.
- Provision of good salaries, and a record of no faculty dismissals at the tenure level.
- Not being pushed into academic reforms they do not want—which are most; not seeing the president's hand too openly in academic affairs.
- Faculty often tend to want a faculty-type person as president, and then, once selected, prefer that he or she stay out of faculty-type problems; a person who, on the job, will be strong externally (raise money) but weak internally (not hassle the faculty).

The alumni test:

Presidential availability to alumni groups, and full and interesting presentations on campus developments.

The students' test:

Most students want friendly interest and concern; political activists want support for their causes, or, at least, a supportive environment.

The public test:

No incidents that run against middle-class morality, and that attract media attention.

Other presidents' test:

Longevity.

History's test:

The long-run advance or retreat of the institution in fulfilling its academic and service goals.

These standard tests of performance are, obviously, quite varied, and they do give a strong overall sense of potential difficulties. Some tests are consistent with each other; for example, all constituencies want a good record on obtaining financial and other resources and a competent administration. Other tests are isolated from each other, for example, the quality of contacts with students stands all by itself. But there also are inconsistencies among tests, and presidents find it particularly difficult when these conflicts become intense:
- When the faculty wants academic freedom and the public wants "100 percent Americanism."
- When the trustees want to balance the budget and the faculty wants a salary increase.
- When the students want to engage in off-campus politics and the public wants the campus used only for academic purposes.

Presidents tend to test themselves by (1) whether relations with all their essential reference groups are going along smoothly, and (2) whether they are making satisfactory progress in whatever goals they have set for themselves for institutional improvement.

The most important aspect of orientation is how the individual president sizes up what he or she faces and develops strategies to meet the various performance tests as best he or she may. Sometimes, there is no successful strategy available. Sometimes, one exists but is not found. Mostly, one is found and followed for some reasonable period of years.

LEADERS, MANAGERS, SURVIVORS, SCAPEGOATS

Presidents all differ in their strategies, in their tactics, in their personalities, in their codes of personal conduct, in what results they leave behind. Yet for purposes of analysis, they can be grouped into broad categories according to their overall strategies. . . .

Pathbreaking leaders. The first category is that of leaders who take charge in moving into new territory. We define such institutional leadership as involving deliberate efforts to create new endeavors, or to improve substantially on the performance and direction of existing endeavors, or a combination of both. The institution, as a result of successful efforts, is clearly different or clearly better or both. Such successful leadership requires both vision and the ability to persuade, or otherwise induce, others to support (or at least not effectively oppose) the vision. It also requires a conducive or, at least, permissive context.

Leaders of this sort may be leaders almost in spite of themselves. They are the founders who must write on a blank sheet of paper; who create something where nothing existed before. They may follow old models in new locations or they may, less commonly, create new or revised models. . . .

Pathbreaking leaders may seek to make revolutionary changes in existing institutions, turning them in quite new directions. . . .

Other leaders make more evolutionary changes, often quite substantial, building on the history of the institution and the changing nature of American society, as have James H. Kirkland at Vanderbilt (1893–1937), James Bryant Conant at Harvard (1933–1953), Herman B. Wells at Indiana (1937–1962), John Hannah at Michigan State (1946–1969), Wallace Sterling at Stanford (1949–1968), Robert Goheen at Princeton (1957–1972), John Sawyer at Williams (1961–1973), Kingman Brewster at Yale (1963–1977), and Sr. Joel Read at Alverno (1968–2003). Some also choose to work at the national level as did Conant on science policy and on secondary education (among other things), and as has the Rev. Theodore Hesburgh of Notre Dame (1952–) on civil rights policy and modernization of the governance of Catholic institutions of higher education (again among other things).

These evolutionary leaders have worked more with persuasion and tend to have taken their time at it, while revolutionary leaders have used more confrontational methods and are more likely to have announced their programs in a manifesto at the start, as did Woodrow Wilson. In his inaugural address, "Princeton for the Nation's Service," Wilson stated his "wish to see every student made, not a man of his task, but a man of the world" for whom "social service is the high law of duty." . . .

Other pathbreakers are saviours of institutions otherwise on the downward slope to extinction as in some of the entrepreneurial liberal arts colleges of today.

A few persons go down in history as great leaders not so much for great changes they have brought about, but because of the force of their personalities, as have Henry Wriston at Brown (1937–1955) and Robert Gordon Sproul at California (1930–1958). Alumni remember them throughout all of their lives.

To be a pathbreaking leader takes a certain type of personality. Personality requirements include the capacity for vision, courage in advancing it, persistence in pursuing it, personal power in overcoming resistance, and a willingness both to endure and to inflict pain along the way. Charles William Eliot believed the president "should live like the captain of a ship, who eats alone. He must never be charged with playing favorites; he must not be tempted by friendship to falter in the service of the institution whose welfare was confided to his care. He must be ready to say No as often as Yes, and to disappoint frequently. . . . To a questioner who asked him, after he had been at the head of Harvard for a few years, to name the quality most essential to a college president, he answered, 'The capacity to inflict pain.' "

The foregoing sets a very high definition for leadership. Most presidents look upon themselves as leaders. They do not, however, use the restrictive definitions of substantial impacts in breaking new ground or leaving a heroic image. Rather, they use the more modest definition of being "out in front" as a guide or conductor on more beaten paths. Some, however, think they are leaders when they are only out in front, as a bellwether in a flock of sheep. One president said, "I should like to be perceived as a leader even as I am being run out of town."

Managerial leaders. Managerial leaders constitute the second category. They are concerned more with the efficient pursuit of what is already being done, of what some constituency wants to have done, or of what circumstances may require to be done. They continue and they react more than they initiate. By contrast, pathbreaking leaders have their own ideas of how to make the institution more effective in serving some great goal or set of goals. A few managers are merely "contented to crawl about in the beggardom of rules," in the words of von Clausewitz. Pathbreaking leaders are more likely to change rules or to operate outside standard rules, and always seek to go beyond existing practices and policies over which such leaders seek to set themselves as "superior." Managerial leaders, as defined by Aaron Wildavsky, are more concerned with "small, repetitive choices that reinforce existing institutions" and pathbreaking leaders with "large, unusual ones that create new designs." In the terminology of James McGregor Burns, pathbreaking leaders are "transforming" and managerial leaders are "transactional." Pathbreaking leaders are concerned more with the long-run effectiveness of the total organization and managerial leaders with short-run effectiveness in the performance of tasks.

Managerial leaders vary greatly in what they choose to manage and how aggressive they are about their management. They may choose to manage the bureaucracy of the institution below them, or the hierarchy of power above and around them, or external relations, or use of resources, or internal community life, or academic programs, or mostly some combination of these and other endeavors. They may choose to drive hard or softly within their chosen realm of concerns. Managerial leaders are defined in detail by the areas they seek to cover and by the intensity of their efforts within them. Along the way they may help, marginally, to change the directions of the institution and, significantly, to improve the efficiency of its operation.

In normal times, boards of trustees and faculty selection committees are more likely to choose managerial leaders than pathbreaking leaders because they usually are more interested in good management than in transforming their institutions. Also, boards and committees want predictability in conduct of the office and a minimum of controversy—a nonthreatening personality. . . .

An intermediate category, between the pathbreaking leader and the manager, is the entrepreneurial manager. This leadership approach is not based upon vision, but upon grasp of nascent and effervescent opportunity in following changing and new chances to attract students or money or both. It calls for sensitivity to the potential markets to be served and to patrons to be cultivated, and a willingness and ability to follow quickly and well where the beacons shine. Quick perception of possibilities and agility in pursuit of them are requisite. Today, entrepreneurial managers are found particularly in the less selective institutions. As market and financial pressures have intensified in recent years, this category of presidents has grown rapidly.

Survivors. Survivors, or timeservers, are the third major type. They are not intent on making their institutions either more effective in the long run or more efficient in the short run; they seek, instead, to continue in their presidencies for as long as they can, at least for a respectable period of time—say five years—and perhaps then move on to another presidency with no one blacklisting them.

Survivors also come in more than one dimension. There are manipulators who "play politics" to keep their positions—adapting to changing constellations of power and to changing institutional needs and imperatives. They survive by their wits and lack of scruples. There are also the willing and even eager servants to power who determine where power lies and then serve it faithfully; and power may lie with the board chairperson, or the alumni, or the governor, or the mayor, or the agricultural interests, or the deans of the professional schools, or the faculty union, among other places. They survive by their shrewdness and self-discipline.

There are, additionally, the low-profile bureaucrats who follow the rules, who seek to make no mistakes, who take no responsibility, who initiate nothing, who lie low, who open and close doors and open and sort mail. They shelter behind union contracts and send all grievances to arbitrators; they welcome detailed state and federal rules that leave little latitude for independent action; they encourage the board or the faculty to make all decisions. They survive by their docility and good temper; and, if the price of survival is to do nothing, that is a price they are quite willing to pay. Some low-profile survivors go into a defensive mode, pulling up the drawbridges to their castles and putting their most loyal vice presidents on the parapets, while they try to wait out the siege—themselves no longer sword in hand. Others just disappear into their offices as invisible presidents, or into jet airplanes to attend every remotely related conference. They survive by not being seen, and they are happy to be forgotten in future history if they can only be forgotten about today; they are permanently "out to lunch." . . .

Scapegoats. A fourth major type is the scapegoat. No president, unless an absolute masochist and few are, starts out with this goal, but many end up in this category. And many know in advance that one role they may play is lightning rod. It is natural for

there to be scapegoats: Many people pass the buck up the line to the president, and board members may blame their own failures downward on someone else, and the president is the likely target. Many current presidents, in turn, blame their immediate predecessor or predecessors, and engage in ex-post scapegoating. This may seem excusable to them, for their successor or successors may subsequently scapegoat them. Entire groups, when excited due to fear and anxiety and when responsibility is ambiguous, may engage in scapegoating against some other group or a chosen individual, even though as Gordon Allport noted, the "victim" may be "wholly innocent." Rosabeth Moss Kanter has observed that "in unmanageable situations with seemingly intractable problems, constituencies can easily scapegoat leaders."

Scapegoating may be not only an emotional response but also a coldly chosen tactic to solve a problem. From an institutional point of view, scapegoating can be highly desirable, however questionable it may be morally. It can have a therapeutic effect by concentrating the blame on one person who then can be eliminated, thus absolving the institution as a whole and particularly other decision makers of a sense of guilt, and it may have public relations value by deflecting blame from those who carry on the responsibilities, allowing them to write on a clean slate. . . .

Other types. There is, of course, an almost endless series of variations of and mixtures within these several presidential types. Also, it should be noted that a single president may not always play the same role: for example, he or she may start out as a managerial leader and end up as a survivor, or begin as a path-breaking leader and end up as a scapegoat, or come in as a hard manager and end up as a soft one. . . .

The four types of roles and their combinations do not, by any means, exhaust the possibilities created by human ingenuity in responding to situations. Among other choices that have been made and are being made are for presidents to be:

- A *royal personage* presiding as titular head over internal and external events with dignity and style, while allowing or encouraging others to make the decisions; the always-present host and master of ceremonies who never forgets a name or remembers a principle to defend; "the mighty gentleman" who "stand(s) on a height" and "squirt(s) perfume on the ensemble."
- A *climber* using each current position as a step on a ladder that hopefully leads higher.
- A faithful *caretaker* holding the institution together, often on an interim basis, and accepting the personal costs with good grace—the "home guard" type with total institutional loyalty who is oriented to institutional rather than personal survival.

Tales of autocratic presidents from the past have lent an aura of authority to the presidential position that lingers, even as actual power has diminished. . . .

One great problem of presidents during the student unrest in the late 1960s was that this perception of omnipotence was held by the public and by alumni and by the press and by legislators and by governors, and also (until they learned better) by the student dissidents and some of their faculty supporters who should have known better (and sometimes did but neglected to share this knowledge).

By the 1960s, this anachronistic perception caused great misapprehensions. . . . Many presidents were held personally and totally responsible for the origins of and the solutions to student problems— both of which lay far beyond their control. The vast gap between perception and reality set them up as scapegoats. They might still look like majestic lions but the best they could be were clever foxes; and many were only hedgehogs burrowing into the ground. They stood closer to impotence than to omnipotence. . . .

OBSERVATIONS

1. Not only the college president but also the President of the United States has lost power, has become more hemmed in (Richard E. Neustadt set "presidential weakness" as "the underlying theme" of his study, *Presidential Power*), and this also is true of most other executive positions. Most administrators have fewer supportive constituencies on which they can reliably count at all times than in the past, and more inconsistent and competitive constituencies; and they encounter less loyalty, less tolerance, and more antiauthority sentiments.

Power has been pulled out of the college presidency by state and federal governments and courts and special interest groups and coordinating councils and trustees and students and faculty and alumni and staff; but the college presidency is not alone in this experience.

2. A strange and significant corollary to this is that the presidency becomes more important to the institution as a whole as the one check and balance on power incursions against the long-run welfare of the institution, whether these incursions come from outside forces or from students or faculty or staff or even individual trustees. The presidency is less influential just at the time it is more needed to defend institutional autonomy, to manage conflict, to integrate separatist forces, to offset small group efforts at inefficiencies and exploitations, and to advance programs over attempted special interest vetoes. One of the most senior and successful of all college presidents said after nearly 30 years in office: "I do not have a tenth of the power I had when I began this job, but I need ten times as much to do it well and particularly to curb the excesses of power in the hands of others—faculty, students, trustees, alumni, the state, the federal government." He also observed that, for the nation as a whole, "the loss of educational leadership on campus and moral leadership in society has been very costly." Another long-term

president said that over the decades his "cannon had become a popgun."

3. All these developments, taken together, led Joseph F. Kauffman to conclude that: "There is not much joy in being a college president today."

Presidents Consider Their Jobs

4. Jill Ker Conway,
True North: A Memoir, 1994

Jill Ker Conway's narrative of being offered and deciding for the presidency of Smith College is unsurpassed in college presidents' writings. Her brief account here is taken from the second volume of an autobiographical trilogy that illuminates a fascinating life. These works describe her "road from Coorain" as a refugee from a girlhood on an Australian sheep station and her education at the University of Sydney (B.A. 1958) in a still-Victorian city to exceptional achievement in American academic life. She traces her graduate life at Harvard (Ph.D. 1969) and commencement of her studies and beginnings of a friendship with Professor John Conway, whom she married and followed to the University of Toronto, where she secured a professorship (1964–75) and later vice presidency of internal affairs (1973–75). She thereafter was the first woman president of Smith College (1975–85), where her tenure verified her conviction of the needs and rewards of higher education for women.

From *True North: A Memoir* by Jill Ker Conway (New York, 1994): 240–48. Copyright © 1994 by Jill Ker Conway. Used by permission of Alfred A. Knopf, a division of Random House, Inc. Further reading: Conway, "Of Jill Ker Conway," *Smith Alumnae Quarterly* (Spring 2002): 25–31; Conway, *Road from Coorain* (New York, 1989) and *A Woman's Education* (New York, 2001); Conway and Susan C. Bourque, eds., *The Politics of Women's Education: Perspectives from Asia, Africa, and Latin America* (Ann Arbor, MI, 1993); and Linda Eisenmann, "One Woman's Education, Jill Ker Conway's Smith College Years," *Harvard Magazine*, May–June 2002, 19.

American educational discussions always focused on social adjustment, and the bourgeois comforts of emotional satisfaction. I thought there was much about the contemporary role of women to which young girls or their male counterparts should never be comfortably adjusted. American society needed a stronger focus on civic virtue, and a greater concern for social service on the part of the young, instead of encouraging early marriage where social service was limited by the boundary between family and society. The pattern of women's voluntarism wasn't a sufficient remedy, for it defined civic concern in gendered terms I thought should be rejected.

It seemed to me that the cozily domestic, introduced too early in youthful development, had the effect of obliterating or muting civic and social responsibility. My nineteenth-century feminist theorists about social evolution had all worried about where and how commercial societies could instill social values that went beyond personal satisfaction and self-interest. I agreed with them that the development of the civic virtues tended to be slighted in exclusively commercial societies, and that leadership and the talent for action came from an education which did not take the paired couple as its social norm. William James, America's greatest psychologist, had worried in the 1890s about how Americans could find the moral equivalent of war, and I thought his worries still entirely justified.

It was touching to read the history of the foundation of Mount Holyoke. Mary Lyon's battle to raise the money for her institution showed a hard marble woman at work, harvesting the pennies New England farm women could scrimp together from within their already frugal housekeeping budgets, coaxing bigger gifts from churches and from large donors. It had taken so long for the pennies to add up to the necessary sum to start the building in South Hadley, where the aim to educate women on their own terms first found architectural expression.

Sophia Smith's benefaction for the college which bore her name had been generous, but there had been the same painstaking scrimping by early classes of Smith alumnae to contribute the extra pennies needed to add up to the cost of building the first gymnasium for women. The endowments that supported women's colleges had grown slowly, and never rivaled their Ivy League counterparts. It troubled me to think of them being casually turned over to male direction, because I knew no male-directed institution would suddenly allow the needs of women to drive financial priorities. And I knew from my daily work at the University of Toronto what efforts of will and political finesse were required to redirect any allocation of resources in times of surplus, let alone in times of scarcity.

In the summer of 1973, Natalie [Zemon Davis, ed.], whose accounts of her life as a student at Smith made the great women scholars who'd given her love of learning seem like household presences, told me that the presidency of Smith would soon be vacant, and that she had written a long letter to the Search Committee setting out why she thought I'd be the right person for the job. She had, by then, become a member of the History Department at Berkeley, after much pondering what would be the most creative choice for the future. Although her departure broke up one of the most creative partnerships of my life, I'd urged her to make the move. It was an indicator of the intellectual environment we lived in at the University of Toronto that neither of us could find a collaborator within our own fields. I knew Natalie was a dazzling scholar, and that she should be teaching in an institution where there was a large cadre of graduate students up to her level of work. Beyond feeling pleasure that my most admired colleague wanted me to be custodian of the institution she cherished, I gave the matter no more thought. I was busy learning to swim in the choppy seas of my new administrative life, rooted in Canada, and far too preoccupied to think of change.

When the letter from the Smith Search Committee turned up on my desk in December, I knew I had to schedule a meeting with them, if only as a courtesy to my friend and collaborator. The few documents which accompanied the invitation tickled my curiosity. Smith's educational budget for its 2,800 undergraduate students was larger by far—than the entire Faculty of Arts and Sciences at the University of Toronto, four times Smith's size in enrollments. I wondered what it would be like to think about educating students drawing on such resources.

I liked the delegation from the Search Committee I met at the Century Club in New York. They were a mixture of trustees, alumnae, students, and faculty —all full of intellectual energy and enthusiasm. They seemed worried about the trend to coeducation among similar male colleges like Williams and Amherst, but energetically convinced that Smith's mission was to educate women. I thought their worries misplaced. I was working with women students in an institution of some sixty thousand students. I taught, by preference, at night, when the part-time women came in droves to the downtown campus. I knew what their battles were, how hard it was for them to feel entitled to take the time for expansive nonutilitarian learning.

One of my favorites was a tiny blond woman in her forties, mother of four, alone in life because of divorce. She worked in a suburban computer center and was often late for class. . . . She continued to arrive at my class white-faced and tired from her long commute by public transport. She needed to change worlds to see herself differently, a vision that could only come from the moral support of her peers, and a counseling service expert in unraveling the conflicts and self-denigration of older women. My few minutes' pep talk after class wasn't enough.

I thought there were thousands of women like her in every major city in North America who would jump at the chance to have four years to devote to self-development. The discussion was lively, but I went away unconvinced that this was the job for me. I thought I could help the cause by what I was writing on the history of education, but I liked what I was doing in Toronto too much to think about the subject more.

Beyond a polite thank-you for making the time to meet with them, I didn't hear from the Search Committee again until April 1974, by which time they had slipped from my consciousness. It was John who insisted that I accept the invitation to visit the Smith campus and learn more about the college. "I know more about this kind of New England institution than you do," he said. "You should take it very seriously. I've had my ten years in Canada. I'll go with you wherever you want to move now. It's your turn." . . .

On my April visit I left a grey city to see a campus ablaze with crocus, daffodils, scilla, and rich strawberry and cream magnolias. Brighter than the spring flowers were the faces of the young women I saw everywhere. I could spend months at a time at the University of Toronto without ever hearing a female voice raised. Here the women were rowdy, physically freewheeling, joshing one another loudly, their laughter deep-belly laughter, not propitiatory giggles. The muddy afternoon games on the playing fields produced full-throated barracking. I was entranced. . . .

My guide was a sophomore from the Midwest. . . . Her house in the Quad evoked a strong response in me, impressive though the science labs, library, art studios, music building, and athletic facilities had been. The space was ample and well furnished, the notice board awash with political notices, the rooms sizable, each door alive with signs, posters, ironic comments, cartoons. There was a notice for a house meeting that evening, and, in response to my inquiry, I learned that each house was self-governing in all but a few respects. Office was elective, and hotly contested. I realized that this was a real alternative society, a place of true female sociability, where women ran things for themselves.

The faculty I met displayed the justifiably wary curiosity of people presented with a total stranger as a potential President. The women clearly fit Natalie's description of the scholarly figures who had transmitted their love of learning to her. The men were more recognizable as academic types, so that I thought I could guess where they'd done their graduate study. I'd recently been spending a good amount of my time at the University of Toronto cutting budgets, scaling down or closing services, thinking about how to make do. This didn't seem to be part of Smith's experience. In fact, the Trustees and the Search Committee spent most of the time I was with them asking what I'd plan to raise money for, what I thought could be improved. They assumed everything was possible, even as they worried about bucking the trend to coeducation.

Educational quality was what everyone cared about, and there seemed to be no limits to the efforts everyone was prepared to expend to achieve that.

What worried them was whether Smith could raise money effectively if it insisted on adhering to its mission to educate women. Could it continue pricing its tuition competitively while not admitting men? What would happen to the quality of its academic life if women from elite prep schools were all counseled to enroll at Harvard or Yale? Would there be enough women of talent to go around in the coming decade of the eighties, when the cohort of young people was dramatically reduced in size?

I thought the case for women's education in an all-female student body was easy to make. One had only to explain the historical trends which had confined middle-class women to domesticity, unravel the ambiguous motivations which inspired coeducation, push people to think whether the classroom experience for young women and young men was really the same, and point to the outcomes in the careers of graduates from women's colleges. In any event, one could also point out that women's

colleges were the only truly coeducational ones so far as faculty were concerned. It was the Harvards and Yales which were single-sex institutions in that dimension. As for the worry about numbers of applicants, that seemed part of the preoccupations of a small segment of American society. A college for women should be concerned with the whole age spectrum of potential students, not just entering eighteen-year-olds. And even among the eighteen-year-old population I thought it foolish to be so preoccupied with entering test scores. That preoccupation was part of the American quest for security in a formless society which eased its anxieties through developing statistical measures for everything. I was from a tradition where one sought to educate not only the very gifted but to expand the potential of those who were not precociously high achievers. There was a very large cohort of women who could benefit from a Smith education, and whose motivation, character, and capacity for growth were as important as the way they tested at age sixteen or seventeen. Smith had always been a leader in women's education, and there was no reason why it shouldn't continue to be so in the changed mores of the 1970s. I was glad that Trustees, students, faculty, and alumnae had all been polled and had voted overwhelmingly that Smith should remain an institution for women. I thought Smith could take the lead in reaffirming that purpose for other women's institutions.

On the plane on the way home to Toronto, reflecting on my two-day visit, I realized that there was a distinct likelihood that I might be invited to become Smith's next President. I had to think seriously about how to weigh that possibility against the other possibilities in my life. If I remained at the University of Toronto there was surely the possibility of heading a Canadian university in the future. I'd be forty on my next birthday, so the question was what to do with my life for the next decade. I knew I wanted to quit administration by the time I was fifty, because my life would never be fulfilled if I didn't do the writing I knew was in me, and if I left it later than fifty, the urge and the energy might begin to fade. . . .

Where would I be most effective? What could one person do to shape events? I'd already begun to be haunted by the time consumed in the bureaucratic processes of administrative life. One had to process so many feelings for others, wait while the people with minds for minutiae fussed over petty detail, listen endlessly to complaints about the human condition. Some days I would count how many hours closer I was to my death, hours in which nothing had happened but the same repetitive human complaints, or ritual committee maneuvers that were substitutes for thought.

I could write the script for most academic committee meetings. My most hated ones were devoted to nit-picking about the hours of credit assigned a course. How many minutes of a chemistry experiment were the equivalent of learning to conjugate six French or Russian verbs? I couldn't care less about such silliness. It was the total conspectus of a student's experience that mattered. Then there were the budget discussions. How to equate books and journals to microscopes to ensure exact similarity of treatment between departments. I always wanted to shred the pettifogging papers on the subject and focus the discussion on how students learned. But for many of my academic colleagues these were subjects worthy of countless hours of discussion. . . .

In worldly terms, most people would assign a higher value to running a university, but I wasn't interested in the empty forms of status. I wanted to know that whatever form of service I took up would matter, not just as a notch on a list of achievements, but because there was some contribution I could make that would warrant setting aside the private pleasures for a life of ceaseless activity. . . .

The most important consideration was where my work would have the greatest impact on women's education. It might touch greater numbers of women indirectly if I ran a Canadian university, but the influence would be fleeting, and the institution would revert to type the minute I left, like some hybrid iris or daisy lacking cross-fertilization. If I went to Smith I might be able to prove to a doubting public that a women's institution could thrive in the modern world, that in itself it embodied important aspects of modernity. If I were successful, it might be possible to make it an intellectual center for research on women's lives and women's issues, research that could have influence far beyond Smith's lyrical New England campus. . . .

In June, John and I were invited to dine with the Smith Trustees in New York, an occasion I took to be another stage in vetting the various candidates' backgrounds. In fact, it was the Trustees' point of decision. The next morning, while we were at breakfast, the phone rang, and I heard myself saying yes to the job. . . .

5. Derek Bok, *Beyond the Ivory Tower*, 1982, and *Universities and the Future of America*, 1990

In two of his several books, Derek Bok (1930–) urged the social responsibility of the modern American university. He confronted this issue in terms of academic leadership. *Beyond the Ivory Tower* presented the roles of the president and deans in a university's shared governance, describing their authority and its limits and their responsibility to initiate and encourage teaching and research in socially vital new programs. In *Universities and the Future of America*, his Terry Sanford lectures at Duke University, he critically returned to this theme to point out specific areas where academic officers and trustees could do much more to face up to some of the country's largest problems. He defined how administrators in alliance with an engaged faculty can work creatively for the public good.

After his bachelor's degree at Stanford (1951) and law degree at Harvard (1954), Bok devoted his career to Harvard University, first at its law school (1958–71) where he

was dean (1968–71), and then became president of the university (1971–91). Thereafter he was appointed 300th Anniversary University Professor at the John F. Kennedy School of Government. Personifying the kind of leadership he advocated in these excerpts, Bok collaborated with William G. Bowen, president of the Andrew W. Mellon Foundation and former president of Princeton, to publish *The Shape of the River* (1998), a landmark statistical study of the results of affirmative action in higher education. Thereafter he continued to publish works on higher education (II, 20).

Reprinted by permission of the publisher from *Beyond the Ivory Tower: Social Responsibilities of the Modern University* by Derek Bok, pp. 84–88, Cambridge, Mass.: Harvard University Press, Copyright © 1982. And Derek Bok, *Universities and the Future of America*, pp. 106–11, 118–22, Durham, NC: Duke University Press, Copyright © 1990, used by kind permission of Duke University Press. All rights reserved. Further reading: Jeffrey J. Williams, "The Post-Welfare State University," *American Literary History* 18 (Spring 2006): 190–216, valuably summarizes a growing critical literature on institutional control, support, and the situation of academic workers within "academic capitalism" entering the twenty-first century.

THE ROLE OF LEADERSHIP IN THE UNIVERSITY

Unlike armies, corporations, and other hierarchical organizations, universities are communities in which authority is widely shared instead of being concentrated in the hands of a few leaders. Individual professors are largely immune from administrative control over their teaching and research by virtue of the doctrine of academic freedom. Acting collectively, faculties typically have the power to fix the content of the curriculum, set academic requirements, search for new professors, and shape the standards for admission. Students do not have much power to initiate policy directly. Nevertheless, they do exert considerable influence on policy—not so much by collective action but by their ability not to attend institutions they do not like and to force changes in curriculum and teaching methods by the slow, silent pressure of apathy and disapproval. Alumni likewise have considerable power to block developments they oppose by withholding contributions or by voicing their discontent through boards of trustees or in other embarrassing ways. Finally, of course, government agencies can influence institutional policy through their ability to provide subsidies, or to resort to outright regulation, or in the case of state legislatures, to approve or disapprove budgets covering most expenditures made by public universities.

In this environment of shared authority, presidents and deans have limited, though significant, powers. To begin with, they generally have the means to block particular programs or initiatives that they consider unwise or improper—either by refusing to allow the institution to sponsor the activities or award the necessary degrees or, indirectly, by declining to assist in obtaining funds or providing other forms of essential support to the enterprise. There are various reasons for exercising such power. A president or dean may block a program because he believes that it does not meet accepted standards of quality, because it invades the jurisdictional prerogatives of other units in the university, because it permits outside influence over matters of academic policy, or because its administration and financing seems inadequate.

In addition, academic leaders have a responsibility to curb activities and programs that promise to violate generally accepted norms of society or to inflict unwarranted harm on others. This obligation raises difficult issues both in defining the proper ethical standards and in deciding how to reconcile such moral duties with the need to preserve institutional neutrality and academic freedom. These problems will crop up repeatedly in the chapters that follow. Although the conclusions reached will often differ sharply from those of many activists of the late 1960s, these critics were surely correct in insisting that many university programs do raise serious moral issues that are a proper and important concern of the administration.

All the grounds for intervention just described are fully consistent with the traditional and accepted responsibilities of academic leaders. In exercising such authority, of course, presidents and deans must avoid intervening arbitrarily or indiscriminately. In particular, they must refrain from using their authority to impose their private political views on the university. Any attempt to do so would threaten to violate the academic freedom of individuals holding contrary opinions. Such action would also constitute an abuse of office, since academic leaders are appointed to serve the interests of a wide variety of groups who support the university and benefit from its activities. Finally, efforts to use the university for particular ideological goals would jeopardize the independence of the institution by inviting the intervention of outside groups who will respect the university's autonomy only so long as it does not seek to become a mechanism to achieve specific political reforms. It is in this sense that the university administration must be neutral. Any president or dean who ignores that principle not only will violate his trust but will almost certainly be stymied by the opposition of faculty, alumni, and trustees.

In addition to their power to block unwise initiatives, presidents and deans can also exert a positive influence to encourage new ventures, since their position gives them special opportunities to present proposals, have them considered carefully by the faculty, and find the funds and the facilities to carry them out. These advantages are considerable. Yet the extent of a president's influence is limited by the fact that his proposals will succeed only if they command the genuine interest and support of the professors who must put them into practice and the funding agencies that must provide continuing financial support.

In the exercise of this positive influence, the activist critique once again is relevant, though not in precisely the way that its proponents may have intended. Activist critics often exaggerate the monolithic nature of the existing power structure and overstate its effects on the activities of the university. After all, there are many sources of funding in the United States and some are quite hospitable to unconventional proposals. Professors can often write books, give speeches, and offer courses without much need for money. Hence, universities need not be dominated by a single point of view, nor have they been in practice. What is true, however, is that no unseen hand exists to ensure that every important opportunity for education and research is automatically recognized and supported by the society. As a result, if universities are to discharge their responsibilities to the public, academic leaders must actively seek to find neglected opportunities and important new initiatives for valuable work. Of course, this responsibility must be exercised with proper regard for the limits and capabilities of the institution and for the maintenance of high academic standards. With more than three thousand colleges and universities in the country, there is no need for each institution to initiate every socially valuable program that comes to its attention. But most presidents and deans can still find room to search for promising new ventures without overburdening their institutions or asking them to take on inappropriate tasks.

We must recognize, of course, that the search for such opportunities has undeniable political overtones. . . . It is one thing to encourage research on poverty and quite another to take an institutional position on appropriate government policies toward the poor. Efforts to stimulate teaching and scholarship on important social problems do not interfere with academic freedom any more than a decision to found a business school infringes on the rights of professors who oppose the free-enterprise system. If each new venture can be debated by the faculty, if participating scholars are chosen purely on their academic merits, if curricula and research projects remain a prerogative of the professors, presidential efforts to launch new initiatives are not likely to evolve into programs that use the institution for predetermined political ends. Nor will such ventures be regarded by the outside world as inappropriate for the university. On the contrary, initiatives of this kind have long exemplified the kind of academic leadership that is essential if the institution is to use its resources to respond creatively to a full range of social needs and opportunities.

In sum, a form of social responsibility exists quite distinct from the vision produced either by traditionalists or by social activists. Those who hold this position recognize that universities have an obligation to serve society by making the contributions they are uniquely able to provide. In carrying out this duty, everyone concerned must try to take account of many different values—the preservation of academic freedom, the maintenance of high intellectual standards, the protection of academic pursuits from outside interference, the rights of individuals affected by the university not to be harmed in their legitimate interests, the needs of those who stand to benefit from the intellectual services that a vigorous university can perform. The difficult task that confronts all academic leaders is to decide how their institution can respond to important social problems in a manner that respects all of these important interests.

Universities and the Future of America

THE ROLE OF LEADERSHIP

Can anything be done to help universities respond more quickly and fully to society's needs? Some would argue that there is no cure for the status quo that would not be worse than the disease. Although universities could doubtless do more to help society overcome its difficulties, no one can be sure what patterns of teaching and research are truly ideal. Hence, the interplay between individual teachers and scholars pursuing their intellectual interests and a diverse group of funding sources may provide a marketplace of sorts that yields results better than any substitute that human ingenuity could devise. Individual professors can do their best work only insofar as they are allowed to choose the subjects that interest them the most and seem most susceptible to systematic thought and investigation. The presence of many autonomous funding sources permits scholars to search for opportunities that strike them as promising and important while minimizing the risk that any deserving subject will go unrecognized and unsupported. The results of this process may not be perfect. But will they not be far superior to any system that fixes priorities to fit a set of predetermined social needs?

Such arguments make a convincing case against any solution that relies on central planning to set the agenda for higher education. It is the penchant for such planning, after all, that has made most other systems of higher education even less responsible and effective than our own. Nevertheless, there are steps far short of centralized. control that could help universities respond better to society's needs.

The most obvious key to progress is effective leadership from those who preside over universities and their faculties. Presidents and deans are in a better position than anyone to perceive the social problems that will benefit most from education and research and to encourage faculty members to respond accordingly. No one else can so readily secure the necessary funds, either by reallocating internal resources or by persuading outside sources that the cause is worth supporting. Granted, such leadership will have to be resourceful and tenacious in order to succeed. . . .

Opportunities for leadership exist in the field of moral education as well. It does not take prohibitive sums of money to mount successful courses in professional ethics, develop community service programs, or set a high example of institutional behavior to affirm the importance of ethical standards. Rather, the challenge is to muster the cooperation of faculty and staff by persuading them to recognize the need to help students develop a stronger commitment to ethical standards and a stronger sense of responsibility to others. Individual colleges, such as Haverford and Notre Dame, have shown how far one can succeed in this endeavor by sustained, determined effort. . . .

Of course, leadership has its limits, especially when the task at hand is large enough to require the transformation of an entire faculty or professional school. The most enthusiastic president cannot conjure up tens of millions of dollars to strengthen areas of work that command no interest in the outside world. Provosts cannot build great faculties in subjects where the supply of outstanding scholars is very small, nor can deans attract large numbers of talented students into fields where pay and prestige are less than adequate. Still, effective leadership can usually make a difference great enough to make the effort worthwhile, especially when the obstacles are not too severe. By reallocating internal resources or by determined fund-raising, presidents and deans can develop robust programs of international business, production engineering and design, or poverty research. With persuasion and modest financial help, faculties can be induced to improve their offerings in other languages and cultures or to build programs of moral education. With exceptional skill and dedication, it is even possible to build a strong school of public policy or education.

The key question is whether such leadership will emerge. As costs continue to rise and government spending lags, university presidents must devote more time to lobbying public officials and funds. Meanwhile, faculties have extended their control over academic policies, relegating presidents even more to administrative and external duties. Quoting from a survey of 700 university presidents, William Bennett reported in 1984 that less than 2 percent "described themselves as playing a major role in academic affairs." These trends all serve to weaken the tenuous links that connect the needs of society with the priorities of the university. Even if presidents do play a stronger role in shaping academic programs, they will also have to swim against the tide in order to launch serious efforts to address the practical problems of society. For though competition drives university leaders and their faculties to intense and unremitting effort, what competition rewards is chiefly success in fields that command conventional academic prestige rather than success in responding to important social needs. The media, with their primitive ratings and polls, only serve to strengthen this tendency. All in all, therefore, though it is still possible to lead a university toward higher levels of social responsibility, the obstacles are substantial and seem to be growing all the time.

THE ROLE OF OUTSIDE AGENCIES . . .

Government. Of all the outside forces that can affect the behavior of universities the greatest by far is the federal government. Only Washington can perceive the full sweep of problems facing our society. And only Washington commands resources on a scale sufficient to alter the priorities of all higher education.

In science, the federal government has generally used its influence in an enlightened manner to develop a large and successful research effort. True, the record has not been perfect. Because responsibility for research is divided among several agencies, there is no comprehensive review of major, cross-cutting objectives, such as maintaining the basic research infrastructure or developing a larger corps of scientists and engineers from America's youth. At times, politics enters in, as in the recent practice of earmarking money for facilities to designated institutions favored by particular legislators. On the whole, however, Congress has maintained the sustained flow of funds needed to build a first-rate scientific capability, while the National Institutes of Health, the National Science Foundation, and the Defense Department have all done a workmanlike job of supporting research according to its scientific merits.

In the social sciences, on the other hand, there is no real public consensus on the value of research and advanced education so that such work is far more vulnerable to partisan political pressures. As a consequence, the government has been much less successful in developing strong programs of research and training than it has been for most of the sciences. In some fields, such as poverty and education, funding has fluctuated too widely to build as strong a research enterprise as the importance of the subject warrants. In other endeavors that are relevant to America's competitiveness, such as research on the burdens of regulation, the training of school principals, or the development of scholars in international subjects, government funding has tended to be scanty, shifting, and unpredictable. As a result, universities have had difficulty attracting first-rate faculty to work in these fields.

Money aside, the nation also lacks a forum in which public officials and university representatives can discuss higher education as a national resource and search for more effective ways to respond to national problems through research and advanced education. In some states, political leaders and university presidents do talk periodically in an effort to link higher education more effectively to public needs. . . . But at the federal level, the government is too fragmented to consider how universities relate to national needs in any systematic way. Even if this were not the case, university leaders would be ambivalent about such a dialogue, fearing that comprehensive discussions might eventually lead to detailed planning of a distasteful kind. As a result, such dialogue as does exist takes the form of lobbying by countless associations from higher education with countless federal agencies and legislative staffs. The discussions that result are much too self-serving and dispersed to result in coherent policies and priorities that could encourage universities to respond effectively to the full agenda of national needs. . . .

All things considered, then, in the constant interplay between universities and the outside world, neither side has done a satisfactory job of promoting the nation's long-term interests. University leaders have not worked sufficiently hard to bring their institutions to attend to our most important national problems. At the same time, neither trustees, nor the professions, nor foundation officers, nor public officials, nor anyone else concerned with higher education has done enough to urge universities to make greater efforts along these lines or to help them mobilize resources sufficient for the task. . . .

Although the potential exists to respond to almost every issue on our formidable national agenda, the readiness to do so does not. As we have seen, most universities continue to do their least impressive work on the very subjects where society's need for greater knowledge and better education is most acute. . . .

6. Donald Kennedy, *Academic Duty*, 1997

In contrast to those who advise college presidents to regain the public voice that some influential academic leaders exercised in earlier times, Donald Kennedy (1931–) examined the working conditions of the modern president that to him necessitate a guarded approach to public utterance.

Reprinted by permission of the publisher from *Academic Duty* by Donald Kennedy, pp. 281–83, Cambridge, Mass.: Harvard University Press, Copyright © 1997. Further reading: Kennedy's views on other subjects are found at VI, 15; VII, 10; and XII, 9, 11.

Perhaps the most visible and influential presidential role is that of spokesperson. The president of any well-known institution has a "bully pulpit," and there is no shortage of temptation to use it. Students want support from the top on any issue that is deeply felt at the moment. Outside organizations hope for the same. And the presidents themselves, as human beings, have strong convictions that they sometimes want to express in the most public and forceful way. Others, of course, feel differently. Trustees generally hope that their presidents, like nineteenth-century children, will be often seen and seldom heard. They know that any strong view expressed publicly is remembered far longer by those who differ with it than by those who agree. They regularly hear from their friends—in another boardroom, or at the club—whenever "their man" or "their woman" says something controversial. Furthermore, they understand, quite correctly, that when their president tries to take positions as a private individual, members of the public will not make the distinction between person and institution. Most presidents therefore heed these warnings, temper their impulses with judgment, and avoid taking public positions.

When the matter entails a challenge to their own universities or is highly relevant to some institutional interest, academic leaders should be heard. With respect to issues or controversies outside the university, there is more room for doubt. If a matter relates to a specific interest of the institution or of higher education generally, then it is a proper subject for the president to take on in a public way. But if the issue does not matter to the institution itself or to one of its constituencies, then it does not warrant depleting a valuable resource (the public's attention). For example, the institution might not have a direct interest in a particular federal provision regarding student aid if it doesn't affect the university's finances; but if it adversely affects the welfare of its students, the president would certainly be justified in speaking out on their behalf.

It was not difficult to apply these criteria to two of the issues on which I spent the most time during my years as the president of Stanford. One of them was students' engagement in public and community service. It seemed clear to me that it was in the interest of our students, and of our sense of institutional self-worth, to encourage them to seek outlets for helping, both on the campus and in the community outside. With other presidents, I tried to make this a national effort through the founding of Campus Compact. The second was to move universities toward a recognition of their responsibilities for the quality of elementary and secondary public education. The interest of higher education in that subject seems to me self-evident, and I think our neglect of the rest of the educational system contributed to the erosion of public esteem for all our institutions.

On some other important issues, the case for engagement was not so clear. In the mid-1980s, apartheid in South Africa was a hot topic on many campuses, including ours. Students in large numbers demanded that we divest our stock in corporations doing business in that country, to protest human rights violations there. At Stanford we insisted on a case-by-case review, divesting only companies with poor performances under the principles devised by Reverend Leon Sullivan to evaluate corporate citizenship in South Africa. Even then, we divested only after some jawboning to persuade them to improve. Of course this policy did not satisfy many of the students. At the same time, the Congress was considering trade sanctions, and I was urged to comment publicly on those proposals. I did so in the belief that the issue had become so linked to our own institutional policy that it was impossible to separate them.

Finally, there are issues that, even though they do not directly concern the university and fail to meet the criteria I have just suggested, seem of such transcendent importance that the consciences of many people are deeply stirred. A widespread outburst of racial violence, or an episode of unjust and unlawful government action, might justify a presidential statement. If the matter is highly controversial, as it is likely to be, taking a position will entail considerable cost. But the purpose of a self-denying policy, after all, is not absolute constraint. Rather, it serves to remind one of those costs, and to permit only the most carefully considered exceptions.

7. Richard D. Breslin, "Lessons from the Presidential Trenches," 2000

Richard Breslin, experienced as college president and provost, addressed the sometime myth and sometime reality of ancient tensions between professors and those who guide and administer the affairs of a college or university. Conceding the endemic and uneasy presence of a "we/they" attitude on both sides, he reflected upon his own duties and offered prescriptive advice to all. He had many administrative offices: he was an executive vice president and professor of higher education at Saint Louis University, having earlier been a dean at Villanova University, after which he was vice president at Iona College and president of the University of Charleston, West Virginia. He then served as president of Drexel University (1988–94).

Richard D. Breslin, "Lessons from the Presidential Trenches," *Chronicle of Higher Education,* November 10, 2000, B24. Reprinted with the kind permission of the author. Further reading: X, 3.

Several decades ago, on the day I was to assume my first administrative appointment as the dean of a college of arts and sciences, I had breakfast with the outgoing dean. He announced that he was once again assuming the mantle of "we," and that I was about to become one of "them." It was as if I were crossing a threshold that would create a divide, if not an abyss, between me and my fellow faculty members.

Even though I thought his statement was hyperbolic, over time I learned that he was right. As an administrator, I did grow apart from my role as a teacher educator. Despite teaching part time, I quickly became consumed with administrative issues. Instead of educating students about how to become faculty members and administrators, I found myself focused on budgets, tenure decisions, student recruitment, fund raising, and public relations.

Although I realized that I was moving away from issues of concern to academics, I wasn't truly conscious of the distance that I'd traveled until I went full circle and returned to the faculty. Now that I'm back in the ranks as a professor, I'm struck by the wide gulf between faculty members and administrators. In fact, from my new vantage point in the trenches, I can see how both sides suffer from restricted fields of vision.

Presidents and other senior staff members assume that the faculty has little comprehension of the world in which the administration needs to function in order to accomplish institutional goals. In many ways, that assumption is correct. Professors have become so specialized, so focused on their individual disciplines, that they no longer see the institution as a whole.

I realize now, however, that administrators can have equally narrow perspectives. As I served in various senior administrative posts, including the presidency of two universities, I thought I had an intimate knowledge of the workings of higher-education institutions and was in touch with the big picture. However, the more I focused on the "critical issues" of administration, the more removed I became from the day-to-day activities of the typical faculty member. Inexorably, like most administrators, I didn't focus enough on what is known in higher education as "the business of the business."

One does not set out to do this. As administrators, we say that the faculty is our most important constituency and that teaching and research are central to our mission. But as higher education has become more complex, and the bureaucracy has burgeoned, teaching has increasingly lost priority in the hurly-burly of the daily work world. Administrators are so busy planning ahead, seeking the resources that enable our collective dreams to come true, that money is now perceived as the root of all excellence. With our focus on the bottom line, we've increasingly regarded the faculty as an obstacle to our objectives.

Thus, a growing number of decisions are made by senior staff members who see nothing wrong with their control of finances and information. Not only do they "own" the data, but they are comfortable making pronouncements about those decisions as if no one else had been involved in the process. The faculty plays a diminishing role—if it plays one at all.

Although many of us in the faculty see the problems in that approach, as a senior administrator, I viewed it as business as usual. Other presidents and administrators whom I knew also accepted that state of affairs without question. The more time we spent in our own ivory tower, and the higher we went, the more we made decisions in isolation, guided principally by the market forces that were driving our institutions.

Looking back, I also realize that high-ranking administrative officers can lose touch with the realities of life for faculty members. In our senior staff positions, we can receive so many privileges and special perks that we forget to consider that the faculty and others within the institution are not being treated the same as we are and don't have similar resources. Working long hours, six or seven days a week without extended vacations, presidents and senior administrators come to believe that large salaries, cars, club memberships, luncheon clubs, and tickets to special functions are fair compensation for our responsibilities. We can take it for granted that our needs will be met and that the rest of the organization is doing fine.

Additional layers of bureaucracy exacerbate the significant disparity in roles and compensation between faculty members and administrators. In my new academic department, it is virtually impossible to accomplish important goals in a timely manner. To purchase materials requires multiple signatures and lengthy waiting periods—obstacles that I doubt few senior administrators have to endure. Simple requests for guidelines on producing a brochure yield two-page memorandums of single-spaced bulleted statements on the do's and don't's of brochure development.

When I recently received notification of my summer salary, I found five signatures on the form, all originals. Having signed thousands of documents in my professional life, I realized how much time I had wasted—both my own and others'—that could have been put to far better use to pursue the academic goals of the institution.

Although both faculty and staff members have adapted to such an unacceptable state of affairs, the price of conducting business in this way is high. Not only does it sap morale, but it creates the impression that senior administrators do not care about how the institution functions. Among faculty members in the current college environment, numbness has set in.

As an administrator, I had often thought it would be useful if all faculty members could be "dean for a day." Now, as a faculty member, I wish that all administrators would remember the critical role that professors play in the academic life of the institution. In fact, to help bridge the divide between the faculty and the administration, based on my experience, I offer the following eight principles:

Scholars are at the heart of higher education. . . .

Service to the academic community means focusing first on the needs of faculty members and students. . . .

Shared governance means making decisions in concert. . . .

Decision-making needs to be streamlined. . . .

Mutual trust and respect must be earned continually. . . .

Communication must be both "top down" and "bottom up." . . .

Presidents and other top officials should see themselves as leaders who serve their constituencies. . . .

The academic enterprise will function best when the environment is imbued with a "both/and" rather than a "we/they" mentality. . . .

In short, our institutions will flourish, even with a certain natural tension in the air, as long as we seek to achieve consensus. Both administrators and faculty members must reassess the roles that we play so that we can share responsibility and credit in an atmosphere of professional respect. If we remain divided, our institutions will suffer, and we will never reach our most fundamental goals.

8. David Porter,
"A College President Rediscovers Teaching," 2000

After serving as president at two colleges, David Hugh Porter (1935–) returned to teaching newly aware of the comparative roles of professor and administrator. Here he emphasizes the similarities rather than the differing points of view between the two positions. A classicist, musician, and outstanding teacher, Porter, after degrees from Swarthmore (1958) and Princeton (Ph.D. 1962), taught for twenty-five years at Carleton College (1962–87), served there as interim president (1986–87), and then became president of Skidmore College (1987–99). In 2000, he became Payne Visiting Professor of Liberal Arts at Williams College.

David H. Porter, Williams College, "A College President Rediscovers Teaching," *Chronicle of Higher Education*, June 30, 2000, A60. Reprinted with the permission of the author. Further reading: *Swarthmore College Bulletin* (September 2001); and XII, 3, 9.

A refrain from *The Mikado*, "They'll none of 'em be missed," aptly describes some activities I left behind when I returned to teaching after more than 12 years as a college president.

The "Pooh-Bah" presidential responsibilities, for instance: those countless ceremonial occasions when you must "just say a few words," words expected to be graceful, apropos, even witty, but which you know will be immediately forgotten. I certainly don't miss them. Nor do I wish to relive lugging my laptop computer around the country, cracking each hotel's telephone system, and logging on at midnight to read, "You have 45 new messages."

It's also been lovely not to don a tie unless I feel like it, and to spend Sundays with my wife instead of at the office. I've not missed the acute angst a president feels when a fire engine roars past at 3 a.m., headed, one knows, for the campus. Nor those public forums where, even at institutions as generous as those with which I've been affiliated—Carleton College and Skidmore College—Pooh-Bah often feels cast as St. Sebastian.

Some things I do miss: having the college furnish and care for my car and pay the heating bills. Yes, my wife and I enjoyed living in the founder's home at Skidmore, and we miss its beautiful stained-glass windows (if not the cold drafts that came through them). Most of all, I miss working with the colleagues who formed my staff—people who so often gave me credit for their achievements, and so often took the heat for my failings.

It's not that I didn't love what I was doing. Indeed, I wouldn't exchange those years as a president for anything. It was profoundly satisfying to see ambitious goals attained, institutional change realized. But such satisfactions are, by nature, long-term. Especially during a rough stretch, I often contrasted them with the joys of teaching, which I remembered as intrinsic, intense, and immediate. At times, I even dubbed myself a "fallen angel," an image not welcomed by my administrative colleagues.

Now that I'm back in the classroom, however, it's only fair to admit that this Eden has a few more serpents than I recalled. Moreover, I've realized that the best qualities of being a teacher and being an administrator are not mutually exclusive, but surprisingly similar.

To start with the serpents: As a teacher, having time to dig deep into fields I love is as exhilarating as ever, but my Sisyphean efforts to catch up on 12 years of scholarship remind me daily how impossible it is ever to know all that I "should." Playing St. Sebastian wasn't especially enjoyable, but at least by the time I faced the arrows I usually felt as ready as I could be, whether I was discussing the budget, long-range plans, or building costs.

Such topics are finite, but the subjects I'm now teaching—ancient drama, Homer, Greek philosophy—are not. For those, I never will be "as ready as I could be." The very infinitude of their vistas makes our fields, and teaching them, exciting. But I'd forgotten just how close to the edge one sometimes feels.

As for those classroom rewards, they are indeed immediate and intense—but so are the punishments. There are those days when discussion makes the sparks fly, students' eyes brighten with excitement and discovery, and the classroom becomes a field of dreams. But there are also those nightmare times when discussion falters, and those eyes close down rather than light up. Then comes the despairing slog back to the office, the rehashing of what went wrong, the frantic efforts to remedy the disaster during the next class. As a president, I usually had at least a few weeks to savor the illusion that my budget talk had been an absolute smash.

One unalloyed delight is to participate directly in the intellectual life of a college once more. Although the institutions of which I was president were small enough to allow me to interact with students and faculty members—and even occasionally to teach a class—such opportunities remained the exception rather than the rule. And it took just 24 hours as president, at a college where I'd taught for 24 years, to realize from words said and not said, and from colleagues' body language, that I'd crossed the divide and was now an outsider.

It took only a bit longer to recognize that such isolation was both inevitable and necessary. Presidents constantly face tough decisions, many of which involve issues that transcend any one constituency. To make those decisions wisely and dispassionately requires freedom from personal bias and involvement (even though it sure can be lonely).

But what has especially struck me this year has

been not the differences that separate faculty members from administrators, but the similarities that bridge the divide. I'm not even referring to the obvious links, although we tend to forget them: the deep devotion to the institution and its students that motivates faculty members and administrators alike, the long hours they both keep, the tireless efforts that both make to render each year better than the last. I'm thinking rather of basic habits of mind that are as essential to being a good president as they are to being a good teacher.

Start with passion for one's subject. As I saw it, that was about the only qualification that I—a faculty member with little administrative experience—brought to my job as president. Once, when I asked students if I projected enthusiasm for the field that I was teaching, one responded, "Yeah, a bit much. Try mellowing out a little."

As it turned out, that perhaps excessive enthusiasm was tailor-made for an area I initially dreaded when I became an administrator: fund raising. As a classicist and a musician, I had spent years persuading students that they really wanted to study Greek and Latin—and listeners that the Charles Ives and John Cage pieces I was playing were really quite beautiful. After tough sells like those, helping people realize that they really wanted to support a college in which I believed was a piece of cake. It was also very much like teaching.

Add in a sense of humor, a must for both teacher and president. Even my dreadful puns, an addiction fed over years of teaching but carefully hidden from the presidential search committee, came in handy when I became an administrator. I remember, for instance, when several hundred angry students gathered to protest my banning of beer kegs, and I began my remarks by saying, "Well, it seems like we have a real brew-haha." The students looked incredulous that under such crisis conditions I would indulge my habit—but then they laughed and groaned as usual, and the initial tension was broken.

At heart, teachers are mediators, liaisons, people who create connections between their fields and their students, who teach students to converse not only with each other but with scholars in the field, both past and present. I'll count this term's Homer course a success if by its end the students are hearing Homer's voice, not mine, and if they have begun their own dialogue with the legion of other Homerists.

A president constantly plays the same mediating role as a teacher—as do many other administrators. Indeed, my training in Greek and Latin often seemed apt as I found myself cast as interpreter for groups who shared concerns but spoke different languages—trustees and faculty members, faculty and staff members, students and alumni, town and gown, the academy and the business world. With such groups, as with students in a class, one's goal is to bring them to the point where the teacher is no longer needed as intermediary.

Finally, there is a sense of adventure—scary but essential. I've found again this year that the best classes are often those in which, for whatever reason, I move closer to that edge I mentioned. I once launched into a carefully prepared lecture on Euripides' *Medea* only to be informed, "It's the *Bacchae* today, not the *Medea*."

"Oops," I said, or something less printable, and off we went on the *Bacchae*. It was the best class of the term. It helped that I knew the *Bacchae* well, but so did the fact that I was improvising rather than following a script. The students and I had to find our way together. By taking chances myself, I encouraged them to take chances, too.

It was the same when as president—in meetings, talks, and planning sessions—I managed to resist pinning down every detail, plugging every hole in advance. The academy exists to discover new ideas, explore new directions, see the familiar afresh. It is the teacher or president willing to take chances who best awakes that potential, whether in the lab or classroom, the staff meeting or boardroom.

Paradoxically, that sense of adventure, that willingness to court the unexpected, springs only from confidence, knowledge—and, yes, preparation. Franz Liszt apparently played Beethoven with such freedom that each performance felt like a new creation—something he could do only because he really knew those sonatas.

The qualities that I've mentioned as essential to both teachers and administrators are also what we try to teach our students: to be passionate and witty advocates, imaginative liaisons and interpreters, leaders and learners who complement meticulous preparation with the daring to plunge into the unknown. In fact, these words recall a passage from Mann's *Doctor Faustus* that not only speaks to all of us—students, faculty members, administrators—but also evokes the bold energy that our colleges should themselves embody: "To be young means to be original, to have remained nearer to the sources of life; it means to be able to stand up and shake off the fetters of an outlived civilization, to dare—where others lack the courage—to plunge again into the elemental."

9. Theodore Hesburgh, "Where Are College Presidents' Voices on Important Public Issues?" 2001

Still vigorous in 2001, Theodore M. Hesburgh (1917–), C.S.C., president of the University of Notre Dame (1952–87) and recipient of the Congressional Gold Medal for distinguished national service, urged his fellow college leaders to renew what once was "a fellowship of public intellectuals" to speak out on important public issues. His comments can be compared with those of Donald Kennedy (6), Hanna Gray (11), and Nannerl Keohane (10).

Theodore Hesburgh, "Where are College Presidents' Voices on Important Public Issues?" *Chronicle of Higher Education*, February 2, 2001, B20. Reprinted with the kind permission of Theodore Hesburgh, C.S.C. Further Reading: *Chronicle of Higher Education*, March 9, 2001, B17, responses to Hesburgh; Nannerl O. Keohane, "When Should a College President Use the Bully Pulpit?" *Chronicle of Higher Education*, February 7, 2003, B20; and X, 10.

When I was a college president, I often spoke out on national issues, even when they didn't pertain to academic life. Yet nowadays, I don't find many college presidents commenting on such issues on the front page of *The New York Times* or in any of the country's other major news outlets. Once upon a time chief executives in higher education talked to the press about military policy in the same breath as the Constitutional amendment for the 18-year-old vote, but I wonder whether we'd hear them taking stands on similar topics now. I also wonder what that all says about changes in the culture of higher education and how presidents view their roles as spokespersons on important public issues.

My opinion seems to be reflected in a recent American Council on Education report on public perceptions of higher education, which found that "the vast majority of Americans rarely hear college presidents comment on issues of national importance, and when they do, they believe institutional needs rather than those of the students or the wider community drive such comments."

Let me provide a disclaimer up front: American higher education is still one of the wonders of the modern world. Although they may have slipped from view in the news media, the presidents of our colleges are maintaining the country's leadership in educating a citizenry for the responsibilities of a democracy, as well as producing pioneering research in an age driven by science and its applications.

College presidents today, however, do seem to be less involved in public debate than in the past. In the 1950's, for example, President Dwight D. Eisenhower appointed two college presidents to the original five-person U.S. Commission on Civil Rights: John Hannah of Michigan State University, who served as chairman, and myself. Educational leaders strongly influenced public policy and opinion in areas that seemed far from ivory-tower concerns. Yet I recently ran across a comment from William Galston, a former White House domestic adviser and a leader of the National Commission on Civic Renewal, who was less than sanguine about the current lack of national leadership from college presidents. "There are very few voices," he was quoted as saying, "that speak with moral authority today, not just in politics but everywhere. Once university presidents could speak with such authority. Now they're administrators and fund raisers." That may be somewhat harsh, but it is yet more evidence that others have noticed a vacuum.

Where we once had a fellowship of public intellectuals, do we now have insulated chief executives intent on keeping the complicated machinery of American higher education running smoothly?

College presidents may be less present to the American public today because they are less present to one another. In the 60's, I spent one weekend every month for six years at meetings of the Carnegie Commission for the Study on the Future of Higher Education, chaired by Clark Kerr. . . . It seemed nothing to know personally—and well—250 fellow presidents. Collaboration in a common task fostered friendships; we shared birthday greetings as well as platforms. We were quoted on the issues of the day, sometimes in unified chorus, sometimes in agreed disagreement—such as when it came to whether a liberal-arts education should convey moral values as well as facts.

In contrast, today's college presidents appear to have taken Voltaire's advice to cultivate their own gardens—and, as I've said, they are doing that very well. At the same time, however, "assistant to the president" has become such a ubiquitous administrative title that one wonders how much personal contact between presidents, the kind of bonding that grew out of the Carnegie Commission, can still occur.

Presidents now preside over institutions that have grown much more complex and bureaucratic. . . . The rapid and constant changes in new technology demand that presidents be entrepreneurs and visionaries—always keeping an eye on the cutting edge. Many presidents are simply too busy to speak out on issues beyond the immediate concerns of their institutions.

It's also true that presidents must play an ever-larger role in raising money for their institutions—and often from supporters who have strong views on what presidents should or shouldn't say in the press. Getting involved in controversial public issues complicates the already neuralgic life of a college president. It is tough enough to maintain an irenic atmosphere on a campus without inviting criticism for taking stands outside the academy that will inevitably alienate one constituency or another.

Yet John Hannah confronted that risk when he took on the chairmanship of the civil-rights commission in 1957, as did W. Allen Wallis, the president of the University of Rochester, when he was named to the President's Commission on an All-Volunteer Armed Forces in 1969. I am certain that they got angry letters, as I did when I was named to President Gerald R. Ford's Presidential Clemency Board in the 1970's, dealing with "Vietnam offenders" like draft dodgers and deserters.

The 60's and early 70's were contentious times, and college presidents found themselves in the midst of acrimonious and sometimes violent clashes not only over civil rights and the Vietnam War but other societal concerns. Peace and justice issues, as well as the debate over the "military-industrial complex," gain a certain urgency when your R.O.T.C. buildings are on fire, as was the case at more than one institution. In fact, I kept a suit-pocket necrology during the days of the student revolution, noting fellow presidents who were forced from office. Courtney Smith at Swarthmore College even died in his office of a heart attack after confrontations with protesters.

Painful as those days were, however, they taught a powerful lesson: We cannot urge students to have the courage to speak out unless we are willing to do so ourselves. The true antidote to the public's view that colleges are simply ivory towers of intellectual dilettantism is engagement with important public issues—however difficult and thorny those issues may be.

Becoming knowledgeable and articulate on complex social issues is a process that takes time and energy as it imparts wisdom. One must be willing to invest in it. I knew little about immigration, a radioactive issue in American politics, when I began serving on the Select Commission on Immigration and Refugee Policy in 1979, but I knew a lot more after sitting through hearings in nearly every port of entry to the United States. As a theologian who spent 12 years on the National Science Board, I received perhaps the nation's best education in science from the greatest minds in the field.

Today, the issue that would most galvanize me as a college president would be affirmative action in higher education. I applaud . . . William Bowen and Derek Bok, for their 1998 study *The Shape of the River,* which supports racial preferences in higher-education admissions. (As an exception to prove the point, the book and its authors received prominent news coverage in *The New York Times.*) We need more presidents like Lee C. Bollinger of the University of Michigan, who termed his institution's recent defense of affirmative action in the courts "a critical moment for our society."

Another area longing for the attention of college presidents is developing educational programs that seek to improve the status of women—especially in Asia, South America, and Africa, where many are second-class citizens. . . . Only education can break the bonds, primarily of custom, that keep many women worldwide from realizing their God-given dignity and rights.

In fact, technology now gives us the reach—if we have the imagination—to deliver information to any corner of the world. We had a Green Revolution years ago, when we worked to increase and diversify crop yields in less-advanced countries; it fed the stomachs of an impoverished Third World. We now need to feed minds, especially those of the portion of the human race most overlooked. If we can create virtual law schools on the World Wide Web, why can't we deliver elementary education to those most in need?

Of course, those are just my own top concerns.

Our country and world are rife with other important moral and social issues. As the founder of the Worldwatch Institute, Lester Brown, with whom I worked for some years on the Overseas Development Council, said so well, "An affluent global minority is overfed and overweight, but more than half of humanity is hungry and malnourished; some can afford heart transplants, but half of humanity receives no health care at all; a handful of Americans have journeyed to the moon, but much of mankind cannot afford a visit to the nearest city; several thousand dollars are spent on a college education for a young American, while much of mankind lacks the limited resources required to become literate."

I would welcome signs that more presidents of our colleges were willing to take the lead in tackling at least a few of those issues, reminding the public—and perhaps even each other—that they are custodians of institutions where independent, ethical, and compassionate thinking must flourish.

Ruth Simmons Comes to Smith College

10. Leo O'Donovan and Nannerl Keohane, "Sister President: Ruth J. Simmons," 1996

The Journal of Blacks in Higher Education in 1995 applauded the appointment of "Sister President" Ruth Simmons as president of Smith College. To show its hearty approval, it ran the opinions of eighteen well-positioned people in academic life, plus the views of Barbara Bush and Betty Friedan, both Smith alumnae.

Beyond these testaments, in a larger context Simmons's extraordinary record in academic life made her color and gender irrelevant. Her appointment illustrated and propelled a dramatic increase in the percentage of women in college presidencies from 12 percent in 1992 to 21 percent by 2003 (including women leading Ivy League Pennsylvania, Brown, Princeton, and Harvard by 2007). Diversity had increased among undergraduate women at Smith and at similar private institutions. By 2005 the entering class at Smith led women's institutions in its socioeconomic diversity with 19 percent from the first generation of their families to go to college and 29 percent self-identified as women of color.

"Sister President: Ruth J. Simmons," *Journal of Blacks in Higher Education* 10 (Winter 1995/1996): 52–55. Further reading: Carol Christ, "Revealing Demographics: Smith Outshines Its Peers in Economic Diversity of Its Students," *Smith Alumnae Quarterly* (Winter 2005–6): 17; and II, 10–15; IV, 6; V, 7; VI, 6.

SETTING A NEW STANDARD

Leo O'Donovan was then president of Georgetown University.

Ruth Simmons' appointment as president of Smith College means something very special for Georgetown University, which underwent a rebirth more than a century ago under the presidency of Patrick F. Healy, the first African American to lead a major institution of higher learning in the United

States. Patrick Healy was born a slave in 1834 in Macon, Georgia, the son of an Irish father and African-American mother. By age 30, however, he had been ordained a Jesuit priest, and a year later won his Ph.D. in philosophy from the University of Louvain —the first African American to earn a doctorate.

At Georgetown, Father Healy became known as its "Second Founder," as he transformed a very good liberal arts college into a modern university. During his presidency (1874–1882), Georgetown moved closer to founder John Carroll's vision of being open to students of every religious background. President Healy strengthened the science courses and expanded the curriculum across the board while increasing its rigor. He brought Georgetown's aborning law school into early prominence. The campus underwent rapid growth and beautification, and the university's landmark structure—named in his honor as Healy Hall—was built.

But the Healy presidency of Georgetown, successful as it was, proved to be an anomaly. Not until 1995—a span of 113 years—has another African American been asked to lead an elite college which previously had been led, and largely attended, by white Americans. The significance of Ruth Simmons' appointment is that it surely sets a new standard. It is part of a larger, and very recent, pattern in which women and African Americans are assuming the leadership of leading institutions of higher learning. Witness the presidencies of Nannerl Keohane at Duke and Judith Rodin at the University of Pennsylvania.

The greater significance, however, may lie in what the appointment means to a society that, distressingly, is fracturing along racial lines. Here is an example of how the American opportunity system is *supposed* to work. A person of humble origins but huge talent, who happens to be African American and female, works hard, develops her gifts, and reaps the reward, which benefits us all. Ruth Simmons' appointment is a victory for everyone who wants to see this nation function as it is meant to.

My hope is that Ruth Simmons will be remembered years hence, among other things, for having ushered in a new age of African-American leadership in the upper echelon of American higher education, and not, like Patrick Healy, for having served as the spectacular lone exception to the rule. Having heard Ruth speak early in her presidency, I am confident that this will be the case. Congratulations to a marvelous colleague and a superb choice for Smith!

MILESTONES STILL REMAIN

Nannerl Keohane was then president of
Duke University.

Because blacks and women have broken down so many barriers to advancement and are now full participants in most aspects of our society, it may seem that no milestones remain. This view is erroneous, I believe; and I see the appointment of Ruth Sim-

mons as president of Smith College as an important event worthy of celebration, not just in American higher education, but by people everywhere.

For an African American or a woman to serve as president of an institution of higher education surely is not new, since blacks and women have served with distinction in such positions since the nineteenth century. But the idea of a black woman serving as president of one of our nation's most elite predominantly white women's colleges still has the power to capture our imagination and inspire us.

Ruth Simmons did not come to her position at Smith from a family of privilege and a life of plenty; she earned her way through her demonstrated skill, drawing her strength from her upbringing, the love and support of a close family, and the encouragement and guidance of supportive teachers.

For young women, Ruth Simmons' presidency at Smith is a clear signal that an appreciation for the special attributes of single-sex education cuts across racial boundaries, and unites us through our common love of the academic and social strengths such an educational experience can offer. For African Americans, her service at Smith is a welcome reminder that, in our society's best institutions, a person's success is determined more by talent and ability than by race. For all Americans, her presidency should reinforce our determination that our social institutions be guided by those most capable, no matter what their race, sex, or economic background.

Perhaps most important, this latest step in Ruth Simmons' distinguished career bears powerful testimony to how far a person can go with access to educational opportunity, the desire to build on that access, and a commitment to realizing one's full human potential. In weaving together those threads, Ruth Simmons is an example not only for blacks or women, but for all of us.

Greatness Retold

11. Hanna Gray,
"On the History of Giants," 1998

Hanna Holborn Gray's life has been immersed in the academic world. Born in Germany, the daughter of a distinguished historian, she spent her girlhood in New Haven where her father, a refugee from Hitler's Germany, had become a professor at Yale. After graduation from Bryn Mawr (B.A. 1950), where she would return one day as a trustee, she received her doctorate in European history at Harvard (1957), taught there for five years and later served on the Harvard Corporation. She began her long association with the University of Chicago in its history department (1961–72) but moved into university administration as Dean of the College of Arts and Sciences at Northwestern for two years in 1972. She went back to New Haven and Yale in 1974 as provost and for one year (1977–78) as acting president. Gray (1930–) next returned to preside over the University of Chicago from 1978 until 1993. Recognized as an exemplary academic leader and trustee of the institutions with which she had been connected, she was awarded honorary degrees by over sixty colleges and universities. In 1991 she received the Presidential Medal of Freedom from President Bush and the Charles Frankel Prize from the National Endowment of the Humanities in 1993. As a close and keen observer of academic life, she was well prepared in 1998 to sum up the heritage and current condition of the modern American university presidency, as she does in this essay. Her models include her famed predecessor Robert Maynard Hutchins who, for her, was in some ways the last of her presidential "giants."

Hanna H. Gray, "On the History of Giants," in *Universities and Their Leadership*, ed. William G. Bowen and Harold T. Shapiro (Princeton, NJ, 1998): 101–15. Further reading: XII, 3, 6, 9.

One might start by pointing out that a hundred years ago, and indeed well into our own century, presidents were normally expected to have three names. That stately catalog would include Charles William Eliot, Daniel Coit Gilman, William Rainey Harper, David Starr Jordan, Benjamin Ide Wheeler, and later, Nicholas Murray Butler, Arthur Twining Hadley, James Rowland Angell, and Robert Maynard Hutchins. . . .

Regard for the office of president, or for the presidents themselves, has descended a few notches. Where giants once walked the earth and now, deceased, look down from their pedestals, smaller folk are seen to scurry about, tin cups in hand, snuffing out fires here and there, preoccupied with committee meetings, dealing with so-called constituents, and hoping to get through the day without having to think too deeply or face yet another political, financial, or public relations crisis.

In the imagined past, the giants meditated and produced inspiring educational visions that spoke to a larger world. They were wise men, better equipped by character and learning and some kind of spiritual force than was the common run, to forecast the future and to lead the present toward its promise, to teach principles and values, to expound issues ranging from the substance of curricular truth to the prospects for world peace, from prescriptions for curing immediate ills to striking exactly the right balance between tradition and change in a restless and rudderless universe. They were, in brief, the leaders of a secular church who were meant to exemplify the pretensions of high thinking and its consequences for whose sake, after all, existed the institutions over which they presided and for which they were accountable. . . .

The desire that university presidents, and thus their institutions, fulfill . . . expectations indicates the continuing hope for higher education and its works as "creators of the future." The opposite belief, that the university presidency, in its mandate and practice, falls short of past standards, reflects a continuing confusion over the nature of the university itself.

There were indeed giants a hundred years ago,

and we still sit on their shoulders, a position that speaks to indebtedness but also to heightened and widened perspectives and responsibilities. . . .

The most hulking of the late-nineteenth-century gargantuas were founders. Some, like Gilman and White and Jordan and Harper, created new universities; some, most notably Eliot, re-created colleges as universities. Their work directly influenced all of higher education and the larger debates over higher education, its essence, the quality and purpose of its programs, the place of research and scholarship, the goals of knowledge, and the professions of knowledge. They were unrelenting spokesmen for their causes. These presidents were surely not the typical administrators of their time. They were leaders who inaugurated a new era of American higher education. They were in some ways as different from the average "nineteenth-century" president as from ourselves.

These were men, and occasionally women, intent on moving from the model of the small, often sectarian college, itself not far removed from the academy or prep school, to goals less concerned with inculcating personal and civic virtue (although no one opposed these things). Their goals were directed to advancing intellectual life, intellectual training, and the progressive discovery of knowledge. The institutions they created differed from one another in curriculum and in the mix of ideas informing the curriculum. There was constant and intense curricular controversy roiling around the future of undergraduate education and its impact on academic institutions more generally. Yet the impact of the elective system was to some degree common to all, and if its revolutionary force had to do above all with the undergraduate curriculum, it was equally influential for university programs as a whole.

The introduction of the elective system and its accompanying ideas stimulated the very possibility of combining teaching and research, the opening up of new subjects and new methods of learning, the making of research, scholarship, and specialization central in stating the purpose of higher education. It assumed the existence of an organic connection between research and teaching and so provided the charter of the American research university. . . .

Such ideas introduced the characteristic strains of thought that redesigned the vision of academic space and work as animated above all by a set of requisite and enabling freedoms related to both personal and institutional forms of independence. All this tipped the scale of university educational purpose from the assimilation of a common discipline and spirit of service to the development of autonomous minds and judgments and choices. The precise setting of the scale moved back and forth, both then and in succeeding generations. There were always those who feared that the loss of coherence once situated in a curriculum ordered around unifying truth was a sin both intellectual and social—

Woodrow Wilson did, for example, and so, later, did Robert Hutchins. But the institutional framework within which educational goals, however controversially delineated, were to be pursued had altered permanently. The agreement that some basic definition of freedom rested at the core of the collegiate or university enterprise had come to dominate.

A profound change was under way that would construct a new expectation of the presidential role, even though many continued to consider the president the super-headmaster of old or yearned for him to be so—a phenomenon still present in our own day. Eliot's university at the end of his term, as Oscar Handlin has written, had merged the inherited ideal of liberal education with that of scholarship, "ever evolving as knowledge accumulated. Tradition yielded to science as the source of authority.' "

It is evident that the authority of a president for whom the stewardship of tradition came foremost would inevitably be different from that of a president whose goal it became to serve as steward of a realm where the authority of science reigned sovereign. The source, and hence the nature, of presidential authority had moved decisively.

Not all universities became such in the same way or embraced to the same degree the new movements of professional education and of professionalism and greater specialization in academia. The person of the president mattered, as of course did the institutions' particular histories and traditions and governing boards and alumni sentiment, in shaping the pace and the outcome. But the presidents were out in front, planning and arguing and directing. . . .

One must remember, too, the power of appointment that rested in the hands of the founding presidents. . . . These presidents had very busy days indeed, and some had very little wish to pursue the old routines of enforcing discipline or maintaining compulsory chapel. They worked prodigiously, wrote volumes with little secretarial help, and traveled endlessly on long railroad journeys. But if they made do with little support and looked after details unimaginable now, if they persisted in thinking moral discipline a significant dimension of their role in undergraduate education, the founders can scarcely fit under a generic rubric of "nineteenth-century" presidents. The institutional visions they followed and the "university idea" to which they subscribed were set in conscious contrast to the traditions they worked to supersede and to the more conventional aspirations of their contemporaries.

The same presidents, in helping to create the new university, helped also to change the assumptions that had identified their office. Obviously, the rapid growth of numbers (students, faculty, staff, and programs), the proliferation of the disciplines of knowledge and research, the expansion of facilities and of relationships with external entities would guarantee such a result. But more fundamentally, these presidents assisted, with varying degrees of enthusiasm, in developing the forms of governance and shared responsibility that are often seen to have diminished the potential of strong presidential leadership and necessary institutional change and yet are also seen as basic to the idea of a true academic community. A constitutional foundation had been laid, however reluctant the motivations that produced it or partial its actual effects. . . .

In short, while the fullness of the faculty's role in the appointment process took some decades to unfold, the understanding of its foundations and strong presidents' acceptance of its desirability had come to be quite well settled in the leading universities of the late nineteenth century. Future arguments and developments were to revolve around the extent, and not the importance, of such faculty participation. In the newly created departmental structure of universities, it is not surprising to find the swift emergence of the belief that educational policy and judgments of academic need, opportunity, and quality should find their point of origin in the organized faculty.

The presidents, whether out of obedience to political necessity or thoughtful concurrence, helped lay the groundwork for those important attributes of university and collegiate governance and therefore also for another important aspect of presidential leadership: leadership in the interest of sustaining the value of process in institutions of higher education, leadership to preserve what might be called the constitutional norms of a healthy academic community.

The late nineteenth century saw several celebrated episodes that raised acutely the questions of academic freedom, its significance for the integrity of academic institutions, and the responsibility of presidents for maintaining the conditions under which it might thrive. Not surprisingly, these cases and others less dramatic tended to involve professors holding what could be considered heterodox views on economics and social policy, boards with views divided on or even hostile to the changing character of university life, or influential outsiders alarmed by the subversive and anarchic dangers of unfettered thought and expression. It is not, to put it mildly, as though the presidents always behaved like giants on these as on other issues. It is certainly not as though the problem went away. The recurrent crises that have spawned the need for the defense of academic freedom—whether freedom from external intrusion and pressure or freedom from internal orthodoxies and conformities, both implicit and explicit—will never go away. Nor will the concomitant need and opportunity to explore and to explicate the complexities of what universities are about and why their preservation matters. At the same time, it had become clear that the sustenance of institutional independence and of intellectual autonomy, the obligation of maintaining the greatest possible freedom of expression and outlook within an academic community in the interests of the long term and for the pursuit of its educational and scholarly purpose, were, together with the protection of appropriate process and the oversight of an institutions academic and material health, the central mandate given to a president.

Following from this point, we may note yet another shift of emphasis in defining presidential responsibility and presidential leadership, one that has developed far more gradually and is still fiercely debated. If the freeing of individuals to pursue their deepest interests—wherever those may lead within a framework of common commitment to that purpose and its myriad outcomes—is combined with the imperative of institutional autonomy and academic freedom in providing the conditions for pursuing that end, then the president must be vigilant in enabling these values as the *raison d'être* of an institution of higher education.

The president's responsibility has its source in the nature of the institution's mission, always imperfectly realized and always vulnerable to controversy and radical misunderstanding. The president has the obligation of spokesmanship and action on behalf of academic purposes. That being the case, the president cannot become an advocate for other causes that are not germane to that mission, cannot presume to speak for the institution on matters that fall outside its own special functions and competence. To do so would imperil both institutional autonomy and individual freedom within the academy.

The temptation to act the secular preacher is powerful, as is that of benign paternalism in providing moral instruction for the young. Were any of this even possible in the midst of the presidential life that has been described, it would still, I think, be inappropriate for presidents to see the function of moral guidance as their rightful role. There are of course a lot of people who want to see presidents doing just this and who deride their pusillanimous caution. The same people are often infuriated when a president does do what they ask, finding themselves in shock and disagreement and castigating the president's college or university for falling prey to such false and disgraceful opinions.

If a university and the responsibilities of its leaders are defined and judged by the purposes distinctive to that institution and no other, it follows that the ethic of the academy, and the teaching of that ethic, must be based in those purposes and the activities to which they give rise. Ultimately, an institution dedicated to intellectual aims is directly concerned with the priority of one virtue in particular, a virtue that it exists distinctively to teach, to support in practice, and to see constantly renewed and expanded. That is the virtue of intellectual integrity, and this is ideally the quality that education and scholarship and serious debate will aspire to exemplify.

Intellectual integrity is not, of course, divorced from other aspects of character. But its nature and assimilation do have something to do with learning, with the aims of learning, and with the vocation of learning. Critical and independent judgment, respect for evidence, openness to other points of view, tolerance of complexity and uncertainty, willingness to undertake reexamination and to suspend final conclusions, patience with rigorous and even painful analysis, refusal to bend to the fashionable and comfortable, insistence on reasoned explanation-these are among the constituents of principled conduct in the realm of intellectual integrity. The quest for thinking and acting along such lines is the identifying vocation of academic existence, the identifying aim of genuine education, the identifying excellence of first-rate scholarship and teaching. . . .

It is one thing to assert the distinction between exercising the rightful forms of corporate spokesmanship on behalf of academic policies and priorities on the one hand and the inappropriate taking of social and political positions that come to be identified with the corporate academic community on the other. But exactly where that line is to be drawn is, as we all know, often very hard to discover in concrete and controversial cases, as for example in the matter of endowment investment policy. Similarly, the basic requirements of intellectual freedom and of civil behavior may appear at odds and in need of calibration in crucial instances. It is in the capacity to preside over discussion and decision on such matters in accordance with standards imposed by the imperatives of intellectual integrity and principled attention to long-term goals that the contributions and leadership of presidents may ultimately be judged. The ability to sustain that imperative in the daily routine to the greatest extent, and its consequences for institutional integrity over time, sets the ultimate measure. . . .

Hutchins did not, of course, get his way. I would observe that he may have been in some ways the last of the giants to see the academic world in terms of a moral compass that sought to convert and remake the individual and the world. He was a secular preacher and missionary for a faith that believed in regeneration or salvation by grace alone—an intellectual grace to whose acquisition the works of education and reason, mediated through the word of canonical texts, formed a hard and noble path ending in moral renewal. It was, he thought, the president's ministerial responsibility to persuade people of that truth and to that path.

It is also of interest, I think, to note that Hutchins was not entirely one-sided. He represented two strong tendencies in a state of tension: the passionate desire to possess real authority and the equally serious conviction that constitutional and procedural rules, however irksome, should not be violated. He wanted not to undo but to reform and direct an institution for which, despite his impatience with its erring ways and its failure to live up to his grandest visions, he held considerable reverence. He wanted to preserve its fundamental freedom as critic and gadfly together with the freedoms of thought and expression that this required, and no president has ever been more eloquent in stating those values.

The tallest presidents of the late nineteenth or even mid-twentieth century could scarcely have peered so far as to foresee the university of now, of the late twentieth century. The impact of the government relationship . . . is probably the single most important element in the complex of developments that have shaped our present state, as always stemming as much from social and political causes of external origin as from the logic of its own internal development. The lives of presidents are inevitably further removed from the direct participation in every aspect of their institutions that once prevailed, and they devote vast amounts of time to matters like large medical centers and to forms of public service and engagement that earlier generations could not have fathomed. The articulation of shared governance and of the systems of tenure and process in appointments has moved to new levels. The problematic dilemmas seen to intervene between managing to stimulate institutional change and doing so while maintaining the traditions of shared governance appear more formidable than ever, especially in an age of contraction and amid the pressures and expectations of an uncertain environment.

Nor does the presidential role described in this situation appear heroic. As the man hired to mow the lawn at the cemetery was told, "You'll have a lot of people under you, but you won't be able to get them to do much."

The past is always more heroic than the present— we know that. Yet could it be, we ask ourselves, that some pasts really *were* more heroic? Were the giants of the late nineteenth century, human and imperfect as on closer contact we see them to be, not really taller? Was the opportunity to be founders not unique?

My own conclusion is that there were giants then and there have been giants since, the latter harder to identify because the rest of humanity has not yet shrunk to scale. Giants may, of course, be founders. Over time, they are still more likely to be steadfast leaders and renewers, generally under difficult and distracting circumstances that will seem threatening to the requirements of preserving and enhancing the conditions and possibilities of the higher learning and its institutions. Their voices may be quiet, their most important works perhaps invisible as they take place, but cumulative and weighty in their consequence.

In my view, the roles of academic leadership relate above all to what President Harper called "service" and what I would call "enabling," an activity never performed by one person alone in our setting. It means enabling people to meet their own highest standards in an environment at once supportive and demanding, enabling institutions to reach, over the long term, toward their goals. Such enabling, at its best, will rest on a foundation of collegial respect, disciplined restraint, constancy of purpose, and old-fashioned courage, on a willingness to pursue what may be unpopular at the moment and speak out against the merely popular, and on faithfulness to the academic calling itself. Such enabling leadership does not presume to rule but is not afraid to lead, to take decisive positions, and to accept accountability. It recognizes that the president's is but one of the many interrelated roles that together give a degree of form and stability and a reasoned sense of common ends to an academic community that is, by its nature, a society of individualists and questioners.

On the subject of giants, Sir Winston Churchill can perhaps provide us with a coda for these reflections. "I did not," he wrote in his memoirs, "suffer from any desire to be relieved of my responsibilities. All I wanted was compliance with my wishes after reasonable discussion."

And that, I suppose, is probably what giants have always thought, both then and now.

A Brief Concordance of Major Subjects